THE Art & Craft OF BIBLICAL PREACHING

THE Art & Craft OF

BIBLICAL PREACHING

A Comprehensive Resource for Today's Communicators

HADDON ROBINSON

CRAIG BRIAN LARSON

GENERAL EDITORS

ZONDERVAN™

GRAND RAPIDS, MICHIGAN 49530 USA

CHRISTIANITY TODAY

INTERNATIONAL

ZONDERVAN.COM/
AUTHORTRACKER

ZONDERVAN™

The Art and Craft of Biblical Preaching
Copyright © 2005 by Christianity Today International

Requests for information should be addressed to:
Zondervan, *Grand Rapids, Michigan 49530*

Library of Congress Cataloging-in-Publication Data

Robinson, Haddon.
    The art and craft of biblical preaching : a comprehensive resource for today's communicators / Haddon Robinson, Craig Brian Larson, general editors.
    p. cm.
    Includes bibliographical references and index.
    ISBN-10: 0-310-25248-2 (jacketed hardcover)—ISBN 0-310-25249-0 (companion audio CD)
    ISBN-13: 978-0-310-25248-1
    1. Bible—Homiletical use—Encyclopedias. I. Robinson, Haddon W. II. Larson, Craig Brian.
BS534.5.A78 2005
251'.003—dc22
2004015689
CIP

Interior design by Beth Shagene

Printed in the United States of America

06 07 08 09 10 11 12 • 10 9 8 7 6 5 4 3

DEDICATIONS

Haddon Robinson

Sid Buzzell
Scott Gibson
Duane Litfin
Don Sunukjian
Bruce Waltke

Colleagues in ministry whom I am honored to call "Friend"

Craig Brian Larson

To my wife, Nancy, and my sons, Aaron, Ben, Mark, and Brian David,
who have supported this high calling; and to the churches I have
served, who have opened their hearts to receive the Word of Life

A PRAYER OF GEORGE HERBERT
(1593–1633)

Lord, how can man preach thy eternal word?
   He is brittle, crazy glass:
Yet in thy temple thou doest him afford
   This glorious and transcendent place,
   To be a window through thy grace.

But when thou doest anneal in glass thy story,
   Making thy life to shine within
The holy preacher's, then thy light and glory
   More reverend grows, and more doeth win,
   which else shows waterish, bleak, and thin.

Doctrine and life, colors and light in one,
   When they combine and mingle, bring
A strong regard and awe; but speech alone
   Doeth vanish like a flaming thing,
   and in the ear, not conscience, ring.

CONTENTS

PART 3: CONSIDERING HEARERS

How should my approach change depending on who is listening?

PART 5: STRUCTURE

How do I generate, organize, and support ideas in a way that is clear?

PART 6: STYLE

How can I use my personal strengths and various message types to their full biblical potential?

PART 7: STORIES AND ILLUSTRATIONS

How do I find examples that are illuminating, credible, and compelling?

ACCOMPANYING AUDIO CD
Excerpts from Preaching Today *Sermons*

1. Ken Elmer, pastor of Faithful Central Bible Church in Inglewood, California
   "Through the Valley"

2. Gordon MacDonald, author and speaker
   "Repentance"

3. Walter Wangerin Jr., writer in residence at Valparaiso University in Valparaiso, Indiana
   "An Instrument of Peace"

4. Brian McLaren, founding pastor of Cedar Ridge Community Church in the Baltimore-Washington area
   "Sin 101: Why Sin Matters"

5. Rob Bell, teaching pastor at Mars Hill Bible Church in Grandville, Michigan
   "The Goat Has Left the Building"

6. John Ortberg, teaching pastor of Menlo Park Presbyterian Church, in Menlo Park, California
   "Passing the Test"

7. Tim Brown, professor of preaching at Western Theological Seminary in Holland, Michigan
   "I Can Do All Things Through Christ"

8. Max Lucado, pulpit minister of Oak Hills Church in San Antonio, Texas
   "Touch of Christ"

9. The late Bruce Thielemann, former pastor of First Presbyterian Church in Pittsburgh, Pennsylvania
   "Christus Imperator"

10. Haddon Robinson, Harold John Ockenga Distinguished Professor of Preaching at Gordon-Conwell Theological Seminary, in South Hamilton, Massachusetts
    "Good Guys, Bad Guys, and Us Guys."

11. Bryan Chapell, president of Covenant Theological Seminary in St. Louis, Missouri
    "Jesus Wept"

12. Bill Hybels, pastor of Willow Creek Community Church in Barrington, Illinois
    "Who Matters?"

13. Timothy Keller, senior pastor of Redeemer Presbyterian Church in Manhattan, New York
    "Love, Lust, and Liberation"

14. Rick Warren, founding pastor of Saddleback Church in Lake Forest, California
    "Myths That Make Us Miserable"

HOW TO USE THIS BOOK

The chapters in this book have come from four choice sources: the best of the best on preaching from twenty-five years of *Leadership* journal, nearly five years of PreachingToday.com, some twenty years of *Preaching Today* audio (all preaching resources of Christianity Today International), and chapters written specifically for this publication.

A manual like this—overflowing with helpful information—must be managed. Like eating chocolate, the chapters can be so rich that we want to read and read, but the number of insights can be overwhelming. Like attending a week-long seminar, we come to a point when there is too much to assimilate, too much to think about as we prepare and preach.

As with great musicians, men and women in ministry grow over time. We expect this manual is one you will grow with for years to come. You will consciously focus on one important principle from a chapter for weeks or months. Eventually it will become second nature, and you will be ready to focus deliberate attention on another principle.

If you don't have one already, create your personal preaching checklist, which serves as a repository for things you want to remember to do as you prepare and preach a sermon. Add to that checklist as you read this book (noting the page numbers to refer to again later), knowing you won't be able to grow and work on each aspect at the same time. But with a checklist you have peace of mind and a plan for growth you can use and work on as your abilities allow. Perhaps this year you won't be able to implement those great ideas found in an article, but next year you will.

After you prepare a sermon, review your checklist to ensure you have covered at least your essentials. A checklist helps build a normal process of sermon preparation that keeps you from being paralyzed by the complexities of preaching well.

In the manual we have laid out the parts and chapters aiming for a natural flow, but the material does not build like bricks in a wall. Each chapter stands alone. You can begin reading anywhere you like and skip around at will in pursuit of your special interests.

You may especially like certain writers and want to read everything they have written in this book. To do so, check the Author Index in the back for a complete list of articles by each writer.

You may want to read everything on a narrow subject such as delivery or emotion, even when that subject is addressed in only a portion of a chapter. To do so, see the Subject Index.

You may want to see discussions related to particular Scriptures. To do so, see the Scripture Index.

Another way to read, of course, is a chapter at a time, focusing on a more general area of preaching—such as illustrations or style. These chapters cover the waterfront, but you will notice they don't cover it with a blanket. This is not an encyclopedia of preaching. For example, the book does not have chapters on preaching in each of the major traditions.

We commend this book to you with our prayers and faith, believing it can chart your growth and enrichment in the high call of preaching for years to come and hoping you find many articles that end up on your annual *re*reading list.

We offer special thanks to the host of writers whose chapters reside between these covers, for their expertise and permission to use the material. These writers agree about the importance of preaching; naturally they do not all agree about how it should be done. Even within the pages of this book there are healthy differences of viewpoint.

Our thanks also go to Paul Engle, associate publisher for editorial development and executive editor at Zondervan, for his vision and direction for this book over the full course of the project; and to the editors, in particular associate editor John Beukema, and assistants listed on the "Contributors" pages for their diligence, skill, and labor of love.

It has been a joy and honor to serve you in this endeavor.

Haddon Robinson
Craig Brian Larson

CONTRIBUTORS

General Editors

Haddon Robinson
Craig Brian Larson

Executive Editor

Kevin Miller

Associate Editor

John Beukema

Contributing Editors

Kenton C. Anderson
Jeffrey Arthurs
Rich Doebler
Lee Eclov
Mark Galli
John Koessler

Editorial Assistants

Leslie Bauer
Drew Broucek
JoHannah Reardon

Writers

Jay Adams taught homiletics at Westminster Theological Seminary in Philadelphia and is author of *Preaching According to the Holy Spirit* (Timeless Texts, 2000). Now retired, he continues to speak and write.

David L. Allen is W. A. Criswell professor of expository preaching at The Criswell College in Dallas, Texas, and codirector of the Jerry Vines Institute.

Gordon Anderson is president of North Central University in Minneapolis, Minnesota.

Kenton C. Anderson is assistant professor of applied theology at Northwest Baptist College and Seminary in Langley, British Columbia, a past president of the Evangelical Homiletics Society, and author of *Preaching with Integrity* (Kregel, 2003).

Jeffrey Arthurs is dean of the chapel and associate professor of preaching at Gordon-Conwell Theological Seminary in South Hamilton, Massachusetts, and a past president of the Evangelical Homiletics Society.

Craig Barnes is pastor of Shadyside Presbyterian Church in Pittsburgh, Pennsylvania, former pastor of National Presbyterian Church in Washington, D.C., professor of leadership and ministry at Pittsburgh Theological Seminary, and author of *Sacred Thirst* (Zondervan, 2001).

Dan Baty is pastor of Valley Brook Community Church in Fulton, Maryland.

Alistair Begg is pastor of Parkside Church in Cleveland, Ohio, daily radio speaker on "Truth for Life," and author of *Made for His Pleasure* (Moody Press, 1996).

Rob Bell is teaching pastor at Mars Hill Bible Church in Grandville, Michigan, and author of *Velvet Elvis* (Zondervan, 2005). He is also featured in the first series of NOOMA short films.

John Beukema is associate editor of *PreachingToday.com*, preaching pastor of Western Springs Baptist Church in Illinois, and author of *Stories from God's Heart* (Moody Press, 2000).

Paul Borden, former homiletics professor at Denver Seminary, is acting executive minister for the American Baptist Churches of the West in San Ramon, California.

Stuart Briscoe is pastor-at-large of Elmbrook Church in Brookfield, Wisconsin, and author of *Preach It* (Group, 2003).

Wayne Brouwer is pastor of Harderwyk Christian Reformed Church in Holland, Michigan.

Mark Buchanan is pastor of New Life Community Baptist Church, Duncan, British Columbia, and author of *Things Unseen* (Multnomah, 2002).

D. A. Carson is research professor of New Testament at Trinity Evangelical Divinity School in Deerfield, Illinois, and author of numerous books, including

The Cross and Christian Ministry (Baker, 2004) and *Becoming Conversant with the Emergent Church* (Zondervan, 2005).

Noel Castellanos is president of the Latino Leadership Foundation and pastor of Nearwest Connection in Chicago, Illinois.

Bryan Chapell is president of Covenant Theological Seminary in St. Louis, Missouri, and author of *Christ-Centered Preaching* (Baker, 1994).

Rodney L. Cooper is professor of discipleship and leadership development at Gordon-Conwell Theological Seminary, former national director of educational ministries for Promise Keepers, and coauthor of *We Stand Together* (Moody Press, 1996).

Fred B. Craddock is Bandy distinguished professor of preaching and New Testament emeritus at the Candler School of Theology at Emory University in Atlanta, Georgia, and author of *As One without Authority* (Chalice, 2001).

Ken Davis is a speaker and comedian, president of Dynamic Communications International in Arvada, Colorado, and author of *Secrets of Dynamic Communication* (Zondervan, 1991).

Ed Dobson is pastor of Calvary Church in Grand Rapids, Michigan, and author of *Starting a Seeker-Sensitive Service* (Zondervan, 1993).

Richard Doebler is pastor of Cloquet Gospel Tabernacle in Cloquet, Minnesota.

Maxie Dunnam is chancellor of Asbury Theological Seminary in Willmore, Kentucky, and author of volume 31 of the Communicator's Commentary (Nelson, 2003).

Lee Eclov is pastor of the Village Church of Lincolnshire in Lake Forest, Illinois, a consulting editor to *Leadership* journal, and a columnist for *PreachingToday.com*.

Kent Edwards is associate professor of Christian ministry and leadership of the Doctor of Ministry program at Talbot School of Theology in La Mirada, California. He is a past president of the Evangelical Homiletics Society. He is author of *Effective First-Person Biblical Preaching* (Zondervan, 2005).

Richard Exley is a writer and speaker based in Tulsa, Oklahoma, and is author of *Witness the Passion* (Whitestone, 2004).

Richard Foster is professor of spiritual formation at Azusa Pacific University in Azusa, California, and author of *Celebration of Discipline* (HarperCollins, 1988).

Randy Frazee is pastor of Pantego Bible Church in Arlington, Texas, and author of *The Connecting Church* (Zondervan, 2001).

Mark Galli is managing editor of *Christianity Today* and coauthor of *Preaching That Connects* (Zondervan, 1994).

Scott M. Gibson is assistant dean and associate professor of preaching and ministry at Gordon-Conwell Theological Seminary in South Hamilton, Massachusetts, and editor of *Making a Difference in Preaching* (Baker, 1999).

Bill Giovannetti is pastor of Windy City Community Church in Chicago, Illinois.

Stephen Gregory is pastor of Alliance Church of Dunedin in Dunedin, Florida.

Ted Haggard is pastor of New Life Church in Colorado Springs, Colorado, president of the National Association of Evangelicals, and author of *Dog Training, Fly Fishing, and Sharing Christ in the 21st Century* (Nelson, 2002)

Daniel T. Hans is pastor of Gettysburg Presbyterian Church in Gettysburg, Pennsylvania.

Richard P. Hansen is pastor of First Presbyterian Church in Visalia, California.

Wayne Harvey is pastor of First Baptist Church in Sanford, Florida.

Jack Hayford is president of the International Church of the Foursquare Gospel and chancellor of The King's College and Seminary, Van Nuys, California, founding pastor of The Church on the Way in Van Nuys, and author of *The Spirit Formed Church* (Regal, 2004).

David Helm is one of the pastors of Holy Trinity Church in Chicago, Illinois, and a board member of the Charles Simeon Trust.

Bill Hybels is pastor of Willow Creek Community Church in Barrington, Illinois, and author of *Courageous Leadership* (Zondervan, 2002).

David Jackman is president of The Proclamation Trust, director of the Cornhill Training Course, and author of *Opening Up the Bible* (Hodder & Stoughton, 2003).

Darrell W. Johnson is associate professor of pastoral theology at Regent College in Vancouver, British

Columbia, and author of *Experiencing the Trinity* (Regent College Publishing, 2002).

Timothy Keller is pastor of Redeemer Presbyterian Church in Manhattan, New York, and author of *Ministries of Mercy* (Zondervan, 1989).

Jay Kesler is president emeritus of Taylor University and preaching pastor of Upland Community Church in Upland, Indiana.

Matthew D. Kim is a Ph.D. candidate in Christian Ethics and Practical Theology at The University of Edinburgh, Scotland.

John Koessler is chairman and professor in the Pastoral Studies Department at Moody Bible Institute, Chicago, Illinois, and author of *True Discipleship* (Moody Press, 2003).

Craig Brian Larson is editor of *PreachingToday.com* and *Preaching Today Audio*, pastor of Lake Shore Church in Chicago, Illinois, and coauthor of *Preaching That Connects* (Zondervan, 1994).

Greg Laurie is pastor of Harvest Christian Fellowship in Riverside, California, evangelist for Harvest Crusades, radio speaker on *A New Beginning*, and author of *Why Believe* (Tyndale, 2002).

Duane Litfin is president of Wheaton College in Wheaton, Illinois, and author of *Public Speaking* (Baker, 1992).

Crawford Loritts is daily radio speaker on *Living a Legacy*, associate U.S. director for Campus Crusade, and author of *Lessons from a Life Coach* (Moody, 2001).

Grant Lovejoy is associate professor of preaching at Southwestern Baptist Theological Seminary, Fort Worth, Texas.

Dick Lucas is founding chairman of the Proclamation Trust, based in England. In 1998 he retired as Rector of St. Helen's Church, Bishopsgate, in London.

Gordon MacDonald is editor-at-large for *Leadership* journal, teaches at Bethel Theological Seminary and Gordon-Conwell Theological Seminary, and is author of *Ordering Your Private World* (Nelson, 2003).

James MacDonald is pastor of Harvest Bible Chapel in Rolling Meadows, Illinois, speaker on the radio program *Walk in the Word*, and author of *Lord, Change My Attitude* (Moody Press, 2001).

Steven D. Mathewson is pastor of Dry Creek Bible Church, Belgrade, Montana, and author of *The Art of Preaching Old Testament Narrative* (Baker, 2002).

Alice Mathews is distinguished associate professor of educational ministries and women's ministries at Gordon-Conwell Theological Seminary and author of *Preaching That Speaks to Women* (Baker and IVP, 2003).

S. Bowen Matthews is pastor of Brandywine Valley Baptist Church in Wilmington, Delaware.

Dave McClellan is senior associate pastor of Riverwood Community Chapel in Kent, Ohio.

Marilyn Chandler McEntyre is professor of English at Westmont College in Santa Barbara, California, and author of *Drawn to the Light* (Eerdmans, 2003).

Joe McKeever is pastor of the First Baptist Church of Kenner, Louisiana.

Rick McKinniss is pastor of Kensington Baptist Church in Kensington, Connecticut.

Robertson McQuilkin is president emeritus of Columbia International University in Columbia, South Carolina, and author of *Understanding and Applying the Bible* (Moody Press, 1992).

Kevin A. Miller is executive editor of *PreachingToday.com*, vice president of resources for Christianity Today International, and author of *Surviving Information Overload* (Zondervan, 2004).

Jesse Miranda is professor and director of the Center for Urban Studies and Hispanic Leadership at Vanguard University in Costa Mesa, California.

Jim Nicodem is pastor of Christ Community Church in St. Charles, Illinois.

Susan Maycinik Nikaido is senior editor of *Discipleship Journal*.

John Ortberg is teaching pastor of Menlo Park Presbyterian Church, in Menlo Park, California, contributing editor to *Preaching Today*, and author of *The Life You've Always Wanted* (Zondervan, 2002).

Larry Osborne is pastor of North Coast Church in Vista, California.

Bill Oudemolen is pastor of Foothills Bible Church in Littleton, Colorado.

Earl Palmer is pastor of University Presbyterian Church in Seattle, Washington, and author of *Mastering the New Testament: 1, 2, 3 John and Revelation* (W Publishing Group, 1991).

Ben Patterson is campus pastor at Westmont College, Santa Barbara, California, and a contributing editor to *Christianity Today* and *Leadership* journal.

Randal Pelton is pastor of The People's Church, Hartland, New Brunswick, Canada.

John Piper is pastor of Bethlehem Baptist Church in Minneapolis, Minnesota, radio speaker on *Desiring God*, and author of *The Supremacy of God in Preaching* (Baker, 1990).

The late **Ian Pitt-Watson**, author of *A Primer for Preachers* (Baker, 1986), was professor of preaching at Fuller Theological Seminary.

Kenneth Quick is chair of practical theology at Capital Bible Seminary in Lanham, Maryland, and author of *Healing the Heart of Your Church* (ChurchSmart, 2003).

Michael Quicke is professor of preaching and communications at Northern Seminary in Lombard, Illinois, and author of *360 Degree Preaching* (Baker, 2003).

Alfredo Ramos is pastor of Hispanic ministry at Moody Church in Chicago, Illinois.

Eric Reed is managing editor of *Leadership* journal.

Rick Richardson is associate director for evangelism with Intervarsity Christian Fellowship nationally, an ordained priest with the Anglican Mission in America, and author of *Evangelism Outside the Box* (IVP, 2000).

Haddon Robinson is Harold John Ockenga Distinguished Professor of Preaching at Gordon-Conwell Theological Seminary, in South Hamilton, Massachusetts; senior editor of *PreachingToday.com*; radio teacher on *Discover the Word*; and author of *Biblical Preaching* (Baker, 1980, 2001).

Torrey Robinson is pastor of First Baptist Church in Tarrytown, New York, and coauthor of *It's All in How You Tell It* (Baker, 2003).

Ed Rowell is pastor of Tri-Lakes Chapel in Monument, Colorado.

Stephen N. Rummage is associate professor of preaching and director of doctor of ministry studies at Southeastern Baptist Theological Seminary in Wake Forest, North Carolina, and author of *Planning Your Preaching* (Kregel, 2002).

Bob Russell is senior minister of Southeast Christian Church in Louisville, Kentucky, and author of *When God Builds a Church* (Howard, 2000).

Greg R. Scharf is chair of the department of practical theology and associate professor of practical theology at Trinity International University in Deerfield, Illinois.

Jim Shaddix is dean of the chapel and associate professor of preaching at New Orleans Baptist Theological Seminary in New Orleans, Louisiana, and coauthor of *Power in the Pulpit* (Moody Press, 1999).

Emily E. Shive is speech and voice instructor at Western Seminary in Portland, Oregon.

The late **Lewis Smedes**, author of *My God and I* (Eerdmans, 2003), was professor emeritus of theology and ethics at Fuller Seminary in Pasadena, California.

Chuck Smith is pastor of Calvary Chapel, Costa Mesa, California, founder of Calvary Chapel Fellowship, and radio teacher on *The Word for Today*.

Fred Smith is a retired business executive in Dallas, Texas, a board member of Christianity Today International, and a contributing editor of *Leadership* journal.

Andy Stanley is pastor of North Point Community Church in suburban Atlanta, Georgia, and author of *The Next Generation Leader* (Multnomah, 2003).

Chris Stinnett preaches for the Park and Seminole Church of Christ in Seminole, Oklahoma.

John R. W. Stott is rector emeritus of All Souls Church in London and author of *Between Two Worlds* (Eerdmans, 1982).

Joe Stowell is teaching pastor of Harvest Bible Chapel in Rolling Meadows, Illinois, and author of *The Trouble with Jesus* (Moody Press, 2003).

Don Sunukjian is professor of preaching at Talbot School of Theology, La Mirada, California, and a columnist for *PreachingToday.com*.

Chuck Swindoll is pastor of Stonebriar Community Church, Frisco, Texas, chancellor of Dallas Theological Seminary, radio Bible teacher on *Insight for Living*, and author of *The Grace Awakening* (W Publishing Group, 2003).

Barbara Brown Taylor is the Harry R. Butman chair in religion and philosophy at Piedmont College in Demorest, Georgia, and author of *Speaking of Sin* (Cowley, 2001).

Virginia Vagt is former director of research and planning for Christianity Today International.

John Vawter speaks for *You're Not Alone* ministries and is author of *Hit by a Ton of Bricks* (Family Life Publishing, 2003).

Dave Veerman is a partner of the Livingstone Corporation in Carol Stream, Illinois, and primary contributor to the *Life Application Study Bible* (Tyndale, 1997).

Walter Wangerin Jr. is writer in residence at Valparaiso University in Valparaiso, Indiana, and author of *The Crying for a Vision* (Paraclete, 2003) and *The Book of God: The Bible As a Novel* (Zondervan, 1996).

Rick Warren is pastor of Saddleback Church in Lake Forest, California, and author of *The Purpose-Driven Life* (Zondervan, 2002).

Timothy S. Warren is professor of pastoral ministries at Dallas Theological Seminary and ministers to adults at Lake Pointe Church in Rockwall, Texas.

Scott Wenig is associate professor of applied theology at Denver Seminary and leadership development pastor at Centennial Community Church in Littleton, Colorado.

Warren Wiersbe is a writer and speaker, and coauthor of *Preaching in Black and White: What We Can Learn from Each Other* (Zondervan, 2003).

F. Bryan Wilkerson is pastor of Grace Chapel in Lexington, Massachusetts.

Dallas Willard is a professor in the School of Philosophy at the University of Southern California in Los Angeles and author of *Renovation of the Heart* (NavPress, 2002).

William Willimon is bishop of the North Alabam Conference of the United Methodist Church and is editor of *Pulpit Resource* and the *Concise Encyclopedia of Preaching* (Westminster John Knox, 1995).

Paul Scott Wilson is professor of homiletics at Emmanuel College in the University of Toronto and author of *The Four Pages of the Sermon* (Abingdon, 1999).

Mike Yearley is a teaching pastor at North Coast Church in Vista, California.

ACKNOWLEDGMENTS

In part 4, the article "The Big Idea of Narrative Preaching" by Paul Borden and Steven D. Mathewson is adapted from Paul Borden's chapter, "Is There Really One Big Idea in That Story?" in *The Big Idea of Biblical Preaching* (Baker, 1998), edited by Willhite and Gibson. Used by permission of Baker Book House (www.bakerbooks.com), copyright © 1998. All rights to this material are reserved.

In part 5, the article "Lifeblood of Preaching" by Ian Pitt-Watson is excerpted from Ian Pitt-Watson, *A Primer for Preachers*, p. 61. Used by permission of Baker Book House, copyright © 1986. All rights to this material are reserved.

In part 11, the article "A Comprehensive Check-Up" by Haddon Robinson is excerpted from *Biblical Preaching*, Baker Book House, copyright © 1980. Used by permission. All rights to this material are reserved.

Part 1

THE *High Call* OF *Preaching*

How Can I Be Faithful to What God Intends Preaching to Be and Do?

Chapter 1

CONVICTIONS OF BIBLICAL PREACHING

Haddon Robinson

To do the tough work of being biblical preachers, men and women in ministry must be committed to certain truths.

(1) The Bible is the Word of God. As Augustine put it, "When the Bible speaks, God speaks." This is the conviction that if I can really understand a passage in its context, then what I know is what God wants to say. (I don't believe that many evangelicals as well as liberals really believe this.)

(2) The entire Bible is the Word of God. Not only Romans but Leviticus, not only Ephesians but Esther. Not merely the "hot" passages but the "cold" ones.

(3) The Bible is self-authenticating. If people can be exposed to an understanding of the Scriptures on a regular basis, then they do not need arguments about the veracity of Scripture. Therefore, a listener or reader doesn't have to buy into the first two commitments before God can work in a person's life through his Word.

(4) This leads to a "Thus saith the Lord" approach to preaching. I am not referring to a homiletical method here, but to a desire to open up the Scriptures so that the authority of the message rests on the Bible. (This works against the anti-authoritarian spirit of our society.)

(5) The student of the Bible must try to get at the intent of the biblical writer. The first question is, "What did the biblical writer want to say to the biblical reader? Why?" The Reader Response theory embraced by many literary scholars today will not work for the study of the Bible. Simply put, "The Bible cannot mean what it has not meant."

(6) The Bible is a book about God. It is not a religious book of advice about the "answers" we need about a happy marriage, sex, work, or losing weight. Although the Scriptures reflect on many of those issues, they are above all about who God is and what God thinks and wills. I understand reality only if I have an

appreciation for who he is and what he desires for his creation and from his creation.

(7) We don't "make the Bible relevant"; we show its relevance. Truth is as relevant as water to thirst or food to hunger. Modern advertising creates needs that don't really exist to move the merchandise.

Chapter 2

A DEFINITION OF BIBLICAL PREACHING

John Stott

I intend to supply a definition of biblical exposition and to present a case for it. It seems to me that these two tasks belong together in that the case for biblical exposition is to be found in its definition. Here, then, is the definition: *To expound Scripture is to open up the inspired text with such faithfulness and sensitivity that God's voice is heard and his people obey him.*

Now let me draw out the implications of this definition in such a way as to present a case for biblical exposition. The definition contains six implications: two convictions about the biblical text, two obligations in expounding it, and two expectations in consequence.

TWO CONVICTIONS ABOUT THE BIBLICAL TEXT

(1) It is an inspired text. To expound Scripture is to open up the inspired text. *Revelation* and *inspiration* belong together. *Revelation* describes the initiative God has taken to unveil himself and so to disclose himself, since without this revelation he would remain the unknown God. *Inspiration* describes the process by which he has done so, namely, by speaking to and through the biblical prophets and apostles and by breathing his Word out of his mouth in such a way that it came out of their mouths as well. Otherwise his thoughts would have been unattainable to us.

The third word is *providence*, that is, the loving provision by which God has arranged for the words that he has spoken to be so written down as to form what we call Scripture, and then to be preserved across the centuries so as to be accessible to all people in all places and at all times. Scripture, then, is God's Word written. It is his self-disclosure in speech and writing. Scripture is the product of God's revelation, inspiration, and providence.

This first conviction is indispensable to preachers. If God had not spoken, we would not dare to speak, because we would have nothing to say except our own threadbare speculations. But since God has spoken, we too must speak, communicating to others what he has communicated in Scripture. Indeed, we refuse to be silenced. As Amos put it, "The lion has roared—who will not fear? The Sovereign LORD has spoken—who can but prophesy?" (Amos 3:8), that is, pass on the Word he has spoken. Similarly, Paul echoing Psalm 116:10, wrote, "We believe and therefore we speak" (2 Cor. 4:13). That is, we believe what God has spoken, and that is why we also speak.

I pity the preacher who enters the pulpit with no Bible in his hands, or with a Bible that is more rags and tatters than the Word of the living God. He cannot expound Scripture because he has no Scripture to expound. He cannot speak because he has nothing to say, at least nothing worth saying. Ah, but to enter the pulpit with the confidence that God has spoken and that he's caused what he has spoken to be written and that we have this inspired text in our hands, why then our head begins to swim and our heart to beat and our blood to flow and our eyes to sparkle with the sheer glory of having God's Word in our hands and on our lips.

That is the first conviction, and the second is this:

(2) The inspired text to some degree is a closed text. That is the implication of my definition. To expound Scripture is to open up the inspired text. So it must be partially closed if it needs to be opened up. And I think at once I see your Protestant hackles rising with indignation. What do you mean, you say to me, that Scripture is partly closed? Is not Scripture an altogether open book? Do you not believe what the sixteenth-century Reformers taught about the perspicuity of Scripture, that it has a see-through quality, a transparent quality? Cannot even the simple and the uneducated read it for themselves? Is not the Holy Spirit our God-given teacher? And with the Word of God and the Spirit of God, must we not say that we need no ecclesiastical magisterium to instruct us?

I can say a resounding yes to all of these questions, but what you rightly say needs to be qualified. The Reformers' insistence on the perspicuity of Scripture referred to its central message—its gospel of salvation through faith in Jesus Christ alone. That is as plain as day in Scripture. But the Reformers did not claim that everything in Scripture was plain. How could they, when Peter said there were some things in Paul's letters that even he couldn't understand (2 Peter 3:16)? If one apostle did not always understand another apostle, it would hardly be modest for us to say that we can.

The truth is that we need one another in interpreting the Scriptures. The church is rightly called to hermeneutical community, a fellowship of believers in which the Word of God is expounded and interpreted. In particular, we need pastors and teachers to expound it, to open it up to us so we can understand it. That is why the ascended Jesus Christ, according to Ephesians 4:11, is still giving pastors and teachers to his church.

Do you remember what the Ethiopian eunuch said in the chariot when Philip asked him whether he understood what he was reading in Isaiah 53? Did he say, "Why of course I can. Don't you believe in the perspicuity of Scripture?" No, he didn't say that. He said, "How can I [understand it] . . . unless someone explains it to me?" (Acts 8:31).

And Calvin, in his wonderful commentary on this passage in Acts, writes about the Ethiopian's humility, saying that he wished there were more humble men and women in his day. He contrasts that humility with those whom he described as swollen-headed and confident in their own abilities to understand. Calvin wrote:

> And this is why the reading of Scripture bears fruit with such a few people today because scarcely one in a hundred is to be found who gladly submits himself to teaching. Why, if any of us is teachable, the angels will come down from heaven to teach us. We don't need angels. We should use all the aides, which the Lord sets before us to the understanding of Scripture, and in particular preachers and teachers.

But if God has given us the Scriptures, he has also given us teachers to expound the Scriptures. And those of us who are called to preach must remember this. Like Timothy, we are to devote ourselves to the public reading of Scripture and to preaching and teaching (1 Tim. 4:13). We are both to read the Scriptures to the congregation and to draw all our doctrinal instruction and exhortation out of it.

Here, then, is the biblical case that God has given us in Scripture a text that is both inspired, having a divine origin or authority, and is to some degree closed or is difficult to understand. Therefore, in addition to giving us the text, he has given us teachers to open up the text, explaining it and applying it to people's lives today.

TWO OBLIGATIONS IN EXPOUNDING THE TEXT

Granted that the inspired text needs to be expounded, how should it be done?

Before I try to answer that question, let us address ourselves to one of the main reasons why the biblical text is to some degree closed and difficult to understand. It concerns the cultural canyon, or ravine, that yawns wide and deep between the two worlds—the ancient world in which God spoke his Word and the modern world in which we hear it. When we read the Bible, we step back two millennia beyond the microprocessor revolution, beyond the electronic revolution, beyond the Industrial Revolution, back, back into a world that has long since ceased to exist. So even when we read the Bible in a modern version, it feels odd, it sounds archaic, it looks obsolete, and it smells musty. We are tempted to ask, as many people do, *What has that old Book got to say to me?*

Don't resent the cultural gap between the ancient world in which God spoke and the modern world in which we live. Don't resent it because it causes us problems. It's one of the glories of revelation that when God decided to speak to human beings, he did not speak in his own language, because if God has a language of his own and had spoken to us in it, we certainly would never have understood it. Instead, he condescended to speak in our languages, particularly in classical Hebrew and in common Greek. And in speaking the languages of the people, he reflected their own cultures, the culture of the ancient Near East and of the Greco-Roman world and Palestinian Judaism. It is this fact of the cultural conditioning of Scripture, of the consequent tensions between the ancient world and the modern world, that determines the task of biblical exposition and lays on us our two obligations.

(1) The first obligation is faithfulness to the biblical text. You and I have to accept the discipline of thinking ourselves back into the situation of the biblical authors—their history, geography, culture, and language. If we neglect this task or if we do it in a halfhearted or slovenly way, it is inexcusable. It expresses contempt for the way in which God chose to speak to the world. Remember, it is the God-inspired text that we are handling. We say we believe this, but our use of Scripture is not always compatible with what we say is our view of Scripture. With what painstaking, meticulous, conscientious care we should study for ourselves and open up to others the very words of the living God! So the worst blunder that we can commit is to read back our twenty-first century thoughts into the minds of the biblical authors, to manipulate what they said in order to conform to what we would like them to have

said, and then to claim their patronage for our opinions.

Calvin again got it right when in his preface to the commentary on the letter to the Romans he wrote a beautiful phrase: "It is the first business of an interpreter to let his author say what he does say instead of attributing to him what we think he ought to say." That's where we begin. Charles Simeon said, "My endeavor is to bring out of Scripture what is there and not to thrust in what I think might be there."

That, then, is our first responsibility—faithfulness to the ancient word of Scripture.

(2) The second obligation is sensitivity to the modern world. Although God spoke to the ancient world in its own languages and cultures, he intended his Word to be for all peoples in all cultures, including us at the beginning of the twenty-first century in which he has called us to live. Therefore, the biblical expositor is more than an exegete. The exegete explains the original meaning of the text. The expositor goes further and applies it to the modern world. We must struggle to understand the world in which God has called us to live, which is rapidly changing. We must listen to its many discordant voices and especially to the questions it is asking. We must feel its pain, its disorientation, and its despair. All that is part of our Christian sensitivity in compassion for the modern world.

Here, then, is our double obligation as biblical expositors: to open up the inspired text of Scripture with both *faithfulness* to the ancient Word and *sensitivity* to the modern world. We are neither to falsify the Word in order to secure a phony relevance, nor are we to ignore the modern world in order to secure a phony faithfulness. It is a combination of faithfulness and sensitivity that makes the authentic expositor.

But because this process is difficult, it is also rare. The characteristic fault of evangelicals is to be biblical but not contemporary. The characteristic fault of liberals is to be contemporary but not biblical. Few of us even begin to manage to be both simultaneously.

As we study the text, we need to ask ourselves two questions in the right order. The first is, What did it mean? If you like, What does it mean? because it means what it meant. As someone has said, "A text means what its author meant."

So what did it mean when he wrote it? Then we ask the second question: What does it say? What is its message today in the contemporary world? If we grasp its meaning without going on to its message, what it says to us today, we surrender to antiquarianism that is unrelated to the present or to the real world in which we've been called to minister. If, however, we start with the contemporary message without having given ourselves to the discipline of asking, "What did it originally mean?" then we surrender to existentialism—unrelated to the past, unrelated to the revelation God has given in Christ and in the biblical witness to Christ. We must ask both questions, and we must ask them in the right order.

Two Expectations in Consequence

If we are convinced that the biblical text is inspired yet to some degree closed and needing to be opened, and if we accept our obligation to open the text in a way that is both faithful and sensitive, what can we expect to happen?

(1) We can expect God's own voice to be heard. We believe God *has spoken* through the biblical authors, but we also need to believe that God *speaks* through what he has spoken. This was the conviction of the apostles in

relation to the Old Testament. They introduce their quotations from the Old Testament with one or other of two formulas: Either "It stands written," or "It says." Paul could even ask the question "What does the Scripture say?" We could respond to him, "Paul, come on now. What on earth are you talking about *What does the Scripture say?* The Scripture is an old book. Old books don't talk. How can you ask, 'What does the Scripture say?'" But the Scripture does speak. God speaks through what he has spoken. The Holy Spirit says, "Today if you will listen to his voice, do not harden your heart" (see Heb. 3:7). The Word of God is living and powerful, and God speaks through it with a living voice (4:12).

Now such an expectation—that as we read and expound Scripture God will speak with a living voice—is at a low ebb today. As someone has said, "We have devised a way of reading the Word of God from which no word from God ever comes." When the time for the sermon comes, the people close their eyes, clasp their hands with a fine show of piety, and sit back for their customary dose. And the preacher encourages it by his somnolent voice and manner.

How absolutely, radically different it is when both preacher and people are expecting the living God to speak. The whole situation is transformed. The people bring their Bibles to church. When they open it, they sit on the edge of their seat, and they are expecting God to speak. They are hungrily waiting for a word from God. The preacher prepares in such a way that he is expecting God to speak. He prays beforehand and in the pulpit that God will do it. He reads and expounds the text with great seriousness of purpose. And when he's finished, he prays again. In this great stillness and solem-

nity when his message is over, everybody knows that God is present and has confronted his people with himself.

That's the first expectation, and the second is this.

(2) God's people will obey him. The Word of God always demands a response of obedience. We are not to be forgetful hearers but obedient doers. Our spiritual life and health depend on it. Throughout the Old Testament we hear the terrible lamentation of God, "O that you would listen to my voice." God is still saying that today. He kept sending his prophets to his people, but they mocked his messengers, despised his words, and scoffed at his prophets, until the wrath of Yahweh was aroused against his people and there was no remedy. The epitaph engraved on the tomb of Israel was: "They refused to listen."

I fear it's the same often today. Dr. Lloyd-Jones wrote in his great book *Preaching and Preachers* that the decadent eras of the church's history have always been those in which preaching has declined. It's true. Not only the preaching of the Word but the listening to the Word have both declined. The spiritual poverty of many churches throughout the world today is due more than anything else to either an unwillingness or an inability to listen to the Word of God. If individuals live by the Word of God, so do congregations. And a congregation cannot mature without a faithful and sensitive biblical ministry and without listening to the Word themselves.

How should they respond? Response to the Word of God depends on the content of the Word that has been spoken.

- If God speaks to us about himself and his own glorious greatness, we respond by humbling ourselves before him in worship.

- If God speaks about us—our waywardness, fickleness, and guilt—then we respond in penitence and confession.
- If he speaks to us about Jesus Christ and the glory of his person and work, we respond in faith, laying hold on this Savior.
- If he speaks to us about his promises, we determine to inherit them.
- If he speaks about his commandments, we determine to obey them.
- If he speaks to us about the outside world and its colossal spiritual and material need, then we respond as his compassion rises within us to take the gospel throughout the world, to feed the hungry, and to care for the poor.
- If he speaks to us about the future, about the coming of Christ and the glory that will follow, then our hope is kindled and we resolve to be holy and busy until he comes.

The preacher who has penetrated deeply into his text, has isolated and unfolded its dominant theme, and has himself been deeply stirred to the roots of his own being by the text that he has been studying will hammer it home in his conclusion. The preacher will give people a chance to respond to it, often in silent prayer as each is brought by the Holy Spirit to an appropriate obedience.

It is an enormous privilege to be a biblical expositor—to stand in the pulpit with God's Word in our hands, God's Spirit in our hearts, and God's people before our eyes waiting expectantly for God's voice to be heard and obeyed.

Chapter 3

A WEEKLY DOSE OF COMPRESSED DIGNITY

How a sermon gives worth to the soul

Craig Brian Larson

I went to the home of a woman who attended the church I pastored. When I walked into the flat, her husband was asleep on a cot in the living room, a gaunt shell of a man, his substance sucked out by whiskey. His skin was yellow. When he awoke and we met, his voice was rumbly and harsh from smoking, and frighteningly loud. His eyes had something hateful about them that made my blood run cold.

This was the demanding, abusive man whom the woman in our church tried to placate day by day. She had told me chilling stories about him.

They lived on welfare, and their house had poverty written all over it. In the dirt "yard" sat an abandoned tire. The kitchen floor sloped steeply, and the gloomy walls needed paint. In the living room, the fabric on the arms of the chairs was worn through, a chair or two tilted because of a missing leg, the cushions gave no support. Mousetraps were everywhere. Dimly lighting the place were bulbs that could not have added more than forty watts apiece.

But each week something happened in the life of this woman that elevated her to a higher, brighter plane. She would come to church and hear a sermon. That sermon was nothing less than a condensed dose of dignity that saved and ennobled her battered spirit. Regularly I saw the tears of gratitude as she grabbed my hand before she left for home.

No matter what our station, daily life in a fallen world is a walk through a gauntlet of belittlement. Those who attend our churches are daily bombarded by false values and beliefs that cheapen God's creation, by personal slights and insults, by Satan's accusations. Their minds are assaulted by scabrous images in the media and by profanity that is objectionable to God precisely because it debases the creation. They are subject to sins that mar God's image within them. They suffer distorted images of themselves that contradict God's truth.

After such a week, it's a wonder that a person can walk into church with any sense of worth (and the faces of many confirm that).

But then they hear anointed preaching, and gravity reverses as people sense the upward pull of heaven. The sermon reveals the character of God, who infuses all life with meaning and majesty. The sermon tells who we are in God's sight: created in the divine image, beloved beyond description, destined for glory. The sermon uncovers sins—then announces how to be redeemed. The sermon honors the morality that exalts humankind. The sermon assumes that people can think and discern about life and the Book of Life. The sermon appeals to the will, treating people as responsible agents whose choices matter forever. The sermon preaches Christ Immanuel, forever hallowing human flesh, second Adam who will one day resurrect believers in his likeness. A sermon is the most intense dose of dignity any person can receive.

To sit through a quality sermon is something like ascending the Mount of Transfiguration. Prior to that moment, Jesus resembled any other man. He looked and dressed and groomed himself like a common man. But on the Mount of Transfiguration, his appearance changed to display his full divine nature. The glory of God radiated forth, his face blazing like the sun and his clothes becoming heavenly white. The curtain was pulled back, revealing reality.

During a sermon, we are in a sense transfigured. Our true dignity from God shines forth. Nothing else in life treats a man or woman in a way that assumes greater worth or higher powers.

There is no more costly gift I could have given that downtrodden woman than my best and God's best in a sermon. It is a weekly dose of compressed dignity.

Chapter 4

OVERFED, UNDERCHALLENGED

A message must do battle for the will

Jay Kesler

Preaching is distinguished from teaching in that it calls for commitment and attempts to bring people to a point of action.

 For an audio example of this principle see tracks 2–3 on the supplemental CD.

THE NEED FOR CHALLENGE

Somewhere I read about two men. When one man preached, people leaned back and said, "How interesting." When the other preached, they said, "Let's march." To me, preaching is an appeal to the will.

Years ago, Billy Graham said if he preached without an invitation, he felt no loss of energy. But if he preached and gave an invitation, he was exhausted afterward. The demand of preaching toward commitment is much greater. Obviously everyone preaches at times without giving an invitation, but spiritual warfare takes place in a greater way when your appeal could change a person's allegiance.

Someone has said, "Men don't rebel against the idea of God; men rebel against the will of God."

One key sermon resulted in my call to the ministry itself. I was a Christian. I felt an urge to reach others with the gospel, but my father, a labor leader, was anti-church, anti-Christian, but mostly anti-preacher. When I felt the call to

preach, tension was building in my soul over facing a contest between my father and God.

I went to hear a tent evangelist named Pete Riggs. The theme of his crusade was "Let Go and Let God." I remember the almost irresistible pull of the Holy Spirit to follow the voice of God.

I walked forward and was surrounded by people who knew me to help me clinch the nail. That night one of the pastors gave me this verse from the apostle Paul: "For though I preach the gospel, I have nothing to glory of, for a necessity is laid upon me; yea, woe is unto me, if I preach not the gospel" (1 Cor. 9:16, KJV). This has been my sense my whole life—woe is unto me if I preach not the gospel.

Living in the world of higher education the last eighteen years, virtually every meeting I attend lacks real challenge, because many educators have no idea why they exist. Education today is utilitarian. We leave meetings thinking, *I'm giving my life to prepare the workforce for the twenty-first century.* Many educators think of relevance only in terms of materialism and upward mobility.

This is very unchallenging to me. We're not human doings; we're human beings. Helping someone to be is what real challenge is all about.

Worthwhile challenges go back to humans created in the image of God. All purpose in life is tied to that. Anything that makes a person less than that—a means to an end, for instance—I find unworthy.

UNDERCHALLENGING A CONGREGATION

There is tremendous danger of inoculation. As a little bit of cowpox will keep you from getting smallpox, so little doses of the gospel will prevent you from an inflammation of faith. I think it was Tozer who said, "Sermonettes make Christianettes."

A presentation of the truth that doesn't arrive at the place where hearers understand that it involves movement or commitment can have an inoculation effect. This is why many people who are orthodox are not evangelical, and why many who are evangelical are not evangelistic.

When we preach the gospel faithfully, it results in mission, outreach, and evangelistic desire. It has both a vertical dimension of salvation and a horizontal, social dimension of practical charity.

In an environment where people are sitting on the premises rather than standing on the promises, something is usually wrong with the preaching. It starts with the pastor. The easiest thing in evangelism is going down—down to the less educated, down to the youth, down to skid row, down to the impoverished. But unless pastors have a ministry across to their peers—community leaders and so on—they can't browbeat people enough to get them to do it themselves. They have to lead by example.

CHARACTERISTICS OF OVERCHALLENGE

A kid in Youth for Christ camp once asked me, "Would you pray for our pastor?"

I'm cautious of this request, wondering what motivates the criticism or "concern" for a pastor. I asked, "What do you want to pray for your pastor?"

He said, "Every Sunday after he preaches we sing three or four invitation hymns, and it seems like he's not happy until he's got all of us looking at our shoes, until everybody in the place feels reduced to a puddle. I don't understand it."

"What do you want to pray for?"

He said, "Let's pray that my pastor would feel forgiven."

That knocked me out. This kid understands something deep. The pastor is trying to exorcise his own guilt through catharsis of some kind as opposed to understanding grace.

Gilbert Beers said, "Even Moses moving the children of Israel from Egypt to the Promised Land had to move at the speed of the smallest lamb." Pastors need to sense when people are overloaded.

There are certain people you have to take aside and say, "You need to spend more time with your family. I know we've got a church workday this weekend, but I don't think you ought to come. You need to take your kids fishing." You need to know your congregation enough to know which ones need challenge and which ones need rest.

As president of Taylor I drove around the campus in a circle, like Joshua around the walls of Jericho, and I prayed, "Lord, here's the circumference of this place. Please, God, do something. I need you." No pastor can effectively challenge people or move people toward God without the power of prayer.

Chapter 5

THEOLOGY OF POWERFUL PREACHING

Nine beliefs at the heart of biblical preaching

Jay E. Adams

What we truly believe determines what we do. What we believe in our heart of hearts about preaching will determine how we carry it out. In that sense, nothing can be more practical than our theology of preaching. The following nine beliefs are foundational to biblical preaching.

1. THE ULTIMATE AIM OF PREACHING IS TO PLEASE GOD

It is a core belief of the faith that God is sovereign and all things must be done to please him. Pleasing a sovereign Creator means discovering what he desires and, through his grace, doing it. To preach God's Word God's way should be the aim of faithful preachers. As sovereign, God tells us what to preach and how to do so. Ministers of the Word have no right to deviate from his instructions. Human ideas and speculation, therefore, must be foreign to the pulpit.

2. PREACHING PLEASES GOD ONLY WHEN IT IS TRUE TO SCRIPTURE

Christian preaching begins with the Scriptures. Unless preachers acquire and maintain the proper beliefs—and therefore attitudes growing out of these—about the Scriptures, they will fail to preach in ways that please God. Whether our preaching is effective is deter-

mined not by the number of persons who attend it, nor the number of professions of faith, but by the faithfulness of preachers to the message that we are called to preach. Those who do not faithfully proclaim God's Word may claim numbers and supposed professions of faith. And some who do, fail to attract large followings. The sovereign God is the one who produces the results. When he began to preach to a rebellious people, Isaiah was told beforehand that the results would be minimal because the people lacked the eyes to see and the ears to hear. Failure to obtain outward results, however, may never be used as an excuse for flawed preaching.

This message, in every instance, must be true to the Bible. The preacher is a herald (*keryx*) whose task is to convey God's Word to his people and to call the elect from the world into the church. To these ends, we must understand what is required of us and how to pursue it.

3. THE SCRIPTURES ARE THE INERRANT, INSPIRED WORD OF GOD WRITTEN

All true preachers acknowledge the Bible as the source from which to learn and proclaim God's truth. They accept what they read there as inspired and inerrant in the autographs. By inspiration (the term in 2 Timothy 3:16 means "God-breathed") they understand that scriptural words are as much God's Word as if he spoke them by means of breath. If one could hear him speak, he would say nothing more, nothing less, and nothing different from what is written by means of his apostles and prophets. The Scriptures are the very Word of God written.

4. PREACHING IS A SACRED RESPONSIBILITY

The attitude that these beliefs should call forth is one of reverence for the text that the preacher expounds, along with a great desire to learn what each passage means so as to impart this understanding of the message to those who hear. Moreover, trustworthy interpreters of Scripture recognize that they are handling the most important information in all of life and want to be faithful in doing so. We will not engage in shoddy study or inadequate preparation of messages. We will recognize that in all that we say, we represent the God of the universe, and if we fail to understand or faithfully proclaim the truth, we will misrepresent God. To be faithful to the text and the Holy Spirit who caused it to be written is our fundamental concern. In this connection, conscientious ministers keep 2 Timothy 2:15 before themselves at all times.

5. THE SCRIPTURES WERE INTENDED NOT ONLY FOR THE ORIGINAL HEARERS BUT FOR OUR UNIQUE HEARERS TODAY

As heralds who bring a message from God to those who listen, we will not be satisfied with an approach to the text that views it as long ago and far away. We appreciate that the Scripture is for all times, for people in all lands. We keep in mind Paul's words when he declared that "these [Old Testament] events happened as examples for us" (1 Cor. 10:6), and that "they were written for our instruction" (10:11, NASB). Consequently, we will understand that the message of the text is for the edification of our listeners every bit as much as for those to whom it was originally written.

Believing this, we will preach the text as a contemporary message. We will direct the words of the passage to our congregations as if it were written with them in mind. We do so because, as Paul explained, that is the actual fact. Therefore, we will not lecture on what happened to the Amalekites; rather, we will talk about what their experience has to do with our church members. That means that we will not preach about the Amalekites but about God and his people from the account of God's dealings with the Amalekites. Our preaching, then, will be fresh and contemporary in nature.

Preachers today, like the Lord who powerfully wrote to seven of his churches in Revelation 2 and 3, analyze their congregations so that what they preach meets their needs. While preaching may be expository, as one preaches through a book, the choice of the biblical book itself should be made with those needs in mind.

6. THE ORIGINAL INTENT OF THE TEXT CONTROLS ITS MESSAGE TO HEARERS TODAY

Informed preachers will demark portions of Scripture for sermons on the basis of their intent. This intent may also be referred to as the telos, or purpose, of the portion. Every preaching passage, then, is selected because in itself it is a complete message from God. This message may be but part of a larger one, but it is a message that calls on the listener to believe, disbelieve, change, or do something God wishes that ultimately will contribute to the two great purposes of the Bible—to help the members of our congregations to love God and their neighbors.

Throughout the history of preaching, unfortunately, that has often not been the case. Preachers have used the Scriptures for their own purposes rather than for the purposes for which they were given, thus losing the power inherent in any given preaching portion. It is not without reason that the Gospel of John has been used more frequently than any other to bring people to a saving knowledge of Jesus Christ; it was written for that purpose. The Spirit, who produced the Bible, will bless its use when the preacher's intent is the same as his own.

7. The Subject of Every Message Is God and People

Contemporary preaching that proclaims God's message to his people is always personal. That means the preacher will not attempt to preach in a lecture form. We will avoid abstract language and concepts. We will not speak about the Bible, but we will preach about God and his congregation from the Bible. We will "open" the Scriptures as Jesus did (Luke 24:32), informing our listeners about its content, but always making apparent the relevance of the text to them. We recognize that we are not merely giving a speech, but we are preaching to people about their personal relationships to God and their neighbors. That is to say, we will cast our sermons in a second-person mold. The dominant word will not be I, he, she, it, but *you*. We will take our cue in this regard from the preaching of Jesus in the Sermon on the Mount.

8. Clarity Is Paramount

In order to preach effectively, we will adopt a clear, simple style that is easily understood by those who hear. We will recognize that the apostle Paul declared it a duty to be clear (Col. 4:4) and even requested prayer from his readers that God would help him to fulfill this duty. We will not only pray about our preaching ourselves, but will enlist our congregation to do so too.

In our efforts to maintain clarity throughout, we will adopt nontechnical language (unless we explain it). We will avoid "preachy" terminology, obsolete terms, and outdated phraseology. We will proclaim God's message without strange tones, singsong, or anything else that calls attention to itself rather than to the truth. We will keep ourselves in the background as much as possible, thrusting Christ to the forefront of the message.

In order to achieve clarity, we will use illustrations and examples that help listeners to comprehend. These will be culled largely from contemporary experiences so that through them we may be able to demonstrate not only what the passage means in everyday life, that it is practical and not merely theoretical, but also how God expects the listener to appropriate the truth.

God's truth must not be jumbled up in the proclamation. It should flow inexorably from start to finish in a reasoned, logical manner. This means that an industrious preacher will take the time to think not only about content, but also about the form in which this is presented. Caring preachers labor to make God's truth as simple and easily understood as possible (without loss of meaning) so that their people may readily receive it.

9. OUR DUTY IS TO PREACH BOLDLY

Humble preachers resemble the apostle Paul, who asked for prayer that he might "make known with boldness the mystery of the gospel" (Eph. 6:19, NASB). They keep in mind what might be called the preacher's prayer, in which the disciple prayed to speak "the word of God boldly" (Acts 4:29). Such preachers recognize that the word for "boldness" used here (*parremsia*), and throughout the book of Acts, that characterized New Testament preaching means "freedom to speak without fear of consequences."

Chapter 6

PREACHING THAT RAISES OUR SIGHTS
*What sort of preaching—what sort of preacher—
can raise the bar for low jumpers?*

Crawford Loritts

Inherent in preaching is a sense of divine authority that distinguishes it from merely good communication. Great preachers are good communicators, but good communicators are not necessarily great preachers. And the difference is authority. My definition of preaching is it is a word from God for the people at a moment in history.

Every preacher needs to keep in mind three great axioms:

1. *Don't ever dare to stand in front of a group of people with a Bible in your hand and not expect change.* We must have a holy confidence—confidence in God and his Word, confidence that God is going to change lives whenever we speak from his book.
2. *Remember that the goal of all ministry is transformation.* It's not about being liked. It's not about being accepted. God's ultimate goal is to change lives.
3. *At the end of the day, the effectiveness of our preaching will burst forth from the holiness of our personal lives.*

In 2 Corinthians 2:17, Paul says, "Unlike so many, we do not peddle the word of God for profit." In the Greek, the word *peddle* refers to winemakers who had a little scam. They would dilute the wine and pass it off as if it were the real thing. Paul says no, don't violate the integrity of the truth of God's Word. Don't become so concerned about "communication" that the pure content is diluted. Paul goes on to say, "On the contrary . . . we speak before God with sincerity." That tells us to be genuine in our communication, maintaining integrity. Don't be an orator who becomes an actor, who gets so enthralled by saying something in a way that people will give you a standing ovation. Don't be overly concerned with turning a

36

phrase in a way to get the smiles and approval of people.

There is an intoxication about a platform. With increased recognition must come increased brokenness, so that you don't play with people. We have to remember we are dealing with eternal matters, with truth, with things that demand complete transparency and integrity.

Chapter 7

LEADING AND FEEDING
How preaching and leadership intersect

Jack Hayford

We're in a church culture that places a lot of emphasis on leadership. Pastors think not only in terms of pastoring people but also in terms of leading the church, the corporate body of Christ. Yet as we try to be strong leaders and pastors, we have to think about the preaching task. This article examines how leading and preaching intersect.

The discernment between the pastor's roles of leading and feeding are essential. We must discern when we are preaching simply to advance a program and when we are preaching to advance the kingdom. It's important to keep those things clearly distinguished.

The nature of the life of the global church and the nature of the spiritual battle mandate that we recognize our task as not simply to gather people together and teach them the Bible. Small groups can do that—without there being any sort of a congregation or a specifically assigned pastor. People can do that in their home with their own family, and those things ought to happen. But a pastor, by definition, is a person who is not only feeding but is also taking the people somewhere.

Shepherds do that. They lead and feed. That's the essence of pastoral work. Any of us who have pastored have discovered that people would far rather be fed than they would be led. Folks who are hungry for the Word, as good sheep of the pasture of Christ are, like to learn. They like to have freshness, things that warm their soul, encourage them, lift them, give them insight and instruction. But when you start to say, "Folks, it's time for us to move, not just to feed," the flock will begin to grumble and mumble, because the sheep would rather just bed down and eat there for a long time. But there is a place where the pastor's preaching ministry must point the direction for the church to go.

For example, many years ago I preached a series of messages on an issue my church was facing. The elders of the church recommended the acquisition of a large piece of real estate. We bought an entire church campus that was to be in addition to our existing campus. The amount of money involved in the purchase was a big stretch for us.

I had felt the Lord move my heart to purchase this new campus even before anything had been presented to the congregation, and really before we knew for certain we could actually acquire the property. I was moved strongly to bring a series of messages from the book of Joshua. So I preached a series entitled, "Possess Your Tomorrows."

I examined the text in which God said to a group of people in ancient times, "I have a place for you and a promised purpose for you in that place." This purpose was going to require a whole set of steps in order for this to take place. It would not be without struggle. It would not be without vision and faith. It would not be without failures along the way. So that series, "Possess Your Tomorrows," became the calling card for the new campus.

But my role as leader did not trump my role as feeder. When I introduced the series, I did not say, "I'm bringing you this series of messages because we're thinking about buying some property." In fact, that series never once discussed the acquisition of the property. I brought the series of messages because I new that every person in my congregation was in some place in his or her life in which God was beckoning toward new life possibilities. The possession of the tomorrows of their lives had their principles set in taking steps forward to realize the hope and the possibilities of those promises. My first concern was to nurture people, so wherever they were in their lives, they would find something that would feed them with principles for possessing what God had for them.

I believe that series prepared hearts to stretch beyond where they were. When the vision for the additional campus came, I was able to reflect back to that series, and immediately the people were able to make the connection to what God was calling us as a church to do. I was able to help expand their sense of God's readiness to do more than we thought, but also to help them recognize that that would have a price to pay, a path to pursue. For me, that was a classic case of leading and feeding. In a sense,

that sermon series became the stars by which the church could navigate. It became a frame of reference for values, for beliefs, for a way of looking at life so that when they had to take action, they were ready.

THE RESPONSIBILITY OF LEADERSHIP

Every pastor has a leadership responsibility. He or she cannot simply be a chameleon reflection of what the people want. I realize you can get into all kinds of potential political problems, and maybe even lose your job, but there are times when a pastor needs to raise his voice. If I have things I want to say that may have a grating potential on anybody, I usually will meet with leaders in the church first and let them know what I'm feeling. Then I can go before the people with a sense of companionship and the partnership of the recognized leaders and speak with the authority of the Word of God.

Of course, the different degrees of leadership with which each pastor is gifted—and I believe leadership capacities are simply a part of a person's gifting—usually will be commensurate to the dimension of the pastorate to which God will call that pastor to serve. The larger a church, obviously the more demanding the leadership gift.

LEADING GROUPS BY LEADING INDIVIDUALS

The foremost call of the pastor-shepherd as leader and feeder is not only to lead the church as a body, but to lead each individual as a sheep. As it says in Isaiah 40:11: "He will feed his flock as a shepherd; he will gather the lambs in his arms, and carry them in his bosom, and gently lead the mother sheep" (NRSV). The shepherdly task is not just to say, "Hey flock!" and expect them all to follow. There are sheep who need to be carried in the arm at times. There are ones who are like the ewes who are great with young. There's a more sensitive way of leading people who are going through a crisis or transitional times of their lives. There's a personal leadership focus, as well as a group, or corporate, leadership focus.

For me, the primary value has been my call to nurture the creative purpose of God. By "creative purpose" I mean what God invented that person to be, what he or she was made to be. I am called to nurture that process in every individual in the church. In the pulpit, that individual is my target; I want to nurture what God made those individual persons to be and to help lead them through the next baby steps forward of whatever will be God's vision for their life.

I do that hoping that they will, somewhere along the way, capture God's vision for their lives and align themselves with it. I do not see my teaching as simply instructional, educational, and informational. It is always prophetic, pointing forward, calling to some point of advance. It's leading them to stretch.

I lead people with every message. But the target is to nurture the benevolent purpose of God for their lives. It's not to get them to meet some ethical requirement I want to harp on today. It's not to get them to meet some local congregational goal. It's to help that person become what he or she was meant to be.

Within this context, then, the greatest desire I have is—through ministering the Word—to lead people to a conviction of three things. The first is to realize the absolute commitment of God in his love for them, the love that has justified us through the blood of Christ. The second conviction is for them to know that that

same love is the love that is committed to fulfilling God's vision for them. And the third is to come to the assertive confidence that there is going to be a triumph, whatever may be their present environment, their struggle, or their fears. I want them to realize there will be victory. That victory may take on different variations from what the person first thought when he or she started the journey, but nonetheless they are going to come through triumphantly.

So those are my goals: to lead people with those understandings. First, God made you with a specific high purpose and destiny. This throbs through the passion of my preaching. Second, God's love has embraced you and is going to get you there. God is beside you, and he will never leave or forsake you. The Lord is supporting you. Third, whatever is the apparent point of struggle or apparent reversal, there is going to be an ultimate triumph.

Leading people toward that view of themselves is, in itself, feeding, but it is also leading, because our tendency is to think, "You can say I'm a person of special purpose, but I still don't feel it. I know God loves me, but it's just tough to feel that today—and especially as unworthy as I behaved myself this week." They think, "I'm dealing with some tough stuff, and I know you're talking about victory ahead, but you better remind me because it's hard to remember that right now."

Everybody needs to be led constantly through those things. And the essence of the shepherd's doing, as the Isaiah passage says, is to graciously lead the flock, but with a sensitive arm to bear up those who are young and to lead those who are about to bear lambs—those people who are in transition, who are carrying the possibility of new purpose and new life. It's still not a comfortable time for them.

That is the leadership role of the pastor. All feeding should center around those priorities: helping people feel the sense of God's purpose, a sense of his love, and a sense of his commitment to ultimate victory.

SELECTING PREACHING TOPICS FOR LEADERSHIP

Sometimes I pay attention to current events and select preaching topics accordingly. For example, my church is in an area of California with lots of earthquakes. During the earthquake of 1994, which was horribly devastating in our area, I preached on issues like suffering and God's providence. Another example is when I preached on issues related to the Los Angeles riots of 1992.

Those things called for ministry out of the Word of God that addressed a dominating, preoccupying issue of our lives. Any pastor who would continue on some idealistic pursuit of a series he has been engaged in is not being realistic with the Scriptures, not to mention being unrealistic with the world. The Bible addresses people in the need, turmoil, and pathos of their lives. Those moments present the pastor with a leadership challenge: How do I lead the flock during this horrible time of upheaval and respond to the questions this upheaval brings to their minds? How can I lead the ministry opportunities for a thinking believer? What can I be in the environment of this crisis?

When the Gulf War took place, I preached two Sunday mornings on the attitude of believers with regard to war. Leaders address issues at points of crisis.

In this kind of leadership preaching, I've also had to lead at times when we felt God was speaking to us as a congregation attitudinally. I've dealt with such things as ethnic attitudes. I gave a series about how to deal with the face of Los Angeles as it has changed radically in the thirty years I have pastored here. We had to decide whether we were going to make some kind of a flight and relocate and be the white congregation we were when I first took the church. There came a point when I felt we needed to say as a body we would be a congregation that would commit ourselves to multiethnicity in our church. We would make up our minds that we would not be preferential; we'd be tolerant in our church life. We were not on a political crusade to be multi-ethnic, but on a kingdom crusade to be people who model what it means to be "every kingdom, tribe, tongue, and nation."

Thus, I gave a series entitled "Outracing the World." We wanted to outpace society's advance on this and not be controlled by the racial and ethnic attitudes with which all of us have been enculturated. When we do these kinds of messages, we don't just do them on Sunday mornings. They're announced well in advance. They're kind of landmark events, and the church is packed when we do them. And they're long sermons; it's not uncommon for one of our pastors to preach an hour and fifteen minutes or give an hour and twenty-minute message on a significant theme. Preaching on topics of current interest and relevance is a good way to lead with the Scriptures and, at the same time, feed the people. I would encourage pastors to keep foremost in view that you're leading people who have their own challenges to face. We must nurture and then, out of their health, to see the body of Christ move with health toward the realization of their goals.

Chapter 8

JOHN 3:16 IN THE KEY OF C

Why true preachers are worship leaders

Jeffrey Arthurs

An unfortunate trend has occurred in some churches—the separation of preaching and worship. I don't mean that the two no longer occur in the same service but that many people think of them as distinct even when they occur together. The term *worship* has become almost synonymous with singing, especially singing contemporary music. With our healthy postmodern emphasis on experience, worship is valued as more engaging, holistic, participatory, and even transformative than preaching, which connotes cognition and authoritative monologue. Worship is up, preaching is down, and never the twain shall meet.

In contrast to this trend, I contend that the Bible depicts preaching and worship as tightly bound in a symbiotic relationship. First Peter 4:11 captures this concept: "If anyone speaks, he should do it as one speaking the very words of God . . . so that in all things God may be praised through Jesus Christ."

WORSHIP IS REVELATION AND RESPONSE

Worship can be summarized as revelation and response. What that summary lacks in precision, it gains in breadth. It is wide enough to include all that the Bible calls worship, including singing and prayer as well as presenting our bodies as living sacrifices (Rom. 12:1) and sharing with others (Heb. 13:16). It is wide enough to capture the broad expanse of activities and moods characterizing worship in the Bible—singing, shouting, silence, repenting, remembering, serving, giving, tithing, interceding, playing a musical instrument, lifting hands, dancing, kneeling, fasting, and feasting. All of these activities are responses prompted by the revelation of God's character and will.

Two classic texts support the idea that worship is revelation and response. The first is Isaiah 6, where the prophet saw the Lord seated on a throne, high and exalted. The revelation of God's holiness prompted Isaiah to respond, "Woe to me," and "Here I am, send me" (Isa. 6:5, 8). The second text, Micah 6, describes a similar exchange. Micah asks how he should worship: "Shall I come before him with burnt offerings, with calves a year old?" God responds with a reminder of what has already been revealed: "He has showed you, O man, what is good, and what does the Lord require of you? To act justly and to love mercy and to walk humbly with your God" (Mic. 6:6b, 8).

In these texts, God himself (or his commissioned seraphim) reveals his own glory, but even when God uses human instruments—the foolishness of preaching—the process is the same. He reveals himself and prompts response. Therefore, worship is unlikely (dare we say impossible?) without preaching.

I know that my argument has jumped quickly over hedges of objection, so let me qualify the argument. I am not saying that preaching must occur in every worship service. An old fashioned hymn sing can be wonderful worship. Neither am I saying that the only way God reveals himself is through words. He also communicates aspects of his glory through nature, art, and companionship. I've praised God while walking the rim of the Grand Canyon, listening to a concert, and basking in the love of my friends.

I am saying that when God reveals his magnificence, it naturally produces worshipful response—repentance, laughter, works of righteousness, singing, and so forth. I'm also saying that God has chosen to use preaching as a primary channel for his self-revelation, so that the separation of worship and preaching is unnatural at best and harmful at worst. When we reduce worship solely to its experiential, affective, and artistic components, we no longer have biblical worship. True worship is rooted in God's self-revelation—hence, the need for preaching.

Preaching reveals God's character, and it also reveals his expectations for his people. Preaching explains doctrine and applies it to everyday life. As Warren Wiersbe says, "A sermon isn't a picture on the wall, hanging there for folks to admire. . . . The sermon is a door that opens onto a path that leads the pilgrim into new steps of growth and service to the glory of God" (*Preaching and Teaching with Imagination*, p. 218). Because sermons exhort and equip, they are indispensable to the response aspect of worship.

The early church knew this. In *The Reading and Preaching of the Scriptures in the Worship of the Christian Church*, Hughes Old summarizes the *Didache*, a manual of church life from the early second century: The worshiping congregation understood Christ to be present with them "by means of the teaching and preaching of the Word of God." In contrast to the doctrine that developed in a few centuries, "the *Didache* teaches a doctrine of the real presence which is kergymatic rather than eucharistic" (p. 265). When we encounter this lofty view of preaching, we are surprised to see that much of the exhortation in the *Didache* is down-to-earth moral instruction. It speaks of the relations between teachers and students, husbands and wives, and parents and children. It promotes chastity and almsgiving. In the midst of such moral instruction the early church believed Christ revealed himself. Revelation was melded with response.

The union of revelation and response, and the pattern of that ordering, is present in most of Paul's letters. He begins with doctrine and then proceeds to exhortation. That pattern also marks much biblical preaching—explanation then application. It is a time-tested form, and it makes sense.

The pattern is at least as old as postexilic Israel when Ezra read the Law aloud "from daybreak till noon" while "all the people listened attentively" (Neh. 8). In response, the people "lifted their hands and responded, 'Amen! Amen!' Then they bowed down and worshiped the LORD with their faces to the ground." The Levites "instructed the people in the Law while the people were standing there . . . making it clear and giving the meaning." This prompted sorrow as the people realized how far their nation had strayed, but soon Nehemiah and Ezra called for an end to their mourning: "Go and enjoy choice food and sweet drinks, and send some to those who have nothing prepared. This day is sacred to the Lord." Revelation of God's glory and his requirements produced response.

The preacher's role as revealer of God's glory and will is captured in a quotation from Cotton Mather, the New England divine: "The great design and intention of the office of a Christian preacher [is] to restore the throne and dominion of God in the souls of men" (quoted in John Piper, *The Supremacy of God in Preaching*, p. 22).

THE IMPLICATIONS OF PREACHING IN WORSHIP

Two implications arise from my argument that preaching exists in a symbiotic relationship with worship. First, preaching must be thoroughly God-centered (theocentric), not man-centered (anthropocentric).

If a visitor to your church could mistake your sermon for a self-help talk, moral diatribe, or spiritual lecture, you are not preaching biblically. Barth's advice to prepare sermons with the Bible in one hand and the newspaper in the other is helpful as long as we hold the Holy Book in our strong right hand. The Bible must interpret the newspaper. Another way to say this is that the quest for relevance may begin with felt needs, but those needs must be linked to ultimate needs—darkness and rebellion—and solutions must include repentance and faith toward God prompted by a portrayal of his fearsome beauty. Preachers are worship leaders. Our job is to magnify God, explain his decrees, and urge response. This is the essence of worship.

One trend in homiletics, popular among our Reformed brothers and sisters, has understood this implication. That trend is called Christ-centered preaching. You may disagree with some details of that program (I myself have questions about its hermeneutics), but surely all of us applaud its basic stance: Preaching is about Jesus! This stance does not negate our need to analyze the audience, but it will mitigate extreme forms of audience adaptation. The tail must not wag the dog.

The second implication of preaching as indispensable to worship is that preachers should work in concert with the entire worship service.

This takes planning. We should coordinate singing, special music, prayer, testimony, communion, and other elements according to the general pattern of revelation and response as well the specific revelation for that service. Churches in the liturgical tradition have done this for centuries. Perhaps the worship services of those churches would benefit from more flexibility so that they could, for example, follow the sermon with a testimony as a direct response. Churches in the "free" tradition might benefit from more structure. For example, they may want to adopt the tradition of ending each service with a charge to urge response to what has been revealed.

However we work out the details, my hope is that preaching will be seen as indispensable to worship since it both reveals God and urges response.

Chapter 9

GROWING IN YOUR PREACHING
The call to preach demands our very best

Bill Hybels

For those of you who wish to sharpen your teaching gift, whether it's a top-level gift or somewhere lower in your mix, you're desiring exactly what Paul encouraged Timothy to pursue: "Be diligent in these matters; give yourself wholly to them, so that everyone may see your progress" (1 Tim. 4:15). Paul told Timothy to work at improving his preaching. You, in turn, may be asking, "How do I do that? How do I get better?" Here are some ideas that will prove useful.

LISTEN TO GREAT PREACHING AND TEACHING

In almost every discipline, if you want to improve, you need to watch others. If you want to develop your golf game, you need to watch golf. Study tapes showing people swinging correctly and effectively. I'm a sailboat racer. So if I'm not racing a boat myself, I'll watch other people race so I can observe their skills. I study how they trim their sails and how their crew work, and I watch their tactics. The way we tend to get better at anything is by putting ourselves in a situation where we can get more information about what we're trying to improve.

Most of us have two or three communicators who really inspire us. We say, "Boy, I wish I could communicate a little more like her" or "a little more like him." Do more than wish.

Get on their tape lists. Read their stuff. Go hear them when you can. And instead of listening to them casually, listen to them with your work gloves on.

Ask some clear questions. Why did that introduction work so well? Why did that point come across with such power? What was there about the structure of that message that made it so memorable?

In my opinion, the late E. V. Hill was one of the best preachers around. I once watched a tape, marveling at his sense of timing. He came to a very tender part in his message, paused, and then slowly walked around the side of the lectern. He let everything become utterly quiet in the room. Then with a lowered voice he said something with great emotion and gentleness. It was such a moment from God.

That was helpful for me to watch because my temperament is like a machine gunner. I tend to say, "All right, here's the point. Now let's go!" And if I'm not carefully taking time to absorb great preaching and teaching, I'll unintentionally mow people down with my intensity. I have to learn how to pause, shift the level of passion, and vary the tone of what I do.

Some preachers are great storytellers; I just want to get to the point of what I'm teaching. So when I tell a story that's full of potential humor, capable of putting some energy in the room, I'm usually so anxious to get to the lesson

44

payoff that I fail to take the necessary time to embellish it.

John Ortberg recently told a great story about himself and Dr. B. [Dr. Gilbert Bilezekian] winding up in the same airplane. Dr. B. had been upgraded, but John was in the back of the plane. He had fun with that story for several minutes, getting enormous humor out of it with remarks like "I was eating a chicken-like substance in the back while Dr. B. was dining on fine china." The point is this: John had a lot of fun with the story and still made a strong point. It gave opportunity for humor. So listen to great preaching and teaching not with the intent to mimic it but rather to learn lessons that can improve your own preaching and teaching.

This next statement is so obvious that I hesitate to even say it. Develop your own unique style. While you want to learn from great preachers, you don't want to copy their style.

John Maxwell and I teach communications seminars around the country, and we have two very different styles. John will use a music stand, a stool, and have two or three things to drink all around him. He'll wander in and out of the crowd, hide behind plants, throw stuff, and ask people questions. His style is so different than mine that he has fun kidding me about it. One time he took a piece of chalk and drew a line out in front of the lectern. He said, "I'll give you a hundred bucks if you'll step over that line." I tried for two days and just couldn't do it. We laugh at that because our styles are so different. But you know what? I'm comfortable with mine, and he's comfortable with his. There are things we can each learn from the other, but we shouldn't try to copy each other.

A helpful practice we utilize at Willow is brainstorming with other great teachers. People would be shocked if they learned how much we bounce message ideas off one another around here. If I'm stuck on something, I'll drop into Nancy's office or Lee's office or John's. I'll say, "I'm working on this message. I could go at it this way or that way. What comes to your mind?" Great communicators bubble ideas about communication recreationally. When you get the opportunity to do that, don't think you have to sit at your desk in total isolation. Ask people. Say, "I'm preaching on this issue or text. What would you want to hear about it?"

We frequently do this with illustrations as well. We'll just ask someone, "Have you ever had anything memorable happen to you that I could use for an illustration?" It's a great source of fresh stories and we are careful to give credit when we tell one. So remember, you're not in it alone. Listen to great preaching and teaching.

UNDERSTAND THE DYNAMIC OF URGENCY

A second way to develop yourself as a communicator involves understanding the dynamic of urgency. Many years ago when I was trying to take a step toward improving my own preaching, I listened to about fifteen or twenty different sermon tapes while asking, "What are the common denominators of great preaching and teaching?" The one that consistently rose to the top was this sense of urgency. I was repeatedly struck with how the person preaching was talking as though their subject matter was the most urgent issue on the planet. Everything else went away. So I began to analyze that.

If preaching is done right, you live with a text or topic for a week and it builds steam in your spirit. You're thinking about it, talking to people about it, and asking that God will anoint it. So by the time you're ready to preach, this subject is the most urgent item in your spirit. If you've prepared properly, there is an urgency coming out of you that's not manufactured. That becomes compelling communication.

Jesus was the Master at this. At the end of the Sermon on the Mount he says, "You all ought to know there's a tremendous storm on the horizon." That wakes people up, doesn't it? They're looking out in the sky, trying to find the first clouds. He continues, "Now, you can take the words I just spoke to you and disregard them. That would be like building a house on sand. When that storm comes, your life is going to be blown flat. Or you can take the words I just spoke, and build your life on them. And when that storm hits your life, you're going to stand. Either way, you can count on this fact: There's a storm coming" (see Matt. 7:24–27).

Well, people know you're playing for keeps when you preach with such urgency. I think a large measure of Billy Graham's success as a communicator has been his urgency. Don't manufacture it. Live with a text and let it build in your spirit until you're feeling burdened about the issue. Then you're ready to preach.

STRIVE FOR CLARITY

Third, if you want to improve your communication, strive for clarity. When I coach our teachers around here, I always ask them two questions. "What do you want them to know? What do you want them to do?" If they can't answer those two questions immediately, I say, "You're ill prepared. Don't inflict that message on our people."

So much preaching these days is meandering. It's a walk through six or seven different tulip beds, plucking a little flower here and there. You get to the end and you don't know what the preacher wanted you to know or do. You must pass the clarity test.

You must also devote time toward creativity. It is so easy for us to fall into ruts and never vary our styles. We urge our teachers at Willow to drop the spoon-fed approach and shake things up once in a while. We encourage them to use a question-asking style, or some props instead of just standing at the pulpit with a Bible in hand. We've found props to be remarkably helpful. I was talking about the pressures of life once, and I brought out a chemistry set complete with Bunsen burner. When I lit that Bunsen burner and put a beaker over it and stuff started boiling, people were really listening—all because I used that one little prop.

Another time I was preparing to teach on the tenderness of God. The idea occurred to me to preach from the passage that says, "A bruised reed God will not allow to break." So, I got a bruised reed and held it while I said, "Some of you feel like a bruised reed today." I talked to them about the tenderness of God while holding that simple prop.

As I visited the offices or homes of our people over the following weeks, many had a bruised reed on their desk or taped to their refrigerator. It was amazing. People remember that stuff.

THE PERSPIRATION FACTOR

A fourth element in improving your preaching is what I call the perspiration factor. Most of our preaching would improve greatly if we would discipline ourselves to put one more hour into it. Many preachers don't believe work enters into the equation of great preaching. But you don't become good at anything unless you've paid the perspiration price. You've just got to pay it. And when you discover how much you have to pay for the acceptable quality level, then that price must become the "given" in your schedule.

It honestly takes me a minimum of twenty hours a week to put together an acceptable message. So that time becomes absolutely non-negotiable in my week if I have to preach. And if I have a funeral or get called out of town for some emergency, I've been known to get in the office at 3:30 in the morning because I know it takes me twenty hours. I can't cheat that quality rule. If I put the time in, God will usually give me a message. But perspiration is essential.

EVALUATION

Next, evaluation plays a huge part of the improvement process for all growing communicators. If I have developed at all as a communicator in the last twenty-five years, much of it comes from requested evaluations after every single talk I give. Every time I give a message at Willow I have half a dozen people who will evaluate it. We have a system and I rely on these people. I don't ask just anybody to do it because some would use it like an axe. I invite people who love me, but love God and this church more, to give me honest feedback. What worked well? What needed to be improved? I'm specific with my evaluators. "Don't tell me 'Point three stunk' because that doesn't help

me. If you think point three was weak, then tell me how you would make it better." I usually have about an hour until I give the message again, and maybe I can integrate some of that feedback into the next delivery.

I'm often tempted to cut a corner when I'm putting a message together. But I'll think, *That's a logical corner I'm cutting, and attorney Russ Robinson, one of my evaluators, will have me dead to rights if I do it.* I know that "corner" will be first on his list. So, I can't do that.

If I'm tempted to take a little theological shortcut, Dr. B. is going to be waiting for me on the other end. So I think, *Man, I can't deal with that.* And if I miss an opportunity to be a little more artful in my presentation, John always shows me where I could have brought something back at the end that would have made it a more touching thing. There are so many ways to benefit and grow from well-rounded evaluation.

For more from Bill Hybels on evaluation, see chapter 193, "Well-Focused Preaching."

LIVE IN UNION WITH JESUS

Finally, I just cannot end without saying this: Live in such vital union with Jesus Christ that his power and his might flow through your preaching. It sounds as if it shouldn't need to be said but nothing can replace this truth. In simple terms here's how this works. Pray like crazy. Trust like crazy. Expect God to work. And then thank him when he does.

Chapter 10

SPIRITUAL FORMATION THROUGH PREACHING
Four components of preaching that changes lives

Robertson McQuilkin

Recently I was asked to speak at a preaching conference on the topic "Spiritual Formation through Preaching." The first thing that popped into my head was, *Spiritual formation—what else do you do through preaching?* Maybe evangelistic preaching wouldn't qualify as spiritual formation, but it certainly is aimed at starting the process.

My second thought was, *Through preaching? How else would you ever help people grow spiritually?* Oh, I almost forgot—counseling could do it, though it doesn't often intentionally do so. Or teaching, though many a teacher thinks merely of informing the frontal lobe. Writing could surely qualify, though most of it is aimed in other directions. And then there are the newer models aimed at spiritual formation—small group sharing and one-on-one mentoring. Or the latest form of personal discipleship—new for Protestants at least: enlisting a spiritual director. But Holy Spirit-anointed preaching is the means that seems best designed to aid spiritual formation.

There. I've done it, the inexcusable—my musings about the topic have given away my prejudices, my access code! At least that has the merit of enabling you to click delete if we're not tracking. But if you resonate with my understanding of the purpose and potential of preaching, click here, and we may get some clues on how to promote spiritual growth through preaching. Practically speaking, how

do we make sure our preaching results in spiritual transformation?

I suggest four indispensables. Our preaching should be Bible-based, Spirit-energized, verdict-demanding, and audience-connected.

BIBLE-BASED

When I say Bible-based, some people automatically think of expository preaching. Expository preaching is my favorite. In fact, I usually go away feeling malnourished when the message isn't expositional, flowing from the text. But that's not what I mean by Bible-based. Whatever the homiletical structure or approach—every word I speak from the pulpit is under the functional authority of Scripture. It is true to the meaning of Scripture, true to the emphases of Scripture, true to the purpose of Scripture.

The Word of God is designed to function as the controlling authority. That is, every sermon must be developed, consciously and intentionally, under the authority of Scripture so that the Bible—not tradition or a theological system, not my pet theme or contemporary pressures—functions as the control center. The Bible is not just a V-chip to filter out false teaching, but the programmer in charge. So, when it comes to promoting spiritual formation, three grand themes of Scripture will control my content:

1. God's standard for the Christian life
2. God's provision for me to reach that standard

3. Our responsibility in accessing that provision

These themes are pervasive in Scripture, but they are more than pervasive. They are the point of revelation, so if my preaching does not constantly focus on these themes, how can I claim to be Bible-based? Let's consider them briefly.

God's Standard

God's standard is no less than God himself. From Genesis, where we are created in his likeness, to Revelation, where the image is fully restored; from Jesus' command that we are to be perfect as the Father is perfect (Matt. 5:48), to Paul's assurance that the new self is being renewed after the likeness of him in whose image it was originally created (Col. 3:9–10)— our goal is God. We must ever hold before our people in pragmatic detail and specific application God's standard for the Christian life.

I arrived for a missions conference in a dynamic, growing, missions-oriented church in Florida. On meeting the senior pastor, I was surprised to have him say we had met before and even more surprised to hear that first meeting had been ministry-transforming. At the end of a missions week in a major evangelical seminary, Brent told me, he had volunteered to take me to the airport. I had shared with the students the story of God's love for the whole world, clearly revealed from Genesis to Revelation, and the mandate we have for full participation in completing what he began. As a doctoral student Brent apparently hadn't attended the chapels. As we sat over coffee at the airport, I asked about his ministry, and he said he preached the Word. By that he meant verse-by-verse exposition. I asked about the missions program of the church, and he said there wasn't much of one. So I responded,

"And what word is it you're preaching?" In that instant, he testified, his whole life and ministry were transformed.

God's Provision

You might say God's standard produced that response in him. But God's standard could be dreadfully distressing without God's provision. The second great theme of Scripture is God's provision for our salvation in its full splendor— from initial forgiveness through the final denouement when "we shall be like him, for we shall see him as he is" (1 John 3:2). The standard must be coupled always with the provision.

Enter the Holy Spirit, the One who created us on God's pattern in the first place (Gen. 1:27), who convicts us of our hopelessness and helplessness (John 16:8), who breathes new life into us (John 3:6), who changes us into altogether new creations with vastly new potential (2 Cor. 5:17), who takes up residence as our inside companion (John 14:17), who gave us the Book (2 Tim. 3:16–17) and daily illumines its meaning, and who transforms us from one degree of Jesus' glorious character to another (2 Cor. 3:18). The person of the Holy Spirit is the provision of the triune God for living godly in an ungodly world.

Not all teach this. In one church I attended for two years I loved the profound expository preaching. Gradually, however, I began to realize something was missing. The preacher obviously believed strongly in human sinfulness. He also believed in justification and glorification. But I gradually came to understand he didn't believe in much in between. A nationally recognized biblical scholar also attended, but left the church before I did. The other day I met this influential Reformed scholar again, and we spoke of the view of the Christian life we had both been exposed to. "Arrogant pessimism!"

he said. "Those fellows don't offer any hope of power to live the life." By selecting only those passages that advanced his doctrines, we were left with little hope for the interim between initial and final salvation. But God has made full provision in the person of the Holy Spirit for our empowerment to be transformed from one degree of his glorious character to another. Just as the standard is God himself, so the provision.

Our Responsibility

But your congregants will ask, How do I connect? How does it happen? We must be faithful to explain the implications of our personal responsibility for accessing that provision. The access code is simple. The glorious truth is it is available to all! Faith. Faith for initial salvation, faith for transformation, faith for growth toward our goal. "Let us rid ourselves of all that weighs us down, of the sinful habit that clings so closely, and run, with all endurance, the race for which we are entered, our eyes fixed on Jesus, on whom faith depends from start to finish" (Heb. 12:1–2, NEB).

Why do so many church members seem to be spiritually on hold? Of course, a spiritual plateau isn't really possible. We're either spiraling up toward ever greater likeness to Jesus and ever greater intimacy with him, or we're spiraling downward, away from that tight connection, ever less like him. What must we do when the spiral up falters? What's gone wrong? We say faith is the key, but why doesn't it seem to work? Why doesn't the connection seem to produce the promised results?

Perhaps there's a disconnect after all. Perhaps the preacher has only plugged them into the positive pole of faith, neglecting the negative pole of repentance. Bible faith—whether for salvation or sanctification—is bipolar: repentance

toward God and faith toward our Lord Jesus Christ (Acts 20:21). If faith is just intellectual assent to certain essential truths, a person is no more saved than the devils who also believe (James 2:19).

And sanctification? Yield and trust, the same two poles of biblical faith. Neglect one or the other, and growth stops because there's a disconnect. Preach one or the other out of proportion to the need of the people? Disconnect!

These, then, are the themes that must fill the menu of our people's diet if we are serious about nurturing spiritual formation: God's standard—himself; God's provision—the Spirit; and our responsibility—faith.

SPIRIT-ENERGIZED

It's possible to fascinate a congregation so that numbers steadily increase, to explain the Bible text so professionally one's reputation reaches back to the halls of alma mater, to inform the mind so carefully our people are recognized as Bible experts, and still to miss out on spiritual formation. Without the energizing power of the Spirit, fresh each time one enters the pulpit, our people will not demonstrate any miracle quality of life. Family and coworkers will not be impacted by the inexplicable. Any good psychologist could explain their attitudes and behavior in terms of genes, early environment, and present circumstances. And who would go to church in search of such an unsupernatural life?

Unless the fire of the Spirit breaks loose, we can forget about spiritual formation.

Unprepared for Christ's Mission

That's the lesson the disciples had to learn. After three years in Jesus' seminary, after the trauma of their teacher's gruesome death and the exhilaration of his resurrection, they were still on their own agenda—an agenda set by traditions, by centuries of misreading the Scriptures, and by their worldly ambitions. "Is this the time for setting up the kingdom?" they asked (Acts 1:6ff.). (They had in mind throwing out the Romans and, no doubt, putting themselves on twelve thrones surrounding King Jesus.)

Jesus responded, "No, no. That isn't your assignment. I do, however, have an assignment for you. But you're not ready for it." Not ready? After three years in Messiah's School of Theology?

Following his resurrection, over a period of six weeks of final preparation, he'd given his marching orders at least three or four times already (John 20:21; Matt. 28:18–20; Luke 24:47–48; Mark 16:15). And still they didn't get it. So he told them to return to Jerusalem and wait until they were ready. Wait for what? For the Holy Spirit! "Wait till the fire falls—then you'll be equipped to carry out the plan." There's no record he told them to wait on their knees, but I imagine he did tell them because that's what they did. And then the fire fell. Perhaps we're miscuing on what he has in mind for us. We're just plain not ready for his earth-shaking assignment. Is he saying, "Wait. Tarry on your knees. Back to your study till the fire falls"?

Indicators of a Spirit-filled Life

Often the New Testament uses picture language to describe this experience of being Spirit "filled." What will you feel like, what will you look like if you are Spirit filled? The New Testament uses this picture word, *full,* in three different ways. Sometimes it seems to refer to what most contemporaries who specialize in

Spirit filling have in mind—an inner sense of the Spirit's presence—"full with joy in the Holy Spirit," for example (Luke 10:21). God pity the preacher who never has that rush, that ecstatic sense of God's presence.

Sometimes, however, the Bible seems to indicate a relationship more than a feeling—who is in charge? (Eph. 4:29–32; 5:17–18). If the Holy Spirit is in full charge of a relationship, you could say the person is filled with the Spirit. God pity the congregation where the preacher is not unconditionally yielded, fully at the disposal of the Spirit.

By far the most common use of this picture language is to point to the outcome, the evidence of a Spirit-filled life, called "gifts" or "fruit" (1 Cor. 12; Gal. 5:22–23). That is what it means to be filled with the Spirit—being so under the Spirit's control that a miracle life is evident, an abundant harvest of Spirit-fruit that every fruit inspector in the congregation can see. So the only way to explain the results of that man's preaching is to say—Spirit power!

Notice something about those Spirit-filled apostles: Every time a crisis erupted, a new opportunity loomed, or things didn't go according to plan, what did they do? Back to their knees! And what did God do in response? He filled them with the Spirit. Then they preached with boldness, with life-transforming power. Spirit-filled people were filled, the record says (Acts 4:31).

How can that be? I find the analogy of a sailboat helpful. A schooner skimming across the water, sails filled with the breeze, is a beautiful sight. But then a stiff wind comes up from the west and whoosh! Those sails, filled already, are really filled. And so with the Spirit. He may be steady state in charge of our life and ministry, but then comes a special need, a special opportunity. Then comes the time to enter the pulpit. We've been on our knees, we have pleaded for the wind of the Spirit to blow. And that day there is Spirit-filled preaching. If spiritual formation is ever to take place through preaching, that will be the day.

VERDICT-DEMANDING

If I am to preach in a way that results in spiritual formation, my sermon must demand a verdict. This principle of preaching isn't in the same category as the first two principles in this series—that preaching be Bible-based and Spirit-energized—but it does reflect what Bible-based, Spirit-energized preaching is all about.

Preaching for a verdict is one of the things that distinguishes preaching from teaching. Teaching is aimed at the mind, preaching at the heart. "Hold on! When I teach, I'm seeking to move my hearers to action, and when I preach I'm educating my people in the truths of the Word." Of course. Good teaching is aimed at change, and good preaching is solid teaching.

Why, then, the distinction? Several major streams of influence in preaching hold that the correct homiletical approach is verse-by-verse exposition of a text, teaching as many truths as the author may pack into the passage. I would say that is better described as teaching. But when the preacher pulls together the teaching of a passage toward a single goal that calls for response or marshals evidence from various passages of Scripture to drive home a point that requires action, that's preaching, preaching that demands a verdict.

In my student days a favorite teacher used to thunder, "Young men, don't ever fish with a slick line!" Our aim is not merely to fascinate the audience—entertainers do a better job. It should not be our aim just to add to the store of accurate biblical information—a book or computer might serve that end. What we're after is change. If the audience leaves stirred or more biblically literate but doesn't change, there's been no spiritual formation. Spiritual formation is change, and change takes place when choices are made. And so, preaching that demands a verdict is critical to spiritual formation, or, as Paul would put it, to transformation.

Paul is even more specific. He calls us to transform our minds—reformat our mental programs—till more and more we display an accurate depiction of God's good, acceptable, and complete will (Rom. 12:2). How does that happen? "I plead with you by the mercies of God to make a grand presentation"—a sacrifice, in fact (12:1). Paul's charge was verdict-demanding. Change comes by Spirit power when choices are made, so preaching must be verdict demanding if spiritual formation is to occur.

Perhaps you're saying, Bible-based, I can see, and Spirit-energized—those are pervasive in Scripture. But where do you get this requirement to be verdict-demanding? There may not be many instructions to preachers to preach that way specifically in Scripture, but virtually every preacher in the Old Testament and in the New followed this principle. When they opened their mouths, they demanded a response. Their preaching was verdict-demanding.

AUDIENCE-CONNECTED

To connect with our hearers we must translate the message into contemporary language and thought forms.

But isn't our message totally countercultural? That was the thesis of a practical theology professor I spoke with recently. We were discussing over lunch a colleague who has a life-transforming ministry to teens and young adults all over the world. Jack is over sixty, but does he connect! As we talked about the impact of this old man, my lunch mate launched into a strong speech about how Jack belies all this talk about a generation gap: "You have to understand the postmodern mind and connect with it? Rubbish!"

I was astonished to sense the intensity of his feeling about what he felt was the error of trying to be relevant in different ways to different audiences. I was also bemused to think that represented Jack's thinking, so I called Jack to find out.

He laughed. "It's just the opposite," he said. "I study and work hard to understand postmodern thinking and how to connect with a totally different mindset." In fact, he teaches this. He announces to his class they will be tested on the comments he is about to make—that gets their attention—and proceeds to talk in Swahili. Then he tells them there's no point in talking your own language to someone who doesn't understand it. After making his point, he helps them analyze the postmodern mind.

The responsibility of the preacher, then, is to get inside the head, indeed, inside the heart of his audience and communicate in thoughts and words that can be understood, that connect. More than that, thoughts and words that move to action. Jesus didn't drop in for a few weeks in a celestial bubble and talk celestialese. He became one with us.

We need to follow his example and use incarnational preaching. We cannot hide behind the walls of eternal, unchangeable truth, content to pronounce theological jargon with precision, pitching Bible text grenades over the wall into the audience. That's Swahili! Spiritual transformation flows from audience-connected communication.

For specifics by Robertson McQuilkin on preaching to postmoderns, see chapter 43, "Connecting with Postmoderns."

Chapter 11

PREACHING LIFE INTO THE CHURCH
How God uses the ministry of his Word to create and strengthen his body

Jeffrey Arthurs

Of a pastor's numerous activities, sermon preparation ranks as the one that takes the most time. Surveys indicate an average of ten to fifteen hours a week, and that average doesn't include the hours of informal preparation that occur through ancillary reading, observing culture, and interacting with members of the congregation. Preparing sermons is a big part of our lives. Why do we do it? Because we're paid to preach? Because our people expect a good sermon every week? Because we like it?

These reasons have some merit—the merit of duty discharged, people pleased, and the pleasure of study—but they aren't good enough. A better reason, the one I suspect animates most of us, is a conviction that preaching is indispensable to the life of the church. Through preaching God calls forth and grows the church.

Before explaining that thesis, I have one caveat: I am using the term *preaching* in the full-orbed biblical sense. The Bible uses thirty-three words to portray the richness of preaching—heralding, spreading good news, witnessing, teaching, debating, exhorting, and so forth. My usage of the term includes the stereotypical sense of "sermon from the pulpit on Sunday morning," but it's not limited to *public* discourse (preaching can take place with an audience of one), the *form* of monologue (preaching can take place in dialogue; see Acts 17:2–3), or *time and place* (preaching can occur in the home, office, or mall as well as the church building). The Bible's portrayal of preaching is best caught with a general term like *biblical communication* or *speaking in behalf of God*. John Stott's phrase *standing between two worlds* summarizes this ministry.

THROUGH PREACHING GOD CALLS FORTH THE CHURCH

We are born again by the "living and enduring word of God ... the word that was preached to" us (1 Peter 1:23, 25). Faith comes by hearing the Word of God, and hearing demands that someone preach (Rom. 10:14–15); therefore, preaching is the means by which God forms his church. Through preaching, God grants faith, repentance, and new life.

The Bible's depiction of preaching as a mighty power arises from a robust theology of God's Word. By words, God created the heavens and earth. He spoke, and it was so. By words he curses and blesses. He speaks, and it

comes to pass. His words are not merely vibrations of the atmosphere causing sympathetic vibrations in our inner ear; nor are they simply dashes and dots, squiggles and slashes of ink on paper. Rather, they are a creative force that embodies and produces his will. His words break stony hearts (Jer. 23:29), cleanse from sin (Eph. 5:26), pierce the conscience (Heb. 4:12), nourish infants (1 Peter 2:2), bear fruit (Mark 4:20), illumine our path (Ps. 119:105), and show us our true selves (James 1:22–25). Biblical preaching releases the dynamic spiritual power of the Word to enlighten and woo us from the world. By preaching, he makes us his body, the church.

The book of Acts demonstrates how God forms the church through preaching. On the day of Pentecost "Peter stood up with the Eleven, raised his voice and addressed the crowd," and about three thousand were added to the infant church in Jerusalem (2:14ff.). "Those who had been scattered preached the word wherever they went," and the church in Samaria was formed (8:4ff.). "Those who had been scattered ... traveled as far as Phoenicia, Cyprus and Antioch telling the message," and the church in Syria was formed (11:19ff.). "Almost the whole city gathered to hear the word of the Lord ... and all who were appointed for eternal life believed," and the church in Asia Minor was formed (13:44, 48). "As was his custom, Paul went into the synagogue, and on three Sabbath days he reasoned with them from the Scriptures, explaining and proving that Christ had to suffer and rise from the dead," and the church in Macedonia was formed (17:2ff.). "Then Paul stood up in the meeting of the Areopagus" to proclaim the unknown God, and the church in Greece was formed (17:22ff.).

I have a friend who is watching the church form in Cambodia among the Tampuan people. He is watching it happen as God's story is taught systematically with a curriculum called "From Creation to Cross." My friend is a tireless overseer, administrator, translator, teacher, and counselor in that church, so he is well aware that God works through human agency, but he also says he has the remarkable experience of simply watching the church "happen" around him with a life of its own. The seed drops on various soils and sprouts, and in some cases it brings forth fruit. To use a different image, through preaching, God forms his bride, the church. He also uses preaching to make the bride beautiful.

Through Preaching God Grows the Church

The work of salvation *starts* when the Word is preached, and the work of salvation *continues* as the Word is preached. "We proclaim him, admonishing and teaching everyone . . . so that we may present everyone perfect in Christ. To this end I labor, struggling with all his energy" (Col. 1:28–29). The author of that statement, Paul, mentored his son in the faith, Timothy, to adopt a similar "church growth strategy": "Devote yourself to the public reading of Scripture, to preaching and to teaching (1 Tim. 4:13).

Because God sanctifies through his Word (John 17:17), preaching that explains and applies that Word sanctifies the hearers. This is why pastors must be teachers (Eph. 4:11–12; 1 Tim. 3:2; Titus 1:9). They must "correct, rebuke and encourage—with great patience and careful instruction" (2 Tim. 4:2) as they refute false doctrine, explain right doctrine, and

exhort the flock to follow the voice of the Shepherd.

The early church wasn't always pretty, but in this regard they had it right. For example, the *Didache*, a manual of church ethics dating from the early second-century, refers to a host of teaching ministries: bishops, deacons, traveling teachers, apostles, and prophets. The early church had caught the apostles' confidence that through preaching God sanctifies his church.

The emphasis on preaching continued in the second century as described in Justin Martyr's *First Apology* which pictures the "weekly worship of the Christians":

> On the day called Sunday, all who live in cities or in the country gather together to one place, and the memoirs of the apostles or the writings of the prophets are read, as long as time permits; then, when the reader has ceased, the president verbally instructs, and exhorts to the imitation of these good things.

At the end of the second century, Tertullian wrote in his *Apology:*

> We assemble to read our sacred writings. . . . With the sacred words we nourish our faith, we animate our hope, and make our confidence more steadfast . . . and we confirm good habits. In the same place also exhortations are made, rebukes and sacred censures are administered.

In the fourth century, Chrysostom expressed his convictions about preaching in a sermon on Ephesians 6:13. He said that Christ's body, like the human body, is susceptible to disease. Medicine, diet, a change of climate, and sleep help restore the physical body, but what can heal Christ's body?

> One only means and one way of cure has been given us . . . and that is teaching of the Word. This is the best instrument, this is the best diet and

climate; this serves instead of medicine, this serves instead of cautery and cutting; whether it be needful to burn or amputate, this one method must be used; and without it nothing else will avail.

By the Word of God we are born again, and the church is formed. By the Word of God that church grows up to be like the Head. Through preaching God unleashes the whirlwind of his Word.

IMPLICATIONS

Four implications arise from this biblical theology of preaching.

First, "audience analysis" is crucial. (What a cold term! It belongs on Madison Avenue, not in the church, but you know what I mean—we need to think about and get to know our people). If preachers are to explain and apply the Word, they must know how much the listeners understand, agree with, and are practicing that Word. Are the listeners hardened pagans, sincere skeptics, nominal Christians, awakened sinners, apostate scoffers, overzealous new believers, mature disciples, or undisciplined know-it-alls? Are they progressing in the faith, doubting the reality of the supernatural world, or searching for answers? Whether by formal or informal means, preachers must get inside the minds and hearts of the listeners. When we do so, we often discover that we declare too many ideas in one message with too little practical application. I believe it was Spurgeon who said, "Jesus tells us to feed my sheep, not feed my giraffes."

When pastoring a few years ago, I surveyed my congregation with a written questionnaire. I asked them what instruction they personally needed. I expected some of their responses, but some also surprised me: how to discern the

leading of the Holy Spirit, how to be a fully devoted disciple, how to persevere in the faith in trials, and a hunger for basic understanding of the Old Testament. These responses helped me know what pastures to open.

Even if you don't do formal analysis, "empathetic understanding" (Fred Craddock's phrase from *Preaching*, p. 97) will help you feed the sheep: Take a blank sheet of paper and write at the top, "What's it like to be...." Underneath, write one facet of human experience: What's it like to be facing surgery, living alone, suddenly wealthy, rejected by a sorority, going into the military, unable to read, or fourteen years old? From this exercise you will see ways to apply and illustrate the Word.

A second implication arises from the first: The best preaching is done by pastors. These people are best equipped to do "audience analysis." Traveling pulpiteers—I suppose I'm one of them since my primary ministry is teaching in a seminary—can and should do audience analysis, but nothing can replace living, working, playing, grieving, and praying with the "audience." As Ian Pitt-Watson says, "Preaching divorced from pastoral concern is blind. It neither knows what it is talking about nor to whom it is talking" (*Preaching: A Kind of Folly*, p. 58). Elders are soul-watchers, meaning that they "look at" souls (as when we watch TV), "tend" souls (as when we watch the fire), and "guard" souls (as when we stand on watch through the night). By watching the flock, pastors know when to afflict the comfortable and comfort the afflicted.

A third implication is corollary to the first two: preaching and counseling intersect. Preachers must *listen* before they talk. Listening to questions, hurts, and conundrums is indispensable to audience analysis and pastoring. By listening, we get in touch with the experiences, values, and depth of understanding and character our people have. It will show us their spiritual condition, and as Richard Baxter explained in *The Reformed Pastor*, a surprise may await us: Some members of our churches are not converted. Personal ministry shows us such things. Thus, counseling helps us partner with God in forming and growing the church.

In my previous church, the elders began comparing notes on our various counseling sessions and discovered that we were facing an epidemic of marital problems. About 25 percent of the church's marriages were in some stage of dissolving or divorcing! We immediately began to address these issues publicly as well as privately. Of course, the preacher must never reveal private information in the pulpit, but the counselor's office should help guide the pulpit's texts and themes. Ideally, the preacher/ counselor teaches publicly as preventative medicine—when the church is not in the midst of crisis.

A fourth implication is that preaching and leadership intersect. The image of edifying, or "building up," suggests how the counselor/ soul-watcher/preacher can lead: Is the building resting on a weak foundation? Perhaps core doctrinal teaching is needed. Have vandals broken in? Then stolen beliefs must be replaced and security systems activated. Is the building unfinished? Perhaps subcontractors such as evangelists need to be called in. Are storms predicted? Make sure the shutters are tight against the devil's schemes and light and water are on hand to face trials.

Preachers look at the big picture and use the teaching ministry to lead. An important component of this leading is preparing others to do the work of the ministry (Eph. 4:11–12). Preachers teach, facilitate, equip, and model. In this way, preaching is a form of mentoring. God has created the church so that sheep naturally follow shepherds. Yes, I know, some sheep bite shepherds, but most sheep intuitively feel their need for guidance and protection. They instinctively look up to and follow leaders. The result is that churches gradually take on the pastor's values, vision, and even personality.

The preacher is a pastor, counselor, leader, and mentor, not "one without authority." The Bible depicts the preacher as a *witness* (Acts 20:24)—one who both declares the apostolic testimony and who discloses his/her own experience with God; a *father* (1 Cor. 4:14–16)— one who gently disciplines, who is worthy to be imitated, and who has been used by God to bring life; a *mother* (Gal. 4:19)—one who undergoes pain to see her children born and reared; and a *steward* (1 Cor. 4:1–2)—one who dispenses food and material goods to the household in behalf of the Master.

Through the foolishness of preaching God unleashes the power of his Word to form and grow his beloved church. Thus, preaching is indispensable to the work of God.

Chapter 12

MY THEORY OF HOMILETICS

Three ideas shape my approach to preaching

Haddon Robinson

Expository preaching is the communication of a biblical concept, derived from and transmitted through a historical, grammatical, and literary study of a passage in its context, which the Holy Spirit first applies to the personality and the experience of the preacher, then through the preacher applies to the hearer. My approach to homiletics is reflected in the presuppositions of this definition.

1. PREACHERS COMMUNICATE IDEAS

Although preachers may study the words and the grammar of a text and even present some of the study in the sermon, words and phrases cannot be ends in themselves. If preachers are ever to get sermons, they must get them as ideas. Those who have studied and practiced public speaking over twenty-five hundred years have agreed that the most effective way to structure a speech is to build it around a single concept. I build on this and apply it both to the study of the Bible and also to the communication of its truth. The Bible and the sermon are both forms of literature and both communicate ideas.

Therefore, I devote a chapter of my textbook, *Biblical Preaching*, to determining the anatomy of an idea. It comes from asking two essential questions. The first is, "What exactly is this person talking about?" The full, complete answer to this question is the "subject" of a passage or of a sermon. The answer to a second question,

"What is this person saying about what is being talked about?" leads to the "complement" of the idea because it completes the subject. The subject and the complement together lead to the idea of the text and of the sermon.

2. THE IDEA OF A PASSAGE SHOULD GOVERN THE IDEA OF THE SERMON

Ideally the authority for the sermon does not lie with the preacher but in the text. Biblical preaching at its core is more a philosophy than a method. Whether or not a minister does biblical preaching starts with the honest answer to the question: "Do I, as a preacher, endeavor to bend my thought to the Scriptures, or do I use the Scriptures to support my thought?" Taking into account the history, grammar, literary forms and the context of a passage, the expositor ponders what the biblical writer wanted to get across to his original readers.

3. BIBLICAL PREACHING MUST BE APPLIED

After unearthing the biblical writer's thought in its context, preachers then must discern what the Holy Spirit wants to say to men and women in the current generation to whom they preach. The stance of effective expositors is not that they are lecturing to their listeners about the Bible. Instead, they are talking to their listeners about the listeners from the Bible. Application, therefore, isn't incidental to expository preaching. It is essential.

A biblical sermon can take many forms. Just as the biblical writers used many different genres of literature to communicate their ideas, preachers are free to use any form that will adequately represent what the Scripture teaches. In constructing the sermon, the same two questions can also be used to nail down the idea of the sermon. Preachers, too, must know the subject of their sermon and what precisely they are saying about their subject.

Strong biblical sermons must be "bifocal." They reflect both the idea and the development of the text, and they also reflect the concerns and questions of the listener. It is only through relevant, biblical preaching that men and women can come to understand and experience what the eternal God has to say to them today.

Haddon Robinson's approach to preaching is spelled out in his text, Biblical Preaching *(Baker, 2nd ed., 2002), which is used in seminaries and Bible colleges throughout the world.*

Chapter 13

STAYING ON THE LINE

What it means to go above or below the exacting line of truth

David Helm

Years ago I was summoned to give testimony at a murder trial. The clerk had me raise my right hand and said—you know the words—"Do you solemnly swear to tell the truth, the whole truth, and nothing but the truth, so help you God?" I did. I sat down, and I spoke.

There was a day when you took your vow to tell the truth, the whole truth, and nothing but the truth, so help you God. That is the oath we are to uphold—the line of Scripture. It's difficult, isn't it? It's easy to rise above the line by adding your words to God's Word. We're also susceptible to falling below the line, wherein we say less than God is saying. We can either add to his Word or take from his Word, and yet we have vowed to uphold it.

Deuteronomy 4 begins:

And now, O Israel, listen to the statutes and the rules that I am teaching you, and do them, that you may live, and go in and take possession of the land that the LORD, the God of your fathers, is giving you. You shall not add to the word that I command you, nor take from it, that you may keep the commandments of the LORD your God that I command you." (Deut. 4:1–2, ESV, used throughout)

You don't add and you don't subtract, so you might keep the line, the Word. The Word is to mediate. When you add to the Word, the Word is no longer mediating. Therefore, you're no longer keeping. When you take away from the Word, you are no longer mediating. Therefore, you're no longer keeping. Do not add, do not subtract, that you might keep the line, the commands.

GOD'S PREACHER IN THE GARDEN OF EDEN FAILED TO HOLD THE LINE

Now the serpent was more crafty than any other beast of the field that the LORD God had made. He said to the woman, "Did God actually say, 'You shall not eat of any tree in the garden'?" And the woman said to the serpent, "We may eat of the fruit of the trees in the garden, but God said, 'You shall not eat of the fruit of the tree that is in the midst of the garden, neither shall you touch it, lest you die.'" (Gen. 3:1–3)

Before going further I want to make two observations on Satan and Eve. There's a critical distinction. Satan's misuse of God's words is wicked and evil, but Eve's is not. Satan's misuse of God's words is intentional. It's calculated. It is a distortion meant to ridicule God's character. Martin Luther said something to the effect that this is not a question put forward; it's an accusation made.

Think of it this way: I have a fourteen-year-old son. Let's say I tell him he has to be in by 11 o'clock. His friend says, "What time do you have to be in?" He says, "I have to be in by 11." "Did your dad really say you have to be in by 11?" Is he asking a question? No, he's actually impugning my character. He's saying to my son, "Your father's not good"—and that's wicked!

Satan's desire, then, is to get Eve to doubt that God's character is good. And in doubting God's character, she would disobey God's voice. That is consistent throughout the Scriptures, and it is consistent in your life. Satan's tactics are predictable. He will subtly accuse the character of God's goodness that you might leave off the Word. And it's wicked.

Eve's inability to stay on the line, however, is more understandable. Let's face it: Eve was not like Satan. Eve's addition is similar to what parents say to their kids: "If you don't go near the edge of the cliff, you'll never have to worry about falling off." "If you don't ever put your hand on the stove, you'll never have to worry about being burned." Eve thought: *I know I'm not supposed to eat it, so I'm going to tell myself I can't touch it.* That's understandable. She's building hedges. But it has a wicked ending.

Eve is in need of a preacher—not necessarily one who will judge her rebellion, but one who will safeguard her relationship with God. Eve's danger at this point is that she will turn her relationship with God into a religion in which she performs rules to appease God. So where Satan is in rebellion, Eve is on the verge of bringing in religion.

Wouldn't it have been great if a preacher had been there that day? Oh, but there was. See Genesis 3:6: "her husband, who was with her." God, in his providence, knows the world will need a preacher before the Fall, and he secures a preacher. So when the question is raised, he has a man under oath who will judge the Evil One once and for all, and who will safeguard the relationship between his family—which is the church at that point—and keep religion from entering the world.

Notice, the Word given to Adam in Genesis 2:16 is before the creation of the woman in 2:18. So God had seen the need for a preacher, and he had supplied the world with his preacher. All Adam needs to do now is enter into the courtroom. He needs to raise his right hand, and he needs to say, "I do solemnly swear to tell the truth, the whole truth, and nothing but the truth, so help me God. And the truth is this: Satan, your word is wicked and evil. I condemn it and judge it. You now await God's judgment upon you. Eve, your word is deceptive and will bring religion into the world. In my safeguarding of you, I will not allow it. God did not say, 'Do not touch.'"

Adam needs to stand and preach. Does he plow a straight path here? Does he stay on the line? Genesis 3:6 is one of the saddest verses in the Bible: "So when the woman saw that the tree was good for food, and that it was a delight to the eyes, and that the tree was to be desired to make one wise, she took of its fruit and ate, and she also gave some to her husband who was with her, and he"—preached? No—"he ate."

This is God's man, who was created and called to preach. This is God's man, who from this garden was to plant the kingdom of God to the end of the earth. This is God's man, who was to keep God's Word and mediate life through the Word. This is God's man, who was to ascend into the pulpit, close the door behind him, lock himself in, and tell the truth.

Instead of ascending the stairs and speaking for God, he descends into sin. He succumbs to the power of Satan. He participates in the deception of Eve. He gives Satan the victory. He gives religion a foothold. And humanity has been plagued from this moment forth. There are to our day people who do Satan's bidding. They are bent on abject rebellion against God; they hate his character, and they will assail it before all they see. And there are people entrapped by Eve's deception; they are bent on appeasing God by their religious practice.

On that day the line of Scripture is made void. The line is broken. God does not have a preacher in the world. So God becomes his own preacher and defends his own Word. That's what happens in Genesis 3:14–15. God speaks and judges the serpent. He speaks in verse 16 and judges the woman. And in verses 17–19

God speaks to Adam, and he holds him accountable for everything. The ground is now subject to the curse, and the preacher is now subject to the ground. And the garden ground from which Adam was to cultivate the kingdom to the end of the earth is a cemetery plot, which man must leave until he descends into that ground on the day of his death.

GOD'S PREACHERS IN THE OLD TESTAMENT FAILED TO HOLD THE LINE

God was without a preacher in the world in the early chapters of the Bible, outside of a few exceptions. You can go to Enoch. You can go to Noah. But in large part God is his own voice. There is no preacher. In fact, he's still speaking for himself when he calls his people out at Mount Sinai. It's his voice: "And God said. . . ."

On that day the people were terrified when they heard God preaching. They said in Deuteronomy 18: We're going to die if we hear you preach. God says: Then I'll give you a preacher, and it will be a man from your own people, and it will be a prophet. And I'll put my words in his mouth and—what?—he will speak what I command him.

Moses is that great prophet, but even Moses the great prophet falters on the line of Scripture. In Numbers 20:8, God told Moses, "Take the staff and tell the rock. . . ." That's a pretty simple outline. But in verse 11 Moses lifted up his hand and struck the rock twice. He faltered on the line of Scripture. What was the dilemma? Verse 12: "Because you did not believe in me, to uphold me as holy in the eyes of the people of Israel, therefore you shall not bring this assembly into the land that I have given them." Moses' failure was that he did not regard God's word and holiness to hold sway on the people. He cheapened God in the eyes of the people.

So the great prophet faltered. The great priests of the Old Testament faltered. The priests weren't even supposed to speak. They just used sign language. Aaron's sons had that privileged position of sign language before the congregation, but they went in with strange fire, it says in Leviticus 10. *I'm in the privileged position. I'm going to sign this way today.* They presumed on their position.

The great priests failed, and the great kings failed as well. First Samuel 15 is one of the saddest chapters in Scripture: "Now go and strike Amalek and devote to destruction all that they have. Do not spare them, but kill both man and woman, child and infant, ox and sheep, camel and donkey" (1 Sam. 15:3). That was according to the words of the Lord. But in verses 9–11 we read:

> But Saul and the people spared Agag and the best of the sheep and of the oxen … and would not utterly destroy them.… Samuel came to Saul, and Saul said to him, "Blessed be you to the LORD. I have performed the commandment of the LORD."

"I'm holding the line of Scripture," says Saul. Was this a good day for God's people or what? They were happy when they left church.

Samuel asked, however:

> What then is this bleating of sheep in my ears? … Has the Lord as great delight in burnt offerings and sacrifices, as in obeying the voice of the LORD? Behold, to obey is better than sacrifice, and to listen than the fat of rams. For rebellion is as the sin of divination, and presumption is as iniquity and idolatry. Because you have rejected the word of the LORD, he has also rejected you from being king. (15:14, 22–23)

ONLY CHRIST HELD THE LINE OF SCRIPTURE

The great prophets, the great priests, the great kings—they failed to hold the line. It wasn't until the eternal Word of God, who was present with God from the beginning, took on human flesh that the line was held. By Matthew 4 you know this is the Man, when he goes into the desert for those forty days. Whereas Moses sinned by manipulating the Word, bringing water from a rock according to his own desires, Jesus does not succumb to the temptation to make bread from rocks. Whereas the great priests failed because they had presumption in the place of sacrifice, thinking God would not kill them, Jesus does not succumb to that, refusing to throw himself off the high place as if God will obfuscate his Word and save him anyway. Jesus does not succumb to the temptation of Saul and David and every other king. He does not take human kingdoms on his own word. He does not succumb to the temptation to bow to Satan's word to receive the kingdom. He holds the line. He alone does the hard and taxing work of being a biblical preacher.

See how hard it was for him. This was not easy work. In Matthew 19:3 the Pharisees are going away from the line: "Is it lawful to divorce one's wife for any cause?" There's that word *any* again.

Look at what Jesus does in verse 4. First of all, he answers, "Have you not read that he who created them from the beginning made them male and female?" He goes to Genesis 1. He says: I do solemnly swear to tell the truth, the truth of Genesis 1. Then he says: I'm going to tell you the whole truth, the truth of Genesis 2: "'Therefore a man shall leave his father and mother and hold fast to his wife, and they shall become one flesh.' So they are no longer two but one flesh." He tells the truth of God's Word, he tells the whole truth, and then he tells nothing but the truth in Matthew 19:6b: "What therefore God has joined together, let not man separate."

You'd think they'd be grateful for a man who could hold the line of Scripture. But they weren't. Note the words of the Pharisees in verse 7: "Why then did Moses command one to give a certificate of divorce and to send her away?" They're trying to put Jesus' truth statement, which is grounded in Genesis 1 and 2, at odds with Moses' truth statement, which is grounded in Deuteronomy 24. It's sophisticated. The same thing is going on today. This is sophisticated work. People will pit one place in God's Word against another place in God's Word.

Jesus says: I'm not playing that game. We have a lot to learn from him here on how to deal with current dilemmas such as same-sex union. Your apologetic is there in Matthew 19:8: "He said to them, 'Because of your hardness of heart Moses allowed you to divorce your wives, but from the beginning it was not so." He says: I'm going to hold Moses, and I'm going to hold God's created intention, and I will not let them war.

In fact, Jesus continues in Matthew 19:9: "I say to you: whoever divorces his wife, except for sexual immorality, and marries another, commits adultery." What's he doing here? He's saying: You're not going to put me at war with God's created intention and Moses' exception. I'm going to put you at war with both, because your principle is an easy, no-fault divorce, and that's against Genesis 1 and 2, and that's against Deuteronomy 24.

That's what Jesus does. That's what you are called to do, and that is how you hold the line. That is why Jesus could say before Pilate: I've come to testify to the truth. That is why on the cross he is the great prophet speaking, and his resurrection validates that he is God's King.

GOD CALLS HIS PREACHERS TODAY TO HOLD THE LINE

What's amazing is that God gives this ministry to you and me. We are fallen people. We are sons of Adam. But he asks you to preach. Note what 2 Corinthians 4:1–2 says:

> Therefore, having this ministry by the mercy of God, we do not lose heart. But we have renounced disgraceful, underhanded ways. We refuse to practice cunning or to tamper with God's Word, but by the open statement of the truth we would commend ourselves to everyone's conscience in the sight of God.

And then 2 Timothy 2:15:

> Do your best to present yourself to God as one approved, a worker who has no need to be ashamed, rightly handling the Word of truth.

Tell the truth, the whole truth, and nothing but the truth, so help you God. God still needs a preacher in the world.

Chapter 14

HISTORY OF PREACHING
Assessing today's preaching in light of history

Michael Quicke

The history of preaching with its procession of personalities and schools of preaching is as rich and as complex as the story of Christianity itself. This brief survey will identify four types of preaching that have dominated the story. In conclusion, some practical questions will be raised for twenty-first century preachers.

KEY PREACHING TYPES

While it is notoriously difficult to classify preaching styles, it is possible to contrast the defining beliefs and practice of four main types of biblical preaching (though many preachers are composite in practice).

Teacher preachers have a defining belief that hearers should understand Scripture. Such preachers stay close to the text and explain its meaning deductively. Typically doctrinal and instructional, this preaching examines verses in logical order. Some examples of teacher preachers are John Stott, John Ortberg, Timothy Keller, Jack Hayford, and John MacArthur. Often cerebral in style, teacher preachers want to get information across. A sermon form often used by teacher preachers is verse-by-verse preaching.

Herald preachers have a defining emphasis on God's empowering of both Scripture and the preaching event itself. Though such preaching shares deductive and propositional characteristics in common with teaching, it sounds very

different. Herald preachers are often dramatic in style. While teacher preachers are left-brain, referring to small details and building their sermons with many bricks, herald preachers are right-brain, using a few large building blocks. Often herald preachers present a few bold issues with fire and call for a holistic response. Examples of herald preachers include Billy Graham, Gardner Taylor, Jeremiah Wright, Robert Smith Jr., the reformer Martin Luther, and Karl Barth.

Inductive preachers have a defining belief that hearers' needs are most important and that preaching must be relevant to them. In marked contrast with the deductive preaching of teachers and heralds, this style has an inductive dynamic that begins where people are and goes back to Scripture to find appropriate texts. Such inductive preaching may be evangelistic (as with the "felt needs" orientation of seeker-sensitive preaching), apologetic (defending Christianity against false doctrines), pastoral (meeting needs within congregation or society), or political (addressing current issues). Examples of inductive preachers include Bob Russell, John Maxwell, Brian McLaren, Rick Warren, and Bill Hybels.

Narrative preachers have a defining belief that sermons should have a story form that catches listeners up in an experience of God's truth. Though most preachers use stories, this kind of preaching pays particular attention to hearers' listening patterns and plans sermons accordingly. With its roots in Scripture's narrative and especially Jesus' parables, it has recently gained popularity. Notable examples of narrative preachers are Calvin Miller, Max Lucado, Lee Strobel, Barbara Brown Taylor, and Eugene Lowry.

These different types are expressed through preaching history by preachers and schools of preaching.

PERIOD 1: NEW TESTAMENT BEGINNINGS

By the time of Christ, Jewish synagogue worship included readings from the Law and the Prophets followed by commentary in the form of a teaching sermon. However, in Jesus' first sermon in a synagogue teaching context (Luke 4:14–21), he dramatically emerged as a herald preacher, announcing good news in himself— "Today this word has come true" (Luke 4:21). Such strong, propositional, herald preaching lies at the heart of Jesus' ministry, proclaiming the kingdom of God (Mark 1:14; Luke 4:43) and commissioning disciples (Matt. 28:20; Luke 9:2; 10:9). Also we see Jesus as a narrative preacher. His parables remain classic examples of such teaching (Matt. 18:23) and reveal the power of communication by story telling.

When the church was birthed by the Holy Spirit and by a sermon (Acts 2:14–41), herald preaching initiated mission breakthroughs at every turn, as the church moved into the Gentile world, proclaiming God's inclusive grace (as in Acts 10:34–40; 13:16–49; 17:22–34). Apostles defined faith by proclaiming the *kerygma*— core facts about Jesus Christ (1 Cor. 15:3–4)— and preaching took many forms: in formal settings, in homes, outdoors, and on the road. Teacher preaching has a key role in building up

the church (and Paul's letters bear the oral signs of preaching). Forms of inductive preaching also emerged in this period. Paul on Mars Hill (Acts 17:16–31) provides an early model for seeker-sensitive preaching. Note his cross-cultural motivation (1 Cor. 9:19–23). In the period up to AD 150, bishops also seemed to have a key role in apologetic preaching against early heresies such as Gnosticism (similar to more recent New Age phenomenon).

PERIOD 2: CLASSICAL PREACHING

With the church's increasing establishment and acceptability (particularly with Emperor Constantine's conversion in 312), preaching faced a major crisis. How would it respond to the classical high art of rhetoric—the art of influencing an audience by persuasion? Earlier the apostle Paul had warned that clever eloquence might compromise the "foolishness" of the gospel (1 Cor 1:20–25), though he himself was obviously persuasive in his Greek culture (as with his skillful use of the diatribe technique in Romans).

By the third and fourth centuries, through the influence of the church's founding fathers, both teacher and herald preachers had consciously adopted rhetorical principles, especially of forensic speech with its introduction, series of points, and summary conclusion. This has had lasting effect. The Eastern church developed the Greek sermon through Origen (185–254) in Caesarea and Chrysostom (337–407) in Constantinople (present-day Istanbul). Both combined careful exegesis of the text with carefully structured sermons. Similarly, the Western church developed the Latin sermon, reaching its greatest heights with Augustine (354–430) of Hippo, North Africa, who wrote the first preaching textbook, *On Christian Doctrine—Book 4*. Inductive preaching also successfully confronted many current heresies. However, with the decline of Roman civilization into the Dark Ages, preaching also decayed, often taking the form of mechanical repetitions of older sermons.

In the Middle Ages (1100–1500) classical preaching revived through several influences. Universities rediscovered the educational role of sermons and created many teaching aids. Orders of preaching friars, the Dominicans and Franciscans, also had wide impact constructing sermons on a single Bible verse with three points and subpoints, often called the scholastic method. Dissenting preachers such as John Wyclif (1330–1384) reacted against this method and preached extemporaneously verse by verse. Preaching was also impacted by the need to motivate volunteers for crusades against Islam. Such preaching was an unusual and controversial form of inductive preaching, and its most famous example was Bernard of Clairvaux (1090–1153).

PERIOD 3: REFORMATIONS AND PRINTING

The great Renaissance figure Desiderius Erasmus (1466–1536) edited the first Greek New Testament to be printed in 1516 and translated it into Latin. This aided the tumultuous rediscovery of Scripture in the Reformation through Martin Luther (1483–1546), who, trained in an Augustinian monastery, developed a style of herald preaching that prized biblical content, simplicity, and everyday application. His theology of preaching described the Word of God in three forms: the incarnate Word (Jesus), the written Word (Bible), and the proclaimed word (preaching).

Afterwards, Protestants were a new force comprising many other significant preachers, such as John Calvin (1509–1564) in Switzerland, a colorful herald preacher. In a rich time of preaching, Roman Catholics launched their Counter Reformation, and new radical groups emerged, such as the Anabaptists. Several new movements arose in different contexts, such as the Puritans in Britain, who were teacher preachers with sermons that contained two parts: an exposition of a text's doctrinal points and its application to hearers. This so-called plain style remains a significant teaching model today.

Reformation preaching greatly benefited from the invention of movable type printing by Johannes Gutenberg (around 1456). Mass printing enabled sermons to be read, and their teaching gave uniform catechism to mass populations. Printing encouraged deductive sermons with linear forms of points and subpoints. Technology has always impacted preaching, as in today's electronics revolution.

PERIOD 4: EVANGELICAL PREACHING AND INCREASING DIVERSITY

Within Protestantism, explosive preaching fueled the rise of evangelicalism through the eighteenth and nineteenth centuries with many different emphases. George Whitefield (1714–1770) popularized open-air, emotionally charged preaching, and traveling between America and Britain he influenced other important preachers. These included John Wesley (1703–1791), the founder of Methodism, who was a noted herald teacher, and Jonathan Edwards (1703–1758), an intellectual heavyweight whose Puritan teaching led to the First Great Awakening (1726–1750s) in North

America. Whitefield also encouraged black preaching with a notable succession of African-American preachers leading to Andrew C. Marshall at Savannah (1812–1856). Black preachers often used narrative preaching to skillfully retell Scripture stories and intertwine their own.

The nineteenth century was a golden age for herald preaching. Most denominations claimed to possess "star preachers," such as Charles Simeon (1759–1836), an Anglican; C. H. Spurgeon (1834–1892), a Baptist; and Catherine Booth (1829–1890), from the Salvation Army. Charles Finney (1792–1875) and Dwight Moody (1837–1898) used mass evangelism techniques. Herald preaching also flourished among liberal American preachers, as represented by Phillips Brooks (1835–1893), an Episcopalian.

In the twentieth century there was further diversity. The biblical theology movement encouraged theological preaching, as in Karl Barth (1886–1968), who endorsed the herald model. Inductive preaching embraced psychology to counsel people from the pulpit, as with Harry Emerson Fosdick (1878–1969). Others, responding evangelistically to spiritual needs, used mass communication. Billy Graham (b. 1918) became the most heard and seen evangelistic preacher of all time. Martin Luther King Jr. (1929–1968) gained international importance as his preaching addressed poverty, suffering, and oppression.

Most recently there has also been greater analysis of major preaching traditions, such as black preaching (often narrative in style) and the preaching of women (often pastoral), which, though represented by few great figures in the past, like Hildegard of Bingen (1098–1179), has grown dramatically since the 1920s.

The electronic revolution and emphasis on the visual has diversified preaching styles and heightened the use of storytelling.

Megachurch preachers reflect different styles, though currently popular seeker-sensitive worship falls firmly within the inductive model, meeting people where they are.

A WARNING

Often preaching history has been seen from a viewpoint that omits much of the story's richness, including the impact of Latin American and Asian preaching. Today's world church has seen tremendous growth in the southern world—Latin America, Africa, and Asia. Overall, much of the "northern church" of North America and Western Europe seems to be in decline, while the "southern church" (some call it the "majority church") shows significant revival with preaching that resembles the New Testament period for spiritual vitality and missionary impact.

Preaching history is immensely rich, and preachers can learn from each other. It is essential to respond to an increasing range of experiences from the practice of black, Hispanic, Asian, and female preachers as well as to keep open to narrative preaching and other styles.

PRACTICAL ISSUES AND QUESTIONS

Church history shows a vital connection between effective preaching and healthy church mission. From the New Testament on, preaching has spearheaded each missionary expansion. Early preachers "turned the world upside down" (Acts 17:6 KJV). Some preaching has immediate impact. Chrysostom confronted lifestyle issues of his urban congregation and critiqued aspects of the Byzantine Empire; Luther addressed Germans on every issue of moral, political, and social importance. Long-term effects of preaching are often dramatic. The Reformation began the modern era for Western civilization, shaping Christian Europe and seeding the modern missionary movement. It has promoted revival, reformed church life, and affected society.

Preaching is a spiritual matter, marked from its New Testament beginnings by spiritual vitality (1 Thess. 1:5), gospel clarity (1 Cor. 15:3–4), cross-cultural relevance (1 Cor. 9:19–23), and boldness (Acts 4:13; 9:27). All preaching requires spiritual vitality. Is there now less belief in God's presence in the preaching event? Is there less boldness today? Today, the "southern church" seems to be growing through preaching, but the "northern church" faces a critical need for prayerful recovery of spiritual authenticity and courage.

Are there church traditions today that preaching should challenge? At several points of its history, preaching needed to reform the church in its practices or doctrine. The Reformation was partly precipitated by a courageous attack on the wealth and privilege of the Roman church that sold guarantees (indulgences) about shortening purgatory. John Wesley preached out of concern for holy living and founded Methodism.

Churches can easily become sidetracked by wealth, privilege, and complacency to downgrade doctrine. Preaching is involved in leadership as it focuses God's will for his church expressed by correcting, rebuking, and encouraging (2 Tim. 4:2; cf. 3:16). This remains a difficult but necessary task for the twenty-first century.

How much is doctrinal teaching needed today? Reformation and renewal are always associated with personal rediscovery of biblical text and doctrine after a time of biblical illiteracy. The clearest example is Martin Luther's discovery of Pauline convictions about sin, grace, and justification by faith. Whenever preachers are personally committed to live out the Bible by explaining and applying its truth, preaching forms "people of the Book." However, when preaching becomes mechanical and routine, it loses power, as in the Dark Ages.

Where is apologetic preaching needed today? Apologetic preachers seek to understand and confront current false teachings. Early New Age type Gnosticism was followed by a succession of attacks on orthodox beliefs about the divinity of Christ, the nature of salvation, and Christianity's exclusive claims. Augustine remains the best example of a preacher whose intellect, exegesis, and doctrinal perspicacity defended orthodoxy against several rivals, such as the Pelagian heresy that diminished Christ's role in salvation. In today's relativism and spiritual diversity, preachers need to respond to rival opinion formers with clear apologetics for exclusive Christian claims.

Can preachers be more relevant? Evangelistic preaching begins with lost people where they are. George Whitefield developed open-air preaching with great dramatic flair. Like Paul on Mars Hill, more recent seeker-sensitive preaching makes connections with contemporary authorities in order to establish the credibility of Christian claims. Bill Hybels at Willow Creek church represents this approach. Pastoral preaching, in which preachers respond to specific needs within the congregation, as with Fosdick, can engage appropriately. Are there fresh ways to ensure that good news is made relevant?

How does changing media and forms of communication affect preaching? In order to be heard and understood, preachers have always needed to relate to contemporary culture. In Jesus' oral culture, the role of narrative was especially important. Classical preaching adopted rhetoric's principles. Later, Reformation preaching took advantage of mass printing and gained previously unthinkable influence.

There is general agreement that Western modernity, influential for the last 250 years, is giving way to postmodernity, which calls for fresh sensitivity to communication styles. Today, preachers need to use all available technological resources and appropriate means of communication.

How much do preachers make use of preaching helps? Through history, preachers have always benefited from preaching helps. Augustine's textbook was seminal. In the Middle Ages, European universities published large numbers of primers—around 80,000 survive from the two centuries following 1150. John Broadus (1827–95) had influence in the early twentieth century and more recently Fred Craddock (b. 1928) and others have introduced new styles of biblical preaching—especially inductive and narrative preaching. It is important to stay open to valid developments in preaching's theology and practice.

For Further Reading

Brilioth Y. 1965. *A Brief History of Preaching*. Philadelphia: Fortress.

Dargan, E. C. 1954. *A History of Preaching—from the Apostolic Fathers to the Nineteenth Century*. Grand Rapids: Baker.

Edwards, O. C. *A History of Preaching*. 2 vols (forthcoming).

Fant, C. E., and W. M. Pinson. 1986. *Twenty Centuries of Great Preaching: An Encyclopedia of Preaching*. Waco, Tex.: Word.

Mitchell, H. 1990. *Black Preaching—the Recovery of a Powerful Art*. Nashville: Abingdon.

Old, H. O. 2002. *The Reading and Preaching of the Scriptures in the Worship of the Christian Church*, 5 vols. Grand Rapids: Eerdmans.

Wilson, P. S. 1992. *A Concise History of Preaching*. Nashville: Abingdon.

Part 2

THE *Spiritual Life* OF THE *Preacher*

How Should I Attend to My Soul So That I Am Spiritually Prepared to Preach?

Chapter 15

A CUP RUNNING OVER

Why preachers must find deep satisfaction in Christ

Dallas Willard

In my early days of ministry I spent huge amounts of time absorbed in Scripture and great spiritual writers. The Lord made it possible for me to spend whole days—without any issue of preparing for something or taking an examination—soaking up the Scripture. I literally wore out the books of great spiritual writers. This focus was foundational to my spiritual journey, to finding satisfaction in Christ.

Experiencing God in that way leads me to satisfaction in Christ and to speaking to others out of that satisfaction. There is no substitute for simple satisfaction in the Word of God, in the presence of God. That affects all your actions.

CHARACTERISTICS OF DISSATISFACTION

Men and women in ministry who are not finding satisfaction in Christ are likely to demonstrate that with overexertion and over-preparation for speaking, and with no peace about what they do after they do it. If we have not come to the place of resting in God, we will go back and think, *Oh, if I'd done this,* or *Oh, I didn't do that.* When you come to the place where you are drinking deeply from God and trusting him to act with you, there is peace about what you have communicated.

One of my great joys came when I got up from a chair to walk to the podium and the Lord said to me, "Now remember, it's what I do with the Word between your lips and their hearts that matters." That is a tremendous lesson. If you do not trust God to do that, then he will let you do what you're going to do, and it's not going to come to much. But once you turn it loose and recognize we are always inadequate but our inadequacy is not the issue, you are able to lay that burden down. Then the satisfaction you have in Christ spills over into everything you do.

The preacher who does not minister in that satisfaction is on dangerous ground. Those who experience moral failure are those who have failed to live a deeply satisfied life in Christ, almost without exception. I know my temptations come out of situations where I am dissatisfied, not content. I am worried about something or not feeling the sufficiency I know is there. If I have a strong temptation, it will be out of my dissatisfaction.

The moral failures of ministers usually are over one of three things: sex, money, or power. That always comes out of dissatisfaction. Ministers are reaching for something, and they begin to feel, *I deserve something better. I sacrifice so much and get so little. And so I'll do this.* The surest guarantee against failure is to be so at peace and satisfied with God that when wrongdoing presents itself it isn't even interesting. That is how we stay out of temptation.

CHARACTERISTICS OF A SATISFIED SOUL

We are long on devices and programs. We have too many of them, and they get in the way. What we really need are preachers who can stand in simplicity and manifest and declare the richness of Christ in life. There isn't anything on earth that begins to compete with that for human benefit and human interest.

When people hear preachers who are satisfied in this way, they sense that much more is coming from them than what they are saying. When I hear preachers like this, I sense something flowing from them. Preachers like that are at peace. They are not struggling to make something happen.

That is one of the biggest issues for ministers today because of the model of success that comes to us. We get the idea we are supposed to make something happen, and so we need our services to go just right. The concluding benediction has hardly ceased before those in charge are saying to one another, "How did it go?" or "It went really well." The truth is we don't know how it went. From God's point of view it will be eternity before we know how it went. These folks are not at peace if they are trying to manage outcomes in that way.

One mark of preachers who have attained deep satisfaction is they are at peace and they love what they are doing. Peace comes from them. From such preachers I sense something coming to me that is deeper than the words. Hearers sense the message opening up possibilities for them to live. In the presence of this kind of preacher, people find ways of doing the good that is before their hearts.

That is the living water. Jesus brought people that opening up of possibilities. In John 8, when he said to the woman caught in adultery, "Go now and leave your life of sin," I don't think she felt, *I've got to do that.* She experienced Jesus' words as: *That's really possible. I can do that.* That is one characteristic of preaching that comes from a satisfied life.

Another mark of satisfied preachers is they can listen. They can be silent in the presence of others because they are not always trying to make something happen. Such a person has the capacity to listen to people and come to an awareness of the needs that underlie the felt needs. We should be attentive to the felt needs of people, but we should know that the game is at a much deeper level of the soul.

A large part of what the pastor does in preaching and life is to listen and help people feel their real needs, not just superficial needs. The satisfied preacher speaks from a listening heart. Since people often do not know what they really need, such preaching can help them find out. This requires a spaciousness that only comes if your cup is running over because you are well-cared for by God.

STEPS TOWARD FINDING SATISFACTION IN CHRIST

We can take steps to find this deep satisfaction and to preach from the well within us.

I encourage pastors to have substantial times every week when they do nothing but enjoy God. That may mean walking by a stream, looking at a flower, listening to music, or watching your children or grandchildren play without your constantly trying to control them. Experience the fullness of God, think about the good things God has done for you, and realize he has done well by you. If there is a problem doing that, then work through the problem, because we cannot really serve him if we do not genuinely love him.

Henri Nouwen said the main obstacle to love for God is service for God. Service must come out of his strength and life flowing through us into receptive lives. Take an hour, sit in a comfortable place in silence, and do nothing but rest. If you go to sleep, that's okay. We have to stop trying too hard. There may be a few pastors for whom that is not the problem, but for most it is. We need to do that not only for ourselves but to set an example for those to whom we speak.

There is a place for effort, but it never earns anything and must never take the place of God with us. Our efforts are to make room for him in our lives.

Chapter 16

THE PATENTED PREACHER

Every preacher is a limited edition of one

Warren W. Wiersbe

I t doesn't make sense!" said my pastor friend. We were lingering over lunch and discussing the Bible conference I was conducting in his church. I'd just commented that the church was having a strong influence on the students and staff of the nearby university.

"What doesn't make sense?" I asked.

"Where you and I are serving," he replied.

"You're going to have to explain."

"Look, I'm really a country preacher with a minimum of academic training, yet I'm ministering to a university crowd. You write commentaries, and you read more books in a month than I do in a year, yet your congregation is primarily blue-collar and nonprofessional. It doesn't make sense."

The subject then changed, but I have pondered his observation many times in the intervening years. I've concluded it's a good thing God didn't put me on his "Pastor Placement Committee" because I would have really messed things up.

I'd never have sent rustic Amos to the affluent court of the king; I'd have given him a quiet country church somewhere. And I'd never have commissioned Saul of Tarsus, that "Hebrew of the Hebrews," to be a missionary to the Gentiles; I'd have put him in charge of Jewish evangelism in Jerusalem.

All of which brings me to the point of this article: If God has called you to preach, then who you are, what you are, and where you are also must be a part of God's plan. You do not preach in spite of this, but because of this.

Why is it, then, that so many preachers do not enjoy preaching? Why do some busy themselves in minor matters when they should be studying and meditating? Why do others creep out of the pulpit after delivering their sermon, overwhelmed with a sense of failure and guilt?

THE DIFFERENCE A WITNESS MAKES

Without pausing to take a poll, I think I can suggest an answer: They are preaching *in spite of themselves* instead of preaching *because of* themselves. They either leave themselves out of their preaching or fight themselves during their preparation and delivery; this leaves them without energy or enthusiasm for the task. Instead of thanking God for what they do have, they complain about what they don't have; and this leaves them in no condition to herald the Word of God.

One *Christianity Today*/Gallup Poll showed that ministers believe preaching is the number one priority of their ministries, but it's also the one thing they feel least capable of doing well. What causes this insecure attitude toward preaching?

For one thing, we've forgotten what preaching really is. Phillips Brooks said it best: "Preaching is the communicating of divine truth through human personality. The divine

74

truth never changes; the human personality constantly changes—and this is what makes the message new and unique."

No two preachers can preach the same message because no two preachers are the same. In fact, no *one* preacher can preach the same message twice if he is living and growing at all. The human personality is a vital part of the preaching ministry.

Recently I made an intensive study of all the Greek verbs used in the New Testament to describe the communicating of the Word of God. The three most important words are: *euangelizomai*, "to tell the good news"; *kerysso*, "to proclaim like a herald"; and *martyreo*, "to bear witness." All three are important in our pulpit ministry. We're telling the good news with the authority of a royal herald, but the message is a part of our lives. Unlike the herald, who only shouted what was given to him, we're sharing what is personal and real to us. The messenger is a part of the message because the messenger is a witness.

God prepares the person who prepares the message. Martin Luther said that prayer, meditation, and temptation made a preacher. Prayer and meditation will give you a sermon, but only temptation—the daily experience of life—can transform that sermon into a message. It's the difference between the recipe and the meal.

I had an experience at a denominational conference that brought this truth home to me. During the session at which I was to speak, a very capable ladies trio sang. It was an up-tempo number, the message of which did not quite fit my theme; but, of course, they had no way of knowing exactly what I would preach about. I was glad my message did not immediately follow their number because I didn't feel the congregation was prepared.

Just before I spoke, a pastor in a wheelchair rolled to the center of the platform and gave a brief testimony about his ministry. Then he sang, to very simple accompaniment, "No One Ever Cared for Me Like Jesus." The effect was overwhelming. The man was not singing a song; he was ministering a word from God. But he had paid a price to minister. In suffering, he became a part of the message.

The experiences we preachers go through are not accidents; they are appointments. They do not interrupt our studies; they are an essential part of our studies. Our personalities, our physical equipment, and even our handicaps are all part of the kind of ministry God wants us to have. He wants us to be witnesses as well as heralds.

The apostles knew this: "For we cannot help speaking about what we have seen and heard" (Acts 4:20). This was a part of Paul's commission: "You will be his witness to all men of what you have seen and heard" (Acts 22:15). Instead of minimizing or condemning what we are, we must use what we are to bear witness to Christ. It is this that makes the message *our* message and not the echo of another's.

THE MYTH OF "THE GREAT SERMON"

It's easy to imitate these days. Not only do we have books of sermons, but we have radio and television ministries and cassettes by the thousands. One man models himself after Spurgeon, another after A. W. Tozer; and both congregations suffer.

Alexander Whyte of Edinburgh had an assistant who took the second service for the aging pastor. Whyte was a surgical preacher who ruthlessly dealt with man's sin and then faithfully proclaimed God's saving grace. But his assistant was a man of different temperament, who tried to move the gospel message out of the operating room into the banqueting hall.

During one period of his ministry, however, the assistant tried Whyte's approach, without Whyte's success. The experiment stopped when Whyte said to him, "Preach your own message." That counsel is needed today.

Every profession has its occupational hazards, and in the ministry it is the passion to preach "great sermons." Fant and Pinson, in *20 Centuries of Great Preaching*, came to the startling conclusion that "great preaching is relevant preaching." By "relevant," they mean preaching that meets the needs of the people in their times, preaching that shows the preacher cares and wants to help.

If this be true, then there are thousands of "great sermons" preached each Lord's Day, preached by those whose names will never be printed in homiletics books but are written in the loving hearts of their people. Listen again to Phillips Brooks:

> The notion of a great sermon, either constantly or occasionally haunting the preacher, is fatal. It hampers . . . the freedom of utterance. Many a true and helpful word which your people need, and which you ought to say to them, will seem unworthy of the dignity of your great discourse. . . . Never tolerate any idea of the dignity of a sermon which will keep you from saying anything in it which you ought to say, or which your people ought to hear.

PREACHING CHRIST, NOT MYSELF

Let me add another reason for insecure feelings about our preaching. In our desire to be humble servants of God, we have a tendency to suppress our personalities lest we should preach ourselves and not Christ. It is good to heed Paul's warning in 2 Corinthians 4:5: "For we do not preach ourselves, but Jesus Christ as Lord, and ourselves as your servants for Jesus' sake." But we must not misinterpret it and thereby attempt the impossible. Paul's personality, and even some of his personal experiences, are written into the warp and woof of his letters; yet Jesus Christ is glorified from start to finish.

During the past twenty years, I have been immersed in studying the lives of famous preachers of the past. Most of these ministered during the Victorian Era in Great Britain, a time when the pulpits were filled with superstars. If there's one thing I learned from these men, it is this: God has his own ways of training and preparing his servants, but he wants all of them to be themselves. God has put variety into the universe, and he has put variety into the church.

If your personality doesn't shine through your preaching, you're only a robot. You could be replaced by a cassette player and perhaps nobody would know the difference.

Do not confuse the art and the science of preaching. Homiletics is the science of preaching, and it has basic laws and principles that every preacher ought to study and practice. Once you've learned how to obey these principles, then you can adapt them, modify them, and tailor them to your own personality.

In my conference ministry, I often share the platform with gifted speakers whose preaching leaves me saying to myself, *What's the use? I'll never learn how to preach like that!* Then the Lord has to remind me he never called me "to preach like that." He called me to preach the way I preach!

The science of preaching is one thing; the art

of preaching—style, delivery, approach, and all those other almost indefinable ingredients that make up one's personality—is something else. One preacher uses humor and hits the target; another attempts it and shoots himself.

The essence of what I am saying is this: You must know yourself, accept yourself, be yourself, and develop yourself—your best self—if preaching is to be most effective.

Never imitate another preacher, but learn from him everything you can. Never complain about yourself or your circumstances, but find out why God made things that way and use what he has given you in a positive way. What you think are obstacles may turn out to be opportunities. Stay long enough in one church to discover who you are, what kind of ministry God has given you, and how he plans to train you for ministries yet to come. After all, he is always preparing us for what he already has prepared for us—if we let him.

ACCEPTING WHAT WE'RE NOT

I learned very early in my ministry that I was not an evangelist. Although I've seen people come to Christ through my ministry, I've always felt I was a failure when it came to evangelism.

One of the few benefits of growing older is a better perspective. Now I'm learning that my teaching and writing ministries have enabled others to lead people to Christ, so my labors have not been in vain. But I've had my hours of discouragement and the feeling of failure.

God gives us the spiritual gifts he wants us to have; he puts us in the places he wants us to serve; and he gives the blessings he wants us to enjoy.

I am convinced of this, but this conviction is not an excuse for laziness or for barrenness of ministry. Knowing I am God's man in God's

place of ministry has encouraged me to study harder and do my best work. When the harvests were lean, the assurance that God put me there helped to keep me going. When the battles raged and the storms blew, my secure refuge was "God put me here, and I will stay here until he tells me to go." How often I've remembered V. Raymond Edman's counsel: "It is always too soon to quit!"

It has been my experience that the young preacher in his first church and the middle-aged preacher (in perhaps his third or fourth church) are the most susceptible to discouragement. This is not difficult to understand.

The young seminarian marches bravely into his first church with high ideals, only to face the steamroller of reality and the furnace of criticism. He waves his banners bravely for a year or so, then takes them down quietly and makes plans to move. The middle-aged minister has seen his ideals attacked many times, but now he realizes that time is short and he might not attain to the top thirty of David's mighty men.

God help the preacher who abandons his ideals! But, at the same time, God pity the preacher who is so idealistic he fails to be realistic. A realist is an idealist who has gone through the fire and been purified. A skeptic is an idealist who has gone through the fire and been burned. There is a difference.

Self-evaluation is a difficult and dangerous thing. Sometimes we're so close to our ministry we fail to see it. One of my students once asked me, "Why can't I see any spiritual growth in my life? Everybody else tells me they can see it!" I reminded him that at Pentecost no man could see the flame over his own head, but he could see what was burning over his brother's head.

A word from the Scottish preacher George Morrison has buoyed me up in many a storm:

"Men who do their best always do more though they be haunted by the sense of failure. Be good and true, be patient; be undaunted. Leave your usefulness for God to estimate. He will see to it that you do not live in vain."

Be realistic as you assess your work. Avoid comparisons. I read enough religious publications and hear enough conversations to know that such comparisons are the chief indoor sport of preachers, but I try not to take them too seriously. "When they measure themselves by themselves and compare themselves with themselves, they are not wise" (2 Cor. 10:12).

Although we are in conflict against those who preach a false gospel, we are not in competition with any who preach the true gospel. We are only in competition with ourselves. By the grace of God, we ought to be better preachers and pastors today than we were a year ago.

If we are to be better pastors and preachers, we must be better persons; and this means discipline and hard work. The "giants" I've lived with these many years were all hard workers. Campbell Morgan was in his study at six o'clock in the morning. His successor, John Henry Jowett, was also up early and into the books. "Enter your study at an appointed hour," Jowett said in his lectures to the Yale divinity students in 1911–1912, "and let that hour be as early as the earliest of your busi-

nessmen goes to his warehouse or his office." Spurgeon worked hard and had to take winter holidays to regain his strength.

Obviously, we gain nothing by imperiling our health, but we lose much by pampering ourselves, and that is the greater danger.

THE GIFT IS SUFFICIENT

If God has called you, then he has given you what you need to do the job. You may not have all that others have, or all you wish you had, but you have what God wants you to have. Accept it, be faithful to use it, and in due time God will give you more.

Give yourself time to discover and develop your gifts. Accept nothing as a handicap. Turn it over to God and let him make a useful tool out of it. After all, that's what he did with Paul's thorn in the flesh.

Preaching is not what we do; it's what we are. When God wants to make a preacher, he has to make the person, because the work we do cannot be isolated from the life we live. God prepares the person for the work and the work for the person, and, if we permit him, he brings them together in his providence.

God knows us better than we know ourselves. He'd never put us into a ministry where he could not build us and use us.

Chapter 17

I PRAYED FOR MY PREACHING

And got answers I didn't expect

Joe McKeever

I had been preaching for more than two decades, and I should have been at the top of my game. The church I served ran up to 1,500 on Sunday mornings, and the live telecast of our services covered a fair portion of several states. Most of my colleagues thought I had it made, and if invitations to speak in other churches were any sign, they thought I could preach.

But I didn't think that.

My confidence was taking a beating as some of the leaders let me know repeatedly that my pulpit work was not up to their standards. Previous pastors carried the reputation of pulpit masters, something I never claimed for myself. To make matters worse, we had numerous vacancies on staff and my sermon preparation was suffering because of a heavy load of pastoral ministry. But you do what you have to do. Most days, my goal was to keep my head above water. Every day without drowning became a good day.

That's when I got serious about praying for my preaching. Each night I walked a four-mile route through my neighborhood and talked to the Father. My petitions dealt with the usual stuff—family needs, people I was concerned about, and the church. Gradually, one prayer began to recur in my nightly pleadings.

"Lord," I prayed, "make me a preacher." Asking this felt so right I never paused to analyze it. I prayed it again and again, over and over, for weeks.

I was in my fifth pastorate. I owned a couple of seminary degrees. I had read the classics on preaching and attended my share of sermon workshops. I was a veteran. But here I was in my mid-forties, crying out to heaven for help: "Lord, make me a preacher."

I knew if my preaching improved, if the congregation felt better about the sermons, everything else would benefit. I knew that the sermon is a pastor's most important contribution to the spiritual lives of his members. To do well there would ease the pressure in other areas. So, I prayed.

Then one night, God answered.

FOUR SPECIFIC REQUESTS

Without warning, in the quietness of a dark night on the city streets, God spoke within me: "What exactly do you mean by that?"

The question hit with such force that I laughed aloud and said, "What a great question. Wonder what I do mean?"

For the rest of my walk, I pondered God's probing of my too-general prayer. I knew I was not asking for public acclaim or to be on anyone's list of great preachers. I just wanted to be effective, to do well what God had called me to do.

Later that night, at home, I listed four specific requests and began to direct them toward the Father.

I never want to stand up to preach again without a good grasp of the Scripture.

I'm tired of not being clear about the text in front of me.

I want the message from God to have a firm grasp on me, to grip my heart.

I want to preach with genuine passion.

I want a good rapport with the congregation.

I'm tired of that "glazed-over" look on the people's faces. I want to make contact with them, to communicate effectively.

I want to see lives changed.

If the point of preaching is for the Word of God to make a difference in people, then I must be in order when I ask the Father to give me success in doing it.

I learned something about my prayer life. For years, my prayers had been tainted by a curse of generality. It had been "bless this" and "help that" and "strengthen him" and "encourage her." One day I noticed in Luke 18:35–43 this interchange between the Lord and blind Bartimaeus, whose plaintive cries of "Jesus, have mercy on me" had reached the ears of the Lord. Over and over, the beggar of Jericho called into the air for mercy, over the shushing and objections of locals who were embarrassed by his carryings-on.

"Bring him to me," Jesus said. When Bartimaeus stood before him, our Lord asked, "What do you want me to do for you?"

We moderns are tempted to rebuke the Lord for his callousness at this point. "Lord," we would say, "anyone can see what he needs. He's been begging for mercy. He needs his sight." But the question was whether Bartimaeus knew this. He could just as easily have asked for money, for a better begging site, for assistance, for a training program for the blind, or for a hundred other things.

The Lord simply asked the man to be specific in his prayer: "What do you want?"

"Lord," he said, "I want to receive my sight."

"Then, do," said the Savior. And he did.

From that point on, I prayed these four requests in my nightly walks: a good grasp of Scripture, its firm grasp on me, good rapport with my listeners, and changed lives.

Soon I was without a pulpit and without a church.

GOOD NEWS FROM EXIT INTERVIEWS

The conflict in the church I was serving intensified to the point that we brought in a mediator. He interviewed church leaders, watched videos of my preaching, and polled the congregation, then filed his report. "Joe is not a pulpit giant," he said, "but he is a pretty fair preacher." I was encouraged by that. Then he recommended I leave the church.

I agreed. I took a one-year leave of absence, and I waited by the phone. A few invitations for revivals and conferences came in during the year; however, none but the tiniest churches would consider me as a potential pastor. My confidence in my preaching was at an all-time low.

Not by coincidence, the church that called me as pastor a year later was also at an all-time low. It had suffered a disastrous split. Half its thousand members had left, and the remainder was burdened with a great load of debt. Our first five years together were not easy. Gradually, however, we began to see the Lord was up to something special. One day I looked around and realized that we had become a healthy church again, one that is a pure joy to serve.

That's when the other surprise appeared, one just for me. After attending a Saddleback conference on purpose-driven churches, we began sending response cards to church visitors. These notes trickled back into the church office, telling what our guests had noticed first, liked best, and appreciated least about their visit to our church. To my utter amazement, many were impressed by the preaching.

I still recall standing at my secretary's desk reading two cards that had arrived in the morning mail. Both expressed thanks for my sermons. "I am totally surprised," I mumbled.

She looked up from her work. "Pastor, everyone loves your preaching."

"I guess I didn't know it," I replied.

To be honest, I'm still not quite convinced. But I've decided that's all right. The object of my prayers was never that people would like my preaching. It wasn't even that I would like it. It was a prayer for effectiveness in doing what God called me to do.

Good music, it is said, is music that is written better than it can be played. Perhaps that's how it is with the gospel of Christ. The message is far superior to any human expression of it. A gracious Father takes the efforts of his frail servants and uses them to change lives.

Next year marks my fortieth anniversary in ministry, and I still feel inadequate about my preaching. Not only is that all right, I think it's the appropriate way to feel about a calling so far above the capacity of any of us mortals— to proclaim the riches of Christ in human tongue.

It forces me to pray for my preaching.

Chapter 18

HOW DOES UNCTION FUNCTION?

Probing the mystery of "the anointing" in a sermon

Lee Eclov

In his novel *Paul*, Walter Wangerin Jr. has Barnabas describing the great apostle's preaching:

> He had such a thing to tell them, and such a need to say it soon, to say it fast, that the reasonable tone of his voice would change to urgency. So then his sentences got longer, and the words burst from his mouth like flocks of birds, and the faith of the man was a high wind at the hearts of the people, and some of them gasped in delight, and these are the ones who rose up and flew; but others were insulted, and others afraid of the sacred passions. (pp. 115–16)

I imagine unction like that.

Unction means the anointing of the Holy Spirit on a sermon so that something holy and powerful is added to the message that no preacher can generate, no matter how great his skills. At the center of Pittsburgh two rivers, the Monongahela and the Allegheny, come together at The Point to form a new river, the mighty Ohio. That, I think, is how we envision unction working—the sermon and the Spirit meeting to form a spiritual torrent, Jesus' voice "like the sound of rushing waters."

I have occasionally been asked to evaluate

sermon tapes, using a simple set of questions. One question—"Would you describe this sermon as having unction?"—often stumped me. What does unction sound like? What would I hear, exactly? Can unction even be discerned on a tape or do you have to be there in person to sense the Spirit's unction?

Generally we regard unction as the Holy Spirit's anointing of the preacher as the sermon pours from his lips. Surely God does wonderfully and mysteriously anoint preachers, but I've been intrigued with two other "targets" of the Spirit's unction—the very process of baptized rhetoric and the inherent anointing on God's Word itself.

BAPTIZED RHETORIC

We equate unction with a power that lifts words and sends them a-soaring, but there is power something like that in simply good rhetoric. Consider the Gettysburg Address, for example, or the speeches of Winston Churchill. Edward R. Murrow said of him, "He mobilized the English language and sent it into battle." Surely those speeches had something unction-like about them. Or when Dr. Martin Luther King Jr. cried out across the mall in Washington, "I have a dream," was that unction? He was a preacher, after all. But that is also great rhetoric.

Aristotle's classical rhetoric identified three essential ingredients of a great speech: *logos* (what we say), *ethos* (who we are), and *pathos* (the passion we bring to the task). But it is only when the Holy Spirit is added to the equation that we have *unction*. When those qualities are combined in a godly and passionate preacher, steeped in a text of Holy Scripture, great rhetoric is kissed with unction. Kent Hughes, in the

preface to his commentary on the Pastoral Epistles, says these three in a holy combination are in fact what make for "the Holy Spirit filling one's sails, the sense of his pleasure, and the awareness that something is happening among one's hearers."

God's Spirit has surely "filled the sails" of poor sermons and embarrassing preachers from time to time, but for consistency, when logos, ethos, and pathos are baptized into Christ, unction results. When both the sermon and preacher are carefully prepared, the Holy Spirit is poised to pour out his fire.

It appears to me that in the Bible, it is the message that is anointed by God as much as the messenger. Unction seems to live in God-given messages, as fire dwells in lava. The fire is in the message and the warning to the preacher is not to let it cool. Unction is not so much poured out as lifted up and delivered.

Here are four biblical examples where unction is in the message.

The Turning Point

When everything hangs on which way God's people turn next, God's message will have a fiery intensity. People must have trembled to hear Moses boil their choices down to this: "This day I call heaven and earth as witnesses against you that I have set before you life and death, blessings and curses. Now choose life" (Deut. 30:19). Or when Joshua, at the end of his career, cried, "Choose for yourselves this day whom you will serve.... But as for me and my household, we will serve the LORD" (Josh. 24:15). Those words have unction; we tremble before them even today.

It is a preaching truism that every sermon should call for some kind of response, but there are clearly some Sundays, some messages, that are turning points for a congregation. Ahead of them, "two roads diverge in a yellow wood," and it will make all the difference where they step. God may thunder or God may whisper his message, but his Spirit is poured out in pleading and pointing on such Sundays.

Count on it! You will have unction when you speak to God's people with Jeremiah: "Stand at the crossroads and look" (Jer. 6:16).

The Purified Preacher

The ethos of a preacher requires godliness. Every preacher should step to the pulpit with a heart that has been God-tested and blood-bleached. But there are times when preachers have an experience akin to Isaiah's, when it seems as though a burning coal from an angel's hand has cauterized our tongue. The solitary preacher himself has heard a message full of unction, all for him, sterilizing his head and heart. So when he stands to preach—whatever the text before him—he very nearly breathes fire from his own flaming heart.

The preacher has prayed, "Take what I offer thee, O Lord, and teach me to give them all. Breathe on the kindled flame within, O place on my tongue your white coal."

He is the man whose heart has been broken till "all the vain things that charm me most" have been emptied out, and he waits to speak from a holy hollowness, having for the first time a great capacity for God. She is the speaker whose eyes somehow that week saw the undisguised hopelessness of the lost, and she cannot bear any more silence. He has somehow seen the Lord, high and lifted up, till his knees went weak and his tongue tied. Yet when he preaches—gasps, really—the sermon burns with holy oil.

Preaching Christ

Every sermon should preach Christ, of course. After all, what time do we have for small themes and side trips? But there are those times when the glory of Christ, the astonishing accomplishments of the Son of God, come to spontaneous combustion in a preacher.

Such a holy outburst usually comes from long contemplation of the Savior. We stare for long hours on some biblical masterpiece like Isaiah 53—"The LORD has laid on him the iniquity of us all" (Isa. 53:6). Or we circle Philippians 2 like a great monument—he "did not consider equality with God a thing to be grasped" (Phil. 2:6). Or we feed our choked imagination with Revelation's images—"His eyes are like blazing fire, and on his head are many crowns. He has a name written on him that no one knows but he himself" (Rev. 19:12). And we begin to smolder with some inward poetry, some lyric that fairly jumps from our lips on Sunday. In such moments, another's quotes won't do, nor another's verse. We may not speak in rhyme, but we have become poets nonetheless.

There are times, too, when the sole sufficiency of Christ nearly takes our breath away. The Scriptures crack our shell and we see with digital clarity that all else is ashes without Jesus. An urgency comes upon us: "You must—you must!—trust Christ." And we plead as though their lives depended on it. The suits and smiles in the pews fade before our eyes and we see instead prisoners through their bars; we see the sunken cheeks of the famished; we see the pallor of the dead, right there before us where ordinary people sat a moment ago, and we must give them Jesus! They must be redeemed!

Dave Hansen wrote in *Leadership* (Winter 1997) of the suffering of his ministry mentor and friend, Bob Cahill. Pastor Cahill told Dave, "Since my cancer I preach as a dying man to dying men. When I look out at the congregation,

I see people whose lives are passing away and who need Christ. You can't imagine what this does to your sense of unction."

Preach the Word!

In 2 Timothy, Paul does not urge Pastor Timothy to seek unction, but he does say, "All Scripture is God-breathed. . . . Preach the word!" (2 Tim. 3:16; 4:2). The unction is already upon the Scriptures. The Bible is already drenched in sacred oil. When I preach, I love those inexplicable moments when I find myself soaring, when the Word is like honey to me, and fire. But what I have learned from Paul's last admonitions to Timothy is to trust the unction that is always on Scripture even when my words seem clumsy or common.

When we take up the Scriptures for "teaching, rebuking, correcting and training in righteousness" (2 Tim. 3:16), unction is ours. When we show how the Scriptures make one "wise for salvation through faith in Christ Jesus" (3:15), that is anointed preaching. When we offer "careful instruction," we have God's own blessing. That Word, so long as we are faithful to it, is "living and active" (Heb. 4:12).

I told a seasoned preacher friend I was thinking about unction. "It's hard to explain," he said, "but I know when I have it." I know what he means, but I'm not sure he's right. If he means, "I can feel unction when it comes upon me, when my words turn to hammers or lightning or medicine," well, I'm not sure we can always tell. Sometimes unction is simply received by faith, without feeling the wind or the heat. We go home to our Sunday afternoon nap deflated and disappointed that nothing seemed to happen. But when with a pure heart, a Christian preacher declares the Scriptures, or proclaims Christ, or calls for repentance and holiness, his words are surely anointed.

So does any declaration of Scripture carry unction? Does a tedious but true lecture, a plagiarized sermon, or an insincere Bible preacher have the Spirit's anointing? Yes, I think so, but dimly, cooly. It is a fire blanketed, a barely smoldering cinder. The Spirit has been quenched. God has been known to use his Word even in such cases to touch a life. The Word truthfully told always has unction, but when a preacher has ducked the Spirit's holy oil himself, the very Word of the Almighty is muffled and muted. It is a treasure not easily trusted because it is in the hands of a huckster.

STAYING OFF THE MIDWAY

I must admit that unction hasn't always had an altogether positive connotation for me. It is a word that somewhere in my past was hung like a sideshow banner over a sweaty, pulpit-pounder caught up in a frenzy of conviction. He is a preacher I resent—for not preparing well, for running on emotion and guilt, for crying too easily, for thinking there is something superior about being a primitive preacher. He gives unction a bad name: unctuous.

But when we faithfully reiterate Scripture, when our exposition exhales what the Lord has breathed into it, when our hearts are impassioned with Bible truth and our characters are refined by its heat, there is unction.

Chapter 19

SQUEAKY CLEAN

Essential areas of focus for the preacher who wants to do right.

Kenton C. Anderson

This week I met with one of my favorite young pastors. Normally this young man energizes me with his passion and his optimism. This time I found him broken, confused, and embarrassed. His ministry is over, at least for now. He has his excuses and some of them are compelling, but the fact is, he cannot preach the Word when people are not sure they can trust him.

Good ethical practice is foundational to preaching, and good preachers know it. For most of us there is no question about our intent to be ethical in the pulpit. The question is whether we will know what is right and whether we will be able to do it.

PERSONAL INTEGRITY

The foundation of preaching integrity is personal integrity, and we cannot take it for granted. Three areas deserve special attention.

Sexuality

I recently met an old friend while waiting for an airplane. I remember how her preacher husband had left her, allured by the appeal of another woman. Now years later I found her well, growing in her faith and in her person; yet the experience had left her family deeply scarred. I was heartened by her courage but saddened by her pain.

No preacher intends to fall victim to sexual infidelity, yet many do because they do not set up wise boundaries for avoiding straightforward sexual temptation, or they do not understand the relationship between sexual temptation and other nonsexual, emotional desires in their lives, such as the desire for power, intimacy, security, acceptance, and approval. If we are not mature spiritually, emotionally, and relationally, we are more open to sexual temptation.

If we recognize immaturity in ourselves, we should seek guidance from a mature leader, for sexual sin committed in private quickly becomes public. The result is always ugly, as families are scarred and ministries defeated. God himself is dishonored when his servants sin with sex.

Sexuality is of such great concern in human life today that we preachers need to talk about it, but we need to do it appropriately. We must decide in advance that there are things we will do and things we will not do. We will, for example, establish distinct relational boundaries, well clear of danger. We will not indulge in humor laced with sexual innuendo. We will not allow ourselves to let pornography gain a toehold in our consciousness. We will invest our passions in our marriages and make sure our spouses know they can trust us. Remembering Paul's advice in Romans 14 about stronger and weaker brothers, we will be careful in our use of movie-based illustrations because some will have problems with sexual portrayals elsewhere in the movie. We will be willing to pay a price to help people avoid temptation.

Finances

Paul claimed that preachers do not peddle the gospel for profit (2 Cor. 2:17). This has certainly been true for generations of preachers who have labored in poverty. Yet that very poverty can lead underpaid preachers to be tempted by money. The same is true of well-paid preachers who have grown accustomed to money's charms.

Several important actions can keep us from these dangers. Mismanagement of our personal finances can lead us into temptation, fear, or the bitterness that can easily find its way into our preaching. Therefore it is wise to follow a personal budget. Over time we should train our church how to support its pastor. Most laypersons simply lack knowledge on this subject. If our church is not being realistic or responsible in our salary, we should have the courage to negotiate with wisdom but without grasping. When we receive an honorarium, we will do it graciously and not as if it is required. The best way to make sure that people sense we are not driven by money is not to be. We should regularly examine our souls to see if we are marked by contentment.

Accountability

The apostle Paul had confidence enough to invite people to examine his life and character as evidence to the truth of his message (1 Cor. 11:1). That could be a higher level of scrutiny than many of us might welcome. The more we are aware of our own sin, the less we feel competent to stand and preach. Yet privacy cannot be promised to the one who claims to speak for God. Listeners have a right to ask whether we are going to practice what we preach.

Rather than despising this accountability, we ought to welcome and even encourage it. We must resolve to establish strong relationships with people courageous enough to ask us hard personal questions in order to keep us from these destructive impulses. We are well advised to limit intentionally our personal freedom by avoiding even the appearance of evil. Nothing compromises the credibility of the message like a life that denies the words the preacher speaks. Character counts.

An example can be found in the ministry of Billy Graham and his team. In 1948 Graham and his teammates, Cliff Barrows, George Beverly Shea, and Grady Wilson, met in Modesto, California, to determine the ethical parameters for their preaching ministry. The resulting code, nicknamed "The Modesto Manifesto," described four key commitments. They deliberately determined that they would avoid even the appearance of financial abuse. All money would be carefully accounted for and fully disclosed to the public. They determined that they would be absolutely honest in their publication of statistics. They chose to exercise care to avoid the possibility of any perception of sexual impropriety, never appearing alone with a woman not their wives. They agreed to cooperate with any local church that could subscribe to their view of the gospel so as to avoid any sense of competition among churches.

Many would have thought they had taken precautions beyond what was necessary. Yet decades later Graham's ministry stands as a paragon of ethical propriety. The credibility of Graham's preaching has been immeasurably enhanced by these commitments to character deliberately chosen and carefully maintained over all these years.

We will mess up, sometimes spectacularly.

Yet if we mess up, we'll clean up, and we will rest heavily on the grace of God.

TRUTHFULNESS

I have heard preachers share stories from their personal experience and then heard other preachers share the same story as if it had happened to them. I could only assume one of them was lying. Listeners must know they can rely on the preacher's words. Anything that could cause hearers to doubt our credibility is an ethical problem. There are three areas of concern.

Exegesis

Truthfulness begins with sound exegesis. God's Word is given in human language, and language inevitably requires interpretation. This is not to render preaching entirely subjective; it is to say, however, that there is a certain amount of human discretion involved in the preacher's use of Scripture. We abuse that discretion, though, if we knowingly use our position to manipulate meaning for personal purposes: to please or impress hearers, to "improve" the sermon, or to gather a larger following. We are responsible to present the plain truth as it is found in the text.

People should not have to take our words with the proverbial grain of salt. Some preachers are known to embellish stories or to speak "evang-elastically" in the use of statistics, but our points are never enhanced when we bend truth in the direction of our own interest, even when we do it because we think it serves the gospel.

This is not to say we have to be slavish to the details of the stories we are telling. In our use of the Bible, for example, we can imagine a puzzled look on the face of the rich young ruler or a tear in the eye of the prodigal son. The text does not give us those details, but we are not violating the intent of the text when we provide them.

Plagiarism

Plagiarism is a particular concern for the truthful preacher. While many would suggest that the pulpit allows latitude in the use of other people's ideas, unauthorized, uncredited appropriation of intellectual property is theft. Plagiarism occurs whenever we pass along someone else's idea or words as if they were our own.

In my reading I often get excited about the way the writer has put the point. I wish I could have been smart enough to put the matter just that way. The temptation is to use the writer's words in my sermon as if they were my own. If I do it, however, I am not being truthful. A more substantial problem lies in the practice of lifting entire sermons from books or the Internet and claiming them for our own.

Preachers do stand on the shoulders of others. It is good practice, for instance, to benefit from concepts, commentary, and even sermon constructions offered by others. In some of these cases, the ideas are essentially in the public domain and no longer need to be cited. In other cases, where either the ideas are unique to a particular source or where the use is substantial, we will want to identify who it is that we have benefited from. This is not difficult. It can be done orally ("I like the way Rick Warren put it"), on the overhead screen, or in the printed bulletin.

A further area of concern is the use of motion picture content without appropriate permissions. A judiciously used movie clip can add much to a sermon, but just as we have learned to do with music, we must purchase a blanket license allowing limited usage.

Manipulation

I once had a listener stand up, wave his fist at me, and yell, "That's not true." I probably had it coming. I had challenged his point of view, and he had no appropriate way to respond. I was standing in the pulpit, and I had all the power. Ethics in preaching demands that we speak and act respectfully toward our listeners. The pulpit is a place of power if for no other reason than the traditional sermon offers little opportunity for dialogue or interaction. Any half-truths or untruths can be devastating to people unable to defend themselves.

We usually have the best of motives. We preach so that people will find faith in Christ and that the followers of Jesus will serve to bring God's kingdom on earth. Rare is the preacher, though, who does not feel the subtle strains of temptation to manipulate the listener even just a little. Facts can be stretched, stories exaggerated, and rhetoric heated to the point where the listener finds motivation, not simply in the power of the message or the call of God's Spirit, but in the manufactured emotion of the moment. Seminaries don't teach this, but still we learn it well.

We must be careful to motivate people but not to manipulate them. We manipulate when we coerce listeners into beliefs or actions they would not normally accept. Manipulation occurs when we surreptitiously affect an unwitting change in the listeners' thought and life.

Motivation is different. Preachers who motivate lead people to a considered redirection.

This is not to say that the listener fully understands all of the depths and implications but that the preacher leads the listener to a point of intellectual discovery or emotional congruence. The listener is engaged by the moment, not mesmerized by the hype. There is a subtle line between manipulation and motivation, and we must learn to stay on the right side of it.

We must be careful not to use the pulpit as a means to bully people into submission. While we may feel disrespected and maligned, the pulpit is no place to get even or to "set the record straight." Preachers, adept at the use of words, can damage and defame, all the while sounding spiritual and upright. It may be that a pastor is struggling with the church board over a question about strategy, but the Sunday sermon is not the best place to try to win that battle. It is not a fair fight, given that the board has no similar opportunity to express their views.

For two years while studying in Texas, I belonged to a special church. I have never known a pastor to experience such deep respect from the people he was called to serve. The man didn't look much like a preacher. There was little hype or holler in his ways. The people loved him because they trusted him. As he offered them the wisdom he found in God's Word, the people didn't have to question whether or not he was going to live congruently. He lived openly and honestly before his people, and they responded to him like few preachers I have seen.

I aspire to that kind of ministry, for we serve a holy God whom we love and who will hold us to account. "Be holy," the Bible says, "because I am holy" (1 Peter 1:16).

Chapter 20

REQUIRED READING

Why establish a reading plan?

Haddon Robinson

Among the last words Paul wrote in a letter to his friend Timothy are these: "When you come, bring the cloak that I left with Carpus at Troas, and my scrolls, especially the parchments" (2 Tim. 4:13). The apostle was an old man facing death at the hands of the emperor. He was chained in a drafty dungeon in the city of Rome. He needed his cloak to keep the chill off his bones, but he needed his books and parchments to keep the rust off his mind.

Charles Spurgeon took a lead from these words when he observed, "Even an apostle must read. He is inspired and yet he wants books. He has seen the Lord and yet he wants books. . . . He has been caught up in the third heaven, and he had heard things which it is unlawful for a man to utter, yet he wants books. He had written a major part of the New Testament and yet he wants books." Paul had no more sermons to prepare and no more books or letters to write, but he needed to keep on reading. Even though life was running out on him, Paul needed his books.

Ministers must read. We are required to read not as a luxury but as a necessity. We cannot go it alone. Our study of the Bible is enriched by the insights of scholars who have studied sections of the Bible more than we have. Only the lazy or stupid ignore the use of commentaries in their preparation. But we should also open our minds to wider vistas through reading books that are not sermon direct.

Working ministers must try to make this broader reading a top priority, however difficult it may be. Determine to read thirty minutes a day, five days a week. Do that for fifty weeks, and you will have read 125 hours in a year. If you read thirty pages an hour, you will have read over 3,750 pages a year. If you keep up that pace for ten years, you will have read more than 150 books of 250 pages. If those books are well chosen, you can become an authority in any field. As the venerable adage puts it: "Constancy surprises the world by its conquests."

If you have a book in your hand, you are never alone, and reading enables you to have continued education without having to pay tuition.

Chapter 21

RIGHTLY DIVIDING THE PREACHING LOAD

The benefits of developing a preaching team, and how one church is seeing it work

Larry W. Osborne

When I first entered the pastorate, I considered preparing and preaching Sunday's sermon the essence of ministry. Everything else was secondary. The notion of sharing my pulpit was unthinkable, tantamount to a denial of my calling.

But it wasn't long until I discovered that there was much more to being a good preacher than just preaching. From the beginning, people looked to me for far more than a weekly sermon. They wanted from me counsel, administration, vision, recruitment, and a host of other skills that had little or nothing to do with my pulpit prowess.

And to my surprise, all that other stuff really did matter. When it was handled well, our ministry flourished. When handled poorly, we struggled. It was then I first began to think about doing the unthinkable: sharing my pulpit with another preacher. Four years later I decided to go for it.

Here was my thinking: By turning over some of the time spent preparing and preaching sermons, I would be able to give better direction to our overall ministry. That would result in a healthier church and spiritual environment, and in the long run, my sermons would be more effective, even if less frequent.

I was right.

Now, seven years later, I'm more convinced than ever. I doubt I could ever again return to the days of being a one-man show. Sharing the pulpit has been too beneficial. It's proven to be one of the best things that ever happened to our church and to me.

Here's why—and what it took to make it work.

What It Did for the Church

One of the most significant things it did for our church was to make it more stable—by making it less dependent on me.

Let's face it: attendance and giving at most churches rises and falls with the presence of the senior pastor. Any prolonged illness or move to another church usually results in a dramatic drop-off. Sharing the pulpit (which in our case means having a second pastor preach between 20 and 30 percent of the morning messages) has helped mitigate the problem by giving our people the chance to buy into two preachers—and most have.

As a result, when I now leave for a conference, mission trip, or vacation, we hardly miss a beat. There is never an appreciable drop in attendance or giving. Things keep right on going.

That's not to say that my long-term absence or move to another church wouldn't have an effect. Of course it would. As the initiating leader of our ministry and staff, I'm a vital cog in the wheel. But it wouldn't hobble our ministry nearly as much as if I were the only "first-string varsity preacher" our people knew.

Should I be removed from the scene, our people wouldn't be faced with a sudden parade of strangers in the pulpit (or an ill-equipped associate, learning on the job). They'd simply get an extra dose of "the other preacher," someone they've already grown to love and respect.

The church has also benefited in other ways. They've received a more balanced presentation of Scripture than I could ever give on my own. While Mike (the other preaching pastor) and I share the same core theological perspective, we often approach life and Scripture from different angles. I'm more practical and oriented to the bottom line. He's more of an intellectual and a scholar. Thus each of us ends up seeing things and reaching people that the other misses.

HOW THE SENIOR PASTOR BENEFITS

However, the church isn't the only one that has benefited. I have too, perhaps even more so. To begin with, it's given me a chance to regularly recharge my creative batteries.

We each have a reservoir of creativity. For some of us it runs deeper than for others. But for each of us there's a bottom. Unless we're able to periodically replenish it, sooner or later it runs dry. When that happens, the joy goes out of preaching, for us as well as for our listeners.

I once served in a ministry where I was responsible to teach five or six different Bible studies every week. For a while it was exhilarating. But after three or four years I began to fade. It's not that I ran out of passages or topics to teach. I ran out of creative and thoughtful ways to present them. The result was a marked increase in truisms, clichés—and a little plagiarism!—and boredom all around.

Now I use my breaks from the pulpit to rekindle my creativity, to catch up on non-preparatory reading, to reflect, and to dream new dreams. Breaks recharge my creative juices in a way that another week of sermon preparation cannot.

I also use my nonpreaching weeks to regroup emotionally. Preaching is hard work, and it takes its emotional toll. It's no small matter to stand up and presume to speak for God. No wonder we're known to take Sunday afternoon naps and Mondays off. Yet for me, the actual preaching and preparing of a sermon isn't the hard part. I love it. The hard part is always knowing I've got another one due in a couple of days. That keeps me on edge and always pushing.

During my first four years at the church, I preached every Sunday except for my vacations. That meant that, no matter where I went or what I did, next week's sermon was always percolating in the back of my mind. I'd wake up in the middle of the night to scratch out an outline. I'd take note pads on vacation. At conferences and seminars, I'd disappear for a few hours to hammer out that final point or closing illustration.

The result was a slow but steady drain on my emotional reserves. As much as I love study and preaching, it was too much of a good thing. Too often, by the time my vacation rolled around, preaching had become a chore instead of a privilege; I was reading the Bible for sermon material, not personal growth. Furthermore, most of my ministry was on automatic pilot.

That hardly ever happens anymore. I find that my regular breaks from the pulpit get me off the sermon prep treadmill before I've reached a point of emotional exhaustion. Though I often end up working just as hard and even harder during my nonpreaching weeks, it's the change in routine that makes the difference. Preaching can hardly become monotonous when it's periodically taken away. In fact, I always miss it, and I invariably return with heightened enthusiasm for proclaiming God's Word.

Sharing the pulpit has also helped me follow through better on my responsibilities as the church's leader. Like most pastors, I have a love/hate relationship with administration: I love what it accomplishes. I hate doing it. I didn't enter the ministry so that I could juggle budgets, supervise a staff, crank out policy statements, or return phone calls. But that's part of the package, and if I want to do a good job, I have to do those things well and in a timely manner.

Still, they aren't a lot of fun. If I can find half an excuse, I'll put them off until next week. And preparing next Sunday's sermon has always been a great excuse. That's where my weeks out of the pulpit come in. When I'm not scheduled to preach, I no longer have an excuse to let things go. Those important-but-not-urgent administrative matters that have been pushed to the side have a chance to rise to the top of my to-do list. And miracle of miracles, they usually get done.

I've often been told that one of the secrets to our congregation's health and growth has been my excellent administration. But little do people know that what they're so impressed with would never get done if I had my way—or if I had a sermon to prepare every week.

What It Takes to Make It Work

As valuable as sharing the pulpit can be, it can also be a disaster if done poorly or naively.

We've all heard horror stories of an idealistic copastorate gone bad or a trusted associate who turned into an Absalom at the gate. That's probably why so many of my mentors recommended against it, and why so few pastors try it.

But I've found it to be neither difficult nor dangerous as long as I pay careful attention to four key factors.

Mutual Respect and Trust

The first thing I look for in a person to share the pulpit with is someone I can respect and trust. The second thing I look for is someone who respects and trusts me.

The power and prestige of the pulpit is too great to give to someone I'm not sure about. Once they have that platform, it's hard to take it back.

Before turning the pulpit over to Mike, I had known and watched him for four years. Like most of our staff, he was hired from within so his loyalty and integrity had been tested by time and through actual disagreements. I knew I was putting a Jonathan, not an Absalom, in the pulpit.

Bringing in an outsider is a lot trickier. No amount of interviewing and candidating can guarantee that two people will work well together once they're actually on the job. Only time will tell. That's why I'd wait at least one year before starting to share the pulpit with a newly hired staff member. I'd want to confirm that the person I thought I'd hired was the person I actually got.

Make no mistake, sharing the pulpit can be tough on a shaky relationship. That's because people tend to choose sides—even when there isn't a contest. Both Mike and I have found that when some people compliment us, they suggest subtly a criticism of the other person: "Mike, *your* sermons are meaty," or "Larry, *your* sermons are practical." It's not that they are trying to be malicious or drive a wedge between us; it's just their way of saying, "I like you best."

That's no big deal as long as we understand what's happening and share a genuine respect and love for each other. But if either of us lacks that respect and if we begin seeing ourselves as competitors instead of coworkers, those kind of comments would widen the rift, serving as encouragement and confirmation of the ugly things we were already thinking.

Of such stuff coups and church splits are made. And that's why I'll always wait until I'm certain of the relationship before sharing the pulpit with anybody.

Good Preaching

The second thing I look for is someone who'll do a good job in the pulpit. I realize that something as subjective as "good preaching" is hard to define. But for our purposes, let's define a good preacher as someone the congregation thinks is worth listening to.

I know of one church where the senior pastor tried to share his pulpit with a warm-hearted and greatly loved associate. Unfortunately, he was also a pedestrian communicator. Attendance dived.

The best candidates for pulpit time aren't always next in line on the staff hierarchy. They might not even be on the staff. I know of one church where a part-time youth pastor was the one tapped to share the pulpit. I know of another where a lay preacher was clearly the best person for the job. (Obviously, in a solo pastorate it would have to be a lay person, perhaps a gifted Sunday school teacher or someone serving in a parachurch ministry.)

The key is to find someone the members feel good about and who can help them grow. If you do that, people won't care where that person fits in the staff hierarchy.

In a smaller church, it's possible to get by with some on-the-job training. When I first brought Mike aboard, he had never preached a sermon in his life. But I knew from his success as a Bible teacher at a Christian school and various home Bible studies that he had the gift. All he lacked was experience.

Proper Billing

Once I've found the right person, I still have to make sure that he gets proper billing. Otherwise, he'll always be seen as my substitute, someone who's giving them less than the best.

I've found one of the most effective ways to present someone as the other preacher rather than my stand-in is to be highly visible whenever he's scheduled to preach. To do that, I'll often make the weekly announcements. That lets everyone know that I'm in town and healthy. It also sends a clear message that he's not just filling in because I'm unavailable.

That proved to be particularly valuable when I first started sharing the pulpit. In fact, when I went out of town, I often came back early just to show my face. Though it's something I no longer need to do, it paid high dividends during those early days.

It's also important not to give away all the Sundays nobody wants. To assign someone to preach during my vacations and holiday weekends is hardly sharing the pulpit. It's dumping the dogs!

Finally, I'm careful how I talk about our roles. I always introduce myself as "one of the pastors." I never call Mike "my associate." He's the "other pastor" or "one of the other pastors."

None of these techniques are as vital as

mutual respect and good preaching skills. Still, they've gone a long way toward establishing the credibility of the other person in the pulpit.

Meeting Congregational Expectations

Every congregation has expectations (mostly unwritten), tampered with at great peril. To share the pulpit successfully, it's important to know what these expectations are and to meet them or find a way to change them.

For instance, our people expect me to be in the pulpit on Christmas and Easter. I can give away any other Sunday without hearing a complaint. But let me fail to preach on either of those days and I'll have a small uprising on my hands.

How much of the pulpit can be shared will also be dictated by congregational expectations. As Lyle Schaller has noted, churches that place a greater emphasis on the sermon and the personality of the preacher, rather than on the Eucharist and the office of the minister, will have a harder time adjusting to an equal interchange of preachers.

In our case, we're sermon-centered. So when I first started sharing the pulpit, I was pushing it when I was out of the pulpit 15 percent of the time.

Now, I'm out as much as 30 percent, but that's probably as high as it will ever be able to go here. The pastor of one church never missed a Sunday during his long tenure. Even during his vacations he shuttled back and forth on weekends to be in the pulpit. As you can imagine, that built in the congregation some incredible expectations. When a friend of mine became this pastor's successor, the best he could do was to turn over some Sunday nights and his vacation weekends. Anything more would have been interpreted as shirking his duties. The key in any situation is to know what will and won't work there and to adjust accordingly.

Preaching, I've discovered, is only one part of being a pastor. It may be the most important part, but it is still only a part. When I learned to share that part with a trusted and skillful colleague, it not only made me a better preacher but also a better pastor. And it made our church a better church.

Chapter 22

PREACHING THROUGH PERSONAL PAIN

If you have a crisis, should your sermons discuss it?

Daniel T. Hans

"Two days ago my daughter Laura died." So opened the most difficult sermon I have ever had to preach. In that message, titled "God on the Witness Stand," I put myself in the place of Job, who, when assaulted by horrible personal tragedy, declared, "But I would speak to the Almighty, and I desire to argue my case with God."

That morning I preached a dialogue between myself as the prosecutor and God as the defendant. For nine months I had helplessly watched my three-year-old lose her physical and mental abilities to a malignant brain tumor, and I had a strong case against God.

Friends questioned the wisdom of my decision to preach so soon after my daughter's death. Could I withstand it? Could the congregation handle the emotional impact?

But if I did not use my personal life as the basis for preaching during this time of crisis, would I have either an audience or a message for someone else's time of pain?

EXEGETING OUR EXPERIENCE

Those who caution against becoming too personal in preaching raise necessary questions. Does a preacher have the right to carry his or her own confusion and pain into the pulpit? Doesn't such transparency focus more on the preacher than the Lord? Does not personal exposure in preaching turn the pulpit into a soap opera and denigrate the ministry of proclamation into self-aggrandizement? Certainly discretion must be employed in what the preacher says about personal matters from the pulpit. However, in response to these cautions, a counter question must be asked: Shouldn't a human preacher be human in preaching?

That sermon preached two days after my daughter's death was one of many messages composed at my daughter's bedside in the hospital and her deathbed in our home. Those sermons constituted a collection of feelings and convictions as intimate as private prayers. I must confess that little biblical exegesis went into them. My own life became my primary source. My prayers and reflections became my commentaries.

As I preached in the midst of my pain, I was unaware of particular features of my sermons that later proved healing and directive for my congregation. Looking back, however, I can identify four characteristics of preaching that should be present whenever I attempt to preach through pain.

Vulnerability: Admitting the Pain

Vulnerability heads the list. While this has become an overworked word in the jargon of pastoral ministry, it has no suitable substitute. Openly expressing sorrow in the pulpit does not constitute professional sin for preachers. On several occasions, I couldn't keep back the tears. Controlling my pained emotions proved no problem when I stared at myself in the mirror. But somehow my control dissipated as I stood in the pulpit looking out at faces visibly suffering with me. It was painful for my congregation to see me cry, yet it was tremendously healing for them and for me. One member whose earlier years had been clouded by drug abuse confided in me, "Your tears helped free me to face some painful things in my life that I've tried to hide behind a fake wall of strength."

The greatest resource in preaching through my own pain was the Old Testament Prophets and Wisdom Literature. I mined those writings thoroughly, for I found therein faith's best reflections on the injustices of life, placed beside the reality of God and the futility of attempting to categorize and control him.

Arthur Gossip, a Scottish preacher from the early 1900s, lost his wife suddenly. After his return to the pulpit following her death, he preached "When Life Tumbles In, What Then?" In that message, Gossip announced that he did not understand this life of ours. But still less could he understand how people facing loss could abandon the Christian faith. "Abandon it for what!" he exclaimed. Speaking from the darkest storm of his life, he concluded, "You people in the sunshine may believe the faith, but we in the shadow must believe it. We have nothing else."

Honesty: Equal Access for Anger

A second necessary characteristic of preaching in the midst of personal pain is honesty. Honesty holds vulnerability accountable, adding the following caution: We must not talk about our struggles from the pulpit unless the thoughts and feelings expressed truly belong to us. If hope and strength characterize our emotions, let that be known. However, if hope and strength have abandoned us, then in the pulpit we must not pretend to possess them. People will see through our veneer and therefore doubt our integrity.

As grief must be given access to the pulpit, so also must anger and doubt. Here I balked. I had often used the sovereignty of God as an excuse for allowing life's loose ends to remain untied. Now, when I spoke of hope, I found I was ignoring my own strongly felt doubts. Unwilling to face honestly my inner anger toward God, I bailed out when opportunities arose to address my indignation in the pulpit. In the year following my daughter's death, I put together a book that was my "pulpit journal" during those nine months surrounding my family's travail. A counselor friend offered this comment after reading it: "While I appreciated the insights you shared, I think you let God off the witness stand too soon. Your anger was not allowed to present fully its case against God."

In retrospect, I believe I was too polite with God. I've become convinced of two things in this regard. First, God can handle anger, even a preacher's. Second, a congregation needs to hear how the preacher deals with those angry feelings we all have toward God in times of tragedy. When crisis strikes, anger toward God is one of the truly honest emotions we feel. Describing how we as pastors feel in such situations validates the emotion for others and also provides a model of how to deal with it.

Though the expression of my anger was masked in my preaching, a few people discerned it. They told me that the inflamed questions I fired at God in the sermon immediately following Laura's death provided them some emotional liberation.

One mother, who read that sermon nearly two years after I preached it, wrote expressing her gratitude. She said I had given her an invitation to face the anger she still carried over the loss of her son three years earlier. The gist of her discovery was that if a minister could get mad at God, it must be all right for her to do the same. That helped her begin to work through her anger.

Hope: Looking At the Moment and Beyond

A third element in preaching through personal pain is hope. Hope stands as the supreme gift a preacher can offer a congregation while speaking from the shadowy valleys. In its simplest form, God's redemptive hope means that good can come out of bad.

In another sermon following my daughter's death, I looked at the lives of Joseph and Paul. Joseph told his brothers, "You intended to harm me, but God intended it for good" (Gen. 50:20). Despite the pain of his thorn in the flesh, Paul heard God say, "My grace is sufficient for you, for my power is made perfect in weakness" (2 Cor. 12:9).

At Laura's birth I witnessed the serenity of her being placed in her mother's warm arms. At her burial I witnessed the severity of her being placed in the cold arms of the grave. In reflecting on my experience and that of Joseph and Paul, I concluded a message about holding onto hope by saying, "Our faith is built upon a severe mercy—an innocent man being executed on a cross. What person, at the time, thought the death of Jesus was anything but a senseless and severe tragedy? Who now would see it as anything but the mercy of God at work on our behalf? When so many strugglers would seek God's mercy only to deliver them from the severe events, we would do well to seek God's

mercy to teach us through the severe events. These latter works of God, the severe mercies, become the lasting ones."

Near the time of Laura's death, a friend showed me some verse from Emily Dickinson that helped me and my congregation look at the moment and beyond:

> I shall know why—when Time is over—
> And I have ceased to wonder why—
> Christ will explain each separate anguish
> In the fair schoolroom of the sky.

Patience: The Grace of Unanswered Questions

The fourth trait needed is patience. Impatience enticed me to seek a quick and easy explanation for the suffering that befell my family. My greatest temptation in the pulpit is to view my call to preach as a command to offer definitive explanations. I feel far more comfortable concluding a sermon with an inspired call to arms than with an unanswered and perhaps unanswerable question. Personal tragedy has taught me the answer to human suffering is not to be found immediately—if it is to be found at all.

When a parent is confronted with the diagnosis of cancer in his child, the inevitable question "Why?" demands a hearing. How could I reconcile my three-year-old's cancer with an all-powerful, all-loving God who, I believed, ruled this world? In one sermon I addressed the why of evil and the goodness of God by setting forth the classic and contemporary attempts to resolve the conflict. People of faith who encounter a tragic injustice gravitate to one of the following options:

- dualism, with its universe governed by coequal good gods and bad gods
- demotion, in which only one God exists but is

seen as limited, mighty but not almighty, and doing the best he can in the face of evil

- denial, as in religions like Christian Science, which deny the harsh realities of illness, death, and evil
- despair, which gives up on God when he fails to live up to naive and magical expectations of him
- self-damnation, with its guilt-laden question, "Is God punishing me?"

A final option exists, however, which I believe is the only choice consistent with revelation and reality. The simultaneous existence of God and evil is an unsolvable dilemma. Job, Habakkuk, and countless others immersed in personal pain and confusion have attempted to use theology to control the situation, but in the end, our human explanations all come up empty-handed. However, there is a grace in the unanswerable why, for it leads us to the very heart of faith, which is patient trust in God.

I recall a conversation I had with a man several weeks after the sermon in which I "prosecuted" God. This was a compassionate person whose heart had been deeply pierced by Laura's death, and he also wanted answers to the why of her suffering. He reviewed a portion of that sermon in which I accused God of willfully refusing to heal my daughter. Then he confessed, "I have struggled with faith all my life. My conflict with God intensified with Laura's illness. But now I keep thinking back on what you said about us wanting God's absolute control and life's absolute freedom. I never thought of it that way before. We want two things from God that by their nature cannot exist together. I'm beginning to see that to have faith does not mean to have all the answers. Faith is holding on to God in spite of the confusion."

What greater gift can a preacher give a con-

gregation than the picture of trust in the Lord even though grief and confusion remain?

KNOWING OUR LIMITATIONS—AND THEIRS

Having explained some qualities needed when preaching through pain, I must offer a word of caution about when *not* to bring crises into the pulpit. During the three months prior to Laura's death, as her condition rapidly deteriorated, I was unable to make reference to her from the pulpit. At other stages of her illness, tears were somewhat under my control. At this stage, however, my emotions were so strained I feared I might not be able to regain composure if tears began to flow. I knew my congregation would have welcomed my reflections on Laura's status, but when the pain is too fresh or intense, wisdom advises avoiding references to our personal plight.

Another occasion when not to preach occurs after the crisis has passed. I failed to realize that my congregation's grief over my daughter's death did not linger as long as mine. Having conducted countless funerals and having been involved with the grief of many families, I was quite aware of the degrees of grief different people experience. However, when the deceased was my daughter, I somehow thought the rules would change. Surely others would have the same intensity and duration of feeling I carried! Such was not the case.

Following a sermon I preached long after my loss, one church member politely said to my wife, "I think Dan has talked about Laura from the pulpit too long after her death."

When I first heard this, I felt the person was being unfair to my feelings. However, I now realize my prolonged airing of my grief was unfair to my congregation's feelings. Had the Preacher in Ecclesiastes envisioned the theme of this article, he would have added this line to his description of life's cycles: There is a time to preach through our pain, and a time to preach beyond it.

I preached in such a manner on Memorial Day weekend nearly two years after Laura's death. Addressing the necessity of the grieving process after any major loss, I read a note I had received from a young mother. She had lost one child at birth and had a second child who had the same kind of tumor that took Laura. This mother enclosed the following prayer, which serves as a good reminder when we have to preach through our own pain: "Dear God, teach us to laugh again, but never let us forget that we have cried."

Chapter 23

A PROPHET AMONG YOU
What it means to be God's minister

Maxie Dunnam

A couple years ago I was smitten by a message given at a church ordination service. It was from Ezekiel 2:4–5: "The people to whom I am sending you are obstinate and stubborn."

Can you identify with that?

"Say to them, 'This is what the Sovereign LORD says.' And whether they listen or fail to listen—for they are a rebellious house—they will know that a prophet has been among them."

Here's the setting of this passage: Ezekiel is sharing his personal story about how God called him to be a prophet-priest and gave him a vision. The biblical account is complex and vivid, full of imagery. Ezekiel saw the glory of Yahweh coming down from heaven. It was so overwhelming that he fell on his face. (That's the only place for us to be when we're in the presence of the glory of the Lord—on our face.) But the Lord would not let him stay there. God said, "Son of man, stand up on your feet, and I will speak to you" (2:1). Then the Lord spoke.

The message God gave Ezekiel to preach was given in a scroll. Ezekiel received his appointment from God. And it was a tough calling. It wasn't a promising situation—not the opportunity to plant a new church in a rapidly growing part of the city, not an opportunity to serve as the senior pastor of the downtown First Church to which all the influential members of the city belonged, not an appointment to a posh suburban situation. God made this clear: In exercising his prophetic office, Ezekiel would have to preach to deaf ears and dwell among scorpions. There was no prospect for success laid out for the prophet in his initial call to ministry, and the burden of no prospect continued to increase as the Lord continued to speak.

Yet the call carried with it the power of support. Yahweh made the prophet's face harder than flint (Ezek. 3:9). The message of doom

Ezekiel was to proclaim was given to him to eat (3:1), and it tasted sweeter than honey. From that point on the prophet was entirely on God's side; the person and the word were considered the same. Thus, whether the people heard or refused to hear, they would know there had been a prophet among them.

I haven't been able to get away from that text since I heard it a couple years ago. It has been and continues to be a troubling proposition burning in my mind and heart, calling me to assess my witness and ministry, judging my failure, and challenging me to deeper commitment. I keep asking myself: To what degree do people know when I have been with them that a prophet has been in their midst?

Ezekiel was the first prophet consciously to enter this new sphere of activity that may be described as the "cure of souls." Ezekiel's calling was not only a traditional call to speak prophetically to the community and to the nation; it was a call to care for individuals, to play a pastoral role by helping people realize their situation in the eyes of God.

What is a prophet-priest's role—especially when faithfully performed so people will know God's representative has been among them? He or she speaks to the people for God and speaks to God for the people.

A PROPHET-PRIEST SPEAKS TO THE PEOPLE FOR GOD

The prophet addressed this in Ezekiel 36:22–23:

"Therefore say to the house of Israel, 'This is what the Sovereign LORD says: It is not for your sake, O house of Israel, that I am going to do these things, but for the sake of my holy name, which you have profaned among the nations where you have gone. I will show the holiness of my great name, which has been profaned among the nations, the name you have profaned among them. Then the nations will know that I am the LORD, declares the Sovereign LORD, when I show myself holy through you before their eyes.'"

Ezekiel is saying that God's honor must be restored in the sight of the nations, and that honor is connected, in fact is integral, to God's holiness. Ezekiel is speaking to the people for God. We, too, must speak to the people for God. We must call God's people to holiness if we're going to call the nation to God's righteousness.

God's name had been profaned not only by the heathen but by his own people. Today's world is not paying attention to the church, and the world tomorrow will not pay attention to the church until and unless those of us who call ourselves God's people vindicate God's holiness before the world's eyes.

At no other time has there been such great concern for holiness as today. The call is coming from almost every theological tradition, from Calvinist to Catholicism. There has been a rekindling in the concern for holiness because the gospel has been so relativized by those who would revise Christian theology. Is holiness a life-and-death issue in our culture today? This is an important question because our culture has become valueless, almost completely debauched.

That debauchery underscores the need for holiness and supports the Scripture's claim that holiness is not an option for God's people. The prophet-priest must speak to the people for God reminding them of this command to be holy. It's not likely that our prophetic words to the nation will be heard unless there is at least a remnant of God's people who seek to be, as the apostle Paul said, imitators of God—holy as he is holy, and living in love as Christ loved us and gave himself for us, a fragrant offering and sacrifice to God (cf. Eph. 5:1–2).

HOLINESS AND LOVE MUST NOT BE SEPARATED

Holiness without love is not God's kind of holiness. And love without holiness is not God's kind of love. Our prophetic priestly function of speaking to God's people requires us to identify with the people, to have a passion for their salvation, and to have a compassion that will cause us even to suffer for their sake.

To what degree do our people know we really care for them? As Yahweh made Ezekiel responsible, has he not made us responsible for those committed to our care? It was rather dramatic with Ezekiel. If he allowed the people to die unwarned, Yahweh threatened to require the prophet's life. So Yahweh said to him: "Therefore groan, son of man. Groan before them with broken heart and bitter grief" (Ezek. 21:6).

Are you groaning before the eyes of your people? Do they see that kind of passion flowing from your life?

Who are the people in your congregation who, though they may be members of the church, really don't feel they belong? Who are the people in your community who have yet to receive a clear message from you personally and from your congregation that you care deeply for them and that God loves them? What about the poor? Are you committed to the irrefutable truth of Scripture that God has taken a preferential option on behalf of the poor? What about the working poor, chief among them single mothers?

What of the vast segment of folks in every community for whom Christ and his church are really strangers? Are you ordering your life and the worship life of your congregation, your ministry and mission, in a way that goes to their turf and seeks to speak their language, a language they understand? Do you offer something that will meet their needs—not where you would like them to be but where they really are?

What about recovering folks, those seeking freedom from drugs and alcohol? Is your church a community of welcome and hospitality that will help them break the chains of shame and blame?

"Son of man, groan," God said to Ezekiel—and he says this to us. Show the people you care, that you speak for a God who loves us, who forgives our iniquities and heals our diseases, who restores us to wholeness, and gives us joy.

A PROPHET-PRIEST SPEAKS TO GOD FOR THE PEOPLE

Not only do we speak to the people for God, but we speak to God for the people. Our groaning becomes our intercession, our pleading with God on behalf of our people. One of the actions God called Ezekiel to perform was to lie down for a considerable time, first on his left side and then on his right side, in order to bear the guilt of Israel. God introduced that requirement in Ezekiel 4:4: "Then lie on your left side and put the sin of the house of Israel upon yourself. You are to bear their sin for the number of days you lie on your side." It's a powerful call for identification and suffering with and for our people. It's a commanding call to intercession.

The most significant breakthrough I've had in my prayer life during the past decade is a result of my decision three years ago to find a way to pray specifically for our community here at the seminary. At the beginning of each year, I divide our community into subgroups so that before the year has past, I will have had the opportunity to pray for every person in our community. At least, that's my intention. Prior to the week that I'm praying for a particular group of students, faculty, and staff, I write them a letter and invite them to share their joys and thanksgiving so I can celebrate with them. Then I ask them to share their needs and concerns so I might focus my prayer attention in that fashion.

During the past two weeks I have prayed for a young couple who just got engaged and another couple who are struggling desperately to keep their marriage together. I've been praying for the spouse of one of our students. The spouse is deaf, and she's having difficulty getting a job. I've been praying for a baby just conceived, the first baby this couple will have. But I've also been praying for a six-month-old baby who was born nearly blind, is being fed through a tube into her stomach, and has club feet that are in casts—the first child of a student's sister. I've been praying for a student pastor who has had his first conflict with his congregation. (I haven't told him that that's just the beginning!) I've been praying for a group of our students who are on a mission trip to Venezuela. And I've been praying for three of our professors who are in South Africa.

I make no claims about the working impact of my prayers within the lives of these people—though hardly a week goes by that I don't have a dramatic affirmation from someone. But what's really important is that since I began that prayer practice, my life has changed. The way I do my work as the president of this institution has been altered. At the depth of my concern and compassion there is an intensity of spirit, because I speak to God for these persons.

Whether they listen or refuse to listen, they will know a prophet has been among them.

GOD CALLS US TO BE SERVANTS WHO LISTEN AND OBEY

In the record of God's call to Ezekiel in chapters 2 and 3, God gave Ezekiel some direction, some promises we can apply to ourselves. First, God said to Ezekiel: Stand on your feet and I will speak to you. The lesson? We're to listen. Our stance must always be a receptive one. Speak, Lord, your servant is listening.

Second, after hearing God's call to stand on his feet so he might speak to him, Ezekiel said, "As he spoke, the Spirit came into me and raised me to my feet, and I heard him speaking to me."

God called Ezekiel to stand on his feet, but then, as Ezekiel said, "A Spirit entered into me and set me on my feet." God does not call us to a mission that we can accomplish within our own strength and with our own resources, but only with his divine aid. In that way, we're kept on our knees, dependent on him.

Third, Ezekiel 3:1–3 says, "He said to me, 'Son of man, eat what is before you, eat this scroll; then go and speak to the house of Israel.' So I opened my mouth, and he gave me the scroll to eat. Then he said to me, 'Son of man, eat this scroll I am giving you and fill your stomach with it.' So I ate it, and it tasted as sweet as honey in my mouth." We must become one with God's Word. What we say must be matched by how we live. It is only then that people will know a prophet has been among them. Robert Murray McCheyne has observed: "The greatest need of my congregation is my own personal holiness."

AS HOLY AS WE WANT TO BE

Throughout my years of ministry the greatest need of my congregation has been my own personal holiness. I remember a time back in the early sixties when I was confronted with a shocking realization: "I am as holy as I want to be." I was a young Methodist preacher in Mississippi. I was the organizing pastor of a congregation that had known amazing growth and success. The fellowship of that congregation was splintered by my involvement in the Civil Rights movement. I didn't think there was anything radical about my involvement, but many of the folks in the congregation couldn't understand my commitment and participation. I couldn't understand their lack of understanding. The gospel seemed clear.

The pressures, the stress, the tension wore me out. I was physically, emotionally, and spiritually exhausted, ready to throw in the towel when I went to a Christian ashram led by E. Stanley Jones. I'll never forget going to the altar one evening and having Brother Stanley lay hands on me and pray for me. He knew my story. We had been together that week. As I knelt, he asked me, "Do you want to be whole? Do you want to be holy?" That was a sanctifying experience in my life that changed the direction of my ministry.

Through the years since I have constantly asked myself, Do I want to be holy? And I have reminded myself over and over again that I'm really only as holy as I want to be. What about you? To speak to the people for God and to God for the people, your word and life must be in harmony. When what you say to the people for God resonates with how you live among them as an imitator of God, they will know that a prophet has been among them. I hope and pray that every congregation of which you're a part will know a prophet has been among them.

Chapter 24

BURNING CLEAN FUEL

Check the motives and emotions that energize your preaching

Scott Wenig

Well-meaning or not, pastors are in a daily battle, and sometimes we carry that battle into our preaching. Frustrations can bleed into our sermons and affect our passion negatively. We preach with passion, but we are burning the wrong fuel.

I remember preaching after I had been really hurt by someone. I wasn't processing my own feelings properly, and my anger came out in the sermon without my realizing it. People even came up afterward and asked what was wrong—they could hear the anger in my voice.

We can also get into trouble when we use the congregation as a foil to preach to ourselves. I remember an episode of a pastor who preached passionately against pornography, but we later discovered he was entangled in it himself. His preaching resulted from his motivation to work out his own personal issues.

I think also of a time five years ago when I

was fatigued and tried to do a motivational, rally-the-troops sermon. I thought I was trying to cheer the church, but I was really trying to cheer myself. It came out phony; I just didn't have anything to give.

Joe Stowell tells a story of another pollutant. While at a parish in Michigan, he decided certain people in the congregation needed straightening out, and he was going to use the pulpit to get them. But God inevitably protected those people from his ranting—every time he was prepared to give it to them, they missed church that Sunday. He finally realized the Lord was showing him not to berate them, but to love them and to wash their feet. Every congregation has its irritating members, but using the pulpit to go after them is bad motivation.

There's an underlying attitude in Joe's story that is common among us. Preachers can be tempted to think people out there don't care about Christ, the church, the ministry, or the kingdom and its advance—they just come to sit. That sort of thinking creates a temptation to beat them up. We come to God's people assuming they're not what they should be, and unless we get after them with a homiletical stick they never will be.

A colleague of mine, now in his sixties, said this was his approach in his first pastorate right out of seminary. Every Sunday he would beat up the church from the pulpit. It wasn't a hateful thing; theologically he just felt they needed to be motivated by the stick. After six or seven years, he realized they didn't like him, he didn't like them, and he needed to leave. He now looks back on that and tells his students, "Whatever you do, don't go in with that attitude."

The consequence of such preaching is that people don't feel we love them. In most urban areas of North America, if they don't like the tone of your church, if they don't feel cared for, they will go somewhere else. Obviously, that hurts. Moreover, it creates a mentality of guilt. Guilt is a poor motivator for Christian living, and it doesn't inspire true transformational change. Usually you feel bad for fifteen minutes, but then you stop at McDonald's and catch a football game, and it wears off quickly.

Perhaps the most dangerous result of burning bad fuel is that it creates apathy. William Barclay said there's nothing more dangerous than the repeated experiencing of emotion with no attempt to put it into action. Every time one feels a noble impulse without taking action one becomes less and less likely ever to do anything. Discharging passion at the congregation is hurtful if your purpose isn't to encourage them to do something constructive with that energy. Unless you give people something to do, you unintentionally create apathy.

Where do we get the right fuel for our preaching passion? One clean fuel for passionate preaching is a desire to see God's kingdom advanced. Haddon Robinson calls this "preaching the ideal rather than the standard." We raise the bar and challenge people to the highest ideal—until they want to be a part of that, until they want to make their lives count.

Several biblical illustrations show sources of passionate preaching. At the end of Luke 11, Jesus engages a group of Pharisees, and you can almost feel the heat come off the page. The Pharisees were hurting and misleading others, and Jesus attacks their false views on religion. Where God sees false religion or unauthentic spirituality, he gets passionate about it, and we should too.

In the first two chapters of Galatians, Paul gets just as impassioned about doctrine. What we think about God and how he interacts with us matters a lot. It mattered to Paul so much that he was willing to get onto his soapbox and yell a little. It's like the parent who sees his or her child doing something that will hurt them.

British historian Paul Johnson wrote, "Ideas have consequences." If we see people wandering as sheep into the deep end, biblically, theologically, or morally, that should stir a godly passion.

We need to distinguish in our own hearts between righteous indignation and impure anger. When I was preaching on that passage with Jesus and the Pharisees, I became impassioned as I preached about self-centered and self-deceived religion. But I used myself as an illustration, citing cases where I had been self-centered or self-deceived. Instead of pointing a finger and saying, "You are self-centered," I shared from our common human condition.

I also ask myself, "Am I growing in my love for God and for others?" All churches have problems, tangles, and weaknesses. But if I'm growing in love for the church and want to see it become what God intends, and if I have a growing concern for the poor, oppressed, and neglected, my passion will be pure because it's a reflection of the passion in God's own heart.

Chapter 25

BACKDRAFT PREACHING

You've got to reignite the flames Sunday after Sunday

Mark Buchanan

I love preaching. I hate preaching. The best description is Jeremiah's: It is like fire in the bones. It is holy work and dreadful work. It exhausts and it exhilarates, kindles and consumes.

On Mondays, I am charred remains. The hotter I burned on Sunday—the more I preached with fiery conviction and bright hope—the more burned to the ground I am on Monday. I'm restless, but I don't have initiative to do anything or, if I do, the energy to sustain me in it. I'm bone-weary, suffering what the desert fathers called *acedia*: an inner deadness from the hot sun's scorching.

Worst of all, Monday is lived with the knowledge that I am called to do it all over again next Sunday. Mondays are the days I would rather sell shoes.

But then Sunday comes, and the bones burn again. I am once more a firebrand freshly hot in the hand of God. If I don't preach, I am left with an aching sorrow. I chafe worse from not preaching than from preaching. "But if I say, 'I will not mention him or speak any more his name,' his word is in my heart like a fire, a fire shut up in my bones. I am weary holding it in; indeed, I cannot" (Jer. 20:9).

So I love it, and I hate it.

The surprise is that ten years of preaching has not diminished this. It has, instead, heightened and sharpened it. Every Sunday there's the passion if I preach, the aching if I don't. On Monday, either way, there's a daunting road both too long and too short that I must walk to next Sunday. Preaching is not a job. It is fire.

How shall we live with this rhythm of fire and ashes and fire again?

BACKDRAFT PREACHING

Backdraft refers to the phenomenon when a fire subsides because it's burned up all the oxygen in the room—then, if somehow the room is breached—a door is opened or the roof bitten through by the fire itself—oxygen-laden air rushes in and sparks an explosion. Fresh wind meets a dying fire, and all again is fiercely ablaze. That's a backdraft.

Backdraft is a good metaphor for the preaching call. It is exactly what I have described: the fire that burns the insides out and almost burns itself out; then, the fire meets fresh wind and breaks out anew. Knowing that this is the shape of the rest of my life, I have become desperate for disciplines to help me live with it. Here are three.

Look for Divine Interruptions

The Sermon has the hypnotic power of the seductress. It woos me, commands me, compels me. "Come and be with me," the Sermon whispers. When that fails, it gets surly: "Come here now! Or else." It often inhabits my sleep, a vague anxiety scrabbling at the edge of my dreams. Uncontrolled, the Sermon becomes an obsession.

I have no great tale of personal victory to relate here. The best thing I've found is to practice trusting God with my time.

Jesus was always being interrupted—by blind men, lepers, Pharisees finding him at night, desperate fathers with demonized or dying children, sinful women caught in adultery or pouring perfume on his feet. And he was always interrupting others—tax collectors counting money, fishermen mending nets or hauling them up, persecutors riding to Damascus. Much of his life-changing ministry came via interruptions.

Too many of us who preach are the priests and Levites in Jesus' story of the good Samaritan. We're so grimly focused on our temple duty that we miss what God has for us at the roadside. The only cure I know is daily and deliberate commitment to look for God in the interruptions. (As I wrote this, God brought three interruptions into "my schedule." Two were phone calls, one from a man at the edge of saving faith and needing a little extra attention, the other from a man of another faith interested in doing some work for the church. The third was a woman seeking bread. She and her children had nothing to eat. "I came to you hungry," Jesus said. "Did you notice?" In my busyness, I almost didn't.)

Living a theology of interruptions opens my soul to the fresh wind that reignites my fire.

Seek Silence

There is a beautiful line in Carl Sandburg's biography of Abraham Lincoln that describes Lincoln's early years and the secret of his later strength: "In wilderness loneliness he companioned with trees, with the faces of open sky and weather in changing seasons, with that individual one-man instrument, the ax. Silence found him for her own. In the making of him, the element of silence was immense."

Our world is not like Lincoln's; it is cluttered with image, clattering with sound, ceaselessly busy. Wilderness has dwindled away and sanctuary has been crowded out. Now, those who wish to keep silence must seek it out.

Not far from where I live is a river that pours out of a large lake. The river curves labyrinth-like on its way down to the ocean. This is where I go for silence. In summer I swim. In fall, I fly-fish. In winter and spring, I walk along the sandy bank. There I listen.

As a dark night allows the stars to shine

brighter, so dwelling in silence gives words sharpness and brightness. I go to that place word-weary, but I emerge ready again to hear and to speak a word in season.

Connect with the Elements

Preaching is elemental. There is water, wind, earth, fire. Preaching comes from the fire. That fire is fed, not doused, by the water of the Word, stoked by the wind of the Spirit, and then mixed into the earthiness of flesh and bone. To live with the rhythm and texture of fire requires that I live also with earth, wind, and water.

My seeking silence at the river in part serves this. But there is more. I work with wood. I ride my bike. I garden. I swim in swift cold rivers and surging oceans. I touch the earth, immerse myself in water, go into the open spaces where wind caresses or pummels. I reconnect my insides with my outsides, my mind with my body, and my body with its surroundings.

Gardening is wonderful this way. The words "human," "humility," and "humus" share the same root. Gardening is Adamic, touching of the humus from which we were made. It is humbling and humanizing.

There is something about putting seed and bulb in the earth, cutting back branches to the white wood and watching a bead of sap form at the cut, turning compost and seeing the worms writhe in the pungent, steaming dirt, smelling clipped grass or burnt leaves, eating carrots freshly pulled or peaches just picked—there's something about all that that helps me to accept again my humanness.

And there is also something in all that which helps me to meet again, unexpectedly, the risen Christ, like Mary Magdalene thinking he was the gardener.

It doesn't, of course, have to be gardening. Fishing, walking, making bread, building bird-houses, or mudding drywall—it's anything that reconnects our minds to our bodies, and our bodies to the elements.

Monday's Embers

I wrote this on a cold Monday in winter. Before I began, I built a fire in the wood stove near my writing desk. I shaved an inside rind of sap-crusted fir into thin kindling, laid that on last week's crumpled newsprint atop a thick bed of white and gray and black ashes (the remains of many fires), and I struck a match to it. Once I got the fire going, I laid several pieces of fir and yellow cedar in a criss-cross pattern, shut the stove doors, and tightened the dampers.

Then I got down to writing. When I was almost finished, I noticed the room had cooled down. I got up to check the fire. I opened the stove and at first looked into blackness and dark smoke. I had tightened the dampers too much, and the fire was almost out. The logs sat there, charred, inert, smoking. But that only lasted a moment.

Wind from the open doors swirled in, breathed on the wood, and set it to glowing. All at once, it ignited: Flames jumped up, and the wood cracked with the heat of it.

Backdraft

It's Monday, but Sunday's a comin'. I'm not ready. In fact, right now, I never want to preach again. I feel like charred wood on cold ashes. But I don't worry about it. I know God will open the doors again, let the wind rush in.

And me? I'm going out to cut wood.

Chapter 26

WHY I PACE BEFORE I PREACH

Understanding the weekend panic

Walter Wangerin Jr.

On the night before I preach, I pace—back and forth in my room, mumbling sermonic thoughts, testing them, scorning a hundred thoughts, exulting in one or two that shine like coin, investing those.

I grow breathless when I pace. I make strange noises. But the house must be as silent as death. And the mighty God must stand by me to save me, because there surely will come great waves of doubt to drown me, and then I will splutter, "Help me. Lord!" and gasp: "What do you want me to *say?*"

Not all the scriptural interpretation in the world will save me from this nighttime ride on stormy water: I'm going to preach, and I get scared. In the few hours I sleep, I dream. In my dreams I arrive at church too late, and people are leaving. I can't find my vestments, my clothes are shabby, and people are impatient. Or (the second greatest horror) smack in the middle of preaching, I notice that I'm in my underwear. Or (the worst) I've forgotten totally what I'd planned to say.

I wake at 5:00 a.m. I don't eat because I can't. My internal self is as unstable as water. But when I meet the people, my external self has donned a smile, speaks softly, touches everyone, and moves to worship with aplomb. And lo, I preach.

And on any given Sunday, I succeed. No one expects a pastoral collapse. Everyone takes this sermon for granted, while I breathe secret reams of gratitude to God. But when Saturday comes again, I pace again, wild-eyed and terrified.

You too? Does success astonish you as well, since the prospect of preaching had cut you at the gut?

When I was young, I thought experience would calm my fears. It didn't. For years I prayed God would grant me a pre-sermon peace. God didn't, and I accused myself of faithlessness.

But now I wonder: Perhaps the fear goes with the office. Perhaps, because this task requires the whole of the preacher, our entire beings become involved in the tension of preparation, and so our tummies start to jump.

It is—but it is not only—a function of our intellects to preach. We are doing more than passing pure thought to the people. Our souls are required of us, that we believe what we say. Moreover, to believe means that we have ourselves *experienced* what we declare: it's a part of our personal histories, real in our suffering and joy, real in our sin, real in forgiveness and grace and freedom. So we become a standing evidence of what we preach, and the whole of us—soul and mind and body and experience—participates in the holy moment of preaching.

It is Christ who saves. But in human community, it is this particular vessel whose voice, whose person, and whose preaching proclaim that Christ. No, I can't hide in my cape of authority and still persuade the people of a dear, incarnate, near, embracing Jesus.

I can never abstract my *self* from the preaching, nor ever be wholly nerveless before it, since the very purpose and the passion of the task involve my love. I preach because I love, love twice. These two loves define my being.

For I love the Lord my God with all my heart and with all my soul and with all my mind. I've nothing more important in all the world to communicate to anyone than the One I love completely. This is a stupendous responsibility. And it is my own, because I can't divide my beloved from my loving, nor my loving from my self. When I speak of God, my passion is present: In passion do I make God known! But the glory of the Lord makes me self-conscious. Am I worthy to whisper the name?

I have no choice but to try. For I love this people, too—these faces, these eyes—with a sharp, particular, personal love. The best that I have to give, I must give to them. To *them*, in their language, for their individual lives.

And on Saturday night, I worry: Will they hear it? Will they let the hard word hurt them, the good word heal them, the strong word lead and redeem them? Will I speak it so that they receive it from me? *O, people, people, the depth of my love is the depth of my fear for you!*

So I pace.

Chapter 27

PREACHING TO CONVULSE THE DEMONS
Helping people find the hand of Jesus

Craig Barnes

Whenever preachers run across a text that talks about demons, we are tempted to skip that part and keep reading. But when you read through the Gospel of Mark, it gets hard to do that. It starts off in the beginning, in chapter 1. After Jesus calls his disciples, the first thing they do is encounter a man with an unclean spirit inside the synagogue. A few verses later we're told that Jesus took the disciples throughout Galilee, proclaiming the message and casting out demons. Then in chapter 3 Jesus sends the disciples out on their own to proclaim the message and cast out demons. You keep finding those phrases put together in Mark—proclaim the message and cast out demons. They're almost used interchangeably, synonymously. In chapter 5 Jesus heals the Gerasene demoniac, a man driven out of his mind with demons. In chapter 6 Jesus again sends out the disciples to proclaim the message and cast out demons. In chapter 7 he casts a demon out of the daughter of the Syrophoenician woman.

WE ARE POWERLESS AGAINST EVIL BY OURSELVES

If you stay with Jesus, you will find it unavoidable to deal with the demonic. That is because Jesus is a Savior, and it is the nature of the Savior to go to places where evil has taken over, where it is sucking the life and spirit out of people. We may call it by more socially sophisticated names today, but do any of us deny there is an evil at work in the hearts and souls of people both within our congregation and outside? Mark will not allow you to deny that Jesus has called you to do something about it: Proclaim the message and cast out the demon.

In Mark 9, Jesus has gone up to the Mount of Transfiguration with Peter, James, and John—the first string of the disciples. While those guys are away, the other disciples are asked to cast a demon out of a little boy. Though they knock themselves out, they cannot exorcise this demon. When Jesus returns from the Mount of Transfiguration, he finds his disciples arguing with the scribes.

This makes sense, because these disciples aren't feeling good about themselves to begin with. They're the second string. Jesus is away on study leave with the first string on the Mount of Transfiguration. They are left behind. This is their one moment to shine, to do what Jesus commanded, and they're flunking their one moment. They feel powerless to do what they've been told to do.

When the father of the demon-possessed boy sees Jesus, he rushes up to him and says, "Teacher, I brought you my son, who is possessed by a spirit that has robbed him of speech. When it seizes him, it throws him to the ground. He foams at the mouth, gnashes his teeth and becomes rigid. I asked your disciples to drive out the spirit, but they could not" (Mark 9:17–18).

I know what it feels like to be asked to do something Jesus has commanded me to do and not be able to pull it off. As you can imagine, those of us trying to do ministry in Washington, D.C., are in no shortage of pastoral opportunities. I mentioned that once to a friend who

lives in the Midwest. He said to me, "You're not doing much good, are you?" He's right.

We have AIDS all over Africa. We have violence all over the Middle East. We have poverty all over the Third World. Every time I return from a visit to one of our partners in these places of dire need, I know the missionary staying behind in the slums and the violence starts praying, "Lord, I asked your disciple to cast the demon out of this place, but he could not do it. Jesus, you sent me a second stringer."

We cannot cast out the evil all by ourselves. That's the good news. The day you come to that realization is the day you are ready for a Savior. For salvation comes not through your power, not even through your powerful preaching. Salvation comes only through the power of Jesus Christ.

"Bring the boy to me," Jesus says. You ought to underline that three times in your Bible. "And when the spirit saw him, immediately it convulsed the boy, and he fell on the ground and rolled about, foaming at the mouth" (Mark 9:20, ESV). This is quite a scene. The spirit sees Jesus and throws the boy down to the ground, and immediately the boy starts foaming at the mouth, rolling back and forth.

GETTING RID OF EVIL TAKES TIME

Notice that Jesus doesn't rush in to help this kid. In fact, it looks as though he's taking a medical history. This kid is flopping around on the ground, and Jesus looks to his father and says, "Whoa, how long has this been going on? Oh, and does he throw himself into fire? Fire, is that right? And water too?" When we read this, we want to break into the text and say, "Jesus, what difference does that make? Hurry up and fix this kid!"

Jesus never hurries. This drives me crazy. I am hustling for Jesus all the time, every day. I figure Jesus can at least move as fast as I can move. But I'm finally starting to realize the real question is, Can I move as slowly as Jesus moves? Getting rid of evil takes a lot of time. Preaching is never about what you or I make happen. It is always and only about what Jesus makes happen. And apparently Jesus is not in a hurry to get all the evil out of your congregation, is he? He certainly isn't in a hurry to get it out of the world. So the first question the preacher has to ask is not, How do you make people believe in Jesus? The first question you have to keep asking is, Do you believe in him? You get your answer to that question by asking, Are you trying to fix your church or are you bringing it to Jesus? "Bring the boy to me," Jesus says.

The work of Jesus Christ did not end on the cross. He did not abandon you to an overwhelming mission. He doesn't ask you to complete the work for him. Jesus rose from the dead, and he continues his work in the world through the ministry of the Spirit that proceeds from the Son and the Father. The ministry of that Spirit is to bind people to the healing, saving acts of Jesus Christ. So the question is not, Are you an effective preacher? The question is, Do you believe the Holy Spirit is still effective in binding people to the salvation of Jesus Christ?

The father said, "I believe; help me overcome my unbelief!" Who of us doesn't know that prayer? We do have belief, but we cannot deny we have a lot of unbelief and doubt in us. We doubt our sermons are going to make much difference. We doubt they'll do anything to cast out evil. But as honest as we are about these doubts and unbelief, we have to be honest that as tat-tered as it is, there is belief there as well: "Yes. I believe and need help with my unbelief." That's enough. That's all it takes. That is enough of a confession to cast out evil. For as soon as Jesus hears this rather lukewarm confession of faith, Jesus looks at the convulsing boy and says to the demon in him, "I command you, come out of him and never enter him again."

IT GETS WORSE BEFORE IT GETS BETTER

After Jesus says that, notice that the boy's convulsions turn into terrible convulsions. The demon does a lot of damage to this kid on the way out. It gets worse before it gets better. When you start preaching filled with the Holy Spirit, don't be surprised if there's convulsing going on in the congregation. It hurts when evil leaves somebody. It hurts, because most people don't want the demon to be gone. Most people want you to give them tips on how to manage the demon. They want to make the demon their friend. Or if that doesn't work, they want to turn the demon into ambition so they'll at least be successful with all the churning they have going on. Or they want to turn the demon into despair, and they'll grow comfortable with their despair, saying, "This is as good as it gets." They'll trust the demon, because the demon is with them all the time.

When you start talking about hope, they're terrified to hope. If they hope, they're going to have to give up their best friend, the demon. It may be a tormenter, but at least it's always been there for them. That's when the convulsing starts. When you preach hope, convulsing comes. You start hearing things like, "We may need a different preacher here." Or they'll shake your hand and say, "This congregation is used to an intellectual kind of preaching."

They'll do anything they can to get you off the hope subject. Or as someone said to me early in my ministry, "Jesus, Jesus, Jesus—is that all you know?"

Let the convulsing go on. It doesn't matter. Bring the boy to Jesus, and he'll do the healing.

After the demon is finally gone, the boy is laying there cold and stiff, and everybody says, "That boy's dead." That may be what some people are saying about your congregation. It's not what Jesus is saying, because Jesus bends down and lifts the boy by the hand until the kid can stand tall. There it is again. Who is it that turns the dead back to life? Who is it that lifts up a congregation so it can stand tall? Only Jesus Christ. That means that preaching is not about phrases and rhetoric and technique. It's always about helping the congregation find the hand of Jesus, which will lift them up. That's why they're there, whether they know it or not. No other hand will do, only the hand of Jesus.

The disciples are alone with Jesus, still bothered by their performance. They say, "Jesus, what did we do wrong here? Why couldn't we get this demon out?" The Lord responds by saying, "This kind can come out only by prayer"—not through trying harder, not through better legislation, but only through prayer. If you're going to stand up in a pulpit and go after something evil in the world, you better have your spiritual act together. You better know how to pray, because neither you nor I have it in us to take on the demonic. We're not that good. But prayer engages us with all the power of heaven, even if the prayer is as meager as, "I believe; help my unbelief." When you start praying like that, you're going to see some miraculous things happen in your congregation. You're going to see heaven and earth come together in the proclamation of the Word, for in prayer you take your congregation and put it into the hands of Jesus.

Chapter 28

HOLY EXPECTATION

How can we handle dynamite and not expect it to explode?

Haddon Robinson

If I had to make my living with my hands, I would probably starve to death. Living in the tenements of New York City, my family depended on the superintendent to make repairs when things in our apartment broke. So I never learned to fix things myself. A few years ago, a neighbor noting my ineptness asked my wife, Bonnie, "How do you live with a guy like that?" She replied, "Very, very carefully."

Because I don't believe I can fix things, I usu-

ally don't even try. When I do try, I tend to give up whenever I hit a snag. That's normally right after I pick up a tool. I live with low expectations, and Bonnie and I pay a price for it—to plumbers, mechanics, and handymen.

Recently, I purchased some software for my computer and tried to install it myself. I followed the directions closely, step by step, and I was stunned when it worked! I was surprised by my surprise. But that is the result of living with shriveled expectations. You're always taken by surprise.

Our ministries are stunted when we live with diminished expectations. In fact, our surprise when God works is a dead giveaway of our condition.

We preach the Word of God and then are startled when a woman in our congregation hears the gospel and finds it is indeed the best news ever.

We register shock on our personal Richter scale when a young man who was a victim of abuse hears what Jesus says about forgiveness and decides to confront his older brother who had molested him and get things settled.

We can hardly believe it when a husband involved in an affair sits at communion and, faced with taking the bread and cup, decides to end the illicit relationship.

We're handling dynamite, and we didn't expect it to explode.

When we lose the sense of holy expectation, our preaching gets downgraded to a performance in which we are required to say something religious to pass the time between 11:25 and noon on Sunday morning. We make the calls, attend the meetings, conduct the funerals, and officiate at weddings, but we don't expect God will show up. We pray for the sick, but we don't believe our prayers will make much difference. We counsel the bewildered, but we don't count much on the difference God can make. Then one day, surprise! We discover God was at work beyond our most expansive expectations. We had underestimated the reach of God's Spirit.

The Holy Spirit doesn't check in at the church down the street and skip your congregation. He is present, not only someplace else but at your place. Count on him. Expect him. Live with holy expectations. You may be in for a great surprise.

Part 3

Considering Hearers

How Should My Approach Change Depending on Who Is Listening?

Chapter 29

PREACHING TO EVERYONE IN PARTICULAR

How to scratch where people niche

Haddon Robinson

While Grace Chapel in Lexington, Massachusetts, was without a pastor for over a year, I preached there often. The church is remarkably diverse, having Harvard professors and high school dropouts, doctors and lawyers and house cleaners, political activists and those who don't even read the newspaper, people with multimillion-dollar investment portfolios and minimum-wage workers. In addition, members are of many races and colors.

I stood before such diversity each week amazed at the responsibility I had to reach them all. As I prepared my sermons, I stewed over how my sermon could reach the entire cross section.

As men and women who preach, our task can be expressed simply: to become all things to all people. To actually do it is a formidable task.

SACRIFICING WHAT COMES NATURALLY

When we fail to speak to the entire cross section in our churches, we resemble the doctor who knows only how to set a broken arm; if a patient complains of a bellyache, the doctor breaks his arm so she can set it.

Reaching broader audiences demands that we sacrifice what comes naturally to us. When Paul said, "I have become all things to all men so that by all possible means I might save some" (1 Cor. 9:22), he wasn't talking about just evangelism. He was talking also about helping converts grow. "To the weak"—believers who had weak consciences—he became weak; he restricted his freedom for their sake.

Speaking to a broader audience requires a sacrifice from us. We give up our freedom to use certain kinds of humor, to call minority groups by names that make sense to us, to illustrate only from books and movies we find interesting, to speak only to people with our education and level of Christian commitment. Sometimes such sacrifice feels constricting to us.

A pastor who objects strongly to the women's movement, for example, might take a passing shot at its leaders and activities. By doing so, though, he risks needlessly alienating women in the congregation.

But sacrificing what comes most naturally to us is what gives us a platform to speak. Just as a legalistic Jew wouldn't regard Paul as credible if Paul ignored the law, so many women, for example, won't regard a preacher as credible if he shows zero sensitivity to their issues. Why go to all this trouble? Because it is right and because it is wise.

The people we are most likely to offend are those on the edge, those cautiously considering the gospel or deeper commitment but who are skittish, easily chased away by one offensive move from pastors. Those already secure in the fold will probably stick by us in spite of our blunders. The new people we're trying to reach are as easily spooked as wild turkeys.

A young couple moved into a Chicago suburb and attended one church for several months. The church helped them through the husband's unemployment. Several times the pastor met with the man, who had advanced degrees in ecology and was interested in deeper involvement in the church.

Then he and his wife abruptly stopped coming. The pastor repeatedly tried to contact them, and finally after several months, he was able to take the man out for lunch. He asked him why they had not come to church in such a long time. "In several of your sermons," the man replied, "you made comments that belit-tled science. If that is the way you feel, I don't think we're on the same wavelength."

The pastor remembered the remarks, which were either passing comments or rhetorical flourishes contrasting the power of Christ and the weakness of human thought. But the consequence was not passing: A man who showed promise of moving into deeper discipleship had been diverted.

How can we gain appreciation for lives unlike our own, for people as different as security guards and investment bankers? The same way novelists do: by listening and observing. Listen to the people you counsel and the conversations around you in restaurants and stores. Observe characters in movies and common people interviewed on the news. Note how these people state their concerns—their specific phrasing, their feelings, their issues. Get an ear for dialogue.

I know one pastor who holds a focus group each Thursday before he preaches. He eats lunch with several people from diverse backgrounds, tells them the ideas in his sermon, and asks them how they hear these ideas. They often raise issues that had never occurred to him.

After one service a woman told me how she and several other African Americans had taken out an ad in the *New York Times* to explain their resentment of homosexual activists who draw on the black experience to describe their own. "They identified themselves as a minority," she told me. "We're both minorities, but that's the only thing we have in common. They don't know what we've gone through. They don't know the pain of being black." She helped me understand what a disadvantaged minority feels, and someday I'm sure I'll include in a sermon how God can help those who feel the pain of being black in America.

TARGETING PARTICULAR AUDIENCES

In the Gospels we see that Christ never dealt with two people the same way. He told the curious Pharisee that he needed to be born again, the woman at the well that she needed living water. He brought good news to each individual, but at the person's point of contact.

The New Testament letters differ from each other because they brought the same basic theology to bear on diverse problems. In 1 Corinthians, Paul defended the doctrine of the resurrection against those who doubted it; in 1 Thessalonians, Paul brought that same truth to believers who were worried about those who had already died in Christ. From the Bible's beginning to its end, God adjusts the message to the audience without sacrificing the truth. Truth is never more powerfully experienced than when it speaks to someone's personal situation.

Knowing that, some preachers try not to exclude listeners and fall into preaching in generalities. For example, if I say, "Irritation bothers us all," I'm speaking to no one in particular. A sermon full of generalities hits no one in particular.

We do better to focus specifically on two or three types of people in a message (changing who those two or three groups are each week). The surprising thing is that the more directed and personal a message, the more universal it becomes.

I might illustrate a sermon on conflict by saying, "You live with your roommate, and your roommate has some irritating habits, like not cleaning the dishes right after the meal. Or you're married, and your husband comes home and plops himself in front of the TV without any regard for what your day has been like."

Although these two scenarios don't fit all listeners, all can identify with these specific experiences and the feelings they elicit.

To help me speak to what different members of an audience may be going through, I use a suggestion given by a good friend, Don Sunukjian. I prepare my sermons using a life-situation grid. Across the top of the grid, I label columns for men, women, singles, married, divorced, those living together. On the side of the grid, I have rows for different age groups (youth, young adult, middle-age, elderly), professional groups (the unemployed, the self-employed, workers, and management), levels of faith (committed Christians, doubters, cynics, and atheists), the sick and the healthy, to name a few. I develop my grid based on the congregation and community I am preaching to. After I've researched my biblical text and developed my ideas, I wander around the grid, looking for two to four intersections where the message will be especially relevant.

For instance, in one sermon on money, based on the parable of the shrewd branch manager in Luke 16, I went through my grid and thought of a widow in the congregation whose late husband, the president of a major corporation, had left her a large amount of money. She once had said to me, "What a curse it is to have a lot of money and take God seriously." Since I knew others in the congregation had significant incomes, I thought specifically about how someone with money would hear and feel about this passage.

A second intersection on the grid I explored was the working poor. For their sake, in the sermon I mentioned that Christ focuses on the attitude of our hearts, not on the amount we give.

A third group of special concern were visitors

who might say afterward, "All pastors do is preach about money." Seeing them on the grid caused me to include some humor and speak directly to the objection.

(On occasion, I can even preach an entire sermon to one particular group in the church—say, young men or women in business, or teenagers. I might introduce it by saying, "This morning I want to talk only to the teenagers. Some of you adults enjoy a short winter's nap on Sunday morning anyway, but this morning I give you permission to do so. Today I want to talk to young people in junior and senior high. You are an important part of this church, and I'd appreciate it if you would listen." All the application in that sermon would be for young people, but only a rare adult would tune out. In fact, information overheard can be more influential than information received directly.)

ILLUSTRATING BROADLY

Though we preach each week to diverse congregations and need to target particular subgroups, all listeners have these desires:

They want to meet God or run away from him.

They want to learn something.

They want to laugh.

They want to feel significant.

They want to be motivated, in a positive way, to do better.

They want a pastor to understand their pain and the difficulty they have doing what's right, without letting them off the hook.

One of the most important tools for addressing these universal concerns is through illustrations. People identify with people more than ideas. They gossip about people, not principles.

Good stories transcend individual experiences so that people from a variety of situations can gain something from them. When hearing a story, listeners tell the story to themselves, inserting their own experiences and images.

An older woman once said to me, "Sometimes the Christian life is like washing sheets." She described how she washed sheets by hand in a large washing bucket, and when she would push one part of the sheet under water, air bubbles would move to another part of the sheet and float that section above water. "I push it down here, it comes up there," she said. "I can never keep the whole sheet under water."

As she described the scene, her story became my story. My mind jumped back a half century to my boyhood. I recalled my mother's washing clothes in a tub and having the same problem.

To help listeners make emotional connections to my preaching, I try to illustrate broadly. I am tempted to draw many of my illustrations from sports, which may or may not appeal to the majority of women (more than half of most congregations). I intentionally try to include illustrations that more women may identify with, stories focused on relationships and drawn from the worlds of home and family or from their experiences in the workplace.

As I watch TV, I look for illustrations. My own tendency is to draw from what I read, but most people in a congregation do not read the materials I read. They live in a different sphere from mine, and I try to honor that in my sermons. The essential thing about the stories I choose to tell is that all listeners be able to put themselves into the scene, becoming participants in the story.

I heard Gordon MacDonald do this masterfully while preaching about John the Baptist. Gordon presented an imaginative updating of

John's ministry in a story that every listener could enter. It went something like this:

 For an audio example of this principle see tracks 4–5 on the supplemental CD.

Several management types were at the River Jordan as the crowds came to John, and they decided they needed to get things organized. So they set up tables and begin to give tags to those coming for repentance. On the tag is written the person's name and chief sin.

Bob walks up to the table. The organizers write his name on the tag and then ask, "What's your most awful sin, Bob?"

"I stole some money from my boss."

The person at the table takes a marker and writes in bold letters EMBEZZLER and slaps it on Bob's chest.

The next person comes forward. "Name?"

"Mary."

"Mary, what's your most awful sin?"

"I gossiped about some people. It wasn't very much, but I didn't like those people."

The organizers write, MARY—SLANDERER, and slap it on her. A man walks up to the table.

"Name?"

"George."

"George, what's your most awful sin?"

"I've thought about how nice it would be to have my neighbor's Corvette."

GEORGE—COVETER.

Another man approaches the table. "What's your name?" he is asked.

"Gordon."

"What's your sin?"

"I've had an affair."

The organizer writes GORDON—ADULTERER and slaps the sticker on his chest.

Soon Christ comes to be baptized. He walks down the line of those waiting to be baptized and asks them for their sin tags. One by one, he takes those tags off the people and sticks them on his own body. He goes to John, and as he is baptized, the river washes away the ink from each name tag he bears.

As Gordon told that story, everyone in the congregation mentally wrote his own sin and slapped it on his own chest. The illustration was specific but touched on universal feelings.

To come up with images and stories that nearly everyone can own, I sometimes write "idea networks" on a sheet of paper. If I'm talking about home, for example, I'll write the word home in the center of a sheet of paper, circle the word, and then surround it with any associations that come to my mind: "home sweet home," "welcome home," "it's good to have you home again," "home on the range," "going home for Christmas," "stole home."

These associations will inspire other associations and memories, some personal, some cultural. What I'm doing is digging into the phrases and images our culture associates with home. Somewhere from that page I'll come up with one or more images or stories with larger appeal.

TAKING THE LISTENERS' SIDE

I do everything I can to show people I respect them and I'm on their side. It's another way I try to be all things to all people. For instance, in my preaching I cultivate a conversational tone. Many people in our culture resent an authoritarian, lecturing manner. That style is what moderns mean when they use preaching in a pejorative sense ("Don't preach at me!"). They consider it patronizing and narrow-minded.

I also try to show empathy. When I quote

from Malachi 2:16, "God hates divorce," I know there are divorced people sitting in the congregation who may begin to feel that God and Haddon Robinson hate them. So I'll follow up that verse with, "Those of you who are divorced know that better than anyone. You understand why God hates divorce. Not because he hates divorced people but because of what divorce does to people. You have the scars. Your children have the scars. You can testify to what it does. God hates divorce because he loves you."

I've found if listeners know you love and identify with them, they will let you say strong things. Most people are just asking that you be aware of them and not write them off.

Another way I tell listeners I'm on their side is by being careful with terms. Even though you're sure you don't have a bias, a listener may think you do if your phrasing offends them.

I try to use gender-inclusive language. If I'm telling a story about a doctor, I might say, "A surgeon stands in the operating room. As she takes the scalpel in her hand...." I intentionally use she over he in strategic spots.

I also employ terms like spokesperson instead of spokesman. I say "he or she" instead of always saying "he"; or I use "he" sometimes and "she" other times. Even a few female pronouns in a sermon make a difference. (Here's a radical experiment: Try using "she" all through a sermon except when you must use the masculine pronoun. You will get a sense of how much of preaching has a male flavor.)

I call minority groups what they want to be called. This is simple courtesy: If someone's name is Charles, and he doesn't like being called Charlie or Chuck, I'm obligated to call him Charles. I used to say Negroes, then Blacks. I used the term Afro-American in a recent sermon, and afterward a woman kindly corrected me, "It's African American."

NOT COMPROMISING THE TRUTH

Of course, no matter how hard we try, we're still going to offend people. Sometimes we need to apologize from the pulpit. "In last week's sermon, my humor was in bad taste. I described overweight people with a term that was hurtful. I'm sorry. I sometimes say things I don't mean, and you're gracious enough to tell me about it. Bear with me."

While preaching at Grace Chapel, I received at least a letter a week reacting to my sermons. When someone writes me, I always write back. Some people send thoughtful letters, and I owe them a thoughtful response. Sometimes they're dead right; they catch me in a prejudice. I have to admit that.

Sometimes you get letters in which people are vitriolic through no fault of yours. The best you can do is say, "Thank you for writing. I'm sorry I offended you. I wanted to communicate a great truth of Scripture and failed to get that across to you. I'm sorry."

But if we focus too hard on not offending, or if we read too many letters from the offended, we can become paralyzed. We start qualifying every sentence. We end up with weasel sermons that are defensive, cautious, and spineless.

Yes, at Christmas we need to acknowledge that for some people it's the most depressing time of the year, but we can't let that rob the season's joy from the congregation. Yes, on Mother's Day childless women feel extra pain, and we can acknowledge that, but everyone has a mother to honor, and we shouldn't squelch the church's honoring of them.

Although I'm aware of the land mines, I try not to get uptight, defensive, or hostile in the pulpit, for that only provokes people to be more easily offended. Saying, "You shouldn't be so sensitive," or "I get so sick of all this politically correct language," does no one—you or your people—any good.

And there are times when a pastor must preach truth at the expense of some sensitivities, yet we must do so with a burden in our hearts, not chips on our shoulders. There is no greater courage required of pastors than to preach what may cost them their pulpits.

There will always be a healthy discomfort as we try to be all things to all people. It's biblical, but it demands we walk a fine line. We want to be as appealing as possible but not at the cost of compromising the message. When we walk that line well, though, we experience something unequaled: a variety of people with a variety of concerns from a variety of settings all attentively listening to the good news.

Chapter 30

THE POWER OF SIMPLICITY

Lives are changed when we merely read, explain, and apply

Chuck Smith

Nehemiah 8:8 says, "They read from the Book of the Law of God, making it clear and giving the meaning so that the people could understand what was being read." That is as good a description of expository teaching as you can find. They read the Word of God, making it clear. They gave the meaning and caused the people to understand it.

DON'T AIM FOR PERFECTION

We started Maranatha Music several years ago. We produced the first album using an eight-track in a garage that was converted into a studio. It cost us $3,500 to make the first *Everlasting Jesus* album. It was a great success, and it was the beginning of Maranatha Music. As my other obligations increased, I realized it was necessary to turn the management of Maranatha over to others. However, a few years later I learned that Maranatha was losing money. So I reentered management to look things over and see what was going wrong. I discovered that they were spending over $60,000 in the studio to produce a solo album. I realized, of course, that there was no way we could ever recover our production cost for that price tag, especially for promoting a single artist.

So I said, "Fellas, you've gotten your egos involved and are trying to produce the perfect album. About one-tenth of one percent of all people have a perfect ear to appreciate such an album. But these people will probably never listen to the album you're producing for them to begin with. So stop doing that. Create the album for the general public. Create it for people who won't know that in one segment a guitar string was slightly out of pitch.

A lot of times we, as ministers, make the same kind of mistake. We try to develop a sermon so perfect that only one-tenth of one percent can even understand what we said. In doing so, we're not ministering to the general public at all. Exactly the opposite is happening. We are trying to be so precise that we're missing most listeners.

SEE THE CONTEXT

Expository teaching involves reading the Word of God clearly, and if necessary, reading the context around the passage so that hearers see the passage in its context.

Just reading the Word of God alone has tremendous value. As a part of our regular Sunday morning worship we read a chapter out of the Scriptures. Many times people respond by saying, "Oh, the Scripture reading this morning was just what I needed." A lot of things we say just drop and bring nothing back. The Word of God, however, will not return void. So I always try to incorporate a lot of the Word into my teaching because it is always going to affect peoples' lives.

Remember Nehemiah: First, they read the Scriptures clearly, and then they gave the meaning. They explained to the people what the Scripture was saying.

John Wyclif had what he called the golden rule of interpreting the Scriptures. He said, "It shall greatly help thee to understand Scripture if thou mark not only what is spoken or written but of whom and to whom, with what words at what time, where and to what intent, under what circumstances considering what goeth before and what followeth."

In the early years of my ministry, I was introduced to *Halley's Bible Pocket Handbook.* I enjoy it to the present day, especially for his handling of the prophets in the Old Testament. He gives you exactly what was going on that provoked the prophet to say these things. He gives the background to understand what the prophet was saying, why he was saying it, to whom he was saying it, and what preceded and followed.

AIM TO BE UNDERSTOOD

Back to Nehemiah: First of all, the priests read the Scriptures clearly, then they gave the meaning. And then we read they caused the people to understand the meaning. To do likewise we must learn what God was saying then and what he is saying to us today through the passage. Simply put, I ask, *What eternal truth is being spoken here?* so I can apply the Scriptures to the present circumstances people are facing this week on the job, in the classroom, or wherever.

Many preachers would be highly insulted if people said to them, "That message you just preached was something a child could understand. It wasn't sophisticated at all." But I'm not insulted. I'm really complimented when people say, "He preaches so simply." I try to be simple. I can't be anything else.

I know of an autistic patient in a convalescent hospital in Ashland, Oregon, who just lies in bed all day staring at the ceiling. He never speaks to anybody and never shows any awareness that anybody else is around. He's locked up in his own world as he lies there all day long. One day a nurse who happened to be a Christian found a radio in his room and tuned it to our CSN affiliate station in Ashland, so he could listen to Christian music and the teaching of the Word.

One day, there was an alert in the hospital regarding a disturbance in this fellow's room. Because the Christian woman was head nurse of the hospital, she rushed to the room to see what was going on, and found some orderlies trying to hold the fellow in his bed. He was thrashing around and fighting, an uncommon activity for a guy who normally lies still all day. The nurse heard him shouting, "Chuck Smith, Word for Today! Chuck Smith, Word for Today! Chuck Smith, Word for Today!" She realized that someone had tuned his radio to a Western station. She turned it back to our CSN affiliate and immediately the guy returned to staring at the ceiling in a peaceful manner. What does this mean? Simply teach the Word of God simply.

USE THE STORIES IN SCRIPTURE

The Bible says that the common people heard Jesus gladly. What a tremendous compliment to the teaching of Jesus. He was teaching the common people, and the common people heard him gladly. I encourage you to follow the teaching methods of Jesus. Give color in stories. Jesus used parables in order to grab people's attention. Illustrate from the Scriptures as much as possible. They are filled with glorious stories that deal with practically every issue in life. I've always appreciated Spurgeon's preaching because of his use of Bible stories to illustrate the principles that he's dealing with. This was also the method used by New Testament writers.

Seek to illustrate how a precept can be practically applied to people's lives today; look for passages and stories that will illustrate.

After the priests read the Book of the Law of God, gave the meaning, and caused the people to understand the reading, then what happened? People began to weep. They began to repent. They were under conviction because they understood what God had said to them. I have found that if you read the Word of God clearly, if you give the meaning and help people understand, God's Word will bring conviction and repentance to their hearts.

The Word of God is alive and powerful. It is sharper than a two-edged sword. It is able to discern between the soul and the spirit (see Heb. 4:12). So I encourage you, learn to simply teach the Word of God simply, and the Word of God will affect the lives of people powerfully.

Our church is a classic example of what God can do in the teaching of his Word when it is taught simply. I look at the hundreds that have gone out from this church and are simply teaching the Word of God simply, following the model that they learned at Calvary Chapel. I think it is significant that nine of the twenty-five largest churches in the United States today are Calvary Chapels, led by guys who have just gone out and simply taught the Word of God simply. It's a formula that works. Why? Because God said he would honor his Word above his name. God said that his Word will not return unto him void. It will accomplish the purposes for which it has been sent.

So my challenge to you is this: Simply teach the Word of God simply.

Chapter 31

VIEW FROM THE PEW

How to hold the attention of the easily distracted

John Koessler

When I joined the faculty of Moody Bible Institute after nine years of pastoral ministry, I found that my experience of the preaching event changed radically. It took only a few Sundays in the pew to discover how much competition the preacher faces during the message. One Sunday the background noise in the church seemed to be unusually high. It was certainly higher than anything I had encountered during my years in the pulpit. I could barely hear what the pastor was saying above the din of rustling pages, scribbling pencils, and tapping feet. "How can you worship with all this noise?" I asked my wife. She just laughed. "Welcome to the congregation," she said.

In order to impact my listeners, I must first get their attention. Once I have my audience's attention, I must say something worth keeping it, and say it in a way that moves them to respond. My rule for preaching: State your principle, paint a picture, then show your listeners what the principle looks like in their own life situations. Do this for every point in your message, and you will be more likely to carry the audience with you.

STATE YOUR PRINCIPLE

Today's listeners have been conditioned by watching thousands of hours of highly produced, visually-oriented stories that have been neatly packed into segments of fifteen minutes or less. Some of these stories are built on a simple plot structure that raises a problem and resolves it in thirty to fifty minutes.

The obvious response to this cultural trend would seem to be sermons that are short, narrative, affective, and nonpropositional. However, true biblical preaching, even when it is primarily narrative in structure, must be propositional at its core. This is unavoidable because it is the communication of truth. New Testament language is absolutist, repeatedly emphasizing that biblical preaching is the communication of the truth.

In view of this, the first step in preaching must be to determine the propositional core of the sermon. What is the primary truth I hope to communicate to the listener?

We cannot ignore the impact of television on our listeners, but neither can we afford to sacrifice biblical content in an effort to make our sermons more "listenable." The message must be grounded in propositional truth, and that truth must be stated clearly.

PAINT A PICTURE

Propositional truth is foundational to the sermon, but it does not guarantee results. We often encounter those who understand the truths we preach and even affirm them, yet continue to act contrary to what they know and say they believe. Cognition isn't the problem, motivation is.

Visual language and metaphor help to bridge the gap between cognition and motivation. Warren Wiersbe says: "When confronted by a metaphor, you might find yourself remembering forgotten experiences and unearthing buried feelings, and then bringing them together to discover new insights. Your mind says, 'I see!' Your heart says, 'I feel!' Then in that transforming moment your imagination unites the two and you say, 'I'm beginning to understand.'"

Metaphors are important in preaching because they lie at the very core of human understanding. According to George Lakoff, professor of linguistics at the University of California, and Mark Johnson, professor of philosophy at Southern Illinois University: "Our ordinary conceptual system, in terms of which we both think and act, is fundamentally metaphorical in nature." Metaphors help us to understand one thing by pointing to something else and saying, "This is that."

Stories function like metaphors. Just as a metaphor states "a is b" (God is a rock), so stories imply that "individual experience is universal experience" (Moses struck the rock when angry—we act like that too). When preachers use stories, they use holistic communication that touches the mind, imagination, and feelings. Stories capture my interest because they deal with "reality." I may not be interested in theology, but I am interested in real life. A story has the power to touch my heart because I can identify with the problems, circumstances, or emotions of its central characters. Thus, stories can motivate listeners to change their core values.

Show What It Looks Like

The ultimate goal in my preaching is action. To facilitate response in hearers I must help them to see what that response looks like in their own life situations.

With sermon application I struggle between two extremes. When my applications are too general, listeners affirm the truth of what I say without seeing that they need to act on it. As long as Nathan preached to David in parables, David could affirm the heinousness of the sin the prophet had described without referring to himself. It was only when the prophet moved to application and declared, "You are the man," that David said, "I have sinned against the LORD" (2 Sam. 12:7, 13).

Yet when my applications are too specific, it is easy for listeners to disqualify themselves by noting that they do not fit the specific conditions described in my examples. Effective application must be both general and specific. The best way to accomplish this is by using examples. These suggest specific ways to live out general principles, yet they do not exhaust the possibilities.

Above all, application must be relevant. While preparing a message on Hebrews 2, I thought of Joyce, a woman in my congregation who was dying of cancer. Her gaunt face, ravaged by the effects of the disease, came to mind as I meditated on Hebrews 2:15, which says that one of the purposes of the Incarnation was to "free those who all their lives were held in slavery by their fear of death." I had just completed two or three paragraphs of clichés, assuring the congregation that the true Christian does not fear death.

"Do you think Joyce believes that?" an inner voice seemed to say. I could not be certain of the answer. How would I feel if I were dying and had to listen to my own sermon?

The next question was even more disturbing. "Do you believe that?" I had to admit I did not—at least not as a matter of personal experience. I could affirm it as a point of faith. But if I was honest, I had to admit that, even as a Christian, I often struggled with a fear of death. Suddenly the tone of my sermon changed. Platitudes would never do. The thoughtful listener would see through them and know I was only whistling in the dark. If I was going to preach this text truthfully, I would have to spend some time sitting next to Joyce and confront my own fear of death.

To preach effectively I must first take into account the view from the pew.

Chapter 32

PREACHING TO ORDINARY PEOPLE
Many feel like overwhelmed failures

Lewis Smedes

I was just about to bend my six-foot-four frame into our eggshell blue 1952 Plymouth to drive to a little church in the decayed center of Paterson, New Jersey. I was going to be ordained into the Christian ministry, a passage for which I felt tremblingly unprepared.

Before getting into the car, I turned to my friend and former seminary teacher George Stob, who was standing by, and asked him: "George, do you have one last good word for me before I take this plunge?" George shot his answer back, as if it were long coiled tight in his mind, the one thing he thought I still needed to know. "Remember," he said, "that when you preach, you will be preaching to ordinary people."

Thanks a lot, I thought. For this kind of wisdom you get to be a professor in a theological seminary? As if I didn't know! Anyway, I stuffed his bromide into the bulging bag of expendable data I had garnered from seminary teachers and drove off to be ordained as a minister of the gospel.

As it turned out, though, in my early years of arrogant innocence, I did not really know much about ordinary people. I did not know then, not in the depths of my being, not where the issues of a preacher's authentic attitudes are decided. I was ripe with scholarly insights. I was tuned in to my theology. I was tuned in to the craft of sermonizing. But I was not tuned in to the ordinariness of the people who listened to my idealistic preaching.

To be ordinary is to be too weak to cope with the terrible stuff that is too much for mere humanity. Ordinary people are non-heroes—not cowards, just not heroes, limited folk, afflicted with the malaise of too-muchness.

We ordinary people cannot fit our lives into preformed, Styrofoam boxes. We cannot manage life as well as we would like, at least not in our secret places. We cannot get all the strings tied; it won't wrap up the way we want it. For us, survival is often the biggest success story we dare hope for. Ordinary people are people who live on the edge, just a step behind the line that separates us from those who fall apart at the seams. Ordinary people are the ones who cry for a sign, any old sign, that it might still be all right even when everything seems horribly wrong.

What George was trying to tell me was that a lot of people who would be looking to God for help through me would be ordinary in this sense: They would be living, not on the peak of success, but at the edge of failure; not on the pinnacle of triumph, but at the precipice of defeat. He did not mean that everyone who came to me would be a failure. What he meant was that many of them would feel like failures sometime in their lives.

They came to my church on Sunday, ordinary people did, but I did not recognize them in the early days. Now I know that they look like this:

- A man and woman, sitting board-straight, smiling on cue at every piece of funny piety, are hating each other for letting the romance in their marriage collapse on a tiring treadmill of tasteless, but always tidy, tedium.
- A widow, whispering her Amens to every promise of divine providence, is frightened to death because the unkillable beast of inflation is devouring her savings.
- A father, the congregational model of parental firmness, is fuming in the suspicion of his own fatherly failure because he cannot stomach, much less understand, the furious antics of his slightly crazy son.
- An attractive young woman in the front pew is absolutely paralyzed, sure she has breast cancer.
- A middle-aged fellow who, with his new Mercedes, is an obvious Christian success story, is wondering when he will ever have the guts to tell his boss to take his lousy job and shove it.
- A submissive wife of one of the elders is terrified because she is being pushed to face up to her closet alcoholism.

Ordinary people, all of them, and there are a lot more where they came from. What they all have in common is a sense that everything is all wrong where it matters to them most. What they desperately need is a miracle of faith to know that life at the center is all right, and yet that is just what ordinary people often keep behind a locked door.

Keeping Grace Behind a Locked Door

Why? Why is it so hard for the good news to get inside, into our feelings, from whence it needs to percolate to the surface? Why do we need a gift of grace?

I do not think we need a gift of grace because the truth is so hard to understand. It is a mystery, of course, no question about that. But the mystery of Christ is not a secret code that only the elite can unravel. Someone once asked—if the legend is true—the great Karl Barth what it all came down to, all those thick books of his on theology. Barth, teasing maybe, but still serious, said: "It comes to this, 'Jesus loves me, this I know.'" The mystery comes down to something just this simple. Deep, profound, amazing, but simple. God loves you and wills your good forever.

Why do ordinary people lock their doors to this muscular comfort, this sweet reality? We have a galaxy of excuses. I will expose two reasons for keeping my door closed. See if they match yours.

First, we do not want to feel reconciled to God because we will complicate our lives if we are reconciled to him. Something always changes when we believe that life, in spite of everything, is all right, and we dread the change. For instance, we do not want to accept forgiveness because if we feel forgiven, we will have to let go of some prime anger we've stewed up against some lousy people who did us wrong. We do not want to feel loved because if we accept love, we may have to open our lives to someone we want to keep at arm's length. We do not want the joy of discovering that life is all right because if we do, we may have to give up the pleasure of griping about it, and we are just too tight to make that sacrifice. We do not want to live in the hope that God is going to make the earth a splendid place of justice and love because, if we have hope for a new creation, we may feel pushed to help prepare the way by making the world a little better than it is now. Kierkegaard was right: "We choose to lock the door of our hearts because we want to live in the wretched doghouses of our lives."

Second, ordinary people keep the doors closed to their hearts because they are too tired to open them. It is not only as if ordinary people are just too perfervidly wicked to let the light of grace into their lives. Sometimes they are just too pooped. Self-pity drains our energy. We can hurt so much that we have no spiritual push left in us. We feel stuck in a void, sucked down into an empty pit where nothing can make us feel that life is all right. If we cannot locate energy to accept grace for ourselves, we surely cannot feel it for others—not because we are evil, but because we are exhausted.

ORDINARY PEOPLE ARE TIRED

When my wife and I and our three young children moved to California from Michigan, we managed the first few days to get the kids into three separate schools. I started teaching a course at Fuller Theological Seminary I had never taught before, teaching it to 125 students

at eight o'clock, four mornings a week. So far so good. After one week we learned from the hematologists that our youngest son, just turned five, had Gaucher's disease, a rare congenital blood problem with an uncertain prognosis. A week later, two weeks after our arrival in the sun belt, we learned that my wife, Doris, had breast cancer and needed a mastectomy. Those were the first two weeks of our new life in the paradise of Southern California.

I remember getting home from the hospital one night after a visit with Doris, too tired to prepare for the next morning's lecture. I flopped on the bed and opened a copy of *Life* magazine, still coming out every Friday in those days. I paged lazily through it until I came to a section featuring the Nigerian civil war. Pictures of starving Biafran children, skin and bones, bulging empty bellies, knees like hard balls with toothpicks for legs sticking out of them. All the media at the time were throwing these pictures at our almost shock-proof consciences. I shut the magazine tight. I threw it to the floor. I could not look: "I'm sorry, starving children, I am so tired; I need all my pity for myself tonight; I do not have energy to open my heart to compassion for you."

I do believe it would have taken a miracle for me to get the door of my heart open to feel the love of a reconciling Christ for those Biafran kids that night. And it took another miracle to get to feel, to deeply, truly, gladly feel that it was all right with me when everything, everything seemed all wrong. I was too tired to feel it by myself.

Ordinary people feel too tired a lot. They come to church and listen to words about a grace that has made life all right at the core, but they cannot find the extra reserve of power to open their hearts to the reality of Jesus Christ and the fact of his grace. God needs to open the door.

The surprise is that God does give us the gift. Sometimes. And sometimes we accept it.

PREACHING GRACE TO ORDINARY PEOPLE

Sometimes God comes quietly to tell ordinary people that he is around them, above them, under them, in them, and ahead of them, and that with this surrounding shield of strong love, they are going to be all right.

Sometimes people are in the grip of anger that chokes their hearts, stifles their joy, and smothers every intimate relationship. Then God comes in to break the chain of anger and liberate an ordinary person for a new try at love.

Sometimes people live in quiet terror of their own death. Then God comes in to give them a reason for being very glad to be alive just for today.

Sometimes people brood over a depressing memory of some rotten thing they did and cannot forget nor forgive themselves for. Then God comes in to open their hearts to receive the gifts of other ordinary people's forgiveness and so come to forgive themselves.

Sometimes ordinary people wrap themselves like mummies in the suffocating sackcloth of their own self-hatred, and God comes to open their eyes to the extraordinary wonder of their great worth.

All ordinary people have a penchant for sensing that things are in insufferable shape around them. And they often are. Life can be miserable, horrible beyond enduring, the pits. But the secret of grace is that it can be all right at the center even when it is all wrong on the edges. For at the center, where life is open to the Creator and Savior God, we are held, led, loved, cared for, and inseparably bound into the future that he has for every child whom he claims as his.

It took me too long to learn how much I needed George Stob's word about ordinary people. I should have known it a lot earlier. After all, I was one of them. No matter now. The important thing is that an extraordinary gift is available to ordinary people. It is the gift of an open door, the rusty hinged door of angry, hurting, and tired hearts, an open door for a grace that restores us to truth, the truth that, at the depths between ordinary people and God, it is all right and always will be. Preaching that ministers to ordinary people, those overwhelmed failures like you and me, unleashes the grace of God.

Chapter 33

WHY SERIOUS PREACHERS USE HUMOR

Discernment for light moments with a weighty purpose

John Beukema

I once introduced a sermon story by saying, "I don't like this story." Here is approximately what followed:

Fred Craddock tells of a young pastor visiting an elderly woman in the hospital. The pastor finds the woman to be quite ill, gasping for breath, and obviously nearing the end of her life. In the midst of tubes, bags, and beeping medical machines, the pastor reads Scripture and offers spiritual comfort.

He asks, "Would you like to have prayer before I go?" and the lady whispers a yes.

The pastor says, "What would you like me to pray for today?"

The patient responds, "That I would be healed."

The pastor gulps. He thinks *The poor lady can't accept the inevitable. This is like asking God to vaporize the calories from a dozen Krispy Kremes. She isn't facing reality.* The young minister keeps this to himself and begins to intercede, sort of.

"Lord, we pray for your sustaining presence with this sick sister, and if it be your will, we pray she will be restored to health and to service. But if it's not your will, we certainly hope she will adjust to her circumstances."

Have you prayed prayers like that? They're safe prayers. They give God a way out, an excuse, just in case the request is not in his will, and he doesn't come through.

Immediately after the pastor puts an amen

on this safe prayer, the woman opens her eyes and sits up in bed. Then she throws her feet over the side and stands up.

"I think I'm healed!" she cries.

Before the pastor can react, the woman walks over to the door, pulls it open, and strides down the hospital corridor. The last thing the pastor hears before she disappears are the words "Look at me, look at me. I'm healed."

The pastor pushes his mouth closed, gets up, and slowly walks down the stairs and out to the parking lot. There is no sign of the former patient. He opens his car door, and stops. Looking up to the heavens, the pastor says, "Please don't ever do that to me again."

I don't like that story. I don't like it . . . because that pastor is me. I can identify with him.

This anecdote is not hilarious. However, the story is humorously effective. It has the key characteristics of what makes something funny.

THREE CHARACTERISTICS OF HUMOR

Christian author, speaker, and comedian Ken Davis, president of Dynamic Communications, in an interview for this chapter, identified three elements that make something funny: truth, exaggeration, and surprise.

Truth. The story above contains an element of reality that hearers recognize as true. It is an admission of human frailty. People identify with, in this case, praying for things they don't really expect God to supply.

Exaggeration. The whole story is exaggerated, from the overabundance of life-support technology, to the ambiguity of the pastor's prayer, to the immediacy of the woman's recovery. In real life the woman would still be downstairs paying her bill.

Surprise. This is the strong point of the story. As it unfolds, you can't help but wonder what's going to happen. The pastor's reaction is completely unexpected. The final twist is my explanation of why I don't like the story.

Nothing is funny that doesn't have at least one of these characteristics. How painful it is to be under the impression that we are saying something comical when it is not. If your stories fall flat, begin by evaluating them in light of these three categories.

Of course, these are not the only considerations in using humor well, but before exploring further, it is necessary to ask if humor has any place at all in the pulpit.

Is There a Place for Humor in Preaching?

Haddon Robinson, preaching professor at Gordon-Conwell Theological Seminary, in an interview for this chapter, said, "Since preaching deals with life, it has to have some element of humor. We have to look at life as it's lived and see at times how absurd it is."

Consider some of the metaphors and statements of Jesus, and it soon becomes obvious that Jesus was not above introducing a comic element to make a point. Ken Davis gives the example of Jesus' words recorded by Matthew, Mark, and Luke that "it is easier for a camel to go through the eye of a needle than for a rich man to enter the kingdom of God" (e.g., Mark 10:25). Davis pokes fun at attempts to explain the "eye of a needle" as a city gate, where a camel would have to take off all encumbrances and kneel down to enter; or the explanation that the word for camel actually meant "big rope." Such interpretations militate against the point Jesus makes. Jesus presented a picture so outrageous it was funny, and yet the subject of salvation could not have been more serious.

Jesus employed exaggeration. Elton Trueblood was inspired to write the book *The Humour of Christ* when he read Jesus' words about specks and logs in people's eyes, and the description made his four-year-old laugh. Jesus told stories that provoked surprise. When a Samaritan stopped to help the half-dead man after two religious types passed the victim by, it was a shocker. A little research into Samaritan-Jewish relations at the time shows how laughably implausible this must have seemed to the hearers. Jesus spoke truth couched in a smile. Jesus' description of those who "strain out a gnat but swallow a camel" (Matt. 23:24) is as amusing as it is pointed.

John Stott writes, "It seems to be generally agreed that humour was one of the weapons in the armoury of the Master Teacher" (1982, p. 287). If that is accepted, then the question of whether we should use humor is settled. Perhaps a better question to ask is: What types of humor do not belong in preaching?

Unfit Humor

Charles Haddon Spurgeon was renowned both for the power of his sermons and for his wit. Once Spurgeon answered a knock at the door of his home and was confronted by a man holding a big stick.

The man sprang into the hall and announced that he had come to kill Spurgeon.

"You must mean my brother," the preacher said, trying to calm the fellow. "His name is Spurgeon."

But the man would not be dissuaded. "It is the man that makes the jokes I mean to kill" (Warren Wiersbe, 1976, p. 195).

Spurgeon the preacher was no joke teller, but he "had a gift of humor, and at times it came into play as he preached" (Arnold Dalimore, 1984, p. 76). The criticism Spurgeon received prompted him to defend the use of humor in preaching and to clarify which aspects did not belong in the pulpit.

Levity Is Unsuitable

Spurgeon emphasizes that humor and levity are not synonymous. "Cheerfulness is one thing, and frivolity is another; he is a wise man who by a serious happiness of conversation steers between the dark rocks of moroseness, and the quicksands of levity" (*Lectures to My Students*, p. 151). "We must conquer our tendency to levity. A great distinction exists between holy cheerfulness, which is a virtue, and general levity, which is a vice. There is a levity which has not enough heart to laugh, but trifles with everything; it is flippant, hollow, unreal. A hearty laugh is no more levity than a hearty cry" (p. 212).

Spurgeon's differentiations are helpful. Levity is lighthearted to the point of being inappropriate. Flippancy communicates casual indifference or disrespect. Frivolous comments are not suitable in sermons and detract from the grand purpose of preaching. Haddon Robinson feels that "humor is more often misused in preaching than it is well-used . . . because the joke is told for its own sake."

John Piper, author and pastor of Bethlehem Baptist Church in Minneapolis, says, "Earnestness is the demeanor that corresponds to the weight of the subject matter of preaching. The opposite of earnest is not joyful, but trivial, flippant, frivolous, chipper. It is possible to be earnest and have elements of humor, though not levity" (1999).

Of course the line is not always easily drawn, and one person's witty insight might be considered glib or juvenile by another. But levity is the enemy of what Spurgeon and Piper refer to as earnestness. Earnestness give preaching energy, fervency, sincerity, and excellence. Levity tarnishes these qualities, while humor polishes them.

Excessive Humor Is Counterproductive

In an oft-repeated but unverified story, Spurgeon responds to a woman expressing her displeasure over his frequent use of humor by saying, "If you knew how much I held back, you would give me credit." While self-discipline is necessary in all aspects of the sermon, it is most required with humor. John Piper warns, "There is a place for humor in our lives, but there is something deeply wrong that we feel compelled to use so much of it in teaching and preaching and even worshiping" (1986).

John Ortberg, author and teaching pastor at Menlo Park Presbyterian Church in Menlo Park, California, in an interview for this chapter, said he went through a period when he felt humor had become too important to him. Telling a funny story became a predictable part of every message. He used it to relax when speaking and to determine that people were with him. Even though the humor was appropriate and purposeful, Ortberg sensed he was becoming dependent on it. To combat that, he disciplined himself to preach several times in a row using little humor.

Haddon Robinson suggests if we realize we are using humor that doesn't serve the truth, we need to forgo it for a time. "If I'm addicted to it, that means I'm going to tell it for its own sake, or my sake, or the audience's sake, but not for the sake of the truth." "Humour is legitimate," says John Stott. "Nevertheless, we have to be sparing in our use of it and judicious in the topics we select for laughter" (1982, p. 288).

Inappropriate Humor Has No Place

Certain subjects must never be approached in a joking manner. Stories that make fun of a person's weight, ethnicity, age, political views, or physical limitations are off limits. Sexual innuendos, foolishness, what Ephesians 5:4 calls "coarse jesting," are unacceptable.

Sacred things cannot be mentioned in any humorous context without great care. The rite of baptism and the celebration of the Lord's Table should almost always be avoided as topics of humor. Haddon Robinson notes "the most humorous things happen when we are trying to be the most serious." Before mentioning any of those things from the pulpit, you must be sure you aren't "making light of something God takes seriously."

I heard a preacher tell about visiting a woman in her mobile home in an attempt to share the good news. In a single story, he managed to demean baptism, poverty, evangelism, and obesity.

It is unlikely that the Father, Son, and Holy Spirit should ever be invoked in a comedic context. We should not use humor that confirms stereotypes about God, treats him casually, or otherwise portrays him inaccurately.

Some humor that references God can be acceptable. For example, Ken Davis tells about a burglar who breaks into a home only to hear a voice in the darkness saying, "I see you, and Jesus sees you too." After discovering the voice belongs to a parrot, the robber goes to silence the bird, then spots a huge, snarling Doberman next to the cage. At that point the parrot says, "Sic him, Jesus." Davis walks a fine line here, but uses the story effectively by pointing out that this is how many people view God, as ferocious and ready to attack at the first wrong step.

Beware of putting the "ick" in comical. Author and speaker Fred Smith uses as a guideline the old saying, "While the audience laughed, the angels cried." Smith says one test of appropriate humor is "Do the angels laugh too?"

Guided by these cautions, the preacher can be confident that humor can have an important place in the sermon. Phillips Brooks in his *Lectures on Preaching* called humor "one of the most helpful qualities that the preacher can possess"; and John Stott said, "We should press it [humor] gladly into service in the cause of the gospel" (1982, 292). What the preacher must strive for is humor that is appropriate in topic, timing, and purpose.

THE BENEFITS OF HUMOR IN PREACHING

What does the correct use of humor accomplish?

Humor Overcomes Defenses

John Ortberg says he uses humor for the same reason a surgeon uses anesthesia: not to put people to sleep, but to prepare and enable them to receive painful truth they need. Hearers try to defend themselves against hard truth, and humor can smuggle that truth past their resistance and automatic defenses. "No other means can so quickly break the ice, relax inhibitions, and create an attitude of expectancy" (James Cox, 1985, p. 186).

Ortberg says a fast turn from humor to seriousness "catches people off guard, and all of a sudden you're in much deeper than what they were expecting." He gives this example:

> Many years ago, early on in our marriage, my wife and I sold our Volkswagen Beetle to buy our first really nice piece of furniture. It was a sofa. It was a pink sofa, but for that kind of money, it was called a mauve sofa. The man at the sofa store told us all about how to take care of it, and we took it home.
>
> We had very small children in those days, and does anybody want to guess what was the Number One Rule in our house from that day on? "Don't sit on the mauve sofa! Don't play near the mauve sofa! Don't eat around the mauve sofa! Don't touch the mauve sofa! Don't breathe on the mauve sofa! Don't think about the mauve sofa! On every other chair in the house, you may freely sit, but on this sofa—the mauve sofa—you may not sit, for on the day you sit thereon, you will surely die!"
>
> And then one day came the "Fall." There appeared on the mauve sofa a stain . . . a red stain . . . a red jelly stain. My wife called the man at the sofa factory, and he told her how bad that was. So she assembled our three children to look at the stain on the sofa. Laura, who then was about 4, and Mallory, who was about 2 ½, and Johnny, who was maybe 6 months. She said, "Children, do you see that? That's a stain. That's a red stain. That's a red jelly stain. And the man at the sofa store says it's not coming out, not for all eternity. Do you know how long eternity is, children? Eternity is how long we're all going to sit here until one of you tells me which one of you put the red jelly stain on the mauve sofa."
>
> For a long time they all just sat there until finally Mallory cracked. I knew she would. She said, "Laura did it." Laura said, "No I didn't." Then it was dead silence for the longest time. And I knew that none of them would confess putting the stain on the sofa, because they had never seen their mom that mad in their lives. I knew none of them was going to confess putting the stain on the sofa, because they knew if they did, they would spend all of eternity in the "Time Out Chair." I knew that none of them would confess putting the stain on the sofa, because in fact, I was the one who put the stain on the sofa, and I wasn't sayin' nuthin'! Not a word!

But Ortberg turns from that to say, "Here's the truth about us. We've all stained the sofa." The humor opened people's hearts, enabling Ortberg to talk about the serious subjects of sin, guilt, and a holy God.

Fred Smith calls this aspect of humor "lubricating the needle."

 For an audio example of this principle see tracks 6–7 on the supplemental CD.

Humor Relieves Tension

John Ortberg talks about the art of tension management. Communicators gifted at motivation or conviction are able to discern how much tension the audience can tolerate. Too much tension, and hearers start to pull away emotionally. So humor can be a pressure release that keeps people engaged. But we must fight the urge to use humor to relieve the tension prematurely. Ortberg says, "We often underestimate how much tension people are able to tolerate, and we underestimate the use of tension in producing change."

Humor Heightens Interest

Gaining the attention of a congregation and then holding their interest is probably the most common reason speakers use humor. John Ortberg feels that the engagement of the audience can be discerned by the sounds in the room—foot shuffling, coughing, and rustling. When the noise level gets too high, spontaneous humor can often regain the attention of those whose minds have wandered. Ortberg also intentionally injects humor when a section of a sermon has a high information quotient.

Humor Shows Our Humanity

Ken Davis likes the definition of humor as "a gentle way to acknowledge human frailty." Preachers must communicate as real people and not "wholly other" creatures. Humor conveys that perhaps better than anything else. Phillips Brooks declared, "There is no extravagance which deforms the pulpit which would not be modified and repressed, often entirely obliterated, if the minister had a true sense of humor" (*Lectures on Preaching*, p. 57).

If preaching is "a man uttering truth through his own personality," as Brooks described it, then for many the absence of humor would be a denial of who they are. It would be as unnatural to remove all humor from their speech as it would be to eliminate voice inflection. Says author Warren Wiersbe, "*The whole man must be in the pulpit,* and if this includes a sense of humor, then so be it" (1976, p. 197, emphasis original).

Humor Expresses the Joy of the Lord

John Ortberg sees joy as a large component of Scripture, the church, and the experience of being present for the preaching of God's Word. One way we express that joy is in laughter. The willingness of a preacher and congregation to laugh together is a healthy sign of spiritual vitality. Thomas Long implies that laughter indicates good theology. "Because God in Christ has broken the power of sin and death, Christian congregations and their preachers are free to laugh at themselves" (1989, p. 16).

Humor Establishes a Connection Between the Speaker and the Audience

A friend of John Ortberg's visits different churches in his capacity as a church consultant. After listening to many different sermons, the consultant observed that a sense of connection between a preacher and the congregation most often came at the first moment of laughter in a message. Ortberg himself feels humor is a part of who he is, so using it makes him comfortable and helps establish a relationship with listeners.

Humor Encourages a Sense of Community

John Ortberg believes that outward expressions of joy and humor have "the capacity to create a sense of community." Beyond the relationship that humor establishes between speaker and listener, it also sparks something among the people themselves. There is a shared experience that engenders warm feelings. Humor is one way to help break people out of the isolation that comes from sitting in a congregation of strangers, enabling them to feel part of something bigger than themselves.

Humor Draws Attention to the Truth

Spurgeon advised his preaching students to "be so thoroughly solemn that all your faculties are aroused and consecrated, and then a dash of humour will only add intenser gravity to the discourse, even as a flash of lightning makes midnight darkness all the more impressive" (*Lectures to My Students*, p. 189). It is in the flash of humor that truth can sometimes be most clearly seen.

That was my purpose in using this Paul Harvey story.

The Butterball company set up a Thanksgiving hotline to answer questions about cooking turkeys. One woman asked if she could use a turkey that had been in the bottom of her freezer for . . . twenty-three years. You heard me, twenty-three years. The Butterball expert—how's that for a job title—told her it would probably be safe if the freezer had been below zero the entire time. The expert then warned her that even if the turkey was safe to eat, the flavor would likely have deteriorated and wouldn't be worth eating. The woman said, "That's what I thought. We'll give the turkey to our church."

After the laughter subsided, I said, "Sin first shows itself in what you give God."

Ken Davis says, "Laughter helps people see the darkness of their hearts."

Humor Is One Language of Our Culture

Our society craves humor. People love to laugh, and they spend incalculable amounts of money seeking to be entertained. As missionaries to this culture, humor aids in presenting the message in a way people understand. A church or sermon devoid of laughter may not be seen as real.

John Ortberg feels that laughter communicates to those outside the church that this is a place where "they speak my language," a place that has a connection point with today's world.

CHARACTERISTICS OF EFFECTIVE HUMOR

Effective humor follows these principles.

Have a Purpose

John Ortberg believes that since "the ultimate goal of preaching is to have Christ formed in people," humor must always be the servant of the message. If humor does nothing to for-

ward that purpose, then the preacher must be willing to jettison it from the sermon. Haddon Robinson says the "cardinal rule of humor is it must serve the truth." One indication of this is when your audience thinks of the story they think of the truth that lies behind it.

Of the many benefits of humor listed above, some advantages may not be sufficient justification for its inclusion. Humor must serve the greater purpose. We should ask questions such as: In what way does this contribute to the point being made? How will this enable people to hear the truth? Why does this story deserve time in this message? Ken Davis says, "The purpose should be that this humor illustrates a point, clarifies a point, draws people's attention to a point that is going to take them one step closer to the cross."

Effective humor will be entertaining, and there is nothing wrong with that. Entertainment is wrong when it becomes the objective or becomes an end in itself. We can cross the line into that simply by our timing. John Ortberg suggests that when we rush to relieve tension through humor, it indicates a self-esteem issue. Our inability to wait for tension to have its greatest spiritual effect may be because we are too anxious for people to like us. When the preacher is concerned with keeping people happy, truth-telling has been compromised.

Be Neither Offensive Nor Innocuous

Preaching will always offend someone. The solution is not bland speech. Instead, we must strictly monitor those things we intend to be funny. Ask yourself who might consider this offensive and know that your own sensitivities are not always trustworthy.

One high profile speaker told a news story that involved the attempted electrocution of a pig. The speaker told this with glee, even the part where two farmers ended up dead, one was critically injured, and the pig was unharmed. I've learned the hard way that any story involving the endangerment of an animal should only be used with extreme caution. The problem with this story was not that it didn't serve the message—believe it or not, it did. But the real loss of human life should not be a source of casual mirth. The contribution the story made to the point was overshadowed by its insensitivity.

Humor used in the pulpit should not make someone cringe. Hurtful humor can be damaging even if it does not offend the "victim." Ken Davis warns that the preacher may good-naturedly rib a friend, but others don't know this comes out of friendship and take offense for that other person.

Be Selective

John Ortberg says the laws of humor are the same as the laws of real estate—location, location, location. The right story must come at the right time in the message. Fred Smith believes in using it like good spice, "permeating the whole" (2003), but there are moments when humor should be avoided. Ortberg speaks of times when there was a tender spirit in the room, and he realized something humorous he intended to say might disrupt that spirit. Discipline is needed "because there's something else going on that's more important than humor."

Fred Smith writes, "Humor should be used to sharpen the truth, not dull it" (2003). This is a determining factor in the placement of humor. It must not only be in the right place in the message but in the right message. In the rush to use something good, we must resist the urge to wedge it in where it does not belong. Ortberg

says, "When it really fits, it's going to accomplish much more good. I have to discipline myself, wait, and save it for that time."

Be Self-Deprecating Without Becoming Self-Centered

Humor can be an expression of humility if the speaker is secure enough to poke fun at himself. Haddon Robinson writes, "We like people who laugh at themselves, because they are saying, 'What I'm talking about is very serious, but I don't take myself too seriously'" (1989, p. 134). When the speaker is the butt of the joke, this lowers the defenses of listeners even further to the scalpel of truth.

In a sermon from Mark 9, I challenged the congregation to pray impossible prayers. I said I myself was trying to grow in that area. I told of four impossible prayers I had once prayed for daily. Eventually I concluded the answer to the first two prayers was "No," the answer to number three was "Not yet," and prayer number four I gave up on entirely. I said:

I quit my impossible prayer. What a great prayer warrior I am. But in these last few weeks my wife has had four amazing answers to prayer, at least two of which were impossible. One was the exact request I'd given up on. She can pray, she can preach—I think you've got the wrong one of us as pastor.

People appreciated that little insight more than I could have imagined. My wife thought highly of the story also. The caution is we should watch that we don't talk about ourselves too much. Ken Davis says to take care "that the word *self* doesn't become a huge part of our messages."

Practice but Be Open to Spontaneity

John Ortberg warns, "Worse than having no humor at all is forcing humor that isn't funny."

Ken Davis says humor is a tool that we must practice with to learn to operate it well. He believes with a little work just about anything can be funny. Preachers need to look at something that made them chuckle and figure out why it struck them as funny. When that lesson is understood, we can learn to present stories in a way that will produce the same response from our audience.

Practice ways *not* to introduce stories with "A funny thing happened to me the other day." Practice the flow of stories on one or two people until the timing and wording is honed. Humor comes less from what you say than from how you say it.

Practice should not preclude spontaneous humor, which can sometimes be the most effective. A family in our church was moving. The husband told me he was only known in the church as "Kim's husband" because she was so involved and he traveled so much. She would be greatly missed, but he doubted we would know he was gone. With his permission I told that story during a sermon from Romans 12 about significance. I repeated our conversation and began to emphasize his great worth to his family and church. It started to get emotional. Suddenly a thought hit me and I said, "Now if somebody could point this guy out to me . . ." The room went nuts.

Take care, though; these unplanned additions are also the most dangerous because you have only moments to filter and evaluate what you are going to say.

Observe Daily Life

Humor flowing from life experiences always trumps jokes with punch lines. Jokes are what Ken Davis calls high-risk humor. If a joke dies, everyone knows it, and the point may die with it. When a personal story doesn't elicit the laugh you thought it would, it still maintains the power to illustrate the point. That's why Davis calls this low risk humor and suggests this is where someone trying to learn to be more humorous should begin. So avoid joke books and pay more attention to what is going on around you.

John Ortberg says, "The best kind of humor is observational humor, humor that flows out of the incongruities of life and the way life works." Haddon Robinson talks about the power of humor that is "an observation about life that causes me to laugh and at the same time gives me insight."

There is no lack of material. "Life's experiences bring more humor than you could ever use in a million years," says Ken Davis. Preachers need to be aware of how everyday things can be funny—even those things that were not funny at the time. Davis tells a story about a minor car accident that set off the air bag. He says TV doesn't tell you the truth when they picture the air bag coming out like a salvation marshmallow. In his experience the impact painfully bloodied his nose. Davis turns the painful incident into a riotously funny story.

Focus on a Common Truth

Talk about experiences others identify with. Ken Davis ties into a common feeling among men with this observation:

There's proof in the Mall of America that men weren't supposed to shop. The proof is the 180 miles of benches, and there are no women on those benches, only men. I saw an 80- or 90-year-old guy with cobwebs hanging from his head. The sad part was that he wasn't 90 when he went into the mall.

Humor based on truth, in this case exaggerated, gets people nodding and laughing in agreement. It may be something overlooked by the average person until you focus on it.

Be Yourself

While Ortberg and Davis agree that we must work at humor, especially those who are not naturally funny, nevertheless we shouldn't try to become someone we are not. Humor must fit our personality and style. Haddon Robinson says, "If you don't do it within conversation, you are wise to avoid it in public."

Ken Davis says, "It's important to know your own style and ability. My tendency is to be way out there." But Davis admires comedian Steven Wright, who speaks slowly and unemotionally. He simply puts together truths that are rarely observed. For example, Wright points out that if you drop a buttered piece of toast, it will always fall butter side down. And if you drop a cat, he will always land on his feet. "So the other day I tied a piece of buttered toast to my cat's back."

If Steven Wright tried to act like Robin Williams, it wouldn't work. But he delivers lines in a way that fits his personality, and it's hilarious. Davis says, "Humor isn't necessarily that 'lay on the floor and laugh till you're sick' kind of thing. Sometimes it's just a comment that makes people smile and think, *Man, that is so true.* That's humor."

Be Gracious

Poking fun at someone other than yourself is a minefield. Sometimes speakers feel that an infamous celebrity is fair game. That celebrity's lifestyle is so out of line with biblical morality that the speaker thinks little of holding that person up for ridicule. Haddon Robinson uses this guideline, "If that person was sitting in the front row when I made the remark, would they feel it was a cheap shot?"

Humor that is suitable for preaching tears down no one, no matter how justifiable it feels. If a celebrity or anyone the hearer appreciates is mocked, the point being made is lost. "Let your conversation be always full of grace, seasoned with salt" (Col. 4:6).

Be Honest about Exaggeration

Exaggeration is legitimate in humor, and using hyperbole does not cause hearers to stop taking us seriously, if we signal to hearers that we are using humor. Ken Davis says, "It's important to maintain integrity." He says at some point there needs to be something like a wink to the audience. Davis says that with his gestures and tone he becomes bigger than life. This clues in the audience that he's telling the story bigger than it actually happened. He suggests there may be a need to say, "You know it didn't happen quite that way," or to roll your eyes.

Preachers get themselves into trouble when they insist that a story is true when it exceeds the bounds of reality. To qualify with the words, "I don't know if this story is true," doesn't take away anything from it and gives the audience permission to have fun rather than trying to determine the veracity of the speaker.

Keep the Surprise

Introducing something funny by calling it funny is disastrous. It's harder to surprise people. For some people an automatic resistance kicks in. They cross their arms and think *I'll be the judge of that.* The story better be funny or the speaker is climbing out of a deep hole for the rest of the talk.

Credit Sources

Nothing dampens the effectiveness of humor more surely or our credibility more quickly than presenting someone else's humor as our own or someone else's experience as our own.

Giving proper credit does not take away from the enjoyment of the story. I once told a Ken Davis story in a sermon. I acknowledged him at the beginning, and everyone still laughed hard. Afterward a number of people mentioned to me they had heard the story before. Had I failed to give credit, I would have paid for it.

Transition Carefully between What Is Serious and What Is Light

John Ortberg believes it is much easier to transition from light, fun material to serious issues like guilt and sin than it is to move in the other direction.

Ken Davis gives this example of a sudden shift from light to serious:

I read the response of children to what they thought love was. One little child thought love was when "a boy puts on cologne and a girl puts on perfume, and then they go on a date and smell each other." One little girl said, "I think love is when my grandma can't move anymore, she's in a wheelchair, and my grandpa clips her toenails even when he has arthritis and he can't move his hands."

When going from seriousness to humor, in general we should do so gradually, in a step-by-step process. Otherwise, Ortberg says, "I'm going to trivialize everything I've been saying." A sacred moment will be intruded upon and lost.

In a sermon on the supremacy of Christ, I used my personal feelings humorously to make a serious point. I said weddings are my least favorite pastoral duty. There was nervous laughter. I said I felt that way because so much could go wrong. I feared two outcomes: the mother of the bride would hate me, or I would end up on *America's Funniest Home Videos*.

I went on. As a pastor in training I'd been warned about photographers. They were the enemy, seeking to disrupt every ceremony. It didn't take long for me to see this was no idle threat. Photographers ran up and down center aisles, blinded us with flashes, and whispered stage directions during the vows. The worst was the guy who got on his hands and knees and crawled behind the choir rail. I heard him scurrying along behind me, and then every few feet he would pop his head over the rail and snap a few pictures.

I acted all this out. It was a riot. I concluded with these words.

The way I see it, weddings are the legal, spiritual, public joining together of two lives. They are not primarily a photo opportunity. Someday I'm going to grab one of those photographers by the throat and scream, "It's not about you."

You came here today with something on your mind. Maybe you were consumed with your plans, struggling with loneliness, anxious about your marriage, or worried about money. These concerns are all secondary. The gospel shouts, "It's all about Jesus."

This proved to be a powerful story. "It's all about Jesus" is a popular theme in our church. And I'm asked to do fewer weddings.

BIBLIOGRAPHY

Brooks, Phillips. *Lectures on Preaching*. Republished 1989 by Kregel (Grand Rapids) as *The Joy of Preaching*. Quotes are on p. 58 of this volume.

Cox, James W. 1985. *Preaching*. San Francisco: Harper & Row.

Dalimore, Arnold. 1984. *C. H. Spurgeon*. Chicago: Moody Press.

Long, Thomas. 1989. *The Witness of Preaching*. Louisville: Westminster John Knox.

Piper, John. 1986. "Revival and Fasting." A sermon preached on June 6 at Bethlehem Baptist Church, Minneapolis.

_____. 1999. "Thoughts on Earnestness in Preaching." An unpublished lecture at the Bethlehem Institute, Minneapolis.

Robinson, Haddon. 1989. *Mastering Contemporary Preaching*. Portland: Mulnomah.

Smith, Fred. Accessed 2003. "How to Use Humor." www.BreakfastwithFred.com.

Spurgeon, C. H. Undated. *Lectures to My Students*. Grand Rapids: Associated Publishers and Authors.

Stott, John R. W. 1982. *Between Two Worlds*. Grand Rapids: Eerdmans.

Wiersbe, Warren. 1976. *Walking with the Giants*. Grand Rapids: Baker.

Chapter 34

CONNECT HEARERS THROUGH DIALOGUE
A two-way street can be paved with gold

Jeffrey Arthurs

Preaching has a long tradition of one-way communication. You may want to consider experimenting, though, with another alternative well suited to our culture: dialogue. Here are several reasons to consider using two-way communication with your congregation.

BIBLICAL PREACHERS USED DIALOGUE

When Jesus taught, he rarely depended on monologue. The New Testament records that he asked 153 questions. "Whose portrait is this? And whose inscription?" (Matt. 22:20; Mark 12:16; Luke 20:24)? "Which of these three men ... was a neighbor to the man who fell into the hands of robbers?" (Luke 10:36). Jesus, the Master Teacher, engaged in dialogue.

Paul also used dialogue. In Acts, Luke uses the term *dialegomai* at least ten times to characterize Paul's communication. The term means "to discuss, to reason, to argue." Paul "reasoned with them from the Scriptures" (Acts 17:2). "He reasoned in the synagogue ... as well as the marketplace day by day" (17:17). He "argued persuasively about the kingdom of God" (19:8). Apparently Paul felt it was wise for a herald to engage in dialogue.

Some entire books of the Bible are structured by dialogue. Malachi used rhetorical questions, a cousin of two-way communication, to great effect.

WE HAVE DIFFERING FIELDS OF EXPERIENCE.

Listeners hear the preacher's words through their own "grid." For communication to occur, senders and receivers must dance an intricate mental dance to construct meaning.

Max Warren calls this dance "quadruple-think." He says, "Quadruple-thinking is thinking out what I have to say, then thinking out how the other man will understand what I say, and then rethinking what I have to say, so that, when I say it, he will think what I am thinking." Dialogue is indispensable to communicators committed to quadruple-think.

WE LIVE IN A DEMOCRATIC AND PLURALISTIC SOCIETY.

Americans value free expression and believe all human beings are created equal. Every person has a right to hold and express his or her opinion. In this culture, preachers will want to avoid giving the impression of lording it over their listeners.

MANY WAYS TO DIALOGUE

There are various ways to introduce more two-way communication into your sermon. Each preaching situation has its own rules. Preachers who want to try something new need to be brave souls, but maybe one or two of these suggestions will work in your church.

Question and Answer—Audience to Preacher

Speakers often use this method following a message, but we can also allow people to ask questions within a sermon. You may want to use wording like this to prompt feedback: "Have I made that clear?" or "Can I clarify anything?" This puts the responsibility for clarity on the preacher so listeners don't feel stupid for asking.

Question and Answer—Preacher to Audience

We can ask the congregation either closed or open questions. For example, to focus the audience's attention the preacher could ask a closed question: "What is the Great Commission?" Open questions are even more potent, as when Jesus asked, "Who do people say I am" (Mark 8:27)? To teach like Jesus, we might ask a series of questions: "What are people most afraid of? What are you most afraid of? What place does prayer have in your struggle against fear?"

Rhetorical Questions

These are simple to use and can be as effective as "real" dialogue. They engage the audience in mental dialogue with the preacher.

Interviews

Before, after, or even in the middle of a message, why not bring forward a person with firsthand experience in the subject of the message to reinforce the point? Either the audience or the preacher could question the person.

Testimony

Listeners participate vicariously in the ideas and emotions of personal stories. Try following your sermon with a story from someone who has "been there, done that." Rick Warren, pastor of Saddleback Community Church, uses testimony every week to increase the impact of his messages.

Role Play and Drama

This method also creates identification. As a twist on the typical use of drama, I wove a sequence of scenes into a sermon called "A Day in the Life of a Christian." This sermon was designed to show seekers what it was like to be a Christian. The sermon began with a normal introduction but then introduced an actress called Jill Christian. I asked if the audience could accompany her through her day, and as she encountered various trials and triumphs, we dialogued, or I commented directly to the audience on what had just occurred.

Dialogue-Based Sermon Structure

The outline of a sermon can take the shape of questions and answers. Anticipating listeners' questions as you teach on baptism, you might use this outline:

What does baptism mean?

Who should be baptized?

What does baptism do?

How should baptism be done?

Presermon Feedforward

The late Dallas Seminary preaching professor Keith Willhite urged, "Stop preaching in the dark! Gaining feedback isn't enough." Try to gather people's ideas and experiences before you preach and use them in sermon preparation.

Postsermon Feedback

Feedback can show preachers where further teaching is needed. (Warning: you have to be humble to listen to most people's comments. Or it will make you humble!)

Dietrich Bonhoeffer writes, "It is characteristic of the preacher that he simultaneously questions and proclaims. He must ask along with the congregation, and form a 'Socratic community'—otherwise he could not give any reply. But he can reply and he must, because he knows God's answer in Christ" (*The Communion of Saints*).

I think you will find that encouraging more two-way communication in your preaching will invigorate you, your church community, and your sermons.

Chapter 35

SELF-DISCLOSURE THAT GLORIFIES CHRIST
Transparent preaching aims to reveal the light, not the window

Joe Stowell

Observing college students and their reactions to various preachers has been an education for me. Students want to know if the preacher is a fellow struggler or someone who lives on a different planet.

They can quickly sense a "Bible bureaucrat" or someone speaking from a pedestal of perceived perfection, and their hearts shut down. But let them see the reality of a preacher's pilgrimage, and they willingly follow.

But self-disclosure is tricky. Some kinds of confessional preaching erode respect. If in any way self-disclosure lessens our congregation's confidence and respect, we should work on those issues privately. Indiscriminate revelation may diminish our greatest ministry, that of cutting a godly wake by the example of our lives.

Paul's counsel to Timothy helps chart the course for keeping our transparency constructive. In 1 Timothy 4:12, he urges Timothy to live a life that is an example. Paul is quick to indicate that he is not asking Timothy to live a perfect life, but rather that he is to work hard so that his "progress" may be evident to all.

AN EXAMPLE OR AN EXCUSE?

Preachers quick to admit their own faults publicly may, if they are not careful, give the impression that they are stuck in sinful habits and patterns. Wanting not to appear perfect is important—but not if it costs the demonstration of progress in our walk with Christ.

One danger of transparency is that we cease

to be examples to the flock and become instead their excuse. Every pastor eventually becomes one or the other.

Repeated exposure to a preacher's failings may end up only excusing the faults of the flock. Hearing them say "My pastor has this problem as well" without a stimulus from the pastor to remediate the problem is a bad consequence of transparency.

DISCERNING SELF-DISCLOSURE

To be an example in progress demands that we use self-disclosure in discerning ways. Don't talk about the same category of failure year after year. If traffic violations are your besetting sin, the telling of traffic stories throughout your pastorate only tells people that there are areas in which they do not need to grow, since the pastor is obviously satisfied with ongoing failure as well.

When admitting faults, don't trivialize them. Couch them in a context of appropriate shame. Sometimes in the euphoria of connecting with the audience as a real person or in the spinning of a story about ourselves that has some humorous elements, it is easy to give the impression that failure is "no big deal."

Preaching to challenge people to growth and Christlikeness is not enhanced by the impression that we all have problems and after all, "nobody's perfect"—not even the preacher.

Couching the disclosure with disclaimers like "I'm not proud of this," or "This is an area of my life that I am targeting for growth," helps the listener maintain a healthy dose of discomfort with the problem.

Let people see a solution to the struggle. For every struggle there is a biblical pattern of remediation. Weaving that into the story or making it the point of the message places hope in the hearer's heart. They see a definitive way in which they can grow with you.

One way to do this is to balance failure stories with an equal dose of your spiritual successes. We all need people in front of us who are winning victories within earshot of our own lives. If you are uncomfortable with appearing to boast, then keep your reliance on God evident. Add statements like, "I am thankful for the grace God gave me when I. . . ."

Telling about when you went out of your way to be kind, when you said no to temptation, when you captured an opportunity to witness in the face of your fears, or when you responded positively to your spouse or children dramatizes the truth that victory is within reach for everyone. If you share the joy of winning for Jesus, others will want to claim similar joys in their own lives.

Remember that preaching is not about you. It is about him—his authority in our lives, his worthiness to be worshiped and obeyed, the example of his life to be duplicated in our own, the glory of his presence in our lives, and the life transforming power of his Word and indwelling Spirit.

Transparency gone amuck renders the sermon more about us than about him. If listeners leave remembering us and our struggles (or our personal victories!) more than Christ's transforming power, then we have done preaching and our hearers a disservice.

I'll never forget hearing a church member tell his pastor, a gifted communicator, "Bill, ten minutes into the sermon you disappeared, and I heard from God!"

Chapter 36

HOW TO BE HEARD

Mastering five overlooked fundamentals of clear communication

Fred Smith

Every summer you can find advertisements for basketball or football camps where big-name stars, for a fee, will instruct young people dreaming of athletic greatness. I wonder how much actual learning takes place when an all-star quarterback, who spends most of his time reading and outmaneuvering sophisticated defenses, tries to coach a junior-higher who's still trying to figure out how to grip the ball with hands that aren't quite big enough.

Often, I suspect, a similar effect happens to those who want to achieve superstar poise and eloquence in the pulpit. The key is focusing not on the dazzling techniques but on the fundamentals. Improvement comes from concentrating on the basics until we can perform them without conscious thought. Here are some fundamental areas that I find speakers may overlook as they try to improve.

ESTABLISHING A FRIENDLY ATMOSPHERE

To a large degree, the atmosphere we establish will determine how effective our sermon is going to be. Atmosphere is created by both our verbal and nonverbal messages.

I hear a lot of preachers, for instance, who are pretty sloppy in their opening comments. Perhaps it's because they haven't thought about them, but the mood they create right from the start makes it tough to benefit from the rest of the sermon.

Most of us know you don't want to start on a negative note. "I hope you all will excuse my voice this morning. I've had a cold all week."

Or, "I really appreciate you all coming on a miserable, rainy day like today."

Or, "Folks, we just are not getting enough people. When I stand up here and look out at this congregation. . . ."

What kind of impression do these introductions make on the listeners? Probably not a good one. You're not starting from their need. You're starting from your need, and that's not the way to fill people with anticipation for the Word you have to give.

This is why I enjoy starting with something like, "This has been a wonderful week"— people want to know why it's been wonderful. They've had a lousy week. But there are few weeks for which you can't think up some way it has been good—"I haven't been sued a single time this week." And people laugh.

Or, "I haven't had an automobile accident this week, not even a scratch." Little things like that. And then you can say, "No, really. It's been a fine week. I talked to some friends on the phone, and I was just reminded of the marvelous gift of friendship." This builds a friendly atmosphere. It conveys a feeling anybody can identify with. People may say to themselves, *Yes, I talked to some friends this week, too. And sometimes I forget how good that is.*

145

That's one way to help establish a warm, friendly atmosphere. There are other ways, but the important thing is to avoid opening negatively or from self-interest or insecurity. I want to communicate openness, that I'm here to serve these people.

This setting of the atmosphere, of course, begins before I speak my first word. We can show warmth by our demeanor on the platform. I try to pick out certain people and smile at them. This not only affirms those people, but it also shows the whole congregation I'm glad to be there.

People need to know how you feel before you start to speak. They want to know whether you're friendly or worried or mad. For me, the most difficult discipline in speaking is going in with the proper attitude. If I do not want to speak, it is so difficult for me to speak well.

Attitude control is essential. I must go up there with a friendly attitude, with a genuine desire to help those people, to give them something they'll find beneficial.

Encouraging Participation, Not Observation

Another way we all can improve is by remembering that our goal is not simply to have people sit quietly while we talk but to have their minds actively engaged by our subject matter. One of the keys to engaging people is using a conversational style. People listen to it without antipathy. When I raise my voice, people tend to put up a barrier to my increased volume. It's like that story about the kid who told his mother he'd decided to be a preacher.

"Why?" she asked.

"Well," he said, "if I'm going to be attending church all my life, I'd much rather stand up and yell than sit and listen to it."

The minute somebody starts yelling, people mentally distance themselves. Many preachers think they're doing it for emphasis, but generally it doesn't work that way. It deemphasizes.

If I want to say something really important, I'll lower my voice—and people will kind of lean forward to hear what I'm saying. In a sense, you're putting intimacy in a point by lowering your voice. You're saying, "This point means something to me. I'm telling you something from my heart."

What else can we do to encourage participation? Not necessarily by providing entertainment. If people are listening for the next story or next joke, I've become a performer. My goal is not to have people say, "Oh, you're such a great speaker." Then I know I've failed. If they are conscious of my speaking ability, they see me as a performer. They have not participated. My goal is for people to say, "You know, Fred, I've had those kinds of thoughts all my life, but I've never had the words for them. Now I've got words for them." Then I feel I've given them a handle for something. I've crystallized their thoughts and experiences into a statement or story and made it real for them. I've enabled them to give it to somebody else.

Obviously speakers must do the talking, but you can let the audience "talk" too. You talk for them. If I'm making a controversial point, I'll say, "I can tell by your faces that you really don't agree with that." Or, "You're saying to me, 'That's all right for you to say, but that doesn't fit my situation.' And I agree with you, because all of us are not alike."

What I've done is to say their words for them. They're thinking, *He understands. He's not trying to poke this stuff down our throat.* And they want me to continue the conversation. The key here is to make sure we see the process as a conversation and not a performance.

ENSURING I'M BELIEVABLE

I keep a constant watch on my believability. I've got to practice what I preach. Unless I can believe me when I make a statement, I won't make it.

Let's say I've had an argument with my wife before I speak. I will not use an illustration or statement about the marital love relationship because Mary Alice wouldn't believe me if I said it—and I wouldn't, either. Even though the statement is absolutely true, I could not say it and believe it.

Now, if I get with Mary Alice and say, "Honey, I was wrong" or "You were wrong" or "We were wrong," and we resolve the issue, then I can believe me saying some things about marriage. But I won't ask my audience to believe what I can't.

For me, this has meant giving up saying some things I would love to be heard saying. I can't effectively use material that has to do with sudden "miraculous" changes because I'm such a believer in process. While I believe in the miracles of the Bible, I have difficulty teaching people to expect them.

I can't be an inspirational speaker saying, "You can do anything you think you can do . . . and what the mind can conceive, the body can perform." That just isn't me.

Nor am I able to preach effectively on prophecy. While I can listen to others do it and appreciate their ability to do so, I can't do it believably because I have so many personal misgivings. I would not feel on solid ground. I'd have to quote someone else. As credible speakers, we've got to establish some authority or there's no reason to listen to us.

You can establish your authority by being a researcher or a Bible scholar, or by relating certain life experiences. But whatever your authority, you have to be careful of extrapolation—taking a principle from an area you know and trying to apply it to an area you don't know.

Extrapolation is where most speakers show their ignorance, and it undermines their genuine authority. I listen to some preachers extrapolate their knowledge into the business world, and they do it well. Others, however, tell a business story and reveal how little they know about business.

So I'm careful when I extrapolate. Do I stick to things I know? When people see that I'm pretending to be familiar with something I'm not, that hurts my believability.

MAKING MY VOICE INCONSPICUOUS

Few speakers have great voices, but most have ones perfectly adequate if people can understand the words. But I've found people are turned off by preachers who have a seminary brogue, who have developed an intellectual pronunciation, or who preach as if they were reciting Shakespeare. I immediately say, "They're performing."

If I'm conscious of a speaker's voice after listening for two minutes, then the voice has become a distraction. In the first two minutes, people should make a decision about your voice and then think no more about it. It's exactly like your clothing. When you stand up, if people are conscious of your clothes after once seeing you, there's something wrong with your clothes. You're either overdressed or underdressed. You're not properly dressed to speak. The same is true of the voice. It should come across as natural.

But there's more to it than that. The voice should always contain some fire—conviction, animation. Fire in the voice means that the mind and the voice are engaged. There's a direct relationship between an active mind and an active voice.

For example, if I am not really interested in a point I will leave it out, because my voice will be flat. My voice will say, "This point isn't important" no matter what my words say. It will tell the audience I'm really not interested. If I try to fake it, those who are sensitive will know it. So it's counterproductive to try to convince people of a point your voice doesn't believe.

I like to listen to people say certain words. The way people say "God" has always intrigued me. With some, you can almost feel the relationship. It's personal. With others, it's majestic. With others, it's sharp or brittle. The fact that it is so different among different people means there is a different relationship, and the voice is saying what the mind feels.

Fire in the voice has nothing to do with having a good voice or a poor voice. Some of the whiniest voices I've ever heard come from the best speakers. But audiences will listen to a poor voice as long as there's fire, because as soon as the audience realizes the voice is real, they adjust to it.

USING GESTURES EFFECTIVELY

Gestures have a vocabulary all their own. The Spanish painter Goya charged as much to paint the hands as to paint the face, because the hands are the most difficult of all parts of the body to paint. Delsarte studied for several years how the hands show emotion. He got so good

at it that he could sit in a park and tell whether a baby was held by a maid or its mother by the intensity of the hands.

I, too, have become interested in what hands say. When I watch a speaker, I watch the hands. I want to see whether gestures are spontaneous or programmed. I want to see whether the spontaneous gestures are repetitious or varied. My friend Haddon Robinson has one of the finest pairs of hands I know. I've tried to count the different formations his hands make, and the number gets astronomical. Yet they're absolutely spontaneous, and they're in harmony with what he's saying and with the sound of his voice. He has a large vocabulary of both gestures and words.

I've found speakers can't develop mastery of gestures quickly, but they can give themselves permission to improve. Here's one to start with. If you're going to be delivering a climactic statement, instead of getting intense too soon, it's better to relax your body and back away a half step from the audience. Then just before you come into the climactic statement, step toward the audience and straighten up. That way your body as well as your voice projects the message.

Gestures also include giving people your eyes. In speaking, eyes are almost as important as the voice. Everyone knows the importance of eye contact, but the temptation I have is to zero in on a few people up front who are attentive. Maybe I'm insecure, but it's easier to talk to those people. I have to remind myself not to neglect those out on the wings. Like the farmer who's feeding the chickens, you have to throw the corn wide enough for everyone to get some. So I tell myself, Remember the smaller chickens on the fringe. I want them to know I'm thinking of them, too.

Chapter 37

OPENING THE CLOSED AMERICAN MIND
Preaching to skeptics

Ed Dobson

The audience at our Saturday night outreach service is one-third unchurched individuals, one-third church dropouts, and one-third church adherents, so the majority come from a secular viewpoint. At the end of the service, I respond to their written questions; I have no idea beforehand what they will be. Questions range from predestination to masturbation, from abortion to suicide, and my answers aren't always what people want to hear.

One evening someone wrote, "I'm gay, and I've always been gay. Is that okay?"

"What you're really asking," I responded, "is 'What does the Bible say about human sexuality?' The Bible teaches that sexuality is a gift from God to be experienced within the commitment of heterosexual marriage. My understanding of the Bible is that all expressions of our sexuality outside of those boundaries are not within God's creative intent."

"Are you asking me if it's okay to have homosexual feelings? Yes, it is. But Scripture does not permit you to follow through with those feelings as a legitimate expression of sexuality. If you try to ignore that fact, there are consequences, one of which is displeasing God."

Answers like that can irritate people who don't accept an absolute standard of truth. One man said to me, "I really like Saturday night, but when you answer those questions, I wish you would quit referring to the Bible and tell me what you really think."

I congratulated the man on being so perceptive. The point of our seeker-sensitive service is not to tell people what I think but to help connect them with biblical truth. In a culture committed to relativism, hostile toward notions of unchanging, ultimate truth, the gospel can be an offense, no matter how positive my presentation. Sometimes that can't be avoided.

But sometimes it can. I've found that I can gain a hearing for the truth of the gospel, even in a relativistic culture. As I've conducted seeker-sensitive services and befriended non-Christians, I've gathered several principles for reaching skeptics with the truth.

EXPLAIN WHY

The spirit of individualism rather than community dominates our culture, giving relativism a strong appeal. "You believe what you want, and I'll believe what I want" is the spirit of the times. If a couple on a talk show says, "We've been married sixty years, and we're still happy," the audience applauds. But if they say, "We believe everyone should remain married for a lifetime," they'll get booed off the set.

Pervasive individualism has a positive side. People want what enhances their lifestyles, so I can reach them if I demonstrate that the values I teach are truths beneficial to anyone. I must show the modern skeptic the practical wisdom of biblical principles, particularly those principles that appear rigid or intolerant.

For example, to most people on the street, "Don't be unequally yoked" is the most ridiculous, narrow-minded idea they've ever heard. In their mind, if two people love each other, that's all that matters. They would think it silly, even tragic, for religion to interfere with love.

When I'm speaking on this subject, I focus on the logical reasons behind the scriptural principle: "You can't build a house on two sets of blueprints. In marriage, if one person operates on values rooted in Scripture, and the other operates on another set of values, it's only a matter of time until they collide over how to raise kids, spend money, or use leisure time. Sooner or later competing sets of values are going to hit head-on. God understands that. He warns against being 'unequally yoked' because he wants couples to avoid painful conflict."

Secular people usually respond to such reasoning. Once they understand that God is for them, not against them, they are more open to obeying God out of love and submission, not merely because obedience offers cash value in this world.

APPEAL TO CURIOSITY ABOUT THE BIBLE

While many secular people reject the notion of absolute values, they are curious to know what the Bible says. And if they have come to church, I assume they have at least some interest in biblical teachings or they wouldn't be there in the first place.

When answering the questions of seekers and skeptics, I nearly always preface my remarks with, "If you're asking me what the Bible says, here is the answer." If I dodge and weave around the Bible, my audience won't

respect me. Sometimes I must frankly say, "I may not like the Bible's answer, you may not like it, but this is what it says."

One Saturday evening a question read, "I'm a Christian. My brother was not a believer when he committed suicide. I still believe he'll be in heaven. What do you think?"

"What you're asking is whether the Bible gives several options on how to get to heaven," I responded. "I have to be honest with you. Scripture says Christ is the only way to heaven, and there are no other options. You are probably thinking: *So what does that mean for my brother?* Since you are a Christian, you undoubtedly had some influence on him; perhaps before he made this horrible choice, he did turn and commit his life to Christ."

I would have loved to assure him that his brother was waiting for him in heaven, but I couldn't. I concluded, "If you're asking whether people can go to heaven without accepting Christ—no, they cannot. I'd like to tell you it doesn't matter, but if I did, I would be dishonest with the Bible." People respect that level of integrity.

I try to satisfy people's natural curiosity about the Bible in two ways. I preach verse by verse on Sunday mornings, and on Saturday nights I use the Bible to answer topical questions. By going through a book one verse at a time, I'm eventually going to bump into the issue that concerns an individual. The questions on Saturday night force me to deal with listeners' urgent concerns.

KNOW YOUR ESSENTIALS AND NONESSENTIALS

We gain a hearing with a secular audience when we don't confuse essentials with nonessentials. I try to distinguish between three types of truth: absolutes are truths essential to the faith, truths that never change (such as salvation by grace alone); convictions are beliefs over which orthodox Christians may differ (such as the ordination of women); preferences are traditions or customs (such as musical tastes) that may be compatible with the Bible but aren't biblically based, and they may change with the culture and over time.

Naturally, sometimes people will differ about which category a subject belongs to, but most issues seem to fall into one category or another.

Don't Skip the Tough Topics

When you're trying to gain a hearing from a secular audience, it's tempting to water down demanding Scriptures or avoid them altogether. We're afraid people will tune out the sermon.

But I've discovered that's a mistake. Just when I think I know what the culture wants to hear and what it doesn't, I'm surprised all over again. Our most popular Saturday night series was entitled, "What Does It Mean to Be a Christian?" By any measure—attendance, audience response, or follow-up—it was the most successful four evenings in our Saturday history. Until then I had dealt with subjects like depression, bitterness, and forgiving your parents. The last thing I expected was an overwhelming response to such a simple, straight-forward topic.

I learned a valuable lesson. I don't need to trade away forthright, biblical messages for something faddish or trendy. People have a basic spiritual hunger that only faithful biblical preaching can satisfy.

I've found that I can preach even about the most sticky subject, as long as I balance it with

good news. We did a two-part series on Saturday night, one on heaven and the other on hell.

We introduced the subject of the afterlife by telling near-death experiences from popular literature. I wasn't prepared to say these experiences were real, but I pointed out they often paralleled the biblical teachings on death and the afterlife. The evening on heaven was well received.

But the next week, I said, "What I didn't tell you last week was there are other near-death experiences described in the literature that are not so pleasant. In fact, it's incredible how much these experiences parallel what the Scriptures say about hell." I could tell people were uncomfortable in that second session, but they listened intently.

Establish Authority

I suppose in earlier generations most preachers could assume their listeners conferred to them a certain level of authority. Many preachers could also assume their congregations had a minimal level of biblical knowledge. Today I take nothing for granted. I assume almost everyone will question virtually everything I say. Furthermore, I assume most listeners know little if anything about the Bible.

But how do you establish authority with a group that grew up on the maxim, "Question authority"? I've discovered such people will view me as credible if I do the following:

Let the people do some talking. On Saturday evenings, we always take five to eight minutes to let someone share what God has done in his or her life. Listeners will accept my message if they see that it makes a difference for someone who doesn't get paid to spread religion.

I recently renewed the vows of a couple who

had been on the brink of divorce. The husband had been living with another woman for over a year. The divorce decree was about to be granted when they both started attending Saturday night services independently of each other. They both ended up committing their lives to Christ.

The husband soon broke up with the woman with whom he had been living. The estranged couple began talking again. They eventually decided, "Hey, if God can forgive us, we can forgive each other. Let's start over again."

So in front of their unbelieving friends, they renewed their vows. I went to the reception afterward. It was fascinating to hear their unsaved friends try to figure out what had happened to this couple. Out of that experience, several of them began attending our Saturday night service. They couldn't deny the difference Christ had made in the lives of these two people.

Practice what you preach. The Scriptures say we can silence the foolishness of ignorant people by our good behavior. That involves going places Christ would go and spending time with people he would spend time with. I've said from our pulpit that if Christ were in my city today, he probably wouldn't attend my church. He would be down among the poor and dispossessed.

That's one reason we've gotten involved helping people dying of AIDS. When the AIDS resource center of my city hosts its annual Christmas party downtown, some from our church attend. Such events are a great opportunity for ministry. At one of those parties, I met a woman dying of AIDS who had two children also diagnosed with the virus. I was able to talk with her about Christ's love.

Our church donates money to cover burial costs for those who die of the disease with no funds left to their name. In addition, each Christmas the AIDS resource center gives us a list of names of people suffering from the disease and a wish list that we distribute to our people. We gather the gifts, and when we give them the recipients know it's our church that donates the presents.

Our involvement with AIDS sufferers has built credibility. It's not uncommon for our Saturday night services to attract large numbers of seekers from the gay community. Women have stood and said, "I'm a former lesbian. Christ changed my life through this church."

Accept people as they are. One Sunday morning a man walked into our morning service with the F-word printed on his tee shirt. That wasn't easy for many to swallow. As I heard later, when people stood to sing the first hymn, many couldn't get their minds off his shirt.

But as inappropriate as wearing that shirt was, it was important that we accept that man where he was. When the church requires that people clean up their lives, dress, and act a certain way before we will love them, we lose the respect of our culture.

Keep the playing field level. Someone once complained that our church was soon going to be run over with homosexuals. I responded, "That would be terrific. They could take a seat next to the gossips, the envious, the greedy, and all the rest of us sinners."

I try to communicate that same attitude in my preaching: We all stand under God's judgment, and we all are in desperate need of his grace. Letting people know that I'm not speaking down to them from some lofty moral position helps them listen to what I have to say.

Don't pretend to play God. I have to be honest with people when I don't know the answers to their questions. A woman once asked, "Where was God when my father was molesting me?"

"I wish I knew where he was during your ordeal," I answered. "I just don't know. But I do know this: God loves you and wants to heal the wounds of your past." It's ironic, but not having all the answers helps people better trust the answers I do have.

Use the culture to introduce good news. Secular people know popular music, entertainment, and news media. So I've used such worlds to help make the Christian case. In my messages on Saturday nights, I cite secular studies, read from news sources, and quote from popular music to bridge the listener's world to the Scriptures.

One night I used John Lennon's famous song "Imagine." I asked the audience to imagine a world with no competing religions, no wars, and no fights, where complete peace and harmony reigned. "Will there ever be such a place?" I asked. "Such a world is possible only through Jesus Christ, who gives us personal peace and changes hatred into love."

EXPLODE STEREOTYPES

People in our culture hold many misperceptions about Christians. When I explode those negative stereotypes, primarily with humor, and perhaps satirize now and then the real foibles of Christians, I gain credibility.

One Easter morning, knowing many unchurched people would be in the audience, I wore my doctoral robes to the pulpit. I pointed to the various parts of this beautiful robe—the colors, the hood, the sleeves—and explained what each symbolized. Then I unzipped the robe and stepped out in a tee shirt and blue jeans. People gasped.

"On Easter Sunday, we all put on our robes," I said. "By that I mean we all get dressed up. We all put on our best image. But underneath all the hype, at the blue-jeans level, we often are very different people. We need to ask, 'Does Easter make a difference?'"

Reaching out to committed unbelievers is a great challenge requiring creativity and dedication. Sometimes the results are slow in coming; sometimes we have to endure a lot of misunderstanding and hostility. But sometimes the results are remarkable.

Chapter 38

TURNING AN AUDIENCE INTO THE CHURCH
Transforming consumers into the committed

Will Willimon

The dynamics of the modern congregation can be discouraging. Sunday has become just another day to consume. Those who do attend worship nearly demand to be entertained. But they are still a Christian congregation, and we do well to treat them as such. How do we preach to such a crowd week after week? How can we move them from being individualistic consumers to a community of saints responding to God's Word?

IS CHURCH LIFE A LEISURE ACTIVITY?

A number of factors inhibit our Sunday morning crowds from being a congregation, and the first is that our people have adopted many of the values of our consumer and leisure society.

We see this in people's lifestyles. One pastor in Colorado complained because of his congregation's weekend trips. His church is located in a suburb of Denver, and many in his congregation own condos in Breckenridge or Vail. Certain periods of the year—ski season, for example, which can run from early November to the middle of April—many otherwise steadfast members attend irregularly. Trying to sustain a sense of community is hard to impossible.

Second, those attending have fewer strong ties to others in the church. In my last church, for those nearing retirement, the church was their social center. The crowd at a covered-dish social at church would also be the same at a downtown dinner party. If I would have asked them, "Who are your five best friends?" most would have named at least three from the church.

Even a generation ago, the majority attending our churches lived in the same town and got their mail from the same post office and shopped at the same general store. So much of their lives was shared together before they even arrived on Sunday morning. To most of the younger crowd in my last congregation, however, church was only one of many stops along a busy highway. Many commuted twenty to thirty minutes, and they couldn't name even one close church friend.

Third, today's average churchgoer is largely unfamiliar with Christian speech. People arrive on Sunday morning without a working knowledge of Christianity. They hear our words without some fundamental assumptions of Scripture.

A woman recently complained to me about the youth group her seventeen-year-old daughter attends. Her daughter had said something like, "The Trinity is an outmoded concept. We don't need to think of God in such a complicated way anymore."

The youth leader had replied, "Well, that's wrong. That's not the way Christians look at it."

The girl's mother was deeply offended. How presumptuous of this youth pastor to tell her daughter she was wrong!

"Your daughter is extremely bright," I said after listening to this mother. "She's gotten a huge scholarship to the college of her choice. But she's ignorant and uninformed when it comes to basic Christian doctrine. As Christians, we're not here to say, 'I agree or disagree with that.' We're here to be instructed, to be enculturated into a very different way of looking at things."

When people don't know, and don't really care to know, the content of Christianity, it's hard to build a faith community.

A PASTOR'S TWIN TEMPTATIONS

Our fickle congregations can tempt us in two directions. On the one hand, we may pander to their consumer mindset. We avoid the controversial, even if it's biblical, and we strive to make people feel good, designing the service so they're pumped up by the end.

On the other hand, cynicism can set in: "My people don't care about the gospel. They just want to be entertained, to feel good about their miserable little lives." So we preach without expecting any significant change.

A better response requires a fundamental shift in attitude. A congregation's behavior is sometimes deceptive. Though they have a long way to go, there are definite signs they yearn to become a congregation. Here are three attitudes I've developed to remind me of that.

First, I've developed an amazement when people do show up. There are a lot of other things people could be doing on Sunday morning. Many make sacrifices to get to church.

Last winter I was given an assignment by Duke's president to spend more time with students, so early on Sunday morning (2:30 a.m.) after a basketball game with Michigan, I hung

out at a bonfire with several of them. I walked up to one student I knew, who was surprised to see me, and I said jokingly, "Good morning, David. I bet you won't be at chapel later this morning."

"It will be easier for me than it will be for you," he kidded me. "I'm used to this, and you aren't!"

"Oh, David," I retorted. "You're so young and arrogant!" We then spent a half-hour talking about his life. *I can't believe I'm here*, I thought. *In just a few hours, I'm supposed to preach.*

Later that morning, at five minutes to eleven, I was standing with the choir in the back of the sanctuary when in walked David.

"You're up!" I said in surprise.

"Yeah," he said, "and I look better than you do. And you probably got more sleep than I did."

Yeah, I thought. *And I didn't drink what you drank either.*

As he headed for the sanctuary, he said, "You better be good today."

When I think of the five hundred reasons not to go to church, when I reflect upon how archaic preaching must seem to people—and how lousy I preach some days—I'm utterly amazed at the people who do show up consistently.

The second attitude I've developed is that I've learned to relish the serendipities of ministry. When something remarkable happens as a result of preaching, we're tempted to think, *Well, it's about time.* Instead, I want to be thankful, for God's Spirit has been at work creating faith and Christian community.

I once preached a sermon on sex, and the next week I received a call from a father. "I don't know what kind of reaction you got from last Sunday's sermon," he said. "But I just want to tell you my seventeen-year-old son was there." I braced myself for shock and anger.

"Getting my son to church last week was such a hassle," he continued. "I physically forced him to come. When he arrived, he was angry and sat with his arms folded.

"I didn't hear much of your sermon because I was so busy watching my son. But when you started in on sex, his mouth dropped open. He was stunned that you would preach on such a topic. I was so proud that we were there. I was proud of you.

"When you finished, I didn't say a word. But on the way home, my son said, 'Gosh, was this sermon typical of him?' 'Yeah,' I replied. 'That's a typical Willimon sermon.' I lied—all your sermons aren't that interesting—but I just want to thank you for what you said on Sunday."

That's the type of incident I want to be thankful for—sort of.

Finally, I treat those who have shown up for worship with pastoral respect. Many people are coming with burdens for which they are seeking God's help. My first four years at Duke, I solely taught in the divinity school. It was the first time since graduate school I wasn't preaching, so I attended a local church. One Sunday I walked into the church sanctuary and sat beside a middle-aged woman. The organ was still playing the prelude, so I turned to her and asked how she was doing.

"Not so well," she replied. "My husband was killed last week."

"What?"

"A drunk driver killed him," she continued. "What makes his death so hard is that we were separated at the time."

"I'm so sorry." Taken back, I turned to greet an older man who had just sat down on the other side of me.

"George, how have you been?" I asked.

"I haven't been here in a month," he replied.

"Anything wrong?"

"Well, my mother died," he said. "It's just the worst thing that has ever happened to me. I miss her so much."

"I'm so sorry to hear that," I said. Just then the service began, for which I was extremely grateful. I've never since presumed my listeners don't need and want the community created by the gospel.

READING THE CORPORATE CULTURE

Our listeners yearn to be a congregation, but that doesn't mean that becoming a congregation is easy. It requires training. The centrifugal forces of our culture pulling our people apart are strong. We simply can't expect them to arrive on Sunday knowing what they're supposed to do.

I've learned that training them might be easier than we think. In one of the congregations I pastored, I was warned about a member who was considered a "hothead." A couple of months after I arrived, this man approached me after a service. "I just don't see it the way you told it this morning, Pastor," he said. "Maybe I missed something, but I don't think you're right."

I immediately got defensive. "Wally," I said, "I don't know exactly what you heard...."

"Wait a minute," he cut in. "I didn't ask you to take it back. I'm only saying I didn't understand and so I disagree. What kind of preacher are you, anyway? Someone who stands up and says something and then takes it back when someone disagrees?"

Later this man said, "You know, you get to read books all the time. You get to think about all these great things. I run a hardware store, and you can learn to run a hardware store in a year—I've being doing it for nineteen years. Sunday is the only time I can feel like a thinking person."

Wally, it turned out, wasn't a hothead, just a man who was impatient with preachers who didn't take their jobs seriously. I've never forgotten his comments. He gave me authorization to conduct business on Sunday morning. If a hardware store owner was interested in interacting with Sunday's sermon, I knew I could train others to do the same.

A sermon is, first and foremost, about Jesus Christ and what he has done for us and what he calls us to do for him and one another. I want to train people to ask not "Was this relevant to the latest things going on in my world?" but "Was this sermon faithful to the revealed text of Scripture?"

In a recent sermon on Ephesians 5:3–7, which is about not letting filthy talk come out of our mouths, I said, "You know me. I like to preach on the big stuff—sex, war, racism—the large sins. What Ephesians is saying this morning, however, seems so petty. One reason I like to go for the big sins is because it's easier to talk about South Africa's racial problems than what happened at the last board meeting."

I contrasted what I wanted to preach on with the text's clearly stated aims. Then I proceeded to preach the passage I had been given. I sent a clear message that what I preach isn't necessarily my idea; I am bound by Scripture, and this is what people are getting.

If my first task is to get people to hear the Word (versus human words), my second task is to get people to react to the Word, to get them talking about that Word.

I recently preached a sermon on Romans 1. The apostle Paul includes in this passage a laundry list of sins: envy, malice, murder, and the like. After referring to the passage, I gave some statistics on the number of violent crimes in North Carolina.

Then I said, "Paul gives us his list of devastating statistics. But then, after setting up this dismal picture of 'God left us,' he moves to 'God came to us.'"

I illustrated with a story from the *Durham Morning Herald* about a black woman whose brother was shot and killed as he was going to cook a turkey for some poor people before Christmas. Along with the article was a heartwrenching picture of this woman lying prostrate on the sidewalk, screaming with grief.

The article reported her words: "It ain't supposed to be this way." The mother of this man and woman was also there, holding a Bible. Some friends were there as well, and they were quoted as saying, "We're going to find out who did this. We're going to kill him!"

But pointing to the Bible, the mother said, "No, this is my weapon."

I closed the sermon by saying, "I want you to listen to these two women and remember two things: first, it ain't supposed to be like this; we created this mess, and we can change it through Jesus. Second, the Bible is our weapon, not rockets or guns."

I wanted my listeners to walk out reacting, whether they said, "I found that terribly depressing," or "That seemed sort of simplistic. Does Willimon really believe the answer to the crime rate in Durham is Jesus—just accept Jesus and everything will be okay?"

After an exceptional movie or concert, people walk out and find themselves talking to complete strangers because both experienced something so powerful. I want that same thing to happen as a result of my preaching. I want people to react to the outrageous truths of the gospel. As Martin Luther said, "The sermon is the thunderbolt hurled from heaven to blast unrepentant sinners but more so righteous saints."

TURNING PREACHERS INTO PASTORS

Training our listeners to expect something more out of Sunday morning than consumption, however, assumes we understand the world in which they live. This requires our own training. To put it another way, we've got to become pastors if we want our people to become congregations.

I once visited a frail woman from my congregation at her place of employment. The two men she worked for were brothers, both loud and obnoxious. The office air was clouded with cigar smoke. I gasped for air as I walked into the office.

As I was talking to this woman at her desk, one of the brothers shouted from his office, "Where the hell is that report?"

"I don't know where that G—d—report is," shouted the other brother, sitting in his office across the hall. "You get the report."

"Peggy," one of them yelled, "find that damn report."

"I'm talking with my minister," she answered. "I'll get it for you in a couple of minutes."

"I don't care who you're talking to," one of them said. "Just get us the G—d—report!"

She turned to me and said, "This is what I live with eight hours a day, five days a week. I can already hear them yelling all the way down the hall as I arrive each morning." Several months after my visit, I still couldn't shake the memory of her working environment.

Pastoral visitation is great training for the preacher; it's sermon preparation. Many times, when I've struggled with a passage during the week, I've suddenly gotten an "Ah ha!" connection while listening to someone in his living room. It chastens my language and provides me a window into people's souls.

Our pastoral care will affect how we preach.

AN AUDIENCE BECOMES A CONGREGATION

A former student of mine was pastoring a small congregation. One Sunday, just before the pastoral prayer, he asked the congregation for prayer requests.

A woman named Mary stood up: "Joe left us this week, and he's gone for good. I don't know how the girls and I are going to survive. Please pray for us."

The pastor was stunned. How could anybody be so tacky as to lay such a request on people during worship? She's breaking the rules, he thought. We only pray publicly for gall bladder operations or hospitalized mothers-in-law. This is too messy.

"Well, honey," an older woman piped up, interrupting his thoughts, "I don't know that we have to pray for that. When my husband left me, the way I survived was through some of the people right here in this church. We can help you."

Flabbergasted, the minister listened in silence.

"But what am I going to do?" said Mary. "I've only got a high school diploma. I've never worked in my life."

"This is weird that this should happen now," said a man seated further back. "I'm looking for a new employee. I can't pay a lot for this position, but it would be enough to keep going.

No experience is really necessary, and we would train you for the job. Why don't you talk to me afterwards."

The pastor recovered enough to pray and then finished out the morning service.

The next Sunday, however, when the pastor stood up in the pulpit, he said, "Last Sunday when Mary requested prayer was a holy moment for us. Mary made us a church. I'm not sure we were a church before she laid that on us.

"I've often wondered if going to seminary and becoming a minister was worth it. I've questioned whether church was no more than a glorified Rotary Club or Women's Garden Club. I want to speak for all of us and say, 'Thank you, Mary,' and 'Thank you. God,' for making us a church."

My student friend was a touch too humble, because it was his preaching and pastoring—the age-old tasks of the minister—that nurtured virtues that sprang forth in that service. It's just one small example of what can happen in church: It really can become a congregation.

Chapter 39

PREACHING TO CHANGE THE HEART

Paul's example is bold, courageous proclamation

Alistair Begg

In Acts 24, Paul is being kept in a form of house arrest. He is imprisoned on the charge of being a troublemaker, a ringleader of a Nazarene sect. Felix, whose name means *happy*, the governor—you might want to call him Mr. Happy—having listened to Paul's defense, adjourns the proceedings awaiting the arrival of Lysias, the commander. While Paul waits for the inexorable slow, lumbering movement of justice, this encounter, involving Felix and his wife Drusilla, takes place (Acts 24:24–25).

We're not told what motivated Felix and Drusilla to send for Paul and to be prepared to listen to him. Conjecture allows us to imagine that life got a little dull, and perhaps they had the idea, *Well, maybe we could send for the character we've got under house arrest and see what he has to say. People have been saying all* *kinds of things about him, so why don't we see what he has to say for himself?*

PAUL'S AUDIENCE

You have two individuals who in all likelihood would never have attended one of Paul's public meetings. But here, in the providence of God, they are to be confronted with the message Paul brings.

These examples of power in the culture of their day, their background, and all the accoutrements of their lifestyle would be imposing to somebody who had gone through the heartache and beatings that represented Paul's life. He probably had difficulty in walking. He was able to take off his shirt and show the marks of all he experienced as a result of the ministry of the gospel. As they sit in the posture of strength, in comes the apostle Paul in the posture of apparent weakness.

Now how would you have felt going up the stairs? I wonder what would have been going through our minds? We would have thought, *Should I use this as an opportunity for "pre-evangelism"? Will I try and make friends, show them my nice side, tell them about a few dogs that got run over by a train, and let them know I'm a warm and comfortable character? I do have a hard edge, but I'll keep it concealed in the hope that at some later date I may have an opportunity for the cause of the gospel.*

Though I've made light of it, it would be a realistic strategy. It would be a legitimate response to say, *I don't want to take the whole wheelbarrow and dump it on them. Maybe I ought to play it carefully.* That would have been one possibility.

One other would have been, *Maybe God is creating an opportunity for me to negotiate my release. After all, I'm far more useful to God out of here than I am in here. I could certainly do more if I wasn't holed up waiting for the arrival of this character Lysias.* He could have thought in that way.

PAUL'S MOTIVATION AND METHOD

But it is clear that Paul was single-minded in his approach. We can learn from what actually happened about Paul's motivation. What was it that drove Paul? In 1 Corinthians 9 he tells the Corinthians it is his earnest endeavor to win as many as possible. "Though I am free and belong to no man, I make myself a slave of everyone to win as many as possible." He was zealous in the matter of evangelism. His life had been revolutionized by the power of Christ, and

now it was his business to set others on the same journey.

If Paul had been consumed with self-interest or with fear or if he had been keen simply to become friends of the rulers, then he would not have launched into the discourse that follows. No one in his right mind who is trying to make friends with these people would do what he did. We must conclude that something else drove him.

And it did. Paul's conviction was clear. In 2 Corinthians 5:11, he states it well. "Since, then, we know what it is to fear the Lord, we try to persuade men." In verse 14, "For Christ's love compels us, because we are convinced that one died for all." "From now on," in verse 16, "we regard no one from a worldly point of view."

There had to be tremendous temptation to regard Felix and Drusilla from a worldly point of view. The more prominent and powerful and able to alter our circumstances people appear to be, the greater the temptation to show them preferential interest. But what Paul writes in 2 Corinthians 5 he lives in Acts 24. His motivation is clear.

His methodology is equally clear. He discoursed; he reasoned. He did what came naturally to him. *I don't need to try and show off to these people. I don't need to impress them with my background. My significance is in the fact that I have been made a herald, an ambassador, a proclaimer of the gospel. So I am going to declare the message.*

PAUL'S MESSAGE

We also can find his message. He spoke with them about "faith in Christ Jesus." It's striking in its simplicity.

"I want to thank you for having me up, Mr.

Happy and your good wife. I'd like to take the opportunity to speak to you about one thing—about faith in Christ Jesus. I don't want to speak to you about the prevailing crisis in morality that is part of the outlying districts here. I don't want to speak to you about the dreadful things that are happening to children. I don't want to address with you the issues of governmental structures and the various possibilities of political reforms. I want to speak to you about faith in Christ Jesus."

Just in case we're tempted to think that this is some little sugarcoated sermonette to tickle the ears of Felix and make Drusilla feel good about herself, a kind of happy sermon for Mr. Happy, we are given the points, so we can be in no doubt as to the nature of his message.

Righteousness

Not exactly what you'd call a user-friendly point with which to begin. "I'd like to talk to you, Felix and Drusilla, about the fact that God is a holy God, and he has made clear the standards of his righteousness in his law, and that we are lawbreakers. We have sinned against his holiness."

Paul doubtless confirmed for them the standard of God's law, perhaps illustrated it from his own preconversion condition, perhaps looked into their eyes and quoted the psalmist and allowed the power of the Word to reverberate around the massive walls.

He would have preached the Old Testament Scriptures. The Lord is righteous. He loves righteous deeds, and the upright will behold his face.

Paul is not preaching moralism to them but preaching righteousness, so that in the piercing of their armor by the sword of God's law there may be the opportunity for him then to bring the balm of God's healing Word to them.

Self-control

His second point was about self-control. He may have quoted the proverb: "Like a city whose walls are broken down is a man who lacks self-control" (Prov. 25:28). He may have spoke a little about passion and desires, perhaps told them that the world's view of freedom was really a cage, that what is held out as happiness is essentially the embracing of sorrow.

Judgment

His third point was "the judgment to come." "Just in case you're wondering, the wicked are not going to stand. The Lord reigns forever. He has established his throne for judgment. There is coming a day when all of this will be judged. And while you think that I'm standing here in terror of a judgment that awaits me, I'm forced to tell you on the authority of the Lord Jesus, whose ambassador I am, there is a far greater judgment that awaits us all. And, Mr. and Mrs. Happy, it awaits you, too. Therefore, the issue of righteousness and of self-control and of the judgment to come is something to which you must pay most careful attention."

What a sermon.

DOES OUR PREACHING FOLLOW THIS EXAMPLE?

If this approach of righteousness and self-control and the coming judgment is any kind of paradigm of preaching with a view to a change of heart and mind, is this the approach of the church in the West? Is this the sort of thing we're doing?

In Motivation

Take, for example, the matter of motivation. Are some of us tempted to back off on the persuasive element because there is a distrust of persuasiveness? In our generation people fear persuasion. Anybody who is persuaded is regarded as sort of weird or over the top. You don't indoctrinate children. You leave them free to make up their own minds. We don't persuade because it isn't fashionable. Everyone has their ideas, their own space. Who are we to invade their space? Why don't we persuade? It's because we don't fear. "Knowing the fear of the Lord, we persuade men" (2 Cor. 5:11 NASB). There's no part two because there's no part one.

If Revelation 6:16–17 is firmly in my mind, I become persuasive. If I have that picture of my neighbors and friends and unsaved relatives in the day of God's wrath crying for the mountains and rocks to fall on them so they don't have to stand before the judgment, if that grips me and moves me to tears, then I may become persuasive. But until it does, you just got a guy behind a box speaking with empathy.

Our motivation is suspect.

In Methodology

Our methodology is also suspect. O that God would lay on our hearts again a renewed conviction for a methodology that is biblical.

You tell the people, "I know you're feeling lonely. I know you're losing direction and need a little joy. Here's a little joy. Here's a little friendship, and here's a little direction. Now let go of those big, bad sins." That's pragmatism, not theology. That isn't Ephesians 2, "dead in your trespasses and sins" and without any ability to make yourself alive. We have congregations that are smug and self-satisfied. If we don't show human beings their need of a Savior, they may respond to the gospel because they like what it may do for them, not because they have come to recognize they're dead and can't affect their own resurrection.

Preach the Word of God. It's not easy but it is straightforward. When was the last time we heard or preached this kind of sermon? Three points: righteousness, self-control, and the coming judgment.

In Prophetic Voice

We lack a prophetic voice. The church has politicized, psychologized, pragmatized, and trivialized. People may say, "That approach was okay for Paul. But these are different days. Mr. Happy and his wife could handle that. You wouldn't do that to twenty-first-century people."

Did you read any of the history? Felix was a twin. He and his brother were a bad lot. They were born as slaves. They crawled out of obscurity into the limelight. It was said they exercised the power of kings with the disposition of slaves, in savagery and lust. Felix had financial security, power, status, and a good-looking woman. However, he had stolen the woman from her husband.

And Paul says my first point, Mr. Happy, is righteousness. I want to talk to you about doing the right thing. I know you're an adulterer, but I want to talk to you about righteousness. And Drusilla's father killed James. Her great uncle killed John the Baptist. Her great grandfather murdered the babies in Bethlehem. And Paul spoke to her about self-control.

A real user-friendly sermon.

Chapter 40

PREACHING TRUTH, JUSTICE, AND THE AMERICAN WAY

On cultural myths and biblical authority

Rick McKinniss

I had acted innocently enough. Summer was approaching, and I was in need of fresh sermon ideas. So I prepared a bulletin insert asking for suggested texts or topics.

The first one in sizzled like a fuse on a Fourth of July firecracker: "Why don't you ever preach on patriotism? You need to preach on what our flag stands for!"

I felt torn: I didn't want to reject Fred's request out of hand or offend his national pride (he had served his country honorably in World War II), but I do not believe that truth, justice, and "the American way" are triune. I've always considered myself a loyal citizen, and I'm grateful for the liberties I enjoy, yet for me, national loyalties must bow before the Lordship of Christ. So I explained to Fred that I would be more comfortable preaching what the New Testament teaches concerning the duties of believers toward their nation. He understood my position even though his expectation for a patriotic celebration was not met.

The encounter with Fred ended happily enough, with both our relationship and my sense of integrity intact. But his request got me thinking about the larger question of the influence of cultural values on the Christian pulpit. I began to wonder about more subtle and often undetected influences of "the American way" on those of us who are called to preach The Way.

Charles Larson's book *Persuasion: Reflection and Responsibility* provided the tools I needed for thinking through this issue. I realized I wrestle with some cultural myths that are as American as baseball, hot dogs, apple pie, and Chevrolet. By calling them myths I do not mean they are necessarily false—or true. Rather, I mean they are so much a part of the way our culture interprets reality that we often fail to recognize them as anything but axiomatic. We grow up hearing them, breathing them, and thinking them. Though they have scant basis in biblical chapter and verse, I find they often creep unawares into my preaching.

Myth 1: The Possibility of Success

This is perhaps the most easily recognized American myth. It has fueled our country since the age of the earliest settlers. This myth was popularized in the nineteenth century by Horatio Alger, who used this story line as the basis for several novels that told of a young man who through hard work, sincerity, honesty, and faith in the future was able to make good. Sometimes he would make it big and own his own company, gain a beautiful wife, enjoy a good life, and even do good for others. This bootstrap mythology is embodied today in "the American dream."

Positive thinking and possibility thinking thrive as richly in our American soil as corn does in Iowa. And to a certain degree, the appeal of the positive preachers is due to the fact that we are uniquely prepared by our culture to receive these messages. This is not to suggest there is no biblical basis for preaching a positive message—countless verses speak hope, possibility, newness, and encouragement.

The dangers of canonizing Horatio Alger, however, are also apparent. Often "success" means only one thing to many people—health and wealth. Listeners hear that gospel of material success even when the preacher is encouraging them to new possibilities in the spiritual dimension.

Yet there is, I believe, an even subtler danger in employing this motif—a subliminal accusation of failure. I recall one sermon our pastor preached when I was a teenager. After dinner that Sunday I overheard my mother muttering as she washed the dishes.

"What's wrong?" I asked.

"I don't think the Lord is calling me to leave my family to be a missionary hero in Africa," she said, venting frustration. "I'm not likely to make a fortune in the near or distant future. But when I hear a sermon that describes all those heroic and successful people, I feel like a total failure. In what possible way can I do anything of consequence for God?"

The possibility of success had become for my mother the impossibility of significance. The heroes were too distant, the goals too high. She needed images of mothers and homemakers who gained ground for the kingdom in the kitchens where they lived.

The lesson of that episode with my mother has stayed with me, and every time I recruit Horatio Alger for the service of the gospel (which I do as often as any other red-blooded preacher), I try to picture my mother in my congregation. She and the rest of the congregation need to be encouraged to new possibilities but not driven to discouragement with impossibilities.

MYTH 2: THE WISDOM OF THE RUSTIC

One of the enduring legends of our culture is the clever rustic. No matter how sophisticated or devious the opposition, the simple wisdom of the common man or woman wins out. Backwoods figures like Daniel Boone and Paul Bunyan, who outwit their adversaries and overcome great obstacles with clever but simple common sense, fill our folklore. Abraham Lincoln rode this image from the county courthouses of Illinois to the White House in Washington, D.C. The power of this image continues even today. Ronald Reagan developed his reputation as "the great communicator" not only because of his acting experience but because of his uncanny ability to speak the language of the common people.

The flip side of this faith in folk wisdom and reliance on initial instincts is a tendency to distrust the educated or intellectual. The disciplines of scholarship are often seen merely as tools of obfuscation (translation: too much book-larnin' gits in the way of clear-headed thinkin').

Those of us who believe in the simple gospel often find within us an accompanying desire to make simplistic the Bible's subtleties and to codify all the complexities of modern existence. In the small-town church in southern Ohio where I was raised, this was regular Sunday fare. We heard the ABCs of the gospel. We heard the four principles for successful marriage. We mapped the approaching finale of world history with a chart. We were taught to be suspicious of psychiatrists, psychologists, sociologists, anthropologists, and any other "ists" we might encounter.

Several crises of confidence later, I have learned that not all of life is simple, easy, or clear. And when the clear-cut answers I was given did not match the complexities of my own life and the lives of those I was called to serve, I felt a bit betrayed. I began to understand why so many have thrown over the faith when life gets rocky.

Fortunately, I have not done so. Nor have I lost my appreciation for the rustic wisdom with which I was raised. Common sense and intuition often serve quite well. But I have found that God also uses diligent study, solid research, and educated reasoning.

Just as it is our task to explain the difficult, at times our task is also to portray life as complex. Not all wisdom arises from the rustic's simplicity. When the congregation is led to seek wisdom from the learned as well as from the common, when the biblical message is proclaimed in all its mysterious fullness, our people are better equipped to face the world as it really is.

MYTH 3: THE PRESENCE OF CONSPIRACY

Another widespread cultural premise is the presence of conspiracy: a belief that behind most major political, economic, or social problems is a powerful group that has conspired to create them. American history is filled with suspicions of Masonic conspiracies, Populist conspiracies, and international banking conspiracies. In my own lifetime I have heard conspiracy theories connecting John F. Kennedy and the Vatican. The validity of any of these theories is not my point here. I'm only illustrating our tendency to spread such explanations for certain trends and events.

Usually such explanations attract persons or groups who feel threatened. Conspiracy theories

inevitably involve the infamous "they." Usually "they" have labels—right-wingers or left-wingers or humanists or media-types. Labels tend to confirm sinister suspicions and motivate us by our fears. "They" often find their way into our sermons, but only once have I even met one of "them." He is a member of my congregation, a health teacher at the local middle school.

Before I came to the church, Mike was attacked from various local pulpits as one of "those" who taught "values-less" sex education. I discovered that Mike, a committed and sensitive Christian, was trying to walk the tightrope between his Christian values and the realities of public education. In working with those eighth-graders, he was careful to emphasize the church and home as key influences in decision making. But because he was "one of them," more than one local pastor excoriated him from the pulpit, and Mike was besieged with phone calls, letters, and visits from irate parents.

Now, whenever I hear conspiracies preached, I cannot help but think of a disillusioned Mike, harassed and harangued by professing brothers and sisters who were more willing to believe in a conspiracy than in a brother's good intentions for their children.

We are called to proclaim Christ, but by necessity we do so in the context of our cultural assumptions. Since cultural premises are part of the way we think, they can be powerful persuasive tools. Our job is to employ them with an eye toward discernment and fairness—without compromise.

It is not simply a matter of preaching truth, justice, or the American way. Nor of preaching truth, justice, and the American way. But rather it is a matter of preaching in an American way without doing injustice to The Way of Truth.

Chapter 41

PREACHING MORALITY IN AN AMORAL AGE

How can you blow the whistle when people don't believe there are rules?

Timothy Keller

I was in the midst of a series on the Seven Deadly Sins, and today it was time to talk about Lust. This is a difficult subject for any pastor, but preaching in my milieu, the middle of Manhattan, to a group composed roughly equally of non-Christians, new Christians, and renewing Christians poses an even greater problem.

Although we meet in a large auditorium, certain faces were easy to pick out. There was Phoebe, whose red-rimmed eyes still bore testimony to her week of crying. Her boyfriend had broken up with her when he discovered she had been sleeping with another man and another woman, in a *ménage à trois*. She told me, "But what we have is so beautiful. How can it be wrong?"

Laurel's face was a complete contrast—a new Christian, she was eager as a puppy dog. This week she and her husband had brought her former lesbian lover and the woman's current partner to church, promising, "It's really different—you'll see!"

Further back was Fred. He had been brought up attending church and Christian schools, but he moved to New York to get away from family and friends. "I couldn't breathe with all their rules and expectations about how I should live, whom I should date, whether I could go to an R-rated movie. I had to get away somewhere where no one knew me and I could live however I wanted." Fred's freedom hadn't turned out as well as he had hoped, however, and now he was depressed and angry.

They had all been in my office that week, and now their eyes were turned expectantly toward me. What could I say that would be helpful, compassionate, and, above all, faithful to the Word of God?

UNDERSTANDING OUR AMORAL AGE

The contemporary preacher of orthodox Christianity faces an unprecedented dilemma. Despite what you would think from a casual perusal of any video store, bookstore, or magazine rack, we do not live in an immoral society—one in which right and wrong are clearly understood and wrong behavior is chosen. We live in an amoral society—one in which "right" and "wrong" are categories with no universal meaning, and everyone "does what is right in his or her own eyes."

Whether things are worse today than in other periods from an objective point of view—more sins committed, more laws broken—is debatable. But an amoral age presents a problem for preachers who want to expound faithfully God's Word on ethics, morality, and behavior.

In the early twentieth century, skeptics rejected Christianity because it wasn't true—"miracles cannot be." Today, skeptics reject Christianity because it even claims to be true—"absolutes cannot be." Modernity (the mindset of the late nineteenth and early twentieth centuries) said that moral absolutes could be discovered only by human reason and research. Postmodernity now says there are no moral absolutes to discover.

How did we get to this? In the 1950s and 1960s, the existentialism of Camus and Sartre began to collapse confidence in human reason and progress by teaching that truth and morality were completely relative and individually constructed. Today's postmodernity (also led by French thinkers, such as Derrida and Foucault) teaches that truth and morality are socially constructed by groups. In short: "No set of cultural beliefs can claim logical superiority over another set because all such beliefs are motivated by subjective interests."

In this view, all "truths" and "facts" are now in quotation marks. Claims of objective truth are really just a cover-up for a power play. Those who claim to have a story true for all are really just trying to get power for their group over other groups.

In the past, Christian moral absolutes were seen as simply narrow or old-fashioned. But today they are seen as oppressive and even violent.

In America this amoral society is only now arriving in its fullness. Baby boomers were supposedly the first relativistic generation, but most boomers were raised in traditional religion. The next generation is making the sea change. Their understanding is the new hard relativism of identity politics.

In such a new and confusing situation, what is a Christian preacher to say?

TRUTH, NOT PRAGMATISM

I have found we must guide our preaching between two dangers—pragmatism and

moralism—if the radical and fresh Christian message is to be understandable to today's hearers.

The first danger is pragmatism.

I think of Joseph, one of our first and most enthusiastic new converts. Joe announced his new allegiance to Christ to his employees and decreed that henceforth the company's business practices would conform to Christian morality. At a Madison Avenue advertising agency, this was a courageous and potentially suicidal choice. No more lying to clients or the public, no billing of hours not actually worked, no shirking responsibility or blame-shifting for failure—it was a recipe for disaster.

To Joe's delight (and the surprise of us watching this experiment in obedience), his business prospered. Clients who were ready to drop the firm for bigger agencies were delighted with the straight talk they got. One angry client, who had been ready to sue, was so flabbergasted by Joe's honest confession of failure that he reversed his decision and gave him two new accounts. Revenues hit and then passed the one-million-dollar mark. Joe began bringing employees to church, telling them, "You know it's true, because it works."

But when romance with a married woman became a possibility, Joe abandoned his profession of faith. "I know I'm doing something you think is wrong," he said, "but I want to be happy, and that's that. Love is more important than your version of morality."

Joe's early embracing of Christianity shows why pragmatism can tempt a preacher. It reaps quick returns. People are delighted by the practical help they're getting for saving their marriages, raising their children, overcoming bad habits, and fighting off midlife depression. They come back and bring their friends. But without the painstaking work of establishing a changed worldview, their commitment to Christianity will be only as deep as their commitment to any other helpful "product." Allegiance to something that makes their lives easier to manage should not be confused with genuine conversion, which has at its heart surrender to the Creator-God of the universe.

So we must be careful. We can say that morality "works" but only because it corresponds to reality. And we must preach that sometimes Christian morality "works" only in the long run. Looking at life from eternity, it will be obvious that it works to be honest, unselfish, chaste, and humble. But in the short run, practicing chastity may keep a person alone for many years. Practicing honesty may be an impediment to career advancement. This must be made clear to the contemporary listener.

Today's preacher must argue against the self-serving pragmatism of postmodernity. The gospel does say that through it you find your life, but that first you must lose your life. I must say to people, "Christ will 'work' for you only if you are true to him whether he works for you or not. You must not come to him because he is fulfilling (though he is) but because he is true. If you seek to meet him in order to get your needs met, you will not meet him or get your needs met. To become a Christian is not to get help for your agenda but to take on a whole new agenda—the will of God. You must obey him because you owe him your life, because he is your Creator and Redeemer."

This is a critical and difficult balance for the Christian preacher. Every message and point must demonstrate relevance or the listener will mentally "channel surf." But once you have drawn in people with the amazing relevance and practical wisdom of the gospel, you must confront them with the most pragmatic issue of all—the claim of Christ to be absolute Lord of life.

Earlier in my ministry, I often preached about sexual issues with baptized pragmatism. In a sermon fifteen or twenty years ago, I declared, "Emotionally, premarital and extramarital sex destroy your ability to trust and commit to others. Socially, sex outside of marriage leads to family and social breakdown. 'Do not be deceived; God is not mocked. A man reaps what he sows.'"

Nothing about this paragraph is untrue. But it overemphasizes the practical benefits of Christian morality. (It also assumes a respect for Scripture not present in our culture now.) Today, I approach the same theme differently:

"Some people say, 'I reject Christianity because its views on sex don't fit me—they are too narrow for me.' But if a doctor prescribes an unpleasant medicine, what do you do? If you are truly sick, then you take it. It is just as wrongheaded to taste-test Christianity as to taste-test medicines. How silly to evaluate Christianity on its sex ethic!

"The real question is, 'Is Jesus really the Son of God?' Is he really who he said he is—your Way, Truth, and Life? Has he really died for you because you are a sinner? If he is and has, who cares what he asks you to do or not to do? You should do it! In a sense, the gospel does not let you talk about anything else first. It says, 'I won't talk to you about sexuality or gender roles or suffering or anything else until you determine what you will do with him. Who he is determines everything else.'

"You see, until you decide if there is a God, if Jesus is the Son, and other matters, how can you make an intelligent decision about what is right and wrong about sex? Christians believe what they do about sex not because they are old-fashioned, or because they are prudish, but because Jesus is the Way, the Truth, and the Life."

This newer approach takes longer. But it comes closer to my goal to preach truth instead of pragmatism. Christian morality is not true because it works; it works because it's true. But why emphasize truth-as-truth to people who don't believe in standards at all?

First, we do it to be clear. If we argue too pragmatically, we unwittingly confirm the basic postmodern person's view that truth is whatever works; they won't see how radically you are challenging their thinking and life approach. Second, we do it to be penetrating, to get to people's deepest heart. Pascal said, "We have an idea of truth which no amount of skepticism can overcome." What is that? In postmodern people, the knowledge of God sleeps deeper than in previous generations, but it is still there (Rom. 1:18–21).

In *Duke Law Journal*, Arthur Leff, a contemporary nonbeliever, put the postmodern tension perfectly: "What we want, heaven help us, is simultaneously to be perfectly ruled and perfectly free." Only by preaching truth as truth will we throw this inner tension into relief and show that there is a truth that liberates.

GRACE, NOT MORALISM

Deep weariness etched every line of Joan's face and body. "I just can't do it anymore," she said. "I can't live up to what a Christian is supposed to be. All my life I've had people telling me I had to be this or do that in order to be accepted. I thought Christ was supposed to bring me freedom from that, but instead God turns out to be just one more demanding taskmaster—in fact, he's the worst of them all!"

That conversation underscored for me that Christian moral teaching is both similar to, and very different from, that of other moral and ethical systems.

At the end of *The Abolition of Man*, C. S. Lewis demonstrates how the major religions agree on certain moral absolutes. Christians find that in today's culture wars, they often are on the same side with believing Jews, Muslims, and Hindus. The Christian preacher seems to be saying, "Be moral," along with exponents of other philosophies.

But when we ask, "Why be moral?" the other systems say, "In order to find God," while Christianity says, "Because God has found you." The Christian gospel is that we are not saved by moral living, we are saved for it. We are saved by grace alone, but that grace will inevitably issue in a moral life.

Many sermons tell people to say no to immorality. Often the reasons are "it is against the Bible" or "it will hurt your self-esteem" or "it's against our Christian principles," or "your sins will find you out." Those things are true, but they are inadequate and secondary motives. Only the grace of God, Titus says, "teaches" us to say no. It argues with us: "You are not living as though you are loved! As his child! It is not because he will abandon you that you should be holy, but because at inestimable cost he has said he won't ever abandon you! How can you live in the very sin that he was ripped to pieces to deliver you from?"

See the grace of God argument? It is the only argument that cannot be answered.

Earlier in my ministry, I did not rely on it as I could have. When I preached on 1 Corinthians 6:9, I argued, "Sex is a sacred gift of God, and misusing it or tampering with it puts you in the gravest spiritual danger.... Though today many seek to blur these moral lines, the

Bible is most definite and crystal clear about the matters before us."

This statement is true, but sounds implausible in a sexually permissive age. This kind of appeal doesn't explain the why behind every biblical command—the gospel.

Today, I approach it this way: "When Paul lays down the biblical rules for marriage, he says, 'This is all really about Christ's love for us' (Eph. 5:32). In 1 Corinthians 6, Paul hints that the monstrosity of extramarital sex lies in that we become 'one' physically with someone, but we are not 'one' socially, economically, or legally with them. In other words, we have gotten sexual intimacy without becoming radically vulnerable to the other person by making a permanent, exclusive, total commitment.

"When it comes to sex, 'this is a great mystery, but we are talking of Christ and the church.' You must not 'use' God by seeking his intimacy without making a total commitment. You must not use another human being by doing the same thing. Why? Because of his grace, his radical self-giving to you. 'Love one another even as I have loved you.'"

Instead of obeying to make God indebted to them, Christians obey because they are indebted to him. The difference between these two ways of morality could not be greater. I want to preach that Christian morality is a response to grace, not a means to grace.

But why emphasize grace to people who don't believe in guilt?

Postmodern people rightly fear an authority that oppresses and crushes; they long for one that frees. Only the gospel of grace shows how the truth can become a liberating power. Pascal said that every human philosophy or religion will lead either to human pride or to human despair, but only the gospel of grace can deal with both. Some religions use self-esteem and independence as motives for obedience, but that makes people proud and selfish, or proud and cruel.

Other religions use humility and control, but that leads to guilt and despair. Yet the gospel shows us a law that must be fulfilled (destroying our pride) and a Savior that fulfills it completely for us (destroying our despair).

"The Christian religion alone has been able to cure these twin vices," wrote Pascal, "not by using one to expel the other . . . but by expelling both through the simplicity of the Gospel." Preaching morality cannot be the first item on the agenda for any Christian preacher, but it cannot be shirked, either. We have to make the necessary assaults on the underlying anti-absolute presuppositions of our postmodern audience. Men and women need to be convinced that there is a God who has spoken in nonnegotiable absolutes; this God is also our Redeemer. He has paid the price of our failure. Only in this context does the preaching of morality make sense. Today, only in this context can it be heard at all.

Chapter 42

CROSS-CULTURAL PREACHING

How to connect in our multicultural world

Rick Richardson

All of us who preach are involved in cross-cultural communication. We preach to youth shaped by postmodern culture. We cross the bridge to preach to Asian Americans, Latinos, African Americans, Native Americans, whites, and internationals. We speak across gender lines—man to women, or woman to men. The diversity may be so slight that we haven't noticed it before, but it is real. We may also have opportunities to go on short-term missions projects where we will preach cross-culturally. Cross-cultural skills and attitudes are becoming more and more crucial for preaching. Here are seven principles that have helped me to preach to people of different cultures.

HONOR WHAT THEY HONOR

Do they honor time or event? If they care about punctuality, be on time. If they are laid back about the clock, relax. The occasion is what matters, not the time it starts or how long it lasts.

Are they relational or task-oriented? For some cultures the process is at least as important as the agenda. In another, the objective rules. African-American culture is relational, expressive, and event-oriented, and it ascribes honor. So hang out and express your feelings about things.

Do they ascribe honor because of title and prestige, or is honor achieved by accomplishment and experience? Youth don't care about titles, so credibility is built by sharing your experiences with them. African-American culture reveres the pastor and respects titles. That means that when you begin to speak, if you are a guest, you should thank and honor their pastor and leaders. Recognize that as a preacher you will be honored by virtue of your position before you ever say a word.

What do they consider sacred? Something you normally regard as incidental or trivial could be of extreme importance. You might not even be aware that you are being rude. Asian-American culture is honor- and shame-oriented, and honoring elders is crucial. For example, in a sermon I might tell how I've learned a valuable life lesson from my grandparents.

What behavior or dress might offend them? Dress up to speak in a casual culture, and you create a barrier. Dress down, and in many African-American contexts, people will spend 90 percent of the time thinking about why you look the way you do.

How do they feel about women in ministry? This is pertinent whether or not you are a woman. Don't assume they share your convictions.

USE THEIR HEART LANGUAGE WHENEVER YOU CAN, BUT DO SO WITH AUTHENTICITY

The heart language of Native Americans is the language of spiritual experience and of

171

harmony in relationships and nature. Hispanic culture is family-oriented. Talking about your background, your family, and your children speaks to their hearts. "Heart" is communicated in the language itself. I don't know much Spanish, but I use what I can when visiting my friend Pedro Aviles's church.

When I speak to youth, I try to use a little slang and refer to a hip-hop artist, even though I am not fluent in that culture. Music is the heart language of young people today. Referencing that music shows that you are trying to understand their world. A quote from Eminem or 50 Cent can go a long way, especially if you admit your limitations. Genuineness matters most. I might say, "I'm not the world's most knowledgeable fan of hip-hop, but these lines grabbed my attention. . . ." People can smell it when you try to speak their language and it is inauthentic, but they appreciate even a faltering effort to build the bridge.

COMMUNICATE YOUR AWARENESS OF THE TRUST ISSUES BETWEEN YOUR CULTURES

Jimmy McGee, an African-American leader with InterVarsity, told me this detail about America's history of oppression. For three hundred years, Africans were brought over on slave ships through what was called the Middle Passage. Millions died on the way, their bodies thrown overboard, and sharks began following the ships. To this day, sharks travel the Middle Passage, because that was their feeding route for so many years. Christians were involved in rationalizing and manipulating Scripture to support the horrors of slavery. As a white person, when I preach in a black context, the baggage from all that evil lingers. I have to show I am aware of that or I cannot be trusted.

Native Americans experienced genocide at the hands of whites. As a result, only 6 percent of contemporary Native Americans are Christian. The trust issues are immense, and only people willing to recognize the evils of the past can even be heard.

Postmoderns mistrust anyone who believes they know the truth and that everyone else is wrong. This makes preaching to postmoderns a cross-cultural experience.

Recently at Einstein Bagels, which I frequent, a clerk asked me, "Rick, you're not one of those people who believe Jesus is the only way, are you?" The way he said it, I knew that he viewed those who proclaim Jesus as the only way on the level of the 9/11 terrorists. So I said, "Sam, it sounds like you've been hurt by people who excluded you and dismissed you for what you believed." He said, "You're right!" And I said, "I'm sorry that happened to you. I hate it when people exclude and dismiss me because of what I believe. That's why it was so surprising for me when I was drawn to some of the unique elements of Christianity."

Similarly, in a sermon, I acknowledge where the bridge is broken before I try to cross it. I identify with people's fears. I talk about how uncomfortable I am with people who reject others. Then I talk about the hope and love that Christ gives.

BECOME A GREAT STORY TELLER AND A NARRATIVE THEOLOGIAN

Propositions may not translate between cultures, but stories about life, family, and struggles almost always do. Narratives make us feel we can relate to each other. Through storytelling we share pain, apply truth, and build trust. We must become fluent in the universal language of story if we want to preach cross-culturally.

Start with stories of experiences with people from the host culture. Share stories of your attempts to learn their culture as well as stories that recognize the trust issues.

Turn your principles and statements of propositional ideas into illustrations and stories. Tell the stories Jesus told. When you can, choose narrative passages from the Scriptures.

Close with stories that challenge people to appropriate the truths you are communicating.

Do What You Came to Do

After building trust and rapport, don't hold back. Fulfill your calling and speak the truth. The fact that you are from a different culture often gives you tremendous opportunity to challenge people in extraordinary ways. Build the bridge and then *walk across it!* Billy Graham is great at building trust, but he also knows why he's there and what he came to say, and he always says it.

Since you have identified and built trust, you can now give the gift of your cultural practices and the insights you bring. If your culture does altar calls, do them. If your culture challenges people to reflection and thought, do that. People will likely recognize the style of your culture and affirm it.

Avoid Judging Their Response by Your Own Cultural Cues

A group may be with you and not show it in the ways you recognize. When I preach to Asian Presbyterians, who tend to be respectful and quiet, I sometimes wonder if anything I said connected. I need to listen carefully to comments afterward and look for affirmation that goes beyond courtesy to know what happened. When I speak in African-American contexts, I have to be ready to amp it up when they respond. There is a call-and-response that is part of the rhythm of the culture. It's fun, and I must learn to work with it and not ignore it.

What's more, cultural tendencies are only cultural tendencies. We will always find people who don't fit those tendencies at all. We can't make assumptions about individuals based on broader cultural characteristics.

Be a Curious Lifelong Learner and Observer, and Cultivate Cultural "Informants"

My friend Brenda Salter McNeil is a world-class cross-cultural preacher and has shared her expertise with me generously. When she preaches in black contexts, she honors every single person who had anything to do with bringing her there or who is an important leader for that community. Brenda helped me understand that dynamic and respond appropriately.

Find women to help you understand whether you are connecting with women. Find informants among youth who can help you know if you are connecting with youth.

Be immensely curious about other people groups. If you want to preach cross-culturally, you are committing to a long-term adventure that will humble and enrich you. Go for it!

Chapter 43

CONNECTING WITH POSTMODERNS
What to adopt, what to adapt, what to oppose in postmodernism

Robertson McQuilkin

How do we communicate the ancient truth to generations who have been immersed in postmodern thinking from infancy? I believe there are elements of postmodernism we should adopt, elements we should adapt, and elements we are duty bound to oppose.

POSTMODERN ELEMENTS TO ADOPT

The spiritual trumps the material. Of course, we have to help define spiritual, but isn't it great we can champion the prevailing view that the unseen is the important part of our lives? From there it may not be so difficult to move on to the idea that the unseen is what is eternal.

Authenticity is a paramount virtue. We can't get any closer to dead-center biblical truth than that. Of course, the postmodern "authentic" and ours may differ, so we need to help define authenticity in biblical terms. But if we come across as authoritarian, that's perceived as arrogant and the ultimate in nonauthenticity. Our presentation of truth must be humble—the presentation of ourselves in a vulnerable way. Sometimes, with the postmodern, how we stand for the truth may in the end prove as influential as the truth itself.

Reality must be experienced. My experience doesn't alter reality, and there is objective reality that can be known. But when we offer vibrant, experiential salvation and sanctification, we're on solid biblical ground.

I was disciplined in this approach through immersion as a missionary in the Japanese culture. The original "postmoderns," the Japanese were not impressed with logic or evidence when it came to religion. "I believe what you say," was a common response, "but what has that got to do with me?" They weren't interested in propositional truth—which we missionaries incessantly hammered away on—but rather, "What does it do for me?" I was delighted to discover that the Bible is full of exactly what they were interested in: personal experience.

It's hard for me as a thoroughgoing modern to break free from my rational truth-proving long enough to connect with the postmodern in search of life-changing personal experience. But my goal is not proving to be right but rather rescuing my friend, so I've determined to keep in mind that in persuasion, relevance is determined by the receiver, not by the sender. We must not compromise the truth but rather emphasize, especially till the connection is made, the biblical truth that is of concern to our audience. So, yes, reality must be experienced.

How I feel is more important than what I think. We do a grave disservice to this generation if we don't speak to the heart and stimulate feelings, godly feelings. Postmodernism has recaptured the heart and opened us to our emotions. For that we must be grateful, for it leads toward greater biblical reality than what we knew as Enlightenment moderns. It's hard for me to lead with the heart when I've spent a lifetime honing my skills to lead with my head, but I'd better recapture the biblical heart of the matter if I'm to connect with the postmodern.

Relationships are paramount. They want to be connected, as they say. Community trumps our old modernistic individualism. That's biblical enough, but it goes deeper.

You might call it intimacy. We're solidly in biblical territory on this one. In fact, a person's ultimate destiny is to love God and be loved of him forever. And surely horizontal relations are what humanity is all about.

Hope is in short supply. But it is desperately wanted. So we offer hope. Life does have meaning. But we must not offer megahope too soon. Better to offer modest hope, at least to begin with. For example, I could say, "You may not be able to change the course of the history of the world, but you can be instrumental in changing the personal history for some from death to life." Younger generations need that assurance.

POSTMODERN ELEMENTS TO ADAPT

Beware of anti-intellectual sentiment. God is after renewing our minds, and so transformational preaching certainly can't bypass the mind. But we can use the contemporary anti-intellectual mood to dethrone scientific naturalism and a materialistic mindset.

Tell me a story. That has a familiar ring to it. Sounds like the Bible! The Bible is full of propositional truth, of course, and the faithful preacher will proclaim it. But we can capture one element of this mood since narrative, not propositional truth, is the preferred mode of Scripture. Contemporary culture is image-driven. That means visual over verbal, to be sure, but verbal can be visual, too, in metaphor and story. Jesus did both—first he made the invisible world seeable and touchable, but he did more. When it came to talk, he told stories.

I've found that postmoderns respond with excitement when I tell them the story of the Holy Spirit. Jesus' story they know, but the Spirit's story? He's a doctrine at best, right? But when I recast the theological propositions into the form of a story, I've been startled to see the response.

Celebrate diversity. If the only reality postmoderns admit is a combination of what's out there with their perception of it, everyone's "reality" differs. And that's cool. Since everyone's reality differs, embrace it. The only sin is intolerance.

I can attack this head-on—and lose my audience. Or I can celebrate unity in diversity among God's people. I can also teach our solidarity with God's creation while flashing the caution light of biblical limitations to the concept. If I champion unity in diversity, it won't be quite so easy to dismiss me as a hard-nosed, right-wing obscurantist.

Personal fulfillment is the goal of life. No, no. God's fulfillment is the goal. But when we chart the way to God-centered living, we do no wrong in pointing out that the only way to get really filled up is to concentrate on filling others. We can promise true fulfillment to anyone who will stop trying to fill up on fun, stuff, or recognition—an impossibility anyway—and center on bringing joy to God.

Personal freedom is essential to finding fulfillment. Why aren't Christians the chief champions of freedom? Of course, our "freedom" may have a different ring to it—we point toward freedom as power to be what God created me uniquely to be rather than a self-destructive bondage to doing anything I please.

Authority is suspect. Well, postmoderns are right—a lot of it is. So we can stand with them in opposing illegitimate authority or working to purify authority run amok. We must never flinch, however, in advocacy of God's ultimate authority as well as God-ordained human authority. But let's not be caught defending the indefensible or putting institutions (which the postmodern has little use for) ahead of people and "authentic" human relations.

POSTMODERN ELEMENTS TO OPPOSE

Absolute relativism. Not only must we point out the absurdity of this ultimate oxymoron, we must show graphically how it is not a liberating concept, as postmoderns suppose, but how it leads inexorably to dreadful bondage.

Self-sacrifice is bad. It's dishonest, a betrayal of self, destructive, it is said. The God-story of Jesus on the cross is our ultimate weapon to destroy this perversion of the enemy. We must press the theme of love and the joyful fruit of sacrificial love. We must demonstrate how self-orientation is in the end destructive and how self-denial is the affirmation of our true self, the ultimate healing power.

Commitment is stupid. We should find it easy to picture from marriage stories the end results of noncommitment versus commitment. And we can illustrate from all of life how commitment is the glue that holds together that ultimate desire of the X-er and Millennial—relationships, bonding. With one's fellows, yes, but above all with God. You might even persuade them to hope for an ultimate love relationship.

Even for these elements I call us to oppose, however, there is a countervailing mood among postmoderns. There seems to be a yearning for something that seems no more than a fantasy—permanent, self-giving love.

In studying the culture of postmoderns I have felt an exhilarating sense of déjà vu. When we moved to Japan, we were delighted to open a treasure trove of thought and behavior totally foreign to our own. But as we set ourselves to discover elements of that culture to adopt, others to adapt to biblical use, and a few to expose as harmful error, we were overwhelmed to find we could connect at the deepest levels, foreign though we were. I'm determined to do it again with another culture alien to me, postmodernism, a culture that seems to have all but captured our western world.

Chapter 44

PREACHING AMID PLURALISM

Elevating Christ in a culture that sees all religions as equal

Timothy Keller

A Muslim cleric and I were on a discussion panel a few years ago, describing the essence of our two religions to college students. The Muslim explained there is no god but God, and that asserting Christ's divinity is blasphemous. I explained that Jesus Christ's claim to be the unique God is the core of Christianity. But then a student stood and responded, "I don't see any difference between the two."

The cleric and I explained the differences again, but we could not convince the young man that if one of us was right, the other must be wrong. Religious pluralism had taught the student he must never claim that one religion is superior to any other. Such claims are to be categorized quickly as intolerant and exclusionary.

Maintaining my ministry to people of a pluralistic culture requires me to preach in a way that neither forsakes the truth of Christianity nor needlessly alienates those raised to assume a plurality of religions.

ONE OF A KIND

I don't directly make the naked claim that "Christianity is a superior religion," and I certainly don't malign other faiths. Instead, I stress Christianity's distinctiveness.

For example, after the World Trade Center tragedy, between 600 and 800 new people began attending the church I pastor in New York City. The sudden influx of people pressed the question, "What does your God have to offer me at a time like this?"

I preached, "Christianity is the only faith that tells you that God lost a child in an act of violent injustice. Christianity is the only religion that tells you, therefore, God suffered as you have suffered." That's worded carefully as a way of saying, "Other religions tell you many good things, too. But Christianity is the only one that tells you this. If you deny this, then you lose a valuable spiritual resource."

Pluralists get stumped by that because they realize that they want the distinctives of Christianity—a God who has known human pain, salvation by grace, and the hope of heaven—in their times of need. But when I consistently say, "Only Christianity tells you this," their defenses begin to rise. How dare you say your religion is superior to any other?

That's why on occasion I address directly the weakness of pluralism's foundations.

PREACHING THE WHOLE ELEPHANT

About every other week, I confront popular pluralist notions, not with an entire sermon but with a point here and there.

For example, pluralists contend that no one religion can know the fullness of spiritual truth, therefore all religions are valid. But while it is good to acknowledge our limitations, this statement is itself a strong assertion about the nature of spiritual truth. A common analogy is cited—the blind men trying to describe an elephant. One feels the tail and reports that an elephant is thin and flexible. Another feels a leg and claims the animal is thick as a tree. Another touches its side and reports the elephant is like a wall. This is supposed to represent how the various religions only understand part of God while no one can truly see the whole picture. To claim full knowledge of God, pluralists contend, is arrogance.

I occasionally tell this parable, and I can almost see the people nodding their heads in agreement. But then I remind them, "The only way this parable makes any sense, however, is if you've seen a whole elephant. Therefore, the minute you say, 'All religions only see part of the truth,' you are claiming the very knowledge you say no one else has. And you are demonstrating the same spiritual arrogance you accuse Christians of."

ONLY BEING GOOD IS BAD

The young man at the college discussion insisted there was no difference between Christianity and Islam because, he said, "You both say we should just try to obey God and live a good life." Christian preaching too often gives pluralists reason to see it that way.

In the book *Nature of True Virtue* Jonathan Edwards demonstrates that most moral people are complying to ethical standards mainly out of self-interest, pride, and fear. He called this "common morality" and contrasted it with "true virtue," which flows from a life transformed by experiencing God's grace. Edwards discerned a loving and joyful heart that acted not out of superiority of fear of consequences, but out of delight in God for the beauty of who he is in himself.

There is a kind of preaching that exhorts people to moral behavior without rooting its motivation in the joy of God's beauty or Christ's grace. When that is the case, the pluralist sees no distinction between Christianity and other religions. My preaching, therefore, aims for the type of transformation that even a pluralist can't deny.

This shift has changed the content of my sermons. If I had preached on lying ten years ago, I might have said, "Don't lie. Tell the truth because Jesus is truth. And if you have lied, Jesus will forgive you." That appeal stops at changing external behavior.

Today I might preach: "Let me tell you why you're not going to be a truthful person. I lie most often to avoid others' disapproval. If I just try to stop lying, it won't work because my need for others' approval overwhelms my good intentions. I allow other people, instead of Jesus, to determine my worth. If you want to stop lying, you have to find what is motivating your sin—like my tendency to look to others for affirmation—and replace it with the security you can find in Jesus."

The goal is not reformation, but transformation.

FALL OF THE EMPIRE

After September 11, I reread Augustine's *The City of God*. Rome in Augustine's time was facing something similar to what New York faces. The city had been sacked. It didn't really fall; it had just been violated. It's as if the barbarians attacked to say, "See what we can do?" All of Rome, even the Christians, felt that if the barbarians could do that, there would be nowhere safe.

Augustine's point was that people were confusing Rome with the City of God. They were seeking their security from the wrong place. While pagan Romans might run and hide, Christians should be different. As citizens of the City of God, there are no weapons or bombs that can threaten a Christian's home. For Christians it was illogical, even wrong, to flee Rome when there were so many needs to be met and no threat to a Christian's true security.

So I preached five messages on what it means to be a Christian in New York. There are perfectly good excuses for unbelievers to flee this city. But Christians have every reason to stay. That's a distinction anyone can see.

Christianity is indeed distinct from other religions. May God grant us wisdom in knowing how to communicate this to a pluralistic world.

Chapter 45

CONNECTING WITH NON-CHRISTIANS

How to analyze an audience when preparing for evangelistic preaching

John Koessler

Most evangelistic sermons I hear take some form of the four spiritual laws (from Campus Crusade), combine them with a few proof texts, sprinkle in an illustration or two, and then cap it all off with the "sinner's prayer." The sermon's theology is sound, but the sermon takes the same form regardless of the audience. The sermon feels like a suit off the rack. It doesn't take into account the audience's unique size and shape.

To some extent, this is understandable. The fundamental content of the gospel never changes, no matter who the audience is. The life situations and presuppositions of our listeners, by contrast, vary widely and should affect the shape of the sermon. Formulating a series of true propositions and lobbing them in the direction of the audience does not mean we have preached effectively. Genuine communication involves what is heard as much as what is said.

This means if we hope to be understood by our listeners, we must analyze the audience as carefully as we analyze the text. This analysis commonly focuses on the demographics of the audience, their specific life situations, and the occasion of the sermon. Does the audience cluster in a particular age, gender, or economic range? Are they single, married, divorced? Have they come because they are spiritual seekers, or is it a special occasion? Have they come voluntarily or were they "forced" to come?

TOOLS FOR BUILDING BRIDGES

The goal in audience analysis is to identify the experiences, problems, and questions shared by our listeners that can serve as a point of contact with the text. The felt need raised by the preacher must be genuinely related to the need that lies behind the text. The solution offered must correlate with the solution stated or implied by the author of the text.

A sermon based on the parable of the prodigal son, for example, might find a point of contact with the audience in the themes of rebellion, parental heartbreak, and family division that are reflected in the story. But an application that promises, "Trust Christ and he will heal your family relationships," is illegitimate. Jesus' purpose in telling this story was not to provide a model for handling rebellious children or sibling rivalry. He was painting a picture of the kind of person God accepts.

Once we identify legitimate contact points with the audience, we can integrate them into the message in the following ways:

- *Draw the audience into the message during the introduction.* Although your goal is to explain the text, the introduction should not begin with the text. Instead it should raise a felt need consistent with the fundamental concern that lies behind the passage. In the evangelistic sermon, this felt need is not the ultimate need for a personal relationship with Jesus Christ; rather, it is a symptom of sin and the resulting alienation from God and humanity it produces. During the introduction, speak to the audience about themselves and then point them to the text.
- *Use the known to explain the unknown.* Jesus often used stories and parables drawn from everyday experiences to explain divine realities. When he spoke to the woman of Samaria, he capitalized on her natural thirst to make her aware of an underlying thirst that only he could satisfy (John 4:10). He used the relationship between a parent and a child to help his audience understand the nature of God's love (Matt. 7:9–11). Which of your listeners' experiences can help them understand their need for Christ or God's provision of grace?
- *Support the truth with story illustrations.* When Nathan confronted David about his adultery, he used a carefully crafted story to reveal the gravity of his sin (2 Sam. 12:1–7). Story illustrations enable the audience to see themselves through God's eyes.

In a recent sermon based on the parable of the prodigal son, I began by telling the story of Bill. Bill's father was a religious man who sent his son to church and private school, hoping it would teach him the same values. Bill spent most of his life running hard in the other direction. But every so often he would stop just long enough to look at his life and ask himself this troubling question: "What would my father say?"

I transitioned from the introduction to the Big Idea by saying: "It's an old story, isn't it? Sons don't get along with their fathers. That's also true in the heavenly realm. Jesus told a parable in Luke 15:11–32 to illustrate this fact and to help us understand the nature of God's forgiveness. It is a story whose message is essentially this: If you want to understand the true nature of forgiveness, you must ask yourself this question: 'What would my father say?'"

In the conclusion of the message I picked up Bill's story again and described him lying in a hospital bed, his health broken by a lifetime of alcohol abuse: "The picture was bleak. Doctors said his death was inevitable. But in his last hours, this prodigal who had spent a life running from his heavenly Father finally turned for home. 'But while he was still a long way off, his father saw him and was filled with compassion for him; he ran to his son, threw his arms around him and kissed him.' It is never too late. As long as you have breath, you have hope. Even now your Heavenly Father scans the horizon, watching for the first sign of your return. Go to him."

BALANCING THE DIVINE AND HUMAN IN PREACHING

If God does not work with us, our preaching will fall on deaf ears. But our dependence on God's power does not relieve us of the responsibility to make the message clear to our listeners. When the apostle Paul asked for God's assistance in preaching the gospel, he asked for help to "proclaim it clearly, as I should" (Col. 4:4). This prayer reflects the right balance of dependence on divine power and human responsibility.

Effective evangelistic preaching takes a miracle. But it is a miracle mediated through our use of human language. God's Spirit does not ignore the ordinary process of human understanding when he moves listeners to respond to our message. In order to respond, they must first understand us. In order for them to understand us, we must understand them.

Chapter 46

HOW TO TRANSLATE MALE SERMONS TO WOMEN

And connect with what may be the largest half of your congregation

Alice Mathews

All conversation between men and women," according to Roy McCloughry, "is cross-cultural conversation." If he's right, any preacher may communicate well with only part of the congregation and miss the other part. As a woman who has listened mostly to male preachers during the past six decades, I've reflected during many sermons on why some connect with my world and others don't.

How Men and Women Think

Ruth Tiffany Barnhouse compares the male and female thinking processes to two kinds of vision we all use: macular and peripheral. Macular vision focuses on one thing to examine its details. Peripheral vision takes in the larger context. We use both every day; in fact, the two taken together allow us to see more fully what is there.

Barnhouse likens macular vision to the masculine way of thinking. Men tend to analyze problems, figure out their parts, and choose among the options. She compares peripheral vision to feminine thinking. Women tend to consider the context, trying to keep all issues in view. This makes arrival at a "right" answer more complex.

For example, when a couple talks about buying a car, he may check several models and compare prices, horsepower, extras included, and so on. The decision looks pretty straightforward. When he brings up the subject at dinner, his wife asks a new set of questions he may consider irrelevant: What impression would the neighbors have if we start driving such an expensive car? Could Aunt Maude get in and out of the car easily when we take her grocery shopping? Would the pastor think we should increase our giving to the church if we're able to drive such a nice car? He looks at the car; she looks at the context in which the car will be used.

181

From birth, girl babies respond faster to human contact and are relatively uninterested in things. Boy babies like *things* from the start. Carol Gilligan underlines the female tendency to put relationships before other values. In studies of children at play, researchers found that boys' games last longer because they settle disputes by elaborating rules. Girls, by contrast, end the game when disputes break out; relationships are more important than continuing the game.

Roy McCloughry concludes, "Men and women live in different cultures: he in a world characterized by independence, and she in a world characterized by intimacy."

What are the implications of this for preaching? What types of texts or illustrations are most likely to resonate with female listeners? What emphases are they most or least likely to hear?

CARING ENOUGH TO SPEAK OUR LANGUAGE

During the years my husband and I worked as missionaries in Europe, I often served as an interpreter. With practice I could do that without thinking. One time I caught myself "translating" a French sentence into other French words. That was not my job! I was supposed to carry meaning from one language into another.

A woman in the pew goes through that process almost every time she listens to a man preach. Most of the time she isn't aware she is doing it. If she has been active in church, she has developed such skill in translating; it has become second nature to her. But she is still translating. By attending to three areas, a skilled preacher can learn to speak in a woman's

"native tongue" and thus reach the entire congregation.

Translate Masculine Images into Feminine Images

While reworking a series of Bible studies for women, I chatted with Haddon Robinson about the project. He helpfully suggested illustrations for points I wanted to make. One was about a football player, another was a quote from a baseball player. Gratefully, I included them.

But before the book went to the publisher, I took those illustrations out. They just didn't fit. While some women follow sports, others feel that competitive sports violate the values they hold for relationships. The idea of winning is connected with somebody losing. And the violence of sports such as football or hockey does not communicate positively for many women. Unless a woman can translate illustrations from sports or business into relational values and experience, she may not connect emotionally with the point.

Several years ago a large Bible church invited me to speak at their Sunday services. During the first service, I used an illustration from my sewing machine. When I was about halfway through, I stopped and said gently, "I know that this baffles some of you men, but you need to know that this is my sweet revenge for all the sports illustrations I've had to listen to all of my life." There was a titter, and then a roar of laughter, and then applause. Afterward, women came up to me and said, "Thank you for talking about the sewing machine. That connected with me." The experience underscored for me that men and women live in different worlds. But the two worlds can be bridged.

Suppose a male preacher wants to speak on

perseverance or determination, topics for which illustrations from sports would be ideal. He can still connect with women by reaching into the world of the Olympics, where usually an individual competes against a standard. Figure skating, for example, does not require violence against an opponent in order to win (besides, it is beautiful). In a similar way, an illustration from *Chariots of Fire* could show the necessity of discipline in order to achieve, while not being associated with violence.

However, after such an illustration from sports, it would be helpful for women to hear an illustration from another arena of life—for example, professional music. Here, too, great discipline and perseverance are required.

Translate Abstract Principles into Terms of Concrete Relationships

When I listen to a sermon, I want to know how the biblical principles fit my life—not merely as an individual but in my complex web of relationships. How does this point affect me in my role as wife, mother, grandmother, neighbor, church member? How will it change the way I speak to my husband in the car on our way home from church? How will it alter the decisions I make about the use of my time when women in distress call me on the phone? My life is about people, a lot of lonely, confused, and hurting people. I want to know how biblical principles work in *my* world.

Women want to hear the Word of God in a way that applies to our lives in relationship. Effective communicators to women translate abstract principles by using illustrations drawn from relationships.

Consider substitutionary atonement, a principle that can remain abstract for many listeners. Women will relate to it best when the preacher uses human illustrations—for example, a man who donates a kidney in order to keep a family member alive, or a woman who loses her life while giving birth to a child, or a teenager who rescues a toddler from a burning building but dies in the rescue attempt.

Even an abstract principle such as spiritual warfare (Eph. 6:10–18), which many men relate to positively, can be made appealing for women by explaining it in relational terms. If using an illustration from war, for example, it's important to deemphasize the bloodshed and emphasize what was at stake for the people involved. For example, if illustrating from the Second World War, emphasize the freedom from Nazi tyranny it won. Or women might relate to a war for independence that freed people from brutality and gave them security.

Translate Masculine Language to Feminine Language

Much biblical imagery is masculine. Jesus the Son called God "Father," a masculine image. Christian women can hear that and, unless they were sexually or physically abused by a bad father, appreciate the rich image of relationship that Jesus gives us in that name.

But much more than masculine biblical imagery crops up in many sermons. Perhaps twenty years ago, I heard a woman speaker change the noun and pronoun from masculine to feminine as she quoted 2 Corinthians 5:17— "If any woman is in Christ Jesus, she is a new creation; old things are passed away; behold, all things are become new" (cf. KJV). I sat there stunned, then realized that tears were running down my cheeks. This meant *me*. I was included.

Had you asked me ten minutes earlier if I were included in the text of 2 Corinthians 5:17, I would have said, "Of course!" Intellectually, I can grasp that. Emotionally, I cannot. A preacher who cares about communicating to women will not draw back from reiterating the text with feminine pronouns here and there. Saying "men and women" or "women or men," rather than merely "men," helps women feel included.

We understand the need to communicate cross-culturally when we speak to different races or ethnic groups. Do we understand that it also applies when men and women attempt to communicate with one another?

Women in general are good listeners. It's part of being relational. But they are often puzzled listeners. Preachers can make a difference in what women are able to hear as they work to include and affirm both women and men as they speak.

A more complete and nuanced discussion of the wide variety of issues concerning women as listeners is found in Dr. Mathews' Preaching That Speaks to Women *(Baker Academic, 2003).*

Chapter 47

HE SAID, SHE HEARD
Adapting to gender

Jeffrey Arthurs

A friend of mine bought a puppy and named him Zebedee. As Zeb grew he became harder and harder to manage, so my friend went to dog obedience school. There he got a revelation.

He learned his words ("Zeb, you naughty dog, if you do that one more time I'm going to have to spank you") were simply noise to the canine mind. Dogs, he learned, communicate nonverbally. They signal dominance by being "top dog"—literally! The "alpha male" stands over the underlings of the pack, and all canines seem to understand this message.

So my friend was taught to play alpha male. He would roll Zeb on his back, hold the dog's head in both hands, and look him in the eye. Zeb got the message, and so did my friend. To

communicate with Zeb you have to speak canine.

There's a principle here for all communicators: We must adjust to our audience if we hope for them to adjust to our message. We have to speak a language they understand. Missionaries call it "contextualization." Translators use "dynamic equivalence." With communication between men and women, the issue is called "genderlects."

Each of us has a dialect—a Southern drawl, a Midwestern twang—and a genderlect. According to communication scholar Deborah Tannen, genderlects account for much of the mystification between men and women. We try to communicate one thing, but when the message is filtered through the receiver's grid, it takes a new shape.

This article focuses on how to minimize communication breakdown when men speak to women.

TRY A NEW DIRECTION

Since smooth interpersonal relations are a high value for women, they tend to be less direct than men. Women are more likely to avoid confrontation by leaving the other person as many options as possible. Thus, when a woman is hungry, a conversation might go like this:

Michelle: "Do you want to eat somewhere?"

Robyn: "Are you getting hungry?"

Michelle: "Yeah, a little."

Robyn: "Me too. Do you think we should eat?"

Michelle: "Sounds good to me. Where do you want to go?"

A man might say, "I'm hungry, let's eat," but that method would feel confrontational or brusque to a woman. Indirection fosters communion.

This knowledge has saved my marriage (note the hyperbole, irony, and shock value used for effect—a male tactic). My wife uses indirection when deciding what to wear: "Should I wear the blue one or the red one?" These discussions used to frustrate me like a blackberry seed in the teeth. I thought she actually wanted my advice, and as we all know, advice is designed to solve problems. I didn't care which she wore—she looks great in both—so I would arbitrarily choose the red one. And then she would hem and haw and generate reasons against the red one!

The blackberry seed nestled deep.

I would say, "Well, OK, wear the blue one. It looks great too." Then she would object to the blue, and the seed wedged down near the gum line. Little did I realize that she was speaking "female" and I was speaking "male." I wanted to solve the problem, but she wanted me to join her in the trauma of decision making. When she argued against my choices, I thought she was belittling my advice, but actually she was inviting me into her world.

Knowing this phenomenon has revolutionized our talks. Now when she asks about the red one or the blue one, I put a look of consternation on my face and respond, "Well, I don't know. The red one has certain qualities. But the blue one has advantages, too. What do you think?" She catches on to my fumbling attempts to speak "female" and we laugh.

Other tools of indirection are qualifiers (-"you've probably already thought of this"), nonspecific vocabulary ("it's pretty far"), and an upward inflection of the voice so that the statement "Put it over there" sounds like a question. These tools encourage bilateral, not unilateral, decision making.

This isn't just a female phenomenon. Indirection is favored in many parts of the world. Just try starting business negotiation in Japan by saying, "OK, this is what you want, and this is what I'm prepared to give. Do you want to bargain or not?"

However, the male genderlect still dominates most public speaking in America, and women would do well to learn to communicate directly at times. With some audiences they need this arrow in their quivers. Conversely, men need to hear themselves through women's ears and realize that their directness may seem authoritarian or rude. To get the idea, compare these statements:

Male genderlect: "If you want joy, follow these three steps."

Female genderlect: "We all want joy, don't we? I know I do. How can we get it? Maybe the first thing we could do is. . . ."

Here's a direct statement for male readers: Preaching is more than a report of what you discovered in the study; it is also a means of establishing and nurturing relationships.

STOP SPEECHIFYING

Even in interpersonal communication, men tend to make speeches. They "hold forth," displaying their expertise or calling attention to self. Communication establishes the alpha male of the pack. Men interrupt to get in their two cents worth, but women interrupt to show support for the one speaking. They finish sentences, add their own insights, and use nonverbal sounds ("oh," "hmm," "uh huh") to commune with the one speaking. What to men sounds like interrupting, to women is each person in the conversation contributing.

This approach to communication leads a woman to "match" or reflect her partner's statement:

Man: "I didn't sleep well last night."

Woman: "Oh! Me neither. That happens to me all the time."

A man may hear this as one-upsmanship. He may escalate his complaint: "My back ached all night." And the woman, attempting to create rapport may say: "I know what you mean. Mine hurts too." The conversation may cycle downward with the man taking offense where none is meant and the woman not understanding why an argument is forming.

Listening and feedback are usually associated with interpersonal communication, but they have implications for preaching, too. For example, I recommend that preachers incorpo-

rate dialogue into their sermons. (See the article in this volume on that topic.) Sprinkling dialogue into sermons fosters relationship. It avoids an authoritarian tone by showing respect for listeners. I include at least one section of dialogue in nearly every sermon I preach.

PLOTLESS BUT NOT POINTLESS

Men tend to tell stories that are funny, dramatic, and full of remarkable action ("I remember the time I fell off the cliff"). Women tend to tell stories that deal with the everyday and typical ("Last week at the doctor's office, the receptionist was rude to me").

Men's stories emphasize chronology, but women's don't. To men, women's stories seem to meander. A man's story has clear conflict and builds to a clear climax, often concluding with a moral or a punch line, or at least clear resolution. Women's stories (to men) may seem to end with a whimper, not a bang.

These differences are clearly seen in movies—"chick flicks" and "guy movies." I realize I'm in danger of stereotyping (this whole article is guilty of that!), but Hollywood producers don't care if they stereotype. They care about making money, and they seem to know what appeals to men and women. They target audiences.

ANECDOTAL EVIDENCE

Some researchers have found that men often use expert testimony when they want to prove a point. Women often use anecdotes.

This was illustrated for me when I watched two of my students, Ben and Jessica, teach a large lecture class. Ben came to my office the day before the lecture seeking quotations, statistics, and any help I could offer to make his presentation "meaty" (his word). I showed him a quotation from the classical rhetorician Isocrates. Even though he had never heard of Isocrates, he was impressed, and Isocrates showed up in the lecture the next day. None of the students in the class had heard of him either, but that didn't stop Ben. Anybody with a name like Isocrates must know what he was talking about!

In contrast, Jessica quoted no authorities and cited no statistics. She sat on a stool before the class and engaged her peers in dialogue, using her listeners' own experiences to illustrate principles.

Arguing from experience is inductive. It starts from particulars and moves toward a point. Induction is an effective way to argue today since pluralism and relativism have undermined our allegiance to authority. If you want to prove that "it is more blessed to give than to receive," try backing up the authoritative scriptural statement with lots of examples and stories.

Some pastors incorporate testimony into their sermons or in the church service where the sermon is preached. For example, I heard a Valentine's Day sermon on how to better love your spouse. In the middle of the sermon, the preacher played a video of an interview with a woman who had been married more than fifty years. She was now a widow and physically unable to speak to all four services, but the taped interview was quite effective. We laughed, sighed, and yearned for the same kind of marriage this woman had known. My hunch is that the women in the audience were moved even more than I was.

Perhaps the best way to present arguments for mixed audiences is by combining genderlects. Quote an authority (male genderlect), but place the quote in a human context (female genderlect) by giving some details about the person. When quoting Horatio Spafford's hymn ("When Peace Like a River Attendeth My Way"), tell the story behind the words. When quoting Augustine ("Our hearts are restless till they rest in thee"), give some details of his life and conversion. Perhaps the most effective experiences to use are your own.

Genderlects are a fact of life. We need to deal with them just like my friend learned to communicate with Zebedee. We need to hear our words the way others receive them.

Chapter 48

CONNECTING WITH MEN

How to preach to the tattooed

Bill Giovannetti

There's something peculiar about my ministry. God uses me to reach "tough guys." This is the last type of person I would expect to reach. I am decidedly not a tough guy.

I have always gotten good grades and done all my homework. I never cut a class. I graduated with honors. I've never used drugs, gotten drunk, been in a fight, or been arrested. I usually use good grammar. I even watch PBS and listen to Public Radio. A lifetime Christian, my testimony has none of the sizzle of a misspent youth. My sermons are long, doctrinal, and expository.

Nonetheless (see, there's a word tough guys wouldn't use!) ever since age fourteen, I've had an affinity for tough guys, and they seem to respond to me. As a high school student, I directed an Awana club for forty boys. I loved those kids and they loved me. My favorites were the troublemakers, the tough kids. I often wondered why the tough kids were so concentrated in this one local school.

What a shock when I attended the eighth-grade graduation ceremony. The principal passed out awards: valedictorian, most likely to succeed, science-fair participation, literary achievement, and others. To my dismay, I had never met any of the winners. I thought I knew every boy in that school, but those award winners were strangers to me. They had never even visited my Awana club.

Without my realizing it, my club had become a magnet for the school's underachievers. What was going on? How could I—a bookish honors student—attract these nonacademic tough kids? This question perplexed me then, and it still does.

Sunday after Sunday I look over a congregation in which most of the men are blue-collar guys. Yes, we have a couple of financial planners, a few businessmen, a lawyer—but the vast majority work with their hands and bodies: a bricklayer, a few cops, a dry wall salesman, a baggage handler, a furniture mover. This baffles me.

I preach doctrine. I explain the Greek and Hebrew meanings of words. I use relatively few illustrations, and my sermons last at least forty-five minutes. I'm nothing like these men. What is it that draws them to my church?

To find out, I asked some "tough guys" in my congregation what attracted them and what made them stick. Some of them became Christians through our church; some were already Christians when they started attending. I needed to listen to these brothers and learn what God was using in our church and through my sermons to get hold of them.

THE BRICKLAYER

Bernie Ullrich has been a bricklayer for twelve of his twenty-nine years. He has the biggest, strongest hands you've ever seen. Tall, wiry, and muscular, Bernie gets extra points on my tough-guy scale because he recently had his three tattoos removed; I'm told this hurts more than having them etched on!

He didn't finish high school, but he does have his G.E.D. Bernie religiously practices Jeet Kun Do, Jiu Jitsu, Kali, and Muy Thai kickboxing. He's the kind of guy you'd want on your side in a fist fight. He has to take the bus everywhere while he works on getting his license back after a couple of DUIs. Bernie gave his life to Christ four years ago through our church.

When I asked Bernie what initially attracted him to our church, he didn't hesitate: "Three things. The church was very informal. You were preaching on the sin that I was doing the night before—on my level. And there were other people my age that I could relate to." Bernie explained that he does not care for "feel-good sermons." He prefers simple, straightforward teaching, not the loud, bombastic, amen kind of stuff.

I was both humbled and elated. The word "simple" surprised me. I had never thought of my sermons in that way. And yet, by focusing on the one aspect of my ministry that I really delight in—doctrinal teaching and preaching— I was able to connect with him. Maybe, despite conventional logic, this is what tough guys want.

THE TATTOOED THINKER

Then there's Clint Nolan, who has three tattoos—one homemade. He's twenty-six and studies the martial art called Wing Chun. He taught himself computers, dropped out of college after one year, and has his own business as a network engineer. He is a thinker.

His wife and many of his friends have attended our church for years. Before he was saved a year and a half ago, Clint was a staunch critic of Christianity; it didn't appeal to his logical side. After many discussions with his wife and Christian friends and after reading C. S. Lewis's *Mere Christianity*, Clint received Christ at home on a Saturday night. The next morning, he was at church.

I asked Clint what made him initially like our church and what kept him coming back.

"Faith based in logic, the whole thing," he explained. "You don't have to be a moron to be a Christian. After the first week, what kept me coming was the sound, Bible-based doctrine. Nothing more, nothing less."

My ears perked up. This was the second tough guy who found me preaching just the right topic for him on his very first visit to our church—and I preach expository sermons, sometimes taking months to go through one book of the Bible.

THE FURNITURE MOVER

My nickname for Steve James is "Psycho Boy." He has penetrating steel-blue eyes, wears T-shirts and combat boots, and looks as if he could snap at any minute. Forty-two years old, tall, muscular, and hard as nails, Steve moves furniture. I've seen him strap an entertainment center to his back and carry it up three flights of stairs. When he comes home from work, Steve does chin-ups on a bar he has rigged in his tiny apartment.

Steve has been coming to our church for twelve years. What has made him stick with it all these years?

"That's easy," he replied. "You preach grace. Bottom line."

Again, I was humbled. I find myself so often in need of forgiveness and strength and grace that I've decided to make grace my main theme. Steve picked up on this and embraced it.

THE BAGGAGE HANDLER

If you were to visit our church, you'd notice Michael Palomo right away. He's a body builder, and it shows. You'd also notice his uniform. Michael is a union baggage handler at O'Hare International Airport, and he goes straight to work after church. He has a unicorn tattooed on his arm. Though he was saved more than a decade ago, only in the last couple of years has Michael really started getting serious about his faith.

Michael was the only tough guy with an answer when I asked what he disliked about my sermons. "Maybe they could be a little shorter," he said, almost apologizing. He was quick to add: "But really, I like the services as they are." I chuckled and thanked him for being honest.

He continued: "What I like is how you put across the message. There's a compassion and a human side."

REACHING THE TOUGH GUYS

As I thought about my tough guys, four common threads emerged from our conversations.

Don't try to be something you're not. This flies in the face of conventional wisdom, which holds that we should become like the people we're trying to reach—that we should watch their TV shows, listen to their music, read their magazines, wear their clothes. On the contrary, I discovered that tough guys appreciate it when I'm simply myself.

My hunch is that as long as I am comfort-able being myself, the men around me feel permission to be themselves. This makes their move toward God authentically their own, not some superficial attempt to imitate a pastor who is making his own superficial attempt to imitate them.

In Ian Murray's biography of Martyn Lloyd-Jones, Lloyd-Jones observes that the gospel holds out the promise of transformation. People want to believe that they can be changed by coming to Christ. In part, he suggests, the minister represents that change. So he discouraged young ministers from trying to be like the people they were reaching.

Don't assume they won't like doctrine. It's easy for those of us with advanced degrees to lapse into a subtle elitism, thinking that blue-collar guys can't grasp theology. A few days of laying brick with Bernie taught me that tough guys can be very analytical. Tough guys are brilliant in ways that school can't teach. Many blue-collar jobs require a lot of intuitive yet high-level thinking. Anyone who can overhaul an internal combustion engine can hold his own in the intelligence department.

Likewise, these men come to church wanting to know what's inside God's Word, and we should not hold back. Preachers do them a great disservice by assuming they can't handle the deep things of God.

At the same time, *we must be clear in our communicating.* The obstacle is not content but clarity. Many preachers shy away from doctrinal, expository preaching because they feel it will scare people away—especially tough guys. Not so. What pushes tough guys away is fuzzy presentation. Good preaching stands on a foundation of good teaching.

So teach the great concepts of Christianity. Just be careful to explain your terms. Be abundantly clear. Define words. As you begin, assume that your tough guys—and everyone else—know nothing about the text before them. The height of the building is directly proportional to the depth of the foundation. Lay a good foundation, and the tough guys in your church will eagerly go with you all the way to the top.

Clearly structure the way you offer information. The next time you're at an auto parts store, leaf through a Haynes manual. These manuals explain basic car repair for most makes and models. The repairs are described in clearly numbered, distinct steps, with each step building on the step before it. This is how the minds of tough guys work.

So I structure my sermons so that there is a flow, with concisely stated, distinctly enumerated points. In some circles, good preaching means "hiding the skeleton." However, to reach tough guys, let the skeleton show! Have

a clear outline. State your central proposition. Enumerate point one, point two, and point three. Let your sermons show a well-conceived, textually authentic structure, and your tough guys will be right with you.

GOD IS STILL IN CHARGE

This is obvious, but as a preacher, in my pride, sometimes I forget it. What ultimately touches the hearts of men like Bernie, Clint, Steve, and Michael isn't my emphasis on doctrine or my ability to be clear, my love of exposition, or my focus on grace. What draws these guys and keeps them coming back is God's Spirit working within them.

My preaching is just one instrument that God has chosen to use. And I am grateful that he has chosen it to connect with his beloved tough guys.

Chapter 49

CREATING A SINGLES-FRIENDLY SERMON
How to preach to 49 percent of today's adults

Susan Maycinik Nikaido

For me and for many singles I've talked to, Sunday morning can be the loneliest time of the week. Why? Because we see church as a couples' and families' world. Sermons, announcements, even the way Sunday school classes and small groups are structured can communicate that we're not part of the program.

Yet singles make up 40 percent of the U.S. adult population. We are the fastest-growing population group. How, then, can you be sure

your church welcomes single adults? The good news is that the most significant ways don't require a program or a budget. But they may require a change in perspective.

LISTEN AND ASK QUESTIONS

Dan Yeary, pastor at North Phoenix Baptist Church, encourages pastors to gather ten to twelve singles and ask pointed questions: "How can I preach for you? What's the church doing that's helping you, and what could it be doing? Singles will perceive that you care and feel a sense of ownership in the church because they've been given a fair hearing."

As you're talking to singles, be sure to seek out people of different ages who are single for different reasons. The issues and needs important to a single twenty-three-year-old can be vastly different from those of a still-single thirty-nine-year-old, or of someone whose marriage ended in divorce, or of a widow. Singles with children will have different concerns from those without kids or from those whose children are grown.

Use Language Carefully

Like everyone, single adults want to be acknowledged and valued. Yet in some churches, language from the pulpit assumes every adult is married. Illustrations are drawn primarily from marriage and family relationships. Women are referred to exclusively as wives and mothers.

A simple change in wording can draw immense gratitude from your single members. If your sermon application concerns close relationships, refer to "roommates and friends" as well as "spouses and children." When speaking about households in the congregation, say "families and individuals" instead of just "families." Instead of "family picnic," announce "an all-church picnic." You'll show unmarried adults that you know they're there. By varying illustrations, you communicate that the various forms of single life are normal and as valid as marriage.

Many statements meant to encourage families subtly communicate that single life is second-best. The speaker at a church women's retreat declared, "God's highest calling for a woman is to be a wife and mother." The speaker could have affirmed moms, yet avoided injuring the unmarried and childless by saying, "One of God's highest callings is to be a wife and mother."

As you talk about divorce from the pulpit, be sensitive to the fact that some in the congregation are single again—many not by choice. Ask yourself as you prepare a sermon, "If I were divorced, would I feel condemned or rejected if I heard this statement? Have I implied that a divorced person is a lesser child of God? Have I balanced my charge to stay married with the acknowledgment that people fail and that God offers forgiveness for all types of sin?"

Keep Statements Biblical

In movies, music, and family reunions, Christian singles hear the message, "You're nobody till somebody loves you." Even in church, marriage is often seen as the norm, a kind of passage to adulthood. Children and young people hear, "When you get married and have a family," not "if you get married. . . ." Single adults hear, "You're such a nice person. I don't understand why you're not married."

This mindset is more reflective of a culture that exalts romance than of Scripture. The Bible honors marriage, but it gives an equal (or, arguably, higher) place to the single life. Consider Paul's teaching about marriage in 1 Corinthians 7, which comes far from exalting marriage as the ideal. The best thing Paul can say about marriage is, "If you do marry, you have not sinned."

The whole congregation—singles, couples, and parents of future single adults—needs to hear that according to Scripture, staying single is often preferable. It takes courage to promote this counter-cultural but thoroughly biblical view. Jesus and Paul were single adults, as were other Bible leaders. Scripture shows and teaches that marriage is optional, not inevitable.

CHOOSE TOPICS FOR ALL

Most singles expect to hear a family-oriented sermon now and then. But a five-week or three-month series on marriage and family issues gives singles the message: "This church is not for you."

If marriages or families need special attention, consider teaching a Sunday school class or weekend seminar. Or preach more broadly on related topics such as love and forgiveness.

As a single adult, I have seen that what my pastor communicates about marriage and singleness can profoundly affect how I see myself. When the message about singleness is negative, doubts about God's love for me and the wisdom of his plan for my life gain a strong and destructive foothold. When the message is positive, I find it much easier to be thankful for and content in my circumstances. What's more, the church that welcomes me as a single adult is a church I want to commit to and serve within for a long, long time.

Chapter 50

PREACHING TO PRESCHOOLERS

A children's sermon is a time to feed their imaginations, not their egos

Marilyn Chandler McEntyre

I remember going forward for the children's sermon, feeling pleased and shy as I slipped out of the pew. I remember the smiles of the big folk as we gathered at the foot of the pulpit. It can be one of the sweeter moments in a Sunday service. It can also be one of the most uncomfortable.

ASK REAL QUESTIONS

Children's sermons test the skills of the best pastor—and some of the best pastors fail the test. I've seen respectable preachers go slightly pale at the prospect of having to do the children's sermon because the associate (bless her motherly heart) is away. So they take what seems the most cautious strategy, faced with a dozen fidgeting midgets, one of whom is pulling on the vestments, one of whom is showing off her new flowered panties, one of whom looks on the verge of sudden tears. They placate. They talk down. They plead with the children, silently but visibly, not to get out of hand. They ask "safe" questions: "Does God love us?" "Do you sometimes have to say you're sorry?"

Even small children know when they're being set up. A real question invites reflection, and even small children are capable of reflection. One reason kids "say the darndest things," as Art Linkletter put it, is that they do think. They haven't yet dug the grooves of convention so deeply that they don't reason and muse and make surprising connections. If a children's sermon is to start with a question, let it be a real question.

One rich source of real questions is a catechism. Contrary to popular impressions, the material in a good catechism isn't "canned" but a series of durable questions with answers that invite more questions and offer a vocabulary of faith and a storehouse of usable images. A catechism also offers guidance and authority. Children want to be led, directed, and taught. They thrive on the guidance of a confident teacher with authority.

USE THE WORD

For believers, that authority is rooted in the Word. Like any sermon, children's sermons ought to be grounded in the Word. Good questions may be valuable teaching tools, but good stories are even more important, especially when they come from the story we all inhabit. I wonder why pastors so often think they have to rely on the spurious relevancy of "real-life" stories about some boy (just like you) named Jimmy when the real-life stories of Joseph, Miriam, Samuel, David, or Jesus demand and yield so much more.

Bible stories require that even the youngest among us reckon with mystery, moral ambiguity, sibling rivalry, sin, fallenness, and forgiveness. The largeness of such stories is much more invigorating and inspiring. The lasting appeal of fairy tales and folk tales, in which children often figure as agents in real adult dilemmas, testifies to the power of stories that mirror an adult world where there is actual adventure, danger, and moral complexity.

OBJECT LESSONS DO WORK

There is, however, a place for straightfor-ward object lessons, especially lessons from nature. A leaf teaches something about intricate systems and the daily miracle of transformation. An ant farm teaches something about cooperation and community—how to be one body. A sprouting potato has something to show us about life in death, and a bird's feather about beauty in purposeful design. To contemplate such objects is to recognize a Creator who cares for and about little things. It is to be reminded also that we ourselves are fearfully and wonderfully made.

That reminder can have far more lasting value than many of the flat "You are special" messages that come out of fussily reassuring "self-esteem" materials designed by educators with more good will than imagination. A child who has taken a few quiet minutes to reflect on the sprouting potato will not likely eat potatoes again without feeling connected to a web of being whose processes are filled with promise. That child will see a little of the fire in the burning bush.

So here's my plea to those who proclaim the Word to the newly potty-trained: Lead, don't plead; respect their intelligence; feed their imaginations, not their egos; focus on the story they're called into by birth and baptism; give them their first keys to the kingdom by revealing the extraordinary in the ordinary; awaken their curiosity about the world and the one who made it (since curiosity is a form of love). Then maybe, when they go home, they'll head for the garden rather than the video games, and when bedtime comes, they'll want to hear more about Peter leaping out of the boat and walking on the water. They know, after all, perhaps better than we who forget, that anything is possible.

Chapter 51

HISPANIC-AMERICAN PREACHING

Noel Castellanos, Jesse Miranda, Alfredo Ramos

Selena was the Mexican-American pop star killed by a friend at age twenty-three. The movie *Selena* is based on her short life. As her fame in the U.S. increases, one scene shows Selena (Jennifer Lopez) being invited to return to Mexico to perform at an important event. Her father opposes the appearance because he thinks his daughter's Spanish is terrible. When Selena protests that her singing in Spanish is fine, her father says singing is one thing, but interviews are another. He then goes into a tirade about the difficulties of being Mexican American. "The Mexicans think you aren't Mexican enough, and the Americans think you aren't American enough."

This is also a concern in Hispanic-American preaching. There are differences between how Hispanics and non-Hispanics communicate. Keeping both perspectives in balance is crucial, but we need to focus more on the Hispanic than the American. There are several distinctives necessary in good Hispanic preaching.

HISPANIC PREACHING VALUES FAMILY

Hispanic preaching is shaped by the high value Hispanic culture places on family relationships. American culture tends to be individualistic, while we think in terms of *us* more than *me*. The idea of family is not limited to our close relatives but extends to the family of faith and the surrounding community.

This affects preaching particularly during holidays. While some non-Hispanic churches may give little attention to special days, all special days are significant for us. Obviously Christmas and Easter are days of tremendous importance. We also make Mother's Day and Father's Day a great celebration. While it is necessary to clarify the spiritual focus—such as the Fatherhood of God on Father's Day—the connection to family is considerable.

Latino preaching is not content with just an inward focus. It calls people to link our discipleship back into our community. Our preaching calls people to community involvement and service. In the name of Christ we must care about the good of the larger family.

HISPANIC PREACHING LINKS THE BIBLICAL STORY TO THE STORY OF OUR PEOPLE

The circumstance of many Latino people includes limited opportunities and material want. We preach biblical themes that speak to the issues of marginalization, poverty, and liberation. We build bridges between the biblical narrative and the personal story of Latinos through storytelling.

A great example is Jesus and the Samaritan woman in John 4. We connect through the historical-cultural lens of the conflict between Jews and Samaritans. In the sense that Samaritans were not totally Gentile and not totally

Jew, Hispanic Americans have a "Samaritan" identity. We can recognize the inferior treatment of the Samaritans, the otherness of a minority people living in a dominant culture. We can address our sense of inferiority and its relationship to the good news through the lens of Samaria. We show how Jesus crossed the street culturally, socially, politically, and racially with a spiritual agenda. This scene is one way we declare that the gospel goes beyond human limitations and prejudices.

Our preaching addresses the key issues of Hispanic Americans, which include identity, significance, and freedom. With stories like the woman at the well we bring the message of liberation and transformation. The New Testament "Samaritan trilogy" provides a pattern. The trilogy is the woman at the well, the parable of the Good Samaritan in Luke 10, and the Samaritan Pentecost in Acts 8. These accounts provide a paradigm for evangelism, ethics, and ecclesiology. They are a theological basis for intercultural relations.

HISPANIC PREACHING IS PASSIONATE

Latinos tend to be more inspirational than instructional, more emotional than expository. Emotion is extremely important because it is a part of who we are. We speak forcefully, poetically, and with a raised voice. Those familiar with Anglo-American preaching may wonder why the Latino preacher seems to be angry. Our sermon delivery is fiery because we focus more on persuading than informing. This is not for the purpose of manipulation, but a sincere expression of how God made us.

We try to preach in the universal language of love. Whatever else is said, we speak from the heart with love. The mind and logic is not our primary concern; rather the heart is the essential issue.

As with every culture, this can be overdone. Some Hispanic preaching takes emotion to an extreme at the expense of sound teaching. Good Hispanic preaching blends both passion and instruction. The best means to accomplish this is storytelling. In the Hispanic context, stories are a better vehicle for truth than a logical, systematic presentation.

HISPANIC PREACHING IS VULNERABLE

Friendliness and sincerity are part of Hispanic culture. Hispanic preachers communicate that by personalizing our message. We are careful to put ourselves and our feelings into the sermon. Distant, impersonal theories do not reach our people. Latino preachers must be willing to share their own struggles and tie that into the life experiences of their people. We openly admit the tension of living in two worlds and then address the conflict we all face as we seek to follow Christ in this society.

Our vulnerability must be true and natural, authenticated by and consistent with our spiritual life as lived out among the people. Our responsibility is to put the struggle of the people into words. We give expression to the problems they face and offer the hope that is in Jesus.

HISPANIC PREACHING EXPECTS RESPONSIVENESS

We must involve the congregation in our sermons. When we preach, we expect to be answered. Not only does the congregation listen to us, we also listen to them and respond. Hispanic preaching is about give and take and audience participation, much like African-American churches.

That response may not occur if we don't take into account our distinctives. When preaching to Hispanic people in the United States, one size does not fit all. Although we share one basic language, Hispanic congregations are all different. The differences include country of origin, culture, economic conditions, and education. Preachers cannot assume they are communicating clearly when speaking to various groups of Hispanic people. Speech patterns, styles, expressions, and even the meaning of words may be different. We are tied together by language and shared experiences rather than by geographical location.

When Anglo preachers speak to Hispanics, it would be good for them to try to express more passion in their sermons. Work at inspiring the people as you instruct them. Use stories. Be aware of issues faced by our communities and acknowledge the cultural tensions faced by Hispanics. Do not be afraid to address the problems of materialism, racism, oppression, and so forth. As members of the dominant culture, Anglos can make a great impression with Hispanics if they learn to communicate with some of our language and know some of our customs.

In the early days when Noel Castellanos was planting La Villita Community Church in Chicago, they held a potluck supper at Christmas time, and Noel thought he should bring something suitable for the occasion. In a cookbook he found a recipe for Holiday Salsa. The ingredients included pineapple, cranberries, nuts, and chili peppers. He thought people would love his festive salsa but was disappointed to see that no one even tried it. Finally one of the men explained, "Noel, you can't make salsa without tomatoes."

Hispanic American preachers live in two worlds. If we leave out the tomatoes, no one will like the salsa.

Chapter 52

AFRICAN-AMERICAN PREACHING

Rodney L. Cooper

The well-known words of Martin Luther King Jr. tell much about African-American preaching:

> When the architects of our republic wrote the magnificent words of the Constitution and the Declaration of Independence, they were signing a promissory note to which every American was to fall heir. This note was a promise that all men would be guaranteed the inalienable rights of life, liberty, and the pursuit of happiness.

It is obvious today that America has defaulted on this promissory note insofar as her citizens of color are concerned. Instead of honoring this sacred obligation, America has given the Negro a bad check marked Insufficient Funds. But we refuse to believe that the bank of justice is bankrupt. We refuse to believe that there are insufficient funds in the great vaults of opportunity of this nation.

So we have come to cash this check—a check that will give us upon demand the riches of freedom and the security of justice.

We have also come to this hallowed spot to remind America of the fierce urgency of *now*. This is no time to engage in the luxury of cooling off or to take the tranquilizing drug of gradualism. *Now* is the time to make real the promises of democracy. *Now* is the time to arise from the dark and desolate valley of segregation to the sunlit path of racial justice. *Now* is the time to open the doors of opportunity to all of God's children. *Now* is the time to lift our nation from the quicksands of racial injustice to the solid rock of brotherhood. (1968, pp. 157–58)

Dr. King ends his "I Have a Dream" speech with the famous conclusion of celebration: "Free at last, free at last, thank God Almighty, I am free at last."

Black preaching is distinctive in its approach because of the direct impact of racism and the African-American struggle for equality. Preaching to people who feel disenfranchised affects the way you address them. I have had numerous conversations with black parishioners who have stated that Sunday morning is the time to come and "to let go and let God" embrace their pain and encourage their hearts. The atmosphere of people in worship who collectively share their pain and open their hearts to the preaching of God's Word is like a cup of cold water to a parched thirst.

In my own experiences, when I have suffered racial slurs or have been refused to be served in a restaurant, Sunday was a time to regain perspective that "Vengeance is mine, saith the Lord," but that "God is good all the time, and all the time God is good." The black preacher reminds hearers of the present and yet-to-come work of God in behalf of his people.

Dr. King embodies in just a few paragraphs five key ingredients that make black preaching distinctive.

(1) During preparation the black preacher must seek God prayerfully in the Scriptures so the congregation knows the message is from God. He is God's messenger, sent by God—a prophet. Black preaching is built on the reality of the dictums, "Thus saith the Lord" and "God has given me a word for you today." As 1 Peter 4:11 says, "If anyone speaks, he should do it as one speaking the very words of God."

Another key Scripture guiding black preaching is Isaiah 61:1, "The Spirit of the LORD God is upon me because the LORD has anointed me to bring good news to the afflicted; he has sent me to bind up the brokenhearted, to proclaim liberty to captives and freedom to prisoners" (NASB).

We speak prophetically to people whose daily experiences overtly or subtlety produce striving and stress just because of who they are—black. People in the pew want to know the preacher has truly heard from God and is basing what he says on God's Word and principles. Dr. King had power in his preaching because he clearly showed in his messages that racism was not just a moral issue—it was a biblical issue.

(2) The black preacher must be in touch with the people's pain. There is a story about a young black preacher and an old black preacher sitting near the pulpit side by side on a Sunday morning. The young preacher got up and read Psalm 23. The congregation politely said amen.

The old preacher then followed the young preacher and read Psalm 23 again. The congregation wept, clapped, and shouted a hearty amen. When the old preacher sat down, the young preacher asked him why they responded with such emotion to his reading of the psalm. The old man said, "Son, you read Psalm 23, but I *read* Psalm 23. You can read it, but I have *lived* it."

Henry Mitchell, a noted author on black preaching, states that the preacher must "sit where they sit" (1977, p. 7). The authority of the black preacher is built on relationships. It was the slave preacher, one of the slaves, without formal training, who preached effectively to his people because he dealt with issues from inside "their skin and not from some alien identity" (1977, p. 7). Black preaching constantly bridges the sacred to the secular by showing how what those people in the text went through fits what we are going through today. The black preacher constantly points out that salvation is not ancient history—it is current events.

People know whether the messenger has experienced what he is conveying by his use of personal illustrations that show times of distress in his own life.

(3) The black preacher must dispense hope. We must show that "weeping may last for the evening, but a shout of joy comes in the morning" (Ps. 30:5, NASB).

We give this hope by telling the story, a story that is twofold. First, it is the text being preached and what it conveys for listeners today. Secondly, it is the larger story, the gospel story that Jesus has risen from the grave and sits in ultimate authority. No matter what situation the listener faces, there is hope because there is Jesus.

(4) The black preacher must preach with passion and celebration. Our preaching is not animated and enthusiastic for entertainment's sake but as a result of conviction. The black preacher must show that *he believes* he has a word from God. Celebration, the high point of the sermon, is where the preacher raises his voice sometimes to the point of shouting in praise to the God who is one's hope and help in every situation. You know the chord of celebration has been struck when a parishioner says, "We had *church* today!"

(5) Finally, the black preacher is a wordsmith and expert storyteller. The ability to paint a picture with skillful word choice gives pride to the congregation and shows we have come a long way from the slave fields to where we are today. The black preacher was usually the most educated in the congregation, so he needed to paint word pictures for those in the congregation who were not educated. The skillful art of telling the story keeps the congregation linked to the rich heritage of the black church's origin.

Notice the masterful word choice in the message by Rev. Henry Lockyear entitled, "Do You Know Him?" (the message was given at a YWAM meeting in Hawaii):

He's enduringly strong. He's entirely sincere. He's eternally steadfast. He's immortally graceful. He's imperially powerful. He's impartially merciful. Do you know Him?

He's the greatest phenomenon that has ever crossed the horizon of this world. He's God's Son. He's a sinner's Savior. He's the centerpiece of civilization. He stands in the solitude of himself. He is unique. He's unparalleled. He's unprecedented. He's the loftiest idea in literature. He's the highest personality in philosophy. He's the supreme problem in high criticism.

He supplies strength for the weak. He is available for the tempted and the tried. He sympathizes and saves. He strengthens and sustains. He guards and guides. He heals the sick. He cleanses the lepers. He forgives sinners. He discharges debtors. He delivers the captives. He defends the feeble. He blesses the young. He serves the unfortunate. He regards the aged. He rewards the diligent. And he beautifies the meager. I wonder if you know him.

Attention is also given to metaphors, as illustrated in Dr. King's speech when he uses banking terms to show what America owes to her people of color. The use of repeated phrases and just the right words are marks of solid black preaching.

These five ingredients are by no means exhaustive but give a general understanding of the context, content, and uniqueness of black preaching. When my brothers of the lighter hue ask me what their approach might be when preaching to African Americans, I tell them not to try too hard. The best advice is to be yourself and expect a response from the audience. When someone in the congregation responds with an "Amen!" or "Praise God!" just keep preaching and soak it up.

BIBLIOGRAPHY

King, Martin Luther, Jr. "I Have a Dream." 1968. In the *Annals of America* (Vol. 18 of *Encyclopedia Britannica*).
Mitchell, Henry H. 1977. *The Recovery of Preaching.* San Francisco: Harper & Row.

Chapter 53

ASIAN-AMERICAN PREACHING

Matthew D. Kim

In addressing the topic of Asian-American preaching, we must start with the question: Who is Asian American? *Asian American* has commonly referred to East Asians: Chinese, Japanese, and Koreans. This view has unfortunately excluded non-East Asian Americans (e.g., people from Bangladesh, Bhutan, Burma, Cambodia, the Philippines, Indo China, Indonesia, Iwo Jima, Laos, Malaysia, Nepal, Okinawa, Pakistan, India, Singapore, Sri Lanka, Thailand, Vietnam, etc.) and the 150,000 other Asian Americans who do not fit neatly into one of these prescribed Asian ethnic categories. For additional information, see the United States Census Bureau 2000 website at http://www.census.gov.

Like members of other ethnic and racial categories, Asian Americans vary by ethnicity, language, generation, class, and gender. Because of this extensive diversity, generalizations are inevitable, yet for the sake of specificity, I will comment briefly on the preaching of two distinct subgroups of Asian Americans: (1) first-generation Asian Americans, that is, foreign-born Asian immigrants and refugees, and (2) second- and multigenerational U.S.-born Asian Americans.

MARGINALIZATION

All Asian Americans, regardless of the duration of their residence in America, experience marginalization. Sang Hyun Lee of Princeton Theological Seminary states that for Asian Americans marginality is a way of life: "In the Asian world, we are often criticized for not being Asian enough; in American society, we are looked down on for not being American enough" (1999, p. 225). In the words of Asian-American author Mia Tuan, we are perceived by white Americans as "forever foreigners" who cannot and will not be accepted fully in America (1998).

David Gibbons, a biracial Korean and Caucasian pastor in Southern California, shares a personal account of marginalization he faced during his undergraduate days at a southern Christian university: "As I entered his office, the dean greeted me cordially. He proceeded to inform me that I could date only Asian women because I looked Asian. Dating someone of another ethnic origin would be breaking the school's 'biblically based' rule of no interracial dating, he explained. The Catch–22 for the university was twofold. I was both Asian and Caucasian. Yet, my brother, who was of the same birth parents, was given the choice of dating either Asian or white women. Why? Because he looked more Anglo than I did" (1996, p. 7).

Because of such marginalization, Asian-American preachers will often align their sermons with the experiences of biblical misfits like Noah, Joseph, Moses, the wandering Israelites, David, Daniel, the Samaritan women, Paul, and even Jesus himself. The stories of these biblical figures help to assuage some of the psychological distress of many Asians who call America home. Asian-American preachers should ask themselves, *In what ways have I encountered marginalization in America, and how can I assist my congregants to embrace the narratives of biblical characters to cope with their pain?*

FIRST-GENERATION ASIAN AMERICANS

Since most first-generation Asian-American churches serve primarily the people from their own ethnic background and who speak the same language, first-generation Asian-American preachers have an undying commitment to their places of origin. Many such preachers effectively use illustrations and personal stories from their native countries.

The peril for some of them is the lessons their sermons impart may be a hybrid of both Christian and Asian religious and cultural values that are shaped by the country from which they came. Two dominant theological themes in first-generation Asian-American sermons are based on the dualistic relationship between suffering and blessing.

First, the importance of suffering is emphasized in the traditional tenets and practices of Buddhism and Hinduism (Southard, 1989, p. 628). For Christians this suffering mentality is not only a continuation of the first-generation's past experiences of foreign oppression and current discrimination in American society, but it is simultaneously a voluntary suffering as in experiencing oneness with God through Christ who serves as our cosufferer (Southard, 1989, p. 625). Imbalance comes when the willingness to suffer for Christ turns into a need to suffer or into a trust in our suffering as a means of merit before God.

In a recent conversation with my mother, she told me how my parents saw Mel Gibson's film *The Passion of the Christ*. My mother said, "When I saw how much Jesus suffered for me, I cried so much and so did your dad. Jesus suffered so much for me. I must go now and suffer for him." This example illustrates how the Buddhist-Hindu worldview of suffering infiltrates the consciousness of even my first-generation Asian-American *Christian* parents.

While evangelical first-generation Asian-American pastors preach that salvation can only be received through personal faith in Jesus' death and resurrection, many first-generation Asian-American Christians still believe their earthly suffering has some merit.

A second prominent theme for some first-generation Asian-American preachers is the shamanistic concept of blessing. Shamanism originated among Mongolic nations in northeast Asia and in some sections of Siberia. It is a religious faith based on superstition and shamanic ritual.

Engrained into Asian consciousness, the shamanistic ideology of blessing has gradually permeated some of the first-generation Asian-American churches. These Christians may be taught that God blesses his children richly with both material and spiritual wealth, in accordance with the concept of blessing in the Old Testament. Interestingly, this focus on blessings in this life corresponds directly with the immigrant mindset of pursuing the American Dream. Eunjoo Mary Kim, who teaches homiletics at Iliff School of Theology, says: "[Shamanistic] preaching gives the listeners the impression that the gospel itself is a present-centered and success-oriented message" (1999, p. 32).

SECOND- AND MULTIGENERATIONAL ASIAN AMERICANS

While first-generation Asian-American churches are predominantly homogenous and monocultural, second- and multigenerational Asian-American congregations are becoming progressively multi-Asian and multiethnic (Fong, 1999, pp. 205–14). In their quest for cultural sensitivity, many Asian-American pastors deliver sermons that emphasize the ethnicity and culture of no particular ethnic group

(Tseng, 2002, p. 278). These sermons convey orthodox teaching but lack contextualization for varied Asian-American audiences.

The trend among many preachers of multi-Asian and multiethnic congregations has been to discourage the promotion of ethnic culture and tradition within church walls. For instance, one Korean-American pastor expressed that his church was not a Korean church or an Asian church, but rather a place for everyone regardless of their ethnic-racial background. He proceeded to lay down ground rules for the many Korean Americans in the congregation. First, he banned eating *kimchi* and other types of Korean food in the church. Second, he refused to make announcements for any Asian events in the community. Third, according to Michael Luo, he prevented his congregants from going to Korea town for lunch. Luo observes:

> Today, despite [this pastor's] efforts over six years to make people of all races feel welcome, the 250 to 300 worshippers who attend the church's three English services every week are almost all Koreans, with a scattering of other Asians. He has attracted only a handful of whites and blacks. (Luo, www.imdiversity.com)

By deemphasizing ethnicity and culture from the pulpit, some Asian-American preachers prevent ethnic people from being themselves and in a sense reject the beautiful diversity of God's creative workmanship in human differences. Since every person innately possesses an ethnic and cultural tradition, Asian-American preachers should make the most of illustrations that highlight examples from the various ethnicities, cultures, and traditions to which congregants belong.

It is important to contextualize sermons and assist congregants in embracing their ethnicities and cultures. For example, many Asian Americans dislike their physical characteristics and believe God made a mistake when creating Asians. Such ideas should be addressed and corrected through Asian-American sermons. It is possible to overemphasize Christian identity to the complete neglect of ethnic and racial identities. Community will never be built in the Asian-American church by shying away from our differences but rather by acknowledging them head on and conversing sincerely with those who are unlike us.

STRENGTHS

First-generation Asian-American preachers skillfully use biblical narratives that relate to the immigrant and refugee experience. Asian-American preachers know how to communicate stories at heart level. Their hearers respond well to self-disclosure, to hearing personal accounts that represent either triumph or despair experienced by their pastors that reflect on God's immense goodness and grace.

Asian-American preachers in multi-Asian and multiethnic settings are effective biblical expositors who know how to explain theological truths in a cogent style. Many can articulate stories in powerful ways.

During my seminary training, I accepted a part-time position as a youth pastor serving second-generation Korean Americans in Boston. After six months, I looked into my students' disinterested eyes and had a preacher's moment. I realized my sermons had not been addressing the needs of these Korean-American teenagers.

My sermons required a complete makeover. Not only did I need to preach from my life experiences as a bicultural Korean American, but also my sermons needed to be shaped in a

way that my second-generation Korean-American listeners would understand and embrace. I started to use illustrations from my life experiences growing up as a bicultural Korean American and all of the pleasures and baggage that go along with being an Americanized Asian-American Christian. When I began to engage with my Korean and American DNA and my second-generation Korean-American teenage listeners, my preaching took a positive turn.

David Ng suggests, "The church needs to support the search for and the recovery of ethnic and cultural identity and values. . . . Asian North American Christians believe that their identity, culture, language, religious heritage—their whole way of life—is good and is where God is present and at work" (1995, xxiii).

Asian-American pastors must preach in a style that is unique to our culture so that our messages will connect with the minds and hearts of bicultural Asian-American souls. By combining methodical biblical exposition with the exegesis of our Asian-American listeners, we can present sermons with timeless scriptural truths in a contextualized, personal, ethnic, and cultural style.

BIBLIOGRAPHY

Fong, Ken Uyeda. 1999. *Pursuing the Pearl: A Comprehensive Resource for Multi-Asian Ministry.* Valley Forge, Pa.: Judson.

Gibbons, David. 1996. "Introduction," in *Losing Face and Finding Grace*, by Tom Lin (Downers Grove, Ill.: InterVarsity Press).

Kim, Eunjoo Mary. 1999. *Preaching the Presence of God: A Homiletic from an Asian American Perspective.* Valley Forge, Pa.: Judson.

Lee, Sang Hyun. 1999. "Pilgrimage and Home in the Wilderness of Marginality: Symbols and Context in Asian American Theology." In *New Spiritual Homes:*

Religion and Asian Americans, ed. David K. Yoo (Honolulu: Univ. of Hawaii Press).

Luo, Michael, "For Asian-American Churches, Integration Proves Complicated," from http://www.imdiversity.com/Article_Detail.asp?Article _ID=8972

Ng, David. 1995. "Introduction." *People on the Way: Asian North Americans Discovering Christ, Culture, and Community*, ed. David Ng (Valley Forge, Pa.: Judson).

Southard, Naomi P. F. 1989. "Recovery and Rediscovered Images: Spiritual Resources for Asian American Women." *Asia Journal of Theology* 3.

Tseng, Timothy. 2002. "Asian Pacific American Christianity in a Post-Ethnic Future." *American Baptist Quarterly* 21.

Tuan, Mia. 1998. *Forever Foreigners or Honorary Whites? The Asian Ethnic Experience Today*. New Brunswick, N.J.: Rutgers Univ. Press.

Chapter 54

WORK WINS?

How your message can restore their soul

Lee Eclov

I have an old black and white photograph, dated 1909, showing seven Scandinavian young people sitting up straight and solemn in a row, posing for their graduation picture. My grandfather is among them. Over them is a banner with their class motto: "Work Wins." An immigrant creed, if ever there was one. Problem is, I can never look at the picture without taking the sign the wrong way: Work Wins (and You Lose).

The first time I thought of it that way was when I was preaching from Genesis 3 and the curse on Adam in 3:17. "Cursed is the ground because of you; through painful toil you will eat of it all the days of your life." See what I mean? Work wins.

Work, of course, predates the Fall; God gave us work to do that we might reflect his image. Work is good. It is meant to ennoble and enrich. But work was infected with sin, and now it can be not only deadly dull, but just

plain deadly. Work is "painful toil." The "thorns and thistles" God promised Adam now grow in sales meetings, around copy machines and computer servers, and in the Dilbert world of corporate politics.

VIOLENCE TO THE SPIRIT

Studs Terkel begins the introduction to his oral history, *Working*, this way:

This book, being about work, is, by its very nature, about violence—to the spirit as well as to the body. It is about ulcers as well as accidents, about shouting matches as well as fistfights, about nervous breakdowns as well as kicking the dog around. It is, above all (or beneath all), about daily humiliations. To survive the day is triumph enough for the walking wounded among the great many of us....

It is about a search, too, for daily meaning as well as daily bread, for recognition as well as cash, for astonishment rather than torpor; in short, for a sort of life rather than a Monday through Friday sort of dying.

I read that to a couple acquaintances who work for the gas company. "That's us," they said, shaking their heads. One of them said of the climate where he labors, "I can see now why some people bring guns to work."

Not everyone feels that way about work, of course. Certainly Christians whose minds have been bathed by the Holy Spirit often begin to see work differently. Nonetheless, the people who gather before the preacher each week are usually well-acquainted with the violence that work does to the human spirit.

THERE IS A BALM

As with everything vital to people, God tells us the truth in the Bible about work as it should be, and as preachers, we must share God's good news about work with them. But we must do more than preach about work. Worship—and preaching, in particular—must be for these brothers and sisters the Word-soaked balm of our good Shepherd, who "restores my soul." Road weary executives and salesmen need more than a backrub. Nurses and security guards need more than to put their feet up. Secretaries and carpenters need more than some peace and quiet if their souls are to be restored. The old spiritual says, "There is a balm in Gilead to heal the sin-sick soul." That balm works for the work-bruised spirit as well.

God's balm comes in different jars. As physicians of the soul, we preachers must often touch souls with God's different salves.

Apply the Balm of Grace

Christian workers often feel guilty and weak. They show up in church with the baggage of work-a-day sins slung over their shoulders— gossip perhaps, or complaining or loafing. They probably know that "Jesus forgives their sins," but still think he is pretty well fed up with their failures nonetheless. Our sermons ought to have a biblical measure of "thou shalt" and "shalt not" to be sure, but our stock-in-trade— our work product as preachers—is the grace of God in Christ. We come to them as God's own consultants for the heart, always speaking in the dialect and accents of the cross. God forgives you. God loves you. Go in peace!

Apply the Balm of God's Aid

Some jobs are very hard. How often do you hear your people talk about the pressure at work? Doing the work of two or three people? Deadlines that soak up nights and weekends like a sponge? I'm not sure our people always realize how skilled the Lord is at what they do. Part of his gracious provision to them is help. We find God's help when writing a sermon, and they can have his extraordinary help to write a good business plan, to cope with cranky clients, to untangle software problems, or to deal with demanding or demeaning coworkers. Jesus is good at business! And he gladly offers his help to his people.

Apply the Balm of the Beautiful

Old Testament priests only served in the temple occasionally. Otherwise, I suppose, they tended farms or fixed furniture. But when their turn in the temple came, they left their work clothes behind, bathed, and donned white linen. Then they walked into the sacred environs of the Holy One.

Worship and preaching ought to clothe the priesthood of believers in white linen and elevate them to holy privileges. Some sermons give our people work belts and armor for Christlike living in this dark world. But some sermons, and parts of sermons, need to dress them in white and put them to the holy work of awe and adoration. Some sermons ought to put God's golden vessels in their hands and the songs of Zion on their lips. Sermons on the glorious character of God, on the wonders of the cross, on the hope of heaven clothe working stiffs in white and position them amidst the bread of the Presence, the lampstand, and the incense of God. Such preaching is practical, indeed.

THE THERAPY OF THE CURSE

I believe the curses of Genesis 3 were God's ingenious therapy for sin-stubborn hearts. The burdens God pronounced are graciously designed to force people to look toward the God they would otherwise ignore. The struggles that go with work are like that. Work itself is a gift of God, but the weeds and thistles turn it into "painful toil." So each week we remind God's beloved people how to keep their balance and their spiritual sanity where they work. We help them turn from their work to the Master.

A couple of years ago I read in the *Chicago Tribune* that the new head of the Chicago Sewer Department called a big rally for his eight hundred workers. On the wall behind the boss in the Plumbers Union Hall was a banner that read, "Bringing Sewers Above Ground." His pep talk sounded like Vince Lombardi: "Winning isn't a sometimes thing," he shouted. "It's an all-the-time thing!" The sewer workers cheered as if they were going to storm out onto Soldier Field.

On Sunday mornings, Christian workers gather for a rally, of sorts. But they need more for their souls than religious rah-rah and slogans. I sometimes look out on the Sunday-scrubbed saints and think about the dirty, difficult places my people must work every week. Some offices, of course, are filthier than sewers. Some schools are darker than underground tunnels. A lot of folks spend their week trying to keep the gunk off their hearts, trying to keep their souls from smelling like a cesspool. On Sunday mornings, our work as pastors is to help them remember how important their jobs are, for, after all, they work in the same world where Jesus worked. They work for him as surely as we do. And one day we will be promoted to work without thorns and thistles, without sweat in our eyes and sin blistering our souls. Some day soon, we shall serve the Lord in plain sight of his throne!

Chapter 55

ONE SERMON, TWO MESSAGES

How to deliver one sermon at two completely different services

Wayne Brouwer

My church has two distinct worshiping communities. The traditional community meets in the sanctuary. Its design is hushed and Spartan, with subtle gray walls, indirect lighting, white cornices and woodwork, and a choir loft directly behind me as I preach. The pews are long and straight, arranged in Puritan concert-hall fashion. The pulpit, with its clean lines, is a dignified symbol of tradition, authority, and austerity. When you enter the sanctuary, you are quiet. The organ sets the mood of somberness.

Worship here is informed by Enlightenment rationality: God is the wholly Other whom you approach at a distance by the mediated steps of classical artistry in word and song.

The contemporary worshiping community, by contrast, gathers in the sunny Great Room. The chairs are stackables, arranged in a sweeping semicircle of eye-to-eye intimacy. The acoustics in the room are poor, but that doesn't matter, since the praise team is powered by amplified speakers pointed in every direction. There's no pulpit, of course—only a music stand, which I may use if I want to. People tell me I preach better if I don't; I get more "real and personal, not tied to words on a page."

When you enter the Great Room, it's noisy. But noisy conversation and people interaction are the home of spirituality in a post-Enlightenment community. God is not "out there"; he is here, among us.

So each week I prepare doubly for Sunday morning worship. The "feel" and "mind" of the two services are so different that I find it helpful to shape my sermon for the two groups.

SHAKESPEARE OR "ER"?

Often the very things that make a sermon powerful in the traditional worshiping community decrease its effectiveness at the contemporary worship service. And vice versa.

Sometimes I'm crafty with my words. The traditional group loves it—they can see God in the art of wordplay. The contemporary group hates it—they think it is trying to put on a show that isn't real.

For instance, here are a few passages from a message called "Mountain Standard Time," based on Isaiah 2:1–5.

Do you know why you came here this morning? Do you know why you came to this church and wanted to become a member of it? It's because there's something of Mountain Standard Time that whistles through this place. We're bound by the clock out in the lounge that chimes the quarter hour in Eastern Standard Time. But just for a while, in this place of worship, we experience the quickening pace of life on the mountain of God, somewhere beyond the International Date Line. And Mountain Standard Time becomes our wish, and our hope and our prayer.

After I preached this sermon at the traditional

worship service, there was a quiet hush, and then people streamed toward me from all directions. This message spoke powerfully to them. They were moved by the theme and the crafting of the words and scenes that conveyed it.

On the other hand, at the contemporary worship service, I felt as if I were just marking time. At appropriate moments people smiled or laughed a little. But mostly they seemed to tell me I was missing the real world. What was I getting at, anyway? A good friend said to me after the service, "Wayne, I sure like your practical sermons better!"

Shakespeare and the classics speak to those in the traditional worshiping community, while hot television programs hit the button in the other.

THE SIMILARITIES

When I preach best for both communities, I do three things well.

First, I exegete faithfully. The Bible is the Word of God, and nothing in my creativity or rhetorical technique can outdo it in power and significance. When I exegete well, I speak for God—not because I'm such a great speaker, but because he is. He spoke the Word, and he still speaks it today.

Of course, exegeting well doesn't mean I carry all my exegetical work into the pulpit (or to the music stand) with me. It simply means I have found a message worth preaching because it is God's message. And it means that the form of the message rings true to the intent of the passage in tone and substance.

Second, I tell stories. Bible stories. Human stories. Literary stories. I find stories are a powerful way to speak across generations and to different audiences. Storytelling helps me bridge

the psychological and sociological divide separating my two congregations.

Third, preaching needs to create vision. There must be a larger reality that all enter when they are caught up into the kingdom of God. I don't consider Sunday morning preaching to be simply the transmission of cognitive information that empowers someone else by its insight. Preaching, while often encompassing a teaching element, is more of an exercise in frame-building and world-portraying. I call people to participate in a world that is larger than their experiences, one that feeds the craving of their souls, one that always welcomes them at the doorway called HOME.

THE DIFFERENCES

Over the years I've developed a manuscript style that makes it easy for me to read without appearing as if I am closely tied to exact wordings on a page. For the traditional worshiping community, where I am somewhat limited in movement at the pulpit, I basically read the manuscript in an engaging, conversational style.

When I move into the Great Room with the contemporary worshiping community, I usually take the manuscript, though sometimes I jot notes on a slip of paper or even wing it with no notes or manuscript. There I walk back and forth at the center of the crowd, mostly hitting the high points and telling stories. If I have the manuscript, I put it on a music stand and refer to it now and again in order to keep my thoughts focused.

But even the way I use illustrations often differs in each setting. Recently, in a message called "Shopping for a New Wardrobe," based on Paul's teaching in Colossians 3:10–11 to "put off the old self" and to "put on the new," I began by asking people if they liked what I was wearing. In my manuscript, which I used rather closely at the traditional worship service, it came out like this:

Do you like what I'm wearing today?

One of my friends who is a pastor says that his people respond to the different colors of the ties he wears on Sunday morning.

Do you think that's so?!

He says when he wears a yellow tie, they seem to get restless quickly. My friend says that when he wears a red tie, people seem to sing better. They're more attentive. They seem to get the point quicker.

Now, I don't know if he's on to anything. But I do know that clothes make a statement. We look at each other's clothes. Teens check out the gear. Does it have the right labels? Is it the kind all the right kids wear at school? Women look at the cut of a dress. Men go for the insignia on the pocket of the shirt. . . .

Ah! Clothes make a point, don't they?!

When I went to the contemporary worship service, I ad-libbed that entire section. I acted it out, raising my tie in front of the crowd and walking around for them to inspect it.

In both services the same point was made. However, the illustration was tailored to the particular congregation.

TRANSITION TIME

As soon as the worship service ends for the traditional worshiping community, I walk out of the front of the church building and move quickly toward my office. This is the part I dislike about making such a quick turnaround on Sunday mornings. I would rather linger with people for a while and spend moments in pastoral conversations.

However, I need to get away in order to make the transition to the next worship service.

In my office, I take off my suit jacket, role up my shirt sleeves, and sort through the pages of my sermon manuscript. I decide whether I'm going to use the manuscript again, or if I need to make some quick notes on a Post-it note, or if I should try to deliver the message without notes at all.

At the best of times, this exercise taxes my powers of communication, draining the energy out of me. At the worst of times, I feel as if I have failed one of the worshiping communities, and I end Sunday with a terrible headache.

Usually I finish Sunday morning somewhere in between. Still, when I do my preaching right, there is a great possibility for the two congregations to move on parallel paths toward the Parousia. And each, on its pilgrimage, can do effective ministry for Christ.

Chapter 56

THE PLAYFUL PREACHER
Using humor and irony

Richard P. Hansen

Most listeners today are skeptical of power and control. With our culture's commitment to relativism, we have been taught to fear patriarchy and colonialism, not to mention preachers and politicians. To protect ourselves from manipulation, the current generation often uses irony. The shrug and the wink deconstruct power better than argument or confrontation. If we don't take the government, church, university, or media seriously, they can't hurt us, says the postmodernist. Besides, who's to say whose version of "truth" is true, anyway?

While preachers who see themselves as heralds of God's Word must be skeptical of such skepticism, I believe we can plunder the Egyptians by using humor and irony in our preaching. More playfulness can help us communicate more seriously. But that's not easy for me, one whose spiritual ancestors are John Calvin and John Knox.

As I've tried to lighten up, here's what I've discovered.

COLORING INSIDE THE LINES

Playfulness is sometimes misunderstood. One of my early attempts came while preaching about sexuality. To introduce the sermon, I asked both the men and women to read responsively some of the more graphic passages from the Song of Songs. Sure that I had made my point, I playfully asked when they were finished, "Did any of you know this X-rated material was in the Bible?"

I was met with stone-faced, hostile silence. One person's playfulness is another's irreverence. So it is wise to know your congregation's limits.

Another try with my current church brought better results. A guest preacher had described being so excited when his football team scored a touchdown that he jumped off the couch in front of the TV, pumped his arm up and down, and shouted, "Yes, yes, yes. YES!" So I decided to use his antics the following Sunday after a soloist had just sung a deeply moving piece.

"There's just one thing I want to say after James's song," I said in my best preacher's voice. I paused. Then, pumping my arm, I said, "Yes, yes, yes. YES!" Everyone who had attended the previous Sunday roared with laughter.

My former congregation would have seen this as irreverent. But not this church. They considered it playful—and appropriate.

Playful preachers do not try to use reverse psychology. It's not stating the opposite of what I desire. ("Guess what? Our church does not need your money this year.") Such obvious gimmicks are both ineffective and false.

Playfulness does not misrepresent or deny the truth; it creates a new dynamic—within me. "The major effect of playfulness and paradox is on the perpetrator," says Friedman. "It takes him or her out of the feedback position. It detriangles and changes the balance of the emotional interdependency. It is the change in the structure of the triangle that gets the other person functioning or thinking differently."

In preaching, I am the "perpetrator." Becoming more playful affects me more than my audience. I lighten up. Playfulness frees me from trying so hard to make an impact. Hence, the emotional triangle involving me, the congregation, and the message changes. People are free to listen without activating their defenses. The possibility of impact actually increases.

That's the paradox.

AROUND THE MAGINOT LINE

I've found it helpful to identify who in the congregation I feel most responsible to convince. Ironically, these are often the very people I will never touch. Why? They have built a Maginot Line.

The Maginot Line was the impenetrable system of barriers and bunkers built by France to protect itself from Imperial Germany after World War I. In World War II, however, Hitler didn't attack France through the Maginot Line. His Panzer divisions made a sweeping detour around it through Belgium. France fell swiftly.

When preachers try too hard to make an impact, Klaxons sound and bunker walls go up. My people often know what I'm going to say even before I say it (they know the issues I'm most serious about). When facing a Maginot Line, frontal attacks are valiant but ineffective.

Rather than slug it out in a frontal attack, wisdom suggests a detour. What is the last thing they expect me to say on this issue? What would make them laugh? How can I goodnaturedly (not spitefully) be playful?

TO STING LIKE A BEE

Playful preachers do not overemphasize exegetical data. As a young preacher, I was certain that if I marshaled enough exegetical evidence (from the original languages, of course), I could bludgeon my listeners into belief. My sermons were like boxing matches: I didn't always score a knockout, but I expected to win on points.

Since then, I have joined the Mohammed Ali school of homiletics. I must learn to dance like a butterfly if I want to sting like a bee. The footwork of the sermon (how you say it) is just as, if not more, essential than the content (what you say).

Of course, footwork is a means to an end—impact. Playful sermons are not intended to impress the listener (or the preacher) with one's creativity. They are used to communicate truth.

Once I preached about the Lord's Supper as being a prelude to the messianic banquet. I wanted to communicate the joy felt by the early church as they celebrated this event. However, only by coming at the sermon in a lighter fashion could I detour around my church's years of solemn tradition. The sacrament had an aura more of wake than banquet.

I hit on the idea of having eyewitnesses report on their joyful experience. I imagined what caterers present at the meals might have observed.

The sermon opened with two caterers pausing for breath while serving the heavenly banquet. Soon they begin to reminisce about their previous catering jobs for the Lord. They remember the joyful Old Testament feasts in the temple, Jesus' upper room meal with his disciples, the agape meals of the early church, and modern expressions that somehow (in the caterers' minds) lost the intended joy. Finally, the caterers gesture at the people enjoying the heavenly banquet and ask each other, "When they were back on earth, do you ever wonder if they really understood what they were doing?"

This sermon, "Observations of God's Caterers," was my fancy footwork around the entrenched expectations of my listeners. Because it was screened through playful, imaginary characters, most who listened did not feel defensive or threatened.

WITH FRIENDS LIKE THESE

Some of us need permission to be playful. Like my personality, my preaching tends to be serious: to travel well-worn intellectual pathways, expressing the doctrines of the faith in centuries-old imagery. Fortunately, I also have some friends who release me to be playful with the great themes of my faith.

One such friend is Frederick Buechner. Another is C. S. Lewis. While studying, I keep an anthology of one or the other close at hand. I often dip into it for fifteen or twenty minutes as I begin thinking about my sermon. Their playful ideas, even on topics completely unrelated to my theme, push me to play with ideas as well. In their company, I see fresh approaches to the old, old story. Lewis's *Screwtape Letters* is deadly serious, but it's also lots of fun. Lewis shows us his playful stance in the opening quotations: "The best way to drive out the devil, if he will not yield to texts of Scripture, is to jeer and flout him, for he cannot bear scorn" (Martin Luther); and "The devil . . . the proud spirite . . . cannot endure to be mocked" (Thomas More).

PLAYING WITH WORDS

"The difference between the right word and the almost right word," wrote Mark Twain, "is the difference between lightning and the lightning bug." That's a helpful reminder. Words are the raw materials of sermons. The right use of words can inject a sermon with needed doses of playfulness.

Here are a couple of questions I ask myself to add freshness to my words.

Can it be understood in different ways? While preparing an Easter message on the Emmaus road experience, I noticed that when the doubtful disciples were confronted with the risen Christ, they "disbelieved for joy" (Luke 24:41, RSV).

It dawned on me that "I can't believe it" can be understood in two ways: either as an expression of doubt or as an ecstatic expression of joy (as when the 1980 U.S. hockey team won an Olympic gold medal against overwhelming odds: "I can't believe it!"). My sermon traced the journey each of us takes with the disciples. It began with the "I can't believe it" of doubt and despair while trudging down the Emmaus road and ended with the "I can't believe it" of joy, hugging and dancing in the presence of the risen Christ.

Does it have a little-known or surprising meaning? Dr. Ian Pitt-Watson, former professor of preaching at Fuller Theological Seminary, once preached a sermon in which he playfully countered the common assumption that Jesus' beatitude "blessed are the meek" implies wimpish weakness.

He observes of the word meek: "In the French Bible the word is translated *debonnaire*—debonair!—with overtones of courtesy, gallantry, chivalry (remember Hollywood's 'golden oldies' and Cary Grant in his heyday?). Debonair: gentle, sensitive, courteous, modest, unpretentious—yet strong and brave and fun and happy."

Debonair Cary Grant released meekness from the negative images from which I had imprisoned it.

Not every sermon can or should be playful. But when we find ourselves trying harder to lit-tle effect, we may want to try less hard. Loosen up and be playful! Freedom comes to us and our listeners when we say with Bill Murray, an alumnus of *Saturday Night Live*, "Hey, I'm serious!"

Chapter 57

WHAT AUTHORITY DO WE HAVE ANYMORE?
How to bridge the credibility gap

Haddon Robinson

Time has changed the way people view pas-tors. The average preacher today is not going to make it on the basis of the dignity of his position.

A century ago, the pastor was looked to as the person of wisdom and integrity in the com-munity. Authority lay in the office of pastor. The minister was the parson, often the best-educated person in town and the one to whom people looked for help in interpreting the out-side world. He had the unique opportunity to read and study and often was the principal voice in deciding how the community should react in any moral or religious situation.

But today, the average citizen takes a differ-ent view of pastors and preachers. Perhaps we're not lumped with scam artists or manipu-lative fund raisers, but we face an Olympic challenge to earn respect, credibility, and authority.

In the face of society's scorn—or being rele-gated to a box labeled "private" and "spiri-tual"—many preachers struggle with the issue of authority. Why should anyone pay attention to us? What is the source of our credibility? In such a climate, how can we regain the legiti-mate authority our preaching needs to commu-nicate the gospel with power and effect?

Let me identify some guidelines that have assisted me.

ARTICULATE UNEXPRESSED FEELINGS

One way to build credibility with today's congregations is to let people see that you understand their situation. Many people in the pew suspect that preachers inhabit another world. Folks in the pew may listen politely to a reporter of the distant, biblical past, but they won't be gripped unless they believe this speaker speaks to their condition.

This is why, in a sermon, I try to speak for the people before I speak to them. Have you ever listened to a speaker and found yourself saying, "Yeah, that's right; that's my reaction, too"? The speaker gave words to your feel-ings—perhaps better than you could have expressed them yourself. You sensed the preacher knew you. He explained you to you.

We capture the attention of people when we

show that our experience overlaps theirs. For instance, a preacher might say, "There's no good place for a .150 hitter in a championship lineup. No matter where you put him, he's out of place." If listeners know sports, they know that's true. The preacher's speaking their language.

Or the minister may take a punch line from a comic strip, or use material from *Business Week* or *Advertising Age* or *The Wall Street Journal*. A business executive will resonate with that. Obviously this pastor knows a bit more about the bottom line than playing Monopoly. Through illustrations, the preacher has revealed something about his reading, his thinking, and awareness of life. When some areas of a speaker's life overlap with the listeners', they are more likely to listen. He's gained some credibility. An ingredient in effective preaching is using specific material that connects with lives in the congregation.

LISTEN TO THE INVISIBLE CONGREGATION

Another way effective preachers connect with the audience is to sit six or seven specific flesh-and-blood people around their desks as they prepare. I have assembled such a committee in my mind as real to me as if they were there.

In that group sits a friend who is an outspoken cynic. As I think through my material, I sometimes can hear him sigh, "You've got to be kidding, Robinson. That's pious junk food. What world are you living in?"

Another is an older woman who is a simple believer, who takes preachers and preaching very seriously. While I prepare sermons, I ask, "Am I raising questions that will trouble her? Will my sermon help her?"

A teenager sprawls in the circle, wondering how long I'm going to preach. I can make the sermon seem shorter if I can keep him interested.

A divorced mother takes her place feeling alone and overwhelmed by her situation. What do I say to her?

Then there's the unbeliever who doesn't understand religious jargon and yet has come to church but doesn't quite know why.

Another makes his living as a dock worker. He has a strong allegiance to his union, thinks management is a rip off, curses if he gets upset, and enjoys bowling on Thursday night.

The last is a black teacher who would rather attend a black church but comes to a white church because her husband thinks it's good for their kids. She is a believer, but she's angry about life. She's very sensitive about racist remarks and put-downs of women, and she will let me know if my sermon centers on white, middle-class values dressed up as biblical absolutes.

I change the group from time to time. But all of them are people I know. They have names, faces, and voices. I could prepare a vita on each of them. While they do not know it, each of them contributes significantly to my sermon preparation.

SPEAK WITH AUTHORITY

Preachers, of course, have to be more than "fellow strugglers." No one is helped by "You're a loser; I'm a loser; let's keep losing together."

People want to believe you have taken your own advice and, while you've not arrived, you're on the way. You'll never learn to be a .300 hitter by watching three .100 hitters. You study a .325 hitter. Although he will occasionally strike out, he knows how to hit.

Likewise, people want to listen to somebody who knows what the struggle is, has taken the Bible's message seriously, and knows how to hit.

Of course, we identify with the needs and experiences of our people—we're every bit as human as they are. But our task is to speak a word that is qualitatively different from normal conversation. Effective preaching combines the two and gives people hope that they can be better than they are.

When the combination is right, we preach with authority, which is different from being an authoritarian. Preaching with authority means you've done your homework. You know your people's struggles and hurts. But you also know the Bible and theology. You can explain the Bible clearly. We help our credibility when we practice biblical preaching.

The authoritarian, however, is someone who speaks about biblical and nonbiblical things in the same tone of voice. Whether the subject is the Super Bowl or the Second Coming, the verdict is delivered with the same certainty and conviction.

An authoritative tone without genuine biblical authority is sound and fury signifying nothing. When we speak with authority, we preach the Bible's message without embarrassment, but we also communicate that we don't always know how to tailor faith to life.

Be Precise in Descriptions

Authority also comes from a track record of being truthful and not distorting the facts. It's especially important to be precise in our definitions and descriptions, whether we're defining the historical background of the text or delivering an apt illustration. Accuracy builds credibility.

I once used an illustration about snakes and referred to them as "slimy, poisonous creatures." A woman came up afterward and said, "Snakes aren't slimy; they are dry. And most snakes aren't poisonous." She worked in a zoo, so she spotted that I was careless in my description. As a result, I had given her reason for suspecting the rest of what I had to say.

The need for precision is particularly acute with an antagonistic or less than supportive audience. They'll focus on your minor error as a reason for not listening to the rest of what you have to say.

Display Character

For church leaders, perhaps no factor contributes more to legitimate authority and credibility than authentic Christian character. It's what Aristotle called ethos; in New Testament terms, it's being mature, upright. These days, if we want credibility in the pulpit, genuine character has to come through.

Part of effective preaching is the ability to make the presentation match the internal conviction. The image we project will influence our credibility. Appearance in the pulpit will affect the way people respond. I'm convinced inwardly, for example, of the importance of discipline and order in the Christian life. How can I present myself in a way that matches the conviction? In the first thirty seconds, people are deciding whether they're going to listen. God looks on the heart, but people in our culture look on the outside. Am I disheveled? Do my shoes need to be shined? If I'm fifty pounds overweight, they may perceive that I'm not disciplined or that I'm careless about myself.

Obviously one advantage of a lengthy ministry is that the pastor has a better chance to bring perception and reality together. The long-term pastor is judged more on his pattern of behavior than on a specific appearance. People are more likely to say, "The pastor not only talks love; he gives love. He was there in our family crisis when we needed him." A pattern of care can cover a multitude of less-than-stellar sermons.

Of course, the flip side is that we may have things to live down, and that also takes time. A pastor I know lost his temper in a board meeting and spoke some harsh words in anger. Now, months later, when he stands in the pulpit, some people play that record mentally. Another pastor in a similar situation confessed his misuse of anger and publicly asked for forgiveness. He got it. In his case, people learned that the fellow they saw in the pulpit was real and had integrity.

Ethos comes from authentic ministry—praying for individuals, remembering people's names, caring for them in times of crisis. And it comes from recognizing and articulating the struggles people face and offering an appropriate word from God. All this shapes our character, and this character is vital as we preachers strive for our rightful authority among those we serve.

Part 4

Interpretation AND *Application*

How Do I Grasp the Correct Meaning of Scripture and Show Its Relevance to My Unique Hearers?

Chapter 58

WHY THE SERMON?

What is the eternal purpose in this weekly exercise in elocution?

Ben Patterson

A little girl riding on a bus was overheard asking, "Daddy, where will we be when we get to where we're going?"

That question ought to be asked by preachers and congregations regarding sermons. Where will we be when we arrive at the place the sermon is supposed to take us? Confusion over that question has ruined more sermons than all other kinds of homiletic incompetence.

As a matter of fact, I've heard sermons that failed despite sound exegesis and polished delivery. They failed because the preacher had no clear idea of where the hearers should end up.

Where should the sermon take the hearer? To what end was the gospel given? I propose that Paul's answer in Ephesians 1 remains the best. After listing all the benefits of the gospel, he concludes that we have this great salvation

"in order that we . . . might be for the praise of his glory" (Eph. 1:12). If the book of Revelation teaches nothing else, it confirms Paul's assertion. The saints of God in heaven are shown as doing just what Paul said was the purpose of God's saving us in the first place: continually praising, adoring, and thanking God. Eternity appears to be one interminable and joyous concert performed in God's honor by his redeemed people. Both he and they seem to enjoy it immensely.

Sermons are to be preached so that the hearers might praise, adore, and give thanks to God. They are not preached that people should repent. They are not even preached that people should believe the gospel is true. They are preached so that men and women should repent and believe the gospel *so that they may praise God's glory.*

Several methodological implications flow out of this view.

A DIFFERENT KIND OF PREPARATION

Number one on the preacher's agenda should be rigorous preparation to preach. I was told in seminary that good preaching would demand roughly one hour of preparation for every minute preached. That is a good enough dictum, I suppose, but that is not what I have in mind. The men who gave me that guilt-producing advice were academicians, and what they meant was hours of research, writing, honing the manuscript, and practicing delivery until what was said on Sunday morning was worthy of one's dissertation committee. What I have in mind are the personal disciplines necessary to behold the God whose gospel will be preached on Sunday. If the preacher is going to call people to adore God, the preacher had better have been adoring God!

I am weary of books and seminars on preaching these days. Actually, I am weary of seminars period. They betray our fascination with technique instead of substance, methods rather than integrity. In my more sanguine moments I concede the value of learning the techniques that make for excellent writing and delivery. But that is a distant second place to the fundamental imperative of familiarity with the God whose gospel we preach. We must learn to pray before we ever learn to preach.

Jack Sanford tells the story of an old well his family used during their summer vacations in rural New Hampshire. The water was cold and pure and refreshing, and it never dried up, even in the worst summer droughts. When other people would be forced to go to the lake for water, the Sanford family had only to walk out the front door to the old well, which faithfully gave them its cold, clear refreshment.

The years passed, and the family decided to modernize the vacation house. Kerosene lamps were replaced with electricity and the old well with indoor plumbing and running water. The well was covered in order to have a reserve should the occasion ever arise. More years passed by, and one day Sanford became nostalgic for the old well and its water. He uncovered it to look inside and taste again. He was shocked to find the well bone dry.

He made inquiries to discover what had happened. He learned that kind of well was fed by hundreds of tiny underground rivulets. When water is drawn from such a well, more water flows into it through the rivulets, keeping them open and clear. Otherwise, they clog up and close.

Sanford observed that the soul is much like that well. It dries up inside if the living water of God does not flow in. What makes it dry up is not the absence of God's Spirit but disuse. Unless we preachers go often and regularly to the well, unless we draw up the nourishment of God, our preaching will be dry and hollow. It may be brilliant intellectually, it may have the people laughing and crying, it may be filled with marvelous insight and delivered with style and energy, but it will be empty. The objective of the sermon is that God be praised. That will not happen unless the preacher is a beholder of his glory.

THE GOSPEL IN CONTEXT

To declare God's glory, the sermon must face those things that challenge his glory. It must face squarely all the shattering questions of life. It must set the bleak context into which God's glory is made known. The good news of God is not really good news to people until they have come to terms with the bad news of life.

A young couple's first child was stillborn. I went to visit them in the hospital and later met with them in their home to conduct a memorial service for the child. They were understandably distraught and grief-stricken. Again and again they asked, "Why? How could God allow such a thing to happen?"

I am never quite sure what to do in those situations, whether I should attempt to answer their questions or just put my arms around them and pray for peace and comfort. I usually do the latter. But after several weeks of these questions, I began to talk theology with them. Of course I was not able to offer any neat solutions. What began to impress me, however, was how unprepared both the husband and the wife were to think about the problem of evil and suffering in the world. Whatever prior instruction they had received in the faith had not so much as even raised the issue.

I left their home wondering if they had really ever heard the gospel. They were good-looking, affluent young people who had made a connection in their minds between the good fortune they had experienced in life and the god they believed in. When the good fortune left them, so did the god. They dropped out of church.

So much popular preaching today is what I call the "things-go-better-with-Jesus" variety. Like the soft drink that is the perfect complement to the meal or the recreation, so is Jesus to the rest of our lives. He adds just the right touch. That is blasphemy. He is not the complement to the meal; he is the meal. Far too many "practical" sermons are being preached in America's pulpits on how to "win over worry," how to "defeat depression," or how to "make it through your midlife crisis." There is nothing inherently wrong in the church addressing itself to these important issues. But it should be done in Sunday school or a seminar instead of in the sermon. To preach these things is to preach not the Evangel but the Wisdom Literature, not John 3:16 but Proverbs. God gave us his Son not that we might become better people but that we might become the New Humanity, not that we might get on better in this world but that we might be transformed for the next.

The gospel must be preached and heard against the somber background of death, tragedy, world hunger, and nuclear peril. Otherwise it is neither preached nor heard. God's glory does not come to us in a vacuum but in the midst of the pain of living. Those who avoid the pain will also avoid the gospel. There is nothing so sweet as the sound of praise and thanksgiving that comes from the lips of those who have looked unflinchingly at the agony of this present age and have been able to shout, "Nevertheless, I know that my Redeemer lives!"

Praising God's Glory

Because the objective of preaching is that men and women might praise God's glory, preachers must labor with all their might to present the gospel in all its glory. Lord Kenneth Clark, narrator of television's *Civilisation*, once told a reporter, "I still go to Chartres Cathedral each year and to the Parthenon every three years. Very good. Keeps your standards high." That is what authentic preaching does; it keeps people's standards high.

Perhaps that is obvious. But I think not, because of what I hear and read from popular preachers in this country. I give them the benefit of the doubt and assume their motives are good, that all they are trying to do is preach to people in a way that will be understood. As one put it, "I put all my cookies on the lowest shelf so everyone can grab them." It is a sin, they feel, to make the gospel so obtuse or intellectual it cannot be understood.

I don't disagree. But I must add that there is an equal and opposite error, and that is making the gospel too accessible and acceptable. The first error locks up the gospel in obscurity; the second locks it up in familiarity. The gospel and the glory of the God it proclaims are both near to us and far from us. We do God no favors when we so domesticate him that he becomes virtually unrecognizable, indistinguishable from whatever it was we already believed when we walked into church.

Paul spoke disapprovingly of those who "peddle the word of God" (2 Cor. 2:17). The word refers to people who vended wine in the Greek marketplaces. It was usually sold at bargain prices and was often watered down. There could be no question that these peddlers were making their product accessible to the common folk. Some may even have made a case for watering down the wine so as to make it affordable. Of course, all that is self-serving rationalization. In their efforts to make wine available, they were really impoverishing their customers and making themselves rich.

Good preaching should always be a little hard to take, not only because the word of judgment accompanies the word of salvation, but also because it proclaims a gospel that is wilder and richer and more engaging of our minds and spirits than we could ever imagine. People should be stretched in all directions when they hear us preach. God must be looked

at with wonder and amazement before he can be truly praised.

An old Hasidic tale tells of a man named Bontscha. He was called Bontscha the Silent because he had never known anything but blows, loss, pain, and failure and had never complained or expected anything better. When he died, he appeared before the heavenly tribunal. God the Judge declared, "There in that other world, no one understood you. You never understood yourself. You never understood that you need not have been silent, that you could have cried out, and that your outcries would have brought down the world itself."

The Judge then offered him a reward— absolutely anything he wanted. All he had to do was ask. Bontscha opened his mouth for the first time to reveal his deepest desire . . . and told the Judge he would like "every morning for breakfast, a hot roll with fresh butter." Heaven was ashamed and wept.

Bontscha's greatest impoverishment was that he had been rendered incapable of dreaming for anything worthwhile.

The preacher must present the glory of God as clearly and compellingly as human language will permit. Otherwise both preacher and people will be reduced to dreaming little dreams and attempting for God only little things when they could be doing so much more. Otherwise they will succumb to what Annie Dillard terms "the enormous temptation in all of life to diddle around making itsy-bitsy friends and meals and journeys for itsy-bitsy years on end." The trouble with that, says Dillard, is that God and "the world is wider than that in all directions, more dangerous and more bitter, more extravagant and bright. We are making hay when we should be making whoopee; we are raising tomatoes when we should be raising Cain, or Lazarus" (*Pilgrim of Tinker Creek*).

Calling people to praise the glory of God by facing all the shattering questions of life and presenting God's glory in as unadulterated a way as possible will not always be popular. But it will be, pardon the expression, real. It will continue to call out a people who will be salt and light in a world whose own glory is tawdry and fading.

Chapter 59

GETTING THE GOLD FROM THE TEXT

How do you capitalize on the inexhaustible riches of Scripture in your preaching— without sounding like a Bible commentary?

John Koessler

My goal as a preacher is to help the audience understand the meaning of the text, to help them interpret it, and then to understand what the implications are for them. That is because the power of the sermon is rooted in the text. Second Timothy 3:16–17 says the Scriptures are inspired, they are God-breathed, they are useful for equipping the believer for every good work. We work so hard on our sermons that we sometimes forget the power of the message is the Word.

IMPOSTERS FOR A TEXT-DRIVEN SERMON

Several imposters can get in the way of Scripture being the driving force of the sermon. The first imposter is using the text simply as a springboard for the rest of the message, where you start out with a text and then it disappears from the message. I heard a sermon a number of years ago where the preacher began by reading Romans 6, but then he closed his Bible and put it underneath the pulpit, and that was the last we heard of what the text actually said. In

that case, the Scripture was ornamental. It had no meaningful role in the message. He never showed how the main points and the subpoints related to the text. The text gave the appearance that he was preaching from the Bible, but when you listened to what he said, it didn't come from it.

Another imposter is the kind of sermon I sometimes hear in a seeker context. This sermon spends a lot of time establishing common ground with the listener, which you have to do, but perhaps because of an oversensitivity to the way the audience is going to respond, the preacher doesn't even use the Bible. It's biblical in the sense that what's said is consistent with biblical truth, but there's no explicit biblical content in the sermon. That's not a sermon. That's a motivational speech, and it has no place in the church. The authority for the sermon is not made clear. The authority becomes the experiences described in the message or the personality of the preacher, the ethos. All of that is important, but as a preacher my authority and my power are in the Word. They are not in my persuasive ability or in the cleverness of the stories I use. When you remove the Bible from the sermon, you don't have a sermon anymore.

PROPERLY ADAPTING TO HEARERS

One line of reasoning goes, "If I quote from the Bible, my hearers won't respect that authority; if I quote from a current celebrity, they'll believe that."

You don't find the apostle Paul or Peter or even Jesus steering away from God's Word. They're not afraid to base what they say on God's Word or to identify biblical truth as the basis for their authority. Now you do find, with the apostle Paul in particular, a sensitivity to his audience. For example, when he is preaching to the Jews, there is a Jewish flavor to his preaching. And when he's preaching to the Gentiles, he's sensitive to their culture. In one case he even quotes a Greek philosopher. But he always goes back to biblical truth. He preaches the gospel, the message of Christ.

There may be a false fear that because the listeners don't respect that authority I can't lean on that authority. It does give me a greater responsibility to, first, understand their assumptions so I can address the objections they might have, and second, to communicate what biblical truth says in a way that connects with the audience. The fact that the text is the foundation of the sermon doesn't relieve me of the responsibility of exegeting my audience or applying the text.

I can't use the Bible like a magic spell where as long as I just read the text, it's going to have this magical impact on the audience. If that were true we wouldn't need to preach a sermon at all. We'd just read the Bible on a street corner, and when the sound comes out over the audience, something magical will happen and people will change. It would be good in churches if we did have more reading of Scripture. But a process of argumentation and reasoning and understanding the audience is necessary. In his letters, Paul is always anticipating how his readers are responding. He raises the questions for them: "Some of you will say this." "Some of you will say that." "But what about this?" and "What about that?" We have to do that. But his anchor is always God's truth.

One of the preacher's roles is to mediate God's truth to the audience. There's often application explicitly in the text. There is a cultural context the passage deals with. But it may not be the application my audience has to deal with, and it is often not the immediate cultural context my audience finds itself in. So here I have this recorded truth. It is inerrant. It is inspired. Everything it says is true. And then I have my audience. I'm in the middle, and I'm trying to take that biblical truth and show them the implications. But they have to understand what it says, and the things that I urge them to do and the authority of that has to come from God's Word.

It is a valid approach to begin with the authority of someone they respect and then move into Scripture and say, "This is the authority for what I'm saying to you." That is often the function of the introduction, to start with common ground. You start with their experience, or you start with some authority that they recognize. So you quote a statistic on marriage or cohabitation that says cohabitation is a bad idea for a number of reasons.

Or you might quote it to show that most people think it's a good idea, to get them to think about it. And then you take them to a dissenting voice in the Scriptures. But your goal is to move the focus to the Word.

I want my audience to be thinking about what the Bible says and what its implications are going to be for them. I want to anchor it to the text. I don't want to baptize the sermon with the text just because it's a sermon and has to have the Bible in it. We want hearers to be dwelling on what this says.

Grant Osborne talks about a hermeneutical spiral where you go back and forth throughout the sermon: text to audience, text to audience, text to audience. But ultimately what you say in the sermon is God's claim on that person's life. That person needs to know that it comes from Scripture.

Why Sermons Inadvertently Drift from the Text

No one I know sets out to compose a sermon that's disconnected from the text. I suspect if you asked preachers on any given Sunday what they are preaching, they'd answer that they are preaching God's Word. But there are several factors that inadvertently move us away from the text.

One of the most common is that we're driven by application. It's important for me to be relevant to the audience. So I spend a lot of time thinking about the audience and their life situation. But the more I move toward the audience and the more I move out of the life situation that the text explicitly addresses, the greater the temptation to disconnect from the passage.

One common pattern in expository preaching is to begin with the text and talk about what the text says, to provide a kind of commentary for the audience. We talk about the grammar, the syntax, and maybe the cultural background. Then we move to application. But often, when we get into application, we forget about the text. The danger is that the further I remove myself from the text, the more likely I am to press home an application that is inconsistent with what the passage says.

In addition, there's a danger when we are overly familiar with the text to assume that we already know what the text means and what implications it has for the audience. But then I may not do the work of the exegesis because I think I already know what it says. My handling of the text becomes clichéd and shallow.

There's also the temptation to ride a hobbyhorse. Sometimes there's an issue in the life of the congregation we want to address, and that's appropriate. That's part of my role as a preacher, a prophetic responsibility to focus on issues in the church and say things that people don't want to hear. The problem develops when we're so focused on addressing an issue that we fail to notice the passage we're using doesn't really address it.

Recently I was preaching in a church I have attended, and I had become concerned with what seemed to me to be a spirit of legalism. My text was 1 Samuel 16, Samuel's anointing of David where the Lord looks on the heart, not on the outward appearance.

In one of my points I started down an applicational path that I thought was pretty good. I liked it because it zoned in on my concern in that context. But the more I reflected on what the text was saying, I realized that the passage didn't address the issue I was bothered about. I had inadvertently turned the message of the text inside out to make my point. I had to go back and rewrite it, and I didn't end up saying what I wanted to say.

But that's a good thing. That's letting the text control what the message says. It has two advantages. First, if you let the text control the message, sooner or later every problem issue in your church is going to be addressed. Secondly, nobody can blame you for it. Nobody can say that you're picking on them, that you've singled them out, and so it also protects you.

Another way we can abandon the text is by preaching an illustration. An illustration is an important part of the sermon. I spend almost as much time thinking about finding the right illustrations for the message as I do the exegesis of the text. But there's tremendous energy in a good illustration, particularly a story, and we can get caught up in this great illustration and feel the power of it, and then we move to application, but the application may be grounded in the illustration rather than the text.

There's a dimension where that should be the case. It's legitimate to move from illustration to application when the illustration is reflective of what the text says and I'm either pressing home a principle from the text, trying to show you what that looks like in real life, using the illustration as an analogy, or using it to motivate. In those cases, you even want to use the language of the illustration to make the application. Bryan Chappell talks about having the words of an illustration "rain down" through the application.

But when we get caught up in the illustration itself and the illustration is the focal point, then that's what we're preaching. The text then becomes a pretext to introduce the story, and the application points the audience back to the illustration.

"How-to" preaching can also lead us away from text-driven sermons. "How-to" preaching is driven by a legitimate desire to connect with people where they are and to lead them to where God is. But not every text gives a how-to formula for responding to the issues in the text. In fact, few do. If every text gave me a formula, then I could slap it on the sermon and everybody would go home happy. But because the text, in an overwhelming majority of cases, deals on a principle level, I'm left with the responsibility of thinking about the implications for the audience.

I may, as I'm thinking about that, try to translate the implications into a methodology, a step-by-step response. The danger, though, is that it becomes formulaic. The preaching becomes trite. The listener quickly senses that your formula is not a construct that grows out of the text. Often the formulas are superficial.

I like to think of it in terms of diagnosis and remedy. When I look at the text and my audience, and when I am trying to give them something concrete to walk away with, it may not be a step-by-step process. Instead, I need to think in terms of diagnosis. How does the truth of this passage help the audience to understand the nature of the problem? When I preach on a problem that I could point out in myself, I usually already know I have that problem. So then the question is, Why do I have that problem? Try to diagnose the nature of the problem.

Then, in view of that, How should I respond? What is there in the text that helps you to understand the nature of my need for God's grace? And what is there in the text that helps me to understand God's remedy?

Once I've worked through that, maybe I want to think about a concrete strategy for responding to it. That strategy doesn't have to be explicitly mentioned in the text, but it has to be consistent with what the text says.

One of the missing dimensions in relating

text to audience is motivation. We often go for the formula, and we don't think about why. Ask the question, Why should the listener respond that way? The text won't necessarily give a step-by-step formula, but it frequently addresses the issue of motivation.

HOW TO STAY ON TRACK

To ensure that the text has its proper place in our sermon, we must begin with exegesis. You study the text. You try to understand what the author wanted to communicate to his original audience and what application he had in mind for them, either explicitly or implicitly. You have to do the hard work of exegesis before you think about any other issues of style or application.

Second—and I found this to be the most challenging thing as a pastor—you must not rush this phase. When you think of how many messages the typical pastor has to produce on a week-by-week basis, the pressure to produce is phenomenal. But I've found I have to live with a text for a few days before I can really understand it. Discipline yourself so your exegetical work doesn't take place the same week as your sermon preparation. I recommend trying to incorporate that into your devotional life so that you study God's Word for yourself on a deep level before preaching through it.

Because most pastors have multiple prepa-rations to do, you have to prioritize. When I was preaching several messages in a given week, I would do full-blown exegesis, textbook style the way I learned in seminary, on one message. The second one I had to do a bit less. You do the best you can. But the more time you take with a text, the more careful you are, the more likely your sermon is going to be consistent with what it says.

While the text can never be too foundational to the message, it is possible to go to the other extreme in which your handling of the text never moves to application, and then there's a problem. My role as a preacher is not to function primarily as an exegetical commentary or a Bible handbook, but to take biblical truth and apply it to the audience. If you haven't applied the text, you haven't preached. Now if you apply without the text, you haven't preached either. You must have both.

The central issue is not the form or style of the sermon. It boils down to making sure people understand that what God wants them to do came from this text. My confidence as a preacher is in the power of God's Word. That's one of the most exciting things about preaching. It's not because we like to lecture. It's not because people are staring at us and waiting for us to say something. It's because we are driven by the conviction that God's truth that those truths recorded in human language have the potential to transform people's lives.

Chapter 60

FAITHFUL FIRST

The better we understand the text, the more trenchant can be our preaching

David Jackman

Foundational to all good exposition is the conviction that where the Word of God is faithfully taught, the voice of God is authentically heard. In a generation demanding a "now" word from God, as though that would be in some way separate from, or even superior to, the living and enduring Word of Scripture, the expositor believes that everything God has said he is still saying. The preacher's task is not to try to make the Bible relevant; it is relevant, precisely because it is the living Word of the unchanging, present-tense God. Nor is the task to "do something with the Bible," so as to make it palatable to the contemporary scene. Rather, the task is to let the Bible do something with the preacher, so that its truth is incarnated in the expositor's life, as well as with words, which become the channel of its powerful message to the hearers.

Such foundational principles are derived not only from classic biblical, theological propositions about the inspiration, infallibility, and authority of Scripture, but from the logical derivative that such a revelation will also provide its own authoritative key to its interpretation and usage. If the Bible is God preaching God to us, then, as has often been said, the Bible *is* an interpretation. Our part is to be willing both to discover and apply it. We must be prepared to preach the Bible the Bible's way.

That means being governed by the way in which God has put the Bible together, as sixty-six separate but closely integrated units of composition, each with its own specific purpose and major themes. Each constituent sentence of each paragraph or chapter is carefully constructed to play its own role to convey its divinely-intended meaning, in relationship to all the other sentences around it. The same pattern is true of the individual words within each sentence, in their order and emphases as well as in their meaning, so that nothing can be changed without the probability of a change of understanding. It is the same principle that underlies accurate Bible translation work.

These basic convictions in turn lead to the expositor's concern over the purpose and direction of the text, its context in the book of which it is a part and of the Bible as a whole, the distinctive features of the literary genre to which it belongs, and the nuanced meaning of individual words, metaphors, rhetorical devices, and so on. For the expositor's challenge is always to preach his text as "the truth, the whole truth, and nothing but the truth," and that is a harder tightrope to walk than we often recognize.

At Proclamation Trust conferences, a number of "instructions" have been devised and developed to enable participants to sharpen their Bible-handling skills, so that the text is attentively heard and faithfully explained.

1. OBSERVATION

We might describe *observation* as learning to listen by opening our eyes. The problem with a written text, increasing with its familiarity, is the skim-read approach that lacks attention to detail. The Bible is often read publicly and studied privately with nothing more than a wash-over effect. We gain a general idea of its contents, but acquaintance with its meaning is bland and superficial. To be good expository preachers we have to cultivate the skill of reading with our antennas up, to practice not just textual analysis but also the dying art of listening intelligently to an urgent and meaningful communication as the living God addresses us in his Word.

One way to develop this is to read looking for the surprises. What is there in the text that prompts the question *Why?* Why does the biblical author say that? Why does he say it in those words? Why does he say it here? Is there anything that pulls me up with the realization that I would not have put it in those terms, or is there something that challenges my presuppositions by conflicting with my usual way of thinking? Is there anything that will help me to observe what the text is actually saying?

Like a lens sharpening its focus, careful observation enables the reader to see beneath the immediate surface meaning of the words and to begin to grapple with their intended purpose. That in turn will produce clarity in exposition that gives the sermon an edge to penetrate beyond confused half-understandings and generalized notions. It will enable the richness and uniqueness of the detail of a particular passage to have its intended effect, and when that happens, the Bible really does speak.

2. FRAMEWORK

Our *framework* is the enemy of such accuracy. The danger is that certain words in the text will merely trigger ideas in the preacher's memory bank that will then be downloaded and uncritically included in the sermon. While it is inevitable that every preacher will have a unique framework (of theological position, personal experiences, cumulative knowledge, prejudices, and so on), unless the Bible text is questioning the framework every time a passage is under examination, the preaching will soon become a predictable reflection of what the preacher has said many times before. And preaching like that does not challenge the church and will not change the world. It becomes *im*pository of the preacher's world upon the biblical text rather than *ex*pository of the fundamental meaning, with all its unsettling and disturbing challenges to our inherently worldly and fallen ways of thinking.

3. CONTEXT

As we consider the *context* of a text, we must first look at the immediate contextual setting to establish clarity of meaning. Many mistakes are made by taking a verse or paragraph out of its surrounding context and treating it as though it were an isolated, unconnected unit of thought. For example, at times in Christian experience the great assurances of Romans 8:28, of God working everything together for the good of his loved ones, can seem to ring somewhat hollow. But when we see that verse 29 defines the good as "being conformed to the likeness of his Son," the verse is full of promise again. To set the text in its context will rescue it from becoming merely the preacher's pretext.

Then there is the matter of the wider book context, trying to work out how this particular passage fits with the rest of the book and what specific contribution it is making to the overall purpose of the book, the "melodic line," as it has been called. This has been termed "travelling to Corinth," a principle noted from the fact that 1 Corinthians 13, perhaps the most anthologized "purple passage" of the whole New Testament, is actually in its book context a stinging rebuke and indictment of the Corinthian church. What did it mean to them then? That is the question that has to be asked and answered first in every piece of biblical study, if ever preachers and hearers are to stand a chance of working out what it will mean for us now. How does its inclusion here, and in these terms, help forward the writer's purpose? What does it add, or clarify, or correct?

The third level is the whole Bible context, which leads us into the realm of biblical and theological reflection as the expositor compares Scripture with Scripture and seeks to ascertain how the passage under study contributes to the whole in its own unique way. Seeing the whole Bible as one book by one divine author, though written through various different human servants, means we will recognize that the middle page dividing the two Testaments from each other is the only uninspired page in the whole book.

The principle of progressive revelation not only points to Christ as the center and culmination of all the Old Testament, but it establishes the New as the fulfillment motif, so that we see the teaching of Christ and his apostles as the normative control on our understanding of all that preceded him. This also encourages us to reflect on how the perspective of the whole sweep of salvation history impacts and illuminates our understanding of a specific incident or unit.

4. APPLICATION

Application is the purpose that lies behind all this hard work on context. It is never simply for reasons of theoretical or academic correctness that we need to explore the wider field. Rather, it is because working out the meaning and purpose of the text in its various contexts enables relevant application to become much more obvious. It also increases our confidence that we are cutting with the grain of the wood, working with the text as God intended. Much faithful exposition remains at the level of an exegetical lecture rather than crossing the bridge into the world of the contemporary hearers because it is not contextualized.

Ironically, almost every competent contemporary preacher knows the unchanging text must be contextualized into the modern world, but the great mistake that is often made is to start at *our* end of the process. This ensures that our contemporary questions and presuppositions are imported into the text, but they may have little to do with the original author's intention. We may as well criticize the Bible for not teaching the laws of nuclear physics as for not answering the spiritual whims and fancies of the twenty-first century. The good expositor learns to let the Bible ask the questions, which, since they are God's questions, are far more important and immeasurably more significant than any we could ever pose. To do the contextual work at the Bible's end is to ensure that the unchanging text is truly heard in the modern world.

This biblical method of application also delivers both preacher and hearers from the tyranny of the currently fashionable norms of our particular evangelical subculture. So often application is mass-produced in "bolt-on" forms from our current orthodoxies. These are usually in the form of "we ought to . . . are you?" and develop quickly into legalism and soulless duty. Grace is effectively evacuated from a ministry emphasis on doing more Christian things (giving, praying, witnessing), and hearers soon become adept at screening out the all-too-predictable challenges.

Successful, life-changing application is launched from the text and flies under the radar screen to lodge itself in the response center of the listener, with a surprise sense of "So *that's* what it means." The mind is then persuaded of the truth, and the heart is softened to receive and put it into practice. Finally, the will is energized to be obedient and to make the life change in the power of the Holy Spirit, which that same Spirit has been communicating through the Word.

5. LITERARY GENRE

We must attend to the *literary genre* of the material we are preaching. We need to identify the different methodologies of biblical genres and to work with them in the presentation of the sermon. All too often, we have put every text through a particular stylistic or theological mincing machine and laid out its doctrinal content in an identical way, irrespective of whether the original was poetry or prose, proverb or parable. This can become both abstract and boring, and it gets expository preaching a bad name. It also does a grave disservice to the God of the Bible, whose love of variety and ingenuity, reflected in the physical creation, is not

likely to be less evident in his inspired, written revelation.

Thus, the expositor must work with the literary distinctives as God has given them and not try to iron them out into a standard three-point sermon. We will learn to value the intricate arguments and verbal precision of a letter, the twist in a parable, the punch line of a gospel pronouncement story, the provocation of a wisdom saying, the turning point of a narrative, the multiple fulfillments of a prophecy, or the emotive, affective ingredients of a poem.

At Proclamation Trust we do not major in homiletics, since in Phillips Brooks' definition preaching is "truth through personality," and every personality will arrange and present the contents with a proper individuality. Effective expository preaching finds its origin and power not so much in clever construction as in detailed, obedient listening to God's voice in the text. The Bible really is to be in the driving seat, dictating the content of the message, its shape, and its contemporary application.

In serving God's Word in this way, we come to realize that the Bible is a book about God long before it is a book about us, and that its strongest relevance is to teach us his unchanging nature. There will be parallels between his old and new covenant dealings with Israel and the universal church. There will also be similarities between ourselves and the men and women we meet in the Bible's pages, but we are not the focus of the story, and we are not to read ourselves into each and every circumstance or experience. Verse-by-verse exposition seeks to guard and propagate these great revelatory distinctives to the glory of God and for the benefit of his people and the lost world.

Chapter 61

GOD'S LETTER OF INTENT

Six questions that reveal what God meant to say in a text

Greg R. Scharf

What follows rests on three assumptions:

1. All Scripture has two authors, one divine and at least one human.
2. God intends something by what he speaks. He always speaks purposefully.
3. By the grace of God and the illumination of the Holy Spirit, followers of Jesus may adequately discern what God intends to say and do in any passage of Scripture by prayerful, careful, and submissive attentiveness to the words human authors use, in their respective literary, canonical, cultural, and theological contexts.

If any one of these assumptions is false, preachers are on a fool's errand. They have no authoritative, discernable message from God.

Our task as preachers is not to say whatever comes to mind when studying the Bible but to discern what God had in mind, what he intended, when inspiring the human author to write it, and to show how that intent is relevant for our hearers. This article focuses on the first half of that task: discovering original intent. The meaning that the text has for us today must be derived from and be consistent with the meaning it had for its original hearers. To determine that, we must go beyond observation to *interrogation*. We respectfully ask of the text basic questions that focus initial observations and help us discern the intent of the author in the text. At minimum we should ask six questions.

1. WHAT IS THIS TEXT FUNCTIONALLY?

What, on the basis of its content and structure, does the preaching portion seem to want to do (Liefeld, 1984, ch. 7)? Is there a name for that? Is it a reminder, an explanation, a plea, a rebuke, a command, or a description? We discover the answer by prayerful, submissive reading, carefully observing such things as words, their grammatical and syntactical relationships, the literary genre of the passage (whether it is narrative, poetry, letter, etc.), and its textual context. We look for clues concerning what the passage is aiming to achieve.

Imperatives, for instance, point toward a command or exhortation. The presence of negative consequences suggests a warning; positive outcomes may signal a promise. Purpose and result clauses alert the reader to an argument, an explanation, or some cause-and-effect relationship. Other features may lead us to conclude that the text is an example, a description, or a rebuke, or that an event is being reported. Perhaps the text may be a combination, such as an exhortation followed by reasons for obeying it. Asking this question suggests how the preacher will use the passage and helps us resist the temptation to turn everything into an exhortation.

2. WHAT IS THE SUBJECT OF THE TEXT?

Answering this question requires weighing the various things the author mentions and discerning which of them is central (Robinson, 2001, pp. 41ff.). Sometimes in narrative, the subject itself is implicit. The story could be an example of loyalty or divine providence without the words themselves being used. Recalling the themes of the particular book of the Bible may alert us to their presence in the text at hand. Every passage is about God and about humanity, yet for preaching we must narrow down the answer. A valid answer to this question could be a word: *prayer, faith, hope,* or *judgment.* Or it could be a phrase, such as "God's dealings with the nations." The value of this question is straightforward: If the passage is about prayer, the sermon should be about prayer.

3. WHAT IS *THIS TEXT* SAYING ABOUT THE SUBJECT?

If we have accurately discerned the subject of the preaching portion, everything else the passage addresses will relate to the subject in some discernable way (Robinson, 2001, pp. 41ff.). Now we read the text to let it say what it will about the subject. If the subject is prayer, the answer to this third question may be that prayer is essential or too-often neglected. In the process of answering this question, we may conclude that we have failed to answer the second question accurately. What we thought was central we now see to be supportive of something else that is in fact the subject. At this point also, we may conclude that the text is too large to preach; it says more about the subject than can be handled faithfully and clearly in a single sermon. Or perhaps it is too small and

fails to include surrounding text that is an unmistakable part of what the author wants to say about the subject.

4. WHAT RESPONSE DOES *THIS TEXT* CALL FOR?

Accurate answers to the first three questions already incline us to certain answers to this question. So a text that is an exhortation concerning the indispensability of prayer fairly dictates the response a sermon from this text should seek: Pray! The word *response* is used intentionally because too often *application* suggests action. God may want a change in attitude, thinking, feeling, or will, as well as a particular action. There may be more than one response called for.

To ask and answer this question with integrity is to repent of textual abuse, commandeering a text as a pretext for a response we want as opposed to the one(s) God intends. Of course we must not invite this response of others without first letting the text begin to evoke the intended response in ourselves.

5. HOW DOES *THIS TEXT* ELICIT THAT RESPONSE?

This question helps us *expound* the text as opposed to vaguely referring to it. Here we look more closely at the features of the preaching portion, not now for how they develop the subject (question 3) but for how they move the listener toward the response the Author intended (Long, 1989, pp. 44ff.). When preached as God's Word, the Bible goes to work in those who receive it as it is (1 Thess. 2:13).

This question looks for ways this text transforms the life of the believer by renewing the mind (Rom. 12:1–2) and how it sanctifies him or her (John 17:17). Does it appeal to the hearer's mind, emotions, will, conscience, sense of duty, love for God, sense of need, or love of the truth? Does it use questions, examples, reminders, word pictures, Scripture citations, or argumentation? Is the means employed repetitive, hitting the same note again and again, or is it more cumulative, building a case for the desired response by a range of rhetorical techniques?

The sermon may use additional legitimate means of moving people to valid responses, but to neglect those within the passage itself is to rob ourselves of authority in preaching. More important, the Author's intent includes moving to a faithful and obedient response in appropriate ways.

For example, it is valid to challenge listeners from 1 Corinthians 15:58b to give themselves wholeheartedly to the Lord's work. But if we urge them to do so in order to increase the size of the congregation, we have violated the stated reason explicit in the context, namely, that because of the resurrection such hard work is not in vain. Death does not annul our labors because of the victory of Jesus over it.

The goal is not merely for us and our listeners to do the right thing but to do it in the right ways and for the right reasons. To neglect this question risks missing a vital dimension of the Author's intent.

6. HOW DOES THIS PASSAGE CONTRIBUTE TO THE LARGER DRAMA OF REDEMPTION?

The previous steps may lead the preacher to thoughts that are consistent with the text but are inadequate because they are out of touch with how that passage fits into the larger picture, fulfilling a purpose in the whole like a piece in a jigsaw puzzle. Each preaching portion is an integral part of the biblical book in which it is found, but it also contributes to the history of redemption and in some discernable way points to Christ. Our task as Christian preachers is to discover the connections and articulate them.

Thus, for instance, when we preach Psalm 110, we do not speak only, or even mainly, about David but about Jesus, who applies this psalm to himself as do Peter and the writer to the Hebrews (Matt.22:41–45; Acts 2:34–36; Heb. 1:13; 5:6; 7:17, 21). We discover that here the Father is expressing to the Son his unshakable commitment to his (the Son's) lordship. Until we preach that, we haven't really done justice to Psalm 110. Of course other passages are not so clearly linked to Christ, but according to Luke 24:27 all of them serve this Christ-centered purpose in one way or another.

A text may predict and anticipate Christ's first advent, as Micah 5:2 does. It may illustrate the universality of human rebellion that Jesus came to address, as 2 Chronicles 16 does. Or it may reveal how, after Christ's coming, the kingdom is here yet not complete, as Philippians 3 does.

We know, for instance, that the *words* of Genesis 15:6 ("[God] credited it to him as righteousness") were not written only for the sake of Abraham but for our sakes as Christian believers (Rom. 4:22–25). And we know from 1 Corinthians 10:6, 11 that various *events* in Israel's history were written as examples for our instruction. Our task is to discern how other pertinent texts help us to interpret the words and events of our text in ways that reflect God's purposes for including it in Scripture.

There will be times when what an Old Testament text appears to be saying is neglected or overridden by a New Testament writer's use of it. For example, Paul quotes Psalm 68:18 ("you *received* gifts from men") in Ephesians 4:8 as "and *gave* gifts to men." In such cases, good recent commentaries can be a great help (e.g., Peter O'Brien's Pillar Commentary on Ephesians has helpful discussion, pp. 288–93). In principle we must submit to the New Testament use and allow that inspired handling to be a lens through which we gain a greater appreciation of the older text and of how it finds fulfillment in the New.

Is it ever permissible to preach a text for a purpose that supplements and builds on the purpose for which it was apparently written? May we, for instance, preach a sermon on how to listen to Christian preaching from Acts 10:33b? If the handling of the Old Testament by writers of the New is allowed to inform our answer, we may respond with a qualified yes. We may cite and employ a text as *illustrative* of a biblical truth that is not manifestly the subject of that text when the truth itself is plainly taught in other passages of Scripture and the text we are studying is at a minimum reminiscent of it.

So, to return to the example from Acts 10, we know that God is present when people are gathered in his name to hear his Word expounded and that he has commanded the preacher to tell the listeners what his Word teaches, two ideas Cornelius mentions in his invitation to Peter. These abiding realities free us to heed Cornelius's implicit advice and supply a narrative framework from the context in Acts from which to communicate the thought.

We may make valid *inferences* from a text, as the Lord Jesus does in his use of Exodus 3:6 in Matthew 22:31–32 (see D. A. Carson, 1984, p. 462: "If God is the God of Abraham, Isaac, and Jacob even when addressing Moses hundreds of years after the first three patriarchs died, then they must be alive to him"). Note what the Westminster Confession 6.6 says of Scripture: "The whole counsel of God, concerning all things necessary for his own glory, man's salvation, faith, and life, is either expressly set down in Scripture, or by good and necessary consequence may be deduced from Scripture." Such uses, however, must be supplementary and secondary when used at all.

Our calling as preachers, as defined by John Stott, is to discern what God is saying in the text and preach so that his voice is heard and his Word obeyed.

BIBLIOGRAPHY

Carson, D. A. 1984. "Matthew." *Expositor's Bible Commentary*, vol. 8, ed. F. Gaebelein. Grand Rapids: Zondervan.

Liefeld, Walter L. 1984. *New Testament Exposition.* Grand Rapids: Zondervan.

Long, Thomas G. 1989. *Preaching and the Literary Forms of the Bible*. Philadelphia: Fortress.

O'Brien, Peter. 1999. *Pillar Commentary on Ephesians*. Grand Rapids: Eerdmans.

Robinson, Haddon. 2001. *Biblical Preaching*, 2nd ed. Grand Rapids: Baker.

Chapter 62

FIVE BIRD-DOGGING QUESTIONS
FOR BIBLICAL EXPOSITION

How asking the right questions produces a wealth of relevant material
for the sermon

Earl Palmer

To preach with relevance, I suggest you become a commentator on the text. If you develop a method of Bible study in which you work through five great questions, you will put yourself under the text and it will affect your preaching.

The five great questions that make up a commentary are the technical questions, the historical questions, the content-theological questions, the contemporary questions, and the discipleship questions. Bible study is a journey in the text from the technical to the discipleship issues.

TECHNICAL QUESTIONS

The technical questions are those that establish the text. The first half of Bible study is to establish the text. What do the words mean? What is the syntax? What is actually being said? Don't worry about what the overall meaning is at this point. Be sure you understand what's being said. What do the words mean individually, linguistically? If you develop a birddog interest in establishing the text, if you develop a fascination for vocabulary, for words, for the way the sentence is put together, you will have advanced tremendously your ability to do an exposition on the text.

C. S. Lewis says, "When I inquire what helps I have had in this matter of doing literary criticism, I seem to discover a somewhat unexpected result. Evaluative critics come at the bottom of the list for me." That is to say, when I read the evaluative critics of Dante or *Paradise Lost*, they're at the bottom of the list of help to me. Lewis says, "At the top of the list for me comes 'dry as dust.'" That's his coined phrase for the following: "Obviously I have owed and I must continue to owe far more to editors, textual critics, commentators and lexographers than to anyone else."

What's a lexographer? That's your theological dictionary of the New Testament, your Bauer-Danker-Arndt-Gingrich lexicon, your Moulton and Milligan. "Find out what the author actually wrote and what the hard words meant and what the allusions were to, and you have done far more for me than a hundred new interpretations or assessments could ever do."

Lewis felt you should never bypass this technical work. I realize that's hard work. You've got to keep your Greek and Hebrew up. It will pay off as you do the hard work of establishing the text for yourself. I say to Bible students, "Stretch out at least five current translations on every text, because every translation of the text is an attempt to grapple with what the words mean." And as different words or different organizations of the sentence appear, you can see different textual experts struggle with what the words and grammar mean. Even that will give you a clue as to what Lewis calls "a hard word." If you can get that hard word, it will be an important clue that could be the basis of a great sermon, because you may be at the fulcrum point in the development of the text.

HISTORICAL QUESTIONS

There are two types of historical questions.

Historical Material within the Material Itself

If you develop a historical curiosity within the material, it will reap many benefits. If you see any name, pursue it. I was studying about Paul's two-year imprisonment at Caesarea under Antonius Felix, the Roman governor from AD 52–60, and Luke has a one-liner with regard to Felix that captured my imagination. For two years, Felix kept Paul in prison and kept inviting him up to talk to him, "hoping that Paul would offer him a bribe" (Acts 24:25). Ah, but Paul never paid him off. Luke, the historian that he is, is always understated. For instance, Luke mentions that Felix's wife was "Drusilla, who was a Jewess." Actually she's the daughter of Herod Agrippa I, who had been married to another man. Felix stole her by seduction and by using his great power as a governor. That was such a scandal that Josephus goes into detail about how he lost all respect of the Jews.

Josephus said Felix was so cruel that the number of people crucified under Felix was incalculable. In AD 60 Felix was fired by a direct order from Seneca himself, the prime minister under Nero, for corruption, the very thing Luke notes. For two years Felix kept Paul rotting in this prison at Caesarea, because he undoubtedly figured that Paul had access to money, for Paul had brought a large amount of money down to Jerusalem. He had taken an offering through all his Gentile churches for the Jewish Christians in Jerusalem.

It's a tribute to Paul that he sits there and rots. By historical study, you know what Paul is up against.

Historical Questions behind the Material

Scholars call this form criticism. Now, form criticism has dangers when it becomes arrogant, but form criticism rightly handled can be useful. Form criticism tries to understand the setting in the church that produces the documents.

In John 1:1–18, John has a marvelous song to the Word. He begins: "In the beginning was the Word, and the Word was with God, and the Word was God. . . . Through him all things were made." But three times John interrupts the song to say: Oh, by the way, John the Baptist is not the Messiah. Then he goes back to the song.

The historical question within the material says, Who is John the Baptist? Obviously you have to study that. But the form critical question says, Why does John interrupt his song three times to tell us that John the Baptist is not the Christ?

Maybe there's a great controversy. Maybe some people do think John the Baptist is Messiah. Actually, we know that is true from the New Testament. In Luke 3, Luke says some were wondering whether John was the Messiah. Is there still a debate going on about John the Baptist when John writes this book from Ephesus?

I want to get you inside the text just for the sake of the text, because when that happens you're going to end up with so many things to talk about that you're going to have no problem preaching a sermon. In fact, when you get inside the text, the biggest problem in preaching is the narrowing process.

CONTENT-THEOLOGICAL QUESTIONS

With this question we are beginning to move out of the first century. We now ask, What does it mean? That's a big transition, a dangerous one too. That's why it's important you answer the first two questions first. Once you say, *I think it means this,* you're a theologian, good or bad. You have to be a theologian to stay under the text, because the text demands it. I have to come to some judgment as to what it means, not only what it says. And when I do that, I'm at the content-theological core of a commentary.

CONTEMPORARY QUESTIONS

There are two sorts of contemporary issues.

Contemporary within Its Own Setting

I now bring the material into collision with other worldviews around it. For example, after you study John the Baptist, his theology, and his sermons, you could ask, *I wonder how what John the Baptist is expecting collides with what Jesus is doing?* When I try to understand that collision, I'm doing the contemporary question. We know a collision did occur because in Luke 7:20 John the Baptist, in prison, asks: "Are you the one who was to come [the Messiah], or should we expect someone else?"

The contemporary question asks, How would this teaching collide with the Pharisee movement? Or how does it collide with the Sadducees or the Essenes or the Romans or the Greeks? And of course the more you study and develop a curiosity at this level, the better you can do this job.

Contemporary down through the Centuries

Now that I know what this text means, how does it collide with other worldviews down through the generations? For instance, as a sixteenth-century commentator, Calvin does a masterful job of bringing the text into collision with scholastic thought, Roman Catholic theological thought, Aquinas, and Augustine. That's the role of the theologian.

But as great a commentator as Calvin is, you see why we need new commentators in every generation. Because Calvin, as great as he is, doesn't grapple with Karl Marx, with Eastern New-Age mysticism, or with Woody Allen's or Stephen Spielberg's movies, but you have to. The context keeps shifting.

DISCIPLESHIP QUESTIONS

In the discipleship question the commentator dares to ask, What does this text mean to me? Where am I under this text? Where is it rubbing me or challenging me? And then, of course, how does it speak to those who will hear me preach?

If you do this journey for its own sake, when you're finished you're going to have far too many things to say, and your job is going to be narrowing. Because of your study, you will be contemporary, and you will be relevant.

Chapter 63

THE RULES OF THE GAME
Seven steps to proper interpretation

David L. Allen

Preachers today face a formidable challenge: how to communicate God's authoritative Word to the contemporary postmodern mindset. How can we preach in a way that minimizes the unspoken reply, "That's just your interpretation!" Such a statement reflects the popular notion that one interpretation is as good as another.

This, of course, has immense repercussions for biblical authority. Congregations must understand the authority for what we say comes not from our homiletical bag of tools but from Scripture as God's inspired Word. Good preaching may be defined in many ways, but one thing is certain: *There is no good preaching apart from good interpretation.*

This article will use a baseball analogy to identify seven crucial hermeneutical principles for preparing sermons. In baseball, hitters proceed through seven stations to score a run. They begin in the dugout, move to the on-deck circle, then to the plate, first base, second base, third base, and finally home plate again to score.

THE DUGOUT: GENRE

From the dugout a player evaluates the playing field and the pitcher. Good hitters know what ballpark they are playing in: Is the infield grass or Astroturf? How far is it to the left and right field fence? Does the opposing pitcher rely on the fastball, curve ball, or change-up? For the preacher, the dugout position is recognizing the genre of the biblical text.

Genre means literary category. Written discourse falls into four basic genres: narrative, procedural, expository, and hortatory. Genesis is a *narrative* genre. It tells a story with characters, plot, rising tension, climax, and resolution. It follows a time sequence. *Procedural* discourse tells how to do something. For example, sections of Exodus and Leviticus give detailed instructions for constructing the tabernacle. *Expository* discourse explains. This is the dominant genre of New Testament letters, which are characterized not by chronology as in Genesis but by logical relations such as result, means, purpose, grounds, manner, consequence, contra expectation, summary, and a host of other communication relations that primarily explain. *Hortatory* discourse commands. It makes use of imperatives. Most New Testament letters combine hortatory and expository discourse. In fact, most books of the Bible use more than one genre. (For more on genre, see chapter 71, "Fundamentals of Genre.")

We must identify the genre of both the biblical book and the preaching passage since the genre determines the "rules of the game." The principles for interpreting a narrative like Genesis would not be used in interpreting poetry like the Psalms or a letter like 1 John.

First John is obviously a combination of

expository and hortatory, explaining and exhorting. If I were preaching 1 John 2:15–17, I should take note of the dominance of the imperative at the beginning: "Do not love the world." In any paragraph, an imperative verb carries more semantic weight than indicative verbs. Verbs are the load-bearing walls of a text, so the verb structure of any text is one of the keys to identifying its genre. The rest of the paragraph explains why we are commanded not to love the world.

In preaching on this text, the dominance of this imperative should influence the sermon outline.

ON-DECK CIRCLE: CONTEXT

The second station for the batter is the on-deck circle, where we take a few practice swings, get a closer look at the pitcher, and watch the batter ahead of us in the lineup. For the preacher, the on-deck circle is context. Just as all good hitters know who precedes and follows them in the batting order, so good interpreters always pay attention to what occurs immediately before and after the preaching text.

For 1 John 2:15–17, people often view the preceding paragraph (2:12–14) as disconnected to what precedes and follows. The "children," "fathers," and "young men" of this paragraph are unusual Johannine ways of identifying the readers as believers since they are said to "know the Father (God)" and "the word of God abides in you." Actually the description of the believers given in verses 12–14 serves as an introduction to the imperative in 2:15.

The paragraph that immediately follows 2:15–17 begins with the word "children" and continues to identify the readers clearly as believers. Thus, if both preceding and following paragraphs are addressed to believers, it is likely from a contextual standpoint that 2:15–17 addresses believers as well. This interpretation affects our sermon preparation. John was writing to Christians here, not to non-Christians. As we will soon see, this contextual connection helps us correctly interpret the somewhat opaque phrase "the love of the Father" in verse 15b.

AT BAT: SEMANTICS

The issue "at bat" is semantics, the meaning of the text. Semantics is the study of meaning. The heart of interpretation is determining the meaning of the text. All texts have three kinds of meaning:

1. *referential meaning*: that which is being talked about; the subject matter of a text
2. *situational meaning*: information pertaining to the participants in a communication act (environment, social status, and so on)
3. *structural meaning*: arrangement of the information in the text itself; the grammar and syntax of a text

The preacher should look at all three in the process of interpretation. What does 1 John 2:15–17 *refer* to? What is the point, topic, or theme? Our paragraph is a command not to love the world along with two reasons given why we should not do so. This is its main point.

The *situational* meaning is not as prominent in expositional discourse and often has to be gleaned between the lines. We learn that whatever it means to "love the world," John is concerned that some of his readers are already doing so or are in danger of doing so. The text is a warning.

Structural meaning is what is most commonly focused on in the exegetical process: grammar and syntax. Structural meaning is encoded in words, phrases, clauses, sentences, paragraphs, and finally an entire discourse.

Take, for example, the first verb in the paragraph, the imperative "do not love the world." The present imperative with the negative can be translated, "Stop loving the world!" Taking note of the fact that the verb is in the imperative mode and the present tense is significant for properly identifying the structural meaning of the entire paragraph.

Two other structural signals are the conditional particle *ean* ("if"), which introduces a conditional clause, and the subordinating conjunction *hoti* ("for") in verse 16a. The use of "if" introduces a reason for the command in 15a: Don't love the world because love for the world and love for the Father are incompatible; you can't love both at the same time. The "for" in verse 16a introduces a reason for the conditional statement given in verse 15b. The conditional statement in 15b serves as a reason for the command in 15a and the subordinating "for" clause of 16 serves as a reason for the reason given in 15b.

In a command-reason communication relationship, the command is always more important than the reason for the command. And the subordinate reason (v. 16) is less important than what it modifies, which is the conditional clause in 15b.

When we get ready to outline the sermon, all of these aspects of structural meaning come into play.

FIRST BASE: THE BIG PICTURE

A clean hit places the batter at first base. There we take into account that the whole is more than the sum of its parts. Before we analyze in greater depth the bits and pieces of the text (its grammar, syntax, word meanings), we should not miss the forest for the trees. Interpretation should begin at the higher level of discourse, the paragraph, and work its way down to the lower levels: sentences, clauses, phrases, and words.

First John 2:15–17 is a paragraph composed of three sentences in Greek. The first sentence has only one verb, the imperative: "Do not love the world." It is followed by a conditional sentence that begins in verse 15b and ends in verse 16 (note the semicolon as punctuation at the end of verse 15 rather than a period in the Greek New Testament). This is followed by a third sentence that is verse 17.

What is the relationship of these three sentences? Since an imperative carries more semantic weight than an indicative, verse 15 is the dominant sentence in the paragraph and thus contains the topic or theme: Don't love the world or anything in it. Each of the following two sentences provides a ground or reason for not loving the world.

First, one can't love the world and the Father at the same time (v. 15b), and this is true because all that is in the world does not have its source from the Father (v. 16 is introduced by the subordinating conjunction *hoti* in Greek).

The next sentence, verse 17, provides a second ground or reason for the command in verse 15a: the impermanence of the world—it is passing away.

Thus, in the big picture, this text tells us not to love the world for two reasons: (1) the impossibility of loving the world and God at the same time, and (2) the impermanence of the world.

THE Art & Craft OF BIBLICAL PREACHING

From this overall semantic structure, we can construct a basic outline for preaching this text. The outline can consist of one main point (v. 15a) and two subpoints (vv. 15b–16) and (v. 17).

SECOND BASE: GRAMMAR AND SYNTAX

At second base we carefully analyze the grammar and syntax of words, phrases, and clauses. For example, what is the meaning of the prepositional phrase "the love of the Father" in verse 15? What kind of genitive is it: objective or subjective? The choice you make radically alters the meaning of the text. If it is objective, then the phrase means your love for the Father. If it is subjective, the meaning is the Father's love for me.

If it is subjective, the verse means: "If I love the world, the Father doesn't love me," which would probably indicate that John is saying a person who loves the world is not a Christian. On the other hand, if the former meaning is taken, then John is saying: "If I love the world, I can't love the Father at the same time."

Based on the overall structure of the passage, this latter interpretation seems more likely, and most commentators take it this way. In addition, based on the context of this paragraph, the preceding and following paragraphs, it would seem that John views the readers as Christians, as we noted above.

As this shows, the process of exegesis is not strictly linear in practice but is actually multilateral. Each step in the process informs and is informed by the others. Whereas in baseball you have to run the bases in order, in exegesis you generally move back and forth between them or touch more than one base at the same time.

THIRD BASE: WORDS

Third base, the sixth station for the preacher, is the issue of the meaning and use of words in the text. The basic unit of meaning in language is the sentence, not the word. Words mean what they mean in the context of a sentence.

Consider the word *run*. What does it mean? Is it the opposite of walk? What is the difference between a man running, my nose running, and the washing machine running? What about coming in second in the running, having a run in your stocking, running the pool table, leaving the faucet running, or running for office? According to the dictionary, there are approximately eighty possible meanings for the word *run*. The correct meaning is a combination of the root idea in the word plus its use in context.

In 1 John 2:15–17, what does the word *world* mean? Does it refer to the world as the universe, or perhaps the world as planet earth? Does it refer to the world of people as in John 3:16? All of these are legitimate uses of this word, but none conveys the meaning in this passage. Here *world* is used in the sense of the organized world system that is hostile to God.

This is discovered through a combination of word study and context. We use the word in a similar way when we talk about the world of sports or the world of fashion. Word studies of crucial words in the text are essential to proper hermeneutics.

HOME PLATE: APPLICATION

In baseball if you get to third base, you've done well, but if you are left on third base when the inning ends, you don't score a run. Home plate for the preacher is application, getting the meaning from the Bible to the people sitting in the pews in culturally relevant terms. Too often preaching does a good job of explaining the meaning of the text, but then fails to connect the text with the here and now of the listeners.

To apply 1 John 2:15–17, the preacher must move beyond what has traditionally been viewed as "worldly," such as participating in certain kinds of activities like dancing or smoking, to John's broader purpose. A Christian can abstain from certain activities and still love the world.

Also, John's concept of "lust" (1 John 2:16, NASB) must be applied beyond the issue of sexual lust. The word includes that, but is much broader in scope, denoting any inordinate desire contrary to the will and Word of God, as a word study on the Greek *epithymia* demonstrates.

If we keep these seven steps in mind, those who hear us will recognize that our messages are based not merely on our interpretation or ideas, but that we are proclaiming the true message of Scripture.

Chapter 64

WHY ALL THE BEST PREACHERS ARE THEOLOGICAL

Everyone does theology. Do you do it right?

John Koessler

The bones and marrow of the sermon are composed of theology. Yet theological preaching is rare. Listeners fear that too much theology will make the sermon impractical. Many preachers shy away from theological content. Aware of the small window of opportunity given to capture the interest of the audience, preachers are tempted to rush to application. The result is a sermon that begins with the need of the audience, touches lightly on the biblical text, and then moves to concrete implication. In the process, the sermon skips the important step of identifying and stating the theological principles on which the practical application is based. Haddon Robinson has wryly observed: "More heresy is preached in application than in Bible exegesis" (1997, pp. 20–27).

The term *theology* is popularly used to refer to the content of the Bible. I should note that this term can be used in both a broad and a narrow sense. D. L. Baker observes: "A problem arises concerning the validity of using the word *theology* with reference to the content of the Bible. If *theology* is understood to mean the doctrine of God, then it is found only to a very limited degree in the Bible. In conventional usage, however, the word often has a much broader meaning and may include almost any reference to the nature of God and his activity" (1988, pp. 97–98). By this definition, everything in the Scriptures is theological. Any truth statement about the nature of God or humanity or salvation—such as, God is love, humans are sinners—is theological.

Defined more narrowly, however, theology

is primarily a matter of doctrine. A doctrine is simply the teaching of all Scripture on a significant subject—for example, the doctrine of God, the doctrine of salvation, the doctrine of healing. Theology has been defined as "a system of beliefs," meaning that all doctrines are integrated.

THREE TYPES OF THEOLOGY

Three interrelated categories of theology contribute to the theological content of the sermon: exegetical theology, biblical theology, and systematic theology.

Exegetical theology is the theology of the biblical text itself. It is the theological product of the preacher's exegetical analysis of a passage in its context. For example, the exegetical theology of Colossians 3:12–18 includes statements like, "Virtue is both an outcome and an obligation of God's grace." Or, "Those chosen by God to experience the grace of Christ reflect God's transforming power in the way they live, fellowship, and worship." While the passage is itself application oriented, its exhortation to "put on" the virtues of the Christian life is grounded in the theology of grace and election. The Colossians are not told to do these things in order to become God's children but because they already are "God's chosen people, holy and dearly loved" (Col. 3:12). Timothy S. Warren defines exegetical theology as "the statement of universal theological principle that the preacher has discovered in the text through the exegetical and theological processes" (1991, pp. 463–86).

Biblical theology is also exegetical theology, but practiced on a larger scale. If exegetical theology examines a facet of a doctrine from the microscopic view of the sermon text, biblical the-

ology takes a satellite view of the same doctrine. Biblical theology lifts itself above the text and notes the progressive unfolding of a particular doctrine throughout the Scriptures, in a particular portion, or in a single biblical writer. It is the product of collective exegetical analysis.

The biblical data needed to formulate a complete theology of the Holy Spirit, for example, begins with Genesis and continues through Revelation. However, not every book refers to the Spirit, and some passages merely describe his activities. At the very beginning of Genesis the Spirit is portrayed as brooding or "hovering" over the waters (Gen. 1:2). He was an agent of creation. The Old Testament prophetic books describe how the Holy Spirit empowered select believers to speak on God's behalf. The New Testament has a fuller revelation of the nature of ministry of the Spirit. It is there that he is most clearly shown to be a divine person (John 14:16–17). Paul's letters, especially 1 Corinthians 12–14, describe his relationship to the church and its ministries.

Systematic theology is a study of doctrine organized by theme. Instead of looking at the progressive development of a particular doctrine, it attempts to synthesize the theological content of Scripture into a unified summary of the whole of Christian doctrine.

John Calvin's classic *Institutes of the Christian Religion* is a good example of a systematic study of biblical doctrine organized by theme. It is organized into four major divisions. Book one deals with the knowledge of God the Creator and focuses on the nature of God and the ways he has revealed himself to humankind. Book two is concerned with the nature of redemption and highlights both the problem of sin and the work of Christ. Book three looks at the subject of applied redemption by showing how believers receive and live out the grace of Christ. Book four discusses the nature and ministry of the church. Throughout the *Institutes* Calvin supports his assertions with citations from Scripture and interacts with many ancient and (in his day) contemporary theologians.

Each approach has its limitations. The weakness of exegetical theology is its narrow focus. Theological reflection that is limited to what is explicitly stated in one text often results in a one-sided or distorted theology. For example, a theology of works that is based solely on James 2:14–20 will tend toward legalism and may even result in a works-based gospel. On the other hand, a theology of works that is limited to Ephesians 2:8 may not do justice to the transforming potential of the gospel.

The challenge of biblical theology is its immense scope. Few, if any, pastors have the time to do a comprehensive exegetical analysis of every passage that deals with even one of the theological ideas found in a given text.

The danger of systematic theology is it may be used in a way that drowns out the voice of the text. A theological system may incorrectly force the text into a mold it was not intended to fill. The theological system, like a child's Playdough® Factory, pares away everything in the text that does not fit.

Because of these limitations, the preaching task requires attention to all three types of theology.

POOR USES OF THEOLOGY

There is more to theological preaching than adding a few proof texts to the sermon. Some preachers attempt to provide a theological rationale for the sermon by reading a portion of the biblical text, often in support of a main point or subpoint, and then directing the audience's attention to some other passage to explain what has just been read. Instead of discussing the logic and theological implications of the sermon text or showing how its reasoning fits into the bigger picture of revealed truth, the cross-reference is presented as a self-evident explanation.

This approach gives the impression that the preacher's reasoning is circular and creates the potential for bad theology by lifting the meaning of the sermon text out of its immediate historical, grammatical, and literary context. The preacher's first task is always to explain, prove, or apply the biblical author's idea in its context.

Theological preaching isn't a matter of attaching one's pet doctrine to the sermon. Like a congressman attaching special interest legislation to an unrelated bill, this approach is exemplified by the caricature of the preacher who ends every sermon, regardless of the text, by saying, "Now for a few words about believer's baptism."

Theological preaching is not an abstract theological discourse that takes no thought for the life situation or felt needs of the audience. It demands more than simply restating the great doctrines of the Christian faith. In his book *Preachers and Preaching*, Martyn Lloyd-Jones tells of a speaker who gave an address on the Trinity at an evangelistic meeting that targeted elderly women from the poor district of London. "Here was a man, an intelligent trained professional man whom you would have thought would have some idea of addressing people," Lloyd-Jones writes, "but he clearly had not given even a thought to that and probably had been reading an article or book on the Trinity recently." Lloyd-Jones points out that, even though it was sound theology, it was "utterly useless" to his listeners. "You do not give 'strong meat to babes,'" he explains, "you give them milk" (1971, p. 145).

Theology must be applied. This is the pattern of the biblical writers, who regularly move from theological construct to concrete application. Paul's appeal in Romans 12:1 that his readers offer their bodies as living sacrifices, for example, flows out of the theological constructs laid out in the first eleven chapters. It is also grounded in an understanding of the theology of sacrifice outlined in the Old Testament. Peter's first letter follows a similar pattern, repeatedly moving back and forth from theology to application. This same movement should be reflected in the sermon. (For a discussion of the place of application in the sermon see John Koessler, "Getting Gold From the Text," Preaching Today Audio #238).

ANALYZING THE THEOLOGY OF THE TEXT

Theological preaching begins by uncovering the theology of the text. Fundamental questions need to be asked regarding the text, the author, and the original audience. What was the author saying and why? What assumptions about God are conveyed by the text, either explicitly or implicitly? The goal is to identify core theological principles. Once the hard work of grammatical, historical, and literary exegesis is done, it is necessary to utilize the tools and techniques that enable the preacher to fit the theological principles that have been uncovered into the larger context of theological truth.

The theology of the sermon text must be informed by biblical theology. The progressive nature of divine revelation guarantees that no single biblical text will provide an exhaustive treatment of any theological theme or idea. The theology of the text must be placed within the context of the theological scope of its chapter, the book in which it appears, and even the entire Bible.

The difference in what Paul and James say about works, for example, is the result of a difference in perspective, not different theologies. The larger context of Ephesians 2:8 reveals that Paul expected good works to be a natural outflow of the experience of God's grace (Eph. 2:10). Likewise, James does not contrast faith and works but true faith with false faith. Both emphasize the priority of faith and both expect true faith to be reflected in behavior.

Next, especially when there are complex questions, the preacher will want to turn to systematic theology texts, theological dictionaries, and theological journals. Most systematic theology texts arrange their themes under main doctrinal headings and use proof texts to support their assertions. Theological dictionaries arrange their topics alphabetically and go into less depth than systematic theology texts. Theological journals publish scholarly articles that focus on a passage, verse, phrase, or theme.

The result of this analysis should be a theological idea, a single sentence that synthesizes the theological principle of the passage. A theological idea based on John 13:1–17, the account of Jesus washing the disciples' feet, might be: "True divinity is compatible with loving humility and is not afraid to act on it." This is the theological equivalent to what has traditionally been called the sermon proposition or big idea. This statement is built on the foundation of the exegetical idea and paves the way for the sermonic idea or proposition. A flow chart of the process might look like this:

Exegetical Proposition ▶ Theological Proposition ▶ Sermon Proposition

The exegetical proposition focuses on the original audience with its historical and cultural context. The sermon proposition focuses on the cultural context of the preacher's audience. The universal theological proposition provides a necessary bridge from the text to the audience that enables the preacher to combine relevance with authority. Note the words of Timothy S. Warren, citing Walt Kaiser and John Warwick Montgomery:

> The [theological] proposition therefore will be stated in terms of theology rather than history. As a result the preacher will be articulating universal truth that answers the questions, What does this passage tell about God, creation, and the relationship between the two? It is crucial that the theological product be clearly and sufficiently linked to the original passage, for "once the expositor demonstrates that the message is from the text, then the exposition [theology] will carry the authority it must have to be effective in ensuing preaching." Theology then is the "hermeneutical arch that reaches from the text to the contemporary sermon." (1991, p. 478).

The exegetical proposition for a sermon based on John 13:1–17 might be, "Jesus in his divinity did not shy away from true humility because he knew who he was and whom he loved." This is based on John's summary statement in 13:1 that "Jesus knew that the time had come for him to leave this world and go to the Father. Having loved his own who were in the world, he now showed them the full extent of his love."

The theological proposition, stated once again, is "True divinity is compatible with loving humility and is not afraid to act on it."

The sermon proposition takes the theological idea and frames it with the audience in view. In this case, Jesus' humility is presented as an example for the disciples to follow. The idea might focus on the nature of the task: "The greatest thing we can do for God is usually the thing at hand." Or the proposition might focus on the compatibility between humility and greatness: "The surest path to greatness is the lowest path."

BRINGING THEOLOGY TO LIFE

The theological burden of the sermon may require repackaging for postmodern listeners, who feel it is necessary to experience truth to "know" that it is true. When preaching to such an audience, it is often necessary to expose them to theology through the back door of analogy and illustration.

 For an audio example of this principle see tracks 9–10 on the supplemental CD.

One of the best models of this kind of theological preaching can be found in sermons of the eighteenth-century preacher Jonathan Edwards. Edwards was a theological and exegetical preacher. "His sermons," Conrad Cherry writes, "even his most revivalistic ones, were carefully constructed monuments to biblical exegesis, as they followed the tripartite scheme of clarification of biblical text, elaboration of doctrine implicit in the text, and application of text and doctrine to the lives of his hearers" (1985, p. 264).

Edwards was a master of using vivid imagery and concrete analogy so that the theological truths he preached would impact listeners on an experiential level (for more on making the language of your sermon more vivid, see Wiersbe, 1997). Cherry points to Edwards' most famous sermon, "Sinners in the Hands of an Angry God," as a prime example: "The pattern of the scene which Edwards paints in this sermon follows the track of typologizing: from the literal to the symbolic, from the concrete to the spiritual; from beholding an oven and touching a hot coal (common enough experiences for eighteenth-century New Englanders) to eternal consumption by flame; from enduring intense pain a minute, then several minutes, to imagining the torment of constant, unrelieved pain" (1985, p. 268).

Edwards adopted this strategy as a result of his own theological convictions. The seat of true religion, according to Edwards, was not the head but the heart. The chief benefit of the sermon was derived, as Edwards himself put it, from "an impression made on the heart at the time" (Lloyd-Jones, 1987, pp. 348–371).

It is doubtful that theological truth can be communicated completely without stating it in propositional form at some point in the sermon. Not everyone has the same learning style. Some respond to stories, others learn best with a clear outline. The preacher's own ability may be a limiting factor. Cornelius Plantinga Jr. (1999, pp. 16–19) warns of the danger of trying to imitate masters of the narrative form, noting: "Thousands of young preachers have tried to imitate such virtuosity, and without much luck." He goes on to point out how even narrative preachers like Frederick Buechner eventually resort to propositions: "Buechner's own sermons, for all their suggestiveness, usually deliver real freight. In fact, alarmingly enough, a Buechner sermon usually delivers a proposition or two." A dull but clear proposition is often better than an interesting but vague narrative.

Charles Spurgeon once observed that the young preacher is primarily concerned with matters of style while those with more experience tend to focus their attention on content. In effect, the younger preacher asks, "How shall I say it?" while the older preacher thinks, "What shall I say?" The theological preacher must ask both questions. It is by giving careful attention to the theology of the text and the need of the audience that the preacher learns what must be said about it and how to say it.

BIBLIOGRAPHY

Baker, D. L. 1988. "Biblical Theology," in the *New Dictionary of Theology* (Downers Grove, Ill.: InterVarsity), pp. 97–98.

Cherry, Conrad, 1985, "Symbols of Spiritual Truth: Jonathan Edwards as Biblical Interpreter," *Interpretation* 39 (July), p. 268.

Lloyd Jones, Martyn. 1971, *Preachers and Preaching.* Grand Rapids: Zondervan.

_____. 1987. *The Puritans: Their Origins and Successors.* Carlisle, Pa.:, Banner of Truth.

Plantinga, Cornelius, Jr. 1999. "Dancing the Edge of Mystery," *Books & Culture* 5/5 (September/October), pp. 16–19.

Robinson, Haddon. 1997. "The Heresy of Preaching," *Leadership Journal* 18 (Fall), pp. 20–27.

Warren, Timothy S. 1991. "A Paradigm for Preaching," *Bibliotheca Sacra* 148 (October–December), pp. 463–86.

Wiersbe, Warren W. 1997. *Preaching and Teaching With Imagination.* Grand Rapids: Baker.

LETTING THE LISTENERS MAKE
THE DISCOVERIES

Scripture can speak for itself

Earl Palmer

Whenever I stand before a congregation, I have to suppress my natural instinct to preach. We preachers have a tendency—some innate drive—to offer answers to our listeners before they've even heard the questions. We want to help, but sometimes we forget the process required.

No wonder preaching has gotten a bad name. "Don't preach at me!" a teenager shouts at his parents. "I don't need your sermon," a wife says to her husband. And we know exactly what they mean. People resist answers others have found for them. Now-I'm-going-to-fix-you sermons make my congregation's eyes glaze over. When I pontificate, they cannot contemplate.

J. B. Phillips, while translating the New Testament, discovered its truth to be pulsing with life and power. He felt like an electrician, he said, working with wiring while the power was still on. This was no dull routine, grappling with the dynamic, living Word! Phillips felt the awesomeness—both the dread and the excitement—of the electric charge of God's truth.

KEEP THE BIBLE FIRST

Once while traveling, my daughter and I heard a sermon on the radio. The preacher read the text magnificently; it was from Romans 8 and was about hope. The preacher then gave a

series of moving, personal anecdotes about hope.

After the sermon my daughter asked, "How did you like the sermon?"

"It was moving," I said. "In fact, one of the illustrations brought me to tears."

Then my daughter said something I'll never forget: "But Dad, I didn't like the sermon because the pastor basically said, 'Since I have hope, you should have hope.' And that's not gospel."

I was so proud of my daughter. She saw that the good news was something more. I'm glad this pastor has hope. But I need to see how that text in Romans gives me a profound basis for hope whether he has hope or not! In a way, then, the pastor cheated his listeners. We were denied the opportunity to see the text and discover from it the basis of hope for ourselves.

People, of course, desire a human touch—love and compassion and hope. And they need personal stories to show the gospel in action in daily life. The only trouble is, personal stories alone don't connect me to the real source of hope.

Personal witness and stories should be seen like all illustrations—as windows to illuminate, to help people look in on a textual treasure waiting to be discovered. If I make my discoveries through such stories, I may become unhealthily dependent on the storyteller, usually the pastor, for my spiritual growth. But if I can discover hope for myself from Romans 8, I discover it alongside the pastor. Although it takes more time, this discovery is more powerful and longer lasting.

Yes, we must be people-fluent, understanding them and communicating to their needs. But first we must be textually fluent. That means, of course, I must invest time and hard work to know the text. In fact, I have to know a lot just to raise the right questions! Good teaching comes when I understand the content and deeply know the text before I search for its implications. Then people can be connected first and foremost with the text.

LET THE URGENCY COME THROUGH

Letting Scripture speak for itself doesn't mean I'm dispassionate about my presentation. If I want my learners to discover the text, I need to whet their appetite for spiritual things. To do that effectively I need to convey the urgency of the text.

The best calculus teachers believe a kid can't really make it in the world without knowing calculus. Such teachers demand more and challenge more. They also teach more. I want to capture a sense of urgency that says, "This is not just an interesting option. It is essential that you know." Learners catch more than content from such teaching; they catch an enthusiasm for the truth.

This means, among other things, I must be urgent about my own soul. I must be a growing, maturing Christian myself with an appetite for spiritual things. Only then can I communicate with urgency the need for my congregation to grow and mature as well.

DON'T GET TO THE POINT

Although I'm urgent about what I teach, I'm not urgent about getting to the main point of the text. I've learned not to reveal what I know too soon. I've learned not to force the discovery but to let the natural drift of the text unfold. I've got to give people time to wonder, time to ponder, time for questions to emerge, and time for answers to take shape in the text.

When I preach by raising questions that spring naturally from the text itself, I enable the listener to discover meaning for themselves. It's a little like Agatha Christie holding the solution to the mystery until the time is just right.

Take, for example, the text about Zacchaeus in Luke 19:1–10. After Zacchaeus received Jesus into his home, the next line says, "All the people saw this and began to mutter, 'He is gone to be the guest of a "sinner."'" Even though I want to highlight this detail quickly, I don't need to tell the congregation right off why the people murmured.

So first I'll ask them, "Why did the people murmur? Why are they so upset? What's going on that they're so angry with Jesus? And notice, they all murmured—that means the disciples, too. Why are the disciples upset?" I may journey with my congregation through the various kinds of people who'd have been present in Jericho: Why would the Pharisees murmur? Why the disciples? Why the townspeople? What upsets them so? What expectations did they have that Jesus now has dashed? Such an approach retains the text's natural drama.

With this particular story, I can take my congregation on a journey through some Old Testament expectations of the Messiah. I can explore various ideas of what the Messiah would and wouldn't do with a crook like Zacchaeus. I can consider why people weren't prepared for a Messiah who came to seek and to save the lost. I can show why they were so surprised by Jesus.

It's this surprise element in the text that is the wonderful news! When I can help my congregation make such discoveries just a split second before I actually tell them, they get excited about the Scripture and its relevance for their lives.

LET THE TRUTH SELL ITSELF

We teachers are often tempted to say too much all at once, especially at the end of lessons and sermons. We throw in everything we can think of to make someone a Christian, rattling off the most precious facts of our faith—the blood of Christ, the cross, God's love—and reduce them to hasty, unexplained sentences.

Instead, I've found it is far better to let the scriptural text make its own point and sell itself. And we can trust Scripture to sell itself because the Spirit is already working in people before they even come to the text.

People come to the text not as blank slates but as individuals in whom the Spirit is already working. Since the Scripture speaks to people's deepest needs, we can trust that it will get a hearing from people. We can be confident people will discover how good it is once they give it a try.

It's like taking a person to Mount Hood. I've been to Timberline Lodge, and I know how beautiful it is. But I don't have to brag about it beforehand to convince someone of its magnificence. When I get that person there, he'll see its beauty for himself and be impressed. Similarly, all I have to do is bring people to the door of Scripture. Once they walk through the door and see for themselves, they're going to be struck with how relevant Jesus Christ is for their lives.

In our church's small group Bible studies, for instance, we don't try to be evangelistic. Our goal is to let the text make its own point and then enable the group to talk together about what is being read. We consciously try not to cover everything the first week but only what the text for the first week says.

A crusty engineering professor in our city was shattered when his wife died of a sudden heart attack, just before he was to retire. She had been a Christian, and after the funeral, he came to see me. I steered him toward the Gospel of Mark and some additional reading.

After several weeks, I could see the New Testament was gradually making sense to him. My closing comment in our times together was usually, "Let me know when you're ready to become a Christian."

One Sunday after church, with a lot of people milling around, the engineer stood in the back waiting for me. He's not the kind of man who likes standing around. Finally he got my attention, and he called out, "Hey, Earl, I'm letting you know."

That was it; he became a Christian at age sixty-five, convinced by the Scripture of Christ's trustworthiness.

LETTING PEOPLE HEAR THEIR OWN APPLICATION

Creating opportunity for personal discovery sometimes surprises us in the way results come. One pastor struggled with the way his conservative upbringing imposed artificial spirituality on people. He refused to preach on traditional "sins": going to movies, smoking, drinking, and so on.

One Sunday his text gave him ample opportunity to talk of such things: "'Everything is permissible for me'—but I will not be mastered by anything" (I Cor. 6:12). However the pastor still would not mention the sins dictated by his tradition. Instead, he deliberately spoke of other addictions tolerated by his church, things such as overeating and watching too much television.

After the service one woman cornered the pastor, handing him her pack of cigarettes. "It may be lawful," she said, "but I've been mas-tered by these cigarettes. I've never noticed that verse in that way before, so I'm giving these to you. With God's help, I'm going to master them." Without a word about cigarettes or nicotine, the text itself had spoken to this young woman.

I have found that change goes deeper when we make the connection, when *we* discover God's Word to us. When I can help people discover that, then I'm "teaching" a great deal and preaching as I should.

Chapter 66

CONVICTION AND COMPASSION

It takes both toughness and tenderness to rescue people from sin

S. Bowen Matthews

I once preached on divorce from Mark 10: "Therefore what God has joined together, let man not separate.... Anyone who divorces his wife and marries another woman commits adultery against her" (10:9–11).

"Our first reaction to Jesus' words," I said, "is to look for loopholes, to bargain, to soften the blow of his words. That's why we don't hear him speak and race to confess our failure and restore to honor God's will for marriage."

In the next breath, I said, "Many of you here are divorced. Some of you are remarried. What's done is done. It is not my responsibility or my wish to lash divorced and remarried people with Scripture and send them away feeling guilty or aggravated. I suspect all of you who have experienced divorce have had more than your share of guilty feelings. Divorce is not the unpardonable sin. But it is sin. If you have confessed and repented of that sin, then let's get on with your life."

Within hours, a woman from our congregation sat in my office. "You just don't understand what I've been through," she said. She proceeded to tell a horrible story of what her ex-husband did to her. Given her circumstances, my well-intentioned sermon seemed harsh and uncomprehending.

It would be easy to dismiss her complaint. She may have simply refused to own up to her contributions toward the failure of the marriage. But I find that callous. Pastors need to be tough, but toughness without spiritual discernment deteriorates into spiritual abuse. She had come to the sermon seeking bread and found a stone. Why?

THE TENSION

In retrospect I trace that sermon's failure to haste and the lack of passion with which I handled the tension between compassion and conviction. The entire sermon was about divorce and remarriage. But only six short paragraphs developed the tension between the eternal will of God and the experiences of people whose failed marriages have marred that will.

Issues around this tension abound. I can talk (have talked) for hours about some of these issues. Books about them fill a short shelf in my library. But I passed over them that day in haste.

But haste had a more devastating partner in the failure of that sermon. Those six paragraphs were entirely *cognitive*. Rereading them now with that woman's heart-cry in my ear, they seem cut and dried, distant from her pain. She heard no hint of how I had at times struggled to admit that in some marriages divorce actually made more sense than staying together. My words had no taste to her soul; no salt from my tears seasoned them.

If I could preach that sermon again, I would take half the sermon to develop the tension in my commitment to God's eternal plan and my commitment to the people who have marred the plan and who have sometimes been broken in the process.

I'm grateful for that woman. She was one of God's instruments to reshape my heart so I could grow more consistent in preaching God's Word without compromise, but also with compassion.

The following principles maintain the balance for me.

NOT TOO MANY

Too many conviction-driven sermons will make a congregation self-righteous. Nothing makes us feel so righteous as exposing another person's glaring evil, especially if it is an evil we are never tempted to do. My righteous indignation at computer hacking is as pure as the arctic snow, because I have as much interest in the subject as I do in soil samples from Bangladesh.

When pastors preach often and strongly against specific sins, their preaching becomes predictable. It focuses on sins that do not tempt most of the congregation. If it focused on sins they were tempted to commit, the preacher might have a revival on his hands—or more likely, a riot. Since that is usually not the focus, the congregation goes away satisfied, congratulating themselves on how upright they really are.

Furthermore, that kind of preaching raises a question about the pastor and his people: What are they hiding? Is all this predictable condemnation of someone else's sin a ruse to keep them from facing up to some awful truth about themselves?

To counter this danger in myself and in my congregation, there is a small test by which I gauge our spiritual health. If we leave church feeling satisfied with how upright we are, we are flirting with the devil.

I don't ever want to go away from church feeling satisfied with myself. I want to go away feeling satisfied with our Savior, who restores my soul, who leads me in paths of righteousness for his name's sake, and at whose right hand there are pleasures forevermore. Too much preaching against someone else's sin compromises this.

That small test encourages me to remember compassion even when I denounce sin.

ADD YES TO NO

Conviction-driven sermons tell only half the story. "Put off," says the wisdom of the New

Testament, "your old self, which is being corrupted by deceitful desires . . . and . . . put on the new self, created to be like God in true righteousness and holiness" (Eph. 5:22–23). Denouncing sin has a place in pastoral ministry. But in order of intention, it is not first place. Yes, we need to know what to say no to. But above all, we need to know what to say yes to.

In the Ten Commandments series, I pictured each commandment as a doorway in a large wall. We say no to the behavior each forbids in order to pass through that doorway to the other side. There we find paths that lead to joy and union with our God—what older theologians called "the beatific vision."

With this in mind, I preached two sermons on each commandment. The first sermon expounded the meaning of the commandment. The second said, "Let's assume that we obey the commandment. What possibilities for holiness does it open up for us?"

For example, in the second sermon on the first commandment, I said, "You and I have obeyed. We are keepers of the first commandment. We have renounced all pretenders to our ultimate loyalty and affection in order to embrace and be ravished by the living and true God. What is that like?"

I then quoted five statements from the Psalms—for example, "My soul thirsts for God, for the living God. Where can I go and meet with God?" (Ps. 42:2). I asked, "Is there in your experience anything that approaches such passion for God, such delight in God himself?" The rest of the sermon pointed to one path of how to do that.

These first three principles, faithfully applied, restore my perspective when confronted by the evils of our time—and the temptations to become rigid and uncompassionate

about people caught in those evils. They restore in me the realism to focus primarily on our God and not on our evil. They restore in me the realism to consider more carefully the actual people listening to my preaching and what might be going on in their souls as they listen.

I even have the realism to remember that strangest of all creatures in the congregation—me—and my part in the world's evil and my aspirations to holiness. The hills and valleys become a plain, and compassion joins conviction on level ground.

KNOW YOUR SINFULNESS

Balance comes from assuming the position of adulterer. John 8: 1–11 tells the story of Jesus and the woman taken in adultery. Every preacher in whom conviction and compassion are to marry and bear fruit must stand in the position of the woman taken in adultery.

Paul Tournier wrote of her, "This woman symbolizes all the despised people of the world, all those whom we see daily, crushed by judgments which weigh heavily upon them, by a thousand and one arbitrary or unjust prejudices, but also by fair judgments, based on the healthiest morality and the most authentic divine law. She symbolizes all psychological, social and spiritual inferiority. And her accusers symbolize the whole judging, condemnatory, contemptuous humanity."

Corky was my childhood buddy. We grew up in a day when car tires had inner tubes. Several disused ones hung in every garage. We would take them down, lay them out flat, and cut from them wide strips of tubing. The strips looked like giant rubber bands. Next, we cut each strip in half, laid it out lengthwise, and nailed one end to a piece of wood that had a handle. Then, we would walk around and slam those long pieces of rubber down on the street or sidewalk. The sound was louder than a rifle shot.

One day, Corky hit me right across the back with one of those things. I grabbed mine, crying and swearing, and chased him down the street. I hate to think what I would have done to him if I had caught him. I had lost control.

But he was faster. He got to his house and locked the door. I didn't see him for a long time, but I looked for him. I meant to make him pay for what he had done to me.

Many years later, it struck me: What if Corky and I had lived in New York City and had been members of different gangs? Gang wars have been started for less than that. There were no gangs in my neighborhood, but all the passions that start a gang war or a world war were fully operational in my little boy's heart.

Whatever human evil I preach against, I find it easy to imagine myself succumbing to that very evil, if the circumstances were right. I find it easy to see myself in place of the woman taken in adultery: guilty, accused, waiting the final condemnation from him who has all authority in heaven and earth. Standing there in her place does wonders for balancing conviction with compassion.

Use First-Person Stories

Balance comes by using first-person stories. First-person stories from real life put a human face on convictions, and that face invites compassion.

Genevieve was a twenty-something-year-old woman who suffered from Marfan Syndrome, a hereditary disorder that affects the connective tissues of the body, as had her mother before her. She and her husband consulted a world-class authority on the disease about her becoming pregnant. He strongly cautioned her against it. That very week, if not that very day, they received word from their obstetrician that she was pregnant. An abortion was indicated.

No one in our congregation would have blinked if she had gone through with the abortion. Her life was at stake. Genevieve, with the knowledge and consent of her husband, made the unexpected choice of carrying the child to term. About seven months into the pregnancy, Genevieve was hospitalized for tests. Her doctors suggested she be transferred to Philadelphia for more sophisticated tests. She was loaded on a helicopter for the short flight. Just before the helicopter lifted off, Genevieve sat up on the gurney. The arteries of her heart, weakened by the disease, further weakened by the pregnancy, detached from the heart. Death was instant. The doctor, who had just put her on the helicopter, rushed back and delivered a beautiful baby girl, who today is nearing graduation from high school.

Many would say this mother was unwise and unthinking in allowing the pregnancy to continue. We might also say, "Greater love has no one than this that one lay down his life for his friends." I do not say this to praise her. What she did transcends praise. I do not hold her up as an example to be imitated. What she did does not invite imitation. Rather, like some new sun in our sky her act of love serves as a flaming center of gravitation by which the rest of us may in some decisive way be drawn away from the gathering darkness of the old creation.

A story like this moves the sermon beyond the cognitive. Instead of head to head in an intellectual battle, we go heart to heart with our people. The story mediates to the congregation our passion for truth and our compassion for people.

Do I have a story like that for every confrontation between conviction and compassion? Yes, but only after twenty-nine years in pastoral ministry. And I have a lot more as a result of being perceived as someone who cares for people in the jungle of life.

We who wrestle to preach with conviction and compassion in proper proportion need to look to the example of Jesus Christ, rising from his doodling in the dust and towering up over the centuries to utter to the adulterous woman before him the most redeeming words ever to pass human lips: "Neither do I condemn you. . . . Go now and leave your life of sin" (John 8:11).

Chapter 67

THE INADEQUACY OF "YES" THEOLOGY
If saying no makes me narrow, so be it

Ben Patterson

Terror seized me by the throat a few months into my engagement to be married. Ardor turned to horror. Hot pursuit suddenly got cold feet. This came with a fundamental realization: If I had this woman, I couldn't have any of the others. If I said "yes" to one, I was saying "no" to millions. Not that this was the breadth of my options, mind you—but whatever options I might have had before I said my vows, they were no more after I said them.

I gingerly raised some of these concerns with the woman who nevertheless became my wife. That was many years ago. She's forgiven me, I think.

Every yes contains a no. And if you can't learn to say one, you won't learn to say the other. (Maybe that's why we put up with two-year-olds.) It certainly describes the way Christians and churches can drift into heresy and confusion.

I know of a church whose new pastor has led it into serious, even fatal, theological error. The mystery is that his predecessor, a thoroughly orthodox, godly, and beloved man, had pastored the church for more than three decades and had never preached anything but the gospel truth. How could this happen?

I asked a friend who knew the church. She explained, "He told them the truth all those years. What he didn't tell them was what wasn't the truth." He said the yes, but he never said the no, and because he didn't, his people never really heard the yes. They weren't so thoroughly taught after all.

But I empathize with my colleague. It takes intellectual rigor to understand the yes well enough to know the no. It taxes the mind, and it can put a strain on relationships. I once preached on Jesus' command for the rich young man to sell all he had and give it to the poor. Encouraged by some remarks I read by Tony Campolo, I asked my upscale congregation, rhetorically, "May a Christian own a BMW?" Maybe I should have been content just to tell my people that one cannot follow Christ and be a slave to riches. Maybe not. Whatever the case, from the calls and mail I received, I could tell that the message was memorable, if not popular.

Learn to say the yes and the no. Few issues portend so much for the future of the church, because none carries so much potential to fly in the face of the spirit of the age. I speak of the infatuation with pluralism and inclusivism and certain brands of multiculturalism, the belief in the egalitarianism of opinions and feelings— that it is not only wrong, but rude and bigoted to think that some people's ideas and feelings may not be as good or as valid as others. It's the "Who's to Say?" syndrome: Who's to say what is right? The answer is everyone, or no one, or both. Whatever. It's cool.

Faithful stewards of the household of God must practice the discipline of saying both yes and no. It's hard, it's not fun, and it doesn't usu-

ally preach to packed houses. But believers in every age have had to learn it or lose the faith. It wasn't enough for Nicea to say that Christ was begotten of the Father. It had to say, "begotten, not made." It wasn't enough for the signers of the Barmen Declaration to declare that Christ was Lord; they had to add that Hitler was not.

Without declaring the no, we become the church that Machen observed in his day: "conservative in an ignorant, non-polemic, sweetness-and-light kind of way, which is just meat for the wolves."

Saying no is part of the nature of our faith, a faith that Alan Watts, the Anglican-turned-Hindu, found to be "a contentious faith . . . uncompromising, ornery, militant, rigorous, imperious, and invincibly self-righteous." So be it. But its narrowness is the narrowness of the birth canal, or of a path between two precipices—or of a lifetime spent loving one woman.

Chapter 68

WHAT GREAT COACHES— AND PREACHERS—KNOW

How to use positive and negative elements with purpose

Craig Brian Larson

I was coaching gymnasts at a local club for a few hours a week. As I took beginners from basic skills like hip circles on the high bar to more difficult tricks like giants, I repeatedly faced a decision intrinsic to the art of coaching: when to say what the gymnast was doing right and when to say what he was doing wrong.

Both were necessary. I couldn't help a beginner on high bar by ignoring that he was about to swing forward with his hands in an undergrip position—he would peel in the front and fall on his head. "Don't ever do that!" I warned. "You'll break your neck."

But my ultimate goal was not just to avoid

injury; I wanted these boys to become excellent gymnasts someday. So I encouraged them as they developed the fundamentals: "Good stretch. That's the way to hollow your chest. Nice scoop in the front."

Preachers face the same decision weekly. One of our most important decisions when crafting a sermon is whether to frame it positively (what to do, what's right, our hope in God, the promises) or negatively (what not to do, what's wrong, the sinful human condition). The choice between positive or negative in the subject, outline, illustrations, and application powerfully affects the tone of a sermon. It changes the response of listeners.

Surprisingly, it took a friend editing a piece of my writing to make me sensitive to the issue of positive and negative preaching. I found he had written a new conclusion. "I didn't think this ended well on a negative note," he explained, "so I've converted this to a positive conclusion."

I liked my original version, but as I considered the revised version, I had to admit the positive conclusion was more effective. It left a hopeful feeling, and that was appropriate. Thereafter in my preaching, I became intentional about selecting positive or negative elements, and I have seen the difference it makes.

SAME TEXT, DIFFERENT SERMONS

Some time back I preached from Malachi 1:6–14 and had to choose between positive and negative approaches. Malachi 1 scathingly indicts the priests and Israelites for what they were doing wrong. The people were sacrificing to God their blind and lame animals. The priests were sniffing at the altar, complaining that it smelled and that the sacrifices were a burden. God angrily rebuked them because by such "worship" they were showing him contempt rather than honor.

This Old Testament passage forcefully portrays a failing that Christians can have—we may dishonor God by giving him our worst instead of our best.

In writing the sermon, I had several decisions to make. First, the subject could have been framed negatively: How people show contempt for God. I had to develop that theme to be true to the text, of course, yet I decided to do so under the umbrella of a positive subject: How to honor God.

If I had selected the negative approach, my main points would have been: We show contempt for God when we (1) respect a father or employer above God, (2) offer God what we don't value, (3) worship God as if he were trivial.

In the positive approach, I wrote this outline: We honor God when we (1) respect God above a father or employer, (2) give God what we value, (3) worship God in a way that reflects his greatness. I developed the points with contrast, explaining what the Israelites were doing wrong and then illustrating positively how we can do what is right.

That one decision early on drastically changed the application and emotional impact of the entire sermon.

My goal is not a simple fifty-fifty split between positive and negative. Rather, I want to know which approach I am using and why. Finding the right balance of positive and negative preaching leads to healthy Christians and churches and to sermons that people want to hear.

WHEN TO BE NEGATIVE

Both positive and negative sermon elements are especially effective at accomplishing certain objectives. Let's look at four constructive reasons to use a negative approach.

To show our need. Negative preaching takes sin seriously and leads to repentance, thus indirectly bringing the positive results of joy, peace, and life. It is in keeping with the model of Jesus, who clearly honored God's hatred of sin by telling people what not to do.

To seize interest. As journalists know—and radio hosts like Rush Limbaugh make a fortune on—the negative gets more attention and interest than the positive.

To accentuate the positive. The positive feels even more so after it has been contrasted with the negative.

To warn of danger. If my son reaches toward a hot pan on the stove, it's no time for me to tell him what great potential he has. "Don't touch that pan!" is negative—and necessary. In a dangerous world, much of a responsible pastor's counsel is negative by necessity.

WHEN TO BE POSITIVE

At the core, New Testament preachers proclaim good news, a message that brings hope, help, strength, and joy. Jesus sums up the negative commands—don't kill, steal, lie, covet—in positive terms: Love the Lord and love your neighbor.

A positive approach works best when you have the following four objectives:

To show the goodness of Christ. The negative often focuses on what people and Satan do. The positive focuses on God's answer, God's glory, God's nature, God's salvation. Christ-centered preaching requires the positive.

To bring encouragement and hope. God wants people to experience hope, peace, acceptance, courage. Bad news makes people feel bad. So while the negative is useful, it is rarely helpful to leave that as the last word.

To build godliness. People need not only to stop sinning but also to start doing God's will. Preaching is both destructive and constructive, tearing down what's wrong and building what's right. Preaching positively encourages people to do what's right.

To bring resolution. Sermons often have greater emotional impact when we begin with the negative, show the need, and then bring resolution by showing what God can do.

HOW TO CHANGE DIRECTION

As we ponder the purpose of our sermon, we may sense that we need to flip an element from positive to negative, or vice versa. Instead of saying what not to do, we want to focus on what to do. Or instead of illustrating what someone did right, we want to illustrate what someone did wrong. Here's how to make the switch.

Switching from Negative to Positive

In a sermon on James 1:2–4, I wanted to encourage listeners to persevere because it makes them mature in character. I suspected, though, that many of my listeners weren't overly concerned about growing in character. But I also assumed they didn't want to crash and burn morally. So I began by using a negative example, trying to motivate them by showing them what to avoid:

> No one wants to crash and burn.
> On September 8, 1992, Air Force master pilot Don Snelgrove was flying over Turkey in an F–16 fighter. He was on a four-hour mission to patrol the no-fly zone established over northern Iraq to protect the Kurds.

Nature calls even for master pilots. He pulled out a plastic container, set his F–16 on autopilot, and undid his lap belt. As he adjusted his seat upward, the buckle on that lap belt wedged between the seat and the control stick, pushing the stick to the right and sending the plane into a spin.

As he struggled to regain control, the plane plunged 33,000 feet. Finally at 2,000 feet altitude, he ejected from the plane. Moments later the F–16 struck a barren hillside and burst into flames. Neither the pilot nor anyone on the ground was injured. But I'll tell you what: There was one very embarrassed master pilot. That F–16 burning on a hillside in Turkey cost U.S. taxpayers $18 million.

Even inadvertent mistakes are terribly embarrassing. How much worse are the mistakes and failures that result from our weaknesses, flaws, and sins. But we don't have to crash and burn morally. We can develop godly character, and James 1:2–4 shows us how.

My goal was to use negative examples to motivate. But I could have begun the sermon positively. Perhaps the congregation already desired character and needed only encouragement. In that case, I could have begun the sermon with a positive example of someone who inspires us with his or her noble character:

Inside each of us there is the desire to be a better person. Many of us would love to be more like Dr. Elizabeth Holland, a pediatrician from Memphis, Tennessee, who has served as a volunteer doctor for World Vision.

Once she treated patients in the middle of an African civil war, explains writer Robert Kerr. In 1985 she performed one appendectomy in which "the 'operating room' was a mud hut deep in the jungle of Zaire. The anesthetic was an animal tranquilizer, which ran out in the middle of the operation. Outside, MIG jets were dropping bombs." Every time a bomb hit, dirt from the

mud hut fell down on them. She performed a virtual miracle considering the circumstances, and her patient lived.

During the Angolan civil war, Holland routinely saw 400 to 500 patients a day. "I frequently wrapped broken bones in magazines and used banana leafs for slings," she said.

Since food was in short supply, Holland ate a paste made from ground cassava-plant roots. "It tasted like glue," said Dr. Holland. "The first few days, I thought I would die. But then I got to where it tasted pretty good. Sometimes when it rained we could get a few leaves from the trees to cook in with it for variety."

Across the Angolan border was a minefield that often killed or injured civilians; Holland would retrieve them.

She said, "I learned if I got my nose down at ground level and crawled along on my stomach, I could see the mines. So I would make my way across, then throw the injured person over my shoulder and carry them out the same way I had come over."

Maybe we will never be forced to persevere as Elizabeth Holland has, but each of us can grow in character, and James 1:2–4 tells us how.

Notice that this example leaves a positive feeling in listeners; it assumes they want the best and can develop. The negative approach focuses on what to avoid; a positive approach focuses on what to attempt.

Switching from Positive to Negative.

Some Bible passages can be presented with a positive or negative approach, depending on the situation. Take, for example, the story of Peter trying to walk on water.

In his sermon "A Mind-Expanding Faith," John Ortberg draws from the text a positive main idea:

All of us are would-be water walkers. And God did not intend for human beings, his children created in his divine image, to go through life in a desperate attempt to avoid failure.

The boat is safe, and the boat is secure, and the boat is comfortable. The water is high, the waves are rough, the wind is strong, and the night is dark. A storm is out there, and if you get out of your boat, you may sink.

But if you don't get out of your boat, you will never walk because if you want to walk on the water, you have to get out of the boat. There is something, Someone, inside us that tells us our lives are about something more than sitting in the boat, something that wants to walk on the water, something that calls us to leave the routine of comfortable existence and abandon ourselves in this adventure of following Christ.

But the same passage could be used in a negative approach: to point out Peter's mistakes to avoid. It might sound like this:

Peter was able to walk on water for a few steps. But in the middle of that walk toward Christ, something changed in his heart, and it caused him to sink.

Peter isn't the only one who has taken bold steps of faith to follow Christ. Many in this congregation are doing the same. In spite of great fear, you have begun to teach a Bible class or host a cell group or volunteer at the local hospital. Now that you've begun, you are beginning to see how challenging this really is, and you're wavering. You feel like you're going to sink. Let's see if we can learn from this account how to avoid what caused Peter to sink.

To change from positive to negative, look for what a text shows not to do.

My two oldest sons competed on their high school gymnastics team. As the postseason meets began, Aaron, who was a senior, had the goal of qualifying for state. Ben, a sophomore, wanted to make it to sectionals.

In regionals both Aaron and Ben had poor meets, missing several routines. When they got in the car afterward, they were down in the dumps—even though they had both (barely) made the cut for sectionals.

Although after some meets, I have pointed out flaws in their technique, this time I spent the next thirty minutes in the car telling them the bright spots, the specific things they had done well: "Aaron, that was the best double you've ever done off high bar. You were above the bar." "Ben, your plange on parallel bars was unbelievable. You must have held it for five seconds!"

By the time we got home, they were smiling and talking about how much better they would do in the next meet. Their confidence had returned. One week later, Ben hit his routines as well as he had all year, and Aaron reached the goal that he had hoped for all year: He qualified for state.

We coach—and disciple—not only the body but the heart. The choice between positive and negative in our sermons is a critical part of training Christians who have the heart of champions.

Chapter 69

PREACHING THAT OPENS EARS AND HEARTS

The value of taking a more positive approach

Haddon Robinson

The primary emotional element of many evangelical sermons is guilt. People leave feeling guilty. Seldom do they leave feeling they have succeeded.

We can take almost any passage of Scripture and turn it into guilt. Although 1 Peter 1:3–4 says, "Praise be to the God and Father of our Lord Jesus Christ! In his great mercy he has given us new birth into a living hope," the emphasis of our sermon can be, "But your hope isn't as strong as it used to be, is it?" Instead of leaving people with great hope and desire, we keep raising the bar beyond where people can jump.

The problem is people do not change much from guilt. It's not a good motivator.

Many people come from homes where they were seldom affirmed by their parents, or at least by their fathers. They can't remember a time when their fathers took them aside and said, "I think you're great. It doesn't matter to me whether you succeed or fail; you are the greatest thing that ever happened to me." If we grew up feeling we couldn't please our parents, we may carry that into the pulpit. We may think we can motivate others by constantly reminding them how far short they fall.

In addition, conservatives are not always comfortable commending people. In *Alice in Wonderland*, Alice asks the Mad Hatter if there's any cake. He says, "Cake? Well, no. We had cake yesterday, and we'll have cake tomor-row, but we never have any cake today." Similarly, we had cake in the past when God was alive and well and doing things; we'll have cake in the future when Jesus returns; but we treat today like stale bread. Somehow we have a hard time commending the people who are committed and loving and making a difference today.

Negative elements can have a legitimate place in preaching. The Old Testament prophets warned that if Israel did not turn from their sin they would be taken captive. You can't preach the Scriptures without pointing to where failure and danger lie.

But even when warning people, we have to say, "By the grace and power of God, you can be different than you are." And that is not just something to throw at the end of the sermon; it is inherent in the way God gives his message. He is always a God of grace and empowerment. He wants the best for his people. The warnings are given within the broader context of God's delight in and concern for his people.

There are many ways we can include positive elements in our sermons. For example, we can use illustrations. Rather than illustrating a virtue by talking about somebody who does not display it, positive preaching shows someone doing it. If you want to learn how to hit a baseball, don't watch three .100 hitters; watch one .300 hitter. Show someone doing it right. Positive preaching encourages people, shows them they can be better than they are, and suggests ways to improve.

At the same time, positive preaching should not deny the reality of where we are now. You can't preach the good news unless a person senses the bad news. Positive preaching recognizes our depravity, but it also recognizes that there is power from the Holy Spirit that enables us to grow. We are all in a growth process. We are often aware of how far we have to go, but not how far we have come. We need to encourage one another by pointing out progress.

There should be a lot more positive than negative elements in our preaching. I had a formula when raising my kids. I wanted to give them ten that-a-boys for every "you jerk." If I had turned that around, I would have destroyed them. As a seminary president, I was at my best when I caught people doing something right and commending them rather than catching them doing something wrong and criticizing them. If the people know a preacher loves and values them, then when he has bad news to give, they hear it. On the other hand, if every sermon is filled with the negative, people shut their ears.

Years ago when we lived in Dallas, I'd often go to First Baptist Church to hear pastor W. A. Criswell. When he came back from a trip, he would say things like, "I've just preached in a score of churches, and you are the greatest people a preacher could want. When I preach here, you give a response to God's Word that is encouraging." When I was younger, I mistook that for flattery. Now I'm absolutely sure he believed what he said. And the people loved him.

Chapter 70

LEADING HEARERS TO THE TREE OF LIFE
Guiding believers into joyful obedience

Ted Haggard

Some preaching causes hearers to thrive in their walk with Christ. Other preaching seems to make hearers die on the vine. Both use the Bible. What is the difference?

Obedience comes from the working of the Holy Spirit and the Word of God. The power of the Holy Spirit inside of us gives the freedom to obey, and so obedience for a genuine Christian is a delight, a wonderful celebration of a new nature within.

Now, just as Adam and Eve had to make a choice between the tree of life and the tree of the knowledge of good and evil, so must we who preach. If we try to lead others to obey God merely through the knowledge of good and evil, obedience is a difficult load. If we walk in obedience to Christ through the tree of life, by the power of the tree of life, who is Christ himself, then obedience is an incredible delight.

To preach in a way that leads people to the tree of life, we need to understand the invigorating, life-giving power of the Spirit and the authority of God's Word. The Bible is not a tyrannical, religious book. It is a life-giving book that teaches us how—I know this sounds a little unusual, yet it did for those who first heard it from Jesus—to eat his flesh and drink his blood and consume his nature into us.

When we teach people that dynamic, the Scriptures are wonderful. If, however, we use the Bible merely to teach the knowledge of good and evil, we can make people mean. We end up with people who are very good, but they are angry. They fail, hide it, and then blame others. They do everything Adam and Eve did in the garden.

We who preach must be full of life ourselves and the innocence, freedom, and joy that comes from life himself. When we do that, others discover life through our preaching rather than discover merely rules and regulations.

Someone whose preaching leads others to the tree of life probably says a lot of the same things as the person whose preaching leads people merely to the tree of the knowledge of good and evil, but the tone is different. The power is different. The look in the eye is different. The heart love for people is different. The life-giving preacher has an underlying joy instead of anger and frustration.

You always give what you have. The tone and life, or lack thereof, that is in you will be communicated. If we have discovered life, we communicate that as we teach the Bible.

If we are preaching merely from the tree of the knowledge of good and evil, we can be teaching the Scriptures but communicate a dry, deadly, religious thing. We will watch our people slowly die right in front of us. The other guy down the street can be teaching the same Scriptures, but people are loving one another, loving the Scriptures, encouraging one another, repenting of their sin, and growing in beautiful, Christ-centered godliness. On the surface the sermons will look pretty much the same, but they are not.

You can have two churches that believe the same doctrine and teach from the same sermon outlines. One will have discovered the tree of life: obedience, joy, the power of the Spirit within, the authority of God's Word, the victory there is in loving and encouraging one another. The church down the street, which is teaching through the same sermon outlines and believes the same doctrinal statement, can be tense, defensive. There is no one coming to Christ, no joy, no connectivity with one another. They have difficulty in obeying the Scriptures and maybe have a little anger because of it. The differences in those two churches are the different tones, the different rivers flowing through them.

Christian obedience to God's voice is somewhat of a mysterious process. It is not merely, "This is the law. Now obey it." Rather, "This is God's desire for us. Now discover God himself, so you have the power to walk in obedience, joy, and victory."

So the difference is the preacher's own motives toward obedience and the motive he conveys for why listeners should be obedient. That is why Jesus talked about our hearts so much. That is why he talked about being little children. We must have a spirit of innocence.

That is also why he said, "You diligently study the Scriptures because you think that by them you possess eternal life. These are the Scriptures that testify about me, yet you refuse to come to me to have life" (John 5:39–40).

He was constantly struggling to get his followers to understand abiding, being transformed, consuming the nature of God. That is why they objected when he said that you need to eat my flesh and drink my blood. We have been fighting for two thousand years over what that really meant. But those words convey the incredible, delightful mystery of Christianity: It is Christ's nature abiding within that produces a delightful, power-filled obedience to God, in contrast to a harsh, religious discipline of trying to make God happy.

One focus is on God, and the other on rules. I think all Christians start by saying, "I love the Bible, I love God, and I want to grow in him," but the struggle of the Garden of Eden soon presents itself. When Satan approached Eve, he said, "God knows that when you eat of [the tree of the knowledge of good and evil] your eyes will be opened, and you will be like God, knowing good and evil" (Gen. 3:5). He appealed to her godly side.

Christians want to be godly; they want to be like God. But they need to discover the life, love, and joy that comes from Spirit-filled, Bible-centered obedience rather than from religious duty, which does not produce life. Religious duty is desirable for gaining wisdom; it does look good; it is satisfying in many ways; but it does not produce the life of God flowing through us producing the fruit of the Holy Spirit.

When life-giving pastors preach a verse like "Be holy for I am holy," they may say a lot of the same things as preachers who burden people with this verse, but the spirit is different. In a life-giving way, we would say: "God wants us to be holy as he is holy. Therefore during your prayer time let him abide in you, and you abide in him, drinking of him. Let the Scriptures breathe his life into you. Enjoy the Scriptures. Meditate on the Word of God. Let the power of God and the life of God and the will of God grow in you, so that as you walk through your day, you can walk in his holiness, in his life, in his favor for you, in his love for you, and in his power for you.

"Even if you do have to be like Jesus in a situation where you are correcting and confronting someone, turning over the tables of the money changers, you can do that in a way that genuinely reflects the life and power of Christ. It would be Christ-centered. It would be life-giving."

The tree-of-the-knowledge-of-good-and-evil way to tell people to be holy is: "God is holy, and you had better be holy, or he will spew you out of his mouth. He is a holy God who cannot stand to be around unrighteous, undisciplined people. When you fail, you are crucifying the Son of God again. You had better stop it because bad things will happen to you, and it will be God getting your attention. So you had better live a holy life because you are dealing with a God who will not tolerate your foolishness."

Now, both of those are true. Both of those are right. God is a wonderful and a terrible God. But you can say what I said in the second instance in a life-giving way, using much the same words, and still encourage people to love God and want to go pray and fast, love their wives, treat their employees wonderfully, give money away, and volunteer at the soup kitchen. It can all be life-giving. But too often the tone that the preacher uses in the second example makes people fall into a form of obedience that results in disobedience. It stirs up their sin nature. Once their old sin nature is stirred up, they start to cover it up. They become hypocrites. It is not genuine obedience.

Non-Christian obedience is our doing everything we can in our own power to try to be godly, and every time we fall short. Genuine obedience is the life of Christ abiding within us being displayed in our lives.

Chapter 71

FUNDAMENTALS OF GENRE

How literary form affects the interpretation of Scripture

David L. Allen

God chose to give the Bible to us in a diverse collection of literary forms called genres. Each literary category has rules that guide us in its interpretation. In this article we will look at the guiding principles for interpreting and applying five genres in Scripture—psalms, proverbs, narratives, parables of Jesus, and letters—as well as common errors made with each genre.

POETRY

Psalms are at one and the same time both prayers and hymns. They are one example of the poetic genre. They speak to the mind and the heart, expressing a broad range of emotions: fear, anger, comfort, encouragement. Psalms are almost always directed to God, though other forms of biblical poetry may not be.

One crucial facet of Hebrew poetry is the use of parallelism. Ideas are "rhymed" rather than words. For example, Psalm 19:1–2 says:

> The heavens declare the glory of God;
> the skies proclaim the work of his hands.
> Day after day they pour forth speech;
> night after night they display knowledge.

In synonymous parallelism, the second line does not add significant new meaning to the first. Sometimes the meanings are identical; sometimes there is a nuanced similarity. Hebrew poetry sometimes "rhymes" opposite ideas or

uses a lesser-greater pattern. Others have poetic patterns, such as a-b-b-a.

Another feature of biblical poetry is the use of metaphorical language and symbolism, as in the verses above where the sky is said to "speak." The contemporary preacher sometimes needs to explain a metaphor unfamiliar to our culture, but we rob a metaphor of power and life when we take it apart rather than use it.

A common genre error is to press the poetic language of emotion and symbol too far and use them literally as the basis for doctrine—for example, asserting from Psalm 19:1 that God, who is spirit, has "hands." The guiding principle is to allow more concrete teachings of Scripture to interpret scriptural poetry.

PROVERBS

The book of Proverbs is so named because it contains a collection of pithy, practical, "general rule" wisdom. The application of truth to one's life in the light of experience is what Proverbs calls wisdom. Proverbs deliver God-centered principles for successful living in catchy phrases that make the principles memorable. Several literary devices are found in Proverbs, including parallelism, alliteration, acrostics, and numeric sequences.

One of the important interpretative principles regarding Proverbs is understanding the difference between a promise and a general principle. Consider, for example, Proverbs 22:6:

> Train up a child in the way he should go,
>   and when he is old, he will not depart from it.

The fact that godly parents sometimes have ungodly children doesn't refute the general principle of this verse. Proverbs like these are not meant to present an inviolable guarantee, like a law or a promise; rather, they present a principle for living. In general, they are true.

In addition, the abundant use of figurative language indicates that many proverbs express things more suggestively than directly and universally. They should be interpreted in connection with other proverbs and the rest of Scripture.

Preaching the proverbs is a challenge, first because many verses don't refer explicitly to the Lord. Thus sermons on them can sound like a motivational talk at a civic club rather than a sermon. There is also the fact that proverbs are so obvious. They don't require much exegesis or explanation. They generally require more illustrations and examples than other texts.

NARRATIVES

The Bible has more in the narrative genre than any other literary type. More than 40 percent of the Old Testament and almost 60 percent of the New Testament is narrative. The narratives of the Bible are historical, not mythological. The Bible is actually one grand narrative story about God's redemptive plan for humanity comprising hundreds of individual narratives from Genesis to Revelation.

Three critical principles are necessary in the interpretation of narrative. First is the principle of context. Things mean what they mean in context. A given narrative, such as Genesis 22 (the story of Abraham and Isaac on Mount Moriah) occurs in the context of the larger narrative of Genesis, which in turn occurs in the context of the entire Old Testament history. Genesis 22 must be interpreted in light of its immediate context (the story itself, with its message about faith, testing, and obedience), but also in light of the history of the nation of Israel (God's promise to multiply Abraham's descendants), and finally in the context of God's overall plan of salvation (Isaac is a type of Christ). When preaching on Genesis 22, these issues must be recognized and applied to the hearers.

A second principle is that narratives generally illustrate doctrine taught explicitly elsewhere. Hence, while every narrative has theological meaning and intent, we must again carefully follow the rule that Scripture interprets Scripture as we distill theological principles from the text.

Third, interpreters should pay attention to narrator comments. For example, Genesis 22:1 says that the Lord "tested" Abraham. Other interpretive clues are repetition, characterization, point of view, the level of detail in description, and narrative silence.

There are several dangers to avoid in interpreting narratives. The first is allegorizing. It is not the intention of the biblical writers to provide a hidden meaning behind the words of a narrative.

A second danger is moralizing. For example, by giving us the failures of some of the fathers of the Bible, the biblical author does not necessarily intend to tell us how we should be good fathers. That may be a secondary application in preaching, and these stories make effective illustrations, but it is usually not the main intent of the author. Lessons for living drawn from each narrative or from each event in the lives of biblical characters can be a hermeneutical mistake if the preacher does not carefully consider the intent of the passage. Unless the narrative sermon turns the focus on God, the sermon will merely be talks on leadership skills, human bravery, parenting styles, personal relationships, or a host of tangential issues. Such a "sermon" is human-centered rather than Christ-centered.

PARABLES OF JESUS

Parables are fiction. They tell a story, even a story full of truth, but not a historical story. Unlike historical narrative, they may contain exaggerated elements, as when the unforgiving servant in Matthew 18:24 owed 10,000 talents, an astronomical sum; or unusual circumstances, as when all ten virgins fell asleep in Matthew 25:5.

In general, the key principle in interpreting parables is to seek the main point, understanding that the main point may be built on secondary points. To determine that, we should ask three questions: (1) Who are the main characters? (2) What occurs at the beginning (e.g., Luke 15:1–2) and end? (3) What is said in direct discourse?

One important error to avoid when interpreting parables is to allegorize where Scripture does not. In some parables, Jesus identifies how various details correspond to other things. But allegorizing on our own can lead us away from the intended point of the parable. For example, Augustine allegorized the parable of the good Samaritan so that the man going down to Jericho symbolized Adam. The robbers symbolized the devil and his angels. The priest symbolized

the law. The Levite symbolized the prophets. The good Samaritan symbolized Christ. The inn symbolized the church. The innkeeper symbolized the apostle Paul. The promise of return symbolized the resurrection of Christ.

The point of a parable is like the punch line of a joke. It is designed to catch the listener up short—to create that "Ah ha!" moment. Good preaching finds a way to make that twist come to life.

Finally, a parable should always be considered in its context because preceding verses may make it clear why the story is told or what kind of person is targeted.

LETTERS

The New Testament letters are written to specific people or churches dealing with specific issues. Thus, historical context is vital in interpretation. Unlike narratives, this genre follows a logical rather than temporal sequence. The letters explain and exhort.

The first guideline in interpreting a letter is to pay close attention to connectives (e.g., "and," "but," "because," "therefore") to determine the logical relationship of the clauses, sentences, and paragraphs and follow the trajectory of the author's argument. Often the preacher must consult the original Greek (or Greek-based tools) to find these since English translations can obscure them.

One interpretive mistake often made in the letters is to fail to think in terms of paragraphs. Paragraphs generally have a theme sentence around which the paragraph is focused. If one atomizes the letter by looking only at a verse or two here and a verse or two there, misinterpretation often results because context is ignored.

Preaching success requires correct identification of the text's genre, the proper principles used in interpretation, and the avoidance of common errors that lead to misinterpretation.

RECOMMENDED READING ON GENRE

Fee, Gordon, and Douglas Stuart. 2003. *How to Read the Bible for All Its Worth*, 3rd ed. Grand Rapids: Zondervan.

Greidanus, Sidney. 1988. *The Modern Preacher and the Ancient Text: Interpreting and Preaching Biblical Literature*. Grand Rapids: Eerdmans (esp. chs. 9–12).

Kaiser, Walter C., Jr. 2003. *Preaching and Teaching from the Old Testament: A Guide for the Church*. Grand Rapids: Baker.

Larsen, David L. 2000. *Telling the Old, Old Story: The Art of Narrative Preaching*. Grand Rapids: Kregel.

Long, Thomas G. 1989. *Preaching and the Literary Forms of the Bible*. Philadelphia: Fortress.

Chapter 72

FROM B.C. TO 11 A.M.

How to preach an Old Testament narrative with accuracy and power

Steven D. Mathewson

It took a novel by John Steinbeck for me to admit my ineptness at preaching Old Testament narratives. In a scene from *East of Eden*, the banter around a kitchen table turns to the Cain-and-Abel story. A pig-tailed Chinese cook says, "No story has power, nor will it last, unless we feel in ourselves that it is true and true of us."

I thought about the sermon I preached the previous Sunday from 1 Samuel 7, the first I had preached from a narrative book in the Old Testament. Did people leave with a sense that the story was about them? I had to admit they probably didn't. A lady approached me after the service and asked for point number three. "Uh, point number three," I said, "was 'The Resulting Prosperity of God's People.'"

I had preached a sermon full of historical-cultural data in an analytical outline. But that did no justice to the purpose of Bible stories: to lure people into real-life dramas where they run smack into God's assessment of their lives.

Preaching from an Old Testament narrative is like playing the saxophone: It is easy to do poorly. Here are the insights I'm learning that help me do it better.

STUDYING FOR A NARRATIVE SERMON

Stories communicate truth differently than letters or poems do, so I need to study them differently. The features of a story help me identify the author's intent.

Plot

Most plots in Old Testament narratives build on a conflict or a collision between two forces. By the end of the story, the conflict is resolved. Generally, the plots unfold like this: (1) Background, (2) Crisis, (3) Resolution, and (4) Conclusion.

Unfolding the plot frees me from having to find a theological principle behind every paragraph or detail. In Esther, for example, chapters

1 and 2 serve as background. They introduce King Xerxes' anger and compulsive behavior, Esther's secret nationality, and Mordecai's uncovering of an assassination plot. Instead of looking for a sermon theme here ("The Consequences of Anger" or "The Marks of an Attractive Woman"), I simply note these details as clues to the heart of the story.

Usually, a story's central idea comes in the interplay between the crisis and resolution. The crisis in chapters 3–4 (Haman's plot to destroy the Jews) and resolution in chapters 5:1–9:19 (Haman's destruction and the Jews' triumph) show the story's big idea: The Jews were protected from a vicious plot to annihilate them.

Pace

I've learned to observe the pace at which a story unfolds. The time within a story, which scholars call "narrated time," is subject to gaps, delays, and acceleration. Those help me see where the writer places emphasis, creates suspense, or wants to determine my attitude.

In Genesis 22, for instance, as the narrator relates God's instructions to Abraham, four phrases slow the narrated time. With each phrase, the tension builds: "Take your son . . . the only son you have . . . the one you love . . . Isaac." In preaching this story, I need to emphasize, as the biblical text does, the agony in Abraham's faithfulness.

Dialogue

The primary place to look for meaning in the story is in the statements of the characters. In biblical narratives, there is no idle chatter. The speech is highly concentrated and shaped to convey meaning. For example, when Joseph says, "You intended to harm me, but God intended it for good," he summarizes the meaning of his entire life and the story in Genesis 49:29–50:26.

Characters

When studying an Old Testament narrative, I need to discover who is the protagonist (central character), antagonist (force arrayed against the central character), and foil (character who heightens the central character by providing a contrast or parallel).

In 1 Samuel 16, David emerges as the protagonist while Saul functions as antagonist. Thus, in 1 Samuel 17 the conflict is "David vs. Saul" more than "David vs. Goliath." While there is a contest between David and Goliath, Goliath reveals the character of the true competitors, David and Saul. The future king and the present king of Israel respond differently, revealing their fitness to serve. To preach this story well, I must emphasize what the story emphasizes: the difference character makes.

Paying attention to names is also important. Sometimes, a name may be withheld to betray an attitude. David reflects his attitude toward Goliath by referring to him as "this uncircumcised Philistine" (1 Sam. 17:26).

Details

After reading novels, I had to adjust to the sparse writing style of Old Testament narratives. These stories are lean. They don't paint scenes or add extra details, so when details crop up, I now pay more attention to them. They usually foreshadow drama. For example, the reference to Joseph's good looks in Genesis 39:6 anticipates the sexual advance made by Potiphar's wife.

DEVELOPING A NARRATIVE SERMON

Once I've studied the story, I need to develop my sermon differently than I would one from other portions of Scripture.

Tell the whole story. After preaching from books like Ephesians or 1 John, where I expound a paragraph or a couple verses, I had to get used to working with bigger chunks of text. The block of narrative must be large enough to possess a background, crisis, and resolution. Otherwise, my sermon will resemble a fax that is missing a few pages.

Select a vantage point. The most common method is to tell the story as a narrator. Another method is to tell the story through the eyes of a character. For example, Donald Sunukjian tells the story of Esther though the eyes of Harbona, a eunuch who served King Xerxes (Est. 1:10; 7:9).

I watched Sunukjian transition from introduction to monologue by turning his back briefly to the congregation. When he turned around, he assumed the character. Then, at the end of the sermon, Sunukjian again turned his back briefly. When he turned to face the audience again, he spoke "out of character" and shared a few concluding statements.

Build the outline from the story. Instead of proceeding from point one to point two, a narrative sermon unfolds in a series of "moves"— scenes in the story. The outline highlights the story line. (I've made the mistake of resolving the tension too quickly. I'm learning not to give away the ending of the story until the end.)

Outlining a Narrative Sermon

There are three ways to build a narrative outline.

Cue off the story's crisis and resolution. This is the problem-solution approach, using theological points. It is more deductive.

I once preached a sermon from Exodus 5:1– 6:13 by taking off on the crisis in chapter 5 and the resolution in chapter 6:1–13. In the story, Moses' plea to Pharaoh for the release of God's

people results in harsher work conditions. The raw materials are reduced while the production quota is increased. The Israelites then turn on Moses, and Moses turns on God. The story is resolved in 6:1–13 by God's reaffirmation of his original promise to Abraham. The sermon flowed like this:

1. When we follow God, great expectations sometimes end in great disappointments. (5:1–23)
   a. Great expectations sometimes turn into great frustrations. (5:1–21)
   b. Great frustrations can lead to disappointment with God. (5:22–23)
2. God meets our disappointment by asking us to cling to his promises. (6:1–13)

Cue off the scenes of the story. This approach depends more on story-telling skills, because it unfolds in a series of scenes.

I preached an expository sermon on 1 Samuel 16:1–13 that consisted of a series of moves. Notice that several moves were devoted to telling the story, not espousing a particular theological point.

Move 1: Introduction

Move 2: Samuel comes to town. (1 Sam. 16:1–5)

Move 3: Jesse's sons parade before Samuel. (1 Sam. 16:6, 8–10)

Move 4: God rejects these candidates based on their hearts. (1 Sam. 16:7)

Move 5: The youngest son becomes God's choice. (1 Sam. 16:11–13)

Move 6: God is impressed by your heart, not by your image.

Move 7: First implication—Work on your heart, not just your image.

Move 8: Second implication—Don't minimize your potential to impress God.

Moves 2, 3, and 5 tell the story. In Move 4, the big idea begins to take shape, and it clearly emerges in Move 6. The sermon concludes with two lines of application in Moves 7 and 8. With each move about four minutes in length, the sermon lasted a little more than thirty minutes.

Switch from story to idea to story. This combines the first two approaches. The big idea emerges in the middle of the sermon. For example, I preached a sermon on the entire book of Esther from the following outline:

Introduction

Story

    Move 1 (Scene: Esther 1–2)

    Move 2 (Scene: Esther 3–4)

    Move 3 (Scene: Esther 5:9–19)

    Move 4 (Scene: Esther 9:20–10:3)

Big Idea: You can't see or hear God, but he controls your destiny!

Is This Really True?

He controls your destiny in spite of:

    The spiritual insensitivity of people around you

    Impossible people in prominent places

    Unpredictable events

    Circumstances no person can change

Conclusion

Although I gave away the idea after the first major section, I raised the tension again by challenging the idea—"How can you be sure that God is controlling your destiny when you can't see or hear him?"

DELIVERING A NARRATIVE SERMON

Successful sermons from biblical narratives hinge on the ability to present the scenes of a story in vivid color. As David Larsen, former professor of pastoral theology at Trinity Evangelical Divinity School, notes, "When some preachers expound Noah, we can hear it rain."

While Old Testament narratives deliberately spare readers of descriptive details, modern hearers need sensory details to pull them in. In a recent sermon on 2 Samuel 18:24–32 (David waiting to hear about the safety of his son Absalom), I described the scene like this:

> If you have ever waited in a surgery waiting room while your dad, mom, child, or spouse is undergoing surgery, you can appreciate how King David felt. David was on edge. He was a nervous wreck. He paced, and sweated, fumed, and fumbled with his shoes. He waited impatiently in a little guard room between the two city gates. A city guard waited with him, and David kept asking: "Do you see anybody yet?" The guard would scan the countryside and holler down: "Nope. Nobody."

I explained how King David had sent out troops to crush a rebellion, led by his own son Absalom. But his final instructions to his two commanders, Joab and Abishai, were: "Now don't you hurt my boy Absalom!" (18:5).

> The day grew hotter as David waited. The tower guard swore under his breath as he ambled up the rungs leading to the top of the tower. Sweat trickled off his beard. How many times was this? Ten? Twelve? But this time was different. He hollered down to David: "Your Majesty, I see a runner."

The sensory details build suspense. In providing details, should a preacher use anachronisms or colloquial expressions that portray biblical characters as "happy campers" or that describe them "adjusting their sunglasses"? This becomes cutesy when overdone, but at times, it may prove effective. Eugene Peterson once described Shammah in 1 Samuel 16:9 as a "small, cultured man who wore Calvin Klein jeans, listened to Mozart, and hated Bethlehem because he couldn't walk across the street without getting cow-flop all over his boots." Peterson describes the other sons in similar fashion to help readers visualize the irrelevance of outward appearance to a God who looks at the heart.

A few weeks ago, I returned to 1 Samuel 17 and took another shot at the story I had smothered with an analytical outline and historical details. Afterward, a listener commented: "It's exciting to hear God's Word in a real-life way."

That comment reinforced the value of the hard work necessary to proclaim an Old Testament narrative. After all, to quote David Larsen, "We should not do poorly what the Bible does so well."

Chapter 73

THE BIG IDEA OF NARRATIVE PREACHING
What are the clues to interpreting a story?

Paul Borden and Steven D. Mathewson

When Mommy or Daddy began, "Once upon a time," we listened. We learned early that stories caused us to stop what we were doing and to pay attention to the storyteller. Instinctively we knew we lived life in narrative. Story, like breathing or thinking, is an intrinsic part of our existence. We daydream, plot, criticize, hope, and visualize ambitions in story form. No one lives life deductively.

Perhaps this is why our Creator designed much of biblical revelation to be written in story form. Jesus Christ, who preached didactic sermons and taught deductively, was also well known for his stories. The human authors God used to instruct the church about Jesus Christ's life and ministry wisely chose story as their predominate means of communication.

Yet today the preponderance of sermons, especially those preached by individuals who champion biblical authority and integrity, are not given in story form and are seldom based on narrative passages. There often appears to be a studied avoidance of narrative combined with a rhetorical form that communicates ineffectively to audiences saturated by an electronic media.

WHY WE RARELY PREACH STORIES

I believe there are at least two major reasons for the paradox. First, preachers are convinced that abstract truth cannot be communicated well in story form. Our literate technological culture advances that truth cannot be communicated in this manner. Stories may be used to illustrate truth but not communicate it.

While analytical and logical presentation are sometimes required and beneficial, preachers should recognize that the screenwriter and director do more to influence today's North American culture than the philosopher. Perhaps this is why story seems to be God's favorite medium of written revelation. Perhaps he understood that the storyteller communicates truth more widely than the theologian.

Second, many preachers are not trained to discover the big idea of a story and then communicate that story without violating the narrative genre. There are no good models to follow. In the past, preachers tended to treat stories as allegories or illustrations of preconceived theological ideas gained from didactic passages. Such preachers did not understand narrative literature and were not taught to interpret it. This lack of training continues to the present. Seminaries seldom if ever offer required courses in the exegesis and preaching of stories. Most require exegetical courses focused on didactic material, which do not train students to understand and communicate narrative literature. In fact, frequently the methodologies that enable us to understand didactic literature inhibit us from understanding narrative literature or from turning description into prescription.

In light of these observations, I will offer an exegetical method designed to discover the big ideas communicated in biblical stories. This will be covered in the second part of this three-part series. In the third part, I will suggest a way to preach these stories in current-day homiletical styles that will not violate the truth of the story or its development in narrative genre. Before either of these, however, we will look at the important assumptions that underlie my method.

A. My Perspective on Biblical Narratives

Four assumptions underlie this exegetical method.

1. The first assumption relates to the histori-cal orthodox position of inspiration, which holds that God and humans were both extensively and equally involved in the production of Scripture. This means that when God chose to reveal truth through narratives, he selected highly competent storytellers. These individuals developed this form of literature artfully and skillfully.

As a result, we interpreters cannot violate the essence of good narrative when exegeting the text. Stories are not like didactic literature, which can be taken apart verse by verse or paragraph by paragraph. Each story is a unit, whether it is a paragraph long (as in the Gospels) or a chapter or two long (as in the Old Testament). To preach fifteen verses out of a story that is fifty verses long violates the essence of story. It is like reading children the middle of a bedtime story without telling them how the story began or ended. The result is to preach an idea that may be true but is not based on the teaching of that narrative.

2. The narrative portions of Scripture were not written primarily to provide a record of redemptive history as history. This is not to say that these stories are historically inaccurate; they are indeed accurate. An orthodox view of inspiration argues for historical accuracy. However, their primary purpose was to develop a theology through story, not create a historical record. This understanding of narratives seems to be borne out by the New Testament comments about Old Testament stories (Rom. 15:4; 1 Cor. 10:11; 2 Tim. 3:16; Heb. 1:1–2). It is also demonstrated in any comparison of the four Gospels.

There are several crucial results related to the assumption that narratives were not written primarily to record history.

a. Narratives were written to communicate a theology. Each narrative book has as well defined an argument as Romans or any other

New Testament letter. The difference is that each book's argument is developed by a series of stories while Romans is developed through a logical, analytical presentation. Often our inability to recognize this is due to our assumptions coupled with our inability to exegete story as story.

b. An overall chronology is seldom the concern of the storyteller since the purpose is to develop a theological argument, not record a chronological history. If chronology is crucial, the storyteller notes it; otherwise chronology is usually ignored. Older debates over the Bible's authenticity based on chronological issues reflected the fact that both sides assumed that the purpose of narratives was to record history rather than develop an argument.

c. We must see what the narratives have in common, even though narratives may be separated by years. Therefore, outlines of narrative books should reflect theological developments rather than historical, geographical, or biographical concerns. Again, our understanding of the Gospels should convince us that this is true. Knowing Old Testament history is important, but often teaching the Old Testament as history does a disservice to future interpreters. It plants false assumptions.

3. Each narrative communicates a big idea that is unique. Stories, like other biblical literature, contribute to the grand ideas of Scripture. However, each story offers its own unique facet and insight into one of those grand ideas.

The implication of this assumption that each narrative is unique in its teaching means that the idea preached from one narrative fits no other narrative. If a sermon preached from one narrative could be used with a different one, then the preacher's understanding of one or both narratives is incorrect. An infinite God who creates unique personalities, snowflakes, and fingerprints has done the same with stories, including those accounts that are parallel.

This assumption opens up the narratives as never before. Too often our thinking has been confined to just a few themes, while in reality God has placed a wealth of biblical ideas in stories. I frequently find myself addressing issues that are not developed anywhere else in Scripture, except through application.

4. The major moral, spiritual, or theological truth of the narrative can only be understood when one understands the entire story. Other moral, ethical, or theological issues raised in the story may not, and in fact often will not, be addressed by the storyteller.

The implications of the assumption that each story generally speaks to one major issue while ignoring others means that we as preachers must do the same. To focus on other issues either positively or negatively is to treat narrative like allegory. Outlining stories chronologically (as we many times do with the letters) also treats story as allegory, not as story. We must exegete narratives to discover the major truth and then focus on that truth in preaching while ignoring other issues not developed in the narrative.

B. The Exegetical Method

To exegete a biblical narrative, we must first determine where the story begins and ends. This is not always easy to do. Narrative books are like novels. In each one there are several smaller books that make up one complete volume. For example, the book of Genesis has included in it the book of Abraham, the book of Isaac, and the book of Jacob. Within each of these books are chapters or narratives. These narratives may take in one, two, or three chapters. The current chapter divisions are often meaningless in determining individual narratives. Therefore I must read several narratives a number of times, often in different translations, to determine where a particular story begins and ends. Once I have determined the beginning and the ending, I need to recognize that further exegesis may require later adjustments. I am now ready to begin to exegete the story.

We will use the story in 2 Samuel 11–12 to learn how to apply the exegetical method described here. We know the story begins in 2 Samuel 11:1 because of the time marker, "In the spring, at the time when kings go to war." While a new scene begins at the beginning of chapter 12, there is no indicator that a new story begins. In fact, careful reading indicates the crisis in the story has not been resolved. By the end of chapter 12, the crisis has been resolved, and the statement that "David and his entire army returned to Jerusalem" marks the ending. Biblical narrative often signals closure by noting that one or more of the characters has returned home.

1. Design

My first responsibility is to determine the design of the story. Many stories are told in third person, while some are first-person accounts. Some stories begin at the beginning and continue on to the end, while others use flashback. Some stories place the emphasis on plot, while others focus on action or character development. As I note these observations, I am raising questions about why the story is designed as it is. However, these questions cannot be answered until the exegetical process is completed.

In my initial reading, I discover that the 2 Samuel 11–12 story is told in the third person. It appears to move from the beginning to end without any use of flashback. While the

plot is intriguing, there seems to be an emphasis on character development. I will explore this further as the exegetical process continues.

2. Scenes

Next, I divide the story into scenes. It is helpful to imagine you are a movie director shooting a story. Each scene is filmed in a certain way to tell a story, remembering the order of scenes is important. The New American Standard Bible (NASB) paragraph divisions seem to offer the best division of scenes in narratives (this version used throughout this chapter).

Using these divisions, I end up with twelve scenes in 2 Samuel 11–12. The scenes include: 11:1; 11:2–5; 11:6–13; 11:14–21; 11:22–25; 11:26–27; 12:1–6; 12:7–15a; 12:15b–20; 12:21–23; 12:24–25; and 12:26–31.

It is helpful to make a chart for each paragraph or scene using one large piece of blank paper. Exegetical notes, observations, questions, and so on are then written in each section of the chart that corresponds to the appropriate scene. The design of the scenes is best understood through charting.

3. Characters

Next, develop a list of characters. Again, it is helpful to compare the characters in a story to actors in a drama. Who is the star? Who is the antagonist? Who is the protagonist? Who is the character actor crucial to the story's development? Who are the extras? Characters show us how life is lived out and managed in particular situations (the scenes). The living out of life is not announced but accomplished, sometimes successfully, sometimes unsuccessfully, in the conflict of the drama.

In 2 Samuel 11–12, David is clearly the protagonist or leading character. The surrounding chapters confirm this. Obviously, Bathsheba plays a prominent role in the story. However, the narrator portrays her more as a character who is acted upon rather than as a character who acts. Her husband, Uriah, is the other major character in this story. He functions as a foil, that is, as a character who provides a contrast to another character, in this case, David.

Readers often refer to 2 Samuel 11–12 as the story of David and Bathsheba, but it is really the story of David and Uriah. As the story proceeds, Uriah turns out to be the hero. He models a blend of obedience and contentment that David, the leading character, lacks. Nathan emerges in chapter 12 as the antagonist, the character who functions as an opponent or adversary. In Nathan's case, he is an antagonist raised up by God to confront David. Other characters play an important role in the story, but they are the extras. This includes Joab, David's child who dies, David's servants, and Solomon.

4. Action

Then note the action. As events unfold, characters respond and act, which produces further action. In a character study, that action may be thought or dialogue. But even the dialogue or thought is a reaction to events and produces further action that eventually leads to some kind of climax.

As noted above, 2 Samuel 11–12 builds on a contrast between David and Uriah. The actions and responses of these characters develop this contrast. David saw Bathsheba, took her, and lay with her. Then, when Bathsheba ends up pregnant by David, he engages in a cover-up. He calls Uriah home from the battle with the Ammonites under the guise of getting information about the progress of the battle. He then sends Uriah to spend the night at home. But Uriah sleeps at the door of his house! He refuses to sleep with his wife. David responds by getting him drunk the next night, yet Uriah still does not sleep with his wife! The narrator is showing us through the action—rather than telling us directly—that Uriah has more honor in a drunken state than David has while sober! As the story proceeds, David ends up plotting to kill Uriah.

Some expositors end their analysis here, but there is still more action that leads the reader to the big idea of the story. The Lord sends Nathan to confront David. David finally admits his wrongdoing, and Nathan informs him of the consequences, including the loss of the child born to Bathsheba (12:14). David's response is interesting. He prays, fasts, and lies on the ground all night. But once the child dies, David arises, washes, anoints himself, changes his clothes, and worships. David's actions reveal a contrast with his former actions. He has now learned to accept what God has given him and what God has not given him.

5. Dialogue

The next step is to examine any dialogue. (Dialogue may actually be monologue; I am using the term dialogue in its broadest sense.) The major method for developing characterization in narrative is through the words spoken by the characters. The storyteller (in this case ultimately the Holy Spirit) often communicates the major idea through the words uttered by the characters.

Many biblical stories are condensed, meaning the storyteller is functioning as an editor, which makes dialogue important. Note the dialogue to appear first in a story or dialogue that is repeated, especially with minor variations. Such minor variations often have major significance.

Our story in 2 Samuel 11–12 contains a significant amount of dialogue. David's statements in chapter 11 show him to be a man of deceit and treachery at this point in his life (see 11:8, 15, 25). By contrast, Uriah's statement in 11:11 shows him to be a man of integrity. When David asks him why he did not go down to his house, Uriah replies, "The ark and Israel and Judah are staying in temporary shelters, and my lord Joab and the servants of my lord are camping in the open field. Shall I then go to my house to eat and to drink and to lie with my wife? By your life and the life of your soul, I will not do this thing."

In 2 Samuel 12, the dialogue between Nathan and David helps me to zero in on the major idea of the story. One of the key statements occurs in verse 9 when Nathan asks, "Why have you despised the word of the LORD by doing evil in His sight?" In this statement and the ones that follow, Nathan did not separate the sins of murder and adultery and lying and treachery. He viewed them as one big package. The bottom line was that David despised the word of the Lord. Why? In verses 7–8, Nathan recites a list of what the Lord has given to David. It is clear from this dialogue that David has disobeyed God because he did not accept what God's grace gave him and what God's grace did not give him. In verses 22–23, David's statements reveal that he has now learned to accept God's grace, however God chooses to express it.

6. Language

It is at this point that the interpreter employs lexical or grammatical processes. However, in narrative exegesis these processes are usually not needed to determine the idea. Sometimes the idea is developed more through the design, plot, action, and so on than through the dialogue.

This is the case with the story in 2 Samuel 11–12. The interpreter will need to do little, if any, word studies or grammatical layouts. This story turns on the dialogue, plot, and the development of characters.

What makes the interpretation of narratives difficult is that the idea is seldom developed the same way in each narrative. The implementation of exegetical rules may require more artistic flair than needed for didactic materials.

7. Narration

The next step in the exegetical method is to list the statements made by the narrator. Without these statements the story would not make sense because specific motives, thoughts, hidden actions, and the like would not be known. As many have noted, the narrator is omniscient, knowing thoughts, intimate and private conversations, hidden events, and God's mind. These statements are God's entrance as the ultimate Storyteller into the story. Therefore, these comments become decisive in ultimately determining the meaning of the story.

Three such statements stand out in 2 Samuel 11–12:

- "But the thing that David had done was evil in the sight of the LORD" (11:27).
- "Then the LORD struck the child that Uriah's widow bore to David" (12:15).
- "Now the LORD loved him [Solomon]" (12:24).

8. Plot

Next, we must discover the plot. This is not always easy, especially if we know the story well. Look at the story and determine those events that create and intensify the disequilibrium, that is, the instability or imbalance. Then determine where reversal occurs, changing the course established by the disequilibrium. Finally, establish how the story is resolved.

In 2 Samuel 11–12, David's act of adultery with Bathsheba creates disequilibrium, and his attempts to hide this sin intensify it. The process of reversal begins when God sends Nathan to confront David for his sin. The resolution takes place in two phases. First, David admits and confesses his sin. Then the equilibrium (stability) is restored when he responds to a situation—in this case, the loss of his son born to Bathsheba—by accepting what God gives to him and withholds from him.

In developing plot, it is important to determine whether the story is a comedy or tragedy. The literary term *comedy* refers to a U-shaped plot that begins in prosperity, descends into tragedy, and makes a U-turn back to prosperity. A *tragedy*, by contrast, begins in prosperity and descends into and ends in tragedy. The events that develop the plot in a comedy may not be the ones that develop the plot in a tragedy, or vice versa.

The story in 2 Samuel 11–12 is obviously a "comedy." That is, the story begins in prosperity, then descends into tragedy, but then makes a turn back to prosperity.

We must remember biblical stories are not morality plays where good and evil are obvious. Stories have the ability to handle well the ambiguities of life.

9. Tone

After this, examine the tone of the story. You are seeking the worldview being communicated. The way the story is told is often as important as the story itself in determining tone.

In 2 Samuel 11–12, the tone follows the progression of the story as a "comedy." The statement in 11:27 that "the thing that David had done was evil in the sight of the LORD" sounds an ominous note of displeasure. However, the

statement in 12:24 that the Lord loves Solomon brings the tone back to one of acceptance and love. Here is an example of how the various elements of story—plot structure, dialogue, and so on—work together to establish the tone.

10. Rhetorical Structures

The next step is to look for rhetorical structures. Such structures may include chiasm, repetition, contrasts, or a scene that seems out of place with other scenes. Often an anomaly in the pattern or structure points to the major idea being developed in the story. Again, just as certain scenes in movies are pivotal, so certain patterns or deviations from patterns are critical to the story's point.

As noted above, a significant feature of the story in 2 Samuel 11–12 is the contrast between David and Uriah. This is a major key to understanding the story. This story also has a chiastic structure to it. In a chiasm, elements (like words or plot details) are repeated in reverse order. When diagrammed, the chiastic structure looks like this:

A Israel besieges Rabbah without David (11:1)
  B David and Bathsheba conceive a child (11:1–5)
    C David covers up his guilt (11:6–27a)
      D God reveals and identifies David's sin (11:27b–12:12)
    C' David admits his guilt (12:13a)
  B' David and Bathsheba lose a child and conceive one who lives (12:13b–25)
A' Israel besieges Rabbah with David (12:26–31)

The middle element of a chiasm—in this case letter D—functions as a turning point or the focus of the structure. From a literary standpoint, then, the turning point of the story is God's identification of David's sin—the sin of

David's despising God's grace or showing contempt for what God in his grace gave David and what God in his grace did not give David, namely Bathsheba!

11. Context

Finally, the interpreter gathers data from the context. The context is the stories that surround the narrative and create a section. Often, it is best to read the narratives on each side of the one being studied and write a single descriptive sentence title for each. If each story is described accurately in the sentence title, the interpreter begins to gain a sense of how the narrative being studied fits the context. It is crucial at this time to observe how the stories develop ideas rather than focusing on chronology. Remember, narratives are grouped together to create a theological argument.

The story in 2 Samuel 11–12 takes place in the context of David's having consolidated his reign as Israel's king (see ch. 8). The two stories immediately prior to this one show how David reaches out in "loyal love" (Heb. ḥesed) to his enemies—first to Mephibosheth, a potential threat to the throne (ch. 9), and then to the Ammonites (ch. 10). David's reign appears to be built on loyal love or covenant love. But then, out of the blue, the events in 2 Samuel 11–12 take place. David repents and learns a lesson, but chapters 13 and following show how the consequences of his sin play out in his family and his kingdom.

12. Exegetical Idea

Following these exegetical steps, write a single descriptive sentence title for each scene or paragraph. This title should include no interpretation. Again, this is difficult, yet our inability to deal with story as story requires this step.

We must force ourselves to learn what is in the story before we begin to ask why.

Once you have written these sentences, create a single descriptive title for the entire narrative. This sentence should accurately summarize and reflect the paragraph titles. Oftentimes the idea is missed because the major elements of the narrative are not precisely described.

For 2 Samuel 11–12, the title is, What David Learns about God's Grace.

Observe the sentences (paragraph titles and narrative titles) and ascertain the writer's emphasis. No two stories are the same in content and presentation. In each story certain literary aspects are emphasized at the expense of others to communicate the idea. Evidence must be weighed. Sometimes the storyteller may focus on characters, dialogue, and plot. Other times the focus may be design, scene, and the narrator's comments. The formula is never the same. Finding the meaning of stories is like being a detective with a myriad of clues. Only certain clues reveal the mystery while other clues, if pursued, lead to a false conclusion. However, if the correct clues are used to uncover the crime, all the other clues fit in place. Then and only then can the interpreter begin to know the truth communicated in a particular narrative.

Again, the writer of 2 Samuel 11–12 appears to be emphasizing the process through which David learns contentment with God's grace, that is, to accept what God graciously gives and graciously withholds.

After you discover the storyteller's emphasis, determine what the story is about. This determination provides the subject.

The subject of 2 Samuel 11–12 appears to be: What David learns about the grace of God.

Then decide what is being said about the subject, since this provides the complement for the idea.

Now you are ready to take the sentence descriptive title, if it has been stated accurately and precisely, and to supply the interpretation. Add the interpretive elements in order to state the storyteller's idea. State this idea in one sentence, and it becomes the exegetical idea of the story. When this idea is stated accurately and truthfully, it will fit this story alone and no other.

The exegetical idea for 2 Samuel 11–12 is: David learns to accept what the grace of God gives him and what the grace of God does not.

Once you have the exegetical idea, you have completed the exegesis of the narrative. This process, like all exegetical methods, is difficult. You also gain expertise in developing the exegetical idea as you find it, time after time. The important idea to remember is the exegetical method for narratives is different from the methods used to discover God's ideas in letters, poems, proverbs, or parables.

C. The Homiletical Process

For the homiletical process, movies again provide a helpful clue. We distinguish among action movies, character studies, mysteries, period pieces, and classics. A movie based on a work by Tom Wolfe will be developed quite differently than one taken from Tom Clancy. Both movies will have a basic idea to communicate; however, the director will get the idea across quite differently, just as the original author did.

Narrative passages lend themselves easily to narrative-style sermons, either in first- or third-person presentations. However, I wish to describe a process that fits the traditional format while enabling preachers to construct sermons that do not violate the essence of story in their presentations.

First, examine the exegetical idea and determine how you can restate it so it both reflects the historical accurateness and literary intent of the story and uses terms that create a timeless proposition. This process requires much effort and numerous restatements. However, once you have correctly stated the idea this way, you have the eternal theological concept that is true for God's people in any era. This is your preaching idea.

For 2 Samuel 11–12, the exegetical idea can be turned into a timeless proposition by stating it as follows: Believers must learn to accept what God's grace has given them and what that grace has not. Or, the expositor may wish to condense the idea further and state it like this: Believers must learn to be content with God's gracious gifts.

The preaching idea is the precise answer to a specific need, problem, or difficulty in life. The story you have exegeted reveals how an individual or group has dealt with this issue successfully or unsuccessfully from God's perspective. The preaching idea is the remedy; the story reveals how spiritually diseased people embrace or reject this remedy.

Your job as the preacher is to develop for your congregation how people relate, interact, and struggle with the same spiritual disease. You pick those aspects of the story that enable you to illustrate this disease. Rather than thinking of which verses do this, demonstrate how the plot, character development, scenes, actions, design, tone, and so on develop the disease. You use these elements to state, elaborate, and build the first half to two-thirds of your sermon.

This process of developing the spiritual disease means that two things always occur. First, the sermon seldom follows the narrative chronologically. Second, you develop the sermon using disequilibrium. The disequilibrium of the story may be used, but more often it is the disequilibrium of the disease for which the remedy is the preaching idea.

In the case of 2 Samuel 11–12, the sermon will begin by developing disequilibrium created by David's sin of taking more than God had given him. The sermon will note that David experiences God's punishment for committing a sin greater than murder and adultery. The sermon then applies this spiritual disease to the hearers, showing how we can be guilty of not being content with God's gracious gifts and callings.

Now you are ready to develop the second aspect of your sermon, the remedy. You go to the elements of the story that support the exegetical/preaching idea. Again, you will often be moving about the text. You demonstrate how God's people successfully or unsuccessfully embraced the divine remedy for their spiritual sickness. This idea is applied to your congregation. In this way, your preaching idea becomes the reversal (the remedy) to the disequilibrium you have created (the spiritual sickness).

The reversal amounts to David's confession of his sin and his resulting response of accepting what God's grace gives him and what it does not, which is the remedy for his spiritual disease. We then apply that remedy to the hearers, showing how they can accept God's gracious callings and provision today with a spirit of contentment and thanksgiving.

Last, you use the closing minutes to demonstrate the implications of accepting or rejecting this remedy. You show how acceptance brings spiritual health while rejection brings further illness. You appeal to people to choose health (life) over the disease (death).

Preaching this way enables you and your people to feel the story as drama. The sermon, which has its own plot, uses the pieces of the story that reflect the disequilibrium, reversal, and resolution they felt when they first read or heard the story. However, you have used the story as story, and the idea of the story has caused the congregation to wrestle with the disequilibrium of humanness, to understand and feel the reversal of divine truth, and to choose the resolutions that provide life. Both the sermon and the text (a narrative) have been treated as story.

Preaching narratives is a delight. Finding the main idea of the story is a mysterious adventure that results in a wonderful climax. Leading a congregation through disequilibrium is also a grand adventure. Watching people go through an "Aha!" experience as the sermon plot is revealed is awesome. Finally, leading them to resolutions that are real, because they are based on true narratives, is genuinely satisfying. You will preach ideas you never thought the Bible articulated. And as a result, you will see congregations make choices that are astounding.

Above all else, remember that the power in preaching comes from the Spirit's use of God's Word. You and I are instruments through which God often seeks to work.

Chapter 74

LIFE IN LEVITICUS

*Planting this church, I spent a year preaching through Leviticus,
and (surprise!) it worked*

Rob Bell

In February 1999 we planted a church to reach the unchurched and disillusioned people of Grand Rapids, Michigan. For the first year, I preached through Leviticus—verse by verse.

Why start a church with Leviticus? Why not a series on relationships or finding peace? That would be the safer approach.

Leviticus cannot be tamed. Its imagery is too wild. We ventured into its lair and let it devour us, trusting that God would deliver us with a truer picture of his Son.

Why Leviticus? Two reasons. First, I didn't want the church to succeed because we put together the right resources. I wanted the church to flourish on the power of the Spirit alone. I knew opening with Leviticus—foreign words to today's culture—was risky. But the bigger the risk, the more need for the Spirit and the more glory for God to get.

Second, unchurched people often perceive the Bible as obsolete. If that crowd could discover God speaking to them through Old Testament law, it would radically change their perception that Christianity is archaic. I wanted people to know that the whole biblical story— even Leviticus—is alive. The Scriptures are a true story, rooted in historical events and actual people. But many people don't see the connection between the Moses part and the Jesus part.

But Moses' Leviticus is all about Jesus.

THE WHOLE STORY

Every message in my series ended with Jesus. Every picture is about Jesus. Every detail of every sacrifice ultimately reflects some detail of Jesus' life.

This teaching hit home. Many of my listeners wanted to make sense of the Bible, yet they knew only fragments of the story. Leviticus taught us all to ask the difficult questions: How does this connect with entire biblical narrative? How does this event point to the cross? How do I fit into the story?

We discovered that the Bible is an organic whole. These concepts do connect, these images do make sense. For the first time, many in our congregation began to realize, this story is my story. These people are my people. This God is my God.

One middle-aged couple had grown up in church. They'd heard hundreds of sermons. One Sunday they wore a disgruntled look. "How come we never heard this before?" they asked. The Jewish roots of our faith from Leviticus consistently gave them fresh insight into the passages they already knew. Paul, for example, speaks of "offering yourselves" and being a "pleasing aroma." Many of these phrases come from Leviticus and give them their context.

What did the unchurched think about it? I

found out at a high school football game. It was late Friday night. The cheers had subsided, and I was walking home when I heard a man call out: "Hey, Pastor! Leviticus is turning our world upside down. We're getting rocked to the core." The family had just started attending, weren't Christians, and had never been interested in church. But somehow, Leviticus got their attention.

Then two high school kids caught up with me. They too came from pagan backgrounds. "We've been talking about what you said. That was awesome! Can't wait for Sunday. See ya!" These people were excited—by Old Testament law.

Mike was a police officer who came to Mars Hill the Sunday I preached Leviticus 23. The chapter summarizes the feast calendar and gives the Israelites a concrete preview of the first and second comings of Christ. Every verse speaks of Jesus, and for many this was the first time they'd heard it.

Mike later told the congregation: "I was a skeptic. I didn't believe in any kind of god. But that Sunday everything changed. I realized the whole story, the whole Bible, wasn't just a bunch of old books. It all fit together through the whole history. I knew I needed to learn more, and I learned I needed Jesus."

Each week when I invited people to open their Bibles, they cheered! When I said, "Please turn with me to chapter . . ." the congregation erupted, "Five!" and a flurry of page turning began. It's become a tradition.

People were beginning to study ahead and were trying to figure out the next passage. They even egged me on before the service, telling me they were stumped with that week's text and they couldn't wait to see it come to life.

Spontaneous study groups sprang up during the week. My teaching was just a start, the beginning of the wrestling. True transformation begins when people take the Word home to grapple with its meaning.

GRAPHIC IMAGES OF SALVATION

The Leviticus series has been successful in part because it's so visual. We see biblical theology with flesh and blood (literally) in Leviticus. Instead of a treatise on the nature of the kingdom of death and its opposition to the kingdom of life, God instructs people with strange skin diseases to steer clear of the temple until they are clean. Brilliant.

Instead of trying to describe an abstract concept like substitutionary atonement, Leviticus gives instructions on when, where, and how to slit the throat of a lamb.

The picture of blood spattering on your cloak as the lamb is placed on the fire lends vivid imagery to the penalty for sin. The entire sacrificial system becomes one giant prop, a visual aid to explain what it means to be in relationship with the one true God.

We didn't just talk about the pictures, we experienced them. I covered myself with fake blood, built fires on the stage, climbed atop a giant wooden altar. We had "priests" wearing linen ephods marching up and down the aisles and brought in a live goat for the Day of Atonement. We even traced the agricultural cycles to help our city dwellers understand the environmental roots behind the Creator's appointed feasts.

My generation thinks and converses visually. Film is the dominant language of our culture. We relate with images and pictures and metaphors. Leviticus is perfect for us. It's one image after another. Blood, animals, and clothing of certain colors—provocative pictures a person can ponder forever.

Another reason Leviticus is so effective: It speaks to our longing for community. The individualistic culture of the West has deeply affected Christianity. Sermons are more likely to mention a "personal relationship with Jesus" than to call a people to repent for communal sins. Yet younger generations identify with "group guilt." The most obvious example is environmentalism. Leviticus taps this community mindset.

The Day of Atonement was a communal ritual. Certain sacrifices were offered on behalf of the "entire assembly." And one of the gravest punishments in Leviticus? Being cut off from the community.

On the Day of Atonement, the priest placed the sins of the community on the head of a goat and then sent the animal out into the wilderness. So on "Scapegoat Sunday" we reenacted this ritual. A man dressed as the high priest brought in a goat and I explained the instructions in the text. Then I compared these to Jesus and his interactions with Pilate in John 18. We had a vivid picture of Jesus as the ultimate scapegoat.

The metaphor clicked. Awestruck, we saw how Jesus was taken outside Jerusalem to bear the sins of us all. When the goat was taken outside, and the "priest" announced that our sins were forgiven, the place went nuts with celebration. By the time the band broke into "The Blood Will Never Lose Its Power," I thought angels were going to crash through the ceiling to join us!

A year after beginning, the series on Leviticus came to an end, and it was time to move on. Now I'm preaching Numbers.

Chapter 75

APPLY WITHIN

A method for finding the practical response called for in a text

David Veerman

Terry gathers his family and quickly herds them into the station wagon. He has to get to church early to photocopy some handouts for the Sunday school class he teaches. Then there's choir and, after church, several conversations about the committee he serves on. With seemingly boundless energy and enthusiasm, Terry is immersed in church activities. In his quiet moments, however, Terry worries. At home, his briefcase holds a doctor's report telling of a shadow in the x-rays of his lungs.

Ruth is known for her contagious smile and warm encouragement. As hospitality chairperson, she seems to know everyone in church. *How can she always be so up?* people wonder. While Ruth is succeeding at church, she believes she is an absolute failure at home. There is constant bickering with a teenage daughter, and she feels a growing sense of distance from her husband.

An honor student and a varsity volleyball player, Janet is the picture of the all-American girl. She's also actively involved with the church youth group and takes her faith seriously. But she wants to know how to bring what she believes into her everyday life, especially with her boyfriend, who lately has been pressuring her sexually. Janet sits in the back of the church and wonders.

Recognize any of those people? You've never met them, but you probably know many just like them. They fill our churches: men and women and young people, some desperate, looking for answers.

Steven Brown, pastor of Key Biscayne Presbyterian Church in Florida, says that when he preaches, he safely assumes seven out of ten people in the congregation have broken hearts. They especially need a life-changing word from God, something they can *act on* as well as know.

As a communicator, I recognize the value of applications and the difficulty of making appropriate ones. In fact, in many sermons I hear (and some I've preached), the application simply is left out. Yet, as Jay Kesler, past president of Taylor University, puts it, preaching a sermon strong on information but weak on application is like shouting to a drowning person, "Swim! Swim!" The message is true, but it's not helpful.

A friend once said of his former pastor, "The closest he came to application was occasionally to end his sermon with, 'And you?'" I'm sure he wanted to drive home his sermon, but although the spirit was willing, the application was weak.

WHY THE DIFFICULTY?

If applications are desirable, why are they so often lacking? As I've talked about this with pastors, and especially as I wrestled with applications as senior editor of the *Life Application Bible* (Tyndale), I've identified several reasons.

Hard work

This is, perhaps, the main cause of application deficiency. They're tough. They demand time and effort.

When our team began working on the *Life Application Bible*, we wanted (1) to help our readers ask the right questions, and (2) to motivate them to action. That twofold response was our definition of *application*.

I anticipated little difficulty writing application notes. After all, I'd spent two decades in youth ministry challenging young people to follow Christ and teaching them how to grow in the faith. But my assumption was wrong; finding applications was tough work. I found it enjoyable to research and explain textual questions, cultural influences, and theological intricacies, but I couldn't easily make the bridge to real life. Even now, after years of writing application notes, I find it doesn't come easily.

Wrong Assumptions

I used to assume the audience will make a connection between the lesson and their lives, a common mistake. None of us wants to insult the intelligence of our listeners, and so we lay out the Bible story, the theological insights, or the timeless truths and leave the rest to them. But most people, I found to my dismay, can't make the mental jump. Our congregations don't want to be spoon-fed, but they do need to be led.

Fear

We may fear being "too simplistic." We may think we have to speak deep, complex truths or broad, general principles to proclaim properly the Word of God. There have been times when I've subconsciously tried to show off my education. How easy it is to preach to ourselves, splitting the finer points of theology, extrapolating the etymology, or considering the cultural context, while the congregation waits for a life-changing challenge!

I've worked hours crafting sermons I then delivered with confidence, only to have people stare back with a collective ho-hum. It's not that I wasn't prepared or "pre-prayered," or that I stumbled or stuttered. In fact, the congregation probably learned something, and I heard quite a few post-sermon comments such as "That was interesting" and "Good job." But nothing was said about changed lives. For fear of oversimplifying, I simply had been nonspecific. I had failed to move to application.

No Training

I've spoken to many preachers who bemoan their lack of training in applying Scripture. While grateful for the intensive work in other areas of homiletics and theology, they express need for a dose of reality. "I wish I'd been taught how to relate the Word to the needs of real people," said one.

A misunderstanding of what application is can weaken preaching. If I'm unsure of my goal, I'll definitely have trouble hitting it. So what is effective application?

What Application Is Not

Let's begin by listing what isn't application. *First, application is not additional information—simply giving more facts.* Whether in detective work or in Bible study, gathering facts begins the process, but it doesn't complete it. The facts need to be used.

For instance, it's good to know Matthew was a tax collector and that tax collectors conspired with Rome to become rich, exploiting their countrymen. Such information puts Matthew in context and helps us understand the Bible. But to become useful, the informa-tion needs to become wedded to action a listener might take.

Second, application is not mere understanding. Understanding God's truth, the step that must follow fact-collecting, is vital. We need to know what the Bible means, not just what it says. Again, however, a sermon left here is incomplete. Many people understand biblical truths, but the truths make no impact on their lives. I may understand that Jesus quoted Scripture to counter Satan's attacks in the desert and that the Word of God is powerful. But so what? How would I ever do that?

Third, applying the text is not merely being relevant. Relevance explains how what happened in Bible times can happen today. For example, we can describe Corinth as similar to many cities today—wild and filled with idols, violence, and sexual immorality. Relevant description can make us more open to application. But this step still falls short since it doesn't tell us what we can do about the situation we recognize.

Finally, illustration—explaining how some-one else handled a similar situation—doesn't qualify as application. Illustrations shed light on a passage and show us how someone else applied truth to his or her life. But it remains removed from the individual—from us.

If each of these four aspects of Bible exposition isn't application, what is? What steps can we take to apply the Bible to life?

Applications At Their Best

Simply stated, application is answering two questions: *So what?* and *Now what?* The first question asks, "Why is this passage important to me?" The second asks, "What should I do about it today?"

Application focuses the truth of God's Word on specific, life-related situations. It helps people understand what to do or how to use what they have learned. Application persuades people to act.

For example, Luke 5:12–15 reports Jesus' touching and healing a leper. Beyond describing the horrors of leprosy in the first century (information) and pointing out the similarities to AIDS victims today (relevance), application asks the congregation to think about whom they may consider untouchable and challenges them to touch those people for Christ. It asks, "Whom do you know who needs God's touch of love? What can you do today or this week to reach out to them?"

Application moves beyond explaining the text and stating the timeless truths. It makes the message personal and challenges people to act. For this to happen, four steps are necessary:

- The listener must receive the message: Do I understand what was said?
- The person should find reason to reflect on his or her own life: What does the message mean for me?
- The individual needs to identify necessary behavior changes: What should I do about it?
- The person should lay out a plan or steps to make a change: What should I do first?

Keeping these steps in mind during sermon preparation can help us preach a sermon that moves people from receiving the message to taking action. But how do we determine an appropriate application in the first place?

PREPARING FOR APPLICATION

I use what I call a *dynamic analogy grid* to discover possible applications in a Scripture passage (see below). Whether my text is a verse, a paragraph, or a chapter, this tool helps me move from the words and their meanings to

God's word and his message for the people in the pews. Here's how I work through the grid, using my other Bible study tools and my knowledge of people.

Dynamic Analogy Grid

	Humanity's need/problem	God's action/solution	Humanity's response/obedience
Then	1	2	3
Now	4	5	6
Me/us	7	8	9

I work across each horizontal row of three boxes, starting with boxes 1 through 3. These three boxes deal with the information in the text. I decide what the passage says about humanity's need/problem, God's action/solution, and humanity's necessary response/obedience. That helps me put the passage in its cultural-historical context and determine the biblical principle or timeless truth.

If, for example, the passage chastises the people of Israel for idol worship (let's use 1 Sam. 7:3–4), I'd want to know what gods were idolized, how they were worshiped, and what problems ensued for the Israelites. That would fill box 1. Then I'd want to determine God's action or solution for this problem (box 2) and how he wanted the people of that day to respond (box 3).

Next, I move to boxes 4 through 6, a stage that puts the text into a contemporary context. What does God want people to do? This answers the question "So what?" When filled in, these boxes make the text relevant. For box 4: What are the idols today? Of course there are differences, but which of our problems, pressures, and temptations are similar to those of the people of Israel back then? For box 5: How does God's solution for the Israelites parallel his actions for Christians today? For box 6: What response does God want now?

The final step is to fill in boxes 7 through 9. This applies the passage personally as I think of specific needs in my community and congregation. This leads us to answer the question "Now what?" For box 7: What is one example of a similar problem I'm facing now? Or, what are we facing as a church that's similar to idols? For box 8: What is God telling me as an individual, or us as a church, to do about it? For box 9: What, specifically, does God want me or us to do first? What are some steps we should take today to rid ourselves of idols or to reorder our priorities?

PREACHING FOR APPLICATION

Here's how one pastor used the grid. Hebrews 1:1–2:4 introduces the theme of the preeminence of Christ, saying that Christ is greater than the angels. The problem at that time (box 1) was that Hebrew Christians were in danger of falling back into Judaism, and many were fascinated with angels. Simply stated, God's solution (box 2) was to use the author of Hebrews to emphasize the superiority of Christ, that he alone is sufficient for salvation. First-century believers were challenged (box 3) to understand Christ's true identity, to worship only him and not to ignore salvation (2:3).

For the "Now" row, this pastor decided that most people today don't have old religions to fall back into, but several new ones entice us, such as the New Age movement and cults, which permeate all areas of our society (box 4). People easily follow theological tangents. People today need to understand the superiority of Christ over all religions (box 5). Christ is better—the only way. And we need to challenge

believers to keep their eyes on Christ and to trust only him (box 6).

After filling the first two rows, this pastor understood the context, the biblical principles, and the relevance of those principles. He could answer "So what?" The final step was to consider the people of his congregation and what possible actions they should take. He applied the message to both unbelievers and believers wavering in their faith.

For unbelievers, confused by the supernatural talk in society and unfamiliar with Christ (box 7), he emphasized the "great salvation" described in Hebrews 2:3 (box 8) and challenged them to trust Christ (box 9). The Christians sidetracked by theological gurus or fascinated by faddish ideas and theologies (box 7 again) need to reject heresies that diminish Christ and to center their lives on Christ, their only authority and hope of salvation (box 8). One possible way they might do that (box 9) would be to learn more about orthodoxy, perhaps by reading a Josh McDowell book or joining an adult study on the topic at the church.

"Christ is greater than the angels" became more than a truth to affirm. It came alive as a message that challenged people to act.

I usually prepare by working from left to right, as I've illustrated above, but when I speak, I sometimes move down the boxes vertically, one column at a time. That moves from people's problem then, to society's problem now, to my (or our) particular problem; from God's solution then, to God's solution now, to God's solution for me (or us); and from humanity's expected response then, to their expected response now, to my (or our) specific and personal response. That adds variety.

Here's another suggestion: Lloyd Perry, homiletics professor emeritus of Trinity

Evangelical Divinity School, recommends a subpoint of application for every main point in the sermon. In other words, he recommends not leaving all the applications until the end, when people are least likely to be listening because they're tired or thinking about lunch. If we're running late, we're tempted to generalize or skip the challenge to action if it's lumped at the conclusion. Perry suggests we sprinkle applications throughout.

MINING FOR APPLICATIONS

If I want to prepare applications that hit home, I find it best to think through the needs of the people to whom I'm speaking. Needs may be categorized many ways. For example, I generally think in terms of felt needs, hidden needs, and spiritual needs.

As the adjective suggests, *felt* needs relate to what people are feeling. Felt needs include physical and social pressures at the front of their awareness. Hunger is a felt need, as is loneliness or conflict or guilt.

Hidden needs are those things people need but aren't aware of at the moment. An engaged couple needs to know about conflict resolution, for example, but might not recognize it before the wedding. Other hidden needs that a congregation might have include the needs to tithe, to have patience, and to be good stewards of time.

Obviously, such needs can also fit under the heading of spiritual needs. But what I'm calling *spiritual* needs are God's special demands on life and the implications of what it means to call Christ Lord. Involvement in church, sharing the faith with others, studying the Bible regularly, and praying consistently are some of the spiritual needs that come to mind.

Another way to expose a congregation's needs might be to think through the following eight areas of personal application:

- *relationships* (e.g., with family, friends, neighbors, coworkers, fellow believers)
- *conflicts* (in marriage, with children, at work)
- *personal burdens* (sickness, family pressures, death, loss)
- *difficult situations* (stress, debt, hindrances)
- *character weaknesses* (dishonesty, lack of integrity, anger)
- *lack of resources* (in time, energy/money, materials, information)
- *responsibilities* (work demands, church programs, volunteer efforts, home projects)
- *opportunities* (learning, working, serving, witnessing)

Some people study, study, study, and do little about it. They act like a football player who loves the game and knows the plays by heart, but who seldom practices or plays.

Others do, do, do, and spend little time in study. They act like the athlete who runs, throws, and catches footballs by the hour, but who spends no time understanding the rules of the game or learning the play book.

True Bible application involves both studying and doing. It is discovering what the Bible is saying to me and then doing what it says.

We've been given the awesome responsibility of presenting and explaining God's Word. We must be sure to tell our listeners everything they need to know about the text and context—history, culture, archaeology, theology, and etymology. But we must not neglect application.

"Keep putting into practice all you learned from me and saw me doing," Paul writes, "and the God of peace will be with you" (Phil. 4:9, TLB). Our job is to explain what God wants people to know and do about his eternal commands, promises, and truths and then to offer them ways to do it.

Chapter 76

APPLICATION WITHOUT MORALISM

How to show the relevance of the text in a redemptive manner

Bryan Chapell

We preachers face huge questions about why people are not applying what we preach to them. Gallup did a survey that tells us when people claim to be born again, their good behavior actually degenerates. Those who claim to be born again have a higher incidence of drunken driving and divorce than the rest of culture. The incidence of abortion and drug use is not different from the rest of culture among those who claim to be evangelical. So people who say they believe the Scriptures have great difficulties, apparently, applying them.

ETHOS AS A REASON FOR DOING APPLICATION

One reason we need to be doing application in preaching is for our own personal ethos. You probably know these terms: *ethos, logos, pathos. Ethos* is the perceived character of the speaker. *Logos* is the logical content, the verbal content. *Pathos* is the emotive content. Aristotle said the most powerful of these three was ethos. If somebody speaks simply but you believe them to be a person of good character, you listen more than to somebody who is eloquent but whom you don't trust.

The two things that most make up ethos are *credibility* and *compassion*. People will rate us in terms of our ethos based on their perception of these two elements.

Credibility is determined by knowledge and realism. We expect pastors to know facts, but we also expect wisdom and realism. If I as a preacher say, "If you're going to be able to walk with God, you need to learn some Hebrew," I might as well have thrown the sermon out the window, because the average person thinks that would be nice, but it's unrealistic. So we may be intelligent, but we need to base ethos on knowledge as well as realism. Much of what happens in application is saying, "I'm not just knowledgeable about exegesis. I know the world you live in. I am able to be realistic."

Ethos is not just based on credibility but also on *compassion*. The perceived character of the speaker is based on a perception that you care for people other than yourself. If the perception of the person preaching is, *He wants to make an impression,* rather than, *He's caring for the people to whom he speaks,* people will not listen. They certainly will not trust the preacher. They may find his message entertaining, but they will not trust him until they perceive he cares more about the listener than himself.

Difficulties with Doing True Application

What communicates caring? What says, "You care about me; you take it out of the ethereal world that makes you impressive, and you put it in my world, where I can do something with it"? Ethos is tied to the ability to do application that is *realistic* and that is *courageous.*

It surprises me how much God's people truly

want to be challenged in their Christian walk. But we get scared as speakers. We think, *I can't talk about that, because there are people I know who are struggling with that.* Yet the heart in which the Spirit lives desires to walk with God, desires to be challenged. I don't mean people want to be beaten over the head or dealt with tactlessly or angrily, but they desire to be challenged. When the preacher is willing to say things everyone knows are difficult for him to say, they trust him more, because they know he put himself at risk for them.

Think how we joke about pastors who always play it safe: "He's always going to word it politically. He's never going to say anything that upsets anyone." And think how little respect we have for them. So the willingness to say things that put us at risk by doing application that comes into people's real existence, though it is scary, is necessary in terms of being able to have a hearing long term.

It takes courage to be specific. If you look at traditional messages, they move from explanation to illustration to application: Here's the truth; here's the truth demonstrated; now here's the truth applied. But how do people listen to such a message? Typically, if it doesn't go on too long and isn't too dense, people listen to explanation. Then they wake up again when you do illustration.

But when you go to application, this is the breaking point. This is where people often cut it off, because the preacher has now stopped preaching and has gone to meddling. Again, in the hearts of the redeemed there is often a desire for this. But it is also the place that is most risky, because you may say things that are foolish; you may say things that are wise but highly disagreed with; you may simply say things people aren't ready to hear.

Another difficulty with application is the hermeneutics required to be specific: How do I move from that biblical principle to a present imperative? We say things like, "Paul was a missionary, and therefore you should reach out to your neighbors." And "Jesus wore sandals, so you should . . ." What do we say? Where are the exemplars truly instructive and where are they culturally bound? The people in the Acts 2 and 4 passages held all things in common. Are we supposed to do that in our churches? And where does the Bible talk about cloning? We struggle with the hermeneutics required to be specific, even though we talk about the importance of it.

A final thing that troubles us about application is the grace denied, or at least presumed to be denied, by requiring specific duties. I have a number of people who have come out of "grace circles"—the "gracers," as they are sometimes identified today—who don't even let you use the word *duty*. They say it's not biblical to talk about grace and obligation in the same sentence. Is it ungracious to talk about duty?

DUTY AND GRACE

We can talk about duty with grace for several reasons.

(1) To be redeemed from an empty way of life is gracious. First Peter 1:18 says that God has redeemed us from an empty way of life. There are pursuits—in that particular context, ceremonial and religious pursuits—that are wrong, vain, or empty, and to let people continue to go down that path is not a gracious thing. God has redeemed us from an empty way of life.

(2) To teach people to say no to ungodliness is gracious. There are consequences, harm, danger, and personal hurt in doing what God does not allow. Therefore Paul says in Titus 2:11–

12 that it is the grace of God that teaches us to say no to ungodliness and worldly passion.

(3) To lead to the blessings of obedience is gracious. Psalm 1 tells us, "Blessed is the man who does not walk in the counsel of the wicked." It would be ungracious to deny people God's blessings by not saying what God requires. *To teach that there is discipline for disobedience is gracious.*

It is a gracious thing to say, "God disciplines sin, and I want you to know that, because God disciplines those he loves." In Hebrews 12:10 we are told that "God disciplines for our good, that we may share in his holiness." So not to teach about God's discipline is actually to deny people the good he wants to share with them.

These are all appropriate reasons to teach duty and to consider it gracious to do so. But where do we cross the line? *Where does teaching duty become ungracious?*

(1) To teach that there is merit in obedience is ungracious. To say that to walk in God's ways will make him love you more is an abomination to God. Yet we often, by implication if not by direct statement, imply as much. To imply there is merit in moral behavior is against the Scriptures. Luke 17:10 says that when we have done all we should do, we are still unworthy or unprofitable servants.

(2) To teach that God rejects us for disobedience is ungracious. After all, in the parable of the lost son the father ran to the son while he was still a long way off and when it was apparent to all the state in which he had lived.

(3) To teach that God does not require godliness is ungracious. There are consequences to ungodliness. Micah 6:8 asks the question, "What does God require of you?" There are requirements. They do not merit us to God, but they are still required.

(4) To teach the law apart from grace is ungracious. Simply to teach the imperatives is ungracious because of the impression it leaves. You may ask, "I know you have to have grace in the context of the imperatives of Scripture, but do you have to make sure the gospel is there in every sermon?" If you push me to absolute principles, I'll say you don't if the people in the context understand the gospel. But most people do not get the context. Even when we preach grace, people hear law. It's the human reflex.

It is good exegesis to identify a text in its context. Therefore, in my regular preaching and not just occasionally, I make sure the gospel is present. Ultimately, the motive and exegesis determine proper application. We have to make sure the motive is in place at the same time that we're telling people to do or not do something.

THE FIVE QUESTIONS

So, how do we do this? We properly apply duty with a grace perspective by regularly using five standard questions of application: what, where, who, why, and how. You must anchor these questions to do an adequate job of exegesis. It's not enough to say what to do if people don't know why. And if you don't say how, you lead them to despair.

Apply Duty with Grace By Answering *What*

The *what* question is instructional specificity—the specific instructions derived from and proven by the exposition's concepts and terminology.

In answering the *what* question, use consistent terminology. One of the reasons people stop listening to us is we have become essay writers rather than preachers. When I write an essay, I think of my seventh-grade English teacher saying, "Use a different word. Don't be redundant." But we're not writing essays. We're talking to listeners. Therefore, if in my exposition I speak about what it means to be one who loves God, but then in application I use the terminology "we have to show affection for the divine," it's a great essay. It's a terrible message, however, because I've abandoned the terminology I used in the exposition.

One of the most powerful rhetorical tools a preacher has is repetition. When I spend time developing a term and then exchange it for another term, people don't necessarily know I'm talking about the same thing. I'm thinking it's conceptually the same thing, but by changing the term, the listener doesn't hear it as the same thing. So make sure the terms used in explanation are the same terms used in application. This establishes your scriptural rationale and maintains your scriptural authority.

Establish a concept before writing your sermon. I usually encourage students to make application the beginning of sermon writing. Once you've researched the passage but before you start writing your sermon, you need to know what you're going to tell people to do, so you have a target and you know how to form the message of your sermon.

Apply Duty with Grace By Answering *Where*

In application we also need to provide situational specificity. The *what* question was instructional. The *where* question is situational. That is, identify where in real life this concept applies.

When I started preaching, I thought I had to come up with new lists of things people should do every week: You need to go to the bookstore and buy this book; you need to treat your neighbor this way. Yet, before that sermon even I hadn't thought of those things to do.

Situational specificity will make you take the principle of application—we have to be hospitable, we have to be sexually pure, whatever it is—and go to the areas of life in which people are struggling. Instead of saying, "Here's a list of things to do," say, "How does that principle deal with your life?" That makes people think, *You know where I live. You know what I'm going through. You're dealing with the areas of struggle in my life. I see how the Bible applies to my life, not how the Bible gives me a new laundry list of things to do this week that I'm not going to remember thirty seconds after you're done.*

When you think of application, think of it in terms of personal struggle. Think of people you know who are struggling and take the truth to that area. Be concrete. Deal with these real situations in life.

Be Concrete By Going through the *Who* Door

If your principle is, "Be confident because God knows tomorrow," think about who in your congregation needs to hear that. The students deciding where they're going to go to college next year? The guy who has been laid off from work? The couple who got the bad medical report? They need to know that God knows tomorrow. When you go in through the *who* door, you get to the *where*. You think of the people, and you get to their situation.

There's a danger of fencing in the application by mentioning only one situation. We need to spotlight one situation and then quickly unroll to others. Identify other situations people face where the exposition applies, because you don't want to fence it in.

With the first example, you're establishing the reality of this instruction coming into real life. It's like those flashlights that you tighten the lid to focus the beam. You're saying, "Here's the light of truth. To focus that truth I want to show its application to one situation (the person who's struggling with job insecurity)." Now that you've focused the beam so they see what that looks like in real life, you say, "But it's not just job security. There are those of you who have medical issues. There are some of you wondering where you're going to go to school next year." You're trying to keep from fencing in the application.

When you started going to seminary, you thought the hard work was going to be the exegesis, right? In my mind, the exposition is provided to us; the application comes from us, because we have to exegete not the Word but our people. We have to be involved in their lives. We have to know what they're doing. I can't sit in my study twenty or forty hours a week and think I'm going to be a great preacher in the pulpit. I can't do application that way. I have to be involved with people, or I can't bring the truth to bear upon their lives.

Apply Duty with Grace By Answering *Why*

The next question is the *why* question—providing biblical motive. We want to give love over fear as motive; that is, we must take away both self-protection and personal gain as the primary reasons people are doing something. Since we are saved by grace without any merit of our own, why should we do good works? In order that with our whole lives we may show ourselves grateful to God and give him praise—not for our gain but out of love for God.

To answer *Why should I do what God requires?* the mode of hierarchy is this: The first reason is love for God, because of the mercy of his Son. Second is love for others. We tell people to do things because God loves other people, and if you love God, you'll love those he loves. The last reason is love of self. We're children of the king. We've been redeemed by the blood of the Lamb. We're valuable. Recognize the beauty of a proper love of self and teach people that beating on themselves is not holiness. There is a motivation that comes from the joy of proper self-love, and that joy should be part of our lives.

Christ-centered, grace-oriented preaching teaches the reason for doing what you're doing is because you are loved. You will not be loved more, but you'll never be loved less. You're responding to the God who gave his Son for you. Your life is not your own. You were purchased with a price, the precious blood of the Lord Jesus Christ. We're responding to the great love he has given.

Apply Duty with Grace By Answering *How*

Finally, provide biblical enablement. This is answering the *how* question. The Bible provides means. Some of those means are knowing the do's and the don'ts. We teach people what God says to do, and we teach what God says don't do. The disciplines, the means of grace, are also part of the way we teach what God requires. Prayer, reading of Scripture, fellowship among God's people, and the sacraments are ways God gives us for running the race of holiness.

The chief means to do what God requires is consistent adulation of the mercy of God in Christ. People ask, "How do I do that?" They're looking for me to say, "First you put something on your refrigerator door so you can see it. Then you put it on your mirror so when you're shaving you can read it." Those are good aspects of suggestion, but the most powerful means is to have our hearts penetrated with the amazing mercy of God. That is the most transforming thing, and nothing is more powerful than that. Our greatest way of enabling the people God puts in our lives is to adore the mercy of God before them, so they're constantly getting the message of how wondrous and beautiful his love is. Their primary power is the faith God has put in them.

Faith is confidence that I am a new creature in Christ Jesus. My identity is that of a child of God. I have that privilege now. I am a fundamentally different creature. By faith I apprehend that knowledge that I don't have to listen to the lie of Satan that says I can't change. The message of Scripture, by faith received, is that you can change. God has provided the means. It's teaching people that they are new creatures in Christ Jesus; by virtue of their union with him they have power to do what God requires.

Chapter 77

BLENDING BIBLE CONTENT AND LIFE APPLICATION
How to talk to people about themselves

Haddon Robinson

It was a disastrous sermon.

A church in Dallas invited me to preach on John 14. That's not an easy passage. It is filled with exegetical questions about death and the Second Coming. How do you explain, "If I go and prepare a place for you, I will come again, and receive you unto myself?" How is Jesus preparing that place? Does Jesus mean we won't go to be with him until he comes back? What about soul sleep? I spent most of my week studying the text and reading the commentaries to answer questions like these.

When I got up to preach, I knew I had done my homework. Though the issues were tough, I had worked through them and was confident I was ready to deliver solid biblical teaching on the assigned passage.

Five minutes into the sermon, though, I knew I was in trouble. The people weren't with me. At the ten-minute mark, people were falling asleep. One man sitting near the front began to snore. Worse, he didn't disturb anyone! No one was listening.

Even today, whenever I talk about that morning, I still get an awful feeling in the pit of my stomach. What went wrong? The problem was that I spent the whole sermon wrestling with the tough theological issues, issues that intrigued me. Everything I said was valid. It might have been strong stuff in a seminary classroom. But in that church, in that pulpit, it was a disaster.

What happened? I didn't speak to the life questions of my audience. I answered my questions, not theirs. Some of the men and women I spoke to that day were close to going home to be with the Lord. What they wanted to know was, "Will he toss me into some ditch of a grave, or will he take me safely home to the other side? When I get to heaven, what's there?"

They wanted to hear me say: "You know, Jesus said he was going to prepare a place for us. The Creator of the universe has been spending two thousand years preparing a home for you. God only spent six days creating the world, and look at its beauty! Imagine, then, what the home he has been preparing for you must be like. When you come to the end of this life, that's what he'll have waiting for you."

That's what I should have preached. At least I should have started with their questions. But I didn't.

It's also possible to make the opposite error—to spend a whole sermon making practical applications without rooting them in Scripture. I don't want to minimize Scripture. It's possible to preach a skyscraper sermon—one story after another with nothing in between. Such sermons hold people's interest but give them no sense of the eternal. Talking about "mansions over the hilltop" comes from country western music, not the Bible. A sermon full of nonbiblical speculations is ultimately unsatisfying.

Some of the work I did in my study, then, could have helped the people answer their questions. The job is to combine both biblical content and life application in an effective way.

How Much Content Is Enough?

How then can we strike the right balance in our preaching between biblical content and life application? The basic principle is to give as much biblical information as the people need to understand the passage, and no more. Then move on to your application.

The distinction between exegesis and exposition is helpful here. *Exegesis* is the process of getting meaning from the text, often through noting the verb tense or where the word emphasis falls in the original languages. That's what you do in your study as you prepare. But that is seldom appropriate in a sermon on Sunday morning. In fact, an overuse of Greek or Hebrew can make us snobs. Using the jargon of my profession can come across as a putdown, a way of saying, "I know something you don't know." There's an arrogance about that that can create distance between the audience and myself.

I served for ten years as a general director of the Christian Medical and Dental Society. Sometimes physicians would use technical medical terms when they talked with me, and I wouldn't know what they were talking about. Once I said to one of my friends, "I hope you don't talk to your patients as you do me, because I don't know the jargon. I'm an educated person. I just don't happen to be as educated in medicine as you are."

Do you know what he said to me? He replied, "Preachers do that in the pulpit all the time."

I did a lot of that when I first got out of seminary. I used my knowledge of Greek and Hebrew in the study and in the pulpit. One day a woman wounded me with a compliment: "I just love to hear you preach. In fact, when I see the insights you get from the original languages, I realize that my English Bible is hardly worth reading."

I went home asking myself, *What have I done? I'm trying to get people into their Bibles, but I've taken this lady out of hers.*

Spurgeon was right: The people in the marketplace cannot learn the language of the academy, so the people in the academy must learn the language of the marketplace. It's the pastor's job to translate.

While raw exegesis doesn't belong in a Sunday morning sermon, what does belong there is *exposition*. Exposition is drawing from your exegesis to give the people what they need to understand the passage. They don't need all you've done in exegesis, but they do need to see the framework, the flow of the passage. They should be able to come back to the passage a few weeks after you've preached on it, read it, and say, "Oh, I understand what it says."

Does this mean there is no place in the church for exegesis? Of course not. As you study, you may dig out all kinds of material that would help certain people who enjoy detailed Bible study. While including these tidbits in a sermon resembles distracting footnotes, this kind of technical teaching is appropriate for a classroom.

THE "SO WHAT?" OF PREACHING

All preaching involves a "so what?" A lecture on the archaeology of Egypt, as interesting as it might be, isn't a sermon. A sermon touches life. It demands practical application.

That practical application, though, need not always be spelled out. Imagine, for example, that you borrow my car and it has a flat. You call me up and say, "I've never changed a tire on a car like this. What do I do?"

I tell you how to find the spare, how to use the jack, where to find the key that unlocks the wire rim. Once I give you all the instructions, then do I say, "Now, I exhort you, change the tire"? No, you already want to get the car going. Because you already sense the need, you don't need exhortation. You simply need a clear explanation.

Some sermons are like that. Your people are wrestling with a certain passage of Scripture. They want to know what it means. Unless they understand the text, it's useless to apply it. They don't need exhortation; they need explanation. Their questions about the text must be answered.

You may not need to spell out practical application when you are dealing with basic theological issues—how we see God and ourselves and each other. For example, you might preach on Genesis 1, showing that it's not addressing issues of science so much as questions of theology: What is God like? You might spend time looking at the three groups of days—the first day is light, the fourth day is lights; the second day is sea and sky, the fifth day is fish and birds. Each day is followed by God's evaluation: "It was good." But after the creation of man, God observes, "It was very good."

Then you ask, "What do we learn about God?" We learn that God is good, that God has a purpose in creation. We learn that while every other living thing is made "according to its kind," man and woman are created in God's image. What does that say about people—the people we pray with and play with, the people we work with or who sleep on the streets?

The whole sermon may be an explanation with little direct application built into it. Of course, that doesn't mean there's no application. If at the close of this sermon someone realizes, *That's a significant statement about who we are. There are no ordinary people. Every man and woman has special worth*—when that really sinks in—it can make tremendous practical differences as it shapes how a person sees himself and other people.

Or take Romans 3. You might begin by raising in some practical way the question, "How does a person stand right before God?" Then you could lead your listeners through Paul's rather complex discussion of what it means to be justified by faith. If you do it well, when you are finished, people should say, "So that's how God remains righteous when he declares us righteous."

Obviously, this passage has great application. But it's so complex you probably couldn't go through Paul's argument and spell out in any detail many practical applications, too, in the same sermon. And that's okay. If they really understood the problem of lostness, the solution of salvation serves as a strong application.

We need to trust people to make some of their own practical applications. Some of the best growing I've done has taken place when a concept gripped me and I found myself constantly thinking: *How could this apply in my life?*

Of course, you do have knowledge your people don't possess, knowledge they expect you to have and share with them. But you can share that knowledge in a manner that doesn't talk down to a congregation, in a way that says, "If you were in my situation, you'd have access to the same information." If you feel you must make all the practical applications for your hearers, do their thinking for them, you underestimate their intelligence. You can dishonor your congregation if you tell them in effect, "You folks couldn't have figured out for yourselves how this applies."

For me, though, the greater danger lies in the opposite direction—in spending too much time on explanation and not going far enough into application. After preaching I've often come away feeling, *I should have shown them in a more specific way how to do this*. It is difficult for our listeners to live by what they believe unless we answer the question "How?"

REAL-LIFE EXAMPLES: NECESSARY BUT DANGEROUS

To make a principle come to life—to show how it can be applied—we need to give specific real-life examples, illustrations that say, "Here is how someone faced this problem, and this is what happened with her." But as necessary as real-life examples are, they carry a danger.

Suppose, for example, that someone preaches on the principle of modesty. Should a Christian dress with modesty? The answer is yes. But how do you apply that? One preacher may say, "Well, any skirt that's above the knee is immodest." So, he ends up with a church full of knee-length people. In that church, one application of a principle has assumed all the force of the principle itself. That is the essence of legalism: giving to a specific application the force of the principle.

I have a friend who keeps a journal, and it works for him. But when he preaches about it, he makes it sound as though Christians who are not journaling can't be growing. Whenever you say, "If you're not doing this particular act, then you're not following this principle," that's legalism.

How, then, can you preach for practical application if every time you say, "This is how to apply this truth," you run the risk of promoting legalism? Let me answer with a couple of examples.

When my father was in his eighties, he came to live with us. After a while he grew senile, and his behavior became such that we could no longer keep him in our home. Because his erratic behavior endangered himself and our children, we had to put him in a nursing home. It cost me half my salary each month to keep him there. For eight years, until he died, I visited my dad almost every day. In eight years I never left that rest home without feeling somewhat guilty about his being there. I would have preferred to have had him in our home, but we could not care for him properly.

A few years later, my mother-in-law, who was dying of cancer, came to live with us in our home in Denver. It was a tough period in our marriage. I was trying to get settled as president of Denver Seminary. My wife, Bonnie, was up with her mother day and night. She somehow changed her mother's soiled bed six or seven times a day. For eighteen months, Bonnie took care of her in our home. When Mrs. Vick died, we had no regrets. We knew Bonnie had done everything she could to make her last months comfortable.

How should Christians care for their aging parents? Do you keep them in your home or do you place them in a nursing facility? There is no single Christian answer. It depends on your situation, your children, your resources, and your parents.

There is, though, a single guiding principle: We must honor our parents and act in love toward them. To make a Christian decision, you can't start with a selfish premise; you start by asking what is best for everyone involved. How you apply that principle in a given situation depends on a complex set of variables.

The way to avoid the trap of legalism, then, is to distinguish clearly between the biblical principle and its specific applications. One way to do this in preaching is to illustrate a principle with two or three varying examples, not just one, so you don't equate the principle with one particular way of applying it.

When our children were young, I lived under the idea that if we didn't have daily devotions with our children—a family altar—somehow we were failing God. The problem was, family

devotions worked for other people, but although we tried all kinds of approaches, they never worked for us. Our children sat still for them on the outside but ran away from them on the inside. Yet we kept at them because I felt that a family altar was at the heart of a Christian family.

Then I realized that family devotions wasn't the principle but the application of a principle. The principle was that I needed to bring up my children to know and love God. I had mistakenly been giving to our family devotions the same imperative that belonged to the principle behind it.

We then came up with a different approach, one that worked for us. Our two children left for school at different times. Each morning before Vicki left, I would pray with her about the day, about what was coming up. A little later, Torrey and one of his friends came into my study, and we'd sit and pray for five minutes about what their day held.

That may not sound as satisfying in a sermon as saying we had devotions as a family at the breakfast table every morning, but for us it was an effective way to honor the principle. A preacher must make a clear distinction between the principle and its applications.

This is not to say, however, that a biblical principle must sound abstract and vague. Sometimes a preacher merely translates the principle into terms that a congregation understands.

In our American frontier days, there was a settlement in the West whose citizens were engaged in the lumber business. The town felt they wanted a church. They built a building and called a minister. The preacher moved into the settlement and initially was well received. Then one afternoon he happened to see some of his parishioners dragging some logs, which had been floated down the river from another village upstream, onto the bank. Each log was marked with the owner's stamp on one end. To his great distress, the minister saw his members pulling in the logs and sawing off the end where the telltale stamp appeared. The following Sunday he preached a strong sermon on the commandment "Thou shalt not steal."

At the close of the service, his people lined up and offered enthusiastic congratulations. "Wonderful message, Pastor." "Mighty fine preaching." The response bothered him a great deal. So he went home to prepare his sermon for the following Sunday. He preached the same sermon but gave it a different ending: "And thou shalt not cut off the end of thy neighbor's logs." When he got through, the congregation ran him out of town.

It's possible to state the principle in terms the audience clearly understands.

"WE" PREACHING AND "YOU" PREACHING

Another way to view the relationship between explanation and application is to look at the pronouns each calls for. Good preachers identify with their hearers when they preach. All of *us* stand before God to hear what God's Word says to *us*. The letter to the Hebrews says that the high priest was taken from among men to minister in the things pertaining to man. The high priest knew what it was to sin and to need forgiveness. With the people, he stood before God in need of cleansing. In identifying with the people, he represented the people to God.

But that same priest, by offering a sacrifice, could minister God's cleansing to the people.

Not only did he represent the people to God, he also represented God to the people. Somehow, that's also what preaching does.

When I'm listening to a good sermon, there comes a point when I lose track of all the people around me. As the preacher speaks, I experience God talking to me about me. The time for explanation has passed; the time for application has come.

At that point, it's appropriate for the preacher to leave behind "we" in favor of "you." No longer is the preacher representing the people to God; he is representing God to the people. "We've seen the biblical principle; we've seen two or three ways others have applied it. Now, what does this say to you?"

"You've got to decide how you're going to spend your money."

"You've got to decide whether you're going to take your marriage vows seriously."

It's you—not you plural but you singular—you personally who must decide what you will do with the truth you've heard. For the preacher to say "you" at that point isn't arrogant; he's not standing apart from the congregation. He's simply challenging each listener to make personal application.

In the final analysis, effective application does not rely on techniques. It is more a stance than a method. Life-changing preaching does not talk to the people about the Bible. Instead, it talks to the people about themselves—their questions, hurts, fears, and struggles—from the Bible. When we approach the sermon with that philosophy, flint strikes steel. The flint of someone's problem strikes the steel of God's Word, and a spark emerges that can set that person on fire for God.

Chapter 78

SHOWING PROMISE

You want people to obey God's commands. Are you giving them faith to do so?

Craig Brian Larson

While reading Scott Hafemann's *The God of Promise and the Life of Faith* (Crossway, 2001), I came across a passage with profound implications for preaching:

> The promises of God are always organically linked to corresponding commands. Every command of God is built upon a promise from God. Therefore every divine call to action (obedience) is, at the same time, a divine summons to trust in God's promises (faith). The promises of God are commands in disguise, and vice versa. God commands what he commands because he promises what he promises. After the Exodus, God promised Israel that it would rain bread from heaven every day except the Sabbath. God therefore commanded Israel not to gather more than their daily ration, except on Friday.... Disbelief always shows up as an act of disobedience, since every promise carries with it a command. Every time we disobey God it is because we are not trusting him. (p. 87)

God's promises and commands are the stuff of preaching. Most preachers default toward one or the other. Given the confusion in our culture over God's requirements, I probably lean toward preaching God's commands. I want to help people understand what God expects and save them from the terrible consequences of sin. In addition, I typically preach in an expository approach, and the selected text may not state both promise and command explicitly. If I'm not looking for the promise as well as the command, I may miss it.

But Hafemann's insight implies that to omit either promise or command is to break one wing off the airplane. To obey God's command fully, we must see the enabling promise in all its glory and express our obedience as an act of faith. To respond to the promise fully, we must understand how to express our trust in obedience. That doesn't mean a fifty-fifty split between command and promise in every sermon, but each element is there, developed enough to make a significant impression and connected to the other "wing."

We must learn to see both promise and command in the text (or context). For example, in a recent series on stewardship I preached one message on the faithful stewardship of our gifts from 1 Timothy 4:14–16, which includes these words: "Do not neglect your gift, which was given you through a prophetic message when the body of elders laid their hands on you. Be diligent in these matters; give yourself wholly to them, so that everyone may see your progress."

The commands in this passage are clear: "Do not neglect.... Be diligent.... Give yourself wholly...." But where is the promise? What beliefs enable us to obey? This clearly had the potential to be a moralistic, "grit your teeth and do this" sermon.

In search of promise, I decided to focus on the word *gifts*. In order to be faithful managers, Christians must believe God has promised to give each believer spiritual gifts. So I began there, quoting from 1 Peter 4:10 and Ephesians 4:11–16. To ensure that this idea made an impression on hearers, I provided a visual illustration. On our twenty-fifth wedding anniversary I bought my wife a pair of diamond earrings. In his love, God gives each of us spiritual diamond earrings, valuable and intended to display his glory.

I decided to bore deeper still to another promise underlying God's promise to give gifts: God promises to make us fruitful. I quoted from John 15:5, 8. With this promise, the images of a lush garden versus a dry desert were appropriate. (In retrospect, I see one additional avenue of theology I probably should have developed. The word gift is *charisma,* which implies the enabling power of the Holy Spirit.)

After laying the groundwork of God's promises, I turned to the commands. With the promises firmly in place, I and the congregation experienced the commands more for what they are: not burdensome but rather reasonable, righteous, and good. The feeling of synergy between promise and command was palpable. The commands "Do not neglect," "Be diligent," and "Give yourself wholly" told us how to follow through on the promises, how to avoid short-circuiting the loving and gracious promise of God. The promises brought joy, hope, and faith—and thus empowerment. My sermon felt more whole, more like gospel, than it would have otherwise.

In many ways, paying close attention to the relationship between promise and command resembles the classic indicative-imperative sermon form, or gospel-and-its-implications form. In these forms we state who God is and what he has done for us in Christ, and then we apply that to how we should live for him. Although it may just be a difference in terminology, seeing the relationship between promise and com-

mand, and our corresponding faith and obedience, definitely made lights come on for me. For me the emphasis on faith makes everything fit.

As my example from 1 Timothy 4 shows, at times we may need to broaden our horizon from the preaching text to the context of the book or Testament or entire Bible to fill out the theology of promise or command.

Conversely, suppose the sermon text is Philippians 4:19: "My God will supply all your needs according to his glorious riches in Christ Jesus." Here is a clear promise from our God. But what is the obligation inherent in that promise? The immediate context of Philippians 4:10–18 shows us. We must be content in our relationship with the Lord, and we should be willing to give to support the work of God. That, of course, is specifically commanded in the wider New Testament context of Matthew 6:33 and Hebrews 13:5–6.

As we consider the promise side of the equation, the sort of truths that qualify as a promise are not just verses like Philippians 4:19, where God addresses us in the second person, "I promise to do this for you." Promise is broader than that. It includes the truth statements of Scripture that call us to trust. For example, in the affirmation "God is love," God promises "I love you." In the statement "God is righteous," God promises, "I will always act toward you in a righteous way."

Two questions give us the ability to see complementary promises and commands. The lens for finding promises is the question, "What must we believe if we are to have the faith-ability to obey this command?" And the lens for finding commands is the question, "How does God expect us to live based on faith in this promise?"

Answering these questions empowers hearers to obey.

Chapter 79

HELPING HEARERS PRACTICE WHAT WE PREACH
How to avoid adding to people's burdens

Randy Frazee

In Luke 11:46, Jesus said, "You experts in the law, woe to you, because you load people down with burdens they can hardly carry, and you yourselves will not lift one finger to help them." Preachers need to be careful they are not doing the same thing today.

HOW TO KEEP SERMONS FROM BEING BURDENSOME

We must be realistic. The experts in the law gave themselves full-time to the law. The people could not. Often we are not careful in our application to give people sustainable, realistic steps. If people took us at our word and tried to apply everything we asked them to do in just the last eight sermons, they could not achieve that. They would need to quit their jobs and move to a monastery to pull it off. People get exasperated and eventually stop trying.

Give simple and specific application. "Here is one thing you can do." When we prepare our sermons, application is often the last thing on the agenda, and as a result it gets the short end of the stick. We need to ask ourselves, Does the congregation know what I'm recommending?

Balance diagnosis and prescription. It is easier and safer to spend the majority of our time on the problem. But when we spend ninety percent of our sermon diagnosing the problem and little time prescribing, we often fail to make application that is specific.

Be biblical. That means to eliminate man-made stuff that makes it hard on people. The Pharisees made human rules and traditions. Biblical preaching is more grace-filled and accessible.

Preach for impact. Preach to change lives rather than to make an impression. The agenda of the experts in the law was for the people to walk away impressed with them. There is a fundamental difference between wanting to impact people and wanting to hear people say, "Wow, he's got a lot of Bible knowledge," or "He is really spiritual."

Shifting away from impressing people to impacting them will move us away from some of the downsides of the Pharisees. They had a self-esteem, identity thing wrapped up in their preaching. If we are honest with ourselves, we do as well. We are human too, and preaching is a tempting place to try to impress people. Seeking impact fundamentally changes the decisions we make about what we say and what we don't say.

WHAT SERMONS CAN ACCOMPLISH

A sermon can motivate people. The way we motivate, however, affects whether the sermon is empowering or disempowering. We need to major not in what we are against but in what we are for. A sermon disempowers people when we spend an enormous amount of time preaching what we are against.

One of the most significant challenges in my preaching ministry came when a colleague said, "I want you to do something that someone challenged me to do. Listen to a couple of your sermon tapes and diagnose the percentage of time you spend preaching against things versus preaching for things." I consider myself to be a sanguine, positive person, but when I followed through on his suggestion, I was appalled at how easy it was to spend the majority of my time preaching against something. It is much more difficult to say, "Here is what we are going to live for."

For example, it is easy to tell people not to watch TV. It is more difficult to tell them what the alternative is. It is easy to preach against abortion. It is more difficult to give people a vision of the alternative.

A sermon can brag on people instead of scolding them. I think of preaching as similar to raising children. Whenever kids have a success, you stand up and brag on them.

Recently I was encouraged by my congregation's response to community needs. Instead of preaching, "We need to step up to the plate and do more," I said, "I'm overwhelmed by what you have been doing. I just want to say how proud I am of you." That motivates. We are often so busy giving people the next thing to do, we do not stop and celebrate. We may say, "I'm really proud of what you've done, but let's do more." Instead if we will simply brag on the congregation, they leave saying, "My gosh, the pastor said we were doing a good job and didn't give us anything else to do!"

A sermon allows us to be vulnerable about our struggles but passionate about change. We may find it hard to be vulnerable because, again, we are struggling to be impressive rather than to impact. I find there is tremendous

impact when I am vulnerable. But I do not want to leave people just with the sense that I made a mistake; I want them to sense that I am passionate about what Christ can do to bring change in my life.

Recently my daughter lost my wife's cell phone, and I was having a really bad day. I had been trying to call my wife all day on her cell phone, and I found out later—when it was too late for me to get what I wanted—that my daughter had left the phone in the mall somewhere. I told them, "You need to go back and look at every store. I don't care what it takes." I was hard on both my wife and my daughter.

In the car later that day I was not paying attention to my driving as I dialed my cell phone, and my car swerved, hit the curb, and blew out one of my tires, destroying the wheel. The repairs cost me $500. When I later called my wife, she told me they could not find the cell phone. I said, "Put Jennifer (my daughter) on the phone."

She said, "No, Jennifer doesn't want to talk to you." I asked my wife why. She said, "Because she is afraid of what you're going to say." That was reasonable based on how I had acted earlier.

I said, "Put her on the phone." I basically said to my daughter, "The cell phone you lost is going to cost about twenty dollars to replace, and I do think you were irresponsible. But your dad was irresponsible and ruined his car wheel, and it's going to cost five hundred dollars. I will cut you some slack if you will cut me some slack."

Sharing that with the congregation gave people a sense that I was vulnerable but also have a passion to change. We underestimate how powerful that kind of preaching is to our people.

WHAT SERMONS CANNOT ACCOMPLISH

A sermon can't do what a testimony can do. Testimony is powerful. I was part of a team of pastors invited to evaluate *The Prince of Egypt* film a number of years ago. Someone asked Jeffrey Katzenberg, "How did you choose Moses as your first animation for this new production house?"

He replied that Walt Disney taught to do animation only when you cannot adequately depict the picture in real life.

Rick Warren later said, "A similar idea holds true with testimony versus drama. Don't do drama when you have someone in your congregation who is living it out." That hit home with me. We now do about ninety percent testimony and ten percent drama. I found that while drama is great, I prefer live testimony after the sermon that shows somebody who has been struggling with what we have been talking about, and they want to give a progress report. (Never do a "here is a person who has made it" testimony. Always say, "Here is a progress report.")

When we evaluate a worship service, we ask, "What was the inspiration point?" and often, when we have a testimony, the inspiration point was the testimony more than my message. I have to be comfortable with that. While I will share my testimony and try to be vulnerable with inspiring, real-life examples, there is just something about an average person that people often relate to more than to me. They expect me (the pastor) to be good, but when they see a banker or a homemaker talking about it, there can be a greater connection.

A sermon cannot provide what community can. Community gives the opportunity for modeling. Interaction does something life on life that my sermon cannot do. I need to ensure there is an outlet of community for my congregation because without it my preaching will fall short.

A sermon cannot do what the Holy Spirit alone can do. The Holy Spirit certainly works through our preaching, but the Holy Spirit also works through a person's crisis. We cannot expedite the personal crisis that brings about transformation. Preachers need to give themselves a break. We need to realize we cannot manage the disobedience of people in our congregation. That is the work of the Holy Spirit.

First John 5:3 says, "His commands are not burdensome." At the same time, in the Great Commission, Jesus said to teach people to obey *everything* he commanded. We need to find ways to do this without burdening people.

TEACHING PEOPLE TO OBEY

We need to show that we are all in process. On one occasion I told the congregation about how my wife and I once went to our son and asked him to forgive us for a disagreement that broke out between us in his presence. Telling that story did not impress our congregation, but it had great impact on them. When we uncover that even in a pastor's home we struggle and sin emerges, we move away from impressing hearers to transforming hearers. The impact comes from how my wife and I handled it on the other side. Some parents have never gone to their children and said, "Will you forgive me?"

We need to preach theologically, not randomly. If you go to church for ten years and hear six hundred sermons but have no framework to think about what the preacher is saying, it is burdensome. So I try to teach biblical theology in a systematic way, providing thirty categories under which to sort all our thoughts. Systemization helps people assimilate our thoughts into their understanding. People begin to see recurring theological themes.

In every sermon I say something like, "What we are talking about today fits under worship," or some other category. Some people have resisted that notion because they think we are putting God in a box. But the categorization is not the message; it is an educational delivery system to keep people from being burdened.

We must preach biblical morality, not cultural morality. When we confuse biblical and cultural morality, our preaching becomes burdensome. What we have to say about music, movies, TV, and frequency of church attendance can be cultural morals. In addition, if we are not careful, our preaching can develop a political agenda.

Cultural morality is often legalistic and thus burdensome. Biblical morality is not legalistic at all. Biblical morality is filled with grace and freedom. Whenever we address issues of morality, we have to ask ourselves, Is my teaching cultural or biblical?

We must preach being more than doing. Preach, "Here is the vision of what Jesus wants you to become," not, "Here are ten things you should do." Long lists of things to do are burdensome; growing in the fruit of the Spirit is freedom.

We must integrate our preaching with the life and spiritual disciplines of the church in order to empower obedience. Our preaching alone does not provide the full empowerment people need. Preaching can inspire, but our churches need many more components to empower growth.

For example, we encourage personal study by writing study guides. We distribute study guides for nursery children through twelfth grade, as well as for adults, that relate directly to the sermons. Our home groups are another component that complements the preaching.

We are also discovering the benefit of an altar response in wrapping up the preaching experience. I have been pastor at Pantego since 1990, and I have long heard from experts that the seeker struggles with the altar experience. But the secular seeker has now become the spiritual seeker. The spiritual seeker is moved by watching people show their dependence on God publicly. They do not mind it; in fact, they prefer it. They came to see and experience it— as long as they are not forced to participate.

Some people who have come to Christ in our church have cited the inspiration point not as something I said but something I said tied to watching people respond to it. They had to admit that kind of humility and dependence on God is something they did not have, and that was the inspirational turning point for them. Responding to a sermon by coming forward to an area of prayer and ministry is powerful not only for the person who comes forward but also for the seeker witnessing it, if it is done properly. So at the end of the service we provide fifteen minutes or more for this.

And we have done something completely out of the ordinary for a contemporary Bible church: We built three communion stations. People can come forward, kneel, and have someone administer communion to them. We found people will come down and take communion for all kinds of things going on in their lives. Often people feel something urging them in corporate worship to show their dependence publicly on God and to honor him, but without a communion station they would not know what to do once they come forward. Communion has given people something tangible to do. It has also increased the number of people who go to pray with one of our elders or prayer counselors, because the pressure is off—they do not feel singled out, because lines of people are responding in communion.

The response time at the altar is not limited to people who have a moral problem or who are wanting to come to new faith in Christ. I say things like, "You may be coming down to pray for somebody. You may be coming down because you have a job interview tomorrow and need prayer. You may want to come forward on something completely unrelated to what I have said today in the sermon." I often list what I call the four rashes—health, finances, relationships, or career. So I initially present specific things in relationship to the sermon and then make a broad appeal.

The altar response finishes out a sermon by giving an opportunity for people to experience a conscious response of the will while their hearts are still touched. Making room for this is one of the most profound things we have done in the last couple of years.

Chapter 80

THE HERESY OF APPLICATION

It's when we're applying Scripture that error most likely creeps in

Haddon Robinson

More heresy is preached in application than in Bible exegesis. Preachers want to be faithful to the Scriptures, and going through seminary, they have learned exegesis. But they may not have firmly learned how to make the journey from the biblical text to the modern world. They get out of seminary and realize the preacher's question is application: How do you take this text and determine what it means for this audience?

Sometimes we apply the text in ways that might make the biblical writer say, "Wait a minute, that's the wrong use of what I said." This is the heresy of a good truth applied in the wrong way.

For example, I heard someone preach a sermon from Ruth on how to deal with in-laws.

Now, it's true that in Ruth you have in-laws. The problem is, the book of Ruth was not written to give advice on how to solve in-law problems. That sermon had a lot of practical advice, but it didn't come from the Scriptures.

But what's the problem, you may ask, with preaching something true and useful, even if it's not the central thrust of your text or not what the writer had in mind? Well, when we preach the Bible, we preach with biblical authority. As Augustine said, what the Bible says, God says. Therefore, we are bringing to bear on, say, this in-law problem, the full authority of God. A person hearing the sermon thinks, *If I don't deal with my mother-in-law this way, I am disobedient to God.* That's a rape of the Bible. You're saying what God doesn't say. Through this process you undermine the Scriptures. Ultimately, people come to believe that anything with a biblical flavor is what God says.

The long-term effect is that we preach a mythology. Myth has an element of truth along with a great deal of puff, and people tend to live in the puff. They live with the implications of implications, and then they discover that what they thought God promised, he didn't promise.

A week ago I talked with a young woman whose husband had left her. She said, "I have tried to be submissive. Doesn't the Bible say if a wife submits, she'll have a happy and successful marriage?"

"No," I said, "the Bible doesn't say that."

She said, "I've gone to seminars and heard that."

"What the Bible says is you have a responsibility as a wife. A husband also has a responsibility. But the best you may have is a C marriage. There is no guarantee you will have an A marriage."

THE DIFFICULT BRIDGE FROM THEN TO NOW

In application we attempt to take what we believe is the truth of the eternal God, given in a particular time, place, and situation, and apply it to people in the modern world, who live in another time, another place, and a very different situation. That is harder than it appears.

The Bible is specific, but my audience is general. For example, a man listening to a sermon can identify with David committing adultery with Bathsheba, but he's not a king, and he doesn't command armies. We have to take this text that is historically specific and determine how the living God speaks from it to people today.

Preachers can make that journey in different ways. One is to take the biblical text straight over to the modern situation. In some cases, that works well. For example, Jesus says, "Love your enemies." I say to my listeners: "Do you have enemies? Love them."

But then I turn the page, and Jesus says, "Sell what you have, give to the poor, and follow me." I hesitate to bring this straight over because I think, *If everybody does this, we'll have problems, big problems.*

Some texts look as though they can come straight over to my contemporary audience, but not necessarily. I need to know something about the circumstances of both my text and of my audience. For example, I may ask the question, as many Christians did in the last century, "Is slavery wrong?" I go to Paul, who tells slaves to obey their master. But I discover when I get into his world that he's not necessarily answering my questions about the nineteenth century in America, because the slavery Paul talks about isn't the slavery we knew in the United States in the nineteenth century.

In the first century, people sold themselves into slavery because they were economically better off as slaves, protected by their owners, than they were free. Most slaves were freed by age thirty, because in that day maintaining slaves was economically difficult. Roman law said an owner could not handle slaves any way he wanted to. And if you walked down the streets of Rome, you could not tell the slaves from the free men by the color of their skin. If I don't realize that Paul's situation and mine are different, I may apply Paul's advice about slaves in a way it was never intended.

Another difficulty is that Paul talks to people I cannot see or hear. It's like overhearing one half of a telephone conversation. I think I know what the other person is saying, but I can't be sure. I can only guess at the full conversation from what I hear one person saying. The questions the biblical writer answers are not necessarily my questions.

There are signals that may indicate we are confusing the questions. We should remember that a text cannot mean what it has never meant. That is, when Paul wrote to people in his day, he expected them to understand what he meant. For example, we have some thirty different explanations for what Paul meant when he wrote the Corinthians about the baptism for the dead. But the people who read that letter the first time didn't say, "I wonder what he meant by that." They may have had further questions, but the meaning of the subject was clear to them.

I cannot make that passage mean something today that it did not mean in principle in the ancient world. That's why I have to do exegesis. I have to be honest with the text before I can come over to the contemporary world.

LADDER OF ABSTRACTION

I picture a "ladder of abstraction" that comes up from the biblical world and crosses over and down to the modern setting. I have to be conscious how I cross this "abstraction ladder." I want to make sure the biblical situation and the current situation are analogous at the points I am making them connect. I must be sure the center of the analogy connects, not the extremes.

Sometimes, as I work with a text, I have to climb the abstraction ladder until I reach the text's intent. For instance, Leviticus says, "Don't boil a kid in its mother's milk." First, you have to ask, "What is this all about?" At face value, you might think, *If I have a young goat, and I want to cook it in its mother's milk for dinner tonight, I should think twice.* But we

now know the pagans did that when they worshiped their idolatrous gods. Therefore, what you have here is not a prohibition against boiling a kid in its mother's milk but against being involved in the idolatry that surrounded God's people or against bringing its practices into their religion.

If that's the case, it does no good for the preacher to bring this text straight over. You must climb the ladder of abstraction a couple of levels until you reach the principle: You should not associate yourself with idolatrous worship, even in ways that do not seem to have direct association with physically going to the idol.

Let's say you know that a passage can't come straight across. What can you do?

Abstract up to God. One thing I always do when climbing the abstraction ladder is abstract up to God. Every passage has a vision of God, such as God as Creator or Sustainer.

Find the depravity factor. Next I ask, "What is the depravity factor? What in humanity rebels against that vision of God?"

These first two questions are a helpful clue in application because God remains the same and human depravity remains the same. Our depravity may look different, but it's the same pride, obstinacy, and disobedience.

Take 1 Corinthians 8, in which Paul addresses the subject of eating meat offered to idols. *The vision of God*: He is our Redeemer. Therefore, Paul argues, I will not eat meat, because if I wound my brother's weak conscience, I sin against Christ, who redeemed him. *The depravity factor*: People want their rights, so they don't care that Christ died for their brother.

THUS SAITH THE LORD?

Today's preachers approach the task of

application different from that of previous generations. Today, what's prevalent is specific application. In the past, application was often more general—trust God and give him glory. Today, preaching deals with how to have a happy marriage, how to bring up your children, how to deal with stress.

Of course, there are always times I find myself saying, "I wish I hadn't applied a passage quite like that." In my twenties I preached some things I believed deeply then, but now I wonder, *How in the world did I come up with that?* I remember, for example, believing that headship meant the husband ought to take care of the finances. Worse, my wife insists that in one of my sermons on marriage, I made the point that a wife ought not serve her husband instant coffee!

Obviously that particular application came out of the culture of that day more than anything else. It preached well. In those days I used anything that popped into my head that looked like it applied. The awful thing was I said in the name of God what God was not saying. Is it disobedience against God for the wife to keep the checkbook? Of course not. Asking the question, "Does this rank at the level of obedience?" is a good test of sermon application.

Of course, occasionally, you can't say, "This is a matter of obedience to God." We want to have a "Thus saith the Lord" about specific things in people's lives, but we can't always have that. So we need to distinguish between various types of implications from the text. Implications may be necessary, probable, possible, improbable, or impossible.

For example, a necessary implication of "You shall not commit adultery" is you cannot have a sexual relationship with a person who is not your spouse. A probable implication is you ought to be very careful of strong bonding friendships with a person who is not your spouse. A possible implication is you ought not travel regularly to conventions or other places with a person who is not your spouse. An improbable conclusion is you should not at any time have lunch with someone who is not your spouse. An impossible implication is you ought not have dinner with another couple because you are at the same table with a person who is not your spouse.

Too often preachers give to a possible implication all the authority of a necessary implication, which is at the level of obedience. Only with necessary implications can you preach, "Thus saith the Lord."

There are different ways to phrase such distinctions in the pulpit. One way is to say, "This is the principle, and the principle is clear. How this principle applies in our lives may differ with different people in different situations."

For example, the principle of honoring one's parents is not negotiable. But do you keep an elderly parent at home, or do you put the parent in a nursing home? You may want to say, "To honor your parent you ought to keep him at home." But someone may say, "I have three children, and my parent wanders the house in the middle of the night, waking the kids and disrupting the household, and it's hurting the kids." Now we have principles in tension. That application may disappoint many congregations because they like to be told exactly what to do.

It might feel as if we are eviscerating our authority to say, "Think about it." But at times that may be the most effective thing I can do for a congregation because the world that people live in often has conflicting principles. By generalizing, we often miss the contradictions and tensions in the Bible.

For example, the book of Job balances the

theology of Proverbs. Proverbs teaches cause and effect. Job's friends basically recite Proverbs to Job, but there is an ingredient they don't know about—what's going on in heaven.

The Wisdom Literature says, "In general, this is the way God's world works." But we cannot say if a person is hurting and seemingly being punished that he or she must have been disobedient. Disobedience does bring punishment, but not all apparent punishment is a result of disobedience.

The Bible does that kind of thing all the time. We can call it "the balance of harmonious opposites." We all live with that sort of tension. Therefore, when applying the text, it's more important to get people to think Christianly than to act religiously.

HOW GENRE AFFECTS APPLICATION

Bible genres have a direct effect on application as well. The most extensive Bible genre is story. We have to ask, Why does the Bible give us so much narrative? Why didn't God just come right out and say what he meant and not beat around the bush with stories? If I were God and were going to give something that would last until the end of time, I would have said, "Here are five principles about my will." But he doesn't do that.

Therefore, it's dangerous to go into a narrative and say, "Here are three things we learn about the providence of God." That's not the way the biblical writers chose to handle it. If we believe the Bible to be the inspired Word of God, we have to consider the methods used to proclaim God's message.

What is the harm in using a three-point structure or five-principles structure? It may have been foreign to the writer, but it may be helpful to today's listener. It is not a deadly sin.

But what I need to bring out when I preach from stories are the tensions. Here are real people being directed by God and responding to God. The purpose of these stories is not to say at the end, "You must, you should." The purpose is to give insight into how men and women relate to the eternal God and how God relates to them.

In a sermon on Joseph's life, for example, I might say, "A lot of life doesn't seem to make sense. You make plans, but they don't come about. You're true to God, but you aren't rewarded for it. If that's where you are, here's a man who experienced that."

I'm not going to tell people that Joseph's experience will be like their experience. Rather I will say, "The great tension in the life of Joseph is a tension we all feel." I will apply what is a universal experience.

You can deal abstractly with a great principle—God is sovereign—in a way that gets boring. Such a sermon reminds me of a hovercraft that floats eight feet above the ground but never lands into life. Without the human element, you lose the specific, the historical narrative, the emotional interaction.

THE HOLY SPIRIT AND THE WORD

The Holy Spirit has a direct role in the process of applying the text to the listener's life. The Spirit answers to the Word. If I am faithful to the Scriptures, I give the Spirit of God something to work on that he doesn't have if I'm preaching *Reader's Digest*.

I have a formula: Pain + time + insight = change. Sometimes people go through pain over a period of time, but that doesn't change them. But pain and time plus insight will, and that's where the preacher comes in.

This explains why on a given Sunday the sermon is a wide yawn for many. Even with the greatest preachers, not every sermon stirs everybody. But other people will say to you, "You can't imagine how that spoke to me." They didn't come to church neutral; they came with pain suffered over a period of time. They received insight from the sermon, it clicked, and change occurred in their life.

Several years ago I was out of sorts with God. When I came to church one Sunday, the preacher was not particularly good, but he dealt with the biblical text. I did not want to read that biblical text, but I couldn't get away from it. The preacher did not apply the text to my situation, but the Word itself got through to me in such a way that after the service I had to go for a long drive. It was one of those moments when you say, "God has confronted me, and it's going to be dangerous business if I don't listen." It was as though that passage and that preacher and the Spirit had picked me out of the crowd. The sermon was not eloquent, but that passage and his sticking with it drove home the truth to my life.

That's the greatness of preaching. Something can always happen when a preacher takes God's Word seriously.

Chapter 81

PREACHING FOR TRUE HOLINESS
Why we can't divorce theology from application

Randal Pelton

Preaching that produces true holiness is in some ways counterintuitive—even for those committed to sound, biblical preaching. Those who preach in series exposition can be especially vulnerable to preaching an unbalanced message that actually hinders holiness. Preaching that leads to fully biblical obedience has two features.

PREACH THEOLOGICAL TEXTS WITH A VIEW TOWARD THE PRACTICAL

The first step of obedience is not, "Do this," but rather, "Believe this and receive this."

Some texts have both theology and application. For example, 1 Peter 1:1–2 contains a strong connection between theology and application, between who we are as Christians and how we're supposed to live as Christians. Peter writes, "To [those] ... who have been chosen ... for obedience." Preaching this text means preaching both theology and practice, and keeping them together isn't hard.

The problem comes when the link between the theological and practical isn't spelled out. When the text says nothing about how we are to live, it's easy to neglect holiness. To correct this, at some point in the sermon the information about what God has done for us or who we are as Christians must lead to how that gives us the ability to battle temptation and sin and grow in Christlike conduct.

Theological truths are key to practical Christian living because grace and faith are keys to holiness. Bryan Chapell writes: "Grace overwhelms us with God's love, and as a result our heart resonates with the desires of God. His purposes become our own" (*Holiness by Grace* [Crossway, 2001], p. 13). He also writes: "Sanctification is the work of God's grace in us that allows us to receive the benefits and power of Jesus, which in turn enables us to overcome the evil that can so burden our hearts" (p. 41).

The theological sections of the New Testament letters display God's loving grace. Preaching to bring about holiness means asking our parishioners to respond to God's gracious love and care with wholehearted obedience.

Of course, that presupposes that we believe what has been written. John Piper writes, "The way to fight sin in our lives is to battle our bent toward unbelief. Or to put it more positively: the way to pursue righteousness and love is to fight for faith in future grace" (*Future Grace* [Multnomah, 1995], p. 219). Chapell agrees that faith is paramount to holiness: "To find release from the bondage and burden of sin . . . we must believe that we can rely entirely on our union with Christ to make us right with God" (*Holiness by Grace,* p. 41).

Because grace and faith are instrumental to holiness, whenever we preach from theological sections of God's Word, we must ask ourselves and our parishioners to believe what God has done and receive the grace that sets us free to be holy. The text itself may not ask us to turn from sin, but turning from sin is the proper response to the revelation of God's gracious love.

PREACH THE PRACTICAL WHILE LOOKING BACK TO THE THEOLOGICAL

At first glance it appears easy to preach from the New Testament imperatives in such a way that holiness results. If holiness is Christlikeness and if the biblical commands show us what a Christlike life is like, then it makes sense that urging hearers to obey the commands will lead to holiness.

Yes and no. Yes, because by encouraging obedience to Christ, we're on the right track to holiness. No, because by encouraging obedience to the command alone, we may end up creating self-righteousness that leads us off the track to true holiness.

Take, for instance, God's command in 1 Peter 4:9: "Offer hospitality to one another without grumbling." After explaining what it means to be hospitable to each other and to do so without complaining, then comes the task of telling parishioners, "Do that." And for those of us who want God's Word to hit home, we're going to take a shot at helping them see in concrete ways how to be hospitable without complaining. It's at this point we are in danger of moving away from true holiness even though it appears that through application we're moving closer to holiness.

If we neglect the theological side of the equation—who God is and who we are because of what God did for us through Christ—then what are we left with for application-type statements? They might sound like this: Create a list of people you would like to have in your home, then set aside time in your weekly calendar to invite the folks on your list into your home.

Is this helpful? Yes. Spirit-sensitive Christians may find practical help in these suggestions. But notice that the suggestions work for anyone,

Christian or non-Christian. Biblical holiness, then, is not necessarily the result. Piper writes: "Practical, daily righteousness is attained when the law of righteousness is pursued by faith, not by works" (*Future Grace*, p. 220).

Normally, naturally, we attack specific temptations and sin at the point of action. If the specific temptation is Internet pornography, then we address this problem with action steps: Don't randomly surf the web; do not stay up late at night by yourself on the computer. We normally do not fight specific temptation and sin at the point of belief.

But the first step of obedience is not, "Do this," but rather, "Believe this and receive this." To say, "Receive this," is to invite our folks to receive the power that overcame and overcomes sin.

For God to create holiness in us, we must move from the biblical command back to the gospel, especially at the moment of application. Prior to the presentation of practical steps for victory, be sure to help hearers to see what God has done for them through the sacrifice of Jesus Christ. Help them first to respond to his grace and believe it. Then they will be assured of his power to conquer temptation. Otherwise, all we do is help people attempt to live like Christians on their own effort—the opposite of true holiness.

The move from the practical to the theological assures that the modification of a person's character is the result of a heart transformed by grace. Jesus' death, burial, resurrection, and ascension become the motivation and ability for obedience.

Chapter 82

LESS JOE, MORE JESUS
When preaching is too much about us

Joe Stowell

I am passionate about calling followers of Christ to a renewed commitment to focus their lives and aspirations on the person of Jesus Christ. One of the preacher's dilemmas is that preaching is so much about us.

ASKING THE RIGHT QUESTIONS

Preaching has a way of sucking us down into the bog of *To whom am I preaching? Will they like me? Will they listen?* That's the pre-agony.

The post-agony is *Did I do well? Did I get my point across? Oh, I should have said it this way; I should have said it that way.*

If we're not careful, preaching becomes all about the preacher. I have been convicted about that, and though I don't have any easy formulas on how to extract myself from these demons, I do know that my preaching must be more and more about Jesus. I should concentrate on issues like: *Did I lift Jesus up? What would he have thought about my sermon? Did my listeners see him more clearly? Do they find him more compelling because of my sermon? Did I represent him and his calling in our lives in a winsome and yet authoritative way?*

Preaching needs to be Christocentric. Jesus is the story line of the Bible, the Creator of the universe, the pinnacle revelation of God. The Holy Spirit within me does the ministry of glorifying Jesus Christ, and Jesus shows me what God the Father is like. Jesus really is the focal point.

DRAWING PEOPLE TO JESUS

But so often, Jesus gets lost in it all—in our preaching and in our churches. Instead, it's the worship group, the music, the setting, the auditorium, the preacher. Everything is man-centered. I wonder if Jesus feels like the body at an Irish wake: Nobody expects him to sing, but they can't have the party without him.

When Marty and I escape to England every once in a while, we attend a tiny village church where about twenty villagers show up. The pastor stands off to the side. The organ is behind us. The main image that catches your attention is a statue of Jesus on the cross. A woman and a man are on each side looking up in adoring awe at Jesus on the cross. I think that's what we

miss. We haven't worked to create church and to drive our preaching in ways to draw people's hearts and minds to Jesus Christ.

When I turned fifty, I realized I'd been very busy for God, working, working, working. Suddenly I had this longing for God that my busyness had buried. I wanted to go deeper. I wanted to know Jesus like Paul says in Philippians 3, that I would count all things loss—that I would finally get out of the way and know Jesus in my life. I thought, This is what it's really all about, isn't it? That began to impact my preaching. When people hear me preach on a regular basis, my prayer is that they hear more about Jesus than they used to. I want their hearts and minds drawn to him, his character, his call, and the beauty of his holiness in a life-transforming way. At the end of the day in my sermons and ministry, I hope people forget who I am and see Jesus Christ.

I find myself going more to the narrative texts in the Gospels to where Jesus is in action. I'm also more intent to see all of Scripture in its Christological flow, from Jesus as Creator in Genesis 1 to ultimate Redeemer and Consummator in Revelation 21. Whether in the Old or New Testament, I want to end up at the Jesus issue that is in the text and to draw a life-changing application based on him.

Chapter 83

PREACHING THAT PROMOTES SELF-CENTEREDNESS

How to avoid stirring up the wrong motives

Craig Brian Larson

How is a sermon like aspirin?

The answer: You take aspirin with one purpose in mind, but it has unintended side effects, both good and bad. If you take aspirin for a headache, you get pain relief—and a secondary benefit, for doctors say one aspirin a day can prevent heart attacks. On the other hand, you might suffer the side effect of an upset stomach.

Sermons, too, have side effects. One is what we say about motives for obedience.

For example, if the text calls people to use their spiritual gifts, we could offer many reasons to obey, such as the desire to be a faithful steward, to serve God, to build the church, to grow personally, to fulfill one's purpose, to express love to others, to say thank you to God, to imitate Jesus, to glorify God.

Whichever motivations we choose, we teach an important lesson about proper motivations. When your sermon says, "Use your spiritual gift because you will build the church," you say indirectly, "Building the church is a good thing that should motivate you." This is indirect because normally we do not take time to justify that motive.

WHY TEACH WHY

Choosing proper motives is important because righteousness has three characteristics: what we do, how we do it, and why we do it.

If I am a restaurant cook, for example, the what of righteousness is to do what my employer requires: prepare orders according to house recipes. The how of righteousness is to cook in a sanitary way—no putting potatoes dropped on the floor into the pot. Finally, the why of righteousness is to cook to please the Lord. I must not cook motivated by greed and selfish ambition—to curry favor with staff and customers so I can steal them away when I start my own restaurant.

Each week our sermons train believers in the third characteristic of righteousness: why do right, and usually this sermon is unintended. It is the hidden sermon.

UPSET STOMACHS

This indirect sermon can have harmful side effects.

Our greatest challenge in training motives is to change a believer's orbit. Under the full control of their sinful nature, people are self-centered. They have the planetary mass of Jupiter, with God and other people orbiting around them like tiny moons. When people turn to Christ in faith, God begins the revolutionary process of transforming them to be other-centered and God-centered. They begin to see themselves in proper relation to the value of others and the greatness of God. Increasingly they orbit the massive, glorious sun of God's will.

Self-centered deeds do not please God. "All a man's ways seem innocent to him, but motives are weighed by the LORD" (Proverbs 16:2). "[The Lord] will bring to light what is hidden in darkness and will expose the motives of men's hearts" (1 Cor. 4:5).

The harmful side effect of some preaching is that we appeal to self-interest in a way that encourages hearers to continue in an utterly self-centered way of life.

Not that we should never appeal to self-interest. Jesus did constantly. For example, he asked, "What good is it for a man to gain the whole world, and yet lose or forfeit his very self?" (Luke 9:25). While Jesus said to deny yourself and take up your cross, he also said, "Give, and it will be given to you" (Luke 6:38), and "Store up for yourselves treasures in heaven" (Matt. 6:20). Jesus and the New Testament writers teach both a denial of self on the one hand and a sanctified self-interest on the other. With sanctified self-interest we seek what is best for ourselves in a different way and for a different reason. We seek our interests God's way for God's glory rather than our way for our glory.

Theologian Wayne Grudem lists the following as examples of motivations found in the New Testament (*Systematic Theology* [Zondervan: 1994], pp. 757–58):

- the desire to please God and express our love to him
- the need to keep a clear conscience before God
- the desire to be a "vessel for noble use" and have increased effectiveness in the work of the kingdom
- the desire to see unbelievers come to Christ through observing our lives
- the desire to receive present blessings from God on our lives and ministries

- the desire to avoid God's displeasure and discipline on our lives (sometimes called "the fear of God")
- the desire to seek greater heavenly reward
- the desire for a deeper walk with God
- the desire that angels would glorify God for our obedience
- the desire for peace and joy in our lives
- the desire to do what God commands, simply because his commands are right, and we delight in doing what is right

FINDING RIGHT MOTIVES

So how do we select the right motive to emphasize? The good news is the correct motives for obedience are almost always given in our sermon text. God is way ahead of us! Preaching the motives in the text keeps us from defaulting to an appeal either to self-centeredness, to self-interest alone, or unthinkingly, almost as a cliché, to the glory of God. Either way, we may overlook the why in the text. When we fully illumine the text, our hearers are most likely to develop holy motivations.

For example, we might be surprised at the variety of sanctified reasons/motives Paul offers in 2 Corinthians 9 for giving money to kingdom purposes:

- to be a good example to others (vv. 1–5)
- to avoid shame (vv. 1–5)
- to keep your promises (vv. 1–5)
- to delight the Lord (v. 7)
- to see God's grace abound to us, resulting in financial abundance that will both meet our needs and enable us to give even more generously to others (vv. 6, 8, 10, 11)
- to grow in righteousness (vv. 9–10)
- to meet the needs of God's people (v. 12)
- to prove ourselves as obedient followers of Christ (v. 13)

- to enable people to express more thanksgiving and praise to God (vv. 11–13)
- so that others will pray for us (v. 14)

The sermon on this text that appeals to self-centeredness focuses on give-to-get and can foster greed. It ignores the clear principle that we are to replant the increased harvest from the seed of giving. The more we receive the more we give. Further, we give not just for our own benefit but also for God and other believers.

At the other end of the spectrum, the sermon uncomfortable with sanctified self-interest tries to explain away the harvest principle. It suggests that to give in order to receive is ignoble. This, too, distorts the text. We may take this approach because of an either-or mentality about motives. In reality, people rarely make choices for just one reason, but rather, for many.

When we appeal to the motives in the text, we develop highly motivated, God-centered disciples who obey Christ for the right reasons and please God to a fuller degree.

Chapter 84

THE DANGER OF PRACTICAL PREACHING
Why people need more than the bottom line

Lee Eclov

Rob, a stockbroker, thought sermons should be twenty minutes—no longer than that. To him, a good sermon was what others call the conclusion. "Cut to the bottom line," he said. "That's what I expect at work, and that's what I want at church."

Stan, a preacher, didn't see length as the issue, but he was determined every sermon be "practical." He preached on five principles of friendships, six secrets of managing money, and four ways to win over worry. He believed in sound doctrine, but he felt he had to give people something they could take to work on Monday morning.

These men illustrate two fallacies about biblical preaching: The Bottom Line Fallacy and the Practical Fallacy. Both reveal a misunderstanding, not merely of preaching, but of the workings of Scripture.

Picture a wilderness. A pioneer carves out a path, chopping away brush, felling trees, marking the way to a new outpost. As years pass, that path is traveled a thousand times till it becomes a wide, paved road. From it, other trails branch off, leading to other new outposts. Trails intersect, becoming crossroads. More outposts become towns. More trails become roads. More links are made till what was once wilderness is civilized.

Preaching is the work of spiritually civilizing the minds of Christian disciples. Preaching—especially expository preaching—cuts truth trails in the minds of our listeners. Our task is not only to display God's "point" but to instill God's logic—how he gets to that point.

For example, we do not simply preach the conclusion of 1 Corinthians 13—that "the greatest of these is love"—but we move people through the dimensions and definitions of love in that great chapter. We show that Paul intended such love be not only at weddings but also at church meetings. In other words, we not only establish the outpost—"the greatest of these is love"—but the truth trail as well.

But here is where we confront the fallacies.

BOTTOM LINE FALLACY

When our goal is to "bottom line" our preaching, we look in our text for the "so what" and preach that conclusion. For example, our sermon drives home the truth that we need not be afraid. If we have been effective, our brothers and sisters will go home with this outpost of truth established or enlarged in their thinking. But here's the rub. On Tuesday, when some frightening crisis looms in their lives, they may remember, "The Bible says we are not to be afraid," but they don't know how to be strong. They don't know the trail, the process the mind and heart follow to fearlessness. We exposed them to the conclusion without the thinking that makes that conclusion work.

Perhaps you have read an abstract of an article—a short summary of a longer work. After you read it, you know what the article is about. You know what the point is. But you haven't been exposed to the careful reasoning, to the illustrations, to the step-by-step logic, and to careful writing of the author. The abstract may interest you, but without the author's careful development, it is not likely to convince you. Nor is it likely to be important or memorable in your thinking. And you can be sure the author will not think you know what he wrote.

Sermons that are abstracts of Scripture may properly summarize a biblical truth, but they are unconvincing. They do not reorient our thinking. We may know the bottom line, but we don't know how to live what we know. Without a truth trail, people cannot find their own way to the outposts of truth in their own hearts. Sometimes laying down that truth trail, showing the step-by-step thinking of a text, simply cannot be done in twenty minutes.

PRACTICAL FALLACY

I only vaguely recall the world of geometry—axioms, theorems, conclusions. I do remember the inevitable question: "Why do we need to know this stuff?" And I remember Mr. Cermak's answer: "Whether or not you use these formulae, geometry teaches you to think logically."

Some preachers are afraid of the question, "Why do we need to know this stuff?" so they try to make every sermon "practical," meaning it is about everyday issues like money or kids. Doctrinal preaching or the week-by-week exposition of a biblical book appears not to scratch where people itch. People want sermons about things they can use on Monday—like the sophomores in my geometry class.

But Paul tells us, "All Scripture . . . is useful for teaching, rebuking, correcting and training in righteousness" (2 Tim. 3:16). All Scripture! All Scripture is practical. It is practical, not because it all addresses everyday concerns, but because it all "civilizes" our thinking.

As I preached my way through Colossians, for example, we gradually tromped out a wide path to the truth that simply trusting Christ equips us with greater wisdom and righteousness than any counterfeit wisdom can offer. Put that way, it seems like an esoteric, impractical truth, far removed from the water cooler and van pool. But it was Paul's purpose, and therefore mine, to show just how practical this is for the believer. How freeing, simple, and safe. When we eventually arrived at the "practical" passages later in the letter—"clothe yourself with compassion," for example—we could see not only the command but we had come to better understand the spiritual thinking that makes Christian compassion possible.

The Bible spends much more time on shaping the spiritual mind than commanding particular behavior. We need far more training in the ways of grace, of spiritual perceptions, and of what God is really like than we do in how to communicate with our spouse. Understanding the glory of Christ is far more practical than our listeners imagine. Properly preached, every sermon based on a passage of Scripture is fundamentally practical. Every author of Scripture wrote to effect change in God's people. It is our job as preachers to find the persuasive logic of that author and put that clearly and persua-

sively before our people through biblical exposition.

Truth-trail preaching, the careful and persuasive exposition of Scriptural thinking, shapes ready Christian minds for the everyday decisions unscripted in Scripture. When we face an ethical dilemma at work or a discipline problem at home, our minds walk the truth trails we have learned, and we are able to reason our way, by the help of the Holy Spirit, to a biblical conclusion, even when no verse of Scripture directly addresses our situation.

When we preach only the principle, the bullet points, the bottom line, or when we try to make every sermon about an everyday problem, we may set truth in the minds of our hearers, but we do not set the logic and pulse of God into their minds and hearts. By contrast, biblical exposition that lays out the Lord's own logic and heartbeat shapes "doers of the word and not hearers only" (James 1:22, KJV).

Chapter 85

GRACE: A LICENSE TO WANDER?
The need for a balanced message

Bryan Chapell

Talking about God's unconditional love in order to promote godliness is counterintuitive. If all we do is keep assuring people that God loves them, then what will keep them from taking advantage of grace and doing whatever they want?

Without a doubt a grace awakening is occurring, but the new emphasis does not come without varying accents, challenges, and concerns.

Concerns that the new emphasis on grace will result in antinomianism (disregard for the law of God) have become numerous and acute. The history of the evangelical church in North America can partially explain the reasons for these concerns.

Much of the evangelical church finds its cultural roots in the modernist/fundamentalist controversy of the early twentieth century. Not only did those who stood for historic Christianity against modern skepticism fight against disregard for biblical truth, they also warred against the lifestyle changes being adopted by those who discredited the right of Scripture to govern their lives.

Concern about lifestyle issues is necessary for biblical Christianity. Early leaders among the North American evangelicals rightly insisted that the Bible has commands that God's people must obey in order to honor him. Problems came, however, when patterns of personal conduct became almost as much an emphasis in evangelical preaching and teaching as the message of God's grace. As a consequence, people began to think of their conduct as a qualification for God's acceptance.

The result of the strong emphasis on lifestyle issues was the creation of codes of conduct that supposedly distinguished real Christians from the secular world and nominal believers. Strict adherence to these codes became the mark of serious Christianity in many churches, even when the particulars could not be biblically proven. In fact, many of the standards of the evangelical code (e.g., do not play card games, drink alcoholic beverages, smoke, or go to movies) became so much a part of the culture of most conservative churches that few people in them even thought to question whether the Bible actually taught all that the churches expected.

Part of the concern about a renewed emphasis on grace is simply a fear of the loss of evangelical identity as interest wanes in adherence to the codes that have distinguished Bible-believing Christians over the past century. The fear has some merit. The codes have, in fact, kept many Christians from dallying with cultural practices and adopting societal patterns wherein lie great spiritual danger. Those who become strong advocates of a grace emphasis must acknowledge the legitimacy of this concern and show how their teaching will provide protection from secular dangers when the codes of conduct are undermined.

Admittedly, strong advocates of the new grace emphasis may not feel it is their responsibility to deal with the behavior issues that concern advocates of the codes. Preachers of grace typically see the old evangelical codes as destructive forms of legalism to be dismantled. Many of us have been personally wounded by legalistic attitudes in the church and resonate with the need to fight their spiritually corrosive influences.

Still, it is not enough for the advocates of grace simply to react against legalism. We must also respond to the license that always tempts Christians when preachers say, "God will love you no matter what." Legalism makes believers think that God accepts them on the basis of what they do. Licentiousness makes believers think that God does not care what they do. Both errors have terrible spiritual consequences.

Jesus said, "If you love me, you will obey what I command" (John 14:15). Grace should not make obedience optional. When God removes good works as a condition for his acceptance, he does not remove righteousness as a requirement for life. The standards of Scripture glorify God and protect his people from spiritual harm. We cannot undermine the legitimate standards of the Bible without grave consequences.

God does not love us because we obey him, but we cannot know the blessings of his love without obedience. Thus, a grace focus that undermines Christ's own demand for obedience denies us knowledge of and intimacy with him. This is not grace.

Grace that bears fruit is biblical. Grace that goes to seed uses God's unconditional love as an excuse for selfish indulgence. Such egocentric living ultimately burdens us with the guilt and consequences of sin that God has designed his grace to remove.

Resting on God's grace does not relieve us of our holy obligations; rather it should enable us to fulfill them.

Chapter 86

THE RICH SOUND OF GRACE AND HOLINESS
Integrating grace and truth

Kenton C. Anderson

I grew up listening to news radio on my mother's push button AM receiver in her '64 Dodge. When I got my own car, the sound was worse: a single speaker mounted in the back seat delivered my tunes. When I finally installed a new stereo tape deck with dual box speakers under the back window, the sound was incredible. I remember deliberately taking the long way home just so I could keep on listening to the full, rich sound. Moving from mono to stereo is to the ear like moving from two dimensions to three dimensions is to the eye.

The effect is the same when we preach both grace and holiness. Preaching that resonates requires the full play of both polarities. Twisting the balance dial on the stereo to one side or the other produces a diminished monotone at best, and at worst heresy. Jesus' preaching was known to be "full of grace and truth" (John 1:14, 17).

We must integrate grace and truth for three reasons.

(1) The preacher depends on it. I am never sure if I should enjoy the pulpit or run in fear from it. A biblical answer would probably encourage both. Some Sundays I can't wait to climb the platform and let loose with the message God has given. The sheer joy of feeding truth to starving seekers is a passion. The privilege of preaching is exhilarating on those days that I am not overwhelmed by the impropriety of such a thing.

While I am familiar with the joy, I am also acquainted with the misery. I have some appreciation of the sense Moses must have had when he took his shoes off because he was standing on holy ground. I am cognizant that I serve the same God as Aaron, who was under strict instruction even to the extent of his underwear when leading people into the presence of God (Lev. 16:4).

"Who may ascend the hill of the LORD? Who may stand in his holy place?" (Ps. 24:3). I'm not sure my hands are clean enough or my tongue is pure enough to speak for God before the people. It is preposterous to think I would be fit to represent the Almighty. Some suggest that failure (read "sin") enhances a preacher's ability to relate to the congregation's need. Such people need to reread the Pentateuch.

Or perhaps I need to reread Romans 8. I appreciate that I come to the pulpit from this side of the cross. God's grace invigorates me even as it justifies me. Yet, though I preach in the light of New Testament truth, I am challenged by my reading of the Old Testament. The God I serve was awfully particular in Leviticus. I am theologically astute enough to know that he hasn't changed or grown. It is simply that I am privileged to stand at a different vantage point.

Holiness matters. It is not that God decided he had been too hard on us and that if he didn't lighten up there wouldn't be anyone qualified to speak on his behalf. Grace was not a "lightening up." Grace was not cheap. God's standard was not softened; it was satisfied. I am thrilled that God has given me the opportunity to offer his Word as his servant. My awareness of the price tag on that privilege only enhances my appreciation and my passion.

(2) The message depends on it. I love to preach grace. My personal dependence on grace predisposes me to a grace-full preaching diet. I would just as soon leave holiness to the pulpit pounders on TV.

But I am committed to a biblical ministry. The more I study the Scripture, the more I am aware that my affection for grace does not allow a corresponding aversion for holiness. Grace does not do battle with holiness. As Graeme Goldsworthy put it, "The gospel event is not a repudiation of the law; it is its most perfect expression" (*Preaching the Whole Bible As Christian Scripture* (Eerdmans, 2000), p. 159). Paul's apparent light treatment of the law should not be understood as ambivalence. It is, rather, a function of his location in salvation history.

But Goldsworthy also describes moralistic sermons that masquerade as biblical when in fact they are only legalistic. Even texts that offer ethical instruction need to be read in the context of the gospel. Preaching that emphasizes obedience more than grace is not gospel preaching.

> To say what we should be or do and not link it with a clear exposition of what God has done about our failure to be or do perfectly as he wills is to reject the grace of God and to lead people to lust after self-help and self-improvement in a way that, to call a spade a spade, is godless. (Goldsworthy, p. 119)

(3) The listener depends on it. Listeners have an ear for stereo. I can hear a stinging sermon but only for a little while. The harangue as homiletic has a short shelf life. Similarly, a sweet sermon can make my heart soar, but only in moderation. What is sweet soon becomes sticky and beyond my ability to enjoy it or benefit from it.

There are some stilted souls who come to church to be beaten. These are the ones who view the sermon as penance, who have not understood the gospel as grace. There are others who prefer the pastor who believes if you can't say something nice, then don't preach anything at all. These listeners are elderly children who lack the maturity to value the full sound of stereo.

Most listeners have grown to know that sin has its consequences. Helping them appreciate this as part of the fabric of life under God will prepare them to hear that love has its privileges, that grace is the tonic for our inability to obey. Preachers who fulfill the message of holiness with the life-giving message of grace have found the frequency that listeners yearn for.

Part 5

Structure

How Do I Generate, Organize, and Support Ideas in a Way That Is Clear?

Chapter 87

SET FREE FROM THE COOKIE CUTTER
How the text can form the sermon

Haddon Robinson

When we first learn to preach, we learn a form to pour our sermons into, such as a three-point, subject-completed outline. But as we mature in our preaching, we need more flexibility in our sermon forms to stay out of the rut. We must let the text form the sermon instead of vice versa.

GENRE AND THE FORM OF A SERMON

The first step in that direction, of course, is to fully understand the text. You can talk about exegesis, and it can sound cold. Sometimes when people think of exegesis, they think of analyzing words and phrases. But basically what you're trying to do when you exegete a text is to really understand it—understand its flow of thought, how the author is developing that thought.

So when I come to didactic literature, such as Romans or Galatians, I analyze how the thought develops because there tends to be a logical flow. But when I get to a parable, I can't do that. The danger is to go to a letter and see that Paul has three moves in a particular paragraph in which I can trace that development, then move over to a parable and try to say there are three things we learn from this parable. We don't question why Jesus used a story instead of simply stating, "There are three things I want you to know about God's grace."

Part of exegesis is to recognize that the form of literature ought to have some influence on the form of the sermon. A sermon developed from didactic literature (e.g., letters) will be different than a sermon developed from a parable or a psalm or from the narrative literature of the Old Testament, because the writers are using a different form.

For example, if I say to you, "Once upon a time," what do you expect? A story.

If I say, "Dearly beloved, we're gathered here today," what do you expect? A wedding.

323

If I say, "The party of the first part assigns to the party of the second part," what do you expect? A legal document, a contract.

If I say, "There were three men: a Catholic priest, a Jewish rabbi, and a Baptist minister," what do you expect? Humor.

If I say to you, "How do I love thee, let me count the ways," what do you expect? Poetry.

And if I say, "The kingdom of heaven is like," what do you expect? Probably a parable. You pick up from the Bible a certain tone.

Notice what happens. The minute I give you those clues, you set your mind to a whole new hermeneutical development. So if I start by saying, "Once upon a time" and I give you a story, but you respond as though you were analyzing a legal document, we are going to miss each other badly. Or if I start out by saying, "The party of the first part owes to the party of the second part," and I'm trying to establish a legal contract, but you take it as poetry, we're going to have trouble in court. Thus, there are ground rules that immediately get established based on the form.

We see this easily with English. We all carry this hermeneutical grid around with us. Yet somehow when we get to the Bible, we don't understand it. Thus, the first job of the preacher is to understand the text for what it says and how it says it rather than my putting my own grid or mold on it. When I look at a passage, I must say exegetically, *What's going on here? What is the genre? What is the writer doing?* You have to assume the author didn't just choose this genre because any old genre would work. If Jesus tells a parable, then I have to be aware when I preach the sermon that I can't treat it as if it's didactic literature. To be true to the Bible, I have to understand the genre; that's part of exegesis. And different

genres, different kinds of literature, have different rules.

One kind of grid we've put on texts for years has been the three-points grid. If I go to a psalm, I get three things we learn about suffering from the psalm. But the first question you have to ask: Is the biblical writer giving you three things about suffering? We learned four things about stewardship from Matthew 18 in the parable of the unjust steward (about the man who was forgiven the several million dollars he owed but wouldn't forgive his brother's debt). You take something such as that and you can say, "There are three things we learn about our obligation to God because of his grace." But you have to think, *Is that what the biblical writer is doing? Is he giving you three things?* Once you say, *Oh no, that's not what he's doing*, then the question is, *What is he doing? And how does this story carry what he is doing?* That is an important part of taking the genre of the literature, then working to see how you can incorporate that in a sermon.

That is quite a different thing from the cookie cutter approach, where we always fit the content into three parallel points. We always make the text fit that way. Some texts will fit, but some won't. You've got to avoid the cookie cutter syndrome for two reasons. You get bored with your own preaching, and everybody can anticipate your message in terms of what form you're going to use.

SEQUENCING THE MOVEMENTS

How should we sequence the movements in a sermon? Do we always start from the beginning of the text and work our way through to the end? Exegetically, of course, you start from the beginning and you work through. You've got to understand what the writer is doing. That's your homework. Whether you use that in the pulpit or not, you need to do that homework.

In fact, there are two major stages of preparation. The first stage has to do with the studying of the text and getting the idea of the text, and the second stage is communicating that text. It's dangerous to bring those two together; that is, to go to the text knowing you've got to preach a sermon on Sunday. The problem with that is you're going to read the text for the hot buttons. You're going to read it for what will preach. But first you have to understand the text.

Once you understand it—understand its basic idea, its development—then you can think about the best way to get that idea across to a congregation on Sunday. That's where the sermon takes its form and its shape.

If I have a parable, I know my sermon has to have about it the quality of a parable. At times I've taken an ancient parable and put it into the twenty-first century. I retold it in modern dress and spent a significant amount of the sermon doing that, because most of the parables do not depend on the dress they're in. The father welcomes his boy back from the far country and kills a fatted calf. It's not that far from parents who have had a boy go off to San Francisco or Los Angeles and they wait for a letter from him that never comes, and they wish whenever the phone rings that it would be him but he doesn't call. And when he comes back home and they go out to meet him, he may be thin and emaciated and need a suit, and his shoes are worn out, but they come in, call the relatives and friends, and invite them over for a big dinner.

That story doesn't depend on the dressing the Bible gives the parable. Think, *Can I make it into a modern parable? Or can I tell that old parable with a freshness to it?*

When I go to a psalm, I ask myself, *Why did David write this?* (if David is the author of that particular psalm). *Why did he write it? What could have prompted it?* I'm not talking about the historical situation but just why he would write this. I cannot treat that like a logical argument. There will be in the sermon a kind of poetic element in the language I use. Usually I cannot work my way through a psalm—only a few psalms are logical progression—but I want people to feel what the psalmist may have felt and what we would feel in using that particular genre.

I need to look more at emotion and images than logical argument. We're better at this than we think. It's just that somehow we get to the Bible and we think of preaching a sermon. We do better when we think of ourselves as communicating the idea of a biblical text. Sometimes I think we are really hurt by thinking of preaching a sermon because we have a certain form in our head that a sermon takes. I prefer to say that any form you can use that really communicates the idea and development of this text is perfectly legitimate.

But we can't just talk about how the text forms the sermon; we also must talk about the audience and how they form the sermon and sequence the movement. There are two tensions you face: You've got to be true to the biblical text, but you have to be true to your audience. Somewhere along the line you've got to ask, *So what? What difference does this make?*

When a twenty-first-century audience comes to this passage, what are their questions? They may ask of the text, *What does that mean?* Paul may have assumed his audience knew what he meant, but a twenty-first-century audience may not know. Or they may ask, *Is that true? Do I really believe that?* It may seem outlandish to them.

There will be parts of a text I go over quickly because there is another part of that text I really want to spend time on since I know my audience needs that. I can't treat everything in the text with the same emphasis in a thirty-minute message. I often have to determine the thing I really want to come down on are the last verses. I've got to show people how Paul or Peter or James got there, but that's where I want to land because that's the most important thing as I see it for my audience. So, your audience does help to shape the sermon.

After I have worked with the text and have the exegetical idea, that is, what Paul was writing to the Romans, I try to frame it into a modern idea and state it in terms of the twenty-first century. Then I ask myself, *What's my purpose in this sermon? What am I trying to accomplish?* People who do expository preaching often miss that. They don't ask why they are preaching it. Their answer is, "I was in Ephesians 2 last week and now I'm in Ephesians 3." But that's not a purpose; that's just how you got there. Why are you preaching it?

So, I will sketch out quickly what I want to do in the conclusion. I may have to sharpen it and so forth, but I know where I'm going. Then I determine how I want to start. How close can I get to my audience? Once I do that, then I say, *What's the first thing I've got to say? From all the study I've done, what's the first thing I've got to say? What's the next thing? And the next thing?* I jot that down on a piece of paper so I get the flow of thought. Before I ever make an outline, I just want to get the flow, the way that sermon is going to develop.

As I work with that, the flow will take different shape and form, and different sermons have a different flow. The idea of the passage is sort of like a tree. It has its own leaves and fruit. You don't tie oranges onto it. It just develops. So you ask yourself, *How do I develop this to be true to this text, yet do it in the most interesting and engaging way?*

VARIETY

A sermon tends to form itself. As you get a full acquaintance with your audience and with your text, you just have a sense that this has to start and that has to lead to this.

Occasionally I'll look down and say, "Yes, there are three things I'm going to say." So this can be a subject completed. I'm going to raise the subject in the introduction and then each point will be a completing of it.

Other times I look and say I'm going to do it deductively and state the whole idea in that introduction. Then I'm going to either explain it or prove it or apply it. Most often for me I'm going to keep that idea of the text as far along as I can. So it will be at the end or maybe two-thirds of the way through before I state clearly what my idea is because I want to keep as much tension as I can before I state it. That's just the way my mind works.

But sermons will take different forms. Sometimes I will look at a passage and think the best way to get this across is to do a first person narrative.

But however I develop the ideas, I want to delay resolution if possible. If you and I are having a conversation and I say, "I want to tell you what I've learned about the Boston Red Sox," and we're not talking baseball, you might be polite. You might say to me, "Okay. What have you learned?" But almost instinctively I say to you, "I've been in New England and have been rooting for the Boston Red Sox. And I learned something while I've been rooting for the Red Sox that I think is a keen insight into life. It goes way beyond the Red Sox." Now what I'm trying to do is to motivate you to listen to me.

If I succeed in capturing your interest—if you say, "Well, what have you learned?"—I may tell you right away what I learned. But more likely I'll say, "Let me explain the Red Sox to you. That organization has not won a World Series in almost eighty years. Seldom do you meet a fan who was around when they last won a World Series, and if they did they were a babe in their mother's arm."

I'm not going to tell you right off the bat what my lesson is, but I'm going to tell you about all the frustrations the Boston fans have endured. They actually believe there's a curse. They sold Babe Ruth to the cursed Yankees and we got cursed. So as I come to the end of that story, I say, "This is what I have learned. If you believe there is a curse on your life, you will live as though there is in fact a curse on your life."

We instinctively keep that sort of tension when we tell real stories. Those who tell boring stories give you the punch line before they tell you the story.

Chapter 88

SAY AND DO

How to choose a sermon form that helps hearers experience the truth

Fred Craddock

Not all sermons have the same form. There have been great preachers whose sermons usually looked the same. The content and mood varied, but the structure looked exactly the same. Frederick W. Robertson of Brighton, for instance—in my mind the greatest preacher in the English language—preached sermons that almost always had two points; the structure was the same. But most of us shouldn't try to ride the same horse in every race. The sermon form should be congenial to the text, to the message of the sermon, and to the experience to be created.

If I am teaching, the form will be a didactic one that calls for preview, clear statements, summary, maybe a list. Sometimes in a sermon you're just teaching, but in other sermons you're trying to create another experience. Some sermons are to encourage, to challenge, to inspire, to persuade, to correct, to clear up. What is it you're trying to do?

I once had a sermon from a student who was using an either-or text: "Choose for yourselves this day whom you will serve" (Josh. 24:15). The text should have provided the structure for the sermon—either-or—but the student had three points. It was not congenial to the text. It was not congenial to the intention of the sermon.

If one is going to create or recreate the experience of the text, the text provides the form because when we're preaching, we're not just *saying* something, we're *doing* something. Suppose your subject is freedom. We don't just go to the dictionary and get definitions of freedom. We want to preach a sermon that provides the experience of the things we're talking about. Good sermons do what they're talking about and talk about what they're doing.

One goes to forms in the text itself first. Even though some texts are difficult to follow as a form for proclamation, that is always the place to begin. If I don't follow the form of the text in the form of the sermon, I certainly want to choose a form that's congenial to the message and experience of the text.

This is true of any text. Some are more difficult than others, especially Proverbs (because they have such closure). When it's so final, it's hard to get anything going. A proverb is a conclusion, which is a tough place to start a sermon, though many sermons do. You can tell when an introduction was the first thing written in the sermon because just about everything is in the introduction. The rest of the message is a trickle.

To have a narrative sermon form does not mean that the sermon has to be a story, such as the story of David. It does not mean one has to tell stories. Not everybody can tell a story well, though most of us can tell them "well-er" than we do. A narrative sermon is simply one that moves with the proper amount of anticipation. The message can have a structured outline—1, 2, 3—and still qualify as narrative because the movement sustains interest to the end. Such a sermon doesn't have to be full of illustrations or stories to be narrative in its dynamic. It simply has that important ingredient of anticipation built into the structure itself.

The key to having an effective sermon form is to know what you want to say before you start working it into a sermon. In other words, let the study to get a message and the preparation of the form of the material be separate stages. This releases my imagination to ask, *How can I get this across?* The sermon is then free to take a variety of forms. I don't always have the same structure, the same old outline form that results from boiling a text down to its essential point and then outlining that point. That's not always congenial for people's experience of Scripture.

I want to be free with reference to form. *How in the world will I say this?*

Chapter 89

CONNECTING BIBLICAL CONTENT WITH CONTEMPORARY AUDIENCES
A two-stage model

Mike Yearley

How do you make your sermons connect with the culture and yet remain thoroughly biblical? At North Coast Evangelical Free Church, north of San Diego, the lead pastor and I have developed over the years a model for accomplishing that goal that is twofold. We aim our teaching at Christians but work hard to take out the Christianese that we who have been longtime Christians sometimes use, and to make it user-friendly for window-shoppers, the unbelievers who often come to our church. We work hard to put it in their language.

We start each sermon by walking through the passage. That might take ten or fifteen minutes; that connects hearers to the text and to the Bible. Then we talk about the life lessons that we can pull from the text. At that point it gets practical. The points come primarily from the text itself, but they're about how to live the Christian life.

We made one switch years ago that has been helpful to us. In our early years as pastors we saw our goal as to teach the Bible, so we spent a lot more time explaining nuances in the text. But as the years went on, we changed, so that now our goal is to teach people how to live the Christian life with the Bible as our authority. Whenever we're preparing a message, we ask ourselves, *Am I really explaining to people how to live the Christian life on this particular topic?*

As we go through a passage, our main goal is to make sure people can follow the author's train of thought. In a traditional approach you might spend more time talking about the original language or noticing the way conjunctions connect different parts of a verse together. Our goal is less technical. It's to get people in the text so they can understand it, to make it colloquial as we go through. In a message that is forty or forty-five minutes long, after our ten or fifteen minutes of walking through the passage, we have twenty-five minutes to talk about the life principles.

So in most of our messages, you feel that shift. We look at a passage and then apply the life principles. There might be three, five, or six life principles. Those points will be application oriented. Instead of making some comment about the text, we would make a comment about our lives. It would be as if you and I were having a cup of coffee together and talking about that topic of the day, and I had five things I thought were important for you to understand about how to live your life in that area. Each of those points is put in user-friendly language that anyone, regardless of whether he or she is Christian, can understand and appropriate.

You may wonder how we keep people with us when we are focusing on the text for those first fifteen minutes without being overtly relevant to the hearer's felt needs and challenges. We haven't experienced that as a hardship. We often start with a couple of sentences about the topic for the day and why it's important, so there is a hook there at the beginning. As we go through the text too, we often make practical applications, sidebar comments here and there. So it's not as if we're doing a super-deep exegesis of the text.

We may start out by saying, "Today we're going to be looking at a passage that helps us understand five principles of how to live this concept out in our lives." So people are with us from the start; it isn't as if during the expositional part people are bored and looking asleep and then all of a sudden when we get to the practical part—boom—they're with us again. They are with us the whole time.

And we go out of our way to make contemporary analogies with the text. For example, I was speaking a couple of weeks ago on Luke 24. We're doing a series right now on unforgettable encounters with God. I was speaking on "The Road to Aha's," those moments when the light turns on for us in a certain area of our life.

As I went through the text, I talked about how the disciples were depressed. Their world had fallen apart. They had believed in Jesus. They thought he was the coming Messiah, and now he'd been crucified. It was late in the afternoon on Easter Sunday, and they felt maybe as some of us felt after the September 11th tragedy, when we wondered where life was going.

These two disciples were taking a seven-mile trip to—and instead of saying Emmaus, I said the town of Bonsall. In our area Bonsall is about seven miles from us. It's a small town of five hundred or a thousand people. It's the sort of place you just drive through. So the moment I said Bonsall that took them by surprise. There

was a moment of humor there. We laughed together. So going through a passage is not like sitting in a seminary class going line by line. It's more a colloquial storytelling. We're interspersing humor and application as we go.

During the time of looking at the text we will also point out key verses. I might say, "This verse is important. I want you to underline that because we're going to come back to that later." In the expositional time of that message on Luke 24 I highlighted how God had hidden from the disciples' eyes who Jesus was. I talked about how there are times when God hides certain truths from us because we're not ready for them. There are other times when he reveals certain truths, as when the two disciples realized who Jesus was during the breaking of the bread, and also when Jesus appeared in the upper room and opened their minds to understand the Scriptures.

Then I transitioned: "We've seen how aha's worked in the disciples' lives, but now we want to talk about how God uses these aha's in our lives to make us like Christ." This particular message had three points. The first one was that it takes aha's to become a follower of Christ. I talked specifically to the window-shoppers there about how, as we're investigating Christianity, oftentimes we look at it as if we can turn on the light ourselves and make that decision. But in reality every time a person comes to Christ, God is opening their eyes to spiritual truths.

The second point was that it takes aha's to become like Christ. Not only do we need God to turn on the light switch when we first come to Christ, but this is to be an ongoing part of our Christian experience. It's not something that happens two or three times in our life. And at that point I connected with the congregation, because I know that one thing they often say is, "Boy, during that message I felt as if you were talking just to me." So I said, "Sometimes you're in a service and you feel like the pastor is talking right to you. What's that? That's the Holy Spirit giving you an aha moment. There are times when you're reading the Bible. You come across a passage of Scripture that you may have read many times before, but suddenly it comes to life. It's almost highlighted on the page." So I gave several illustrations about how this is a normal part of the Christian life.

The final point of that message was that we need to act on our aha's. Basically when it comes to aha's, you either use them or lose them. I talked about how, when God gives us an aha in a certain area of our life, we have to then act on it, and if we do, God will give us more aha's and we will get more enlightenment. But if we don't act on our aha's, we will lose even the aha that we have.

Some texts do not have an obvious application of something that a Christian can do. Maybe it simply holds up an attribute of God. When I talk about teaching people how to live the Christian life, I mean that in a broad sense. We're not just talking about how to be a better husband or a better employee. We're also talking about knowledge issues, such as who God is, who we are, and how we're to relate to one another. All those theological concepts are critical in talking about how we are to live the Christian life.

Most any truth about life has implications on how life is to be lived, and the task of the preacher is to find those implications and to clearly explain them in a way that people can grab, in the language of today.

There are many benefits to adopting this two-stage preaching model. First, it gets people

in the Bible. One of the challenges we have today is to connect with people who are biblically illiterate, and yet we all believe the Bible holds the path to life for us. So one huge value of this method is it teaches people how to read the Bible.

Second, it's practical and relevant. Especially in our culture today, people are not tolerant of something that is not relevant in the near future. They don't want knowledge just for knowledge's sake.

A third benefit is we spend more time teaching through the Bible. For example, we recently finished a series on 1 Corinthians that was thirty-one messages long. Often after we do a book study like that, we'll follow up with a topical study. But even then it's usually not topical in the sense of "let's talk about marriage." It's topical in the sense that we might talk about great psalms. Or, for example, we look at men and women from the Old Testament who are great examples or bad examples. We called it "Heroes and Bums."

One other benefit is you can't always go back to your pet topics, your eight things that you love to talk about. It forces you to look for relevance in Scripture in ways that you perhaps would not have looked before. So it feeds people a much more balanced diet because you're not just picking out your topics ahead of time and then speaking on those. The text itself is dictating topics to you.

Some expository preachers use an approach whereby if they are teaching on Luke 24, they start by explaining verse 1, and then provide some application or commentary on that verse. Then they move on to explain verse 2, and then give application or commentary on verse 2. So they weave exposition and application verse by verse throughout the passage.

That approach can be done well, obviously. Many have used it successfully. But one of the disadvantages is you can try to cover too many topics in a given message. You talk about verse 1, and it suggests some practical application. Verse 2 suggests something else to you. So you end up talking about seventeen different topics in a message, and you've only gone a minute or two deep into each one of them. The advantage of the method we use is that it helps you to develop a topic in some depth, yet it gives you the ability to talk about five or six different kinds of life applications that can hit a variety of people in the congregation.

We have a luxury of an extended teaching time of forty or forty-five minutes—but at many churches the time for the message is twenty minutes, perhaps twenty-five. In that case you have to limit the number of points, which is something we do anyway. For example, in that aha sermon I had five or six points initially, but after going through them I felt I only had time for three of them because of the way I needed to develop those three. A person with a shorter time might be able to include only one or two. I went through most of Luke 24 in my exposition. With less time, maybe I would just go through twelve verses.

This model requires the skill of making the Bible text contemporary as you're explaining it, the skill of drawing out the line of thought through the entire passage, and the ability to abstract from a larger passage of Scripture two to four application principles.

In addition, we have to develop a passion to communicate in the language of the people. We try to look through our messages and take out anything that sounds "stained glass" or churchy. We would normally not use words like sanctification or illumination. Part of this is a discipline and a skill. When you're planning your sermon, ask yourself, *If I were to explain this to the man on the street, would he understand it?*

This is something that takes work to develop. It involves being up with the culture. I'm always looking for ways to say spiritual truths in the language and sound bites of our culture. Earlier I talked about "use it or lose it." That's a common phrase. We work hard to take a spiritual truth and find a colloquialism that can express that truth.

We want to stay away from oratory. We want to stay away from the feeling of a sermon. We want it to feel as if we're having a conversation, even though we can be directive. If our goal is to have a message that's culturally relevant, then our language and illustrations have to be culturally relevant too.

Chapter 90

CLEARLY

How to preach so everyone understands

Haddon Robinson

When Napoleon sent out his messengers, he gave them three instructions: be clear, be clear, and be clear. There are several challenges facing preachers who desire to do just that.

First, there's a tendency to roam through the whole Bible, bringing in all kinds of things to enhance what we're saying. We end up saying too much and, as a result, communicating too little. We start out stalking bear, but are soon distracted by some rabbits we'd like to chase. Before long, we're chasing this and adding that and missing the bear we started after at the outset. So less is more.

We also deal with the challenge of oral communication. Preachers have to work at clarity because the spoken word lacks some of the built-in aids inherent to writing. When you're writing, you can utilize paragraph divisions, punctuation marks, section headings, and things in quotes. You can't do that when you're preaching. Also, if I don't get what the preacher is saying the first time, I can't go back and mentally review; if I try to, I won't hear what he is saying now. The preacher has the responsibility of helping his congregation think clearly.

Someone who writes out his sermons in an effort to be clear can often cause the opposite effect because of the written style. If that's the case, then how can we bridge the gap between clarity in our notes and clarity in our presentation?

Begin by being clear about your subject. When you've worked through your notes, you ought to be able to answer two questions. First, "What am I talking about?" You ought to be able to state in precise, definite terms what this sermon is about. For example, "Why should I be committed?" or, "Where do I serve Christ most effectively?" We call this the subject, but it's really the answer to the question: "What am I talking about?"

Then, you should be able to answer the next question: "What am I saying about what I'm talking about? What are the major assertions I'm making about that question?" Clarity often fails because we haven't nailed those two things down prior to arrival in the pulpit.

Expository preachers have to ask themselves an additional question: "What's my purpose?" Topical preachers have the advantage of having a purpose, often embedded right in their title. An expository preacher, however, tends to start and end with the text, never answering "Why are you preaching this sermon this Sunday?" The fact that you're supposed to fill the pulpit from 11:25 to 12:00 isn't good enough.

A good outline always helps with clarity. You can use the outline to design the sermon as you would a conversation, so that each point is related to what goes before. For example, if you are preaching a sermon on forgiveness, the introduction might deal with why you're bringing this up. Your first movement could say, "Forgiveness is necessary." The second could be, "But even though forgiveness is necessary, we often find it difficult." Likewise the third could follow, "But I have good news. As difficult as forgiveness might be, Christians can excel at it because we are followers of Jesus Christ."

These major movements in the sermon can be read like a conversation rather than three bare statements. This enables you to have an outline, but it doesn't stick out like a skeleton. It also acknowledges the fact that the "one-two-three things I have to say" type of outline seems to be less popular today. Sometimes that's what you want if your purpose is to be clear. But if every sermon takes this form, it can lead to boredom.

Another way to add clarity to a sermon is, first, to clearly orient the audience to the body of the sermon right in the introduction. A preacher might say at the end of the introduction, "God sometimes keeps his promises to us by performing miracles or performing miracles in us." But if that's all he's going to say, folks already have the sermon. If he asks, "Now what exactly does that mean, to say that God performs miracles or performs miracles in us?" he secures the chance to develop clarity, because the congregation has the whole idea, and the preacher has the opportunity to clarify that idea through the body of the sermon.

You can also add clarity by restating key ideas. Suppose you begin by saying, "We want to talk today about how to know the will of God." Continue by restating this idea several times: "When we are confused about what God wants us to do, how can we determine his direction in our lives? Where would we turn to determine God's will? How do we go about knowing the will of God?" It seems laborious when you're preaching, but restating the sub-

ject several times in different ways makes it stand out in people's minds.

In addition, avoid pronouns requiring the listener to remember the reference. For example, rather than saying, "A second thing we must do is consult the Bible," include the subject it is referencing: "A second thing we have to do in trying to determine God's will is to consult the Bible." It may be clear to you what "second thing" refers to, but such vagueness requires a listener to recall a previous reference, possibly diminishing clarity.

You can also give the audience a map of where you're going. Suppose you are preaching on Christians and government in Romans 13:1–7. You might say, "Christians are to be subject to the government. Christians are to obey what the government demands. I want to talk about the basis for this command. I want to talk about how we show submission to the government; what the implications are in daily life. Third, what exceptions, if any, are there to this command." In beginning this way, you have given the people a road map of your sermon so they can track with you.

If the subject is interesting, people almost automatically begin developing questions. If you anticipate where you're going in the map and promise that before you are through you will deal with that question, it puts that question to rest for awhile so your people can hear the rest of what you're saying.

Visual preaching aids clarity. We use illustrations because they take an abstract concept and ground it in life. A good illustration paints a picture in people's minds; it creates clarity and understanding. Weak preachers constantly say, "Well, in other words," to clarify something that is unclear. Better preachers will substitute "For example," "For instance," or "Let me illustrate." Following an abstract statement with a "for instance" or an example increases its clarity.

It is also critical to use a story that really illustrates the point. Every preacher knows the temptation to follow a story because it is powerful. But if the story doesn't shed light on the point, then it will reduce clarity, because it causes the audience to focus in the illustration's connection to the sermon rather than on the point of the sermon.

Another practice that reduces clarity is the tendency to begin with text and follow with background. Imagine the following scenario. "Do you have secrets? Every single one of us comes to this auditorium with secrets. Some are difficult to carry. Some make you afraid. In Psalm 51, David has a secret. He goes to talk to God about it. He had sinned against a woman by the name of Bathsheba; he committed adultery with her. And he had tried to cover that sin by having her husband, Uriah, killed. As he tried to cover things up, he came to feel very guilty. His secret overwhelmed him. Now in this text he tells us how to handle our guilt." That's a long way of going about it, and it's the wrong way of going about it.

A better approach is to give the background or setting before you announce the chapter and verse. "You have secrets. All of us have secrets. David had secrets. The sin he committed with Bathsheba and the murder of Uriah were David's secrets. He was overwhelmed by guilt because of it. But he had to deal with that guilt. Now, in Psalm 51, we see how David handled the guilt he had before God."

When you refer to a passage, people start turning to it, and they expect you to deal with it right then. But if you're going on and on, giving background about his guilt and how he's going to handle it, and only then getting to the passage, it's a confusing sequence for the listener. You are better off discussing contemporary matters, biblical background, and the subject first. Then announce the Scripture passage and deal with it immediately.

Transitions can be a challenging part of maintaining clarity in sermons. Transitions are difficult because if the message is clear to you, you will tend to not clarify it for the audience. The idea is so evident to you that you don't think it's important to build the bridge. A good transition, however, reviews what has already been said. It takes you back to the subject of the sermon and then anticipates what is coming. A good transition secures the point you're going to make in people's minds.

One way you can transition from one thought to another is by asking a question. Suppose in your first point you've been talking about picking up the cross and following Jesus. In transition, you might say, "Well, that's pretty clear, isn't it? It says we're to pick up a cross and follow Jesus. What does this look like in life if you pick up the cross and follow Jesus? What does it look like in your business or your home to carry a cross?" Transitional questions can help you move into your next point with clarity.

What part can conclusions play in clarity? A strong conclusion brings your sermon to a burning focus. It can help you return to the question you raised in the introduction, giving the audience some satisfaction and closure.

It's difficult, however, for a conclusion to salvage an unclear sermon. Conclusions can salvage sermons in the sense that they make the last five minutes clear, but they usually cannot create clarity in retrospect. It may drive home the point and illustrate it, but your hearers still may not understand what you talked about for the first twenty-five minutes.

Chapter 91

SKILLS OF ORAL CLARITY

Clear writing and clear speaking are two different things

Don Sunukjian

Several years ago I was listening to a student preach in class. In a few minutes I would be leading some class interaction on the message. But I had absolutely no idea what the speaker was talking about! I had a copy of the student's outline off to one side, so I glanced at it, looking for some semblance of order so I could lead a profitable discussion. To my amazement, the student's outline was beautiful—a logical progression, with proper subordinations and overall unity. The student had a first-class brain. Why couldn't I follow him?

That's when I began to discover that clarity in oral communication is different from clarity in written communication. It takes a special set of skills and adjustments to take a message that is clear to a reader and make it clear for a hearer.

As pastors we must have people track with us. They must follow us, know where we're going, and stay with us all the way. I emphasize oral clarity, because oral clarity is a different animal than written clarity. Most of us have been trained to be clear in our writing, and when we write something, such as a sermon, we are writing it for somebody else's eye to read it. That's instinctive in us. We do not realize we are writing for somebody's ear. Oral clarity is vastly different, and there are certain skills of oral clarity that ought to be built in to every sermon.

The reason we need to make these adjustments for oral clarity is because we lose many of the built-in aids to clarity that occur when our material is in written form.

PREACHING WITHOUT PARAGRAPHS

The most powerful aid to clarity in written material is the paragraph. When our eye sees white-space at the beginning of a line—a paragraph indentation—our brain unconsciously says, "You are about to begin a new thought." Our eyes catch some white-space at the end of the line, further down the page, and our brain says, "This new thought you are about to begin will last until you reach that spot further on." Finally, our brain concludes with the voice of our high school composition teacher, "As you begin this new thought, the first sentence you read will be the topic sentence that tells what the whole paragraph is about."

We have not yet read a single word of the paragraph, but all these things have been powerfully and clearly organized in our mind. Nothing in oral communication corresponds to the white-space of the paragraph indentation. (A lengthy pause is not the same—the listener will simply think you forgot!)

There are other aids to clarity built into written communication. Readers can go at their own speed. They can reread a page if they didn't get it the first time. They can look up unfamiliar words and return to find the page in the same spot they left it. And they can benefit from visual cues such as italics, bold print, center headings, and punctuation.

SAY IT AGAIN, SAM . . . AND AGAIN

Since oral communication has none of these things, a speaker must make an important adjustment for the message to remain clear for a hearer. The greatest skill of oral clarity is to restate something you just said. Immediately say the same thing in different words.

You have to know where to do that in the message, and there are two major guidelines. First, use restatement any time you come to a new content point or a new concept. There are probably five or six times during a message when you do that. The second is any time you transition. Restate transitions before moving to a new point, and then restate the new point.

Whenever you come to a key sentence in your message, restate such things as:

- the central truth of the whole message
- a Roman numeral main point
- a significant subpoint
- a sentence that summarizes the point of several examples
- a key sentence that also reveals organizational structure
- a preview in the introduction that lays out the flow of the message to come
- a summary of previous concepts in the message
- a transition between points that connects concepts to each other

Restatement is God's gift to oral communicators. Whenever you have a key sentence of either content or structure, give the listener more than one chance to grasp it aurally. It will add clarity to your preaching.

CONSISTENTLY USE KEY PHRASES

Another skill is to use the same key phrases all the way through the message. The words ought to be consistently used so that they rain down through the message. For instance, a recent message of mine was on the filling of the Spirit from Ephesians 5:18, where Paul says "Do not get drunk on wine . . . instead, be filled with the Spirit." After an introduction, I asked the questions I said I wanted to answer in the message:

I. What do we mean by being filled with the Spirit?
II. What does it look like?
III. How do we get it?

That was my outline. When I came to Roman numeral two, I used exactly those words: What does being filled with the Spirit look like? And when I got to Roman numeral three, I used the same words: How do we get filled? I was sure to repeat that same key phrase.

It's that tracking of the same word all the way through that's important. Getting those words in as the message proceeds is one way of gaining clarity.

ASK A RHETORICAL QUESTION AT TRANSITIONS

As you transition from one point to another, use a rhetorical question. Ask a question your next point is going to answer. I could say, "We've seen what it means to be filled with the Spirit. Once we are filled with the Spirit, certain things begin to show up in our lives." And I could begin to talk about what it looks like. But it's much better if I transition between those points by asking a question. I could say, "We've seen what it means to be filled with the Spirit. Now, what does it look like? How does it show up?"

Why is that a good oral clarity skill? Because the rhetorical question gives the listener a chance to refocus on the message. It enables the listener to think, I've been fogged out the last two or three minutes. But I bet for the next four minutes you're going to answer that question. It immediately brings the mind back to a point of, "Yes, I'm with you again. Thanks, you picked me up again." It's a way of making the flow of thought stand out.

USE PHYSICAL MOVEMENT TO KEEP THE LISTENER'S ATTENTION

A final oral principle is that physical move-ment has a benefit to keeping a listener. If I have three things I'm going to cover during the message, my hand is going to move from one to two to three. In fact, my body will turn from one to two to three.

An interesting tip is to put the past on the speaker's right and the future on the speaker's left, because from the standpoint of the listener, that's the way things move. The past always moves from the listener's left to the listener's right. If you're counting off points, start from your right and end up on your left, because that's how the listener reads.

If you put these things together, you can be clear.

Chapter 92

QUESTIONS THAT PUT MUSCLE ON BONES
What to ask when developing an idea

Don Sunukjian

How do you expand fifteen sentences into thirty minutes? How do you go from the biblical outline (the Scripture writer's flow of thought) to your Sunday message?

You ask three developmental questions. Probing each statement in the outline with these questions causes the biblical text to expand and develop into a full sermon. While there are many ways to phrase these developmental questions, they all get at the three essential areas of understanding, belief, and behavior regarding the biblical assertions:

Understanding
- What does this statement mean?
- What do I need to explain?
- What won't my listeners understand?

Belief
- Is this statement true?
- Do we believe it?
- Do we buy it?
- Why is this statement true?
- Why does the cause-effect relationship hold true?
- What could cause my listeners not to accept or act on this statement?
- Do I need to prove or defend this statement?

Behavior
- What difference does this statement make in our lives?
- What does it look like in everyday situations?
- Where does it show up in real life?

- What are the implications, the practical applications?
- How, exactly, would my people carry this out in the daily events and circumstances of their lives?
- How can I specifically visualize this for my listeners?
- What ought to happen?
- What ought to change?

As you ask these questions of each assertion in the biblical outline, you discover what needs to be said further about each point to make it intelligible, convincing, and practical to your contemporary listener. Let's begin with the first developmental area.

UNDERSTANDING

In the following outline on Colossians 1:9–12, some things obviously need to be explained:

We should continually pray for our Christian friends to know God's will.

- Paul continually prays for the Colossians to know God's will (1:9).

  - More than anything else, he wants them to know fully God's will through all spiritual wisdom and understanding.
  - He continually prays, therefore, for this to happen.
  - We should continually pray for our Christian friends to know God's will.

When our friends know God's will, they will live worthy of and pleasing to the Lord in every way (1:10–12).

- When they know God's will, they will live worthy of the Lord (1:10a).
- When they know God's will, they will live pleasing to the Lord (1:10–12).

  - They will please him by being productive in good works.

  - They will please him by growing in knowledge.
  - They will please him by developing endurance and patience.
  - They will please him by giving thanks.

The first and biggest thing that needs to be explained is what Paul means by "God's will." Does he have in mind the behavioral statements of Scripture, such as, "It is God's will that you should be sanctified" (1 Thess. 4:3)? Or does he mean the sequence of events God has in mind for your life/church, such as, "Those who suffer according to God's will should commit themselves to their faithful Creator and continue to do good" (1 Peter 4:19)? Obviously we need to explain whether "God's will" is objective or subjective in this passage.

Another big thing that needs to be explained is the meaning of "continually pray." Listeners might be thinking, "Pastor, I can't continually pray; I have to go to work."

Other areas for explanations might include:

- Paul's relationship to these people whom he has never met (see v. 9)
- the precise meaning of "spiritual wisdom and understanding" in verse 9
- the difference between "worthy of" and "pleasing to" (the former may be a horizontal assessment by others, while the latter may be a vertical assessment by God)
- the difference between "endurance" and "patience" in verse 11 (the former may relate to events, the latter to people)

When we give explanations, we should be as "picturesque" as possible. Avoid dictionary definitions and abstract descriptions that cause eyes to glass over. Instead, create a visual picture in the listener's mind. For example, explain trust or faith by asking a member of the audience to stand rigid and fall back, trusting your promise to catch them. See if they really will trust you, or whether at the last minute they will thrust back one of their feet to protect themselves from falling.

Matthew 10:29 can be explained in picture terms: "Tomorrow morning, downtown, a pet store owner is going to open shop. He'll go to the glass area against one of the walls, take out two parakeets, and put them in a cage with a sign, 'Sale, 2 parakeets, $5.95.' Later that morning a woman will come into the store to buy a pet for her grandchildren. Because her son-in-law will not tolerate dogs or cats, she'll settle on the parakeets. She'll write out a check, put the cage in the back seat of her car, and drive off. A few blocks later a car will suddenly swerve in front of her. To avoid a collision, she'll jam on the brake. And in the back seat of the car the cage will tumble to the floor amid a flutter of 'brreet, brreet, brreet.' And God in heaven will know that it happened. Isn't that what Jesus says in Matthew 10:29? 'Are not two sparrows sold for a penny, yet not one of them will fall to the ground apart from the will of your Father?'"

As preachers, we're usually good at this first developmental question. Explanation is easy; it's our strong suit. Our hours of study in the passage and the commentaries provide us with the information we need to develop this area, and we can usually think of illustrations or pictures to make it vivid and interesting.

But explanation is not enough to cause spiritual change in our listeners. "If we explain it, they will do it" is an inadequate approach to preaching. Knowledge alone does not produce godly behavior. Until listeners can see why the statement is true, it will have no motivating power in their lives. That brings us to the second developmental question:

BELIEF

Knowing something does not necessarily mean that we buy it or do it. Our own experience confirms this. For example, many of us probably had some secular theory or body of knowledge explained to us in college. Maybe in a class on child psychology the professor explained that spanking was the least desirable method of discipline for a child. At worst it was child abuse; at best it taught the child that might makes right and that he could impose his will on others by force. The professor may then have gone on to advocate distraction or isolation as preferable methods of child discipline. As we listened to his explanations, however, something in our spirit said, That's not true. The Bible says, "He who spares the rod hates his son, but he who loves him is careful to discipline him" (Prov. 13:24).

When the time came for the final exam, and we saw the question, "Compare and contrast different methods of child discipline," though we knew the answer, we didn't buy it. (We got our A on the exam while preserving our integrity by writing something like, "According to the material presented in class...." That meant, "I know what you want me to know, but I don't necessarily accept it as truth for my life.")

In a similar way, our people know many biblical teachings: that wives are to be submissive to their husbands; that husbands are to treat their wives with consideration and respect; that we all are to avoid lustful fantasies, give generously to the Lord's work, marry Christians, intercede for others, and on and on. In fact, our people probably already know 90 percent of any biblical instruction we plan to give them. The reason they're not yet obeying biblical truth is not because they don't know it, but because they don't yet buy it.

We could simply explain it to them again for the eighteenth time, but this probably won't have any more effect on them than the previous seventeen times. Instead, along with our explanation we should begin to probe whether they buy it. Do they accept the biblical statement as an authoritative and energizing truth for their lives? Do they own it deep in their souls?

In order to probe and expand the biblical outline points with this second developmental question, it helps to know the three reasons why a person doesn't buy something. Whatever we need to say to convince them to own God's truth will depend on the reason why they may not yet have accepted it. *There are at least three reasons why people don't buy something.*

People Don't See the Cause-Effect Connection

For example, in the statement, "Be nice to your grandfather, it will help you have babies," the meaning of the individual words and phrases is obvious. But the validity of the cause-effect relationship is not. Until the listeners can see why the statement is true, it will have no motivating power in their lives.

In such situations the listeners are not hostile or argumentative. They are willing to be persuaded if the speaker can simply answer the question, "Why is this statement true? What does being nice to that old man have to do with getting pregnant?" Until the listeners buy the truth of the cause-effect relationship, the statement as a whole will have no authoritative or energizing force in their lives.

In order for the listeners to be truly motivated to be nice to their grandfathers, the speaker could point out that their grandfather's secret recipe for BBQ sauce is an aphrodisiac, and if they are nice to Grandpa, he may give them his secret recipe, which will help them have babies.

More likely, the speaker will remind his listeners that "the prayer of a righteous man is powerful and effective" (James 5:16). He will then explain that their kindness to a godly grandfather may lead him to pray on their behalf for the Lord to open the womb and that such a prayer may enable them to conceive.

Our preaching must inevitably cover the many cause-effect statements of Scripture. The Bible continually uses language that implies causation: "This leads to this"; "This results from this"; "This produces this"; "This follows from this"; "This brings about this."

For example, 1 Timothy 5:1 teaches that it is detrimental to a young man's ministry to harshly rebuke an older man. This is essentially a cause-effect statement: Harshly rebuking will cause the effect of a weakened ministry. But why is this true? On the surface, a young pastor may nod in agreement. But later, under pressure, he will blow up at an elder in a meeting, justifying it by thinking, *Somebody needs to tell this man the truth.* And from then on the young pastor's ministry suffers because he never did see or buy the connection between a harsh rebuke and a diminished ministry. We need to show why the statement is true.

But what if our text doesn't give the answer? How do we surface the correct cause-effect connection when neither our passage nor a cross reference spells it out?

Several sources can yield the insight we are looking for. Our own life experiences sometimes reveal the connection. There may have been a time, for example, when we harshly rebuked an older man and saw why it set back our ministry. Quiet reflection, combined with prayer for the Spirit's help, can often yield understanding. Friends, wives, older pastors, devotional commentaries, outside reading, or members of small groups can have insights that are helpful. For example, a *Newsweek* issue might feature an article on how human relationships affect health and longevity.

We should offer our cause-effect insights in language more tentative than "Thus saith the Lord." Since the text itself does not amplify the connection, we will lead into our explanations with such phrases as: "Perhaps the apostle has in mind ...""; "It seems to me that ..."; "One explanation might be ..."; "Maybe the biblical author has observed what you and I have observed, that...." This kind of language helps convey that we are giving our best attempt to explain God's inerrant Word.

Granted, we will not have absolute certainty that our connection is the one the biblical writer had in mind. But as the insight satisfies our heart and as the Spirit affirms it during the sermon to the hearts of God's people, we will have a high degree of confidence that we are presenting God's truth.

The Biblical Statement Seems Contrary to Real Life

Some people hear the Scripture and think, *That's not how it is in the real world!* For them, the statement is simply not true because their experiences contradict it.

For example, a woman's response to 1 Peter 3:1–2, "The way to win your husband is through a gentle and quiet yieldedness" (my paraphrase), might be: "I tried that, and it didn't work. When I let him do what he wanted, he joined five different softball leagues, and the kids never saw him at night. Instead of my winning him, he got worse. And if I let him handle the money, he'd take our savings and

invest in the dumbest Ponzi schemes you ever heard of. Our family would be bankrupt. Maybe some other woman can win her husband that way, but not me. I have to lay down the law and then stay on his case."

In such situations, listeners flat out disbelieve the biblical truth. Based on their life experiences, the statement is simply not true, and therefore they have no intentions of living according to it. We must address these unspoken objections, or we will not accomplish anything in the message. Listeners sit with a "yeah, but" attitude, and the "but" deflects anything from entering their hearts.

Here are two steps for answering objections.

1. *Define your terms.* Make sure you and the listeners have the same meaning in mind for key words. Make sure, for example, that when the wife hears yielding, she hears it as something that she should do after she has fully explained her position to her husband, countered his objections, and even pleaded with him. Explain that yielding does not mean "keep your mouth shut and do as you're told."

2. *Explain why Scripture is true.* Even after you've made concepts clear, objections may remain. Therefore the second and more critical step in dealing with objections is to show that people's experiences do not contradict biblical truth.

This does not mean we deny people's experiences. We can't imply, "Oh, it wasn't that bad." They would respond, "Were you there?" But we can show that while their life experiences and attitudes may be real, they do not invalidate God's truth. For instance, if they have chosen to walk a different path than what God says, we can show that this will lead to worse consequences than those they hoped to avoid. Or we can show that the experiences of doing it God's way need more time to arrive at the desirable outcome. One way or another, by reflecting on their experiences we can show they actually reinforce what the Word teaches.

For example, we might show that when a wife fails to yield to her husband instead of winning her husband, she actually drives him farther away. We might say: "When a man and woman come to marriage, each has expectations deep within. A man expects to be the leader in his marriage. That's strange because he doesn't have that thought in most other areas. Unless he is president of his company, a man doesn't go to work and say, 'I'm supposed to direct this company.' He doesn't look at the government and say, 'I'm supposed to be in charge of the country.' He doesn't go to church and say, 'I'm supposed to lead the congregation.' But when a man marries, something deep within says, 'I'm supposed to lead this marriage.' God has put that thought inside him; it is part of his maleness.

"Similarly when a woman marries, she expects that this man will be her protector. She wants him to be her knight in shining armor. When children come and she's vulnerable with them to the world, she wants him to stand guard. She wants to count on him to keep the family safe. These thoughts are part of her femininity, created by God.

"Now, because we are sinners, we often don't act consistently with these thoughts. Because a man is a sinner, he sometimes doesn't lead as he should. Instead of caring for the best interests of his family, he may think only of himself. And because a woman is afraid of the consequences to the family when she sees this happening, she may try to force the man to act as he should. But by trying to compel his right behavior, she adopts a morally superior position. In essence, she stands over him with a scolding finger and says, 'I will tell you what to do; I know better than you do.'

"But this raises the man's hackles because now she is taking the leadership position in the marriage. She is acting as his mommy, telling him what to do. But she is not his mommy; she is his wife. Therefore in the early stages, a man will resist her attempts to compel his behavior. 'Don't tell me what to do,' he will shout. He will argue, fight, and slam doors, and if he is really a sinner, he may even strike her. Though he is doing a bad job of being a leader, he will still do everything he can to hang on to that role.

"As this fighting continues over months, eventually, the Bible says, a man will kick into a second response. He will shut down and become passive. In the words of Solomon, he will conclude, 'Better to live on a corner of the roof than share a house with a quarrelsome wife.' He will retreat to his hobbies or the television. He will pour his life into his career. His attitude will be, 'I don't want to argue any more. I want peace. You can do whatever you want. You can decorate the house any way you want, send the kids to whatever schools you want, join whatever clubs you want. I don't care.' And the wife will have lost her knight in shining armor. Instead of winning him, she drove him away.

"And as the wife listens to us, she may start thinking: *My husband never talks to me anymore. Whenever I suggest something or ask something, he just shrugs and doesn't comment much at all. I can't get him to interact. But I'm afraid to let him take the lead. I'm afraid of what he'll do. I'm afraid of bankruptcy.*"

At this point we as preachers are ready to go further into 1 Peter 3:1–6. We admit that her fear is real, but also we can show how holy women of the past, like Sarah, put their hope in God, submitted to their husbands, and did not give way to their fears. We explain how Abraham twice put Sarah in fearful and compromising circumstances, but show how God acted both times to save her from the consequences of his poor leadership. Then we continue:

"When you stand in a morally superior position over your husband, you essentially get between him and God. God can't get at him. God says, 'Stand aside, honey. Let me take care of him.' But when the woman follows God's plan, God will hit him with a four-by-four. The man will stagger, look into the heavens, and ask, 'Whaddaya want, God?' A man will take from God what he won't take from his wife. And God will deal with him.

"It may involve bankruptcy. But you can come back from bankruptcy; you can't come back from divorce. Afterwards your husband will say to you, 'Honey, you were right. I'm sorry.' And instead of saying, 'I told you so,' you'll say, 'You're my man. We did it once; we can do it again.' And you will have won your husband.

"In this way, a husband's folly does not remain an obstacle to God's truth. The wife can 'buy' yielding as an action that will lead to God's blessing."

For us to search out how hearers' experiences line up with biblical truth, we ourselves must begin with the conviction that God's statements are always true. We must have the spirit of Paul: "Let God be true, and every man a liar" (Rom. 3:4). Whatever God says is true, and anyone who says something contrary is wrong. We start with the conviction that no one's experience invalidates Scripture.

Then we can find motivation in the thought that while it is accurate to say, "Something is true because it's in the Bible," it's even more accurate to say, "Something is in the Bible because it's true." Our job is to explain the ultimate truth, or reality, behind the biblical words. When we show what God knew that led him to say what he said, we help listeners really believe it.

Our insights into this ultimate truth come with experience, through reflection and prayer, from friends, spouses, older people in the congregation, or from members of a small group who help us think about each week's sermon.

Something "More Important" Comes Up

On Sunday, our listeners may seem to assent to a particular truth. But during the week other factors come up that outweigh the biblical statement and prevent them from acting consistently with it.

In a vacuum, all things being equal, they buy the biblical truth. But real life is not a vacuum, and all things are not equal. People hold to a hierarchy of beliefs, a ladder of truths. Some values are higher on the ladder than others. They are more important; they matter more; we buy them ahead of others.

Suppose, for example, I detest rhubarb pie and essentially buy the statement, "Rhubarb pie is to be avoided." But suppose also that I'm invited to a friend's house, and as we're waiting for the hostess to bring in the dessert, the husband says to me: "Don, you're in luck. My wife has prepared her secret-family-recipe, county-award-winning rhubarb pie. She doesn't do this for many people, because you have to drive two hours to get decent rhubarb and it takes four to five hours to soak, peel, and bake the pie. But for you, she's done it."

Now, I may buy the statement, "Rhubarb pie is to be avoided," but I also buy the statement, "You don't insult the efforts of a loving hostess."

Whichever one of these statements I buy the most is the one I'm going to act on in that situation. And you can probably guess that I'll choke down a few swallows before I announce, "I'm too full to eat another bite."

A teenage girl may prayerfully commit herself in a Sunday school class "to dress modestly to the glory of God." But you may then see her at a pool the next Saturday wearing a bathing suit that doesn't fit anybody's definition of modesty, and you see her twined around some college guy. This doesn't necessarily mean she's a hypocrite. It may simply mean that while she buys dressing modestly to the glory of God, she also buys having a boyfriend or getting appreciative signals that she is attractive in her femininity.

To get her to value God's truth most of all would require bringing up the other values on Sunday, acknowledging their tug on her, and then showing either the superior benefits of acting according to God's truth or the dangerous side-effects of acting according to contrary values. One way or another, the goal is to help her see the biblical truth as more important.

Suppose a woman named Helen is listening to you preach about being honest at the job. Let's imagine that Helen works for an entrepreneur named Sam who has developed a software program for the medical industry. Hospitals can use the program to track medical supplies, schedule operating rooms, handle payroll, and so on. Once a central hospital adopts the program, most doctors' offices in the community follow suit so as to be compatible with the hospital. Sam is the creative genius behind the program and markets it throughout the state. Helen is his business manager, holding down the fort and supervising two other women in the office.

Helen is a godly woman. Her husband is on the church board. They have a high school daughter and a junior high son, both active in the church youth groups. You wish every family in the church could be as this family.

Helen also appreciates Sam as a boss. He pays her well. He lets her take off a few hours to watch her son's soccer game or attend her daughter's after-school theater presentation.

As Helen listens to you preach about being honest at the job, she buys it. She nods at your applications: She doesn't take office supplies home for personal use, she doesn't call in sick unless she's really ill, she promises accurate delivery dates to clients. On Sunday, in church, she buys the biblical truth.

But then Tuesday at 1:30 in the afternoon, she gets a call. It's Sam. Before he can say anything, she blurts: "Sam, where are you? Did you forget about your 2:00 meeting with Dr. Shiller, the Hospital Administrator at St. Jude's?"

"Helen, that's why I'm calling. I accidentally double booked. I'm in a hotel an hour away getting ready to demonstrate the program to the heads of the major teaching hospitals in the country. If they go for it, we'll go national! We may even get a write-up in the *New England Journal of Medicine*."

"But what about Shiller? He's going to be here in a few minutes. What should I tell him?"

"Tell him I'm caught in traffic, and I'll be there any minute."

"Sam, I can't tell him that. By the time you demonstrate the program, answer their questions, and then drive across the city, you won't be here until 4:00."

"Helen, you've got to tell him that. If he finds out I double booked on him, he'll storm out and we'll never get him back for a demonstration."

"Sam, I can't lie for you."

"Helen, you tell him that, or I'll get someone at that desk who can tell him that."

Now, Helen buys being honest at the job. But she also buys having a job. Whichever one she buys the most will determine what she'll do when Shiller shows up at 2:00.

To help listeners buy God's truth above all other factors, we must surface on Sunday the competing beliefs or attitudes. We must help listeners feel their full force, and then we must show why acting on the biblical statement is even more desirable. We must bring up the potential conflicts that could arise, visualize them honestly, and walk our people through them to a commitment to God's truth above all else.

For example, we might say to Helen: "Even though it might mean losing your job, you should still be committed to honesty at work. Trust God's promise: If we are persecuted for righteousness' sake—we act with integrity, and pay a price for it—we are blessed."

At this point Helen probably thinks, Okay, Pastor, you just got me fired. Could you work with that "blessed" part some more?

And so, to help Helen buy honesty more than keeping a job, we might continue along the following lines: "One way or another, you'll be blessed. God may give you a better job—higher pay, closer to home, better hours. I can't guarantee that, but the Bible says he feeds the ravens and clothes the lilies, and if you need the new joy, he'll give it to you.

"I can guarantee you a clear conscience. You'll walk out of the office that Tuesday afternoon thinking, *God, you're up to something in my life. I'm not sure what, but I just did something that pleased you.*

"Maybe the blessing will be the impact on your junior high son. Maybe Wednesday morn-ing he'll see you at breakfast in your robe and slippers and come to a wrong conclusion: 'Do you guys have a holiday and we have to go to school? No fair!' 'No, honey, no holiday. I'm just not going to work today.' 'What's the matter, Mom, are you sick?' 'No, honey, I'm not sick. To tell you the truth, I got fired yesterday.' 'You did! What did you do?' 'Well, the boss wanted me to say.... But I wouldn't lie for him.'

"On his way to school your son excitedly tells his best friend, 'My mom got fired because she wouldn't tell a lie.' On Sunday, as he shares a hymnbook with you, he looks at the pastor, and thinks, *You don't know what happened at our house this week—my mom got fired for telling the truth!* This stuff must be real. Helen, if getting fired will turn your junior high son into a man of God for the rest of his life, would that be a blessing? You bet!

"Maybe the blessing is the impact it will have on someone in the office, perhaps even Sam. After you tell the truth and Shiller storms out, maybe you decide to make it easy on Sam by cleaning out your desk and leaving early. As you're putting your personal effects into a card-board box—family pictures, plants, Far-Side Cartoons—Sam shows up sooner than expected. 'Helen, what are you doing?' 'Well, Sam, you said—' 'Never mind what I said. Put that stuff back! Sit down! Work! You're not going anywhere.' Then, as he goes into his office and starts to return a telephone message, he looks back through the door and thinks to himself, *That's one classy lady.*

"A few months later, when Sam is having trouble with his teenagers and he needs to talk to someone who has her head screwed on straight, he may wander out into the office: 'Hey, Helen, how long has it been since I've taken you to lunch? You like that Italian place around the corner, don't you? How about tomorrow? Good! Maybe my wife will join us.' And over lunch Sam is going to work his family situation into the conversation and receive godly counsel.

"Maybe the blessing is that God wants you home for the sake of your teenage daughter. He's been trying to get you to quit, but since you haven't, he's getting you fired instead. Your family doesn't need the money as much as your daughter needs you. Have you noticed that her bedroom door is closed every evening, and she's on the phone for hours talking to her girlfriends? You knock on her door. 'Who's there?' your daughter says. 'It's me, Mom.' 'What do you want?' 'I have your laundry; can I bring it in?' 'Okay.'

"While you're in the room, she's silent, phone cradled to her chest, waiting for you to leave. As you exit, she says, 'Close the door, will you, Mom?' And then you hear her talking again. Your daughter is going through some heavy stuff right now, and she's getting all her advice from non-Christian teenagers. What she needs is a mother who's home. What she needs is to help with dinner, so that while she's peeling carrots she can casually drop that oh-so-important question into an everyday conversation. And your daughter, still peeling carrots, gets the wisdom of a godly mother to help her through life.

"One way or another, you'll be blessed."

And Helen, listening to us preach, thinks to herself, *I'll take any one of those results! Any one of those blessings is better than lying to keep my job.*

By bringing up the competing beliefs or attitudes within the message itself, acknowledging their force and attraction and showing why God's truth is even more desirable, we help our listeners to buy the biblical value more than anything else.

BEHAVIOR

Relevance occurs when the listener *sees* how the biblical truth applies to a specific situation. The word *sees* should be highlighted, underlined—with little red hearts drawn around it!

Unless listeners have a mental picture—a video running in their minds—of some real-life situation, the biblical truth remains an abstraction, vague and unhelpful. The message has no apparent bearing on their lives until they visualize some person, event, or circumstance in their everyday world.

Our discussion of this third question is not limited to the conclusion of a message. We are not necessarily talking about giving the listener at the end of the message "three tangible steps you can take to put this message into practice." Instead, this question focuses on a relevancy that pervades the message; all through the message our listeners see the concepts in terms of everyday life.

For example, suppose we say in the introduction, "Did you ever obey God and have the bottom fall out of everything? Did you ever do exactly what God told you to do and have disaster occur?" We then suggest immediately what this might look like, how it might show up in everyday life:

"You obey God and move to another city so you can study at seminary. A few months after the move, however, life seems to fall apart: Your home church is unable to continue its pledged financial support because of an economic downturn. Your kids come home from school crying because they are being ostracized and teased by the longtime cliques. Your wife has developed undiagnosed allergies in the new community. You receive an F on your first language exam. And you find out your car has a cracked block.

"Or another example. You obey God's prompting to honor your mother by taking her into your own home after your dad died. Everybody seems in agreement. The kids double-bunk so Grandma can have her own room. But after six months the house is in an uproar. Your wife comes to you and says, 'It's her or me. Decide which woman you want in this house. She doesn't like the way I cook. She criticizes the way I keep house. She's rearranged my kitchen so I can't find anything.' Your kids are walking on eggshells because Grandma's constantly down on them: 'You shouldn't be listening to that devil music. You can't wear that to school—put on something decent.' And you're thinking, *God, what are you doing? All I wanted to do was honor my mother, and my home is a disaster.*

"A man is convinced God is leading him to marry a certain woman. His parents and church friends confirm what the Spirit has been telling him—that this is God's will. So he obeys. But in the months that follow, his life is in constant and tumultuous upheaval. He sympathizes with the young husband in one story, who returns to the minister who conducted their marriage and says, 'When you married me, you said, "Son, congratulations. You're at the end of all your troubles." But this last year has been the worst year of my life. You told me I was at the end of all my troubles.' The minister replies, 'Son, I didn't tell you which end.'

"Sometimes we obey God, and the bottom falls out of everything."

All through the message—from the opening and all through the concepts—we constantly ask, "What does this look like in real life? How does it show up in everyday situations?"

Our ultimate goal in speaking is not simply to add to the listener's biblical knowledge. Such knowledge can seem irrelevant. Our ultimate goal is not to "teach the Bible." Our ultimate goal is to teach how the Bible's message fits our lives. The reason we are teaching Genesis 11 and 12 is because God may come to one of our hearers and say the same thing he said to Abraham: Leave what is comfortable, leave what you're familiar with, and come with me without knowing what I will put in its place. Follow me without knowing in advance how it will turn out. God may say that to

- a couple he wants to minister cross-culturally
- a wife struggling over a cross-country move, leaving family, long-time friends, doctors, and neighborhood shops
- a man wondering if he should leave IBM, with its secure paycheck, benefits, and retirement, and pioneer his own start-up company
- a teenager who needs to leave the circle of friends who have become a bad influence on him, for the unknowns of "Whom will I hang out with? Whom will I go to the mall or movies with?"
- a comfortable bachelor, who is afraid to pop the question
- a fiancée who needs to break up her engagement because God is saying, "Fred is a good man, but he is not the one for you; I have someone else in mind." "God," she prays, "I'm thirty-three years old; Fred is the best thing to come into this small church in ten years. If you have someone else in mind, how about you bring him in the front door so I can take a good look at him before I let go of Fred."

Though knowledge alone is irrelevant, it is nevertheless possible to develop a large following from an information-oriented ministry. People get pleasure from learning something, like the Athenians in Acts 17:19–21:

Then they took him and brought him to a meeting of the Areopagus, where they said to him,

"May we know what this new teaching is that you are presenting? You are bringing some strange ideas to our ears, and we want to know what they mean." (All the Athenians and the foreigners who lived there spent their time doing nothing but talking about and listening to the latest ideas.)

But Scripture passes judgment on any preaching that is primarily information-oriented. That kind of ministry produces an arrogant people, exactly like the Athenians:

"Now about food sacrificed to idols: We know that we all possess knowledge. Knowledge puffs up, but love builds up" (1 Cor. 8:1). Knowledge produces a Pharisaism that knows the law but is unable to see how deeply it should be changing their lives.

Our ultimate goal in speaking is not to convey knowledge but to stimulate godly behavior. The purpose of our ministry is not information but Christlikeness: "The goal of this command is love, which comes from a pure heart and a good conscience and a sincere faith" (1 Tim. 1:5).

Our primary intent is not that our listeners learn something, but that they use the Scriptures for all the practical ways intended in everyday life: "All Scripture is God-breathed and is useful for teaching, rebuking, correcting and training in righteousness, so that the man of God may be thoroughly equipped for every good work" (2 Tim. 3:16–17).

Until our listeners see how the truths of Scripture apply in the concrete situations of life, their Christianity is meaningless, and they are deceived about their spiritual growth: "But everyone who hears these words of mine and does not put them into practice is like a foolish man who built his house on sand. The rain came down, the streams rose, and the winds blew and beat against that house, and it fell with a great crash" (Matt. 7:26–27).

"Do not merely listen to the word, and so deceive yourselves. Do what it says. Anyone who listens to the Word but does not do what it says is like a man who looks at his face in a mirror, and, after looking at himself, goes away and immediately forgets what he looks like. But the man who looks intently into the perfect law that gives freedom, and continues to do this, not forgetting what he has heard, but doing it—he will be blessed in what he does" (James 1:22–25).

In order for relevance to occur and godliness to form, *we* must make the applications. The listeners usually will not make them for themselves. This is not a criticism of them; rather, it is a realistic assessment based on my own experience when I am on vacation and listening to another preacher. At the end of his message—when the music is playing, the congregation is dismissed, and people are trying to step past me to get to the aisle—if he has not given me some concrete pictures of how the truth bears on my life, am I going to stay seated in my chair, blocking others, saying to my wife, "Honey, let me have a few minutes alone. I want to think of how this applies to my life." No. I'm going to rise like the others, turn to my wife, and say, "You want to go to McDonald's or Wendy's? You get the girls, I'll get the boys. I'll meet you at the car."

So the next time you find yourself saying, "May the Spirit of God apply this to your hearts," what you are really saying is, "I haven't the vaguest idea of how it fits; maybe you'll think of something." But they won't.

We must make the application. Our sermon must be an extended meditation on God's truth, which will result in an understanding not only of *what* is said, but also *why* it is good wisdom, and *where* it is operating or can operate in our lives (covering all three developmental questions).

FINDING RELEVANT PICTURES

But how do we come up with these relevant *pictures*? What skills help us to surface and describe how it *shows up* in their lives? Let me suggest four things to do.

1. Examine Your Own Life

Think where something would show up in your own life. Ask yourself, *How have I experienced this? How am I experiencing it? How might I experience it?* (Think in all three tenses; imagine *realistic* situations in the future as well as *actual* ones in the past and present.)

For instance, suppose you're talking about the kind of anger that erupts or explodes when we're impatient, irritated or frustrated. Ask, "When might this kind of anger show up in my life?"

- When you head to the "15 items or less" check-out line at the grocery story, only to find yourself behind a cart that has forty-five items in it. Then the offending shopper waits until all the items have been scanned before fumbling for coupons.
- When someone cuts you off on the freeway and almost drives you into the guardrail.
- When one of your church board members, in a knee-jerk reaction, throws cold water on one of your suggestions without even trying to understand its advantages.

Wherever it shows up in your life is probably where it also shows up in their lives, and you can visualize the situation for them. For example, the board member situation could correspond to when an in-law pooh-poohs some idea you have, or a coworker ridicules a suggestion at work.

2. Present Life Circumstances of Others

Run the truth through an expanding grid of the various groups and life circumstances in your audience. Visualize the different kinds of people you'll be talking to—men, women, children. Break them down into subcategories and rummage around to see if your biblical truth shows up in some situation.

Break these subcategories down further, into sub-subcategories and sub-sub-subcategories. Not all husbands or fathers are the same, for example. What are the different kinds of husbands? How do the men differ in their fathering?

Husbands
  How long married
    One year
    A twenty-year-old married one year, first marriage
    A forty-year-old married one year, first marriage
    Fifteen years
    Forty years
    First marriage or a subsequent one for either spouse
    Whether they had role models for husbanding in their own fathers
Fathers
  How many children
  How old the children are
  Whether the children are boys, girls, or both
  Whether he's the biological father or a step-dad

Let's probe the work category. See if your biblical truth strikes fire with one of the scenarios:

Owns the business and is the boss
  Bottom line; profit
  Employees
  Hiring, firing, training
  Morale
  Fringe benefits
  Government regulations, OSHA, Worker's Compensation, competition; obsolescence of the product/service

Works for another; is an employee
   Dead-end job, no advancement
   Boring job, routine
   Boss
      Demanding, critical

      Incompetent

      Plays favorites, guilty of nepotism

      Harasses, is crude, immoral
   Fellow employees
      Lazy

      Incompetent

      Obnoxious
   Safety concerns, health hazards
   Salary, benefits
   Commuting time or distance
   Production pressures; stress; feeling in over
      one's head
Retired and on Social Security
   Still consulting; a different part-time job
   Struggles over self-worth, purpose in life
   Adequate pension, retirement funds
   What now fills up the time
Unemployed
   How long between jobs; economic impact on
      the family
   Self-image concerns
   Age discrimination; likelihood of finding
      another equivalent job
   Retraining necessary; new schooling

If nothing strikes fire in the work area, you would switch to another—their dwelling situations, or the different stages of marriage, still asking, Does my biblical truth show up in any of these circumstances?

3. Find Applicable Pictures

Use pictures that apply the biblical concept, not ones that simply illustrate it. I define an illustration as a picture or analogy from an area outside our personal lives. By this definition you would be illustrating if you told of the courage of a Civil War general whose horse was shot out from under him, yet he grabbed his sword from the ground and shouted to his men, "Follow me." To urge our listeners to have a similar courage may leave them unmoved since they can't identify with the situation. It's an illustration, not an application.

Stories of Victorian widows, accounts of Indonesian prisoners being persecuted, analogies of geese flying in formation, explanations of how to make a dress—they are all illustrations. They may clarify, they may entertain, but they don't apply—they don't help the listener to *see* how it shows up in *their* lives.

In contrast, an application is a picture from the exact situation in your listeners' lives that the biblical author is talking about. For example, suppose you're preaching on 1 Timothy 6:9–10, and your central idea is "The love of money can be your downfall." An illustration would be to tell the story of King Midas or of Yusef the Terrible Turk—a true story. In the 1940s Yusef came to America to participate in a heavyweight wrestling tournament. One by one he defeated all his opponents and won the grand prize of $10,000.

Two days after winning, he was ticketed on a ship to Europe and his native Turkey. He told the promoters that he didn't want his prize in the form of a check; he insisted on gold coins— a universal medium of exchange. He bought a money belt and stuffed the sixty-five pounds of gold coins into the belt around his waist.

The ship's personnel offered to store the gold in the ship's safe, but Yusef preferred to have the gold on his person at all times. A few days out at sea, however, an engine malfunction caused the ship to be stranded. Another vessel was sent to transfer all passengers on board.

Yusef tried to jump on board the new vessel, but he missed by a few inches and plunged into the water below. And that's the last anyone ever heard of Yusef the Terrible Turk.

After telling this story, you then solemnly warn your people, "The love of money will be your downfall." And someone in the audience thinks, *I'll remember that the next time I win a wrestling championship and am crossing the Atlantic on a ship.*

Would I tell this story in church? Probably. But I wouldn't deceive myself into thinking I had been relevant. I've been entertaining, but I haven't helped people *see* how it fits in *their* lives. So if I tell that story, I also need to picture how the love of money leading to a downfall might show up in my listeners' experiences. I need to talk in concrete images about

- working eighty hours a week to make money at the expense of your family
- playing the lottery at the expense of the family's economics
- incurring large credit card debt in pursuit of a lifestyle
- engaging in unethical practices that pay a lot but corrupt the soul
- withholding your tithe and experiencing God's displeasure

An illustration brings interest and clarity. An application brings interest, clarity, and relevance.

4. MAKE DETAILED APPLICATIONS

Make your applications detailed and extended, not vague and brief. Paint the picture. Visualize specifics, create conversations, act out the actions you want the listeners to do. Rehearse out loud the internal thoughts or reasoning process you want them to go through. Nothing happens in our listeners apart from specific pictures. No godliness forms unless the truth is related to concrete situations of life.

Suppose I'm teaching a fifth-grade boys Sunday school class, and I say, "Guys, what does this mean to your everyday lives? It means, 'Be a good Christian.'"

"Uh, Mr. Sunukjian, what does that mean?"

"Okay, it means, 'Respond to those over you.'"

But *respond* is not a picture-word, and when you're in the fifth grade, everybody is "over you." So I try again. "It means, 'Obey your parents.'" *Parents* is a picture word, but *obey* is not.

I must not be content with such vagueness and brevity. I must visualize in extended detail some situations in their lives, so that they can see what godliness would actually look like in their lives. For example: "Guys, it means when your mom gives you sixty-five cents and tells you, 'Use this at school to buy milk,' you use the sixty-five cents to buy milk and not Cheetos."

Now the boys have a picture, and some small godliness can form in their lives as they anticipate pleasing God in some concrete situation.

The biblical narratives present truth through these kind of extended, detailed pictures. Since God uses extended pictures from the biblical world to present the truth to us, we should use equally extended contemporary pictures to carry forward the truth into our world.

Chapter 93

BETTER BIG IDEAS

Five qualities of the strongest preaching ideas

Haddon Robinson

What's the purpose of "the big idea"? In other words, why put blood, sweat, and tears into developing the best one possible?

First of all, I need to be clear as to what I'm talking about when I talk about a big idea. I'm talking about the major idea of the sermon, the proposition of the sermon, the basic principle you're trying to get across. The reason "the big idea" has become popular as a way of talking about it is that when I was trying to establish it in the minds of my students I would say, "What's the big idea?" It was a slang expression, but I was trying to get it to stick in students' minds. I did well, because that's the way people refer to it today.

A sermon has many ideas to it, but all of them should grow out of the major idea of the sermon. That's not new with me. Go back as far as Aristotle, Plato, and Cicero, and you'll find that they talk about having a proposition around which a speech is developed. Often this gets lost in sermons. So when I talk about a big idea, I'm talking about an organizing factor. Take all the parts of a sermon and put them together into a whole, and that whole is the central idea—the big idea—in the sermon. So, one purpose of the big idea is that you organize the sermon around it.

A second purpose is that you want to leave something lasting in the minds of the congregation when a sermon is over. The truth is, people don't remember outlines. They may not even refer to them again. I don't know of anyone who's been moved to God with an outline of the book of Galatians. What people do live for, what they do die for, is an idea, some great truth that has gripped them.

I can't expect that every congregation is going to remember every idea I try to get across, but there's a better chance they'll take something away and remember it a week or two or even a month or two later if I can stamp that central thrust on their minds. The rest of the sermon is often like the scaffolding: It's important, but the major thing is for people to get hold of an idea or have an idea get hold of them that can in some way shape the way they respond to life.

CHARACTERISTICS OF THE BIG IDEA

 For an audio example of this principle see tracks 10–11 on the supplemental CD.

There are five characteristics of a powerful central idea. *(1) The idea has to be narrow enough to be sharp.* It has to be narrow enough to get under your skin as a preacher. It's a clear answer to the question, *What exactly am I talking about?* If you have a vague idea, if it's too broad, too general, too abstract, it doesn't do anything for you. But when you get one that's sharp enough to get into your soul, that's important.

For example, a colleague of mine at Gordon-Conwell, Dr. Peter Kuzmic, was speaking about hope, and he took an idea from Augustine. He said, "Hope has two daughters: anger and courage—anger at how things are, and courage to try to change them." That's a great idea. I heard it several weeks ago, and I'm able to remember it. And the more I think about it, the more it has gotten under my skin.

Another idea is about hope: "Hope is hearing the music of the future, and faith is having the courage to dance to it." That, too, is an idea—the relationship of faith and hope. You could state that in a lot of blah ways. You could say, "Hope helps us to think about the future, and faith is to live in the light of that thought." But it doesn't have the power of, "Hope is hearing the music of the future, and faith is having the courage to dance to it." It gets under your skin.

(2) The next characteristic of a powerful idea is that it has an expanding force. It's like the yeast in dough; it has a way of fermenting. Often when you start, you wonder if you have enough to say to fill thirty minutes. But when you get hold of an idea or it gets hold of you, you wonder if you can get it said in thirty minutes. If you ask, "What has to be said about this idea? What do I have to say to get it across? What's it really mean?" you discover it has a powerful force. It cries out for development.

(3) A third characteristic of a good idea is that it has to be true. I'm not just talking about true because it's found in the Bible and we believe the Scriptures are true. I'm talking about true, deep in your own bones. If you get an idea that gets hold of you and you sense it's true, it creates passion in you. The single most important ingredient in effective preaching is passion. It's not enthusiasm, not loudness; it's the sense that this matters. When you sense this is true to life, this is true to God, this is true to my experience, this is true in the fundamental part of life, then that enables you to want to work on a sermon and give it your best and give it some time. When you sense this is true, it makes it worth your while to prepare it and preach it.

(4) The next great idea grows out of the third: It ought to be filled with the realities of life. Some preaching explains doctrine. That's important, but people sit in the audience and ask, "So what?" If theology doesn't explain life, it's probably not worth the time it takes to study it or preach it. Theology isn't some abstract thing we put on the blackboard at a seminary and look at and argue about. Real theology is about how God intersects with our lives and how life looks when we take seriously that the God of the Bible is really there. So a good idea is loaded with the realities of life. It's concerned with deep and universal problems. It wrestles with questions like life and death and courage and fear and love and hate and trust and doubt and guilt and forgiveness and pain and joy, the awful emotions of shame and remorse, and the great emotions of compassion and hope.

You have a great idea when you've gotten to the cross, when it's true in your own soul and people sense it. The trivial sermons try to get out on the edge and talk about some esoteric doctrine, but the great sermons go back to the center, to the great fundamental issues, where people live and love and hurt, the kinds of issues the Bible speaks to.

(5) This brings me to the fifth characteristic of a great sermon idea: It is true to God's Word. The first four characteristics are true of any idea, but fundamental to a sermon idea is that it's true to the Scriptures, true to the Word of God. We are not simply philosophers as preachers. We are

not motivational speakers. We are people entrusted with God's Word. One of the great things about working with Scripture is that it's a book of great ideas, because its words reflect the reality of God and how God intersects with us. We go to the Scriptures to get our ideas.

That means when I come to the Bible, I have to recognize that's what it is. It's a book of ideas—not just a book of words or phrases or isolated verses. The biblical writers were attempting to get across ideas, and I have to see that when I come to a biblical text. I have to look for it, and you don't get trivial ideas in the Bible. The more you work with the Scriptures, the more you recognize you're dealing with depth and greatness.

Years ago when my son Torey had gotten out of seminary, I was joshing him. I said, "Torey, you're only in your middle twenties. What's a kid like you got to say to somebody like me?" He turned the conversation to seriousness and said, "Dad, that's why I've got to be a preacher of the Bible. Quite frankly, I haven't lived long enough to think deeply and strongly enough about things. But the biblical writers have. And if I can understand biblical truth and preach it, I'll have a wisdom beyond my years." And then he said with a wink, "And by the way, it's still beyond your years too."

DEVELOPING THE BIG IDEA

We must follow an exegetical and homiletical process to come to the point of writing the big idea. First of all, the exegetical idea is what the biblical writer was saying to the biblical readers. The Bible cannot mean what it has not meant. So one of the things I have to ask is, When the author of Genesis was writing his story, what was he intending to say to the people who read the account? What was Paul trying to say to the people in the town of Colosse when he wrote his Colossian letter? That's the exegetical idea.

It may sound obvious when I say you look for ideas when you study the Bible, but when I went through seminary I didn't get that. I'm sure there were professors who were saying it. I just didn't get it. So when I got out of seminary, I didn't know when to quit studying, because I didn't know what I was looking for. I would parse the verbs, decline the nouns, diagram the sentences. But I didn't know when I was through, because I didn't know I was looking for ideas.

The homiletical idea is the idea from Scripture as I phrase it and shape it for a twenty-first-century audience. That is, if somebody came into my study, how would I express that concept to the person sitting across the desk from me? The homiletical idea is based on the work you do in exegesis, but you haven't preached if you leave people in the past, two thousand years ago. The homiletical idea is to take this great truth of Scripture and state it in a way people today will hear it.

One challenge in understanding and communicating the central idea of the text is working with exegesis to get it. I often end up in exegesis with a lot of parts. But I've got to come back to synthesis to put it together. In a way, as I study it's like an hourglass. There's the top of the hourglass, in which I read the text, usually in several versions. Then I use my commentaries and whatever else I can get hold of to look at the details of the text. Then I come back and put it together in a strong exegetical idea.

Many of the commentaries explain the particulars but don't tell you the universals. That is, they tell you about the individual words and phrases but don't trace the argument of the passage. So one challenge I have is to be able to say, *This is what the biblical writer is talking about.* There are two parts to that.

The first part of this challenge is to ask: *What is the author saying?* This must be a complete idea; it can't be a single word. We call that the *subject,* and the subject is the answer to the question, *What is this writer talking about?* You can state the subject in terms of a question. That is, you can't preach a sermon on forgiveness. You can preach a sermon on, *Why should we forgive?* or a sermon on, *How do we go about forgiving other people?* or, *When should we forgive? Should we do it immediately? Should we do it when the other person apologizes or repents? Who should forgive?* One of those questions will dominate, and you have to think that through: *What's the biblical writer getting at? What's he talking about?*

The second part of this first challenge is what we call a *complement.* It completes the subject and answers the question, *What's this writer saying about what he's talking about?* If the subject is a question, then the complement is the answer to that question, and the two together become the idea. So one task I have is nailing that, getting the sense that I understand the text and the major idea the biblical writer is trying to communicate.

The second major challenge I have is to ask: *I have this biblical idea. How does it apply to life?* For example, the book of Leviticus tells me how to give a burnt offering. I could probably summarize in a complement how to give a burnt offering. But having done that, the question is, *What's that got to do with people in the twenty-first century?* Nobody will come into your study and say, "I'm interested in giving a burnt offering to God. Can you tell me the way I should go about it?" It's not hard to under-

stand Leviticus, but it's difficult to understand how you take this passage and apply it to people today. Crossing the bridge from the ancient world to the modern world is a difficult process at times.

A third challenge I wrestle with when I'm working with a text is to state it in modern terms, in ways that people will get. For example, suppose you were preaching on the baptism of the Holy Spirit. If you're going to state it as a theological principle you might say, "The baptism of the Holy Spirit is the act of the Holy Spirit when we're converted that puts us into the church, which the biblical writers call the body of Christ, and gives us a relationship to every other Christian and to Jesus Christ, who is the head." That's theologically accurate, but nobody will be able to take that idea home with them. It's too long, too vague. Even after you've explained it, people will have a hard time remembering it.

You might decide to apply that to your audience and say, "The baptism of the Holy Spirit is the work the Holy Spirit did for you in placing you into the church and giving you a relationship to every other Christian and to Jesus Christ himself." This is a little better, because at least you're talking to the people in front of you about them.

I might, though, work with the implication of that and say, "The baptism of the Holy Spirit means if you belong to Jesus Christ, you belong to everyone else who belongs to Jesus Christ." Now that's a better idea. It gets under my skin. I sense it has great implications. There's a lot to be said about it. There's great truth. And instead of building walls between myself and other Christians, it has a way of tearing them down. But it's only when I state it that way that I sense, *Yes, that's worth preaching.*

It doesn't come easily. And some Sundays it doesn't come at all. But those are the things I wrestle with to have a strong central idea at the throbbing heartbeat of the sermon.

GOOD IDEAS AND GREAT IDEAS

There are many ideas in the Bible, and yet all the ideas are not equally great. There are overarching ideas. There are probably only eight or nine great ideas in the Scriptures. They recur again and again and come in different shapes and forms.

For example, one great idea of the Bible is that the just shall live by faith. You get it in Habakkuk. You get it three times in the New Testament. It's a great central truth. It's abstract. The just shall live by faith. They don't live by their experiences. They don't live by what they see. They live by faith. The just live by faith in the way they come to Jesus Christ. You become a Christian by putting your faith in Christ. We often miss the fact that after you become a Christian you live by faith. It's the argument of the book of Galatians. Ultimately, when we see Christ, we'll be there because of faith. It's a great principle of the Scriptures, and that's a great idea because it captures so much.

Not every sermon idea can be a great idea, but there are a lot of good ideas. They are not as overarching, but they are often the stuff that makes our sermons. And every so often you can hit a homerun with a great statement of a great truth, but the difference between a good big idea and a great big idea has to do with the magnitude of what the idea is about.

Once we have a great big idea, we need to use it for maximum benefit in the sermon. *It must become the organizing principle of your sermon.* Whether the sermon is developed deductively, where you state the idea up front and then question it, or inductively, where you lead up to the idea, it is the organizing center of the sermon. Everything leads up to it or everything develops out of it.

You have to say it several times. Even if you lead up to it and put it at the conclusion, then you state it and restate it. And to restate it you usually put it in other words. But then you come back and repeat it again. In the sermons I have preached that have been most effective, I will have stated my central idea five, six, seven times. The preacher with skill repeats the idea sometimes through an illustration and other times through the quotation of a hymn. You want to drive it home. It's what a congregation is to remember. People will not remember it if you only state it once. If you don't state it at least three or four times, they will not get it.

There have been times when I have pounded home the idea. I mean, I have really hit it. And at lunch, I'll say to my family or to trusted friends, "I'm curious. If you were to sum up what I was saying in the sermon today, what would you say?" Sometimes they get it. If it's a memorable statement, sometimes they get it. Many times they have gotten the thrust of the sermon, but it's in a ragged, vague sort of way. I've learned that if you don't drive it home, if you don't take time to do it, if you don't say it over and over and over again in different ways in different parts of the sermon, people will not get it. It's amazing how little people are able to carry home from the sermon and remember a day or two later. The way you get maximum benefit from the idea is to lay it down, explain it, prove it, apply it, and show people where it is in the biblical text, but always try to get them to remember it.

Chapter 94

THE POWER OF SEQUENCE
Should you use parallel points or sequential points?

Craig Brian Larson

The sermon form I cut my teeth on uses parallel points. Every point in the sermon bridges out of the transition in the introduction, so that all the points are parallel. For example, in a sermon on Luke 12:22–34, the transition sentence could be "Jesus gives us five reasons not to worry." The key word is "reasons." Every point offers a reason not to worry, and so every point is parallel in logic, bridging from the one transition. Here is a possible outline:

Jesus gives us five reasons not to worry:
- God intends life to be much more significant than just getting food and clothing.
- We can depend on God to provide for us better than he does for plants and animals.
- Worry accomplishes nothing.
- Worry makes us like those who do not know God.
- God promises to provide for those who seek his kingdom.

This form of preaching—keyword with parallel points—has the advantage of clarity. In addition, it suits texts that have parallel ideas or lists. But not all texts have that shape, especially narratives, psalms, and longer sections of letters. When we try to force a text without parallel ideas into the grid I describe above, we may distort the text. Or we may neglect important ideas in the text that do not fit the logic of our parallel points (or may shoehorn them into our outline).

In the example above, what can I do with an important idea in the text that does not give a reason to avoid worry? Verses 32–34 do not provide straightforward reasons not to worry, but they climax what Jesus says. Life is not just food and clothes; life is ultimately about experiencing the kingdom of God. In the satisfying life of the kingdom, we are so free from seeking food and clothes that we can actually seek ways to give our things away!

If I feel bound to my parallel points, I might not include verses 32–34 in my sermon text, which would truncate this Scripture's full, intended message. Another downside of parallel points can be predictability. Once we have given the transition sentence in the introduction, everyone knows where the sermon is going. What we gain in clarity we may lose in suspense. If hearers are passionately interested in every reason not to worry, predictability is a positive; if they are not interested, it is a negative. Whatever is predictable can bore both us and our hearers.

SEQUENTIAL POINTS

But there is an alternative. Our points don't have to be parallel; they can be sequential. Each idea can flow into the next rather than all flow out of the transition sentence in the introduction. Point 1 leads to point 2. Point 2 leads to point 3. Point 3 leads to point 4. It's simple, logical, compelling.

Here is a topical sermon with points that follow sequential logic:

- God loves every person.
- But not every person responds to God's love.
- People can reject God's love because God gives people the freedom to choose.
- Our free choice has consequences.
- And so, I urge you to respond to God's love.

Notice how each point in this topical sermon flows out of the preceding point and leads to the next point. The points cannot be rearranged, as they could be in a parallel structure.

Here is a sequential outline based on the exposition of a single verse, 1 Peter 4:10:

- Each of us has received a spiritual gift from God.
- These spiritual gifts come in many forms.
- No matter what our gifts are, they place on us the responsibility to be faithful managers of them.
- Identify and use your gift!

Or again, using the longer Luke passage above (Luke 12:22–34), if I develop points in sequential logic I might have the following outline:

- Sometimes we are tempted to worry about our daily material needs (v. 22).
- Such worry can make "making a living" the primary focus of life (v. 30).
- Jesus says life is more than making a living (v. 23).
- Worry actually prevents us from experiencing what God intends life to be (vv. 29–30, 34).
- We can trust God to provide for us (vv. 24, 27–28).
- We find real life in seeking and experiencing God's kingdom (vv. 31–34).

One great advantage of sequential points is that they keep the interest of listeners. Sequential points follow patterns that people instinctively respond to, such as a problem-solution or question-answer pattern. Notice in the Luke example that points 1, 2, and 4 explore the human problem, creating interest. Point 3 hints at an answer, and 5 and 6 give the full answer to our human need. The sequential approach follows an inductive rather than deductive logic, delaying the full discovery to the latter part of the sermon.

OVERCOMING CHALLENGES

One significant difference between preaching in parallel points versus sequential points is the transitions. With parallel points we typically transition between the points by numbering them and repeating the keyword. "The first reason not to worry.... The second reason not to worry...." Calling attention to parallel points in this way brings clarity. It is simple for people to follow our structure because we mark points with a flashing light.

With sequential points, things get foggy if we do not carefully highlight the shift between points. Numbering and key words do not suit this form as well. (Although sequential point sermons can use the often-heard keywords *principles* or *points* or "things I want to say," and we can number those, this usually makes for awkward transitions.)

The solution is to repeat and rephrase points. As we conclude each point, we should repeat or rephrase the point, then state the next point and repeat and rephrase it two or three times before proceeding to develop it.

For example, in the Luke sermon above, after I finished explaining and illustrating point

1, I could say, "And so we do worry sometimes about our daily material needs. Now, such worry has a huge drawback. Worry can make 'making a living' the primary focus of life. We live to earn a paycheck. Our reason for being is nothing more than paying the bills." Then I can develop the idea.

After I have developed point 2, I can bring closure and move to point 3 by saying, "Because worry consumes our thoughts, it makes 'making a living' the primary focus of life. But Jesus says life is more than making a living. God created us to set our hearts on more than money, food, and housing payments." This is a natural, conversational way to transition between points.

One additional thing to watch for with sequential points: Be sure to stay on one subject. If we are not careful, a sequence of ideas can begin on one subject and three points later end on another subject. This is especially likely in a topical sermon drawn from various texts. For example:

- God loves us.
- We should love others.
- We may not feel like loving others.
- Our feelings can lead us astray.
- False teachers can also lead us astray.

All points must be subordinate to one overarching subject. In the Luke text above, my overarching subject is "How to experience God's highest purpose for your life."

You will probably not use sequential points in every message, but for many texts they produce interesting, biblical sermons. If parallel points has been your only form of preaching, sequential points can open a whole new sermon world.

Chapter 95

OUTLINES THAT WORK FOR YOU, NOT AGAINST YOU

How to write sermon points that follow the way people think

Steven D. Mathewson

Twenty students and two professors stared at the handwriting on the wall. One by one, students in a seminary preaching class were to project on overheads their first attempts at a sermon outline from an assigned passage. I waited apprehensively for my turn. My friend, Rod, was up first. Rod looked at his transparency and read aloud his main points for a potential sermon on 1 Samuel 17, the David-Goliath story:

Goliath Challenges God's People.

Saul Cowers with God's People.

David Conquers for God's People.

After a pause, Haddon Robinson, the lead professor, growled: "That sounds like it came out of a book called *Simple Sermons for Sunday Evening.*" The class erupted with laughter. Nervous laughter. Sympathetic laughter. "Nobody talks like this anymore, except in the pulpit," he continued. Duane Litfin, guest professor, chimed in: "What Haddon is saying is that he's afraid you might go out and actually preach that sermon!" More laughter.

The outline stage in sermon preparation is, for some, the most intimidating step in the process. Homiletics author Bryan Chapell says, "In the classroom and in seminars around the country, I find that preachers have more questions about structure than they do about any other aspect of preaching." So how do we write sermon outlines that are not trite, communicate in a natural way, and present our ideas clearly? Here are three strategies.

Use Complete Sentences

One of the key purposes of a sermon outline is to track the sermon's flow of thought. Out of this purpose flows the first strategy: State your outline points in full sentences. According to Haddon Robinson, since each point in the outline represents an idea, it should be a complete sentence. When words and phrases stand as points, they deceive us because they are incomplete and vague. Partial statements allow thought to slip through our minds like a greased football.

Writing an outline is a way of thinking. You will short-circuit the thinking process if you do not write out your points in complete sentences. You can't evaluate clarity of thought or the logical progression of your ideas if all you see are lone words.

Don't Try to Make It Memorable

The second strategy is: Don't try to create outlines people will remember. It took me years of preaching to figure this out. I sincerely believed that listeners would be better for taking my outline points home with them—either in their heads or, better yet, on paper. Without a "captioned survey" of either the passage or the principles in it, how would people get the text into their lives?

The problem is modern listeners are not used to getting information in a captioned survey format. Neither Dan Rather nor Dan Patrick communicate information like this. Their presentation follows a conversational flow.

A few months ago, Lisa, a close family friend, called and asked me what appendicitis pain feels like. Her husband, Eric, was on a business trip in California and was feeling an excruciating pain in his lower abdominal region. Because I had my appendix removed about three years earlier, Lisa wanted my input. Imagine how canned my reply would have sounded if it had followed this outline:

The Character of Appendicitis Pain
- It is an excruciating pain.
- It is an enveloping pain.

The Context of Appendicitis Pain
- Its locus is abdominal.
- Its focus is appendicital.

The Cancellation of Appendicitis Pain
- It requires reflection by the doctor.
- It requires removal of the organ.
- It requires rest for the patient.

The advantage of this kind of presentation is that Lisa could easily follow it. Alliterating the three main points with the letter C (Character, Context, and Cancellation) provides a memory aid. But obviously, this kind of communication is unnatural. It's boring, and it doesn't work the way conversation usually flows.

As a preacher of God's Word, your goal is to communicate the ideas in a text and to point out the controlling thought or "big idea." Ideas gel in people's minds through words and pictures. I want people to go home with God's truth in mind, particularly a picture of what that looks like when lived out in their lives. I need my outline to help me communicate the ideas and pictures. But hearers don't need to see my outline any more than they need to see the two-by-four studs supporting the drywall in my living room.

In fact, when I preach, I may or may not say the statement exactly as I have it worded in Roman numeral I. The key is, by the time I'm done with Roman numeral I, the idea it expresses will have formed in the hearers' minds.

Like a map, an outline gives directions. It provides a preacher with a communication plan. It says, "Here's the concept to communicate first; here's the concept to communicate second," and so on. Writing an outline for yourself helps produce a flow of thought that is logical. As you look at an outline on a page, you'll be able to spot any muddled thinking. You'll be able to evaluate whether your sermon has a sense of movement or progress. You'll see gaps or inconsistencies in your thinking.

In the following outline from a sermon on Psalm 137, notice the two main points:

Unfair experiences leave people, who are designed to praise God, wondering how they can ever praise him again (vv. 1–6).
- The believer's life is supposed to be a life of praise (Psalms 135 and 136).
- But unfair experiences ruin a person's appetite for praise (137:1–3).
- This puts believers in a dilemma since what they can't do is what they should do (137:4–6).

(Big idea) Trusting in God's justice restores a ruined appetite for praise (137:7–9).
- The psalmist's solution appears to be vindictive.
- The solution is trusting in God's vindication.

The first point states the idea I want to communicate from verses 1–6, but I don't state it directly when I begin developing the idea. The idea will emerge by the time I'm done developing this section of the sermon. At some point I may say, "Verses 1–6 teach us that unfair experiences leave people, who are designed to praise God, wondering how they can ever praise him again." However, I won't try to make this statement prominent. I'll communicate the idea by restating this concept in various ways. For example, I'll say something like, "The operative question in verses 1–6 is, how can I restore my appetite for praising God when he allows unfair experiences into my life?"

The second major point is a statement of the sermon's big idea, so I will state it verbatim two or three times, and then I'll find a couple of other ways to restate it. However, I won't preface it as "point number two." I'll simply work the statement into the flow of my material. The trick to keeping people on track when your sermon is more conversational is to craft effective transitions. Transitions stitch blocks of ideas together, showing relationships between them.

Now having said this, there may be times when you want people to remember the points in your outline. This happens when the biblical writer offers a list. Usually a sermon giving "four keys to a strong marriage" or "three ways to avoid anger" reflects the preacher's convention, not the Bible's. However, a passage like 1 Peter 4:7–11 certainly contains a list. The writer begins by saying, "The end of all things is near." Then he uses the word "therefore" to introduce some implications. The main idea of the paragraph is: Last days living requires God's people to get serious about prayer, love, sharing, and serving. The main level outline points for a sermon on this text look like this:

- Last days living requires God's people to get serious about prayer (v. 7b).
- Last days living requires God's people to get serious about love (v. 8).
- Last days living requires God's people to get serious about sharing (v. 9).
- Last days living requires God's people to get serious about serving (vv. 10–11).

MAKE IT AN ENDING, NOT A BEGINNING

Here's a final strategy for creating sermon outlines that help a sermon without taking on a life of their own: Sometimes view main points as endings, not beginnings. Use this whenever you want to present your material inductively. In an inductive presentation, you deal with the details first and then present your conclusion at the end. The advantage is the creation of suspense.

Typically a preacher will move out of an introduction and state point I. After stating point I, the preacher moves to subpoint A, then to subpoint B, and so on. However, in an inductive presentation of point I, the preacher will move out of the introduction into subpoint A, then subpoint B, and so forth. Only at the end of the subpoints does the idea or point in Roman numeral I emerge.

This is precisely what I do when I preach Psalm 137 according to the above outline. Go back and look at how the subpoints build to express each of the two main points. When you prepare your outline, indicate which main points will be developed inductively. Put "develop inductively"—in parentheses and in italics—after the statement of the main point.

Try out these strategies as you prepare your sermon outline this week. You should end up with an outline that makes for a clear and conversational message.

Chapter 96

THE TENSION BETWEEN CLARITY AND SUSPENSE
How to choose between inductive and deductive logic

Don Sunukjian

Distinguishing between inductive and deductive preaching can be difficult. Inductive preaching essentially asks a question and arrives at the answer toward the latter part of the sermon. Deductive is the opposite: You give the declarative statement up front and then support it. So the styles differ by whether the listener hears the point you're going to make up front, or they hear the question and then arrive at the answer through a progression.

We make serious choices between induction and deduction in four places of a sermon.

1. THE OVERALL SERMON PATTERN

Is the overall sermon pattern going to be deductive or inductive? Will the listeners get my central truth up front, or will they learn it as I progress through the message?

The advantage of a deductive structure is

that the big idea is up front. It's clear. It's early so the listener grabs onto it. The disadvantage is you give away all the cookies at the start. The listener can say, "Got it. I'm out of here. I can catch the football game in the first quarter instead of waiting till the fourth quarter."

The inductive structure advantage is the flip side. You sustain the interest of listeners because you have not yet arrived at that central theme. They're going through a journey with you. They're learning with you. The climax is yet to come. The tension is still there. The disadvantage is that unless you're really clear, by the time you get to it, you may have lost them.

So with deduction we have to ask, "How do I use it in a way so there's still some reason for the listener to keep listening?" When I use induction, we ask, "How do I really know that I'm being clear orally?"

Now, let's come back to deduction. When would I use deduction? When would I give away all the cookies at the start and still know that I can keep the listener with me? The answer is when my deductive statement automatically raises questions in the listener's mind. Somehow it's provocative.

Let me give you an example. "Today we're going to talk about the fifth commandment, 'Honor your father and your mother.' Some of you say, 'Oh, good. I hope the kids are listening.' That commandment wasn't given to kids. It was given to adults standing at the base of Mount Sinai. We think of it in terms of kids because of what Paul says in Ephesians 6:1, 'Children obey your parents,' but originally God was talking to a nation of adults. Honor takes the form of obedience when we're children. But what did God have in mind at the other end of life when adults were looking at parents who were entering the last decades of life?"

Now, here comes my deductive statement. "Today we're going to see that to honor our parents in their latter years is to support them financially. When God said 'Honor your father and your mother,' more than anything else he meant be ready to assist them economically in their retirement years. See that they lack for nothing in the way of housing, medicine, clothing, or anything necessary for a comfortable life."

Now there's my deductive statement, yet nobody's saying, "Got it. I'm out of here." They're saying, "Wait a minute. Where did you get that from? I've been reading the Bible for years. Honor—you preachers find money everywhere. How much money are you talking about? I can barely support my own family. I've got kids going to college. How old do my parents have to be? What about my siblings? Should they help out?" They've got all kinds of questions they hope I'm going to address in the message.

So the first way to use deduction is when your central truth in the introduction raises questions in the minds of the listeners. The listener has a reason to keep listening. Other than that we probably will want to go inductive since most biblical materials are written inductively.

So once you have developed your main idea, it would be helpful to stop and ask, "What are the questions that I'm going to raise by this? Does it really raise questions or not?" The answer to that will determine whether you're going to go deductive or inductive.

Often the passage of Scripture has a natural flow to it. I'm surprised at how many times a narrative passage places the central truth at the end. But I still may start with it. For instance, I might be preaching on the life of Jacob and say, "Today we're going to see from the Scriptures that even though you have messed up God's plan for your life, God still has a way of making it possible." And I know the listener is saying, "I hope that's true. Convince me of it." Even though there is enough listener interest to hold the truth until the end, I want them to know at the start what comfort the Lord is going to give them in this message.

2. The Preview

In the preview paragraph of the introduction, you tell the listener, "Here's where I'm going to go with this sermon." In the preview you often make statements or raise the questions you're going to answer. So right away you're dealing with induction or deduction.

Any sentence is an idea. If I say, "This podium was made by a master craftsman," that's an idea. There is something I'm talking about (the podium), and there's something I'm saying about it (it was made by a master craftsman). It has a subject and a complement. When we make a deductive statement, we are giving the subject and the complement up front. When we raise a question, we are raising only the subject. So when we come to the preview sentences, we have to decide if we're going to be deductive or inductive.

Let's say I start my introduction by saying, "Early in geometry we learn that the shortest distance between two points is a straight line. Well, that may be true in geometry but not with God's dealings in our life. Today we're going to see that the shortest distance between two points is a zigzag. God will lead us in his own route to get us safely to his intended destination for us. Now, where do I find that in Scripture? We're going to turn to a time in Israel's history when God led them deliberately on a zigzag path."

Now, that's a deductive statement. I've given you what I'm going to talk about. But I've got some questions to answer about that. The listener is thinking, *Is that true? Would God lead me on a zigzag path? I've been on my zag so long I don't know whether point B is God's destiny or I psyched myself into it.* The movement of the text will follow that inductive development. I take them to Exodus 13, where it shows that God led Israel on a zigzag path. It tells them why he did that and how he kept them encouraged when they weren't moving in a straight line.

I want the listener to say, "Oh, I've got to keep listening to that. You're going to prove to me that God does do it." That's deductive. "Then you're going to explain why. I need you to answer me that, and help me to know how I stay encouraged." That's inductive. So I've used a combination of deduction and induction in the preview elements to mark off the big chunks of the message while keeping the listener in a state of tension over unanswered questions.

3. Within Each Main Point

The third area where induction or deduction shows up is in the main points, or what we might call the Roman numerals. There are certain ways to decide whether I should handle each Roman numeral inductively or deductively.

When you're in a major point, look at your subpoints. If the subpoints are a list, then go inductive. You can say, "All right. Finally we come to Roman numeral three. What are the rewards of obedience?" Then answer that question in your subpoints. "The first reward of obedience is joy. The second reward of obedience is long life. The third reward of obedience is children who know the Lord."

It wouldn't make sense to say, "In Roman numeral three we're going to see that the rewards of obedience are joy, long life and children who follow the Lord." Why give it all away like that? Look at the subpoints. If they're a list, go inductive.

With some lists, there's no priority. Item five could be item one, while item two could be item three. But most biblical passages are not lists. They are a chain of thought or a progression. What if I said, "Roman numeral three: What is the reward for obedience? We notice in verse 14 that Israel is prosperous. But in their prosperity Israel turns to the fertility gods of the land. Because of this, God lets an oppressor come in and take over Israel. The Midianites come and eat Israel's food, reducing them to poverty." Though I'm going through my progression, by now you've forgotten what my question was. "What was this Roman numeral about?" You haven't heard anything about obedience.

Whenever you have a sequence in the subpoints, you cannot go inductive. The listener will lose you because there is no connection in the first three or four subpoints to the inductive question you ask.

I need to be deductive when I've got a sequence. "In Roman numeral three we finally come to the reward of obedience. And we will see in verses 17–24 that the reward for obedience is a restoration of the years that were lost. Let's follow Israel's history to see that when they returned to God, he restored what they had lost." And now I go into my sequence, but you know where it's headed. I have reached to the last subpoint and put it into the major Roman numeral. I have made a deductive statement of everything that I'm going to cover.

So in the Roman numerals, if the subpoints are a list, go inductive. But if the answer to your question is way down on the bottom of a list of eight subpoints, you've got to go deductive.

4. WHEN READING A SCRIPTURE PASSAGE

The choice between induction or deduction also shows up in our reading of a text. We ought to read the Scripture deductively. Always tell the listener before you read the text what they will find in the verses. Too often preachers say, "Let's see what Paul says next in verses 17 to 24," and then we start reading. And the listeners glaze out on us real fast. We know what we're looking for there but they don't.

So instead you would say something like, "In verses 17 to 24, Paul tells us the third time that we are vulnerable to temptation. Just when we have done something for Christ, Satan has his best chance to get at us. Paul says right after he had preached with great response, he found Satan lifting him up to pride. Read with me to see how we are vulnerable after a spiritual victory." Now as the listeners read verses 17 to 24 they know what they're looking for. They listen intelligently. They say, "Yes, there it is. I see it."

In all the choices we make at every level of the sermon between induction and deduction, there is a tension between clarity and interest level. There are times you choose a style because you've got to be clear. The issue isn't whether you have everybody on the edge of their seat. At times you're just trying to keep people interested. You've got to balance this tension at every point.

Chapter 97

LIFEBLOOD OF PREACHING

Why emotions matter as much as outlines

Ian Pitt-Watson

A sermon's "cardiovascular system" or "bloodstream" is its emotive flow.

Every counselor knows that what we feel is often more important than what we think. In consequence, the emotive cardiovascular system of a sermon is certainly no less important than the conceptual skeleton. Indeed, cardiovascular disease, in sermons as in people, causes more fatalities than broken bones do.

When the truth communicated in preaching is only thought to be true but not felt to be true, we have not heard the full gospel. The Bible does not tolerate the separation of the head from the heart. The heart has its reasons. Felt truths are not to be despised.

Preaching involves a kind of passionate thinking. Sometimes the preacher is giving conceptual expression to what the hearer had previously only felt to be true, but at other times the preacher is expressing as a felt truth something the hearer had previously only thought to be true. Both tasks are equally important, and for both a healthy cardiovascular system is required that can express felt truths and carry the affect (the feel) of these truths to every limb and organ of the sermon. This is the lifeblood of preaching.

Chapter 98

ALLITERATION DOWNFALLS

When sound-alikes turn good preaching bad

Don Sunukjian

Woody Hayes, legendary football coach at Ohio State (1951–1978), ran an offense that sportswriters dubbed, "Three yards and a cloud of dust." When someone asked, "Why don't you ever throw a forward pass?" Hayes replied, "Three things can happen when you throw a forward pass, and two of them are bad."

In that same vein I say: Four things can happen when you alliterate, and four of them are bad. Alliteration is the literary device of repeating the same initial sound or letter several times in close succession: conspicuous consumption, or nattering nabobs of negativism.

Preachers most frequently use alliteration in the major points of their outline. Sometimes alliteration is appropriate and effective in a sermon outline. Succinct and accurate words can crisply communicate the concepts of a short outline. For example, "Today we're going to look at the cause and the cure of our problem." But when a sermon outline has more main points, alliteration runs the risk of four bad things.

USING THE WRONG WORD

Alliteration may cause the speaker to use a word nobody knows and thus be unclear. To sustain the same letter, the speaker searches a thesaurus. Unfortunately the only word that accurately conveys the concept is a word few listeners are familiar with. Look at the points in this sermon entitles "A Perspective on Prayer":

The purpose of prayer

The power of prayer

The perspicacity of prayer

The outline may accurately convey the text, but it is unclear to the listener.

CONVEYING THE WRONG MEANING

Alliteration runs the danger of changing the biblical author's meaning. Speakers who resolve to alliterate with only familiar words may manipulate the true meaning of the text to remain intelligible to the listener. The outline may be clear, but now it is biblically inaccurate. Consider "The Characteristics of a Leader" based on 1 Samuel 17:17–54:

Cooperative (17:17–24)

Curious (17:25–27)

Consistent (17:28–30)

Courageous (17:31–37)

Careful (17:38–40)

Confident 17:41–47)

Conclusive (17:48–51)

"Cooperative," "Consistent," and "Careful" do not accurately reflect what is happening in the text. "Obedient," "Persistent," and "Wise" come closer to describing David's actions in those verses.

Worse than changing the meaning of a paragraph within the text, alliteration sometimes violates the author's entire flow of thought as the speaker turns the biblical progression of ideas into an artificial, David Letterman-list of parallel points.

It is doubtful the author of 1 Samuel said to himself as he came to chapter 17, I will now write about the seven characteristics of leadership. Such an approach to preaching is far from the intent of the author, which was to show how a young man from the tribe of Judah, believing the covenant promises of God, finished the task God gave his tribe by removing the uncircumcised from Gath, thus qualifying himself for leadership among God's people.

Alliterated preaching by lists can not only violate the author's theological intent but also present supposed truths that are contradicted elsewhere in Scripture. In contrast to the above list, abundant examples can be found of biblical leaders who were uncooperative (Peter's refusing the Sanhedrin), inconsistent (Joshua's changing strategy at Ai), fearful (Gideon's preparing for the Midianites), rash (Jonathan's charging the Philistine outpost), and uncertain (Daniel's friends' explanation to Nebuchadnezzar of their refusal to bow to a statue).

CREATING THE WRONG FOCUS

Alliteration runs a third danger. It may suggest that the most important thing in the message to remember is the outline. What listeners really need to get is the central truth and its relevance for their lives. They should walk away from the message not with an outline but with an awareness of how a biblical truth bears on life. Their minds should be engaged not with "points" but with how they are going to think or act differently in some concrete way.

Worse yet, the alliterated outline all too often communicates no content. If listeners do manage to remember it, they still don't know anything. This is true of the following outline of a sermon entitled "Preaching the Gospel":

The process for preaching

The practice in preaching

The product of preaching

Based on 1 Thessalonians 1:4–8, the sermon from which this outline comes conveys the following thoughts:

We must remember that God elects and the power of the Spirit saves.

We must practice what we preach.

The gospel cuts through human suffering, causing joy and growth.

But you can't access any of these thoughts by remembering the alliterated outline. Rather, that outline is an unnecessary middleman the listener must jump over to form the concepts in mind.

If remembering the outline is important, a set of points that is not alliterated but full of content—that is, written in complete declarative sentences—would be more effective:

We don't need to sell the gospel.

But we must live it.

It will change lives.

THE WRONG ATTENTION

With an alliterated outline, our listeners' attention may be drawn more to our cleverness than to God's Word. They may appreciate our skill more than they absorb God's message. The words of an ancient divine still ring true: "No man can at one and the same time give the impression that he is clever and that Christ is mighty to save."

Chapter 99

MODULATING TENSION

How to maintain interest throughout a sermon

Craig Brian Larson

We preachers know how to inject tension into a sermon. We may pose a question that cries out for an answer, or paint darkly some aspect of the fallen human condition that can be redeemed only by the good news of God's grace. We may tell a story.

We also know, though, that such tension doesn't last long. Listeners lose interest once the question is answered, the need is met by the gospel, or the story is ended. How can we sustain tension and interest throughout the sermon?

A sermon by Haddon Robinson shows one way to meet this challenge. Here is how I would outline the tension of his sermon "Life and Death Advice," based on Psalm 49:

- Robinson develops the idea of riddle and presents not only the riddle of the text but a contemporary riddle of his own, piquing our curiosity.
- Then the sermon explores the problem of why the evil seem to have it better in the world than those who try to live righteously.
- The sermon offers the first taste of resolution, showing that evil people ultimately have no advantage, for they die like everyone else.
- Then Robinson adds new complication by exploring the ultimate human problem—death—which even the good must experience. This creates a sense of need.
- Then the sermon offers some resolution by saying that death is not the end. There is an afterlife.
- But this raises a new complication: The sermon elaborates on what happens to the wicked, that death feeds on them forever.
- Finally, there is full resolution as Haddon tells of the blessed life that awaits the righteous.

He preaches the good news of Christ and the hope of resurrection.

- The message ends by tying together the good news with the riddle developed in the introduction.

This sermon demonstrates how we can sustain tension throughout a message: by measuring out complication and resolution, in degrees, from beginning to end. The tension in this sermon is not in two simple stages: problem and solution. Rather, as in a vintage Hitchcock movie like *Rear Window*, there are degrees of problem and solution, and they overlap. Describe a problem, later describe further aspects of the problem, later still present even further aspects of the problem. Follow the same design with the solutions.

We can sustain tension in a sermon from beginning to end. One secret is to mete out complication and resolution by degrees throughout the message. The complication and resolution can overlap, or we can use a series of discrete cycles of complication and resolution, one following the other. Each measure of resolution should lead to another round of complication.

Chapter 100

THE PURPOSE-DRIVEN TITLE

Evaluate yours with four questions

Rick Warren

Writing a great sermon title is an art we must continually work on. I don't know anyone who has mastered it. We all have our hits and misses. But if the purpose of preaching is to transform, not merely inform, or if you're speaking to unbelievers, then you must be concerned with your titles. Like the cover of a book or the first line of an advertisement, your sermon's title must capture the attention of those you want to influence. In planning appealing sermon titles, I ask myself four questions.

Will It Capture Their Interest?

Will this title capture the attention of people? Because we are called to communicate truth, we may assume unbelievers are eager to hear the truth. They aren't. In fact, surveys show the majority of Americans reject the idea of absolute truth. Today, people value tolerance more than truth.

This "truth-decay" is the root of all that's wrong in our society. It is why unbelievers will not race to church if we proclaim, "We have the truth!" Their reaction will be, "Yeah, so does everybody else!"

While most unbelievers aren't looking for truth, they are looking for relief. This gives us the opportunity to interest them in truth. I've found that when I teach the truth that relieves their pain, answers their question, or solves their problem, unbelievers say, "Thanks! What else is true in that book?" Showing how a biblical principle meets a need creates a hunger for more truth.

Titles that deal with the real questions and hurts of people can attract an audience, giving us an opportunity to teach the truth. Sermon series titled "How To Handle Life's Hurts," "When You Need a Miracle" (on the miracles of Jesus), "Learning to Hear God's Voice," and "Questions I've Wanted to Ask God" have all attracted seekers.

Is It Clear?

I also ask myself, "Will this title stand on its own—without additional explanation? If I read this title on a cassette tape five years from today, would I instantly know what the sermon was about?"

Unfortunately, many compelling evangelistic messages are hampered by titles that are confusing, colorless, or corny. Here are some sermon titles from a recent *L. A. Times*: "On the Road to Jericho," "No Longer Walking on the Other Side of the Road," "The Gathering Storm," "Peter Goes Fishing," "The Ministry of Cracked Pots," "Becoming a Titus," "Give Me Agape," "River of Blood," and "No Such Thing as a Rubber Clock."

Would any of these titles appeal to an unchurched person scanning the paper? And do they clearly communicate what the sermons are about? It's more important to be clear than cute.

How Appealing Is It?

Is the title good news? In his first sermon, Jesus announced the tone of his preaching: "The Spirit of the Lord ... has anointed me to preach good news" (Luke 4:18). Even when I have difficult or painful news to share, I want my title to focus on the good-news aspects of my subject.

For instance, years ago I preached a message on the ways we miss God's blessing because of our sinfulness. I titled the sermon, "Why No Revival?" Later I revised the title to "What Brings Revival?" It was the same message, only restated in positive terms. I believe God blessed the latter message in a far greater way.

Here are sermon-series titles I've used to communicate good news: "Encouraging Words from God's Word," "What God Can Do through Ordinary You," and "Enjoying the Rest of Your Life," an exposition of Philippians.

IS IT RELEVANT?

Does the title relate to everyday life? Some people criticize life-application preaching as shallow, simplistic, and inferior. To them the only real preaching is didactic, doctrinal preaching. Their attitude implies that Paul was more profound than Jesus, that Romans is deeper material than the Sermon on the Mount or the parables.

The "deepest" teaching is what makes a difference in people's day-to-day lives. As D. L. Moody once said, "The Bible was not given to increase our knowledge but to change our lives."

I have been criticized for using sermon titles that sound like *Reader's Digest* articles. But I do it intentionally. *Reader's Digest* is the most widely read magazine in the world because its articles appeal to common human needs, hurts, and interests. People want to know how to change their lives.

Using sermon titles that appeal to felt needs isn't being shallow; it's being strategic. At Saddleback, beneath our "how-to" sermon titles is hard-core gospel truth. A casual observer will not know that the series "Answering Life's Difficult Questions" was a study of Ecclesiastes, "Stressbusters" was an exposition of Psalm 23, "Building Great Relationships" was a ten-week exposition of 1 Corinthians 13, and "Happiness Is a Choice" was a series on the Beatitudes.

We have the most important message in the world. It changes lives. But for people to be attracted to it, the titles of our sermons must capture their attention.

Chapter 101

WHY SHOULD I LISTEN TO YOU?
Principles of effective introductions

Kent Edwards

Within the first seven seconds of meeting, people begin to form opinions about each other—opinions that often go on to influence the long-term nature of the relationship. The same thing happens with sermons. It does not take long for people to form an impression about a preacher and the sermon about to be delivered. An impression that the audience forms in the first few moments often determines whether they will listen to what follows.

Introductions play a critical role in helping preachers gain a hearing. They answer the question every listener asks of every preacher: "Why should I listen to you?"

Good introductions compel listeners to listen by succeeding at two major objectives. First, they *indirectly* relate the audience to the speaker. The major impressions that a listener has of a speaker are gained during the first moments of the sermon. Audiences decide during an introduction if the speaker is likeable, knowledgeable, and trustworthy. They decide if the preacher is the kind of person that they want to listen to. Good introductions also compel listening by *directly* relating the audience to the main idea of the sermon. They show how the subject of the sermon is relevant to the life of the listener.

How do preachers create these compelling introductions? By observing the following principles.

Begin with a clear understanding of the idea of the sermon. Effective preachers start by writing out the single idea that the sermon will address. It is impossible to introduce a vague or ill-defined concept. Preachers must know exactly what they are going to say before they can effectively introduce it. Until you know exactly what you are saying and how you will be saying it, you cannot create a truly effective introduction.

Develop interest. While gaining the attention of listeners is important initially, keeping this attention is even more important—and difficult. Momentary attention is transformed into continued interest when preachers show listeners why it is in their best interest to listen. People give their attention to what they perceive is important to them. Unless they understand early on in a sermon what difference it will make in their lives, they are unlikely to give the message the attention the preacher would prefer. Generally, the more abstract an idea, the more time is required to help people understand its relevance to life. Good introductions take whatever time is necessary (and no more time than necessary) to explain why this particular sermon is important to this particular audience.

Write well. This is no place for wandering words and vague thoughts. The wording should be striking, specific, and direct. Effective first sentences could be paradoxical statements, twists on familiar quotations, or even rhetorical questions. Whatever the specific approach may be, carefully crafted introductions help listeners give their attention to the content that follows.

Match the mood of the introduction with the mood of the sermon. The first words the preacher speaks are not simply those that happen to stand on the top of the first page. They are the beginning of a new experience. They must grip the mind of the listener and begin to mold his or her mood. Effective preachers ensure that the emotions evoked by the introduction contribute to the overall mood of the message.

Adapt to fit the structure of the sermon. In *deductive* sermons, the introduction will contain a clear statement of the biblical idea. By the end of that introduction, the audience should know not only what the preacher is going to talk about in the sermon, but how the idea will be developed (whether the idea will be explained, proved, or applied).

In an *inductive* sermon, however, the introduction is structured much differently. Rather than telling the audience exactly what they can expect, these introductions intentionally create tension in the mind of the listener through an exploration of the subject of the sermon. The complement(s) will not be revealed until much later in the sermon. An effective introduction of this type of sermon will compellingly lead the audience to the first point.

Don't overlook delivery. Dressing appropriately, moving confidently to the pulpit, pausing a moment, and making eye contact can be very engaging. Delivery should be authentic and have variety as well as energy. The audience should feel that the speaker is in control. It is easy to stumble during an introduction. Wise preachers take the extra preparation necessary to avoid giving an introduction that appears choppy or uncertain.

Be yourself. Don't try to be someone you are not. Be honest. Be authentic. Be who God made you to be. If you have a natural sense of humor, utilize it. If you don't, don't pretend.

A good introduction is to a sermon what an appetizer is to a gourmet meal. It whets the appetite for the rest of the meal. It creates a hunger for the food that follows. Good sermon introductions can accomplish the same result. They stimulate a hunger for the Word of God and are an important part of a good sermon.

Chapter 102

SATISFYING CONCLUSIONS

Kent Edwards

Conclusions do more than simply end a sermon, they bring a message to a *satisfying* finale. Conclusions are to sermons what the final chapter is to a good mystery novel. What the final two minutes are to a great basketball or football game. What a great cup of coffee is to a gourmet meal.

OBJECTIVES FOR EFFECTIVE CONCLUSIONS

Reinforcing the Main Idea of the Sermon

Good conclusions should enable the listener to understand with even greater clarity what the sermon is all about. It should bring all of the information of the message into burning focus. To achieve this level of intellectual precision in the conclusion, the wise preacher will do the following.

Avoid introducing new concepts. By this time in the sermon, all of the relevant concepts should have been presented and adequately developed. Serving up leftover thoughts will only diffuse the clarity you have worked so hard to achieve.

Review the main points. Briefly draw the points together into your central idea. While restatement is often more effective than rote repetition, the results of this review can be profound. In oral communication, it is almost impossible to repeat yourself too often. Repetition leads to clarity in the mind of the listener, and clarity is a critical component of legitimate behavioral change. People cannot obey a biblical passage they do not understand.

Avoid an exhaustive review of the sermon. It is more effective to hit the highlights. Those who try to repreach their sermon during the conclusion risk dissipating any interest they may have generated.

Use appropriate emotion. Good sermons crescendo as they conclude. They end with a bang, not a whimper. A dull, anticlimactic closing can ruin an otherwise excellent message.

Emphasizing Application

Effective conclusions reach beyond the listener's mind to the will. They call listeners to embrace the action that the sermon calls for. While some application will usually be given during the main body of a sermon, it is in the conclusion where the clearest and most compelling call for response often occurs. This is where the answer to the question "so what?" is communicated with maximum clarity and specificity.

Many of the sermons recorded in Scripture conclude with strong applications. Joshua climaxes his sermon to Israel by saying, "Choose for yourselves this day whom you will serve" (Josh. 24:15). Jesus, in his Sermon on the Mount, finishes by exhorting his listeners to build their lives on the rock of his words (Matt. 7:24–27). The preachers of Scripture conclude their sermons with a call for concrete behavioral change. We need to do the same.

METHODS OF CONCLUDING A SERMON

Give suggestions concerning the ways and means that the central idea can be carried out. Take the time to give specifics of what should take place because of the truth. Good preaching occurs when a sermon is shaped and spoken with a consciousness that the weekend will soon end. Monday morning's world must be brought into harmony with Sunday morning's truth.

Paint a picture. Visualization can intensify desire and lead to action. Preachers can place their audience into a plausible scenario that allows them to experience the benefits of applying God's truth. Or, they can select a situation that highlights how bad things will be if the listeners choose to ignore the biblical concept. What is important, however, is that the preacher's visualization stands the test of reality. To be effective, the conditions chosen should be probable. To be highly effective, the preacher must make the situation so vivid that it touches the senses of those listening. The audience should be able to see, hear, taste, and smell God's Word in action.

Give an illustration that applies the truth. More than just a heartwarming story to close out the message, this is a slice of life that embodies the big idea of the sermon. It shows either positively or negatively (although positive illustrations are often more effective) how the biblical idea has worked itself out in the lives of people past and present. This testimonial approach allows congregants to "connect the dots" of theory and practice.

Use a poem or hymn. Although this approach may have been overused in a previous generation, it can still be utilized with great effect. Preachers need not restrict their poetry search to old high school textbooks. Lyrics from a contemporary song or a line from a well-known movie may be appropriate. If concluding with an older hymn, it is worth the effort to quote it from memory.

Employ a contrasting truth. When the biblical text presents an idea in the negative (e.g., "do not commit adultery"), the preacher may choose to apply that idea positively: "Build a strong marriage."

Be audience specific. Do the research necessary to learn how to best apply the truth to the individuals whom you will be addressing. Ask questions such as: How old are they? What education level? What work situation? What ethnicity? What gender?

Part 6

Style

*How Can I Use My Personal Strengths and Various Message Types
to Their Full Biblical Potential?*

Chapter 103

DETERMINING YOUR STRENGTHS AND WEAKNESSES

This self-test can help you understand your gifting as a preacher

Duane Litfin

The spin cycle had just begun when the washing machine began to vibrate badly. It danced a jig briefly, then a raucous buzzer signaled that the machine had shut down. The problem: Its burden was off-center.

Like the load of that dancing washer, many of us preachers are off-center. Although we have enough equilibrium not to shut down, we aren't perfectly balanced.

In one sense, this is keen insight into the obvious. Like everyone else, preachers are finite creatures who have strengths mixed with weaknesses. Unfortunately, in preachers this mixture has extraordinary implications.

Common wisdom has it that churches tend to take on the character of their leaders. This is worrisome enough when we consider matters of style and personality, but it becomes fright-

ening when we realize that churches may take on not only the strengths but also the shortcomings of their pastors. Where a preacher is strong, the church likely will be strong; where the preacher is weak, the church also may become weak. And even strengths can become weaknesses if they're imbalanced.

I may not be able to become a fully balanced preacher like Jesus, and I may not be able to correct my weaknesses completely. But simply being aware of my eccentricities—my strengths and weaknesses—has given me a better understanding of my ministry.

To help me identify my own eccentricities, I developed a diagnostic self-evaluation tool, the TEMP matrix. It is not a scientific instrument. It is simply one way to analyze preaching. This TEMP matrix is made up of four scales combined into a grid. The four scales correspond to what I believe are four spiritual gifts that shape the preacher the most: Teaching, Exhortation, Mercy, and Prophecy (hence, TEMP).

For our purposes, let's think of these as simply four tendencies or natural strengths among different preachers. Read the descriptions below and then rank your preaching ministry in each area.

Avoid ranking yourself as you think you *ought* to be; rather, rank yourself as you *are*. (That's the only way, in fact, this tool will become useful.) Rank yourself on a scale of 0–10, with 0 representing "That's not me at all," and 10 representing "That's me exactly."

T SCALE (TEACHING)

You are drawn to Jesus, the great teacher, who lived and taught the truth effectively and whose truth sets us free.

You are a good student who finds study stimulating. You possess an organized mind. You tend to thrive on the world of ideas and principles. Grasping the meaning of things ranks high with you. You don't mind the abstract; you work well at that level and have come to appreciate the usefulness of broad principles. Yet, you shy away from oversimplifications and overstatements and often qualify the statements you make.

You believe strongly in the power of God's Word to change lives. Passages such as Hebrews 4:12 and 2 Timothy 3:16, which you know by heart, shape your ministry. You have full confidence in the power of Scripture to transform people into godly disciples.

Furthermore, you delight in understanding detail and the harmony of Scripture. You can spend hours alone with it, enjoyably. In fact,

you often are moved by the sheer elegance, depth, and relevance of God's truth.

You believe God has called you to expound his truth, to help others understand. Clarity of thought and communication is among your greatest assets. You say exactly what you mean, and want your listeners to understand fully and accurately. Moreover, you want to present the whole counsel of God. Thus, you prefer to stay with the text in your preaching. That's the only way people consistently can hear from you a word from heaven.

Because you love the truth, you are greatly troubled by the presence of biblical and theological error. You realize that such error leads to sick lives. You view both misunderstanding and deception with great seriousness. Thus, you strive to guard and preserve sound doctrine, the faith once for all delivered to the saints. You view this body of truth as a wonderful stewardship and desire to pass it on to other faithful men and women undistorted.

Rank yourself by circling the number that best represents you on the T(eaching) Scale. (0 = Not at all like me; 10 = That's me exactly.)

0   1   2   3   4   5   6   7   8   9   10

E SCALE (EXHORTATION)

You are inspired by Jesus, the Son of Man, who lived with, understood, and ministered to people's needs. You are touched by his ability to relate to people through down-to-earth stories taken from everyday life.

You are gregarious, friendly, and well-liked. You are generally positive and tend to be optimistic, but you are also effective at confronting or rebuking when necessary. You have a strong practical side. You are perceptive and possess a high level of common sense and practical wisdom. You don't mind innovation and change; in fact, in some ways you thrive on them. In addition, you are an active person, who maintains a high energy level. You are committed to being a doer of the Word, not merely a hearer.

Furthermore, you delight in seeing people come to know Jesus and grow in the faith, and you willingly invest yourself to help them do so. You are effective at coming alongside others and getting involved in their lives. You know the power of one life upon another, and you enjoy being used in this way. You love to encourage people and to help them solve their problems. You tend to emphasize God's spiritual resources and ways Christians may use them.

Though you see the value of study, you do not enjoy study for study's sake. Study for you is a means to an end. You would rather spend your hours with people than with books. When you do study, you tend to take regular breaks. To stay in touch with the people you are ministering to, you feel sometimes that you would do better to prepare your messages in a restaurant or on a busy boulevard than in your office.

In your preaching you take naturally to the narratives of the Bible, which portray men and women dealing with the common problems of life. You are also drawn to the book of James and wisdom literature such as Proverbs. Your sermons tend to be practical, topical, and direct, with perhaps one main idea memorably worded and thoroughly illustrated. Your sermons typically stress application, the practical "how to's" of the Christian life. You are strong on using concrete, real-life illustrations and examples.

Rank yourself on the E(xhortation) Scale by circling the appropriate number.

0 — 1 — 2 — 3 — 4 — 5 — 6 — 7 — 8 — 9 — 10

M SCALE (MERCY)

You are inspired by Jesus, the great physician, who comforted the bereaved, restored the sick, gave sight to the blind, and finally gave himself to heal a sin-sick race. Because of his own suffering, you know that Jesus understands the needs and pain of this life and offers redemption to men and women.

You are sensitive to the needs of people. You do not have to work to identify with the pain of the poor, the dispossessed, those who are suffering. You naturally seem to speak to that pain, perhaps out of your own experience. People see you as warm and caring.

While you are strong at comforting others, you do not enjoy confrontation. You prefer an indirect approach, using a carrot rather than a stick. Your inclination is to handle people with gentleness; you would never want to hurt them. You are flexible and easygoing, and you tend to stress a relational approach to ministry. It is not difficult for you to make room for human imperfections. You are willing to overlook weakness and shortcomings in others because you are all too aware of your own.

The ambiguities and gray areas of life do not bother you. Sometimes other people seem too dogmatic, a tendency you consciously seek to avoid. You are troubled that systems, programs, procedures, and structures get in the way of the needs of people. Your initial inclination is to put people first. You view yourself as a nurturer.

You delight in the message of God's forgiveness and you emphasize it regularly. You are moved by the truths of redemption and grace. In your preaching you regularly stress hope and the potential for restoration and healing. The notion of unconditional love inspires you. Your preaching is typically warm and gracious, filled with life-affirming truths and anecdotes.

Rank yourself on the M(ercy) Scale by circling the appropriate number.

0 — 1 — 2 — 3 — 4 — 5 — 6 — 7 — 8 — 9 — 10

P SCALE (PROPHECY)

You are inspired by Jesus Christ, the righteous Judge and King, who calls men and women to the highest standards of righteousness and self-sacrifice. His strong demands are not a burden but your greatest challenge and delight. Some of his hard sayings are among your most familiar passages of Scripture. You note that he did not lower his demands for anyone, even when listeners refused to follow him as a result.

You are inspired by people who take difficult but godly stands for what's right and true, even at great personal cost. If you must choose, you would rather be respected than liked. You are ready to confront when necessary, even if the prospect of doing so is unpleasant. You stress that a life of deep personal holiness and prayer is the most important starting point for a preacher.

"'Be holy, for I am holy,' says the Lord," is a command you take seriously. You have high expectations, both for yourself and others. It is hard at times for you to be patient with those who seem to willingly make wrong choices. You truly are offended by sin, whether in yourself or others; yet you are equally moved by the majestic beauty of God's holiness and righteousness. A passion to see others come to share this beauty is one of the wellsprings of your ministry.

You know we all make an infinite number of choices in life, choices both large and small, and

God holds us responsible for how we choose. You believe the most loving thing you can do as a preacher is to call your listeners to the best choices, choices for Christ and against self, Satan, and the world. You have a low tolerance for worldliness, whether in yourself or others, because you see it for what it is: spiritual adultery. Accountability, repentance, obedience, and faithfulness to God's revealed will are some of the consistent themes of your ministry. You do not sidestep addressing the matter of God's judgment.

You are conscious of the potential for harshness and hypocrisy in proclaiming God's righteous standards, but you are determined not to let these potential pitfalls deter you from preaching the unrelenting call of God. You are hesitant to pull your punches. You believe you have been called to serve as a voice for the Lord and his ways, and you are determined to avoid waffling or giving an uncertain sound from the trumpet.

Rank yourself on the P(rophecy) Scale by circling the appropriate number.

0 — 1 — 2 — 3 — 4 — 5 — 6 — 7 — 8 — 9 — 10

Now that you have ranked yourself on each of the four scales, plot your ministry on the TEMP matrix by drawing vertical lines through the numbers you picked on the T(eaching) and E(xhortation) scales, and horizontal lines through the numbers you picked on the M(ercy) and P(rophecy) scales. Extend the lines until they intersect, forming a box on the matrix. The size, shape, and location of the resulting box will indicate your eccentricities as a preacher.

For instance, see the sample for a preacher who scored himself a 7 on the T scale, a 3 on the E scale, a 4 on the M scale, and a 5 on the P scale.

A blank matrix is provided for you to plot your own pattern. On this one, you'll notice I've also added four terms to various quadrants of the grid: Proclaimer, Motivator, Healer, and Counselor, which I will explain in the next section.

ANALYZING YOUR PREACHING

I believe Jesus would score high on each of the four TEMP scales. He excelled in all areas. His ministry would be represented by a large, square, centered box. As a less-than-perfect, less-than-balanced imitation of Christ, I cannot match that pattern. The size, shape, and location of your box and mine, however, will tell us about our eccentricities as preachers.

Size: The larger the box, the more gifted you feel you are.

Shape and location: The more square and centered your box, the more balanced you perceive your ministry. Rectangular boxes indicate you sense strengths and weaknesses.

TEMP Matrix

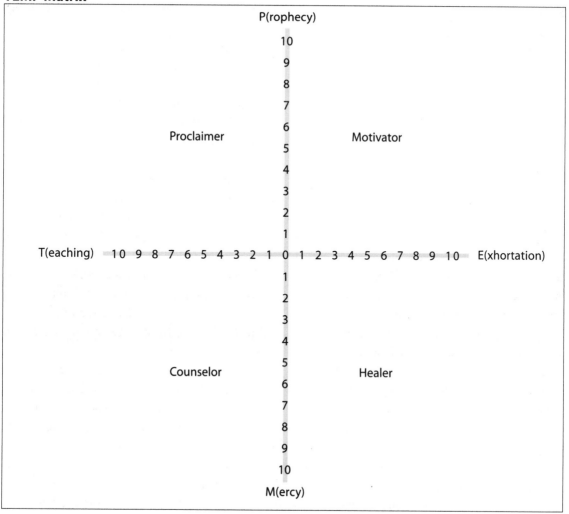

Thus, if your box is a large, centered square, it suggests you are gifted in all four areas and are maintaining a balanced ministry like Jesus. May your tribe increase! But if your box is a long, thin rectangle, sitting to the right of center, on top of the T-E line, you are highly gifted in one area (Exhortation) and are eccentric accordingly.

Or, if your box is nearly a square, and slightly shifted left and up (as in the example), you are a preacher gifted at teaching and, to some degree prophecy. Exhortation and Mercy, on the other hand, are relative weaknesses. Since most of this box is in the Proclaimer quadrant, this is probably how such preachers would describe themselves.

Naturally, if most of a box was located in the upper right quadrant, those preachers could be described as Motivators, and so on.

WHAT IF I'M OFF CENTER?

Since I began using this simple tool, I've gained several insights into my preaching ministry.

No quadrant is the right one. Each one represents important biblical priorities present in the earthly ministry of Jesus. Wherever my box is located and whatever its shape, it can represent a valid, biblical emphasis.

If that applies to my preaching, it applies also to my evaluation of other preachers. I listened recently to a tape of a pastor who was spelling out his church's philosophy of ministry. I don't know the fellow, but his approach to ministry and his personal style indicate he'd score high on the Exhortation scale.

At the same time, he valued little the strengths of the Teaching and Prophecy scales. "In our church," he said proudly, "we always keep our message positive." He was careful to stay close to the core truths of the gospel, he said, but he didn't want to "divide people over doctrine." Instead, his philosophy of ministry was task oriented, rooted in "real life" and kept constantly before the people. In short, it was an Exhortation emphasis.

Since my own box is well skewed toward the Proclaimer quadrant (I'm high on the Teaching and Prophecy scales), I was irritated with this preacher's lack of appreciation for such strengths. Not surprisingly, I dismissed his approach as lightweight. Then I caught myself. I was doing to his strengths what he was doing to mine. Aware of this, I listened to the tape again, this time trying to learn from someone who had strengths in areas I do not.

Likewise, those who rank high on the Prophecy scale may be tempted to criticize as sentimental those high on the Mercy scale. Counselors may feel that Motivators are pushy. Healers may think that Proclaimers are harsh. The combinations of criticism are many—as any pastors' conference gossip proves. Each of us tends to define ministerial strength in our own image, forgetting that all four emphases are valuable and biblical.

Everyone has natural strengths. This exercise makes my uniqueness graphic. I don't have to be like other preachers. While remaining faithful to God, I just have to be the preacher God has gifted me to be.

Some preachers struggle, not because they preach poorly, but because their listeners don't appreciate their particular preaching strengths. In some cases, that might suggest the pastor should seek another church. There is no sense in vainly beating one's head against a pulpit.

Bill's problems started soon after he began serving a new church. It was too late before he realized the people didn't like his preaching. In the end, he was asked to leave. Naturally, he was devastated, and he contemplated leaving the ministry altogether. "Am I really an incompetent preacher?" he once asked me forlornly.

At the time, I didn't know what to say, but now I see the problem was almost certainly not his lack of preaching skills, but a poor match. Actually, Bill is a good preacher, but he is a Proclaimer. His former church apparently wanted a Healer. Since leaving that church Bill has taken a different congregation. He has regained his composure and gone on to an effective ministry in a setting where his strengths are appreciated.

Then again, unheeded does not necessarily mean unneeded. Perhaps, as with Jeremiah, a preacher's strengths are precisely what the Lord has ordered, whether the people want to hear it or not and whether it is popular or not.

In either case, the preacher's strengths don't become weaknesses by being unappreciated. They remain genuine strengths whether a particular congregation appreciates them or not.

Strength doesn't mean balance. Preachers are tempted to define ministry to fit their peculiarities. We say, "This is what the church is about, and this is how the work should be done," not realizing that we may be defining the church in our image. A look at my box quickly reminds me that the church needs to be bigger than my strengths.

We are also tempted to mistake the strengths of other preachers, especially those we envy, for balance. Some popular preachers and churches intentionally lift up their styles as universal. Others recognize that every church should fashion its own purpose and direction. But the very popularity of "successful" ministries inclines us to think these ministries are real ministries—balanced and biblical—and ours are something less.

To rid ourselves of this delusion, we need to run through the matrix of the preachers we envy. We soon see that even people we idolize are skewed in one way or another.

An associate pastor in one such church said to me, "In our church, you hear constantly the theme that we are all forgiven sinners. The appeal is, 'Come join us, and let us meet your needs.'" Then he added, with something less than full approval, "What you never hear is, 'Deny yourself, take up your cross, and follow Christ.' That puts people off." This church, large and growing, was held up as a model for others. But like most churches, it is skewed in a particular way.

Different churches have different gifts; different preachers have different strengths. There is nothing wrong with being limited or skewed, as long as we don't mistake our eccentricity for balance.

Strengths bring dangers. I also recognize the pitfalls inherent in my strengths. A piece of ancient wisdom says that within our greatest strengths lie the seeds of our greatest failures. Wise preachers will be aware of where their natural strengths might take them, especially for ill.

I have a friend, for instance, who demonstrates a high Mercy profile. John is sensitive and empathetic, constantly reaching out to those who hurt. John, of course, is also committed to God's Word and assures his congregation that the Scriptures must be our only rule of faith and practice. However, during the tough judgment calls of pastoral ministry, John invariably falls into the trap of the Mercy preacher—he goes with his feelings. He tends to take positions or give counsel based on his emotions rather than God's truth. John is the type who might sympathize with the rich young ruler, softening the impact of Jesus' abrupt instructions to sell all.

Likewise, a preacher high in Exhortation may lack biblical substance, just as a strong Teacher may tend to preach from an ivory tower, the Proclaimer may become merely harsh, and the Healer may become sentimental. Each of us needs to guard against the liabilities inherent in our strengths.

Balance within reason. It's uncomfortable to notice the eccentricity that this matrix makes so plain. I naturally want to offer my church a balanced fare. So, as long as I recognize I am who I am by the grace of God (perfect balance is impossible for anyone but Jesus, after all), then this matrix can highlight areas I can work on.

For example, one preacher high on the Exhortation scale told me he had to relearn the discipline of study. Though he has a good mind, serious study has never come naturally to him. He did well in college and seminary, but only because he had been forced to study. Once he was out in the pastorate, he'd allowed that discipline to slip.

He would actually be relieved when interruptions cut into his study time. For awhile, he even chose a public place to study. Supposedly this was to keep his preaching in touch with real people and real needs. Actually, he said, it was little more than an excuse to avoid those long hours of serious mental work. As a result, his preaching lost substance, and both he and his people suffered.

Thankfully, this preacher recognized what was happening before it was too late, and he took steps to discipline his study time. He set up firm study hours and asked his wife and secretary to help him keep them. He enlisted the help of coworkers to hold him accountable. To this day, disciplined study does not come easily for him. He never will score high on the Teaching scale. But he is working faithfully against this weakness, and his preaching is the stronger for it.

In larger churches, of course, preachers can strengthen their weaknesses by adding staff members who complement them. Last year, we added an executive pastor to our staff. In one sense, an executive pastor must share a common vision and work in harmony with the senior pastor. Yet I was also looking for someone who would compensate for some of my weaknesses. God gave us a man who could do just that; his box on the TEMP matrix nicely complements mine. My task now is to give Rob the freedom to counterbalance my influence where necessary.

In addition, teammates in ministry can use the TEMP matrix to plot their own ministries, and one another's, to discover the strengths and weaknesses of the team. In the same way, churches looking for a pastor might plot the church's ministry and ask prospective candidates to plot theirs to see if the two fit.

No Cure-All

The TEMP matrix, of course, doesn't analyze every aspect of preaching. It can't evaluate the effectiveness of delivery, the appropriateness of illustrations, or the coherence of sermon structure. It's a limited tool, but helpful.

It may not have stopped me from wobbling like a washing machine from time to time. Nor has it made me all things to all people. (I'm not sure I want to be.) But recognizing my tendencies through the TEMP matrix, I know I'm a more effective and more confident preacher—even though I remain a bit eccentric.

Chapter 104

INTERESTING PREACHING

How to avoid talking in someone else's sleep

Stuart Briscoe

Gerald Griffith, a pastor and Bible teacher in Toronto and a good friend of mine, said to me one day, "Every week God gives me bread for his people."

I looked him straight in the eye and replied, "That's true, but you spend a lot of time in the kitchen!" He had to agree. Those hours "in the kitchen" are among the most important of my week. Why? Because in the kitchen I prepare what God gives me to feed his people, and they can be picky eaters.

People are distracted by all kinds of things—legitimate things, for the most part, but sometimes not. Pain fills a lot of hearts. People are unhappy at work. Or their homes are less than ideal. Or they feel great economic stress. Or they strain under the demands of a job. When troubled people come to church, their thoughts suppress the appetite for God's menu. My job as a preacher is to overwhelm the careworn with the aroma of the gospel.

So when I preach, I'm continually thinking. *How am I going to hold and use the attention so tenuously lent me?* I don't have it long. When I listen in on conversations in the church foyer any Sunday, I'm amazed at how quickly thoughts skirt from divine worship to talk about the Bucks and the Brewers, or making a buck and what's brewing in politics. So one of my major responsibilities of the week is to grab their attention with the sermon.

Consequently, I pass my sermon material through what I call the "So what?" test for relevance. There's no problem with the Scriptures. They're relevant. But I have to do my part to make the sermon as relevant as the Scriptures, because I want people to leave saying, "I see!" and not "So what?"

The way to do that, I've found, is to preach to the mind, the will, and the emotions. Donald English once said: "When I leave a church service, I ask myself the question: Which part of me need I not have brought here today?" That's why I try to touch every part of the person through the material I use in the sermon. If I'm preaching to mind, will, and emotions, people won't go away saying, "So what?"

PREACHING TO THE MIND

Theology challenges the mind. I admit not many people think in theological terms. Perhaps that's the problem: They haven't looked at the worldview—the philosophy of life—behind their lifestyles. So I intend to keep them thinking about it when I preach.

For instance, I often point out the flip side of a proposition or belief. Most issues have at least two sides, so when I make a strong point about something, I'm anxious to point out that others believe differently. Often I'll spell out the opposing beliefs. I'm not being wishy-washy,

385

but getting people to *think*. Those with tunnel vision need someone to open up for them a broader view.

Once I was preaching a series on the Apostles' Creed: "I believe in God the Father Almighty. . . ." To get at the opening phrase fully, I stepped back and tried to help my congregation understand why the concept of God as *Father* disturbs many in our society. How does the radical feminist feel? I'd done my reading on the matter, so I quoted some feminists. I also mentioned those people who have been abused by their fathers. For them, unlike many of us, *father* does not have good connotations.

If we have a high view of Scripture and God, I continued, we have to beware of inflating images of our fathers to explain God; otherwise we will be left with a heavenly Father with ballooned faults. When we say, "God the Father," I concluded, we surely mean something more figurative and less literal than a polished-up version of our dads. I wanted people to accept the transcendent concept of God that Scripture communicates by the term *Father*.

I try to stretch people through my preaching. I did that in the Apostles' Creed series when I preached on "Maker of heaven and earth." Most people in our society view the universe as a closed system operating on set laws that are empirically discernible. So where does a "Maker of heaven and earth" fit in? Because materialists and naturalists populate our society, I found it necessary to explore an alternative to a closed system. By preaching good, hard science and theoretical physics along with sound theology, I was able to capture their attention.

Our access to people's minds is a terrible thing to waste, so I try to engage the mind. When I can snag their thinking and broaden their understanding, I've wrested their attention for the gospel.

PREACHING TO THE WILL

When I preach to the will, I'm looking for response. I want people to act on what is said. As a pastor, I'm apt to be gentler and less demanding than I might be as an itinerant preacher, because I'm going to be with the people for many years. I don't need to get all or nothing in one shot.

I'm usually looking for minor movement in the right direction rather than a gargantuan step. It seems that people's wills move incrementally. So I try to choose words and illustrations that *encourage* movement, even if slight, in the right direction.

I use the word *encourage* purposefully. Usually people respond better to encouragement than to "challenge." Most people need inspiration and courage more than a kick in the pants. So I try to give people bite-sized and good-tasting pieces to chew on.

For instance, when I preached on "By this all men will know that you are my disciples, if you love one another" (John 13:35), I didn't instruct people to go out and swamp their world with love. Instead, I said, "Think of one person close to you. How well do you love that person in light of what we've talked about today? If *agape* love is concerned primarily with the well-being of others, irrespective of their reaction, then practice that love this week. See if your love makes any difference."

When I preach an evangelistic sermon to the will, I want people to understand that repentance might be a simple step rather than a big leap, but it nonetheless needs to be ventured.

A woman wanted her pastor to pray with

her because she no longer felt Christ's presence. When he asked about her problem, she said, "I don't want to talk about it. Just pray for me. That's all I want of you."

He probed gently anyway, and eventually she began to cry: "I'm living with my boyfriend, and I really have no intention of moving out." She wanted to sense Christ's presence while she lived in disobedience. She needed to repent, of course, and end the disobedience if she were to feel close to God again. Without that step of the will, her spiritual life would remain stale.

The will is a wily creature. Sometimes it needs to be encouraged, sometimes challenged. The trick to preaching to the will is to find which kind of stimulation best works for the people to whom you're preaching.

PREACHING TO THE EMOTIONS

Awhile back, I was preaching about Christ being rejected. Such a familiar theme is prime material for a yawner of a sermon. So how did I add interest?

Emotions! I told the story of Winston Churchill's post-war experiences. I'm a Churchill fan, and I recalled his tremendous impact during the Second World War. I said as a little boy I listened on a crackling radio to his famous speech—"We will fight them on the beaches. . . . We will *never* surrender!" All the time bombs were dropping, and the sound of anti-aircraft guns and the glare of searchlights split the night. His bulldog-like determination got us through that dreadful period.

Churchill was the man of the hour during the war. But at the end of the war, an election was held, and, surprisingly, Churchill lost. After all he had done, he was turned out of office by the British people.

The congregation looked shocked when I reminded them of that bit of history. Then, very quietly, I said, "He was a broken man." I just left it there for a moment. While that thought stirred within them, they felt deeply what rejection means.

I'd engaged their emotions. Churchill's rejection really bothered them. From there it was a short step to move those feelings to the rejection of Jesus Christ.

Some rightly object that we can address the emotions at the expense of the mind, but that's not my problem. I'm not as prone to manipulate people's emotions as I am to forget them. Purely intellectual matter can get extraordinarily dry, but emotions add life. Emotions move people to response. People identify with them.

Humor, because it elicits emotion, plays an important part in my preaching. Humor can be a wonderful servant or a dreadful master. But if Philips Brooks's definition of preaching is right—that preaching is truth communicated through personality—then I need to communicate through humor, because I enjoy humor.

A fellow once said to me, "I've been listening to you for quite a long time now, and sometimes when I go home from church, I find a knife stuck in my ribs. I always wonder. *How did he do that?* So today I decided to watch you closely, and I found out how you did it. You got me laughing, and while I was laughing, you slipped the point home.

He wasn't suggesting that I was manipulative. Instead, it was a warm-hearted compliment. He was saying that humor puts us off guard, and at those times we are highly receptive to penetration by the Word.

Once in a sermon I spoke about a purported memo written to Jesus by a management consultant. It evaluated the aptitude of the various disciples. Predictably, it panned the qualifications of most of the disciples—too unrefined, no credentials—but it lauded the great potential of one: Judas. People laughed. They could feel the irony. In a humorous way, I made my point: The unrefined and ill-qualified disciples were transformed into sterling men of character by the Resurrection.

Humor also allows the mental equivalent of a seventh-inning stretch in a sermon. People's minds need a break now and then, and humor can supply it in a way that enhances the sermon. After momentary laughter, people are ready for more content. Or when something disturbs the sermon—such as a loud sneeze—a good-humored retort can bring attention back to the preacher.

Fear also can be used for good or bad. I hesitate to motivate people with fear. I would rather love be their motivation. Fear, however, can be used to bring interest to well-worn passages, for fear grabs people.

When preaching about the security that the presence of the Friend brings, I recalled an invitation to speak at pastors' conferences in Poland. When I arrived at the Warsaw airport, nobody came forward to greet me. I had no names to contact, no addresses, no phone numbers, no Polish money. So I just stood in the middle of the airport while people collected their bags and the lobby emptied. Soon workers began to close down the area, and I was left standing there very alone.

My loneliness turned to fear when I heard a voice behind me say, "Briscoe." I turned to see a fellow in a long, leather coat, the type I'd seen in too many pot boilers about the Second World War. I thought. *Hey, don't look at me! I didn't want to come here in the first place!* But before my panic was unleashed, he came over, grabbed me, kissed me, and said warmly, "Brother Briscoe!" Then he leaned over and said, "Quickly, we must get on the tram car," and we rushed to catch it.

On the tram he told me, "Speak loudly of Jesus. You can use English and any German you know. They'll understand." So as we hung on the straps in that tram, I began to broadcast my love of Jesus, and everybody started to listen. Suddenly I was enjoying myself. The difference between being lonely and afraid a few minutes before and being comfortable on the tram was this: A friend was with me. I used fear that was transformed into fun to illustrate Jesus' words: "I am with you always, to the very end of the age" (Matt. 28:20). As people felt my fear, they hooked into the relief Jesus brings.

If I don't preach to the emotions, I'm missing a good part of the person sitting in the pew. Since people bring that part of themselves to church, the least I can do is address it with my sermon.

When you get right down to it, preaching is like farming. I often say, "Lord, here I am. As far as I can tell, I've tried to fill my sack with good seed. I've done my homework, I think my attitude is right, and it's the best, most interesting seed I've got. I'm going to scatter it now. Lord, so here goes. We'll see what comes up in the field." Then, once I've sown the seed, I do what farmers do: I go home and rest.

Over time, I get to watch that seed sprout and grow. A lot depends on the soil. God has to give the seed life. But eventually, I see the results of the good seed I've sown.

Chapter 105

CRAFTING AN EXPERIENCE
How to engage listeners fully

Rob Bell

A lot of pastors, when they approach the text, have in their heads a list of rules. There are hermeneutical and exegetical rules. It's a good idea to get close to what the Bible actually might be saying. There are rules like "God is God, and we're not." But a lot of them have rules about the methodological and execution part of the preaching task.

What we need are people who will approach the text and say, "God, what do you want to unleash here?" The guiding principle is the text, and you've encountered the living, sacred Word, and you're going to explode if you don't share what's happened in you, as opposed to *Well, I guess I have to start it this way.* You don't. *I have to have an intro.* Prove it. Maybe some teaching people have no idea where you're going until the last minute, and maybe that's why it works.

When Jesus tells the parable of the good Samaritan, everybody thought it was going to be a Pharisee who stops, but a Samaritan stops. Get it? He has them. He's working them over.

Sometimes I intentionally have three teachings going at the same time. I want you to be wondering, *That has nothing to do with what you're saying now. I have no idea....* And then at the end, *oooh.* If you don't get that *oooh,* you're in trouble.

THE HISTORICAL DIMENSION

We swim in a deep stream. There are all these different dimensions. When I approach the text, I am part of a historical movement of people who said yes to God—to the revolution. I want to connect people. The Scriptures are accounts of redeeming. It's a story, and I get to be part of the continuing story.

Abraham left and set out from Haran. My mind immediately thinks, *Okay, Haran, where was it? Can I get slides? Can I get pictures of it? What else happened there? What was Mesopotamian society like at that time? Are there other documents from Haran? What's the landscape like? What were the people like? What language did they speak? What was the currency? Are there other writers from that time?* If you actually believe he's a real dude leaving a real place, then what was Haran like? If I knew something about Haran, would it help me understand the text?

It's not that you need this. It's not like you need the Bible—plus. But if we're serious about bringing it to life, maybe up comes a slide of Haran. "Let me tell you about this place." Especially for the person who's never been in church. *Oh, okay, this is real people.*

A friend of mine did a teaching on the sociopolitical climate of Gath. It sounds exciting, doesn't it? He walked through the god Dagon. He walked through the cult of Dagon. Here was Dagon currency. Here were Dagon's cultic rites. Here was the way Dagon was organized. Here was Philistine society. Here were the four Shephelahs that led from the Philistine region to the Israel region. David and Goliath battled in the Valley of Elah. What was the Valley of Elah known for because it was one of the four Shephelahs? Why do David and Goliath battle here? What did Goliath believe about Dagon?

When he got to David and Goliath, he's reading the text, and people are, like, *wow*. If you understand Dagon and the things Goliath says, why does David say, "So the whole world will know"? Well, that's because of the Valley of Elah and what it was known for.

We swim in a deep stream, and there's a historical dimension. When I approach a text, I immediately want to know what's going on here. *Why does he say this? And why does she say that? And why does this guy go here?*

It's real people in real places at real times. When you come to the text, you've got all of these different things to draw from. That's my central idea. How do I connect these people in the third row who—their kid is sick, he lost his job, and her mother is in failing health? How do I connect them with real people in real places at real times who struggled with the same kinds of stuff?

Here's an example. King Herod is escaping from the Parthians. He's fleeing south of Jerusalem, and he finds out he's been rescued, and he's going to have his kingdom. He decides, *I want to mark this place by building a mountaintop palace.* The only problem is there's no mountain there. So Herod builds a mountain in the middle of the Judean wilderness and calls it the Herodian. It had a lower pool—in an area where it hasn't rained in eight hundred years—with a gazebo in the middle that you could only get to by boat. Unbelievable. There's a little town in the shadows of the Herodian called

Bethlehem. When Mary and Joseph come to Bethlehem, this giant mountaintop palace would have been right there.

What's interesting about this is we don't know where he got the dirt for this mountain. All we know is somewhere there isn't a mountain. It's like Archaeology 101. Even to this day it's dry, loose dirt at the top.

The reason why I say this is if you're on the Mount of Olives and you look south, you can see the Herodian, and then way off in the distance you can see the Dead Sea. Jesus, leaving Bethany, going into the Temple Mount, which means he crossed over the top of the Mount of Olives, turned to his disciples and said, "If you have faith [like a mustard seed] ... you can say to this mountain, 'Go, throw yourself into the sea,' and it will be done" (Matt. 21:21; cf. 17:20).

What else was Herod known for? Herod built a stadium. They've excavated 350,000 seats. They believe it sat 500,000 people. He built the second temple. Bill Gates has a paper route compared to Herod. And Jesus turned to a group of post-pubescent Talmudean disciples and said: Hey, by the way, you have faith? You can do greater things than Herod.

In teaching and preaching, when you can capture this element of real people in real places, it does amazing things.

THE EXPERIENTIAL DIMENSION

These are questions I ask myself. *How can I make it as hard as possible for somebody to sit with a holy stare? How can I make it so you have to engage? How can I create an experience such that it becomes harder and harder for people to stay spectators? What's happening in this text? What could I have people do? What could I have them say to each other? What can I have them feel, hold, or look at? Is there something I could hand out?*

When I talked about how Ephesians says we're God's handiwork, the word is *poiema*, which means artwork. I purchased a lump of modeling clay for everybody. When you walked in, you were handed a chunk of clay. I did the whole teaching around *forming*. "You're God's art." The title of the sermon was "You're a Piece of Work"—which is a biblical phrase. What can you hand out?

I've handed out honey. The rabbis used to place honey on a kid's finger and say, "May the words of God be as delicate. . . ." When you walk in and you're handed a honey bear, people are engaged.

I was thinking about Jesus being tempted in the wilderness: *What if I could convince our whole congregation to fast on the Saturday before our Sunday services? What if everybody could come to the Sunday services having not eaten on Saturday, and when they walked in they were handed a rock? And what if the whole teaching was Satan saying to Jesus, "Turn this rock into bread"?* How can I let them know we're going somewhere today? "I want to take you somewhere, so here's this rock."

Last Christmas, I had somebody buy everyone in the church a little chunk of myrrh. We talked about how myrrh was used to ease people's suffering when they were being crucified. At Jesus' birth the parents are given myrrh. Real hopeful gift there.

If people can smell it, the kids can chew it, if you can create as many different dimensions as possible—many of us are tactile—if we can feel it, it makes more sense.

How can I get people out of their seats? One Easter, we built a tomb. I gave people sheets of paper and talked about how Jesus rose from the dead.

If somebody died and came back to life, that is a dangerous person because they're not scared of much. You can chuck your flannel-graph, white-bathrobed Jesus, because this is one dangerous dude. He survived death. People who aren't afraid of death are frightening to be around because they'll do anything. If you have given your life to Jesus, you have trusted your life to somebody who knows what they're going to do. Whatever you're scared of you need to write it on a sheet of paper. We're going to spend some time worshiping. You need to take whatever it is you fear and throw it into the tomb and leave it there.

And to see on Easter Sunday people walking up and spouses sobbing and then throwing it into the tomb. . . .

I did this message on "The Gospel According to Salsa" and talked about how my wife makes the best salsa in the world. And I will arm-wrestle you about that. Everything in my wife's salsa was living at one point. The tomato was living. The parsley was living. The cilantro was living. The onion was living. But in order for it to be made into salsa, it had to be plucked from its life source. The tomato had to be cut from the vine. All of your food was living at one point, but it had to be severed. It had to die in order for it to make it to your plate. If you're at a restaurant and your food is not dead, leave immediately. But there's this principle in which we have to eat to live.

What's interesting about your food is that everything that you eat—and food gives you life—it had to die first. Death is the engine of life. The worm is eaten by the bird, which is eaten by the cat, which is eaten by the wolf, which is eaten by the grandchildren of the worm. Even in the physical realm, death is the engine of life. That's why a Twinkie isn't good for you, because it was never really alive.

Here's the idea. Death is what gives life to the physical universe. When God sends his Son to give us life, his Son has to die. So the cross isn't just true sacramentally. Death is life all over the place. God's giving us life through Jesus' death isn't a new idea in the history of the world. It's God working in the flow of what he's already created. I started thinking, *That's what Jesus keeps saying about really living. To be fully alive you have to deny yourself, take up your cross, become a servant. It's still true that in order to live I have to die.* We had this cross set up, and we said, "What do you need to die to, so you can really live? We're going to spend some time worshiping. Come up and kneel at the cross and take whatever is on that sheet of paper and jam it into the rocks at the bottom of that cross."

I'm always trying to think, *How can we engage people, and they can do something?*

One of the problems for preachers is when they're thinking, *What am I going to say about this text?* The question should be *What does the text want to say? And how many different dimensions can I get going?* In my message "The Goat Has Left the Building," I had slides talking to you, I read the text, the goat came in, the high priest in his outfit, and I said at one point, "Turn to the person next to you" and say such and such. Hopefully you were engaged at multiple levels. You were engaged visually. You were engaged auditorially. There were multiple things going on that carried the thing along. We're like artists.

We have all of these different tools at our disposal. We have this massive world God has created, and the Scripture leaps to life with truth that can't be kept down. Think about the exam-ple of Jesus: Check out those birds . . . check out those lilies . . . a man had two sons.

What's Jesus doing? He's saying, "Look at the world. You can learn about God from that." So I want to pull from those many different things.

Another thing we do is assume teaching is about me talking. There are times when the worst thing I should do is talk. I heard a teaching the other day; a guy told the most unbelievable personal story. It was an overwhelming story. The problem was, previous to that story was a lot of talk, and immediately following the story was a lot of talk. Mark Twain said, "If I would have had more time, I would have said less." That story was brilliant, but it got steamrolled by the stuff before and after. You don't have to talk the whole time to be preaching.

What I'm learning is there are times when the worst thing I can do is talk. For me, in my message "The Goat Has Left the Building," when the high priest was walking toward his seat, it was a sacred moment. I can't explain it. The problem with some of our preaching is you can explain it. You got your four points, your three applications, and this is what the text means.

At the end of the parable of the prodigal son, is Jesus saying, "Okay, here's the deal—God is the father figure"? What if at the end of *Gladiator*, Ridley Scott, the director, came out and said, "My intention was that you identify with Russell Crowe"? Great stories tell themselves. What we need are the storytellers.

THE "CELEBRATE A MYSTERY RATHER THAN CONQUERING IT" DIMENSION

One of the things that helps people is, when we've explained enough, we should let it sit. I have mystery on my side.

John 3:16 says: "For God so loved the world that he gave his one and only Son." Why did God give his Son? Because God loved the world. You mean God loves everybody? No matter what they've done? God loves everybody the same. His love is unending. God's love is expansive. It's unlimited. It endures forever. Do we have God's love now? I'm just scratching the surface. Why does God love the world? God *is* love. *Okay, sure. That fixes it.*

The nature of mystery is that when you get an answer, it raises a whole new set of questions. You know the foundations of our faith, the Trinity? *Yeah, sure, the Trinity, I got that one nailed.* We believe as orthodox Christians, and yet the nature of believing and placing our faith in the Trinity raises new questions. *How could God be Three in One? How can God be a community of self-giving love, of oneness?* The nature of truth is that it brings up more questions. That's why sometimes you heard sermons and thought, *I've heard that all before.* The person was preaching the doctrines of the faith, and yet you knew something was missing. A friend of mine says, "If you study, and it doesn't lead you to wonder and awe, then you haven't studied." Abraham Joshua Heschel said, "I did not ask for success; I asked for wonder."

There's a time when words fail and you simply have to worship. When you are preaching, there are moments, when we stop and say, "We're just going to sit in awe of God."

THE "YOU BE YOU" DIMENSION

You be you. I always think about the dimension of new identity. You aren't who you were. *Where in this teaching is God's message to the people that I'm leading or teaching at this moment about who they are in Christ? How is this teaching going to paint for them a more beautiful, compelling picture of who God says they are in Christ?* I want to create these pictures. I want to create teachings that are so beautiful that people are pulled into the ways God created them to live. How do I do this? Where is the empowerment element?

THE "THERE ARE NO RULES" DIMENSION

There are no rules. Other than basic things like doctrine: God and Jesus. But in terms of how you're going to do it, maybe there's no intro. Maybe the whole point of the teaching is it comes at you and people are just, like, *wow!*

I did a teaching one time on silence where I put the whole teaching on slides and stood there for forty-five minutes. At the end I said, "Let's stand for a benediction." Up came "May the Lord bless you and keep you," and I waved and walked off.

Maybe you read a whole book of the Bible. Sometimes reading the story is better than anything you could say. *What does it take to bring it to life?*

THINGS TASTE BETTER WHEN THEY'VE BEEN MARINATED

I work on teachings for as long as four to six months, a year. You'd think I was obnoxious because if we go out to lunch, I'll be diagramming on a napkin.

If you're married and I said, "Tell me about your wedding day," you could tell it to me. You wouldn't say, "I forgot my notes." No, you just tell me.

Those of you who have kids, if I asked, "How old are your kids, and what are their names?" You won't say, "I have my notes some place. I don't have my PowerPoint with me." No. Boom, boom, boom, these are the ages. Why? Because it's a part of you.

What if your teaching was such a part of you it was like telling about your wedding day or like telling about your first job? What would it be like if you could tell it like it was a story you told two hundred times?

That's my passion. I have found the harder I work and the farther out I've been working on it, the more freedom I have.

The people who are listening to you, they know when it's become a part of you. They can feel when the speaker is just giving some information and observation, and they know when it is coming right through your soul.

We don't need people who sing the notes off a chart. We need soul singers. We need prophets. We need poets. Our generation needs people who have had an experience. They've got their hair set on fire. They're wild-eyed, and they can't wait. *I got to say this, or I'm going to explode.*

I've been wrestling with this lately. God makes the world in six days; rests on the seventh. Six days, seven. Six, one. Six, one. There is a rhythm to six days on and one day off. I started thinking about drummers and how drumming is all about the spaces. It's all about hitting it and then backing off. Music and beat and meter and drum are a reflection of how God made the world. If you don't take that day and live according to the beat God has put in creation, your song isn't going to be good. When the drummer is off, the whole song falls apart. Rhythm is something that's built in; it's elemental to life.

Everybody I come in contact with, I say, "Check this out. Think about this. Sabbath and drums." I get something like this, and I can't shut up about it. By the time I get to share it with people, I will have told the person at the gas station. I will have told the person at 7/11—everybody I come in contact with. "Check this out. Sabbath . . . drums."

I invite you to become thoroughly unbalanced like me.

Chapter 106

SEVEN HABITS OF HIGHLY EFFECTIVE PREACHERS
How to speak so listeners can't forget

Craig Brian Larson

What's the difference between these two sentences?

"Washington is not an efficient, charming city."

"Washington is a city of southern efficiency and northern charm" (John F. Kennedy).

The first is flat. The second has flair. One is prosaic, the other artistic.

Artistic speech is interesting, fresh, appealing. It fires the imagination. It speaks to the heart. It reaches corners of the human spirit that plain, literal speech misses.

While the strength of literal speech is clarity, the strength of artistic speech is depth. An artful phrase communicates at more than one level. It resonates with the soul more than Webster's-accurate prose ever will.

No wonder artistic speech is used by the best contemporary communicators in speech or in print. It was certainly used by Jesus: "No one lights a lamp and hides it in a jar or puts it under a bed. Instead, he puts it on a stand so that those who come in can see the light" (Luke 8:16).

Few of us, though, have the time to do any more than salt our messages with artistic elements, primarily at the strategic points: the introduction, key sentences and paragraphs, and conclusion. Yet even a light sprinkling of artistry can add flavor. Here are seven ways to interest listeners.

COMPARISON

Good comparisons enliven the imagination and stir emotions. At a practical level, word pictures keep the interest of today's visually oriented listeners.

Scripture is full of comparisons, both metaphors ("The LORD is my rock, my fortress and my deliverer," Ps. 18:2) and similes ("As the deer pants for streams of water, so my soul pants for you, O God," Ps. 42:1). Metaphors can enliven an already dramatic scene and help make abstract topics tangible.

In his sermon "Tide Riding," the late Bruce Thielemann accomplished both of these effects in one short passage:

> My first pastorate was in McKeesport, Pennsylvania, which was famous at that time for having the world's largest steel-tube rolling mills.... Many was the time I stood in one of those great

machines ... with the man operating the machine. I'd see a great serpent of molten metal come slithering down into the machine, and it would be chopped off. Then the machine would grab it by its end and begin to spin. By centrifugal force, that bar of metal would open from the inside out.... I asked the men directing those machines, "What's the most important ingredient in the process?"

> The answer was always the same: "It's the temperature of the metal. If it is too hot, it will fly apart; if it is too cold, it will not open as it ought. Unless you catch the molten moment, you cannot make the perfect tube."

> Unless we catch those molten moments when character can develop, we miss our opportunities just as the disciples did.

Thielemann heightens our interest in the steel mill by introducing the snake metaphor, and then he uses "molten moments" as a tangible way to talk about the abstract concept of opportunity.

It's easy to misuse comparisons, however. Too many of the following mistakes, and listeners suffer confusion.

Mixed Metaphors

Multiple images in close proximity confuse rather than enlighten: "She charged into my office like a bull and fired one rocket of criticism after another."

We are most prone to mix metaphors when using "dead" metaphors (ones so common we no longer recognize them as metaphors): "If you can't take the heat [a dead metaphor referring to the discomfort of standing by a kitchen stove], start firing back [a military metaphor]."

Overreaching

We reach too far when a comparison is illogical, weak, or nonexistent, or we stretch the imagination just a tad too far: "Love is the tree sap of human relations. It nourishes the leaves of our soul."

Adverse Associations

"The gospel is as powerful as a nuclear bomb." Though both things are powerful, the simile fails because it compares something glorious and life-giving—the Christian message—with something fearful and destructive—nuclear holocaust. Neither would you say, "Joy is as infectious as the bubonic plague" or "The devil prowls the streets like Mother Teresa, looking for the weak and dying."

CONTRAST

Contrast accentuates and intensifies, just as a match unnoticeable in the sunlight burns brightly in a deep cave.

In the conclusion of his sermon "Tide Riding," Bruce Thielemann used contrast well:

> Please don't say anything to me about tomorrow. *Tomorrow* is the word the Bible does not know. If you can find me any place in the Scriptures where the Holy Spirit of God says 'tomorrow,' I will step down from this pulpit and never step into it or any other pulpit for as long as I live.
>
> The Holy Spirit's word is the word *today*. "Now is the accepted time; now is the day of salvation.' 'Today, if you will harden not your heart and hear my voice....'"
>
> Don't say *tomorrow* ... The word is *today*. Come to Christ today. Grow in Christ today. Serve in the name and in the spirit of Christ today.

Christ used contrast to underline the difference between past and present, between his teaching and other teaching: "You have heard that it was said, 'Do not commit adultery.' But I tell you that anyone who looks at a woman lustfully has already committed adultery with her in his heart" (Matt. 5:27–28).

Some of the most effective epigrams are merely clever contrasts: "War talk by men who have been in a war is always interesting; whereas moon talk by a poet who has not been in the moon is likely to be dull" (Mark Twain).

PARALLELISM

Parallelism is memorable. "Never in the field of human conflict was so much owed by so many to so few" (Winston Churchill).

People would not decorate their bedroom walls with the Beatitudes if Christ had said, "Blessed are the poor in spirit, for theirs is the kingdom of heaven. Mourners will be comforted, so they're blessed as well. The meek, who will inherit the earth, are blessed. God will bless those who hunger and thirst for righteousness by filling them full."

Parallel structure highlights special distinctions of thought. "That comfort is not a knowledge that everything will be all right, but a knowledge that everything is under control" (John Hannah, in his sermon "Is There Any Comfort?").

Or consider Haddon Robinson's phrase about the proud Pharisee praying in the temple: "In the presence of God, he had a good eye on himself, a bad eye on his neighbor, and no eye on God."

In his sermon "Living a Life of Integrity," George Munzing uses parallel structure to show the relationship between abstract ideas. "Sow a thought, reap an act. Sow an act, reap a habit. Sow a habit, reap a character. Sow a character, reap a destiny."

When a speaker piles up sentences and phrases in parallel structure, a tremendous sense of drama and emotion builds. "We shall not flag or fail. We shall go on to the end. We shall fight in France, we shall fight on the seas and oceans, we shall fight with growing confidence and growing strength in the air, we shall defend our island, whatever the cost may be, we shall fight on the beaches, we shall fight on the landing grounds, we shall fight in the fields and in the streets, we shall fight in the hills; we shall never surrender" (Winston Churchill, in a speech about Dunkirk in the House of Commons, June 4, 1940).

REPETITION AND REFRAIN

Repetition and refrain are another way to bring power to a sermon. Jesus used them not only in the Beatitudes but also when he chastised:

"Woe to you teachers of the law and Pharisees, you hypocrites! You shut the kingdom of heaven in men's faces" (Matt. 23:13).

"Woe to you teachers of the law and Pharisees, you hypocrites! You travel over land and sea to win a single convert" (Matt. 23:15).

"Woe to you teachers of the law and Pharisees, you hypocrites! You clean the outside of the cup and dish, but inside they are full of greed and self-indulgence" (Matt. 23:25).

Or take a modern example, Martin Luther King Jr.'s speech, "I Have a Dream":

> Even though we face the difficulties of today and tomorrow, I still have a dream. It is a dream deeply rooted in the American dream. I have a dream that one day this nation will rise up and live out the true meaning of its creed: "We hold these truths to be self-evident that all men are created equal."
>
> I have a dream that one day on the red hills of Georgia the sons of former slaves and the sons of former slaveowners will be able to sit down together at the table of brotherhood. . . . I have a dream that my four little children will one day

live in a nation where they will not be judged by the color of their skin but by the content of their character. I have a dream today.

> I have a dream that one day . . . little black boys and black girls will be able to join hands with little white boys and white girls as sisters and brothers. I have a dream today.
>
> I have a dream that one day every valley shall be exalted, every hill and mountain shall be made low, the rough places will be made plain, and the crooked places will be made straight, and the glory of the Lord shall be revealed, and all flesh shall see it together.

This is one of the most dramatic speeches of the twentieth century, and the wave upon wave of "I have a dream" has embedded itself in the national consciousness.

(Of course, using repetition when the subject or setting doesn't warrant only backfires. Don't try it without passion. It will feel as awkward as wearing a tuxedo to a small group Bible study.)

HYPERBOLE AND UNDERSTATEMENT

Ironically, understatement emphasizes a point.

"Dying is bad for you" (Russell Baker).

"Nothing in life is so exhilarating," said Winston Churchill, "as to be shot at without result."

Understatement is a national sport for the British, while overstatement—hyperbole, exaggeration—is the American preference. Chuck Swindoll combines hyperbole and understatement to humorous effect in his sermon, "Reasons to Be Thankful":

> When my wife and I were at Dallas Seminary back in the early 1960s, we lived in a little apartment that was a part of a small group of apartments that have since then been destroyed, I am

happy to say. Hot and cold running rats—all the joys of home were there. In the summer the weather came inside, and it was hot. Hot? Hotter than you can imagine. Like a desert.

That hot fall, we began to pray for an air conditioner; we didn't have one. I remember through the cold, blowing winter—strange!—we were praying for an air conditioner. Through December, January, and February, we told nobody, we made no announcement, we wrote no letter; we just prayed.

The following spring, before we were to have another summer there, we visited my wife's parents in Houston. While there, one morning the phone rang. We hadn't announced our coming; it was for a brief visit with her folks and mine before we went back to seminary. The phone rang, and on the other end of the line was a man I hadn't talked to in months. His name happened to be Richard. . . .

I said, "How are you?"

He said, "Great! Do you need an air conditioner?"

I almost dropped the phone. [Up to this point Swindoll's delivery has been typically enthusiastic. Before the following line, however, he pauses and then calmly says,] "Uh, yes."

"Well," he says, "we have just put in central air conditioning here, and we've got this little three-quarter-ton air conditioner that we thought you might like to have. We'll bring it over and stick it in your trunk and let you take it back, if that's okay."

[Again Swindoll pauses and answers calmly]

"That'll be fine, Richard. Bring it on over.'"

We put that thing in the window, and we froze winter and summer in that little place!

As Swindoll shows here, using understatement in tandem with overstatement can help listeners "get it."

Overstatement can be humorous—"Always do right. It will gratify some people and *aston-*ish the rest" (Mark Twain). Or it can have an edge to it: "If your right eye causes you to sin, gouge it out and throw it away. . . . If your right hand causes you to sin, cut it off and throw it away" (Matt. 5:29–30).

Explaining understatement or hyperbole to listeners is a mistake, though. Much of the impact comes from listeners' getting it for themselves, and if they don't, explaining only highlights failure. Another error is to commonly use adjectives such as *rather*, *somewhat*, *very*, *super*, or *mega* to under- or overstate.

ALLITERATION

Alliteration—using words that begin with similar sounds—accents comparison or contrast. "This time through a similar whirlwind, God brings not *ruin* but *revelation*, not *disaster* but *disclosure*."

When we alliterate the key words of a sentence—the subject and verb, the verb and the direct object, a series of parallel words—the words fit, and the sentence sounds right.

"If you accept Christ, righteousness can be a reality."

"His career was ruined through laziness and lying."

"The end of sin is sorrow."

Alliteration is both a tool and a temptation. We've all abused alliteration in sermon outlines, forcing words to fit the scheme, even at the risk of confusing the meaning. If we find we have to explain an alliterative outline for listeners to get it, we've probably gone too far.

PERIPHRASIS

One general rule of good communication is to keep it simple. Sometimes, though, saying something in a roundabout way can be more interesting. It's called *periphrasis*.

Many biblical phrases could be shortened, but the periphrasis appeals to the heart and imagination. Instead of saying "David loves me and is a righteous man," God says, "I have found David son of Jesse *a man after my own heart*" (Acts 13:22).

Describing a source for one of Shakespeare's plays, instead of saying "a disorganized play," Northrop Frye, in his book *On Shakespeare*, says, "A messy dog's breakfast of a play."

One common structure for periphrasis is a hyphenated phrase used as an adjective: "They lived in a cockroaches-have-the-right-of-way tenement house."

Turned phrases—based on movie, book, or television titles, cliches, familiar quotations, Bible verses, or advertising slogans—make for arresting titles:

"When the Roll Is Called Down Here" (Fred Craddock).

"Glory to God in the Lowest" (Bruce Thielemann).

"Levi's Genes" (Vic Pentz).

Turned phrases also draw an effective contrast: "How many times have you heard it said that in this world it's not what you know but who you know that counts? And that is often true. But in God's world, it is not what you know but who you are that counts" (George Munzing).

Wordplay can be used for serious purposes. Jack Hayford described in one sermon a divine message he received regarding his finances: "The reason things are so tight is because you're too tight."

Wordplay can highlight a comparison or contrast. "You're very careful about your actions," said one preacher. "Character is revealed by your *reactions*."

Explaining a wordplay, or any artistic element, patronizes listeners. While clarity is a virtue in communication, so is subtlety, which allows listeners the pleasure of figuring things out.

"For I am convinced that neither death nor life, neither angels nor demons, neither the present nor the future, nor any powers, neither height nor depth, nor anything else in all creation, will be able to separate us from the love of God that is in Christ Jesus our Lord" (Rom. 8:38–39).

Redwood-solid substance like this—expressed with contrast, repetition, parallelism, balance, variation, and climax—was written by an apostle who said, "I may not be a trained speaker, but I do have knowledge" (2 Cor. 11:6). He said he "did not come with eloquence or superior wisdom" (1 Cor. 2:1). He clearly could never be accused of putting style over substance.

The lesson for us is that we don't have to choose substance over style or style over substance. For as biblical writers such as Paul and David and Isaiah and John knew, in the hands of serious communicators, artistic style is substance.

Chapter 107

THE SERMON'S MOOD
The spirit of a message is like the tune of a song

Fred Craddock

Everyone knows a sermon has points, but not everyone knows a sermon also has a tune.

I applied the term *tune* to preaching a few years ago when I began to wonder, *Why do I especially like certain sermons? What makes certain ones really work?* There was some important ingredient in effective sermons that went beyond the normal considerations of content. That ingredient, I realized, was the tune.

A sermon's tune—its mood or spirit—is not easy to define precisely, but it's unmistakable. Hearing some sermons, I think of seventy-six trombones coming down Main Street. Other messages make me picture a violin and a crust of bread.

We don't often think of the tune we'll play when we're preparing a sermon, because our preparation tends to focus on the content. But afterward, when we evaluate how we spoke it and how people responded to it, *then* we recall the tune: the subtle atmosphere that was projected, the mood that filled the sanctuary as the sermon was preached.

Complicating matters is that not just sermons but preachers have tunes. I ask my students to imagine what sound track would best complement their preaching, and they give me answers ranging from Willie Nelson's music to something majestic from Handel's *Messiah*.

In fact, when I open my ears, I find tunes all around me. Churches have their tunes. Communities do too. In Appalachia, most of the tunes are somber: "We're Going Down the Valley One by One," "'Tis Midnight, and on Olive's Brow," "The Old Rugged Cross." Pathos flows through these tunes. If I want to preach to Appalachia a greater sense of Easter, I can't fuss at them for not jumping up and down the first Sunday I sound that unfamiliar refrain. Joy is a strange tune to their ears. They need time to catch the beat.

So I've realized I need to be aware of the tunes of preaching. My sermon, the text it's based on, my church, and my own personality—each has a distinctive "sound." A sermon's tune may not play well in every situation. The idea is to harmonize our preaching with the notes being sounded around us.

YOUR PREDECESSOR'S TUNE

Preachers new to their church need to discover their predecessor's favorite tunes. It's especially important if the predecessor had a lengthy tenure, because that preacher's style has defined the word *sermon* for that congregation. In the minds of the hearers, any variation from that tune has to struggle even to qualify as a sermon.

Suppose for twenty-three years my predecessor said each Sunday, "I have four things I want to say about the text this morning. In the first place ..., and the second ...," and so on, and at the end summarized the sermon. That's a precise, ordered tune, like a military march. The congregation is accustomed to a methodical, logical sermon—major premise, minor premise, and conclusion. Thus, when I come in singing another song, I can't expect everybody to ooh and aah. If I don't preach that way, I can expect, at least for a while, that the congregation will not accept my "talks" as sermons. They'll probably say, "Well, it just didn't seem like a sermon."

This is not unreasonable. For many listeners, a change in *form* is equivalent to a change of *content*. Preach a narrative sermon, and the people who have been used to hearing Reverend Outline preach "One, two, three, four" will say, "Well, it was real interesting and all, but we like more Bible." You may have included more Bible in your sermon than he ever did, but the only way listeners have to register the different tune they heard—even when the content or theology of the sermon was virtually identical—is listing some vague problem with the contents. They couldn't take their usual notes on the sermon, so they figure it must have had an unbiblical melody.

In a new church I wouldn't try to imitate the previous pastor. Nobody preaches well enough to imitate, and no one can sing someone else's tune anyway. However, I need to prepare the people to hear a new tune. And that takes time, just as it took me time to get used to new translations of the Bible. I first memorized Bible verses from the King James Version, so I *talked* about using other translations long before I was comfortable with them emotionally.

Second, I must respect how hard it is on a congregation when I change the *form* of the sermon. If the form is always new and different, congregations don't hear it as well. It's like hitting them with a hymn with unfamiliar words and tune. But if the basic form of a sermon remains predictable and clear, I am allowed to work creatively within it.

Most congregations can handle only one variable at a time. So if I am going to vary the form of my preaching, my message had better be familiar. Or if I plan to hit them with a novel message, then my preaching style ought to be predictable.

That rule extends to the service itself. If I plan to preach a different kind of sermon, the rest of the service ought to be straightforward and predictable, and if I'm going to experiment with the service, I'm wise to preach my standard sermon.

Since visually and vocally I'm a new variable to the congregation when I first come to a church, I try not to add a lot of clever innovations initially. Once they get accustomed to my voice and appearance, then I can make some changes. Whether I like the waiting period or not doesn't matter. What they're accustomed to has shaped the ear.

The Congregation's Tune

I work with not only my predecessor's tune but with my congregation's. I analyze a congregation somewhat like I would a group of people going down a street. I ask myself, *What are they doing? Is it a parade? Are they just out for a stroll? Or is it a protest march?*

For some congregations, every Sunday is a protest march. Some issue must be taken on: arms control, taxes, poverty—whatever. They're marching to city hall, and you can almost hear the drumbeat of protest, protest, protest.

Certainly there are things to protest. But if you protest all the time, people get weary of that tune: *Here we go again to city hall.* It's not effective. I may thump my suspenders and say, "I'm a prophetic voice in this age!" but the point is, I'm not getting anything done.

Some congregations are on parade. You get a sense of John Philip Sousa. It's triumphant. Every day is Palm Sunday, and everything is grand and glorious. But there are always people recently widowed or hurting or whose daughter is on drugs or whose job just disappeared. These people are not in the parade.

That means the music has to vary. Some sermons need the feel of a friendly stroll down the street, just a couple of you talking. Then the parades and protest marches provide a different beat, a new sound that catches one's attention.

THE TEXT'S TUNE

The tune of a sermon also needs to be appropriate to the tune of the text. With some of the Psalms, you're excitedly on the way to Jerusalem. With others, you're sitting in a trash dump, saying, "I just want to die." There are some where you're sitting in a circle with your kids. In some of them you're all by yourself: "My soul is quieted within me." So sometimes the biblical material itself may say, "Don't play the wrong tune here. This is a penitential psalm, so don't try to inspire people."

Once I listened to a pastor preaching on the beatitude, "Blessed are those who hunger and thirst for righteousness, for they will be filled" (Matt. 5:6). But he started hitting people with what was wrong with them. "You're out hungering after this and thirsting after that," he fumed, "when it should be *righteousness* you're after!" He said some good things, but the words *hunger* and *thirst* did not flavor the sermon, and as a whole it never came across as a blessing. He turned a beatitude into an exhortation and thus changed the music entirely.

Later I asked him, "Do you have other words for *blessed*?"

"I don't like the word *happy*," he said. "I would rather just say *blessed.*"

"That's an important word in the Bible," I said, "but blessed are those who live within earshot of the Beatitudes." I wanted him to know that somehow the soft oboes of blessing needed to be heard.

YOUR WEEKLY TUNE

My personal experiences during the week—my work, my prayers, my study, my attending all kinds of events—have set up a certain rhythm, a tune, in my own life. And I may discover my tune doesn't fit that of the text. My tendency at times like that is to tell the congregation, "When I chose this text with its stately marching cadence, it echoed the way I felt. But this week I've had 487 committee meetings, and everything is still hanging. I'm exhausted. Yet this passage arrives so beautifully in Jerusalem that I wish it were my experience today. So if you detect in my voice some longing, some wishing, it's really there."

That's the course I take when my personal tempo is out of sync with the text. It works better than saying, *Fred, get up to that text!* That's often unrealistic. I say to the people, "I'm down here, and the text is up there. If anyone wants to try to reach up to it, let's give it a try."

I want to understand my personal tunes, but unless they prove unhealthy, I don't feel obliged to alter them. If I'm constantly sucking melancholy out of every situation, however, then I may need some help. But within the normal variations of my life, it's wise to recognize my own tunes and share from them.

Most often, people will be able to pick up our tunes. There will be days when we show up with a violin and everybody else brings drums, but most people can adapt. And next Sunday will probably be better.

Your Dominant Refrain

Although we will play variations on our theme, most of us settle into a dominant refrain. The gospel playing in our lives for years has created in us a distinctive sound. Congregations usually accept the theme to which their pastors return. But it's dangerous to assume that ours is the tune everyone must play. In the best of circumstances, we know and the congregation knows that ours is not the only tune the gospel will play, but it's what it plays best through us. Others will have their distinctive tunes as well. Understanding individual tunes can help avoid a lot of heartache and jealousy. When we invite guest speakers, we can say, "We're bringing in a set of tympani, folks. You've been listening to this little ol' clarinet, but the gospel in this person's life sounds with extraordinary resonance, and you'll love it!"

That little speech helps keep people from saying, "This preacher is better than that preacher," because that's like saying a drum is better than cymbals. You can't compare them. It's also a good way to get people ready for a new minister.

Over time our tunes become like theme songs. Thirty years later, people will recall my ministry and say, "He was the violin we had way back before we brought in the trumpet." And once my tune becomes a theme song, I can talk about it at points where I know there will be dissonance, like at the beginning of a difficult sermon: "This is a tough one today, folks, so I'm going to bring out the violins."

Of course, overuse turns it into a ploy. But it's useful every now and then when I know my experience and theirs are at cross-purposes, or the text and I are on different wavelengths. And it sure beats getting mad because they are not in tune with me.

Beginning with the Ear

Often I go into the sanctuary and sit in the pews to do part of my sermon work. There in the quiet, I ask myself, *How would this part sound? If I heard this tune in the sermon, what would I think?* I want to be sensitive to the tunes of preaching, to operate from the ear to the mouth.

Isaiah writes, "The Sovereign Lord has given me an instructed tongue, to know the word that sustains the weary. He wakens me morning by morning, wakens my ear to listen like one being taught" (Isa. 50:4). Preaching, like music, begins with the ear. If I get the tune right, people will not only understand my words but sing along.

Chapter 108

TEACHING THE WHOLE BIBLE

Six reasons to do expository preaching

D. A. Carson

Puritan theologian William Perkins wrote that preaching "has four great principles: to read the text distinctly, from canonical Scripture; to give it sense and understanding according to the Scripture itself; to collect a few profitable points of doctrine out of its natural sense; and to apply, if you have the gift, the doctrines to the life and manner of men in a simple and plain speech."

There is something refreshingly simple about this statement. Our aim as preachers is not to be the most erudite scholar of the age. Our aim is not to titillate and amuse. Our aim is not to build a big church. Rather, our aim is to take the sacred text, explain what it means, tie it to other Scriptures so people can see the whole a little better, and apply it to life so it bites and heals, instructs and edifies. What better way to accomplish this end than through expository preaching?

Some use the category *expository preaching* for all preaching that is faithful to Scripture. I distinguish expository preaching from topical preaching, textual preaching, and others, for the expository sermon must be controlled by a Scripture text or texts. Expository preaching emerges directly and demonstrably from a passage or passages of Scripture.

There are a number of reasons why expository preaching deserves to be our primary method of proclamation.

1. It is the method least likely to stray from Scripture. If you are preaching on what the Bible says about self-esteem, for example, undoubtedly you can find some useful insights. But even when you say entirely true things, you will likely abstract them from the Bible's central story line. Expository preaching keeps you to the main thing.

2. It teaches people how to read their Bibles. Especially if you're preaching a long passage, expository preaching teaches people how to think through a passage, how to understand and apply God's Word to their lives.

3. It gives confidence to the preacher and authorizes the sermon. If you are faithful to the text, you are certain your message is God's message. Regardless of what is going on in the church—whether it is growing or whether people like you—you know you are proclaiming God's truth. That is wonderfully freeing.

4. It meets the need for relevance without letting the clamor for relevance dictate the message. All true preaching is properly applied. That is of extraordinary importance in our generation. But expository preaching keeps the eternal central to the discussion.

5. It forces the preacher to handle the tough questions. You start working through text after text, and soon you hit passages on divorce, on homosexuality, and on women in ministry, and you will have to deal with the text.

6. It enables the preacher to expound systematically the whole counsel of God. In the

404

last fifteen years of his life, John Calvin expounded Genesis, Deuteronomy, Judges, Job, some of Psalms, 1 and 2 Samuel, 1 Kings, the Major and Minor Prophets, the Gospels in a harmony, Acts, 1 and 2 Corinthians, Galatians, Ephesians, 1 and 2 Thessalonians, and the Pastoral Epistles.

I'm not suggesting we organize ourselves exactly the same way. But if we are to preach the whole counsel of God, we must teach the whole Bible. Other sermonic structures have their merits, but none offers our congregations more, week after week, than careful, faithful exposition of the Word of God.

Chapter 109

DRAMATIC EXPOSITORY PREACHING
Sermons that are both stirring and faithful to the text

Haddon Robinson

There are folks who think of expository preaching as a dull plodding through the text that gives out information nobody wants and answers questions nobody's asking. There's nothing dramatic about it because there's no tension. If that's what people mean by expository preaching, I can understand why they walk away from it.

But that's a wrong definition. Expository preaching is more of a philosophy than a method. It's the answer to the question: Do you bend your thought to the text, or do you bend the text to your thought?

Preaching that takes the text seriously can be dramatic. The Bible is filled with drama. Paul didn't sit down one day and say, "Well, I haven't written to the folks at Galatia in a while. Let's see. What will I write about? Oh, I'll write about legalism. I haven't covered that topic." No, he was upset when he wrote. He saw them giving up the gospel. That's why he begins without any introduction and just says, "Even if we or an angel from heaven should preach a gospel other than the one we preached to you, let him be eternally condemned" (Gal. 1:8). That's dramatic. He's concerned about what's happening to those people. If you can pick up the spirit of Paul, it will not be a pedantic plodding through the text, sentence after sentence as though there were no great issues at stake.

True, if you preach nonexpository sermons, it may seem easier to preach dramatically because you don't have to bother with the text. You can take your own stories and fashion them and handle the text any way you want that has dramatic flare. The problem with that is if we take seriously our calling as preachers, we haven't been called to entertain people, we haven't been called to tickle their ears or to get them to say, "Wasn't that a magnificent sermon! Wasn't that dramatic!" We are called to proclaim the Word of God.

Thus, while there may be an easier route to being more dramatic—that is, ignoring the text—ultimately, it causes us to be unfaithful to God. If it's not expository and not solidly biblical, I don't care how wonderful the sermon is, I don't care how people line up at the door to tell you it's a great message, and I don't care how many people break down in tears as they listen—if it's not faithful to the Scriptures, forget about it. You're not called to be an actor; you're called to be a preacher.

Historically some have approached expository preaching in a way that can cause it to be more cerebral and less moving. The more cerebral sermon says the main object of preaching is to inform people. But the main object of preaching is to change people's lives through the use of the Scriptures.

If I think of the sermon as an information dump, it moves me away from being dramatic, and it moves me away from the mood of the text. A good expository sermon is true to the text, its basic idea, its general development, its tensions—and also its mood. If you capture the mood of that text, that can be moving.

Expository preaching requires that we take time with the text, but how much time can we spend talking about the words of the text and still keep the dramatic level high? It strikes me that most sermons don't spend that much time in the text. I have not heard many sermons in which I thought this passage of Scripture is opening up in front of me. But it is possible to spend too much time in the text, if you spend all your time on content and don't think about the audience.

There are two basic parts of preparation. The first part is to ask what the text is saying, what the purpose of the author is, and what the biblical writer was saying to the biblical readers. The second part of preparation is to discover what this text says to people today. How can I get this text across to people in the twenty-first century in a way that grips them?

When I do that, I will move towards drama because all drama consists of conflict. A TV movie starts off, somebody is shot, and they can't explain the murder. The police are called in, and they try to unravel the crime. They work all the way through the evidence until at the end, they discover the murderer was the maid and not the butler.

Sermons can be that way. They start off by raising an issue important to the audience. I am not teaching people the Bible; I'm talking to people about themselves from the Bible. And so I want to talk about issues they have that are reflected by the issues in the biblical text. If we can put sermons together with a sense of conflict, with problems that need to be solved, questions that need to be answered, needs that must be satisfied from the Scriptures, then we will have a dramatic sermon.

Chapter 110

VERSE-BY-VERSE SERMONS THAT REALLY PREACH

While God is certainly in the details, he is uniquely and stirringly at work in the organic flow of ideas.

Steven D. Mathewson

Verse-by-verse preaching possesses a long, storied tradition. It finds biblical precedent in Ezra's reading of the book of the Law, after which the Levites gave the sense so that the people could understand (Neh. 8:8). It traces its origin to the commentators at Qumran, who cited a few words of the biblical text and then commented on their significance. Origen (185–254) incorporated the running commentary approach in his sermons, as did John Chrysostom (about 347–407) and Augustine (354–430). Both Martin Luther (1483–1546) and John Calvin (1509–1564) preached verse-by-verse sermons. In more recent times, preachers like Harry A. Ironside and Martyn Lloyd-Jones have employed this approach.

Basically verse-by-verse preaching is the proclamation of a Scripture passage by unpacking one verse after another. The sermon moves through the text much like a Bible commentary does—proceeding phrase by phrase and analyzing select words. Some homileticians refer to verse-by-verse preaching as *continuous exposition* or *the running commentary method*.

An analysis of more recent masters of the verse-by-verse approach reveals a variety of styles. Harry A. Ironside showed more interest in providing application and illustration than in giving exegetical details. J. Vernon McGee's sermons typified the running commentary method and offered a blend of exegetical insights and application to life situations. John MacArthur Jr., who considers himself a verse-by-verse expositor, preaches sermons that concentrate more on providing exegetical and doctrinal insights than application ideas. Even though MacArthur's sermons proceed verse by verse, they cover one unit of thought. Thus his verse-by-verse sermons reflect a sense of unity and order lacking in sermons that settle for a running commentary style. MacArthur also frequently examines cross-references to illumine the verse he is explaining. Martyn Lloyd-Jones showed as much inclination as any verse-by-verse preacher to probe the depth of the words and theological ideas resident in a particular verse. As a result, he often moved slowly through biblical passages.

The preachers just cited represent the more conservative wing of evangelicalism. But two recent mainline preachers, Ronald J. Allen and Gilbert Bartholomew, advocate the use of this method in their book, *Preaching Verse by Verse* (Westminster John Knox Press, 1999). In their model, the sermon unfolds like a commentary on the Bible and interprets the passage unit by unit.

THE RELATIONSHIP TO EXPOSITORY PREACHING

One of the key issues involved in understanding verse-by-verse preaching is its relationship to expository preaching. Some homileticians equate verse-by-verse preaching with expository preaching. However, it is best to view verse-by-verse preaching as one of the methods of expository preaching.

What, then, is expository preaching? Premier homileticians like Haddon Robinson and Bryan Chappell use different wording to craft their definitions, but they agree on those elements that make a sermon expository. Basically, an expository sermon exposes the meaning of a particular Scripture passage and applies the meaning to the listeners' lives.

Two elements are critical. First, both Robinson and Chappell stress the need for an expository sermon to work through the biblical text. Robinson's definition stresses the need to communicate a biblical concept that is "derived from and *transmitted through* a historical, grammatical, and literary study of a passage in its context" (italics added for emphasis). Chappell's definition proposes that the expository sermon will "cover the scope of the passage."

The question is, does the need to work through the biblical text require a verse-by-verse approach? The answer is, in some cases yes, and in some cases no. For example, an expository sermon on Ephesians 2:1–10 or Psalm 100 can proceed verse-by-verse and still cover the entire unit of thought. However, an expository sermon on Genesis 38 or Revelation 17–18 will require the preacher to proceed paragraph-by-paragraph. It is impossible even in thirty to fifty minutes to expound on every word, phrase, or even sentence in either of these texts. So then, a sermon may be expository without preaching verse-by-verse. This is why many homileticians see verse-by-verse preaching as a subdivision of expository preaching.

This distinction raises an important question.

Why not preach three sermons on Genesis 38 or four sermons on Revelation 17–18 to enable the expositor to proceed verse-by-verse? The answer is that a sermon must be based on a unit of thought. A preacher who opts to prepare a sermon on Genesis 38:1–11 is not working with a complete unit of thought. In narrative, a complete unit of thought requires a complete story or an episode (a story within a story). The story begun in Genesis 38:1 is not completed until Genesis 38:30.

Likewise, while Revelation 17–18 could be preached legitimately in more than one sermon, the two chapters together definitely constitute a unit of thought as they describe the fall of Babylon, the city of man. If the expositor chooses to preach the entire unit, then it will be difficult, if not impossible, to proceed through the two chapters verse by verse. The point is that a commitment to preach through complete units of thought may sometimes lead expositors to preach large blocks of text that will require some summarizing—a paragraph-by-paragraph development rather than a verse-by-verse development.

A second element that is critical to an expository sermon is the application of the author's intended meaning. Both Robinson and Chappell stress that if a verse-by-verse sermon fails to apply the text to the listeners' lives, then the sermon, by definition, fails as a truly expository sermon. Therefore, not all verse-by-verse preaching is true expository preaching.

STRENGTHS AND WEAKNESSES

At this point, we can begin to see the strengths and weaknesses of verse-by-verse preaching. Three unique *strengths* of verse-by-verse sermons deserve mention.

(1) Verse-by-verse sermons dig deeply into the text. They provide an in-depth analysis that feeds people who are hungry to know what the Scripture says. They counteract the tendency in twenty-first-century America towards biblical illiteracy.

(2) Verse-by-verse sermons lead the preacher to follow the contours of the text rather than an artificial outline. That is not to say verse-by-verse preachers use no outline. Nor is it to say all verse-by-verse preachers avoid the trap of pressing their material into an artificial outline. But the very exercise of working through the words and phrases of one verse and then moving on to the next will shape the sermon according to the shape of the passage.

(3) A third strength is the tendency of the verse-by-verse sermon to reveal the author's intent rather than to impose an idea on the text. This strength flows from the first two. Walking over the same set of tracks left by the biblical writer is more likely to lead the preacher to the biblical writer's destination.

Preachers who use a verse-by-verse format should also be aware of four potential *weaknesses*. These weaknesses may not be inherent in the form itself. But a careful evaluation of verse-by-verse sermons preached over the last several decades shows that the form can be misused.

(1) The verse-by-verse approach does not serve all literary genres of Scripture equally well. Many narratives and certain psalms take a large amount of text to form a complete unit of thought. Preachers who insist on going verse-by-verse through the David-Uriah-Bathsheba story in 2 Samuel 11–12 will be forced to end their sermon (or sermons!) before the full idea of the story emerges.

(2) The verse-by-verse approach sometimes results in sermons that lack unity. Such sermons discuss the details of the text but fail to paint the big picture. That is, they analyze but do not synthesize. Helping people think biblically means helping them trace the flow of the author's thought. A verse-by-verse approach does not automatically produce Bible readers who can follow the development of an argument in a text. Verse-by-verse preaching can obscure the development of the argument when preachers lose their listeners in a pile of details or when they feel free to stop whenever their allotted time is finished. Then, they begin next week's sermon where they stopped. But as homiletician Richard Mayhue argues, expository preaching "is not a commentary running from word to word and verse to verse without unity, outline, and pervasive drive."

(3) A third weakness of verse-by-verse preaching is its tendency to overload the sermon with raw data and short-change application. Of course, listeners want and need exegetical information—lexical, grammatical, historical, and cultural insights. But expository preaching involves more than backing up the exegetical dump truck and unloading it on a congregation! If expository preaching, by definition, attempts to apply the text to the lives of the hearers, then verse-by-verse sermons must invest time not only in probing the details of the text but in probing its implications for Christian living in modern culture.

(4) Verse-by-verse preaching sometimes slows the preacher's pace so much that a congregation does not get to hear the whole counsel of God over a period of time. A strict verse-by-verse approach may require three years of sermons to preach through Romans. Might it be better to devote one year to Romans, and the other two years to a few other books of Scripture?

SUGGESTIONS FOR EFFECTIVENESS

In light of the strengths and weaknesses of verse-by-verse preaching, here are four suggestions for using this approach effectively.

(1) Keep the big picture in mind. Remember, you are preaching a unit of thought, not just individual verses. So think paragraphs! Or, think preaching units. Verse-by-verse preaching is a strategy to serve a larger goal—the exposition of a thought unit in Scripture. Even though you move verse-by-verse, highlight the overall idea that the individual verses work together to express. Make a commitment to work through a block of text, not just to stop wherever you run out of time.

(2) Highlight the contours of the text. Don't settle for a bucket of exegetical nuggets as you move from word to word and phrase to phrase. Point out the connections between phrases and between verses. When preaching a verse-by-verse sermon on Isaiah 9:1–7, show your listeners that the term "for" at the beginning of verses 4, 5, and 6 (cf. NASB) tells us how God will accomplish the promises he has made in Isaiah 9:1–3. Or, when expounding Matthew 5:38–42, inform your listeners that verse 38 contains what people were hearing, that verse 39a contains Jesus' standard, and that verses 39b–42 offer four illustrations from Jesus' culture of the standard he has just set.

(3) Determine which details to cover in-depth and which to summarize. Even when handling three to five verses, a preacher cannot provide a systematic theology on every word. You must think about your audience to know what needs to be explained, what needs to be validated, and what needs to be applied. Your listeners only need explanations of words they do not understand. They need an apologetic only if they tend to doubt a particular statement or concept. They need application ideas when they are unsure of how to flesh out a principle in their everyday lives.

(4) Use verse-by-verse preaching in concert with paragraph-by-paragraph preaching. When preaching through a particular book of the Bible, vary your pace. Some sermons will tackle larger units and will need to move paragraph by paragraph. Other sermons will handle smaller units and can move verse-by-verse. Still other sermons can use a combination of both approaches.

For example, if you have worked slowly through Romans 1–2, then perhaps preach a single sermon on Romans 3:1–20. Part of the sermon may proceed verse-by-verse, and part of it may summarize particular groups of verses. Then, slow down and work verse-by-verse through Romans 3:21–26. Strike the balance between giving people breadth and depth. Preaching through "too few" verses too often will result in listeners who cannot think through the argument of a passage. Preaching through "too many" verses too often will result in listeners who cannot grasp the depths of what the Bible teaches.

AN EXAMPLE FROM PSALM 100

What follows is an attempt to track the development of a possible verse-by-verse sermon from Psalm 100. Notice what happens at the level of ideas. While the sermon proceeds phrase by phrase and verse by verse, it also maintains a sense of unity. The introduction will raise the question, "What is corporate worship supposed to be?" To frame it another way, "How should people behave when they gather to worship?" This question derives from a careful exegetical study of the text. That is, the question reflects the text's subject.

Verse 1 says: "Shout for joy to the LORD, all the earth." The sermon unpacks this verse by discussing the command "shout for joy," the person to whom this shout is directed (Yahweh, as indicated by the rendering "LORD" in small capital letters), and then the anticipated participants who will fulfill this command ("all the earth").

At this point, a transition to verse 2 will note that Hebrew poetry resembles stereo sound. So the two lines in verse 2 add texture to what verse 1 says by restating the same concept in different words. The first line in verse 2 reads: "Worship the LORD with gladness." The sermon will discuss the term *worship,* a common Hebrew verb for *serve,* as well as the term *gladness.* The expositor will also point out that Yahweh is still the focus of this response.

Then, the second line of verse 2 reads: "Come before him with joyful songs." The preacher can note that *come* is a general term for approaching a person or place and that this approach is (1) directed to Yahweh as indicated by the pronoun *him* and (2) accompanied with "joyful songs."

Here the preacher will do well to stop and summarize what the three lines say in stereo or surround sound: Worship is supposed to be an enthusiastic expression of honor to God. To frame it another way, verses 1–2 tell us *what* to do (attribute worth), *to whom* we do it (Yahweh), and *how* we do it (with enthusiasm). Theoretically, the preacher could front-load the discussion of verses 1–2 with this summary. However, to retain the poetic flavor of the text, it seems advisable to let the text build to this conclusion. The point is, the verse-by-verse movement in the sermon shows an overriding concern for seeing the unity of the text.

At this place in the sermon, a verse-by-verse preacher committed to the unity of the passage will want to do more than say, "Now, let's look at verse 3" as a strict running-commentary sermon would do. Rather, the expositor will tell the listeners that this psalm follows a pattern in which the psalmist follows up a call to praise with a cause to praise. So the shift is from what to do in verses 1–2 to why we should do it in verse 3.

Verse 3 tells us who God is and who we are. It begins by declaring: "Know that the LORD is God. It is he who made us." A pastor who does careful exegetical work will notice that the Hebrew text makes two assertions about Yahweh, both starting with the pronoun *he.* First, he is God. Second, he made us. The remainder of the verse makes three assertions about us: (1) "and we are his"; (2) "we are his people," (3) "the sheep of his pasture." The sermon will touch briefly on each assertion, taking time to develop the sheep/shepherd image utilized in the last phrase. Thus, the three assertions are really the same assertion stated poetically with each one building on the one before it. At this point, the preacher can summarize the flow of ideas so far. The reason for giving an enthusiastic expression of honor to God is based on our relationship with God. He is the One who created us. We belong to him.

Moving into verse 4 requires another transition. The preacher will have to refer again to the pattern that this type of praise psalm follows. The psalmist is about to offer a renewed call to praise. This renewed call in verse 4 fills out our answer to the question, "What is corporate worship supposed to be?" It begins with the command: "Enter his gates with thanksgiving and enter his courts with praise." The expositor will note that a new element has been added in this renewed call to praise. Two terms—*gates* and *courts*—point out that a place of worship is involved. So, corporate worship is in view in this psalm. This is the exegetical support, by the way, for the question raised at the beginning of the sermon.

As the sermon continues, the preacher will spend time defining *thanksgiving* and *praise*. These terms show that this worship has some substance. It is more than raw emotion. Thanksgiving is public acknowledgment of what God has done. Praise is excited boasting over who God is and what God has done. Then verse 4 concludes with a command: "Give thanks to him and praise his name." The expositor will point out that the repetition provides emphasis.

The preacher must negotiate one more transition to negotiate move into the final verse of the psalm. The psalmist is now offering a renewed cause for praise. Some additional facets of the answer to the question "why offer this kind of worship" will emerge. The first line of verse 5 declares: "For the LORD is good and

his love endures forever." The sermon will observe that the term *for* signals the movement from what to do to why it should be done. The sermon will develop the two attributes of God in the first line of verse 5 that motivate the kind of worship described in this psalm: God's goodness and his enduring love. The last line of verse 5 adds a third attribute: God's faithfulness—"his faithfulness continues through all generations." An astute expositor will see a reflection of Exodus 34:5–7, where each of these three qualities is prominent.

At the end of the sermon, the preacher can drive home the main idea that has emerged: Worship should be nothing less than an enthusiastic response to God because God is so great! Note that the idea of greatness is an abstraction, that is, a way of summarizing the attributes of God expressed in this psalm—he is creator, shepherd, good, loving, and faithful.

The above example shows how a preacher can and must move from words and phrases to ideas that have an organic relationship.

Chapter 111

WHAT MAKES TEXTUAL PREACHING UNIQUE?

And how do we use this sermon form, with its great rhetorical potential, biblically?

Steven D. Mathewson

Textual preaching dominated the homiletical landscape in the latter half of the 1800s and the first half of the 1900s and remains popular in some circles today. The list of preachers who have employed textual preaching effectively, though not exclusively, includes Charles

Haddon Spurgeon, Frederick W. Robertson, and Rick Warren.

At the dawn of the twenty-first century, when topical preaching and expository preaching get most of the press in America, what is the role of textual preaching? That question can be answered only after defining what textual preaching is.

A Definition of Textual Preaching

The question about what constitutes textual preaching resembles the question about who killed John F. Kennedy. Even the experts disagree. Some homileticians distinguish it from expository preaching, while some view it as a type of expository preaching or even equate it with expository preaching. Others argue that the length of the passage to be preached determines whether the sermon is textual or not. Others disagree and claim that the relation of the divisions of the sermon to the divisions of the text is what classifies a sermon as textual or places it in another category.

So what is textual preaching? A good place to begin a quest for definition is the classic homiletics text by John Broadus, *On the Preparation and Delivery of Sermons* (first published in 1870). Broadus, premier Southern Baptist preacher and seminary president, classified sermons in three forms: (1) subject-sermons (what most contemporary homileticians describe as topical), (2) text-sermons (what this article refers to as textual), and (3) expository sermons.

According to Broadus, a subject—or topical—sermon is structured according to the nature of the subject rather than the biblical text(s) on which it is based. He notes that the Bible does "not present truth in a succession of logical propositions," so when the preacher needs to present a doctrine or moral issue, the topical form works well. While the sermon must of course be faithful to Scripture, its structure does not take its cue from the biblical text(s) on which it is based.

In both textual and expository sermons, the sermon's structure takes its cue from the biblical text. The preacher draws the "topic and the heads"—that is, the subject and its divisions—from the passage. What, then, is the difference between a textual sermon and an expository sermon? Broadus sees a gradation from textual to expository sermons. The difference lies not so much in the length of the sermon text as in its details. He explains: "If we simply take the topic and the heads which the passage affords and proceed to discuss them in our own way, that is not an expository sermon but a text-sermon."

Broadus distinguished between two types of textual sermons: those that present a single subject and those that discuss several subjects. In a single-subject textual sermon, the details relate to one definite and comprehensive subject. However, in a textual sermon with several topics, the points or topics of the sermon are much more diverse, although Broadus argues that they should have some kind of "internal connection."

While the length of a passage to be preached does not define the form of the sermon, it appears that textual sermons are generally based on shorter passages. Broadus observes that an expository sermon may be devoted to a long passage, a short one, or even part of a sentence. Likewise, in theory, a textual sermon could be based on a long passage. The bottom line is how the details develop. An expository sermon will explain and concentrate on the details of a given biblical text. A textual sermon will take its leading ideas from the text but then look elsewhere in Scripture for much of its development. In a sense, then, a textual sermon is a hybrid of a topical and an expository sermon. As Broadus's two categories for textual sermons suggest, a textual sermon may lean more in one direction than another.

Here are some examples cited by Broadus. In the following sermon on Luke 23:43, the preacher will take the successive words or clauses of the text and enlarge on them.

I. Thou shalt be in paradise
II. Thou shalt be with me in paradise
III. Today thou shalt be with me in paradise

The following sermon on Romans 5:1–2 describes the believer's happy estate:

I. He may have peace with God
II. He may stand in the grace of God
III. He may exult in hope of the glory of God

Still another sermon from Ezekiel 11:19–20 attempts to explain the particulars of genuine religions. Notice that these points are not characteristics as in the sermon on Romans 5:1–2. Rather, they are labels or categories for analyzing what the text says about genuine religion.

I. Its author
II. The disposition it produces
III. The obedience it demands
IV. The blessedness it assures

How have other homileticians understood textual preaching? In 1881, Austin Phelps defined a textual sermon as "one in which the text is the theme, and the parts of the text are the divisions of the discourse, and are used as a line of suggestion." His last phrase—"used as a line of suggestion"—aligns his understanding of a textual sermon with John Broadus. In 1955, Merrill Unger suggested that the only difference between a textual sermon and an expository sermon is found in the length of the text. A textual sermon expounds a passage of shorter length. H. Grady Davis mentions textual preaching only twice in his 1958 classic

work, *Design for Preaching*. In the first discussion, he seems to link textual preaching and expository preaching. In the second discussion, he cites a sermon by Karl Barth on Matthew 11:28 as an example of a textual sermon, which he defines as one that "draws not only its idea but also its structural elements from the text."

In 1990, Sidney Greidanus proposed that all textual preaching be understood as expository preaching since "textual preaching is preaching on a biblical text and expounds the message of that text." Al Fasol contributed a fine essay in 1992 on textual preaching in which he seemed to concur with Greidanus in arguing that a textual sermon is not defined by the length of its text but rather by its practice of drawing both its topic and divisions from the biblical text. In 1994, Bryan Chappell published *Christ-Centered Preaching: Redeeming the Expository Sermon*, now a standard textbook in many evangelical seminaries. His taxonomy of sermon forms, which resembles the understanding of John Broadus, is helpful for grasping the uniqueness of textual preaching. Here is a summary of his distinctions:

- A *topical sermon* takes its topic from the passage and gets its organization from the nature of the subject rather than from the text's distinctions.
- A *textual sermon* takes its topic and main points from ideas in the text, but the development of those main ideas comes from sources outside the immediate text.
- An *expository sermon* takes its topic, main points, and subpoints from the immediate text.

The following definition attempts to describe the textual sermon as it has been defined and practiced over the past 150 years. *A textual sermon derives its topic and main ideas from a biblical text—usually a verse or two—and then develops these ideas theologically from other biblical texts.*

It seems helpful, then, to maintain Broadus's distinction between and gradation from topical to textual to expository sermons. At the very least, a textual sermon should be viewed as a specific type of expository sermon, if not a category by itself.

THE VALUE OF TEXTUAL PREACHING TODAY

What is the use to biblical preachers of textual sermons in the twenty-first century? While people need expository preaching to help them think through and track the arguments developed in Scripture, textual preaching can supplement exposition to meet two specific needs.

(1) Textual preaching provides an effective vehicle for preaching on some of the Bible's grand statements. Even in a course of expository sermons on a particular book, these grand statements are worth examining under a microscope. They may be "mountaintop" texts like Jeremiah 33:3; Romans 8:28; or 1 John 1:9, which believers memorize and turn to in times of need. Or they may be texts that summarize some of the Bible's grand themes. Some texts which fall into this category include individual proverbs (such as Prov. 15:1); Ezra 7:10; Mark 12:30; Romans 12:1–2; and Hebrews 12:1–2.

For example, the three infinitives in Ezra 7:10 ("to study . . . to practice . . . and to teach," NASB) can form the heart of a sermon on the task of a Bible teacher or preacher. The idea of the sermon will be that effective teachers of Scripture will commit themselves to studying the Bible, obeying the Bible, and then teaching the Bible to others. The preacher will develop these points theologically by appealing to other

Scripture and will describe what this process looks like for Christians living in the twenty-first-century.

For another example, an adaptation of a Rick Warren sermon on Mark 12:30 takes the first half of the "Great Commandment" and explains how God wants his people to love him. The sermon outline would look like this:

   I. God wants you to love him thoughtfully (with your mind)
  II. God wants you to love him passionately (with your heart and soul)
 III. God wants you to love him practically (with your strength)

One reason the textual form is well suited for the Bible's grand statements is that it lends itself to more dramatic, rhetorical, and artistic development. Since preachers can turn elsewhere in Scripture for the subpoints of the sermon, they can arrange these subpoints in ways that deliberately employ artistic features like contrast, climax, storytelling, parallelism, refrain, and metaphor.

(2) Textual preaching provides an effective vehicle for evangelistic preaching—that is, preaching to unbelievers. It allows a preacher to combine the benefits of exposition and topical preaching. As in an expository sermon, it leaves the listeners with a passage that will serve as a reference point. Because the passage in a textual sermon is usually one or two verses long, this reference point is something that listeners can grasp and remember. At the same time, as in a topical sermon, the preacher is free to cover key ideas that reside in different passages and genres of Scripture.

Passages that lend themselves to textual sermons for unbelievers include John 3:16; John 14:6; Romans 4:5; Galatians 4:4–5; and

Ephesians 2:8–9. For example, Larry Moyer preaches an evangelistic sermon on Romans 4:5 in which the main idea is: "You will stand perfect before God if you trust Jesus Christ and not your works." The sermon could proceed either as an expository sermon or a textual sermon, depending on whether the details emerge from the immediate text or from the whole sweep of Scripture. Here is a possible outline adapted from Moyer's sermon:

I. God is not asking how many good works you have done ("to the man who does not work")

II. God is not asking how well you have behaved ("but trusts God who justifies the wicked")

III. God is asking whom you are going to trust ("his faith is credited as righteousness")

The following guidelines will help preachers prepare and preach textual sermons effectively.

(1) Pay attention to the context. Context determines meaning. Preachers who select a small preaching unit like a verse or two run the risk of isolating a statement from its context and thus missing the author's intent. For example, Revelation 3:20 has been a favorite text for evangelistic sermons. But when viewed in its context, the statement is made to Christians about restoring their relationship with Christ—not to unbelievers about entering a new relationship with Christ. Legitimate textual preaching makes the effort to locate the selected verse(s) in the larger flow of material.

(2) Use the textual sermon form strategically and sparingly. People pick up a methodology for studying the Bible from the sermons they hear. A steady diet of textual sermons will teach people to look for "hot" statements instead of tracing the flow of thought through a paragraph, a chapter, and an entire book. Further-more, listeners will never get the opportunity to work through major blocks and books of Scripture. In general, reserve textual sermons for the defining statements of Scripture or for times when you need to address a huge issue and a single verse or two captures the heart of what you need to communicate.

(3) Include synthesis as well as analysis. Some homileticians complain that textual sermons take things apart but never put them back together again. Like any other type of sermon, a good textual sermon must have unity. A preacher must show how the pieces relate to the whole. For this reason, writing outline points in complete sentences is a helpful discipline. This practice will help preachers think through their ideas clearly as they attempt to synthesize them.

(4) Avoid trite, cleverly packaged outlines. Recent homiletical thought suggests that outlines resemble skeletons. They are vital for providing structure, but they do not need to be seen. Textual preaching in the past—like expository preaching in the past—sometimes focused too much on cleverly worded outlines, especially ones developed with alliteration. But in the twenty-first century, verbal communication shies away from this approach.

AN EXAMPLE FROM HEBREWS 12:1–2

Here is a more detailed example of a textual sermon outline that derives its main ideas from the text but takes its subpoints from other Scripture. The text is Hebrews 12:1–2:

Therefore, since we are surrounded by such a great cloud of witnesses, let us throw off everything that hinders and the sin that so easily entangles, and let us run with perseverance the race marked out for us. Let us fix our eyes on Jesus, the author and perfecter of our faith, who for the joy set before him endured the cross, scorning its shame, and sat down at the right hand of the throne of God.

I. God calls us to run the race in which he has entered us with endurance
   A. The race in which God has entered us is the Christian life here on earth
      1. One church leader, Paul, likened his own Christian life and service to a race (Acts 20:24; Gal. 2:2; 2 Tim. 4:7)
      2. Paul also likened the lives of other Christians to a race (Gal. 5:7)
   B. The race metaphor helps us understand why Christians need endurance
      1. Like a race, the Christian life requires stamina over a long period
      2. Like a race, the Christian life contains difficult challenges
      3. Like a race, the Christian life has a prize at stake (1 Cor. 9:24)
II. We can run with endurance when we adopt Jesus' strategy of focusing on future joy!
   A. Jesus serves as our model for how to run the race and win
      1. Qualification #1—He is the pioneer who finished the course
      2. Qualification #2—He finished the course as a winner
   B. What we learn from Jesus is to endure misery by focusing on future joy!

1. Future joy includes a life of beauty (Rev. 21:2, 4, 18; 22:1)
2. Future joy includes a life of intimacy (Rev. 21:3, 7, 16)
3. Future joy includes a life of adventure (Rev. 22:3, 5)

Notice how this sermon unfolds. First, the second main point is the main idea of the sermon. Of course, a skilled preacher will want to work on another way or two of restating this. A catchy way of restating it would be: Like Jesus, you can endure your present misery when you focus on future joy!

Notice that the sermon follows the text in first explaining what God is asking you to do (verse 1) and then explaining how God says you can do it (verse 2). Yet the subpoints come either from other Scripture or, in the case of subpoint I. B., from the race metaphor. Here, preachers can use their imaginations—as controlled by Scripture!—to probe the metaphor as a means of understanding the text. Notice that subpoint II. B. is derived entirely from the description of heaven in Revelation 21–22.

When employed thoughtfully and strategically, textual sermons can take listeners through specific texts of Scripture and still cover the grand sweep of biblical theology.

Chapter 112

CAN TOPICAL PREACHING ALSO BE EXPOSITORY?

If handled rightly, the two forms can complement one another

Timothy S. Warren

If I were a golfer, I would use every club available to get the ball in the hole. I'd use my driver, irons, putter, and any other club I could master. I can't imagine limiting myself to a three iron. Unfortunately many preachers unnecessarily limit themselves by using one style of expository preaching exclusively.

This is an appeal for topical expository preaching. I'm not suggesting that every sermon be topical, only that some topical preaching supplement textual and verse-by-verse exposition. I realize some homileticians speak against topical preaching. The problem with topical preaching, however, is not that it's topical. The problem is when it isn't expositional.

WHY TOPICAL?

I can think of at least three reasons for preaching topically. While none carries biblical sanction, each adds substance to my appeal.

(1) People like topical preaching. The relevance engages them. Most listeners like to hear about things that immediately concern them.

(2) Sometimes issues arise that demand a biblical response. Waiting for that subject to surface in a verse-by-verse exposition through the Bible could take years. Whether it's a preliminary to church discipline or a response to a killer tornado, topical preaching addresses the issue at hand.

(3) Topical preaching is modeled in the Scrip- *tures.* I don't recall any preachers other than Ezra in Nehemiah 8 or Jesus in Luke 4 who started with a text. The individual books of the Bible and the sermons in them address topical issues rather than expound texts. Granted, texts were often expounded along the way, but a text was not usually the starting point. And, like Peter's topical sermon in Acts 2 or Paul's in Acts 13, multiple texts on the major topic were woven into a single exposition.

WHAT IS TOPICAL EXPOSITION?

While I am committed to the use of a topical style some of the time, I am committed to expository preaching all of the time. By expository preaching I mean the communication of a biblical proposition discovered from a Spirit-directed exegetical/theological interpretation of a biblical text (or texts) and applied by the Holy Spirit through a preacher to a specific audience.

Although definitions vary, this gives us a starting point. Two elements of this definition are especially crucial to any discussion of expository preaching. Preaching must be centered in a biblical text that is authoritative, and they must focus on relevance for particular listeners. I want to be both text-centered and audience-focused. Following this definition of expository preaching, topical preaching does not represent a different method from expositional. Topical is simply a subset, one among several styles, of expository preaching.

Even when what a preacher says about a topic is true and perhaps biblical in that it appeals to some great theme of the Bible, if there are no means of confirming the message from a text or texts of Scripture, the message is not expositional. That common lack of connection to textual authority is why some expositors reject all topical preaching. They allege there is only one style of preaching that is expository: verse by verse. Within the perimeters of my definition, however, there are at least three styles of expository preaching.

(1) Textual expository preaching finds its message in a single verse or sentence. For example, Proverbs 28:13 could generate the following sermon:

I. Hiding sin results in failure (13a)
II. Confessing sin results in forgiveness (13b)
III. Therefore confess your sin

(2) Verse-by-verse (for lack of a better title, but also called paragraph or through-a-book) expository preaching finds its message in two or more verses in a literary unit. Whereas the textual preacher finds the sermon's message in a sentence, usually taken arbitrarily, the verse-by-verse preacher works from a literary unit, like a paragraph or pericope, while moving consecutively through a whole book of the Bible. Ephesians 1:3–14 could generate this sermon:

I. Praise the Father who chose you (1:3–6)
II. Praise the Son who redeemed you (1:7–12)
III. Praise the Spirit who sealed you (1:13–14)

(3) Topical expository preaching finds its message in two or more different texts or units in their individual contexts that share a common subject. For example, several biblical texts address the topic of dealing with sinning believers. While each passage addresses the same general topic, they all contribute different, but compatible, complements that fill out the biblical teaching on the subject.

A topical expository sermon could emerge as follows:

I. Restore a sinning brother or sister (James 5:19–20)
II. Restore a sinning brother or sister gently and humbly (Gal. 6:1)
III. Follow the Christian steps to restoration (Matt. 18:15–17)
   A. If he sins, confront him privately
   B. If he doesn't listen, confront him with one or two others
   C. If he refuses to listen, confront him before the church
   D. If he refuses to listen, treat him as an outsider
   E. When he listens, restore him

THE EXPOSITORY METHOD

Topical expository preaching is the same kind of preaching as all text-centered, audience-focused expository preaching. The difference is that topical exposition deals with more than one text or literary unit in their different contexts. All styles of expository preaching, whether starting with a text and moving to a relevant topic/application or starting with a relevant topic and moving back through several texts to application, follow the same method.

Once you grasp the expositional process, you will see how topical preaching can be expository. John Stott's *Between Two Worlds* employed the metaphor of "bridging the gap" between the world of the ancient text and the world of the contemporary audience. This bridging process makes possible the connection between text-centered authority and audience-focused relevance.

Over time I've tried to fill in more details of the expositional process. Whether by intuition or intent, whether in brief, broad strokes or in comprehensive, specific steps, all expository preaching proceeds in four movements.

(1) The first movement progresses from a text to an exegetical interpretation. An exegetical interpretation seeks to understand and state the meaning of the text from the perspective of the original author, audience, and situation. I work through the exegetical process using a historical/contextual, grammatical/syntactical, normal/literal, literary/rhetorical hermeneutic. I state the original meaning of the passage according to its own outline/structure, culminating in a proposition or big idea statement. For example, "The purpose for which Paul commanded the Corinthian believers not to eat meat offered to idols was so that they would not cause their weaker brother in Christ to eat against his conscience" (see 1 Cor. 10:28).

(2) The second movement in the expositional process is the theological. I generalize away from the particulars of the exegetical statement and seek to express the text's timeless message. In Leviticus 4, for example, Moses, the Israelites, and the sin offering give way to a universal truth. I must consider the progress of revelation. The sacrificial system of Leviticus was appropriate until superseded by Jesus. As a Christian expositor I must factor in Hebrews 9–10.

I also test my theological proposition against my systematic theology. If something doesn't "fit," I go back through my exegetical and theological processes to discover my misunderstanding. Then I either restate my theological proposition in acceptable terms or I adjust the way I think about and express my theological system.

Ultimately I will state a timeless biblical truth abstracted from my chosen text. "Love for a fellow believer limits the expression of Christian liberty" (1 Cor. 10:28), or "Without the shedding of blood there is no forgiveness" (Lev. 4).

(3) The third move in the expositional process is the homiletical. Having articulated the timeless message of my text, I ask the following questions of that theological proposition with my particular audience in mind. First, what does this theological truth mean? Will my audience understand the message of the text? Second, is it really true? Will my listeners actually believe it? Third, what difference does it make? Will they know how this theological truth applies to their lives?

I may argue, for example, for the 1 Corinthians 10 passage, "Since your attending gratuitously explicit movies causes your sister to attend such movies against her conscience, do not attend gratuitously explicit movies." Or, with Leviticus 4, "Trust Christ alone for forgiveness."

(4) I will not have completed the full expositional process until I and my listeners follow the demands of the text in our own thinking, feeling, and doing. Paul had this concept in mind when he called the Corinthians "living letters read by men." Biblical truth applied to real life completes the full expositional process.

Expository preachers move through the expositional process step by step and in order. They remain aware of their theological biases and homiletical situations, setting aside those influences, as much as possible, during exegesis. They do not allow a rush to relevance to twist the theologically intended message of the text.

When the topical preacher fails to let the text speak its original and timeless message, he opens himself to legitimate criticism. Without careful adherence to the expositional process, the preacher who starts with a relevant topic is likely to find that topic in a text whether it is there or not. Such preachers do not preach with biblical authority. By contrast, preachers who start with a topic and then find that topic addressed in a text or texts through the exegetical-theological-homiletical process are legitimately preaching expositionally.

Chapter 113

THE BIBLICAL TOPICAL SERMON
How to keep topical preaching truly biblical

Don Sunukjian

Topical preaching that is truly biblical is the communication of a biblical concept, derived from several different passages related to one another through a common subject and through either parallel or progressive assertions about that subject.

Let's unpack each of these elements. (1) A topical message, as all good preaching, attempts to communicate a single idea—one central truth, one dominant sentence that expresses the sermon in a nutshell. (2) This central truth is formed from several different passages, each of which genuinely addresses the same specific subject.

It is at this second point that many topical messages go biblically astray, as the preacher makes a passage speak about a subject other than the one intended by the biblical writer. For example, a preacher who delivers a message on "How to Parent Teenagers" might be tempted to include James 1:19 among his main points: "Be swift to hear, slow to speak, and slow to become angry." But James is not talking about parenting teenagers. Instead, his flow of thought through chapter 1 is:

1. If we persevere under a trial, we will gain maturity and reward (1:1–12).
2. If we sin because of the stress of the trial, it is not because God has pushed us too far—God is too good to do that—but because of evil desires within us (1:13–18).
3. Instead of blaming God for our sin—an attitude that will never bring the righteous life God desires—we should instead be quick to listen to the Word, slow to speak our alibis, and slow to become angry against God (1:19–25).

The danger in topical preaching is that we may short-cut the exegesis of a passage, fail to get the true point of the biblical author, and instead attach his words to a topic far different from what he had in mind. For example, in a sermon on "A Man after God's Own Heart" (1 Sam. 13:14), the preacher might be tempted to highlight three characteristics of David:

I. Fearless trust (1 Sam. 17)
II. Generous devotion (1 Chron. 29)
III. Genuine confession (Ps. 51)

But none of these passages is intended by the biblical author to explain what made David a man after God's own heart. The selection is purely arbitrary on the part of the preacher, who could have just as inappropriately listed David's "skillful songwriting" and thus eliminated most of us from ever qualifying as a person after God's heart.

Instead, the context of 1 Samuel 13–15 clearly shows which of David's traits the biblical author has in mind. David, in contrast to Saul, will "keep the LORD's command"; he will obey everything God says (13:14; 15:19–27; Acts 13:22). This unswerving obedience, and not any of the factors above, is what made David a man after God's own heart.

Biographical sermons are especially vulnerable to this abuse of using verses to establish points unintended by the biblical author. For example, a sermon on "What Are the Marks of a Spirit-Filled Man?" based on the life of Philip (Acts 6:3–5), would certainly be suspect if its main points were:

I. A Spirit-filled man will leave a successful ministry and labor unknown in a desolate region (Acts 8:4–8, 26–40)
II. A Spirit-filled man will channel his daughters into celibate ministries (Acts 21:8–9)

There is no suggestion in the text that Philip was struggling with the decision to relocate. For all we know, he had completed God's mission in Samaria and was anticipating returning to his home in Jerusalem. Nor is his Gaza road assignment a posting to a desolate region. Instead, he is walking just outside the Jerusalem city limits, on the road that leads south through the desert to Gaza, and is being overtaken by the traffic exiting from the city.

The point of Acts 8 is not the ministry choices a godly man should make, but rather how the Spirit is expanding the church into previously excluded countries and social classes.

And, obviously, point II is an absurd extreme of what can result when we incorrectly attach biblical statements to our chosen topics.

Topical preaching that is truly biblical thoroughly studies each individual passage in its context to make sure the biblical author is genuinely talking about the speaker's chosen subject. Properly done, topical preaching will result in profitable messages, such as "How to Be a Good Husband"

I. Live considerately (1 Peter 3:7)
II. Love sacrificially (Ephesians 5:25–33)

Or, in a message on "Honor Your Father and Mother"

I. In our early years, we honor our parents by obeying them (Eph. 6:1–3)
II. In our middle years, we honor our parents by respecting them (Lev. 19:3, 32)
III. In our mature years, we honor our parents by assisting them financially
  A. Assisting our parents financially comes ahead of commitments to the Lord's work (Matt. 15:1–9)
  B. Assisting our parents financially shows our own genuine godliness (1 Tim. 5:3–8)

Sometimes a speaker may be tempted to use a general verse to speak to a specific topic. For example, in the above message on "How to Be a Good Husband," the speaker may be tempted to include "Forgive freely" (Col. 3:13) as one of the main points. Or, in the message on "Honor Your Father and Mother," the speaker may be inclined to make the point, "We honor our parents by being kind and compassionate toward them" (Eph. 4:32). While such statements may be true, the listener senses: We're supposed to do this to everybody; that Scripture is not uniquely about husbands, or parents.

In such cases, it is better to preach a passage

exposition on the specific verse rather than a topical exposition on a subject. In a passage exposition on Colossians 3:13, the speaker would explain what it means to freely forgive and then apply this to many relationships in life—husbands, wives, parents, coworkers. Similarly, for Ephesians 4:32, the speaker would explain kindness and compassion and then illustrate how we could show these to many different people—parents, spouses, children, harried sales clerks, and so on. In this way the topical speaker saves specific verses for their specific subjects, and the result is a message that has greater focus, penetration, and impact.

Finally, in biblical topical preaching, the subject will develop into a central truth by means of either parallel or progressive assertions. The assertions will be parallel when each individual passage answers the same specific question about the subject. For example, in a sermon on "God Speaks to You," each of the main points answers the same question, "How does God speak to us?"

 I. Through creation (Ps. 19:1–6; Rom. 1:18–20)
 II. Through conscience (Rom. 2:14–15)

 III. Through Christ, the incarnate Word (Heb. 1:1–5)
 IV. Through Scripture, the written Word (2 Tim. 3:16–17; 2 Peter 1:20–21).

The assertions will be progressive when each individual passage answers a different question about the subject. For example, a message on "Fasting" might address the questions,

 I. What is fasting?
 II. How should we do it?
 III. Why should we do it?

The main point assertions would progressively develop into a central truth along the lines of:

 I. Fasting is a voluntary refraining from food and drink
 II. Fasting is done in secret (Matt. 6:16–18)
 III. Fasting is for the purpose of obtaining God's direction (Acts 13:1–3; Judg. 20:26–28)

Done correctly, topical preaching can lead to a more comprehensive understanding of a biblical doctrine or subject. But done incorrectly, it can lead to ideas the Bible never intended to say. We need to study thoroughly and organize carefully in order to be sure we can say, "Thus saith the Lord."

Chapter 114

TOPICAL PREACHING ON BIBLE CHARACTERS

*How to preach expositionally when focusing on what God teaches
through a biblical person*

Timothy S. Warren

Stories work because they talk about people. People with their character traits and constant struggles invest stories with interest and value. Even stories about the natural elements, man-made objects, or animals give people-like personalities to their characters. The sun competes with the wind to cause a traveler to remove his coat. Herbie saves the day and the girl for his friend. Babe wins the prize to help keep the farm. Stories work because of people.

Sermons work because of relevance. No one seeks information simply for information's sake. Even a trivia guru gains a sense of superiority over the ignorant masses. Our culture, especially, finds the value of preaching not so much in a knowledge of truth but in relevance, the application of truth.

When people and relevance come together, as they do in topical biographical sermons, a preacher can anticipate an enthusiastic response. Perhaps the most popular form of preaching today is the topical biographical sermon.

YOU DON'T HAVE TO ABANDON FAITHFUL EXPOSITION TO PREACH ON BIBLE PERSONS

Like all topical expository sermons, topical biographical expository sermons follow the expositional model. Exposition takes a preacher progressively through an exegetical understanding of a text/paragraph, through a theological interpretation of the passage, through a homiletical application, and into practice. Topical expository preaching is a subset of exposition that takes two or more passages through this same process.

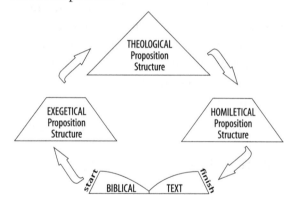

Topical biographical messages are based on a biblical character, the biblical story/stories that include that character, and especially the biblical author's intended use of that character in the story/stories.

Two questions may help clarify this definition.

1. Is a sermon topical if it does not expound two or more different texts/paragraphs in their

own contexts? No. By definition topical preaching expounds two or more passages.

2. Can we preach biographical sermons that are not topical? Yes. There must be hundreds of biblical characters that show up in one story line and then disappear, never to be mentioned again. Some of those characters, because of the specifically intended roles they play in the narrative, provide legitimate expositional material. Achan's story takes place in Joshua 7:1–26. His name appears only once after that, in Joshua 22:20, and only as a sermon illustration. Achan's biography, short as it is, intentionally models how to avoid God's judgment: Don't covet, steal, or deceive. True topical biographical expository sermons, however, deal with characters that appear in more than one passage, one unit of Scripture.

To Be Expository, Your Sermon Must Have a Biblical Mandate

Some biographical sermons begin with the selection of a character from a biblical passage(s)—Abraham, David, Herod, Peter—and then develop a character trait that the chosen individual's life mandates: faith, a heart after God's heart, submission, discipleship. Others start with a characteristic topic—dependence, loyal-love, repentance, or leadership—and then find a biblical character whose story mandates that trait: Jacob, Hosea, John the Baptizer, Paul.

No matter where the preacher starts the process, the challenge of topical biographical expository preaching will seldom be relevance; rather, it is the demonstration of a biblical mandate for what is being preached.

Two things are worth noting here.

1. God uses other means than expository preaching to evangelize the lost and edify believers. I've heard many "talks" based on biblical characters that were interesting, relevant, true, even biblical. Many of those "devotionals" were beneficial and challenging. But they were not expository because their messages were not developed from, nor were they shown to be the intended exegetical/theological message of, a specific passage or passages. Thus, you can "talk about" many helpful topics, but you shouldn't confuse that with, or substitute it for, expository preaching.

2. The only way to demonstrate the intended message of any passage is to interpret it fully in preparation and then expound it sufficiently in presentation. If a preacher doesn't show that the subject of his message is the subject of the passage(s), and if he doesn't explain that the relevant application of that message is, at some level, intended by his passage(s), then he shouldn't call it preaching. In summary, you need not take a biblical text/paragraph to say many interesting, relevant, true, even biblical things, but if you call it expository preaching, you'd better be able to demonstrate that your sermon idea is the intended message of your text(s)/paragraph(s).

As a result, when you begin sermon preparation with the selection of a character, you have to ask why and how that character was included in the story. Does your character merely help carry the plot along so that the author can develop the theological message, or does your character intentionally model a mandated behavior? The role the character plays in the story will determine the way the character can be preached.

 For an audio example of this principle see tracks 12–13 on the supplemental CD.

I don't think Potiphar, a mere agent, was placed in the biblical record intentionally to model compassion when he imprisoned rather than executed Joseph (Gen. 39). I'm certain that Matthew's intent in 4:1–11 was not to use Jesus, though he is a major character, to mandate a strategy for resisting temptation. Matthew's intent was to prove that Jesus alone, unlike any other, could resist all temptations, a victory validating his messianic claim.

On the other hand, I could demonstrate that Judges intentionally used Jephthah, a major character in chapters 11–12, to warn against succumbing to pagan influences (foolish vows, human sacrifice, extreme violence) that taint true worship. Mark intentionally contrasts the disloyalty of the religious authorities, major characters, with the loyalty demonstrated by the widow, a mere agent, who gave two coins out of her poverty (Mark 12:38–44). She is more than an illustration; she is held up as a model to imitate. The question every biographical preacher must ask is whether the character is an incidental illustration or an intentional model. I'm afraid that in our typical rush to relevance we often find more than the author intended.

Starting a biographical sermon with a character trait and then searching for a biblical character who's role in the narrative mandates that trait requires a preacher to ask the same question. Is this trait merely illustrated in the life of this character, or is this trait mandated by the author's intent?

Caleb, for example, serves as more than an illustration of complete devotion to God. Three different texts report that "he followed the Lord fully" (Num. 32:12; Deut. 1:36; Josh. 14:14). Caleb's complete devotion enabled him (1) to trust God to give Israel the Promised Land, (2) to escape God's judgment on Israel in the desert, and (3) to inherit the blessings of the Promised Land. The biblical evaluations of Caleb's biography do more than illustrate devotion, they mandate complete devotion.

WHAT I LEARNED WHEN I PREACHED ON THE TWELVE DISCIPLES

Preaching through Matthew pericope by pericope, I came upon the list of disciples in Matthew 10:2–4. I thought a biographical series might provide a welcome change of pace. I was sure there would be many biblical principles to expound through topical biographical expositions on each of the disciples.

I found that the amount of material on each disciple varies enormously. Peter's name appears nearly 150 times in the New Testament, while Thaddaeus appears twice. Even James manages to do only one thing by himself: he's martyred in Acts 12:2. I quickly decided I wouldn't preach on Thaddaeus. And I had far too much material for a single, focused sermon on Peter.

I'm smiling as I think back on how I handled Peter and James. Most of what I preached in that series was not topical biographical exposition. Instead I preached textually, using the disciples as illustrations. My key text for Peter came from his last recorded words, "Grow in the grace and knowledge of our Lord and Savior Jesus Christ" (2 Peter 3:18). Peter says grow, Peter spent his life growing (lots of illustrations here), and you should grow. My text for James was John 12:24, "Except a grain of wheat falls into the earth and dies, it remains by itself alone, but if it dies, it bears much fruit." What a leap!

I am much more pleased to tell you about the

true topical biographical expository sermon I preached on Thomas. Except when he appears in lists with the other disciples, Thomas shows up on only three occasions—all of them in John and all related to the subject of believing. I knew the purpose of John's Gospel was that his readers might believe in Jesus (20:31) and that believing was a key theological theme (the Greek verb *pisteuo* is used nearly one hundred times in John). I had decided on my character, Thomas, and identified the three key passages I needed to study (in John 11, 14, and 20). I also had a general notion that each passage emphasized belief. The question was whether my exegetical/theological interpretation would confirm or negate that notion.

In my judgment, John used Thomas on all three occasions to model a believing disciple. Granted, he has been known as Doubting Thomas, but I discovered that as a misrepresentation. Unquestionably Thomas demonstrated the struggle of coming to belief, but that

was John's point. Ultimately each story/pericope shows Thomas finding substantive reasons for believing in Jesus. My theological proposition went something like, "Believing disciples conquer all obstacles with belief." My homiletical proposition stated, "Keep on believing in Jesus." My outline (here abbreviated) developed as follows:

I. Keep on believing in Jesus when circumstances paralyze (John 11:1–16)
II. Keep on believing in Jesus when questions perplex (John 14:1–7)
III. Keep on believing in Jesus when skepticism plagues (John 20:19–29)

As in all topical expository preaching, a biographical sermon must find its topic/character in two or more passages. It must also convincingly demonstrate the author's intended use of the character to mandate a legitimate application. People and relevance make biographical sermons work. Genuine exposition makes them authoritative.

Chapter 115

TOPICAL PREACHING ON CONTEMPORARY ISSUES

How to preach expositionally when a current issue is the talk of the town

Timothy S. Warren

After more than four years of pastoral ministry at a church, I thought it would be helpful to let my congregation choose a series for the summer. Over those four years my paragraph-by-paragraph expositions had covered several New Testament letters, the Minor Prophets, Genesis, and a few selected Psalms, and these

had been supplemented along the way by textual messages for special occasions. I had preached what I thought were the most critical themes. That approach had been well received.

So I passed out three-by-five note cards and invited all regular attenders to write down what they wanted to hear preached. The results? The only book study suggested by more than three people was on Revelation. All other requests were topical. And almost all touched on a contemporary issue: "Talk about AIDS." "Is welfare biblical?" "Are computers Satan's tool?" "What about evolution and the Bible?" Saying something about these relevant issues would be no problem; speaking with biblical authority would be the challenge.

A truly expositional preaching method made it possible. Since it is text-centered, expository preaching gives the sermon a "Thus says the Lord" authority; and because it is audience-focused, it provides contemporary relevance. The message of an expository sermon must clearly emerge out of the intended meaning of a biblical passage or passages. That meaning must then be applied anew for the immediate audience. Without both biblical authority and contemporary relevance, a sermon, by most definitions, is not expository.

MANY ROADS TO THE SUBJECT

There are at least three different styles of exposition. Textual exposition bases its message in a single verse or sentence of Scripture. Verse-by-verse, or paragraph, exposition bases its message in two or more verses in a literary unit. Topical exposition bases its message in two or more different biblical units that share a common subject.

Within topical exposition there are at least three divisions. Theological topical exposition finds its subject in a theological topic specifically addressed in the Bible: marriage, temptation, forgiveness, and so on. Biographical topical exposition finds its subject in the original author's intentional use of a biblical character to reveal a divine truth. Contemporary issue exposition finds its subject in the context of current culture and then moves back to Scripture to discover what passages address that issue.

Whether the preacher starts with a text, a paragraph, a theological topic, a biblical character, or a contemporary issue is not a question or concern for the person committed to expository preaching. What is crucial is that the preacher—wherever he has discovered his sermon subject—move into and then through the exegetical-theological-homiletical process (see "Can Topical Preaching Be Expository?"). Preachers cannot speak with biblical authority unless they have discovered the original and intended meaning of the passage(s), identified the timeless theological message of the passage(s), and only then sought to apply that truth with immediate relevance to a contemporary audience.

Sometimes theological and biographical expositions are initiated with a topic from a contemporary setting (e.g., the need for church discipline or a challenge to wholehearted devotion to the Lord) and then move to relatively easily identifiable biblical passages that address that subject. On other occasions the theological or biographical expositions begin with a passage (e.g., Matt. 18:15–20 or Num. 32:12) that suggests the topic. The contemporary issue exposition, however, always begins with a question, problem, or struggle that has emerged from within the context of contemporary culture (e.g., air or water pollution, weapons of mass destruction, homosexuality, abortion, capitalism).

CHALLENGES OF PREACHING ON CURRENT ISSUES

I find contemporary-issue exposition a greater challenge than theological or biographical exposition, though the latter two have their own challenges. One reason: current issues have multiple viewpoints with multiple arguments. The question of our present response to crime illustrates this challenge. The problems of unreliable witnesses, convictions based on circumstantial evidence, and an overextended judicial system make the question of capital punishment a complex topic. How can a preacher hope to know, understand, and address the multitude of related arguments?

The expositor who expects to maintain integrity will research the topic sufficiently enough to know its major questions, and only then strategically and candidly narrow the sermon's subject. Reading the "experts" or those with different and opposing views can expose blind spots and fill in gaps. It is presumptuous to speak on God's behalf without knowing the basic facts.

Another reason I find contemporary-issue exposition a greater challenge than other forms of exposition is because of the typical preacher's rush to relevance. When a topic surfaces in the give and take of everyday life, it is easy to get caught up in the need for an immediate, relevant answer. Preachers may find themselves preaching an audience-centered and audience-focused message simply because the popular "fix it now" and "how to" mentalities tempt them into sliding past the exegetical and theological interpretation of relevant biblical passages.

Sometimes there seems to be no biblical passage that addresses the topic, at least in the way it is shaped by contemporary culture. No texts address the topic with any explicit intent. For example, there are passages that deal with the creation of the world as we know it, but none that specifically address the debate between creationism and evolution. To make Genesis 1 and Genesis 2 argue the contemporary issues is to

misuse the text and miss the intent of its author, resulting in a lack of biblical authority and a compromise of integrity. To say, however, that Genesis has nothing to offer the debate would be to fail to consider some significant inferences from what Moses did intend.

RANGES OF BIBLICAL MEANING

As we try to address current issues like this from Scripture, we need to answer two crucial questions.

1. What ranges of biblical meaning lead to legitimate authority in preaching? My friend Ramesh Richard taught me that biblical texts communicate over three ranges of meaning: *statement*, *implication*, and *extrapolation*. When the Bible says, "You shall not commit adultery," that's statement. This statement could lead to a meaning implied by the Exodus 20:14 text: Marriage is sacred. That's implication. The condemnation of all sexual activity outside marriage would be an extrapolation, a further drawing out of meaning, from the text.

Application is another issue. "Never have sex with anyone other than your spouse" is an obvious application of the biblical statement. "Cultivate your own marriage" is a possible application of that text's implication. "Avoid pornography" is a legitimate application of the extrapolation. All may be preached with authority. The issue is not whether the applications are legitimate but rather whether all the ranges of meaning have been legitimately validated. Expositors of contemporary issues must move with caution through the ranges of meaning to keep from finding implications or extrapolations that cannot be proven consistent with the original intent of the passage.

2. How do contemporary-issue preachers

signal the level of meaning from which they are preaching? I suggest we simply state, "This passage does not specifically address our topic, at least not in the same way we are considering it. However, there are some implications (or extrapolations) we can legitimately draw from this passage that will help us decide how we should respond to today's issue."

God has spoken explicitly and absolutely on some subjects. On many subjects the Scriptures are not explicit; we are left with implications or extrapolations. Knowing the difference and expressing a proper tentativeness seems prudent.

A CRIME IN MY COMMUNITY

A few years ago a paroled sex offender raped and killed a child, provoking outrage in our community. I prepared the following message knowing I couldn't say everything, but that I should say something:

Child sex offenders are criminals
- Exodus 22:16
- Deuteronomy 22:25–29

The community must be provided justice and protection
- Exodus 21:22
- Deuteronomy 24:16–17

Accused child sex offenders deserve due process
- Deuteronomy 16:18–20; 17:2–7; 19:15–21

(Ultimately, we must...)

Restrict the rights of convicted child sex offenders
- Society has the right to punish (Deut. 25:1–3; Rom. 13:4)
- Society has the right to put them to death (Ex. 22:22–24; Lev. 20:2)
- Society has the right to isolate/incarcerate them (Lev. 20:3, 5–6, 17–18)

Once my topic found me, I chased down close to fifty passages. A concordance and topical index proved invaluable for my initial search, then cross-references guided me to further texts. I started exegeting each text in its original context to determine its intended meaning. When a passage seemed not to address my topic even by implication or extrapolation, I dropped it. Since no text provided a statement about child sex offenders specifically, I worked with implications and extrapolations. It seemed that several passages made legitimate contributions by addressing sex crimes and justice in general.

Theological propositions often address more than one topic at the abstract level. For example, in Deuteronomy 17:2–7, Moses speaks to the specific issue of providing idolaters due process. Few people in my culture wrestle with how to handle idolaters. But by taking Moses' message to the theological level we can generalize a message for any criminal violation. "Any accused criminal deserves due process." That truth applied to idolaters in Moses' day. It applies just as authoritatively to any contemporary issue of supposed criminal behavior. It is at the level of the theological abstraction that ancient and contemporary particulars meet. That's why it's essential to move through the exegetical and theological processes—to ensure a proper understanding of biblical meaning. Only then may new applications of timeless truth be affirmed.

I'm certain my message left much unsaid. In fact, I always have that nagging feeling when I preach a contemporary issue. However, when an issue so captivates a congregation that not to speak would signal indifference, contemporary issue topical exposition enables the preacher to address the issue with authority and relevance.

Chapter 116

TOPICAL PREACHING ON THEOLOGICAL THEMES

How to preach expositionally when a theological idea is the order of the day

Timothy S. Warren

I entered my first pastorate with enthusiasm, confident I could preach for several years using paragraph-by-paragraph, through-a-book exposition. I'd start with Ephesians. That would take a good year, maybe longer. Ephesians was theologically solid and relevant. Then on to 1 Corinthians. That would take two years at least. I'd do some Psalms along the way and preach through a narrative like Genesis or Matthew. Of course I would break away to expound some key texts for special occasions: Isaiah 9:6 at Christmas, for example.

Then reality visited, an incident that demanded church discipline. I should have known. Ours was a new church plant and had no experience in or policy for discipline. It was simply in the bylaws that church discipline would be practiced in a biblical manner when necessary.

Ready or not, it was time for a topical theological expository sermon. Our congregation needed a biblically based message on what church discipline was, why we practiced it, how we would do it, and what we could expect as a result. Since no single text or paragraph covered all those questions, I preached several passages topically.

A few weeks later, as prelude to a baptismal service, I preached a topical message on baptism. I pulled together a unified sermon based on several passages dealing with the subject, a topic no single text or paragraph covered exhaustively. I was learning not only the necessity of preaching topically, but also how to preach a topical theological sermon expositionally.

Exposition takes a preacher progressively through an exegetical understanding of a text/paragraph, through a theological interpretation of the passage, through a homiletical application, and into practice. Topical expository preaching is a subset of exposition that takes two or more passages through the same process.

I divide topical exposition into three kinds: theological, biographical, and contemporary issue. To address what the Bible says regarding a theological topic—church discipline, baptism, marriage, divorce, temptation, trials, forgiveness, and hundreds more—I use topical theological exposition. Here are five essentials for preparing topical theological expositions.

(1) Decide on the theological topic you want to preach. Sometimes a topic just shows up, as in the case of church discipline, or a funeral, or a building dedication. Otherwise we can discover topics through personal devotional studies, praying about key doctrines, knowing your congregation's theological strengths and weaknesses, and being sensitive to people's questions and struggles. Sometimes a key word or concept surfaces during a book exposition.

While an endless supply of theological topics will likely come to your attention through these means, you must decide which are essential and guard against preaching on a few favorite doctrines again and again. Topical preaching demands discipline to remain objective, comprehensive, and balanced with other styles of exposition.

(2) Identify all passages you want to explore. While preaching through Matthew, I came across Jesus' command, "Be of good cheer" (9:2). I discovered the phrase was but a single Greek word, *tharseo.* I thought there might be something theologically significant about the use of this term and decided to locate all its uses.

Ultimately, each passage in its context must address your theological subject. In addition, each passage must contribute something to the topic the others don't. At this point, however, be as exhaustive as possible. If your topic is church discipline, you'll discover only a few passages on the subject. If you wanted to preach on forgiveness, however, you'd have to select a workable handful from more than one hundred passages that speak about forgiveness.

I usually start my search with a concordance, both English and Hebrew or Greek. Computers have made this work much easier. I also use topical books like Torrey's *The Treasury of Scripture Knowledge* or Lockyer's *All the Holy Days and Holidays,* reference Bibles with topical indexes on the margins and in the back, and theological dictionaries or wordbooks. Often I'll look up the topic in a systematic theology to see what passages are considered essential. I usually have little trouble finding multiple passages to study. The challenge is in deciding how many and which ones to study further.

In the "Be of good cheer" message I found the term *tharseo* used eight times in the New Testament, but only four times by Jesus. One of those four was a Synoptic repetition. That meant I had only three passages to take through the expositional process. Thirteen or thirty passages is more usual.

(3) Discover the exegetical and theological meaning of each passage in context. To maintain biblical authority, sermons must fully expound each passage preached. Doing full expositions for multiple texts/paragraphs simply takes multiple amounts of time and work. There is no substitute. Many preachers avoid topical exposition for this reason. Others skip the discipline of exposition—but compromise their authority along the way.

As you get into your exegetical/theological exposition, you may discover that a certain passage doesn't really deal with your topic after all. Scratch that text and go on to the next. Your increasing understanding of each passage may also cause you to narrow the subject of the sermon. Instead of preaching one sermon on rewards, you may decide to preach a series of sermons on rewards: What are rewards, who gets rewards, who gives rewards, on which basis are rewards given? Preaching a series can help cut your weekly preparation significantly.

As I exegeted the three "Be of good cheer" passages in their different contexts, I found that Jesus consistently used the imperative to encourage: a sinner he was forgiving (Matt. 9:2), the disciples for whom he had just appeared (Matt. 14:27), and the apostles he was sending into the world (John 16:33). From a theological perspective I determined these three commands of Jesus were not merely accidental parallels. They were clearly intended words of encouragement to the readers of the Gospels.

The question of what biblical passages mean and whether they are intentionally speaking to the proposed sermon topic will be answered in your exegetical/theological exposition. While different interpreters will discover different meanings and intentions for the same passage, your use of a text/paragraph must be honest and defendable.

(4) Articulate a single, unified theological proposition. Until you can express the synthesized message of all the passages you've pulled together under the same topic, you cannot expect to preach a clear, single-subject, topical exposition.

My first try at a theological proposition for my topical message was, "The good cheer of God's forgiveness, presence, and victory encourages needy sinners, disciples, and apostles." I abstracted it further to, "The good cheer of God's blessing encourages needy people."

(5) Follow the usual homiletical process. Apply the single, timeless truth to your own and your listeners' lives. Try to keep your homiletical proposition simple. Simplicity isn't always possible because topical sermons often have multiple complements to the same subject.

My homiletical proposition was longer and more complex than I prefer, but taken point by point, I think it was clear. The way to get God's good cheer of encouragement into your life is:

I. Trust Jesus as your Savior
II. Obey Jesus as your Lord

III. Go, tell of Jesus' victory

I had noted that the sinner's problem was guilt, the disciples' problem was fear, and the apostles' problem was despair. These three needs were relevant to my contemporary audience. In fact, these needs are universal. Those universal needs and the specific responses to those needs lead to this outline:

I. Get God's good cheer of forgiveness into your life (Matt. 9:2)
   - Sinners have a problem with guilt
   - Jesus says, "Be of good cheer; your sins are forgiven"
   - Trust Jesus as your Savior
II. Get God's good cheer of presence into your life (Matt. 14:27).
   - Disciples have a problem with fear
   - Jesus says, "Be of good cheer; it is I"
   - Obey Jesus as your Lord
III. Get God's good cheer of victory into your life (John 16:33)
   - Apostles have a problem with despair
   - Jesus says, "Be of good cheer, I have overcome the world"
   - Go, tell of Jesus' victory

In pastoral ministry, topical preaching on theological themes is unavoidable and, if done expositionally, invaluable.

Chapter 117

MAKING THE MOST OF BIBLICAL PARADOXES

They offer a refreshing and deeper alternative to "how to" sermons

Richard P. Hansen

Carl Sandburg captured well the human condition: "There is an eagle in me that wants to soar, and there is a hippopotamus in me that wants to wallow in the mud." That's a paradox—seemingly contradictory statements that are nonetheless true. Recently paradox has become more important in preaching.

A new worship attender came to see me. A believer, she vulnerably shared some of the mud in which she was currently mired. Then she blurted out: "I got so frustrated at the church I used to attend. Everything was five easy steps! I need to hear something more than pat answers." I am finding more and more people recognize that a steady diet of "how to" preaching has left them spiritually anemic.

What's the alternative? For those who aren't helped by "three easy steps," a better alternative is to preach the power of paradox.

Paradox is the wild territory within which most ministers live and work.

- We see unseen things.
- We conquer by yielding.
- We find rest under a yoke.
- We reign by serving.
- We are made great by becoming small.
- We are exalted when we are humble.
- We become wise by being fools for Christ's sake.
- We are made free by becoming bondservants.
- We gain strength when we are weak.
- We triumph through defeat.
- We find victory by glorying in our infirmities.
- We live by dying.

With the passage of time, most preachers clear land, build a homestead, and try to tame this paradoxical wilderness. We are told that we're vendors in a spiritual street market clogged with competitors. People pause only a moment before strolling on to the next booth, so we've got to grab them with snappy "How to . . ." titles. People are looking for answers to make a difference in their lives—yesterday. So we must hit felt needs quickly, cut to the chase, offer "spiritual principles" and "practical handles" that plug directly into people's pragmatic expectations.

Is any attention still being paid to Baron Von Hugel's observation: "The deeper we get into reality, the more numerous will be the questions we cannot answer"? Addressing the person who asks, "How will Christianity improve my life?" C. S. Lewis replies:

Frankly, I find it hard to sympathize with this state of mind. One of the things that distinguishes man from the other animals is that he wants to know things, wants to find out what reality is like, simply for the sake of knowing. When that desire is completely quenched in anyone, I think he has become something less than human.

Foolish preachers, by always telling you how much Christianity will help you and how good it is for society, have actually led you to forget that Christianity is not a patent medicine. If Christian-

434

ity is untrue, then no honest man will want to believe it, however helpful it might be; if it is true, every honest man will want to believe it, even if it gives him no help at all.

Raising questions that might not have easy answers—leaving the security of the homestead to venture deeper into life's wilderness, beyond the sight lines of reason into the mystery of God—would seem to be the kiss of death to attracting customers. What preacher in his or her right mind will raise thorny questions when people already have too many burrs under their saddles?

And yet, when pat answers no longer satisfy, paradox, paradoxically, can reach the depths of the soul.

What to Do with Paradox?

C. S. Lewis goes on to distinguish two kinds of readers. One reader receives from books, while a second does things with books. Of the second reader's misguided motives, Lewis writes: "We are so busy doing things with the work that we give it too little chance to work on us. Thus increasingly we meet only ourselves."

This is the contemporary preacher's temptation. We are so busy doing things with Scripture (especially things that address the need of the moment) that Scripture has little chance to do its work in us. We come to Scripture faithfully and genuinely, yet increasingly meet not God, but only satisfy our current want.

What about the truths of Scripture that do not come in easily digestible spoon-size bites? What about truths that need to be gnawed on? We find it hard to do things with paradox. Yet paradox is often a window into the deeper mystery of God.

Enlightenment rationalism was no friend of paradox, but postmodern appetite for mystery is insatiable. People pound away at computer terminals all day, visit their aroma therapist to unwind on the way home, and then read *The Celestine Prophecy* by candlelight.

Do we realize that we Christians sit atop the mother lode of all mystery? A God who is Wholly Other yet graciously reveals himself to human beings in Jesus Christ is the unsurpassed mystery of the universe! How are we inviting contemporary people to touch this Mystery, even as we present God as the answer to their felt needs?

Exploring the wild territories of paradox helps us see God less as our personalized AAA map for life (with hazards highlighted), and more as the purpose of the journey. Tramping through these regions, I've identified three distinct types of biblical paradox that open doors to the mystery of God.

Paradox Reframes the Issue

Have you ever noticed Jesus' preaching does not have the point-by-point "fill in the blanks" directness so popular today? Jesus was often intentionally paradoxical. His open-ended sermons sent listeners away scratching their heads, with dangling loose ends for them to tie together. (How long would most modern preachers last if our key leaders regularly asked, as Jesus' disciples did, "Tell us, what were you trying to say this morning?")

Jesus' use of paradox shakes us by the shoulders to see familiar things from a fresh perspective. This type of paradox, like a good picture frame, doesn't call attention to itself but focuses attention on the magnificence of the painting.

When Jesus says, "Those who save their lives will lose them, and those who lose their lives for my sake will save them," our attention is quickly drawn away from the paradox per se, because it reframes all that we have ever thought about hedging our bets, playing it safe, being conservative—in short, "saving" our lives. We look through this new window where losing becomes saving. What "saving" behaviors might be hindering my spiritual growth? What do I need to lose for Jesus' sake?

Such use of paradox prods us to ask questions of ourselves. It reveals and yet hides, asserts yet invites reflection. "The last shall be first, and the first last" not only asserts a truth but prompts me to ask: Am I thinking and acting in ways that make me "first" or "last?"

If we try too hard to explain it, such paradox loses its heuristic value. Snappy applications ("Go home this week and . . .") are insufficient when dealing with Jesus' use of paradox, which is transforming largely because it works below the waterline.

Framing paradox can be preached effectively through story—not story illustrations hung like coat hangers on a deductive outline, but a story comprising the bulk of the sermon. Narrative sermons move preaching away from analysis to experience.

Stories draw us in. We suspend judgment and are more open to change. We move from detached observers to involved participants. The story creates a role for us and we try it on for size. Especially when left open-ended, as many of Jesus' stories were, narrative sermons offer the opportunity for listeners to put themselves in the story and create their "own" ending. Rather than sitting back to evaluate the preacher's truth, listeners discover truth for themselves.

In a sermon addressing the paradox of faith and works, I created a sermon-length story about a woman on a hijacked airplane who must decide whether to identify herself as a Christian when passengers are told all non-Christians are free to leave. Tension builds as the terrorists move toward her seat, forcing each passenger into a bizarre rite of denial by spitting on a picture of Jesus before being allowed to exit to safety.

In her mind, the debate continues—how much action/effort/commitment does faith demand?—until the hijacker finally arrives to shove the saliva-pocked face of Jesus in front of her and bark, "What about you?" Quietly, I asked the congregation, "What about me? What about you?" and sat down. Each was forced to confront the cost of faith and add his or her own ending.

PARADOX THAT HARMONIZES

Consider a tuning fork. It delivers a true pitch by two tines vibrating together. Muffle either side, even a little, and the note disappears. Neither tine individually produces the sweet, pure note. Only when both tines vibrate is the correct pitch heard.

Like a tuning fork, harmonious paradoxes declare their truth when two sides of the paradox vibrate in unison. This requires care and honesty. Unlike the tuning fork, which is forged by highly controlled mechanical processes, the paradoxes of Scripture must be forged by the words of highly subjective preachers. Yet despite our biases toward one tine or the other, neither side of the paradox should be muffled, even a little.

The paradox of divine sovereignty/human responsibility offers an excellent example of finely tuned tension. Is my salvation God's election, or is it my free response to the gospel message? Does God's choice of me negate my choice of God? Can two choices (mine and God's) exist without one inevitably determining the other?

Job and his friends do not face the sovereignty/responsibility tension as an abstract theological debate but as a painful flesh-and-blood dilemma. Job has lost everything. Who is responsible: Job or God? How can Job accept that God is both all-powerful and perfectly good? Is God transcendently aloof from Job's pain or somehow personally involved?

Job keeps both tines vibrating: God is both transcendently all-powerful and personally involved. In fact, refusing to mute one tine is what allows Job to argue with God. Who could argue with the impassive God of the deists?

Ultimately Job realizes no simple solution is possible. The paradox opens the door to a mysterious and unsearchable God. "Surely I spoke of things I did not understand, things too wonderful for me to know" (Job 42:3). Yet living in this paradox has clarified for Job whether his faith is in God or in what he knows about God. In the end, it is significant that Job cries out, not "I understand" but "I repent" (Job 42:6).

Something similar happened to a woman in our church who tragically lost her middle-aged husband. She began the grief process questioning many of the timeless truths she thought she knew about God. Over time, these questions were not so much answered as shown to be side issues. Like Job, she realized that her faith could ultimately rest only in God, not in understanding God. Mystery reveals, even as it obscures. She came to know God better when she acquiesced to God's mystery.

Something similar happened to Job. At the end of his wrestling with God, Job admits God is unfathomable but also (paradoxically) indicates that he now knows God better than he did before: "My ears had heard of you but now my eyes have seen you" (Job 42:5).

Intellectual debate or Job-like personal circumstances can devastate believers who have never explored the wilderness beyond easy, five-step answers. Regular exposure to paradox challenges Christians early on to exchange faith about God for faith in God, a God who is trustworthy even if often inscrutable. What a relief to realize that both tines of the tuning fork are necessary for the admittedly elusive note of truth to be heard!

The two-headed monster on Sesame Street uses exactly this strategy to teach children phonetic pronunciations. One head of the monster says "C...."; the other, "...AR." Each head pronounces its syllable with ever-shortening time intervals until the two sounds meld together into a new word: "C.....AR," "C...AR," "CAR!" Sermons using this method follow an inductive path: first showing the inadequacy of either side of the paradox by itself, then heralding the new note they create when held in tension with each other.

For example, in a sermon on God's being perfectly just, yet also perfectly loving, I bounced listeners' attention back and forth between the two sides of Mr. Beaver's description of Aslan in *The Chronicles of Narnia*: "He isn't safe ... but he's good." Like "C...AR," judgment and love melded together by the end of the sermon in a way people may not have heard in the beginning.

PARADOX THAT'S TWO-HANDLED

While the tension of the harmonious paradox draws opposites together to complement one another, a third type of paradox, the "two-handled paradox," consistently pushes the poles apart.

G. K. Chesterton saw that orthodoxy must exalt extremes: "It has kept them side by side like two strong colors, red and white, like the red and white upon the shield of St. George. It has always had a healthy hatred of pink. It hates that combination of two colors which is the feeble expedient of the philosophers. It hates that evolution of black into white which is tantamount to a dirty gray."

I often watched my grandfather dig postholes on his farm with an old-fashioned auger. Turning the giant corkscrew, the farmer needed both strength and balance to push on one handle while pulling on the other. Under his practiced hands, every push/pull half turn caused the auger to bite deeper into the hard Nebraska soil.

Nothing is more useless than a one-handled auger! Maximum effect is achieved when you position your hands at the very ends of the handles. Slide your hands toward the middle, and the auger becomes proportionately less effective. Likewise, we do ourselves no favor by whittling down opposing extremes of a two-handled paradox—for example, God's transcendence and immanence, separate from the world yet actively engaged in the world. The transcendent but uninvolved clockmaker God of the eighteenth-century deists, and the New Ager's immanent, pantheistic God swallowed up within the natural world, both grasp only one handle.

Christian history's greatest heresies whittled down the handles of paradox: God not fully three or completely one, Jesus Christ not fully divine or completely human. In both the Trinity and Incarnation, theology's danger has forever been the coalescence of opposites into a dirty gray.

Types of Paradox

	Reframing	Harmonious	Two-Handled
Visual symbol	Picture frame: "reframes" reality as we look at it	Tuning fork: both tines vibrating together create a new note	Auger: performs best when hands are far apart on opposite handles
Characteristic tension	Startles us, but ultimately dissolves	Pushes polarities together	Keeps polarities apart
Representative examples	Faith vs. works Judge vs. judge not (e.g., Matt. 13:24ff.) Great reversals (e.g., Matt. 20:1–16; 25:29; Mark 9:35)	Eternal life: present possession vs. future inheritance Predestination vs. free will	Jesus: God yet human God: transcendent yet immanent God: three yet one Humanity: sinful yet in God's image
Opens the door to:	Mysteries of life in God's kingdom	Mysteries of relationships: God's actions and purposes	Mysteries of being: God's and ours
Strategies for preaching	Narratives/stories Playfulness Let listeners connect the dots	Unravel "double binds" Back and forth vibration ("C…AR")	Emphasize contrasts between opposite sides
Risks to avoid	Trying too hard to make listeners "get it"	Emphasizing one pole over the other upsets their delicate balance	Allowing black and white to coalesce into "dirty gray"

How might the black and white of the two-handled paradox be proclaimed in all its stark clarity, leading us with awe and silence into the presence of the divine mystery? Both sides of the paradox must be maintained in all their contrary distinctiveness. No pink must intrude into the crisp red on white of St. George's cross. Different facets of one side of the paradox are counterbalanced by opposing facets of the other side. Each pull on one handle is balanced by a push on the other. The shifting back and forth adds movement and retains interest.

One approach I have used is a "Paul Harvey" strategy. The first half of the sermon argues only one side of the paradox. Astute listeners begin to wonder: "This isn't right. What about the other side?" Then "the rest of the story" presents the opposite in equal detail.

I have also used imaginary characters to represent opposite handles of a paradox, taking on different personas for contrary positions. For instance, in one sermon I played two roles endorsing the opposing views "Jesus is human" and "Jesus is God." The two characters began their conversation side by side, then I gradually took steps apart as it became increasingly apparent that, for the whole truth to be heard, each position must maintain its distinctive identity.

As I presented evidence for each viewpoint, they gradually separated until I was shuttling fifteen feet back and forth across the chancel as I played each role.

BIGGER THAN WE IMAGINE

In a pragmatic age, persistent in finding the quickest route to whatever works, we preachers find little to do with paradox. Yet, like unusual stones found in the bottom of a prospector's pan, we keep discovering biblical paradoxes, rolling them over in our palms, pondering their secrets.

Paradox beckons us into mystery and offers a wholesome reminder that God is infinitely greater than our ideas about God.

Chapter 118

GETTING THE MOST FROM THE SERMON SERIES
How to take full advantage of the unique strengths of series preaching

Craig Brian Larson

Recently I decided to fix a basement leak and had a contractor give an estimate. Wanting to remove some paneling, he asked, "Do you have a pry bar?" I retrieved two: a small, thin lever about five inches long and a Superbar more than a foot long. The contractor grabbed the Superbar and removed the paneling in minutes.

The contractor chose the tool with more leverage. In the same way, many pastors, wanting greater leverage, choose to preach primarily in series.

But we may not be using all the power inherent in the form. When we understand how a series differs from a single sermon, we can take full advantage of the unique strengths a series affords. Here are six differences, along with suggestions on how to capitalize on them.

DEEP DEVELOPMENT

The more an idea is developed, the greater is its impact. If I preach a thirty-second sermon—reading John 3:16, saying, "God loves you so much he sent Jesus to die for your sins. Believe in Jesus and you will be saved," and then sitting down—that will have less effect (all things being equal) than if I give a thirty-minute sermon in which I explain why God had to send his Son, illustrate with stories showing human sinfulness, give examples from the Gospels of people turning to Jesus in faith, and so on. As long as there is movement, not redundancy, more development means more power.

Series offer much more time for development; a four-part series gives us several hours. We can explain more principles, dig deeper theologically, answer more objections, paint images in greater detail, offer more examples, tell longer stories, address the full scope of application (who, what, where, and how), and expose more Scripture. Instead of one drama or testimony in support of the theme, there can be many. We can preach sequential expository sermons through books of the Bible. Such breadth and depth and focus will more likely change lives.

To harness the power of deep development:

- Plan a series with the big picture in mind. In many cases, we can view the entire series as a single large sermon, having one main subject *and* one big idea needing development. In this mega-sermon perspective, each week's sermon is like a main point developing that big idea.
- Ask yourself: What is the overall purpose of the series? What Scriptures do I need to cover? When the series is over, what do I want people to know, do, and feel? What objections will I

need to answer? At what point in the series will I deal with these various aspects?

A series is not four sermons gathered loosely under a general topic (a wide series), but rather four sermons working together to accomplish one aim (a deep series).

MOMENTUM

A series that gathers momentum can be a landmark in church life. I recently preached through Galatians, and midway through it one man prayed in the service, "Lord, thank you for leading your pastor to preach through Galatians. You have spoken to us through this book. Continue to guide him as he plans his preaching in the future." Another woman told me, "Make sure you are taping these." Others asked me to email my sermon notes that week, and one woman came up after church and asked for my printed notes. This series coincided with a renewed sense of God at work in our church, leading in new people and bringing back people long absent. God gave us a spiritual momentum that was not there when the series began.

In the sports world it is called Big Mo, and it can make a season. Momentum in a sermon series is just as powerful. People get curious and excited. They learn new things that change their lives forever. They stand up and tell how God is working. They invite others.

Series build momentum because of connection. What happens today is tied to what happened last week and what will happen next week. A series resembles a giant flywheel, still spinning from spiritual energy applied before, accelerating more from energy exerted today.

Series have far more potential than single sermons to increase attendance and visitor flow. After the first sermon, hearers know what to expect in future sermons, and if they are helped, they are motivated to attend and to invite others.

One reason people like series is they give a sense of mastery of a subject. Serious Christians do not want to be shallow novices. Spirit-filled people yearn to learn and understand.

To take full advantage of the power of momentum:

- Sweat over titles and announce them with enough lead time. Use titles that promise something, stir curiosity, create tension. Do not release all tension and answer all questions before the last sermon.
- As you answer questions in one sermon, raise new questions by saying things like, "Notice that so and so is true, but what about such and such? We'll talk about that next week." Media land calls those "teasers," and they are extremely effective. Plan the series before you begin so you can use teasers effectively.
- Over the course of a series, aim for a pattern of crescendo rather than decrescendo. I am prone to give my best stuff up front and make the first sermon the climax, but then the following sermons simply let the dust settle. Instead, like a novelist writing a mystery, we should plan what tension will be maintained and resolved at what points of the series.
- Tell people who should attend in the future. "If you know someone with an addiction problem, you will want to bring him for the next two weeks." And lest we overlook the obvious, tell people to invite their friends. "Has God been helping you through this series? Who do you know who needs the same thing?"
- Pray. The Spirit of God is the primary source of kingdom momentum.

WIDE RESEARCH

When we study for a series that will last four weeks or more, we have added time, reason, and motivation to research thoroughly our subject. We know our spadework will pay higher dividends.

When preaching through a book like Genesis or Revelation, expanded research is critical. We must make decisions about how to interpret texts early in the book, and we don't want to have to pull an about-face in chapter 20.

David Jackman, a leader of Proclamation Trust in England, says when he decides on a book for exposition, he begins to read it devotionally, and he focuses his side reading on related commentaries. This process begins six months or more before he starts preaching the book.

Bill Hybels says when he takes his month-long summer study breaks, he brings a pile of books on topics he knows he will preach in the year ahead. He culls stories, statistics, and principles.

To take full advantage of wide research:

- Build margins in your preparation.
- Plan for several weeks or months between when you decide on the subject of a series and when it begins (some preachers plan preaching calendars six months to a year ahead). This usually means we will research future series at the same time as we do final study for a current series.
- Plan your research. Once you decide on a series, list the must-read works on the subject. In order to prevent procrastination, set due dates for completion.

PLANNED RESPONSE

Many people will not respond to a significant appeal for action on first hearing. As I recall, one study said the average Christian heard the gospel something like seven times before responding. Urging people at the end of a sermon to pray more may not require much consideration, and people may respond on the first request. But asking people to sign up for a two-week missions trip to Haiti, or to fast and pray for lost neighbors, is another matter.

Series preaching enables us to prepare people thoroughly for a significant response. In the first sermon we can announce the specific commitment we seek during the series. For example, one church I know has a three-week stewardship series every year, and the pastor asks early on that every church member give a percentage of his or her income to the church, and for members already thus committed, to increase that percentage.

After we announce a desired response, we can carefully lay the groundwork and make our appeal for action at the opportune time.

Nevertheless, we may feel that stating the desired application up front will scare people away for the rest of the series. In that case, we can prepare the soil, and then near the end of the series plant the response we want hearers to consider in the weeks remaining.

To take advantage of the significant responses that series make possible:

- Ask for one unfamiliar response.
- Appeal for something specific, concrete, and large.
- Challenge people. If the topic is familiar, like Bible reading, challenge hearers to join a churchwide reading program that aims to cover so-many chapters a day, records progress, uses a buddy system, and so on. A series implies that the subject is important, and so a murky, minimal response is an anticlimax that can trivialize what has gone before.
- Plan application as thoroughly as the rest of the content.

- Arrange content with the response in mind. Know before the series begins what response you will present in every sermon.

REPETITION OVER TIME

For five weeks I have been preaching a series on walking in the Spirit, and I have had one overarching objective: to help people learn to pay attention to the Holy Spirit every day. A stand-alone sermon may have inspired some to attempt that in the following week, but most people probably would soon have changed their focus because of the different application of the following week's sermon, the different topic of the next Christian radio program or devotional reading, the demands of life pressing upon them.

But in this series I repeated my objective weekly, and as the series progressed, I noticed the power of repetition over time. Some who did not pay attention the first Sunday did on the second. Based on conversations, I discovered that those who tried to pay attention to the Holy Spirit grew in their focus and learned from experience. Some have established new thought *habits* as over thirty-five days they have again and again tuned in to the Spirit.

Author Stephen Covey says, "To establish a good habit takes about twenty-one days." Another author says, "Positive change that lasts usually takes anywhere from thirty to ninety days." When I teach something week after week, my people are more likely to apply it day after day, and habits will more likely form that continue after the series ends. Repetition over time is one of the biggest wrenches in the series tool bag.

To take full advantage of repetition over time:

- Make the main application visual with a picture, illustration, or object lesson that you allude to throughout the series. In my series on walking in the Spirit, I asked one man to walk across the room with me twice. One time I looked away from him as we walked, and as a result we did not walk in step. The second time I watched his feet and marched in cadence with him. My point: in order to walk in step with the Spirit I have to pay attention to the Spirit. I acted out that object lesson in two sermons. As the series progressed, I asked, "Do you remember when I walked across the room with Sam? What was the point?" People answered immediately.
- Write memorable, engaging statements that sum up the main application of the series.
- Prepare enough before beginning the series to know what idea and application will take center stage.

Blanket Coverage

The great frustration of preaching stand-alone sermons is that on any given Sunday 25 to 50 percent of the congregation is absent. We preach a sermon "everyone needs to hear," and everyone—especially the one who needs it most—is not there. Series preaching ensures that a higher percentage of the church hears the series theme.

In a series on the book of Galatians, the chief idea was that human performance of moral codes cannot make us acceptable to God; that happens only through faith in Christ. I made that statement in some form in nearly every sermon. After several months of sermons from Galatians, even casual attenders got that principle in their bones.

To take full advantage of the power of blanket coverage:

- For each message, assume this is the only sermon in the series some will hear.
- Find ways to present the key series idea in each sermon.

A powerful sermon series is more than four sermons with a common theme, and it is more than the sum of its parts. A powerful series is a team of sermons that work together. Take advantage of series synergy, and you will multiply sermon power.

Chapter 119

TRENDS IN SERMON SERIES
How they are changing to keep up with the times

F. Bryan Wilkerson

In a recent *New York Times Magazine* interview, three TV executives commiserated over the pressure to come up with a new, blockbuster sitcom or dramatic series. A successful series not only captures a large audience for that time slot, but serves as an anchor show that secures viewers for the entire evening and positions the network in the marketplace. In the words of one of these media moguls, "Everyone's looking for the next *Friends*."

Preaching pastors feel their pain. We're always in search of the next sermon series. For me, the most vexing question in preaching is not, How will I preach this text? but, What will I preach next? Like those executives, we know that an effective sermon series not only captures the attention of the listeners for thirty minutes a week, it breathes life into other ministries and shapes the culture of the church.

Series preaching is not a new idea. I grew up under a pastor who routinely preached his way through books of the Bible or relevant topics, and I have followed his lead from my first days of preaching. But over the past twenty years of preparing preaching calendars, I have discerned several changes in my approach to series preaching.

SHORTER

The length of a typical sermon series has gotten progressively shorter. Forty years ago it was common to spend many months or an entire year in a particular book of the Bible.

When I first began preaching, I settled on three or four major series for the year, allowing wiggle room for holidays and a stewardship message. A series in those days was roughly the length of a school term: about twelve weeks. But somewhere along the way, America's collective attention span shortened, and twelve weeks felt like a long time to talk about anything.

The pace of life continues to quicken, the cultural attention-deficit increases, and things change more rapidly and unpredictably than ever. Shorter series allow us to be more nimble in responding to the changing mood of the nation or to the needs of the congregation. Shorter series also provide frequent entry points

for a transient population, and multiple opportunities in a year connect with a variety of felt needs.

Seeking people are more likely to commit to a few weeks than up to three months. Most of my series now run from three to seven weeks. If I want to cover a book of the Bible, I'll deal with it thematically—pulling out the highlights—or else cover it in two or three installments spread out over a year or two.

SHARPER FOCUS

It used to be that a simple, generic title was enough to capture interest and give a sense of movement through the year. Series titles like The Miracles of Jesus, or The Church in Action (Acts), or Beginnings (Genesis 1–12) worked just fine. Sometimes I would dive into the series not even certain where it would lead. In this age of specialization and consumerism, I find people want to know exactly what they're getting and why it is worth their time.

Packaging the series with clear, compelling titles and subtitles is more important than ever. A dozen years ago I did a rambling series from the Sermon on the Mount entitled simply, Kingdom Living. This time around I called it, The Life God Wants for You, and each week I introduced the listeners to a specific dimension of life in the kingdom of God. Summer in the Psalms was enough to capture attention in the 1980s. In 2001 a similar study became Real Life, Real Prayers.

MORE STRATEGIC

A pastor's goal used to be simply to give a balanced offering of Old and New Testament books, covering the major points of Christian life and doctrine in the course of a year. Now I find myself much more intentional in my series selection, looking to cast vision, reinforce ministry values, and shepherd the congregation strategically throughout the year.

Typically I lead off in the fall with a pacesetting series that casts a specific vision for the ministry year to come. A series from Romans 12–16, entitled Discovering the Joy of Authentic Community, sets the tone and direction for a year in which community-building is a primary objective. As the year unfolds, I'll do a series for each of our four core values—worship, community, discipleship, and outreach—but that first series in the fall gives us momentum in a particular direction that carries us throughout the year.

While we try to be seeker-friendly throughout the year in our worship and preaching, we are especially sensitive to times of the year when visitors are most likely to attend and our people are most likely to bring friends, such as Advent and the Easter season. I usually do a seeker-oriented series for three weeks following Easter, speaking to a felt-need like Faith for Monday Morning or When Life Gets out of Control.

I have found the summer months to be rich with newcomers—people moving into the area or wanting to make a change in their lives—so I preach pre-evangelistically in the summer, often working out of the Gospels or the Psalms. During the Lenten season, I preach devotional texts and themes appropriate to the season, being especially sensitive to nurturing the believers' intimacy with God.

Multidimensional

In recent years we have discovered that sometimes a sermon series can be much more than simply another sermon series. That is, the messages become one of many components in a broader campaign to effect change in the lives of people or the church.

Chapel of the Air pioneered this approach several years ago with the 50-Day Spiritual Adventure, in which a thematic preaching series of eight messages was complemented by daily study guides, small group materials, and learning activities designed to personalize and reinforce the messages from the pulpit. The idea is to engage the congregation on a variety of levels, appealing to multiple learning styles over a long enough period of time to allow real transformation to begin.

We took a multidimensional approach to our pacesetting series this fall. Our vision is for Grace Chapel to become A Church You Bring Your Friends To. This fall we wanted to challenge our people to be building genuine friendships with unbelievers and to be praying for opportunities to invite them to an event at church. In order to accomplish that, we planned a church-wide campaign we called People Bringing People.

In partnership with our evangelism pastor, I laid out a five-week preaching series from the Gospels, looking at stories of what happened when people brought other people to Jesus: Andrew and his brother, the four men who lowered their friend through the roof, Jairus and his daughter (presented as a dramatic monologue), a group of townsfolk who brought the deaf and mute man, and the Samaritan woman bringing her neighbors. Each message was supported by a drama, an interview, or a faith story.

In addition to the Sunday services, we offered a personal study guide with daily readings and action steps. We also custom-designed small group studies that explored the preaching texts and applications in greater depth. A logo for the series reinforced the message visually on the weekly worship folder and on posters and banners around the facilities.

On one of the Sundays, we invited people to go to banners on the side walls in the sanctuary and write the names of people they were praying for, asking God for the opportunity to strengthen those friendships and to invite them to some upcoming outreach events. We made bookmarks available as prayer reminders.

The series culminated in an Open House Sunday in which we encouraged people to bring friends to services designed especially to introduce them to the church. I spoke that day on True Friends, exploring the spiritual dimension of friendships from the story of Philip and Nathaniel. What could have been a simple sermon series became a culture-creating event by engaging the entire congregation in a variety of learning activities.

As the TV executives wound down their conversation, one of them suggested that "the hardest thing to do in show business, by far, is to create and execute a high-quality, successful, long-running television series." They all agreed that the relentless pursuit of the next big thing was essential to their effectiveness as leaders and to the success of their networks. In some measure, I feel the same way about sermon series.

Chapter 120

THE COMPELLING SERIES

An interview with John Ortberg

How do you title individual messages and the whole series to connect with people?

In our congregation titling is very important. The main thing a title needs to do is explain why someone needs to hear this topic addressed. Periodically I look at the religion page in the newspaper for the titles of messages given at various churches. Usually the titles are clever wordplays that make sense if you know the text, but the average person wouldn't have a clue what it means.

I'm going to do a series on the kingdom of God. The title is "If Jesus Ran the World." At the anniversary of September 11 and for other reasons, people are aware of how messed up the world is. That kind of edge between the world as it is and what it might be if the kingdom were realized makes the title interesting. When there's an edge to a title, when there's a sense of tension or you feel as if there could be some controversy here, the title is far more attractive than the bland and predictable. You don't want people to read a title and think, *I expect a preacher to say that kind of stuff.*

So a title has to have an edge. It has to stir curiosity. Should there be an element of promise?

Yes, but tension is the main issue.

A title also needs to have clarity, so that people get the concept. They need to know what the message is going to be about and feel that this is a topic they would like to hear more about.

Even so, it must have an edge. If the title is bland, it suggests to people that the talk is going to be predictable and bland. Why should I come hear this? I've heard it before. If you just say you're going to talk about "Prayer," the average person has heard messages about prayer before. There's no promise in that title that says they're going to learn something they don't already know.

The edge to "If Jesus Ran the World" causes people to think, *Isn't he running the world? Or is he not running the world? How am I supposed to think about that?* It forces you to think about what you assume to be true about God.

For this series I put in three or four hours coming up with titles. I had conversations with numerous people. It took a long time, but there was a huge payoff.

Recently you preached an extended series that was an Old Testament survey. What did you learn?

People's hunger to learn is going up. People want to have a sense they are mastering new material.

One challenge I encountered was when you preach shorter series, there are natural on-ramps to tell folks who haven't been coming regularly that a new series is starting. When you preach a long series, you don't have those kind of natural incentives. You have to work harder to invite folks to come.

How did you handle long portions of text?

I learned the importance of effective summarizing and about the need to be clear with where the sermon is going, so I know how much time to give to various parts of the story. It's like what the Scripture writers had to do when they wrote history for theological reasons. Their theological agenda drove decisions about what material to include, what not to include, and why. I had to decide, How much information can people tolerate? When do they overload?

I was doing one message from the book of Judges, and there was some rich stuff about Samson. But then, because I was trying to go through the Old Testament, I wanted to hit Ruth in the same message. As a teacher and student, I was excited about all the wonderful stuff in there. I felt this need to talk about it all. But I had to force myself to remember if I try to pack too much in, they're going to miss it anyhow because it gets too diluted for them to remember. With a long text, the editing process becomes much more important.

What are the best and worst series you have preached?

Some of the best series are those I learn from and can translate that passion of learning into teaching. For example, I gave a series on the parables and found there had been much study and thought on the subject of the parables since I was in seminary. I was excited about what I was learning and then excited to be able to teach it.

Other great series are those where there's a sense of momentum in the congregation. When a series is clicking, people go from one week to the next saying, *I've got to come back next week because I want to see where this is going.* Those are the best ones.

The worst series are those where I came up with what sounded like a clever concept or metaphor, but there wasn't clarity in how it was going to preach out from one week to the next. Then I got stuck with a series that didn't have logical flow.

What have you learned about connecting sermons in a series?

When there's a sense of momentum and flow, it feels to people as if they are taking a good class at school. If you're taking German, by the end of the class you should feel not that you have heard a series of individual lectures but that you've learned German.

For my series on the kingdom of God, I'll know it has worked if at the end people sense, *I have an understanding of the kingdom, and I have a love for it, and I've learned how to live in it. My mind has shifted. I'm starting to think kingdom thoughts.* That can happen through a series over a period of weeks in a way that can't happen in a single message.

Chapter 121

FIRST-PERSON NARRATIVE SERMONS
Taking advantage of the power of drama and the pull of story

Torrey Robinson

Any preacher worth an honorarium knows the challenge of preaching on Christmas and Easter. How can I add special force to my sermons on these important days and bring some spice to a few other Sunday sermons throughout the year?

I offer one suggestion that has consistently worked for me. At Christmas, Easter, and once or twice during the year, I have my congregation approach the Bible through a first-person expository sermon.

The essential distinctive of a first-person sermon is that we tell the story from the vantage-point of one character in the narrative. For example, the biblical story of Ruth was written from a third-person perspective, in which the unnamed narrator stands outside the story as he tells it. To preach Ruth from a first-person perspective you enter into the story and retell it from the vantage point of Boaz, Ruth, Naomi, or any other eyewitness to what transpired.

First-person sermons are highly effective because they combine the personal presence of drama with the power of story. This makes first-person sermons well-suited for communicating the message of Scripture to audiences who may know *TV Guide* better than their Bibles.

A first-person sermon gains people's attention and holds it. Nevertheless you as the preacher still need to say something significant based on God's Word. But how? To demonstrate how you might go about preparing a first-person sermon, let me show what I did to prepare my Easter message this year.

A first-person sermon starts with either a character or a text. A Scripture passage may suggest an individual, or your interest in a character may lead you to a text. This year I started with a character. I have long been fascinated by Cleopas, one of the two disciples who encountered Jesus on the road to Emmaus. The story raised questions in my mind: Who was he? Where was Emmaus located? How could

Cleopas and his companion spend several hours walking with Jesus without recognizing him? These questions drew me to Luke 24:13–35.

After selecting a text and character, it's time for further study. A survey of several key passages where the character is mentioned may reveal some helpful information about that person. You may consult a Bible handbook, Bible dictionary, Bible commentary, or even books of historical fiction to learn more about your character.

In your study of the text, the main objective is to understand what the passage is talking about, its main idea. In Luke 24:13–35, I found the central idea on the other side of a forest of questions. What kept Cleopas and his companion from recognizing Jesus when he first caught up with them on the road? Since Cleopas and his companion had expected Jesus to redeem Israel, what was Cleopas's understanding of redemption? Why did Jesus disappear when they finally recognized him? What is significant about their recognizing Jesus in the breaking of the bread?

Determining the central thought of a biblical text is often the hardest work in sermon preparation. Narrative passages can make this work especially challenging because seldom does the narrator state his idea directly. However difficult it may be, it is essential to determine the focus of the passage. To tell a story without understanding it is just blowing fog. After some study, I was able to clearly state Luke's idea: *Cleopas came to see that the suffering and death that he thought had disqualified Jesus as Messiah, in fact uniquely qualified Jesus to be the Messiah.*

Once you've grasped what the biblical writer is saying, you are ready to identify your purpose. Why are you preaching this sermon? With a clear purpose in mind, a sermon will have the unmistakable ring of relevance. I wanted my sermon to do three things. First, I wanted non-Christians to see that Jesus' suffered on the cross for their sin. Second, I wanted the congregation to feel the hope of God. Third, I desired for my listeners to have a burning heart experience with Jesus.

Keeping the purpose and idea of the biblical story in mind, it is important to determine the stance of your character in relation to the audience. The character's stance is where he or she stands in time to retell the story. In my Easter sermon, I had to decide whether I would take the audience back to the first century or whether I would bring Cleopas forward to our day.

Determining the character's stance is fundamental to the logic and consistency of your sermon. Where you position a character in time affects what he or she knows about the modern world. If you take the audience back in time, the character speaking in his day would know nothing about our day or many of our contemporary issues.

You may choose to bring the character forward into the present. Given this stance, it seems reasonable that he or she would be at least somewhat aware of the modern world. This stance may make it easier to speak directly to the audience, but be careful. The power of narrative comes in part by its indirect impact. When you tell a story, the audience lets down their guard to listen. If a first-person portrayal is too direct, your listeners may become defensive. What they hear is a thinly veiled sermon.

Whatever stance you choose, be consistent with it. If your character stands in the biblical world, be careful to avoid anachronism. That is, make sure all the references made in the sermon are consistent with what someone in that day would have known. Even if you bring a character forward in time, think through the details. How familiar is this person with our day? Consistency is key.

All this talk about stance may sound like much ado about nothing, but many first-person sermons unravel at this point. Poor attention to stance will either confuse your listeners or frustrate their imagination. Clarity and consistency of stance will significantly affect the believability and ultimately the impact of your message. For the stance of my sermon, I decided to bring Cleopas to the modern world to tell his story.

Now you are ready to state the homiletical or preaching idea. This involves stating the idea of the passage in a way that is relevant to your audience. Here's the homiletical statement for my Easter sermon: *That Easter, when I finally saw who Jesus was, I discovered that it really had been a "Good" Friday after all.* Although this idea is stated from the perspective of Cleopas, I tried to keep my audience in mind with references to Easter and Good Friday.

Now it's time to bring structure to your sermon. There are at least three ways to organize a first-person message. You may choose a chronological, a psychological, or a dramatic structure. Chronological structure follows a sequence of time. You retell the events in the story in the order they happened.

A psychological structure begins the story at a point in time but interrupts the chronological continuity of the story to recount earlier episodes in the character's life. These episodes are not necessarily retold in the order they occurred but in the way they stand out in the character's mind. The episodes within the narrative skip around in time. A psychological structure may prove helpful in tightening the climactic strings of a story.

In the dramatic structure, it may be more helpful to think of the movement of the sermon like the scenes of a play. The book of Ruth is organized by scenes. The opening scene tells us Naomi's dire situation. The next two scenes, in chapters 2 and 3, complicate the situation. Then the final chapter and closing scene resolves the action.

To look at these three structures another way, first-person sermons may be organized either by unfolding events, by psychological episodes, or by scenes. I chose to develop my Easter sermon psychologically.

Once the sermon is structured, you are ready to write a sermon manuscript. A manuscript strengthens a sermon in three ways. First, a sermon manuscript helps to polish wording. Words are powerful. Choosing words well can make a good sermon great. Second, writing the sermon helps make sure that important details in the story are included. Finally, the process of writing forces you to think through the sermon. When you stand up to tell the story, you already know where you're going.

Once you have planned what you want to say, you are ready to think about how you will present it. There are three aspects to the presentation of a first-person sermon: physical movement, delivery, and costuming.

In any kind of sermon—traditional or first-person—our movements communicate. Whether they communicate what we want them to say is determined to some degree by our understanding of movement. As you read through your sermon manuscript, decide where you will position yourself in each scene. Make sure your placement on the stage supports what you are saying.

We must deliver a first-person sermon without notes. Notes get in the way of an authentic presentation. But preaching without notes does not require that you memorize your manuscript. Word-for-word memorizing also hinders an authentic presentation. Rather, try to experience the story as you tell it through the character's eyes. Eye contact, movement, and gestures will all be more natural if you relive the story in your imagination rather than recite a memorized script. Let your vocal and physical response come from within and be appropriate to the character you are presenting.

If you are going to be intentional in your movement and confident in your delivery, then some rehearsal is essential. I try to set my manuscript aside and talk through the entire sermon at least once before I preach. Think through the structure of the sermon. In doing so, it can be beneficial to position yourself on the platform as you picture each scene, episode, or event. If that is not possible, then picture the stage in your mind and imagine where you will position yourself as you talk through the sermon.

Costumes, make-up, and props all deserve consideration as you plan your presentation of a first-person sermon. While a costume is not essential to the success of a first-person sermon, a well-designed costume may enhance your presentation. I own several costumes that have been made for me over the years. In most cities you can rent quality costumes from costume shops. You can use props along with a costume or sometimes in place of a costume, but props can also get in the way.

You may want to consider using make-up if it can be applied effectively and if it enhances your costume. In my portrayal of Cleopas I made use of a beard. I have found that, used wisely, costumes, make-up, and props have the potential to make a memorable sermon unforgettable. At the same time, I can say from hard experience, "If in doubt, do without."

Next Easter, or Christmas, or maybe next month, why not climb into a story and tell it from a first-person perspective. It may just make an average Sunday special or a special Sunday great!

Chapter 122

BIBLICAL PREACHING IS ABOUT LIFE CHANGE, NOT SERMON FORM

If people aren't enabled to respond, something is wrong with the sermon.

John Ortberg

The core value of preaching that changes lives is that it's biblical. You and I don't change lives; God changes lives. For two thousand years, he has used the power of this Word to convict stubborn hearts of sin, to move cold spirits to repentance, and to lift faltering lives to hope.

The question that causes a fair amount of controversy is: What makes preaching biblical?

IT'S NOT ABOUT FORM

Often people think what makes preaching biblical is a particular style or structure. Where

I grew up, people talked about three categories for preaching: topical, often regarded as not very biblical; textual, where the main point comes from a Scripture verse, which was considered more biblical; and expository, which is difficult to get a clear definition of. Expository is a word that gets thrown around a lot. Some people think of it as verse-by-verse preaching, or where points and subpoints are from one text in Scripture.

There are a number of problems with thinking one particular style or structure of preaching is the only kind that's biblical. One problem is Jesus didn't do that kind of expository preaching. Mostly he told stories and the implications for listeners' lives. The apostles didn't do that kind of expository preaching. In the New Testament you don't see any sermon that goes verse by verse through an Old Testament text. I'm not saying that kind of preaching is a bad thing. It's important that people become biblically literate. But what makes preaching biblical is not its structure. To be biblical does not mean the preacher follows a particular form that, after all, human beings created.

IT'S ABOUT RELEVANCE, APPLICATION, AND ENABLEMENT

William D. Thompson, author of *Preaching Biblically*, writes: "Biblical preaching is when listeners are enabled to see how their world, like the biblical world, is addressed by the Word of God." It is important not to be superficial when it comes to what makes preaching biblical. How many Bible verses a sermon has does not determine whether or not it's biblical. You can have a hundred verses in a sermon and misinterpret every one of them. It is not the structure. Biblical preaching occurs when

people listen, are able to hear that God is addressing them as God addressed the world of the Scriptures, and are enabled to respond.

Far too many sermons have lots of information about the Bible but are not really biblical preaching because they do not call and enable people to respond to the Word. There is lots of information about the Bible—exegetical, historical, or theological—with maybe a few applications tacked on the end.

IT'S ABOUT WORKING THE SOAP OF THE WORD DEEPLY THROUGH THE STAINED FIBERS OF HEARERS' HEARTS

What happens when the Word addresses people? In Ephesians 5:25–26, Paul has a wonderful metaphor. He says, "Husbands, love your wives just as Christ loved the church and gave himself up for her in order to make her holy by cleansing her with the washing of water by the Word." The church is to be made holy by being cleansed with the washing of the water of the Word. Why do you wash something? Because it's dirty. What happens when you wash something? Soap and water move through the fibers and lift out impurities from the fabric.

When we and our congregations come before God, our hearts are like that. They are cluttered with false beliefs, attitudes, misguided intentions, and wrong perceptions.

I could tell you what a few of mine are. I'm walking down the street. Somebody wants money. I find myself looking away from him because I don't even want to be reminded of that need, and I don't want to feel guilty by not giving him something. Or I'm at a convenience store in a line of people, and the person behind the counter doesn't speak English well, and my reflexive thoughts are, *I'm in a hurry. Why can't they get somebody that speaks English well around here?* Or another time I'm in church standing next to somebody who's important and the thoughts that run through my mind are, *This is an important person. I wonder what I might be able to say to make a connection because he or she is important.*

Those are just a few thoughts in my mind that are dirty. They equip me for bad works. They make bad feelings and behaviors almost inevitable. Imagine having a mind cleansed of all that. Imagine when you're with somebody, your first thought is to pray for them and bless them. Imagine that if you're challenged, your first thought is to look to God for strength.

That's what it would be like to have a mind washed by the Word, and that's your goal for the people to whom you speak. That's the goal of biblical preaching. The goal is not to get vast amounts of exegetical information into people. My goal is not to get people all the way through the Bible. My goal is to get the Bible all the way through people.

Biblical preaching answers three questions: What must hearers know, feel, and do? To do that I ask three questions. What do I want people to know? What do I want people to feel? What do I want people to do? I think about these questions for every message I preach because if I don't address the mind and heart and will—if I can't answer those questions— then I need not deliver this message because it's not going to wash their minds in the Word.

Your goal is to wash the minds of your people in the Word so that Christ is formed in them. That's biblical preaching.

Chapter 123

SEVEN PRINCIPLES FOR REACHING LOST PEOPLE
How Paul preached to skeptics

Dick Lucas

What does it take to be a preacher to pagans, whether of the religious or irreligious variety? My answer is the ancient patterns are still the best for the modern preacher, as long as they come from the Bible. We find a prime example in Paul's sermon to the men of Athens. One of the happy changes to occur in my lifetime has been the rehabilitation of this great discourse in Acts 17 as rightly a model for today's Christian evangelist. I pinpoint here seven characteristics of preaching, based on Paul's message, that will speak for God in an idolatrous world.

POWERS OF REASONING

Note the verbs Luke uses to describe his hero's preaching. For instance, arriving in Thessalonica (Acts 17:1–4), Paul "reasoned" or "argued" with members of the synagogue on three Sabbaths, "explaining and proving" that Christ had to suffer and rise from the dead. So convincing was his proclamation of Jesus as the Christ that some Jews "were persuaded" and joined Paul and Silas, along with many God-fearers as well as "not a few prominent women." In Acts the Christian converts are often described as the "persuaded"; this is hardly common parlance today.

After leaving Athens, there is no suggestion that the great missionary apostle changed his normal practice. Acts 18:1–4 tells how Paul lodged with fellow tentmakers, plying his trade and presumably paying his way while he made regular visits to the synagogue, where once again he "reasoned" with the people, seeking to "persuade" Jews and Greeks. Acts 19:8 continues the same story, which extends right through to the end of this book, with Paul in a rented house, still "explaining" and "convincing" all but those whose minds were closed and who would never believe (28:23–31).

The old suggestions that "failure" in Athens caused Paul to jettison all intellectual skills thereafter, forsaking rational arguments in his preaching, in order simply to placard "Christ and him crucified" before his hearers, has had a long life—understandably perhaps in the light of 1 Corinthians 2:4 ("not with wise and persuasive words"). But it is the subtle and beguiling persuasiveness based on this world's wisdom, which his opponents were later to use with so much numerical success, that Paul always hated (Col. 2:4).

One textual reading of 1 Corinthians 2:4 inserts "human" before "wisdom," and though this must be accepted as a secondary reading, it exactly makes Paul's point. He would not enforce his proclamation by "the wisdom of the world" (1:20), for by this wisdom no one ever came to a knowledge of God. Of this fact a century of liberal and rationalistic theology, and such preaching as it produces, should finally have persuaded all but those whose prejudices are invincible.

So, whether it was this world's wisdom or this world's ways of persuasion as practiced by the Corinthian superstars (2 Cor. 2:17; 4:2), Paul renounced them both. Nevertheless, since he knew what it was to fear the Lord, he still sought to persuade people (2 Cor. 5:11); this was at the heart of his ministry of reconciliation.

What was heard that day at the Areopagus was emphatically not "the wisdom of this age"; the Athenians knew all about that, but this new teaching was different. Reading Paul's words today, however, we cannot miss the relentless logic, the close reasoning, and the irresistible conclusion. If verses 22–31 record the structure of Paul's sermon, it is marvelously tight, ordered, and clear. The argument, beginning with Athenian ignorance of God, is as follows:

Introduction (Acts 17:22–23)
- I see how religious you are.
- I see how ignorant of God you are.
- I will now tell you of him.

Body (17:24–28)

Paul overturns the ignorant assumptions of his audience with three great denials, after which he builds a right understanding by proclaiming God as creator, sustainer, and goal of all human existence.

Conclusion (17:29–31)
- Their idolatry is unthinkable.
- Their ignorance is intolerable.
- Their judgment is inevitable.
- Thus, their immediate duty is to repent.

Preaching to pagans today demands similar coherent, discriminating outlines that will lead, by sound reasoning, to the refutation of error and the establishment of the truth. The "therefore" of verse 29 is a hammer blow, just because the preceding links in the chain have been so well made. Everyone has been made to think. The fact of Christ can no longer be ignored.

It is not that the language used is sophisticated or complex—the "superior wisdom" of 1 Corinthians 2:1, so loved by the proudly intellectual. Our doctrine of inspiration guarantees that Luke's report accurately mirrors the sort of terminology used. All is straightforward and clear. Luther's maidservants in Wittenberg would have understood every word. It is the conscience that Paul is out to reach—not just the intellect—and plain speaking is necessary in order to reach it (2 Cor. 4:2b).

In a little book on *Pastoral Work*, dated 1890 (written by a previous rector of St. Andrew Undershaft, W. Walsham How), there is a chapter on preaching. It includes the following delightful if unflattering paragraph:

> You cannot believe too firmly in the ignorance of your listeners. Take nothing for granted. Explain what to you seems simple, and do not be afraid of repetition. It is by no means a bad plan to look round your congregation and single out the most dense-looking among them, resolving to do your best to make that particular person understand you.

It seems that this is exactly what Paul did when addressing his distinguished audience in Athens.

DEMOLITION SKILLS

During my time in the city of London, I regularly witnessed the demolition of office blocks. Often these enormous buildings were of no great age or had been newly refurbished. But down they came. What the developer paid his millions for was not the building but the site. So it is in preaching to pagans; the ground is already occupied, religious or irreligious opinions firmly in place. We cannot start to build, as Paul demonstrates in the Athenian sermon,

without first demolishing the old, well-established structures.

In a different context (2 Cor. 10:3–5) Paul describes the weapons with which we fight such spiritual battles. They are not the weapons of this world (as discussed in point one), yet they have "divine power to demolish strongholds." So the preacher, in his special work, must of necessity demolish arguments and every pretension that sets itself up against the knowledge of God.

How effectively before the men of Athens did Paul set about this work of demolition! Consider as two examples Acts 17:24–25, where the apostle's skills in engaging with his Epicurean and Stoic hearers are frequently commented upon. Far more important, however, is the way in which he subverts everything that Athenian religion stood for, with two great negations.

First (v. 24), God does *not* dwell in temples made by human hands. The Greeks had created magnificent structures in honor of their deities, the remains of which modern tourists still see with wonder and admiration. Paul was no wandering tourist, yet he did not deny the costly and beautiful materials, nor the prodigies of imagination and skill that went into these architectural marvels (v. 29). It was Athenian thinking, not craftsmanship, that was all wrong; to create deity in our human image was to turn reality upside down.

Far from living in man-made temples as, for instance, did golden Athena in the Parthenon, the Lord of heaven and earth created this beautiful world, and everything in it, for human habitation. It is he who builds a home for us.

Second (v. 25), God is *not* served by human hands, as if he needed sustaining by his creatures. Yet, round the clock, devoted Greek hands performed their worship obligations to their gods and goddesses at innumerable shrines. It seemed that ceremonies would never cease, nor the hunger of the gods for offering ever be satisfied. If religious zeal is in question, the people of Athens could not be faulted. Yet they have no understanding that it is the true God who has given help to them, as to all men everywhere, sustaining them in existence each moment by every breath and providing for them all things necessary for their enjoyment in the world he has created for them as their present home.

It is a powerful exposition of foundational Bible truths; as such, it destroys finally and forever the claim of religion to bring us near to God. Nevertheless, God is not far from any of us, as the failure of the Athenian religious search had suggested.

Such demolition work, such great denials, are the very stuff of New Testament teaching. We cannot be Christian teachers of integrity if we accept all the apostles affirmed but refuse to acknowledge what they denied. Positive statements are regularly interpreted by negative ones. In the famous John 14:6, for example, to celebrate verse 6a yet disregard verse 6b is to empty Christ's words of their original force, and by implication reject his authority.

"Negative" teaching has a bad press in today's church, yet it is inevitable. For example, in a fallen world where human beings are naturally idolatrous, murderous, and adulterous, the Decalogue is bound to be given in a negative form. We are not to bear false witness, because it is the easiest thing in the world to do.

Just so, sinful men and women naturally think and believe about God that which is erroneous and absurd. Thus the trustworthy teacher must expose and rebuke senseless and false thinking, as Paul did in Athens.

Paul is wonderfully faithful in this unpopular ministry. Do not all men, religious or not, seek to establish their own righteousness? Then Paul must insist that salvation is "*not* of works" (Eph. 2:9), and "*not* because of righteous things that we have done" (Titus 3:5). Such great denials are an indispensable part of the proclamation of God's free grace in Christ.

Perhaps surprisingly, it is not Paul but John, the apostle of love, who is the demolition expert of the New Testament. From the prologue on, with its repeated denials (John 1: 3, 5, 8, 10, 11, 13, 18), John enforces divine truth. Preachers will gain much from a study of this remarkable characteristic running through the entire Gospel of John (for a preliminary crash course, try John 3 on the new birth, or John 6:25–59 on the bread of life).

It is here that acceptable, easygoing preaching falls short. It is agreeable to be known as a "positive" preacher; and if, as my thesaurus suggests, this means "clear, definite, direct, precise, unequivocal, and real," we are right to applaud. If "negative" means harsh, sour, ill-natured, unfeeling, and ungracious, who would wish to defend so distasteful a spirit of bitterness? But in the Christian revelation, there is a no as well as a yes. And if Paul on this occasion in Athens had not been the trusty voice of his Master, neither the Athenians nor we would have heard the shocking truth about man-centered religion and its dire consequences.

FEARLESSNESS

Demolition work of the spiritual variety can never be popular, so it leads us naturally to the third characteristic necessary for preaching to pagans, namely, courage. From the start Paul seems to have been a dauntless ambassador for

Christ (Acts 9:22–27). Soon afterward, debating with Hellenistic Jews in Jerusalem involved risking his neck (9:28–29). Throughout Acts the picture is always the same (13:46; 14:3; 19:8).

As most of us know from experience, speaking out for Christ, especially in hostile situations, is beyond natural resources to sustain for long. We would not be like Peter (Mark 14:31). Or rather, we would be like him after Pentecost (Acts 4:8, 13). According to Acts, it is one of the distinctive ministries of the Holy Spirit to nerve those whose responsibility it is to speak the Word of God (4:31). Regularly this indispensable enablement is prayed for (Acts 4:29; Eph. 6:19–20).

The Greek words used, *parresia* and *parresiazomai,* are of special interest. The redoubtable Bauer-Arndt-Gingrich has for *parresia* the following: "outspokenness, frankness, plainness of speech, that conceals nothing and passes over nothing," as well as "courage, confidence, boldness, and fearlessness, especially in the presence of persons of high rank." This latter clause is significant, for we are easily overawed by the "wise" of this world, the "influential" and those of "noble birth," few of whom pay any serious attention to the gospel (1 Cor. 1:26–31). As for *parresiazomai,* BAG suggests "to speak freely, openly, fearlessly, to express oneself freely." In the contemporary Greek world "free speech" of this order was seen as a presupposition of democracy; it marked a free people and has been prized ever since by those who enjoy its benefits.

But how quickly, under any sort of tyranny, this freedom disappears! So the courage of those many Christian people who have spoken up for Christ under the tyrants of the past century is deeply impressive to us who live in untroubled places. Ought we not to be thoroughly ashamed of ourselves if, with our heritage of freedom, we fail to speak out because of the petty and contemptible tyranny of political correctness?

What then of the speech before the Athenian Court, as a result of which (according to Longenecker) Paul "might either receive the freedom of the city, or be censored and silenced"? Was the apostle's approach tentative and carefully guarded, full of equivocal statements, avoiding clarity that might offend, obscure rather than open on sensitive issues, in the style of modern ecclesiastical negotiators?

Of course not! Words of conspicuous force were given him. He will tell them of what they do not know. Their religious zeal is entirely misdirected. Their ignorance is culpable. Even their own poets know better. The Judge of the whole world has already been appointed, and his appointment confirmed. The call to all men is going out, and proud Athenians are not excepted. Repentance is heaven's command for them, and that without delay.

If this is typical, no wonder Paul so often landed up in trouble. Similar ministry at any time will hardly avoid hostility, and worse. This is Paul's theme in his last letter to Timothy. Everyone is deserting him; only a few brave and loyal friends are standing with him. Will Timothy, too, be ashamed of him and his preaching? Can he be sufficiently strong so as not to disown his spiritual father? A confident answer for Timothy, as for us, is impossible apart from the power of God (2 Tim. 1:8) and the grace that is in Christ Jesus (2:1).

PERSISTENCE IN EVANGELISM

As we have seen, Paul's was an undaunted spirit. However inconvenient the time, however unpropitious the circumstances, he persisted in doing the work of an evangelist (2 Tim. 4:5). Who but this man could have turned a defense of his position, before such an audience, into so direct a call for repentance?

Inevitably there will be resistance. But I am reminded of Charles Simeon's first visit to (Great) St. Mary's Cambridge in 1786 to preach before the University. He was then twenty-five years of age.

> The greatest excitement prevailed on this occasion. St. Mary's was crowded with gownsmen; and at first there seemed a disposition to disturb and annoy the preacher, in a manner at that period, unhappily, not unusual. But scarcely had he proceeded more than a few sentences, when the lucid arrangement of his exordium, and his serious and commanding manner, impressed the whole assembly with feelings of deep solemnity, and he was heard to the end with the most respectful and riveted attention. The vast congregation departed in a mood very different from that in which it had assembled; and it was evident, from the remarks which were overheard at going out, and the subdued tone in which they were made, that many were seriously affected, as well as surprised, at what they had heard. Of two young men who had come among the scoffers, one was heard to say to the other: "Well! Simeon is no fool however!" "Fool!" replied his companion, "did you ever hear such a sermon before?"

> It would surprise me if on that day long ago in Athens none among Paul's hearers reacted rather as did those undergraduates.

The question is often asked as to how adequate this sermon was/is as an exposition of the Christian gospel. "Repentance towards God"—yes—but where is the mention of "faith in our Lord Jesus" (Acts 20:21)? And how do we relate Paul's sermon in Athens to his resolve in Corinth to preach "Christ and him crucified"?

Two possible solutions have commended themselves to me.

(1) If we take Acts 10:42–43 as a standard summary of the gospel, as taught by the risen Lord himself after his resurrection, we get the following pattern:

- v. 42: the apostolic testimony (New Testament), which points forward to the coming of Jesus as the God-appointed judge of all men
- v. 43: the prophetic testimony (Old Testament), which points forward to the coming of Jesus as the Savior of the world, so that all who believe in him escape condemnation at his hand. Our refuge from Christ the righteous Judge is found in Christ the crucified Redeemer.

Logically, then, the "whole Bible" message begins with an announcement of the Last Day, the significance of this for the whole human race, and the name of the one in whose hands our destiny rests. The church's doctrine of salvation makes little sense unless the reality is acknowledged of that final revelation of the "wrath of the Lamb" (Rev. 6:15–17). Man's greatest need is a favorable verdict on that day, enjoyed, by God's grace, in this life (Acts 13:38).

According to this solution Paul was interrupted as he discoursed on "judgment to come," just as, at a later date, Felix stopped him in full flow (24:25). So too did Festus (26:24).

The reference to resurrection aroused vigorous objection and scorn, so that further instruction had to wait until later, when those who wanted to hear more could be told of the divine remedy for sin. This was to result in a few serious learners becoming disciples.

(2) Alternatively, if we take Luke 24 to be a standard pattern of how the resurrection of Christ is to be preached, as in part a vindication of the one who had to suffer (vv. 7, 26, 46),

then it would be all but unthinkable to preach Christ's resurrection from the dead without having explained the unique significance of that death, from which it pleased God to deliver him. Indeed the intriguing factor in Luke's resurrection chapter is the central place that the sufferings of the Savior occupy. It seems that the best evidence for the fact that Jesus is risen today is that "Christ and him crucified" is being preached to all nations.

The one inference we should not draw from Paul's Athenian sermon is that the resurrection, without the cross, was the heart of the earliest gospel preaching. This will not square with the brief summaries of Acts 3:18; 17:3; and 26:23. Nor will it do to ignore the famous "tree" passages (e.g., 5:30; 10:39; 13:29) with the background of Deuteronomy 21:22–23 (see Gal. 3:13).

Paul persisted in preaching the gospel to pagans because he was convinced that it was the power of God for salvation (Rom. 1:16). One of the clearest lessons of Acts is that the Word of God on the lips of his servants is the supreme secret of missionary advance (Acts 6:7; 12:24; 13:49; 19:20).

A Heart for God

John Stott, commenting on Acts 17:16, asks whether we can speak as Paul spoke if we do not feel as Paul felt. It is a helpful reminder. Festus was right to acknowledge Paul's great learning (26:24), but Paul also had a great heart.

At regeneration when we received the spirit of adoption, we were given a renewed heart, from the depth of which we began to cry out "Father, dear Father." Ideally, as Jesus taught, the first desire of our hearts should be that the Father's name be hallowed on earth as in heaven.

Some years ago, a son of Stanley Baldwin (a pre–WWII premier) wrote a book to restore his father's battered reputation—Baldwin had been blamed for complacence in the light of the growing menace of Hitler's military build-up. As I recall it, the title of the book was *My Father—The True Story,* which might well be a fitting title for the four Gospels, indeed for the entire New Testament. To tell that story is the great priority for Christian preaching, so that the devil's lies, spread abroad since the beginning of creation, might be exposed for what they are.

One evidence of a heart for God is a replacement of man-centeredness by God-centeredness in our preaching. The old advice for a young preacher to "preach about God and about twenty minutes" may produce groans for its frequent repetition, but it will not produce groans in our listeners. There is a deep, unrecognized hunger for God, and although the apostles may not have managed the twenty-minute limit, they certainly did satisfy that hunger. Consider how the sovereign purposes of God control Peter's Pentecost sermon (Acts 2:22, 23, 24, 32, 36, 39). The same is true of Paul's magnificent discourse in Pisidian Antioch (13:16ff.). It is the same story in Athens, where every single verse from 17:24–31 centers on God and his relation to his world.

A heart for God, therefore, will also be a heart for lost humanity, and that leads us to the next essential.

A Missionary Mindset

The God of the Bible wants all to be saved (1 Tim. 2:3), and preachers to pagans discover within themselves the same desire. With its repeated emphasis on "all men" (Acts 17:25,

30, 31) Paul's sermon in Athens is very much a missionary sermon.

It may be that this mindset in Paul explains his brief sojourn in Athens. How he made his plans seems to have depended on many circumstances: a night vision (16:9, 18:9), hindrance from the Spirit (16:6), or simply a human desire to see how young converts and new churches were getting on (15:36; 18:23).

But perhaps the commonest reason why Paul moves on to fresh places is because he is compelled to—by opposition. The same is true of the Lord's journeys, where rejection, divinely overruled (particularly in Mark), dictates the pace and direction of advance. So in God's providence, the early Christians were forcibly thrust out of Jerusalem to begin their outward march to Samaria and the end of the earth.

The Athenian sermon was not without fruit; names of a few converts were well known in later years. But the clear impression is that the message and the messenger were not acceptable to the city's establishment. All was done politely no doubt, since the mob did not control policy in Athens. But one suspects that somewhere in the official files Paul's name was listed as persona non grata. So, on to Corinth (18:1).

But here too the same principle applies. Acts 18:6 is important, as a comparison with 13:46 and 28:28 will show. So urgent is the need to reach those who have not heard that the evangelist is not permitted to remain for long with those who will not listen.

The exercise of a settled pastorate does not remove from us the obligation to seek out the lost sheep. The ninety-nine without cannot be left to perish because we are busy at home feeding with the finest of pasture the remaining little flock. This we all know. But it is possible to err in the opposite direction, spending too much time with those who will never listen. Bashing one's head against a brick wall does not seem to be a pattern for New Testament evangelism. When we reach out to people who spend their time doing nothing but discussing the latest ideas (17:21), it is probably time to move on.

After all, God's elect are everywhere to be found, as Paul discovered in Corinth (18:10). They are to be recognized by the fact that they honor the word of the Lord when they hear it (as the fascinating 13:48 makes clear), so that's the place to stay for a while and build up the believers. Rejection by people who don't want the truth is painful of course, and pastors are bound to experience that pain from time to time. But the next move may be different. It was a dark night when Paul was hustled out of Thessalonica, but the next day was one of the brightest in his experience (Acts 17:10–11). Who knows when we might meet some noble souls like the Bereans who are eager for the truth? That's the romance of preaching to pagans.

A WIDE CULTURE

This is a tricky one if disheartenment is to be avoided, since few if any of us can hope to be as well equipped in this area as Paul, Hebrew of Hebrews, Roman citizen, master of Greek philosophy and literature.

So let's start by avoiding exaggeration. The preacher to pagans does not have to be a glutton for pagan culture, especially of the present-day variety. An easily neglected apostolic imperative says, "In regard to evil be infants, but in your thinking be adults" (1 Cor. 14:20). In whole areas of modern life it does us no harm, rather the reverse, to be "innocents." Late night television viewing is not necessary for the preacher, anxious to be relevant. We may be better employed in learning from our forefathers and leaving most modern movies off our schedule, especially since in our ministry we recommend a particularly painful kind of spiritual surgery (Mark 9:43–48).

What matters is wide sympathies and an interest in all things human. In our approach to pagans, the possession of this often makes the difference between success and failure. For then people quickly understand that we are not isolated from the world in which we all live.

So it was not just that Paul could mix it with Epicureans and Stoics, or that he knew their own poets as well, if not better, than they did. It had more to do with his "becoming all things to all men" in order that "by all possible means" some might be saved (1 Cor. 9:22).

Chapter 124

EVANGELISTIC PREACHING IN THE LOCAL CHURCH

How to preach sermons that engage non-Christians

Haddon Robinson

For pastors preaching on Sunday, sometimes it's important to preach an evangelistic message, to lay out to a congregation the central issue of the Christian faith, namely, how does a man or woman come into a right relationship with God through Jesus Christ? It might be helpful to announce to a congregation, "Two weeks from now, if you've got non-Christian friends, folks who are still on the way to faith, have them come. I want the whole service to be devoted to getting across this basic message."

Not every sermon can be, in that sense, an evangelistic sermon, or you'll ignore great truths of Scripture. But sometime, in the course of the year, there ought to be time set apart when you directly address that issue. Even for the Christians who come, it's always good to be reminded. You ought to preach an evangelistic sermon with non-Christians in mind, stated in terms they can understand and illustrated in ways that would be true to their lives.

A second thing you can do as a pastor is, within any sermon, bring in an element of the gospel. For a non-Christian who attends church, the most attractive thing is to get a glimpse of what Christians know and the assurance they have. Several years ago, a friend of mine, who was not a Christian, said, "You folks don't realize how what you have seems so warm and good to those of us who are on the outside." He went on to say, "I think you're fooling yourselves, but you've got to know the most attractive thing you've got is a hope, and all I look forward to is the grave. You have a purpose. You have something to live for. I go to work and come home, but I don't know what I live for. You can't imagine how good that can look to somebody like myself as I get older." Later, this person did come to faith in Christ.

So, often when we're going through the passage and pointing out what Christians have, we need to remind people how you get it. You can bring in the gospel and say, "As wonderful as this is, it can be true for you."

When you preach a sermon specifically targeted to those who are not yet believers in Christ, your purpose is clear: You want to bring people to a point of decision. You can't force that or manipulate them, but they've got to know there's an issue before them and a decision they have to make. I try to speak as I would to a person on the street. I don't want to get theological jargon into it. Also, evangelistic messages should be filled with illustrations. Evangelistic preaching is a good place, if it's natural to you, to use humor, humor that fits your point and advances your argument. I don't want the person to think this is a grim and awful business. I want them to believe I want the best for them.

Then, of course, you are headed for decision. Someone has said, "You haven't preached the gospel until you've given people something to believe." I would add, "something to believe and someone to trust and the need to make that decision." I don't think, as an adult, you ever just drift into faith. As an adult, there comes a place where you cross the line and you have to lay that down.

When I have done evangelistic preaching and we've invited people to bring their non-Christian friends, we hand out cards. Everybody in the church signs the cards, so nobody feels odd. On the cards we have them write their name, address, and phone number, and then they can check either "I trusted Jesus Christ this morning" or "I'd like to know more about Jesus Christ," and then something like, "I'd be interested in a Bible study I can do at home." That's a way for people to say, "I'm opening myself up to somebody talking to me about this issue. You can call me and visit me, and you won't be intruding in my life and space."

In evangelistic preaching, we should use the Bible as much as we can. One of the problems we face in the Bible is passages that raise the right questions but give a difficult answer. For example, a man comes to Jesus and asks, "What must I do to inherit eternal life?" Jesus says, "What is written in the Law?" "Love God with all your heart, soul, strength, and mind, and love your neighbor as yourself." Jesus says, "You keep doing that and you'll live" (see Luke 10:25–28).

That's a great question, but it's not quite the answer I want to give, because the immediate response is, "I can't do that." The question is developed, but the answer isn't there. I could get the answer from Romans 4:5, which says, "To the man who does not work but trusts in God who justifies the wicked, his faith is credited as righteousness." I could show that Abraham, who was a major league saint, never came to God on the basis of what he did.

Sometimes you get a passage in which the answer is given, but you've got to go back and establish the question because the text itself, at least in the immediate context, doesn't raise the question. There are not that many texts in the Bible where you have the question and the need raised and the answer given. You either have to preach a whole book, or you have to tell people what the question is and then show them, from this passage, what the answer is.

But they have to take your word for the fact that that's the question. Most people will. In fact, often when you do evangelistic preaching outside the church, they don't have Bibles, so you can't do exposition the way you might do it for a congregation that's used to doing that.

To get non-Christians to open the Bible and look at it is difficult. They tend not to be able or willing to follow the argument of the passage. I wish I could say you do exposition every time you do evangelism, but I don't think you can do it as well in the light of the people you're trying to reach.

Instead you will have more illustrations to relate to hearers in their world. If you listen to somebody like Billy Graham, that's what he does. He uses some Bible, then he talks about the modern world, some Bible, the modern world. He seldom leaves the modern world for long, because that's where people are. You're saying, "I'm talking about Jesus Christ, who can meet you in the twenty-first century." What I often have to say to people is, "The thing you think is your problem isn't really your problem. It's much deeper than that." I can't make light of their problem, but many of the problems people wrestle with are a symptom of a disease, a rash on the skin. I have to convince them that the problem is in their bloodstream, that there's something fundamentally wrong.

I start with where people are at, but I can't sell the gospel on the basis that it'll make them happier persons. I can't sell the gospel on the basis that it'll give them a well-adjusted life. If they trust Jesus Christ, it can make life miserable. They can get into all kinds of difficulties they wouldn't have gotten into without it. I can't lie to them, but I can tell them there are certain things they can be absolutely confident of when they put their trust in Christ, and that it's worth it. I want to be honest. I want to be a person of integrity when I preach the gospel. I can never represent the God of truth by lying to people. I have to be careful I don't imply something I know isn't going to be true.

Should we use apologetics in an evangelistic sermon? There was a time in which apologetics had great force. I don't think that's as true today. In a postmodern age, to use that cliché, people aren't as impressed with evidences that demand a verdict. That's not just my opinion. It's the opinion of a lot of people who are skilled at reaching non-Christians, who have, in the past, used apologetics. Usually apologetics are more forceful for those who have come into faith, and having come to faith, have all kinds of questions.

Often a church that has small groups, that has warm fellowship, that draws people to an atmosphere of love, has something going for it. People are drawn to that, and then they want to talk about the gospel. People want relationships; they want to know there are people who care about them. When they find that, then they will hear the gospel, but I don't think apologetics is as strong and as needed today as it was twenty-five years ago.

What has taken its place is people telling their story. I'm not talking about the modern theology that you have your story and I've got my story, but there's no great story, no meta-narrative. I'm talking about giving your testimony, what's happened to you along the way. You're telling how coming to trust Jesus Christ has made a difference in your life. When someone hears that story, and it overlaps their story, there's a way in which that can connect. That's truer today than in the past. We've always used testimonies, but today the witness box has an appeal to people because, in a way, that's the way life comes to them.

In an evangelistic sermon, the style of delivery is especially important. When you're trying to reach people in the community, you can't yell at them. The reason preachers yelled a hundred years ago was they didn't have public address systems. If they wanted to talk with a person in the back row, they had to yell so they could be heard. In some traditions, yelling is equal to preaching. But we've discovered the public address system. I can raise my voice, as I might in any conversation when I'm animated, but to shout is counterproductive.

For example, if you are telling me about a recent Chicago Black Hawks game, and four people come up and join us, you'll raise your volume and increase your gestures. But then, suppose a class lets out and thirty people join us, you'll raise your voice and widen your gestures even more to bring them all in, but there will always be a conversational tone about what you're saying. You'll vary the rate and force and pace. That conversational element in delivery is far more appealing to people today.

Chapter 125

FELT-NEEDS PREACHING

How a sermon addresses the real need of the hearer

An interview with Duane Litfin

PreachingToday.com: What's the difference between felt needs and real needs, and how should this distinction affect our preaching?

Duane Litfin: Often there isn't a difference. The felt need is a real need. Our difficulty comes when a distinction is to be made between the felt need and the real need; in other words, when people have a felt need but that's not their real need.

Good preaching speaks to both of them, but sometimes the felt need is where you need to begin. Or you may zero in on the real need and raise it to the level of a felt need. A good introduction will often do that. People walk in on a Sunday morning, and they don't start out with this as a felt need. But by the time you're through with your introduction, you have taken the real need your text is going to speak to, and you have raised it to the level of a felt need. You'd be hard pressed to find a better definition of what an introduction is supposed to do.

In this culture, people are talked into certain kinds of felt needs that bypass what their real needs are. The Scriptures are not speaking to the superficial. They are always speaking to the real needs. We let the text determine for us what the real need is, and then we seek to surface that in our introduction.

Sometimes people speak with derision about felt-needs preaching. You're saying all needs are real needs.

Yes, although there are ways in which, for example, advertisers create false needs to sell their product. The Bible is always dealing with the deep needs people have. Often those deep needs are the most profoundly felt needs of all. Those are the needs we're going after. So I don't disdain the felt need, although we always want to be going after the real need.

C. S. Lewis and others have over the years made a strong point that all of our sinful lusts and desires are really misplaced attempts to answer deep-seated needs. The human is driven by some of those large needs. Again, those are the needs the Scriptures regularly speak to. Our task is to come to the text, to understand at a profound level what needs it's speaking to, and then to help the listener get in touch with that need.

I don't like talking about creating a need. Again, that's what advertisers do. We're talking about bringing it to the surface so it becomes a felt need. If you can bring the need to the surface in your introduction, and then the passage speaks to that need so that by the time you're through, people come away genuinely impacted. They're impacted by the passage of Scripture that is speaking to their needs, and they're reminded again that the Scriptures are relevant to where real life is lived. All of that comes when we think our way through to the needs this truth is speaking to and let the text address that need.

That is a primary goal of a good introduction, but it's hard to do on a consistent basis. People come in with their minds and hearts all over the place. It's hard to corral their thinking and emotions in the space of that introduction and bring it to bear on this particular need, so by the time you're through they're saying, Boy, am I glad I showed up this morning; this is going to speak to me. That's what a good introduction does, but I don't have any illusions it's easy to do.

It's a matter of attention or consciousness. There are all sorts of things going on in my life that I'm not thinking about right now. You begin helping me think about it and raise it to the level of consciousness and focus, and by the time you're through I am genuinely back to feeling that real need. You didn't create it; you simply surfaced it for me in those few moments.

I have sometimes threatened to do an experiment with seminary students where we would take students' sermons on videotape. Then we would take another set of students and have them watch those tapes and evaluate the introductions. We would stand over to the side and watch how many of those student evaluators, once they finished the introduction and accomplished their assignment, would keep watching the tape. If they would think, *My assignment is over, but this is speaking to me and I want to hear what this is about,* that would be the mark of a good introduction.

Is it possible to overemphasize felt needs or not deal with them in a proper way?

It is. Felt needs can distract us because of the misdirection of our society, the pop culture, the advertising. People think they need all sorts of things they don't need, and they are distracted from the things they do need. It's almost a mistake to be asking, What are the felt needs of my audience? and use those as my take-off point. As an expositor, I work the other way around. I come to the text, and I ask, What is this passage saying? What is the truth here? Why does God want us to know this? What is the need in our lives this passage is speaking to? That is the need I'm going to try to raise in my introduction.

I don't start with my audience. I'm big into preaching to needs, but I don't begin with my audience and ask, What are their needs? I start with the passage and say, This is the answer. Now what question might someone pose to me where I would say, "Let's turn to this passage and look what God has to say"? In other words, you let the passage determine what the need is. Then that's the need you raise in your introduction and deal with.

That comes out of a confidence in the profitability of all Scripture. All the *graphai*, all the writings, are profitable for teaching, correction, reproof, instruction in righteousness (see 2 Tim. 3:16–17). God wants to grow us into the people he wants us to be through the sacred writings, through the Scripture. It is God-breathed, profitable for us. Now the question is: Here's a passage. How is this profitable? What needs to be reproved, corrected, and instructed? How do we need to grow in our walk with the Lord? How is this passage helping us do that? What is it speaking to? Why does God want me to know this? When I've answered that question at a deep level, I'll know what to do in my introduction.

I remember a student preaching a sermon on the Gospel of Mark, where Jesus is casting out demons. The student preached a sermon basically on how to cast out demons. When he was through, we began probing what he had done with the text. I asked him, "Do you think Mark was trying to tell us here how to cast out demons?"

He said, "Mmm, no, probably not."

"What do you think Mark was doing?"

"Well, Mark was teaching us about Jesus."

"What was he teaching us about Jesus?"

"That he had power over the occult, the forces of evil, and the universe."

I said to him, "Why didn't you preach it that way?"

He said, "I couldn't think how to apply it."

And I said to him, "How about if we apply it this way: 'Let's all get down on our knees and worship Jesus'?"

And he said, "I didn't think of that."

That's what I mean about felt needs. He's thinking he's got to have some sort of how-to, so he's going to what he thinks are felt needs. Our society has taught him you have to have some how-to, three things to do on Monday morning, whereas the real felt need is to get down on our knees and worship Christ. He was missing the force of the passage and the profound difference it needs to make in our lives.

Should we approach this any differently when we're dealing with non-Christians in evangelistic preaching?

Yes. There are those who do expository evangelism, and I've heard it done. Larry Moyer is a fine evangelist who does expository evangelism. That's unusual. Usually when you're doing evangelism, you are not expositing Scripture. You're dealing with people who have not yet embraced the authority of the Word of God.

When you have a passage of Scripture in front of you, you let the Scripture tell you what need it's addressing. By definition if you move into evangelism, you probably aren't working with a passage of Scripture. Now you're coming with the fundamental issue of the gospel and the human needs to which the gospel speaks. Again, you're letting the message determine the need you're speaking to, but the message in this case is the gospel and the profound need every human being has to come and acknowledge Jesus Christ as Lord and Savior.

So there is a place with unbelievers to first have a subject we're going to talk about, and that subject is going to take us to various texts or a text? Rather than beginning with the text and working backwards, we're beginning with the people and their needs.

Yes. It's a lot trickier when we're talking about evangelism, because I can see doing evangelism and not doing exposition of any passage at all. Billy Graham is famous for saying, "The Bible says... The Bible says..." You're citing Scripture all the way through, even in good evangelism. When you're dealing with evangelism, it's much more legitimate simply to start with where the people are, to capture their attention and say, "I'm going to speak to things you're interested in." But where you're always headed is to make a beeline for the gospel. Just giving them various moralistic messages isn't what their real needs are.

We think of a seeker church model in which the sermon talks about how to have a happy marriage, how to have a happy home, how to raise your kids, how to get your finances under control. You would see these as legitimate doorways that speak to the needs those unbelievers feel right now, and then you would move them in a direction toward the cross, not just toward how to have a happy financial situation. Would you agree with that?

Yes, I would, although that's not preaching as the Bible would talk about it. It's not even *didaskein*; it's not teaching. You're dealing with seekers and unbelievers, and you're giving them a how-to-live-a-more-effective-life thing. It's more a form of pre-evangelism; that is, wooing them toward something, giving them little glimpses into something stronger and better than anything they know.

I think of the Willow Creek seven-step strategy: To build a friendship, give a verbal witness, but early on get them to the seeker service. That's one of the early steps. The goal is to move them toward new community, so they would come to understand the gospel, embrace the gospel, and want to start growing as a Christian. The whole thing you do in a seeker service is early on in this process. It's a form of pre-evangelism rather than evangelism itself.

Chapter 126

PREACHING TO THOSE RIPE FOR CONVERSION

An interview with James MacDonald

At Harvest Bible Chapel you're seeing a lot of people come to Christ. You've had hundreds of people baptized for several years in a row. Before we talk about evangelistic preaching, talk about your view on how churches should do evangelism.

Of course, there are lots of different kinds of churches and lots of different ways to get the good news out. I wouldn't want us in any way to posture ourselves as saying, This is the way to do it—except as the things we're doing are informed by Scripture. I think God has said

some things about the way he wants the good news to be given. I'm mindful, for example, of 1 Corinthians 2:4–5, in which the apostle Paul said: "My speech and my preaching were not with the persuasive words of wisdom, but in demonstration of the Spirit and of power, so that your faith would not rest in the wisdom of men but on the power of God" (NASB).

There's a school of thought that practices getting out the good news by elevating the role of human persuasion in evangelism, in which a lot of the talk about sharing the gospel gets down into nitty-gritty kind of marketing terms, as though we're some sort of eternal Mary Kay. And everyone is strategic about it. Yet as I've wrestled with the Scriptures, I just don't see it that way.

I see proclamation as a supernatural event. I see the conversion of a lost person as a supernatural thing. And I think it comes about in a kind of strange way. The Bible calls it "the foolishness of preaching." You would never go about it this way. You would never stand up and herald the good news. You'd get strategic and "markety," and sort of "how to win friends and influence people," and get real sociological about it. I don't believe that is the biblical model. I think the biblical model is the foolishness of proclamation. There's great power in that, and God blesses that proclamation supernaturally.

I draw a distinction between red apple evangelism and green apple evangelism. I believe the Bible teaches clearly that God uses the circumstances of life to ripen some people to the gospel. There's no point in sharing the gospel with a person who isn't ripe. We would call a person who isn't ripe to the gospel a green apple. Your next-door neighbor, the guy down the street—he is just some guy, and he's not open about it. He's not thinking about God. He doesn't care about God. If you share the gospel with him, he's likely to say, "I don't care about this, I don't need this." He's not ripe to the gospel yet. Only God can ripen a person to the gospel, and he uses the painful circumstances of life to do that in the hearts of the people he's drawing.

When green apples—those people who weren't ripe to the message—came to Jesus, he would say radical things. They'd say, "We'll follow you wherever you want us to go." Definite green apple statement. And Jesus would say, in essence, "Get away from me; you're not ready." But the scriptural terminology he used was,

"Go, sell everything you have and give to the poor" (Mark 10:21). Now, is that really how you come into the kingdom of God, by selling everything you have and giving it to the poor? That's evidence of a person in the kingdom, but that's not how you get in. So what Jesus was really doing was revealing to the green apple that he was, in fact, green.

Jesus would say, "Foxes have holes and the birds of the air have nests, but the Son of Man has no place to lay his head" (Matt. 8:20). Christ would hold the cost up to the green apple, and then the green apple would walk away. When we pull the cost out of the gospel, we are in great danger. When we are so interested in appealing to people and meeting them on their level—"felt-need" evangelism—what we're really doing should be subtitled, "How to fill your church with tares." What we're doing is filling our church with green apples—all the while all around us are hurting people who are desperately looking for something else, people whom God has ripened to the gospel. In our church we teach our people to go out in the world and look for the people God is ripening to the gospel.

A lot of our approach to evangelism today is that we want to reach the people we want to reach. Instead of looking for the people God is breaking down and bringing them to a place of humility, where they can accept the powerful message of the cross of Christ, we want to reach whom we want to reach. Jesus went to the down-and-outers; we're a lot of times—and certainly in suburbia—looking for the up-and-outers. That's just not where the gospel is penetrating.

So what we've done is built a philosophy of ministry that will allow us to get green apples in and out of church without offending them, and we call that evangelism. Eventually some of those green apples get ripened to the gospel in

God's sovereignty, and they come to know Christ. We praise God for every one of those decisions. But we could be seeing far more conversions if we skipped the dog and pony show and just went straight to the heart of the matter, which is reaching people whom God's trying to reach with a bold proclamation of truth. Red apples. They're ready to hear the good news.

When they hear it, it's a wholesale response?

It is! It's phenomenal. You just can't believe the responsiveness in the hearts of people when they hear the good news. They're looking for something. Like the person who found the pearl of great price, they are ready and willing.

We work hard at speaking directly to people in a language they'll understand in a simple way. Our church's Bible teaching radio ministry has as its theme: Igniting passion in the people of God through the proclamation of truth. The power is in the proclamation. That's what the Spirit energizes and uses.

There's a great move coming back in the church to the power of proclamation. Stand up and get your head filled with truth, get your heart filled with passion, and speak for God. So that when people have forgotten what you said this week or last week or next week, when they've forgotten the details of the sermons, they'll remember that here's a place they can go to hear from God. That's when we and our personality fade out of the picture, and God becomes the One who is lifted up in that Sunday morning worship context.

How often do you preach with unconverted people solely in mind?

I believe the church is for believers. We don't have an evangelistic service, per se. We encourage our people to bring their nonbelieving friends. We believe, as 1 Corinthians 14:22–25 says, that there is evangelistic power in a red

apple, in a person ripe to the gospel, who observes sincere, Spirit-filled, passionate worship. That is a powerful evangelistic message. We see the proclamation portion of the service as part of the worship.

One of the pillars of our church from the very beginning was preaching the authority of God's Word without apology. We believe God is at work in this world, and God is looking to get people to places where he knows they're going to hear his heart. We believe that if God in his sovereignty brings some people to this place, they're going to hear his heart. And if God's trying to reach that person, then we're going to get the privilege of partnering.

So to answer your question specifically about the gospel: We preach Christ every weekend. It would be seldom that we don't have the gospel in whatever passage of Scripture I'm teaching. But our "target," as people like to say, is the believer. We're building up the believers, as Ephesians 4:11–16 commands us to do. Once every month or every other month, we'll lead in a sinner's prayer. We don't often give a public invitation, though sometimes we do. And we have concurrent new believers' classes running, to which we funnel people who have made decisions for the Lord.

Maybe once or twice a year I'll dedicate a whole service to the proclamation of the gospel. I did that this year at Christmas. I preached on John 3:16 on a Sunday morning.

I'll never forget when a lady in the church wrote me a letter. I didn't like what she said, but she was right. I had preached a message from somewhere in the Pastoral Letters talking about the roles of men and women and the roles of employers and employees. She wrote me a letter and said she could have heard the same message in a Muslim mosque. It was just behavior teaching, and I didn't preach Christ.

After I was done being mad at her, the Lord pursued me about that. And the more I thought about it, the more I saw she was right. I made a change, and I think God's used that.

When we talk to unbelievers, how direct or indirect should we be?

Preaching is truth communicated through personality, and we all have different personalities. I see three preaching types:

The shepherd preacher has a predisposition toward comfort, encouragement, and mercy. The shepherd preacher brings emotional support and encouragement for the discouraged. I celebrate that.

The teacher preacher has teaching gifts and brings enlightenment and understanding for the mind. This preacher is able to explain things, to make them clear and understandable.

The prophet preacher is more in line with my giftedness. While the teacher preacher addresses himself to the mind, and the shepherd preacher addresses himself to the emotions and the place of encouragement, the prophet preacher addresses himself to the will.

All these are important. How direct you are in your preaching will relate to the gifts God's given you. I believe, however, that whether you're a teacher or a shepherd or a prophet in your primary giftedness, the biblical model is boldness. Whatever your message, the biblical model is boldness. It's clear in the early chapters in Acts. The people took note of the apostles because they were bold. They were beaten and threatened, and they went back to a prayer meeting and said, "Lord . . . enable your servants to speak your word with great boldness" (Acts 4:29). Paul said in Ephesians 6:19, "Pray also for me that whenever I open my mouth, words may be given me so that I will fearlessly make known the mystery of the gospel." Now

what could be any clearer than that? God is not looking for messengers who mince words and beat around the bush. People shouldn't think, *What's he really trying to say?* With boldness, that's not a problem.

Some people are going to walk away from our messages and think, *I don't like that; I didn't want to hear that.* Well, they walked away from Jesus' teaching and said, "This is a hard teaching. Who can accept it?" (John 6:60). And I've told our young pastors here at the church that if we don't have people walking away from our ministries saying, "This is a hard teaching; who can accept it?" then we don't have a ministry like Jesus had. Remember when Jesus turned to the disciples and said, "You don't want to leave too, do you?" And, of course, they were the red apples. They said, "Lord, to whom shall we go? You have the words of eternal life" (John 6:67–68). Those are the people preachers are trying to reach.

So I believe strongly in a bold, direct proclamation of truth within the framework of your giftedness.

Do you regard yourself as an expositor?

Yes. The great commitment of my life is the teaching of God's Word. But I'll tell you what. If you can't get from your passage to the cross, then you don't understand the passage yet. There's been great things written lately on Christ-centered preaching. Those are good books, and they bring an important balancing statement.

When I'm speaking into people's lives, I don't just expound the text. I don't believe in "break the bread and close in prayer." You need to be just as conscientious about your application preparation as you are about your interpretation preparation. When the preacher goes into the pulpit—not just with an understanding of

God's Word but with an equally clear understanding of where this penetrates the life of the listener and what the listener's genuine needs are that this truth about God meets—then it's not hard to get from that point to helping them see that maybe they're not willing to receive this truth yet. You can at that point share that maybe they've never made that first-time decision to turn from their sin and to embrace Christ, whom to know is life eternal. And—boom—you've just moved right into the gospel.

That resonates not just with unbelievers—that's the great blessing—the preaching of Christ is a blessing to all who know him. And when you really love the Lord, you're never tired of hearing that message. I think pastors need to be encouraged to keep on speaking the gospel.

You said you don't give many altar calls. Is that true?

Well, we don't often invite people to come to the front in response to a gospel message. I have a different perspective on that. I believe the real coming to the front is in baptism. That's going public. I know from the parable of the sower that there are four professions for every genuine conversion. I think sometimes walking the aisle can tend to promote shallowness, in that some people haven't really wrestled with the gospel. But I'm not opposed to coming forward.

The way we use public invitations in our church is that we'll frequently invite people to come to the front for prayer and to be ministered to. We leave it open also for anyone who has questions. But I just don't ascribe to that historic, hard-sell, heavy close: "Here comes the gospel. Did you pray that prayer? If you did, raise your hand. If you did, please stand. Now that you're standing and you don't have any way out, please come to the front. If you walk the aisle, you really meant it."

We certainly promote crises, but we don't necessarily look to collect and count all those at the point of decision. We do, however, offer many ways for people to access Christ. We say, "If you've made this decision today, you could do this or this or this after the service is over." We believe if the heart was genuine, there will be a desire to do that.

Chapter 127

HOW TO PREACH BOLDLY IN A "WHATEVER" CULTURE

An interview with Greg Laurie

What is bold proclamation, and what is it not?

Bold proclamation is not speaking loudly, with more emotion, or even with more passion. It means working through Scripture, rightly dividing it, and then bringing it with unction from the Holy Spirit.

Some preachers try to study for insight, while others pray for passion. Bold proclamation is finding the balance between the two. A bold proclaimer gives the listener a lot to think about, but he delivers it with an energy that keeps listeners engaged.

Bold proclamation shows the relevance of God's Word to what the culture is grappling with, and it does not cower. It is uncompromising in stating the truth. The classic example of a bold proclaimer is Paul on Mars Hill in Acts 17, where he assessed the local culture, understood the philosophy of the day, and then tactfully but powerfully brought the message of the gospel.

So bold proclamation needs to be tempered by knowing the audience?

Very much so. In Acts 2 Peter addressed a people conversant with the Scriptures, and in Acts 17 Paul proclaimed to a largely pagan culture. Their gospel was the same, but their ways of presenting it were different.

How is proclaiming boldly to believers different from proclaiming boldly to an unbelieving audience?

When we proclaim God's Word to the church, we need to trust the authority and inspiration of Scripture and not in any way feel we are "trying" to make the Bible relevant. Rather, we understand it is relevant. Everything we need to know about God is in its pages. We can step into the pulpit with boldness and confidence because of the sufficiency of Scripture. We are just letting the lion out of the cage.

I once asked Billy Graham, "If you knew as a young preacher what you know now, how would your preaching have been different? Would you have emphasized something more?"

Billy looked at me with those steely blue eyes and said, "The cross of Christ and the blood. That's where the power is."

Paul said when he preached the gospel to the Corinthians he wanted to know nothing else except Jesus Christ and him crucified, and then he warns us not to shroud the message of the gospel with flowery words or human wisdom (1 Cor. 2:1–5). We can deprive the gospel of its power when we try to add to or take away from it. The cross resonates with energy when it is proclaimed in its simplicity.

What else weakens proclamation?

The first thing that comes to mind is a fear of offending people. We cannot let the cultural mythology of moral relativism and the mandate of tolerance water down the gospel. We have to believe that Jesus Christ is the only way to God, and we have to say that sooner or later.

We also have to beware of preaching through too much personality. People are looking for a preacher who is confident, who can hold their interest—those are assets—but also for an authentic person, not a pulpit personality. Many unbelievers are turned off by preachers with exaggerated inflections, dramatic speech, and an on-stage persona. I want to show instead that I'm a real person with the same struggles as everyone else, but God is changing my life through his Word.

Would you agree that many people associate bold proclamation with flamboyance?

Yes, but I don't advocate flamboyance. Nor do I advocate dullness. I advocate biblical accuracy coupled with an attempt to engage the audience's interest and hold it. That can be done in the same tone of voice I normally speak with. Instead of focusing on my performance, I focus on my listeners.

For example, I watch for signs that I'm losing people: watch-checking, fidgeting. When that happens, I shift gears with an illustration or a touch of humor.

How else can the preacher keep unbelievers engaged with the bold proclamation of Scripture?

When Paul was on Mars Hill, he began by saying, "Men of Athens! I see that in every way you are very religious" (Acts 17:22). He was building a bridge to his audience. I likewise put a lot of preparation into my introductory remarks to build bridges.

We also have a great responsibility to preach in a way that people can hear. We, like Paul, have to speak in the language of the people. Today when I speak outside my congregation, I no longer assume my listeners know biblical terminology. So instead of saying, "You need to repent and give your life to Christ," I say, "You need to repent, which means doing a U-turn in the road of life, to turn away from how you've been living and toward Jesus Christ."

Do preachers have to frame their sermons within the philosophy of the current generation—postmodernism, for example?

Yes and no. We do want to use terminology that people understand and show how it applies, but we cannot change the message to cater to an incorrect worldview. Instead, we need to reeducate people to a biblical worldview.

People develop an appetite for what you feed them. If you cater to their non-Christian viewpoints, you strengthen those views. Rather, I try to bring them to a new place.

On Mars Hill, Paul acknowledged their worldview, their worship of an "unknown god." But then he told them their view was missing the good news of a knowable God. This God, he said, "I am going to proclaim to you."

Chapter 128

PREACHING WITH A LEADER'S HEART
Both roles require our best

Jim Nicodem

I'm a senior pastor, and that makes me both a preacher and a leader. There is such an emphasis being put on the need for a pastor to be a leader that the preaching role is being diminished in its importance. I understand where this is coming from. Seminaries tend to produce preachers; then they go out into the real world of pastoring a church and discover that a lot is demanded of them as leaders, and many pastors feel ill-equipped for that task.

LEADERSHIP AND PREACHING ROLES

I agree there is a need to raise the bar on the leadership emphasis. It doesn't hurt to try and move those in pastoral positions in the direction of being better leaders. I do believe there's a danger that it has subtly begun to diminish the importance of the preaching role. It almost forces a dichotomy in our thinking: Are you going to be a leader or are you going to be a pastor? You can't do both well, so you have to choose which you're going to gravitate to.

The second danger is that in trying to focus on leadership and shore up one's leadership abilities, there is the potential for neglecting God's Word. This is not only something that gets neglected in the preparation for Sunday's sermon, but by giving oneself to leadership and organization building, you can crowd the Word out of your own personal life and not make the time that's needed for it.

I probably lean toward preaching more than leadership, but in my gift mix they run neck and neck. My greater passion is preaching, and leadership is something I do to give myself permission to preach. But there is a constant tension. I've talked with my leadership team, my elders, about this on a regular basis, saying I am feeling pulled in two different directions. I feel as if I've got two full-time jobs. But, to be honest, both are necessary. I don't see how I can give up either one. I have to figure out a way to do both well because biblically we are called to do both.

Some might think, *Why live with this tension? Just gravitate toward whichever one you want, and let somebody else do the other.* I don't think you can separate the two. In Acts 6, the early leaders of the church are presented with an administrative problem, and they delegate it to others. The core leaders of the church say: Our primary responsibility is in the Word and prayer, and that's what we have to give our attention to. So they're leaders, they're point people for the church, and yet they have this responsibility to be guardians of the Scripture and teachers of it.

LEADERSHIP TASKS ACCOMPLISHED THROUGH PREACHING

The first leadership task that I accomplish in the pulpit is diagnosis. I see myself as a doctor of the church, trying to figure out what my church needs from me, where we are at as a congregation, what attitudes need to be corrected, what challenges we need to face. As I diagnose where my church is, I direct the emphasis of my preaching in that direction. Because of that, when I go to preach that same message in another context, almost always I have to redo the message. If I'm doing a family camp in the summer and then I go to preach in Moscow, I have to rework that message. Even if I preach it to another suburban congregation, I have to redo it, because I have taken a passage and directed it toward the needs and the challenges we face as a congregation.

A second leadership role I'm able to address through my preaching is vision casting. We as a church have a mission. It's not original to us, but it's carved in the cornerstone of our church: "To know Christ and to make him known." We play that out through four megagoals:

We want people to experience the *Master*, to come to a relationship with Christ.

We want them to grow in *maturity*.

We want them to discover their *ministry* in the church.

We want to engage in the *mission* of getting the gospel to the world.

As a preacher, I tend to preach seasonally along the lines of one of those four *m's*. For example, the last ministry season was on that second *m*: maturity. We did three or four series throughout that ministry season, but they were all geared to people growing in maturity.

A third component of leadership in the pulpit would be that you have to reiterate some themes again and again. The most obvious is stewardship. Every pastor knows stewardship is part of leading, seeing the resources come in to make ministry happen.

You can do it in several ways. We've done it as a series. Typically in the course of a ministry year, we'll have at least one series on a stewardship topic. It's also done within a series. If you're doing a topical series on disciplines of the Christian life, stewardship can be one of those messages. Or if you're doing a parenting series, teaching your kids how to be good stewards of the things God has entrusted to them can be one of the messages. Or, within a message itself, there may be an opportunity for a stewardship illustration: "Now let me illustrate this point with . . . ," and you can give an illustration on someone who gave a generous gift to the Lord's work. So you take a theme like that, and as a leader you're constantly thinking, *How do I work that through my preaching?*

Evangelism is another issue I emphasize to build the corporate body, because evangelism is one of those primary focuses of a church that get "backburnered" easily. Before you know it, you've taken your eyes off the fields that are ripe for harvest, and you're no longer making a priority out of reaching lost people. So at every turn I'm working in evangelism. I'm using illustrations that tell of a recent contact I had with a spiritually lost person and how I directed him or her to the gospel. We also work in evangelism series.

There are other corporate issues I gravitate toward. One of our *m's*, as I said, is discovering your ministry. So this fall has been given to helping people find their way out of the grandstands and onto the playing field. That is a corporate emphasis—how people discover their giftedness and employ it in service within our church. We did a series called "It Takes a Team to Win a World," in which we looked at half a dozen spiritual gifts and how they contribute to building a successful team.

Still another quality is motivating. As a leader it's my job to motivate the troops, and that can be done best through preaching. If you're excited, if you're enthusiastic, if you're highly motivated about the things God's teaching you, that will come through in your teaching.

As a leader you have no more important role than to be a model to the flock, and that comes through in your preaching. As you work in illustrations of how you've put into practice the theme from the Scripture that day, the congregation sees that you're a person who lives it. That is both an important preaching and an important leadership role you play.

When you put leadership and preaching together, you have a double whammy. You have a great impact, because the person who is doing the communication is leading, and the person who is leading is doing the communication.

Chapter 129

CRITIQUE OF THE NEW HOMILETIC

Examining the link between the new homiletic and the new hermeneutic

Scott M. Gibson

The new homiletic is new in that it turns away from traditional preaching and the kerygmatic preaching of Karl Barth. The first concentrated on the transmission of an idea, while the second focused on mediation (Lowry, 1997, p. 31).

The new homiletic has its roots in the hermeneutical work of Gerhard Ebeling and Ernst Fuchs. For them, the alleged separation between the theology of the pulpit and the people in the pews was a threat to preaching. Both writers insisted on practical relevance in today's world (Ebeling, 1966, p. 15). How does language, particularly the language of the Bible, hit home to the modern listener? How may its words reach through the preacher's own understanding so that when they are repeated, they will be the listener's words? How may the Word of God become a living word which is heard anew? (Thiselton, 1986, p. 78).

The emphasis on practical application as opposed to a biblical proposition has connection with the work of Rudolf Bultmann, who asserted that the risen Christ comes to listeners in the words of preaching and calls men and women to faith. The desire was for the gospel to speak anew to the listener, to speak a new world into existence. Along with philosopher Martin Heidegger, Bultmann held that language itself is an interpretation and therefore cannot be understood in reference to ancient texts as somehow embodying objective truth. Under-standing is existential, involving a "hermeneu-tical circle" in which the self and the text come together in daily life (Thiselton, 1986, p. 90).

This means that the preacher does not simply restate the text but says it in a new way for the new situation because the language of the text can at times obscure the meaning of the text. One need not paraphrase the text into the present, but one must interpret the text and the present situation and then attempt to merge these two "horizons" in what Fuchs called a "language-event" (1964, p. 196). Ebling used the term "word-event" (1966, 28–29).

Both Fuchs and Ebeling had been pastors for several years where relevance and effectiveness in preaching was tested. Fuch's central question was, "What do we have to do at our desks if we want later to set the text in front of us in the pulpit?" Therefore, the key question in the new hermeneutic was, "How does the New Testament speak to us anew?" (1964, pp. 196–206).

The connection between the new hermeneutic and the new homiletic cannot be overstated. Ebeling and Fuchs gained inspiration from Bultmann's perspective that people today can understand the Bible as a word addressed to *them*. They were also influenced by the work of Friedrich Schleiermacher and German philosopher Wilhem Dilthey, father of modern hermeneutics. Schleiermacher strove to inter-pret the Bible and Plato in terms that would be meaningful to modern people (Randolph,

1969, p. 17). As philosopher Heinz Kimmerle observes: "The work of Schleiermacher constitutes a turning in the history of hermeneutics. Till then hermeneutics was supposed to support, secure, and clarify an already classical understanding [of the Bible as theological hermeneutics; of classical antiquity as philological hermeneutics]." In the thinking of Schleiermacher, hermeneutics achieves the qualitatively different function of first of all *making understanding possible* and deliberately *initiating understanding* in each individual case" (Thiselton, 1986, p. 82).

The new hermeneutic is further expressed in the way reality and language are understood (Ebeling, 1967, p. 15). The impact on homiletics is profound. The new homiletic introduces a new way of listening to the Bible, a new way of understanding reality and the expression of this new reality in practical situations, and it suggests a new way of understanding preaching. The central concern is not what a sermon *is*, but what a sermon *does* (Randolph, 1969, p. 19). There is a shift from traditional homiletics based on determining the original meaning of the text, to the sermon as a speech-event that discloses its meaning through its relationship to its context, to the faith, and to the listener and community. The sermon is seen as an event or experience.

As the new hermeneutic advocates, the new homiletic has given much attention to the parables. Ebeling was interested in the person of Christ and observed Jesus' ability to arouse in his followers the certainty to meet all of life's situations.

David James Randolph coined the term *new homiletic* and formalized the teachings of Ebeling and Fuchs in his 1969 landmark book, *The Renewal of Preaching*. He defines the new homiletic as follows: "Preaching is the event in which the biblical text is interpreted in order that its meaning will come to expression in the concrete situation of the hearers" (p. 1). Randolph further remarks:

> The sermon is becoming understood as *event*, and event means encounter, engagement, and dialogue: the end of "monologue" in the pulpit. Preaching as a one-man affair is a thing of the past, to be replaced by that kind of participatory experience in which those present know themselves involved, even though only one man may be vocalizing at the time. The sermon is being understood as event, and the consequences of this are beginning to be understood in a new way. (p. 14)

Some of the key advocates of the new homiletic—with similarities and differences—include Fred Craddock, David Buttrick, Eugene Lowry, Charles Rice, Edmund Steimle, Morris Niedenthal, Richard Jensen, Lucy Rose, Thomas Troeger, and Henry Mitchell. A few are highlighted below.

Following Randolph was Fred Craddock, whose 1979 book, *As One Without Authority*, further expanded the possibilities of the new homiletic. Craddock's background in New Testament was influenced by Bultmann (p. 42). On a sabbatical at Tübingen he studied under Ebeling. Later he was put onto the writings of Søren Kierkegaard (Craddock, 1990, pp. 6–14).

Like Ebeling and Fuchs, Craddock's concern was "not of understanding language but understanding through language," (1979, p. 42). He further states: "In this encounter with the text, the Word of God is not simply the content of the tradition, nor an application of that content to present issues, but rather the Word of God is the address of God to the hearer who sits before the text open to its becoming the Word of God. Most importantly, God's Word is *God's Word* to the reader/listener, not a word about God gleaned from the documents" (p. 114). Preaching is an experienced event.

For Craddock, the preacher and the listeners are cocreators of the sermonic experience. More important than imparting knowledge, the sermon seeks to affect an experience by cultivating the surprise of the gospel through the preacher's ability to embed the experience in the familiar world of the congregation. Craddock's shadow in the field of homiletics runs long. His emphasis on induction, plot, and movement in the sermon has inspired preachers in their conception and practice of sermon structure.

David Buttrick advocates the phenomenological approach (1987). His concern is what happens when language in a sermon interacts with the consciousness of listeners. Buttrick asserts, "Homiletics can emerge from the objective/subjective split in which it has been trapped—either objectively rational or subjectively romantic—by moving toward the notion of consciousness where objective and subjective meet" (1994, pp. 88–104). His sermon style consists of a sequence of five or six plotted ideational units culminating in a conclusion. This sequencing is called movement.

Like other new homiletic advocates who embrace movement, Eugene Lowry emphasizes what he calls "the homiletical plot" (1980). Lowry also views the sermon as an experience. He comments, "As evocative event, the sermon's sequence follows the logic of listening, not just the consistency of conceptual categories" (1997, p. 59). His intention is the ordering of experience within a narrative plot.

These representative examples of the new homiletic strategically do not announce a conclusion. Instead, there is an intentional delay of the preacher's meaning. As Randolph underscored, "Preaching is understood not as the packaging of a product but as the evocation of an event" (p. 19). These preachers rely on plot, induction, experience, imagination, performative language, metaphor, story, narrative—but evocation of an event or encounter is key.

The influence of the new homiletic in later twentieth century and early twenty-first century preaching is widespread. Although there are different expressions of it, the common feature is sermon as experience.

PRESUPPOSITIONS OF THE NEW HOMILETIC

1. The Interpreter and the Text

The interpreter realizes that he or she comes to the text with presuppositions. The text is not considered to be the object with the interpreter as the subject. Instead, the interpreter is himself or herself the object of interpretation. The text then is spoken into and creates the community of faith. The center of authority does not lie in the text but with the listener or listeners in the context of community. Authority, then, is not located in a particular place but rather in the relationship between the preacher, the text, and the congregation.

Some advocates of the new homiletic appear to dispense altogether with the use of the biblical text: "We must not say that preaching from Scripture is requisite for sermons to be the Word of God" (Buttrick, 1987, p. 458). Certainly there are varying views of authority within the new homiletic. This perspective leads to the second presupposition.

2. The Superiority of the Self

The emphasis on application has caused a shift from the objective use of the Bible to the subjective. Craddock argues, "It is, therefore, pointless to speak of the gospel as Truth in and of itself; the gospel is *Truth for us*" (1979, p. 71). As one observer astutely wrote: "The belief that preaching, created by the living Word of Scripture, may itself under God's sovereign grace become God's Word can only be sustained by an existential impression and response which is *auto-pistic* or self-validating" (Woodfin, 1970, p. 411). In light of the first two points, the final presupposition is as follows.

3. The Authority of Experience

Whereas in classical homiletics the preacher brought the meaning and application of the text to the congregation, in the new homiletic the listeners and preacher together create the experience of meaning. One advocate boldly states:

> One of the reasons we must alert our eyes to keener sight and feel the bodily weight of truth is that if we do not ground our sermons in the actuality of experience, the authority of what we say will be suspect. Appeals to the Bible or tradition do not carry sufficient weight in themselves. (Troeger, 1990, p. 122)

Yet there are those in the movement who are not afraid to critique it. One new homiletician reflects on the new hermeneutic and observes, "The movement came and went with startling dispatch. Probably the fatal flaw was a lurking assumption—namely, that the gospel addresses human beings in their existential self-awareness" (Buttrick, 1994, p. 101). Another comments: "The real question comes: Is Word-event really happening? What appeared to be a most promising homiletical theory has not produced, in spite of all the scholarly care that has gone into its formulation, a significant new movement in preaching" (Skoglund, 1967, p. 57).

The emphasis on experience certainly raises questions about the movement's dependence on the modern liberal paradigm and presuppositions.

WHAT EVANGELICAL PREACHERS CAN GAIN FROM THE NEW HOMILETIC

1. We Benefit from an Emphasis on Language and Its Evocative Nature

The interest in language prominently featured in the new homiletic gives rise to the limitations of literary criticism. If one embraces literary criticism's emphasis on the multivalence of texts, preachers may be uncertain about controls in interpretation while one attempts to keep interpretation in line with the text itself. In addition, the new hermeneutic manifests a one-sided view of the nature of language and places emphasis on language that is imperatival, conative, and directive as opposed to the language of description or information.

Evangelicals can benefit from this shift concerning the use of language in the sermon—the language of the biblical text and the language used while preaching the sermon. Being aware of the nature of the language of the text and its mood as reflected in the sermon will enhance one's preaching.

However, the preacher must be aware that behind the emphasis on language in preaching advocated by the new homiletic is a presupposition about the nature of Scripture. No longer is the Bible considered to be the objective authority. Instead, inspiration is shifted to the actual preaching/hearing of the spoken word. Whereas evangelicals regard the Bible as the revelation from God, the God-inspired Book, advocates of the new homiletic emphasize the preached word as event/experience with the listener encountering God in the spoken word. This understanding raises serious questions about the nature of inspiration and biblical revelation. In addition, this perspective limits sermonic language as primarily a symbolic expression of experience.

2. We Benefit from the Conception That a Sermon Is a Movement, a Plot, or "Plotted"

This way of looking at sermon design allows the preacher flexibility and variety that otherwise might not be considered when constructing a sermon. Related to movement is induction. Induction is arguably the way in which the parables and some sermons chronicled in the New Testament were preached. Keeping inductive sermon structure in mind—especially when the passage selected is inductive—will keep the preacher from the rut of habitually preaching deductively shaped sermons. This insight from the new homiletic gives preachers the opportunity to explore different sermon shapes that may enhance interest.

Much has been made in the new homiletic about the narrative or *storied* nature of the gospel. The difficulty here is that advocates tend to underplay the nonnarrative passages of Scripture "to narrow the communicational range of preaching to a single method." The narrative form may not be the best way to preach a given text.

3. We Benefit from a Concern for How the Listener Hears a Sermon

The experience of the listener is crucial to preaching. The new homiletic has made preachers aware of the importance of connecting with one's listeners and being aware of the importance of application.

Like the new homiletic's use of language and the misplaced emphasis on inspiration, however, an undue concern for the listener can cause imbalance and a misdirected focus for the preacher.

4. We Benefit from Giving Attention to the Affective Experience of the Audience

Evangelicals would not disagree that the listener experiences a sermon. The new homiletic contends that the weight of preaching rests on the actual, affective experience of the listener. Although the experiential encounter is important, especially since the listener is called on for a response, the preaching does not become any more or less authoritative.

In addition to the issue of inspiration in the new homiletic, there are questions about the role and work of the Holy Spirit. Little is mentioned in new homiletics literature about the Holy Spirit in preaching. The responsibility seems to rest on the preacher to replicate the text or even "regenerate the impact" of a biblical text so it actually becomes the Word of God once again in the new situation.

Of equal concern is the new homiletic's emphasis on what the sermon may do in the experience of the listening congregation. Instead of the sermon conveying the content of the text, doctrine, or biblical teaching, the emphasis is on experience. For the new homiletician, what is important is not what a sermon is but what it does.

What we see is a shift away from the truth of the biblical text to the experience of the text—possibly (most likely?) away from the intended idea. The responsibility of the preacher has moved from teacher of truth to director of happenings. One advocate of the new homiletic has warned, "There is a deep theological danger in measuring preaching by its capacity to generate religious experience."

The difficulty here for evangelicals is the focus of the sermon becomes human experience rather than the God of the authoritative biblical text and what the text teaches. In addition, there is an overconfidence in homiletical method to bring about transforming experiential events rather than a confidence in the power of scriptural truth applied to the heart by the Holy Spirit. The new hermeneutic in the new homiletic has essentially lost biblical meaning because of the overemphasis on the role of the hearer.

Through a complicated theory of language, the new homiletic has shifted the focus of homiletics from the traditional understanding of the preacher preaching from the authoritative Bible, to the experiential event of hearing the text in the life of the listener. There is much to appreciate from the methodologies and concerns expressed in the new homiletic. However, preachers should not naively or uncritically accept the new homiletic—or its practices—at face value.

BIBLIOGRAPHY

Buttrick, David, 1987. *Homiletic: Moves and Structures*. Philadelphia: Fortress.

_____. 1994. "On Doing Homiletics Today." Pp. 88–104 in *Intersections: Post-Critical Studies in Preaching*. Ed. Richard L. Eslinger. Grand Rapids: Eerdmans.

Craddock, Fred B. 1979. *As One Without Authority*. Nashville: Abingdon.

_____. 1990. "Inductive Preaching," a paper presented for the Societas Homiletica meeting at Stetson University, August 20–23 (pp. 6–14).

Ebeling, Gehard. 1966. *Theology and Proclamation: A Discussion with Rudolf Bultmann* London: Collins.

_____. 1967. *The Problem of Historicity*. Philadelphia: Fortress.

Fuchs, Ernst. 1964. *Studies of the Historical Jesus*. London: SCM.

Lowry, Eugene L. 1980. *The Homiletical Plot: The Sermon as Narrative Art Form*. Atlanta: John Knox.

_____. 1997. *The Sermon: Dancing the Edge of Mystery*. Nashville: Abingdon.

Randolph, David James. *The Renewal of Preaching*. 1969. Philadelphia: Fortress.

Skoglund, John E. 1967. "Towards a New Homiletic." *Princeton Seminary Bulletin* 60 (Fall): p. 57.

Thiselton, Anthony C. 1986. "The New Hermeneutic." P. 78 in *A Guide to Contemporary Hermeneutics: Major Trends in Biblical Interpretation*. Ed. Donald K. McKim. Grand Rapids: Eerdmans.

Troeger, Thomas H. 1990. *Imagining a Sermon*. Nashville: Abingdon.

Woodfin, Yandall. 1970. "The Theology of Preaching: A Search for the Authentic." *Scottish Journal of Theology* 23: p. 411.

Part 7

Stories AND Illustrations

How Do I Find Examples That Are Illuminating, Credible, and Compelling?

Chapter 130

3-D STORYTELLING

How to make sermon stories come alive

Kevin A. Miller

A host of books and articles have been published recently telling us that the key to reaching today's congregations is to use narrative, storytelling.

I actually was a writer first and a preacher more recently. I'm not gifted with natural dramatic flair, but I found that a lot of the skills I learned as a writer transferred beautifully into the pulpit, and I could use the same principles as those that make a story work in print.

One thing I've taught writers for years in workshops and now I use in my own preaching is a system called 3-D storytelling. It's a simple way to remember three things that help make your stories more vivid, since they all start with D.

DETAILS

The first thing that helps improve your stories is details, concrete details. As a writer

you're always asking yourself, *How can I describe this scene in a way that people can see it?* You can describe the sounds as well as the sights involved.

For example, let's say I'm writing a scene that's happening at the ocean. I will describe the sound of the waves crashing on the shore and the squawk of gulls. I will talk about things you can see, like circling gulls in the sky or mounds of seaweed along the shoreline. When I tell a story in the pulpit, I want to do the same thing. I want to select some key details that help people visualize themselves in that situation.

On the one hand, the description should be concrete. It should be something that everyone in the audience knows. It adds that sense of a specific, immediate item they can see, hear, taste, or touch.

Bill Hybels did a sermon a number of years ago called "The Character Question." He compared leaders starting ministry to cars starting the Indianapolis 500. Now, a lot of preachers, because we're in a hurry and we don't have time to prepare, would just say something like, "You know, Christian leaders are a lot like Indianapolis cars. They've been dropping out of the race." And that would be a pretty interesting analogy. But hear how much better it is when you use specific details. Here's how Bill started his sermon, and he preached this on Indianapolis weekend, so it was well-timed:

> If it hasn't started already, in just a short period of time the green flag will drop at the Indianapolis Speedway signaling the start of the world's most celebrated auto race. Thirty-three gleaming, low-slung, turbo-charged weapons will shoot out of the fourth turn and scream through the starting gate at almost 200 miles an hour.

I don't know whether he's been to Indy or not, but he knows there are thirty-three cars in the race. He knows they start out of the fourth turn. He knows they go two hundred miles an hour. And those specific, concrete details make the story much more vivid for the listener.

On the other hand, you can bog down a story with too many details, so you have to ask yourself, *What is the main point of the story? Does this detail help bring forward the main point of the story? Does it show an aspect of that person's character that's important to the story?*

For example, if I want to talk about someone who gave so sacrificially that he didn't have enough money for himself, I might point out that the shirt he was wearing was worn at the cuffs and elbows. But I wouldn't include that detail if I was telling a story that had nothing to do with his not having enough money for new clothes. Pick the detail that brings out the point you're trying to make.

DIALOGUE

Writers and preachers can bring stories to life by using dialogue. Dialogue allows your listeners to eavesdrop on a conversation. People naturally like to eavesdrop on interesting conversations. They do it in restaurants. They do it at Starbucks. So when you tell a story that uses the actual words of the characters in dialogue, it makes everybody else want to listen in.

Recently on *Preaching Today* Josef Tson used dialogue to help bring the story alive.

> I was interrogated for six months, having to go every day for eight to ten hours Monday through Friday. After about three months, the interrogator told me they were muckraking. You go through the life of a person and find everything dirty there. "We have many ugly things from your past, and we are going to spread them to all the churches. Your Baptists will come to smash your windows."
>
> I became pale. Power left me. I started to tremble because there was dirt in my life—my past, those years when I was away from the Lord. He looked at me and was afraid I had a heart attack. It was eight o'clock in the evening, and he called but couldn't find a car available [to take me home]. He said, "I don't want you to die here." He took me into the street, stopped a taxi, told the driver my address, and said, "Take him home." I went home, and for two days I couldn't walk. I was crushed.
>
> That Saturday morning, in my morning devotion Jesus was in front of me and said, "Josef, let me tell you how you imagined your martyrdom, going with your cross to be crucified but passing among two rows of Christians applauding. 'Bravo, Josef!' But what if I make those brothers and sisters of yours as you pass with your cross stoop down, take mud, and throw it on you and your cross? Will you accept a cross with mud on it?"

"Lord, even this is from you. Then I accept it."

It came like lightning. It hit me in the head and went through my legs, and at that moment I was able to stand up. When they called me back the following week and the man started gently to tell me something, I snapped [a response]. With each sentence he said, I retorted. At one point he stopped and said, "Mr. Tson, who visited you this weekend? I have in front of me a different person than the one who left here. Somebody came and changed you completely. I have to know who came and visited you."

"Jesus visited me and made me ready for the battle again, and I accepted even the mud as coming from him."

This story is powerful not only because it is on an emotionally compelling topic, namely, persecution, but because the actual words are used: "Mr. Tson, who visited you this weekend?" You can get a sense for that character. And even when he talked about his time of prayer to the Lord Jesus, he used exact words: "Jesus was in front of me and said, 'Josef, let me tell you how you imagined your martyrdom.'" It's compelling. You want to listen in on that conversation. By retelling the dialogue, you can move the inflection of your voice to create the emotion inherent in the words.

 For an audio example of this principle see tracks 14–15 on the supplemental CD.

A lot of people tell a story using indirect rather than direct address. In Josef Tson's story, for example, instead of using Jesus' exact words they might say something like, "And during prayer I had a sense that I was imagining my martyrdom this way, and I really should be seeing it another way." That could be compelling, but it's much richer when you give the actual words of the characters in the story.

As with details, it's possible to overdo dialogue. You want to use dialogue when it reveals something of who that character is, of what they're thinking and feeling. You don't want to use dialogue to communicate something that is a basic fact like "the sun was up" or "it was ten o'clock." You don't need to put that in the direct words of characters.

DENOUEMENT

Here is a word you may not have heard since college English class. Denouement means the ending, the conclusion, the wrapping up of all the elements in the story neatly at the end. The third D for stories, actually, is delayed denouement. Leave the ending for the ending.

Sometimes when we're preaching, without meaning to, we tip off what's going to happen in the story. For example, let's say I want to tell a story about human folly to demonstrate the waywardness of people apart from God's Spirit, and to illustrate that I want to use a story from my college days. I could start that story by saying, "Let me tell you about the time the dean kicked me out of college and suspended me for three days because of what I had done." But as I'm setting up that story, I've already told my listeners the punch line.

It's much better for me to say, "It was 2:00 a.m., and there I was hanging on the ivy, clinging to the downspout of Houser dormitory as I got ready to make my raid." Well, now everybody is listening. They want to hear what happens in the story, and eventually of course will come the punch line: "The dean suspended me, and I learned a lesson about the perils of human folly." But sometimes, because we're focused on the point the illustration makes, we tip off listeners where it's going to go.

I've heard people start a sermon with an illustration of a person facing a dilemma, and you don't find out how it's resolved until the end of the sermon. Joseph Stowell at Moody Bible Institute recently gave a sermon in which he talked about how we have to follow Christ even though it may cost us comfort. In the opening of that message he talked about a man in his congregation who had a highly placed job with a cable company, and he said to Dr. Stowell, "I don't know whether as a Christian I can continue to work here because our cable system puts out channels I think are completely antithetical to my Christian faith. And I'm not sure what I should do about that." Dr. Stowell then carried on with the message. He left the congregation with that tension, while the story remained unresolved. At the end of the message he came back around and told what happened to that person, what decisions he made. It's an effective technique.

If you do that, though, your story needs to be compelling enough that people will remember it by the time you get to the end of your message.

I think all stories will work better with the right details, the right dialogue, and a delayed denouement. The only thing I would add is that sometimes it takes a little practice to determine exactly how many details to use and where to put them.

God has wired people to want to tell stories and hear stories. People instinctively love stories that have details, dialogue, and an ending that doesn't come until the end.

Chapter 131

PREACHING PYROTECHNICS
Why some illustrations work better than others

Craig Brian Larson

At any Fourth of July fireworks display, some rockets capture more attention than others. There are the delicate sprays that gently "puffph," sending to one side a dozen streaks of red or blue. There are the dazzling sky-fillers that radiate spokes of fire into a gigantic wheel of light. Then there are, what I called as a boy, the "boomers." Their launch sounded a bit louder. I would spot a small flash in the sky; a moment later the intestine-vibrating concussion thundered over the golf course, kids squealing with ear-aching delight.

Like fireworks on Independence Day, illustrations put light, color, and excitement into our sermons. They celebrate the sermon's ideas and principles. The small ones—allusions, analogies, and clever turns of phrase—are designed to support small points. But when we want to drive home the major theme, we best send up our most powerful and illuminating illustration.

As a preacher and as editor of PreachingToday.com, I've reviewed literally thousands of illustrations, and I've noticed seven elements of the most powerful.

SPECIFIC RATHER THAN GENERAL

Being specific means saying *Luger* rather than *weapon*; *'89 Taurus* rather than *vehicle*; *adultery* rather than *sin*; *the nails through Christ's palms* rather than *Christ's sufferings*; *Bob, the 45-year-old overweight Chicago detective with the scar on the back of his hand* rather than *the officer*. The gunpowder is in specifics—the more precise the better.

Terry Fullam, in his sermon "Life on Wings," tells how mother eagles force their young to fly. If he had spoken in generalities, he would have said, "When their fledglings are old enough, eagles actually destroy their own nest to force the offspring to fly." But Terry used specifics:

> The mother eagle stands on the edge of the nest and begins to pick up the feathers and the leaves from the lining and cast them over the edge. There they go.
>
> "Mother, what are you doing?" Mother eagle pays no attention. She takes out the interior of the nest. She takes the great sticks, and with her strong beak she snaps them in two. She turns them up on end—pulls the place apart.
>
> "Mom, what are you doing?" She pays no attention. She begins to disassemble the nest, and the branches go plummeting down the face of the cliff.
>
> "Mom, we're not old enough to go out into the world." But she doesn't pay any attention. Is she trying to break up housekeeping because she doesn't like her children anymore? Not at all. She understands something they don't know. They weren't made to perch in the nest. They were made to soar, and they will never soar as long as they are in the nest.

Three specifics have dramatically improved this illustration. First, Terry details the destruction of the nest, with branches being snapped in two and feathers, leaves, and branches tumbling over the side. Second, he offers the thoughts of the young eagles. By articulating their fears and objections in direct dialogue, we enter the story. Third, instead of *fly* Fullam uses *soar*, which communicates the nobility of the eagle's flight. One strategically specific word can make or break an illustration, turning a fluorescent light into a laser beam.

General words stir as much excitement as generic products; specific, as brand name. Specifics explode because listeners can better see, hear, feel, and experience the thing. Specifics command attention, enticing listeners.

We tend to use generalities for compelling reasons. Specifics often take research and extra thought, precious commodities to a pastor. Generalities are safe; no one accosts us after church arguing that the nails were put through Christ's wrists not his palms, for example. We can't help but use generalities when we can't remember details of a story or we want anonymity for someone. Still, speakers communicate better the more specific their language.

ABOUT PEOPLE RATHER THAN THINGS

In his sermon "What about Shaky Marriages?" Stuart Briscoe says that men and women often cannot understand each other. He could have used computers to illustrate this: "Your IBM computer requires IBM-compatible software. If you try to run Apple software on it, your IBM computer simply can't read the program." That illustration would make the point, but it lacks the power of the illustration Briscoe actually used:

> Clint Eastwood made a movie called *Heartbreak Ridge....* There is a side story in that movie where Eastwood—the 24-year-veteran marine gunnery sergeant, Congressional Medal of Honor winner—has lost his wife, who doesn't want anything to do with him. This big macho man is quite pathetic. He doesn't know what to do, so he starts buying women's magazines. You have a remarkable picture of Clint Eastwood reading women's magazines to find out what on earth his wife really wants. The tragedy is that it's perfectly obvious to everybody else, but not to Clint.

This seizes our interest. The average church attender finds *People* magazine more engaging than *PC User*. Listeners identify with people's emotions, thoughts, opinions, appearances, problems, successes, strengths, and weaknesses. While illustrations drawn from nature, mechanics, or mathematics can help clarify, people illustrations are more likely to stir emotion. They are alive.

STORY RATHER THAN IMAGE

Images, which make abstract ideas concrete, are crucial to good preaching. For example, in his Christmas sermon "Glory to God in the Lowest," Bruce Thielemann says:

> We have an observatory in California called Mount Palomar, where there's a great telescope that can look out into space and pick out light so far away that it takes one hour of focusing upon that light for it to make even the faintest impression upon a photographic plate—tremendous capacities for focus in that telescope. But that is nothing compared to the way in which God focused himself in that baby. One little girl said

Jesus was the best picture that God ever had took.

While such images can be effective in sermons, when it's time to make a larger impact, a story works better. Howard Hendricks tells this story:

> There's a running controversy in art circles as to who is the greater: Michelangelo, the pupil, or Bertoldo, the teacher. The great teacher Bertoldo knew gifted individuals are prone to ride rather than develop. He warned Michelangelo repeatedly, but with no effect.
>
> One morning he walked into the studio and watched Michelangelo as he was piddling on a little piece of statuary. Bertoldo went over and picked up a sledgehammer and batted it into a thousand pieces that ricocheted all over that room. In the stunned silence, he shouted, "Michelangelo, talent is cheap; dedication is costly."

Stories even more than images provide impact through their plot, conflict, resolution, curiosity, human interest, climax, life, and surprise.

BOTH EMOTIONAL APPEAL AND LOGICAL APPEAL

In his sermon "The Wisdom of Small Creatures," Haddon Robinson says:

> A while ago I was trying to fix our garage door. I came to that one screw I had to get loose, and the more I worked to loosen that screw, the tighter it seemed to get. A neighbor came over and saw my plight. He looked for a moment or two and said, "Oh, this has a left-handed thread. It's a reverse screw. You have to tighten or loosen it going in the opposite direction."
>
> It took me fifty years to find out how screws work, and now they change the rules! There's a sense in which all of the Bible is kind of a reverse

screw. Everything in the culture that seems right, in the Bible comes out wrong. The way up is the way down.

This story is effective emotionally and logically. We identify with Haddon's frustration over the stubborn screw and his surprise that a reverse screw exists. When he ties these common human emotions to a grand truth, the story is complete for us.

Less powerful would have been a merely logical illustration: "American League hitters struggle if and when they are traded to the National League. They've been accustomed to a higher strike zone, so for a while, they tend to get a lot of called strikes on low pitches, which they have trained themselves to lay off. It's the same way when you first read the Bible; God seems to change the rules. What was once a ball is now a strike, and vice versa."

Emotion alone can be as empty as cotton candy. Logic alone can be clinical, a tasteless meal of vitamin pills. Together, though, they are a full course meal.

True Rather Than Hypothetical

Again, in his sermon "The Wisdom of Small Creatures" from Proverbs 30:24–28, Haddon Robinson is describing the destructive power of locusts. He could have said, "Imagine a plague of locusts sweeping through the breadbasket of America, consuming all the wheat and corn standing in the fields. They would leave behind a natural disaster costing millions of dollars." Instead he said:

> What the locust and grasshopper cannot do alone, it can do in community with others. Back at the turn of the century there was a plague of locusts in the Plains of the United States. In a matter of a few days that swarm of locusts swept over

the states of Nebraska, Iowa, and Kansas. In less than a week they did over 500 million dollars worth of damage (in the currency of that time).

Robinson's true story rings with authority. It's interesting. While someone can argue or doubt a hypothetical situation, a true account "proves" its point.

Show Rather Than Tell

Instead of standing between listeners and the story, *telling* people what to think, a preacher can *show* listeners what happened and let listeners learn for themselves.

"Johnny was mad," is telling; "Johnny turned red, clenched his teeth, and pounded his fist on the table" is showing.

At the beginning of one sermon, one preacher told this story:

> A few years ago, I had the opportunity to spend time with some well-known winners—professional athletes, best-selling authors, renowned business leaders, financial authorities, televangelists, and even a few political leaders—winners, by anyone's definition. What surprised me about my interaction with many of these celebrated winners was that their victories had not seemed to satiate their desire to be winners. On the contrary, I came to understand that in many cases their victories had merely whetted their appetites to continue to succeed no matter what the cost.

This is better than no illustration at all, but it's a bunt single rather than a home run. Why? We never see the mannerisms and hear the words of these athletes for ourselves. We are forced to accept the speaker's assessment of their lopsidedness.

The illustration would have grabbed us, though, if he had let us see one of those unsatisfied winners, perhaps with dialogue like this:

I bumped into one guy who towered over me (and his biceps were as big as my thighs), and we started talking. I asked the obvious: "Are you in pro sports?"

"No more," he said. "But I played linebacker for the Pittsburgh Steelers a few years ago."

For the next forty-five minutes I sat nodding my head and saying nothing. He talked about himself, his records, his big plays, and he proudly showed me his Super Bowl ring.

Finally, I interrupted him. "So tell me about your family."

"Well, to be honest," he said, "I'm separated from my wife, and she has custody of the kids."

"That must be pretty tough."

He glanced away. "Yea, sometimes it really bothers me," he replied quietly. Then he looked me in the eye. "But in order to win you have to pay a price," he said sternly. "I worked long and hard to play in the Super Bowl. Nothing and no one can ever take that away."

With such dialogue, the curtain is pulled back. *Showing* lets listeners gain insight for themselves. It raises curiosity and brings immediacy. If that jock spilled his drink, every person in the church would get wet.

DESCRIPTIONS RATHER THAN ALLUSIONS

One preacher said, "Think of it. One maverick molecule running loose in this universe outside the sovereignty of God could be the very thing that disrupts every promise God has ever made to his people!"

He illustrated with this one-sentence allusion: "A grain of sand in the kidney of Oliver Cromwell changed the course of western civilization."

Allusions to stories have built-in limitations. First, ignorance: The majority of listeners would not know how Cromwell died. Listeners would understand the point but miss the emotional impact. Second, proportion: Even if listeners do know a story, a glancing reference impacts less than a developed story, unless well-known allusions are piled up for cumulative effect, as in Hebrews 11. With an allusion, the listener's mind is like a flat stone skipping across the surface of a river and landing on the opposite shore; it gets wet but not submerged. The idea needs to be fully described.

The more developed an illustration, the more its details are allowed time to sink in, the more a listener's senses and memories and emotions are engaged, and the greater will be its effect. Listeners need to get interested and care about the people involved, all of which takes time to craft into a story.

In the following illustration, the preacher does more than briefly allude to Diocletian's unsuccessful attempts to stamp out the gospel of Christ. He describes them:

In one wave after another that continued until AD 298, it looked as if Emperor Diocletian, the last persecuting emperor, was going to destroy the Christian faith from the earth. When you look at Eusebius's church history, you find they took Christians at Alexandria, North Africa, cut their tongues out, boiled them in oil, and threw them into the sea. In the Roman Coliseum, they threw Christians to the lions. Diocletian imprisoned the preachers, murdered the Christians, and took their books and burned them to ashes. In fact, he erected a column in the city of Rome, and on that column was written in Latin *Extincta Nomina Christianorum*. It proclaimed in triumph the name of Christ extinct. But a strange thing happened. Diocletian divided his empire up, and the fellow who came after him in AD 312 looked up and said there at Milvian Bridge, "I see something strange in the sky." It was the cross of the Lord Jesus Christ, and next to it the words, "Under this sign, conquer." Whatever you think about Constantine and his conversion, I'll tell you this: Jesus cannot be hid.

On the Fourth of July, the explosive celebrations across our land are not staged by amateurs. Professional pyrotechnic engineers, thoroughly trained and following strict safety guidelines, plan the show, design and pack the missiles, arrange and load the mortars, and finally light the fuses. Because these technicians can anticipate the patterns and effects of their gunpowdered art, we enjoy a fabulous show and, more important, celebrate a notable holiday.

Following these seven guidelines, preachers likewise can add both fire and light to their sermons.

Chapter 132

PREACHING AS STORYTELLING

How to rely on stories to carry spiritual freight

Fred Craddock

A story, if it's a good story, is tailored and contoured to the audience. It's never repeated exactly. It's fitted in. A different condition calls for a reshaping of the story that will address appropriately the new condition; you have to put the grease where the squeak is.

I was at a family reunion, and I was seated on the patio on a very cold seat. All the other seats were wooden, except this one, and it was cold. Someone said, "Don't you recognize that?"

I looked at it and said, "I don't recognize this. Why should I?"

"That was the bottom step at the old home place where we were born." Then I remembered the old rotten wooden steps, and how someone replaced the bottom one with a piece of marble. Then the person said, "Turn it over."

We turned it over and on the other side were burial inscriptions appropriate for someone named George Washington Duncan who had died in 1792. A piece of marble became a gravestone, then a step, and now a patio seat.

That's the way a story goes: It's the same, it's not the same. The Bible uses, and good storytellers use and reuse, the basic stuff of the story in many ways.

DIFFICULTIES OF STORYTELLING

Storytelling is difficult because all communication is difficult. Communication is difficult because taking what is profoundly important to me and moving it into the public arena is like holding open house in a prayer room. Therefore it is important that I reexperience that story at the time I'm telling it.

Storytelling assumes that value is put upon continuity. A story has continuity. We have gone through a period of existential influence in which the great accent was on the moment, the now. A story is not important in a culture where there is general disinterest in what happened before I was born and in what happens after I'm gone.

491

Scott Momaday, American Indian writer, professor of literature in Southern California, tells this story. When he was a small boy, his father woke him early in the morning and said, "I want you to get up and go with me." His father took him by the hand and led him, sleepily, to the house of an old squaw, and left him saying, "I'll get you this afternoon." All day long the old squaw of the Kiowa tribe told stories to the boy, sang songs, described rituals, told the history of the Kiowa. She told the boy how the tribe began out of a hollow log in the Yellowstone River, of the migration southward, the wars with other tribes, the great blizzards, the buffalo hunt, the coming of the white man, the starvation, the diminished tribe, and finally, reservation, confinement. About dark his father came and said, "Son, it's time to go." Momaday said, "I left her house a Kiowa."

When youngsters leave our church building, do they leave Christian? To be Christian is to be enrolled in a story, and anybody who can't remember any farther back than his or her birth is an orphan.

Stories must be trusted to carry the message. The greatest difficulty in storytelling is the matter of whether or not we trust a story to carry the freight. Do you trust the kingdom of God, the message, to something as fragile as a story?

Some believe that telling stories to change the world is like trying to break up concrete by throwing light bulbs against it. I've been present when someone threw light bulbs against concrete walls, and the walls cracked and fell.

I do believe there is in many of us a lack of trust in the power of the word that's spoken. Jesus compared words with seeds. A seed carries its future in its bosom. The farmer does not put it in the ground and then scream over it. He leaves it alone. When preaching, many of us operate out of caution, hesitation, fear, and defensiveness. We can reflect our lack of trust in the very thing we're saying.

CHARACTERISTICS OF GOOD STORYTELLING

Think about what goes on in telling a story. *The storyteller is not speaking to people, but speaking for them.* In preaching we don't just speak to those people; we speak for those people. We don't tell them what they want to hear. We've all been warned about that. But now and then why not tell them what *they* want to *say*? The unused treasure of preaching is the experience, the faith, the commitment and love of those people, all of whom have a story to tell but they can't articulate it. You can speak for them.

The mark of a good story is that when it's over people say, "As you were talking I was thinking about when. . . ." Ah, now you're stirring the story. You're not just tapping more in; you're calling more out. Good storytelling speaks for the congregation and evokes their own stories. Good preaching is an act of the people.

Stories must be realistic. If your stories are all shaped into homiletical contortions, then nobody can identify because they're unrealistic. The tragedy is stories are bent out of life's shape to fit some homiletical enterprise. Let the story stand up on its own. Stories must have the smell and sound and taste of life. When you tell a real story, everybody is relaxed. It's not confrontation time. It's not challenge time. "Once upon a time. . . ." Everybody relax. And in that relaxation you're drawn into the story, and identification begins to take place. The great single power in storytelling is the power of identification. And things that have long been in the head, known, begin to move toward the heart, and that's when life is changed.

Stories create an experience. It's a long trip from the head to the heart. A sermon is full of information. The substance is there. But preaching is not just transferring information. It's creating the experience of that information.

If you are preaching on freedom, what's going to be the size, the sound, and the shape of that experience? There's freedom and then there's *freedom*. There's bombs-bursting-in-air, Fourth-of-July-parade, firecrackers, drums, 76-trombones, John-Philip-Sousa-down-Main-Street freedom. You can also preach freedom that's as quiet as six female voices outside a county jail humming "We Shall Overcome." Don't just say you're preaching on freedom. What experience are you going to create?

The way you put the words together creates it. I hear some powerful passages used in sermons as though it were information. "There was this beggar sitting at the gate." Wait a minute. Give me a chance to experience the beggar at the gate. See the rags, smell the odor, hear the coins in the tin cup, see the hollow eyes. Don't rush to the destination. Take the trip.

The fit of a story is important. Have you had the experience of telling a story in a sermon and then later you say, *I wish I would have saved that story?* Most of the power of a story is not somebody's particular ability to tell it. Most of the power in a story is in its appropriateness. The Word of God is appropriate. Therefore the fitting of a story to Scripture is extremely important.

Select stories with size and quality—not little, bumper sticker, cute things—but big things. Then move among them with the magnet of the text to be appropriate, not just to the text, but also to the listener and the experience.

This appropriateness applies not just to the selection of stories for the sermon but the location of the stories within the sermon. Take the egg out of the nest and set it out on a limb, and it's a different story. What makes the story powerful is the taking of time to build the context in which it is told and then placing it. The people have to be given time to get on the bus before you go roaring off.

Be careful in the preparation of an introduction. How can you prepare an introduction to what you don't have? For most of us it should be prepared last. Then you will not unload too soon your strong material and stories that need contexting.

Stories have movement. The key to the power of the story depends much in its movement. Forget structure. Stories are to be heard not seen. That is my best counsel about a sermon. Forget about getting an outline. Get the movement. Masterful storytellers do it that way.

Picture an old man peeling an apple for his grandson. "Grandpa, will you peel this apple for us? Momma thinks I might get choked some on the peeling."

"Okay," and he pulls out an old Barlow that he uses for everything, opens it up, rubs it on his britches. After all, it's his grandson. He doesn't want any germs. Then he starts peeling real slow, and the curl begins to drop. And he says, "You know one time I peeled thirty-five of these before I ever broke a peel." And what's happening to the kid? The juices are flowing. The stomach is saying, *I thought I was going to get an apple.* The saliva is flowing; the body is getting ready for the apple. Getting ready for the apple. And it just keeps going, *When is he going to get through?*

Finally the peel drops at his feet. I made it. The kid starts to lunge. "Wait, just a minute." And then he lays it down. "Let me get the core out for you." And just taking forever. When the kid gets the apple, it is the best apple in the world. Now contrast that to walking up to a machine, putting in a quarter, pulling a lever, grabbing an apple, and eating it on the way to something, when the stomach is saying, *I didn't ask for an apple.*

Now think of the movement of your preaching. Do people get prepared to come to the conclusion when you come to the conclusion? It's just a matter of saying I respect the listener and I want to take them with me.

GATHERING STORIES

Where do we get stories?

You can create stories. In the creation of stories one gives clues to the listeners that the story was created. "Once upon a time...." The way Jesus usually started them was with two statements. One, "Which of you...?" You knew it was a parable. Or "There was a certain man..." and you knew it was a parable. Little clues that don't detract from the power of the story should be given to release people from engaging in the things in the wrong way. But create stories.

Stories are mostly in observation and experience. The stories of life, the things that happen, are as available to you as to me. Some of us have by negative adaptation lost our capacity to pick up on the sights and sounds of our world. Or if we notice it, we don't make any notes to ourselves, and therefore, it's lost.

I keep a journal. I enter the way I feel about experiences; I reflect on the day and the context of things I heard or saw. Then I can recover the experience, not just the information. Observation. Just listing things. If you have freedom to think about yourself and your own experiences, that will be a grand source of stories.

Kind of sad thing, funny thing, happened once. I don't get to go to New York often. I spent my money on the room and was in a place getting a hot dog. And there were only two customers besides myself. The elderly woman waiting on us was in her seventies. Her name was Anna. There was an old man in a booth. He wasn't being waited on. I could just see the top of his head. I knew he was an old man. Later I heard his voice. And so I was just listening, and suddenly conversation started between the old man and Anna. I don't know his name. She never called him by name. He said to her, "The boss wants me to stick around in case you get busy. I can help you."

She said, "Who's busy? Three people."

He said, "Well, you may get busy."

"I won't get busy."

He said, "Well, just in case."

She said, "Okay, if you want to stick around."

He said, "And then when you close, I can walk you home."

She said, "Ah-ha, now I know why you're staying."

"I just want to walk you home."

She said, "You'll not walk me home." She was, I would say, seventy-five years old. "You'll not walk me home."

He said, "I will walk you home. You need somebody to walk you home."

"Yeah, you want to walk me home. Pretty soon you walk me home, and I will be great with child."

He said to her, "What are you talking about, Anna? You passed that point years ago."

She said, "Huh? You don't know about Sarah?"

He said, "Sarah who?"

She said, "Sarah in the Bible. Sarah in the Bible was older than I, and she was great with child."

He said, "Well, how did she do that?"

Anna said, "She believed in the man upstairs.

And the mother of our Lord before she was ever married, before she ever knew a man, was great with child."

And he said, "How did she do that?"

And she said, "She believed in the man upstairs."

And this old man said, "Well, if I were a woman I wouldn't believe in the man upstairs."

Chapter 133

HOW TO TELL A MOVING STORY
The purposes of the beginning, middle, and end

Craig Brian Larson

To tell stories well (biblical stories or otherwise), make sure they have a beginning, middle, and end. This is especially true of the lean stories, lasting from one to five minutes, that we normally use in sermons. Each part—beginning, middle, and end—is essential, each different in purpose.

BEGINNINGS

The beginnings of lean stories have three fundamental purposes.

Orient Hearers

We must provide a minimum of information that sets the story in time and place. Who are the people that begin the story? Where and when is the story happening? When hearers get insufficient information, they are distracted and often frustrated. They won't fully follow the story or appreciate the story's resolution. (Ever see the first *Mission Impossible* movie?)

However, too much information bogs the story, diminishes interest, and frustrates hearers. Give no more information than necessary. From beginning to end, a story needs movement.

"Jesus said: 'A man was going down from Jerusalem to Jericho, when he fell into the hands of robbers. They stripped him of his clothes, beat him and went away, leaving him half dead'" (Luke 10:30). In the two-sentence beginning of this lean story, Jesus gives the minimum information hearers need. How many children "the man" had, what his name was, what he looked like—none of that affects the point of the story, so Jesus omits it.

Audiences like to know whether a story is fact or fiction, so with true stories include specific names and dates, conveying authenticity. With imagined stories tip off hearers with a phrase like "The story is told of . . ." or "In a certain town, a man lived with his elderly mother. We'll call him Bill. . . ."

Establish the Complication

Complication (also variously called conflict, disequilibrium, tension, problem) is what makes a story a story. A mere chronicle of events is not a story: "I went to the store. I bought some eggs. I came home. I watched TV. I went to bed."

A story has plot, and a plot has dramatic tension. "Yesterday morning I went to the store, and when I walked into the fruit section I realized I had forgotten what my wife asked me to pick up for her. *Uh oh,* I thought. *She's away from the phone all day, and tonight we're having her parents over for dinner.*"

We must establish the complication in the beginning of the story, because that is what gets attention and interest, and that is where the significance of the story begins.

When possible, though, we precede the complicating event with a brief description of what was happening before things got sticky. "A man was going down from Jerusalem to Jericho"—this sets up a dramatic contrast. Disequilibrium feels more jarring if listeners have had at least a brief sense of equilibrium. Stories go the full cycle: from normal circumstances to problematic, then to reversal and resolution, and then back to normal.

Be careful, though, to keep this setup brief, without telling some of the ending in the beginning and thereby letting all the tension out of the story. "Yesterday we had my wife's parents over for dinner, and my neighbor, who always has what I need, saved my neck. I went to the store in the morning, and when I walked into the fruit section. . . ."

Show What Motivates the Key Person

This adds interest and depth to a story. When hearers know why the main person in the story dearly wants to resolve the complication, it increases the tension and the sympathies of the hearer for that person. In other words, hearers care more about what happens.

"Yesterday morning I went to the store, and when I walked into the fruit section I realized I had forgotten what my wife asked me to buy for her. *Uh oh,* I thought. *She's away from the phone all day, and tonight we're having her parents over for dinner.* Now, my wife's parents have not spoken to me in four years, ever since I made a sarcastic remark about their perfectionist tendencies at a Thanksgiving dinner."

When presenting characters, remember that no one is all good or all bad, perfect in faith or doubt. Real-world ambiguity adds authenticity to the story and keeps it interesting.

"Now, my wife's parents have not spoken to me in four years, ever since I made a sarcastic remark about their perfectionist tendencies at a Thanksgiving dinner—ironically, they had forgotten to bring the apple pie."

One exception to this is when you turn the tables on what hearers expect. "A priest happened to be going down the same road, and when he saw the man, he passed by on the other side. So too, a Levite, when he came to the place and saw him, passed by on the other side. But a Samaritan, as he traveled, came where the man was; and when he saw him, he took pity on him" (Luke 10:31–33).

Middle

The middle of a lean story has two basic purposes, which I will discuss together: (1) Prepare for and (2) present a strong reversal.

The reversal is the action, insight, decision, or event that triggers the climax. In some stories, the reversal is the climax; in others the reversal leads directly into the climaxing scene that releases the tension of the story. "But a Samaritan, as he traveled, came where the man was; and when he saw him, he took pity on him."

As the word *reversal* implies, it should have an element of the unexpected. Usually, the stronger the surprise, the stronger the story. But, a reversal should not be a complete surprise or entirely incongruous with what has come before; otherwise the story seems unreal. When needed, subtle foreshadowing can make for a more satisfying reversal and climax.

To prepare for the reversal, an effective middle narrates one or more failed attempts to resolve the complication. "A priest happened to be going down the same road, and when he saw the man, he passed by on the other side. So too, a Levite, when he came to the place and saw him, passed by on the other side." If there are no failed attempts, the story ends with a whimper.

In addition, the middle prepares for the reversal by adding important information: chronicling the necessary chain of events leading to the reversal, adding necessary information about people, elaborating on the complication, introducing new people, foreshadowing the reversal. In terms of drama, the best preparation of all are elements that make the complication progressively worse.

"This dinner was so important I decided to do whatever it takes. I filled my shopping cart with salad items, fruits, meats, breads, desserts. Somehow we would be able to put a decent meal on the table with this mountain of food! But when I got to the checkout counter and reached for my wallet, my heart stopped: My pockets were empty. Had I dropped my wallet in the parking lot? Had I left it at home?"

The best stories prepare for and present the reversal and climax in a way that makes them understandable, believable, satisfying, moving. For that reason, the reversal and climax will usually be the most fully developed elements in the story. Here you often use the most dialogue, a fuller description of the setting, a prop that symbolizes an important element of the story, the most detailed chronicling of action (without going overboard and killing the pace). Fuller development conveys the message that this is the most important part of the story.

"He went to him and bandaged his wounds, pouring on oil and wine. Then he put the man on his own donkey, took him to an inn and took care of him. The next day he took out two silver coins and gave them to the innkeeper. 'Look after him,' he said, 'and when I return, I will reimburse you for any extra expense you may have'" (Luke 10:34–35).

ENDING

The ending of a lean story has three basic purposes.

Present the Climactic Scene

The climax resolves the complication. If the reversal is not the actual climax, then the climax follows immediately on its heels and begins the end of the story. In the parable of the good Samaritan, the actions of the Samaritan are both the reversal and the climax.

Show Consequences of the Reversal and Climax.

In story parlance, this is called the denouement. Briefly show that the reversal and climax did result in a return to equilibrium. In addition, although the story has come full circle, show how people or circumstances have changed.

"That family dinner was a fiasco. Who would have thought it would end up with my father-in-law and me becoming great friends? Hardly a week goes by that he and I aren't on the phone about something."

Give a Sense of Closure

Make sure no loose ends hang from the story that leave people wondering. They will feel the story isn't over. But be careful not to touch the airplane down on the runway and then take off and land a few more times. Everything in the ending should be brief. The story has been told, the tension resolved, the consequences shown.

End the story with one strong sentence that has a feeling of finality, and then bridge back into the flow of the sermon in one or two sentences.

"Which of these three do you think was a neighbor to the man who fell into the hands of robbers?" The expert in the law replied, "The one who had mercy on him." Jesus told him, "Go and do likewise" (Luke 10:36–37).

Effective storytellers select from myriad available details which to include in a story and which to omit. Understanding the unique roles of the beginning, middle, and end will help you purposefully select the data that make for life-changing stories.

Chapter 134

BRINGING BIBLE STORIES TO LIFE
How to paint the scenes that engage modern audiences

Steven D. Mathewson

What's the difference between the style of John Grisham and that of the Bible's storytellers? The answer hit me one day when I read a section from Genesis and then later read a section from one of Grisham's novels.

In John Grisham's novel *The Testament*, lawyer Nate Riley searches for the surprise heir to an eleven billion dollar fortune—a missionary named Rachel Lane. Riley finally finds her deep in the jungles of Brazil. At their initial encounter, a group of tribesmen escort her to Riley. Notice how Grisham describes her:

Rachel was with them; she was coming. There was a light yellow shirt in the midst of the brown-skinned chests, and a lighter face under a straw hat.... She was slightly taller than the Indians,

and carried herself with an easy elegance.... Nate watched every step. She was very slender, with wide bony shoulders. She began looking in their direction as they grew closer.... She removed her hat. Her hair was brown and half-gray, and very short.

By contrast, notice how the writer of Genesis describes the first time Rebekah lays eyes on her fiancé Isaac:

Rebekah also looked up and saw Isaac. She got down from her camel and asked the servant, "Who is that man in the field coming to meet us?"

"He is my master," the servant answered. So she took her veil and covered herself.

Then the servant told Isaac all he had done. (Gen. 24:64–66)

The difference between the style of a modern novel and that of a Bible story is in the detail. While the writers of Bible stories were first-class literary artists, they wrote with a spare, lean style. Compared to John Grisham or Charles Dickens or Jan Karon, the biblical writers provided fewer details.

This presents a challenge to those who preach Bible narratives. A modern audience often requires more sensory details for a story to come to life. Preachers must imagine the scenes in a Bible story and then paint vivid pictures. Otherwise the retelling of the story will come across as bland and boring.

In *Leap Over A Wall,* notice how Eugene Peterson paints the scene when David encounters Saul in the desert cave near En-Gedi:

> David and a few of his men are hidden in a cave cut in the cliffs above the Dead Sea. The day is hot and the cave is cool. They're deep in the cave, resting. Suddenly there's a shadow across the mouth of the cave; they're astonished to see that it's King Saul. They didn't know that he was that close in his pursuit. Saul enters the cave but doesn't see them: fresh from the hard glare of desert sun, his eyes aren't adjusted to the darkness and don't pick out the shadowy figures in the recesses of the cave. Besides, he isn't looking for them at that moment; he has entered the cave to respond to the call of nature. He turns his back to them.

Peterson's description reveals a couple of strategies. First, he does not resort to flowery language. He uses strong words, but he strikes a balance between economy and detail. Furthermore, he lets his exegesis control his imagination. He doesn't go beyond the text and splice his conjectures into the scene. He simply places himself in the story and describes what any character would see.

Painting scenes like this gives you an edge especially when it comes to communicating historical-cultural data. As you tell a Bible story, you may need to explain geographical details, marriage rituals, Canaanite religious beliefs, or warfare practices unfamiliar to your contemporary audience. It's easy to convey such information in a bland way that detracts from the story.

Suppose you are preaching a sermon on Joshua 6. To make the story come alive, you will probably need to explain a bit about siege warfare. If you take the typical approach, you might introduce the information by saying: "Based on archaeological data, Bible scholars can describe with accuracy how the ancients conducted siege warfare." At this point, you've likely bored part of your audience. However, turning the information into a scene conveys the information in a more interesting way. In a recent sermon on Joshua 6, I presented the data on siege warfare like this:

> The city of Jericho is tightly shut. That's what you expect, but it's not what you want to hear. It's tough to attack a fortified city once the gates have been closed and the people are holed up inside. Perched high upon the walls are guard towers or stations with guards, ready to shoot arrows, pour hot oil, and dump boulders on you if you get close to the wall. Guards watch the entrance from their towers. Since the gate system is potentially the weakest part of the wall, the entrance consists of a series of two or three gates. Punch through one, and you still have one or two left. So you hope to get some battering rams close enough to start whacking at the wall. But punching a hole through can take weeks, even months. Scaling the wall is horribly difficult, too. Like General Custer, you'll be wearing an Arrow shirt before you climb very far up the wall.

You can paint scenes like this by culling information from Bible dictionaries, encyclopedias, atlases, or books on archaeology. You'll get help on how to shape this material into a scene by reading some of the masters of the craft. Try Eugene Peterson's *Leap Over a Wall: Earthy Spirituality for Everyday Christians* for scenes from the life of David. In his book *Peculiar Treasures: A Biblical Who's Who,* Frederick Buechner breathes color into Bible characters. Sometimes his imagination transcends the text, but reading his material will exercise your creativity. In addition, get a copy of James Michener's tome *The Source.* It sweeps back and forth from the fictional account of an archaeological excavation in western Galilee to the ancient stories behind the artifacts it uncovers. The first 373 pages supply vivid images from Jewish history through 605 BC, particularly of the daily routines of family life, farming, and Canaanite religious practice.

When you paint scenes, pay attention to word choice. "Going up the wall" sounds bland to listeners. "Scaling the wall" engages their interest. Sometimes a thesaurus will get you out of a verbal rut. But be careful to choose an appropriate word. Specific nouns and verbs help, too. Some communicators use adjectives and adverbs to pick up the slack left by weak verbs and nouns. Instead of trying to boost a noun like *rock* with a generic modifier like *big,* use a word like *boulder.* Instead of *flowers* select the appropriate designation like *daisies* or *lilies.* When it comes to verbs, try "punched the wall" or "whacked the wall" rather than "hit the wall." Just make sure the verb accurately describes the action. Again, exegesis must set the limits for your creativity.

Generality drains the life out of stories. So when you preach, shoot for a style with enough sensory details to engage your readers. Painting vivid scenes will bring Bible stories to life.

Chapter 135

SUSPENSE

Why everybody—including your Sunday audience—loves a mystery

Dave McClellan

Many preachers are taught a well-organized sermon requires a clear preview and review. Tell the audience what you will say, say it, and then tell them what you said.

Hogwash! I can't think of a more tedious way to communicate the good news than to sap it of all intrigue.

Movies, novels, stories, even jokes—every effective communication medium uses suspense as part of its appeal. Every one, that is, except the sermon. In an effort to be clear and concise, many sermon writers have jettisoned the element of suspense, leaving their outlines with all the wonder of a dishwasher instruction manual.

Suspense keeps listeners involved. Who walks away from a joke half-told? Anticipation of the punch line grips the listeners. Yet people routinely tune out in the middle of sermons. Why? There's no suspense!

Master storytellers can speak much longer

than a preacher, yet maintain the rapt attention of their audience. Garrison Keillor, for example, knows how to keep the audience hooked by "letting out" his story one incident at a time. He doesn't announce what a story will be about, who will be involved, or how it will end.

You don't need to be as gifted as Garrison Keillor to make good use of suspense in preaching. Suspense is simply the withholding of information followed by its strategic release. As the word implies, it's a "suspending" of the communication process. Incorporating a variety of tension and release moments involves the listeners, intellectually and emotionally, throughout the message.

We can learn the art of suspense from storytellers, but be warned: Their lessons may contradict what the experts taught you.

DON'T SAY TOO MUCH

Preachers often structure their sermons like an academic lecture—three bullet-points and an illustration for each. Thinking of the sermon as a story, however, creates the potential for building suspense. I don't mean adding stories to the sermon. I mean thinking of the entire sermon as a story, a novel slowly unwinding.

Stories build suspense because the ending is withheld. So look at your sermon. Is anything being withheld? Or are you giving away the ending too early? Like a good novelist, a pastor who conceals a plot twist captures the listener.

Even familiar passages become riveting when given a suspenseful twist. For example, if the first half of a sermon on the Golden Rule from Matthew 7 stresses not the "do unto others" part, but instead the importance of knowing your own needs, you can raise the possibility that this teaching of Jesus sounds

self-centered. That's the idea. It's part of the suspense.

After making the case for knowing your needs, the preacher can throw in the sudden plot twist. "Now that you've discovered how to identify your needs, realize Jesus' purpose was not for you to get them met, but for you to meet that need in someone else. Your own needs are the seeds for serving others."

The sermon that announces instead, "Today, we'll examine how to identify our needs in order to discern the needs of others," squanders the opportunity to keep the listeners baited for the application. The simple suspending of the communication process is more likely to keep listeners' attention.

Oddly enough, it is possible for a sermon to be too clear. Jesus was willing to trade clarity for mystery, knowing a mystified person will be more affected by the truth than a bored one.

In John 16:16, at the Last Supper, Jesus teases his disciples with "In a little while you will see me no more, and then after a little while you will see me." His message is cryptic. He lets the disciples turn that teaching over in their heads and speculate about what he might mean.

"Some of his disciples said to one another, 'What does he mean by saying, "In a little while you will see me no more, and then after a little while you will see me," and "Because I am going to the Father"?' They kept asking, 'What does he mean by "a little while"? We don't understand what he is saying'" (John 16:17–18). He waits until they're really hungry for answers before he offers his meaning.

Long before cultural gurus were analyzing postmodern thinking process and concluding that people don't want to be told all the answers, Jesus was cultivating questions in the minds of his hearers. Gnawing questions led them to pursue answers. May we be as subtle, and as bold.

Jesus also avoided a common pitfall that saps suspense from many sermons. His preaching struck images that made his audience acutely uncomfortable. He issued strong warnings laced with hyperbole. Yet today's sermons are often so balanced and innocuous that few can protest. Scarcely does a strong statement slip from a preacher's lips before he begins backpedaling and explaining away its power.

When preaching about the prosperity of the righteous from Psalm 1, we could balance it right away by acknowledging that Scripture does not promise constant prosperity, but that would rob the message of its suspense. If, instead, we preach uncompromisingly about how God does bless the righteous, a tension fills the room. People wrestle with the idea, examine their theology against their experience, and wonder how the preacher intends to apply this teaching. And isn't the goal of preaching to cause people to wrestle and examine and apply?

Once the issue has been successfully framed, then it can be counter-balanced if necessary. We can say something like: "Now at this point some of you are thinking, *Wait a minute. It doesn't always work that way.* . . ."

Suspenseful preaching allows Scripture to make strong statements without dousing them too quickly. Audiences need to squirm a little under the heat.

THE SOUND OF SYMBOLS

A sermon doesn't have to be simply an auditory experience. The more sensory experiences built into the sermon, the more engaging it becomes. After all, Jesus said, "Show me the coin used for paying the tax." And when they

brought him a denarius, he asked, "Whose portrait is this? And whose inscription?" (Matt. 22:19–20). Can you imagine the curiosity that asking for a coin aroused? Jesus had their undivided attention.

I recently started a sermon with a battered, old chair to the left of the pulpit. It was there throughout the worship, leaving people to wonder who forgot to take out the trash. But when it came time to preach on God's passion for restoring broken-down lives, I had the visual cue right beside me. The tension, which had been building since I started, was released.

Many pastors are realizing that object lessons are no longer just for Sunday school. But if we wait to bring out the prop until it's needed, we've missed an opportunity to utilize suspense.

I started another sermon with a Styrofoam cup and a hand-crafted ceramic mug sitting on top of the pulpit. I offered no explanation for their presence. Later in the sermon, I used the cup to illustrate a mass-produced object designed only for temporary use. The handmade mug demonstrated the lasting value of God's individual workmanship. I challenged the congregation not to be Styrofoam Christians. Instead I called them to demonstrate the creativity and thumbprint of the Potter.

BAITING THE HOOK

A final tool for preaching with suspense is the sermon title. Typically, this is the congregation's first glimpse of the message. If they see "Five Ways to Improve Your Marriage" or "God's Passion for Good Marriages," they already know the topic and tone and can probably guess what the conclusion will be. Little curiosity is aroused.

On the other hand, a title like "What Marriage Seminars Will Never Teach You" starts to build suspense before the preacher utters a word. A suspenseful title leaves people wondering what they might miss if they don't "tune in" on Sunday.

From the cover, to the illustrations, to the plot itself, a suspenseful story captures attention and imagination. Suspense in a sermon can do the same.

Chapter 136

HOW TO PREACH LIKE JOHN GRISHAM WRITES
I needed to move from principle to plot

Bill Oudemolen

During a recent vacation, my wife and I ventured across town to another church. The jammed parking lot and crowded lobby suggested a scintillating sermon. The preacher was articulate and entertaining. His sermon was biblical, with four crafted principles from the text. But as we left that morning, I realized, as William Willimon has said, I got the sermon, but it didn't get me.

Fast-forward to a couple of days later, same vacation: Sitting under a thatched umbrella on a beach, I'm reading John Grisham's *The Chamber,* a novel about capital punishment. Toward the end of the story, Grisham describes Sam Cayhall, the death-row inmate, taking off the clothes he has worn for so many years. His new clothes lying on the bed are for his execution in the gas chamber. The portrayal overwhelmed me, and I began to weep. As a tear rolled down my cheek, I silently asked the Lord to forgive me for my past hatred of death-row inmates.

It struck me that Grisham's novel had "got" me in a way the principled sermon I'd heard hadn't. I began studying what makes a good story work. As I applied the elements of plot to

my sermon structure, they revolutionized the way I create and deliver a sermon.

STARTING WITH SURPRISE

A plot-based sermon is not one with more stories in it. It is not created by cramming more illustrations into a sermon or seeing the sermon as one lengthy illustration. Rather, the very structure of a plot-based sermon is different. The difference between a plot-based sermon and a principle-based sermon is not hermeneutical but homiletical. A plot-based sermon still requires traditional exegesis; I still have to immerse myself in the text. But once I do my exegetical spadework, I head in a new direction. I steer away from principles and launch out into the realm of surprise, tension, and disequilibrium.

Obviously, this is easier with narrative literature, but every text is set in a context, in a story and a situation. And every situation has some disequilibrium or tension.

As I begin thinking about my sermon, I ponder what my audience might expect from this text. Then I do my best to avoid their expectations. As I start the sermon, I want people to wonder, "Where is he going with this?"

In *The Homiletical Plot,* Eugene Lowry illustrates with the old *Quincy* TV show (a more recent example is *CSI*). Both shows start with a dead body—no surprise there. The interest factor is the uncertainty—"Who did it?" "How did they do it?" "Why did they do it?" "How will Quincy or Jessica figure it out?"

In a recent sermon on the parable of the rich fool in Luke 12, for example, the congregation expected I would oppose the rich fool. So I showed how much I identified with him. I viewed him as a financially fortunate farmer: "The rich fool seems wise to us. He earned his money honestly. He was hard-working. He invested and expanded. He used his surplus to plan for his retirement. *Money* magazine would profile him as a financial genius."

I used a quote: "If this man is a fool, then a lot of Americans are fools!" I told my audience I had recently calculated the money I'd have for retirement in twenty years if, instead of giving to the church and missionaries during the past four years, I had invested it. The tally was more than $200,000. I then asked them to decide whether having $200,000 less at retirement was wise or foolish.

To my suburban congregation, that created disequilibrium, tension, and surprise.

BUILDING TENSION

In the exegetical phase of sermon preparation, I search carefully for any textually-based disequilibrium.

While preaching on the life of Paul, for example, I found some delicious disequilibrium in Acts 27. Luke tells about riding out a storm with Paul. The storm rages with no word from God. Luke writes in 27:20 that they finally "gave up all hope" of being saved.

I could have ruined the sermon at that point by chiding my audience, "But of course, we all know the doctrine of omnipresence, so we know God was there—the principle of his presence!" The temptation is to play down disequilibrium in the text, as if it's my job to make God look good. One commentator on this passage used the four anchors from Acts 27:29 as "four anchors to keep us from shipwreck during life's storms." But the problem here is not only homiletical but theological—Paul's ship does shipwreck!

My goal is to play up the tension. In all good stories, things unravel, creating more tension until the climax. My tendency has been to reach the last chapter too quickly. But the heart of the sermon, like the heart of a novel, is a thickening plot.

While preaching a series on the life of Abraham, I used him as an example of what it's like to be a friend of God. To build tension, I asked my audience whether they would treat a friend as God does.

Abraham and Sarah waited twenty-five years for God to give them the promised child. I told my audience I could understand what Abraham was feeling during those years. Although God didn't promise me a son, I know what it's like to wait to have a child. My wife, Jan, and I are still waiting. We have been married for twenty-four years. We planned to have children, raise a family, and joyfully serve the Lord. We are now a childless couple in midlife.

I told the audience that when I read the news account of a mother who drowned her two children in South Carolina, anger welled up in my heart. My passion was not as much toward her as toward God. Why allow her to have children and not us? I'd never do what she did.

There is power in a sermon that asks some questions.

Wrapping It Up

But the tension created by the disequilibrium eventually has to be released. The time clock runs out in the fourth quarter of the game. The book of Revelation resolves the tension between God and Satan. In good stories and sermons, the denouement (or resolution) is brief. Using the TV-drama analogy, a sermon's denouement should not take more than five minutes.

This part of the sermon feels most like traditional preaching to me. It is the time for propositional statements about God. It is the time to explain the "rest of the story." But it must not drag on and on.

In my sermon on the parable of the rich fool, the denouement was simple—"If you're not careful, your money can make a fool out of you. Storing wealth is foolish, but sharing wealth is wise." I mentioned the $200,000 less I'll have for retirement and reminded the audience that even though someone may say, "What a fool!" God says, "How wise!"

This was a stewardship sermon in preparation for a campaign banquet. I suggested to the audience that as they filled out a pledge card the next week, someone might look at their card and judge them a fool. I hoped it wasn't God.

Finally, I told about two little girls named Kaylee and Whitnee, who had sold caramel apples and cookies the week before. A little sign at their booth read: "Everything we make is for our new church building." I held up the envelope they gave me earlier that morning. Scrawled in a little girl's handwriting was the figure $36.75 and then: "For the new church. Love, Whitnee and Kaylee." I concluded by asking my audience whether God's response was "What fools!" or "What wise little girls!"

Producing sermon principles is easy; creating sermonic plot is arduous. To help me produce better plot-based sermons, I read fiction, take in movies and dramas, listen carefully to the stories of those who see me for pastoral care, and pay attention to the lyrics of country music—"Sometimes you're the windshield, sometimes you're the bug."

But fueling my creativity more than anything, perhaps, is the disequilibrium of my own story.

Chapter 137

GOOD TENSION

The role of timing in telling a gripping story

John Ortberg

Much of the energy of a sermon comes from tension-producing statements.

I heard a message by author and speaker Ken Davis that shows how to use tension-producing statements well. Here is an excerpt:

> Kids don't like it when you say, "I love you," and try to hug them. But don't stop saying it.
>
> With my daughter, I would try to coerce her. I would say, "I love you." She would reply, "Me too." I would say, "Say it." She would say, "I just did." When she was 14, 15, 16, I did not hear the words "I love you" from her.
>
> It doesn't matter whether you sit at the top of a corporate tower or drive a tractor on a farm, it doesn't matter whether you're a teenager or an adult—all of us are born with this desperate need to be loved, and we will do things that destroy our lives trying to heal that wound in our hearts.
>
> When my daughter was 16, I cornered her in the kitchen one day and said, "Honey, I love you. I love you." She said, "Whatever." She might as well have pulled a knife and run it through my heart.
>
> When she was 18, I was about to leave her in her college dorm room. With tears streaming down my face I grabbed her by the shoulders and established eye contact and said, "Tracy, I love you." And at 18-years-old she said, "Me too." I drove 800 miles weeping because I wanted to be loved. I just wanted to be loved.
>
> Several months later I was invited to speak at her school. I enjoy speaking, but that day I was terrified because she was in the audience and I

> didn't want to embarrass her. I gave my speech, and afterward the college chaplain invited me out to lunch. My daughter went to class. We went to a nice Italian restaurant. He pulled from his briefcase a stack of several hundred response cards. He read to me some of the things the kids had written about my message.
>
> I was gratified. I took a bite of spaghetti. He reached into his pocket and grabbed a single card. He said, "Here's a card that I think will interest you." I looked at the card and written on the front of it was my daughter's name, Tracy Lynn Davis. And I couldn't turn it over.
>
> I've jumped out of an airplane at 8,000 feet. I love driving fast cars. I have an airplane of my own that I flew to Alaska and landed in places where people have never landed. There is a guide up there who said he'll never fly again after riding with me. I love danger, but I couldn't turn the card over.
>
> There's only one thing worse than knowing that wound exists. That's taking the chance someone will rip it open even more widely. Finally I just turned the card over. Written on the other side in huge round letters were these words: "I love my daddy." I spit spaghetti all over the table.
>
> I was so embarrassed that I ran from the room and found a little bathroom and closed the door. There was a latch. I can still see it. I slammed that latch shut, and I cried like a child. I said, "Oh Jesus, she loves me."
>
> I didn't know there was a guy in there.

In Ken's story, the tension-producing statement was "I didn't hear the words 'I love you' from my daughter." When he said, "I said to my daughter, 'I love you,' and she said, 'Whatever,'" his audience became real quiet. That's tension. People are wondering, *How's that situation going to end?*

When we make a tension-producing statement, we sometimes make the mistake of releasing the tension too soon. Tension gives energy. When people experience tension, they are motivated to find resolution.

Davis artfully tells his story, maintaining tension throughout. He describes how he spoke at his daughter's college, and afterward he got the card from his daughter. We all know there's something on the other side of that card. We want to know what it says.

What does Davis do? He doesn't turn the card over! He starts talking about his willingness to take risks: "I've jumped out of an airplane...." What's he doing there? He's increasing the tension, elongating the time. It takes a lot of skill to do that because if you try

to increase the tension and it's not effective, people just get irritated. What's on the other side of the card?! Davis delays the resolution with a skillful ability to discern how much tension people can take.

Think of a rubber band. If it's too slack, there's no tension at all. If you stretch it too much, it's going to break. But if you have it at the right distance, there's tension—energy.

When Davis turns the card over and it says, "I love you," the impact—because of the tension—is enormous. That partly explains why the audience exploded with laughter when they heard there was a guy already in the bathroom listening to Ken bawling, "She loves me." If the tension wasn't there, there wouldn't have been nearly that degree of response to the humor.

Tension is important not only in stories but also when challenging a congregation to some area of obedience. You do not want to let them off the hook too soon. Preachers and teachers need to be willing to live with tension.

Chapter 138

ILLUSTRATING FROM POP CULTURE
How to refer to popular culture in a way that is appropriate and connects with hearers

Kevin A. Miller

THREE ASSUMPTIONS

In my sermons I use illustrations from movies, TV shows, popular magazines, and the celebrity culture. I do that based on three assumptions.

(1) All teachers and communicators must take people from the known and move to the

unknown. In other words, we start with what is known and make comparisons or contrasts so people can understand what they don't already know. This is a universal law of education. It is the reason behind every metaphor and simile and analogy.

For example, the parables of Jesus are filled

with the known world of his listeners. There are many references to sheep. I've hardly ever been around sheep in my life, and I don't know anyone who herds sheep, but that was common for Jesus' listeners. That was part of their known world, so he used it. He referred to fig trees and oil lamps, common things in first-century Palestine. Why did he do that? Jesus wanted to teach about the unknown world of the kingdom of God and couldn't immediately start talking about something completely unknown without a reference point in what hearers knew.

When I preach about heaven, the inspiration of the Holy Spirit, or the indwelling presence of Christ, these are unknowns to many of my listeners. The only way I can do that is to start talking accurately and convincingly about the world they already know. In order to do that I need to know about politics, business, and the way families work, and I must know something about pop culture.

Some people in our congregations assume what preachers have to say is totally irrelevant. I chip away at that assumption by showing that Christianity directly applies to the world they know.

(2) Pop culture is the known world for an increasingly large number of people today. The majority of people age forty-five and under have grown up with TV, video games, and a celebrity culture. That is what they know thoroughly.

For example, a young woman was employed at Christianity Today International who was working on her doctorate in English, an extremely bright and literate person. She and some others were standing around in the hallway talking about a friend of theirs who is a TV-watching junkie. I was listening and said, "Yeah, some people actually know the name of every person J-Lo has ever dated." The conver-

sation stopped dead. This young woman looked at me and said, "I know the names of every person J-Lo has ever dated." Suddenly I realized I had accidentally insulted this person I cared about. I had looked down on her world, which is a pop culture world.

A friend of mine is a professor at a Christian college, and we were talking about which websites, newspapers, or TV shows he watches to stay engaged with the world. He said, "I don't really follow all the national news."

"Why not?"

"That doesn't affect me," he said.

"National news doesn't affect you?"

"No," he said. "What I need to know about is pop culture because that's what my students are talking about. If I'm going to teach and connect with my students, I need to know pop culture."

That conversation brought home to me again that for an increasing percentage of people today, pop culture is the known world. If I want to take them from the known world to the unknown world, I have to know something about it.

Obviously this approach carries danger for those of us who pursue holiness and separation from the world. An appropriate acquaintance with popular culture requires prayer and discernment.

When John Wesley decided to preach outdoors to the masses, the coal miners, the poor and ragged people of England, that was a radical thing in his time. He said, "I consented to become more vile." In other words, I was willing to rub shoulders with the messiness of the world in order to bring the gospel there. That being said, again, we need a lot of discernment on how to use pop culture appropriately and well.

(3) I can gain or lose credibility by using pop culture references in a sermon. It all depends on how I do it. For example, Paul refers to the culture of his hearers in Acts 17 when he goes up on Mars Hill and speaks to the pagan, Athenian philosophers. He says, "I was walking through your city, and I noticed this statue dedicated to an unknown god." Later he quotes the Athenians' own poets. So at two points in that message Paul refers to things that are true in Athenian culture. Notice the second one—"as some of your own poets have said"—he cites approvingly, indicating that what those poets said is actually true. He does not refer to the statue dedicated to the unknown god approvingly, but he does so graciously.

Acts 17 is an example of what Paul says in 1 Corinthians 9:22: "I have become all things to all men so that by all possible means I might save some." It's also a good example of how trying to make a connection point to the pop culture world doesn't mean we need to embrace or affirm everything we find there. Obviously we can't. Paul doesn't affirm this statue to an unknown god; he simply uses that as a jumping off point.

Billy Graham does this. He spends the first portion of most of his evangelistic messages talking about problems in our contemporary culture. He'll reference headlines, social problems, divorce rates, and suicides. He is leading up to the fact that Christ is the ultimate answer to those things. He makes a connecting point with the people in the stadium.

Two Principles

To use pop culture illustrations with credibility, I must answer two questions important to the person immersed in pop culture: Do you know about my world? and Do you care about my world?

(1) The preacher must know about the pop culture world. People don't expect me to be a cultural expert because they know I'm a pastor. They expect me to be knowledgeable about the Bible, God, prayer, and other spiritual matters. But they appreciate when I make a comment that shows I know at least something about their world, and they respect my effort.

For example, on a summer vacation in Wisconsin, our family went one day to a Go-Kart track. Standing next to me in line was a young man with a T-shirt that said "Flogging Molly," (which sounds sort of sadistic). I asked him, "Hey, is that a Celtic punk band?" He nodded, and I asked, "Are they sort of like Drop Kick Murphy?" His eyes got wide, and he looked at me with astonishment, like *Hey, you look a little old, but you know something about Celtic punk music.* I think he was wondering, *How do you know about the world of music that I like?*

That's the kind of bridge I want to make in a sermon. I want to know enough about the hearers' world that they start to think, *Oh, well, if you know that about my world, then maybe I can trust you when you talk about spiritual things.*

If I don't know about that world, I can lose points. It's okay if I admit I don't know, but if I act as though I know and I don't, then I lose points. For instance, I saw a great quote by Johnny Depp in the *Preachingtoday.com* illustration database, but I decided I couldn't use it because I had not seen Johnny Depp's films. If I tried to talk about him, I couldn't talk for ten seconds without my ignorance showing. What if I had called him *John* Depp, which would be like calling Michael Jordan *Mikey* Jordan! It just betrays my ignorance of the subject.

What could I do in that case? I could go online (*imdb.com* is one site that gives extensive background information on films) and learn enough to speak intelligently about Johnny Depp and introduce that quote. Or I could drop the name and say, "Recently a famous actor said ..." and just use the quote, sidestepping the fact that I don't know much about Johnny Depp.

The details make all the difference. For example, one Sunday I used an opening illustration from *The Lord of the Rings*. I know that some people are absolute fanatics about *The Lord of the Rings*. They've seen every scene in it many times. They've read the trilogy many times. When I used that illustration, I looked up those pages in the book. I checked some of my understanding with my son, who is a *Lord of the Rings* nut, and somebody else who is even more of a *Lord of the Rings* nut to make sure I had all the details right when I retold that story. When you get it right, people think, *You know my world.*

Another resource I use to become more knowledgeable about pop culture is the magazine *Entertainment Weekly*. It covers a lot, especially film, and helps me learn about it without having to go see everything, particularly those films that are a morality problem. It helps me know the important names and topics.

ChristianityToday.com has a free email newsletter that reviews movies every week and summarizes what Christian reviewers are saying about them. It helps me know where a movie falls in terms of its worldview and how salacious or redemptive it is. It's concerned with what this movie is trying to say and how well it is saying it.

When a preacher refers to a movie, it comes across as an implied endorsement of that movie. I may use just one scene that is morally impeccable, but I can't assume my listeners will hear it as my using only one scene. They'll think, *Oh, he went to that movie. He must have liked it because he's talking about it.* There may be something morally reprehensible in another scene of the movie, and I don't want that implied endorsement to come across. Faced with that dilemma, what am I going to do?

I should know the rating and general worldview of the movie before I use an illustration from it. Movie sites like *Screenit.com* tell me what the movie is about, how violent it is, how sexually oriented it is, what the worldview is, and so on. With that knowledge I determine whether I can reference the movie—or will regret it if someone sees it as a result.

Although it would be easier to say, "This particular scene is great, but I don't recommend the overall movie," you don't want to do that often because it comes across as *I can see it, but you can't.* Or it communicates that I don't practice what I preach about lifestyle selection, holiness, and discernment. Either one of those is a bad message to send.

(2) The preacher must care about people in the pop culture world. This is the most critical point because tone is even more than content. The tone of the pop culture reference will make or break your ability to connect with people.

Recently I visited a church in another state and attended a Sunday school class prior to the worship service. In this adult class of ten or twelve people, as we sat around the table talking about different themes, several people referred to the "pagans out there," or talked of "how awful the world is." I thought to myself, *I'm glad I didn't bring a non-Christian friend with me because that non-Christian friend would be feeling judged, put down, or looked down upon.* A non-Christian would feel alienated. That happens in sermons unintentionally.

For example, let's say you want to use a quote by Madonna that is antithetical to the gospel in your sermon. The use of quotations as a point of contrast or a foil to the truth can be effective. It would be easy to introduce the quotation by saying something like, "I heard Madonna say something the other day. It's just what you would expect from her. . . ." That's an understandable emotion, but it immediately distances you from anyone in your church who has a Madonna album and who likes her. They think, *Why is he beating up on Madonna?*

A more productive approach would be "I heard Madonna say something that really made me think." I haven't said I agree with the statement; I've just said it made me stop and think. Or I could say, "I heard Madonna say something that perfectly expressed how many people feel today." Through the rest of my message I may show how her view is completely the opposite of the gospel, but I've done it in a way that doesn't tear her down. I simply say her words represent a worldview shared by others. I want to talk in such a way that Madonna herself could be in the room and not feel as though she was walked on.

I reserve the right to fully and forcefully disagree with the values expressed in the quotation, but I want to do it in a way that respects the person. That way the pop-culture oriented person feels, *You care about the people in my world.* Jesus was a friend of sinners. I want to have that same attitude and tone.

For example, a recent Easter sermon of mine was about the resurrection of the body. Here is what I had originally written in my sermon notes: "*Rolling Stone* interviewed Natalie Port-

man, who plays Queen Amadala in the *Star Wars* movie, and they asked her about the afterlife. And Natalie said, 'I don't believe in that. I believe this is it.'" In my notes I originally wrote, "She may be a good actress, but she's a terrible theologian."

When I was reviewing my message before I preached it, I thought, *That's kind of a slam. It may be accurate, but if she were in the room how would she feel? If one of her fans was in the room—and a lot of people like Natalie Portman as an actress—how would they feel? Would they feel distanced or brought near to what I want to get across?*

So I softened my words to: "She may be a good actress, but on this point it's not the movies we're talking about. This is not something you film on a soundstage or in front of a big blue screen. This is real life with a new and better reality coming." That was better, but there still seemed to be a tone of *She doesn't know what she's talking about.*

Here is what I finally said: "I wish I could have been in the room during that interview and asked Natalie some more questions. I would have said, 'Natalie, are you sure? Are you 100 percent confident that it is physically impossible for an afterlife to exist?' And then I'm sure she would have asked me, 'Well, Kevin, what makes you so sure that there is one?' And then I would have said. . . ."

From there I went on to the text. I presented it as if I was conversing with her. I didn't preach down at her. I didn't use her as a cardboard caricature. I engaged her viewpoint and treated her as a person. Then I showed the contrasting message of the Bible. It took three revisions to get there. I kept working until I followed my own advice and showed that not only did I know something about the culture, but I cared about the people in that culture and respectfully engaged their viewpoint even when I disagreed.

People are saturated in pop culture; it is the only world many of them know. I want to take them to a new world, but it's going to take time. I need to do as Jesus did: He entered our messed-up world to bring us to heaven. I need to follow that incarnational journey.

Chapter 139

ADAPTING ILLUSTRATIONS SO THEY FIT YOU

Six recipes for changing ready-made illustrations to fit your style and purpose

Craig Brian Larson

When someone special whips up a home-cooked meal for you, does the cook make everything from scratch? Not likely. Those zesty baked beans, for example, probably came from a jar, but they were prepared to the personal requirements of the chef by adding ingredients: bacon, pepper sauce, and some extra brown sugar.

Those who preach weekly often cannot prepare enough illustrations from scratch to consistently create well-illustrated sermons, but they can always personalize the ones they find ready-made. Here are six ways to adapt illustrations available on *PreachingToday.com* or other quality sources to your personal style and unique purposes.

CHANGE TONE

Sometimes the wording of an illustration clashes with our personality or viewpoint. Perhaps the writer is too sentimental or too detached. There may be slang, purple prose, or regional idioms. Perhaps the illustration contains stuffy, academic transitional words and phrases such as "moreover," "furthermore," or "in con-clusion." We can fix this with a bit of nip and tuck or by adding some signature phrases.

Here, for example, is an objective, journalistic illustration:

The publisher's review of a recent book describes it as "a thoughtful, detailed discussion of every aspect of considering, preparing for, beginning, and conducting a successful and emotionally fulfilling extramarital affair." The book is called *Affair! How to Manage Every Aspect of Your Extramarital Relationship with Passion, Discretion, and Dignity* (by Cameron Barnes, UPublish.com, 1999). For just $19.95, plus shipping and handling, you can get a practical summary of the deception in our culture on the subject of sexual relations outside of marriage.

Let's change that to a passionate perspective on the illustration:

Believe it or not, there is a publisher that has the gall to promote one of its new books as "a thoughtful, detailed discussion of every aspect of considering, preparing for, beginning, and conducting a successful and emotionally fulfilling extramarital affair." Sadly enough, this depraved book is called *Affair! How to Manage Every Aspect of Your Extramarital Relationship with*

Passion, Discretion, and Dignity. For $20 you can buy the lies that the devil would have you believe concerning adultery.

Or we could use a slang-filled street voice:

> Get this. There's a bottom-feeding publisher who is promoting a new book as "a thoughtful, detailed discussion of every aspect of considering, preparing for, beginning, and conducting a successful and emotionally fulfilling extramarital affair." Whoa, am I hearing that right? This sick book is called *Affair! How to Manage Every Aspect of Your Extramarital Relationship with Passion, Discretion, and Dignity*. Yeah, right. For just $19.95, plus shipping and handling, you can stuff your brain with the lies that the devil wants to sell you about sex.

Notice in these different versions how much a slight shift in wording changes the tone.

BEEF UP

Some illustrations are too spare for our tastes. We like to draw hearers in and have an emotional impact. For instance, we may find a story does not develop a scene enough to make it moving. It may lack physical setting and sensory appeal. What this illustration needs is more body.

One way to beef up an illustration is to use our imagination to fill in incidental sensory details that are lacking. This is not dishonest as long as we do not exaggerate, change, or add significant events or dialogue to a true story.

When Max Lucado enhances a Bible story, for example, he stays within the boundaries of what the Bible says but imagines what we could reasonably expect to experience if we lived the story. In *Six Hours One Friday*, Lucado writes: "'Lazarus, come out!' It took only one call. Lazarus heard his name. His eyes opened beneath the wrap. The cloth-covered hands raised. Knees lifted, feet touched the ground, and the dead man came out. 'Take the grave clothes off of him and let him go.'"

In addition to sensory details, we may add a description of what we can reasonably expect people to feel, often with a qualifying statement like, "I imagine that at that moment tremendous fear welled up in her heart."

Tony Smith of Gainesville, Georgia, tells this story:

> I was sitting at my desk in my study after having scolded my 4-year-old daughter for misbehaving. I heard a gentle knock on the door. "Come in," I said. Bethany entered and then matter-of-factly said, "Daddy, sometimes I am good, and sometimes I am bad. And that is just the way it is." Then she left the room just as summarily as she had come in, acting as if she had completely explained her misbehavior for all time.

When I tell this story, I want Bethany's words to have a stronger impact right when they are heard, so I choose to set them up more. My enhancements are in italics:

> Tony Smith writes: I was sitting at my desk in my study after having scolded my 4-year-old daughter, *Bethany,* for misbehaving. *Unknown to me, my little girl was sitting in her room doing some serious thinking. She felt guilty for what she had done, and she was searching for a way to justify herself.* Soon I heard a gentle knock on the door. "Come in," I said. In walked Bethany, *cute and innocent, yet with a determined look in her eyes.* She matter-of-factly said, "Daddy, sometimes I am good, and sometimes I am bad. And that is just the way it is." Then she *turned and* left the room just as summarily as she had come in, acting as if she had completely explained her misbehavior for all time.

Another way to beef up an illustration is to

add important or enhancing facts from research. Let's see what we can do with this spare illustration:

> The Ken Burns PBS series on jazz music has a terrific quote by jazz great Duke Ellington. Duke was asked about his feelings at not being able, as a black man, to stay in the guest rooms of the hotels he and his band performed in because of segregation. He said, "I took the energy it takes to pout and wrote some blues." (source: "Jazz: A Film by Ken Burns," Part 4)

One way to add muscle to this illustration would be to find an anecdote that describes a scene in which Ellington and his band were denied accommodations in a particular hotel. Short of a true story, we could say, "I can imagine Ellington walking into a hotel and. . . ." Through the story behind the quote, hearers would feel the pain of segregation and realize what strength of character Ellington must have had to overcome self-pity.

SALVAGE

On occasion, instead of abridging an illustration, we may only want to salvage a key element: a quote, image, or metaphor. For example, suppose in the following illustration I want to focus less on the writer and more on the words of the man to whom he is speaking:

> D. A. Carson, an author and professor at Trinity Evangelical Divinity School, used to meet with a young man from French West Africa for the purpose of practicing their German. He writes:
>
> Once a week or so, we had had enough, so we went out for a meal together and retreated to French, a language we both knew well. In the course of those meals we got to know each other. I learned that his wife was in London, training to be a medical doctor. He was an engineer who

needed fluency in German in order to pursue doctoral studies in engineering in Germany.

> I soon discovered that once or twice a week he disappeared into the red-light district of town. Obviously he went to pay his money and have his woman.
>
> Eventually I got to know him well enough that I asked him what he would do if he discovered that his wife was doing something similar in London.
>
> "Oh," he said, "I'd kill her."
>
> "That's a bit of a double standard, isn't it?" I asked.
>
> "You don't understand. Where I come from in Africa, the husband has the right to sleep with many women, but if a wife is unfaithful to her husband she must be killed."
>
> "But you told me you were raised in a mission school. You know that the God of the Bible does not have double standards like that."
>
> He gave me a bright smile and replied, "Ah, le bon Dieu, il doit nous pardonner; c'est son metier [Ah, God is good. He's bound to forgive us; that's his job]. (*Bibliotheca Sacra* [October 1999])

Here is one way to salvage just one quote from this story:

> Author D. A. Carson tells of a conversation with a friend who was committing sexual immorality. When Carson confronted him, the man replied, "Ah, God is good. He's bound to forgive us; that's his job."

I accomplished this by summarizing only what was needed to set up the quote and by changing from a first person to a third person account.

SHORTEN

Sometimes a relevant illustration is too long for our purposes. A five-minute story does not suit a minor point. What we need to do is abridge the illustration.

Here, for instance, is a long movie illustration I have shortened. In *italics* are the words I can delete without losing the essentials of the story. In **bold** are words I am adding.

The movie <u>Glory</u> chronicles the true story of the first noncommissioned black regiment to fight for the North during the Civil War. *The formation of the 54th Regiment of Massachusetts is not taken seriously from the beginning. Most doubt that enough soldiers will volunteer. Others suspect that even if enough enlist, the regiment will whittle away deserter by deserter. But the white abolitionist officer from Boston, Robert Shaw, played by Matthew Broderick, idealistically agrees to command the 54th, believing that blacks should be given the right to fight for their freedom.*

From the beginning, Shaw, tries to treat his men like soldiers, not like the slaves they once were. Even though the Union doesn't consider the 54th equal in status with other white regiments, Shaw wants his soldiers equipped as every other soldier is in the North: with firmly soled shoes, Union uniforms, and sturdy weaponry. Lobbying on behalf of his regiment, however, he increasingly understands how little his men are valued, even by those Northerners who maintain that blacks should be emancipated.

Throughout the film **the white abolitionist officer who commands the black regiment, named Robert** Shaw, faces the dilemma of standing up for his men or staying quiet amongst his superiors to save face. This dilemma is strikingly portrayed when Shaw must inform his soldiers that the Union recently determined that black soldiers would receive a smaller salary than white soldiers. *Standing on a high, commanding platform, Shaw hesitantly announces to his troops, "You men enlisted in this regiment with the understanding that you would be paid the regular army wage of 13 dollars a month. This morning I have been notified that since you are a colored regiment you will be paid 10 dollars a month."*

His regiment grumbles at the injustice, but they fall out by company to receive their pay. *Some pay, no matter how little, is better than no pay at all.* But there is one dissenter, a runaway slave named Trip, played by Denzel Washington, who stridently protests the pay cut.

"Where you goin', boy?" Trip asks one soldier.

"To get paid. Ten dollar, lot of money," his comrade replies.

Trying to garner some support, Trip asks his elderly bunk mate, Rawlins, played by Morgan Freeman, "Hey pop, are you gonna lay down for this *too*?"

When Rawlins ignores him, Trip files up and down the forming lines struggling to get someone to join his protest. *He hollers, "A colored soldier will stop a bullet just as good as a white one and for less money too. Yeah, yeah, Ol' Unc Abe has got himself a real bargain here."*

Soon other soldiers join **in** the protest. *One yells, "That's right, slaves. Step right up. Make your mark. Get your slave wage." Another says, "All you good colored boys, go ahead and sign up."*

One by one, soldiers join the outcry, and Trip incites the regiment to tear up their paychecks. "Tear it up. Tear it up. Tear it up," he shouts.

The regiment repeats the same words: "Tear it up. Tear it up. Tear it up."

"Pow!" A shot instantly silences the clamor. The soldiers turn their attention to their commanding officer, Shaw, expecting to be disciplined.

"If you men will take no pay," Shaw sternly announces, "then none of us will." He proceeds to tear up his check as well.

Recovering from their shock, the soldiers uproariously celebrate, tossing their tattered paychecks in the air like confetti.

These changes cut the illustration more than half, from 563 words to 265. With a word processor, abridging an illustration is a snap.

With printed text, use a yellow highlighter on the words you want to keep. With each phrase and sentence, simply ask yourself, "Is this absolutely necessary for the illustration to be understood or emotionally compelling?" If not, cut it. Sometimes if we cannot cut a segment, we can summarize it.

GENERALIZE THE SOURCE

Illustrations may come from a source our hearers will not relate to. What would happen if you serve a largely blue-collar congregation and have a great excerpt from Dostoevsky, or your classical music crowd receives an anecdote from Garth Brooks?

Some try to overcome this by owning the illustration: "I once wrote a story about a one-legged man obsessed with killing a great white whale." Not a good idea.

The right way to solve this problem is to generalize the source. Instead of "In *Les Miserables*, Victor Hugo wrote...," make it "A great writer tells this timeless story...." Rather than, "In AD 400 Augustine wrote...," say, "One of the best-known leaders of the church once said...."

PARAPHRASE

Nip and tuck will not always put an illustration in our voice. The entire approach to the story may clash with our style. Other illustrations are in a written style—complex, long sentences, stiff-sounding transitions, formal wording—that will not connect with hearers in spoken form.

We need a total overhaul, a paraphrase. To do that, reread the illustration several times, fixing important details in your mind. Then,

either immediately, or after letting it percolate through your subconscious a while, retell the illustration from memory out loud (preferably with someone listening—maybe at the dinner table). I suggest taping your retelling and then having an assistant type it for your notes. Finally, reread the original illustration and add to your paraphrase any important details you missed.

Here is an illustration I would feel awkward presenting in a sermon as is:

If you become an evangelical Christian in Laos, the communist neighbor of Vietnam and Cambodia, you likely will be "asked" to sign a fill-in-the-blank form. And it's not a membership card at your neighborhood church. The form reads, in part:

I, (name), who live in (location), believe in a foreign religion, which the imperialists have used for their own benefit to divide the united front and to build power for themselves against the local authorities. Now I and my family clearly see the intentions of the enemy and regret the deeds which we have committed. We have clearly seen the goodness of the Party and the Government. Therefore, I and my family voluntarily and unequivocally resign from believing in this foreign religion.

If you sign, you promise not to participate in this "foreign religion"—Christianity in every reported case—under punishment of law. If you don't sign, you can expect humiliation, harassment, and persecution, including probable imprisonment and torture.

The document's widespread use by Laotian officials has been authenticated by the World Evangelical Fellowship's Religious Liberty Commission and other sources. Hundreds of rural Christians reportedly have been forced to sign the form in public, then compelled to participate in animistic sacrifices. (Baptist Press [10–9–2000])

Here is my paraphrase:

Laos, as you know, is a communist country bordered by Vietnam and Cambodia. If you become a Christian in Laos, communist officials may come to you with a form and demand that you sign it. The form basically says, "I know that I've been deceived, that this religion is just a weapon used by our enemies against us, and I turn away from it completely." If you sign that form, you are promising to stay away from Christianity, under penalty of law. If you don't sign the form, you can expect to be persecuted, harassed, perhaps imprisoned and tortured. The communists have forced hundreds of Laotians to sign and then to participate publicly in pagan sacrifices.

One advantage of writing out a paraphrase is that it fixes the illustration in our mind, so we can tell it from memory rather than by reading it.

We might consider these techniques for adapting illustrations as spices in our cabinet. With them, we can adapt the recipe of any illustration to our own tastes and purposes. When we do, we have thousands more illustrations available and a far greater ability to connect with our hearers.

Chapter 140

OVEREXPOSURE

Transparent preaching is not without risks

Richard Exley

Several years ago I participated in a seminar about sex and dating held at a Christian college. The other speaker was a well-known minister whose vision and ministry have influenced thousands of young people. Unfortunately, the subject of sex and dating was not his forte.

Attempting to relate, he shared a personal temptation experience in graphic detail. He was so explicit the students responded with embarrassed amusement. Instead of identifying with him in a positive way, they later turned his disclosure into a campus parody.

While risky, transparent preaching is still worthwhile. Our family struggles, for example, uniquely prepare us to speak to one of the deepest concerns of our congregations. When people see that we wrestle with similar life issues, they inevitably see our preaching as more authentic.

But how do we use personal experiences constructively? What are the secrets of making our sermons truly transparent and not just emotional exhibitionism? How can we draw on the rich experiences of family life without humiliating our family members?

DISCLOSE IN THE PAST TENSE

For successful transparent preaching, I concern myself both with what I share and the way I share it. When I relate personal temptations, for example, I am careful to disclose them in such a way that the worshiper's attention is focused not on my struggle but on the grace of God. That means the personal struggles and failures I disclose in the pulpit should be in the past tense. If I admit sinful actions, they should be ones I've repented of and, if possible, made right.

I heard of one pastor who opened his sermon by confessing that he and his wife had a fight in the car on the way to church. "I hope we can settle the issue after the service," he said, and then launched into his text.

That pastor's confession may have been therapeutic for him, but it certainly didn't help his wife or the congregation feel better. No one could concentrate on the rest of the sermon; they were wondering how seriously damaged the pastor's marriage was.

My preaching should inspire hope, not amusement or sympathy, or worse yet, doubt. When we make our congregations privy to our present temptations, we inevitably threaten them.

Despite what's said to the contrary, our listeners still expect us to rise above the average person's struggles. And if we have not, they reason, we should at least have the good taste not to mention our spiritual shortcomings in the pulpit.

Keeping my temptations in the past tense accomplishes three things:

- Because I have already worked through the problem, rather than threatening my congregation, the positive outcome gives them hope.
- Because I've had time to reflect on the past experience, I can provide practical insights for helping them deal with their own temptations, thus reinforcing their faith.
- Even though the situations are not current, they're still real. Because I share life experiences common to us all, they find my preaching more real, more helpful.

GIVE HOPE

I do at times share some of my current conflicts. If I bare my soul in a hopeful way, often my transparency can have a healing power unlike any other type of preaching.

I know one minister who returned to his pulpit ten days after his son committed suicide. Under duress he read his text: "And we know that in all things God works for the good of those who love him, who have been called according to his purpose" (Rom. 8:28). Visibly struggling, he said:

> I cannot make my son's suicide fit into this passage. It's impossible for me to see how anything good can come out of it. Yet I realize that I only see in part. I only know in part.
>
> It's like the miracle of the shipyard. Almost every part of our great oceangoing vessels are made of steel. If you take any single part—be it a steel plate out of the hull or the huge rudder—and throw it into the ocean, it will sink. Steel doesn't float! But when the shipbuilders are finished, when the last plate has been riveted in place, then that massive steel ship is virtually unsinkable.
>
> Taken by itself, my son's suicide is senseless. Throw it into the sea of Romans 8:28, and it sinks. Still, I believe that when the Eternal Shipbuilder has finally finished, when God has worked out his perfect design, even this senseless tragedy will somehow work to our eternal good.

Because the congregation was struggling with the same painful questions about his son's suicide as he was, his transparency was timely and appropriate. He did not deny or make light of his unspeakable grief. He affirmed his unconditional trust in the wisdom and sovereignty of God. As a result his witness was authentic, and his faith became a source of hope for his congregation.

STANDING IN BOTH GOOD LIGHT AND BAD

Revealing too much, too soon, however, is not the only pitfall the preacher faces when drawing from personal experience. I also resist the temptation to present myself only in the best possible light. If my congregation always sees me as the hero—riding through life on a white horse, conquering every foe—they will find my preaching self-serving and my credibility suspect.

Not long ago I preached a series of sermons on parenting, and one of the messages was titled "Mistakes Parents Make." I was concerned that my message might sound accusatory or condescending, so I decided to relay this story:

> The first time our future son-in-law visited in our home, I humiliated our daughter. Leah had made us coffee, and when she went to pour it, she discovered that the handle on the coffee pot was too hot to hold. Instead of getting a potholder, she grabbed the handiest thing—a kitchen towel with fringe on the ends. When she picked up the coffee pot, the towel touched the gas flame and caught on fire. Screaming, she dropped both the burning towel and the coffee pot. She wasn't burned, but we had quite a mess.
>
> I lost control and berated Leah right there in front of Todd. "What were you thinking?" I demanded. "You know better than to use a fringed towel around the stove."
>
> Once I got started, I couldn't seem to quit. "You're lucky you didn't burn the house down." With a few more words, I reduced her to tears, and she ran from the room.
>
> My wife Brenda gave me a look that clearly said, "You are one of the world's most insensitive fathers." Without a word she followed Leah upstairs.
>
> I risked a glance at Todd, who sat uncomfortably in the living room not knowing what to do. Not knowing what to say, I went to the kitchen to clean up the mess. By the time I finished, I knew what had to be done.
>
> I went upstairs to find Leah. When she heard me coming, she turned her face to the wall and tried to stifle her sobs. Sitting down on the edge of her bed, I put my hand on her trembling shoulder. She cringed beneath my touch, and I thought my heart would break.
>
> I was tempted to explain my behavior, tempted to say something like "I'm sorry I lost my temper, but you know better than to use a towel around the stove." Somehow I realized that I would still be pointing the finger of blame at Leah.
>
> Finally I managed to say, "There was absolutely no excuse for what I did. Please forgive me. If you'll come back downstairs, I will apologize to Todd as well."
>
> Leah agreed to come, and that emotional scene had a happy ending. But had I been unwilling to admit my mistake and make restitution, our relationship might have been seriously wounded, perhaps for life.

By sharing this painfully embarrassing incident, I showed the congregation that, like all parents, I, too, make mistakes. Without accusing anyone I highlighted the common parental mistake of losing one's temper. By owning my mistake publicly, I encouraged other parents to accept responsibility for their own mistakes and then presented a model for making restitution for parental failures.

ATTENTION TO THE ORDINARY

I avoid the temptation to overlook the ordinary experiences of life in search of the extraordinary. While examples of dramatic spiritual experiences have their place, our congregations often have difficulty relating.

For the most part, my listeners live lives that can best be described as ordinary—not unlike my own. Their problems, too, are ordinary—trying to make ends meet, finding time for the most important things, dealing with the death of a beloved parent or the empty nest when their last child leaves home.

Frederick Buechner says, "In the last analysis, all moments are key moments, and life itself is grace." If I miss the "little" moments, I will be the poorer for it, and so will my preaching.

I often use other people's material to introduce my own. It helps set the context and shows the significance of the everyday occurrence. On Mother's Day I began by reading Mary Jean Irion's "Gift from a Hair Dryer," a mother's reflection as she dried her seven-year-old daughter's hair following a Saturday night bath:

> Comb and dry, comb and dry. *Soon I won't be able to do this any more*, you say to yourself, knowing that the little straight bob must inevitably yield to grown-up coiffures and ugly curlers. What will she be like at fourteen? Where will her hair be blowing then? And sixteen and eighteen—you suppose boys will love to watch her hair blow as you do now. And some of them will feel it on their faces, and one of them will marry her, and her hair will be perfect under the veil, and there will be her hair spread out on his pillow ... oh, you hate him a little and wonder where he is at this moment and whether he'll be good to her ... they will grow old together ... the gold-brown hair will be gray, and you will be gone, and then she will be gone ... this very hair that now your fingers smooth ...
>
> All the tears of the world swim for a second in your eyes as you snatch the plug out of the socket suddenly and gather her into your arms burying your face in the warm hair as if you could seal this moment against all time.

For a moment we were all there, mothers and fathers alike. It was our children who were growing up faster than we ever thought possible. Soon they would be gone, and their precious childhood years would be just a fading memory.

Then I told my congregation how deeply I was moved the first time I read Irion's account. How I put my finger between the pages while tears ran down my cheeks. How she made me realize the many times I had lived moments like that without ever realizing it. How I asked God to forgive me for missing so many of life's special moments. How I vowed to slow down, to spend more time with my family, to live life to the fullest.

Finally, I told them how I got up and went to the door of my seven-year-old daughter's room and watched in wistful silence as she played Barbies. My heart swelled with love and thanksgiving as I realized—maybe for the first time—that this was abundant life. Leah sensed my presence and glanced a question in my direction. I smiled, spread my arms wide, and said, "I love you big—this much!"

Leah returned to her dolls, as if nothing special had happened, while I thanked God for her and for all the special moments we had shared.

I addressed a common concern, and it grabbed the attention of everyone in our church. It not only spoke to their intellect but to their hearts as well.

MAKING MY STORY THEIR STORY

Perhaps the greatest challenge in transparent preaching is to avoid focusing on ourselves. By its very nature, transparent preaching is autobiographical, filled with personal experiences. How can we help but focus on ourselves?

I've discovered that I must communicate my experiences so that the hearers get in touch with their own story, not just mine. In a recent seminar conducted by my wife, Brenda, and me, I told how for years I had frustrated Brenda with advice and exhortations.

"Whenever she shared a problem or worry with me," I confessed, "I had a ready answer. The things that troubled her seemed so insignificant to me, so easy to solve. Yet it was not my 'wisdom' she sought, but my understanding. Not realizing this, I continued to advise her. I was a 'fixer,' but what she needed was a compassionate husband who would accept her and listen."

By then, several husbands had sheepish looks on their faces. My story was their story. A number of the wives, identifying with Brenda, were nodding their heads.

"Needless to say," I continued, "my insensitivity was not without its consequences. After a while Brenda stopped sharing her needs and concerns. I hardly noticed, so busy was I in my own world. My easy answers and constant advice had only made her feel silly, inadequate, and angry. So she suffered alone. Over the years this silent suffering took its toll, and she grew depressed. She was careful to hide it from me, for I had not proved worthy of her trust.

"One winter evening I came home early and found her in the bedroom crying. Reluctantly she poured out her hurts, fears, and self-doubts. For once I listened with compassion and didn't try to fix everything. After her grief had spent itself, we sat for a long time that night in silence."

I noticed that several wives in the audience were weeping. This was their story, too. Some of the men, too, were realizing how they had hurt their wives.

"That night was a turning point in our lives. Brenda wasn't suddenly free from her depression, but a bit of the loneliness was gone. She began to believe I might be able to understand her. Little by little she began to trust me with her feelings again. As I responded with compassion and understanding, our relationship deepened."

After the session, several couples shared similar experiences with us. More than one wife said, "That's exactly how I feel, but I've never been able to put it into words." Our story had become theirs. Several were moved to renew their commitment to their marriage.

Jesus told the man out of whom he had cast a legion of demons, "Go home to your family and tell them how much the Lord has done for you, and how he has had mercy on you" (Mark 5:19). That, in the final analysis, is how I view the moments of transparency in my preaching. I am describing the grace of God in my life.

Chapter 141

ILLUSTRATING WITH INTEGRITY AND SENSITIVITY

Seven questions for staying above reproach

Wayne Harvey

Several years ago I heard a sermon illustration I thought was great for demonstrating determination. I decided to use it. Here's the story:

On the last day of the 1956 Olympic Games, Austria had yet to win a gold medal. Its only hope was in a young Austrian named Johann who had entered the rapid-fire pistol competition. His teammates weren't disappointed. As he fired his last shot, he gave his country their single gold medal.

When Johann returned to his homeland, his country gave him a warm welcome and a huge parade in his honor. Tragically, only a few weeks later, his right hand, his shooting hand, was blown off in an accident.

But this didn't stop Johann. After his body had healed, he walked out the back door of his home one day with something stuffed under his shirt. His wife noticed the bulge and followed him to a place where she saw him loading a pistol, holding it between a tree and his leg. Shot by shot, he emptied the pistol with his left hand and reloaded. After months of this daily practice Johann became proficient. Almost miraculously, he went to the 1960 Olympics where his determination paid off for himself and his country as he won a second Olympic gold medal in the pistol competition.

Isn't that a great story?

If only it were true.

When I heard this story about Johann, I was so impressed I decided to learn more. In an Olympics book, I found, to my surprise, little of what I had heard in the sermon was accurate. The man's name wasn't "Johann" but Karoly Takacs. He wasn't Austrian but Hungarian. The years he won gold medals were not 1956 and 1960 but 1948 and 1952, years in which his country won not one gold medal but ten and sixteen, respectively. And his right hand wasn't blown off between the Olympic games but during World War II, after he'd won the European championship.

I was amused after I learned the truth about "Johann," so I called the pastor who had preached the recorded sermon and told him what I'd discovered. After we had a good laugh, he told me he had gotten the story from a well-known preacher, who in turn had received the story from a nationally known writer and pastor. Who knows how many people have been impressed and inspired by an almost entirely fictional man named "Johann"?

But telling half-true or untrue stories to our congregations can threaten our integrity. Accuracy is critical also because our listeners will remember illustrations far longer than our sermon points. So I have created a checkup to ensure my illustrations stay healthy.

Am I inserting myself into someone else's illustration? A cartoon showed several church members giving three large volumes to their pastor. The caption reads: "Pastor, since you've been with us for a year now, we wanted to give you a copy of your biography that Mrs. Smedley has put together from all that you've told us about yourself in your sermons."

To take someone else's personal experience and make it yours is theft. If you find someone else's good personal illustration, don't say that it happened to you. Attribute it accurately, and it can still be effective.

In the illustration, is someone described as "a member of my former church"? This phrase may irritate present church members, who tire of hearing about people in "that other church." It also broadcasts this message: "I'm telling this story about something confidential a former parishioner told me. If you confide in me, I may tell your story at my next church."

Just say, "I once knew someone who. . . ."

Should this illustration be checked for accuracy? Some illustrations are like investments: If they seem too good to be true, they probably are.

For years I've enjoyed using an illustration about the introduction of Coca-Cola in Korea, to show how easily we can misunderstand one another. I found the story in a sermon magazine, which said that when the soft drink was first introduced, the company wanted to use Korean letters and words that sounded as much like "Coca-Cola" as possible, so they used "Ko Ke Ko Le." However, sales were flat because that set of Korean words means, "Bite the wax tadpole." So Coca-Cola changed the name to "Ko Kou Ko La," which means, "May the mouth rejoice," and sales increased.

I planned to use this illustration recently, but because we have a number of internationals as members, I decided to confirm it. When I showed the two Coca-Cola names to a Korean member, she informed me that neither set of words means anything in Korean. On bottles in Korea, "Coca-Cola" is "Ko Ka Kol La," which means nothing but sounds just like Coca-Cola.

I won't be using that one anymore.

Will this illustration be sensitive to people in the congregation? It's simply good manners to be sensitive to gender, age, and ethnic groups. The phrase "little old lady" will turn off at least some older women; so will "girls" when talking about women. One man in my church told me how offended he was when he read in our local newspaper about an "elderly man" who was listed as sixty-five, just his age!

Will this particular congregation relate to the illustration? Do most of your listeners read *Vogue* or *People*? Do they watch professional wrestling or public television? Do they prefer jazz or country? Every church is different, so some illustrations will work better than others.

If you have a story about a king, you might make the character a CEO, a business owner, or a union boss, if the illustration can be adapted. Your listeners will be better able to put themselves into those stories than stories about people from another age and setting.

Relate also to local people, events, and places when possible. For example, if a member of your church has overcome cancer and gives permission to use the story as a sermon illustration, that will have great impact.

Is this illustration too detailed? Early in my preaching ministry, I thought the only good illustration was a detailed illustration. If I told about a day in May, I would describe the weather, the color of flowers, how much rain had fallen during the month, and more.

What adds impact, though, are *relevant* details. One of my favorite sports stories is about Glenn Cunningham, a student at the University of Kansas who set an American record for the indoor mile run in 1932. What makes him even more remarkable is that at age eight, his legs were so severely burned that his doctors said he would probably never walk again. Yet with hard work and perseverance, Cunningham became a winner.

The details make the story better than just, "A young man once won a record in the indoor mile run even though his legs were burned as a child and doctors told him he might never walk." Details do have an important place if they're the right ones and they aren't too numerous.

Am I clearly differentiating true and imaginative stories? Sometimes we add unsubstantiated details to true stories: "As David gathered the stones to fling at Goliath, he gathered the smallest from the stream, knowing that even one of these, aimed by God's unerring hand, would be enough to knock down the giant." These kinds of details can alter a story's substance (and make the story saccharine).

However, imagined details that don't change the substance of the story can help listeners. I recently heard a Bible teacher tell the story of

Hosea buying back his prostitute-wife. The only biblical description of this incident is in Hosea 3:2–3: "So I bought her for fifteen shekels of silver and about a homer and a lethek of barley. Then I told her, 'You are to live with me many days; you must not be a prostitute or be intimate with any man, and I will live with you.'"

This teacher embellished the sparse story this way: "Imagine Gomer, Hosea's wife, standing on the auction block, about to go to the highest bidder. Dressed in rags. No makeup or pretty clothes to attract men as she had done before. Looking at the crowd of bidders and seeing the grinning faces of men who'd had her. But then among the crowd she sees the face of her husband she'd abandoned. Imagine how

stunned she would have been to see him come for her, his rightful wife, to buy her back with all he had. All for one woman who had rejected him, left him, and been with her many lovers. *How can he love me so much?* she must have thought."

I liked this illustration, in spite of the license the teller took with the story. He has brought a simple transaction to life by dramatically portraying the important scene—yet he never presented his version of the story as if it really happened. He asked us only to imagine his version, and that exercise painted a beautiful picture of God's grace.

 For an audio example of this principle see tracks 16–17 on the supplemental CD.

Chapter 142

FOOTNOTES IN THE PULPIT
How to credit your sources without distracting your hearers

Chris Stinnett

Now, what was that first book you mentioned? I read the other three, but I never heard of that one."

In a sermon, I mentioned four recent books in which university professors expressed some belief in the concept of intelligent design behind existing life. Now one of my friendly critics wanted information about the first. I knew he wasn't exaggerating about having read the other three. I was glad to be able to recite the author, title, and publication year. I knew he would read that book—and check to see if my attribution was accurate and fair.

To provide arresting and relevant sermon illustrations demands that preachers read widely. When we use others' material in the pulpit, integrity demands that we give proper attribution. But how do we strike the proper balance between too much information and too little in a verbal footnote? The trick is to give our hearers enough background so they can understand, accept, and recognize the importance of the quoted material, but not to bog down or distract from the truth we're trying to communicate.

From my failures and occasional successes, I offer a few suggestions.

Keep it short. If brevity is the soul of wit, it likewise is the heart of helpful attribution. If I give more than one or two sentences of reference, the audience gets lost prior to the quotation.

Consider this example: "Presbyterian preacher and theologian Timothy Keller wrote a three-part series called 'A Model for Preaching' which was published in the *Journal of Biblical Counseling* back in 1994. In the second part, Fall 1994, on page 42, he wrote, 'The goal of communication must be change, not performance or ritual.'"

Kind of numbs the brain, doesn't it? By the time the pertinent line is delivered, my hearers are trying to guess how many of these details matter. Is the publication date significant? Is the journal title a clue? Is the source's denomination and theological stance leading me to agree or disagree with him?

These details are essential in written footnotes, but only clutter oral presentations. If I want to point out that preaching aims for life change, I could say, "Preacher and theologian Timothy Keller put it like this: 'The goal of communication must be change, not performance or ritual.'" A name and professional credential will often be enough. Should a hearer request fuller citation, I can provide it. The important thing is that the quote is heard honestly and full force, unobscured by irrelevant facts.

Anticipate doubters' questions. If the hearers are likely to question the material, I include the source where I found the information and the date it was published.

Details help in this case. A vague "many experts believe" or "current studies show" as a preface to a startling idea will generate skepticism among hearers. They assume that if many experts actually believed it, I'd be able to name one. Without attribution, this sounds like just another opinion. Remember, we preachers don't like it when someone brings us a bad report that begins, "A lot of people are saying...."

Consider this approach to a report on the power of prayer: "In a 1992 interview in *Christianity Today*, senior government researcher Dr. David Larson revealed that scientific studies on the effect of prayer showed that it had a clear beneficial effect on physical and mental health." The date and source of the article, and the professional credentials of the scientist all lend credibility to the information.

Some things are better left unsaid. If my hearers are likely to have access to the source from which I quote, the writer's name and the source are usually sufficient: "In last Tuesday's newspaper, the columnist Thomas Sowell wrote...."

Skip the reference altogether if most people know the source. Quotes from *Poor Richard's Almanac* or *Aesop's Fables* shouldn't need attribution.

But make sure when you cite a source that you get it right. While preaching once in Michigan, I attributed a humorous line to the wrong man. One sister nailed me. "That was Dr. Will Kellogg, the cereal maker, who said that," she grinned. "He was from Battle Creek, you know, and quite famous long before your time." She hastened to add, "And mine, of course!"

Even accurate attribution can backfire, though, when the source is actually a source of irritation! Briefly a hero to many in Detroit, Lee Iacocca made some unpopular decisions in later years. I once began an illustration by pointing him out as the source. Before I could complete the story, an uneasiness washed across the congregation and several people turned and whispered to their neighbors. My point was sabotaged by the crowd's feelings toward Iacocca. I should have left the story anonymous.

This concept brought to you by.... Footnotes in sermons prove we've done our research. They can lend credibility and power. They allow us to tap the best of expert opinion and the most brilliant wording of ideas. If I am forced to rely solely on my own ingenuity in weaving memorable tapestries of words, I cheat my hearers.

A stirring line like "slip the surly bonds of earth" is stronger when we remind people that President Reagan uttered those lines in eulogizing the Challenger astronauts. Or, "The final test of a leader is that he leaves behind him in other men the conviction and the will to carry on" is made more poignant because it comes from Walter Lippman's tribute to FDR in April 1945.

In a sermon, a few well-chosen words of introduction can prepare our hearers for a quote that really drives home the point. And a little research can allow us to respond with the appropriate information when challenged at the door, "What was that first book you mentioned?"

Chapter 143

AVOIDING SELF-CENTERED SERMONS
Why limit the number of personal illustrations?

Craig Brian Larson

A few months ago I was talking about preaching over a pancake breakfast with Lee Eclov, pastor of Village Church of Lincolnshire in Lake Forest, Illinois, and he surprised me with this observation: "Personal illustrations are cheap."

Preachers know the effectiveness of using stories from their own experience, so my eyebrows raised, and I asked, "What do you mean, 'cheap?'"

Lee explained we often use personal illustrations because they are easy to come by. Though easy and close to home, they are often weak stories, metaphors, or examples. If someone else tried to quote our personal illustration, we would immediately see how lame it is. Even so, because the illustration is immediate and concrete and we need something, we use it rather than search for something better.

Since that breakfast I have thought a number of times about what Lee said and realized I have indeed often used cheap personal illustrations in my sermons. They had the interest of the congregation because of our relationship, but they really didn't add to the sermon anything beyond a breather.

I thought of another conversation with a preacher I talked to years ago who, when I asked where he found good illustrations, said, "All my illustrations come out of my daily life."

That may sound good—I don't stoop to using "canned" illustrations!—but there is a danger there. Doesn't that become narrow for his congregation after a while? Don't his people tire of hearing about his hobby, his kids, his feelings? After a few months or years, won't people roll their eyes at excessive autobiography even from someone they love dearly?

Certainly well-crafted personal illustrations are some of our best illustrations, but they can never meet the majority of our needs. I must illustrate from a world bigger than my own. My listeners don't relate to everything in my life. They relate as well to the pervasive world of media and the experiences of other people.

What can make an illustration "canned"— ineffective—is a cut-and-paste approach. Skillful communicators know that just because a sermon and an illustration are both about love does not mean the illustration will suit the sermon. When you consider using an illustration, I suggest weighing the following factors:

- tone and associations
- suitability and relevance for your audience
- the purpose an illustration must serve at that point of the sermon
- whether the illustration fits who you are

I've also found when I use a prefabricated illustration, I have to do extra work to become familiar enough with it to where I can deliver it with authority and sincerity. The point is, such illustrations usually take more work, not less, but they are worth it.

Chapter 144

ILLUSTRATING WITH SLICES OF LIFE

Finding powerful sermon illustrations in the stories and scenes of the everyday

John Ortberg

EXEGETING LIFE

There is a knack for finding just the right illustration to fit the message. I want my illustrations to communicate to people that I live in the same world they live in. The single largest source, then, is the people themselves—staying immersed in the lives of people and telling stories about people, because story communicates deeply.

In part, that means watching for things in the spheres of government, business, and the arts. I also look at things like *USA Today, The Chicago Tribune,* and *Time.* Especially for the people who are outside the church, I want to communicate that I live in the real world, their world.

But the best method I've found came from a great homiletics professor in seminary, Ian Pitt-Watson. He taught us the preacher has two tasks: exegesis of the text and exegesis of life. If Christ really is present in all of space and time, then I can find him in all kinds of moments in life if I learn to look diligently and creatively enough.

I've always tried to think less about illustrating a point and more in terms of exegeting life. There's a little piece of my mind that is always doing that, looking for ways to teach.

Those moments in life are the slices of life that make good teaching.

I'm not just focused on the series I'm working on now. I've taught myself to be alert to moments that communicate something deeper. I hear things people say, or I pick up a story, and it strikes me: "That'll teach."

Some people keep a file of these illustrations and stories, but I don't do that. Occasionally I've tried, but I find it difficult. I prefer to immerse myself deeply in whatever the message is and wait for the right slice of life to resurface. Whether it's my mind, the Holy Spirit, or some combination, the right thing tends to come up at the right time.

LOCATION AND DEPTH

A big temptation is after we find something that feels like a great story, we try to wedge it in somehow. Almost all of us have had the experience of hearing somebody share an illustration in a message, and then we try to do it and it just doesn't work. I can remember early on in preaching being really confused by that.

They say the three laws of real estate are location, location, location. Illustrating is the same way. When an illustration is right in the flow of what we're talking about so that it becomes deeply, intrinsically, organically connected, it works. If it doesn't fit, you're much better just waiting for when it does.

I've discovered, for instance, that an ordinary insight from life that many would devote three sentences to can be strung out for four minutes so that it builds and takes on a life of its own. One way that happens is to ask, "What is the doctrinal truth that is present in this situation?" Thinking about basic theological themes already there—like brokenness or persistent love—and asking how these things are present in the story causes the illustration to deepen.

The vast majority of us as teachers and preachers don't squeeze nearly all the blood out of the turnip. It requires the discipline of forcing yourself to sit down and think about it again and again to get the maximum mileage. A lot of people don't take the time to think creatively about connections between everyday stories and theological truths.

Years ago a group of us were playing *Trivial Pursuit* when the board game first came out. We were playing with some pranksters, and one of them made up an unanswerable question, "What is the color of Mona Lisa's necklace?" But Mona Lisa didn't wear a necklace.

That story later became the primary theme of a message I was doing on Ecclesiastes. The game was hot, everyone was talking about it, and I preached the idea that all life is vanity, a trivial pursuit. The phrase "trivial pursuit" kept playing over and over as I preached how the busyness of life, running errands and such, is a trivial pursuit. Then there's the trivial pursuit of Ecclesiastes: learning, achievements, wealth, and pleasure. You can chase these things as long as you want, but you eventually find this too is just a trivial pursuit. The story and the phrase start on a light, easy-to-relate-to level, and then get deeper and deeper.

I also invert the idea, give it a twist. Out of the whole universe there's this one little planet of fallen, bent people, and yet God decides they are worth sending his Son to the cross. And the gospel becomes a story of trivial pursuit. The God of the whole universe goes after this one little bent planet, but in God's mind, it's not a trivial pursuit.

ADAPTATION OF ILLUSTRATIONS

Part of what I'll look for with an illustration is language and images that work on multiple levels. There's where the adaptation and the depth come in.

But there are some stories that don't really work. Just because something is a slice of life does not mean that I should use it as an illustration. The biggest rejection factor, again, is fit. I have to discipline myself all the time to say, have enough trust in God not to use that illustration now; save it for another time. That's the number one criteria.

Another factor is taste or appropriateness. I remember one time I was at an InterVarsity meeting at Harvard. A Gen-X student was explaining Paul's argument in 1 Corinthians 15. It was a fascinating combination of theological language and Gen-X language. The climactic moment was when she declared, "Basically what Paul is saying here is if Christ be not raised from the dead . . . we're screwed." It was hilarious. At one level it was deeply true, but I just couldn't use that at my church because of the language.

A huge third factor is tone. Does it feel church-y, or pastor-y? There are many stories in this business where the story, its language, and the voice it assumes sound like a "pastor story." It breaks down the authenticity; it doesn't relate with people.

I enjoy using historical illustrations. But I'm aware of how it will sound to people and whether I need to make it accessible to them. I won't assume the people I'm speaking to know who Gregory the Great was. I might describe him in contemporary language so I'm bridging this world to that world. If it feels to people as though I'm showing off my historical knowledge, then it gets in the way.

To talk about Gregory the Great, for example, and quote some of his statements on humility and pride, I might say, "Here are some terrific insights on the nature of humility that, ironically, come from a guy whose nickname was—Gregory the Great." It would just be something to warm him up a little bit.

IDEAS FOR IMPROVEMENT

Exegeting slices of life involves long-term skill development. But there are some practical things preachers could do to help them improve right now.

First, become a student of people who preach well. When I first started preaching, I listened to Tony Campolo and thought I needed to tell stories like that. I listened to Swindoll, and I wanted to have that kind of folksy, warm quality. I listened to Ian Pitt-Watson, and I wanted to be artistic. I was influenced by a ton of people, and it's a trial-and-error process of discovering your own voice.

I admired the late Lew Smedes's artistry when he used images multiple times at multiple levels. I remember Lew telling a story from the old PBS series *Upstairs, Downstairs*, the story of a wealthy family living upstairs and the servants downstairs. There was a vast social chasm between the two. He told of a time when he was in England, and the woman who lived downstairs would serve him but would not consider him a friend. Then he developed it into the gap between us and God—while humans don't normally cross financial gaps, which are relatively small, Jesus crossed the infinite chasm between God and man. And then he said the gospel is Jesus Christ coming all the way downstairs, "and he brought his toothbrush and his jammies, and he came to stay." It was such a creative, vivid, compelling way of expressing the beauty of incarnation.

I love art in preaching. Not for art's sake, but because it can communicate truth in a way that penetrates both heart and mind.

A second thing is to teach narrative material. Illustrations are about story, and narrative material is story. Large chunks of Scripture come with the illustration prepackaged. The slice of life is already set up for you. Practice telling an ancient story and give it a contemporary color that folks will understand.

Finally, get evaluation. When you're done preaching, ask people which illustrations worked, why they worked, and what kept the others from working well.

Chapter 145

POWER OF EVERYDAY-DISCIPLE ILLUSTRATIONS
What kind of examples influence hearers most?

Craig Brian Larson

What kind of illustration is an "everyday-disciple" illustration? And why would you want to use these kind of illustrations in your sermons?

Let me give you an example, then explain. Dave Goetz writes:

My wife, an experienced nurse, recently switched jobs. The change had been a long time coming. Jana was excited to join up with two doctors whom she had worked alongside previously. She was back with "family"; she had come home.

Her first evening at the clinic a young mother came with her 18-month-old son. He needed his final shot for a routine immunization; his mother came for a physical. Both patients were new to the clinic.

Jana gave the boy his shot, and his mother took him back to the waiting room, where his sister and grandmother sat. The mother then went back to the room for her physical. When Jana went to record the vaccination on the boy's chart, she noticed that the seal on the vial inside her lab coat was unbroken. Quickly Jana realized that she had given the boy the wrong vaccine.

She had given him a shot from a different vial—a routine vaccination for children, but the boy had already completed that series of shots months earlier. Jana told me she gasped when she realized her mistake and then went into shock, physically numbed by the fierceness of what raged within. Here is the sequence of her thoughts, according to what she told me later:

"No one will ever know. No harm done."

"I can't tell the doctor."

"This is my first day on the job."

"The doctor will think I'm incompetent."

"It can't hurt him, can it?"

"It doesn't hurt to be immunized twice for the same thing."

"But he needs the right vaccine."

"What will the mother say?"

"But I will always know, and so will God."

Meanwhile, the doctor was examining the boy's mother. Jana weakly paced outside the room.

When the doctor walked out of the room, Jana told him her mistake, almost vomiting her confession. "Whoa. Let me think about this for a moment," he said. After a few moments, he walked back in the room, told the mother what happened, and asked her to schedule another time for her child's immunization. Jana's anxiety released, she was now free.

Notice six characteristics of this everyday-disciple illustration:

(1) The essence of everyday-disciple illustrations is that they give an example of how to live the Christian life. They let people see how to obey a particular Scripture. They flesh out a virtue. After hearing an everyday-disciple illustration, a person should think, *Oh, that's how I put that Scripture into practice,* or *That's what humility is.* The above example illustrates honesty and integrity.

(2) Everyday-disciple illustrations don't necessarily show someone doing it right, as Jana did, but if the person stumbles, the illustration can show how he or she learned through the experience. In fact, everyday-disciple illustrations should not have a "hero" story feel to them. The story of someone deciding to sell everything and become a missionary has a valuable place in preaching, but most people also need to see ordinary people living for Christ in everyday circumstances. People have trouble identifying with someone doing everything right because their own lives are a churning jumble of doing right and struggling and sometimes blowing it.

(3) People must identify with an everyday-disciple illustration. For that reason, most such illustrations will be contemporary, not historical. On rare occasion a historical illustration will work if we can tell it in a way that it doesn't feel dated and is in a setting people can relate to.

(4) For the sake of identification, everyday-disciple illustrations will most often be about a noncelebrity. If the story is about a celebrity, it must be in a situation that normal people face. We can identify with a story about Steven Curtis Chapman overcoming temptation while watching a TV show; we identify less with him as he struggles with the temptation to be proud as he sings on stage before thousands of people.

(5) Everyday-disciple illustrations will be stories, not an image, quote, or statistic. Stories give the most compelling examples.

(6) The stories will be applied literally, not figuratively as a metaphor. The story about Jana is a literal one about honesty. It would not be an everyday-disciple illustration if we used it figuratively, as in: "Just as Jana accidentally vaccinated the child, so we may accidentally vaccinate someone against the good news of the gospel."

Thus, everyday-disciple illustrations are literal stories that hearers can identify with, that flesh out what it means to follow Jesus. Your preaching will gain power to change lives as you use illustrations that share these characteristics because they will show—not just tell—people how to obey God, in ways that are relevant to hearers.

Part 8

Preparation

How Should I Invest My Study Time So I Am Ready to Preach?

Chapter 146

WHY I PAT THE BIBLE ON MY NIGHTSTAND

One pastor's greatest regret, and how he is making up for lost time

Ben Patterson

A few years ago Bill, a retired pastor and seminary professor, convinced me and Tim, another pastor friend, that it would be a good idea for the three of us to memorize the book of Revelation and recite it before our church on a Sunday evening. I mention that he was retired because a few days before the event—when I was scrambling to prepare and fearing I would make a complete fool of myself in front of a lot of people (one thousand people turned out)—I was thinking it was easy for him to talk about memorizing a third of a book in the Bible; he had time, for heaven's sake. But I didn't. *What was I thinking*, I was thinking.

On the night of the event, just before we went out and did this terrifying thing, Bill reminded us that no matter how poorly we might do in the memory department, God was pleased with us and would bless his Word. He was right: For two and a half hours all the people, children included, listened as three men simply recited the Word of God from the last book of the Bible, beginning to end. The Word was all it says it is: a hammer, a sword, rain, light, truth, and bread.

I was stunned, and when my persuasive friend later suggested we do the same thing with the book of Mark and then Romans, we agreed and saw the same results. Each time, the people sat in pregnant silence and listened to the naked Word of God, "unplugged" as musicians might say, with no frills, no illustrations, and virtually no visual aids. Alone, it was more than enough. I'll never forget how whistles and applause erupted spontaneously from the audience when one of us came to the closing lines of Romans 8: "For I am convinced that neither death nor life, neither angels or demons, neither the present nor the future, nor any powers, neither height nor depth, nor anything else in all creation, will be able to separate us from the love of God that is in Christ Jesus our Lord."

A HERMENEUTIC OF SPEAKING

One of the surprising benefits of all this memorization was the way I was forced to think in new ways about what a biblical text means. It was one thing for me to check the commentaries and pore over the critical apparatus and do the exegesis. It was another thing for me to think of how I would say Scripture if I were its author. Emphasis, pause, and inflection of voice can have a powerful effect on how a passage is heard and understood. Since then I have been practicing a kind of hermeneutic of speaking, and I have been dazzled at the creative impact it has had on how I think about a passage. It isn't always first I think it and then I speak it. Sometimes I have to speak it before I can think it! All this now happens in concert with commentaries, language study, and the rest. Memorization with a view to speaking has become a chief way I meditate on Scripture.

As I have done this, I have thought often of something Rabbi Abraham Heschel said to the people in his synagogue who complained to him that the liturgy did not express what they felt. He said it was not that the liturgy should express what they felt, but that they should feel what the liturgy expresses. The liturgy was there to train, not merely express, their spiritual sensibilities. Memorizing Scripture can have that effect. Even as I try to think of how I would say a passage if I had written it, what I am forced to do is think of how Paul or Moses or Jesus would have said it. It isn't me saying it my way, but me saying in my way what they meant. My thoughts are most certainly not God's thoughts, but in learning to say a passage his thoughts may become my thoughts.

IMPLICATIONS FOR PREACHING

My preaching has also changed. When I started saying the text, I noticed how people seemed to pay so much more attention than when I just read it. This probably shows I should have paid much more attention in the past to the way I read the biblical text. In any case, I and those to whom I speak are discovering the Bible is really quite wonderful. In fact, if the words of the Bible are heard clearly, the sermon may fail, but the time isn't wasted!

My view of myself as preacher has also changed. I used to think, quite presumptuously, that I had to make the Bible interesting to those who heard me. For instance, if there were no great illustrations, there was no sermon. I've repented of that. Again, I have discovered the Bible is really quite wonderful! It doesn't need my help. Now when I preach, I think of myself more as a docent in an art gallery. My job is to say just enough and then get out of the way so people can see for themselves the glory of what God has given us in his Word. I still use illustrations, of course, but more sparingly, less gratuitously.

The Bible is really quite wonderful! One of my greatest regrets in life is that I waited so long to memorize large chunks of Scripture, to meditate on the Word by learning to say it. But it's never too late. Francis Schaeffer said of the Bible:

> I don't love this Book because it has a leather cover and golden edges. I don't love it as a "Holy Book." I love it because it is God's Book. Through it, the Creator of the universe has told us who he is, how to come to him through Christ,

who we are, and what all reality is. Without the Bible we wouldn't have anything. It may sound melodramatic, but sometimes in the morning I reach for my Bible and just pat it. I am so thankful for it. If the God who is there had created the earth and then remained silent, we wouldn't know who he is. But the Bible reveals the God who is there; that's why I love it.

After I read those words, I put a Bible on my nightstand for just that purpose.

Chapter 147

BUSTING OUT OF SERMON BLOCK

Having to speak doesn't always mean you have something to say

Haddon Robinson

Preaching well is hard work. We're expected to be witty, warm, and wise. And then next week, we have to do it again.

The great science fiction writer H. G. Wells reportedly said most people think only once or twice in a lifetime, whereas he had made an international reputation by thinking once or twice a year. Lots of pastors have to think once (or more) a week! More often than we would like to admit, we begin preparing a sermon with the feeling not that we have something to say, but that we have to say something. Only one time in twenty do I start my preparation feeling that this sermon will go well. The creative process is accompanied with a feeling of ambiguity and uncertainty, of trying to make the unknown known.

Like the homemaker whose goal of three nutritious meals a day is complicated by toddlers making messes, demands of a part-time job, overflowing baskets of laundry, and a phone that won't stop ringing, the multiple demands of pastoral life make fresh thinking and sermon writing even more difficult.

People never die at convenient times. The administrative load preoccupies pastors with scores of details that won't go away. Emotional weariness from dealing with people problems drains creative energies. And speaking several times weekly outstrips your capacity to assimilate truth fully into your life.

Just as savvy homemakers find resourceful ways to feed their families—a deft combination of ten-minute recipes, healthy snacks, a microwave special, and a few full-course evening feasts—pastors, too, can find ways to keep tasty and balanced spiritual meals on the table.

DISTINCT PHASES

When we feel we don't have anything to say in a sermon, it's usually because we've gotten ahead of ourselves. We're thinking about the sermon before we've understood the text. Instead, we need to divide our sermon preparation into two distinct phases.

What Am I Going to Say?

I start the process by focusing on content, not delivery. Approaching a text with the attitude *How am I going to get a sermon out of this?* pollutes the process. We can end up manipulating the text for the purposes of an outline instead of first trying to observe, interpret, and appreciate the text.

For one message based on the story of Christ's calming the storm, I began my study assuming my sermon's main idea would be that we can count on Christ to calm the wind and waves in our lives. But as I studied the text, I realized I couldn't promise people they would never sink just because Christ was with them in the storms of life.

This passage has to be seen in its broader context. Jesus has called the disciples and told them about the nature of his kingdom: It will start small but spread wide. In that early stage, everything depended on the men in that boat—Jesus and the disciples. If they go under, the kingdom is gone. The point of the passage is that those who have committed everything to Christ's cause can know that the kingdom will ultimately triumph because of the power of the King. This is an eternal truth that shifts the emphasis from the personal storms in my life and whether I will sink to the eternal kingdom that will never fail. If I promised that Christ would calm every storm, I would have twisted the text to say what I wanted. Instead I preached what the text taught me.

I have learned to let understanding the text dominate the sermon process early and later let sermonizing dominate. I have more material than I can preach when I first try to understand and interpret a text for its own sake. I ask, *What is the biblical writer doing?*

Then I study the context for the flow of thought. (I usually get more preachable insights from context than from studying the grammar and word structure of the original language.) By studying the context, for example, I came up with a major lead for a sermon on 1 Peter 5. "To the elders among you," writes Peter, "I appeal as a fellow elder, a witness of Christ's sufferings and one who also will share in the glory to be revealed" (v. 1). In my study, I found the theme of suffering accompanied by glory runs throughout 1 Peter. Whether in marriage, government, family—or church—when we suffer for Christ, we experience the glory of Christ. My sermon therefore pointed to this theme as it applied to leaders in the church.

How Am I Going to Say It?

In this phase, I move to the communication question. How will I get the ideas I've uncovered in the passage across to people in a way that interests, informs, motivates, and changes them? Out of all that I could say about this passage, what will I choose to say?

This part of the process can also provide us with something significant to say. Early on I ask, *Which of the following tacks is the biblical writer taking here: Is he primarily (a) explaining, (b) proving, or (c) applying?*

(a) If the passage majors in explanation, then my sermon will major in teaching. In the parable of the Pharisee and the tax collector (Luke 18:9–14), the primary purpose of this passage is to teach that the person who sees God as God and humbles himself before him is justified and exalted, and the person who exalts himself before God remains in his sins.

Accordingly, my sermon majors in explanation, not exhortation. I dig beneath the assumptions we have about Pharisees and tax collectors, helping my listeners get into the minds of these two men. What did they think about themselves? What did others think about them? How would these roles look today? I talked about the nature of the sins of hypocrisy, self-righteousness, and disobedience.

(b) One of the best ways to overcome "sermon block" is to think through *What's hard to believe about this passage?* We can underrate the need to prove the truth of a text. Even if there isn't a skeptical bone in our body, we need to ask, *Will those who hear me believe this? Does this conform to my and their experience? If not, why not?*

Our experience doesn't govern the Bible, but we need to explain perceived discrepancies between what the Bible says and our reality. Suppose someone hears the passage, "If two of you on earth agree on anything, it will be done for you." She wonders, *What if I want a blue Cadillac? If I can get two of the elders to agree with me in prayer, is that a done deal?* Like most people, she questions, *Do I believe that?*

In my sermon, I try to be an advocate for that person. She won't raise her hand and interrupt me, but like most people in the pews today, she listens to sermons with a keen sense of skepticism. The preacher who ignores that is ignoring reality. C. S. Lewis has been popular in recent decades largely because he deals with the "Is this really true?" question. He assumed people needed to be convinced.

(c) Good ideas for preaching also emerge as we apply the Bible's truths to people's lives. Sermon ideas ignite when the flint of people's problems strikes the steel of God's Word. Sometimes we can't come up with much to say because our thinking is too steely; it's all God's Word, but we don't link it to specific situations in contemporary life. Other times we come up short because we're too flinty; we're people-oriented, but we lack the authoritative content that only Scripture can bring.

But we almost always spark a preaching flame if we strike those two elements together. So part of my preparation is to ask these application questions: *What difference does this make? What are the implications for our lives in this text? If someone takes this truth seriously and tries to live it on Monday morning, how will he or she live differently?*

KITCHEN HELPERS

Like labor-saving devices in the kitchen, there are ways to write a sermon that can relieve the pressure of finding something to say. Here are six "kitchen helpers."

Develop a Preaching Calendar

Many pastors set up a plan for what they will preach over the next quarter, half-year, or year. We can take a retreat for several days and ask ourselves what the needs of the congregation are, what subjects we sense God impressing on our hearts, what themes we have an avid interest in.

A preaching calendar doesn't have to confine us. If some brilliant stroke from God strikes us, we can always change our plans. But if not, when we walk into the study, we have a sense of well-thought-through, well-prayed-through direction. My calendars have been based primarily on expository series through complete books of the Bible (which provides more than enough grist for any mill).

Once a calendar is set, we can set up file folders for each series of sermons, which become repositories for the relevant material we come across in the weeks and months before the sermons are preached. When the time finally comes to begin preparing the sermon, we already have a file of illustrations, quotes, and insights.

Work on Sermons in Ten-Day Cycles

The purpose of a longer cycle is to provide simmer time. On the Thursday ten days prior to the Sunday I will preach, I do my exegetical study. I read the text and think about it till I hit a wall. Then I write down what is holding me up: *What words don't I understand? What issues can't I solve? What ideas don't make sense?* If you can't state specifically where your problems are, you won't get answers.

Thus, ten days before I preach a sermon, I know what I need to be thinking about, which I do while driving the car, taking a shower, or laying awake at night. This also directs my reading. I know where the gaps in my understanding are, and I can more quickly find the answers. I can cull twenty commentaries in an hour if I know the key questions. Often, when I sit down to resume study the following Tuesday, the issues in the passage are much clearer. I wonder, *What in the world was I so hung up about?*

When I preached a sermon on the seven churches of Revelation, I grew curious about the seven cities and how they affected the churches. I did some extra research that added significant insights. If I had been writing this sermon the day or two before preaching, I couldn't have done that.

My next study time in the cycle is five days later, on Tuesday, when I finish up my exegetical work and organize the sermon. By the end of Tuesday, I want at least to have the sermon's homiletical skeleton and introduction completed. I may also have begun shaping the main movements.

My final writing installment takes place on Friday. I finish writing and actually have time to rearrange and polish.

Get Double Duty off Study

Duane Litfin, president of Wheaton College, first introduced me to the idea of preparing two sermons from research on one preaching passage. When he was pastoring in Memphis, if his Sunday morning message primarily explained or proved the truth of a passage, on Sunday night he focused on application. Or, on Sunday night he developed a subtheme of a passage that couldn't be given justice in the Sunday morning message. In Philippians 2:1–11, for example, he might preach in the morning on Christlike humility and on Sunday night, the doctrine of Christ's humanity.

Think Visually

Think of words on a spectrum, with abstract words and ideas at the top of the ladder and concrete ideas at the bottom. Scholars climb up the ladder of abstraction; communicators step down to get as close to specifics as possible. When I have an idea without a specific picture in my mind, nothing interesting happens in me. But my mind starts to roll when I have an image.

When I study a text, I ask, *What image was in the biblical writer's mind as he wrote this?* If the subject is reconciliation, he didn't write about some abstract doctrine; he was thinking about enemies who made peace. As I study such a passage, I pose questions that keep me close to real life: *What's it like to have an enemy? Why is it so hard to make peace?* I'll think about countries in the Balkans, where people who have lived together for decades suddenly begin killing each other. What happens when neighbors turn into enemies?

I don't think about abstract ideas like "parenting." I think of bouncing a baby on my knee, of getting up in the middle of the night and staggering to a crib to a child who won't stop crying, and of the feelings of love and anger that go along with all this.

Work on a Sermon Out Loud

My family learned that if they walk by my office and hear me mumbling, I'm working on a sermon. I get in imaginary conversations with people I want the sermon to help:

"Robinson, you say God wants us to love our neighbors, but what do you do when you go to wash their feet and they kick you in the mouth? How many times do you get kicked before you say, 'Forget it'?"

"You have to get kicked three times," I'll continue out loud to myself, "and then you can break his toes. No, I wouldn't say that. What would I say?"

Working through a sermon aloud helps crystallize our thinking. It also gives us a feel for the flow of thought in the text.

Borrow

God doesn't give us any points for originality. He gives points for being faithful and clear. To have sitting on our shelves books from the great teachers of the world, people who have spent years of their lives studying a book like Romans, and not use them is to deny the many contributions of Christ's church. To think that in three hours of exegesis we're going to match the insights of those who've spent years studying a book is a mistake.

But save commentaries for later in the process. If we go to the commentaries too quickly, they frame our thoughts. But once I have read through a passage and know where my difficulties lie, commentators become my teachers.

TRIBUTARIES FOR HIGH-WATER PREACHING

I have developed habits that help me collect material for sermons on an ongoing basis (not just for the sermon I will be preaching this Sunday). They are tributaries for high-water preaching.

Observe and Interpret Daily Life

Helmut Thielicke said, "The world is God's picture book." We can waste a lot of experiences. There are lessons in every day's events, in things as mundane as getting stuck in traffic or hearing a joke.

This is especially so when something happens that touches us emotionally, either positively or negatively. Even if I don't immediately grasp its significance, I write the anecdote down on a 3x5 card and reflect on it. It's a piece of life that someday will fit some insight, illustration, or sermon.

Reading books and magazines and watching movies and television—even commercials—is another way of observing life. I recently watched the Italian movie *Jean de Florette*, which begins with a city dweller inheriting a farm, moving to the country, and trying to learn farming from books. Wanting the farm for themselves, some unscrupulous neighbors block a spring that irrigates the farm. The new owner, unaware that he owns spring water, prays for rain. Storm clouds gather, but the rain falls on the other side of the mountain, never watering his land. Eventually the man dies, and the corrupt men buy his farm for next to nothing. There the movie ends.

I turned off the VCR profoundly depressed. I said to my wife, "That's the way many people see the world. Evil triumphs—The End." If I ever preach on Ahab stealing Nabal's vineyard, though, that movie will be a part of my introduction.

The questions I ask about ads are, *What do they want people to do? And how are they motivating them?* Marketers spend millions of research dollars to learn what motivates people. Watching their ads, we see the results of their research.

In one recent ad, a school appealed for new students, stating repeatedly that their graduates make more money. The school didn't promise its classes would make students deeper, better people or open the door to a more fulfilling career. The carrot being dangled was money. In preaching, I can use that ad to raise the question of whether money alone is ultimately going to satisfy.

As another tributary for high-water preaching, I make it a point to converse with people different from me. I've learned to make the most of the power of questions: *How do you make your living? In your field of work, what are your biggest problems? Who are the successful people in your world? What makes people winners or losers to you? What do you have to worry about? If you could have anything in the world, what would it be?*

One of the most meaningful conversations I've had recently was with a person who has AIDS. He had been involved in a homosexual relationship with a man with whom he thought he had a "love-bonding relationship."

"He didn't tell me he had AIDS," he said sadly. He described his fears of dying in a few years and his anger that someone he loved had done something that would kill him. He talked about his feelings of regret, of being ostracized, of wanting others to care but not sensing their care, of being sexually frustrated yet at the same time hating sex for its drawing power. "I couldn't do to another human being what that man did to me," he said.

Through all of this, he had become a Christian. Talking with him helped me better understand people in such situations. Such conversations feed my soul and add richness to preaching.

Soul Attention

The more full our souls, the more we can preach without running dry. Of the many spiritual disciplines that enlarge spirit, mind, and soul, we need to find the ones that benefit us the most.

I have a friend whose son has joined a monastery in pursuit of spirituality. He finds great benefit from the vow of silence and from long periods of meditation on Scripture. Such disciplines have less benefit for me. But it is impossible for me to overstate how much my friendships with certain people have challenged me. Although being with large groups does more to drain me than stimulate me, I will rearrange my calendar just to spend a day or two with a friend.

There's a difference between someone who derives great pleasure from meditating on a sunset and someone who meditates on sunsets because that's what "deep" people do. We can read in *Preachers and Preaching* what Martin Lloyd-Jones says about the importance of urgency in preaching, but if we try to be more urgent without having the values and passions that produce urgency, our preaching will strike listeners as affected. The ideas, themes, experiences, virtues, authors, and art that have gripped our souls are the ones that fill our preaching cup.

The number of issues that need to be addressed is so vast, the quantity of preaching material in Scripture so great, the needs of people so inexhaustible, a preacher couldn't finish the job in ten lifetimes. If we organize our sermonic work and stay full of God, more often than not, as we sit down to work out our sermons, we will not only have something to say, we will have more to say than time allows.

CENTERED

How prayer brings authority

Richard Foster

What is it about prayer that links it to preaching? Why would a person like Martin Luther set down as a spiritual axiom that "he who has prayed well has studied well"? Why would E. M. Bounds, the great Methodist preacher and pray-er of a century ago, say, "The character of our praying will determine the character of our preaching. Light praying makes light preaching. . . . Talking to men for God is a great thing, but talking to God for men is greater still."

IN TOUCH WITH GOD

Prayer gets us in touch with God, causing us to swing like a needle to the pole of the Spirit. It gives us focus, unity, purpose. We discover serenity, the unshakable firmness of life orientation. Prayer opens us to the subterranean sanctuary of the soul where we hear the *Qol Yahweh*, the voice of the Lord. It puts fire into our words and compassion into our spirits. It fills our walk and talk with new life and light. We begin to live out the demands of our day perpetually bowed in worship and adoration.

People can sense this life of the Spirit, though they may not know what it is they feel. It affects the feeling tones of our preaching. People can discern that our preaching is not the performance of thirty minutes but the outlook of a life. Without such praying, our exegesis may be impeccable, our rhetoric may be magnetic, but we will be dry, empty, hollow.

We are told that when the Sanhedrin saw the bold preaching of Peter and John they perceived them to be men who had been with Jesus. Why? Because they had a Galilean accent? Perhaps. But more likely it was because they carried themselves with such a new spirit of life and authority that even their enemies sensed it. So it is for us. If we have it, people will know it; if we don't, no homiletic skills will take up the void.

What does prayer of this kind look like? What do we do? Intercede for others? Perhaps, but primarily we are coming to enjoy his presence. We are relaxing in the light of Christ. We are worshiping, adoring. Most of all, we are listening. François Fénelon counseled, "Be still, and listen to God. Let your heart be in such a state of preparation that His spirit may impress upon you such virtues as will please Him. Let all within you listen to Him. This silence of all outward and earthly affection and of human thoughts within us is essential if we are to hear His voice."

Add to those words this perceptive observation of Sören Kierkegaard: "A man prayed and at first he thought prayer was talking. But he became more and more quiet, until in the end he realized that prayer was listening."

Prayer involves centering down, becoming genuinely present where we are, what the devotional masters often called "recollection." It cultivates a gentle receptiveness to divine breathings. We do not do violence to our rational faculties, but we listen with more than the mind—we listen with the spirit, with the heart, with our whole being. Like the Virgin Mary, we ponder these things in our hearts.

Perhaps one meditation exercise will illustrate how we practice centered listening. I call it simply "Palms Down, Palms Up." Begin by placing your palms down as a symbolic indication of your desire to turn over any concerns you may have to God. Inwardly you may pray, "Lord, I give to you my anger toward John. I release my fear of the dentist appointment this morning. I surrender my anxiety over not having enough money to pay the bills this month. I release my frustration over trying to find a baby-sitter for tonight." Whatever it is that weighs on your mind, just say, "Palms down." Release it. You may even feel a certain sense of release in your hands.

After several moments of surrender, turn your palms up as a symbol of your desire to receive from the Lord. Perhaps you will pray silently, "Lord, I would like to receive your divine love for John, your peace about the dentist appointment, your patience, your joy." Whatever you need, you say, "Palms up." Having centered down, spend the remaining moments in complete silence. There is no need for hurry. There is no need for words, for like good friends you are just glad to be together, to enjoy one another's presence.

And as we grow accustomed to his company, slowly, almost imperceptibly, a miracle works its way into us. The feverish scramble that used to characterize our lives is replaced by serenity and steady vigor. Without the slightest sense of contradiction, we've become both tough with issues and tender with people. Authority and compassion become twins and infiltrate our preaching. Indeed, prayer permeates everything about us. It is winsome, life-giving, and strong, and our people will know it.

IN TOUCH WITH PEOPLE

Some of the richest times in my pastoral ministry came when I would go into the sanctuary during the week and walk through the pews praying for the people who sat there Sunday after Sunday. Our people tend to sit in the same pews week after week, and I would visualize them there and lift them into the light of Christ. I would pray the sermons on Friday that I would preach on Sunday. Praying for their hurts and fears and anxieties does something inside you. It puts you in touch with your people in a deep, intimate way. Through prayer our people become our friends in a whole new dimension.

In our congregation in Oregon was a little fellow who underwent two serious brain operations. The times of prayer we shared during those six weeks built a bond between us that was like steel. Twice I stayed in that hospital all day with his mom and dad waiting to see if Davey would live or die. Davey was only five years old, and he had Down's Syndrome, but I value him as one of my closest friends. And would he listen to me preach! No children's church for him; he would perch himself up on that pew, eager, attentive. I do not know if he ever understood a word I said, but I would preach my heart out because I knew Davey was listening. If we have prayed with our people—really prayed with them—they will listen to us preach because they know we love them.

PEOPLE CAN TOUCH US

Prayer gets our people in touch with us. I want my people to know they have a ministry of prayer to give me. My people know I want them to come into my office and pray for me.

People need to sense our confidence and spirit of authority, but they also need to know us in our frailty and fear. They need to know that we hurt too. We need their help. The religion of the stiff upper lip is not the way of Christ. Our Lord knew how to weep. In his hour of greatest trial he sought the comfort and support of the three, and he went through that night in unashamed agony. Many times our stiff-upper-lip religion is not a sign of piety but of arrogance.

Beyond that, it is important to help our people understand the ministry of prayer they can have for and in our worship services. I would meet every Sunday at 8:00 a.m. with all the platform people and remind them that perhaps the main ministry they would be having that morning would be to pray for the people. Sometimes I would have people sit on the platform for no other reason than to pray. One dear brother would sit through both worship services every Sunday bathing the people in prayer, praying for the power of Christ to conquer, praying for truth to prosper. When you know someone is doing that, you can really preach.

Prayer is an essential discipline for preaching because it gets us in touch with God, it helps get us in touch with our people, and it helps people get in touch with us. As John Wesley said: "Give me one hundred preachers who fear nothing but sin and desire nothing but God, and I care not a straw whether they be clergy or laity; such alone will shake the gates of hell and set up the kingdom of heaven on earth. God does nothing but in answer to prayer."

Chapter 149

A LONG, RICH CONVERSATION WITH GOD

The joy of depending on the Lord for a sermon

Darrell W. Johnson

Over the years the Lord has nurtured the sense that preaching ministry emerges out of an ongoing conversation, an ongoing communion, with God. The call to preaching is first and foremost a call to listen and intercede. Effective preaching emerges out of a life of prayer.

PRAYER IN THE PLANNING STAGE OF PREACHING

I pray, *God, what text of Scripture do you want opened up for your people? What are you wanting to say to your people? And which texts are the texts that will say that? I'm always* asking that question, and many texts come. Then I try to plan at least one year in advance, so I have a sense of the various texts that could be opened up. All the while I'm asking, *Lord, what are you saying? What does the church need to hear in our time?*

For instance, when I go home after Easter Sunday, when family is there for dinner, I pray, *What do you want preached next Easter?* I find that's the best day to ask it, because I'm still caught up in all the feelings of Easter, the wonder of it and the joy. And I'm also aware of what I didn't say, what else could have been said about the resurrection. So I try to get a sense that day of what God might want to have preached next year.

Because I try to have the text way out in advance, I've got a lot of soaking time. In my mind I've got this closet with fifty-two hangers in it, and I think ahead about the texts for each of those hangers, each of those Sundays. I also have a file for each of those where I collect any thoughts that come.

Christmas Eve is the best night of the year. I come home late from service, at one or two in the morning. I'm still putting presents under the tree for the kids, and before I go to bed I try to ask, *So what would you want preached next year?* I don't always stay with the answer I get, because I can get corrected as I go along between now and next Christmas, but for the most part, it's there.

PRAYER IN PREPARING THE MESSAGE

I begin by asking the Spirit to open up the text to me: *Help me understand why you inspired this text in the first place.* And right on the heels of that I pray, *And open me up to what you open up.* That prayer asks God to

open the text, but then also to open my eyes and ears to receive it. He always honors that. I base that on Paul's prayer in Ephesians 1:17–18: "I keep asking that the God of our Lord Jesus Christ, the glorious Father, may give you the Spirit of wisdom and revelation, so that you may know him better. I pray also that the eyes of your heart may be enlightened...."

Then I do the exegesis and the hard work. But it begins with, *Will you open this text, and will you open me up to what you open up?* Then I pray through it as part of an ongoing conversation: *How am I going to craft this to make sense? What is the word you're speaking out of this Word? What homiletical structure does this best?*

I'm also praying, *Help me love the people who are going to hear this.* I can think of six, seven, or eight people offhand whom I care about, and I ask the question, *What does this text sound like to them?* But more than that: *Lord, help me love Steve*, or, *Help me love Jane the way you do, and, Help me speak this word to them out of your love.*

- Monday is my day off, so I just try to look at the text devotionally. I don't worry about whether my thoughts are exegetically sound or not. *Lord, what are you saying to me? What does this say just for my own soul at this time?*
- On Tuesday morning, I get to exegesis, praying, *Help me understand these constructions in the text. Help me understand the background. I don't know what this place is or who this person is.* Then as the day goes on, it's all percolating.
- Wednesday morning I try to tie up that exegetical work and begin to think about how this can be illustrated.
- Thursday morning I try to get an outline. I pray, *How can this be made accessible? How*

can this be made clear? That's the word I'm always after: How is this clear? I shoot for mid-Thursday afternoon to have a working outline.

- Then Friday morning I sit down at eight o'clock and write until quarter till twelve, and that whole time is, *Please, help me to write this clearly.*
- Saturday is polishing day. I know I have to move from the written English to oral English. I hate Saturday. It's an agonizing day. Saturday night I pray, *Please, now, just help me trust the power of the text and the power of your Spirit. Help me not to ride on my personality. Help me not to ride on my carefully crafted words. Help me to trust that this text is powerful in and of itself and that you, Holy Spirit, will show up and do your work.* So it's much more soul work on Saturday night.

Through the exegetical, hermeneutical, and homiletical work I ask and pray, *Lord, can you make this an act of devotion?* And that's what I try to coach the students here, too. When you write a research paper, yes, you've got to do all that hard academic work, but just say, *Lord, can I make this an act of worship, too?* I think we do better work when we do that. It's an ongoing devotional communion.

Scriptures that mold my prayers for preaching are:

- John 17:17, Jesus' prayer: "Sanctify them by the truth; your word is truth."
- Matthew 8:5–13, when the centurion comes on behalf of his servant and says to Jesus, "Just say the word, and my servant will be healed." How the centurion knew that I don't know.
- Ezekiel 37, the vision of the dry bones. This is the biggest one. Ezekiel is simply told to speak, and when he does, lives are changed. In fact, the dead are raised.

THE RELATIONSHIP BETWEEN PRAYING AND EFFECTIVE PREACHING

I find great joy that just about every time I do a sermon someone will say, "You wrote that for me, didn't you? You were in my living room, weren't you?"

I say, "No, I wasn't," and, "No, I didn't," but somebody else was. And I rejoice in that. In fact, most of the people who say that to me after the sermon are people I didn't have in mind while I was writing. And the people I did have in mind often don't come.

Here at the college, too, students will say after a message, "I just needed to hear that," and "It got into my soul." And I think, *O Lord, you spoke again.*

The Word not only informs; it transforms. I see the power of the Spirit effect more than a cognitive exercise, even more than a devotional exercise. God makes preaching something deeper, a further conforming into the image of Christ.

The most powerful experience came when I was pastor of Union Church of Manila in the Philippines from 1985 to 1989 and lived through the People Power Revolution. The sermons I preached on Sunday mornings were broadcast on the Far East Broadcasting Company throughout Manila and the Philippines the following Sunday. So the October 6th sermon was broadcast October 13.

It turned out that though the sermon on October 6 was in the Union sanctuary, it was really for the people who were listening by radio on the 13th. The revolution broke out on Saturday morning and went through Monday. That Sunday the radio broadcast my sermon from the week before, while three million people were out there in the revolution. I was blown away. That's when I began to realize,

You don't know what is really going on in the crafting of a sermon, who it's for and when it's for. You think it's for this group of people and for this time, but it may also be beyond them.

The sermon was on when Satan took Jesus to the mount of temptation and showed him all the kingdoms of the world, tempting him to be king without being the Suffering Servant. Satan offered him a way to power that didn't involve the cross. The sermon moved to the end of Matthew when Jesus said, "All authority has been given to me." The message was, "It's through the cross that Jesus gained the power that Satan tempted him with." I ended the message with Tony Campolo's "It's Friday but Sunday's Coming." That was exactly what people needed to hear as the revolution was unfolding.

PRAYER AND THE PREACHING EVENT

I expect Jesus to speak. I sit in the front pew before I go up to preach, and I regularly find myself praying, *If you don't show up, Lord, this is just so much moving of the wind. Please speak. You're the only one whose speech makes any difference.* And he comes through. I don't think I've ever been let down on that prayer. Even in my sermons that I judged weren't good, he spoke to somebody.

If I pray and it doesn't go well, I get discouraged. Still, within a day or two I can say, I prayed, so something must have been happening. I just didn't see it, or I won't see it for a while.

When I haven't really prayed and worked that hard, and God works, I take that as the sovereign grace of God. These are his people we're serving. The Good Shepherd just decided he was going to feed the sheep that day in spite of me. When those times happen, I thank him,

I rejoice in it, and I'm humbled. *Well, Lord, you are in fact in charge of this, aren't you?*

In the last few years I've prayed, *Lord, after I get through with this, help me retreat. Help me do this and then choose the way of hiddenness. Help me to walk away from this and thank you and rejoice in you and go on to the next thing.* Adulation is more powerful than criticism in what it does to your soul.

Throughout the whole process I can see the people who are going to be there. During the singing, before the preaching, I look around at people, and I'm aware of what they're struggling with, so I will be praying for them. Often it's, *O Lord, thank you, you've got a great word for them today.* When I'm thinking of people who are suffering or angry at God, I pray, *Lord, please help them stay with me long enough to hear the good news at the end of this.*

During the sermon, I'm typically focused on the manuscript. But when I see somebody angry with me, I might pray, *Lord, protect me. I don't want to get shot at afterwards.* Or if I see somebody beginning to tune it out, *Lord, don't let him do that. Catch him.*

The Holy Spirit comes to help us in our prayer. Prayer is a Trinitarian reality. Prayer is to the Father, through the Son, in the Spirit. So it's the Holy Spirit who empowers prayer. Praying in the Spirit, then, is praying dependent on him. I'm not alone in praying; I am working with the Spirit in this. I'm joining him as he prays, as he works in these people's lives.

TEACH ME TO PRAY

I learned to pray out of my weakness and inadequacy. Even when my sermons seem to me to be wonderful and well-crafted, I can get up there before the message and suddenly realize,

This isn't going to fly at all unless you show up, Lord. So a profound sense of inadequacy led me here.

There was also one man who took me under wing as a young preacher. Peter Joshua was a Welsh Presbyterian pastor. At the time he was probably ninety, and I was twenty-two. He was living in the Ventura, California, area where I was serving. He'd take me out for tea a couple of times a month and taught me how to drink tea with cream in it as the British do.

I told him I was struggling with pride. People were very affirming of the sermons I was preaching, and I wanted the affirmation. I wanted people to think well of me. I told him I was trying to push this down.

He said to me, "Don't try to push it down. You will never succeed. Humility is not a function of putting yourself down. Humility comes with putting Christ higher. So don't try to put yourself down; just lift Christ higher."

I asked, "What do I do practically?"

He said, "As you walk up the steps" (and this pulpit had big steps), "pray, *Lord, I want these people to think well of me.*"

"What? Actually pray that?"

"Yes. And then just before you get to the pulpit pray, *But I want them to think more well of you.*" And that works. I'm free, and I'm still praying that in one form or another. *Lord, help me to look good, but more than that, I want you to look good.*" And I'm free.

Chapter 150

A MYSTERIOUS IMPULSE TO PRAY

You are preparing a sermon. You suddenly feel led to talk to God. What is happening and what to do.

Lee Eclov

One thing preachers don't talk much about is how they pray while they prepare their sermons. I'm curious about it both because I know it is vital and because I don't think I'm very good at it. But I know that it is yeast to a sermon. A message will never rise without it.

That old firebrand, E. M. Bounds, intimidates me when he writes:

> The power of the preacher lies in the power of prayer, in his ability to pray so as to reach God and bring great results. The power of prayer is rarely tested, its possibilities seldom understood, never exhausted. . . . Every part of the sermon should be born of the throes of prayer; its beginning and end should be vocal with the plea and song of prayer. Its delivery should be impassioned and driven by the love from the furnace of prayer.

Yikes! Don't get me wrong; I agree. But when I read that, I'm pretty sure I'd disappoint E. M.!

Any sincere sermon preparation has some inherent elements of prayer. For one thing, concentrating on Scripture, trying to think out what it means and how to express it, is a kind of prayer. After all, in the Scriptures God speaks a living word to us, and we're trying hard to listen. We study like someone trying to tune in a short-wave radio, picking up a static-y truth and then delicately tuning spiritual dials till it comes in as clearly as possible. That surely qualifies as a kind of prayer.

Furthermore, we're usually consciously or unconsciously dedicating what we do to the Lord throughout the process and trusting him to use his Word through us. Surely I don't have to stop, bow my head, and fold my hands for it to become "official."

There's no question that all of sermon preparation can be an act of prayer—just like Brother Lawrence's familiar dishwashing. But there is something to be said for stopping now and then throughout the process to bow our heads and pray. D. Martin Lloyd-Jones wrote:

> Above all—and this I regard as most important of all—always respond to every impulse to pray. The impulse to pray may come when you are reading or when you are battling with a text. I would make an absolute law of this—always obey such an impulse. Where does it come from? It is the work of the Holy Spirit.

There are some distinct benefits to obeying that impulse.

PRAYER PERSUADES ME OF A TEXT

Like you perhaps, I believe everything I read in the Bible. I'm an inerrantist. So I don't need to be persuaded that a passage is true. But that isn't enough. Sometimes I need to be persuaded that it matters that the text is true. No, more than that: I must believe that it matters to me. And for that to happen, I must pray.

After I've come to understand the passage as thoroughly as I can, I have to talk to God about it. Sometimes I honestly can't see myself in the Bible mirror. After the first pass, some passages just don't seem to have much to do with my life.

(Which is a problem I assume others will have with that passage, too). So I ask the Lord to help me tilt the mirror till I find my own soul in its reflection, till I know what it has to do with me.

Sometimes the passage is so familiar—so overly familiar—that it is like looking at a postcard of the Grand Canyon instead of the real thing. It is easier, of course, and quicker to look at a Bible postcard, but all it really says is, "Wish you were here." So I bow and ask God to help me see the beauty, the wonder, the reality of his Word.

Then there are the passages that tell me how to behave as a Christian. I know it sounds audacious, but I'm almost always doing what they say—somewhere in my life! But not everywhere. Invariably there is a relationship untouched, a door still locked, a tension the Lord has just been talking to me about. Prayer is where I cannot dodge God any longer, where I admit the sin, and ask for grace or wisdom or help.

My sermon preparation must wait while I pray to be persuaded. If I try to press on to the end with just an occasional whispered, "Bless this," the sermon might still be true, but it won't persuade my listeners, because it hasn't persuaded me. Somehow, they will know.

PRAYER HELPS ME SEE THE IMPENETRABLE

Sometimes, no matter how well we study, a passage will baffle us. The commentators seem to be on another wavelength, and our old professors are not answering their phones. Prayer is how we sit, Mary-like, at the Lord's feet and ask him to teach us. C. H. Spurgeon wrote, "Texts will often refuse to reveal their treasures till you open them with the key of prayer." He also wrote:

> Often when I have had a passage of Scripture that

I cannot understand, am I in the habit of spreading the Bible before me, and if I have looked at all the commentators, and they do not seem to agree, I have spread the Bible on my chair, kneeled down, put my finger upon the passage, and sought of God instruction. I have thought that when I have risen from my knees I have understood it far better than before; I believe that the very exercise of prayer did of itself bring the answer.

I recall the time I was attempting my first first-person sermon, about blind Bartimaeus. I was studying hard to try to picture the scene and feel the story, but I was frustrated. As I prayed, it dawned on me: "I'm talking to Someone who was actually there that day! Surely he will help me capture the spirit and importance of this story." And I think he did.

Prayer Helps Me Edit My Sermon

I'd prefer we not let this get back to my congregation, but I know that I'm long-winded. Praying is a way I can give the Lord an editor's blue pencil. I can get so close to my material—to all the interesting details and drama, to the delicate reasoning and dynamic illustrations—that I can't see a way to cut a single precious word. When I pray with the sermon before me, reviewing it line by line before the Lord, he shows me how a certain illustration isn't right on the point, or how a detailed section could be simply summarized. He helps me see that something I've written is cliché-crusted, or that I'm belaboring something that isn't worthy of people's time.

Prayer Brings Artistry to My Sermons

I like it best when a sermon has something beautiful about it—a kind of poetry or color or drama. Prayer, on the one hand, keeps my imagination in check so that I don't obscure God's word with my gaudy paints. On the other hand, I find that in prayer, God the Creator collaborates with me! Often it is only when I'm praying that my mind makes imaginative connections. A fragment of a conversation, an article I read somewhere, another passage of Scripture, something I saw on TV—the Lord connects two different ideas, and I see what I would have surely missed.

Occasionally as I sit there, praying over a point, talking it out with the Lord, it begins to feel like a great two-way brainstorming session. "What if you told about the time . . ." he seems to whisper, eyes gleaming. "Oh, you've got a great idea there. Now put that with. . . ." We forget sometimes that God not only speaks the truth to us, he also does it with imagination and beauty. Preachers can collaborate with him in that artistry, but for me, at least, it doesn't seem to happen if I don't stop to pray.

Prayer Purges the Preacher

Sometimes when I'm praying through a sermon I realize how spiritually dangerous something I've planned to say is. I remember a few times when it was only in prayer that I realized I was about ready to pop off out of frustration. Other times, it dawned on me while I prayed that I was more excited about telling a funny illustration than I was about sharing God's truth. Not long ago I was planning on using something foolish a colleague had said as an illustration when I felt God nudge me and say, "You know, I really love that guy, even if he said something unwise. Why don't we just leave him out of it."

I don't like dealing with my own soul, and I likely wouldn't do it often—if I didn't have to stand up there and preach. But I just don't dare preach without cleaning house. Let's just say I learned that lesson the hard way. I also picked up a few pointers from Samson. I'm terrified of pulling off feats of homiletical weight-lifting that would make Philistines flee and of untangling biblical riddles to the delight of the faithful, only to stand up some Sunday shorn and oblivious to the Spirit's exit. The only way I know to avoid that is to pray—soberly—about both my sermon and my soul, trusting that our merciful God will not let me be deluded by some Delilah or trimmed to helplessness by some unseen razor.

PRAYER GETS ME PSYCHED TO PREACH

Have you ever seen behind-the-scenes footage of some singer or actor a few moments before he goes out on stage? The nervous pacing, eyes closed tightly in concentration, silently mouthing words. I feel something like that while the worship service moves toward the sermon. I've got to get psyched up to preach well. Prayer helps me do it the right way.

When I pray through a sermon, I try to worship God for the truths I have learned. Often I have seen angles and intricacies in Scripture that I'd never seen before, wisdom and applications that I'd never considered. Simply marveling at them in a conversation with God is like heating up the meal. And when those abstract truths become personal, I get excited about preaching them.

As I've looked for help on integrating prayer into my sermon preparation, I found a D.Min. thesis by Stephen Ratliff, a pastor in Manhattan, Kansas. (All the quotes I've used above were drawn from his work: "The Strategic Role of Prayer in Preaching," Trinity Evangelical Divinity School, May 2002.) I appreciated something Ratliff said:

> Those who have a high view of Scripture must not settle for a low experience of Scripture. . . . God is not looking for preachers who will merely parrot his truths. God seeks preachers who share his love for the flock of God and his compassion for sheep without a shepherd. Since God alone can bring about such depth of conviction, the preacher should consciously appeal to God for this work of grace.

Chapter 151

PREPARING THE MESSENGER

A strong delivery results from getting our whole person ready to preach

Gordon Anderson

In 1986 I had a series of experiences that turned my preaching around. I came to realize that the ability to help or stir people depends primarily on preparing the heart of the preacher.

I found in myself that the pull toward religious Pharisaism is a constant, a given. That's why I need to respect the manna principle. I need fresh bread every day, fresh oil every day, fresh water every day. If it's left over from yesterday, it's stale and stinky.

I also found it is a given that the emotional and physical realm of my person is largely sealed off from the Holy Spirit by the activities and busyness of life. I start with that assumption, as opposed to thinking that I am always "in the Spirit" unless I do something really bad.

For all these reasons, I need to prepare the messenger as much as I prepare the message. My philosophy of preparing the messenger arises out of the nature of the human person. The Bible talks about loving God with all our heart, soul, mind, strength. So I see four parts of my person that I need to prepare before I preach: my physical body, my emotions, my will, and my intellect. A person is a composite of all these characteristics.

Before preaching, I need to provide enough time and opportunity for God to affect every element of my personal makeup: my mind, emotions, body, and will. The exegetical, theological, and homiletical work are mainly the preparation of the message. But preparing the physical, emotional, and volitional elements of the messenger are required as well before the sermon is truly ready.

If I don't have my own emotions stirred by the message, for example, to the point of laughter, tears, anger, then I have not yet allowed the message to interact with the whole person. The message is more than a body of truth. The idea that preaching is just the distribution of ideas is a Western intellectual notion of what communication is all about. Preaching is much more than a cognitive experience.

My assumption about myself is that I am not generally hearing or feeling or moving in the Spirit. I need to "get in the Spirit," that is, to let all the human personal makeup be affected by God's Spirit. This means my emotions must be stirred so that I feel deeply about the message to be preached. It means submitting my will to God's Word. And it means the physical expression of worship and enthusiasm. The work of preparing the messenger is to allow the Holy Spirit to touch all of that. The tether that runs from the heart of the hearer to the throne of God passes through the heart, not the head, of the preacher.

I have some disciplines I follow in the preparation process to get in the Spirit. After the message is entirely prepared, I usually schedule two hours to allow the Spirit to affect the messenger.

You've got to get on fire before you can set a fire. You can't give what you don't have.

Chapter 152

LIFTED BY THE ACCOMPANYING PRESENCE

*An interview with Bill Hybels about how he experiences the Holy Spirit
in the preparation and delivery of a message*

Bill Hybels

***Tell a story of a memorable time when you felt
you preached in the power of the Spirit.***

For me, being moved by the Holy Spirit in
preaching is often more dramatic when I'm
preparing a sermon than when I'm in the pulpit
delivering it.

I can think of a time recently when I was
anchored out on a boat and I had been praying
and studying a text, and the ideas began to
flow. I grabbed pen and paper, and I wrote as
fast as my hand would allow me to write for
probably an hour and a half. In one setting I
put an entire message together, got down on my
knees on the deck of the boat, and said, *The
greatest miracle of this sermon has already
taken place.* This was a gift I didn't deserve—
the spiritual gift of preaching and teaching
deposited in my life—and the Holy Spirit energized that gift that afternoon. That it worked
as mysteriously and supernaturally as it did still
overwhelms me.

***Have you ever thought about why that greater
sense of inspiration may occur at times?***

A lot of men and women can read a text, formulate a few thoughts, and speak sort of off the
top of their heads, but in thirty years I've never
been able to do that. The greater miracle happens in my study as opposed to in the delivery
process. Usually in my case the delivery of the
message is less mystical or supernatural.

***What suggests to you that you are preaching
in the power of the Spirit?***

Thoughts come into my mind that I know
were deposited there by a power other than my
own. Sometimes I'll be reading a text, and I'll
be prompted by the Holy Spirit: Hang with this
text, Bill. Read it again. Read it slower. And
while I'm ruminating on it, reading and rereading it, it's like something comes off the page or
drops from heaven and intersects in my mind.
A thought comes that I quickly try to put on
paper, and then that leads to a next thought and
a next. When additional thoughts begin to
flow, I know that's not just the work of the
flesh. I'm not that good. That's a supernatural
thing.

One way to know you have the preaching
and teaching gift is that this supernatural
dynamic occurs, and you learn how to go with
the flow. You learn how to prepare your heart
for that flow to occur and to capture it when it
does.

***What have you had to unlearn about this,
things you expected were supposed to happen
when you preach in the power of the Spirit but
perhaps they didn't.***

Certainly I've had to unlearn the idea that
preparation is always going to be easy, as
though you're going to sit down and God's

going to appear and it's always going to flow and be mysterious.

Like your experience on the boat.

Yes. Probably the reason that came to mind as vividly as it did is because of how unusual that is. Usually I have to invest a lot more in research and preparation of my spirit. I make progress in thirty-minute increments. My administrative assistant would assure you that my study sounds more like a dentist's office than some great artistic revelation happening.

This is a factory, not the symphony center?

Most certainly. My average weekly preparation is taxing and requires more discipline than I thought was going to be required when I started many decades ago. Once you get accustomed to that, you settle into the routine. That becomes the norm, and you thank God like crazy when it goes easier or flows more dynamically than that.

When we think of preaching in the Spirit, we often use impersonal metaphors like wind, fire, or power. What personal, relational aspects of preaching in the Spirit have you experienced?

Sometimes in the pulpit, I'll make eye contact with someone in the auditorium who is going through what I'm talking about at that exact moment. When your eyes meet the eyes of someone at a decision point, that is a powerful experience. The Spirit can make connections in the crowd that you weren't aware could be made. I think that's supernatural.

Regarding the Holy Spirit, do the terms presence or manifest presence describe what you experience?

I refer to an Accompanying Presence. When I'm in the flow of the Spirit as best I can yield myself to be so, it's as though I have an awareness of the accompanying presence of the Spirit saying, *You're doing it just right, Bill. You're saying it just the way I gave it to you. You're being true to yourself, true to the Word, true to my promptings. Just keep going. Way to go.* And when I feel that, it's like time stands still, and you go, *This is a great thing to be doing right now.*

Of course, there are other times when for whatever reasons—and that's another whole subject matter—I don't feel that Accompanying Presence as strongly. I've laid awake nights wondering about that. I will probably never know why I feel it more strongly sometimes and not other times. But it's greatly appreciated when it's there.

Would you describe that sense of God's Accompanying Presence as rare or frequent?

I would say it's frequent. Again, if you're living a yielded life, and if you have the preaching and teaching gift, and if you're yielding that to God on a continual basis, that's one of the signs that you're in the right place doing the right thing for the right reasons.

If you're doing something in the kingdom and you rarely feel that, that would be a red flag to me. Something needs to be looked at. Are you using the right gift? Are you using it in the right way? For the right reasons? At the right time? In the right context? If I didn't feel it consistently, it would be quite troubling to me.

Scripture portrays two sides to our experience of the Spirit. Ephesians 5:18 says, "Be filled with the Spirit," and Ephesians 6:18 says, "Pray in the Spirit," suggesting there are things we can do that put us in a place where God's Spirit can be manifest in us. Then again, Jesus says, "The wind blows wherever it pleases" (John 3:8). What observations have you had on that?

The texts indicate we should do what we can

to prepare ourselves for the work of the Spirit in the preparation and delivery of a message. Every great communicator I know could tell you how they "get in the zone." Michael Jordan had a strict regimen of what he did before every big game to get himself in a prepared state to do his best.

I've been fascinated by this. When I'm together with other speakers, I ask them, "What do you do to get in the preparation zone? How do you pray? When do you prepare? Do you prepare in the same place? Do you listen to music? How do you prepare yourself just before the delivery of your message?" Great communicators can say precisely how they up the probability that the Spirit will be strong in their life.

Having done all of that, then, the wind blows where it wills. Sometimes it blows stronger than others. I can only do the part that depends on me. I can fast and pray and kneel before God and invite others to pray with me. Sometimes the messages get lifted to fifteen thousand feet. Sometimes they get lifted to twenty thousand, sometimes to twenty-five thousand. Why there are those altitude differences, I don't know.

What have you learned from Scripture and experience about preaching in the power of the Spirit?

It has a lot to do with courage. Look at the great messages delivered in Scripture. Joshua stands before the people in Joshua 24 and says, "Choose this day what you're going to do. Here's what I'm going to do." Peter stands up in Acts 2 and says, "Here's what you did to the One who was sent from God."

Preaching involves an inordinate amount of courage. You have to be willing to take heat and backlash if you're going to say the words God gave you to say in the Spirit he gave you to deliver it. In my own experience, the messages that turned certain corners at Willow and the messages that were greatly used in conference settings were ones that I walked toward the lectern with knees knocking, thinking, *There is no way I'm going to be able to say these words to these people.* God says, *Here we go,* and you say them. You feel alone in the moment, and you have to die to audience response, realizing they are probably not going to carry your picture in their wallet anymore. But you know, *This is precisely what God wanted me to say.* That's a refining, character-building, intensely spiritual process.

Does anything else stand out as an integral part of preaching in the power of the Spirit?

Authenticity. In my opinion one of the downfalls in classic preaching has been an unwillingness for preachers to admit how their sermon is playing out in their own personal lives. People sit in pews and listen to someone wax eloquent, and they think, *There's no way he lives that as well as he's talking it. It's just not believable.*

I need to be conscious of this in my preaching. So I need to right-size my personal track record. If I make a strong statement, I need to follow it up by saying, "Now if you're wondering if I live this as well as I'm preaching it, I can only say I wish I did. It's in my heart to want to. I am asking God to help me with this. But I am not batting a thousand, and if you're not, I'm in good company with you. But this is what we need to move toward. This is the way God needs to work in our lives. These are the commitments we have to make and keep."

Courage and authenticity are twin strengths of powerful preaching.

Paul speaks in 2 Corinthians 12:7–10 about the power of Christ resting on him when he

was weak. What have you experienced in this regard?

Some of the best preaching I've done came out of times when I was desperately needy. One message I've probably given five hundred times around the world came to me in the slums outside of Soweto in South Africa when I was supposed to speak to several thousand illiterate people about the nature of the church of Jesus Christ. I realized this is an impossible task. How can I communicate complex theology to an uneducated, simple-minded, large group of people who have probably never seen what it is that they want me to describe.

I woke up at four o'clock in the morning and prayed, "God, I'm going to stay in this humble, kneeling position until you give me a way to talk about your church in a fashion that these folks can understand." I put together a unique message in which I brought people up on the stage and posed them in certain stances to give listeners pictures of the church. When I delivered the message that day, I knew I had that Accompanying Presence. People got it. It changed their understanding of what a church could be. That message came out of an exhausted, desperate situation where unless God had moved, I was done for.

Chapter 153

THE HARD WORK OF ILLUMINATION
Why hearing the Spirit in the text can seem so difficult

Lee Eclov

I've always suspected that there are other preachers—better men and women than I—who sit down to study for a message, and just out of sight on the other side of the desk, the Holy Spirit pulls up a chair and leans forward eagerly. The preacher dutifully and earnestly begins to study. Then he looks across the desk at the Spirit, just a shadow out of sight, and says, "Speak, Lord, for thy servant is listening." And—boom—with a kind of shiver, the pastor begins to write as fast as he can—the sermon almost leaping out of his pen, full-blown with lucid outline, transforming insights, gripping illustrations. The preacher then sits back, gasps, wipes the tears from his eyes, and heads home to supper, armed and ready. And the Spirit smiles.

Now with me it is an entirely different story. If I didn't know better, I'd guess that the Holy Spirit pokes his head around the corner at some point on Friday afternoon and says, a little rushed, "So how's everything going in here?" like a supervisor with too many workers to check on. Before I can lift my bleary eyes and weary shoulders, he says, "Good. Good. Glad everything is coming along," and he's off to someone else's cubicle.

I know it isn't really like that, of course, but that's how it feels.

Gospel preachers must—must—know the Holy Spirit as their constant help and power, but don't you ever wonder why preparing has to be so tough, so slow, so painstaking?

Considering we're in league with God himself, it just seems like it all ought to come a little easier. After all, God brought forth all creation with just a word. So couldn't he cut us a break on sermon preparation?

POOR RECEPTION

Difficult preparation is guaranteed, of course, if our hearts are out of sync with God. There's no doubt that we can be like a cell phone when the battery is on its last legs. The Voice on the other end keeps cutting out. The psalmist said, "If I had cherished sin in my heart, the Lord would not have listened" (Ps. 66:18). I'll tell you something else: Not only does the Lord not listen when we cherish sin, he doesn't talk much either. A pastor's study can take on an unearthly, ominous silence when there's sin in the air.

Even when I've settled things with the Father, I have noticed that study is often harder after a time of rebellion. It is almost like my receptors have been sin-dulled. It is almost as if, in my sin—radio-like—I tuned God out and began listening to some other voice, and now it is hard to find the station again. I suspect it is simply that God pulls back a bit, perhaps reminding me of Samson's haircut, and giving me a taste of the awful weakness I'd know if he really were silent. The message comes, but harder and with the sober reminder, "You really don't want to try this work without my help."

PROSPECTING

There are lots of times, though, when neither sin nor spiritual apathy seem to be the problem. That's when the study struggle really mystifies me. Do you remember Jesus' promise in Luke 12:11–12? He said: "When you are brought before synagogues, rulers and authorities, do not worry about how you will defend yourselves or what you will say, for the Holy Spirit will teach you at that time what you should say." Every Christian who lives on the cutting edge of life has had times when, in standing up for Christ, the right words just came—with no preparation.

So why not when we preach? Maybe you're one of those folks who have stepped to the pulpit some Sunday to say, "I had a different message prepared, but the Lord gave me this sermon on the way to church today." But that has never happened to me. Not once. Every single one, I think, has been hard work.

But how rich I've gotten digging! Sometimes I feel like one of those legendary prospectors from the Sierra Madres, all dust and grizzle and poverty-patched pants, but with a secret stash of gold tucked away deep in my soul from all those hard hours of mining Scripture. It seems as though there have been hundreds of times, as I've wearied of the hard work of preparation, that I've begged the Lord to let me be done, to let me go home. Sometimes he does. But most of the time I've felt as though God has said, "There's treasure waiting for you! Dig and scrape a little longer, and you'll be glad you did. There's gold in them thar hills!"

CAN YOU HEAR ME NOW?

I'd like it if there was a sermon prep technical help line. I'd plug away in preparation till I got stuck. Then I would just bow my head and dial up the help line. "Yeah, hello. Is this the Holy Spirit? Good. Just a quick question: I can't seem to find a good outline on chapter 12. What would you suggest? By the way, how much should I make of that chiasm in verses 3 and 4? Oh, and one more thing. Got any good stories about humble kings?"

That doesn't usually work, obviously, but I have learned to recognize the Holy Spirit's help in other ways.

When Archimedes, sitting in his bathtub, realized the principle of displacement, he is said to have run naked into the street, yelling, "Eureka!" Discovery invigorates all good students, but when we're studying Scripture, the kick of discovery becomes the bowed head of worship.

For example, I recently considered Jesus' statement to the paralyzed man, "Son, your sins are forgiven" (Mark 2:5). Jesus then said that compared to healing, forgiveness was a far more difficult miracle. Why is that? I wondered. I sorted through my mental files of Bible study and theological training and began to list all that Jesus' grant of forgiveness entailed. I'm sure the Holy Spirit was clarifying my thinking in those moments, but the mental process was that of any good student. As the truths began to line up, my heart filled with wonder, and my sermon gathered electricity—my "Eureka!" became "Hallelujah!" Every student knows the shout, but only the Holy Spirit gives the hymn.

Another similar evidence of the Holy Spirit's work is when I'm nourished by the Scripture I study. Who but lovers of Scripture can understand how the Bible feeds us? As the hours of study pass, in spite of a weary mind and body, there is a sense of nourishment, of strength. I think of it sometimes like Popeye's spinach. That ability to digest Scripture, to sense it like the pulse of blood in my heart, to sense wisdom forming in my mind—all that is a sure sign of the feeding of the Spirit.

Another way the Holy Spirit works: I've read

how spacecraft run the risk of "losing their balance"—of starting to wobble out of control. I have that capacity in sermon preparation. Being angry makes me wobble with the desire to "give 'em a piece of my mind." Being tired or pessimistic makes me wobble by cutting corners. In those times, the Holy Spirit is like those complex gyroscopes that keep satellites from wobbling into oblivion. He helps me to cool down, to check my words, to persevere, to pray, to check my heart, so that I don't crash crazily into my congregation on Sunday.

I used to see a fellow named Mike at the bagel shop I frequent. We got acquainted through crossword puzzles. He found out I had a knack for finishing the last few words that he couldn't get. He said he was the starter and I was the closer. That is what the Holy Spirit does for us all on Sunday mornings. I've filled in all the blanks that I can and erased things two or three times, till the sermon is paper-thin. But we get up there, open our Bibles, and preach a finished sermon. Mike would always shake his head when he'd see the right answers I penciled in. "Of course," he'd say, "why didn't I think of that?" That's how I usually feel after a sermon. People tell me how the sermon helped them, or I reflect on how a thought jelled right there in front of God and everybody, and I shake my head and think, *How did he do that? Why didn't I think of that in the first place?* Because I'm the starter, and the Holy Spirit is the Closer.

Don't Forget Who You're Dealing With

When we get to feeling that the Spirit is making preparation a whole lot harder than it needs to be, we're forgetting our pneumatology. We forget just who we're dealing with, or rather, who is dealing with us.

We forget sometimes that the Holy Spirit who helps me is the same Spirit who gave Isaiah both the truth and the language to describe the Suffering Servant's comfort and the redemption, the same Spirit who inspired Moses' rock-inscribed law, David's soul-singing poetry, Paul's intricate doctrine, and Jesus' own parables and sermons. And now the same Spirit whispers to me and through me. My words do not carry the authority of Scripture, of course, but the Spirit works with me to find my words for his Word and to pour his truth through my heart till God's message carries something of the flavor of my own soul. It makes me wonder what would happen if I listened even a little more intently, prayed even a bit more silently!

We forget sometimes, when it seems the weight of the sermon rests heavily on our shoulders, how deeply invested the Spirit is in what we do. He is no passive observer, no busy supervisor. He does not stroll the aisles of studying preachers like a stern, silent professor looking over the rim of his glasses, seeing if we know our stuff. Fact is, he desires far more to come from our sermons than we do.

He is, we know, the very author of Scripture, so when Scripture is preached he is intensely involved. He knows every nuance of theology and exactly how far every word and metaphor is to be stretched. And he wants me to know, too, if I'll dig and listen at the same time. He'll tell me if I'm trying to make more of a text than God intends, or less. I never need to study alone.

But more. He is Christ's own champion, devoting all his infinite ingenuity, authority, and power to showing forth the glory of Christ. Every sermon we preach is, to him, another light to shine on Christ. Surely he will give us lustrous words and gleaming insights if we share his goal of showing forth Christ from the text before us.

There is yet another reason for his help, for the Spirit loves the church. He is her earthly Companion and Coach, Hearer and Helper. He has poured out every spiritual treasure on this Bride of Christ, and we "are being built together to become a dwelling in which Christ lives by his Spirit" (Eph. 2:22). When we earnestly desire to nourish and build Christ's church, the Holy Spirit stands close by our side.

Sermon preparation will almost always be a difficult work. Our world-warped minds do not easily grasp the Lord's logic or the King's decrees. Nor does God often leave his treasures lying about on top of our desks. He doesn't usually cast his pearls before preachers, unless we dive for them. But we need never doubt the Holy Spirit's eagerness to help us in our work. He is never reluctant to do such work through us. When we want nothing more than for Scripture to be clear, the Spirit is our sure ally. When we burn to show the glory of Christ, the Spirit will certainly aid our feeble light. And when we eagerly desire to spread a feast of God's own truth before his beloved people or to proclaim good news to the lost and blind, the Holy Spirit stands ever ready with words and wisdom, with passion and purity, to set our sermons a-gleaming.

Chapter 154

HEART-TO-HEART PREACHING

How to tap authentic emotions, both yours and the listeners'

Dan Baty

Several years ago I endured one of the worst Bible studies ever.

I wasn't in the audience.

The musicians concluded the worship service, and I stepped onto the stage alone. As I adjusted the podium and laid out my notes, I heard the familiar rustling of Bibles, pens, and notebooks.

After a brief introduction, I delved into my message. Suddenly, though my lips were moving and words were sounding forth, my neatly typed notes blurred into classical Greek. My carefully planned message had no energy. Before long I'd lost the entire congregation to purse-fishing, watch-peeking, heavy eyelids, and blue-sky daydreaming.

Though the dead of winter, I was sweating profusely. I wanted to die!

When it was over, I was so embarrassed I quickly slipped out of the building—and into depression. I didn't want to show my face at the church office the next day. I had bombed, and I feared I had raised serious questions about my teaching ability.

Finally I shared my grief with a fellow pastor. He listened empathetically and offered consolation: "That happens to all of us."

That didn't help. I had long been a believer that anything worth saying is worth saying well. I hadn't done well, and that, in my mind, was inexcusable.

Where had I gone wrong?

GETTING REAL

The problem with that message, I've since discovered, was not that I hadn't prepared enough; rather, I had neglected preparation in a vital area.

Over the past fourteen years, I've often wondered. *How can one message stir the listeners' souls while another leaves them stirring restlessly in their seats? How can I become consistently persuasive for Jesus Christ?*

A strong case for any number of factors could be made: adequate preparation of both my heart and the audience's hearts by the Holy Spirit, my daily walk with the Lord, the amount of time spent in study and preparation. One additional factor, however, has made the difference for me. Lives change only when hearts have been affected, and hearts are most deeply affected when the speaker exposes his own.

 For an audio example of this principle see tracks 18–19 on the supplemental CD.

In other words, what people want and need most from a communicator is authenticity. This wasn't a new revelation to me. I had read and heard much about "being real." But authenticity seemed to be a mysterious and elusive quality with a will of its own. Without it, people might offer polite comments: "I enjoyed your message." But when authenticity appeared, they would say, "*God* spoke to my heart this morning." I liked the effects of authenticity, but I had no idea how to express it.

Then one speaking opportunity turned out to be a watershed moment.

HEART EXPOSURE

In 1986 I spoke at a conference for young people. I had prepared for months and was delivering my message with great passion. They were listening attentively and taking notes, but their eyes and posture told me I hadn't really connected.

Then I paused for a moment and considered the importance the subject had for their lives. Suddenly I was completely overcome with emotion. Unbidden tears welled up and overflowed the banks of my eyes. It took me by surprise (I don't cry often), and for a few minutes I stood there silently, head bowed. When I regained my composure, I looked up, surprised to find many tissues and handkerchiefs drying tearful eyes.

Afterward I mused about what had happened. *I'd been speaking for hours trying to affect those people, and they were moved most when I was unable to speak at all.*

What touched hearts was not my tears per se but my giving people the opportunity to peer into the window of my heart. They not only heard what I *thought*, they experienced what I *felt*. Sometimes emotions are more persuasive than eloquence. And sincere emotions expressed *with* eloquence make for honest persuasion.

People want to know not only what I think about the subject, but also how I *feel* about it. That's why I now use the phrase *heart exposure* rather than *authenticity*. Authenticity seems passive; heart exposure suggests an active choice on my part to disclose. Heart exposure

reminds me of my goal each time I speak: I want to reveal not only my thought and theology, but my heart and soul as well.

THE POWER OF STORY

I accomplish heart exposure primarily through storytelling. God gives all his leaders many stories, and he wants us to share them with the flock—not from a heart of pride but from a genuine desire to *model* how one responds to the promises and mandates of God. Peter exhorts elders about "being examples to the flock," and stories allow me to do that. Whenever I stand before a group, I assume their implicit question is, *How has this truth touched your heart and life, Dan?* I ensure that I am answering that question when I DARE myself.

DARE PREACHING

To DARE means that I describe the story with sensory detail, attach specific emotions, reveal why I feel as I do, and explain what it means.

Describing the Story with Sensory Detail

Because we experience the world through our five senses, when I tell a story I try to let my audience see, hear, smell, touch, or taste what's in the story scene. Even weak stories are greatly strengthened when I provide such details.

I employed all four DARE components at the beginning of this article. In the opening story, I described the scene, letting you hear the "rustling and bustling of people retrieving their Bibles, pens, and notebooks." These details aren't trivial. By them I transport my audience into the physical environs of the story. You don't have to use many, but a few choice details enliven your stories.

Attaching a Specific Emotion

In my story I said, "I wanted to die," and I was so embarrassed "I didn't even want to show my face at the church office the next day." Feelings are the common denominator of us all. I strive not only to offer relevant subject matter but to be emotionally relevant.

It is often much easier for me to report the facts of a matter than to disclose how the matter affects my heart. But as the acronym DARE implies, all true heart exposure involves daring to take a risk. Time and again I've found that I connect with my audience's hearts to the degree that I am willing to expose my own.

Revealing Why I Feel This Way

This is the most critical element for connecting with the audience emotionally. Simply saying "I was embarrassed" won't provide enough basis for my audience to share my feelings. For their hearts to be affected, they must see and identify with what caused me to feel embarrassed.

"I had bombed, and I wondered if my failure had raised serious questions about my teaching ability." I give my audience enough specific information to understand the depth of my feelings so they can experience the emotion with me.

When I'm not the subject of my stories, I still concentrate on how I feel about the people and events in the story. In effect the story becomes my own.

Explaining What It Means

This final component is the "therefore," the connection, the point. Here people pick up their pens and write. I tell them how they can respond in their own way to the truth in the story.

The message of my opening story was "The problem with that message, I've since discovered, was not that I hadn't prepared enough; rather, I had neglected preparation in a vital area. . . . Lives change only when hearts have been affected, and hearts are most deeply affected when the speaker exposes his own."

Is this manipulation? I consider it thorough and effective preparation. I'm getting in touch with my own sincere emotions, not performing or selfishly manipulating the emotions of others. Heart exposure helps me walk among the people instead of floating out of reach above them. I show them the Christian life in action as one who experiences it with them.

The DARE components can be used with stories of different intensity and length. Sometimes they involve serious themes such as envy or anger, but many times they are on the lighter side, funny comments and awkward situations. I don't make every story one of earth-shattering impact. My goal is simply to let the stories humanize me.

Whatever my message, I usually have a story because I always have feelings about my topic. If I don't feel something about a subject, I won't speak on it! In fact, many times, by asking myself what I really feel about a portion of Scripture and why, I find the nucleus of my story.

Chapter 155

IMAGINATION: THE PREACHER'S NEGLECTED ALLY

When listeners are starving for a meal, creativity is what ensures
there will be more than a recipe

Warren Wiersbe

Few speeches are as monotonous as the average stewardess's flight announcements. When I hear, "This is Helen, your chief attendant . . ." I either settle down for a long nap or open my book to read. I could make the speech myself.

But Frank was different. "My name is Frank," he began as we left Detroit, "and this plane is going to Chicago. If you aren't going to Chicago—well, you're going anyway!"

After a dramatic pause, he continued. "Please be sure your seat belts are fastened. If they aren't, and I discover it, I will belt you into your seat *upside-down*." A chuckle rippled throughout the cabin.

"There will be no smoking—I emphasize, *no smoking* in the aisles or the lavatories. If I catch you smoking in either place, I will take your lavatory privileges away from you." We laughed out loud; but we got the message.

At the close of the flight, we bounced hard on the runway as we landed. But Frank was ready: "That was our Easter evening hippity-hop landing at O'Hare Field. The Easter Bunny says, 'Welcome to Chicago!'" Almost the entire plane broke into applause.

Frank reminded me of something that Easter night: No matter how important your message, people will miss it unless you get their attention. Information needs imagination if there is to be communication. And no area of communication has a greater need for imagination than preaching.

IMAGINATION: FRIEND OR ENEMY?

Whenever I mention *imagination* in a homiletics class or a preaching seminar, people glare at me as if I had just denied the Virgin Birth or the responsibility of a church to pay its pastor. The fact that we misunderstand imagination is one reason why we neglect it. People tend to confuse *imagination* with *fancy* or the *imaginary*. We are so wedded to the historic faith that we want to defend it against anything invented by humans. To most people, *imagination* belongs to the Brothers Grimm, Walt Disney, Tolkien, and little children who have no playmates.

But imagination and fancy are not the same. Fancy helps me escape reality, while imagination helps me penetrate reality and understand it better. Fancy wrote "Mary Had a Little Lamb," but inspired imagination wrote Psalm 23. Fancy creates a new world for you; imagination gives you new insight into the old world.

Great preachers have, for the most part, valued imagination as an ally. Alexander Whyte called it "nothing less than the noblest intellectual attribute of the human mind." He even felt that the imagination was stronger than the will and could be used to reach the will. The blind preacher George Matheson prized imagination as "the highest power of man."

Listen to the testimony of Henry Ward Beecher in the first series of Yale Lectures on Preaching: "And the first element on which your preaching will largely depend for power and success, you will perhaps be surprised to learn, is *Imagination*, which I regard as the most important of all the elements that go to make the preacher."

But our misunderstanding of imagination is not the only cause for its neglect. Another factor is our emphasis on *content* rather than *intent*. In recent years, the preacher has become a lecturer, and the sanctuary has become a classroom. The most important preparation for hearing a sermon is not a keen mind and a clean heart, but a clean notebook and a sharp pencil.

Lest I be misunderstood, let me make it clear that sermons must have biblical content. But if that is all they have, they are not sermons. The preacher needs to spend time on exegesis, but merely taking words apart will never put lives together. We need to obey the rules of hermeneutics and homiletics, but we also need to use our imagination so our listeners get something more than a recipe when they are starving for a meal.

There are times when preaching must emphasize only doctrinal content. Fine; but even then, let the preacher use imagination in presenting the material. I believe in the immediacy of preaching. I believe God wants something to happen in the hearts of people *while the preacher is delivering the Word of God.*

There may be a place for a cassette rerun or a review from a notebook, but these can never replace the immediate impact of the Word as the sermon is being preached. While I do not agree with Harry Emerson Fosdick's theology, his philosophy of preaching was excellent: "The purpose of preaching is not to explain a subject, but to achieve an object."

It has well been said that the human mind is not a debating chamber but a picture gallery. The prophet Nathan did not approach David with a lecture, complete with charts, on Levitical sacrifices. He told the king a story about a stolen ewe lamb, and he reached the king's heart. Nicodemus wanted information about Jesus and his miracles, but the Lord used imagination and talked with him about birth. The Samaritan woman tried to argue about rival religious doctrines, but Jesus kept talking to her about her thirst and God's living water.

Perhaps the greatest cause of the decline of imagination in preaching is right there: We have forgotten that the Bible is an imaginative book. It contains every kind of literature, from funeral dirges and pastoral poems to epigrams, parables, allegories, and creative symbols that have captured poets, artists, and composers for centuries. For some reason, our views of inspiration and inerrancy have robbed us of a living book, a book that throbs with excitement and enrichment. Instead of entering into the literary genre of the passage, we treat all passages alike. David's poems sound, to our ears, like Paul's arguments, and our Lord's parables like Moses' genealogies. Shame on us!

Let me suggest a final cause for this neglect of imagination: Too many preachers refuse to be themselves and, instead, imitate the books and cassettes of better-known preachers. Why fear to be yourself? God made you as you are and wants you to deliver his message *your* way. Imagination leads to originality, and originality leads to variety, power, and excitement.

WHAT CAN IMAGINATION DO?

To begin with, imagination can help us understand and interpret the Word of God. Imagination is as essential to the science of hermeneutics as the lexicon and interlinear. I once asked D. Martyn Lloyd-Jones if he had any trouble preaching non-Pauline passages. He replied, "Folks said I wouldn't do a good job with the Gospel of John because Paul didn't write it. But I was able to enter into John's mind as easily as I entered into Paul's."

We do not degrade Scripture when we come to its pages with a sanctified imagination. Rather, we accept the Scriptures as they were given to us, in simile and metaphor, in parable and allegory, in poetry and narrative, in song and proverb. The preacher who masters a book like *The Language and Imagery of the Bible* by G. B. Caird (Westminster, 1980) will discover a new touch to both his hermeneutics and his homiletics.

While preparing a message on Hosea 14, I decided to read the entire book again and especially note the similes. I was amazed to find the brokenhearted prophet painting one picture after another. "Israel is stubborn, like a stubborn heifer" (4:16, NASB). "For I will be like a lion to Ephraim" (5:14). "And He will come to us like the rain, like the spring rain watering the earth" (6:3). "For your loyalty is like a morning cloud, and like the dew which goes away early" (6:4). Simile is piled upon simile!

No wonder Spurgeon preached one of his most effective sermons from Hosea. The title is "Everybody's Sermon," and the text is Hosea

12:10—"I have multiplied visions, and used similitudes" (KJV). "In addressing myself to you this morning," said Spurgeon, "I shall endeavor to show how every day, and every season of the year, in every place, and in every calling which you are made to exercise, God is speaking to you by similitudes." The preacher who questions the value of imagination in preaching ought to study this sermon, and then go quietly and repent.

Many preachers try to use their imagination only in reconstructing Bible scenes, and this has its place when done with accuracy and insight. The better the preacher's imagination, the shorter the description and the more vivid the strokes in the picture. But I am not encouraging reconstruction so much as identification: entering into the spirit of the passage, the mind and heart of the writer, and being true to the literary genre. It would be difficult to conceive of an interpreter understanding Ezekiel 1 or Isaiah 40 without the use of sanctified imagination.

Imagination also helps us identify with people and apply the Word to their lives. (If all you want to do is explain a subject, you need not worry about meeting needs.) Halford Luccock wrote, "Nothing is more central to a genuine ministry than the faculty of feeling one's way into the lives of others.... It is more than sympathy; it is *empathy*, the imaginative projection of our consciousness into another's being."

Imagination helps you anticipate people's questions and objections. As you put yourself in their place, you discover mental obstacles that must be removed, prejudices that must be exposed, and objections that will need answers if the listener is to receive your material. Again, Harry Emerson Fosdick was the master of answering the listener's questions before they were even voiced. As you read his sermons, you note such phrases as "Some may be saying . . ." "Do not misunderstand me . . ." "Now, when somebody says . . ." "'True enough,' you reply, 'but what about . . .'" Phrases like these indicate preparation with the congregation in mind.

Your imagination can help you present the truth in ways that encourage reception. "Don't just throw the seed at the people!" Spurgeon said. "Grind it into flour, bake it into bread, and slice it for them. And it wouldn't hurt to put a little honey on it."

Though we often deal with abstract truth, the best way to get it across is to incarnate it in pictures and illustrations. "You may build up laborious definitions and explanations," Spurgeon told his students, "and yet leave your hearers in the dark as to your meaning; but a thoroughly suitable metaphor will wonderfully clear the sense."

It amazes me how some preachers can make Bible doctrine so dull! Each of the key doctrinal words in our New Testament is part of an exciting picture. *Justification* belonged to the courtroom before it moved to the seminary. *Redemption* was born out of Greek and Roman slavery. The phrase *born again* was familiar to the Greeks and carried meanings that would illumine any sermon today. The preacher who does not study words—including English words—is robbing himself or herself of an effective tool for communicating truth. It is not accidental that some of our most effective preachers were students of words, readers of dictionaries, and lovers of crossword puzzles.

Literary critics have led the way in studying the significance of metaphors in human life. I recommend the books by Dr. Northrop Frye, especially *The Educated Imagination* and *The Great Code: The Bible and Literature*. If you

want to do postgraduate study with Dr. Frye, tackle his classic, *Anatomy of Criticism*. I also recommend *Metaphor and Reality* by Philip Wheelwright, and *Religious Imagination* by Robert D. Young. Perhaps you studied all these in college or seminary. I did not, so I had to get them the hard way—or maybe the easy way, now that I see how important they are.

Imagination enables you to see the universal in the particular, and that universal is often expressed in a simile or metaphor. The Bible is saturated with this kind of language. Paul used dozens of different images to describe the church (see Paul S. Minear's *Images of the Church in the New Testament*), and most of these images are still part of human thinking today.

We must have information; otherwise our preaching is but noise. However, that information reaches the heart and mind of the listener with greater impact if it is coupled with imagination.

Preaching is an art as well as a science. Hermeneutics and homiletics can give us the skeleton, but it takes imagination to put flesh on the bones. Homiletical scientists may be good at textual autopsies, but they cannot raise the dead. As Goethe once remarked, "The artist who is not also a craftsman is no good; but, alas, most of our artists are nothing else!" Imagination is what transforms a craftsman into an artist.

This means preachers are more than organizers of ideas. They are not carpenters who nail together a number of miscellaneous boards, the doctrinal driftwood that has floated ashore during their studies. Sermons grow; they come from the seed of the Word, planted in the mind and heart, nurtured by meditation and prayer, cultivated by sanctified imagination. A sermon is a living thing that produces fruit, and that fruit has in it the seed for more fruit. Some sermons can be preached (or read) over and over, bringing blessing and opening up new horizons of thought each time.

"The sin of being uninteresting," wrote Bishop Quayle, "is in a preacher an exceedingly mortal sin. It hath no forgiveness." If you want your preaching to be both interesting and penetrating, learn the power of metaphor and the genius of imagination.

CULTIVATING YOUR IMAGINATION

Children seem to be imaginative by nature. True, their imagination usually runs to fancy, but even that is not all bad. Once you get a grip on reality, fancy and imagination can live together and even help each other.

Why does the passing of years destroy imagination? *I am not so sure it does.* I think it is a fable that children have great imaginations but adults do not. So perhaps the first step is to rid ourselves of this defeatist notion that our imagination is dead and cannot be revived. Perhaps it is only hibernating. What happens when your grandchildren show up? You think of all sorts of fun things to do! Novelist W. Somerset Maugham wrote, "Imagination grows by exercise and contrary to common belief is more powerful in the mature than in the young."

The preacher, of all people, has the greatest advantages when it comes to developing his imagination. To begin with, he is expected to be a student, a reader. *Imagination must be fed.* The mind grows by taking in just as the heart grows by giving out. The preacher who reads only the approved books and never faces truth on many fronts will have difficulty developing his imagination.

Read widely, especially those classics to which time has given its seal of approval. Read poetry and children's stories as well as history, biography, and theology. All truth is God's truth, and (as Phillips Brooks reminded us) all truth intersects. You cannot confront truth without gaining some new insight into your Bible.

But the ivory tower bookworm will never meet the needs of people. Education is important, but so is *experience.* The preacher must live! He must mix learning and living, the library and the marketplace. He must be among his people, with the publicans and sinners as well as the preachers and saints. Emerson said, "If you would learn to write, 'tis in the street you must learn it.... The people, and not the college, is the writer's home." Substitute the word "preacher" for "writer" and take it to heart.

Martin Luther used to say that prayer, meditation, and suffering made a preacher, and he was right. Sermons are not made from books so much as from battles and burdens. Hermeneutics professors take note: Some in the Bible who suffered most gave us the most imaginative pictures of spiritual truth—Moses, David, Ezekiel, Jeremiah, John, and Paul ... not to mention our Lord Jesus Christ.

Certainly an important part of living is creative communion with people who truly live. Every preacher needs to be a part of a brain trust where ideas are debated and neat systems shattered. The minister who has all truth filed on pages in a notebook needs a fellowship like this to help him turn some of his periods into commas and perhaps some of his exclamation points into question marks.

Cultivate a sense of humor. There are exceptions, of course, but generally speaking, creative people have a sense of humor. After all, a humorist has been defined as a person who can see more than one thing at a time—and that is what imagination is all about. If you know how to laugh—and *why* you laugh—you can feed your imagination on humor.

Most of all I recommend a childlike sense of wonder at life. Spend your days with your eyes and ears open, your mind constantly inquiring. Beware of coming to a place in life where you feel you have learned it all and done it all. When you come to that place, you are entering a dead-end street. "What is experience," asked advertising magnate Alex Osborn, "but a wealth of parallels upon which our imagination can draw?"

It takes time to develop a creative imagination, and most preachers are too busy to work at it. Creative people need times of incubation as well as times of investigation. Your best ideas may come when you least expect them, provided you have been doing your homework. We must get away from things in order to see them clearly.

This means the busy preacher, who often cannot use his time as he wishes, must set aside periods for relaxation and meditation. Each person must know his own creative cycle: when to study, when to get away from the desk, and how to make the best use of free time. We need parentheses in our lives. This means setting *priorities*. Creative people know how to say no.

Imagination is the preacher's neglected ally, waiting to serve if we will let it. If we determine to be creative, there is a price to pay; but there is a greater price to pay if we are not.

Our listeners will know the choice we have made.

Chapter 156

PREACHING THAT MAGNIFIES GOD

It's not about taking down other gods, but raising up our own

Lee Eclov

Those who cling to worthless idols forfeit the grace that could be theirs" (Jonah 2:8).

Preaching against idolatry is not what it used to be. Idolatry isn't less of a problem today than it was in the Old Testament days of gilt godlets, when prophets could rail at the worshipers of Baal and Molech, because sin and sinners don't change that much. Of course, there are still idolaters today of the first magnitude—the modern pagans who really do worship gods who will swallow up their children. But we rarely preach to them. Most of the time we

speak to people who believe in the true God and who confess salvation through Christ. We're hard pressed to consider them Idolaters with a capital *I*.

Nonetheless, when idolatry comes up in our texts, we carefully string yellow "crime scene" tape around the ordinary-looking idolatry that just seems to be "culture." We try to show TV and credit cards as today's household gods, and workaholism and consumerism as the gold-plated, wooden Baals that are no substitutes for the "Lord of the Angel Armies."

567

But it is a hard go. If the truth be told, most of our people cannot conceive that even their gross indulgences, their over-doings ("Too much TV, I know") are anything like biblical idolatry. After all, for them there is no worship, no rituals, and no depending on such things for rain or health, let alone heaven or salvation. "Call it a fault, if you must," they seem to smile back at us while we preach, "but idolatry? Puhlease!" And, frankly, it is a tough sell for me, too.

Yet idolatry has not gone away, even among God's people. But our greatest threat may not be the little wooden gods of TV and leisure, work or money, but the great God—the Lord God Almighty, El Shaddai—minimized. We certainly don't deny God's greatness. We would never do that, nor do we believe it in our darkest heart. But we too often let our view of God grow small, like our snapshots of the Grand Canyon or a Mount Rushmore paperweight.

"Well, that is certainly not the way my people hear about God," we protest. But the problem isn't that we fail to affirm the saving God, the powerful God, the holy God. Our sermons are most certainly orthodox; but often, they just aren't rich. God is captured, again and again, in oral nutshells. He is usually summed up. Many sermons take us to the woodshed, or to the great Physician, or to Mount Nebo where we can see God's promises stretching out before us, but seldom do sermons dwell well on the Lord himself.

DULLING DOWN GOD

The sorry fact is this: Sometimes in our sermons we unwittingly dull our bright, vivid, vital God till the picture we preach looks like it came over a bad fax machine.

One way we dull the glory of God is to surrender to our theological clichés in speaking of him. It is surely difficult to continually find fresh language to describe the Lord and his works. But when we resort to overfamiliar language ("God is so holy," "Jesus is more powerful than anyone else," "God is . . . God!") our words become almost "white noise"; the listeners don't go home having really thought about the Lord. We do the same when we use predictable illustrations (the father sacrificing his son in the drawbridge, God in the courtroom) or when we use our favorite metaphors for God repeatedly, having never worked to mine fresh language.

Another way we deaden the living God is to resort to scholastic, technical jargon in describing him. For example, if you were to preach on the great Christological hymn in Colossians 1:15–20, what would you do with the phrase, "He is the image of the invisible God"? Of course, it would help our people to know that the word "image" is the Greek "icon," and we may want to mention that God is invisible because he is spirit. To explain and illustrate these things may have people nodding in understanding, but shouldn't there be more? Shouldn't they come to the end of such a sermon wanting to sing and eager to pray? To reduce our message to term-paper language won't make that happen. At the end, they'll be thinking only of lunch.

A third way we fog God's glory is by not showing how he stands behind texts that are not explicitly about him. When I see a play I like, I'm invariably curious about the playwright. What of her is written into the story? What prompted him to give such a powerful speech to that character? Many Bible passages don't have explicit statements about the attributes of God, but there is no text that doesn't reveal something wondrous of God. We don't do the text justice if we don't help people see God standing in the wings.

POLISHING THE SPOTLIGHT'S LENS

Preaching, of course, is supposed to bring glory to God. I think of myself preaching as being like a spotlight operator. Our spotlight is the Bible. We need to point the spotlight accurately lest we become like one of those amateurs who jerk their light beam all over the stage till they find the star. We need to know when the light should be wide to give room for God to move and when it is focused tightly so that we hear every syllable God says. And we'd better be sure the lens is polished so the light shines as brightly as possible. Here are two ways to polish and point the lens.

(1) Most important is to scour the text for all it can tell us about the Lord. I read a mystery recently about a forensic scientist who solved a disappearance by meticulous examination of fibers, soil, and chemicals. He regarded everything as a clue, and he made lists of every clue, reading the lists over and over till they revealed their secrets. We need to have that diligence in searching for evidences of God in a text. Even texts that are explicit in their statements about God need to be scrutinized lest we miss the most important details in the brightness of the obvious.

Like a forensic scientist, when we look at the evidence of a text we want not only to gather every detail we can find, but we also want to know what they mean. What do these details collectively tell me about our God? When I preached on the Old Testament tabernacle, I spent a lot of time thinking about what a table

with bread in the Holy Place told me about God. When I studied Colossians 1:16, I thought hard about what Paul meant by saying, "In him all things were created." And when I was working on yet another Christmas sermon from Luke 2, it took me a long time to sort out how the manger was a sign. All these passages told me things about the Lord that I would have missed had I not gotten out my official Sherlock Holmes magnifying glass and crawled around on the floor of the text looking for clues.

(2) Pray for your own poetry of praise. As mentioned before, preachers must not always describe God in "cool" terms (academic, factual, unemotional). Our talk of God must be rich in fact, but also warm and beautiful in language.

As I've struggled to craft a sermon point that exalts Christ, I've often wished I had worked to be a poet. I have favorite places I look for quotes from others who have a flair for the well-turned phrase—the sermons of Charles Spurgeon or Alexander Maclaren, writings by the likes of Eugene Peterson or Frederick Buechner. When Vance Havner wanted to communicate that Christ is preeminent, he found a fresh way to say it: "Jesus is all we have; he is all we need and all we want. We are shipwrecked on God and stranded on omnipotence." I was glad I could use his words.

But I have also learned that God can give me a kind of poetry in my own tongue. I remember years ago searching in vain for just the right quote when I felt as though God said, "Write your own quote! I'll help you. You can say things beautifully, too." It is hard artistic work to say something about the Lord in well-crafted words. Not too flowery or ostentatious, but our own soul's poetry. We find our poet-voice when we pray a text into our heart; when we take that one fresh clue we have found about the Father, the Savior, or the Spirit, and wonder over it in prayer, like a Boy Scout blowing on a spark till a flame flares up.

"O God," I prayed, "what does it mean to know a Savior who was born in a manger? Why was the manger a sign?" Gradually, as I pondered that in prayer, I came to these words for my sermon: "Most saviors—rescuers—save by might or by trickery. But God's Savior would not save that way. He would save from a kind of weakness, by a kind of surrender. Here was born a Savior who would take on the very nature of a servant, who would touch our outcasts and dine with our failures, who would wash our feet and submit to our unjust systems, who would surrender to our most heinous and humiliating death. And he would save us that way! The manger was the first sign of a Savior who would be born among animals and die between thieves" (a phrase I borrowed from New Testament scholar Darrell Bock).

It wasn't great poetry, but it was the poetry of my soul, and I think it was moving to the people who heard me, because God had breathed it into flame during my prayers.

GRINDING THE GOLDEN CALF

When Moses discovered the Israelites had cast the golden calf, he ground it to powder and made them drink it like an anti-idolatry potion. But he also delivered to them the plans for the tabernacle that they might see what a poor substitute that bull-god was for Jehovah, who wanted to make his home among them. Sometimes our preaching takes us to texts that grind up the golden calf again and pour the metallic-tasting stuff down the throats of God's people so they won't chase after such imposters. But more often the Scriptures will combat the lurking idolatry of the Lord's people by setting before them the beauty and grace, the transcendence and immanence, of our Triune God.

Let us preach in words warm with the Spirit's breath, brought recently to life in our prayers. We cannot leave the "beautiful words, wonderful words, wonderful words of life" to the songwriters and worship leaders. Preachers must be lyricists of the Lord, too. Such sermons are the most practical and useful of all. For people who have been brought near enough to the holiness of God to yank off their shoes and close enough to the cross to receive back their ring and robe and sandals are Christians who are alive.

Chapter 157

WHEN IS A SERMON GOOD ENOUGH?

Sometimes you wish you'd had more time to prepare

Stephen Gregory

The phone rang at 10:00 a.m. on Sunday. Generally I would have long since been at the church. But this Sunday morning I was caring for our sick son while my wife taught her Sunday school class. Our game plan was for her to finish early and come home. Then I would rush to church for the morning service.

The call was from one of our lay leaders at the church. "Steve, the district superintendent just walked in. He mentioned he was in the area and wanted to worship with us today. Did you know he was coming?"

"No, I sure didn't," I replied. "I'll be there shortly."

Oh, no, I thought. *What a lousy day for the district superintendent to show up.*

My thoughts raced ahead to my message. I had some misgivings about my sermon. Besides my Sunday rhythm being thrown off by a sick child, the previous week had been filled with interruptions, meetings, and necessary paperwork. The time I'd planned to fine-tune my sermon had vaporized. Now I faced preaching a "best I could with the time I had" sermon with the D.S. sitting in the second pew!

After the service, the D.S. made several kind remarks about the service and the message. But I mentally dismissed his comments, moaning to myself, *Why didn't he come a few weeks ago when I had a good sermon?*

Afterward I pondered my feelings and asked myself some hard questions: *What is a good sermon? How can I preach with confidence a message I have not had time to polish? Who am I seeking to please, anyway?*

THE CONGREGATION'S CRITERIA

In the past, I've promised myself never to get caught without being fully prepared. *No matter what it takes,* I vowed, *I will be at my best.* So the next week I meticulously crafted my message, doing the biblical spadework my seminary profs would applaud. But is that a good sermon? The real grade, I've concluded, comes not from what my profs would think, but from the congregation, and ultimately, from God.

My congregation judges a sermon based on two criteria. *(1) Is the message specifically for them?* Being their pastor allows me to know my audience as other speakers cannot. They want this close relationship reflected in my words.

I became painfully aware of this when I preached in a nearby city. I used a sermon that had been well received in my home church. In an unfamiliar setting, however, it bombed. My delivery seemed fine, but the message did not connect with the audience. It lacked the personal element.

(2) How well have I pastored them? They respond better if I've ministered to them personally. If I have been with a family going through a crisis or gone out of my way to make a visit or phone call, they get more out of my

homiletical efforts. If, however, my pastoral care has disappointed them, their ears close to even my best sermon.

THREE MEASURES OF GOOD ENOUGH

Even though my congregation's love will normally transcend my mediocre sermons, I still struggle with perfectionism. When is my less-than-best effort still good enough? I am learning that on those infrequent occasions when I haven't had adequate time to prepare, I can still enter the pulpit with confidence and a clear conscience if I have accomplished three things.

(1) If I have done my best under the limitations I have providentially experienced. Like the two-talent person in Jesus' parable, I must accept what God gives—in this case, the schedule God allows in a given week. A pastor can only be faithful with what he has been given. But whatever amount of time that is, I must work my hardest.

Failing to maintain this perspective, I become anxious with those who interrupt me. As I sit in the hospital with a parishioner, I catch myself watching the clock. But if I accept that God may give me certain weeks filled with pastoral care rather than extensive exegesis, I don't have to begrudge my time at the hospital. And I can enter the pulpit with peace, knowing I've put as much time into my sermon as God intended.

(2) If I have been honest with the text. When time is tight, a preacher can be tempted to use a biblical text as a springboard to whatever random thoughts he wants to communicate. Such a sermon is not "good enough." I rarely have time to research every aspect of a passage. But

I can almost always focus on one aspect of a passage, and research and develop that well enough to speak with confidence and integrity about its application.

(3) If I have anticipated listeners' questions. Even though I can't address every issue, a sermon is "good enough" if I can identify and address the issues important to my people.

In my preparation I frequently use an inductive study method and ask many questions about the text. As I have matured in the ministry, I realize that often the congregation does not ask the same questions. Theirs are far removed from the academic understanding of the text.

GOD'S PERFECT PREPARATION

My greatest confidence comes when I rest in the sovereignty and calling of God.

Once in a message on body life, I explained we all have a ministry of encouragement and, at times, confrontation. I mentioned how people sometimes ask me as their pastor to do the dirty work of correcting a fellow church attender.

During this part of the message, I struggled because my example didn't seem to fit anyone in the congregation. Later that afternoon, however, a member revealed she had been on the verge of asking me to talk to someone else in the congregation about a problem between the two of them. Later she spoke to the person on her own, and they resolved the problem.

Preaching God's Word is a serious task, yet one I also want to enjoy. With a dose of realism and a recognition of God's sovereign work in my life and my congregation's, I am more at ease as I stand to deliver God's Word.

Chapter 158

MAKING THE MOST OF YOUR COMPUTER

I can't imagine preaching without my electronic research assistant and sermon coach

Richard Doebler

Our culture has become tied to technology so that computers play a serious and ever-increasing role in my ministry, especially in my preaching.

I can hear the skeptics: "God won't send his anointing through a Pentium processor." Something so blatantly material seems unspiritual. If I become too consumed with my PowerPoint, might I miss God's power?

Yes, it's true. Computers can impoverish my soul while improving my image. I must continually remind myself that new software will not help me preach with greater power or stronger conviction. Electronic wizardry cannot replace spiritual gifts. Microsoft does not open the windows of heaven. In short, computers cannot substitute for ministry basics—a heart for God, spiritual disciplines, personal and professional integrity, and diligent study.

However, despite the hazards, I remain committed to using technology in ministry. Computers have done two things for my sermons: (1) improved my study and preparation methods, and (2) polished my delivery techniques.

TURBO-CHARGED STUDY

I still use my books, but technology has beefed up my study and cut my prep time.

Better Bible Research

Everyone uses Bible software differently. Some focus on original Greek and Hebrew studies. Others use CD commentaries, vast libraries crammed into small spaces. I use Bible software in simple, utilitarian ways, mostly comparing translations. Software can provide me with twelve, sixteen, or more versions, side by side. My books can do that, but only with a desk the size of a Ping-Pong table.

Software performs concordance-like searches for topics or words, only faster and more comprehensively. I can print verses containing a word, several words, or a specific phrase, or copy verses into sermon notes in my word processor.

Better Sermon Illustrations

I subscribe to a couple of Internet services that offer collections of illustrations. It's almost like having a research assistant collecting and organizing stories. I can search for a specific word or topic among a huge database and view contemporary anecdotes, quotations, historical items, or humorous stories.

The only downside I've encountered is information overload. On occasion, I've collected up to fifty pages of (mostly) relevant stories for a single sermon. I've had to set limits, otherwise I could spend more time than ever on sermon preparation.

Better General Research

If a network news program reports a quote I'd like to use, I can usually retrieve the exact quote through news archives or transcription services available on the Internet. The Internet offers quick access to otherwise obscure information. Late one Saturday night, I realized that a reading I'd seen more than twenty years ago would be an ideal addition to my sermon. The next morning, I did a quick Internet search and found "One Solitary Life."

Better Filing

I used to collect illustrations in notebooks and file folders. No more. Now I save them in a computer file. This works for me because I recall stories more by a name or detail than by the topic. I won't remember whether I filed it under "perseverance" or "persistence" or "patience" or something else. If I remember some story was about Frederick the Great, I let the computer do the searching.

I store my sermons on disk and can easily refer to an old sermon. Some search tools do word searches through an entire directory or drive. In other words, I don't have to open each file separately to search for a particular word. This is especially helpful when I want to find a story I've already used.

Better Notes and Manuscripts

If you still prefer a typewriter or legal pad, fine. But drafting and editing sermon notes on the computer works better for me.

BUFFED-UP DELIVERY

When it comes to preaching, nothing can take the place of divine anointing, deep passion, and a commitment to speak authentically. But I can still improve my speaking skills by tapping new technology.

Preaching to the Eye

Presentation software allows me to show key sermon points to listeners. I've also projected poignant quotes, Scripture texts, even photos, drawings, and maps. The congregation's attentiveness and comprehension improve when I connect with their eyes as well as their ears. When I first started using presentation software, one man told me, "I never realized how much of a visual learner I am."

Even before we got a video/data projector, I improved my sermons by generating overhead transparencies of sermon points with my computer. Using Bible software, I made color transparencies of Bible maps and photos of archaeological sites.

An unexpected bonus of using presentation software has been a more disciplined editing of my sermon. Rambling sentences don't communicate well on screen. Concise, logical points reduce my tendency to be wordy.

Preaching to the Heart

The computer sparks my creative energies. I no longer think merely words and outlines. I also consider photos, video, and graphic designs. For instance, I might accentuate a message with a musical montage. On Independence Day we laid the words to America over a series of patriotic and historic photos. The congregation not only read and sang the words, they made an emotional connection with scenes of the Statue of Liberty and Vietnam Memorial.

Chapter 159

HOW TO BUILD A FIRST-RATE LIBRARY
Investing in quality, not quantity

Jim Shaddix

I would be a rich man if I had a dollar for every time someone has walked in my office and asked, "Have you read all these books?" I made a big mistake when I started in ministry. Thinking that more books meant better preaching, I began collecting volumes from anywhere and everywhere. I set out to build as big a library as my shelves would hold—and then some. I took pride in stockpiling volumes of books that served no purpose other than to look impressive. After lots of wasted money (not to mention a strained back from moving my library several times!), I'm now giving books away. Through this experience I learned two helpful principles to guide the development of my library.

(1) I build my library *functionally*. I now take time to identify and collect only those works that will directly inform my Christian walk and preaching ministry. Most of us can't afford to be book collectors. So avoid cluttering your shelves with inferior books donated by well-meaning friends or acquired on sale tables at discounted prices.

(2) I build my library *economically*. I use discount booksellers,[1] and I am disciplined in acquisitions. I try to include my wife in planning for acquisition as well as each individual purchase. Such a simple discipline is not only courteous, but it also prevents unneeded stress in our home and provides her with another opportunity to share in my ministry. I also try to keep a wish list of materials in order of priority. That list is a handy way to provide potential gift-givers meaningful ideas for birthdays, Christmas, and other occasions.

A carefully assembled collection of library resources is as essential for preachers as the professional tools of a dentist or medical doctor. Paul charged Timothy to "be diligent to present yourself approved to God, a worker who does not need to be ashamed, rightly dividing the word of truth" (2 Tim. 2:15, NKJV).

I need a library for:

- *Inspiration*. Reading challenges both my heart and conscience, calling me to higher planes of spirituality, morality, and integrity.
- *Stimulation*. As with physical exercise, I'm strengthened through mental gymnastics that stretch me intellectually.
- *Cultivation*. My preaching is enhanced by people who enlarge my vocabulary, teach me to think, and instruct me in the art of compelling speech.
- *Information*. Reading is my primary means of keeping abreast of the age and remaining well-informed in my field.
- *Communion*. I can fellowship with the greatest and godliest masters of all ages through their writings. One of Paul's "deathbed" requests of Timothy is, "Bring ... the books, especially the parchments" (2 Tim. 4:13, NKJV).

What should be in the preacher's library? Most preachers' libraries have both glaring voids as well as overkill. To overcome that, plan your objectives and priorities for acquisitions. I suggest developing your library according to the following essentials and priority:

- *Computer and software.* A computer helps you study more proficiently. Consider getting a comprehensive and expandable Bible study software program[2] that includes word study and language tools, commentaries, multiple translations, as well as libraries of computerized books.[3]

  With a computer and Internet access, you can also take advantage of Internet sites with Bible study search engines, illustration databases, periodical and book indexes, libraries of various institutions, general reference works, and powerful search engines.[4]

  A simple search of "Bible study resources" or "preaching resources" on an Internet search engine usually will produce many available links to helpful resources. Lists of online resources for preaching and Bible study also can be found on websites maintained by many seminaries and Bible colleges.[5]

- *Books.* To determine a potential book's usefulness before I buy, I lean heavily on personal recommendations, book review articles in periodicals, best-seller lists, as well as book introductions, footnotes, bibliographies, conclusions, publishers, dust jackets, and author information. I buy the best book or books on a given subject first. When acquiring commentaries for the study of a particular Bible book, I have made it a practice to contact four or five respected preachers or teachers and ask them to suggest their top five favorite works on the subject. In addition, read the books that evaluate commentaries and other Bible study tools.[6]

- *Periodicals.* The list of magazines and newspapers we can read is long,[7] but it and the reading of theological journals and the like keeps us on top of the most current thinking.[8]

Although the lion's share of our study should be given to biblical and theological pursuits, our libraries ought to expose us to a variety of fields. I like to regularly read works on history, biography, leadership, communication, political and social issues, and of course preaching.

I have a friend who keeps a Lazy Susan bookcase on his desk containing one book each from a variety of fields. During scheduled reading times, he rotates the shelf and reads a chapter or so in each book. The development of a working knowledge in various fields will not only sharpen your intellect but enable you to engage the church and the culture from an informed perspective.

NOTES

[1] *Some good distributors include Christian Book Distributors, P.O. Box 3687, Peabody, MA 01961–3687; Christian Publications, Inc., P.O. Box 3404, Harrisburg, PA 17105–3404; Scripture Truth Book Co., P.O. Box 339, Fincastle, VA 24909; Great Christian Books, 1319 Newport Gap Pike, Wilmington, DE 19804–2895.*

[2] *Some of the better programs include* Logos Series X *for PC;* Bible Works *for PC;* Accordance *for Macintosh.*

[3] *An annual review of available software programs can be found in the September–October issue of* Preaching *and at www.preaching.com.*

[4]*Surely one of the best and most standard is Google at* google.com.

[5]*One example is the Virtual Reference Room on The New Orleans Baptist Seminary website at* www.nobts.edu/library/virtual_ref.shtm.

[6]*Guidance in acquiring the most needful and useful commentaries and other Bible study tools can be found in the following: Daniel L. Akin,* Building a Theological Library *(Louisville: Daniel L. Akin, n.d.); Tremper Longman III,* Old Testament Commentary Survey, *3rd ed. (Grand Rapids: Baker, 2003); D. A. Carson,* New Testament Commentary Survey *(Grand Rapids: Baker, 1986); Gordon Fee and Douglas Stuart,* How to Read the Bible for All Its Worth *(Grand Rapids: Zondervan, 1981, 2003), 265–75; Bruce Corley, Steve Lemke, and Grant Lovejoy,* Biblical Hermeneutics *(Nashville: Broadman & Holman, 1996), 385–416; James F. Stitzinger, "Study Tools for Expository Preaching" in John MacArthur Jr.'s* Rediscovering Expository Preaching *(Dallas: Word, 1992), 188–208. Stitzinger's list is updated periodically on the Master's Seminary website at* www.tms.edu/850.asp.

[7]Christianity Today *magazine;* Leadership *journal;* Preaching *journal;* World *magazine;* In Other Words *illustration newsletter;* Newsweek *magazine;* Time *magazine;* USA Today *newspaper;* The Wall Street Journal *newspaper.*

[8]*The preacher who wishes to go deeper in biblical and theological studies might consider* Banner of Truth, Biblical Archaeology Review, Bibliotheca Sacra, Criswell Theological Journal, Grace Theological Journal, Interpretation, Journal of Biblical Literature, Journal of the Evangelical Theological Society, Review and Expositor, The Master's Seminary Journal, *and* Themelios.

Chapter 160

WHAT MAKES A SERMON DEEP?
The sources of wisdom preaching

Lee Eclov

Have you noticed that some preachers seem to think more deeply about a text than others? Their exegesis isn't necessarily better, and the depth isn't just from their lucid outline, revealing illustrations, or practical applications. But they see implications in the text others miss, connections to human experience others haven't pondered before. It is as though, in surveying the starry wonders of the passage, they have a telescope and others have binoculars.

I call that *wisdom preaching*. I think it is accomplished through what Eugene Peterson calls "contemplative exegesis."

Wisdom preaching begins with careful exegesis and exposition. We must study hard—parse verbs, track context, consider the theological themes, and grasp the author's logic. If we turn contemplative without thorough exegesis first, we will not think clearly or deeply. Our natural mind, even in considering a sublime subject, will take us astray or not take us deep enough. So first we indoctrinate our mind with the text. Only hard study is likely to force our minds out of their spiritual clichés and allow us to think in fresh ways.

But as we study, and after we study, we must

think. Of course, we are thinking all the time about how to explain words or concepts, how to apply and how to structure our message. But there is a deeper kind of thinking involved here.

I was in high school when I set out to think "deep thoughts." Seeking to separate myself from "shallow" classmates I would go for long walks at night, preferably in a drizzle, and brood. But I kept running into a problem in my pursuit of deep thoughts—I couldn't think of anything.

Sometimes I feel that way in sermon preparation. I know I ought to be "deep," but I can't seem to think of anything. But at other times I find ways to think about a sermon that take me beyond shallow clichés. Here are the tools that guide me in the spelunking of a text.

Don't substitute endless fact-finding for thinking. Folks who love to study never want to stop. There is always one more word to trace, one more commentator to check out, a leftover handful of cross-references to read. But there is limited time to prepare a sermon, and if we take all our time in research and writing, we leave no time to ponder. We are not preparing a term paper or a dissertation; we are preparing our hearts as much as our heads.

Pester the passage. Things I read in Scripture generally do not surprise me anymore. My first reaction is often, "Oh, I know that." But I've learned to assume that, in fact, a text probably doesn't say what I expect. It almost surely goes deeper and takes more unexpected turns than meet even my practiced eye. So I've learned to think of a passage as something like a professor I know who will just answer my question if I ask, but who will tell all kinds of wonders if I pester him a little. So I pester the text each week.

I'm amazed that often none of my commentaries answers the questions I have. That means I must pester the passage for answers. Actually I'm pestering the Holy Spirit to help me understand. "But why did you use this word? I don't see what this verse has to do with the one before it. Didn't you just say this? Why did you say it again? What would be missing if this weren't here?"

Let the passage pester me. This is a form of prayer for me, listening prayer. I pray, of course, for understanding as I study and for help with concentration. But after I've done my exegesis, I try to pray—weave the text into me.

"Lord," I once prayed, "the text says, 'Apart from you I have no good thing.' Where don't I live like that's true?" Some things came to mind. Then I had to decide if it was just my overcritical personality coming after me or if the Bible was exposing a weakness. That process of consideration helps me grow wise in the text. The Bible passage has just burrowed into me, and I have learned something of how the heart responds to this truth, and that will help me be a more penetrating preacher.

Mental doodling. I like words. I find I think better as I write out my observations, so I fill several pages of musings each week: fragments of outlines, half-ideas, questions, running reflections, private prayers. Some of these things are ultimately useless; after I preach I throw most of them away. But this mental muttering helps me go deeper. I extrapolate the text: "If this is true, then. . . ." I find fresh words to say familiar things, and I find that the fresh words and metaphors help me see things I had missed in all my exegesis.

 For an audio example of this principle see tracks 20–21 on the supplemental CD.

Know when to hold 'em; know when to fold 'em. Books, I mean. We have all learned that insights we come to ourselves are more alive when we preach than those we get from someone else. There's something about the inner transformation of personal discovery that comes through to our listeners. So there is a time to study and a time to stop.

Many pastors have learned the benefits of doing a serious amount of study before we turn to commentaries. We may use lexicons, other translations, and the like to be sure we are getting our facts straight, but we try to do our own thinking about the theology of the text, the structure, the importance of words. Then, when we turn to the books, they can test our conclusions and explain questions we just couldn't untangle.

But something else happens then, too. When we are full of the text and we begin to read someone else's thoughts on it, their words springboard us to fresh thoughts of our own. The same kind of thing may happen when we just talk with someone else about what we've been studying. But if I haven't done considerable thinking on my own first, the books I read rarely stimulate my own ideas. I am a passive rather than active receiver.

Mine the metaphors. Most Bible passages are rich in metaphors. Some are obvious ("the full armor of God"), and others are hidden in the original languages and lost in translation. Sometimes the metaphor is really the Bible story or parable. The power of metaphors is the power of suggestion. They are implicit, not explicit, truth. As a picture, they are worth a thousand words. Good preachers don't dissect metaphors; they frame them like beautiful pictures, so people see the wisdom hidden in them.

On *Preaching Today* Audio Tape #206, Timothy Keller preaches on Jacob's marriages to Leah and Rachel from Genesis 29:15–35. At one point, he says, "No matter what your hopes for a project, no matter what your hopes for marriage, no matter what your hopes for a career, no matter what you hope in, in the morning it will always be Leah. No matter what you think is Rachel, it will always be Leah." That is wisdom preaching in a metaphor.

Death to clichés. One reason I write out a manuscript is to fight the clichés that seem to dominate my sermon without it. A cliché is verbal shorthand. Some are overused phrases ("lead, guide, and direct"), and others are overused ideas ("This Christmas, let us, like the wise men, lay our treasures before the Lord"). It isn't that they are untrue, but that they are unheard. They become like white noise. They don't communicate much any longer. Wisdom preaching startles us with fresh phrases that arrest our thinking. In that same sermon by Tim Keller, he concludes by driving home the truth that though we may be ugly like Leah, God loves ugly people. Well, that is the clichéd way of saying it. What Keller actually says is, "Is there anybody here who feels ugly? The only eyes that count are ravished by you."

Browse the library of lives you have known. When I am working through a text, people I've known come to mind. I test the verses against their stories. One Sunday morning years ago I had spoken on a text of great encouragement. After the sermon, a grieving mother came through the handshaking line and ambushed me. "It doesn't work," is all she said. So now when I have a passage like that, I think, *What would keep someone from believing that this works?*

Once when I was preaching about Moses' excuses to God in Exodus 3, I called a pastor I know who stutters. "For Moses, stuttering was an excuse," I said to him. "Why wasn't it for you?" His answer helped me make the sermon more practical. Many times, I've pushed God in my prayers, "Lord, I think I know what this text says, but I just don't see how it will make much difference to Dave or Marjie. I really don't think people will go home moved by this. What am I missing?" Crash-testing the text against the walls of real lives helps me find the weaknesses in my sermons and make them strong enough to keep people safe in real life.

Often on Sunday mornings, when I come to the end of a sermon, I inwardly marvel at the wisdom of God that I have been privileged to study and explain. By the gracious help of God's Spirit and Word, not only can we reveal the deep thoughts of God to our people, but those thoughts become our thoughts. From the flax of our foolishness God spins for us the gold of wisdom.

Chapter 161

BEFORE YOU PREACH

Questions you ask yourself now may save your sermon later

Ed Rowell

When I go to the store without a list, there's no telling what I'll bring home. Same with preaching. Without a list to go by, there's no telling what I'll deliver.

I have a three-by-five card taped to my desk with a list of questions on it. Once I've done my biblical spadework, I break for caffeine, then start in with the first question. I ask these questions every time I prepare a sermon.

In one sentence, what is this sermon about? When, on Tuesday, someone asks, "What are you preaching about Sunday?" I hope I can answer with one clear sentence. It may be similar to the big idea of the text, but it's more relevant.

What theological category would this fit under? Am I being theologically faithful? If the sermon is not theological on some level, what is it?

What do I want my listeners to know? This question causes my sermon to engage the mind. What information does a listener need to know before he or she can act?

What do I want them to do? This is the application question, which focuses on my listeners' hands and feet. I must be as specific and practical as possible.

What do I want them to become? Now I'm going for the heart. What attitudes, priorities, and adjustments in lifestyle will this sermon address?

How does this sermon fit with the larger vision? This question helps me focus on the long view: How does this week's message move us toward our long-range goals? How does it fit into our church's vision statement? Is there a cohesiveness with what I've previously preached? A sense of direction?

So what? That is the relentless question of pragmatists: So what if the Philistines stopped up the wells dug by Isaac's father, Abraham? I didn't sign up for a class in ancient Middle Eastern history.

Oh really? Many people are conditioned by life to discount every promise they hear by about 90 percent. I try to imagine the broken promises and empty assurances people have had to face.

Do I believe this message will make a difference? Without this question, I could drift a long time before I'm conscious of growing cynicism or hopelessness. I can fake sincerity pretty well, but contrived passion is ugly to watch.

Has this sermon made a difference in my life this week? By this stage of preparation, I've spent many hours engaging the text and thinking about its implications for life. If it has not yet touched me, dare I believe it will touch anyone else in the thirty minutes I'll be in the pulpit?

Have I earnestly prayed for God to speak through me? As my friend Dennis Baker says, "Even a church service can get pretty interesting when God shows up." Have I met with him in the study? Am I expecting him to show up this Sunday?

Have I tried to make myself look better than I am? Who else besides us preachers can tell stories about ourselves without getting interrupted? If I'm not careful, I can abuse the privilege and select excerpts from my life that make me look smarter, funnier, and kinder than I'll ever be.

Will my listeners know I care about them? Love does cover a multitude of pastoral sins. If my flock recognizes my voice as that of a loving undershepherd, they will listen with ears of trust and faith. They'll know instinctively I have their best interests at heart.

Chapter 162

INSPIRATION POINTS

Planning the high moments in a message

Lee Eclov

You have probably driven up a mountain road through tall trees with only glimpses now and then to tell you what lies beyond. Then comes a scenic overlook where the advantages of your climb are spread before your wondering eyes. You pause nearly speechless and let time stop while you look at the beauty before you, hoping somehow to videotape that moment into your memory to replay on some future, dreary, desk day. Sometimes that scenic overlook has a name: Inspiration Point.

Sermons should have inspiration points, scenic overlooks where our climb through a Scripture stops to allow us to look with wonder at the spiritual scenery.

THE LACK OF INSPIRATION POINTS

I have occasion to listen to dozens of sermon tapes by as many different preachers each year, and I have been struck by how seldom preachers invest in the hard work of developing inspiration points in their sermons. There is much explanation, some illustration, occasional passion; but there is little beauty, few breath-catching moments, seldom need for a moment of silence to take it all in.

We are wary of oratory and suspicious of the overwrought, overheated language of grandiloquence. But too often we are not eloquent at all. We just want to "put the cookies on the bottom shelf." Our motto is K.I.S.S.: "Keep it simple, stupid." We want so badly to preach plainly that our sermons are sometimes no more memorable than a phone call.

To be sure, inspiring language comes more easily to some than others. Some preachers have the soul of a poet. Language for them is a palette, a keyboard, a block of marble. Some of us find inspiration points a waste of precious Bible time. "Just the facts, Ma'am." That mindset likely does not care for poetry either, or *Pilgrim's Progress*, or *Screwtape Letters*.

The main reason our sermons lack inspiration points, though, is that developing them requires such hard work. We are taught to exegete and research and to marshal thoughts into an outline, but professors never upped our grade in seminary for writing something beautiful, for painting a word masterpiece, for setting a text a-singing. As we guide our listeners up the mountains of Scripture, however, we misguide them if we do not stop at some inspiration points.

After we have done our study to rightly understand a text, we must pause to think about what is before us. Where is the beauty, the poetry, the wonder in this text? If I do not see it, I haven't stopped long enough to look at the view, for no passage of Scripture is a mere parking lot. All Scripture is inspired by the same God who tosses off sunsets every night. Even genealogies have inspiration points!

CRAFTING INSPIRATION POINTS

Look for a truth that has become too familiar. Look for a phrase everyone takes for granted. Look for a metaphor that puts a paintbrush into your hand and a canvas before your people. Look for a moving photo where you can point out what people might have missed in the black-and-white of print. What is the melody of this passage? What would a poet see? Ask God to heal your blindness and release your tongue!

Scenic overlooks don't just happen to be along the highway. Someone saw the possibilities and engineered a wide spot in the road, cut away the brush that hindered sight, and put out signs telling us what is coming. Preaching an inspiration point takes some rhetorical engineering also. Several different tools are at our disposal:

Story

We should illustrate off and on throughout a message, but for this purpose a story must do more than clarify a point; it must inspire. It needs to be a story with pathos, but it cannot be sappy. A story that tastes like syrup is nothing more than a sugar rush. An inspiring story must have the ring of truth, and it must have first truly inspired us as a window into this biblical truth.

Quotation

As with illustrations, some quotations are tools we use only to clarify—a pithy definition, for example, or a well-worded summary by a recognized authority. But sometimes we come across a jewel of eloquence that will help our listeners see the beauty in the Word. I occasionally read Alexander Maclaren for just that reason. We have all benefited from favorites like C. S. Lewis and Spurgeon, and among the contemporary, Frederick Buechner, Max Lucado, and Martin Luther King Jr.

Stacking

That's what I call the method I learned listening to African-American preachers, where a series of several clauses of similar sentence structure are stacked one upon another.

C. L. Franklin (father of soul singer Aretha Franklin) was a noted preacher. In a sermon about Doubting Thomas, he chose as an inspiration point Jesus' statement to the disciples when he appeared in the upper room, "Peace be unto you" (John 20:21, 26, KJV). You can hear the "stacking" cadences of these words: "He knew how doubtful some of them were. And he knew how afraid some of them had been. And he knew how their faith had been tried. And he knew what a terrible ordeal they'd gone through. And think about how consoling his address was. Listen at him: 'Peace be unto you.'"

Extrapolation

This is a simple tool of the imagination where we take a biblical phrase and state some of the wonderful implications. It becomes an inspiration point when we paint pictures rather than explain.

Billy Sunday could have said, "In heaven we will live forever." Instead he turned that truth into an inspiration point: "In heaven they never mar the hillsides with spades, for they dig no graves. . . . In heaven no one carries handkerchiefs, for nobody cries. In heaven they never phone for the undertaker, for nobody dies."

Expanding a Biblical Metaphor

Many word pictures run throughout the Bible. If we come across such a metaphor in our text, pick up its strain from the rest of Scripture. For example, Ephesians 2:20 says Christians are "built on the foundation of the apostles and prophets, with Christ Jesus himself as the chief cornerstone." The preacher might say:

There, deep beneath us is the great foundation stone of Jesus Christ, the Son of God, his mighty cross and his powerful resurrection. Locked up against that stone is God's covenant with Abraham and the stone-carved law of Moses.

There are the great granite blocks of the prophet Isaiah: "His name shall be called Wonderful Counselor, Mighty God, Everlasting Father, Prince of Peace"; and of the apostle Paul: "It is by grace you have been saved, through faith"; and John the Revelator: "See, the Lion of the tribe of Judah, the Root of David, has triumphed."

And there, atop those great blocks, the blood-red bricks of the martyrs and the fire-baked bricks of the Reformers. And then, above them, rise our forefathers in the faith, and finally, our own lives, for we too are part of this great temple that rises to God—for we "are being built together to become a dwelling in which God lives by his Spirit."

I love calligraphy, the visual art of words. I have framed on my office wall a portion of a prayer written by James Weldon Johnson in *God's Trombones*, because it reminds me to be an inspiration point preacher:

And now, O Lord, this man of God, who breaks the bread of life this morning . . . put his eye to the telescope of eternity and let him look upon the paper walls of time. Lord, turpentine his imagination. Put perpetual motion in his arms. Fill him full of the dynamite of thy power. Anoint him all over with the oil of thy salvation, and set his tongue on fire.

Chapter 163

SIMPLIFY

Harnessing the power of economy

Charles Swindoll

The scene was thick. The clouds were heavy and dark gray. The mood was tense. It was no time to take a walk in the park or stroll down Pennsylvania Avenue. The smell of death was in the air. A decision was essential. With paper and pen in hand, the long, lank frame of a lonely man sat quietly at his desk. The dispatch he wrote was sent immediately. It shaped the destiny of a nation at war with itself.

It was a simple message—a style altogether his. No ribbons of rhetoric were woven through the note. No satin frills, no enigmatic eloquence. It was plain, direct, brief, to the point. A bearded Army officer soon read it and frowned. It said:

> April 7, 1865, 11 a.m.
> Lieut. Gen. Grant,
> Gen. Sheridan says, "If the thing is pressed, I think that Lee will surrender."
> Let the thing be pressed.
> A. Lincoln

Grant nodded in agreement. He did as he was ordered. Exactly two days later at Appomattox Court House, General Robert E. Lee surrendered. "The thing was pressed" and the war was ended.

Simplicity. Profound, exacting, rare simplicity. Lincoln was a master of it. His words live on because of it. When assaulted by merciless critics, many expected a lengthy, complex defense of his actions. It never occurred. When questioned about his feelings, he answered, "I'm used to it." When asked if the end of the war or some governmental rehabilitation program might be the answer to America's needs, he admitted quite simply, "Human nature will not change." In response to a letter demanding the dismissal of the postmaster general, he wrote, "Truth is generally the best vindication against slander."

When encouraged to alter his convictions and push through a piece of defeated legislation by giving it another title, he reacted with typical simplicity, "If you call a tail a leg, how many legs has a dog? Five? No, calling a tail a leg doesn't *make* it a leg!"

Simplicity. The difference between something being elegant or elaborate. The difference between class and common. Between just enough and too much. Between concentrated and diluted. Between communication and confusion.

Between: *"Hence from my sight—nor let me thus pollute mine eyes with looking on a wretch like thee, thou cause of my ills; I sicken at thy loathsome presence...."*

and: *"Scram!"*

Simplicity. *Economy* of words mixed with *quality* of thought held together by *subtlety* of expression. Practicing a hard-to-define restraint so that some things are left for the listener or reader to conclude on his own. Clear and precise, yet not overdrawn. Charles Jehlinger, a former director of the American Academy of Dramatic Arts, used to instruct all apprentice actors with five wise words of advice: "*Mean more than you say.*"

It has been my observation that we preachers say much too much. Instead of stopping with a concise statement of the forest—explicit and clear—we feel compelled to analyze, philosophize, scrutinize, and moralize over each individual tree—leaving the listener weary, unchallenged, confused, and (worst of all!) *bored.* Zealous to be ultra-accurate, we unload so much trivia that the other person loses the thread of thought, not to mention his patience. Bewildered, he wades through the jungle of needless details, having lost his way as well as his interest. Instead of being excited over the challenge to explore things on his own, lured by the anticipation of discovery, he gulps for air in the undertow of our endless waves of verbiage, clichés, and in-house mumbo jumbo.

One dear old lady said of the Welsh preacher John Owen that he was so long spreading the table, she lost her appetite for the meal. I particularly like the way William Sangster put it: "When you're through the pumpin', let go the handle."

The longer I study Jesus' method of communicating, the more convinced I am that his genius rested in his ability to simplify and clarify issues others had complicated. He used words anyone could understand, not just the initiated. He said just enough to inspire and motivate others to think on their own, to be inquisitive, to search further. And he punctuated his teaching with familiar, earthy, even humorous illustrations that riveted mental handles to abstract truths. Best of all, he didn't try to impress. Such a captivating style led others to seek his counsel and thrive on his instruction.

As a fellow struggler earning the right to be heard Sunday after Sunday, let me offer this summary:

- Make it clear.
- Keep it simple.
- Emphasize the essentials.
- Forget about impressing.
- Leave some things unsaid.

Luther made it even more simple: Start fresh. Speak out. Stop short.

We've got the greatest message on earth to declare. Most people have either never heard it or they've been confused because someone has garbled the issues. Jesus implies, "If the thing is simplified, they will surrender."

Let the thing be simplified.

Chapter 164

USING SOMEONE ELSE'S SERMON

What is plagiarism?

Haddon Robinson

Plagiarism is stealing other people's material. In the world of scholarship, when things are put in print, any idea taken from someone else must be credited in a footnote. In the world of preaching, a pastor who takes sermons from other preachers—word for word—without giving credit is guilty of plagiarism. That is stealing what is not yours. If my regular sermon preparation consists of going online and getting a sermon from somebody else and preaching it as is, that is an ethical problem.

Motives and honesty are the key issues. We quote others for two reasons: Either the person has more authority than we have, or the person said it better than we can. The second case requires that we give credit. If I get Timothy Keller's sermon and deliver it as if it came from me, that's deception. If I quote him word for word, I should give him credit. The general rule we should follow is, whenever our motive for using someone else's material is that they said it better than we can, then honesty requires that we give them credit. You are not diminished by quoting somebody else.

This is not to say that we should not draw from many sources in sermon preparation. Occasionally the thrust of someone else's sermon, the main idea, or the development works for you, and you think it will help your hearers. But somehow you have to make the sermon your own. Using someone else's material cannot take the place of our own study and meditation on the biblical text. The sermon must be in your words. It may be someone else's idea, but it is in your words. Do you make it your own, or do you claim it to be your own when it really belongs to somebody else? It must fit your experience.

When we make someone else's ideas our own, the line between what is "original" (nothing is truly original) and what is plagiarized is difficult to discern. But clearly if we take most of our material for a sermon from another preacher, then it is a matter of honesty and integrity that we give credit.

In the cases where we use most of someone else's material, it would be wise to discuss this with church leadership. They ought to be part of our conscience, understand why we want to do this, and agree to it.

The requirements for footnoting differ greatly between writing and preaching. If a sermon is put into print, the footnoting should be more extensive.

When we use someone else's sermon outline, one way we can give credit is: "I came across an approach to a sermon by so-and-so, and I want to share it with you."

Chapter 165

PLANNING FOR A RICHER, DEEPER SERMON SERIES

Expository preaching requires thinking ahead

Haddon Robinson

Only with advanced planning can you preach a wide assortment of biblical material. It's hard to imagine someone tackling the book of Jeremiah starting on a Saturday night. So how can we develop a preaching plan for a three- or a twelve-month sermon series?

Most pastors who plan their pulpit work get away by themselves for at least a week. First, they ask themselves and others, "What would we like to accomplish through preaching and teaching in the months ahead?" On the basis of the answer, they think about different books of the Bible that might speak to those goals.

On the study retreat, take your Bible and a few good commentaries on the selected book (or books) of the Bible. Read the biblical text several times (usually in different translations) and if possible in the original languages as well. Look for the major divisions and subdivisions of the biblical material and determine the preaching passages and what each passage is about. It helps to give each passage a general title that summarizes its subject. Commentaries can help you nail down the broad and narrow subjects in a book as well as help you discover what each passage is about and how it develops. You want to understand the biblical writer's flow of thought, his audience, and his purpose in writing.

Then take several sheets of paper and mark out the Sundays for the months ahead. Then put down the dates, and note any special days that are on or around each date (Labor Day, Father's Day, Mother's Day, Advent, and so on). Then plot your sermon calendar. A long series can be broken up with special days.

Even though you are preaching a series, each sermon must stand alone. (It is a rare congregation these days that shows up with the same people each Sunday. A pastor can't assume that everyone has heard the previous sermons or even that those who have will remember what was said.) It may help to give the series a title that promises what each sermon in the series will be about.

If you make out a folder for each Sunday on your calendar, you can take any material that you come across in the weeks ahead that seems pertinent and put it in the folder. If you have done enough homework so that you are familiar with the book you plan to expound, material pops up at you that you might not have noticed. When you get down to preparing each sermon, you will often have illustrations and articles that will help you teach and apply the passages.

Planning your pulpit work gives you "simmer time" that makes your sermons richer and deeper.

Part 9

Delivery

How Do I Speak in a Way That Arrests Hearers?

Chapter 166

THE SOURCE OF PASSION

Focusing on emotion does not produce truly passionate preaching

Paul Scott Wilson

Most preachers who desire to be more passionate make a common mistake: They think of passion in preaching as primarily an emotional issue rather than a theological one. Passion in preaching is primarily a theological issue arising out of a preacher's strong awareness that God wants to accomplish something through the sermon. Preachers have good reason to be passionate when they facilitate an encounter with God and when they offer the congregation what they are longing for: an experience of God judging and reconciling the world in love and grace.

Obviously no one has the ability to offer God apart from the Holy Spirit working in and through the sermon. Because this is the case, preachers might be tempted to conclude they can do little to help the Holy Spirit in this regard, when in fact there is much they can do.

Preachers must try to focus on God instead of continually focusing on humans and what humans are expected to do before God. Many sermons are man-centered. They may sound as if they are talking about God, and the congregation may think they are getting the help they need, but generally the preacher is casting them on their own resources to accomplish what God requires instead of offering God's help as it is revealed in the biblical text. This help is not separate from the cross, resurrection, and ascension of Jesus Christ.

Focusing on God in itself is often not sufficient, though, for the sermon easily can become more like an essay than a word of proclamation. We can present God in a manner that suggests that the most important thing for the congregation to receive is information about God rather than communication from God as an event in their lives. We can present God as an abstract idea the congregation must apprehend or as a theological doctrine they must accept—both of which are important and have their place in a sermon—rather than as God known in three Persons, who seeks a relationship with his beloved creatures.

Passion certainly includes exhortation but ought not be restricted to it. Passion in preaching also needs to communicate God's love and delight in the Lord.

I am convinced that God cannot adequately be the subject of the sermon unless God is the subject of the theme sentence of the sermon. Since it represents the sermon in microcosm, where the theme sentence focuses, the sermon will focus.

For example, Paul writes, "Therefore, since we are justified by faith, we have peace with God through our Lord Jesus Christ" (Rom. 5:1). Because Paul has humans as the subject of his sentence, we may naturally decide to keep humans as the subject of our sermons on this text. As long as human actions are the focus, it is hard for preachers to become passionate in anything other than exhortation, for the message quickly becomes an effort to prove a point, in this case Paul's point that we are justified by faith. To make that argument has merit, but the sermon need not focus exclusively there when it

can also offer something more. As preachers we are called to proclaim the power, mystery, and saving grace of God. The potential for passion rises when the preacher puts on theological lenses and brings God into focus. Paul is saying this: God justifies us through Jesus Christ.

When we get to a place in the sermon where we talk about God's power, greatness, activity, and purpose, then we have something more to be excited about. Then too our people have something to get excited about. They can leave church buoyed by the Spirit, not weighed down by their sins and failures. It is not that the latter have not been mentioned but rather they have not been allowed to have the last say, just as the cross was not the end of our story.

I recently heard a former student preach. He and his family had been through hard times since I knew him, and it showed. There was a reverence in his pulpit manner, a deep respect for his task, a deep feeling for the words of Scripture as he read them. His sermon was not eloquent, but he was sincere, his humor was natural, and he had a wonderful, hopeful message focused on Christ. This preacher was passionate in the best sense of the word: authentic, exhortative at times, but also rejoicing.

Chapter 167

PATHOS NEEDED

Why reasonable preachers have regard for emotion

Jeffrey Arthurs

Pathos means "feeling or emotion" (Conley, 1990, p. 317). When used in discussions of persuasion, it is "all those materials and devices calculated to put the audience in a frame of mind suitable for the reception of the speaker's ideas" (Thonssen and Baird, 1948, p. 358). Pathos deserves a central place in homiletical theorizing and practice—a higher place than it currently receives.

I will argue that claim in the first section of this article and make some suggestions in the second section, but first I need to make a disclaimer: I do not pit pathos against logos. Preaching must include a strong cognitive element, or else it is not preaching. Without a dominant idea derived from a biblical text, supplemented with other ideas, a sermon is merely "sound and fury signifying nothing."

However, while preaching cannot be less than the communication of a biblical idea, it should be more. De Quincey compared the two arts of rhetoric, logos and pathos, to rudder and sail. The first guides discourse and the second powers it (Thonssen and Baird, 1948, p. 358). Even a traditionalist like John Broadus argued that preachers need "the capacity for clear thinking, with strong feelings, and a vigorous imagination" to produce "forcible utterance" (McDill, 1994, p. 10).

Since emotional appeal is the stuff of demagogues, let me extend my disclaimer to say that no ethical communicator uses pathos to induce an audience to act contrary to reason. That is manipulation, not persuasion. Jonathan Edwards wrestled with this issue in response to charges of sensationalism in the Great Awakening. His answer sets the tone for this article: "I should think myself in the way of my duty, to raise the affections of my hearers as high as I possibly can, provided they are affected with nothing but truth, and with affections that are not disagreeable to the nature of what they are affected with" (Piper, 1986, p. 80). Ethical (and effective) communicators use pathos to prompt people to act in accord with the truth.

My argument is not a plea to discount or circumvent logos. Neither is it a plea to bypass the role of the Holy Spirit in preaching. It is my conviction that the Holy Spirit converts and sanctifies the whole person, not just the mind, and the Holy Spirit appeals to the mind and emotions to move the will.

PATHOS INFLUENCES DECISION-MAKING

The old dichotomy between logic and emotion, the head and the heart, does not reflect how humans actually make decisions. As rhetorical scholar Roderick Hart argues, "To contrast people's 'logical' versus 'emotional' tendencies is to separate human features that should not be separated in analysis since they cannot be separated in fact. When people react to anything...[they] react with all of themselves"

(1990, pp. 121–22). Arnold and Wilson state simply that "people do not reason or feel, they reason because they feel, they feel because they think they have reason" (1963, p. 318). The dichotomy between pathos and logos may be useful in the academy, but in the marketplace the two cannot be separated.

Even if we allow the dichotomy to stand, we find that pathos influences the will more than logos. This was Cicero's observation: "Mankind makes far more determinations through hatred, or love, or desire, or anger, or grief, or joy, or hope, or fear, or error, or some other affection of mind, than from regard for truth, or any settled maxim, or principle of right" (Thonssen and Baird, 1948, p. 360).

What is "reasonable" for listeners depends more on how well they believe the proposal will fulfill their desires or how congruent it is with their current attitudes than on canons of formal logic. C. S. Lewis states, "People don't ask for facts in making up their minds. They would rather have one good, soul-satisfying emotion than a dozen facts" (Martindale and Root, 1989, p. 482).

GOD IN SCRIPTURE USES PATHOS

Pathos is primary in human decision-making because God made us to respond to emotional appeals, and he himself uses pathos. He motivates us through awe of his immensity, fear of his holiness, confidence of his goodness, and joy of his grace. Pathos is crucial, not incidental, to God's communication. As Robinson says:

> Some passages are alive with hope, some warn, some create a sense of joy, some flash with anger at injustice, others surge with triumph. A true expository sermon should create in the listener

the mood it produced in the reader. . . . The task of the poet, the playwright, the artist, the prophet, and the preacher overlap at this point—to make people feel and see. (1999, pp. 82–83)

From the earnest pleading of Charles Spurgeon, to the pastoral warmth of Jack Hayford, to the exuberance of E. V. Hill, effective preachers represent God—his ideas and emotions. When preachers use pathos (and logos and ethos), they handle the Word skillfully.

Before turning to suggestions of how preachers can incorporate more emotion into their preaching, one other observation helps establish the place of pathos in preaching.

TODAY'S CULTURAL SHIFT

The well-documented shift to postmodernism in Western culture includes skepticism toward rationalistic logic. Modernists trusted logic and were comfortable with propositional truth, but postmoderns are more likely to adopt an "imaginative/feeling perspective that sees 'feeling' and 'imagining' as a more integrating key to the whole of reality than either 'knowing' or 'willing'" (Sims, 1995, p. 332). Postmoderns desire an experience of reality, not simply statements about it. In this way, postmodernism is closer than modernism to biblical Christianity.

Unfortunately, most of our training equips us to exegete and communicate the ideas of the text, not the feelings. Therefore, in the following section, I suggest three ways to upgrade the place of pathos in our preaching so that our sermons will not be, as Ralph Waldo Emerson described his own lectures: "Fine things, pretty things, wise things, but no arrows, no axes, no nectar, no growling, no transpiercing, no loving, no enchantment" (Larsen, 1989, p. 71).

UPGRADING PATHOS

The three suggestions relate to three standard areas of sermonizing: exegesis, delivery, and arrangement.

Including Identification of Mood As Part of Exegesis

Biblical literature prompts emotions as well as communicates ideas. Effective heralds attempt to embody all of God's message; therefore, they should identify the dominant mood(s) of the text. "While the emotion of a writer may be more difficult to pin down than ideas and their development, every passage has a mood" (Robinson, 1999, p. 82).

We can identify that mood by reading slowly and imaginatively. Even though hermeneutics texts offer few tools for exegeting the affective quality of texts, I believe that most preachers possess enough sensitivity to identify the dominant mood of the passage. Simply by keeping in mind that the text aims to create an experience, not just transmit an idea, preachers should be able to identify the dominant mood of the passage.

However, if a preacher feels "literarily challenged," I suggest reading in the disciplines of rhetoric and oral interpretation. Rhetoric identifies a writer's purpose and symbolic agency for achieving that purpose, and oral interpretation deals with embodying that purpose for an audience. Also helpful are works that show how to determine and communicate affective content. Two other fields to pursue are "the Bible as literature" and reader-response theory (although much maligned in evangelical circles, reader-response criticism helps interpreters identify the effects texts prompt in readers). Sources on these fields are listed in the appendix to this chapter.

But to reiterate, I believe that specialized study in "affective exegesis" is not necessary for most preachers. We simply need to add a few more questions to our checklist when doing exegesis: "What is God trying to do with this text," and "How does pathos help achieve that goal?" We should ask not only "What does it mean," but also "How does it make me feel?" Identification of the mood is the first step toward communication of that mood, and the next step is to embody the mood in delivery.

Embody the Mood in the Sermon

Once the preacher has identified the affective content of the text, then he or she should embody it. I use the word "embody" because much of the communication of pathos occurs nonverbally. When preachers genuinely feel the mood(s) of the text, the audience will more likely respond. Rhetorician and preacher Hugh Blair writes, "The only effectual method [of moving the listeners' emotions] is to be moved yourself. . . . There is an obvious contagion among the passions" (Thonssen and Baird, 1948, p. 364).

Oral interpretation scholars explain this "contagion" by the theory of "empathy." When a performer "feels with" the literature, physical response occurs. The audience perceives this response (although the perceiving is often unconscious) and adopts the same attitude (Lee and Gura, 1987, pp. 126–128; Aggertt and Bowen, 1963, pp. 146–150).

This "contagion" is indispensable to preaching. Dabney says that the "law of sympathy" is the preacher's "right arm in the work of persuasion" (see Sacred Rhetoric section in Hogan). Effective heralds demonstrate that the truth has gripped them and that it should grip the listeners. Effective heralds embody the text.

But this is easier said than done. Each of us

has his or her own habitual emotional state. This state may or may not correspond with the mood of the text. A mellow preacher will have trouble embodying the climax of the ages described in Revelation 21. A stern preacher who does not "submit to the atmosphere and spirit of" 1 Peter 1:3–9 will turn radiant hope into guilt for not having that hope (Robinson, 1999, p. 83).

In addition to the problem of habitual moods, the preacher's varying moods may or may not match the tone of the text. One week we are depressed, another week we are thankful. The only solution is to think and pray and imagine ourselves deeply into the text so that it rules our hearts and minds, and then we must speak naturally, not fearing to reveal our feelings in public.

Of course, embodying the mood of the text will look different for each of us since preaching is truth through personality, but listeners will still be able to tell if we are emotionally attuned to God's message.

Can "embodying" be taught? Yes and no. There is some value in drills that refine delivery, and exercises can help speakers be more comfortable projecting emotion, but the key is not technique. It is genuinely feeling. Teachers should raise consciousness about pathos in preaching, help their students identify the affective elements of the text, model "embodying," and exhort student preachers to "let it out." They need to know that "ordinary people listen for a preacher's feelings as much as his ideas, perhaps more. That is simply part of the power of the spoken word" (Shelley, 1998, p. 102).

Surface Need

To upgrade the power of pathos in our sermons, we should give special attention to surfacing need in the introduction. This suggestion, like the previous one, is simply a reminder, but it is a reminder worth making. Early in the sermon, the audience must feel their need for the Word, otherwise the engine of pathos stalls.

Classical rhetoricians spoke of the need to rouse emotion in the "peroration" (the finale), but modern theorists such as Monroe with his "motivated sequence" argue persuasively that listeners grant attention only to what interests them, and what interests them is what they feel they need. Therefore, to bring the world of the text into the world of the listeners, the preacher must demonstrate early in the sermon how the truth addresses felt needs. All learning begins at the feeling level.

What tools are available for identifying need? Many, such as soliciting "feedforward," but perhaps the most powerful tool is simply imagination. Henry Ward Beecher went so far as to argue that "the first element on which your preaching will largely depend for power and success ... is imagination, which I regard as the most important of all elements that go to make the preacher" (Larsen, 1989, p. 108). We should imagine the emotions of the text, and we should imagine the needs of our people. Imagination increases identification, and identification is nearly synonymous with effective communication.

Pathos deserves a high place in homiletical theory and in preaching. When it works hand in hand with logos and ethos, powerful and holistic communication occurs. Effective heralds identify and embody the moods of the text while they speak to needs. Effective preachers value pathos and use it to the glory of God.

SOURCES CITED

Aggertt, Otis J., and Elbert R. Bowen. 1963. *Communicative Reading*, 2nd ed. New York: Macmillan.

Arnold, Carroll, and John F. Wilson. 1963. *Public Speaking as a Liberal Art*, 3rd ed. New York: MacMillan.

Buttrick, David. 1994. *A Captive Voice: The Liberation of Preaching*. Louisville: Westminster John Knox.

Conley, Thomas M. 1990. *Rhetoric in the European Tradition*. New York: Longman.

Hart, Roderick P. 1990. *Modern Rhetorical Criticism*. Glenview, IL: Scott, Foresman & Little, Brown.

Hogan, William L. 1997. "White Guys Can't Preach (What I Have Learned From African American Preachers)." Unpub. paper presented at Evangelical Homiletics Society, October 1997, South Hamilton, MA. Electronic transcript.

Larsen, David L. 1989. *Anatomy of Preaching: Identifying the Issues in Preaching Today*. Grand Rapids: Kregel.

Lee, Charlotte I., and Timothy Gura. 1987. *Oral Interpretation*, 7th ed. Boston: Houghton Mifflin.

Martindale, Wayne, and Jerry Root. 1989. *The Quotable Lewis*. Wheaton, IL: Tyndale.

McDill, Wayne. 1994. *The 12 Essential Skills for Great Preaching*. Nashville: Broadman & Holman.

Piper, John. 1986. *Desiring God: Meditations of a Christian Hedonist*. Portland, OR: Multnomah.

Pitt-Watson, Ian. 1976. *Preaching: A Kind of Folly*. Philadelphia: Westminster.

Reid, Robert Stephen. 1995. "Postmodernism and the Function of the New Homiletic in Post-Christendom Congregations." *Homiletic* 20/2, pp. 1–13.

Robinson, Haddon W. 1999. *Making a Difference in Preaching*. Ed. Scott M. Gibson. Grand Rapids: Baker.

Shelley, Bruce. 1998. "The Big Idea and Biblical Theology's Grand Theme." Pp. 95–107 in *The Big Idea of Biblical Preaching: Connecting the Bible to People*. Ed. Keith Willhite and Scott M. Gibson. Grand Rapids: Baker.

Sims, John A. 1995. "Postmodernism: The Apologetics Imperative." Pp. 324–43 in *The Challenge of Postmodernism: An Evangelical Encounter*. Ed. David S. Dockery. Wheaton, IL: Victor.

Thonssen, Lester, and Baird A. Craig. 1948. *Speech Criticism: The Development of Standards for Rhetorical Appraisal*. New York: Roland.

Walzer, Arthur E. 1999. "Campbell on the Passions: A Rereading of the Philosophy of Rhetoric." *Quarterly Journal of Speech* 85: pp. 72–85.

Appendix

On rhetoric, specifically speech act theory, see John L. Austin, *How to Do Things with Words* (New York: Oxford Univ. Press, 1970). On oral interpretation, see Charlotte I. Lee and Timothy Gura, *Oral Interpretation*, 7th ed. (Boston: Houghton Mifflin, 1987); Todd V. Lewis, *Communicating Literature*, 2nd ed. (Dubuque, IA: Kendall/Hunt, 1991). On determining and communicating affective content, see Michael A. Bullmore, "Re-examining Author's Intent: The Nature of Scripture, Exegesis, and the Preaching Task," unpublished paper, Evangelical Homiletical Society (Oct. 1997); Jay Adams, *Preaching with Purpose* (Phillipsburg, NJ: Presbyterian and Reformed, 1982); Mike Graves, *The Sermon as Symphony: Preaching the Literary Forms of the New Testament* (Philadelphia: Judson, 1997); and Thomas G. Long, *Preaching and the Literary Forms of the Bible* (Philadelphia: Fortress, 1989). On the Bible as literature, see Leland Ryken, *How to Read the Bible As Literature* (Grand Rapids: Zondervan, 1984). On reader-response theory, see Stanley E. Fish, *Self-Consuming Artifacts: The Experience of Seventeenth-Century Literature* (Berkeley, CA: Univ. of California Press, 1972).

Chapter 168

PREACHING WITH INTENSITY

How to communicate so listeners feel your passion

Kevin A. Miller

I couldn't wait to preach this sermon. The text, from 1 Samuel 20, captures one of the most poignant moments in all Scripture—David saying good-bye for the final time to his dearest friend Jonathan. "Then David bowed to Jonathan with his face to the ground," the Bible relates. "Both of them were in tears as they embraced each other and said good-bye, especially David" (v. 41, NLT). I got a lump in my throat as I studied the passage. The previous month I had helped one of my best friends load a big, yellow Ryder truck with his every belonging. The truck's metal back door had rolled down with a metallic thunk. Then my friend had driven away to another state, and I knew I would not see him again for a long time.

In preparation for the message, I had studied much of 1 Samuel to gain the context. I had poured through commentaries. That morning, I was like a sprinter in the blocks, waiting for the service to come to the moment when I would be able to deliver this message from the Bible and from my burning spirit.

As I preached, I included illustrations from current events, from history, from my life. I even choked up a little while telling the story of losing my close friend to a long-distance move.

The following week, in a bit of preacher's bravado, I sent the sermon tape to *Leadership's* audio series, *Preaching Today*. One of *Preaching Today's* expert screeners duly evaluated my sermon, and because I worked as editor for *Leadership*, I got to see the comments. The sermon was good, the screener said, though not quite good enough to earn a slot on *Preaching Today*. The content generally got high marks. But the delivery, my sermonic report card went on to say, was a little flat.

Flat? I couldn't believe it. Later that week I popped the sermon tape into my car's tape player and gave it another listen. As I heard the sermon from this distance, surprisingly, I had to agree: It lacked sizzle. Even though I had felt the message so deeply, somehow my conviction and emotion did not come across with the intensity I wanted. I puzzled over that.

Why is it that sometimes we as preachers feel a message so deeply, yet our listeners don't feel that? Why is something that's so intensely meaningful to us not always communicated in a way that grips the congregation as intensely?

WHY INTENSITY DOESN'T TRANSFER

At least four factors keep a preacher's passion from moving the congregation.

The Personality Factor

When I listen to sermons by many of the best-known preachers in this country, I am gripped and moved. Part of the power comes from the insight, the skill with which these ministers communicate God's truth. But part of the reason their sermons are so effective is because these preachers are so intense. Their energy draws me in.

In my work with *Leadership*, as I've interacted with some of these gifted communicators, I've discovered something surprising: They are just as intense out of the pulpit. Even talking to them one-on-one, they leave you a little breathless and feeling you must act now. The bottom line: These are high-energy people. Their intensity for the gospel message comes through, in part, simply by virtue of their God-given personalities.

I'm a quieter sort. I can't expect my personal demeanor to adequately communicate how deeply I believe God's Word, how much I love Jesus Christ, how critical it is that people obey him. I must learn and use the time-tested means of communicating to a group so they feel the same conviction, emotion, and energy I feel inside.

The Time Factor

By the time I step into the pulpit, I have studied for this message all week. I meditated on the text. I read commentaries. I prayed about the message. I gave this sermon from eight to twenty hours of my best thought, prayer, and energy.

But the people listening to me are hearing the sermon cold. What's become so meaningful to me has had no time to sink in to them. I can't expect the truths that have gripped me during hours of study to automatically grip a congregation—unless I practice the skills I will describe below.

The Position Factor

The way a preacher experiences a message and the way a listener experiences that exact same message are poles apart. For example, when I pause while speaking, it seems as if I'm pausing forever. But when I play back the tape, what seemed like a ten-second pause actually lasted only two or three seconds. In the same

way, what seems like a big and important point to me may not come across as big or important to my listeners.

Why? I'm standing in front of dozens or hundreds of people, which makes the speaking moment intense for me; adrenaline races through my system, heightening my emotion, energy, and memory. Sorry to say, my listeners do not find simply listening to a sermon an adrenaline rush. Sunday morning is probably not the emotional peak of their week, and they have dragged in tired from yard work the day before and movies the night before. They aren't bringing intense focus and emotion on their own, so they need me to communicate in a way that conveys intensity.

The Distance Factor

A sermon is like a stone dropped in a pond—the ripples flow outward from where the stone hit the water, getting weaker as they go. A preacher's facial expression of intense emotion looks powerful up close but like a blurry squiggle to the guy sitting in the last row (and the woman who closed her eyes for a second didn't even see it). The arm motion that seemed like a major sweep to you looked like a small finger wave to the people farthest from you.

QUESTIONS OF CONVICTION

To help compensate for these four factors, I've developed some questions I ask about my preaching to ensure my conviction communicates forcefully. I ask these questions as I look over my manuscript.

The Boldness Factor

Am I keeping the bold statements bold? Few elements in a sermon pack as much punch as a simple declarative statement or command. But read through a few recent sermons and you may find precious few of them. Why?

Educated people—and ministers are some of the most highly educated people in the world—are taught throughout college and graduate school to qualify their statements. For example, if you write in a seminary term paper that "In his Ninety-Five Theses, Luther attacked indulgences with ferocity," the professor will circle the statement in red and write in the margin, "But at this early stage of his theological development, Luther attacked only the abuse of indulgences, not the very idea of them—see Thesis 73." After you get two or three such comments, you start to shy from making bold declarations, because you don't want to be looked down upon as making sweeping statements or oversimplifications. You want to show that you have done your homework and understand the nuances and subtleties.

It's easy to take this ingrained academic practice into the pulpit. Instead of boldly saying, "If you have two coats, you should give away one" (Luke 3:11), we manage, "This text cautions us from excessive indulgence. It's important to realize, though, that this doesn't mean we have to quit enjoying life, or that we must all become monks in the desert." The nuances of the second statement might seem necessary, but they can also snuff the fire of John the Baptist's words.

Every nuance and qualifier, though it may add technical accuracy, also blunts the force of the statement we're trying to make. Even if we believe something intensely, we can drain the energy out of our statement so that the congregation doesn't sense that. It's good to be accurate, to use nuance, to balance. But we must never let those good practices dull the sharp edge of the Bible's two-edged sword.

I've decided that if simple boldness turns off some of the more educated people, so be it. Martin Luther once said, "When I preach, I regard neither doctors nor magistrates, of whom I have above forty in my congregation; I have all my eyes on the servant maids and on the children. And if the learned men are not well pleased with what they hear, well, the door is open."

If a desire to be technically careful can sometimes lower our intensity, so can our God-given love for people. We feel awkward saying "God hates divorce" (cf. Mal. 2:16) because we look out and see someone in the third pew who just went through a rough divorce after years of unfair treatment from her husband. Or we back off the simple phrase "Do not store up for yourselves treasures on earth" (Matt. 6:19) because we don't want to unnecessarily put off a member who is a certified financial planner and spends his days helping people do just that. We must show compassion, but we lower our intensity and effectiveness as preachers if we allow oversensitivity to keep us from making bold statements.

The Volume and Emotion Factor

Am I varying my volume and emotion enough? Not doing this is one of the main reasons, I concluded, that my sermon on David and Jonathan felt flat. When I was explaining background information about the text, I spoke in a moderate volume and even emotional tone. But when I got to the poignant core of the text, when David bows on the ground before Jonathan and rises to hug him, weeping—I still spoke in the same moderate volume and even emotional tone.

One reason African-American preaching hits home is it draws on the full range of human volume, from whisper to shout, and the full range of human emotion, from rage to joy. One of the most powerful sermons I've ever heard is the now-famous message "When Was God at His Best?" by E. V. Hill. In typical African-American style, Hill begins the sermon speaking slowly, in a deep, quiet voice—almost with an emotional neutrality and distance. Through the sermon, as he examines different possible moments when God was at his best—when he created the world, when he created human beings, when he led the children of Israel out of Egypt, and so on—Hill gradually builds with intensity. By the end of the sermon, when Hill reveals the moment when God was truly at his best—"when God saved a sinner like me"—Hill tells his own story of conversion joyfully and at the top of his voice, with a shout.

I ask myself, "What is the most important section of this sermon? What is the peak moment?" Then I try to make sure my greatest intensity is communicated at that spot.

The Expansion Factor

Am I making my motions expansive? Have you ever noticed what you do when you're talking to someone and you want to say something that's critically important or highly sensitive? I find myself moving my head a little lower and closer to the other person, lowering my voice, and pulling my hands in to the center of my body. Even my neck and upper back hunch over slightly, because I want to get close and personal to communicate this news. All this is natural and perfectly appropriate when we're talking intensely one-on-one.

It's easy, though, to use instinctively the same body language when we're talking intensely to 175 people. And when we pull in our hands and lean our head a little lower, we can end up looking smaller and cramped, at just the moment

our bodies should be communicating, "This is big news! Listen to this!"

Haddon Robinson, author of *Biblical Preaching*, wisely counsels preachers to make sure their motions are natural. But within your natural range of motions, try to open up. When you want to communicate the wideness of God's mercy, stretch your arms to full length. When you want to communicate the poignant moment when Jesus cried, "*Eloi, Eloi, lama sabachthani,*" tilt your head back and look far up into the blackened sky.

The Speed Factor

Am I speaking fast enough? It's true that speaking slowly can be a powerful tool for emphasis. It's also true that a sermon works best when there's variety: fast, slow, and medium tempos. But as a general rule, I can increase the intensity of my communication if I turn up the default setting on my metronome. The increase in speed should not be a great deal, nor should it be beyond what feels comfortable. But a quicker tempo conveys energy, excitement, and thus, importance. It can be one more way to make sure that the intensity you feel comes through to your congregation.

The Life Factor

Finally, and most importantly, I ask this question: *Am I trying to live what I'm about to say?* The most powerful intensifier of our communication is not our content and it's not our delivery. It's our life.

If we have visited people in the hospital, then when we preach about showing compassion, our statements will hit the mark. If we have weathered faithfully a tragedy—a car accident, the death of a child—then whatever we say thereafter about trusting God during suffering will go straight to the heart of our listeners.

I suppose that since Roe v. Wade in 1973, hundreds of thousands of sermons have been preached against abortion in this country. Some have described the gruesome physical process of late-term abortions, which one would think would easily make them the most intense sermons preached on the topic. But I think the most intense sermon ever leveled against abortion was a plain-spoken, halting message delivered by a shriveled, elderly, Albanian woman who spoke at the National Prayer Breakfast in 1994. Her sentences were painfully simple: "Please don't kill the child. I love the child. Give me the child." Her words hit with the intensity of a laser because her name was Mother Teresa.

Chapter 169

NO NOTES, LOTS OF NOTES, BRIEF NOTES
The pros and cons of extemporaneous and manuscript delivery

Jeffrey Arthurs

The Montagues vs. the Capulets; the Hatfields vs. the McCoys; the House of Lancaster vs. the House of York. Clan spats are not limited to literature, folk lore, or history. Homiletics has its own spat: preaching with a manuscript vs. preaching extempore. Each side has its champions, and each holds its turf with fervor.

This article tries to bring some balance to the spat by adopting Fred Craddock's stance:

> Every method pays a price for its advantages. Those who prefer the freedom and relationships available to the preacher without notes will not usually rate as high on careful phrasing and wealth of content. Those who prefer the tightly woven fabric of a manuscript must . . . accept the fact that a manuscript is less personal and its use is less evocative of intense listener engagement. (185, p. 216)

This article describes the pros and cons of each method as well as some pointers for each. Before looking at the three methods—no notes, lots of notes, and brief notes—three clarifications are needed.

Clarification 1: No one recommends that we preach *entirely* without notes. Even the no-notes clan allows us to bring statistics and quotations into the pulpit. If nothing else, we will have our Bibles with us, which we may have marked for preaching.

Clarification 2: This article does not deal with two methods of delivery often discussed in public speaking texts (memorized and impromptu), since neither should be the pastor's staple method. Memorizing takes too much work for too little return. As John Stott says, "The labour of [memorizing] is enormous, the risk of forgetting our lines considerable, and the necessary mental energy so great that the preacher has to concentrate on the memorized script instead of on his message and the congregation" (1982, p. 256). Stewardship tells us to use our time elsewhere.

Impromptu messages are occasionally necessary in the ministry of the Word to answer questions and speak during crises, but this method is not well suited to a regular teaching ministry. An IV is necessary during triage, but it shouldn't replace a balanced diet.

Clarification 3: The term *extemporaneous* is sometimes used interchangeably with *impromptu,* but in this article I am following the majority of homileticians who define it as a method of speaking that uses careful preparation but which chooses much of the language at the moment of delivery (e.g., Jay Adams, 1975, p. 113).

No Notes

Why Use This Method?

(1) Jesus and all biblical preachers seem to have used it. While this fact may be more descriptive than prescriptive, it is still a fact worth considering. We should develop our theology of preaching from the affirmations *and* examples in the Bible.

Not until the Reformation did a considerable number of preachers bring a manuscript to the pulpit. This occurred in part because the values of typography influenced oral communication in the post-Gutenberg world. Sermons became closely reasoned, complex, and permanent works of art, but today we are post-post-Gutenberg. Some scholars call our day *secondary orality.* We no longer communicate with the bookish style of the sixteenth and seventeenth centuries. In secondary orality, public speakers don't sound like essays. They sound like conversation.

(2) It appeals to the audience. With few exceptions, listeners prefer sermons that are direct, conversational, and possess an air of spontaneity. They don't like to be read to. Watch the popular lecturers on public TV on subjects like success and spirituality, and you will never see one read to the audience. To be sure, the talks are well planned and rehearsed, but the speakers use no visible notes. In the post-post-Gutenberg world, audiences have been socialized to expect extemporaneous speaking so that even when speeches are delivered from manuscript, such as the evening news or the State of the Union Address, communicators use teleprompters to appear extemporaneous.

(3) It enhances communication and persuasion. Part of the power of no-notes stems from eye contact. Humans send and decode scores of messages with the eyes. Babies instinctively look in the eyes to discern relationship and intentions. Animals do too. Poets consistently describe the power of the eyes with statements like "Drink to me only with thine eyes, and I will pledge with mine" (Ben Jonson), and he "holds him with his glittering eye" (Samuel Coleridge). Consider the sobering statement in Luke 22:61 when Peter betrayed Jesus: "The Lord turned and looked straight at Peter. Then Peter remembered … went outside and wept bitterly."

Preaching demands eye contact, and the method that best lends itself to eye contact is to use no notes.

> Preaching, after all, is conversational in character. … Those listeners, if you truly look at them, will affect you. Their attention will quicken your concentration. Their apparent agreement will kindle your conviction. Their seeming bafflement will slow you down and may cause you to speak in a more reflective and less assertive tone. … You cannot look at your listeners and "read" their responses to you, to what you are saying, and how you are saying it, without in some way being moved. (Charles Bartow, 1980, 99–100)

While it is possible to use effective eye contact when using lots of notes, it is difficult. Few preachers read well, a point I will emphasize below.

Besides unleashing the communicate power of eye contact, no notes also lends itself to oral style in language and syntax, and people in secondary orality have higher comprehension when hearing messages in oral style than written style (Adams, 1975, p. 113). While it is possible for lots-of-notes preachers to write in an oral style, few do so (see below).

(4) It inspires careful preparation. Preaching without notes demands ruthless simplicity of organization. Idea *must* flow into idea, or else you won't be able to remember what comes next. As seasoned preachers know, developing simple (not simplistic) messages is more demanding than developing rambling collections-of-thoughts-that-include-the-kitchen-sink. Illustrations that marginally illustrate, analogies that don't quite fit, and micro rabbit trails that are interesting but ancillary are taboo when preaching without notes.

The result of this ruthless simplicity is more powerful preaching. In fact, I believe this is the primary benefit of no notes. When the preacher thinks himself or herself clear, the hearers get the benefit.

(5) It enhances freedom. No notes gives freedom to add or subtract ideas at the moment of utterance. Which of us has not been promised thirty minutes to speak but then ended up with twenty-two after the other portions of the service went long? Furthermore, no notes gives freedom to move away from the pulpit, giving physical as well as psychological freedom.

This issue of freedom is crucial to lively, impassioned preaching. Jay Adams uses the term *jelling* to describe it:

The jelling factor is the culmination of careful preparation and long thought prior to the delivery of the sermon. During the full concentration due to the tension of the preaching experience, at the moment of delivery certain ideas jell. Jelling gives a spontaneity and sparkle to speaking that the calm composition of a full manuscripts done solely in the study is unable to bring. (1975, p. 114)

Why Avoid This Method?

(1) You might forget! As we all know, that's a bad feeling! Worse yet, your deletions may hinder the clarity and impact of the message. Advocates of no notes tend to minimize this fact, but facts are stubborn things. Those who preach without notes, even when long experienced, *will* forget some things. Of course, the no-notes clan is quick to tell us that it rarely matters, and they are right. Usually you are the only one who knows when you leave out a point, but you may leave out a *crucial* point, or your forgetfulness may lead to fumbling and mumbling.

(2) It leads to glib or imprecise speech. Once again, this pitfall is not certain, but it is more likely than when we preach *with* notes. We revert to clichés when scrambling for phrases, and clichés rarely find their mark in the human heart.

How to Use This Method

Koller (1962, pp. 85–97) suggests a three-stage process for preparing to preach without notes.

(1) Saturation. This takes about 50 percent of your total prep time. The key is to study well, and think and pray yourself deep into the text. As Haddon Robinson says, we must "think ourselves clear." Similarly, Cicero stated, "No man can be eloquent on a subject he does not understand" (in Koller, p. 85). When you do good exegesis and have prayed over your sermon, you will be surprised at how deeply

you have internalized the message. You're halfway to the goal of preaching with no notes!

(2) Organization. This takes about 40 percent of your prep time. The key is to organize your sermon so simply and naturally that the flow is easy to remember. The better the outline, the less likelihood of its being needed in the pulpit. This stage takes 40 percent of your time because it is hard to be simple! Commenting on this issue of organization, Lloyd-Jones said:

> The preparation of sermons involves sweat and labour. It can be extremely difficult at times to get all this matter that you have found in the Scriptures into this particular form. It is like a ... blacksmith making shoes for a horse; you have to keep on putting the material into the fire and on to the anvil and hit it again and again with the hammer. Each time it is a bit better, but not quite right; so you put it back again and again until you are satisfied with it, or can do no better. (1972, p. 80)

A friend recently told me he is getting ready to preach from Revelation with this flow of thought: (1) God wins. (2) Satan loses. (3) It isn't even close. (4) It is permanent. I was able to remember that flow of thought from a single email, and I'm not even the one preaching the sermon!

Here are some natural patterns of thinking that make simple patterns of sermon forms:

- Chronology (such as past–present–future).
- Space (such as inner–outer).
- Cause–effect (such as symptoms–disease).
- Problem–solution (such as disease–cure).
- Antithesis (such as not this–but this).

To help you remember your main points, use an illustration with each one. Also consider using literal images such as objects and slides. These will remain in listeners' minds after the sermon, and they will remain in your mind before it.

One of the easiest ways to preach without notes is by doing narrative sermons. With their causal flow of events as well as their psychological flow of mounting tension, stories are easy to remember. Alan H. Monroe's "Motivated Sequence" and Eugene L. Lowry's "Homiletical Plot" provide narrative shape even to didactic sermons.

Memorization. This takes about 10 percent of your prep time. The key is to practice out loud without notes and see where you draw a blank, then go back and fix those places in your mind.

If you've never tried not using notes, why not give it a whirl? Put an outline in the back of your Bible as a security net, but I suspect you won't need it. You may be surprised at how easy this method can be, and you may be surprised at how it improves your impact.

LOTS OF NOTES

By "lots of notes" I mean preaching from a manuscript or a very detailed outline. Preachers such as Jonathan Edwards, John Henry Jowett, and Richard Baxter used this method with great effect.

Why Use This Method?

(1) It creates security. What a wonderful feeling to walk into the pulpit knowing exactly what you will say! What a wonderful feeling to know within a minute or two how long your sermon will run!

(2) It yields precise wording. This is the reason cited most often by the lots-of-notes clan, and it is a powerful argument. Some preaching occasions, such as enforcing an instance of church discipline, demand such careful language that the use of a manuscript is not only permissible but advisable. Just as the President of the

United States would not dare to make a policy statement without a manuscript lest his spontaneous comments later bite him, just so should preachers sometimes prepare precise statements for the church. Even the no-notes clan affirms the importance of exact wording in portions of the sermon such as the introduction. Presumably, this clan recommends memorizing (or nearly memorizing) the introduction.

The desire for exact wording takes various forms. The person with a gift of language takes joy in the right word in the right place; the meticulous person is compelled to include everything from the sermon plan in the sermon utterance; and the conscientious person doesn't want to cheat the listeners. These motives are understandable and praiseworthy.

(3) It gives you a permanent record. The labor of preparation is captured on paper and is available for future revision and preaching. Of course, some members of the no-notes clan recommend writing a manuscript as part of your preparation, so these folks also have a permanent record, at least a permanent record of what they *planned* to say.

Why Avoid This Method?

(1) Most readers cannot read with skill. The fact is (and remember that facts are stubborn things) most people sound as if they are reading when they read, and reading is not conversing. One of the signs of reading is a steady pace. The pace usually is not too fast or too slow, but it is too steady. Listen to people conversing and you will hear the rate of their speech in constant flux as their voices reflect heart and mind. But when we read, our rate become as steady as a metronome, communicating each word as our eyes scan lines of print. As word follows word with the regularity of a train's clickity-clack, listeners drift. They cannot pick out which ideas

are central and which are subordinate, so they fade. Charles Finney said that "any monotonous sound, great or small, if continued, disposes people to sleep" (in Duduit, ed., 1992, p. 413).

While mono-pace can be overcome with practice, the fact still stands that most readers do not read well. Furthermore, we are often unaware of how our voices influence reception of the message. Since the message is clear to us, we assume it is clear to others. But it isn't.

(2) Eye contact is difficult or impossible. Another instance of poor reading relates to lack of eye contact. In Switzerland in 1667, the problem of eye contact was considered so grave that church authorities instituted the "Bern Preacher Act," which stipulated that ministers must preach extemporaneously: "They must not read [sermons] in front of the congregation from notes on paper, which is a mockery to have to watch and which takes away all fruit and grace from the preacher in the eyes of the listeners" (in McDill, 1999, p. 137).

Like the problem of mono-pace, this problem can be overcome, but most manuscript preachers do not overcome it because we do not perceive ourselves as the congregation perceives us. Wayne McDill tells of a man who asked a preaching professor to evaluate his sermon. When they later discussed the sermon, the professor asked the preacher how many times he thought he had looked at his notes during the sermon. The preacher guessed maybe twenty to twenty-five times. He was shocked to learn that the professor had counted 161 times (1999, p. 142).

(3) Most writers write in a written style. Of course they do! How else would you write? In an *oral* style. We need to transcribe spoken language, but this is difficult to do. Alistair Cooke, patriarch of radio broadcasting, learned this early in his career:

During the end of the war, the BBC in New York invited various famous exiles, Frenchmen mostly, to come and talk to the underground in France; famous, famous, great literary men. And I had the privilege of sitting in the control room, and I thought that I will learn about broadcasting from listening to these men. . . . What I learned is that they were dreadful broadcasters. They wrote essays, or lectures, or sermons and they read them aloud. And I suddenly realized there was a new profession ahead. Which is writing for talking. Putting it on the page in the syntactical break-up and normal confusion that is normal talk. ("Letter from America," Nov. 19, 1998)

As with the other problems, the problem of written style is not endemic to manuscript preaching. It is just pandemic. I give suggestions below on how to write in an oral style.

(4) Reading a sermon is a barrier to rapport. I can hear the lots-of-notes clan objecting, "Not in *my* church; my people know me, love me, and know that I love them." You may be right. Your church may have unusual taste, but most people in most churches desire the preacher to converse, not read. We live in secondary orality. The norms of typography are fading.

(5) It limits comprehension and retention in the audience. Koller cites a study where psychologists measured retention when material was read and when it was expressed by direct address: 49 percent versus 67 percent (1962, p. 39). I suspect that the readers read normally (i.e., poorly), but the lots-of-notes clan still must wrestle with this fact.

(6) It hinders adaptation, spontaneity, and interaction. "Paper is a very poor conductor of electricity" (McDill, 1999, p. 145).

In summary, I'm afraid that the cons outweigh the pros. The skills below can help mitigate the weaknesses, but I cannot recommend that you use lots of notes as your normal mode of delivery.

How to Use This Method

(1) Write in an oral style. Your writing will seem redundant and choppy, but that is how we talk. On the page your sermon will seem wordy. Furthermore, remember that your voice—*how* you say something—carries much of the meaning. When C. S. Lewis first published his "Broadcast Talks," he simply transcribed the talks, using italics for words he stressed with his voice. Afterwards, he felt this was a mistake, "an undesirable hybrid between the art of speaking and the art of writing," so he revised the broadcasts into written style for the book *Mere Christianity*. He felt that "a 'talk' on the radio should . . . be as like real talk as possible, and should not sound like an essay being read aloud" (preface to *Mere Christianity*).

To write in an oral style, listen to yourself as you write your manuscript. For advanced preachers this listening can take place in the mind, but most preachers should speak aloud as they write. Here are some marks of orality:

- Less formal than written; uses colloquialisms, contractions, sentence fragments, and greater percentage of short sentences
- Assumes face-to-face encounter; uses first and second person, and dialogue/response
- Designed for listening, not reading; uses much repetition and restatement (see Sunukjian's article "Skills of Oral Clarity" in part 5 of this volume) and paralanguage (sounds, not words, that communicate, such as "hmmm" and "shhhh")

(2) Prepare the manuscript for easy reading. Use different fonts, colors, and spacing to help your eyes focus quickly and your voice emphasize meaningfully. Develop your own set of marks such as the use of brackets for illustrations and red asterisks for applications. Number your pages. Type the notes so that you don't

have to turn the page in the middle of a sentence.

(3) Practice! Work on rate and eye contact. "You must look at people! The eyes can spit fire, pour out compassion, and preach Christ in you. When you deny people your eyes, you really deny them yourself. No one ever talks to them without looking at them—unless to insult them." (Chapell, 1994, p. 319).

BRIEF NOTES

By "brief notes" I mean very limited, skeletal notes.

Why Use This Method?

The majority of preachers use this method, and for good reason. It is the best of both worlds, combining the strengths of no-notes and lots-of-notes and minimizing their weaknesses. This method enables you to remember your points; it lends itself to oral style, yet can employ occasional lines of exact wording; prompts spontaneity and "jelling"; and so forth. To be sure, any method can be used poorly (you could be glued to your half-page outline!), but in this article I have tried not to caricature the methods.

Why Avoid This Method?

I can't think of any reasons, especially if you write out a manuscript as part of your preparation or save your extensive exegetical notes.

How to Use This Method

Put the notes on a single page that fits in your Bible. You won't even need a pulpit, if one is unavailable or you choose not to stand behind one. Use a Post-It note, a 4 x 6 card, a half sheet of paper, or one $8^{1}/_{2}$ x 11, but no more than this. That is all you will need. Some preachers simply mark their Bibles. Also consider using Power Point slides or placing notes in the bulletin. These will keep you on track.

Develop your own system of marks. Make the notes easy to read with the same tools as I suggested above under Lots of Notes. I have heard that Billy Sunday used to write his notes in bold letters almost an inch high. Thinking that Billy might have had poor eyesight, someone asked his wife, "Ma" Sunday, why the letters were so big. She replied, "Well, Billy didn't pass by the pulpit very often, and he had to catch his next point when he had the chance."

No notes, lots of notes, or brief notes—the choice is yours. The Bible does not stipulate one method. Make the choice wisely according to your own gifts and the needs of the occasion.

BIBLIOGRAPHY

Bibliography

Adams, Jay. 1975. *Pulpit Speech*. Phillipsburg, N.J.: Presbyterian & Reformed.

Bartow, Charles. 1980. *The Preaching Moment*. Nashville: Abingdon, pp. 99–100.

Chapell, Bryan. 1984. *Christ-Centered Preaching*. Grand Rapids: Baker, p. 319.

Craddock, Fred. 1985. *Preaching*. Nashville: Abingdom., p. 216.

Duduit, Michael. 1992. *Handbook of Contemporary Preaching*. Nashville: Broadman, p. 413.

Koller, Charles. 1962. *Expository Preaching without Notes*. Grand Rapids: Baker.

Lewis, C. S. 1952. *Mere Christianity*. New York: Macmillan, Preface.

Lloyd-Jones, Martyn. 1972. *Preaching and Preachers*. Grand Rapids: Zondervan, p. 80.

McDill, Wayne. 1999. *The Moment of Truth*. Nashville: Broadman & Holman.

Stott, John R. W. 1982. *Between Two Worlds*. Grand Rapids: Eerdmans, p. 256.

Chapter 170

IN THE EYE OF THE HEARER

Visuals that support rather than distract from the Word

Kenton C. Anderson

The primary tool of preachers is their voices. Nevertheless, effective preachers have always understood the added power of a well-chosen visual aid. Jeremiah once hid a linen belt under a rock to help his audience visualize the spiritual decay of Jerusalem (Jer. 13). Today's visual methods are more technologically advanced, yet they serve much the same purpose.

POWERPOINT

How it can help. Projecting still images helps the preacher to focus the attention of listeners on key ideas. It can assist us in sharpening focus, deepening impact, and enhancing listener retention.

How it can hinder. Building an effective PowerPoint presentation takes a lot of time. For many, the time and energy taken to develop these presentations comes at the expense of sermon study. In the end, we might have a pretty presentation without much worth presenting.

In addition, people are accustomed to viewing professional quality presentations on their televisions and in their workplaces. Few churches can come close to matching people's visual expectations without investing huge amounts of time.

The answer might be to delegate the task, but this is not as easy as it sounds. Effective presentations require the integration of technical, graphic, and theological acumen. A computer geek might not have a good eye for graphics. A graphic designer might not have the theological insight necessary to know how to enhance the sermon. In the end, preachers may decide it is easier to do it themselves at the expense of other aspects of sermon development.

How to use it well. Despite the challenges, still image projection is likely to grow in use. Preachers can make it work for them if they pay attention to a few basics.

(1) Start with the sermon. The best way to build a great PowerPoint presentation is to have great material. Garbage on the page will be garbage on the screen. A good presentation starts with a good sermon, clearly conceived and carefully constructed. Be sure you have a clear grasp of the *big idea* of the sermon. PowerPoint will expose any fuzziness in sermon design, so the words have to be sharp. Theme statements ought to be short (twelve words or less), simple (no conjunctions), declarative statements (not phrases) that can be spoken by the preacher. The heading for this paragraph, "Start with the sermon," is an example of the kind of focused wording that will communicate on screen.

(2) Create visual metaphors. Preachers need to use fewer words and more visual metaphors in their PowerPoint presentations. Images come from a variety of sources. Some images can be found online for free. Other fee-for-service websites like *photos.com* or *worshipphotos.com* can be helpful.

Some preachers will take their own digital photos in order to get just the right image. PowerPoint is the software that allows you to present that image. The best slides are often created using Adobe Photo Elements (the cheaper version of Photoshop) or some other image production software that allows the designer to creatively merge words with images in ways that communicate an overall concept. The completed image can then be imported into PowerPoint.

(3) Less is more. Like a child with a new toy, preachers initially want to make use of all the bells, beeps, and transitions the technology offers. But more is not necessarily better. Simple images and constructions are almost always stronger. As a general rule, twenty-five words on a single slide should be a maximum, and twelve to fifteen slides in a presentation should be a ceiling. For further hints on slide construction, see *powerpointers.com.*

(4) Aim to be seen. All our efforts will not be worth much if the slides cannot be seen. Try sitting in the back row with normal Sunday morning lighting and see how easily you can read the screen. Font sizes of less than 28 points might be difficult for some to read. Generally, white fonts against dark backgrounds read well. Colors ought to contrast without clashing. Sometimes the technology itself causes a problem. A weak projector that offers images too dull to be seen from the back row will frustrate more than it will help. If you're going to spend the money, spend enough money. An 1800 lumen projector is a minimum standard for a small church building.

(5) Team up. Few preachers bring expertise in homiletics, theology, computer technology, and graphic design. A team approach, however, could bring all of these together. Rather than seeing this as a burden, we can view this as an opportunity for collaborating on sermon development. The design team could serve as a sermon consulting group, giving us helpful feedback on the sermon while the cement is still wet.

(6) Keep the visuals secondary. Throughout the sermon, the preacher needs to retain the focus of the listener. The technology must always be in the service of the human event, that is, the sermon. For instance, we shouldn't ignore the screen. Referring to the image, pointing at the screen, and reading from the screen can help to keep the listener focused on the human preacher while still making use of the projected image. In addition, the screen does not always have to be illuminated. It may, in fact, enhance the dramatic flow of the presentation to have the screen darken at strategic moments, such as when we call for response.

VIDEOS

Computer projection units also offer the preacher opportunity to show motion picture clips, either those prepared in-house or taken from popular movies and other public sources.

How it can help. The use of video allows us to connect with listeners on their terms. Video is the language of contemporary culture in just about any part of the world. Not only does it add variety, color, and motion to the preaching experience, it shows that the preacher is relevant and in-touch with the culture.

Inexpensive access to digital video cameras and editing software allows churches to customize sermons with locally produced "on the street" interviews, dramatizations, and music-video style enhancements. Such approaches allow the preacher to involve people in the process of putting truth into the context of life. Digital video cameras can now be found for less than $400. Simple video editing packages start at less than $100. Apple Computers bundle *iMovie*, a simple, intuitive, editing package, with their computers for free.

How it can hinder. A video clip is a supercharged sermon illustration, subject to all the strengths and weaknesses of such illustrations and then some. Video can eat precious time and interrupt carefully designed sermon flow. Further, a video clip creates a world for the listener to inhabit. Many times that world is more compelling than the world of the sermon itself. Listeners can get lost there, losing touch with the intent of the sermon itself. Preachers need to be particularly careful with clips taken from movies that can be seen to give license to listeners to view things that might be substantially less than the pure and lovely things of good report that Paul describes in Philippians 4:8.

How to use it well. Preachers who want to make good use of video should keep a few simple principles in mind.

(1) Keep it legal. We must respect copyrights. Using clips taken from copyrighted motion pictures without consent of the rights holder is theft. Gaining consent usually requires paying a fee. Blanket licenses can be easily and inexpensively obtained from the Motion Picture Licensing Corporation. Whatever the fee, it will not equal the cost of losing integrity.

(2) Keep it short. Using a movie clip often requires contextual set-up for the scene, how it fits into the overall plot. If the clip requires too much explanation, it probably isn't worth using. A clip of more than two or three minutes (10 percent of the sermon duration) will probably damage the sermon itself. Shorter is always better.

(3) Keep it flowing. Smooth transitions in and out of the video are critical. In most cases it is best to use the video clip as a lead-in to the sermon or as a post-sermon piece. Either way, videos need to fit the flow of the overall worship experience, or they could be more trouble than they are worth.

(4) Keep it clean. Remember that showing a movie clip in church is equivalent to offering a blanket recommendation for the whole movie. The clip we show might be clean, but what about that graphic sex scene forty-five minutes later in the movie? If we can't recommend the whole movie, then we should not use it at all.

OTHER MEANS

Still and video projection are only two of the more contemporary uses of visual enhancement in preaching. While perhaps not as trendy, a good old-fashioned object lesson still has power. Using real human beings in the sermon is another low-tech way of enhancing the sermon experience. Through brief dramatic sketches, personal testimony, or interview, the preacher can use the experience of real people to humanize, contextualize, deepen, and accredit the ideas the sermon presents.

Visuals are valuable, but they should be used with the confidence that the greatest visual effect inherent to preaching is the image of the preacher standing and delivering. Preachers are going to have difficulty competing with Hollywood, but no one excels the preacher in standing up and speaking the truth of the gospel. The strength of preaching is that a human being, having heard from God, helps others hear the same. The energy and passion of such a preacher can be visual stimulation enough.

Chapter 171

NO VOICE, NO PREACH
Safeguarding and improving your voice

Emily Shive

Many ministers fill their weeks with sermons, committee meetings, and countless conversations. Unintentionally, they abuse their voices. Voice fatigue sets in. Even if they don't develop chronic hoarseness, weakness, or vocal nodes, their effectiveness as speakers may be diminished by weakened or forced voices.

Not everyone has "golden pipes," but everyone can improve the sound of his or her voice. The point is not to develop a "stained-glass voice" but to strengthen the natural voice we've been given. Here are some things to improve the voice.

GOOD POSTURE

Since our bodies house our voices, good posture becomes an important prerequisite for the best use of our vocal instruments. Proper *external* posture means your head lines up with your back, causing your rib cage (not your shoulders) to lift. Your feet will be flat on the floor with the weight evenly distributed, your knees unlocked. Poor posture crowds the breathing process. After adopting good posture, one speaker's voice stayed strong to the end of his sermon for the first time.

The *internal* posture maintains a space inside your mouth for a perpetual "Ahh." This helps relax your jaw and tongue and opens your throat. The volume of speech determines the size of the "Ahh"—the softer your voice, the smaller the "Ahh."

REDUCED MUSCLE TENSION

Tension is an enemy of good performance, whether we're speaking, singing, or trying to sink a putt. Reduced tension means we'll be free of tightness in our bodies generally, tightness in our shoulders, jaws, and tongues specifically. If the muscles above and below the vocal cords relax, then the breath can freely vibrate the vocal cords in the larynx or voice box.

Incidentally, a mirror works well as an effective, but inexpensive, teacher. Speakers can use a mirror daily as they practice monitoring posture and watching for signs of tense muscles.

PROPER BREATHING

The vocal process that produces sound can be divided into three basic areas: (1) the breathing technique—the activator of the sound; (2) the vocal cords—the source of the sound; (3) the resonators—the reinforcers of the sound, adding quality, volume, and control.

Breathing should be free and silent with no obstruction in the way. Any tightening of the muscles above or below the larynx can inhibit the breath and keep it from carrying the sound into the resonators. Here are some steps that can help ensure effective use of the breath:

- Open your throat as if to begin a yawn ("Ahh").
- Relax, then open your jaw, inhaling through both your nose and mouth.
- Think of aiming the moving air about three feet in front of you. This helps keep the sound from hanging in the back of your mouth, projecting it out instead.
- It also helps to imagine your lips not touching your teeth. This keeps the muscles around your mouth from tightening and allows enough room for consonants to flow over your tongue and for vowels to resonate in the chambers.

GOOD VOCAL HEALTH

Friedrich S. Brodnitz, M.D., says, "To no group should the preservation of physical health be more important than to men and women who make professional use of their speaking and singing voices." Here are some things to do to keep your body and voice in good condition:

- Get enough rest to restore body energy.
- Never yell or force your voice.
- Drink lots of liquids, preferably not too hot or too cold. Many speakers request ice water, but tepid water would be better. Cold contracts muscles—and vocal cords are muscles. They will do better if kept warm and flexible.
- Avoid clearing your throat. Often this is simply a nervous habit, but it irritates your vocal cords.
- Avoid medicated lozenges, mint, or menthol. These dry the throat and tend to create more phlegm. Drink warm tea or water instead.
- Avoid extended time in a loud environment, such as basketball games. When I attend a Portland Trail Blazers basketball game, I wear ear plugs. This protects both my hearing and my voice. Ear plugs automatically cause me to cut down the volume of my voice. Because I hear it louder inside my head, I'm not so apt to push my voice to be heard above the noise.
- If there seems to be a chronic voice problem, consult a throat specialist.

EXERCISING YOUR VOICE

Vocal exercises will help develop your voice. They should be done consistently, even on days when you have no sermon to preach. Spend five to ten minutes doing the following exercises before speaking or singing:

- Loosen your jaw. Take your jaw between your thumb and index finger and shake it up and down rapidly without moving your head. Repeat, "Yah, yah, yah" vigorously. Move your jaw from side to side.
- Massage your face from the hinge of the jaw to the temples. Place a finger at the jaw hinge on each side, move your fingers in a circular motion from there, up to the side of the forehead.
- Move your head slowly to one side as far as possible and then back to the opposite side. Drop your head slowly back to the shoulders and then on to the chest. This isometric exercise should be done often. I do this in the car when I stop for red lights or at my desk.
- Maintaining good posture, inhale slowly. Then let out a slow, breathy sigh, starting in a high voice and going down, much like a descending fire siren.
- Do the same descending breath exercises as a short sentence: "How are you? I am fine." If you produce these sounds freely, you should have the sensation that your vocal cords are doing nothing at all. Your breath should move your voice, and the resonators should reinforce the sounds. Learn to trust these sensations. When you can visualize the correct technique, the sound will take care of itself.

- Practice humming a scale (from high to low) maintaining a relaxed jaw and tongue, keeping an "Ahh" space inside your mouth. Keep your lips together, but not tightly. If your breath freely moves your voice, your lips will vibrate noticeably. My husband, a preacher, always hums during a hymn before his sermon to make sure his lips tingle. This assures him he has the correct room for the breath to bring his voice forward in the mouth.
- Read aloud when practicing a sermon or speech. This helps make the procedures a natural part of your speaking process.

With daily practice on these techniques, your voice can be strengthened and revitalized. You might wish to evaluate your progress by recording your voice.

Rick, a pastoral student, listened carefully to his voice on tape. As a result, he gained new appreciation for the value of good vocal technique. His voice felt more relaxed the next time he preached, and his wife noticed a marked difference in its sound.

If possible, studying with a voice teacher can provide another set of ears to listen for things you cannot hear. Because the techniques for singing are so similar to those for speaking, singing instructors can often help speakers.

RECOMMENDED READING

Jerry Vines and Jim Shaddix, *Power in the Pulpit* (Chicago: Moody, 1999), pp. 263–90.

Chapter 172

ELIMINATING MY UM, UM, ANNOYING PULPIT MANNERISMS

I can't let personal quirks get in the way of the message

Kenneth Quick

As a bored lad in the pew, I remember counting the number of times the pastor pushed his glasses up his nose—one Sunday more than fifty, averaging one every thirty seconds. I also remember the young pastor who said "God" as though the word had three syllables, and the pastor who pronounced "worship" as "war-ship."

Like static on the telephone line, annoying pulpit mannerisms can make hearing the message difficult. I feel responsible to remove distractions that affect how people hear the

gospel, so I've taken pains to reduce mine as much as possible.

WRESTLING PERSONAL DEMONS

I've learned that I can't let my insecurities prevent me from facing embarrassing mannerisms. I struggled for years with a painful self-consciousness before I stood to speak. In college, I almost flunked a required speech class.

Something changed after I met Christ; I received the gift and call to communicate God's

Word. But it took years for me to become emotionally comfortable with my gift. Every time, I feared my sermon would turn out like my speeches in college. Beforehand, I regularly doubled over with excruciating cramps. At times, I almost fled the platform for the bathroom.

But the moment I stood to speak, the pain stopped. So I've had to work hard not to look self-conscious on the platform. My hard work, however, became the breeding ground for distracting, nervous mannerisms.

Who is this guy with the goofy grin? That's what one of my (soon-to-be) best friends thought when I candidated at my second church. I had sat on the platform with a grin plastered on my face. Only a passionate commitment to communicate the Word put me on the road to overcome my insecurities.

INVITING FEEDBACK

In preaching, we need people who love us enough to tell us the truth, even if it hurts. But loving people tend not to point out to their pastor his distracting mannerisms.

I once used an interactive style of teaching on Sunday evenings. While someone responded to questions, I would lean on the pulpit and rest my chin on my hand. I had the habit of laying my index finger on the bridge of my nose. (This was definitely better than in my nose, but not much.) One day I observed the chairman of our elders leading a study and doing the same thing—on purpose. Everyone laughed, for they knew whom he was imitating. I had to admit: It looked ridiculous!

It's difficult for someone to overcome fear and be honest with me. This should be easier with my wife, but it's not. Not long ago she asked, "Why do you always sit on the platform with your chin up in the air? You look like you are stuck up."

"Say what you mean, dear," I replied testily.

"For some reason," she explained, "whenever you sit on the platform, you elevate your chin. You don't do it when you speak, but you almost always do it beforehand."

I didn't have an inkling of this, but I began to catch myself with my chin lifted to jaunty heights. I have had to make an effort to keep it lower. It's distressing to think I may have been doing that for years. I encouraged my wife not to wait so long to say something the next time.

She immediately said I look better when my coat is unbuttoned.

TWO WAYS TO PAIN

Here are two sure-fire ways to identify annoying preaching mannerisms.

Tape yourself—either audio or video. While listening to a tape, I noticed that when I began a message, I would fill every pause with an "ah": "I was thinking the other day ... ah ... about the nature of the media's influence ... ah...." I felt the need to fill every empty space with sound, a common distracting mannerism.

Three or four sentences into the message, as soon as I got rolling, I would stop the "ahs." I wonder how many church youngsters have snickered to each other, "He 'ah-ed' fourteen times today! It's a record!"

Use anonymous questionnaires. A few will abuse this, using the opportunity to criticize, so anything too negative I dismiss out of hand. One way to limit the overly negative is by giving the questionnaire only to the church leaders as part of your yearly job evaluation.

In the questionnaire, I ask for an honest response about my length of messages, issues they'd like addressed in the future, and their favorite series I've done and why. Then I add: "Because I want to be the best communicator I can be in the Holy Spirit, are there any distracting mannerisms (jingling coins in my pocket, clearing my throat in the mike, etc.) that bother you? If you have trouble thinking of these, imagine someone parodying me: What mannerisms might they exaggerate? Thanks for helping me to be the best I can be for Christ."

TAKING PREACHING TO HEART

To eliminate a mannerism, I focus on one per month. Sometimes the solution is a simple mechanical change, like applying no-slip pads to my glasses. I work up a sweat just blinking. In the summer, even with my jacket off, I perspire profusely. That requires wiping my face regularly with a handkerchief—another distraction. I have threatened to preach in a sweat band. Then someone suggested an alternative—a small fan to circulate the air around me.

Voice changes are harder. I have always had a wide range of volume. My voice projects well when I'm speaking normally or loudly, but sometimes the bottom falls out; I get so soft that our sound man turns up the mike. Everyone leans forward to catch what I'm saying.

I have worked on my voice control for years with only moderate success, trying to become more conscious when the drops occur and strengthening my diaphragm. I'm learning I have limits to my God-given abilities, and only so much time; I refuse to hammer myself for not being able to communicate with the world-class preachers. Even so, I work hard to remove distracting mannerisms that prevent people from hearing the message.

Chapter 173

READING SCRIPTURE IN PUBLIC
How to present a good read of the Good Book

Jeffrey Arthurs

Devote yourself to the public reading of Scripture" (1 Tim. 4:13).

As a long-time church planter, Paul knew the essentials for the growth of the body, and he urged young Timothy to concentrate on those things. Public reading of Scripture is one of the essentials. In the first-century, public reading was indispensable to the Christian life because few people had Bibles. Texts were rare, so God's Word had to be transmitted orally. Today, of course, we have plenty of Bibles (I have seven in my office), but the command is still essential because most people do not read their Bibles. This includes believers.

Just as we preach and teach expositionally, so should we read expositionally. We should "lead out" the ideas and emotions God has put into the text. We do so by matching our nonverbal communication with the verbal message—the words of the text. The term *nonverbal* literally means "not dealing with words." How we say words (tone of voice, and so on) is a nonverbal matter. I divide nonverbal communication into two parts: what we look like and what we sound like when speaking words.

What Research Shows

What we look like and sound like influences how listeners react to the words. The power of nonverbal communication is well documented in communication scholarship. For example, in a 1968 article in *Psychology Today,* Albert Mehrabian argued that when the verbal and nonverbal channels seemed to contradict, listeners decided what the speaker meant by observing facial expression and listening to tone of voice. Listeners based only 7 percent of their interpretation on the words themselves. If we scowl through Psalm 23, sigh through 1 Thessalonians 4, or listlessly describe the escape from Egypt, we perform oral eisegesis. We add foreign elements to the text.

Nonverbal communication affects not only perception of the *content* of what is read but also the *context* of the reading. If the Scripture reading is done in a church service, listeners make judgments about the entire church based on what the reader looks and sounds like. Communication scholars estimate that 65 percent of all "social meaning" and 93 percent of all "emotional meaning" come through the nonverbal channel. People get impressions like "this is a friendly church," or "they value excellence," or "this is a solemn occasion" based on the nonverbal channel of the Scripture reading and other communications that take place.

Two Qualities of Effective Public Reading

Knowing the power of delivery and desiring to "devote ourselves to the reading," how should we read? Two qualities mark effective public reading.

Read conversationally. The old days of orating are gone. Large gestures, orotund voices, and exaggerated inflection were necessary in lecture halls, but they are out of place in a world dominated by the intimate media of television, movies, and radio. Audiences have been socialized to expect all public communication to sound like TV—conversational. Today's public communicators should adopt a style that is conversational and natural.

Read with conviction. While public reading should be conversational, it should not be casual chatter. One-way communication intended for a group demands more energy than chatting. Effective public delivery displays deep conviction. Readers should internalize the ideas and feelings of the text so that when they speak, they speak out of the fullness of their own hearts.

Silence, Phrasing, Eye Contact

The general principles of conversation and conviction can be exercised with three specific techniques: silence, phrasing, and eye contact.

Silence. Silence is a powerful but underused tool for reading expositionally. It gives listeners time to think, allows time for response, increases tension, and separates ideas. Readers tend to neglect silence because it makes them feel exposed, but readers need to get over this feeling. Audiences are comfortable with silence. It helps them process and imagine.

Silence, for example, can be used to lead out the ideas and moods of Genesis 22 (Abraham sacrificing Isaac) by inserting a pause after the first line: "Some time later, God tested Abraham." Since this line serves as a headline to the whole story, a pause will set this idea apart from the details of the story itself that follow. A pause will also allow the audience to internalize the sobering truth that God tests his friends.

Phrasing. Phrasing is crucial in helping audiences understand the ideas of the text. Effective readers spend enough time preparing to read that they know how the subordinate ideas relate to the main ones. By using a louder voice, higher pitch, or slower rate, they emphasize the main ideas. A brief pause before and after a key idea sets it apart from subordinate ideas that should be expressed more quickly or with a lower voice.

Listen to a conversation, and you will see that this is how we talk naturally. But public readers often sound as if they are reading because they lack natural changes of pace. Only a few readers are monotoned, but many readers are monopaced.

Eye contact. Eye contact is a most difficult technique to utilize when reading. But it must be done. Of all the channels of nonverbal communication, eye contact may be the one we attach most significance to. By eye contact we judge preparedness, sincerity, poise, and interest in the listener. Communicators should use lots of eye contact even when reading.

How much? Your eyes should relate to the audience more than to the page. This obviously demands practice, but it may take less work than you think. If you read the text out loud five to ten times, you will have it half-memorized, and you should be comfortable looking away from the page for a few seconds. When making eye contact, look directly in individuals' eyes for a second or so. Longer contact is usually unnecessary and may even distract the listener. For large auditoriums, look at individuals in each section. Each person in that section will feel contact with you.

Occasionally eye contact is not appropriate, as when the text is a prayer or highly personal like the psalms of lament. In these cases look just over the heads of the listeners or focus within the audience without looking into anyone's eyes. That technique allows the audience to "overhear" the personal ideas and feelings.

W. E. Sangster said, "When the Book is well read and made to live for the people, it can do for them what sermons often fail to do: it can be the very voice of God to their souls" (in Fasol, *A Guide to Self-Improvement in Sermon Delivery*, Baker, 1983). By giving thought and a few minutes of practice to our public reading of Scripture, we can embody God's mind and heart for our parishioners.

Chapter 174

THE IMPORTANCE OF BEING URGENT
Overcoming things that defuse sincere passion

John Ortberg

One of the ways carnality plays itself out in me is to be automatically focused too much on *How am I doing? Is this connecting? Are people being attentive? Do they think it's going well?* One area I want to grow is to be able to let go of that. I want my goal to be simply to help people take their next step toward God.

When I can do that, on the one hand it relieves a lot of personal anxiety because it's no longer my well-being or sense of value on the line. On the other hand, it makes preaching much more important because if preaching is just about trying to convince people they should like me, that's a trivial task. But if it is

about the proclamation of the Word of God and allowing the Spirit to form Christ in people's hearts, then it is an authentically urgent task.

When preaching is at its best, it is not a series of compartmentalized statements. "Here is a didactic proposition. . . . Here's an example. . . . Here's a joke to relieve tension. . . . Here's application. . . ." That approach to preaching often feels stilted, canned, and artificial. When preaching is done at its best, it all melds together, and the heart is deeply stirred. Often there's a sense of fierce joy and deep challenge combined with each other.

When that happens, that's preaching.

Chapter 175

THE DAY I LOST MY NERVE
And how I got it back

Lee Eclov

One Sunday, in the middle of the third point of my sermon, I lost my nerve. For two days, doubts about the usefulness of the message had whispered darkly in the back of my mind, but I pushed ahead, ever the good soldier, ever mindful that Sunday was coming.

But on Sunday, at a precise point in time, I mentally bolted! Outwardly I kept preaching—faster, I think, and, perhaps, in a lifeless manner; I was gunning for the benediction. Inwardly, though, I was AWOL. I checked out.

What happened?

I had lost faith—the willful act of believing God is in the sermon—that he can use even my words. I lost my nerve.

After the benediction I made a beeline down the aisle and through the foyer to my study, without so much as a nod at an usher. I closed the door, locked it, and crumbled. Another service started in a few minutes, and I didn't know what to do. What I did, of course—what all preachers do—was preach once again, as well as I could with renewed dependence (a desperate dependence) on God to make his Word clear out of the jumble of my sermon.

Time and again I have reflected on that experience, and several things are clear. *(1) It isn't preaching if there is no active faith at work.* Then it's a lecture, a talk. Preaching is, by definition, an act of faith. That means there must be room for doubt and failure. Part of preparation, as surely as exegesis and outlining are, is activating our faith that God will work through this message by his Spirit. That involves not only believing God can work in the sermon as a whole but also in its individual parts. I now pray through each sermon element, testing it before God, and then trusting him with it.

(2) Feeling vulnerable is part of the package. That is one reason preaching can be so powerful. It isn't a scholarly lecture reporting research results. A sermon is our personal response to the "living and active" Word of God. A loss for words—and thus an exposure of our hearts—must be expected.

(3) Confidence comes from outside us. Even the most Bible-devoted preacher can traffic too much in the realm of personal thoughts and musings. Such thoughts may be theologically solid and pastorally wise, but it's the biblical text that is our stock in trade. Our task is to make the text's meaning clear and then let God speak for God.

Preaching is not for the faint of heart. Preaching nerve doesn't come from self-confidence but from Word-confidence. When I forget that, I start sinking, wide-eyed, into the waves of doubt. When I remember that, I can walk on water.

Part 10

Special Topics

*How Do I Speak on Holidays and about Tough Topics
in a Way That Is Fresh and Trustworthy?*

Chapter 176

WHEN YOU DON'T LOOK FORWARD TO SPECIAL DAYS

Addressing holidays secular and religious with delight

John Beukema

It was Mother's Day. I knew the two well-dressed elderly ladies glaring at me were visitors because they sat in the front row. In the middle of my sermon, one said aloud to the other, "This isn't about mothers." The other responded, "What kind of church is this?" and together they looked down the row disapprovingly at the family members who brought them.

Choosing not to focus an entire sermon on a special day, as I sometimes do, can create a stir. By contrast, some may avoid church on a special day because of the strong negative emotions attached. One man told me, "I skipped last week because it was Mother's Day." When I asked why, he replied, "It was pointless. My mother's been dead for years."

SPECIAL DAYS PRESENT PREACHERS WITH SPECIAL CHALLENGES.

(1) When we ignore a special day, we may suffer the consequences of disappointing people. My experience has been that if you choose not to address a given holiday, most people will be happy provided it's a good sermon. But as the above story shows, that isn't always the case. Depending on the day, we encounter expectations from several sources:

- *Congregational expectations.* Members of the congregation may be disappointed if there is no patriotic sermon on July 4 or Christmas sermon for every Sunday in Advent.
- *Visitor and irregular attender expectations.*

Some holidays mean an influx of visitors or an appearance by sporadic attenders. They are there because of the holiday and find it strange if it is not addressed. At other times the holiday means fewer people in worship, which can disrupt a sermon series.

- *Denominational expectations.* Beyond the days on the average calendar, your denomination has its own expectations about special themes to be addressed, projects to be plugged, and offerings to be raised.
- *Liturgical expectations.* Although I have never been part of a liturgical tradition, one year an elder called a hasty meeting to uncover why we had ignored Pentecost that Sunday. Depending on your church, you may not want to skip Reformation Sunday, or Martin Luther King Jr. Day, or St. Patrick's Day.

(2) People may focus on the holiday rather than on God. This is probably the greatest danger of any special day. Humanism, hyper-patriotism, and outright idolatry can hijack worship. Biblical preachers must avoid dressing the gospel in patriotic clothes, tying the flag to the cross on July 4, or turning Christmas into merely a sentimental family affair.

After one worship service, a member met me at the door with a mild rebuke: "I was a little disappointed not to hear a sermon about mothers today."

"Why was that?" I said as casually as possible, dismayed that so many in the narthex seemed to be listening.

"It is Mother's Day," she replied. "Shouldn't mothers get one Sunday a year?"

In a flash (of what I hope was inspiration) I responded, "Nope. God gets 'em all."

That is the heart of the matter. There are many holidays and special events that demand attention, but the only thing that matters is that God be honored. As Stephen Rummage writes,

"The purpose of the special day sermon is not to glorify the special day but to glorify Jesus Christ" *(Planning Your Preaching,* 2002, p. 124).

(3) The celebration pushes the sermon off to the side. A word from God can be overshadowed by a musical extravaganza, a powerful drama, or cute children waving palm branches. Recognition of the oldest father present or the presentation of a lengthy special music number leaves less time for preaching. One Easter our platform was filled with so much staging I had to preach from the aisle.

(4) We may use Scripture wrongly to address the holiday. When we try to speak to a special day, we may make a text mean what it never meant. For example, we may offer biblical characters as case studies in parenthood when that was not the intent of the text.

- "A cord of three strands is not quickly broken" (Eccl. 4:12) is not the right text for Trinity Sunday.
- "But for those who fear you, you have raised a banner to be unfurled against the bow" (Ps. 60:4) does not refer to our nation's flag and a call to patriotism.

(5) The holiday theme is not what we sense God wants preached at this time. Have you ever faced a holiday and sense the theme seemed opposite to what God wanted? The calendar season was not the spiritual season of the church. It was Thanksgiving, but you felt the mind of the Lord was to deal with broken relationships. The holiday mood was celebratory, but you sensed the need for repentance.

Rather than automatically jettisoning either, try to wed the two. How does what you sense relate to the holiday? Another option is to ignore the holiday and explain why. This only adds to the urgency of the message.

(6) We have run out of fresh things to say. Of all special days, the most significant are Christmas and Easter, and that makes them also the most challenging. Since each of those days tends to arrive every year, a pastor must find ways to declare powerfully the basic message of Christ's incarnation and resurrection to the same audience. The preacher must be able to do more than declare "ditto."

How to Keep from Running Dry

Here are nine suggestions for producing fresh material for any special day.

(1) Plan and study ahead. When you suddenly realize Palm Sunday is a week away, it's hard to come up with something fresh. Planning ahead gives you time to think, pray, and be creative.

It also allows for mid-course corrections. Several years ago I spent the summer preaching through 1 and 2 Thessalonians. As I planned the series, I realized 2 Thessalonians 3:6–15 (on idleness and work) was scheduled two weeks prior to Labor Day weekend. I decided to take a two-week break in the middle of the series so the passage would line up with the holiday. I never gave a Labor Day sermon before or since, but that one was unexpectedly powerful.

(2) Glean from others. After a few years at the same church, preaching five Advent sermons each year, I started to worry about running out. In desperation I tried to discover how others had preached these themes. As a result I heard and read some great sermons that pointed me in new directions. Titles alone proved helpful. Two that stood out to me were William Willimon's "Blood in Bethlehem" and Bruce Thielemann's "Glory to God in the Lowest."

(3) Capture content all year. Gather material this Christmas for next Christmas. What you don't use now, store for next year. Set up folders in your computer or file drawer for special days. Throughout the year file away material that will fit holidays months down the road.

(4) Preach topics related to but not about the holiday. The topic of "Living Above Our Fears" can fit in at Christmas or Easter, for example, because fear is consistently referenced throughout the nativity and resurrection narratives. For either holiday, Hebrews 2:14–15 could serve as the text, declaring freedom to those enslaved by the fear of death. Or instead of addressing felt needs, we can explore various facets of the character and works of God related to the holiday, such as God's humility or providence at Christmas, God's power at Easter, God's tenderness on Mother's Day.

The result may not be a typical holiday sermon, but it may be more effective.

(5) Expand the range of your preaching styles. If you are like me, you tend to use one preaching style the majority of the time. A special day may be a good opportunity to broaden your horizons.

Textual preachers could try a topical approach—changing from the study of a pericope to a thematic study of peace, for example. Sequential expositors might consider attempting a first-person narrative—complete with robe and sandals. Those who preach doctrinal sermons could try a verse-by-verse approach.

This variance in style will give you different options as you select the text. It will challenge you and enliven your congregation as they experience the presentation of truth in a different manner.

(6) Use uncommon texts. Some texts are so familiar that people glaze over from the reference

alone, so keep your eyes open for infrequently used texts that speak to these major holidays.

While we must not neglect the narratives of the birth, suffering, death, and resurrection of Jesus, words from an unexpected text can cast new light on the truth. One I have never heard preached is "The Christmas Dragon," from Revelation 12:1–6. Have you used Genesis 3:15 to preach the death and resurrection of Christ, or explored the many other Old Testament prophecies concerning him? The story of Ruth suggests the coming of the Kinsman Redeemer.

(7) Speak from different viewpoints. Even using the most familiar texts, we can consider the same event from another perspective. We can tell the Christmas story through the eyes of angels, shepherds, or Herod, and the Easter story through Peter, Pilate, or Simon of Cyrene. However, to keep the emphasis on Christ, I avoid placing the focus on the minor characters; they are simply the viewpoint from which I look at the Savior. And to maintain biblical authority, I don't create imaginary, extrabiblical ones.

I once preached from Matthew 2 on "Grinches That Threaten Christmas." King Herod threatened the birth of Christ out of fear while the religious leaders responded to Jesus' birth with indifference, not bothering to travel five miles out of Jerusalem to check out the prophecy. Similar grinches of the soul are alive and well today. Our own fear of a loss of power threatens the place of Jesus in our lives. Indifference born of religious complacency threatens the reality of Christ to us.

(8) Clarify the objective. The questions of *What am I trying to do?* and *Why am I doing it?* are necessary for every sermon, but on special days we may neglect to ask them. "Because it's Christmas" is not a worthwhile response.

For example, for a time I went through an apologetics emphasis in my Christmas and Easter sermons, spending several holidays defending the virgin birth and bodily resurrection of Jesus. Certainly there is a place for that type of preaching on occasion, but few of my hearers seemed as blessed by it as I was. Suddenly the thought came to me, *Stop trying to prove the resurrection and talk more about what it accomplished.* That is a subtle but significant shift in purpose.

Have you focused primarily on evangelizing the visitors on those special days? Switch your emphasis and encourage the saints. Have you seen the holiday as a time to bring comfort? Shift your approach and aim for conviction and cleansing. Perhaps the mood has always been joyful, and a more solemn tone would be effective.

(9) Use the holiday as a bridge. When I am in a book study or a topical series, I prefer not to break the flow for a special day. But I have found I can use the special day as a bridge into the sermon. For example, on Father's Day I could begin a message from a series in Proverbs by saying, "One thing that fathers need most is wisdom. We find that in our text today on the subject. . . ."

Since Christ's work is the focus of the most important special days and every sermon should connect to the gospel, bridging to or from the holiday should be a natural crossing.

THE SPECIAL OPPORTUNITIES

Although special days have their challenges, they have far greater opportunities. There is an air of expectancy that can be used by God. Visitors are present who may never have heard the gospel. It is rarely business as usual.

On the fourth Sunday of Advent one year, I preached from 2 Corinthians 1:20, on the Yes of Christ. My big idea was, "Everything God promised us was delivered with Jesus." Afterward, one woman told me that though her divorce was long in the past, she struggled with feelings of loneliness and abandonment by God. That day she knew she needed to trust in God's promises. Grandparents came to relate how glad they were that their visiting children and grandchildren had come that day. They had been tempted to stay at home and celebrate the holiday, but in coming they had heard from God. A young couple came to tell me that they were believers visiting from another state and had convinced their unbelieving relatives to visit our church with them. The couple was elated that their relatives had heard the good news.

Those who preach on special days can do so with the confidence that God truly can make a holiday a holy day.

Chapter 177

PREACHING THE TERRORS
When your text is bad news

Barbara Brown Taylor

Not long ago, I was invited to address a senior citizens' group on "Women in the Old Testament." They had been studying various biblical characters and wanted me to introduce them to some of Israel's heroines, so I did.

I told them about Jael, "most blessed of women" (Judg. 5:24), who drove a tent peg through Sisera's temple with a mallet.

I told them about Esther, who won permission for the Jews of her husband's Persian empire "to destroy, kill and annihilate" 75,000 of their enemies (Est. 8:11).

By the end of my talk, my audience's eyes were very large, and I was feeling a little queasy myself. They thanked me very much and have never asked me back.

Granted, I could just as easily have talked about Sarah, Ruth, and the widow of Zarephath, but there comes a time in every preacher's life when the queasy-making parts of the Bible can no longer be ignored, when it is time to admit that the Bible is not a book about admirable people or even about a conventionally admirable God. It is instead a book about a sovereign God's covenant with a chosen people, as full of holy terrors as it is of holy wonders, none of which we may avoid without avoiding part of the truth.

On the whole, we do not do so well with the terror part. It does not fit the image of the God we wish to publish; it goes against the good news we want to proclaim. Who is eager to remind the congregation how the prophet Elisha cursed a crowd of jeering boys in the name of the Lord and how two she-bears trundled obediently out of the woods to maul forty-two of them (2 Kings 2:23–25)? Or how Ananias and Sapphira were struck dead for withholding a portion of their cash from the early Christian community and lying about it (Acts 5:1–11)?

Fortunately or unfortunately, there is little reason to tangle with such peripheral texts of terror when we have many more central texts of terror readily at hand. In the Old Testament, God asks Abraham to roast his only son; in the New Testament, obedience to God's will puts another only Son on a cross. In these two worst-case scenarios, and all their derivatives, the issue for us remains the same: How do we preach a loving God who does such unloving things? How do we preach the terrors?

TERROR AT THE CENTER

Because I am addressing biblical texts in this article, I am taking the biblical view, which is that God's will is at work in all the events of our lives. While there are good theological reasons and even better pastoral ones to approach the terrors as stray bullets outside God's plan, the Bible leans the other way. "I form light and create darkness," says the Lord, "I make weal and create woe; I the LORD do all these things" (Isa. 45:7, NRSV).

In practice, we tend to preach the terrors by making them less terrible. Of course God sent a ram to take Isaac's place at the last moment, we say; of course God raised Jesus from the dead and made him Lord of all. Thus, the first story becomes one about how obedience results in rescue and the second one a story about how obedience results in resurrection.

But what is lost while such morals are being made is the very real terror of obeying God without the least idea how things will turn out in the end—which is, after all, the human situation. Things will turn out according to God's

will, certainly, and in faith we confess that to be enough for us. But insofar as God's will is so radically different from our own, there is plenty of room left for terror in our lives.

Every preacher has his or her own canon of terror. My own includes three kinds of texts: first, those in which God sanctions violence—killing every firstborn in the land of Egypt (Ex. 11:5) or ordering Saul to slaughter the Amalekites down to the last woman, child, and donkey (1 Sam. 15:3); second, those in which God aims to separate me from my stuff—suggesting that I surrender my last handful of meal (1 Kings 17:11–13) or sell all that I own to follow (Mark 10:21); third, those texts in which God exercises final judgment—refusing to open the door to the foolish bridesmaids (Matt. 25:12) or banishing the ill-clad wedding guest to outer darkness, where there is weeping and gnashing of teeth (Matt. 22:13).

They are terrible to me because they expose my vulnerability. If God can condemn Amalekite babies for the sins of their parents, then there is no hope for me. Nor can I find safety in following Jesus, if selling all that I own is the way. So, of course, I will find myself on the wrong side of the door when the time comes, hearing my muffled sentence pronounced through the latch: "Truly, I tell you, I do not know you."

These terrible texts remind me how helpless I am, how frail and not in charge I am. While there are clearly things I can do to improve my life and things I can do to cheapen it, my fate is ultimately out of my hands. I cannot control God's disposition toward me, and that is terrifying.

One way to hide from such knowledge is to take refuge in righteousness, suggesting that those who behave properly are terror-exempt. Obey God and avoid the sword. Give generously and prevent misfortune. Be good sheep and dodge the outer darkness. Congregations are relieved to hear sermons like these and preachers are glad to preach them because they offer some leverage in an otherwise frightening universe, but they finally fail to meet the test either of human experience or biblical witness. Job stands on one side of the pulpit shaking his head and Jesus on the other, both of them confirming our fear that righteousness does nothing to dissuade God from trying the faithful by fire and by ice.

Jesus' own death is the chief terror of the gospel. Here is God's beloved, who has done nothing but right all his life, and what is his reward? Not ripe old age with grandchildren hanging on his sleeves but early, violent death on a cross. This death ruins all our efforts to turn the Bible into a manual for the good life.

No one who has heard the story of Jesus Christ can mistake where following him will lead, which makes the gospel itself a text of terror for all who wish to avoid suffering and death. The good news of God in Christ is heard loudest and best by those who stand on the far side of a fresh grave. That, finally, is what makes a text terrible to me: not what it exposes about me but what it exposes about God—a sovereign God who is radically different from me, whose mind I cannot read, whose decisions I cannot predict, and whose actions I cannot control.

"It is a dreadful thing to fall into the hands of the living God," writes the author of the letter to the Hebrews (10:31). But it is not as if we had a choice. That is whose hands we are in; our only choice is how we will handle our fear.

Hidden Consolations

As preachers we have an additional choice, and that is how we will address the fear of those who listen to us. Jonathan Edwards, the great eighteenth-century American pastor and theologian, was one of the most frightening preachers of all time. In his book *Thoughts on the Revival of Religion in New England*, he rose to the defense of those who were being blamed for "speaking terror to them that are already under great terrors." It was, he said, a matter of saving those who were drowning in full sight of land.

It is an alarming image, and yet it is what texts of terror do. They pry our fingers away from our own ideas about who God should be and how God should act so that there are only two things left for us to do with our fear: Use it to propel us toward the God who is or let it sink us like a stone.

Preaching texts of terror calls for the same kind of choice. We may try to protect ourselves and our congregations from them by tossing out inflatable bits of comfort and advice, or we may find the courage to forsake those twigs and swim for our lives toward the living God. As fearful as that may be, it is finally less fearful than the alternative.

In a paradoxical way, texts of terror carry their own consolation inside of them. Several nights ago, a friend and I watched Laurence Olivier in Shakespeare's *King Lear*. Neither of us had ever seen the play before, so we were unprepared for the relentless tragedy of it, with fathers rejecting children, children betraying parents, brothers plotting against brothers, and sisters poisoning sisters. By the end of the last scene, the stage was littered with bodies—Lear, Cordelia, Goneril, Regan, Edmund—all dead. As the lights went down and the credits rolled, my friend turned to me with tears in his eyes and said, "What could be more wonderful than that?"

When I asked him to explain himself, he could not, except to say that he recognized his own life in the play, and that it helped him somehow to see his worst fears acted out. It was *real*—that was the best he could do—and it was redemptive for him to witness real pain suffered in a way that seemed true to him.

In the same way, I believe, texts of terror are recognizable to us. Judgment, violence, rejection, death—they are all present in our world, if not in our lives, and there is some crazy kind of consolation in the fact that they are present in the Bible as well. They remind us that the Bible is not all lambs and rainbows. If it were, it would not be our book. Our book has everything in it—wonder and terrors, worst fears and best hopes—both for ourselves and for our relationship with God.

The best hope of all is that because the terrors are included here, as part of the covenant story, they may turn out to be redemptive in the end, when we see dimly no more but face to face at last. That is the fundamental hope all texts of terror drive us to: that however wrong they may seem to us, however misbegotten and needlessly cruel, God may yet be present in them, working redemption in ways we are not equipped to discern.

Our fear of God's method may turn out to be like our fear of the surgeon's knife, which must wound before it can heal. While we would prefer to forego the pain altogether—or at the very least to perform our own surgery, thank you very much—our survival of the terrors depends on our trust in the surgeon's skill. If we believe the One to whom we surrender ourselves is competent, then "all shall be well, and all shall be well, and all manner of thing shall be well" (Julian of Norwich).

If we are open to this possibility in our interpretation of Scripture, then we open the possibility of its being true in the interpretation of our lives as well. Whether the terror is heard on Sunday or lived on Monday, the hermeneutical question remains the same: Do we trust God to act in all the events of our lives, or only in the ones that meet with our approval?

Several summers ago, I spent three days on a barrier island where loggerhead turtles were laying their eggs. One night while the tide was out, I watched a huge female heave herself up the beach to dig her nest and empty herself into it while slow, salt tears ran from her eyes. Afraid of disturbing her, I left before she had finished her work but returned next morning to see if I could find the spot where her eggs lay hidden in the sand. What I found were her tracks, only they led in the wrong direction. Instead of heading back out to sea, she had wandered into the dunes, which were already hot as asphalt in the morning sun.

A little ways inland I found her, exhausted and all but baked, her head and flippers caked with dried sand. After pouring water on her and covering her with sea oats, I fetched a park ranger, who returned with a jeep to rescue her. As I watched in horror, he flipped her over on her back, wrapped tire chains around her front legs, and hooked the chains to the trailer hitch on his jeep. Then he took off, yanking her body forward so fast that her open mouth filled with sand and then disappeared underneath her as her neck bent so far I feared it would break.

The ranger hauled her over the dunes and down onto the beach; I followed the path that the prow of her shell cut in the sand. At ocean's edge, he unhooked her and turned her right side up again. She lay motionless in the surf as the water lapped at her body, washing the sand from her eyes and making her skin shine again.

Then a particularly large wave broke over her, and she lifted her head slightly, moving her back legs as she did. As I watched, she revived. Every fresh wave brought her life back to her until one of them made her light enough to find a foothold and push off, back into the water that was her home.

Watching her swim slowly away and remembering her nightmare ride through the dunes, I noted that it is sometimes hard to tell whether you are being killed or being saved by the hands that turn your life upside down.

WRESTLING OUT THE BLESSING

Our hope, through all our own terrors, is that we are being saved. Whatever we believe about why things happen the way they do, we are united by our hope that God is present in them, working redemption in light and darkness, weal and woe.

To hope this does not mean we lie down before the terrors, however. For as long as we have strength to fight, it is both our nature and our privilege to do so. Sometimes God's blessing does not come until daybreak, after a full night of wrestling angels, and sometimes it takes much longer than that. As preachers and as believers, it is our job to struggle with the terrors, refusing to let go of them until they have yielded their blessings.

If we are tempted to draw back from this task and seek an easier way, we are not alone. The world is full of former disciples. "Do you also wish to go away?" Jesus asks the handful who are left with him at one point (John 6:67–68, NRSV).

"Lord," Simon Peter answers him, "to whom can we go? You have the words of eternal life."

Chapter 178

PREPARING PEOPLE TO SUFFER
What expectations do our sermons create?

John Piper

If the aim of preaching is the glory of God through Jesus Christ, and if God is most glorified in our people when they are most satisfied in him, and if the universal human experience of suffering threatens to undermine their faith in the goodness of God and thus their satisfaction in his glory, then preaching must aim to help our people be satisfied in God while suffering. Indeed, we must help them count suffering as part of why they should be satisfied in God.

We must build into our people's minds and hearts a vision of God and his ways that helps them see suffering not merely as a threat to their satisfaction in God (which it is), but also as a means to their satisfaction in God (which it is). We must preach so as to make suffering seem normal in this fallen age—purposeful and not surprising.

The forces of American culture are almost all designed to build the opposite worldview: Maximize comfort, ease, and security. Avoid all choices that might bring discomfort, trouble, difficulty, pain, and suffering. Add this cultural force to our natural desire for immediate gratification and fleeting pleasures, and the combined power to undermine the superior satisfaction of the soul in the glory of God through suffering is huge.

If we would see God honored in the lives of our people as the supreme value and deepest satisfaction of their lives, then we must strive with all our might to show the meaning of suffering and to help them see the wisdom, power, and goodness of God behind it, ordaining; above it, governing; beneath it, sustaining; and before it, preparing. This is the hardest work in the world—to change the minds and hearts of fallen human beings and make God so precious to them that they count it all joy when trials come, exult in their afflictions, rejoice in the plundering of their property, and say in the end, "To die is gain."

Preaching is about doing the impossible: making the rich young ruler fall out of love with his comfortable lifestyle and into love with the King of kings so that he joyfully sells all that he has to gain that treasure (Matt. 13:44). Jesus said, "With man this is impossible" (Matt. 19:26). The aim of preaching is impossible. No techniques will make it succeed. "But with God all things are possible."

We must preach to prepare our people for suffering because coming to Christ means more suffering, not less. Suffering is normal, not exceptional. Suffering is certain. Most American Christians are not prepared in mind or heart to believe or experience this. Therefore the glory of God, the honor of Christ, the stability of the church, and the strength of commitment to world missions are at stake. If preaching does not help our people be satisfied in God through suffering, the church will be a weakling in an escapist world of ease, and the completion of the Great Commission, with its demand for martyrdom, will fail.

Consider the certainty of suffering that will come to your people if they embrace the Savior:

- "The Son of Man has nowhere to lay his head" (Matt. 8:20).
- "A righteous man may have many troubles" (Ps. 34:19).
- "If they persecuted me, they will persecute you also" (John 15:20).
- "Christ suffered for you . . . follow in his steps" (1 Peter 2:21).
- "Do not be surprised at the painful trial you are suffering, as though something strange were happening to you" (1 Peter 4:12).
- "We must go through many hardships to enter the kingdom of God" (Acts 14:22).
- "[Let no one] be unsettled by these trials. You know quite well that we were destined for them" (1 Thess. 3:3).

What does a pastoral heart of wisdom do when it discovers that death is sure, life is short, and suffering is inevitable and necessary? The answer is given in Psalm 90; it's a prayer: "Have compassion on your servants! Satisfy us in the morning with your unfailing love, that we may sing for joy and be glad all our days" (Ps. 90:13–14). In the face of toil and trouble and suffering and death, the wise preacher cries out with the psalmist, "Satisfy us in the morning with your unfailing love." He prays this both for himself and his people: "O God, grant that we will be satisfied with your steadfast love always, and need nothing else." Then he preaches to that end.

Why? Because if you leave your people where they are, seeking satisfaction in family and job and leisure and toys and sex and money and food and power and esteem, what will they do when suffering and death strip it all away? They will be embittered, angry, and depressed. And the worth, beauty, goodness, power, and wisdom of God—that is, the glory of God—will vanish in the cloud of murmuring, complaining, and cursing.

Preaching involves timing. Preach the whole truth about suffering and the sovereign goodness of God while it is day, and when the night comes and you stand beside the suicide victim's pool of blood, or the ice cold, ivory body of a one-year-old boy, you won't have to say anything. This will be a time for embracing. At this point the suffering saints will be glad that your suffering has taught you to preach the hard things and then, at the right time, to be silent.

Chapter 179

PREACHING HELL IN A TOLERANT AGE

Brimstone for the broad-minded

Timothy Keller

The young man in my office was impeccably dressed and articulate. He was an Ivy League MBA, successful in the financial world, and he had lived in three countries before age thirty. Raised in a family with only the loosest connections to a mainline church, he had little understanding of Christianity.

I was therefore gratified to learn of his intense spiritual interest, recently piqued as he attended our church. He said he was ready to embrace the gospel. But there was a final obstacle.

"You've said that if we do not believe in Christ," he said, "we are lost and condemned. I'm sorry, I just cannot buy that. I work with some fine people who are Muslim, Jewish, or agnostic. I cannot believe they are going to hell just because they don't believe in Jesus. In fact, I cannot reconcile the very idea of hell with a loving God—even if he is holy, too."

This young man expressed what may be the main objection contemporary secular people make to the Christian message. (A close second, in my experience, is the problem of suffering and evil.) Many today reject the idea of final judgment and hell.

Thus, it's tempting to avoid such topics in our preaching. But neglecting the unpleasant doctrines of the historic faith will bring about counterintuitive consequences. There is an ecological balance to scriptural truth that must not be disturbed.

If an area is rid of its predatory or undesirable animals, the balance of that environment may be so upset that the desirable plants and animals are lost—through overbreeding with a limited food supply. The nasty predator that was eliminated actually kept in balance the number of other animals and plants necessary to that particular ecosystem. In the same way, if we play down "bad" or harsh doctrines within the historic Christian faith, we will find, to our shock, that we have gutted all our pleasant and comfortable beliefs, too.

The loss of the doctrine of hell and judgment

and the holiness of God does irreparable damage to our deepest comforts—our understanding of God's grace and love and of our human dignity and value to him. To preach the good news, we must preach the bad.

But in this age of tolerance, how?

HOW TO PREACH HELL TO TRADITIONALISTS

Before preaching on the subject of hell, I must recognize that today, a congregation is made up of two groups: traditionalists and postmoderns. The two hear the message of hell completely differently.

People from traditional cultures and mindsets tend to have (1) a belief in God and (2) a strong sense of moral absolutes and the obligation to be good. These people tend to be older, from strong Catholic or religious Jewish backgrounds, from conservative evangelical/Pentecostal Protestant backgrounds, from the southern U.S., and first-generation immigrants from non-European countries.

The way to show traditional persons their need for the gospel is by saying, "Your sin separates you from God! You can't be righteous enough for him." Imperfection is the duty-worshiper's horror. Traditionalists are motivated toward God by the idea of punishment in hell. They sense the seriousness of sin.

But traditionalists may respond to the gospel only out of fear of hell, unless I show them Jesus experienced not only pain in general on the cross but hell in particular. This must be held up until they are attracted to Christ for the beauty of the costly love of what he did. To the traditional person, hell must be preached as the only way to know how much Christ loved you.

Here is one way I have preached this:

Unless we come to grips with this terrible doctrine, we will never even begin to understand the depths of what Jesus did for us on the cross. His body was being destroyed in the worst possible way, but that was a flea bite compared to what was happening to his soul. When he cried out that his God had forsaken him, he was experiencing hell itself.

If a mild acquaintance denounces you and rejects you—that hurts. If a good friend does the same—the hurt's far worse. However, if your spouse walks out on you, saying, "I never want to see you again," that is far more devastating still. The longer, deeper, and more intimate the relationship, the more torturous is any separation.

But the Son's relationship with the Father was beginning-less and infinitely greater than the most intimate and passionate human relationship. When Jesus was cut off from God, he went into the deepest pit and most powerful furnace, beyond all imagining. And he did it voluntarily, for us.

HOW TO PREACH HELL TO POSTMODERNS

In contrast to the traditionalist, the postmodern person is hostile to the very idea of hell. People with more secular and postmodern mindsets tend to have (1) only a vague belief in the divine, if at all, and (2) little sense of moral absolutes, but rather a sense they need to be true to their dreams. They tend to be younger, from nominal Catholic or nonreligious Jewish backgrounds, from liberal mainline Protestant backgrounds, from the western and northeastern U. S., and Europeans.

When preaching hell to people of this mindset, I've found I must make four arguments.

1. Sin Is Slavery

I do not define sin as just breaking the rules but also as "making something besides God our ultimate value and worth." These good things, which become gods, will drive us relentlessly, enslaving us mentally and spiritually, even to hell forever if we let them.

I say, "You are actually being religious, though you don't know it—you are trying to find salvation through worshiping things that end up controlling you in a destructive way." Slavery is the choice-worshiper's horror.

C. S. Lewis's depictions of hell are important for postmodern people. In *The Great Divorce*, Lewis describes a busload of people from hell who come to the outskirts of heaven. There they are urged to leave behind the sins that have trapped them in hell. The descriptions Lewis makes of people in hell are so striking because we recognize the denial and self-delusion of substance addictions. When addicted to alcohol, we are miserable, but we blame others and pity ourselves; we do not take responsibility for our behavior or see the roots of our problem. Lewis writes:

> Hell . . . begins with a grumbling mood, and yourself still distinct from it: perhaps even criticizing it. . . . You can repent and come out of it again. But there may come a day when you can do that no longer. Then there will be no you left to criticize the mood or even enjoy it, but just the grumble itself going on forever like a machine.

Modern people struggle with the idea of God's thinking up punishments to inflict on disobedient people. When sin is seen as slavery and hell as the freely chosen, eternal skid row of the universe, hell becomes much more comprehensible.

Here is an example from a recent sermon of how I try to explain this:

> First, sin separates us from the presence of God (Isa. 59:2), which is the source of all joy (Ps.

16:11), love, wisdom, or good thing of any sort (James 1:17). . . .

> Second, to understand hell we must understand sin as slavery. Romans 1:21–25 tells us that we were built to live for God supremely, but instead we live for love, work, achievement, or morality to give us meaning and worth. Thus every person, religious or not, is worshiping something—idols, pseudo-saviors—to get their worth. But these things enslave us with guilt (if we fail to attain them) or anger (if someone blocks them from us) or fear (if they are threatened) or drivenness (since we must have them). Guilt, anger, and fear are like fire that destroys us. Sin is worshiping anything but Jesus—and the wages of sin is slavery.

Perhaps the greatest paradox of all is that the people on Lewis's bus from hell are enslaved because they freely choose to be. They would rather have their freedom (as they define it) than salvation. Their relentless delusion is that if they glorified God, they would lose their human greatness (Gen. 3:4–5), but their choice has really ruined their human greatness. Hell is, as Lewis says, "the greatest monument to human freedom."

2. Hell Is Less Exclusive Than So-Called Tolerance

Nothing is more characteristic of the modern mindset than the statement: "I think Christ is fine, but I believe a devout Muslim or Buddhist or even a good atheist will certainly find God." A slightly different version is: "I don't think God would send a person who lives a good life to hell just for holding the wrong belief." This approach is seen as more inclusive.

In preaching about hell, then, I need to counter this argument:

> The universal religion of humankind is: We develop a good record and give it to God, and

then he owes us. The gospel is: God develops a good record and gives it to us, then we owe him (Rom. 1:17). In short, to say a good person, not just Christians, can find God is to say good works are enough to find God.

You can believe that faith in Christ is not necessary or you can believe that we are saved by grace, but you cannot believe in both at once.

So the apparently inclusive approach is really quite exclusive. It says, "The good people can find God, and the bad people do not." But what about us moral failures? We are excluded.

The gospel says, "The people who know they aren't good can find God, and the people who think they are good do not." Then what about non-Christians, all of whom must, by definition, believe their moral efforts help them reach God? They are excluded.

So both approaches are exclusive, but the gospel's is the more inclusive exclusivity. It says joyfully, "It doesn't matter who you are or what you've done. It doesn't matter if you've been at the gates of hell. You can be welcomed and embraced fully and instantly through Christ."

3. Christianity's View of Hell Is More Personal Than the Alternative View

Fairly often, I meet people who say, "I have a personal relationship with a loving God, and yet I don't believe in Jesus Christ at all."

"Why not?" I ask.

They reply, "My God is too loving to pour out infinite suffering on anyone for sin."

But then a question remains: "What did it cost this kind of God to love us and embrace us? What did he endure in order to receive us? Where did this God agonize, cry out? Where were his nails and thorns?"

The only answer is: "I don't think that was necessary."

How ironic. In our effort to make God more loving, we have made God less loving. His love,

in the end, needed to take no action. It was sentimentality, not love at all. The worship of a God like this will be impersonal, cognitive, and ethical. There will be no joyful self-abandonment, no humble boldness, no constant sense of wonder. We would not sing to such a being, "Love so amazing, so divine, demands my soul, my life, my all."

The postmodern "sensitive" approach to the subject of hell is actually impersonal. It says, "It doesn't matter if you believe in the person of Christ, as long as you follow his example."

But to say that is to say the essence of religion is intellectual and ethical, not personal. If any good person can find God, then the essential core of religion is understanding and following the rules.

When preaching about hell, I try to show how impersonal this view is:

> To say that any good person can find God is to create a religion without tears, without experience, without contact.

The gospel certainly is not less than the understanding of truths and principles, but it is infinitely more. The essence of salvation is knowing a Person (John 17:3). As with knowing any person, there is repenting and weeping and rejoicing and encountering. The gospel calls us to a wildly passionate, intimate love relationship with Jesus Christ, and calls that "the core of true salvation."

4. There Is No Love Without Wrath

What rankles people is the idea of judgment and the wrath of God: "I can't believe in a God who sends people to suffer eternally. What kind of loving God is filled with wrath?"

So in preaching about hell, we must explain that a wrathless God cannot be a loving God. Here's how I tried to do that in one sermon:

> People ask, "What kind of loving God is filled

with wrath?" But any loving person is often filled with wrath. In *Hope Has Its Reasons*, Becky Pippert writes, "Think how we feel when we see someone we love ravaged by unwise actions or relationships. Do we respond with benign tolerance as we might toward strangers? Far from it. . . . Anger isn't the opposite of love. Hate is, and the final form of hate is indifference."

Pippert then quotes E. H. Gifford, "Human love here offers a true analogy: the more a father loves his son, the more he hates in him the drunkard, the liar, the traitor."

She concludes: "If I, a flawed, narcissistic, sinful woman, can feel this much pain and anger over someone's condition, how much more a morally perfect God who made them? God's wrath is not a cranky explosion, but his settled opposition to the cancer of sin which is eating out the insides of the human race he loves with his whole being."

A God Like This

Following a recent sermon on the Parable of Lazarus and the rich man, the post-service question-and-answer session was packed with more than the usual number of attenders. The questions and comments focused on the subject of eternal judgment.

My heart sank when a young college student said, "I've gone to church all my life, but I don't think I can believe in a God like this." Her tone was more sad than defiant, but her willingness to stay and talk showed that her mind was open.

Usually all the questions are pitched to me, and I respond as best I can. But on this occasion people began answering one another.

An older businesswoman said, "Well, I'm not much of a churchgoer, and I'm in some shock now. I always disliked the very idea of hell, but I never thought about it as a measure of what God was willing to endure in order to love me."

Then a mature Christian made a connection with a sermon a month ago on Jesus at Lazarus' tomb in John 11. "The text tells us that Jesus wept," he said, "yet he was also extremely angry at evil. That's helped me. He is not just an angry God or a weeping, loving God—he's both. He doesn't only judge evil, but he also takes the hell and judgment himself for us on the cross."

The second woman nodded, "Yes. I always thought hell told me about how angry God was with us, but I didn't know it also told me about how much he was willing to suffer and weep for us. I never knew how much hell told me about Jesus' love. It's very moving."

It is only because of the doctrine of judgment and hell that Jesus' proclamation of grace and love are so brilliant and astounding.

Chapter 180

PREACHING FOR TOTAL COMMITMENT

*What does it take to convince people to become fully devoted
followers of Jesus Christ?*

Bill Hybels

Recently a man commented on the "tough topics" I'd taught on over the years—hell, money, sex, relational confrontation, self-discipline. He asked, "Of all the topics you've preached on, which has been the hardest to get across?"

I didn't even have to think about it: "Becoming Totally Devoted to Christ." My greatest teaching challenge is to convey what Paul was driving at in Acts 20:24 and other places where he conveyed the idea: I no longer count my life as dear unto myself; I have abandoned my personal aspirations and ambitions; I have offered myself as a living sacrifice to Christ. When I teach that to secularly minded people, they think I'm from Mars. The thought of living according to someone else's agenda is ludicrous.

To many people, living for Christ is a kind of fanaticism the world could do without. *Who, they wonder, would be foolish enough voluntarily to suffer loss, refrain from pleasure, or impinge on the comfort level of his life?* They think total devotion to Christ means squandering the only life they have.

A man from my church provides a perfect example. His biggest problem, as I perceive it, is his successful company. Clients whose business he's not even seeking are lining up for his services. Just responding to them is tyrannizing his life. Several months ago I asked him why his

heart didn't seem to be as warm toward things of God as it had been.

"Business has been dominating my life," he admitted, but added in defense, "but I'm not seeking it. I'm just trying to handle what's coming in. I mean, what do you expect me to do?"

I suggested he could say, "Enough is enough." He looked at me as if I were insane. What businessman in his right mind would say no to a client whose order would produce a bigger profit? You don't do that in this world. More is always better; it's the American way. The desire for more had a greater pull on this man than his desire to follow Christ, use his spiritual gifts, serve his wife, or be father to his kids.

If it's so hard to persuade people to commit themselves unreservedly to Christ, why bother? Why not settle for church attendance, or membership, or at least periodic service?

As ministers, we all have to come to terms with the quality of fruit we're producing. We have to decide what level of commitment we expect from the people we're leading.

Church history has taught us that a leader can do more through a handful of totally devoted believers than through a church full of halfhearted ones. So we're left with a tension: How can we teach in such a way that we produce fully devoted followers of Jesus Christ, when we know that most people don't want to hear about radical discipleship?

Let me suggest five principles that guide me when I preach for 100 percent commitment.

DESCRIBE TOTAL COMMITMENT

The first step is to develop a clear understanding of total commitment. A teacher constantly has to define and redefine: What does it really mean to be completely devoted to Christ? If it doesn't mean simply showing up for services, putting in a check, and going home, then what does it mean?

Several Bible passages define total commitment for me and shape my preaching on the subject.

Paul's words in 1 Corinthians 15:31: "I die every day." I've never met a fully devoted follower of Christ who didn't have to die daily to a host of things that would like to have a grip on him—personal ambition, worldly pleasures, people's applause, greed. This culture ferociously maintains that "you can have it all," but that slogan is foreign to the mind and teaching of Christ. It's difficult for me to stand in an affluent, suburban congregation and tell people what they need to die to, walk away from, or give up, but I have to do it.

Jesus' command in Luke 10:27: "Love the Lord your God with all your heart and with all your soul and with all your strength and with all your mind." This means we must obey God's Word and order our lives in such a way that we can live in the constant awareness of his presence.

John's comment, "Anyone who does not love his brother, whom he has seen, cannot love God, whom he has not seen" (1 John 4:20). We live in an age in which hate is routine, and too often that attitude spills over into the church.

Yet Scripture makes it clear that total devotion to Jesus Christ includes being at peace with our brothers. True Christians, particularly leaders, need to take Matthew 5:23–24 (the need to be reconciled with our brother before coming to God) more seriously. We need to make relational integrity a priority and actively seek reconciliation whenever a problem arises. That should be a prerequisite to ministry.

Jesus' constant teaching on the use of time, talents, and treasures. After a person spends thirty years devoting all of his or her time and talents to the marketplace, it's hard to start devoting it suddenly to the Lord. It's hard to hear verses like "Seek first the kingdom of God," or "Always abound in the work of the Lord," or "Set your mind on things above," or "What does it profit you to gain the whole world and lose your soul?"

It takes time to develop personal spiritual disciplines—Bible study, journaling, praying, fasting, reflecting. It takes time to be in a small group of brothers or sisters who will provide challenge and accountability. It takes time to advance the kingdom in practical service. But those commitments of time are a good measure of our devotion to Christ.

A medical professional from our church has decided to work a four-day week so he can devote the other three days to his lay-leadership role and his relationship with his family. The work time he has given up costs him substantial income every week. But he has decided to die to that so he can live to what Christ has called him to do apart from his vocation. Already he had been using his skills to serve needy people; but now, in addition, he's able to use his gifts of administration and leadership within the church in significant ways. He's putting his time, talents, and treasures at God's disposal.

MODEL IT

The second step in preaching on total commitment is tougher: to live it ourselves. It's clear, I think, that we can't lead a congregation into total commitment unless we're attempting to model it.

Every pastor has been on the wrong side of the total-commitment fence at one time or another. It's like asking an athlete, "Have you always been in superb condition?"

Inevitably, the answer is, "Not always."

When you ask, "How'd you feel when you weren't?" they say, "Sluggish. Under par. Less than professional."

Recently I read about a top leader who was asked, "What is your main objective in leading your organization?"

He said, "To intercept entropy." That fascinated me, because that's what I try to do in my own life. I look at myself and say, *Where is there slippage? Where am I getting out of condition? Where am I becoming sluggish?* Before I pay attention to the spiritual condition of others, I examine myself.

One of my great frustrations is not being able to manage my life so that I'm always fully committed. But if I'm willing to hear the truth about myself, the Spirit will point out areas of carelessness and inconsistency. Then I can repent and intercept the entropy at a fairly early stage.

In addition to trying to model total commitment, we need other congregational leaders who are fully devoted followers, who can uphold the standard. Last night I looked around the table at our elders' meeting and thought, *Every elder in this church is committed to Jesus Christ and would take a bullet for him right now.* That means when I preach about total commitment, they're the first ones to cheer me on: "Don't ever settle for less.

We're with you 100 percent." It would be pretty hard for me to bring a strong call for deeper discipleship if the elders and other key leaders weren't in agreement.

What's exciting is that the more fully devoted the pastor and lay leaders become, the more fully devoted the congregation becomes. The growth in the congregation then inspires the leaders to deeper commitment, and that prompts a continual cycle of growth. Total discipleship becomes contagious and exhilarating.

There's one man in our church whose only day off is Wednesday; he comes in that morning and cleans our water fountains. Another man comes in on his day off and services our vacuum cleaners. Other volunteers weed and cultivate various flower beds on the church property. I recently saw a young mom tending one of the beds. Her baby sat in a stroller, while she listened to a cassette tape and dug around the flowers. When I see discipleship manifested in service like that, I become motivated to be a more devoted servant myself.

PREACH FROM EVERY ANGLE

The third step is to preach on total commitment from as many creative angles as possible. Here's what I mean.

Select series that lead naturally to a call for commitment. In a sense, every sermon I preach defines some aspect of commitment, whether it's about marriage, character development, caring for our bodies, or whatever. Still, I believe the call to devotion is best presented overtly, and some series don't lend themselves to that as naturally as others.

For example, I preached a series that dealt with honesty in relationships. It was a helpful series, but it didn't provide a good opportunity for calling people to a deeper commitment to Jesus Christ. To do that would have been somewhat manipulative, a bait-and-switch for people who came expecting something else. With some topics, if I want to have integrity, I need to stick with the subject matter and wait for another time to talk about discipleship.

But other topics naturally lead to a call for 100 percent commitment. Last year I preached a series called "Alternatives to Christianity," in which I discussed the New Age Movement, Mormonism, Jehovah's Witnesses, Hinduism, Islam, and Buddhism, and contrasted them with Christianity. Following an honest comparison of these belief systems, I ended the series by saying,

> After you've heard all this, wouldn't you agree that the Christian message is absolutely compelling? When you line it up against the other belief systems, doesn't it prove to be a more excellent way? If this series has convinced you that Christianity is compelling in its truths, in the person of Jesus Christ, and in what it produces in individual lives, if, in fact, it's the clear winner, then embrace it with all your heart, soul, mind, and strength. Don't hold back.

That series naturally lent itself to a call for commitment, and I didn't shrink from presenting it. As I plan my preaching, I monitor the series I'm selecting as to whether they lead without manipulation to a message on all-out Christian commitment.

Present committed service as a joyous response to what God has done for us, not as a means to earn salvation. We ministers have to make sure our people realize that discipleship is a way to say thank you to God, not a way to gain merit.

At times I've stopped myself during a call to commitment and said, "If you're outside the family of God, please understand that discipleship is a response to God's amazing grace. It's not an attempt to improve your status before God. Paul says you can 'give your body to be burned,' but you can't save yourself through discipleship. Commitment is a means to express gratitude, not to win entrance into heaven."

Illustrate the alternatives to wholehearted commitment. When I'm trying to challenge the secularly minded person to be a devoted follower of Jesus Christ, I find it effective to play out the opposite scenario.

For example, in a series called "Rare and Remarkable Virtues," the closing message was on contentment. I began by saying:

> All he ever really wanted in life was more. He wanted more money, so he parlayed inherited wealth into a billion-dollar pile of assets. He wanted more fame, so he broke into the Hollywood scene and soon became a filmmaker and star. He wanted more sensual pleasures, so he paid handsome sums to indulge his every sexual urge. He wanted more thrills, so he designed, built, and piloted the fastest aircraft in the world. He wanted more power, so he secretly dealt political favors so skillfully that two U.S. presidents became his pawns. All he ever wanted was more. He was absolutely convinced that more would bring him true satisfaction. Unfortunately, history shows otherwise.

Then I went on to describe how this man concluded his life—emaciated; colorless; sunken chest; fingernails in grotesque, inches-long corkscrews; rotting, black teeth; tumors; innumerable needle marks from his drug addiction. "Howard Hughes died," I said, "believing the myth of more. He died a billionaire junkie, insane by all reasonable standards."

By depicting the path of the self-centered life, we can show its emptiness and ultimate futility.

We can say, "Friends, it's madness. Can you see that? Maybe these men traveled further down the road to deception than you have, but play it out. Think about where you're headed. Sooner or later you'll get so tired of drinking cups of sand, and you'll say, 'I'm ready for some living water.' You can do that fifteen years from now, after you've gone through two or three more marriages and left a trail of broken children. Or, you can learn from the madness of others, and bow right now and trust Christ."

I go on to ask, "Has your most recent acquisition quenched the thirst in your soul? Has your most recent thrill, your promotion, your marriage, your new child, your published book, left you totally satisfied inside?" People need to admit that what they thought would satisfy them, when once attained, usually doesn't do the job.

For the currently satisfied, offer your help for a later date. Sometimes people say, "Hey, I'm happy with who I am. I'm not hungry or thirsty for anything. I have no major problems, and I'm doing okay." To people who are that self-deceived, there's nothing I can say. It does no good to try to convince them of their need. But publicly or privately I can offer my assistance for the day they finally realize they need Christ.

For several years I was chaplain for the Chicago Bears and taught a weekly Bible study at Halas Hall, where they practiced. One player used to walk by the door, shake his head and wink at me, and then move on. One day I said to him, "You're on top of the world right now. You've got all the money and fame you could ask for. So you go by and wink, and think I and the rest of the guys in there are fools." He just smiled.

I said, "I'm not trying to be a prophet of doom, but sometime the roof is going to cave in on your life. All of a sudden you're going to realize you don't have it all. When that happens, call me."

Three weeks later, he called. "My only brother just had his first child. It was born deformed. My brother's devastated, and so am I. I don't know what to do or say. Can I talk to you?"

With the currently satisfied, our best strategy is to advertise our availability for the day they realize their need.

PATIENTLY LET THE SPIRIT WORK

Bill Hybels speaking on patience is like Imelda Marcos speaking on frugality. But I've had to learn to be patient, to preach on discipleship and allow the Spirit to bring it to pass.

Becoming wholly devoted is a process. Colossians 1 says people need to become complete in Christ, but 1 Corinthians 3:1–4 reminds me that they start out as spiritual babes. My responsibility is not to push the growth but to monitor the diet. Does the menu I'm offering provide the nutrition that will lead them to maturity? Is the diet too meaty, so that it chokes them? Or is the diet junk food that tickles the taste buds but fails to sustain health?

All believers ultimately should abandon themselves to full commitment to Christ. However, all believers cannot do that at the same pace. Some people in our body are, by temperament, timid and methodical. If they take tennis lessons, they go forty-five minutes a week, and in eight years they'll play a good game. When it comes to full commitment to Christ, they follow the same pace. They're not fighting God or being rebellious; their slow progression toward commitment is in keeping with the overall speed of their lives. With them, I have to slow down and move accordingly.

Other people are just the opposite. Not long ago, a man wrote to me: "I own two businesses. I became a Christian at one of your services two weeks ago. I have already found two men to run my businesses. I am ready to devote the rest of my life to serving at Willow Creek Community Church. Call me."

We called him immediately—to make sure he wasn't moving too fast. His speed made us nervous, but some people are like that by nature. He probably knew his wife a week before he proposed!

Because of these differences in personality, I never say, "Decide by next Sunday." Ultimatums and specific time frames may not be consistent with individual temperaments. Instead, I say, "You've heard truth from Scripture today. Please don't be hearers only, but doers. As for me and my house, we've decided to do this (whatever I'm preaching). You, too, have decisions to make. May the Holy Spirit have freedom in you as you make the right ones."

BE READY TO LIVE WITH OPPOSITION

I must point out a painful fact of pastoral life. Preaching sold-out Christianity draws the disapproval of snipers who will try anything to persuade us to lower the standard.

Halfhearted believers respond to messages on total commitment the way rebellious sinners respond to messages on repentance. Suppose you stood before one hundred thousand kids at a rock concert and said, "You're on the wrong road. Please reconsider the direction of your life. Fall to your knees, repent of your rebellion against God, and receive Christ as your Savior." You can bet you'd see hostility.

I've found similar resistance when I've challenged halfhearted, cosmetic Christians to be dedicated completely to Christ. Whenever you expose someone's addiction to gratification, you can expect a defensive reaction.

Pastors feel it. We preach a tough message on discipleship, and the reaction tells us it's "thirty-two degrees and falling." The next week we preach on rebuilding self-esteem, and suddenly it's "eighty-five degrees and sunshiny." What are we inclined to preach about the third week?

How do people couch their resistance? "You're being too harsh. You're being unrealistic. We're not ready for that yet. What about 'God loves you as you are'?" If I didn't have support from my elders, I couldn't keep it up, because sometimes the resistance gets too strong.

Not long ago we surveyed our committed core people. One question we asked was, "Are you using your spiritual gift in this body for God's glory on a weekly basis?" About 53 percent said they were. Scripturally, that's not good enough. So, in a message I cited that statistic and said, "I thank God for those of you who are using your spiritual gifts. And I pray for those of you who have been so deeply wounded in the past that you need a time of healing before you can begin to serve. But to the rest of you, I have to ask a tough question: What's going on? If you've been redeemed and welcomed into the family of God, you should be lying awake nights thinking of ways to show God your gratitude. One way you can do that is by identifying and using your spiritual gift. If you're not doing that, something is wrong!"

I have to confess I even used the word *parasites* for people "who eat and run, who enjoy the benefits of the body of Christ but don't contribute to its well-being."

One of the elders stopped me afterward and said, "Great word. It had to be said." I needed that kind of support, because the next day the missiles started arriving in the mail: "Just because I choose not to serve in this body does not make me a parasite."

"You had no right to pressure us that way."

"You're an egomaniac who thinks you can tell everybody else how to live."

I answered every letter and offered to talk further. I did, however, affirm my understanding of 1 Corinthians 12: If you claim to be a part of the body, then you need to function as a part of the body.

The point is, when we feel we have to confront the congregation, that's when we need to be surrounded by elders who can say, "That's the right message, given in the right spirit. Don't let the missiles get to you."

Because of that, I alert the elders when I'm thinking of preaching a particularly challenging message. Sometimes they say, "Bill, that sounds more like your personal pet peeve than our collective concern. Be careful." Then I usually drop the issue or wait until I have a better perspective on it.

Other times, they confirm my desire to preach the message, and I can step into the pulpit with confidence.

WHY I KEEP PREACHING THIS MESSAGE

What helped me overcome my hesitation to preach the genuine, all-or-nothing gospel of Christ? The realization that living a genuine, all-or-nothing life for God is the only path to satisfaction.

Every day I journal, write out my prayers, and resubmit myself to God. I say with the hymn writer, "Take my life and let it be consecrated, Lord, to thee." Or, "You are the Potter; I am the clay. Hold over my being absolute sway." Then, with the help of the Holy Spirit, I try to follow those commitments during the day.

I have never regretted my attempts to be yielded to God. In fact, my times of greatest yieldedness have been my times of greatest joy. They've prompted me to ask with the psalmist, "What can I render to the Lord for all of his benefits to me?"

By contrast, I have paid dearly for the times I have *not* been yielded, when I've been self-willed, carnal, rebellious, or timid. Remembering that helps me when I reach the point in the message when I call people to full commitment to Christ. It's easy to feel tentative when I realize I may be asking a man to give up a six-figure income, or a woman to forsake a relationship she depends on, or a teenager to be rejected by his peer group. The evil one clouds my mind and makes me think I shouldn't lay such heavy challenges on people.

Then I remember: It's in total commitment that we find the blessedness, peace, thrill, and adventure we were meant to enjoy. It's in the pursuit of radical discipleship that we experience the constant companionship and smile of God. Remembering that makes me want to shout from the mountaintops, "The best thing you can do is drop to your knees right now and say, 'Lord, here I am, wholly available. I pour myself out for you.'"

I've never met anyone who regretted his or her decision to become a devoted Christian. I could fill a stadium, though, with people who shipwrecked their lives because they refused to respond to God's call. People write me saying, "If only I could roll back the clock; if only I hadn't been obstinate in my relationship with God; if only I'd listened."

Radical commitment to Jesus Christ is a tough challenge, but it leads to life in all its fullness. Since we know that's true, we need to ask ourselves only one question: Will we shrink back from calling people to do what will serve them best and give God the most glory, or will we be faithful servants who speak the powerful, life-changing truth?

Chapter 181

SPEAKING INTO CRISIS

What we can learn from two pastors—Bonhoeffer and Thielicke— who ministered in terrible times

Gordon MacDonald

I have long been romanced by the story of Paul's bold intervention among the soldiers and sailors in charge of a ship that is breaking up in the middle of a Mediterranean storm. Having exhausted their routine responses to severe conditions, they had given up hope of being saved.

Enter Paul! "Men," (and I'm paraphrasing here) "you should have listened to me earlier when I said not to leave port, but you didn't. But don't be afraid. I've received a word from God. The good news is that no life is to be lost; the bad news is that the ship has made its last voyage. Keep courageous, men; God will do as he's promised."

Here was a voice speaking confidently into crisis, offering a message that steadies people and provides reliable direction. It's an apt subject for our times in which people are scared, wonder about the future, and speculate on their personal security. Not always the most important issues, ultimately, but nevertheless the ones on people's minds.

In times of crisis, people listen for a voice.

They're tuned to receive messages of hope, courage, God's purposes, and meaning. Augustine's was such a voice when Rome was coming apart. Luther's was heard when the Holy Roman Empire was crumbling. Wesley's spoke into the turbulent times of industrial revolution.

More recently two insightful voices spoke into the crisis in Germany during the 1930s and 1940s. Amid the economic, political, and military upheaval, only a few stood to speak for God—among them, Dietrich Bonhoeffer and Helmut Thielicke. The two stand like human bookends at the beginning and the end of World War II. Bonhoeffer's greatest years were from 1932 to 1945 while Thielicke ascended to his prime in the mid-war years and those that followed.

It was given to Bonhoeffer to warn the German people of the political and moral consequences should they select Hitler as their national leader and then follow him to his grave. Thielicke's task was to challenge the German people to the task of spiritual and moral reconstruction. Both men did their jobs admirably.

THE COST OF DIETRICH'S DISCIPLESHIP

In 1933, just two days after Hitler became Chancellor of Germany, Bonhoeffer preached on the radio, warning of a leader "who allow(s) himself to succumb to the wishes of those he leads, who will always seek to turn him into their idol, then the image of the leader will gradually become the image of the 'misleader'.... This is the leader who makes an idol of himself and his office, and who thus mocks God."

Bonhoeffer was cut off the air as he spoke, presumably by Hitler sympathizers, and he was forced to publish the talk in print to make sure that his audience heard everything he had to say. But he'd made his stand, and soon there were those who questioned his patriotism.

His preaching and his instruction to student preachers took on an increasingly confrontive tone. "Do not try to make the Bible relevant," he said. "Its relevance is axiomatic.... Do not defend God's Word, but testify to it.... Trust to the Word. It is a ship loaded to the very limits of her capacity."

Bonhoeffer's greatest books came out of this era. *The Cost of Discipleship* calls for one to pursue the selfless life; to use a more modern phrase, Bonhoeffer was trying to say, "It's not about me!"

"The cross is laid on every Christian," Bonhoeffer wrote. "As we embark upon discipleship ...we give over our lives to death."

In 1939, Dietrich Bonhoeffer visited New York, and friends in the church world passionately tried to keep him there for fear that if he returned to Germany, he would lose his life. But Bonhoeffer chose to sail back to Germany. "I will have no right to participate in the reconstruction of Christian life in Germany after the war if I do not share the trials of this time with my people," he said.

"Christians in Germany will face the terrible alternative of either willing the defeat of their nation in order that Christian civilization may survive, or willing the victory of their nation and thereby destroying our civilization. I know which of these alternatives I must choose; but I cannot make that choice in security."

In the wartime years that followed, Bonhoeffer's logic led to relationships with people (including members of his extended family) who plotted to take Hitler's life. When they were almost successful, many were arrested throughout Germany, including Bonhoeffer, and he spent his last years in prison before being executed at Flossenburg in 1945, shortly before the war ended.

Even in prison, Bonhoeffer was ever the preacher. At one point he reflected on the hope generated in a fresh Christian marriage. "Welcome one another, therefore, as Christ welcomed you, for the glory of God," he quoted from the Scriptures, then expounded: "In a word, live together in the forgiveness of your sins, for without it no human fellowship, least of all a marriage, can survive. Don't insist on your rights, don't blame each other; don't judge or condemn each other, don't find fault with each other, but accept each other as you are, and forgive each other every day from the bottom of your hearts."

The larger significance of these comments is that Bonhoeffer never accepted the notion that life is only about the crisis. Rather, life goes on, and the more hopeful, new-start-oriented statements we can make—like marriage—the better.

Bonhoeffer was one tough preacher, and he called people to resistance against evil, to courage, to nobility of life and witness, and to pure fellowship among Christ-following people.

"Who stands fast?" Bonhoeffer wrote in

1943. "Only the man whose final standard is not his reason, his principles, his conscience, his freedom, or his virtue, but who is ready to sacrifice all this when he is called to obedient and responsible action in faith and in exclusive allegiance to God—the responsible man, who tries to make his whole life an answer to the question and call of God. Where are these responsible people?"

Bonhoeffer was even preaching when they came to take him away to the place of execution. In his last hours, he was asked to speak to the prisoners. At first reluctant, Bonhoeffer relented. The text, from Isaiah, was "by his stripes we are healed."

Then he was led to the gallows, where after his execution, his biographer records, "his body was taken down and burned, along with his suitcase and manuscript." His manuscript! Bonhoeffer never stopped preaching and writing, even in the worst of times.

SERMONS IN A BOMBED-OUT CHURCH

If Bonhoeffer's calling was to warn the German people of the consequences of Hitler's political philosophy, Helmut Thielicke's calling was to sustain people through the war and then to help them rebuild their lives spiritually and morally afterward.

In 1936 Thielicke was awarded a professorship at the University of Heidelberg. But four years later he lost his position when the Nazis became sensitive to his growing criticisms of the Hitler regime. He eventually moved to St. Mark's Church in Stuttgart, where he preached despite changes in venue from week to week because of damage from Allied bombing. John Doberstein, Thielicke's English translator, says that, after each sermon, "hundreds of volunteer

stenographers remained and took down dictated excerpts, which they then duplicated privately. Printing was forbidden, but these copies of the Christian message, handed from person to person, found their way to thousands of eager readers."

At one point during the war Thielicke felt in desperate need of rest. He reasoned that some weeks spent in a quiet village in the countryside would be good medicine. Yet the retreat to the country failed to restore him, and he soon returned to the city. Yes, the village had been peaceful. But something was missing, which left him restless.

He concluded that people in the village were of a different mind, not deeply touched (yet!) by the war. And he craved to return to the city where people were clawing for survival. Among them he found a spiritual strength and vitality that was far more restorative than the "escapist" life of the countryside. So Thielicke returned to the bombs, the damage, and the suffering, because there he found reality and courage and community. That became the seedbed of much of his preaching.

"I have been interested in the theological question of what change takes place in a man," writes Thielicke, "when he finds God and so also finds himself. For of one thing I was always sure, that when a man seeks himself, he fails to find himself, and that he gains and realizes himself only when he loses his life in God."

He was bold when he called men and women to Christ. "I believe," he said, "that one can do justice to the seeker only if one leaves him under no illusions about the existence of a steep wall at which decisions must be made. He must be led to face the granite greatness of a message that brooks no evasion."

In another place: "Anybody who looks

downward and measures himself by the weaknesses of his fellow men immediately becomes proud." And again: "When a man really turns to God with a burdened conscience, he doesn't think of other people at all. There he is utterly alone with God."

Are his comments out of date? Or do they call us back to something that may be lost in our time of sermons that smack more of self-help than deep-spirited and thoughtful gospel? When we look for the voices that have spoken out most eloquently and spiritually since September 11, will we hear any of the substance that these two "bookends" gave to the German people?

Some time after the war Thielicke visited the United States and toured the United Nations building in New York. When he was shown the "chapel" in the UN building, he was appalled. It was a room decorated by spotlights and little else.

> The spotlights were ignorant of what they were illuminating, and the responsible men who were invited to come to this room were not shown to whom they should direct their thoughts. It was a temple of utterly weird desolation, an empty, ruined field of faith long since fled. . . . Only here, where the ultimate was at stake, only here was emptiness and desolation. Would it not have been more honest to strike this whole pseudo temple out of the budget and use the space for a cloakroom or a bar?

The man was a prophet.

WHAT DO THEY SAY TODAY?

What can we say of these two World War II "bookends"? Certainly they in fact did speak into their crises. They were tough on their hearers; they expected much from the people to whom they preached and wrote. Their preaching was not parochial, pandering to the fears and superficial patriotism of their people, and they were willing to accept the consequences that came from proclaiming biblical truth.

For Bonhoeffer, this meant not just proclaiming but living out the message that ministry is more important than security. Instead of escaping the place of danger, he stayed where he could do the most good and paid the ultimate price for doing so.

Likewise, I hear Thielicke saying that the greatest preaching is most likely to come from the lips of a preacher who suffers alongside his or her people. We are not called—neither preacher nor hearer—to run fearfully from affliction or to curse it (and those who cause it), but rather to stand and face it, to squeeze from it everything God might like to say to us.

Speaking into crisis means focusing on themes such as:

- hope because people wonder if there is a tomorrow
- courage because people succumb too easily to fear
- nobility in the normal Christian life because living for the glory of God is our calling every day, but especially in times of crisis, and because loving (and forgiving) one's enemies is imperative
- repentance in those circumstance where we have come across as an arrogant and materialistic nation
- biblical justice because so few of us really understand what it is
- what substantial prayer looks and sounds like—praying for the leaders of this world, for peace, for those who suffer far more than we do

But the most important theme to speak into crisis is theological at its base. It is to preach the sovereignty of a great and powerful God, of a

Christ who weeps over the city (or the country, and not ours only) and who longs to come again to create a new heaven and a new earth. This kingdom-dream leaps off the pages of Scripture from beginning to end and tells us that life and relationship will be better, much better than we know today, when everyone shall bow to confess him as Lord of All.

What a day that shall be! And what a privilege to preach about it in the midst of crisis.

Chapter 182

WHEN THE NEWS INTRUDES

What do you say from the pulpit about national crises and tragedies?

Eric Reed

When President Kennedy was assassinated November 22, 1963, Walter Cronkite interrupted "As the World Turns" with the tragic announcement.

Pastor Gene Boutellier climbed the tower of his Fresno church and began pulling the bell rope. Much later, exhausted from his tolling, he descended and found the sanctuary full of weeping people. Tear-streaked faces turned upward, wondering what he would say. Boutellier told his story to Joseph Jeter Jr. in *Crisis Preaching* (Abingdon, 1998). The scene was repeated the following Sunday in virtually every church in the nation. People needing hope turned to their pastors. Preachers of that generation called it "The Sunday with God."

When President Kennedy's son died in a plane crash in 1999, the news media climbed their towers and sounded the alarm. After witnessing a week of nonstop coverage, pastors ascended their pulpits wondering, *What should I say? Should I say anything at all?* And if they're like me, they wondered, *How do I preach to the endless tide of natural disasters, terrorist attacks, celebrity deaths, and political intrigue? Why does this seem to be happening so often?*

Preaching At the Speed of Satellite

I watched the famed low-speed Bronco chase from a Holiday Inn in Tallahassee, Florida. Returning home from a week-long vacation, I had turned on the television to see what my congregation might be talking about. What I found was a major shift in the way news is processed and presented.

With their interminable reportage of O. J. Simpson's murder trial, the networks discovered an insatiable public appetite for the mindless repetition of scanty facts. With the proliferation of satellite news channels and up-to-the-minute online news, tragedies once distant now unfold without interruption in our living rooms and offices. And senseless acts, once given some context by those reporting them, are increasingly presented raw, leaving listeners the endless task of sorting and weighing headlines.

Are there more wars than there used to be?

Or is it that we all have cable access to every rumor of war? Are the earthquakes more severe? Or are we harder rocked by sensurround accounts of them? Whichever the case, the world as seen on TV makes less sense than it ever has. Do parishioners with countless hours of news and analysis rumbling around in their heads come to church on Sunday hoping that the preacher will make sense of it all?

TO SPEAK OR NOT TO SPEAK

As a journalist turned pastor, I have regularly used the news to illustrate my sermons, but only once have I preached a whole sermon on a news event. In one memorable week, our city was shaken by the drive-by shootings of several children, one of them in our neighborhood; a suspected drug dealer was found slain execution-style four blocks from our church; and police reported that New Orleans once again led the nation in murders. I had to address the fear that gripped us all.

We must deal with tragedies when they are our own, but even if they are distant, terrorist attacks or faraway wars may force the preacher to reconsider the sermon schedule. If my conversations with pastors are any indication, few are comfortable doing so.

Timothy Keller pastors Redeemer Presbyterian Church in Manhattan. "Some of my folks here have said they wish I'd talk more about current events," he says candidly. "I'm not sure I'm wise enough to pull it off."

Keller has two concerns. One is that the news will overshadow his message: "When you talk about something that is making headlines, the illustration becomes the point," Keller tells his listeners, including non-Christians. "They want to hear eternal truths, not an interpretation of news events." He wonders too about the unreliability of early reports. He usually waits a year or more before referring to a news event. "It often takes months to get perspective," Keller says.

Keller points to the sermons of the old masters as examples. The only sermons of Jonathan Edwards and others that seem irrelevant now are those preached about national events, Keller says. "It is remarkable how poorly reasoned those sermons are. That is what originally made me hesitate about preaching on current events."

"But who says a sermon has to last for five hundred years?" counters Joseph Jeter Jr., professor at Brite Divinity School at Texas Christian University and author of the book *Crisis Preaching*. "All of us would like to preach a five-hundred-year sermon, but it would have to be a very general sermon."

In his research, Jeter found many preachers who refused to speak to news events. "Some said they don't know what to say; others don't want to sensationalize. But if your people bring to church a concern they're confused and disturbed about and nothing is said, that is like looking for bread and getting a stone." Choosing to address a news event requires discernment: of the likely lasting impact of the event, of the emotional needs of the congregation at the moment, and of the Spirit's leadership in sermon preparation.

LESSONS LEARNED

A tornado ripped through Goshen (Alabama) United Methodist Church during the Easter drama on Palm Sunday 1994. The building just exploded, says Pastor Kelly Clem, burying worshipers crowded in the sanctuary under three feet of rubble. When the debris was cleared, twenty were dead, including Clem's four-year-old daughter Hannah. The media descended on the tiny community outside Birmingham.

"They asked us 'Why?'" Clem says. "Isn't the sanctuary supposed to be safe? Isn't this going to shatter your faith?" And the larger and harder question: "Why would God let this happen to a church? During the crisis is not the time to ask the why question," Clem goes on. "The real question is 'What am I going to do with the life I have today, with the family members I have today, with the church I have today?'"

Clem's words to her congregation on Easter morning a week later spoke to the need of the moment: How can we be the comforting church when we're all suffering? Help with the why question came later.

The pastor's temptation in a crisis-prompted sermon is to offer answers. Although the people may say they want answers, what they really need is help dealing with overwhelming emotion.

A little more than six months after the shooting deaths of fifteen students at Columbine High School, nearby West Bowles Community Church continued to wrestle with the catastrophe while at the same time watching a great revival in Littleton and in their church. "Some wanted to make sense of (the deaths)," says Pastor George Kirsten. "I don't think we can. Others would say, 'Where can I turn? Is there any hope? Is there any comfort?' That's the issue we addressed loud and clear."

Kirsten's church became a clearinghouse for wise counsel. Many Columbine students came to West Bowles two days after the shootings to talk through their trauma. They didn't seek out the counselors sent by the school system,

according to Kirsten, but went instead to other teens, youth from the church who were willing to listen and to cry with them.

Both Kirsten and Clem approached the preaching task as fellow strugglers. They expressed what their people were feeling and what they themselves were feeling. "Sometimes that's all we can do—cry with our people," Jeter surmises.

Craig Barnes calls this "emergency room talk." Barnes, an author and pastor, recommends the E.R. approach to emotionally wrenching crisis. "You don't do a lot of constructive theology in emergency rooms. You just remind people that we live in the hands of God, and that's a wonderful place to be. The constructive preaching comes in the second wave."

BREAKING NEWS CAN WAIT

"Crisis rips the veneer off," Barnes says. "It can be very helpful." Yet in twenty years of pastoral ministry, Barnes counts only a handful of occasions when national news became sermon fodder. Most he treated briefly—the deaths of Princess Diana and Mother Teresa in the same week produced two paragraphs to close a message on the cost of following Christ.

Pastoring for nine years in the nation's capital, Barnes felt pressure to speak to the news. He resisted. For many months he refused to address the investigation that led to the impeachment of the president. "I told my congregation I was taking the high road, but when everything finally came out, I had to speak."

News anchor Peter Jennings called while Barnes was preparing his sermon. "He was taking a survey on how churches were handling it. He wanted to know whether I was calling for the head of the president or the head of the special prosecutor. Those were my only two options.

"I explained that the gospel is a little bit larger than that. My intent in this kind of sermon is to transcend the options. I want to say something that is clear and useful as people work their way through the issue. The crisis sermon should draw them to Jesus as Savior as opposed to leaving them with the 'right' answer.

 For an audio example of this principle see tracks 22–23 on the supplemental CD.

"We live for those moments when we can stand on the stump and say, 'I have a word from the Lord.' If it's truly the word of the Lord, then it's not just for the president or the prosecutor. It's for all of us."

The preacher's temptation is to exegete the crisis rather than the Scripture. Barnes avoids this by starting with his congregation's emotions and moving quickly to the text.

"All preaching has to maintain both sides of that sacred conversation," Barnes says. "You have to tell the Lord how it is down here. The people need to hear that. They need to see you as Moses, as the person who is speaking on their behalf before the Lord, in order also to hear the word of the Lord from you."

For the most part, Barnes sticks to his preaching plan. He has found that his text, selected as much as a year in advance, has spoken to the need on the few occasions when he has preached on a crisis. Like Keller, Barnes usually waits awhile before referring to traumatic events. "There are some pretty heroic stories that emerge in the second wave of media coverage. I think there is more valuable information there for the preacher."

While crises that directly affect the local church must be addressed immediately, others, more often national or world events, can wait until more information is available and the lasting impact of the event has been determined. A real crisis will still merit attention in a few weeks or months. Until then, inclusion in the pastoral prayer will suffice to acknowledge awareness of the congregation's feelings.

Other crises—and many of the incidents generating nonstop news coverage fall in this category—are simply distractions.

GRIEVING FOR PEOPLE YOU DON'T KNOW

"I'm surprised by how much that hurts me," my wife said, some months after the death of John Kennedy Jr.

"That it hurt at all? Or that is still hurts?" I asked.

"Both, I guess. I see their pictures at the magazine stand, and I ache, deeply. Some celebrity deaths you expect to affect you. Diana, certainly. [My wife had stayed up overnight so she would not miss the royals' wedding on television.] But I didn't expect to feel this one."

I understood her feelings. In our star-eyed culture, we keep electronic vigils by many bedsides, and the deaths of people we've never met become very real to us. Our listeners need help mourning losses both real and imagined. But do tragic, widely reported deaths merit attention from the pulpit?

Some instances should be referenced, but most are distractions from the real issues, according to Argile Smith, preaching professor at New Orleans Baptist Theological Seminary. "What separates them from truly catastrophic events is that they are everyday events that happen to famous people." People are born, live, and die, and except for their fame, most would not make the news. Neither should they make the pulpit.

Still, Smith admits, the emotions of his listeners must be considered. "I had prepared to preach on death and resurrection one Sunday. The night before that sermon, Princess Diana was killed. Because that was what everybody was talking about, I scrubbed my introduction and started with her death. The message wasn't about Diana, but it spoke to some things people were thinking about."

Smith is watchful when invoking the names of the famous. "Be careful not to make value judgments on dead people or speculate on their salvation," he warns. "The preacher can help his congregation with their emotions without expressing opinions about the deceased." In other words, don't say anything you wouldn't say at the celebrity's funeral. In time, Smith says, the preacher develops an internal mechanism for deciding which events are worth talking about.

THAT'S THE WAY IT REALLY IS

The danger of preaching to the crisis too frequently is that the temporal rather than the eternal begins to drive the preaching schedule. The preacher becomes reactionary, Chicken Little in the pulpit. On the other hand, ignoring crisis, whether real or perceived, may be seen by our listeners as failure to speak to their needs.

By preaching appropriately when the news intrudes, we can show our listeners that God still cares and that he can still be trusted even in catastrophe's aftermath. Our goal, always, is to help people view the issues of life and death in the light of Christ. "If this world is going to make sense," Smith says, "it will only be when we see it through the eyes of Jesus."

Chapter 183

REDEMPTIVE SERMONS FOR WEDDINGS AND FUNERALS

When the sermon is the last thing on your hearers' minds

Stephen N. Rummage

One honor of being a minister is to be welcomed into the lives of people during deeply personal moments. One such honor is preaching sermons for funerals and weddings. These messages are different from almost every other type of sermon because they are directed at specific people—the wedding party or the grieving family—as well as being intended for the larger congregation.

Though the services are vastly different in tone and purpose, the principles for preaching at weddings and funerals are surprisingly similar. As we prepare sermons for weddings and funerals, we should pray for a word from God that fits these unique people and this special day and strive to craft messages demonstrating the following qualities.

BIBLICAL CONTENT

When we are called upon to preach at a wedding or funeral, we are more than a master of ceremonies; we are God's messenger for that hour. We should resist the temptation merely to eulogize the deceased or to give the bride and groom commendations for a happy life together. While there is a time and place for the aforementioned types of speeches, our sermon should aim for a deeper purpose: to communicate a timely message from God's Word. Though the sermon for the wedding or funeral service will be short, it must be biblical.

PERSONAL APPEAL

Some aspects of weddings and funerals are present each time the services are performed. In every wedding, however, two unique persons are being joined together before God. We should honor the individuality of the bride and groom with a wedding sermon tailored especially for them. In the same way, each funeral sermon deserves a distinctive and personal treatment. Subjects and texts for sermons will be repeated, but we should avoid the impression we are pulling out an all-purpose wedding or funeral message from the file and reciting it once again, with only the names changed.

To make the sermon personal, we might include a brief mention of how the couple met, the couple's faith in God, or some other personal reference. The message should include application directed toward the couple, in which we address the bride and groom by name.

We can personalize a funeral service by quoting one of the deceased's favorite passages of Scripture or by relating an experience we had with the departed. We can share some of the family and friends' memories and impressions of the deceased. Even if we did not know him or her, we can gather personal remembrances from the family in preparation for the funeral. We should take care to refer to the deceased and the closest family members by name in the sermon.

The delivery of the sermon also can make the message more personal. Recognizing the emotional significance of these services, we should speak conversationally and with warmth. Though we might consider using brief notes in order to control the sermon's length, we should deliver the sermon with as much eye contact and empathy as possible.

Making the sermon special does not require preparing a message from scratch every time we preside at a wedding or funeral. In fact, the ceremonies may be better served if we modify existing messages that have been refined over time. One pastor makes it a practice to keep on file a dozen good funeral messages that clearly and concisely set out the Christian view of death and hope in Christ. He has preached some of these messages previously in regular church services but then condensed and polished them for use in funerals. Using this method allows us to prepare a personal message quickly, customizing the sermon to suit the particular occasion with relevant personal details.

ABBREVIATED LENGTH

Sermons for weddings and funerals should be relatively short. The sermon is not central in the attention of most who attend. Few people—

especially the bride and groom or the mourning family—go to these ceremonies thinking, *I wonder what the pastor will preach about today?* A well-planned wedding or funeral sermon *can* have impact on the listeners, however, if we bear in mind that the message tends to increase in effectiveness as it decreases in length.

In most cases, we should aim for the entire wedding or funeral service to last about thirty minutes. Ceremonial elements and music will require more than half of that time, especially for weddings. For that reason, the wedding sermon should be no longer than five to seven minutes. The funeral sermon can last a little longer, but generally should not exceed fifteen minutes.

A wedding sermon should normally not have multiple points. Instead, it is better to draw one major idea from a passage of Scripture, which we then explain, illustrate, and apply. For the funeral sermon, we may use a more conventional sermon outline. Even then, however, we should condense the sermon's content. Because listeners are unlikely to have Bibles with them at weddings and funerals, we should limit the details of technical exposition.

REDEMPTIVE PURPOSE

In many congregations, weddings and funerals are among the largest groups we address. Moreover, there are often greater numbers of non-Christians present for these occasions than at typical church services. Ultimately, the goal of wedding and funeral sermons should be the same as in any sermon—to point listeners to Jesus Christ. All of the biblical themes associated with wedding and funeral sermons can be readily connected to faith in God's Son. We should find opportunities to focus on Jesus throughout the sermon and to proclaim the redemption available through faith in Christ.

Chapter 184

THE LANDMARK SERMON

A clear word at the right time can keep the church from pulling apart

Jack Hayford

Whatever a pastor's position on wine drinking, it's not hard to marshal proof texts. And it's for sure some people will disagree with whatever conclusion you come to. Despite the disagreement I knew we'd uncover, several years ago I faced the need to deal directly with this subject with our "Servants Council," a group of several hundred key people in our congregation.

As I wrestled with the issue in my study, I felt the internal pressure of being responsible for these leaders and their influence on our whole congregation. They needed a shepherd-like spirit instilled in them for rightly guiding all whom they taught and touched. This had to be explained in a loving way, rather than legalistically. My heart whispered, *You better help them see this clearly. Most of our people are going to* decide what's right and wrong based on what you say and how you act.

I also was concerned with external pressure, about the larger Christian community, that others might pass judgment on me. I could hear some saying, "Hayford is soft on drinking" (for not declaring a teetotaling stance) or "Hayford is a legalist" (because I concerned myself with the issue).

Strong leaders are known for their landmark sermons (and sometimes lynched for them). Landmark sermons are the defining moments of a church and a pastor. Without them there are no boundaries, no banners in the sand; there is nothing to communicate vision and goals, policies and practices, beliefs and standards.

Like Joshua's landmark recitation of the law with its blessings and curses at Mount Ebal, landmark sermons are memorable, weighty, conclusive. Some will regard your landmark sermon as a familiar "oak tree" on the church landscape, guiding them in the way they should go; others, deeming the sermon a garish neon sign, will wish it didn't mark the land. But no one can ignore such sermons or their consequences.

THE PURPOSES OF LANDMARK SERMONS

Landmark sermons are highly visible for good reason. They tower above the normal weekly sermon because they accomplish at least one of six purposes.

To address questions that weigh on people's consciences. Ethical and theological questions bear heavily on many people.

Dozens of women who have had an abortion have committed their lives to Christ in our church, for instance. Sooner or later most accept God's forgiveness, but they wonder, *If that really was a person who was aborted, where is he or she now?* Their guilt and concern can be unbearable. Those who have suffered a miscarriage can raise the same question.

After counseling several women, I decided to preach a sermon on what happens to the soul of an aborted child. In a message titled, "Short-Circuited into Eternity," I took a clear sanctity-of-life stance but was not condemning. I made it clear that the child had not reached an age of accountability.

Many Christians worry in silence about other troubling issues: Have I committed the unforgivable sin? Will God forgive my divorce and remarriage? Can a "backslider" be forgiven? What if my job requires me to work on Sunday? Preaching on such subjects can clearly guide people through their confusion.

To prepare the congregation for a church project. Several years ago we purchased an eleven-million-dollar church complex as a second facility. Before I proposed this move, I preached for ten weeks in the book of Joshua on the subject "Possess Your Tomorrows." The main idea of this series—God promises us many things, but we have to move in and "possess" them—became part of the spiritual rationale for buying the property. Of course, it also encouraged individuals to "possess" what God had ordained for them.

Whether it's building a church, beginning more children's ministries, or launching small groups, people in the congregation need the motivation, insight, and challenge that can come only from their pastor's sermons.

To put landmark moments in biblical perspective. When the big earthquake hit San Francisco in 1989, I heard some say God was judging the homosexual community of that city. Landmark moments beg for landmark sermons, whether the issue is God's judgment, end-times prophecy, or the morality of war.

The week after the earthquake, I chose as my text Christ's comment on two tragedies: the collapsing tower of Siloam that killed eighteen and Pilate's mixing some of his victims' blood with their sacrifices. The consensus was that these victims were more sinful than others. But Jesus refuted the conventional wisdom (Luke 13:1–5).

My sermon's main point was, "If God is judging San Francisco, we all better dive under our chairs right now." I acknowledged that while such a catastrophe could be an expression of God's judgment, it is a mistake to conclude it happened because some people are more deserving of judgment than others. Although I had expressed many of that sermon's ideas in bits and pieces before, the landmark moment made it a landmark message.

To change policies. Over time, a church may shift its membership policies, leadership qualifications, positions on whom to marry or bury or baptize, or to whom to serve the sacraments. Such controversial topics beckon for a landmark sermon or series of sermons.

In the early 1970s, the predominant stance in my tradition had been that the Bible prohibits all divorced persons from remarrying. Wrestling with the whole truth of the Scriptures, being driven there by tough questions that were raised in my soul as I talked with broken people, I came to a different conclusion: that persons divorced prior to their decision to follow Christ were eligible for marriage on the grounds that their past was forgiven by God.

I preached a sermon on the subject on a Sunday night and concluded the message by performing the wedding of a couple who had each been divorced under those conditions. (Our policy, though, is not simplistic or arbitrary;

there are specific stipulations governing each situation.)

To confront cultural trends. A year after the PTL scandal and five weeks after Jimmy Swaggart's problems came to light, I decided to preach a sermon on restoring fallen leaders. I had heard so many advocate that because God forgives a fallen leader, his sins should not disallow him from continuing in ministry, that if he repented, he could continue in leadership without a period of probation. I challenged that.

In my sermon I made what I feel is a biblical distinction: God forgives us instantly, but being forgiven isn't the only qualification for Christian leadership. Being forgiven isn't the same thing as rectifying character. Scripture says that potential leaders must be tested and proven over time to see whether certain essential qualities are present in their lives. I concluded that a leader who violates the qualifications of leadership must again be proven and tested over time before being restored to a position in the church.

To bring healing at times of human failure. When a key member falls short of biblical morality, it shakes the church. Several years ago the daughter of one of our elders gave birth to a child out of wedlock. Later, when the issue of her immorality had been resolved, she asked for the child to be dedicated in church. We did so on a Sunday night. I preached a sermon on justice and mercy, asserting that we are obligated to stand on the side of mercy even when we run the risk of appearing to have sacrificed righteousness.

I concluded that sermon by calling the girl and her child forward, and the congregation joined me in dedicating this child to the Lord. No one felt standards had been sacrificed, and everyone recognized God's mercy was being manifest.

I also called to the platform the baby's grandfather, our elder. "John (not his real name) has submitted to the board his resignation as an elder," I announced. "We did not ask for his resignation, but he knew that at this time his family required his special attention, and so he did the right thing in submitting it."

There wasn't a dry eye in the place.

MISTAKES TO AVOID

Landmark sermons have their own special temptations. Here are some mistakes I try to avoid.

Sensationalism or exploitation. When the news first broke about Magic Johnson having the HIV virus, I considered preaching on sexual morality. The more I thought about it, though, the less I liked the idea.

It was a judgment call; many ministers did preach on it, of course, and I may have missed a landmark moment. But especially since I serve in the Los Angeles area where Johnson lives, I felt I would be sensationalizing the subject or capitalizing on someone else's tragedy.

To test whether I'm tempted to sensationalize a theme, I ask myself these questions:

- *Am I concerned with this theme mainly to draw a crowd or to truly edify the flock?*
- *Am I dealing with it substantively and biblically, or merely "grabbing a topic" and then glossing over the problem and only giving a superficial solution with a quick text or two?*
- *Is the issue crucial to the moment? Can I wait—should I wait—until a more profitable moment*

Giving the message to the wrong group. Some messages are suited for smaller circles within the church because of the differences between followers and leaders, males and females, children and adults, new Christians and mature Christians, the young and the old, the committed and the peripheral. What will be a landmark for a small group in the church may be irrelevant or confusing to some of the Sunday-morning-only attenders.

I did, in fact, deliver a message at the time of the Magic Johnson incident but only to our men's group. I felt the message was more appropriate there.

Imbalance. When I spoke to our leaders on the subject of wine drinking, I showed them the Scriptures that support both sides of the issue, but then I took my position: "I can't make a biblical case against wine drinking, but I feel this is one of those rare times when the Bible has a double standard for leaders and followers. That is why, personally, I have made a commitment never to drink alcoholic beverages of any kind."

I'm always concerned about touching all the bases and have found that people respond to that. Several of the elders in our church are attorneys, and some have specifically commented, "Pastor, I appreciate the way you cover all sides of these controversial issues. I feel we can make valid decisions because the whole case is presented." A balanced message shows respect for people's intelligence and confidence in their spiritual decision-making abilities. This doesn't mean I don't draw a conclusive point, but I do speak with respect toward positions I oppose.

KEYS TO EFFECTIVENESS

I have a strong sense of anointing as I prepare and deliver landmark sermons. I sense that these messages are more than simply teachings or exhortations; they're prophetic. I'm presenting the counsel of God conclusively and categorically on a critical issue.

Still, I recognize the human dimension. Many factors can make people more or less receptive to what I'm going to say. Here are some of the things I do to make my landmark sermons more effective.

Maintain the tensions. Our tendency is to try to resolve the dynamic tension of truth, to oversimplify or go to extremes. I have found, however, that the truth is found in tension.

Ten years ago one member of our singles group worship team had a recurring problem with severe depression. He took medication to counteract it, but at times he would neglect his prescription, and the chemical imbalance would bring terrible suffering. At one such time, he took his life—jumping off a building near downtown. Although only a fraction of the congregation knew him, he was a significant leader to enough singles that I felt I had to address the subject of suicide.

In my sermon, I emphasized the comforting grounds of our salvation—the grace of God and the death of Christ—but I also stressed our moral responsibility as stewards of God's gift of life. Such tensions may make landmark sermons controversial—but they also become inescapably confrontational and memorable.

Point to the overarching principles of Scripture. Universal principles are crucial to every issue, question, or problem that landmark sermons address. My job is to find the big picture in a particular situation, for overarching principles provide the deepest insights and broadest perspectives.

In 1990 and 1991 as the Persian Gulf crisis dominated the headlines, I preached on such issues as, "Does God Desire War?" "How Patriotic Should I Be When My Country Is at War?" "What Is My Christian Responsibility During a War?" I can't answer big questions about war without touching on great themes: how God views the nations and how God views secular authority. Landmarks are built with huge stones and deep foundations.

Take adequate time. There are no landmark sermonettes. My landmark sermons take an hour to an hour and fifteen minutes to deliver (I usually give them on Sunday night). When I'm preaching a definitive word, I can't be sloppy or shallow, and I can't be brief, superficial, or simplistic. I take pains to exegete Scripture, select and define terms, frame the big questions, and focus the issue. I distinguish carefully between what I mean and don't mean.

While preaching through a five-installment overview of the book of Ezekiel on Sunday nights, I decided to spend an entire sermon on chapter 18 (fathers and children should be punished for their own sins, not for the sins of the other). I had become increasingly concerned about the trend to rationalize our failings by blaming our family of origin or assigning blame for one's sin or immaturity to abusive people in the past. I frequently saw people using these ideas as an escape instead of vigorously pursuing a transformed life in Christ.

I didn't want to appear to oppose Twelve-Step programs or support groups (I don't). Nor did I want to seem impatient with spiritual "turtles," God's slow-grow children. But I did develop a fourteen-point contrast between God's system of healing and the world's system of healing (for example, "Justify or forgive yourself" versus "God has justified and will forgive you," and "Break codependence and liberate yourself" versus "Submit to repentance and God's deliverance"). When I gave the message, we distributed a chart summarizing the points.

Such thoroughness is also necessary when discussing awkward subjects. I once did a sermon about masturbation. Although I normally go to the pulpit with only an outline, for that sermon I wrote out nearly a full manuscript. The possibilities for unintentional double-entendres or awkward moments was so great, I spent the extra hours to ensure that I had not only the right ideas but the right words.

Although this is hard work for me—and the congregation—I have found that people will listen to a more didactic message patiently and with interest if they care deeply about the subject.

After my Ezekiel message, as I was preparing to dismiss the service, I leaned on the pulpit and said, "I need to tell you, at times like this I feel a real heaviness. I don't apologize for anything I said, but I'm sorry for keeping you so long tonight." The message was over ninety minutes, and virtually no one moved. After the service and over the following week, I received a flood of comments from people who appreciated my taking the time to do the subject justice.

Consider a series. Sometimes I just can't say all I need to in one sermon. So I occasionally preach a landmark series. Some especially nettlesome subjects are best approached in stages, that is, with months or years between sermons. I may need to nudge the congregation into the truth, to let them process the Scriptures one step at a time.

That's the way it turned out with my divorce and remarriage sermons. The first sermon addressed the subject of Christians divorced before their conversion; the second sermon, three years later, addressed rare instances when Christians divorced after their conversion may

remarry. I didn't calculate this development, but time and understanding helped people digest the teachings.

When appropriate, I branch off into related issues and application. Since so much groundwork has been laid, it's a perfect time to show how this subject relates to other doctrines and practices.

In the message from Ezekiel that addressed the family-of-origin "escape clause," I applied the truths about Christ's power to transform us to how and why we do "altar calls" and "altar services." We have found these times, when we call people to come to the front of the church to make or renew their commitment or for the laying on of hands, to be one of the most life-transforming steps a Christian can make. I was able to develop the subject more meaningfully than if I had preached "The Purpose of Altar Calls" as a standalone message.

Relieve the tension. Landmark sermons address serious, sensitive, sometimes awkward subjects. The tension can be exhausting both for me and the congregation. Relieving that tension two or three times in a long message can make the waters much easier to navigate, and that increases the congregation's ability to receive.

Discreet and timely humor not only breaks the tension but also keeps me human and personable. On the occasion I dealt with a particularly delicate sexual topic, I preceded it with a reading that illustrated the confusion of a camp director: A Victorian prude inquired too obliquely regarding the "Water Closet" (the restroom facilities) at the camp. The woman's undue caution in not risking suggestive speech set the scene for a hilarious exchange of letters; absence of directness brought no answer whatsoever. It set the atmosphere for me to be direct and also created a sense of "humanness" in the room as we approached a very human subject.

When humor would be inappropriate, I ask people to turn to their neighbor and repeat some positive affirmation. I began the suicide message by announcing to the congregation the title of my sermon and explaining about the death of the individual. I knew everyone was feeling heavy. So I said, "Although we're going to talk about the sin of suicide, I want to remind you that we serve a mighty and merciful God. I'd like for you to turn to the person next to you and gently say, 'We serve a mighty and merciful God.'"

As they said those words, all across the auditorium you could see faces relax somewhat and people shift into more comfortable positions. Everyone was emotionally better able to face what we had to talk about after that.

Sometimes we'll pause for fifteen seconds of praise and thanksgiving for some encouraging truth: "Let's take a moment and praise God for the hope of eternal life with Jesus."

Relate personal experience. Sometimes divulging personal experiences that triggered my message help make the sermon more personal, authentic, and powerful. When I discussed wine drinking with our leaders, I told them why. I was raised in a teetotaling environment. Years ago, however, I realized how moderate amounts of wine with foods such as pasta or red meat benefited my digestion. I occasionally drank a glass of wine for this reason.

One Saturday morning, about three years after I began this practice, two events changed my habits. First, early in the morning as I was in prayer, the Lord "spoke" clearly to me: I was no longer to drink wine. Nothing I knew of had prompted this "word" to me. It was pointed, and my response was absolutely unhesitant. But,

a few hours later the same day, I went to a counseling session not knowing why the wife of a young leader in our congregation had scheduled the appointment. She related how a Christian leader whom we both knew had gone to a restaurant with her husband, drank too much wine, and convinced her husband to think nothing of it. She was understandably troubled.

I didn't say anything to her about how the Lord had dealt with me just hours earlier, but the coincidence of those two events happening on the same morning was not lost on me. I felt God was unmistakably saying, "I'm dealing with you first."

When I recounted this to our leaders, I didn't mandate they act on the basis of my experience; I presented the Scriptures. But my story illustrated the heart of my message and showed how the Lord was teaching about the "cost" of leadership.

Choose the opportune moment. Since a landmark sermon is a prophetic moment, I can't pencil it on the calendar as I would any other message. Several factors signal when the time is ripe.

Sermons of mine that have proven to be landmarks have been delivered with a strong feeling for God's heart. Often we sacrifice God's love on the altar of his truth. But I have sought to bring both passion for God's holy truth (reflecting his righteous nature) and his endless compassion (reflecting his merciful and loving nature). If either is lacking, the message falls short.

As I prepare a landmark message, I also have a growing sense of anointing best described as a sense of mission and authority. Even before I come into the pulpit, I feel clothed with a mantle of grace to declare a vital word. The message, fully gestated, is ready for birth.

However, events may demand immediate

response. When that worship leader in our singles group committed suicide, I felt I had to bring that message within two weeks. World or local events also call for a landmark word on short notice. When responding to the headlines, I must hammer while the iron glows red.

Landmark messages are extraordinarily demanding. They strain my emotions and study time. They force me to wrestle with great issues. They draw criticism. And I know I will have to face some repercussion for people incorrectly following what I say (usually people who didn't listen to all I said).

Despite these pressures, however, as I prepare and deliver landmark sermons, I commonly have as deep a sense of God's presence as at any time in ministry. As a result, I view landmark sermons as one of the highlights of my pastoral ministry. Shouldering pressure is a small price to pay for a sermon that serves as a can't-miss-it, unshakable oak tree in our church for years to come.

Chapter 185

YOU HAD TO BRING IT UP
Every faithful preacher must sometimes raise controversy

Stuart Briscoe

I have twice passed out cards to my congregation with the following words: "I would like to hear a sermon no longer than ____ minutes on the subject: What the Bible has to say about _____." Self-appointed comics took advantage of this. One fellow said he'd like to hear a sermon no longer than five minutes on what the Bible says about God.

But many times people request the tough issues. People want to know if the Bible's message can stand up to modern pressures. I want to assure them it can.

It would be easier if we could preach a lifetime without ever touching on sin, morality, sexuality, lifestyle, or any number of other adrenaline inducers. Controversy makes preaching a more difficult proposition. But, as any pastor knows, a congregation needs the spicier issues if for no other reason than that God fills his Word with just such fare. However, a crisis is not inevitable. We can preach controversial topics without picking a fight.

TURN THE HEAT OFF AND THE LIGHT ON

We need to credit people with enough maturity to handle the balanced presentation of an issue. Over the years I've addressed the role of women, eternal security, Spirit baptism, various issues of sexuality, and the church and politics. I've concluded that what's crucial is not so much the topic as the method.

When diving into an area of controversy, I don't expect total agreement. That's why there's a dispute in the first place. People's belief systems are complex. Much more is at stake than the particular issue at hand. I recognize from the start that I'm probably not going to change anyone's mind.

Thus, I try to broaden thinking rather than change it. Although people probably won't budge from their position, they may at least acknowledge the other side. That's progress. Maybe, over the years, they will change. Maybe not. In any event, I agree with Oliver Wendell Holmes, who said, "Once a mind has been stretched by a new idea, it never returns to its original shape."

When I try to *change* people, however, I only add heat and dim the light. For instance, I have strong feelings about the way the talents of women have been wasted in the church. So I must be careful when I talk on the subject. People often say I feel this way because of the wife I have. I usually answer, "Has it ever occurred to you that I may have the wife I do because I feel this way?" That doesn't always go over too well!

Preaching out of anger may feel good at the time, especially when we've built up a good head of steam. But in the long run, it doesn't accomplish what we're after.

I also have to point out that I was at the same church for nearly twenty-five years. That gave me a level of credibility that a fresh seminary graduate doesn't have. I would think carefully before I preached controversial themes in my first few years at a church. It's a matter of sensing the needs and maturity of the congregation. But I never provoke controversy just for the sake of controversy.

Drumming up a controversial topic is not hard. Currently American Christians are debating the relationship between church and state. Some Christians believe the state is working its way into church matters and trying to take away freedoms. Others insist believers must be more politically active. The issue of abortion is a prime example: The extent to which the church should be challenging the state on its laws concerning abortion is highly controversial. In many instances, people's spirituality is measured by their level of involvement on this issue.

Recently I addressed this in a message on the church and politics. I opened by saying that the politics of many Christians are often more determined by economics than theology. I pointed out that we live in a particular country in a particular socioeconomic group and that people living in other countries in widely differing socioeconomic groups may look at the Scripture differently.

I gave an example: If we live in a comfortable, upper middle-class suburb in the Midwest, then we probably don't spend much time in the Old Testament where it talks about God's concern for the poor. But if we had grown up in an impoverished Asian or African country, we would. If we lived under a totalitarian regime or right-wing dictatorship, then it's quite possible we would be interested in what the Bible says about liberty.

To further provide context, I mapped out the historical background, from the days of the early church when the state controlled the church to the modern period where the church and state live in an uneasy relationship. I concluded that the church and the state should be separate but mutually respectful and influential. I also concluded the church should encourage individual Christians to recognize the limitations of participatory democracy and to exercise their Christian citizenship responsibly in a less-than-ideal situation. I gave specific ways they could do this.

I could tell I had touched a nerve that Sunday by the debate stirred in our congregation. Our church is filled with thoughtful people unafraid to debate controversial topics. In fact, that's one way I gauge the impact of my sermons: Does it generate discussion? Discussion is an indicator that the lights have been turned on.

Do Your Homework

Few controversies in the church are new. Whenever I touch on eternal security, I remind folks that if Whitefield and Wesley struggled with this for a lifetime, I'm not likely to end the debate in a thirty-five-minute sermon. However, if I prepare well, I at least can give them an overview of the issues involved. A preacher who handles controversial subjects must do adequate research.

To prepare for a recent sermon on values, I read *A Question of Values*, a book that delineated three ways people arrive at a system of values. One is the individualistic approach—the it's-nobody's-business-what-I-do approach. The second is what society thinks—for example, the Supreme Court's debate over defining pornography. It finally decided that pornography is that which offends local community standards. The third way is based on the assumption of a sovereign Lord, in whose character and nature reside absolute values.

In addition to *A Question of Values*, I also found helpful Robert Bellah's *Habits of the Heart*. Since in the last few years a tremendous amount of material on this subject has been published—in *Time*, *Newsweek*, and the *Atlantic Monthly*—there was no shortage of resources. Preaching effectively on controversial issues requires a lot of spadework.

Touch the Funny Bone

Humor is a tension-reliever, though you always run the risk of offending someone. Still, I like the odds, so I occasionally weave lighter stories and quips into a controversial sermon.

I recently preached on a passage that preachers either harp on or avoid: "'Therefore come out from them and be separate,' says the Lord" (2 Cor. 6:17). I spoke on the issue of separation. "What Paul meant," I said, "is that identification is clearly wrong—but that isolation is totally counterproductive." I explained how Christians often develop subcultures that determine what is and isn't appropriate separation.

To illustrate, I told the story of the Dutch elders who sent people to check on the moral condition of the American church. The observers were horrified. They reported to the Dutch elders that American women wore makeup and wore expensive clothes. The Americans also drove big cars, had carpets in the sanctuaries, and had a piano as well as an organ. It was obvious to the Dutch the tremendous amount of money Americans were expending on themselves. And as the old Dutch elders heard this report, some of them burst into tears—and the tears ran down their cigars into their beer.

One time that story backfired on me, however. Several people said, "Those Dutch elders couldn't be Christians because they smoked and drank. You're not suggesting they really were Christians, are you?"

Other times, though, humor has served me well. In the sermon I mentioned on church and politics, I ended it by saying, "The church playing politics is not unlike Michael Jordan playing baseball." That time, everyone laughed.

GIVE BALANCED TREATMENT

When I preach on a disputed topic, I think it's only fair to present more than one side. I don't mean setting up a straw man only to knock him down, but trying to present both sides with honesty and empathy.

Often, after outlining both sides of the issue, I can present what I feel is a biblical point of view. Other times I can't. In that case I challenge people to come to their own conclusion. I have to remind myself that these people believe the Bible. If I present what it says, then Scripture remains the authority over us all, and we all have to wrestle with the implications. If I set up myself as the authority, then they wrestle with me.

I preached on Ephesians 5, with particular reference to the phrase, "Wives, submit to your husbands." I struggled to prepare for the message, because in some extreme instances men abuse their wives and rationalize it based on this verse. And many women find any talk of submission distasteful.

So to be balanced, I first pointed out that in Ephesians 5:22, the Greek word "submit" is not there. Paul uses ellipses; the phrase is dependent on the previous verse, which says, "Submit to one another out of reverence for Christ." Literally, then, the passage reads, "Submit to one another out of reverence for Christ, wives to your husbands," which means it is appropriate to add *submit* in verse 22, but inappropriate to separate verse 22 from verse 21. Grammatically, you can't do that.

"Whatever it means that wives should submit to their husbands," I said, "it cannot be divorced from two other kinds of submission— both people submitted to the Lord, and both

submitted to each other. Now that puts it into an entirely different context." Careful exegesis helped me give what I believe is a more balanced view on the controversial issue of submission.

CONSIDER PASTORAL NEEDS

Whenever I preach a controversial topic, I try to keep in mind that more than theory is at stake. Real people in my congregation are struggling with the implications. Some have had abortions. Some are confused about homosexual desires. Some are alcoholics. I can't just leave the issue "out there." I have to think through the situation well enough that I can suggest a sensible course of action.

When I spoke on God's plan for marriage, I took into consideration the couples in the congregation who were living together out of wedlock. I could have told them it's simply not God's will. But I realized some of these couples have overextended themselves financially. They can save several hundred dollars each month by doubling up. In that case, they need to hear that the church will help them locate inexpensive housing.

Sure, they should separate anyway. But if I can communicate to them that I understand their situation, they're more likely to change.

I also try to remember that behind topics such as abortion, divorce, or child abuse is an enormous amount of pain. I must be sensitive to people's experiences without blasting them with the truth. It took a while to learn this.

When I started addressing touchy subjects, the issue of abortion was causing a great deal of turmoil. It seemed everyone in the church was discussing it. Although our members were in basic agreement, some were confused about the details and proper biblical response. I decided it was time to confront the issue, however controversial it might be.

So I studied the appropriate passages, read the current literature, and delivered what I thought was an inspiring message on the sanctity of life. I felt fine about it until I heard the honest reservations of a good friend. "You know," he said, "by the law of averages, you probably spoke to three or four unmarried women who were contemplating abortion." Then he said, "I feel that what you said this morning will only add to their dilemma."

I had powerfully challenged them to make the right choice but failed to show sensitivity to their painful situation and the shame they probably felt. I'd offered no help in dealing with the heavy responsibilities of carrying a baby full term. It was a vivid reminder of how easy it is to wound people with the truth. The truth can be cutting, but we don't have to be.

SEIZE THE OPPORTUNITY

I don't want to give the impression I announce controversial topics every month. If I did, I'd be guilty of sensationalism. I don't want my sermons to be the ecclesiastical equivalent of supermarket tabloids. Most of the time, I deal with controversial issues while preaching on some other subject.

When I did a series on the Israelites' settling of Canaan, we came to the passage in Deuteronomy that speaks of the sins of the fathers being passed down to the children. I saw this as a beautiful opportunity to address the trend in some church circles where parents are blamed for their children's faults and where people fail to take responsibility for their sin. When I preached on that topic, no one came expecting a controversial sermon, but they got one nonetheless.

I once preached a sermon based on Colossians 3:16 and Ephesians 5:19, which speaks of singing psalms and hymns and spiritual songs. I had to address the controversy over musical styles in worship. I said:

> In the sixteenth century, Zwingli would not allow any music. Luther had to have music but said it must be simple. Calvin said that only psalms should be sung but used modern music that was disparagingly called "The Geneva jingles."
>
> In the seventeenth century, Pietists said that there ought to be singing, but it needed to be unaccompanied. In the eighteenth century, Christians had orchestras, but no violins, because they were called "the devil's fiddle." In the nineteenth century, the organ came in and began to push the orchestra out.
>
> Then William Booth came along and said, "Why should the devil have all the best tunes?" so he started brass bands. The Scandinavians came over to America and brought guitars. In the twentieth century, the youth culture brought rock; from the South, we got folk music; the charismatics began to emphasize praise songs; and from Britain we got the celebration marches.
>
> So what is your position on what is appropriate for worship music? Is it based on your theology or is it based on taste?

Certainly preaching on controversial topics carries a risk. However, I've learned that if I ignore controversial issues, I also ignore a timely opportunity to argue for the relevance of Christianity. And that's an opportunity I don't want to miss.

Chapter 186

PREACHING ON CONTEMPORARY ISSUES

How to preach social trends and topics with wisdom

Grant Lovejoy

Preaching on contemporary issues can cover a lot of territory: modern medical technology and life, issues that arise through crises and catastrophes, social trends, public policy debates, and contemporary theological issues. In addition, there are issues that arise in a specific congregation that threaten its fellowship and witness but wouldn't be an issue elsewhere. We dare not be silent on such issues.

The process involved in preparing sermons on such issues begins by asking what our audience's relationship is to the issue. "What do they know about it? What is their involvement in this issue and the nature and extent of their involvement? How are they likely to react?"

Ask, too, how they view you and your ministry. Ministry depends to a great deal on your own credibility and trustworthiness. If you don't have that kind of trust, the chances of your making a significant impact are diminished. The issue may be important, but you may not be the right spokesperson, or this might not be the best time.

Then ask, "Is this an issue that would divide church members or affect your church's witness to the surrounding community?" The issue may still need to be addressed, but it is wise to choose carefully the hill you die on.

Obviously you ask, "What does the Bible say?" In fact, it would be best to think, *I'm not really going to preach on an issue, I'm going to preach on the Bible as it relates to this issue.* If a congregation perceives your message is rooted in the Bible, they are more willing to give you a hearing. But if the sermon resembles the editorial page with the Bible tacked on, they may treat it as only your opinion.

WHERE ARE YOU AIMING?

There may be a range of aims you are trying to accomplish when you preach on an issue. You may say, "I know my congregation holds a view that is not what a Christian should believe." You then may want to preach periodically on different aspects of the topic in order to move them through stages of change. Initially, get them to acknowledge, "There may be another view a Christian could hold." Then move them to the next stage, seriously considering your view as more truly Christian. In time, they may come to say, "Now I realized that what I've believed all along may not be right." Then you may be able to move them to actually endorse the view that is Christian. Finally, you may get them to accept it and to act in ways consistent with it.

You may find that your congregation is any place along that route and may want to target your sermon to accomplish one of those aims. Of course, there are times you also address issues of agreement, aiming to reinforce what they already believe.

CHOOSING YOUR ROLE

One way to help you plan a sermon on a contemporary issue is to ask, "What role do I envision myself playing as the preacher?" There are four possibilities.

First, there is the *principlist*, who talks about biblical principles: "Love your neighbor"; "as you would that others should do to you, do also to them"; "hate what is evil, cling to what is good." Sermons that remain at the level of abstraction allow the hearers connect the issue to the principle. The main risk of this approach is that the principlist may be viewed as irrelevant if the congregation isn't making the connections between the principle and the specific problem.

Second, the preacher can engage the issue more as an *analyst*. In this case, the sermon serves to pick the issue apart, trying to find strengths and weaknesses in one approach to the issue. This gives people more help in thinking Christianly about the issue but still requires them to think.

Third, the *catalyst* works especially well where there are people in the congregation who understand the issue better than the preacher does. The catalyst lays out general principles but then says, "Some of you are in a position to act on this. You have specialized knowledge or access to decision-making powers. You can, and ought to, do something about this."

The fourth role is that of the *strategist*, who not only knows what the problem is but plans on endorsing a specific course of action. In this mode, it is especially good if you can use the sermon to point people toward a specific ministry within your church or community that addresses the problem. It is frustrating to church members when the pastor moves them to get involved in an issue but doesn't give them

a way to apply what he's said. It's like a steam engine that builds a full head of steam but doesn't have any track: It can blow its whistle but can't move anything. However, when the action called for is in the realm of public policy and legislation, the only realistic options may involve compromise. When a preacher endorses compromise, some may say, "You have left the high idealism of Scripture and become a theological compromiser."

DOWN TO BRASS TACKS

Here are some principles that will help you tackle contemporary issues wisely.

Don't ambush people with a controversial subject. Most congregations don't like to be surprised. If speaking on a controversial subject, contact the church leadership and put an article in the church newsletter, saying, "Please be praying for me as I prepare to speak on such-and-such an issue in a couple of weeks." People may not agree with you, but at least you will not have blindsided them.

Keep the channels open. When you come to the end of a controversial message say, "I realize not all of you agree with this view; however, I believe it is a Christian view, rooted in Scripture. I'd be glad to talk with you about it, and I want to assure you that I love you, whether we agree on this or not." That kind of statement is powerful and important to retain your pastoral relationship. Also, if you haven't convinced them in this sermon, you want them to come back to continue the process; for most people, change will be a process.

Give people opportunity to interact. After a controversial Sunday morning message, for example, allocate time in the Sunday evening service for interaction, schedule a special class for the purpose, or invite letters or emails. Having an arena for discussion helps people feel they've had a hearing, and that enables them to live with disagreement more easily.

Use concrete, local examples whenever you can. To talk about world hunger is one thing. To talk about a guy named Bill in your community who doesn't have enough to eat helps bring it home. It helps people say, "I can't feed a billion hungry people across the ocean, but I could help Bill." "Think globally, act locally" applies here.

Use statistics sparingly and carefully. On many contemporary issues you can bury people in an avalanche of statistics. A few statistics used carefully are better.

Assume those who disagree with you are acting in good faith. Don't demonize those who happen to disagree with you. People usually will respect the preacher who says, "I believe you are well-intentioned and will do what's right when you understand what is right." That makes people more amenable to change. I like the adage, "Turn up the light and turn down the heat."

State what you are for as well as what you are against. So often in prophetic preaching we only condemn societal wrongs in the strongest language possible. While the prophets did that, they also used vivid, powerful language to describe the world as it could be. This will help Christians move beyond being viewed by society as largely negative and convey that we are constructive. So often we end too soon by saying, "These are all the things we are against, so cut it out." We're not clear on what *could* happen.

Martin Luther King Jr.'s sermon, "I Have a Dream," drew a lot of its power from this very thing. He said, "This is my dream. This is the day I'm longing for." He made that quite concrete, quite specific in its imagery, so people could say, "Oh yes, this is why we must change. We need what you are describing." The power to paint images of what could be if God's will were done give a drawing quality that is powerful and effective.

Chapter 187

PREACHING THAT OH-SO-DELICATE SUBJECT
Speaking about sex clearly and redemptively

Bill Hybels

I once had a professor who asked, "How often do you entertain thoughts about prophecy?"

One student answered what most of us were thinking: "About twice a year—once around Christmas, and again some time around Good Friday when I hear Isaiah 53."

"Okay," the prof replied. "Now, how many times in a given *day* do you have sexual thoughts?" Silence. The professor had accomplished his purpose. How many times do you hear biblically relevant preaching on human sexuality—something people are thinking about all the time?

That question stuck with me, and when I

began ministering with youth, I put his advice to work. After all, what's on the mind of teenagers?

But as I got older, it occurred to me that I was still interested in sexuality, even though I was married and pastoring a church and years removed from the hormonal battles of puberty. I know I'm not alone, because every time I preach on a sexual matter, the church grows quiet in a hurry.

Sex is on our minds. Anything that occupies that much of our thought life and powers that much of our personality ought to be addressed from the pulpit, because some of those thoughts are misguided and in need of God's correction. Not to preach about sex would be to desert my post at one of the most active battlefronts in our culture.

WHY RUSH IN WHERE ANGELS TIPTOE?

I realize preaching about sexual matters is fraught with possible problems. I could offend people. I might embarrass somebody, including myself. I might even distract the thinking of those listening.

Yet I can't ignore the topic. Marriages are struggling because of misleading information about this subject. Young people are making mistakes because they're getting behavioral cues from all the wrong sources. Singles are wrestling with sexual dilemmas. Sex is a subject begging for a clear Christian word.

For example, if we were to ask the married couples sitting in church on Sunday morning, "How many of you at this point in life are having a great physical relationship with your spouse?" my educated guess would be that 30 percent or less would say they have a vital relationship. If that's true, and my study and expe-

rience would say it is, 70 percent of deacons and Sunday school teachers and trustees and churchgoers and pastors are experiencing a measurable amount of sexual frustration.

People can tell themselves, *I'm not going to let my sexual frustration affect me.* But some way, somehow, sometime, it will seek an outlet. What I'm trying to do through my preaching and our other ministries at Willow Creek is to spark dialogue, because talking can be an acceptable outlet. I say, "Let's talk about it. Let's not let frustration build until someone runs off with a willing partner, because that's a terrible way to solve the problem." We're committed to talking about sex responsibly as opposed to ignoring it until it causes unnecessary damage.

I preached a sermon series titled "Telling the Truth to Each Other," and one sermon illustration told of a husband talking openly with his wife about the sexual frustration he was feeling in the relationship. That illustration telegraphed the message that it's legal in marriage to talk about sex in that way. Frustrations don't need to be pushed underground until they emerge in the wrong place. Yes, telling the truth can get messy and complicated, but we need at least to try. The response I read in the congregation was agreement. Talking about it from the pulpit, daring to bring sex into the open, gave them the sense that such communication could happen in their marriages as well.

My hope is that such frank talk on Sunday morning can lead to more open expressions throughout the week, so people can get the help they need.

Besides making sex a permissible subject of conversation, my overarching concern is that people understand human sexuality as one of God's good gifts, part of his grand design for us. I preach each week to non-Christians who are seeking Christ in our fellowship. Many have stereotyped Christians as rather Victorian—joyless, repressed people who think of sexuality as dirty and vulgar. I want them to know that sexual impulses—even strong ones—are not in and of themselves evil.

When I talk openly and without embarrassment about God's wonderful design for human sexuality, speaking positively and in a God-glorifying way, that's big news for many. It breaks open their stereotypes of dreary Christianity and accusatory preachers.

Of course, I continue on to explain that sexuality is a highly-charged, God-designed drive that we need to understand and submit to the lordship of Jesus Christ because it can be used for great good or enormous destruction.

DIRECT AND INDIRECT PREACHING

I preach about sex in two ways: directly and indirectly. If I'm going to do justice to the many aspects of human sexuality, I need to take a direct approach. I dive into the subject, develop it, explain it. That's why occasionally I'll devote a whole series of sermons to the subject.

For example, I have tackled such topics as sexual fulfillment in marriage, romance, unfaithfulness, homosexuality, sexual abuse, pornography, unwanted pregnancies, and sex and the single person.

However, although sex is not a taboo subject at Willow Creek, I do limit the subjects I cover. Because I have many young ears present in worship services, I have never approached topics such as masturbation or sexual experimentation by married partners or sexual aberrations. These are doubly volatile since perhaps 90 percent of parents have never talked with their

children about such topics. I don't want to be the first to bring them up with children present. That would violate the parents' rights. Instead, I encourage people to read suggested books on the topics or to stay after the services and talk with me or one of our counselors. And in private settings like that, people will be candid.

The second method I use in preaching about sexual topics is more indirect, what I call maintenance statements. These I sprinkle through the rest of my preaching to remind people. In the midst of a sermon on, say, the woman at the well, I'll throw in a maintenance statement: "The woman was floundering; she had lost the meaning of faithfulness to her spouse, just as she had never known faithfulness to her Lord."

This double-pronged approach keeps me from thinking, *I handled human sexuality in that sermon on David and Bathsheba.* I'm able to cover topics substantially through direct sermons and then reinforce my points continually through asides in other messages.

Even with ample reason to preach about sex, however, I still approach the pulpit with fear and trembling, because I know how difficult it is. But I've found help from five principles I've learned over the years.

Putting Sex in Perspective

Whenever I speak about sex, there is one impression I definitely do not want to leave—that misappropriated sex is the one sin the church and God cannot tolerate. I don't want to give it that kind of press, because I'm not sure Scripture does.

When I preach about illicit sex, I do call it a sin, as I do any other sin. I say it's wrong to break God's sexual code. But my main emphasis is on the downside of disobedience: Not "God will never forgive you for that!" but rather, "If you don't obey the Lord in this area of life, eventually you'll find yourself in deep weeds." I deemphasize obeying rules for rules' sake alone and emphasize instead the dire consequences of breaking God's rules. "God gave us the rules for our protection. You break them at your own risk. In fact in these days, you can die from promiscuity."

I paint as vivid a picture as I can of sexuality run amuck, and I never have a problem with attentiveness at this point. People have stumbled enough to know I'm not exaggerating. It's not uncommon for people to cry during such sermons. They know.

But then I always hit the positive side: "If you keep those benevolent rules and experience sex within God's well-defined boundaries, it can be a wonderful gift of intimacy and ecstasy."

Unfortunately, preaching this way isn't easy. It's relatively simple to preach against some sin, but I have to work overtime to develop positive and edifying messages on sexuality. For instance, preaching on "You shall not commit adultery" is a lot easier than giving a message on the positive side: "How to Affair-Proof Your Marriage."

If I'm short of sermon-preparation time and really scrambling some week, my temptation is to develop a "thou shalt not" message. But if I'm a better disciplinarian of my schedule, and if I'm truly thinking and praying about my people and how they will receive the sermon, I'll put in the extra work to show the rewards of the righteous, inspiring people to obedience rather than just castigating them for wrongdoing.

Being Sensitive to Pain

People are sensitive about their sexuality. For instance, try questioning my masculinity, and watch what I do! I'll throw up emotional walls, if not my fists. We're like that when our sexuality is impugned. So I try to be tender when I talk about these matters of the heart. Since people's understanding of their sexuality—and their practice of it over the years—touches so close to their personal core, they are particularly aware of their shortcomings and sin.

In the area of sexuality, the guilt is unbelievable. I simply cannot talk about "sins against your bodies" or spout "thou shalt nots" without being sensitive to the depth of pain most people already feel concerning sex. If I cannot include a word of grace, I may do irreparable damage.

In addition, if the women in my church are typical—and I have no reason to believe they aren't—as many as half of them have had a destructive or unwanted sexual experience forced on them. Several studies bear this out. That means whenever I speak about sex, as many as half the women must deal with the pain, guilt, and unresolved feelings brought by these episodes. Therefore, I dare not treat the subject lightly.

Early in my ministry, I was naive about this reality and rather oblivious to the heightened sensitivities. I would speak on how wonderful human sexuality is. I'd go on about what a pleasurable experience it is and why God designed us as sexual creatures.

Finally a few women were thoughtful enough to pull me aside and say, "Bill, that's great for most people to hear, but the truth of the matter is, some of us have been scarred by this 'wonderful gift of God.' Frankly, we think sex was a rotten idea."

That was hard to hear. Such attitudes were foreign to me. In the sheltered Dutch enclave in which I was raised, the men would have hanged anyone who laid a finger on a girl! But today we run across the ugly scars of misappropriated sex all the time.

I had to learn that whenever I talk about the beauty of human sexuality, I have to qualify my words: "But some of you have seen the other side of this good gift; you've been victimized by those displaying their depravity by the abuse of sex." And I must speak many words of comfort and understanding.

Providing a Means of Grace

Reassurances that God's grace covers sexual sin are fine, as are other expressions of comfort. But I have another responsibility when I preach about sex: I need to offer tangible ways for people broken by adverse sexual experiences to find healing.

A while back I studied the problem of pornography prior to preaching on it. As I neared the end of a protracted preparation period, I realized how many people are addicted to porn. I had to look in the mirror and say: *Am I going to handle this subject with integrity, or am I going to pontificate about it and leave a bunch of trapped and wounded people feeling even worse about what they're doing?* Giving them the word of grace—telling of God's forgiveness—was one thing, but actually dropping a rope to pull them out of the pit was something else.

I decided to ask a Christian counselor to put together an Alcoholics Anonymous-like support group for those who were ready to deal with their pornographic addiction. Such a group would need to function under close supervision because of the nature of the problem. When I preached on pornography, I announced the forming of the group "to hold one another accountable in breaking free of that harmful addiction." More than fifty people gathered. The group has continued and has had an effective ministry.

Unless I give people something to grasp as they let go of sexual problems, they have only their disoriented equilibrium to keep them from returning to their problems. Marriage-enrichment groups, counseling programs, mutual-accountability groups, discipleship programs with mature leaders—these offer people a way to begin to remedy their denatured sexuality.

Injecting Humor

I work hard at humor; it's one of the toughest parts of sermon preparation. As long as it's used appropriately, its importance when preaching can hardly be overemphasized. Some people come to church not expecting to find themselves enjoying the experience. If I can get them laughing, they relax and become more open to what I'm about to say.

Particularly in preaching about sex, humor is the perfect counterbalance to the weightiness of the topic. With all that pain and guilt and sin-talk floating in the air, with people feeling nervous or perhaps expecting to be offended, anything I can say that disarms them for a moment is precious.

In one sermon I wanted to communicate the idea that sometimes even the best-laid plans in marriage go awry. I told the story of one anniversary night when I took my wife, Lynn, to the honeymoon suite of a luxury hotel. I told how I bought her flowers, took her out to dinner, had a special treat brought up to the room—the works. Of course, I was looking forward to the romantic agenda I had in mind. When we finally turned off the light, Lynn noticed a crack in the curtains letting in light from the parking lot. She got up in the dark, crossed the room, closed the curtain, and returned across the even darker room. But just as she got to the bed, she stumbled into the bedpost and gashed her forehead. The cut was so bad I had to take her to the emergency room for stitches, which sort of took the twinkle out of my eye that night.

Our people laughed, and I was able to reach into their lives at that time because I had touched a universal point of connection: humor.

Yet humor must be appropriate. Once in an attempt to communicate with nonchurched males in the congregation, I let slip a flippant remark. I was referring to an ostensibly successful man, who doesn't think he needs Christ because "he's got a big home, a high-paying job, a condominium in Florida, a nice wife and two kids, and a little thing going on the side." I said it matter-of-factly and went on from there to make my point.

What I had neglected, and what I was reminded of by a number of women in our church, is that being the victim of an extramarital affair is a devastating experience. Many never get over it. My offhand remark about "a little thing going on the side" showed how drastically I had underestimated the impact of the words. We can't wink and make light of something that painful. I would rather not use humor than use it at someone's expense.

Being Transparent

One sure-fire way to ruin my effectiveness when preaching about sex is to speak as if I'm not subject to sexual sin: "I've got this sexuality thing all figured out. It's not much of a problem for me, and I'm going to straighten out you people in the next twenty minutes so you can get your passions under control as I have." That's pontificating, not communicating.

In the years before I started Willow Creek, I don't recall once hearing a pastor make reference to his own sexuality. Does that mean pastors aren't sexual beings? Is that an area of our lives we don't want others to emulate? The longer we're silent, the larger those question marks become. When I preach about sex, generally I want to be able to say, "Friends, here's who I am. I love you more than I value your impressions of me, and we've got to talk about some important things here."

I include myself in the conversation, because as a pastor, I'm called not just to feed the flock, but also to model as best I can the kind of life Christ would have me lead. Since part of that life is my sexuality, I'll occasionally make reference to personal subjects, like the fact that Lynn and I have had a physical relationship that sometimes is satisfying and sometimes is not so satisfying. Then I point out the factors behind a satisfying relationship.

People tell me such candor is appreciated. It says we don't always have to have wonderful sexual experiences even if we'd like to brag that we do. I like to give people the sense that we can be men and women together who have cut the pretense and stopped pretending.

There remain, however, seasons in my marriage when, because of pressures and difficulties in our relationship, it would be destructive to me personally to try to address the subject of sex. When I am in turmoil about it, I don't need the added pressure of speaking about it as if all were well.

That's not to say I dare speak only out of my strength, because there are times when I speak out of my weaknesses, too. But I need to be fairly healthy before I preach, or I find I begin to launch into thunderous "thou shalt nots" only out of my own frustrations. I'll be more pastoral and effective if I wait until I have cooled down a little and can be more balanced.

Perhaps one other caution is appropriate: Personal transparency is for a purpose—identification with the congregation—not for mere verbal exhibitionism. Before I use personal references, I obtain Lynn's permission, because I would never share an illustration that would violate the intimacy and integrity of our marriage. I also pass questionable illustrations by our elders and ask them how they feel about them. They veto any personal anecdotes that are inappropriate.

But they encourage me to be open. They, along with me, want my messages to say authentically: "I need to hear this message as much as I need to give it, because I live where you live. I'm listening to myself as I preach."

THE PAYOFF

Preaching on the subject of sex is one of the hardest things I do, so it would be much easier to dodge it. Then I'd have no personal soul searching, no controversy, no possibility of offending people. But there would also be no rescuing people from the devastation of misused sexuality and no leading them to the joy of God's intentions for this gift.

I've discovered when I preach on sex, invariably I go home encouraged. The last time I spoke about marriage, I talked afterward with numerous couples who echoed what one said: "We're not going to settle anymore for less than a satisfactory sexual relationship. We're going to work on this, with a counselor if necessary, until we flourish in our physical relationship. We don't want to frustrate each other to the point that we have an affair we may never get over."

When I preach about sexual purity, I often hear from people who have been convicted by the Holy Spirit and have determined to put impurity away. I spoke with a new Christian from our fellowship who had been living with a woman for three years. I told him that as painful as it would be, he really had no other choice but to separate. I listened to him and prayed with him and promised to help him walk through the experience.

As he left, he said, "I can't thank you enough for forcing the issue, because there's one side of me that's screaming, *I don't want to cut this off!* and the other side of me says, *But I have to.* I just needed someone to put the pressure on me. Thanks for doing that."

That's what happens when we preach—humbly, prayerfully, and lovingly—the truth about sex.

Chapter 188

PREACHING SEX WITH COMPASSION AND CONVICTION

How to communicate the biblical view of sex without becoming Dr. Ruth

Craig Barnes

It's on most everyone's mind, yet the subject of sex often gets little press in the church. No big surprise why. To preach well on that oh-so-delicate subject takes courage, compassion, and conviction.

To begin with, I don't want to make angry denouncements, but I want to make clear that within the church there's a lot more sexual activity outside of the biblical norms than people want to admit. Many have had or are having premarital sex. Some have had affairs they've not admitted to anyone. Some are spending enormous amounts of time on the Internet looking at pornography. When I talk about sexual immorality, I'm not talking about those who don't come to church. I want people to know these are really our issues.

It does no good to media bash. When we do that, we miss the real point of preaching, which is to say something redemptive for those who have sexual longings, sexual confusion, and enormous sexual guilt. The Christian preacher must provide hope. Otherwise, if the statistics are accurate that say 70 percent of people who are religious have had premarital sex, we are only clobbering them. I assume the people in the pews want to be righteous.

I also assume that my hearers are confused about sexuality. People think if you're not sexually active, you are less than whole. That's part of the whole homosexual debate—"Because I've got a sexual yearning, it must come from God. And if it comes from God, he wants me to use it." But people are more than sexual beings. Much of the debate about sex has reduced people to their sexuality. That's true whether they're gay or heterosexual.

We're created as sexual beings, but that doesn't mean we have to be sexually active.

DON'T OVERDO IT

Typically I bring up the topic of sex in a series of sermons on a larger theme. That way it's seen as part of the larger picture of our lives. If we become preoccupied with talking about sex, then the preacher is also guilty of reducing people to their sexuality. The temptation for the preacher is either to ignore it or to be preoccupied with it.

For example, when we preach on loneliness, we also have an opportunity to speak on sex. Most people I've talked to who have engaged in sex outside of marriage are not promiscuous, but they are lonely. The mistake they make is thinking that sex will take care of the loneliness. But it just complicates their lives.

The doctrine of the body is another larger theme; so is the topic of choices. Sexual activity, for example, is fundamentally a question of choices. I've also spoken on sex as a subtheme of stewardship.

The least helpful way to speak about sex is as an *issue in and of itself.* You may end up just provoking your congregation. I want to talk about it pastorally through some of these human themes, giving people relief from their struggles.

Be Careful!

There are wrong ways to approach this delicate subject. For example, it is dangerous for the preacher to talk too much about his or her own sexual temptations or longing. I understand the value of personal illustration, but you're begging for trouble if you do that on this topic. It's too much vulnerability for a congregation to handle. Vulnerability by the preacher on the topic of sex simply says, "Come see me with your longings."

In speaking about sex, I refuse to limit the discussion to the lectionary of secular society. I don't need to approach it with the world's terms. It is best to stick with the biblical images and the church's own theological language. That's why I have used the term *sacrament* to describe intercourse. I don't say sex itself is a sacrament, but it's sacramental in that it's given for a holy and sacred purpose.

I prefer to use the church's language not only because it's our own but also because it's beautiful. For example, I can use either the word "intercourse" or the phrase "one flesh," but the biblical phrase "one flesh" is much more elegant than the other.

I have a high view of sex, and I make the assumption that people don't value sex enough. I'm trying to raise their value of sexuality— that's why I don't want to use earthy language. I also assume many have been hurt sexually, and they've never seen the magnificence of it.

When we proclaim the Word of God, we call people to something higher while recognizing their brokenness. The preacher must find a balance between compassion and conviction. We always have to carry on both sides of the conversation.

Chapter 189

THE EVER-MORE-DIFFICULT MARRIAGE SERMON
In an age of divorce and remarriage, how can you preach graciously about lifelong commitment?

Bob Russell

I never used to speak on marriage. As a young preacher, I didn't have much personal experience in the matter, and I had grown up with parents who truly loved each other. I had no idea how stressful marriage was for many people.

As I began speaking about marriage, though, I discovered hurting people had been sitting in church for years, putting up a front, and wondering, *Is our marriage abnormal?* After a sermon on marriage, I'd hear, "It's so good to know we're not the only ones who struggle."

I've concluded that most people want help with their marriage, even when they believe there's nothing more to do, so I've decided to preach more intentionally about the subject.

THE CHALLENGES

As I did, I found that it's easy to preach about marriage but difficult to do it well. And it's getting more difficult. One major challenge is how to make everyone in today's congregation feel included. Some have happy marriages, others have seen a divorce lawyer that week; some have been married three times, while others have never married.

Another difficulty is how to illustrate the message. Stories carry emotional impact, and everyone in the congregation holds strong feelings about marriage—either their own, their parents' marriage, a failed marriage, or a marriage they wish they had.

A third challenge is how to talk about my own marriage without making myself look better or worse than I am and without invading my family's privacy. Some preachers wrestle with the need to preach about marriage when their marriage is struggling or when they are not married.

PRINCIPLES

Here are some principles I've found helpful.

Use positive examples, without glamorizing. In a day when so many marriages break up, it's more important than ever to hold up successful marriages as examples. One idea, which I got from a friend, is when preaching on marriage to say occasionally, "I'd like for everybody who has been married for more than fifty years to stand." As they stand, I say, "These are heroes of our church." People burst into applause.

I tell of men and women who have stuck by their spouses. I told the story of Jim Irby, preacher at the church where I served as youth minister years ago. I saw him and his wife at a convention a while back. An elegant woman, his wife now has a disease that has deteriorated her muscles until she can barely walk. As I saw this dignified couple in their late seventies walk into the room, Jim was walking at the same slow pace as his wife, bent in the same places she was bent, so he could hold onto her in support. "That's what we all want," I said. "A companion who really believes what he or she said—'I'll stand by you in sickness and in health.'"

I also use strong examples of fidelity. When my friend Russ Blowers retired recently, somebody asked him, "What's the greatest accomplishment in your ministry?" He was president of our convention of Christian churches. His was one of the largest churches in Indianapolis. He headed the Billy Graham crusade there. Yet he didn't mention any of those things.

Russ said, "I'm most proud of the fact that I never had to go into my children's bedroom and try to explain to them why I had been unfaithful to their mother."

Yet it's possible to glamorize marriage too much. I've used a cartoon I found years ago of a beautiful girl driving an Italian sports car. The top is down on her convertible, she's smiling, her long hair is blowing in the breeze. There are two haggard, miserable looking women, with babies on each arm, looking at her saying, "Poor Nancy. She could never find a husband."

Include everyone. When preaching about marriage, it's easy to make certain people feel excluded. I used to hear comments like, "Why is it you never say anything about divorce?" or "How come you never preach to singles?"

In recent years I haven't heard that as much,

because I now do two things. (1) I listen to the experts. I've never been through a divorce, but that doesn't mean I'm not authorized by God to preach on divorce. Since my experience is limited, though, I go to those who've experienced it. A few years ago, I preached a sermon on divorce and one on remarriage. To prepare, I gathered six or seven people who have wrestled with those issues firsthand and said, "I've got some questions to ask you." Later, when I preached, I said, "I've never been through a divorce, but I have some friends who have. Let me tell you what they said to me."

In addition, I scan periodicals geared for singles, divorced people, and single parents. There is an avalanche of information available on these issues. I have no excuse if I come across as ignorant. Recently two women came to me and said, "We are a part of a support group for women who are abused physically. Could you address this subject a little more in preaching?"

I was hesitant. The topic was so foreign to my experience. But two weeks ago, while talking about forgiveness and overcoming the pressures of the past, I said, "Maybe you have a husband who has beat you up." We could have heard a pin drop. After the service, a woman came to me and said, "I'm in an abusive situation right now. I don't know where to turn. Can you help me?"

(2) Include specific, one-line illustrations of various situations. People need to know that I know they are present, and that the message is for them too.

It's easy to be generic in preaching: "Maybe you need to forgive somebody in your family." It may take me another fifteen minutes of thought to come up with a specific illustration: "Your dad ran out on you and your mom when you were six years old. When will you forgive him?"

By being more specific, I communicate, "I know you're out there. This sermon is for you, too." Such one-line illustrations also communicate, "I recognize that your parents got a divorce. There are others here just like you, and you are welcome and accepted here."

Balance hero and goat. I try to balance illustrations in which I'm the hero, or our family is ideal, with illustrations that show me as the goat or that highlight us in our day-to-day struggles.

Once I told about a time we were traveling on the East Coast and disagreed about whether I was driving in the right direction. Judy said, "You're going west."

I said, "I'm not either. I'm going east. We're going in the right direction." Each of us was convinced the other was wrong.

Then I saw a sign that she didn't see that told me I was going in the wrong direction. I drove past the next two exits trying to think of some way I could get off for gasoline and get back on without telling her I had changed directions.

Often, it's harder for me to use an illustration that reveals the tenderness of our marriage. Several years ago, we went through a difficult period with Judy's health. That time of our lives was too tender to talk about for some time, but I finally got to the place where I could tell it without tearing me up. One of the first times I made more than a passing reference to it was with this story:

> When we celebrated our thirtieth wedding anniversary, I wanted to get Judy a ring that cost more than I felt I could afford. I'd always been a little embarrassed about the ring I gave her when we got engaged. Even after I took her engagement ring and the new ring to have the stones set, I kept debating whether I should have spent so much money.

But just a few weeks later, when Judy lay in the hospital bed after a stroke, her left hand partially paralyzed, I looked down at her hand and said, "That sure is a pretty ring on your finger."

She replied, "I think it is too."

I wanted the story to remind people to demonstrate love before it's too late.

Sometimes, of course, a preacher may not be able to use personal illustrations because of marital struggles. I have a preacher friend who has been holding on to his marriage with his fingertips for more than twenty years. He dreads preaching on marriage, because he feels like a hypocrite. But he grits his teeth and looks for illustrations from the marriages of others. He might say, "My friend, Bob Russell, tells the story. . . ." That technique may limit his effectiveness, but I respect him, because he rises above his situation to preach on a subject that needs to be addressed.

Bring up sex—discreetly. When anyone talks about problems, needs, and expectations in marriage, sex always is near the top of the list. I preach on the topic because I believe in preaching the whole counsel of God and because I want to speak to real life.

We encourage parents to put their kids in children's church, yet I'm more discreet about how I discuss sex than I was fifteen years ago. Back then I might have used the word "intercourse" in a sermon. Now I use the word "intimacy." That may seem counterintuitive, given our exposure to the subject from pop culture. For example, fifteen years ago, many people recoiled at hearing the word "condom." Few are shocked by it anymore. But it's because people get the full frontal approach from television and movies that I want my approach to be tasteful.

I use personal illustrations on this topic only with caution, discretion, and permission. I've shared that one thing I love about Judy is she is really affectionate. She's kind of formal in public, and it surprises some people that she would be that warm at home.

One night, Judy and I were eating pizza with the youth after church in the church kitchen. Judy really looked pretty that night. She looked my way, and I winked at her. She looked away like she was embarrassed, but later that night at home, as I was sitting in my chair reading, she came up behind me and put her arms around my neck. She asked, "You know what it does to me when you wink at me like that in public?"

"No, not really."

Well, I found out, and I'm going to do it more often!

A story like this has an important purpose: It signals to married people that it's okay to be affectionate, to desire your spouse, and to initiate intimacy.

Point to practical help. I want a sermon on marriage to point people to the Source of hope. But many people need additional, practical assistance. Whenever possible, I point people to that. In one message, I brought up the subject of being a single dad. I said:

> Our society is becoming more sensitive to single moms; when you hear of single dads, it's usually deadbeat dads and dads who have abandoned their families. But statistically, fourteen out of one hundred custodial parents are fathers. Then there are dads who wish they could go back and relive their situations, but they can't. So if you're in that situation, there's a support group here that can help you.

Believe in preaching's power. Despite the challenges, I keep preaching on marriage.

One couple, now married for more than twenty-five years, was in deep marital trouble about six years ago. They were not members of our church. They were separated, he had been running out on her, and a divorce was in the works. Somebody gave the wife a tape of one of my sermons on marriage, and she listened to it. When the husband came to pick up his things, he saw the tape on the counter and said, "What's this?"

She said, "It's by some preacher at Southeast Christian Church."

"Do you mind if I listen to it?"

"You can have it," she replied. "I'm finished with it." He headed to his apartment and started listening to the tape. He kept driving around until it was over. Then he drove back home and said to his wife, "I want to work on our marriage again."

They started coming to our church regularly, worked through their issues, and today are still together. They are so happy. They recently stopped me to introduce me to their daughter.

When I see God's Word turn around a marriage, that makes the hard work of preaching worthwhile.

Chapter 190

WHEN THE SERMON GOES TO WORK
Life on the job is too important to give it light treatment

Haddon Robinson

Does selling insurance, running a laundromat, driving a cab, or delivering mail matter to God? Judging by our preaching, the answer is "not much." In one survey 90 percent of Christians said they had never heard a sermon that applied biblical theology to work. Yet Christians may spend between 40 and 75 percent of their lives in work-related tasks. Unfortunately, they have reason to suspect that, as far as God is concerned, their work-life is a vast wasteland.

Several years ago I had breakfast with a group of Christian businessmen. Perhaps because I was there, they began talking about their pastors. They respected their ministers and appreciated their dedication, but they also felt their pastors were out of touch with them. Their preachers had visited them or members of their families when they were in the hospital, and a couple of the ministers had visited two of the men in their homes. Two others reported that their preachers had played golf with them. Yet, none of the clergymen had ever spent a day with them at work or even visited them at their place of employment. As one of the men put it, "I enter his world once or twice a week, but he doesn't bother much about mine."

If ministers do preach about the workplace, they may speak of it solely as a platform for evangelism. The idea here is that the dock worker or the tailor should find significance in their labor by sharing the gospel with fellow-workers.

Some Christians have bought into this attitude. "I earn my living as an accountant," they say, "but my real work is telling people about

677

Jesus Christ." Is it? Does God care nothing about how the books are kept?

Would it be out of line for pastors to ordain men and women to the work of the ministry in the marketplace? Would it be sacrilegious to send them out not simply as evangelists but as witnesses who honor Jesus Christ by the way they do their jobs?

Whom do we honor? When someone leaves the workplace to go to the mission field, have they always made a more godly choice? Or suppose a pastor leaves the church to run the jewelry store. Is it possible that he hasn't really left the ministry at all?

REMEMBER THE WORKDAY

Read again the passages in the New Testament directed to slaves. Paul affirms them. They are doing the will of God; they are serving their Master, Jesus, and they will receive their reward from him for what they do in their work. Don't those passages alone challenge our silence about labor?

The line of penetration should be from the pulpit to the pew to the pavement. We need to break down the wall between the sacred and the secular. We must help those who are Christ followers to "remember the workday to keep it holy."

THE WORLD OF THE BOTTOM LINE

When one of the executives in that Bible study commented that in all the years he had been in business his pastor had never visited him at his office, another man said, "It's just as well. A minister would feel out of place in my office." Since I consider myself a minister, I pressed him to explain.

"Most ministers I know come across best visiting the hospital or working in the church environs. That's their turf." He went on to say he saw the world of the pastor and the world of business people as very different: "The pastor is used to working alone or with a small staff, and his interest is relationships. The world of business is a more impersonal atmosphere dominated by people who emphasize the bottom line.

"Pastors do pretty well with issues of grief and loneliness and interpersonal ethics—not stealing, coveting, fornicating, and so on," he said. "But I don't know too many pastors who address the problems of the individual's conflicting loyalties in groups and organizations."

Another man, who helps run a large construction corporation, agreed and offered an example: "A fellow owed us $500,000 when he died. He and his wife owned a house worth $150,000. The question is, do we sue the estate for the money we're due, even if it costs the woman her house as part of the payment for her husband's debt?"

He continued, "If you own the company, you can make a compassionate decision if you want to. But when you are responsible to stockholders and your job is to collect bad debts, where is your higher loyalty? Now, you might argue, '$150,000 isn't worth it.' But suppose the house is worth $500,000; now do you go after it? Or a million? Is it ethical to go after a $500,000 house but unethical to go after a $150,000 house?"

The businessmen agreed—rarely in church do they hear anybody even mention these kinds of issues. Yet that is the common stuff of life. Tough, morally ambiguous issues are where some business people have to live out their faith. "While the preacher talks about absolutes of right and wrong," one man said, "most of us deal with gray situations."

Another said, "My pastor talks about 'the good being an enemy of God's best,' but people in my world aren't dealing with first or second moral choices. They're down to the twelfth or thirteenth choices.

"As much as I appreciate my pastor and enjoy his sermons," the businessman concluded, "it's not often that he speaks about my world."

I was dismayed by the conversation. Not everyone would agree with these businessmen; some people attend church expecting their minister to say something that will help them understand the broad issues of life a little better. But not many expect the preacher to be able to speak with insight to the particular world in which many of them live.

SERMONS THAT TALK ABOUT THE HARD QUESTIONS

Let's face it. Life is complex. But we sometimes preach as though it were not. Here's an example from one of my sermons. One time after I had preached a sermon on love, a man came up and said, "You said that love means always seeking other people's highest good."

"Yes."

"That's fine, but my business puts me in competition with another man in this congregation. I run an efficient operation that lets me sell my product cheaper than his. What's the loving thing to do—underprice him and take some of his customers? Or should I keep my prices roughly equal?"

Before I could respond, he went on.

"But that's not the toughest part. A large corporation has just moved into town selling the same product. I'm going to have to scramble to stay in business myself. I may have to cut prices so drastically it will drive my fellow church member into bankruptcy.

"I want to love this man. We're in the same Sunday school class. I coach his kids in Little League. I want to do what's best for him. But the name of the game out there is survival," he said. "Why don't preachers talk about these kinds of things when they talk about love?"

For us to communicate with authority, we've got to step into the shoes of those Christians who are in the home and marketplace. No matter how gray the issues, we've got to be willing to say, "As a pastor, I must talk about the hard questions." In our preaching, we must recognize the complexity of the issues. How do we do that?

First, it's helpful simply to admit the tension and point it out. All truth exists in tension. God's love exists in tension with his holiness. Skillfully applying love and justice is not easy.

I believe God honors an honest try. People need to know that. Sometimes I'll point out that we will make a wrong decision with the right motive, which is different from making a right decision out of a wrong motive. As far as I know, the Bible never calls any action, in itself, right. No action is right apart from its motive. Obviously there are some acts the Bible calls wrong: murder, lying, adultery. But it's not as easy to classify right behavior.

For example, Jesus talks about two men who went to the temple to pray—which sounds like a good religious act. But only one was justified, the other was not. Jesus talks about people giving—and that's a good thing—except some give to be seen by others. That's not good.

So in God's economy, motive is a key factor. One of the things we preachers can say to people, with authority, is: "In these situations, it's important to handle life skillfully, to make the right decisions. But the prior and more important decision is *What's motivating you? Are you willing to be God's representative in* this situation? Sometimes those decisions are confusing. We need wisdom. That's what Christian friends and Christian counsel give you."

Chapter 191

BRIDGING THE MARKETPLACE GAP

How can we church insiders get a hearing from our people—the marketplace experts—about bringing Christ to work?

Andy Stanley

Most of us spend the majority of our waking, productive hours at work. Even our students think about careers and getting into the marketplace. It's so incredibly relevant and there is so much material to draw from, I feel this is a theme I need to address annually.

BIBLICAL CONTENT

There are only a few passages of Scripture that deal specifically with work, but rather than focusing only on those, I ask myself, *What biblical principles are challenging to apply in the work environment?* The issue for most men and women is not, "What do I believe?" or, "What ought I do?" but, "How do I do it in an environment hostile to my Christian values?" It's hard enough to live consistently at home, where everyone is pretty much on the same page spiritually, but how do you walk into a neutral or sometimes hostile environment and live out Christianity?

So I preach the passages that deal with basic Christian principles and apply them specifically to the marketplace. I talk about competence, doing your best, character, and how to work under authorities you disagree with. There are many principles we need to take into the marketplace, but without handles on how to do that, the tendency is to leave those values in the car.

The texts I preach on I have used before in different contexts, but viewing them again through the lens of the marketplace gives them new application, fresh relevance. When you force the old principles through a specific grid, in this case the business world, they take on new life.

ESTABLISHING CREDIBILITY

In every such message, usually in the middle, I show a five-minute video interview with someone in our church whose life and stories from work illustrate the principle being taught. For instance, a woman in our congregation owns a real estate firm. I interviewed her about how to be a Christian employer and how to evangelize without running off your business or employees.

One of the reasons I use those videos is

because most business people look at a pastor and think, *What do you know? Pastors don't deal with stockholders, market share, economics. We don't answer to a boss nine hours a day.*

I feel I have to build credibility early. And I cannot make the mistake of saying, "I understand what it's like," because I don't. So I take the other approach and say, "I don't understand. I don't work in your world, and I won't pretend. But here are some people who do—CEOs, small business owners, middle management." The video testimony brings credibility to what I am saying.

Seeing Marketplace As Ministry

In those interviews, I want to make sure I have women and men, middle management and executives. I wanted to show that these was principles that apply across the board because we're to live out our faith with the same honesty, diligence, and so on regardless of where we work or fit into an organization.

I've learned that we need to remind people constantly that they are ministers, with a calling and opportunity to minister at work. For most people, their neighbors are no longer the people who live near them, but the people they are intimately acquainted with at work, people they're with day in and day out. It's not necessarily the guy next door anymore, but the people at work who are the mission field. When men and women begin to see their marketplace responsibilities as ministry, it energizes them. Any talk of the professional ministry being a unique "called ministry" in contrast to everybody else destroys motivation.

One of the topics we talk about is how to leverage your influence in your company for ministry. One of my interviewees, for example, pays for his coworkers' lunch if they'll come to the conference room and watch a DVD of our worship service. He calls it "Life Lessons over Lunch." That sparked all kinds of creative thinking in our congregation.

I'll do a whole series on the fears of the marketplace. I'll focus on the tension between work and family. We need to preach annually on prioritizing family over work, because the long-standing trend in our culture is to make work number one.

I have a good friend whose employer wanted him to move, but he didn't want to because of his wife. His boss said to him, "Well, get another wife!" In other words, you're only going to get one opportunity like this, but there are lots of wives out there. That's the kind of pressure people are under.

Chapter 192

SERMONS ON GIVING THAT PEOPLE ACTUALLY LIKE!

It's all in your approach

Bob Russell

For years I boasted to our congregation that I only preached on stewardship once annually. When that dreaded sermon came, I apologized at the beginning: "If you're visiting with us today, please understand that we only preach on giving once a year." In essence I said, "I'm sorry you've chosen to come today—I know this subject is a downer. Please come back anyway, and I promise you'll not hear another sermon on money for fifty-one weeks!"

It's easy to understand why we tiptoe around the subject of stewardship. Money is still a god to many church members, and many visitors are skeptical of the church's motives. Certain spiritual con men have fleeced their congregations and given preachers a bad name, and we don't want to be identified with them.

Even though preaching on money turns some people off, some are turned off when we preach on adultery or forgiveness, too. But we don't apologize: "If you're having an affair, please understand we seldom talk about sexual purity. Come back next week and you'll be more comfortable." We don't print a disclaimer in the bulletin: "The preacher will be talking about releasing resentment today. Please understand this sermon is for our members only. If you're visiting today you aren't expected to forgive. If you're currently harboring a grudge, earplugs are provided."

About a decade ago I changed my philosophy from apologizing for teaching on a touchy subject to making it an essential part of my preaching calendar. Now nearly every January I preach a series of three or four sermons on stewardship.

The result have surprised me—attendance has been good, the number of people coming to Christ has actually increased during the stewardship month, and offerings have improved as much as 15 percent annually! My transition taught me several lessons about preaching on stewardship without alienating the audience.

THE $6,000 SERMON

Many immature believers and visitors are alienated when we preach on stewardship because many preachers speak almost entirely about the need to give to the church. Our sermons are erroneously viewed as self-serving—a necessary evil to generate church income—but not spiritual or helpful.

But when the preacher encourages families to get out of debt, to refrain from extravagant luxuries, to avoid wasting money on credit card interest rates, to be generous with their children, or to learn contentment with less, the congregation regards the message as helpful. It's not viewed as a fundraiser but as a relevant, biblical, and much-needed challenge. A discussion of giving against the backdrop of total stewardship of resources is much more effective than preaching on giving alone.

Once, in a sermon on hoarding, I pointed out the foolishness of waiting until we die to give our children their inheritance. I explained, "When we die, our children will most likely be in their fifties or sixties. They likely won't need our money then! And so, until our deaths, we hoard it from our grandchildren.

"The time to help our children is when they're young and need the money. Our children will actually benefit from it, and we can hear them thank us instead of wondering if they quietly hope we croak early! And since we can transfer as much as $10,000 per child annually without the recipients paying taxes on the gift, it's wiser to transfer resources when we're living."

Several weeks after the sermon I received a thank-you letter from a young couple whose parents happened to be visiting that weekend. The wife explained that after hearing the sermon her parents sent her and her brother checks for $6,000. Nothing even close to that had ever happened before! The young woman wrote, "My brother and I call that the $6,000 sermon! Please preach more sermons on stewardship—especially when my parents are in town!"

THE BEST TIME TO TEACH

The timing of a stewardship sermon dramatically affects how it is received. If people are reconsidering their spending priorities, they're more likely to welcome biblical teaching on money. But if they're overwhelmed with charities, events, and school expenses, for example, they'll likely resent a church asking for more money, too.

For forty years, our church's fiscal year ran from July 1 to June 30. We voted on the proposed budget and made pledges the third Sunday in May. That was when I preached the dreaded sermon on stewardship.

But few people were interested in reviewing their financial commitments in May. We competed with the Kentucky Derby (which is huge in Louisville), Mother's Day, and Memorial Day weekend. Other things demanded our people's time, thoughts, and commitment.

January proved a much better month for us to consider stewardship. During January people make New Year's resolutions, they're chastened by Christmas bills to be wiser money managers, and they feel little pressure from other church and community activities.

And even though we moved our fiscal calendar to begin in January, we stopped asking for pledges toward the budget. We don't want people to regard the sermons as fundraisers. We want them to consider their attitude toward possessions as a personal and spiritual matter, vital to their relationship with God. For us, the beginning of the year is the best time for that.

PEOPLE WANT TO GIVE

When I stopped asking for pledges, it signaled a change in how I preach on money. Most people aren't motivated to give their best so that they can meet a church budget. Instead of saying, "We need every member to step up their giving so we can meet our budget," I now say, "When you give, your money will be used to take the gospel to unreached people in Third World countries; it will buy food and clothing for the poor in our inner city; it will enable our children to learn about Jesus at Christian camp." I remind people repeatedly that they are giving to the ministry of Christ, not just to meet a budget.

The examples I use are more often about the poor who have sacrificed, not the rich who have given huge amounts. Even the wealthy are moved more by genuine sacrifice than by big gifts from the well-to-do.

Jackie Nelson gave a moving testimony years ago that I've often repeated. Jackie said, "I am a single mother of three teenagers. My ex-husband does not help. I barely get by. We really want to do our part in this three-year campaign so our new building can be built. But when we discussed it as a family, we realized that we can't give any more than a tithe. So we decided that our gift would be to pray every day for the success of this program.

"But in the middle of our discussion my oldest son said, 'Mom, we've got cable television. We don't have to have that.' So we've decided to give up our cable TV for three years so we can do our part."

The congregation realized, "If she can make that kind of sacrifice to give a little, we who are so blessed can do even more." Like the five loaves and two fish that Jesus used to feed a multitude, God took Jackie's small gift and multiplied it many times over.

I also seek examples that teach through conviction rather than guilt and obligation. For example, I've preached:

> When my first son was born, we were blessed to have an excellent babysitter who lived next door. Patty not only babysat, she washed dishes, folded clothes, and looked for ways to help around the house. She was dependable, and my son loved her.
>
> When she first started babysitting, I asked Patty how much she charged, and she said, "Fifty cents an hour." (Obviously this was a long time ago!) I gladly paid that amount.
>
> A few years later our second son arrived, and I said, "Patty, your responsibilities have increased

significantly now. What do you charge for taking care of two children?"

> By this time we had a good relationship, and she said, "Oh, Mr. Russell, just give me what you want to give."
>
> Do you think I gave more or less than 50 cents an hour?
>
> In the Old Testament, God commanded his people to tithe—10 percent of their crops and flocks were returned to God. In our era he has given us Jesus Christ, the indwelling Holy Spirit, the fellowship of the church, the privilege of living in the most affluent nation in the world, plus so many personal blessings. Yet when we ask how much we should give, he just says, "Give as you have been prospered. You decide whether that should be more or less than a tithe."

Most people want to be generous. So I don't hesitate to use that as a motivation for wise stewardship. When I say, "When you are a wise steward, it honors God, relieves tension, gives you self-confidence, eliminates guilt, enhances your witness, and enables you to give more generously," people are not offended. They understand I'm not talking about fundraising but about a better stewardship of life.

When Still They Complain

No matter how hard you try to make the subject of stewardship helpful and palatable, some people will still object. Many just love money too much, and when you touch a nerve, you elicit strong emotions. But I often remember an old proverb, "If you throw a rock into a pack of dogs, the one that yelps is usually the one that got hit."

Criticisms need to be evaluated as objectively as possible, but they should not discourage us from preaching the truth. On the contrary, criticism often illustrates the need for preaching on stewardship more often.

Jesus talked a lot about money, but not everyone responded favorably. When the rich ruler asked, "What must I do to inherit eternal life?" Jesus didn't try to develop a long-term relationship with him before discussing the subject of generosity. He said up front, "Go, sell everything you have and give to the poor, and you will have treasure in heaven" (Mark 10:21). That wasn't very seeker-friendly, and the rich young ruler turned and walked away because he had great possessions. But the problem was with the young man's greed, not Jesus' message.

Jesus made it clear there's a close tie between people's pocketbooks and their hearts. He didn't say, "If a person's heart is right, they will give." He said, "When you invest your money in something, your heart will follow." When we motivate people to give, we're helping them to put their heart in the right place.

Despite the occasional criticism, some of the most gratifying experiences I've had in ministry have occurred during times of stewardship emphasis. Jerry Nichter, for example, who now serves as chairman of our elders, points to a sacrificial financial commitment he and his wife made as the turning point in his walk with Christ. "That was the single most deepening spiritual experience of my life," he admits. Many others echo his testimony.

After making a sacrificial commitment to a major capital campaign, Bill Beauchamp, another elder, wiped tears from his eyes and said, "I just gave away money I don't have, for people I've never met, for a God I love very much."

Get Ready: I'm Preaching on Money

Here are five ways to prepare your people for a stewardship sermon.

Don't apologize. A preacher who subscribed to our tape ministry was disgruntled that I had preached four straight sermons on sacrificial giving. "If you don't stop preaching about money, there won't be any people left to fill up the new building you're trying to finance," he wrote.

My wife replied to him, "Dear sir, during the month Bob preached on giving, enthusiasm was high, and twice as many accepted Christ as do in a regular month. Over half of Jesus' parables concern use of material possessions. Maybe if you preached more often about money, your church would do better. In Jesus' love, Judy Russell."

We are ambassadors of Christ, not negotiators. Have confidence that preaching about money is God's will and that it will strengthen people's relationship with Christ.

Gain the support of the church leadership prior to the series. An endorsement from church leadership gives you confidence, support, and credibility with the congregation. It also includes and silences some of your most potentially hurtful critics—the leaders themselves.

Include stewardship examples in non-stewardship sermons. A line or two in a sermon unrelated to stewardship reminds the congregation that faithful living always involves giving.

Last Easter in a sermon on heaven I talked about our rewards there: "The young Christian woman who remains pure will receive a greater reward than the young woman who yields to temptation. The husband who cares for his sickly wife receives a greater reward in heaven than the husband who takes his healthy wife for granted. And the couple who tithes every paycheck from the beginning of marriage will have more treasure in heaven than the couple who gives God the leftovers."

No one could say the Easter sermon was about giving. But stewardship is such a vital part of life that it should be naturally included on a regular basis.

Emphasize that church funds are administered with integrity. "We want to avoid any criticism of the way we administer this liberal gift. For we are taking pains to do what is right, not only in the eyes of the Lord but also in the eyes of men" (2 Cor. 8:20–21). During every stewardship series, I explain how donations are administered.

The offering is deposited in a safe. The next morning it is counted and recorded by a volunteer committee. Then it is taken to the bank by the treasurer, who is accompanied by a policeman. Two people must sign all checks, and the preacher is not one of them. The minister has to go through the same red tape of budget requests, purchase orders, and receipts as others do. Our church is a member of the Evangelical Council on Financial Accountability, and there is an annual, independent audit of our books. The church staff is reminded to spend church funds more frugally than if the money were their own.

People are motivated to give when they are confident they are giving directly to legitimate needs.

Title sermons to communicate they're about more than giving. Message titles that reflect an emphasis on helping people understand money, instead of giving more of it, takes the dread out of money messages. A sermon series on "Money Matters" could include: "How Can You Make the Most of What You Have?" "When Is Enough Enough?" and, "Can You Earn More Than Your Neighbor and Still Be Christian?"

Part 11

Evaluation

How Do I Get the Constructive Feedback I Need to Keep Growing?

Chapter 193

WELL-FOCUSED PREACHING

Taking a clear picture of your preaching requires both wide-angle and zoom lenses

Bill Hybels

When I first began teaching publicly as a youth minister in the early 1970s, I taught in a conversational, dialogue style. After all, there were just twenty-five kids. When my material wasn't all that useful, one of the students would raise a hand and say, "Can we move on?" Then I'd realize I was missing the mark, or I had overstayed my welcome in the book of Leviticus, and we would move on.

I stayed with that style for more than a year, but then we started outreach programs, and all of a sudden the group jumped from twenty-five to 150. My teaching style soon became inappropriate for the larger group; I actually had to start putting together formal messages. In a panic, I went to a senior pastor friend and said, "I have to start giving full-blown messages to 150 high school students. What do you suggest?"

He said, "Well, if I were you, I would get a copy of Berkhof's *Manual of Christian Doc-*trine and just start at chapter 1 and teach these kids." Sounded fine to me. So I read the first chapter of Berkhof, did some underlining and preparation, and that night began delivering it to a roomful of students.

Five minutes into that talk, I started to see glazed expressions. Students were looking around the room to see who was there. Others were looking at their watches, passing notes to each other, drawing on the backs of the chairs in front of them.

Right then, I knew this teaching was not useful. I was so disheartened by what was happening that I stopped about a third of the way into the message.

"I have to apologize," I said, "for the fact that I am missing the mark tonight. What I prepared to say is obviously not on target. And I want to make a commitment to you students. If you'll come back next week, I'm going to talk about something straight out of the Bible that is going to make a difference in your understanding of God, in your appreciation of the Christian faith, and in how you live your daily life. And if you'll give me another opportunity, I'd like to prove that to you."

The next week most of them returned, graciously, maybe just to humor me. But from that day on, I have lived with a sanctified terror of boring people or making the relevant Scriptures irrelevant. That experience helped me die to pride on the issue of having my teaching evaluated.

Every preacher is evaluated, one way or another, by every listener. I want to get evaluation that will help me be most effective in reaching people with God's truth. I consider getting accurate evaluation part of my job.

THE RIGHT QUESTIONS

Constructive evaluation won't happen, though, no matter how willing I am to receive it, unless I'm asking the right people the right questions at the right time.

By *right people* I mean people with great discernment whom I have learned to trust. It will only distract, confuse, or harm me to get input from everyone. Instead, I want to go to wise counselors.

By *right questions* I mean that I want to find out how I'm communicating at a variety of levels:

- Each illustration—did it communicate what I intended?
- Each message—did it serve its function in the series?
- A year's worth of messages—are they covering the topics and passages this congregation wants and needs to hear?
- My preaching as a whole—is it helping to accomplish the goal of my ministry?

Finally, by *right time* I mean I want to receive evaluation when it's most effective. Obviously, that's when I can do the most about it. Finding out after I deliver a message that it was slightly off track is somewhat useful. But how much more productive it is to find out *before* I put twenty hours into something that wasn't well aimed. So increasingly, I ask "evaluation" questions during the planning stages before I preach. Each weekend, for example, I preach the same message three times—once on Saturday night and twice on Sunday morning. I try to get evaluation immediately following the Saturday night service, so I can make adjustments before I preach the same message two more times. As a result, some Sunday mornings have found me in my office at 5:30. But getting evaluation early keeps me from making a mistake multiple times.

Asking someone to evaluate your preaching is a delicate operation, and the people, questions, and timing are going to vary with each pastor and church. But let me share how I have tried to gain the information that has made my preaching better.

EVALUATING ONE SERMON

The elders at Willow Creek always responded truthfully when I asked them about the accuracy or relevancy of my preaching. But unless I asked, they didn't say anything.

So over the course of time, we have formalized the process. Now the elders evaluate every message that I preach, and they give me a written response to it within minutes after I complete the message. One elder—our most discerning when it comes to preaching evaluation—collects responses from the other elders, summarizes them, and writes them on the front of a bulletin and gives it to me before I leave.

For example, on a recent Wednesday night I gave a strong call to honoring the lordship of Christ. One elder called me (though usually his comments would just be written on the bulletin) and said, "I really do appreciate all of what you said and the style and the tone of what you communicated Wednesday night. Now that you've made that emphasis, I feel it's important for you to remind the people regularly in ensuing messages of the assisting work of the Holy Spirit. We need his power to submit consistently to that kind of lordship."

I said, "Good word." That's the kind of correction I need, because sometimes I will feel so strongly about a subject that the sheer force of my personality causes complications I didn't intend. People think I am angry about something. And so hearing how my tone and demeanor come across is very important to me.

This past Wednesday night, I again spoke on the lordship of Christ, and several elders remarked that they appreciated the spirit and tone with which I spoke. In this message, they said, I was not strident, but gave a loving call to discipleship. That meant a lot to me.

I realize the thought of having elders evaluate every message—or any message—is a frightening thought for many pastors. I confess that the primary reason this system of accountability and evaluation works in our setting is because of the enormous trust and love that has been built between my elders and me. When I work sometimes twenty-five or thirty hours on a sermon, I pour my life into it, pray over it, and write out three drafts. If the evaluation were not done with great sensitivity and with no ulterior motives from the evaluators, the system would be imperiled. If I ever, even once, sensed a private agenda or a hobby horse one particular elder wanted to ride, this form of evaluation we enjoy might unravel.

Having said that, however, we have taken several steps to ensure effective evaluation.

(1) I freely admit to my elders I'm sensitive about having my preaching evaluated. I have told them probably a hundred times, "I am extremely vulnerable about these evaluations in the first four minutes after I get down from the pulpit. I would appreciate very much if whoever's doing the evaluating would put a lot of time into thinking about how to present constructive criticisms to me." The elders have understood that and worked hard on it.

(2) We filter all the evaluations through one person. It used to be that if I had said something a little off the mark in an illustration, by the time I got to my office, I'd heard about it seven or eight times. After the third elder would say something, I would say, "Enough already; I got the point." But each one felt responsible to say something. So finally I went to the elders and said, "Time out. The seven pats on the back when I preach well are nice, but the seven slaps when I blow it are excruciating. Let's filter all the comments through one elder so I'll hear things only once."

We chose as the person to collect responses a man who has a rare ability to affirm that which should be affirmed. The agreement is this: If an elder senses a message was right on the mark, then there's no need to find this elder appointee and say anything. If the message was incredibly insightful—I think it's happened once or twice—then make a point of telling the appointed elder. And if there's a problem in the message, naturally, the elder appointee should hear about that. But there isn't a formal caucus after each message, because over the years this particular elder's evaluation has been recognized as almost always illustrative of the feelings of the group. Usually he will talk to two or three elders before he talks to me.

(3) There's give and take on the evaluations. A lot of times, the elder appointee will say something like this: "You might reconsider the use of such-and-such word, given the fact we have so many former Catholics." I'll ponder that and say, "I didn't realize that would set them off. It's no big deal to replace a word there. I can use another word, and everybody's happy."

But other times he'll say, "Might you consider not making reference to the football player?" And I'll say, "If this is one of those 'might you reconsider,' I think no, it's very important for the unchurched men I'm trying to reach." As many times as not, the elder will say, "I can understand that."

Of course, periodically, there are the comments such as, "Please change this; please delete the use of that word; please delete that illustration. We can talk about it later, or call me at home, but we have strong reservations about that concept." And in those cases, I change it. The elders (and board members and staff people, whom I occasionally ask for evaluation) are discerning people who know when I hit the mark and when I forgot to load the gun.

For example, I used an illustration one time about sitting next to a black attorney on a plane returning from Washington, D.C., and went on to talk about our conversation. One of the board members stopped me on the way out after the service, smiled, and said, "Was it necessary to say that attorney on the plane was black? Were you proving that you're impartial? What were you saying there?"

"It never crossed my mind," I said. "I was just reporting the facts. He was black."

He said, "I would guess that as many people wondered why you noted that he was black as benefited from the point of your illustration."

I said, "Now that's a good insight." To me, I was just reporting the facts, but reporting that fact clouded my illustration in many people's minds; that one word made them miss the whole point of the illustration.

I know I've heard other speakers mention off-handedly in an illustration, "I saw this obese woman," and I'm painfully aware that if I said that, many people in my church would have their self-esteem destroyed. They would be out of commission the rest of the sermon and not hear anything else I said. And that offhanded comment had nothing to do with the point of the illustration!

In fact, I got so tired of having ancillary issues become the dominant issues in my preaching, simply because of carelessness, that I now write my sermons in three drafts and include every word of every illustration. Now, I'm not suggesting for a moment that other preachers inflict themselves with a discipline that I have chosen willfully and joyfully to submit to. I just got sick of reading, "Did you realize who might have been hurt by your reference to that? Your off-the-cuff remark about this may have meant this...."

If, after reading the sermon I'm preparing, I still have a question about the appropriateness of a certain point, I may talk it over with an elder. This is especially true of messages for Wednesday night, when there's no second chance to fix them. The elders and I meet to pray before services, and if there's a troubling issue I'm going to get into, I'll say then, "I feel I have to mention this certain topic, and I was planning to handle it this way. Are you all going to feel comfortable with that?"

Having elders or other trusted people evaluate each sermon sounds like work. It is. But this evaluation has saved me so many times from saying something I would regret later, that I have reached the point where I wouldn't want to preach without it.

EVALUATING A YEAR'S WORTH OF SERMONS

Sometimes, though, I need to step back and look at more than one message or series. The zoom lens is fine, but sometimes you need to use a wide-angle lens to get everything in. I've found it natural to look at a year's worth of messages at one time.

The only way I can do this, though, is to get away from the church for an extended period in which I can pray, read, and look back over my previous year's sermons. I have started taking a summer study break each year, and I'm convinced it has improved my teaching. Only when I'm away from the crush of the daily routines can I see patterns of strengths or neglected areas. Suddenly I notice topics or themes that have gotten lots of attention and others that have been overlooked.

But when a year's worth of preaching is at stake, I don't want to wait until it's over to listen to people in the congregation. After a hundred messages, evaluation comes almost too late. What I need more is to hear people's interests and concerns before I start the year. As a result, I have developed a three-step approach to planning a coming year's sermons, and I get input from people at every step.

In April, I select eight or nine people from the congregation. I choose people who are members of our main target audience (suburban business people who wouldn't feel comfortable in many traditional church settings). Sometimes I'll add someone who is highly creative or who represents a large segment of the congregation in terms of his or her age, career, family situation, or whatever. I give these people an assignment: "Circulate in your social circles and find out on what issues people would like clear teaching from the Word of God. Then, based on that, put together what you feel would be an ideal sermon series addressing those needs. Come up with a series title, how you would break down the topic, and what your emphasis would be. You can work with anybody you want, and you have thirty days to do it."

People think, *Hey, this might change what I have to listen to!* and they get motivated. They talk to their friends and people they work with. Some of them invite groups of people to their homes for input.

Then this group and I go away together for two and a half days. We meet from 8:00 a.m. till midnight, with a few hours off to eat and let the jets cool. The main thing I do is listen and take notes. I ask the first person, "Read me one of your series titles and the sermon titles that would be a part of that," and we discuss it. Usually one idea will trip another idea, and we'll end up with thirty or forty viable sermon series.

For example, I just finished a series entitled "Seasons of a Spiritual Life" that included four messages: "The Season of Spiritual Seeking," "The Season of Spiritual Infancy," "The Season of Spiritual Adolescence," and "The Season of Spiritual Adulthood." That title and breakdown of messages came straight from this group.

This spring I'll be preaching a series about Jesus entitled "Someone You Should Know."

What a great title! Later I'll work on still another idea from this group: "Families in the Fast Lane."

During the month following this meeting, I go over all the ideas the group came up with. I rule out any topics I just covered in the past few months as well as any that are extraneous to the scope of Willow Creek's ministry. From the remaining proposed sermon series, I choose twenty I feel I could really work with or that stimulate some interest in me.

Then I convene a second group made up of elders and senior staff members. We go away for three days and make the final selections for the coming year—which of the twenty contenders we will preach, and in what order.

It's amazing to me the wealth of wisdom that comes out of a plurality of godly people who look at life differently than I do. Last year, in the first planning session, someone had proposed a series of sermons on fear: a message on the fear of failure, another on the fear of living alone, another on the fear of dying, and so on. When the person proposed it, I thought, *That series will never make it.* Those fears were simply not things that kept me awake at night. But I did leave it in as one of the twenty contenders for the second planning group to consider. When the elders and senior staff began to discuss it, I told them frankly I just couldn't see it working. But these highly discerning people looked at me and said, "Bill, just because you don't wrestle with these fears doesn't mean other people don't. People have these fears—normal people. Take our word for it that this subject is pleading to be spoken to."

So I agreed to preach the series, even though it wasn't one I would have chosen. But as they suspected, it was tremendously beneficial for our church. In fact, "The Fear of Dying" was one of the most highly requested tapes in recent years!

How Well We Meet Our Overall Goal

So far I haven't mentioned the usual barometers we use to measure our preaching: informal comments from people after services, letters they send, the number of tapes ordered, or comments from our spouse at home. Not that I don't think these measures are important. The problem is that I (and other preachers, I suspect) tend to put too much importance on them. And if we're not careful, that can lead to a subtle imbalance in our preaching.

It happened to me. Here's how.

Over the period in which Willow Creek has developed, society has fragmented at a frightening pace. When we started the church, maybe five percent of our congregation was made up of people who were so badly wounded they were dysfunctional. They grew up in homes with alcoholics, or were sexually abused or verbally abused, or were abandoned, divorced, or victimized in one form or another. Now, as a result of trends in society, that percentage has multiplied.

During this time, I have been careful to use the normal ways of listening to people and getting feedback about my preaching. I have a commitment to stay after a service as long as anybody wants to talk. After a typical service, I'll have serious conversations with probably thirty people. In addition, people write to me; I'm contacted by between 100 and 150 people a week.

But what I have not been sharp enough to pick up on, until recently, is that this sample of conversations and letters doesn't reflect the total congregation. It's skewed. Why? Because the people who will take the time to stay after a service in order to talk, or who will take the time to write a letter, are from the segment of the congregation that tends to be dysfunctional. They are so wounded that they write impassioned letters, and they are so hurting they are willing to stand for forty-five minutes in order to talk to me.

What I didn't notice, because it happened so subtly over time, was that I was not being contacted by the 85 percent of the congregation who are fairly functional, normal people who want to get on with their lives and grow. The preponderance of my interaction was with the 15 percent: wounded, needy people who were screaming out for me to be helpful. They did not want me to talk about picking up a cross and carrying it to serve Jesus Christ. They did not want me to talk about denying themselves. They did not want me to talk about making a difference with their lives. They wanted to be helped and loved and encouraged and nurtured.

So when I would give a message on "God will be with you even in your pain," or something like that, all the normal indicators of preaching effectiveness would go sky-high. Letters and phone calls would start coming that said, "Thank you for that tremendously helpful message." People would stand in long lines to tell me that message was just what they needed. I looked at all that and thought, *If I really love the flock, if I'm here to serve the flock, that's the kind of preaching I'm going to do.*

Then I went on my summer study break. As I evaluated the past five years of sermons, I began noticing subtle shifts. *Five years ago,* I realized, *70 percent of my messages were what I would call firm discipleship or gospel-oriented messages. Only 30 percent were more general,*

helpful messages. But over the years, those numbers have almost flipped. I was floored.

I reread *Loving God,* and when I finished, it dawned on me, *Chuck Colson thinks we ought to be producing fully devoted followers of Jesus Christ in our churches. All I'm trying to do is patch up people's lives. All I'm trying to do is lift burdens off sagging shoulders.*

I began to ask myself, *What about the 85 percent? Who is challenging these people to full discipleship? And who is asking these people to become kingdom men and women? Who's asking these people to lay down their lives for the cause of Christ? I'm not. And I'm the only preacher they have.*

I could say honestly I had not done anything consciously to preach a cheap gospel. I was trying to proclaim a compassionate gospel. Let any sensitive pastor talk with 125 people a week, the preponderance of whom are wounded, victimized, and crying out for help, and it takes a toll. You begin to think, *How can I add the burden of kingdom responsibility onto the shoulders of people who are bent over already? I don't have the heart for it.* My authentic motivation for that subtle shift was to be more responsive to a broken people. But as I spent days earnestly seeking the mind of God, it became clear to me that even though the motivation for the subtle shift was admirable, continuing down that path would be disaster.

When all this crashed in on me, it was both exhilarating and devastating. For weeks, I wrestled with what had happened. I came back and talked to the elders about it, and the minute I alerted them to this, everybody could see it. They said, "We knew something was happening, too." But no one had the luxury that I had of spending several weeks trying to hear what God was saying. The elders are godly people; I only had to mention the change in a cursory fashion and they said, "That's it. It's got to change."

Our solution has been to offer regular seminar and workshop teaching and therapy on all of these areas of victimization and pain. We are able to say to the 15 percent, "There is a place for you; there's hope for you; there's a context for you to receive the nurturing and expertise that are going to really solve your problem." But it's primarily in our counseling center, not in our Sunday service. And that makes sense. Allan McKechnie, the head of our counseling center, has pointed out to me that lasting change rarely comes out of large-group therapy, which is what I was attempting. It comes in the context of small groups or one-on-one discussions.

That frees me to be able to do the kind of teaching that exhilarates me and fulfills me and that is a true representation of who God made me to be. It's with the 85 percent.

Take, for example, a recent Wednesday night message. A theme of this whole ministry, coming out of Luke 15, is "You Matter to God." During that recent message, the first or second after my study break, I said, "We talk a lot around here about the fact that you matter to God. That's right, and that's true. But let me ask you this: Does God matter to you?"

It's interesting what has happened as a result of our sharpened focus. I used to drive home on a Sunday feeling as though I had been run over by a truck. I would talk after the service with dozens of people who were struggling to make it through another day, and I would feel totally defeated. I would come in the house, and Lynne would say, "That was a great message this morning." And I'd say, "What message? I don't even remember preaching."

But since this whole understanding has come, I talk to just as many people, but because of the subject matter I'm preaching these days, the conversations invigorate me. People are wrestling with what it means to be a man or woman of God. Even the wounded people see their need in a spiritual way. I'm not doing therapy; I'm doing discipleship. And that kind of talking doesn't exhaust me; it infuses me with energy.

From this experience, I have learned some important lessons. First, for my preaching to be effective, it's imperative I know—and stay riveted to—the overall goal of my ministry.

At Willow Creek, we ask ourselves, "What do we want the end product to be? There's this enormous machinery—buildings and staff. But after the people finally come through our ministry, what are they supposed to look like?" We have answered that: "We want to develop fully devoted followers of Jesus Christ. They should think Christianly, act Christianly, relate Christianly."

I know I haven't drawn that target on the wall often enough. Too often I've been caught preaching as if the goal of my ministry were to help people lead happy, well-adjusted lives and be more helpful to each other. Baloney! We have to shoot much higher than that. I want to preach in such a way that I help produce people who can rise above petty scrapes and get on with following Jesus Christ.

Second, I rigorously and regularly have to measure my preaching against this bull's-eye. Are the messages I'm preaching contributing to that? Are they really leading people to become more devoted to Christ? It's so easy to drift, incrementally and unconsciously, from that goal. But when that happens, my preaching, no matter how clever or prayed over or prepared, is undermined.

Why Fool with Evaluation?

Sometimes I'm tempted to think, *It really would be so much nicer if I didn't have the elders reproving me every time I slip up, and if I could just preach the way I want to preach and forget about anybody's evaluation.*

But then I realize why I have to take evaluation seriously. It's because I preach, as every pastor does, before a righteous and holy God, and I know he evaluates my work. Every time I take out a new pad and write a new sermon title with a passage under it, I pray, "Lord, I would like this to be an unblemished lamb, a worship sacrifice that you would really be proud of. I'm not going to be happy, and you're not going to be happy, with a sick, dying, blind, diseased, ravaged lamb. I will not offer it; you will not receive it." So to me it's a holy thing to start a new message. If God has given you speaking gifts and called you into the ministry, he expects unblemished lambs.

But that's also a good, freeing realization for me. I give a lot of messages that I don't think meet the standard I would have liked. But then I can go back and say. *Did I really do my preparation effectively? Did I pray on my knees as I should have? Was it biblical? Did the elders say that it was approved?* If I can say yes to those questions, then I'm done with the message, and I can walk away from it, no matter what anyone thinks. If those who came through the line said they didn't appreciate it, and if I got ripped apart by an extremist on either side of the message, it doesn't affect me. I did the best I knew how in trying to offer an unblemished lamb. That's the extent of my responsibility.

The rest is God's. I never have the final word on any passage or on any topic. When I get to the end of myself, that's where the real message starts. My prayer, when I'm driving home from church, is "Now, Holy Spirit, that I'm done and out of the way, do your real work. I tried to give you enough truth and opportunity to work with. But the result in these people's lives is up to you."

Chapter 194

THE AGONY AND ECSTASY OF FEEDBACK
What sermon evaluations taught me

John Vawter

My preaching was getting better and better. People were captivated by my sermons every Sunday. I was nearing my maximum potential as a Christian communicator—at least I thought so.

My wife brought me crashing back to reality. "Darling, you have developed a couple of bad habits during your sermons that really detract from your content and presentation."

Feedback . . . ouch!

I genuinely recoiled at the suggestion that I needed improvement. I was not at all certain I wanted to hear what she had to say. It was easier to see the church growing—almost every

Sunday—than to acknowledge I needed to refine my skills.

Yet feedback is necessary, and we grow through it. But it is not always pleasant.

When I finally listened to my wife, I realized she was right. I had developed a habit of clapping my hands together to emphasize points. It seemed a nice touch, but I was hitting one ring against the other and creating a loud, irritating clank. And to help people through difficult points of Scripture, I was pointing to my head and saying, "We've got to think through this truth together."

Hey, those were terrific gestures! I developed them myself. I had not stolen them from anyone! I really liked them. Little did I know they were driving the congregation crazy. And no one would tell me except my wife.

IN SEARCH OF EVALUATION

With this in mind, and as part of a study program, I asked for evaluation of my preaching skills. I mailed evaluation forms to thirty-five people in the church whom I thought would be candid. Each one had heard at least two years' worth of my sermons. The cover letter explained the project and emphasized my commitment to anonymity—no names on the surveys, stamped return envelopes.

My initial reaction to the feedback was anger and hurt. Though most of the feedback was positive, I saw only the negative. *Why would these people hurt me like this? Who do they think they are? What do they know about preaching?*

But once I began to think maturely about the situation, I realized they had done exactly what I'd hoped they'd do—give honest feedback. They cared enough about me to help me grow,

even if the process hurt momentarily. Proverbs 27:6 helped me at this point: "Faithful are the wounds of a friend, but deceitful are the kisses of an enemy" (NASB).

Also, I realized I had asked the opinions of perceptive and intelligent people who observe many public speakers in their careers. They were not about to give me answers that would not be direct and helpful.

I asked for evaluation of six areas:

- Do my introductions make a good first impression?
- Do I establish rapport with the audience?
- Do I reflect humility?
- Are my presentations conducive to learning?
- Am I logical?
- Am I biblical?

In each category my evaluators made helpful suggestions that would improve my sermons. Here is a sample of what they said and how I refined my sermon presentation accordingly.

A number of people said I needed to project my voice more during the introduction.

I decided to give up some of the "service duties," such as the offering, so during the early part of the service I could concentrate on my first few words. Through my friends' feedback I realized I was not single-minded about the sermon when I walked to the pulpit. I now make a concerted effort to grab everyone's attention during the introduction. I know this is basic, but I had lost sight of it.

I needed to improve my initial rapport with the audience by not talking down to them.

So I became careful to smile throughout the introduction, use anecdotes that did not point to the audience's frailties, and use the pronoun *we* instead of *you*. I did this by reminding myself during preparation time that we are in this growth process together.

The reactions were mixed on whether I reflected humility. But since a number of people commented on my lack of humility, I took their word for it. I asked God to purge me of any pride over the church's health.

As I prayed and thought about this area, I also realized some people misunderstood my humor. My friends tell me my sense of humor is sardonic, bordering on caustic, and sometimes misunderstood by those who don't know me well or don't see the twinkle in my eye. I thought I was being witty, but I was perceived as sarcastic. For example, one day when I was stumbling over my words and not explaining my point well, I said, "Intelligent people will understand me." I meant it to be funny because I obviously was at fault, but many in the audience interpreted it as a put-down. I began to delete some things that were better left unsaid.

There were no negative comments on how conducive my sermons were to learning. People said I was honest in admitting my shortcomings. They perceived me as wanting to learn, and this inspired them to learn. This confirmed I was on the right track in sharing myself in my sermons.

The evaluators also perceived me as being biblical and careful to delineate between my insights and God's wisdom. They considered me logical and structured in what I had to say. This positive feedback actually made me work harder to ensure I remained on track.

BREAKING OUT OF A CLOSED SYSTEM

Scott Peck, in *The Road Less Traveled*, says, "A life of total dedication to the truth also means a life of willingness to be personally challenged. The only way that we can be certain that our map of reality is valid is to expose it to the criticism and challenge of the other map-makers. Otherwise, we live in a closed system . . . rebreathing our own fetid air, more and more subject to delusion."

People tell me I have become a better preacher since I asked for evaluation. The feedback pointed out areas where I did not know I needed to grow and confirmed strengths I thought I had. Indeed, the process has been so helpful I am compiling another list of people to survey. I intend to have people evaluate my preaching on a regular basis for the balance of my ministry.

Oh, by the way, I have broken those two habits to which my wife alerted me. But just to make certain she is still paying close attention, I'm developing a couple of new annoying habits. I'll see if she can spot them.

Chapter 195

GETTING THE FEEDBACK YOU NEED

How to invite a constructive critique

William Willimon

Nice sermon, preacher."
For most of us, that is the extent of the feedback we receive on our preaching. Yet we yearn for something more substantial: How do we come across to people? What aspects of our preaching style, delivery, organization, and biblical interpretation need to be improved to communicate the gospel more effectively?

To grow, we need honest evaluation, but how can we move beyond the haphazard, off-the-cuff "Nice sermon, preacher" without getting ambushed by pet peeves of chronic complainers?

CREATING GOOD LISTENERS

A number of years ago, Dr. John K. Bergland, who at the time was teaching at Duke Divinity School, conducted scores of interviews with people in rural North Carolina United Methodist Churches, asking them to evaluate their preachers' sermons. Bergland discovered that these laypeople were extremely reluctant to criticize a pastor's preaching. They assumed, apparently, that since the pastor has been called by God to preach and has studied preaching to prepare for ministry, the comments of ordinary laypeople are out of place.

People also hesitated to criticize their pastor's preaching because, according to Bergland, even though the preacher may not be the world's best, he or she is our preacher. Most

church people tend to be intensely loyal to their local congregation; they want to be proud of it. Drawing attention to the pastor's weaknesses only reflects negatively on their church.

Over the years I have tried, sometimes successfully and sometimes not, to elicit honest, usable reaction to my preaching. Sometimes laypeople are not sure the minister really wants their criticism, so initial responses tend to be positive. However, as time passes and people understand that I sincerely want their responses, even their critical responses, they become more honest.

For instance, when I gave out the standardized questionnaire that accompanies this article and asked people to complete it each Sunday for a few weeks, my scores actually went down in a number of areas!

Why? People were becoming more candid. Their initial "Nice sermon, preacher" was becoming a more straightforward "Nice sermon, but. . . ." Because of my persistence, they realized that I was determined to get honest reactions, even if the reactions were negative.

Plus, in the process of evaluating my sermons, people were becoming better listeners. For instance, a number of them, when first asked, "Was this a biblical sermon?" quickly responded, "Yes." Of course the sermon was biblical: A Bible text was read at the beginning of the sermon.

However, as week after week they continued

to evaluate my preaching, they stepped back and asked themselves, *Was this really a biblical sermon?* They began noticing that, though some verses were read at the beginning of the sermon, the text sometimes didn't control the movement and the thoughts of the sermon.

In urging my laypeople systematically and carefully to react to my preaching, then, I was making them better listeners. Critical listeners consider sermons with certain criteria in mind. Although I was receiving truthful, and sometimes (to me) painful, responses, I had given them criteria to help them have "ears to hear."

A Questionnaire That Helps

In the early 1970s, Boyd E. Stokes, as part of his doctoral work at Emory University, performed many months of research, interviewing scores of laypeople, preachers, and professors of homiletics, asking them what they looked for in a "good" sermon. He then selected the criteria most frequently cited. The result was the "Sermon Reaction Questionnaire," a version of which is shown here.

I have used this questionnaire in three different congregations, with good effect. It's easily understood. It can be completed in just a few minutes, and it offers standardized scores, whose results can be compared over a period of weeks or months.

This questionnaire has helped me focus on particular problems. For instance, since I had always prided myself in not referring to my notes, I was surprised to see my listeners thought I looked at my notes too often. So over the following few weeks, I disciplined myself to look even less at my notes, and my scores improved.

The questionnaire has also helped me see how different groups within the church react to my preaching. In general, younger respondents like my preaching better than do older respondents, and women are more positive about my preaching than are men. I'm not always able to make changes in my preaching based on what I learn, but knowing how I come across has made me a more sensitive preacher.

I've used the questionnaire in a couple of different ways. In one church, I gave the questionnaire to a selected group of laypersons to evaluate my sermons my first two weeks with the congregation. Then, two years later, I gave the same questionnaire to the same laypeople for two more weeks. That helped me gauge my progress over the long term.

I've also randomly selected a group of about twenty laypeople, asking them to attend worship every Sunday for five weeks. (That's important because even one absence can skew the scores.) I gave them questionnaires and asked them to fill them out and return them at the end of each service.

After five weeks, I met with all of the respondents and shared the results of the research. Together we looked at individual sermons and the scores they received, and I asked the people to clarify some of their responses. This discussion greatly increased the value of the questionnaire for me.

In either case, the questionnaires are scored by totaling and then averaging the scores on each item and on the questionnaire as a whole.

Some items (3, 5, and 7, for instance) are stated negatively to keep respondents from simply going down the questionnaire and mindlessly checking off the same number on every question. That means, though, when I tally the scores, I need to reverse the scores: for instance, a score of 1 on item 3, "did not inspire me," would be scored as 5. That way all the results "move" in the same direction.

To remain faithful to Christ, sermons are accountable to Scripture and a church's tradition, but they must also to some degree be accountable to the church, and that means the men and women sitting in the pews each Sunday morning. Through this questionnaire such men and women have improved my preaching and strengthened the church.

Sermon Reaction Questionnaire

Do not sign your name.

Supply the following information:

Sex: male_____ ; female_____

Age: under 20_____ ; 20–29_____ ; 30–39_____ ; 40–49_____ ; 50–59_____ ; over 59_____

Regarding the sermon you just heard, indicate whether you agree or disagree with these statements. Circle 1 if you strongly agree, 2 if you agree, 3 if you're uncertain, 4 if you disagree, 5 if you strongly disagree.

Your honesty and frankness will be appreciated.

1.	My interest was maintained.	1 2 3 4 5
2.	The sermon was integrated into the service of worship.	1 2 3 4 5
3.	I was not inspired.	1 2 3 4 5
4.	The preacher's personality came through.	1 2 3 4 5
5.	The Scripture text was not used or illumined.	1 2 3 4 5
6.	The preacher used contemporary language.	1 2 3 4 5
7.	The preacher did not evidence a personal faith.	1 2 3 4 5
8.	The sermon was too long.	1 2 3 4 5
9.	I did not understand the sermon well.	1 2 3 4 5
10.	The preacher referred to notes too often.	1 2 3 4 5
11.	The preacher sounded like he/she loved us.	1 2 3 4 5
12.	The sermon spoke to some of my personal needs.	1 2 3 4 5
13.	The sermon did not sufficiently emphasize the greatness of Christ.	1 2 3 4 5
14.	The preacher showed self-confidence.	1 2 3 4 5
15.	The sermon did not make me eager to serve God any more than I'm already serving him.	1 2 3 4 5
16.	I identified with the preacher.	1 2 3 4 5
17.	The preacher spoke down to us.	1 2 3 4 5
18.	The sermon did not have a sufficiently forceful conclusion.	1 2 3 4 5
19.	The sermon did not help me encounter God.	1 2 3 4 5
20.	I can remember most or all of the sermon points.	1 2 3 4 5

Chapter 196

A COMPREHENSIVE CHECK-UP

Questions to ensure you are covering the essentials

Haddon Robinson

ORGANIZATION

Introduction

- Does the message get attention?
- Does it touch some need directly or indirectly?
- Does it orient hearers to the subject? Or to the main idea? Or to the first point?
- Is it the right length? Is there a specific purpose?

Structure

- Is the development clear? Is the overall structure clear?
- Does the sermon have a *central idea*? Can you state it?
- Are the transitions clear? Do they review?
- Is there a logical or psychological link between the points?
- Do the main points relate back to the main idea?
- Are the subpoints clearly related to their main points?

Conclusion

- Does the sermon build to a climax?
- Is there an adequate summary of ideas?
- Are there effective closing appeals or suggestions?

CONTENT

- Is this subject significant? Is it appropriate?
- Is the sermon built on *solid exegesis?*
- Does the speaker show where he or she is in the text?
- Is the analysis of the subject thorough? Logical?
- Does the speaker convince you that he or she is right?
- Does the content show originality?

Supporting material

- Is the supporting material *logically* related to its point?
- Is it *interesting? varied? specific? sufficient?*

Style

- Does the speaker use correct grammar?
- Is the speaker's vocabulary concrete? Vivid? Varied?
- Are words used correctly?
- Does the choice of words add to the effectiveness of the sermon?

DELIVERY

Intellectual Directness

- Does the speaker want to be heard? Is the speaker alert?
- Do you feel the speaker is talking to you?
- Is the speaker friendly?
- Does the delivery sound like lively conversation?
- Are words *pronounced* correctly?

Oral Presentation

- Is the voice easy to listen to? Is there clear articulation?
- Is there vocal variety? Does the *pitch* level change?
- Is there a variety of force? Does the *rate* vary enough?
- Does the speaker use *pauses* effectively?

Physical Presentation

- Is the speaker's entire body involved in the delivery?
- Does the speaker gesture?
- Are the gestures spontaneous? Wide? Definite? Are there distracting mannerisms?
- Is the posture good? Does the speaker look alert?
- Is there good facial expression?

AUDIENCE ADAPTATION

- Is the sermon adapted to hearers' interests? Attitudes?
- Is the message related to hearers' knowledge? Does it meet needs?
- Does the speaker look hearers in the eye?
- Do you feel the speaker is aware of audience response?

Chapter 197

THE SCIENCE OF SURVEYS

Formal procedures lead to more objective results

Virginia Vagt

To be most effective, a survey requires careful planning and analysis.

Surveys provide not only comments on where to improve but also two uplifting results: what your people gained from your sermons, and representative feedback. Representative comments—from a cross-section of church people—help keep you from placing undue weight on the scathing individual comment that comes to every pastor from time to time.

SAMPLE SURVEY

To get started, I recommend a written, one-page, anonymous survey focused on a specific sermon. It is easiest for people to respond to something concrete, such as this morning's sermon. And you will gain specific feedback. Here is a sample survey. (An actual survey would allow space for answers.)

Sermon Survey

The pastor is seeking feedback from people within the congregation. Please take a minute or two right now to complete this survey. Thank you.

1. Overall, how would you rate today's sermon?

   Excellent   Good   Fair   Poor

2. How would you compare today's sermon to most of the pastor's sermons?

   Better   About the same   Poorer

   If today's sermon seemed better or poorer than usual, why?

3. What are the *main points* you remember from today's sermon?

4. What, if anything, did you *gain* from the sermon?

5. What, if anything, did you think was *weak* about the sermon?

6. Do you think today's sermon will change your life in any concrete way? (For example, change an attitude, cause you to do anything differently, and so on)

   Definitely yes   Probably yes   Maybe   Probably not

   If yes, what do you think will change?

7. If you could tell the pastor one positive thing about his/her sermons, what would it be?

8. If you could give the pastor one suggestion about sermon content or delivery, what would it be?

9. Please add any other comments you may have about today's sermon or other sermons.

10. Are you: Male_____ Female_____

11. Your age: Under 30_____ 30–49_____ 50 or over_____

12. How long have you attended this church?

    Less than 1 year   1–3 years   More than 3 years

SUGGESTED PROCEDURES

Number of Surveys

Regardless of the size of your church, fewer than twenty returns may not be enough feedback, and more than fifty per Sunday is not necessary to get representative opinions. You won't get every survey back, so pass out twenty-five to fifty.

Distribution

Pick one or more personable and trustworthy people to distribute the survey. I suggest these people approach individuals as they leave the sanctuary, asking them if they would like to help the pastor by taking a few minutes to complete a survey on today's sermon. (It will be most accurate and helpful if people complete the survey *right away*.)

The persons should hand them out to a mix of young and old, men and women, leaders and nonleaders, and new and long-term members. The survey distributors can personally collect the surveys or tell people where to place them. A cardboard box nearby marked *Surveys* would ensure anonymity.

The distributors should thank people for their time.

It's possible that a few people may not be honest or fair, so I recommend surveying a cross-section of church members on at least three or four Sundays.

Tabulating and Analyzing the Results

While you may want to just read through all the survey forms, tabulating the answers gives you a better understanding of what the feedback really means. You will see what percentage of your respondents felt positively or negatively about the sermon.

Some tips:

- Use a blank copy of the survey to record your tabulations and analysis.
- If you see major differences in the way people answer based on age, sex, or length of time at your church, you may want to tabulate each group separately. For example, separately tabulate surveys from male and female respondents, or those under thirty and those over thirty.

- On questions 1, 2a, and 6a, find percentages for each answer. Save these percentages and compare them to the answers from your next sermon survey. If the next message is a different type, and you receive a significantly higher or lower score (more than 10 percentage points), you can conclude something about your congregation's receptivity to these two types of sermons.
- On the remaining questions, it would be helpful to count the number of times a response is repeated. For example, on question 3, count which point in your sermon was remembered by the *greatest* number of people and which was remembered by the *least* number of people.
- Throughout the tabulation, pay attention to the repeated comments. These represent the typical response to your sermons. Don't place lots of weight on the single complaint. Perhaps you can't help taking such comments to heart, but remember, they represent only one person's view, not the church's as a whole.

Using the Results

Think back. Using question 3 again, was the most remembered point the first point? Did it have the most graphic image associated with it? There may be more than one reason why it was most remembered. These reasons will tell you something about your congregation and how to best communicate with them.

The results may make intuitive sense to you. They may not. If there is something truly baffling about the results to any question, you may want to talk it over with an elder you trust. It's always helpful to have more than one interpretation of survey results.

Chapter 198

LESSONS FROM *PREACHING TODAY* SCREENERS

Ten criteria used by our experts to choose the best sermons

Lee Eclov

I have the privilege of being one of the sermon screeners who review about 250 sermon recordings sent to *Preaching Today Audio* each year. It is a rare opportunity to hear a wide variety of the best of American (usually) preaching. What follows are the ten questions by which we evaluate all the sermons received by *Preaching Today*, and some of the lessons we've learned from listening.

IS THIS SERMON GROUNDED IN SCRIPTURE?

Most sermons we hear are scriptural, but many do not "keep their finger on the text." Listeners are not taken to Scripture frequently through the sermon. The effect is subtle—the source of authority seems to shift quietly from the Bible to the preacher. Too few sermons actually try to follow the reasoning—the logic—of a text.

I carry a PDA—one of those little hand-held computers. The screen is bright and colorful, but if I don't touch the screen the light goes off after about a minute. The words are still there, but there's no light. It is hard to read. Sermons are like that. We need to keep tapping the Scripture as we preach—reading the next sentence in the text, pointing to a phrase explicitly, asking people to look at a certain verse—if we hope to keep the light on the Bible and not ourselves.

IS THE EXEGESIS AND THEOLOGY SOUND?

My most frequent reaction to this question after hearing a sermon is, "Sound?" Yes. Deep? No. A few sermons unload so much exegesis that you'd think this was an oral final exam in seminary. But most sermons, while true, do not display well the surprises, ingenuity, or depth of Scripture. I suspect the preacher didn't study well.

To the natural mind (versus the spiritual mind), the Bible is always counter-intuitive. Good sermons reveal how the text teaches us to think differently, showing us how God's truth and logic challenge our "old man" way of thinking.

Screener Jeffrey Arthurs, associate professor of preaching and communication at Gordon-Conwell Theological Seminary, notes another issue: "I am sometimes concerned with 'how-to' sermons typical in the seeker-sensitive movement. These often take verses out of context and elevate other sources of authority (especially ethos) on a par with Scripture."

As to the theology in a sermon, preachers are sometimes surprisingly careless in their choice of words, belying fuzzy theology. But more often, I have the feeling the preacher didn't realize the rich nuances of theology in the text before him, like someone looking at the Grand Canyon and preaching, "Boy, is that big!" We shortchange God's people when we shade their eyes from the glory of theology.

Would You Describe the Sermon As Having Unction/Anointing?

This is the most difficult question to answer. Screener Scott Wenig, associate professor of applied theology at Denver Seminary, says, "If the sermon really 'connects,' then I'll answer yes. I would guess that less than 15 percent of the sermons I screen meet this specific criteria."

A sense of passion is a possible tip-off to unction, but sometimes that is more a matter of personality and style than the work of the Holy Spirit. Ultimately, the most sure sign to me is if Scripture speaks loud and clear; if not only the full sense of a passage is made clear but also the passion of the biblical writer. When it seems the preacher and the original writer are in synch with each other, that is a unique work of the Holy Spirit, and on that sermon there is unction.

Did It Engage Your Mind from Beginning to End?

Scott Wenig says, "Most sermons I listen to don't do this. The sermon must move and hum to keep attention." One of the benefits to manuscript preachers is that their sermons tend to be tighter, better edited. But most preachers are more extemporaneous. Their sermons tend to bog down somewhere. A stale illustration will do it, or belaboring a point that is already clear, or trying to milk some humor from a story.

Screener John Koessler, chairman of the pastoral studies department at Moody Bible Institute, puts another factor very simply: "Are the ideas interesting?" One thing that will certainly engage our minds and hearts are great biblical ideas, expressed well. It takes work and time to hone an idea to vivid expression.

Is the Sermon Fresh?

Think garden-fresh. The sermon doesn't have to be something you've never heard before, but it needs to come across as crisp, tasty, and newly-harvested. It seems that sometimes preachers are telling their folks things they surely already know and believe, and doing so in terms the congregation would probably find overly familiar.

Koessler identifies one key test of freshness: "I want the speaker to avoid clichés." Clichés come when a preacher hasn't thought too much about how he will say something and so naturally reverts to road-weary words and phrases. I listened to a fine sermon recently and found myself thinking again and again, *That man thought hard about how to say that well.* As a result, a familiar theme was fresh.

Is the Sermon Well-Structured and Clear?

John Koessler explains that he wants to "be able to discern the major movements within the sermon. I prefer to have the outline points stated and emphasized. I think it is clearer if they are stated as complete sentences rather than phrases. In a narrative I want to be able to follow the plot clearly and have a smooth transition to application."

Jeffrey Arthurs adds, "The key to clarity is restatement, review, and repetition. The key moments in sermons where those techniques are needed are the transitions."

Is the Sermon Well-Illustrated?

Koessler responds, "My first question is whether it is illustrated at all." Many sermons are not well-illustrated, and I think the reason is that illustrating takes time and work, added to all the other elements of sermon preparation. Many illustrations we hear are easy; they came quickly to the preacher's mind and are not sharpened well. Quite often it seems that the illustration isn't quite focused enough—a little too general. It fits the sermon like those baggy jeans on a teenage boy. Increasingly, we're hearing video clips as illustrations. Some work very well, but they tend to be general; sometimes I wonder what a pastor was doing watching that film.

It is rare to hear *metaphors* used well. They take time and imagination, but they are such wonderful windows. The Puritan John Owen was a past master from whom we can learn. For example, he said in one sermon, "The world is but a great inn where we are to stay a night or two and be gone. What madness it is to set our heart upon our inn as to forget our home!"

Analogies work well for giving a fresh understanding of an idea. For example, I recently filed away a news story about a whale carcass exploding on a city street under "life gets messy." That is an illustration by analogy. It will bring smiles *and* nods of understanding.

Examples are stories of people actually working out the sermon's principle—how God provided for a generous giver, for example, or a quote from someone who feels life crashing in on her. Koessler adds, "I want to hear the speaker apply the illustration—tell me its significance."

DID THE MESSAGE CHALLENGE YOU?

Sermons that challenge listeners who are as tough as we screeners are pretty special! Again, a rule of thumb is, the more biblical it is, the more challenging. Good sermons have a kind of time-delay medicine pushed into my subconscious mind that keeps treating my soul, keeps dosing me hours and days after I've finished listening.

I often wonder how well a sermon I'm hearing was prayed for. Though I don't know how to gauge it, I think a sermon that has been prayed well carries a long-term potency. Prayer is a means of unction.

For a sermon to challenge us, it has to have a great-heartedness, a grand idea about it. Some sermons feel lightweight.

IS THE DELIVERY EFFECTIVE?

All the screeners note something most preachers don't usually think about—the sound of our voices. Scott Wenig says, "Most sermons I listen to for PT leave much to be desired here." He points to "a lack of variety in terms of voice, inflection, and pacing."

I listen for a good command of language and emotion. Some preachers are so casual that they undersell weighty subjects. In an effort to "put the cookies on the bottom shelf," they drop them on the floor. A sermon about sin, for example, that is funny is missing something. Sermons can be warm and human without sacrificing dignity.

Underneath our listening is the subconscious question, "Is this a godly person? Do I discern a Christlike heart and mind?" Somehow we discern that in a preacher's delivery.

IS THE APPLICATION TRUE TO SCRIPTURE AND TO LIFE?

Many preachers work hard at this, but John Koessler warns, "Do not tell me the obvious. If it is something that I already know that I should do, help me to understand why I am not doing it. I especially want the preacher to help me explore the nature of the problems I face in implementing the application."

We usually think of application in terms of what we should *do*, but much of Scripture addresses how we should *think*. Romans 12:2 says we will be "transformed by the renewing of [our] *mind*." Show people how their typical thinking is contrary to the truth of Scripture, and then bring sanctified tools of rhetoric to persuade them to think with the mind of Christ. That is application even if we do not speak of *doing* something.

Chapter 199

HOLDING HEARERS CAPTIVE

Three things that make it hard for listeners to escape a sermon

Craig Brian Larson

What makes a sermon captivating—a message not just true and biblical, but one people must listen to? As we evaluate our own messages, especially by listening to them on tape, this is one of the important criteria we should be listening for.

Of course, if we address painfully felt needs, people listen, but what about all those important sermons that ground believers but do not address torment or ambition? How do we engage hearers no matter what the topic?

After listening to hundreds, perhaps thousands, of sermons on tape for *Preaching Today*, I think I know. Hearing a sermon on tape is the acid test. On tape preachers lose the benefit of their winsome facial expressions, physical movement and gestures, the excitement of a crowd, and the presence of God in the meeting. Taped sermons strip preachers down to their voice and words. I have heard many sermons in person that I thought were world class, only to listen later on tape and be unmoved. So if you can captivate hearers on tape, then in person you can really preach.

What grabs hearers even on tape is energy.

When you listen to yourself preach, do you sense an electricity in the message? I have observed three types of energy in sermons. If you have at least one type, your messages can capture hearers so they might fully hear the Word.

EMOTIONAL ENERGY

 For an audio example of this principle see tracks 24–25 on the supplemental CD.

Rarely can I turn off a preacher who speaks with heart—even when the sermon lacks organization. Passion overcomes a multitude of preaching sins. (Of course, passion also raises red flags. But just because manipulators and heretics abuse emotion does not mean ethical speakers must avoid it. Quite the opposite!)

Emotional vitality springs from the feelings of both the speaker and the listener, as heart touches heart. In my observation, emotional energy comes from the following sources:

- I sense that the preacher's heart pulses with Christian virtues: faith; love for God and people; passion for holiness; zeal for the church, the lost, and the kingdom. In other words, the preacher is filled with the Holy Spirit.

- The speaker talks about an important subject, clearly believes it is important, and shows me why it is critically important to me. The greater the consequences of a sermon, the greater the emotion.
- The speaker expresses feelings at an appropriate and mature level. The speaker's expressed emotions work like an emotional thermostat in the congregation. The congregation must sense that speakers have their feelings under control, though. Otherwise, they grow uncomfortable and think more about their preacher needing help than they do about the message. Obviously the speaker's feelings must also be authentic.
- The speaker appeals directly to the will. "Today I call you to focus your resources on helping needy people." Asking others to change electrifies a message because the thought of change both traumatizes and excites a congregation. Challenging the congregation also energizes the preacher because seasoned ministers know the stakes.
- When suited, the sermon offers an inspirational story of love, hope, mercy, perseverance, courage, faith, overcoming obstacles. We must not toss in a story gratuitously. If, however, the story genuinely fits our heart, the text, and the sermon, we should not shy from using it.

INTELLECTUAL ENERGY

 For an audio example of this principle see tracks 26–27 on the supplemental CD.

Some preachers think particularly interesting thoughts, and I have to listen because I must know what they think. They form sermons in a way that makes ideas hum.

Intellectual dynamism comes naturally from a growing mind and from meditating long on a text and its application to today's hearers under the leading of the Spirit. Here are some personal disciplines and message preparation steps that increase mental energy in sermons:

- Seek truth, wisdom, and understanding all the days of your life. Ask honest questions, prayerfully pursue answers, journal your thoughts—and not just for your current sermon.
- Provoke curiosity. Some preachers fail to build tension or raise questions.
- Watch for extremes. We may skid into one of two ditches: We oversimplify issues, making them black or white; or we overemphasize complexity and ambiguity, rarely coming to strong, clear resolution. Intellectual energy comes from the pull of two poles, equal regard for the tension between ideas and for conviction. (Yes, that is a both-and answer!)
- Like a novelist, write sermons with an eye for conflict and contrast. That is not hard, for the greatest struggles in the world rage over the battlegrounds of truth: doubt versus belief; Satan versus God; good versus evil. Preaching on gentleness, for example, can put people to sleep, until we contrast gentleness with an uncaring, selfish heart.
- Be creative. Imaginative elements ignite bottle rockets in the mind. Insight thrives in the realm of image and metaphor. This does not require Mensa-level genius. Ask the Creator how to express the main elements of the sermon in ways you have never heard before.
- In devotions and sermon preparation, read Scripture slowly, prayerfully. Observe everything in the text. Ask questions. When you commute, exercise, or daydream, meditate on the meaning and implications of Scripture.
- If God has blessed you with a sense of humor, use it (judiciously and purposefully), for it too has inherent energy.

• Stick to what matters most. Must-hear preachers resemble a savvy CEO who weighs every business decision in terms of the big-picture mission of the company. Through their reading and conversations with God and people, preachers with energetic ideas have a gut sense of what is important, what is at stake, what matters to hearers, what matters to God.

VOCAL ENERGY

 For an audio example of this principle see tracks 28–29 on the supplemental CD.

My idealistic side wants to say we can present the Word in any vocal delivery, and the preaching will bear fruit. But preaching involves both divine and human dimensions, and of the human factors one of the most influential is the voice.

Forget whether your voice is high or low, strong or weak, or whether you speak in a conversational or speaker mode. What a preacher's voice must have is not beauty but vitality. Some preachers with surging emotions and thoughts have a disconnect between that inner energy and their voice, and so they must work on vocal energy.

The following factors affect vocal vitality:

Aiming only to comfort. When you try to soothe hearers, you risk losing them. One preacher I know who has energetic ideas speaks in intimate tones from beginning to end. His sermons just lie there because when we soothe, we lower our volume, smooth the edges off our enunciation, slow down—in other words, stop doing everything that energizes our voice.

I often hear preachers throttle-back in the same way in the conclusion, even when they are not trying to comfort. They intend to wind up the sermon, and unconsciously, perhaps, they

start to wind down their delivery. The moral: Use soothing tones for variety, but not for long.

The use of vocal dynamism.

• Volume. Even with a public address system, in preaching we need to speak louder than we would in normal conversation. It helps me to think more about projecting my voice to those in the back of the room than speaking loudly.
• Pitch. We all speak in a melody, in movement up and down in pitch. Compare the melody of your voice with that of speakers with a dynamic voice.
• Rate. Like a fast car, word speed is dynamic and exciting. Even a slight increase in speed does wonders. The older we get, the more we need to push ourselves to keep the tempo alive.
• Emphatic enunciation. Emphasizing some sounds and not others is one of the lesser-used secrets of dynamic speaking. We emphasize sounds through volume, pitch, pauses before or after, and articulation.
• Variety in all of the above. For example, used sparingly, a pause in the midst of rapid speaking can be the most charged moment in the sermon.

Formality. Preachers who try to speak in a serious manner often lose the life in their voice. They get stiff. If we use our speaker's voice, it still has to be our voice raised to another level, not someone else's voice.

On a recent commute home, I listened to a sermon on tape that stirred my heart and mind deeply. When I pulled into the driveway, the message had not yet finished, but I put the car in park and kept listening, my cheeks wet with tears. When the preacher concluded, I turned the key and sat in the car thinking and praying. The Spirit and the Word changed me to be more like Christ through a sermon that had an energy I could not escape.

Chapter 200

MY WORST AND BEST SERMONS EVER
How I was set free from the need to judge my preaching

Barbara Brown Taylor

The worst sermon I ever preached was in Canajoharie, New York, the chewing-gum capital of the world, where I was invited to address what was described to me as an ailing congregation.

The Gospel lesson for that Trinity Sunday was John's story about Nicodemus's search for new birth. It was a promising sign, I thought, and I proceeded to construct an eight-page masterpiece on faith and doubt. Sunday morning arrived, the processional hymn began, and I marched into a church with three people in it—five, including me and my host.

Two were elderly women, still weepy over the loss of a friend the day before. The third was a heavy, angry-looking man who occupied the other side of the church all by himself. When the time came for the sermon, I crept into the pulpit, wondering what to do. I tried the first page of my manuscript and abandoned it; it was like reciting poetry to a wall. With a fast prayer to the Holy Spirit, I put my notes away and tried to summarize what I had planned to say. The result was five minutes of pure gibberish. The Holy Spirit never showed up, and as my congregation stared blankly at me, I rapidly confirmed all their worst fears about women preachers.

OUT OF THIN AIR

One of the best sermons I ever preached was at the funeral of a baby girl. Her death, which came just three months after her complicated birth, tried the faith of everyone who knew her and her parents, including me. I worked and worked at something to say, but everywhere I turned I ran into the dead-end of my grief. When it came time for the service, I walked into a full church with nothing but a half page of notes. I stood plucking the words out of thin air as they appeared before my eyes. Somehow, they worked. God consented to be present in them.

When I received a transcript of the sermon later, it was as if it had been written in disappearing ink. Nothing was there but a jumble of phrases and images, trailing off at the end into awkward silence. While the Holy Spirit was in them, they lived. Afterward, they were no more than empty boxes, lying where the wind had left them.

TIN INTO GOLD

These two experiences remind me not to take myself too seriously. They also make me reluctant to talk about "best" and "worst" sermons. Something happens between the preacher's lips and congregation's ears that is beyond prediction or explanation. The same sermon sounds entirely different at 9:00 and 11:15 A.M. Sermons that make me weep leave my listeners baffled, and sermons that seem cold to me find warm responses. Later in the week, someone quotes part of my sermon back to me, something she found extremely meaningful—only I never said it.

More is going on here than anyone can say. Preaching is, finally, more than art or science. It is alchemy, in which tin becomes gold and yard rocks become diamonds under the influence of the Holy Spirit. It is a process of transformation for both preacher and congregation alike, as the ordinary details of their everyday lives are translated into the extraordinary elements of God's ongoing creation. When the drum roll begins and the preacher steps into place, we can count on that. Wherever God's Word is, God is—loosening our tongues, tuning our ears, thawing our hearts, and making us a people who may speak and hear the Word of Life.

Chapter 201

LEARNING FROM GIANTS

Although I can't just imitate great preachers, I can benefit greatly from their example.

Kevin A. Miller

How do we learn from outstanding preachers and still be ourselves? That question is one I've wrestled with over the years, and I've come up with some principles that have been helpful to me.

CAUTION

The first principle is counterintuitive: Don't apply what you first notice in a great preacher. That is because what you first notice in a great preacher is their strongest gift.

For example, when I listen to John Ortberg, I am awed by his sense of comic timing. The guy has an ability to deliver the punch line at just the right moment. Or I listen to Haddon Robinson. Haddon has these incredible hands. He uses his hands better than anybody I've seen in preaching. They're perfectly timed and apt.

Or Timothy Keller. He's got these subtle, nuanced, intellectual distinctions, and when I hear him I think, *I want to preach like that.*

We all have these kinds of responses to great preaching, but you don't want to apply that first thing you notice about the great preacher. You don't want to look at their greatest gift, because you don't have a gift that great—at least I don't in those three cases I gave—so I want to look not at their charisma but at their craftsmanship, something I can duplicate.

Right. I don't want to ask, *What is their amazing gift?* because I may not have that. I want to look at their craftsmanship: *How do they achieve a good effect?*

I'll give you an illustration. Over the years I've listened to many sermons by Bill Hybels, and one of the first things I notice is his great passion. He's a jet-fuel drinking, high octane, intense person, which comes through in his preaching to great effect. That is Bill's charisma. That's one of the gifts he brings as a preacher, but I don't have that same kind of temperament. I'm intense, but not to that level of intensity, so I can't apply that to me. But here's what I can apply. One craftsmanship technique Bill does well is that in the first five minutes or so of the sermon he will convince you why you absolutely must listen to this sermon. This topic is of such importance that you cannot afford to ignore it. This is for you and will affect your life. So he spends a lot of time at the beginning of a message setting up the importance of the topic.

I could do that, even though I don't have the same level of intensity in my temperament as Bill does. For example, recently I taught on forgiveness. And rather than launching into the subject and assuming people knew how important it is, I said:

> Forgiveness is one of *the* most important topics in the Christian life. If you do not learn how to forgive, you will become a bitter person. You will become swallowed by anger. You will become self-absorbed. You will damage your relationship with God. But if you learn how to forgive and you courageously make the choice to forgive, you will become a more gracious person. You will become a person of life and joy. You will become the kind of person other people long to be around, and you will become the kind of person God can use. Would you like to learn how to forgive this morning?

I essentially said: "This is such a critical topic, you must listen to it. You cannot afford not to listen to it." All of a sudden I have added passion to my message, I've added a level of intensity, and I learned that from Bill Hybels. I can't imitate his charisma, but I can learn from his craftsmanship.

ADOPTION

The second way we can profit from great preachers is, rather than borrow everything they do or reject everything they do, ask, *How much can I adopt certain approaches to preaching from them?* The way you know how much you can adopt is to ask yourself one question: *If I do this, will I feel good about it and will my people feel good about it?*

Not long ago on *Preaching Today* audio we had a wonderful sermon by the late E. K. Bailey, in which he took on the role of the prophet Hosea. And he went into a burst of rhetorical fireworks that was absolutely amazing. It went something like this: "What concord hath the prophet and the prostitute? What unity can there be between the sacred and the secular? What intercourse can there be between purity and profanity?"

And he was just getting warmed up. He went on from there to have at least three more of these alliterative contrasts between the holy and the unholy. I was moved. I could feel the impact of that. I loved it, and there was something inside myself that said, *Oh, if only I could preach like that.*

But the truth is that if I got up on Sunday in my congregation and started saying, "What unity is there between the prophet and the prostitute? Between the sacred and the secular?" people would look at me and scratch their heads. They'd say, "What's wrong with him today? Is he trying to show off?" because they know that's not part of my usual style. So even though it works brilliantly for E. K., I couldn't do it and have my people feel comfortable. They'd start to focus more on the technique than on the message. Now—and this is my main point—rather than reject that out of hand

and say, *I could never use anything from that,* I ask, *What amount of this could I adopt and still feel good about it and have my people feel good about it?*

I'll tell you how much in my particular example I could adopt. I'm preaching this Sunday on the parable of the persistent widow from Luke 18. I want to adopt from E. K. Bailey a certain amount of the power of alliteration, so I'm going to use in that sermon the phrase "the power of persistence." I could go on from there and say something like "the potency of perseverance." I'm not going to do that, because that wouldn't feel natural to me, but I will use that one alliterative phrase, "the power of persistence." In addition, I'm going to use a triplet of phrases about the persistent widow in which I will say, "She won't give up. She won't back up. She won't shut up." I feel comfortable with that amount of rhetoric, and it will work for my people. If I tried to push it beyond that, it wouldn't work.

So you want to have a level of approaches that is measured by what feels comfortable to you and is acceptable to your people.

ADAPTATION

The third principle of learning from the great preachers deals with knowing how much content you can adapt from them. *What kind of content could I borrow or adapt and it would work for me?* So my third principle is that you have to know who you are before you can know what content you can adapt.

I have to accept the fact that there are certain types of illustrations I will be able to use effectively, but there are other types of illustrations I will not be able to use effectively. I used to think any preacher could use any type of

illustration and it would work. I have since realized that, no, there are certain categories of illustrations I can use with great effectiveness and others I can't.

For example, I cannot tell in an effective way what I call "Johnny stories," which are these homespun, country stories that involve young boys, dogs, grandpas, moms. Bob Russell, however, has a warm, folksy approach when he preaches, and he can tell stories like that powerfully. They have this elemental power, this mythic quality to them, and I love it when Bob does it. When I try to do it, it sounds cheesy. It doesn't work for me.

But there are certain illustrations that do work well for me. I use stories out of business well. I use stories from current events well. So I need to know what illustration types work for me and not try to go far beyond that in adapting or borrowing content from other messages.

Let me give you one more area where this is critical. That is, I need to ask, *What kind of tone does this content have as presented by this preacher, and is that consistent with my tone?*

Let me give you an illustration of this. I love the way James MacDonald preaches, because he burns with a prophetic flame. He just says it. I remember one sermon he did on repentance that was on *Preaching Today* audio. He said, "You say to me, 'But, pastor, I've repented over and over, and I haven't changed. How come?'" And MacDonald says, "Because you haven't really repented. If you had truly repented, you'd be different." He just says it. He gets in your face, and he wins people through this bold, prophetic challenge.

I loved it when I heard him do that, and I thought, *I wish I could get up and say it like that, just let it fly.* But you know what? If I did that, it would be out of character with my tone.

The people would say, "Kevin's a little angry today," because I have a different tone. I have more of a mercy tone, so I win people less through bold, prophetic challenge and more through an encouraging tone that says, "You can have a lasting change in your temperament and behavior and attitude, and let me show you how." It's a different approach.

So I've learned from James MacDonald to challenge people and, when you do challenge them, to be bold. But I need to not wholesale adopt his tone; I need to challenge people in a way that fits my tone. So it's challenge with a flavor of mercy. It's challenge infused with practical strategies. So I can't adapt things without understanding what my tone is.

APPLICATION

In addition, you need to make sure you apply what you want to learn. I will never incorporate another person's craftsmanship or content into my sermon or into my life unless I make it part of my sermon preparation process. It's so easy to listen to a great tape, think about it, and then forget about it. So I've created a file on my computer that has a preaching checklist. I write in there ideas or strategies I have learned from other preachers. Before I get up and preach, I'll look down that checklist and say, *Am I including one clear, simple big idea in this message, or am I trying to do too much?* And then I go to the next thing: *Am I telling people in the first five minutes of this message why it's important that they listen to this?* And I'll include all these different things I've learned from other great preachers. I don't slavishly do everything on my checklist every Sunday, but it's a refresher and a reminder that is now part of my sermon preparation process.

So if you've listened to a great preacher and you go, "I love the way they did this, and I would love it if I could do something like this," then figure out what that is and write it down somewhere. Maybe put a post-it note on your computer screen, or put something in the front of your Bible that says, "A reminder. Am I doing this?" If you don't do that, you'll be impressed, but you won't apply it. You need some system or strategy or reminder or checklist so that you'll make it part of your routine.

ATTITUDE

The last thing I want to talk about is the attitude we have as we listen to great preachers. I want to never be satisfied, but I want to always be secure.

Let me explain. When I'm 65, 66, 67 and, Lord willing and he tarries, I am still preaching the gospel, I hope I'm still improving. I'm still adding to my checklist. I'm still trying out new things and trying to become more effective. So I never want to be satisfied with the level of preaching skill I'm currently exercising. But I always want to preach from an attitude of security. I know God has given me this level of gifts, and I'm comfortable with that level of giftedness. I am not trying to be somebody I'm not.

Not many people know this, but almost every time I prepare to preach I hit a dark, difficult emotional point where I think, *This sermon stinks. This is not coming together. This message is not going to happen.* And then it turns into, *I'm not sure I'm a good preacher. I don't even know why I'm doing this.* There's this doubt and self-criticism. It's a difficult thing for me, and a few times I've asked my daughter, Anne, to pray for me at those moments. I say, "Dad's struggling with the sermon for Sunday.

Will you pray for me?" It's happened enough that Anne calls it "Dad's freak-out moments." She says, "Oh, Dad, you're just having another freak-out moment. Don't worry. It always goes well."

So recently I was praying about it. I said, "Why, Lord, do I have these freak-out moments?" One of the realizations God gave me is that I was still too focused on what people would think of me. Would they like the sermon? Would they respond enthusiastically? Would they be eager to hear me again? And that is not a basis for security in preaching.

As I prayed and meditated about it, I felt as if God showed me there are only two pillars on which you can be secure as a preacher. Here they are.

One is the pillar of obedience. I am preaching because God called me to preach. He commanded me to preach his Word, so if I don't preach the gospel, woe unto me (as says Paul in 1 Cor. 9:16). I have to do it. I'm doing it out of obedience. And whether it goes well or badly, I have to preach God's Word because I have to obey. So the first pillar of security is obedience.

The second pillar is confidence that God's Word has a power beyond my own skill level. In Isaiah 55:10–11 God says, in effect: My word will never go forth and come back empty. It will always accomplish what I send it out to do. It's unfailing. My word has an inherent power to change, shape, and affect things. It will always make an impact.

Honestly, the last time I preached it was not a very good sermon. I got into it and realized it wasn't connecting with the congregation. I quickly tried to scramble and condense a lot, leave a lot out. I went to the closing story, which went over not as well as I had hoped. I finished the sermon. Nobody came up to me and said, "Great sermon." Nobody said, "Boy, that was a powerful message today."

Normally, I would have gone down into an emotional spiral of frustration and doubt and discouragement. Instead, I held myself in check and said, *Did I preach this sermon out of obedience, because God has called me to preach?* Yes. *Did I go in with confidence that God's Word will never come back void and that it will accomplish what God sent it out to do?* Yes. And you know what? I walked away free. I didn't rehash that message. I didn't beat myself up with recriminations or doubt. I felt a freedom and a lightness in the Spirit. It was a security.

So whenever I look at other great preachers and think, *Boy, they preach so wonderfully, and it would be great to preach like that,* I never want to lose my security. I never want to be satisfied, I want to grow, but I always want to be secure.

So we compare ourselves with others in a way that is constructive rather than destructive. It's liberating to be able to learn from them without the insecurity of, *Why don't I preach better?* Instead, if I can learn from them from a position of security, then I can learn from these people with a tremendous sense of liberation. I can rejoice in their great giftedness. It's greater than mine. It's probably greater than mine will ever be. But that doesn't mean I can't freely and securely learn from them and grow.

BOOKS THAT HAVE SHAPED THE PRACTICE OF PREACHING

An Annotated Bibliography

Kenton C. Anderson

The development of biblical preaching can be traced through a study of the books that have shaped its practice. In some of these cases the authors have set the pace, stimulating fresh thinking about the shape of preaching. In other cases the works were merely descriptive. In either case, contemporary readers gain insight into both the practice of preaching and the historical antecedents of the method under observation.

THE HISTORY OF PREACHING

Dargan, Edwin Charles. 1968. *A History of Preaching, Volumes I and II*. Grand Rapids: Baker.

Turnbull, Ralph G. 1974. *A History of Preaching, Volume III*. Grand Rapids: Baker. First published in 1905, Dargan offers the most comprehensive history of preaching detailing the life and practice of most of the preachers of significance up to the end of the nineteenth century. The third volume, edited by Ralph Turnbull covers the first two-thirds of the twentieth century. While many of the more interesting developments in the history of preaching have occurred in the last three decades, Dargan and Turnbull offer insight helping preachers understand where their models come from.

ANCIENT RHETORIC AND EARLY WRITINGS

Saint Augustine. 1958. *On Christian Doctrine, Book 4*. Trans. D. W. Robertson Jr. New York: Macmillan.

The first Christian author to write directly about preaching was St. Augustine. The fourth volume of *On Christian Doctrine* is devoted to the discussion of the shape and form of Christian preaching. Augustine, steeped in the ancient rhetoric of Cicero and Aristotle, sought to describe how such influences might be most effectively appropriated. Why, he wondered, should the sophists be allowed to use their rhetorical skills while Christians were left ignorant of such persuasive techniques? Augustine, setting the stage for centuries to come, shows how ancient rhetoric under the authority of Scripture can birth persuasive preaching.

Alan of Lille. 1981. *The Art of Preaching*. Cistercian Fathers 23, trans. by Gilian R. Evans. Kalamazoo: Cistercian Publications. For almost one and a half millennia since Augustine, little was written on the subject of preaching. Dargan shows that much preaching took place during this period with many sermons available to be read today. However, little formal thought seems to have been given to the subject during this time. What writings there are seem to have followed Augustine. Alan of Lille (1128–1202) focuses on listener "formation." "Preaching is an open and public instruction in faith and behavior whose purpose is the forming of men"; he writes, "it derives from the path of reason and from the fountainhead of the 'authorities.'"

Robert of Basevorn. 1971. *The Form of Preaching*. Trans. by Leopold Krul O.S.B., in James J. Murphy, ed., *Three Medieval Arts*. Berkeley, Los Angeles, London: Univ. of California Press. We have Robert of Basevorn (1322) to thank for the three-point sermon. Again, following well-developed rhetorical patterns, Robert counsels three points because it is Trinitarian, and because it is the most convenient for the set time of the sermon. "A preacher can only follow up just so many members," he writes, "without tiring his hearers."

William Perkins. 1979. *The Art of Prophesying*. Grand Rapids: Baker. The Puritan William Perkins (1592) counseled the plain style of rhetoric as best for biblical preaching. Straightforward, simple explanations of the truths of Scripture were understood to be the hallmarks of solid biblical preaching.

THE DEVELOPMENT OF MODERN HOMILETICS

Broadus, John Albert. 1979. *A Treatise on the Preparation and Delivery of Sermons*. Revised by Vernon L. Stanfield. San Francisco: Harper San Francisco. Broadus's *Treatise* (1870) was the first modern homiletics textbook. Professor of preaching at Southern Baptist Theological Seminary, Broadus followed the Augustinian lead, building his method from ancient rhetorical roots. From Broadus we derive the classic taxonomy of homiletical forms (textual, topical, expository). Here we also find the familiar threefold sermon structure common to so many contemporary sermons: explanation, illustration, and application.

Brooks, Phillips. 1964. *Lectures on Preaching*. New York: Seabury. Brooks (1877) defined preaching as "truth through personality." Few have been able to match this definition for simplicity. Brooks's approach effectively combined the human element of preaching with an objective sense of truth. His method was responsive to the listener even as it was respectful to God himself. It is this integrative element that continues to give Brooks's definition its relevance.

Dodd, C. H. 1964. *The Apostolic Preaching and Its Development*. New York: Harper & Row, 1964. Dodd (1936) sought to understand the purpose of preaching through analysis of the preaching of the early church. It was his conviction that preaching (*kerygma*) ought to be distinguished from teaching (*didache*). Further, he suggested that much of what passes for preaching today would not have been recognized as such by the early Christians. Preaching,

he asserted, proclaimed the death, resurrection, and salvation made possible in Jesus Christ. Anything less is not kerygma. Dodd may not have settled the argument, but he certainly raised a question that has been pivotal: What is preaching?

Stewart, James S. 2001. *Heralds of God*. Vancouver: Regent College Publishing. Stewart (1946) was rated by the *Preaching* magazine editorial board as the greatest preacher of the twentieth century, largely because of the pervasive influence of this book. Stewart urges his readers to ask of their listeners, "Did they hear from God today?" He constantly encourages his readers to preach expectantly as if God were present and active in the preaching process, to preach as if something crucial or decisive could happen for people as they gain a vision of Jesus this very day.

NEW HOMILETIC APPROACHES

Davis, H. Grady. 1958. *Design for Preaching*. Philadelphia: Fortress. The first book to rethink the classic rhetorical roots of biblical preaching was Grady Davis's *Design for Preaching*. Davis brought life to preaching by suggesting a more organic way of thinking about the task. Preaching is something that grows, he said, rather than something that is constructed. The form of the sermon, then, could take various shapes. It could be "a subject discussed," "a thesis supported," "a message illumined," "a question propounded," or "a story told."

Fred B. Craddock. 1969, 2001 (rev. ed.). *As One Without Authority*. St. Louis: Chalice. The first to take full advantage of the gains made by Davis was Fred Craddock. Craddock counseled an inductive approach to preaching, welcoming the listener into the process of discovery along with the preacher. Why, Craddock wondered, should the listener be denied the same joy of discovery experienced by the preacher every week in his or her study. Craddock developed a variety of potential sermon forms all designed to encourage listener attentiveness and engagement through induction.

Lowry, Eugene L. 1980. *The Homiletical Plot*. Atlanta: John Knox. Lowry represents a variety of homileticians who, building out of Craddock's work, have championed narrative preaching. While preaching narrative sermons from narrative texts only makes sense, Lowry described a way of treating every biblical text narratively. We live our lives in story, moment by moment, place by place. Through use of Lowry's five-part "loop," a sermon can serve as an "event in time." Instead of sermons serving as static propositional structures, Lowry's approach allows sermons to come alive.

Buttrick, David. 1987. *Homiletic*. Philadelphia: Fortress. David Buttrick's massive homiletic study describes how sermons can take shape in the listener's consciousness. Describing sermon building in terms of "moves" and "structures," Buttrick's method depends on ideas taken from phenomenology. Looking at point of view, imagery, and modes of consciousness, his method suggests a variety of possibilities for shaping the listener's thought through renovating the architecture of the sermon.

FRESH VISION FOR EXPOSITION

Stott, John R. W. 1982. *Between Two Worlds*. Grand Rapids: Eerdmans. While some were exploring new directions in preaching, others were renewing a vision for biblical exposition. John Stott, for one, reminded preachers that the task of the sermon is to build a bridge between the ancient text and the contemporary situation. Stott sought a new generation of preachers who would show determination to bridge the chasm between God's unchanging Word and the ever-changing world. He challenged preachers to be faithful to the Scriptures while remaining pertinent to today.

Robinson, Haddon. 1980, 2001 (rev. ed.). *Biblical Preaching*. Grand Rapids: Baker. Assigned as required reading in more than 160 colleges and seminaries, Robinson's *Biblical Preaching* has become the primary text for contemporary exposition. While maintaining faith with Broadus's concern for historical-grammatical exegesis, Robinson also borrows from Davis ("story to be told," "proposition to be proved") and others in the desire to find creative, genre-sensitive forms that remain faithful to the intent of Scripture. Perhaps Robinson's greatest contribution, however, is his insistence that every

sermon offers one "big idea." Sermons can take a variety of structures, but they ought to intend the proclamation of one big idea, which the Holy Spirit applies first to the preacher and then through him or her to the hearers.

Chapell, Bryan. 1994. *Christ-Centered Preaching*. Grand Rapids: Baker. The subtitle of Chapell's book declares his intention to "redeem the expository sermon." The choice of the word "redeem" is intentional as the author counsels a traditional rhetorical sermon structure for the presentation of a Christological redemptive theology. Every sermon must declare God's redemptive intention in Jesus Christ. C. H. Dodd would be pleased. So would John Broadus. Chapell's homiletic form is straight out of Broadus's work, detailing the threefold structure of explanation, illustration, and application. Perhaps the most important feature of Chapell's work is his emphasis on "The Fallen Condition Focus." "But God doesn't leave his children without hope?" Chapell asks. Preaching ought to offer that hope in Jesus Christ.

Goldsworthy, Graeme. 2000. *Preaching the Whole Bible as Christian Scripture*. Grand Rapids: Eerdmans. Goldsworthy would agree with Chapell's contention for the centrality of Jesus Christ. Representing a biblical theological approach to preaching, Goldworthy argues that every sermon must point to Christ. He champions a brand of preaching that moves away from a bland moralism toward a healthy engagement with the revelation of God in Jesus Christ as it is represented in different ways throughout the whole of the Bible.

READING LIST OF OTHER SIGNIFICANT BOOKS IN PREACHING

Just as the development of preaching can be traced through a study of the books written on the subject, searching a bibliography of current books on homiletics will show the diversity in approach and conviction that has ensued. The following sources represent some of that diversity.

Anderson, Kenton C. 2001. *Preaching with Conviction*. Grand Rapids: Kregel.

_____. 2003. *Preaching with Integrity*. Grand Rapids: Kregel. These two Anderson books utilize a narrative form to describe an integrative approach to preaching.

Bartow, Charles L. 1997. *God's Human Speech*. Grand Rapids: Eerdmans. Bartow seeks to describe the mysterious way in which divine and human speech are mingled in preaching.

Eslinger, Richard L. 1987. *A New Hearing*. Nashville: Abingdon. Eslinger describes and critiques the emergence of a new homiletic in the preaching of David Buttrick, Fred Craddock, Eugene Lowry, and others.

Galli, Mark, and Craig Brian Larson. 1994. *Preaching That Connects*. Grand Rapids: Zondervan. The authors take a journalistic approach to developing compelling sermons.

Greidanus, Sidney. 1988. *The Modern Preacher and the Ancient Text*. Grand Rapids: Eerdmans. Greidanus offers a genre-sensitive, biblical/theological approach to expository preaching.

Johnston, Graham. 2001. *Preaching to a Postmodern World*. Grand Rapids: Baker. Johnston points to ways in which preaching might reach a new generation of listeners.

Kaiser, Walter C. Jr. 1981. *Toward an Exegetical Theology*. Grand Rapids: Baker. Kaiser describes a helpful way of exegeting Scripture for preachers.

Long, Thomas G. 1989. *The Witness of Preaching*. Louisville: Westminster John Knox. Long reframes the task of preaching through the metaphor of "witness."

McLaren, Brian, and Leonard Sweet. 2003. *A Is for Abductive*. Grand Rapids: Zondervan. Inductive, deductive, and now *ab*ductive? McLaren and Sweet seek to describe preaching in the emergent church.

Mathewson, Steven D. 2002. *The Art of Preaching Old Testament Narrative*. Grand Rapids: Baker. Mathewson counsels creative preaching that is sensitive both to the message of the sermon and to its form.

McClure, John S. 2001. *Other-Wise Preaching*. St. Louis: Chalice. Moving well beyond an evangelical view of Scripture, McClure takes the new homiletic to an extreme, offering "a postmodern ethic for homiletics."

McDill, Wayne V. 1999. *The Moment of Truth*. Nashville: Broadman & Holman. McDill helps preachers to a more effective process of sermon delivery.

Miller, Calvin. 1995. *Marketplace Preaching*. Grand Rapids: Baker.

_____. 2002. *The Sermon Maker*. Grand Rapids: Zondervan. Miller brings creativity and conviction in his descriptions of the transformations possible through biblical preaching.

Pitt-Watson, Ian. 1986. *A Primer for Preachers*. Grand Rapids: Baker. Pitt-Watson counsels preaching not only from the "text of Scripture" but also from "the text of life."

Wiersbe, Warren W. 1994. *Preaching and Teaching with Imagination*. Grand Rapids: Baker. Wiersbe counsels imaginative preaching on the basis of a rich array of biblical examples.

SCRIPTURE INDEX

NAME INDEX

SUBJECT INDEX

Effective First-Person Biblical Preaching

J. Kent Edwards

A practical text to help students and pastors understand why and how first-person sermons can be preached with biblical integrity. While following Haddon Robinson's "big idea" preaching methodology, the author walks the readers through the steps they can take to prepare an effective first-person message.

Hardcover ISBN: 0310263093

Preaching Re-Imagined

Doug Pagitt

What is the role of preaching in the postmodern church? Doug Pagitt takes on this pivotal question as he invites you to reimagine the goals and roles of preaching. Using a few questions as guides, learn how to create followers of God who thrive amidst the complexities of life. Perfect for pastors and emergent thinkers, this book is a hopeful look at the present and future of preaching.

Hardcover ISBN: 0310263638

Pick up a copy today at your favorite bookstore!

ZONDERVAN™

GRAND RAPIDS, MICHIGAN 49530 USA

WWW.ZONDERVAN.COM

Preaching God's Word

Terry G. Carter, J. Scott Duvall,

and J. Daniel Hays

This user-friendly practical textbook helps preachers and homiletics students develop and deliver biblically based expository sermons relevant for the twenty-first century.

Hardcover ISBN: 0310248876

More Movie-Based Illustrations for Preaching & Teaching

Craig Brian Larson & Lori Quicke

If you've used the original *Movie-Based Illustrations for Preaching and Teaching,* you already know why this sequel is a must-have. If not, you're about to discover why *More Movie-Based Illustrations for Preaching and Teaching* is one of the most effective people-reachers you can add to your tool kit. Movies have become the stories of our culture, and they can help you communicate God's Word with power—if you have exciting, movie-based illustrations at your fingertips.

Softcover ISBN: 0310248345

Pick up a copy today at your favorite bookstore!

GRAND RAPIDS, MICHIGAN 49530 USA

WWW.ZONDERVAN.COM

We want to hear from you. Please send your comments about this book to us in care of zreview@zondervan.com. Thank you.

GRAND RAPIDS, MICHIGAN 49530 USA

ZONDERVAN.COM/
AUTHOR**TRACKER**